WHO DONE IT?

A Guide to Detective, Mystery and Suspense Fiction

WHO DONE IT?

A Guide to Detective, Mystery and Suspense Fiction

by Ordean A. Hagen

R. R. BOWKER COMPANY • New York & London • 1969

Published by R. R. Bowker Company (A XEROX COMPANY),
1180 Avenue of the Americas, New York, N.Y. 10036

Standard Book Number: 8352-0234-8
Library of Congress Catalog Card Number: 69-19209

Manufactured in the United States of America.

THIS BOOK IS DEDICATED
TO MY LOVING MOTHER
Mrs. Martha Hagen

Acknowledgments

Although my name appears on the title page as the author, it is virtually impossible for a book to be written by one person alone. I wish to take this opportunity to thank the persons and groups who have helped me in every possible way.

First, to my wonderful family, without whose help and understanding this book would never have been finished. To my sisters, Clara Ostmo and Orpha Partlow for their active part in checking copy and doing research work; to my brother Trigve who helped in indexing the E. T. Guymon library in San Diego; to my nieces Gloria Meier and Dianne Nelson for the hours they put in typing the manuscript; and to my nephews Gary Allen and Ronald Partlow for their valuable contributions.

Second, to the Chester Fritz Library and the staff. To Mr. Donald Pearce, the Head Librarian, for his interest and cooperation, and to Mrs. Anna Kueneman, Mrs. Sady Cady, Mrs. Mary Lonsky, and Miss Pam Halvorson who gave up hours of their free evening time to come back to the library and do the typing for me. To the University of North Dakota, especially to the Faculty Research Committee and Dr. Edwin Olmstead for their solution to my problems.

Third, to E. T. Guyman of San Diego for the time spent in indexing his fine library in San Diego, California. To Mr. Allen J. Hubin of White Bear Lake, Minnesota, for the use of his fine personal library, and his assistance on the Bibliography. And to Nigel Morland of Bognor Regis, England, for offering to check the English part of the Bibliography and for giving me good advice which I was smart enough to follow.

Fourth, to John N. Berry III, my editor, and Mrs. Maureen Enos, the Assistant Editor, for all their help and interest.

Contents

Foreword

I was first put in touch with Ordean Hagen through the Mystery Writers of America in January of 1967. Then came my first glimpse into his incredible project: to provide a complete bibliography of the broad genre of mystery fiction. I don't know if he fully appreciated at that time the forbidding difficulties standing in his way—difficulties which probably explain why such a bibliographic venture had not been carried out long before.

Consider these obstacles: the primary references down through the years are sprinkled with errors of omission and commission; the bibliographies of some authors are so complicated that the writers themselves don't have accurate accounts; there is no adequate record of very early paperbacks, particularly in England; a host of pseudonyms have never been uncovered and the books attributed to the right authors; many early mysteries had unrevealing titles, virtually necessitating a look at the actual volume in each case to determine whether inclusion in the bibliography was warranted; some early non-mysteries had mystery-like titles, requiring the same nearly impossible personal inspection; the primary references do not always clearly distinguish between adult and juvenile mysteries; the lines of demarcation between various forms of fiction are indistinct, so the incorporation or rejection of hundreds of books becomes a matter of painful judgment.

I feel the present book is a truly remarkable achievement. The bibliography is the result of diligent examination of the records of the years 1841–1967, of consultations with mystery writers, of examinations of large collections of criminous fiction and personal inspections of thousands of volumes. And to this basic bibliography have been added a host of useful features: run your eye down the contents page to see the wealth of information not previously collected in one volume.

The task of providing a bibliography for mystery fiction will probably never be complete in the ultimate sense, but Ordean A. Hagen has here provided what will surely become the single most indispensable book in the field for thousands of writers, reviewers, editors, students and aficionados of mystery fiction, and a must in every library collection of reference works.

Allen J. Hubin
December 11, 1968

Key to Abbreviations of Publishers

NOTE: *Where two publishers are listed following the abbreviation, the first is either an affiliate or an imprint.*

Abelard Abelard-Schuman, Ltd.
Ace Ace Books and Ace Star Books
Adelphi Adelphi Co.
Airmont Airmont Publishing Co., Thomas Bouregy & Co., Inc.
Albatross Albatross Publishing Co.
Aldine Aldine Publishing Co., Ltd.
Aldor, F. Francis Aldor, Publisher
Aldus Pub. Aldus Publishing Co.
Allan, P. Philip Allan & Co., Ltd.
Allen & Unwin George Allen & Unwin, Ltd.
Allen, T. Thomas Allen, Ltd.
Allen, W. H. W. H. Allen & Co., Ltd.
Alliance Alliance Book Corp.
Allied Newspapers Allied Newspapers, Ltd.
Altemus Henry Altemus Co.
Amalgamated Press Amalgamated Press, Ltd.
Ambassador Ambassador Books, Ltd.
Amer. News American News Co.
Angel Island Publications Angel Island Publications, Inc.
Anglo-Eastern Anglo-Eastern Publishing Co., Ltd.
Angus Angus & Robertson, Ltd.
Appleton Appleton-Century-Crofts
Appleton-Century D. Appleton-Century Co., Inc.
Appleton, D. D. Appleton & Co.
Arcadia Arcadia House, Inc.
Archer Denis Archer, Search Publishing Co., Ltd.
Arco Publications Arco Publications, Ltd.
Arena Arena Publishing Co.
Arkham Arkham House
Arlington Arlington House, Inc.
Arnold, E. Edward Arnold & Co.
Arrow Books Arrow Books, Ltd.
Arrowsmith J. W. Arrowsmith, Ltd.
Art & Educ. Pubs. Art and Educational Publishers, Ltd.
Atheneum Atheneum Publishers
Austin Austin Publishing Co.
Austin-Phelps Austin-Phelps, Inc.
Australasian Book Society Australasian Book Society, Ltd.
Authors Authors & Newspapers Association
Avalon Avalon Books
Avon Avon Book Division, Hearst Corp.
Award Award Books Division, Universal Publishing & Distributing Corp.

Badger, R. G. Richard G. Badger & Co., The Gorham Press
Baker Stanley Baker
Baker, J. John Baker Publishers, Ltd.
Ball Ball Publishing Co.
Ballantine Ballantine Books, Inc.
Banner Banner Press Publishers
Bantam Bantam Books, Inc.
Banyan Banyan Press
Barker Arthur Barker, Ltd.
Barmerlea Barmerlea Book Sales, Ltd.
Barnes, A. S. A. S. Barnes & Co., Inc.
Barrie & Rockliff Barrie & Rockliff, Barrie Books, Ltd.
Barse & Co. Barse & Co., Grosset & Dunlap, Inc.
Barse & Hopkins Barse & Hopkins
Bart Bart House Pocket Book
Beacon Beacon Press
Beadle Beadle & Adams
Bear Bear, Hudson, Ltd.
Bell Bell Publishing Co.
Bell, G. George Bell & Sons, Ltd.
Bellevue Bellevue Books
Belmont Belmont Books
Ben Hur Ben Hur Press

Benn Ernest Benn, Ltd.
Bentley Richard Bentley
Berkley Pub. Berkley Publishing Corp.
Bernard Pub. Bernard Publishing Co., Inc.
Black Walter J. Black, Inc.
Blackie & Son Blackie & Son, Ltd.
Blakiston The Blakiston Co.
Blackwood William Blackwood & Sons, Ltd.
Bles Geoffrey Bles, Ltd.
Blond, A. Anthony Blond, Ltd.
Blue Ribbon Books Blue Ribbon Books, Inc.
Boardman Clark Boardman Co., Ltd.
Boardman, T. V. T. V. Boardman & Co., Ltd.
Bobbs Bobbs-Merrill Co., Inc.
Bodley Head The Bodley Head, Ltd.
Bonde, A. Arthur Bonde, Ltd.
Boni Albert & Charles Boni, Inc.
Boni & Liveright Boni & Liveright
Bonner Robert Bonner's Sons
Bookman Associates Bookman Associates, Inc., Twayne Publishers, Inc.
Books Books, Inc., Publishers
Books for Today Books for Today, Inc.
Bouregy Thomas Bouregy & Co., Inc. (formerly Bouregy & Curl)
Bowden James Bowden
Bradbury Bradbury & Evans
Brandon Brandon House Publications
Braziller George Braziller, Inc.
Brentano Brentano's, Inc.
Brewer Brewer, Warren & Putnam
Brimmer B. J. Brimmer Co.
British Book Centre British Book Centre, Inc., Pergamon Press
British Book Service British Book Service
Brown J. & C. Brown
Brown, Watson Brown, Watson, Ltd.
Browne & Nolan Browne & Nolan, Ltd.
Bruce Pub. Bruce Publishing Co.
Buckles F. M. Buckles & Co.
Burke J. W. Burke Co.
Burke Pub. Burke Publishing Co., Ltd.
Burleigh, T. Thomas Burleigh
Burns Burns, Oates & Washbourne, Ltd.
Burt A. L. Burt Co., Inc.
Burton Pub. Burton Publishing Co.
Butterworth, T. Thornton Butterworth, Ltd.

Calder, J. John Calder Publishers, Ltd.
Cameron & Kahn Cameron & Kahn, Inc.
Canaveral Canaveral Press
Cape Jonathan Cape, Ltd. (formerly Jonathan Cape and Harrison Smith)
Capper Capper, Harman, Slocum, Inc.
Carleton Carleton Printing Co.
Carleton, G. George W. Carleton & Co.
Carlton Carlton Press, Inc. (formerly Comet Press Books)
Carlyle Carlyle House, Publishers
Carrick Carrick & Evans, Inc.
Carrier Louis Carrier & Co., Ltd.
Carrier & Isles Louis Carrier & Alan Isles, Inc.
Cassell Cassell & Co., Ltd.
Caxton Caxton Printers, Ltd.
Cayme Press Cayme Press, Ltd.
Century Century Co.
Century Press Century Press, Ltd.
Chambers W. & R. Chambers, Ltd.
Chapman Chapman & Hall, Ltd.
Chatto Chatto & Windus, Ltd.
Chelsea House Chelsea House, Street & Smith Publications
Cheshire Cheshire House, Inc.
Chilton Chilton Book Co.
Christopher Christopher Publishing House
Clark, Irwin Clark, Irwin & Co., Ltd.
Claxton Claxton, Remsen & Haffelfinger
Clay & Sons R. Clay & Sons, Ltd.
Clerke Clerke & Cockeran, Ltd.
Clinic Clinic Publishing Co., Abbott Press
Clode Edward J. Clode
Coker J. Coker & Co., Ltd.
Collier P. F. Collier, Inc., Collier Books, Crowell, Collier & Macmillan, Inc.
Collingwood Collingwood Bros.
Collins William Collins Sons & Co., Ltd.
Columbine Columbine Publishing Co., Ltd.
Comet Comet Press Books, Inc.
Commercial Commercial Service Co.
Constable Constable & Co., Ltd.
Consul Consul Books
Convoy Convoy Publications
Copp Copp, Clark Company, Ltd.
Corgi Corgi Books, Transworld Publishers, Ltd.
Corinth Corinth Books, Inc., Citadel Press
Cosmopolitan Cosmopolitan Book Corp.
Cotton Press Cotton Press
Covici Covici, Friede, Inc.
Coward Coward-McCann, Inc.

Creative Age Press Creative Age Press, Inc.
Cresset Cresset Press, Ltd.
Crest Crest Books, Fawcett World Library, Inc.
Crombie Andrew Crombie
Crowell Thomas Y. Crowell Co.
Crown Crown Publishers, Inc.
Crowther John Crowther, Ltd.
Cupples Cupples, Upham and Co.
Cupples & Leon Cupples & Leon Co., Inc.
Curl Samuel Curl, Inc.

Dakers Andrew Dakers, Ltd.
Darling Darling Brothers & Co.
David The C. W. David Co.
Davies Peter Davies, Ltd.
Davis Davis Publications, Inc.
Day John Day Co., Inc.
Delacorte The Delacorte Press
Dell Dell Publishing Co., Inc.
Dent J. M. Dent & Sons, Ltd.
Deutsch André Deutsch, Ltd.
Devin-Adair Devin-Adair Co.
Dial Dial Press, Inc.
Diamond Press Diamond Press, Ltd.
Dick & Fitzgerald Dick & Fitzgerald
Dickson Lovat Dickson & Thompson, Ltd.
Digby Digby, Long & Co.
Dillingham, G. W. George W. Dillingham Co.
Diprose Diprose & Bateman
Dobson Dennis Dobson, Dobson Books, Ltd.
Dodd Dodd, Mead & Co., Inc.
Dodd, Eyton Dodd, Eyton, Co.
Dodge Dodge Publishing Co.
Dodge, B. W. B. W. Dodge & Co.
Dolphin Dolphin Book Co., Ltd.
Donnelly R. R. Donnelly Corp.
Donohue Donohue & Henneberry & Co.
Donohue, M. A. M. A. Donohue & Co.
Doran George H. Doran Co.
Dorrance Dorrance & Co.
Doscher C. S. Doscher & Co.
Doubleday Doubleday & Co., Inc.
Doubleday, Doran Doubleday, Doran & Co.
Doubleday, Page Doubleday, Page & Co.
Downey Downey & Co., Ltd.
Drane Henry J. Drane
Duckworth Gerald Duckworth & Co., Ltd.
Duell Duell, Sloane & Pearce, Inc.
Duffield Duffield & Green, Inc.
Dufour Dufour Editions, Inc.
Dunkerley W. A. Dunkerley
Dutton E. P. Dutton & Co., Inc.

Eagle Pub. Eagle Publishing Co.
Earl William Earl & Co., Ltd.
Earle, P. Philip Earle, Ltd.
Edinburgh Pub. Edinburgh Publishing Co.
Educ. Pub. Educational Publishing Co.
Edwards, W. Walter Edwards, Publishers, Ltd.
Eldon Eldon Press, Ltd.
Elek Elek Books, Ltd.
Emerson Emerson Books, Inc.
Epworth The Epworth Press
Estes Dana Estes & Co.
Estes & Lauriat Estes & Lauriat
Euphorion Euphorion Books
Evans Evans Brothers, Ltd.
Everett Everett & Co.
Evergreen Evergreen Books, Grove Press, Inc.
Excelsior Excelsior Publishing House
Exposition Exposition Press, Inc.
Extension Press Extension Press
Eyre Eyre & Spottiswoode (Publishers), Ltd.

Faber Faber & Faber, Ltd.
Faber & Gwyer Faber & Gwyer, Ltd.
Falcon Press Falcon Press, Ltd.
Farrar Farrar, Straus, & Cudahy, Farrar, Straus, & Giroux, Inc.
Farrar & Rinehart Farrar & Rinehart, Inc.
Farrar, Straus Farrar, Straus & Co., Inc.
Fawcett Fawcett Publications, Inc., Fawcett World Library
Federal Federal Book Co.
Fell Frederick Fell, Inc.
Fenland Fenland Press
Fenno R. F. Fenno & Co.
Fiction League Jacobsen Publishing Co.
Field House of Field, Inc.
Findon Findon Publications, Ltd.
Fleet Pub. Fleet Publishing Corp.
Fleetway Fleetway Press, Ltd.
Fly H. K. Fly Co.
Fontana Fontana Books, Wm. Collins & Sons Co., Ltd.
Forbes Robertson Forbes Robertson, Ltd.
Fortune Fortune Press, Ltd.
Fortuny Fortuny's, Publishers, Inc.
Foster, W. William Foster
Foulsham W. Foulsham & Co., Ltd.

Four Square Four Square Books, New English Library, Ltd.
Frank-Maurice Frank-Maurice, Inc.
Funk Funk & Wagnalls Co., Division of Reader's Digest Books, Inc.
Funk, W. Wilfred Funk, Inc.
Furman Lee Furman, Inc.

Gabriel Samuel Gabriel Sons & Co.
Gale Gale & Polden, Ltd.
Galleon Galleon Publishers, Inc.
Garden City Pub. Garden City Publishing Co., Inc.
Gardner Wells Gardner, Darton & Co., Ltd.
Gardner, A. Alexander Gardner & Co., Ltd.
Garnett Peter Garnett, Ltd.
Gateway Gateway Book Co.
Gifford John Gifford, Ltd.
Ginn Ginn & Company
Glen Kelvin Glen
GM Gold Medal Books, Fawcett World Library
Gold Label Gold Label Books, Inc.
Gollancz Victor Gollancz, Ltd.
Grafton Grafton & Co. (Frank Hamel), Copic House
Gramol Gramol Publishers
Grant, E. Eric Grant, Ltd.
Graphic Graphic Books
Gray Arthur Gray
Grayson Grayson & Grayson, Ltd.
Green William Green & Son, Ltd.
Green Circle Green Circle Books, Lee Furman, Inc., Publisher
Greenberg Greenberg, Publisher, Inc.
Greening Greening & Co., Ltd.
Greenwich Greenwich Book Publishers, Inc.
Gresham John Gresham, Ltd.
Grey Walls The Grey Walls Press, Ltd.
Greystone The Greystone Press, Inc.
Grosset Grosset & Dunlap, Inc.
Grossman Grossman Publishers, Inc.
Grove Grove Press, Inc.
Gryphon Gryphon Books, Ltd.

Hale Hale, Cushman & Flint, Inc.
Hale, R. Robert Hale, Ltd.
Halle, A. A. Halle, Ltd.
Hamilton John Hamilton, Ltd.
Hamilton & Co. Hamilton & Co. (Stafford), Ltd.
Hamilton, H. Hamish Hamilton, Ltd.
Hammond Hammond, Hammond & Co., Ltd.
Hampton Hampton Publishing Co., Inc.
Harborough Harborough Publishing Co., Ltd.
Harcourt Harcourt, Brace & World, Inc.
Harlo Harlo Press
Harper Harper & Brothers
Harper & Row Harper & Row, Publishers, Inc.
Harrap George G. Harrap & Co., Ltd.
Harrison-Hilton Harrison-Hilton Books, Inc.
Hart Hart Publishing Company, Inc.
Hart-Davis Rupert Hart-Davis, Ltd.
Hartney Hartney Press, Inc.
Harvill The Harvill Press, Ltd.
Hay, W. William Hay
Hayes Robert Hayes, Ltd.
Heath Heath, Cranton, Ltd.
Heinemann William Heinemann, Ltd.
Henkle Rae D. Henkle (Publisher) Co., Inc.
Henry Henry & Co.
Herald Herald Publishing House
Herder B. Herder Book Co.
Heritage Heritage Press
Heritage, J. John Heritage, The Unicorn Press, Ltd.
Heywood John Heywood, Ltd.
Hill & Wang Hill & Wang, Inc.
Hill, H. Harold Hill & Son, Ltd.
Hillman Hillman Brothers
Hillman-Curl Hillman-Curl, Inc.
Hodder Hodder & Stoughton, Ltd.
Hoeve W. Van Hoeve
Hogarth Hogarth Press, Ltd.
Holden Robert Holden & Co., Ltd.
Holt Holt, Rinehart & Winston, Inc.
Holt, H. Henry Holt & Co.
Home & Van Thal Home & Van Thal, Ltd.
Hopkins & Son John H. Hopkins, Inc.
Horizon Press Horizon Press, Inc.
Houghton Houghton Mifflin Co.
Howell, Soskin Howell, Soskin, Inc., Publishers
Humphries Bruce Humphries, Inc.
Hurst Hurst & Blackett, Ltd.
Hutchinson Hutchinson & Co., Ltd.

Innes A. D. Innes
International Fiction Lib. International Fiction Library, World Syndicate Publishing Co.
International Pub. International Publishing Co.
Invincible Invincible Press, Macdonell House
Isbister Isbister & Co., Ltd.
Ivers M. J. Ivers & Co.

Jacobs George W. Jacobs Co.
Jacobsen Jacobsen Publishing Co.
Jarrolds Jarrolds Publishers (London), Ltd.
Jay Jay Books, Ward, Lock & Co.
Jefferson House Jefferson House, Inc.
Jenkins Herbert Jenkins, Ltd.
Joseph, M. Michael Joseph, Ltd.
Judd Orange Judd Co.
Juniper Juniper Press, Publishers

Kearney & Co. John E. Kearney & Co.
Keen W. B. Keen, Cooke & Co.
Kelly Hector Kelly, Ltd.
Kemp David Kemp & Co.
Kendall Claude Kendall, Inc.
Kennerley Mitchell Kennerley
King, A. H. Alfred H. King Co., Julian Messner Inc., Publishers
Kinsey H. C. Kinsey Co., Ltd.
Knopf Alfred A. Knopf, Inc.

Laird Laird & Lee
Lancer Lancer Books, Inc.
Landsbrough Landsbrough Publishing Co.
Lane John Lane, The Bodley Head, Ltd.
Langdon John Langdon, Ltd.
Lantern Press Lantern Press, Inc.
Laurie T. Werner Laurie, Ltd.
Lawrence Lawrence & Bullen, Ltd.
Lee & Shepard Lee & Shepard Co.
Lehmann John Lehmann, Ltd.
Lever Lever Brothers
Lewis, C. Clifford Lewis & Co.
Lippincott J. B. Lippincott Co.
Lit. Society Literary Society
Little Little, Brown & Co.
Liveright Liveright Publishing Corp.
Lloyds House of Lloyds
Locke Hennel Locke, Ltd.
Locker R. & L. Locker
London Book London Book Co.
London House London House & Maxwell, British Book Centre
Long John Long, Ltd.
Long & Smith Ray Long & Richard R. Smith Corp.
Longmans Longmans, Green & Co., Ltd.
Lothian Lothian Publishing Co.
Lothrop Lothrop, Lee & Shepard Co.
Lounz Gregory Lounz, Books
Lovell, Coryell Lovell, Coryell & Co.
Lovell, F. F. Frank F. Lovell & Co.
Lovell, J. W. John W. Lovell Co.
Low Sampson Low, Marston & Co., Ltd.
Loyd Alex T. Loyd & Co.
Luce, J. W. John W. Luce & Co.
Lutterworth Press Lutterworth Press, United Society for Christian Literature, Proprietors
Lymanhouse Lymanhouse, Bookhaven Press

Macaulay Macaulay Co.
McBride Robert M. McBride & Co.
McClelland McClelland & Stewart, Ltd.
McClure McClure Co.
McClure, Phillips McClure, Phillips & Co.
McClurg A. C. McClurg & Co.
MacDonald & Co. MacDonald & Co. (Publishers), Ltd.
Macfadden Macfadden-Bartell Corp.
MacGibbon MacGibbon & Kee, Ltd.
McGraw McGraw-Hill Book Co.
McKay David McKay Co., Inc.
McKinlay McKinlay, Stone & MacKenzie
McLeod George J. McLeod, Ltd.
Macmillan The Macmillan Co., Crowell Collier & Macmillan, Inc.
McNaughton Wayne L. McNaughton, Inc., The Parkwood Press
Macrae Smith Macrae Smith Co.
MacVeagh Lincoln MacVeagh, Dial Press
Macy-Masius Macy-Masius, Vanguard Press, Inc.
Mandrake Mandrake Press
Manthorne Manthrone & Burack, Inc.
Marquis A. N. Marquis & Co.
Marshall, P. Percival Marshall & Co., Ltd.
Marston Marston & Co., Ltd.
Mason The Mason Publishing Co.
Mathews Elkin Mathews & Marrot, Ltd.
Meador Meador Publishing Co.
Mellifont Mellifont Press, Ltd.
Melrose Andrew Melrose, Ltd.
Menzies John Menzies & Co., Ltd.
Mercury Pub. Mercury Publishing Co.
Meredith Meredith Press
Meridian Meridian Books, Ltd.
Merit Books Merit Books, Ltd.
Merle Merle Armitage Editions
Messner Julian Messner, Inc., Publishers
Methuen Methuen & Co., Ltd.
Metropolitan Metropolitan Press, Ltd.
Mill M. S. Mill Co., William Morrow & Co.
Mills & Boon Mills & Boon, Ltd.
Milne John Milne, Ltd.
Minton Minton, Balch & Co.

Mitre The Mitre Press, Fudge & Co., Ltd.
Modern Age Modern Age Books, Inc.
Modern Fiction Modern Fiction, Ltd.
Modern Lib. Modern Library Inc.
Modern Pub. Modern Publishing Co., J. Coker & Co., Ltd.
Moffat Moffat, Yard & Co.
Mohawk Mohawk Press, Inc.
Monarch Monarch Books, Inc.
Moring Alexander Moring, Ltd.
Morrow William Morrow & Co., Inc.
Muller Frederick Muller, Ltd.
Munro George Munro
Munsey Frank A. Munsey Co.
Murray & Co. Murray & Co.
Murray & Gee Murray & Gee, Inc.
Murray Hill Murray Hill Books, Rinehart & Co.
Murray, J. John Murray, Publishers, Ltd.
Museum Press Museum Press, Ltd.
Mussey Barrows Mussey, Inc. (formerly Loring & Mussey)
Musson The Musson Book Co., Ltd.
Mycroft & Moran Mycroft & Moran, Arkham House
Mystery House Mystery House, Thomas Bouregy & Co., Inc.
Mystery League Mystery League, Inc.

Nash J. Eveleigh Nash Co., Ltd.
Nash & Grayson Eveleigh Nash & Grayson
Natl. Mag. National Magazine Co.
Neale Neale Publishing Co.
Neely F. Tennyson Neely
Nelson Thomas Nelson & Sons, Ltd.
Nelson, Foster & Scott Nelson, Foster & Scott, Ltd.
Nevill Peter Nevill, Ltd.
New Amer. Lib. New American Library, Inc.
New Amsterdam New Amsterdam Book Co.
New Authors New Authors, Ltd.
New Directions New Directions Publishing Corp.
New English Lib. New English Library, Ltd.
Newnes George Newnes, Ltd.
Nicholson Ivor Nicholson & Watson, Ltd.
Nisbet Nisbet & Co., Ltd.
Nod Nod Publishing Co.
Nonesuch The Nonesuch Press
Norman, Remington Norman, Remington Co.
Norton W. W. Norton & Co., Inc.

Obolensky Ivan Obolensky, Inc.
Oceana Oceana Publications, Inc.
Odhams Odhams Press, Ltd.
Ogilvie J. S. Ogilvie Publishing Co.
Oldbourne Oldbourne Press, Oldbourne Book Co., Ltd.
Oliphant & Co. J. H. Oliphant & Co.
Osgood James R. Osgood & Co.
Ousley, J. John Ousley, Ltd.
Oxford Oxford University Press
Owen, P. Peter Owen, Ltd.

Page L. C. Page & Co., St. Botolph Society
Pageant Press Pageant Press, Inc.
Paladin Press Paladin Press, Ltd.
Palmer, C. Cecil Palmer & Hayward
Palmer, F. N. Frank N. Palmer
Pan The Pan Press
Pantheon Pantheon Books, Inc.
Panther Panther Books, Ltd.
Panther Pub. Panther Publications, Inc.
Paperback Lib. Paperback Library, Inc.
Parrish Max Parrish & Co., Ltd.
Parsons, L. Leonard Parsons, Ltd.
Partridge Publications Partridge Publications, Inc.
Paul Kegan Paul, Trench, Trubner & Co., Ltd.
Paul, S. Stanley Paul & Co., Ltd.
Payson & Clarke Payson & Clarke, Inc.
Payson, W. F. William Farquhar Payson Co.
Pearson C. Arthur Pearson, Ltd.
Pellegrini Pellegrini & Co., Ltd.
Pellegrini & Cudahy Pellegrini & Cudahy, Inc., Farrar, Straus, Giroux, Inc.
Pendulum Pendulum Publications, Ltd.
Penguin Penguin Books, Ltd.
Penn Penn Publishing Co.
Permabooks Permabooks, Pocket Books, Inc.
Philosophical Lib. Philosophical Library, Inc.
Phoenix Phoenix Press
Pillar Pillar Publishing Co., Ltd.
Pilot Pilot Press, Ltd.
PB Pocket Books, Inc.
Poe Pub. Poe Publishing Co.
Popular Lib. Popular Library, Inc.
Prentice-Hall Prentice-Hall, Inc.
Price, McGill Price, McGill Publishing Co.
Putnam G. P. Putnam's Sons

Pyramid Pyramid Books, Pyramid Publications, Inc.

Quadriga Quadriga Press, Ltd.
Quality Quality Press, Ltd.
Queensway Queensway Press

Rand Rand McNally & Co.
Random Random House, Inc.
Readers' Club Readers' Club
Readers' Lib. Readers' Library Publishing Co., Queensway Press
Redman Alvin Redman, Ltd.
Regency Regency Press
Regnery Henry Regnery Co.
Reilly & Lee Reilly & Lee Co.
Reinhardt Max Reinhardt, Ltd.
Reinhardt & Evans Reinhardt & Evans, Ltd. (now Max Reinhardt, Ltd.)
Renaissance Renaissance Book Co.
Review of Reviews Review of Reviews Co.
Reynal Reynal & Hitchcock, Inc.
Rich Rich & Cowan, Ltd., Eclipse Press Service, Ltd., Proprietors
Richards Grant Richards, Ltd.
Richards Press Richards Press, Ltd.
Rickey William Rickey & Co. (successors to B. W. Dodge & Co.)
Rider, W. William Rider & Son, Ltd.
Rinehart Rinehart & Co., Inc.
Rivers Alston Rivers, Ltd.
Roberts Roberts Bros.
Robinson & Birch G. Heath Robinson & J. Birch, Ltd.
Robinson, C. C. S. Robinson & Co.
Rockliff Rockliff Pub. Corp., Ltd.
Routledge G. Routledge & Sons, Ltd.
Routledge & Paul Routledge & Kegan Paul, Ltd.
Roy Pubs. Roy Publishers, Inc.
Rudkin Rudkin Press
Ryerson Ryerson Press

S & S Simon & Schuster, Inc.
Saalfield Saalfield Publishing Co.
St. Martin's St. Martin's Press, Inc.
Sands Sands & Co., Publishers, Ltd.
Saunders, Otley Saunders, Otley & Co.
Saunders, S. J. R. S. J. Reginald Saunders & Co.
Scientific Pub. Scientific Publishing Co.
Scribner Charles Scribner's Sons
Sears Sears Publishing Co., Inc.
Secker Martin Secker, Ltd.
Secker & Warburg Martin Secker & Warburg, Ltd.
Seltzer Thomas Seltzer, Ltd.
Selwyn Selwyn & Blout, Ltd.
Shasta Shasta Publishers
Shaylor Harold Shaylor, Ltd.
Sheed Sheed & Ward
Sheldon Sheldon Press
Sherbourne Sherbourne Press
Sheridan Sheridan House, Inc.
Sherman, French Sherman, French & Co.
Shoe Lane Pub. Shoe Lane Publishing Co., J. Coker & Co., Ltd.
Sidgwick Sidgwick & Jackson, Ltd.
Signet Signet Books, New American Library, Inc.
Simpkin Simpkin, Marshall, Hamilton, Kent & Company, Ltd.
Skeffington Skeffington & Son, Ltd.
Sloane William Sloane Associates, Inc.
Small Small, Maynard & Co.
Smart Set Smart Set Publishing Co.
Smith & Durrell Smith & Durrell, Inc.
Smith, Elder Smith, Elder & Co.
Smith, H. Harrison Smith and Robert Haas, Inc.
Smith, R. R. Ray Long and Richard R. Smith, Inc.
Smithers Smithers & Bonellie, Ltd.
Sonnenschein Swan Sonnenschein & Co.
Souvenir Souvenir Press, Ltd.
Sovereign Sovereign House
Spearman, N. Neville Spearman, Ltd.
Spectator Spectator Co., Inc.
Speller Robert Speller Publishing Corp., Inc.
Stackpole Stackpole Sons
Staples Staples & Staples, Ltd. (formerly Staples Books, Ltd.)
Staples Press Staples Press, Ltd.
Stein Stein & Day
Stevens B. F. Stevens & Brown, Ltd.
Stitt Pub. Stitt Publishing Co.
Stockwell Arthur H. Stockwell, Ltd.
Stokes Frederick A. Stokes Co.
Stone, H. S. Herbert S. Stone Co.
Stratford The Stratford Co.
Street Street & Smith Publications, Inc.
Stuart, L. Lyle Stuart, Book Publisher
Sully George Sully & Co.
Sun Dial Sun Dial Press, Inc.
Superior Pub. Superior Publishing Co.
Svenska Borforlaget Aktiebolaget Svenska Borforlaget
Swain Roland Swain Co.
Swan, G. G. Gerald G. Swan, Ltd.
Swift, J. Jonathan Swift, Ltd.

Talbot Talbot Press, Ltd.
Tallis Tallis Press, Ltd.
Taplinger Taplinger Publishing Co., Inc.
Taylor John A. Taylor & Co.

Telegraph Telegraph Press
Thacker Thacker & Co., Ltd.
Thornton J. Thornton & Son
Thorpe & Porter Thorpe & Porter, Ltd.
Tinsley Tinsley Brothers
Todd Todd Publishing Co.
Torquil Torquil & Co.
Tower Tower Press
Transatlantic Transatlantic Arts, Inc.
Transworld Transworld Publishers, Ltd.
Treherne Anthony Treherne & Co., Ltd.
Triangle Triangle Books, Garden City Publishing Co.
Trident Trident Press
Tudor Tudor Publishing Co.
Turner Herbert B. Turner & Co.
Tuttle Charles E. Tuttle Co., Inc.

Univ. of Tex. Press University of Texas Press
Unwin T. Fisher Unwin
U.S. Book U.S. Book Co.

Vallancey The Vallancey Press, Ltd.
Vanguard Vanguard Press, Inc.
Vantage Vantage Press, Inc.
Vaughan Vaughan & Gomme, Alfred A. Knopf
Verschoyle Derek Verschoyle, Ltd., André Deutsch, Ltd.
Victoria Victoria Press
Viking Viking Press, Inc.
Visionary Pub. Visionary Publishing Co.
Vixen Vixen Press

Walker & Co. Walker & Co.
Ward & Downey Ward & Downey
Ward, E. Edmund Ward, Publishers, Ltd. (now Kaye & Ward, Ltd.)
Ward, Lock Ward, Lock & Co., Ltd.
Warne Frederick Warne & Co., Ltd.
Washburn Ives Washburn, Inc.
Watkins John Maurice Watkins
Watt W. J. Watt & Co.
Watt, G. G. Howard Watt
Watts, F. Franklin Watts, Inc.
Weidenfeld George Weidenfeld & Nicolson, Ltd.
Wessels Wessels & Bissell Co.
Westbrook The Arthur Westbrook Co.
Westhouse John Westhouse, Publishers, Ltd.
Westminster Westminster Press
Wetzel Wetzel Publishing Co.
Weybright & Talley Weybright & Talley, Inc.
White F. V. White & Co., Ltd.
White House White House Publishers, Inc.
Whitman Whitman Publishing Co.
Willett Willett, Clark & Co.
Williams The Temple Bar Publishing Co., Ltd. (Lincoln Williams)
Williams & Norgate Williams & Norgate, Ltd.
Wingate Allan Wingate, Publishers, Ltd.
Winston John C. Winston Co., Inc.
Wishart Wishart Books, Ltd.
Witherby H. F. & G. Witherby, Ltd.
Withy Grove Withy Grove Press, Allied Newspapers, Ltd.
World Distributors World Distributors, Ltd.
World Pub. The World Publishing Co.
World Syndicate World Syndicate Publishing House
World's Work The World's Work, Ltd.
Wright & Brown Wright & Brown, Ltd.
Wyn A. A. Wyn, Inc.

Yates Pub. Dennis Yates Publishing Co.
Yoseloff Thomas Yoseloff, Inc.

Zenith Zenith Press
Ziff-Davis The Ziff-Davis Publishing Co.

PART I

A Comprehensive Bibliography of Mystery Fiction, 1841-1967

INTRODUCTION

The Bibliography which follows is a listing of the most important books in the field of mystery, detective and suspense literature from 1841 to the present. Included here are adult novels and short stories in collections. Juvenile novels also appear; sometimes because they have an interest for the adult reader, and sometimes inadvertently when there was no way of distinguishing them from an adult novel. The choice of titles is solely mine, but I have followed the advice of many persons in the field who have been kind enough to make suggestions. Some science-fiction is included, as well as ghost and supernatural stories when they have a murder or mystery background. Some true stories are even included, especially very early ones which had a big influence in the development of the genre.

Every attempt has been made to be as accurate as possible, but mistakes will happen in a work of this size. The job of checking the individual titles was made doubly difficult by the fact that the various sources consulted did not always agree with each other. The *Library of Congress Catalog of Printed Books, The British Museum General Catalogue of Printed Books,* the *British Catalogue of Books,* and the *Cumulated Book Index* among others, disagreed as to the exact listing of titles and dates. Even having a copy of the book in hand did not always solve the problem. Many copies of the books actually examined had neither dates nor publishers in them. This is especially true with certain pocket editions. However, supplements and revisions are planned and readers catching errors and wishing to help with the corrections, are urged to send them to the author or the publisher, and they will be included in future editions.

It will be quite apparent that many of these books listed in the bibliography are no longer available. They are out-of-print, which means that copies may no longer be purchased from the original publishers, many of whom have long since gone out of business. This should pose no problem for the collector however, as many of the first editions are still available in second-hand bookstores and especially in places such as the Salvation Army, Goodwill Industries and St. Vincent De Paul.

In recent years, especially since World War II, pocket editions have become an important part of the book trade. Many of the authors represented here have never written for anything but the paperback trade. These books can be found second-hand in bookstores and salvage stores and pose no real problem of collecting. It should also be noted that paperbacks, like hardcover books, are becoming collector's items and will soon be as difficult to obtain as their counterparts in the hardcover editions. In the Bibliography, in most cases, only one paperback edition is listed. This does not mean that others do not exist. Numbers for the various editions were omitted as editions come and go so fast that they would have been meaningless by the time the book was printed. Authors like Agatha Christie, for instance, have gone through dozens of editions and it would have been impossible to have listed the various changes here. Another reason for the addition of pocket book titles is to indicate that the books can probably be obtained in these editions.

Books have been classified as (D) detective, (M) mystery, and (S) suspense, but these classifications are arbitrary and my own. Purists may argue with them, but they were placed here originally as a guide for librarians who do not have much knowledge of the field. Many of these books appeared at a time when no such labels were attached to them. What is labeled a suspense story might originally have been called a story of adventure or even a love story. Many of the love stories of yesterday have come back into popularity today as Gothics.

There may even be books in this Bibliography which are not mystery, detective or suspense titles. Although every attempt has been made to weed such titles out, it is practically impossible to be sure some have not crept in. Titles, I learned, can be meaningless. Titles with death in them do not have to be mysteries, and titles with love in them can be some of the most thrilling detective stories.

NOTE: Pseudonyms are listed following the author's name. A pseudonym follows the title when (1) an author has used two or more pseudonyms or (2) he has written some books under his own name and some under a pseudonym. When a pseudonym is given for an author and does not follow the title, it may be assumed that all of his books were written under the pseudonym. This form has also been followed in the case of two authors writing under a joint pseudonym.

A Comprehensive Bibliography, 1841-1967

AARONS, EDWARD SIDNEY (S) (Pseudonyms: Paul Ayers, Edward Ronns)
The Art Studio Murders. Macfadden, 1950, 1963
Assignment - Angelina. GM, 1958
Assignment - Ankara. GM, 1961
Assignment - Black Viking. GM, 1967
Assignment - Budapest. GM, 1957
Assignment - Burma Girl. GM, 1961
Assignment - Carlotta Cortez. GM, 1958
Assignment - Cong-Hai Kill. GM, 1958
Assignment - Helene. GM, 1959
Assignment - Karachi. GM, 1962
Assignment - Lili Lamaris. GM, 1959
Assignment - Lowlands. GM, 1961
Assignment - Madelaine. GM, 1958
Assignment - Manchurian Doll. GM, 1963
Assignment - Mara Tirana. GM, 1960
Assignment - Moon Girl. GM, 1967
Assignment - Palermo. GM, 1966
Assignment - School for Spies. GM, 1961
Assignment - Sorrento Siren. GM, 1963
Assignment - Stella Marni. GM, 1957
Assignment - Suicide. GM, 1957
Assignment - Sulu Sea. GM, 1964
Assignment - The Cairo Dancers. GM, 1965
Assignment - The Girl in the Gondola. GM, 1964
Assignment to Disaster. GM, 1955
Assignment - Treason. GM, 1956, 1967
Assignment - Zoraya. GM, 1960
Black Orchid, by Edward Ronns. Panther, 1959
Catspaw Ordeal. GM, 1950
Come Back, My Love. GM, 1953
The Corpse Hangs High, by Edward Ronns. Phoenix, 1939
Dead Heat, by Paul Ayres. Bell, 1950
Death in the Lighthouse, by Edward Ronns. Phoenix, 1938
Death Is My Shadow, by Edward Ronns. Bouregy, 1957; Macfadden, 1965
The Decoy. GM, 1951
The Defenders. GM, 1961; Jenkins, 1962
Don't Cry, Beloved. GM, 1952
Escape to Love. GM, 1957
Gift of Death. McKay, 1948; Macfadden, 1950
Girl on the Run. GM, 1954
Glass Cage, by Edward Ronns. Pyramid, 1964
Hell to Eternity. GM, 1960
I Can't Stop Running, by Edward Ronns. Moring, 1958
Murder Money, by Edward Ronns. Phoenix, 1938
Nightmare. McKay, 1949; Macfadden, 1963
No Place to Live, by Edward Ronns. Macfadden, 1947, 1964
A Passage to Terror. Moring, 1958; GM
Point of Peril, by Edward Ronns. Ace, 1956; Bouregy, 1956; Ryerson, 1956
Say It with Murder, by Edward Ronns. Berkley Pub., 1960
The Sinners. GM, 1954
The State Department Murders, by Edward Ronns. GM, 1958
Terror in the Town, by Edward Ronns. McKay, 1947; Musson, 1947; Invincible, 1948; Macfadden, 1964
They All Ran Away, by Edward Ronns. Graphic, 1955

ABBEY, KIERNAN, pseud; see REILLY, MRS. HELEN KIERNAN

ABBOT, ANTHONY, pseud; see OURSLER, CHARLES FULTON

ABBOTT, A. A., pseud; see SPEWACK, SAMUEL

ABBOTT, ELEANOR HALLOWELL (Full name: Mrs. Eleanor Hallowell Abbott Coburn) (M)
Rainy Week. Dutton, 1921

ABBOTT, ROSA (D)
The Young Detectives, or Which Won? Lee & Shepard, 1870

ABBOTT, SANDRA (S)
The River and the Rose. Signet, 1967

ABDULLAH, ACHMED, pseud; see ROMANOFF, ALEXANDER NICHOLAYEVITCH

ABRAHAMS, DORIS CAROLINE (D) (Pseudonym: Caryl Brahms)
A Bullet in the Ballet. Doubleday, Doran, 1938; Joseph, M., 1937
Casino for Sale; see Murder à la Strogonoff
Murder à la Strogonoff, with S. J. Simon. Doubleday, Doran, 1938 (English title: Casino for Sale. Joseph, M., 1938)

ABRAHAMS, ROBERT DAVID (M)
Death After Lunch. Phoenix, 1941
Death in 1-2-3. Phoenix, 1942

ABRO, BEN (S)
Assassination. Morrow, 1963; Crest, 1965 (English title: July 14 Assassination. Cape, 1963)

ABSINTHE, PÈRE, pseud; see KELLY, GEORGE C.

ACHESON, EDWARD CAMPION (D)
Dead Men Can't Walk; see Grammarian's Funeral
Grammarian's Funeral. Macrae, Smith, 1935; Hutchinson, 1935. (Serial title: "Dead Men Can't Walk")
Murder by Suggestion. Hutchinson, 1933
Murder to Hounds. Harcourt, 1939; Harrap, 1941
Red Herring. Morrow, 1932

ACLAND, ALICE
Person of Discretion. Collins, 1958

ACRE, STEPHEN, pseud; see GRUBER, FRANK

ADAIR, DENNIS, pseud; see CRONIN, BERNARD

ADAM, RUTH (Mrs. Kenneth Adam) (M)
Fetch Her Away. Chapman, 1954
I'm Not Complaining. Chapman, 1938; Liveright, 1938
Look Who's Talking. Muller, 1960
Murder in the Home Guard. Chapman, 1942
Set to Partners. Chapman, 1947
So Sweet a Changeling. Chapman, 1939
There Needs No Ghost. Chapman, 1939
War on Saturday Week. Chapman, 1937; Lippincott, 1937

ADAMS, CHRISTOPHER (S)
Amateur Agent. Boardman, T. V., 1964

ADAMS, CLEVE FRANKLIN (M) (Pseudonyms: Franklin Charles, John Spain)
And Sudden Death. Dutton, 1940 (Magazine title: "Homicide Honolulu Bound")
The Black Door. Dutton, 1941
Borderline Cases; see Contraband
Contraband. Knopf, 1950; Signet, 1951 (English title: Borderline Cases. Cassell, 1950)
The Crooking Finger. Reynal, 1944
Death at the Dam. Cassell, 1945
Death Is Like That, by John Spain. Dutton, 1943
Decoy. Dutton, 1941
Dig Me a Grave, by John Spain. Dutton, 1942
Escape to Death, by Franklin Charles. Collins, 1951
Evil Star, by John Spain. Dutton, 1944; Swan, G. G., 1950
Gallows for a Fool, by Franklin Charles. Collins, 1952
Girl in Shadow, by Franklin Charles. Collins, 1955
"Homicide Honolulu Bound"; see And Sudden Death
Maid for Murder, by Franklin Charles. Collins, 1951
Mark of Kane, by Franklin Charles. Collins, 1950
One Night to Kill, by Franklin Charles. Collins, 1950
Perchance to Kill, by Franklin Charles. Collins, 1954
Play with Death, by Franklin Charles. Collins, 1953
The Private Eye. Reynal, 1942; Grosset, 1944; Signet, 1964
Sabotage. Dutton, 1940; New Amer. Lib., 1952
She'll Love You Dead, by Franklin Charles. Collins, 1950
Stop That Man, by Franklin Charles. Collins, 1954

Storm in an Inkpot, by Franklin Charles. Collins, 1949
The Stranger Came Back, by Franklin Charles. Collins, 1953
Up Jumped the Devil. Reynal, 1943
The Vice Czar Murders, by Franklin Charles. Funk, W., 1941
What Price Murder. Dutton, 1942

ADAMS, CLIFTON (S)
Death's Sweet Song. GM, 1955
Whom Gods Destroy. GM, 1953

ADAMS, ELIHU (M)
Operation Homicide. Mill, 1947

ADAMS, EUSTACE LANE (M)
Death Charter. Coward, 1943; Crowther, 1945
Gambler's Throw. Dial, 1930; Hamilton, 1932; Grosset, 1932

ADAMS, FRANK DAVIS (S)
The Life and Times of Buckshot South. Dutton, 1959

ADAMS, FRANK RAMSAY (M)
Help Yourself to Happiness. Macaulay, 1929; Newnes, 1929
The Long Night. Paul, S., 1932

ADAMS, FREDERICK UPHAM (M)
Bottom of the Well. Dillingham, G. W., 1906
The Kidnapped Millionaires. Dillingham, G. W., 1906

ADAMS, GERALD; see FITZSIMMONS, CORTLAND

ADAMS, HERBERT (M-D) (Pseudonym: Jonathan Gray)
The Araway Oath. Collins, 1942
The Black Death. Collins, 1939, 1940, 1941
The Bluff! Collins, 1938
The Body in the Bunker. Collins, 1935; Lippincott, 1935
By Order of the Five. Methuen, 1925; Newnes, 1930
Caroline Ormesby's Crime. Lippincott, 1929; Methuen, 1930
The Case of the Stolen Bridegroom. Collins, 1940
The Chief Witness. Collins, 1940, 1941
Comrade Jill. Methuen, 1926; Lippincott, 1926
The Crime in the Dutch Garden. Lippincott, 1930; Methuen, 1931
The Crime Wave at Little Cornford. MacDonald & Co., 1948
The Crooked Lip. Lippincott, 1926; Methuen, 1926
Damned Spot. Collins, 1938, 1939, 1940
The Dean's Daughters. MacDonald & Co., 1950
Death of a Viewer. MacDonald & Co., 1958
Death off the Fairway. Collins, 1936
Death on the First Tee. MacDonald & Co., 1957
Diamonds Are Trump. MacDonald & Co., 1947
The Empty Bed. Lippincott, 1928; Methuen, 1928; Grosset, 1930
Fate Laughs. Collins, 1935; Lippincott, 1935
Four Winds. Collins, 1944
The Golden Ape. Lippincott, 1930; Methuen, 1931
The Golf House Murder. Lippincott, 1933 (English title: John Brand's Will. Methuen, 1933)
John Brand's Will; see The Golf House Murder
The Judas Kiss. MacDonald & Co., 1955
The Knife. Collins, 1938, 1955
Lady So Innocent. Methuen, 1932
Murder Without Risk! Lippincott, 1936
Mystery and Minette. Collins, 1934, 1938; Lippincott, 1934
The Nineteenth Hole Mystery. Collins, 1939, 1940, 1941
Oddways. Lippincott, 1929; Methuen, 1931
The Old Jew Mystery. Collins, 1936
One to Play. MacDonald & Co., 1949
The Owl, by Jonathan Gray. Harrap, 1937; Lippincott, 1937
The Paulton Plot. Lippincott, 1931; Methuen, 1932
The Queen's Gate Mystery. Grosset, 1927; Lippincott, 1927; Methuen, 1927
The Queen's Mate. Lippincott, 1931; Methuen, 1932
Roger Bennion's Double. Collins, 1941
Rogues Fall Out. Lippincott, 1928; Methuen, 1928
Safety Last. Muller, 1936
Secret of Bogey House. Methuen, 1924; Lippincott, 1925
Signal for Invasion. Collins, 1942
A Single Hair. Collins, 1937
Sleeping Draught. MacDonald & Co., 1951
Slippery Dick. MacDonald & Co., 1954
Sloane Square Mystery. Methuen, 1925; Dial, 1926
Spectre in Brown. MacDonald & Co., 1953
Stab in the Back. Collins, 1941
Strange Murder of Hatton, K. C. Lippincott, 1933
Victory Song. Collins, 1943
Welcome Home. MacDonald & Co., 1946
Woman in Black. Lippincott, 1932; Methuen, 1933

A Word of Six Letters. Collins, 1936
Writing on the Wall. Collins, 1945

ADAMS, LETA ZOE (M)
The Mirror Murder. Phoenix, 1937

ADAMS, NATHAN (S)
The Fifth Horseman. Random, 1967

ADAMS, SAMUEL HOPKINS (D)
Average Jones. Bobbs, 1911; Grosset, 1913; Palmer, F. N., 1913
Flying Death. McClure, 1908
Secret of Lonesome Cove. Bobbs, 1912; Hodder, 1913; Grosset, 1915

ADAMS, SHIPLEY (M-D)
Money by Menaces. Fiction House, 1948
Murder in the First Person. Boardman, T. V., 1948
Murder Unsolved. Boardman, T. V., 1947
Murder Well Begun. Boardman, T. V., 1950

ADAMS, WILLIAM T. (M)
Living Too Fast, or, The Confessions of a Bank Officer. Dillingham, G. W., 1876
Way of the World. Lee & Shepard, 1867

ADAMS, J. CLEFT-; see CLEFT-ADDAMS, J.

ADDIS, ERIC ELRINGTON (M-D)
(Pseudonym: Peter Drax)
Crime to Music; see Tune to a Corpse
Crime Within Crime; see Death by Two Hands
Death by Two Hands. Hutchinson, 1937 (U.S. title: Crime Within Crime. Appleton-Century, 1938)
Tune to a Corpse. Hutchinson, 1938 (U.S. title: Crime to Music. Appleton-Century, 1939)

ADDIS, HUGH (M)
Dark Voyage. Dodd, 1944; Jarrolds, 1947
Night over the Wood. Dodd, 1943; Jarrolds, 1944

ADDISCOMB, JOHN, pseud; see HUNTER, JOHN

ADDISON, H. R. (M)
Diary of a Judge, Being Trials of Trial. Ward, Lock, 1860

ADDISON, IRVING BACHELLER, pseud; see BACHELLER, IRVIN A.

ADE, GEORGE (M)
Bang! Bang! Sears, 1928

ADEE, DAIRD GRAHAM (M)
No. 19 State Street. Cassell, 1888

ADKINS, CLEO (D)
Case of the Ebony Queen. Arcadia, 1955

ADYE, SIR JOHN (M)
A Flash of Lightning. Methuen, 1927

AFFORD, MAX (D-M)
Blood on His Hands. Long, 1936
The Dead Are Blind. Long, 1937
Death's Mannikins. Appleton-Century, 1937; Long, 1937
Fly by Night. Long, 1942
The Owl of Darkness. Angus, 1942

AFTEREM, GEORGE (M)
Silent Threads. Cupples, 1885

AIKEN, ALBERT W. (D)
California Detective; or, The Witches of New York. Beadle, 1878
Chin Chin, Chinese Detective. Westbrook, 1927
Joe Phoenix, Private Detective. Westbrook, 1927
Joe Phoenix, the Police Spy. Westbrook, 1927
Spotter-Detective; or, The Girls of New York. Beadle, Vol. III, No. 27
Wolves of New York. Westbrook, 1927

AIKEN, CONRAD (M)
King Coffin. Dent, 1935; Scribner, 1935

AIKEN, JOAN (S)
Beware of the Bouquet. Doubleday, 1966
Dark Interval. Doubleday, 1967; Dell, 1968
The Fortune Hunters. Doubleday, 1965; Bantam, 1967
Hate Begins at Home. Gollancz, 1967
The Silence of Herondale. Doubleday, 1964; Ace, 1965; Gollancz, 1965

AIKEN, RALPH (M)
The Ghost Hunters. McBride, 1934

AINSWORTH, CYRUS (M)
The Disappearance of Nicholson. Ousley, J., 1908

AINSWORTH, ED (M)
Death Cues the Pageant. Arcadia, 1954

AINSWORTH, HARRIET
Shadow on the Water. Hodder, 1958

AINSWORTH, WILLIAM HARRISON (M)
The Lancashire Witches. Privately printed, 1849; Nelson, 1937

AIRD, CATHERINE, pseud; see Mc-INTOSH, KIM HAMILTON

ALAN, MARJORIE, pseud; see BUMPUS, DORIS MARJORIE

ALAN, ROY (M)
My Bonnie Lies Under the Sea. Jenkins, 1964

ALBERT, JEAN; see RENARD, MAURICE

ALBERT, MARVIN H. (S) (Pseudonyms: Nick Quarry, Anthony Rome)
The Girl with No Place to Hide, by Nick Quarry. GM, 1960
The Hoods Came Calling, by Nick Quarry. GM, 1958
The Lady in Cement, by Anthony Rome. PB, 1960
Miami Mayhem, by Anthony Rome. PB, 1960 (Also published as: Tony Rome. Dell, 1967)
No Chance in Hell, by Nick Quarry. GM, 1960
Party Girl. GM, 1958
The Pink Panther. Bantam, 1964
Some Die Hard, by Nick Quarry. GM, 1961
Till It Hurts, by Nick Quarry. GM, 1960
Tony Rome; see Miami Mayhem
The Trail of a Tramp, by Nick Quarry. GM, 1959

ALBRAND, MARTHA, pseud; see LOEWENGARD, HEIDI HUBERTA FREYBE

ALDANOV, MARK (S)
For Thee the Best. Cape, 1947

ALDERSON, ALFRED JAMES (M)
Crime of Wilfred Hanson. Stockwell, 1942

ALDERSON, JAMES (M)
Harding Mystery. Grey Walls, 1949

ALDHOUSE, ERIC (M)
The Crime at Quay Inn. Allan, P., 1934

ALDING, PETER (S)
The C.I.D. Room. Long, 1967

ALDIS, MRS. DOROTHY KEELEY (M)
Murder in a Haystack. Farrar & Rinehart, 1931

ALDRICH, EARL AUGUSTUS (M)
(Pseudonym: A. B. Leonard)
The Judson Murder Case. Clode, 1933

ALDRICH, RHODA TRUAX (M) (Pseudonym: Rhoda Truax)
The Accident Ward Mystery. Little, 1937

ALDRICH, THOMAS BAILEY (M)
Out of His Head. Carleton, 1862
Stillwater Tragedy. Houghton, 1880

ALDRIDGE, JAMES (S)
A Captive in the Land. Hamilton, H., 1962; Doubleday, 1963
The Diplomat. Bodley Head, 1949; Little, 1950
The Hunter. Bodley Head, 1950; Little, 1950
The Last Exile. Hamilton, H., 1961; Doubleday, 1961
The Sea Eagle. Joseph, M., 1944; Little, 1944
Signed with Their Honour. Joseph, M., 1942; Little, 1942
Statesman's Game. Doubleday, 1966 (Sequel to A Captive in the Land)

ALEXANDER, COLIN JAMES (M)
(Pseudonym: Simon Jay)
Death of a Skin Diver. Doubleday, 1964
Hank of Hair. Harper & Row, 1964

ALEXANDER, DAVID (M-D)
Bloodstain. Lippincott, 1961; Longmans, 1961; Boardman, T. V., 1962
Dead, Man, Dead. Lippincott, 1959; Boardman, T. V., 1960; Dell, 1960
Death of Daddy-O. Boardman, T. V., 1960; Lippincott, 1960
Death of Humpty-Dumpty. Random, 1957; Boardman, T. V., 1959 (Also published with Another Man's Murder, by Mignon G. Eberhart. Published for the Detective Book Club by Black, 1957.)
Die Little Goose. Random, 1956. (Also published with Death Keeps a Secret, by Clarence Buddington Kelland. Published for the Detective Book Club by Black, 1956.)
Hangman's Dozen. Boardman, T. V., 1961; Roy Pubs., 1961
Hush-a-bye Murder. Random, 1957; Boardman, T. V., 1958 (Also published with Poor Harriet, by Elizabeth Fenwick and Death of an Ambassador, by Manning Coles. Published for the Detective Book Club by Black, 1957.)
Madhouse in Washington Square. Lippincott, 1958; Boardman, T. V., 1959; Collier, 1962
Most Men Don't Kill. Random, 1951
Murder in Black and White. Random, 1951
The Murder of Whistler's Brother. Random, 1956; Bantam
Murder Points a Finger. Random, 1950; Boardman, T. V., 1955
Paint the Town Black. Random, 1955; Boardman, T. V., 1957
Pennies from Hell. Lippincott, 1960 (Also published with Murder: One,

Two, Three, by John Creasey and Death-Wish Green, by Francis Grane. Published for the Detective Book Club by Black, 1960)
Shoot a Sitting Duck. Random, 1955; Bantam, 1957; Boardman, T. V., 1957
Terror on Broadway. Random, 1954

ALEXANDER, GEORGIA; see ALEXANDER, GRACE

ALEXANDER, GRACE CAROLINE and GEORGIA ALEXANDER (M)
Prince Cinderella. Bobbs, 1921

ALEXANDER, HOLMES M. (M)
Shall Do No Murder. Regnery, 1959

ALEXANDER, IAN (M)
The Disappearance of Archibald Forsyth. Hutchinson, 1933

ALEXANDER, IRENE (M)
Crooked Alley. Penn, 1933; Burt, 1934
Ninth Week. Penn, 1935; Burt, 1936
Revenge Can Wait. Allen, T., 1941; Putnam, 1941
Villa Caprice. Penn, 1932; Burt, 1933

ALEXANDER, JOHN, pseud; see VLASTO, JOHN ALEXANDER

ALEXANDER, RUTH (M)
Ghost Train. Arrowsmith, 1927 (Novelization of play by Arnold Ridley)

ALGER, HORATIO, JR. (D)
Dan, the Detective. Carleton, 1884
$500; or, Jacob Marlow's Secret. Donohue, 1890

ALGREN, NELSON (S)
The Man with the Golden Arm. Doubleday, 1949; Crest, 1964
The Neon Wilderness. Doubleday, 1947; McClelland, 1947; Berkley Pub., 1965
Never Come Morning, Harper, 1941; Musson, 1942

ALINGTON, CYRIL ARGENTINE (M)
(Pseudonym: S. C. Westerham)
Archdeacons Afloat. Faber, 1946; Ryerson, 1946
Archdeacons Ashore. Faber, 1947
Blackmail in Blankshire. Faber, 1949
Crime on the Kennet. Collins, 1940
Gold and Gaiters. Faber, 1950
Midnight Wireless. MacDonald & Co., 1947
Mixed Bags, by S. C. Westerham. Christopher, 1929
Mr. Evans: A Cricketo Detective Story. Macmillan, 1922
Nabob's Jewel. Faber, 1953
Ten Crowded Hours. MacDonald & Co., 1944

ALLAIN, MARCEL (D)
Bulldog and Rats. Paul, S., 1928
The Exploits of Juve, with Pierre Souvestre. Paul, S., 1916
Fantômas, with Pierre Souvestre. Paul, S., 1915
Fantômas Captured. McKay, 1926; Paul, S., 1926
Juve in the Dock. Paul, S., 1925; McKay, 1926; Burt, 1927
The Limb of Satan, with Pierre Souvestre. Paul, S., 1924
The Long Arm of Fantômas, with Pierre Souvestre. Macaulay, 1924
The Lord of Terror. McKay, 1925; Paul, S., 1925; Burt, 1926
Messengers of Evil, with Pierre Souvestre. Brentano, 1917; Paul, S., 1917, 1926; McKay, 1926
A Nest of Spies, with Pierre Souvestre. Paul, S., 1917; McKay, 1926
The Revenge of Fantômas. McKay, 1927; Paul, S., 1927
A Royal Prisoner, with Pierre Souvestre. Paul, S., 1919
Slippery as Sin, with Pierre Souvestre. Paul, S., 1920
The Yellow Document; or, Fantômas of Berlin. Paul, S., 1920; Brentano, 1919

ALLAN, A. W. (M)
Devil's Dive: A Tale of Four Bad'uns. Dodd, Eyton, 1910

ALLAN, DENNIS, pseud; see DENNISTON, ELEANORE

ALLAN, FRANCIS K. (M)
First Come, First Kill. McClelland, 1945; Reynal, 1945
The Invisible Bridge. McClelland, 1947; Reynal, 1947

ALLAN, LUKE, pseud; see AMY, WILLIAM LACEY

ALLARDYCE, PAULA, pseud; see TORDAY, URSULA

ALLEN, A. J. (M)
Good Evening, Everyone. Hutchinson, 1929

ALLEN, ADDISON J. (M)
New England Gothic. Chilton, 1960 (Also published as: Thunder over South Parish. Dell, 1964)

ALLEN, AUSTIN (M-D)
The Dead Mouse. Bles, 1930
The Live Wire. Bles, 1931
The Loose Rib. Bles, 1932; Kinsey, 1933
Menace to Mrs. Kershaw. Bles, 1930; Harper, 1930; Burr, 1932

ALLEN, CHARLES GRANT BLAIR-FINDIE; see ALLEN, GRANT

ALLEN, CLIFFORD (M)
Dark Places. Redman, 1958

ALLEN, ELISABETH (S)
This Tangled Web. Bouregy, 1966

ALLEN, ERIC (M) (Pseudonym: Eric Allen-Ballard)
Canaries Also Sing. Hammond, 1960
Death on Delivery. Hammond, 1958
The Man Who Chose Death. Hammond, 1959
Passport to Murder; see Perilous Passport
Perilous Passport. Hammond, 1958 (U.S. title: Passport to Murder)

ALLEN, ERICKA VAUGHAN (S)
Voices in the Wind. Signet, 1967

ALLEN, F. (D)
Whitechapel Murder. Ogilvie

ALLEN, GRANT (Full name: Charles Grant Blairfindie Allen) (M)
African Millionaire. Richards, 1897
The Beckoning Hand and Other Stories. Chatto, 1887
Hilda Wade. Richards, 1900
Ivan Greet's Masterpiece. Chatto, 1893
The Laws of Death. Chatto, 1893
Miss Cayley's Adventure. Richards, 1899
This Mortal Coil. Chatto, 1887
Twelve Tales. Richards, 1899
Under Sealed Orders. Collier, 1894

ALLEN, HERBERT WARNER (M-D)
Death Fungus. Constable, 1937
Mr. Clerihew: Wine Merchant. Methuen, 1933
Trent's Last Case, with E. C. Bentley, Nelson, 1913 (U.S. title: The Woman in Black. Century, 1913; PB, 1944; Ballantine, 1963)
Trent's Own Case, with E. C. Bentley. Constable, 1936; Knopf, 1936; Grosset
The Uncounted Hour. Constable, 1936
The Woman in Black; see Trent's Last Case

ALLEN, HUGH, pseud; see MORRIS, CHARLES

ALLEN, LESLIE (M)
Murder in the Rough. Five Star, 1946

ALLEN, MABEL ESTHER (M)
Murder at the Flood. Paul, S., 1957

ALLEN, MARCUS and ANNE FULLER (M)
Blood on the Common. Dutton, 1943
Death on the Outer Shoal. Dutton, 1934

ALLEN-BALLARD, ERIC, pseud; see ALLEN, ERIC

ALLERTON, MARK, pseud; see CAMERON, WILLIAM ERNEST

ALLERTON, MARY, pseud; see GOVAN, CHRISTINE NOBLE

ALLINGHAM, MARGERY (Mrs. P. Youngman Carter) (M-S-D)
The Beckoning Lady; see The Estate of the Beckoning Lady
The Black Dudley Murder. Doubleday, Doran, 1929; Macfadden, 1962 (English title: The Crime at Black Dudley. Jarrolds, 1929; Penguin, 1960; Heinemann, 1967)
Black Plumes. Doubleday, Doran, 1940; Heinemann, 1940; Penguin
Cargo of Eagles. Chatto, 1967 (Completed by P. Youngman Carter)
The Case Book of Mr. Campion. American Mercury, 1947
The Case of the Late Pig. Doubleday, Doran, 1937; Hodder, 1937; Penguin
The China Governess. Doubleday, 1962; Macfadden, 1962; Chatto, 1963
Coroner's Pidgin; see Pearls Before Swine
Crime and Mr. Campion. Doubleday, 1959
The Crime at Black Dudley; see The Black Dudley Murder
Dancers in Mourning. Doubleday, Doran, 1937; Heinemann, 1937; Macfadden, 1962 (Also published as: Who Killed Chloe? Avon, 1943)
Deadly Duo. Doubleday, 1949; Avon, 1961 (English title: Take Two at Bedtime. World's Work, 1950)
Death of a Ghost. Doubleday, Doran, 1934; Heinemann, 1934; Penguin, 1960; Dell; Macfadden
The Estate of the Beckoning Lady. Doubleday, 1955; Macfadden (English title: The Beckoning Lady. Chatto, 1955; Penguin, 1960)
Fashion in Shrouds. Doubleday, Doran, 1938; Heinemann, 1938
The Fear Sign; see The Kingdom of Death
Flowers for the Judge. Doubleday, Doran, 1936; Heinemann, 1936; Avon, 1961; Macfadden, 1966
The Gyrth Chalice Mystery. Doubleday, Doran, 1931; Macfadden, 1963 (English title: Look to the Lady. Jarrolds, 1931, Penguin, 1960)

Hide My Eyes; see Tether's End
The Kingdom of Death. Doubleday, Doran, 1933 (English title: Sweet Danger. Heinemann, 1933; Penguin, 1961. Also published as: The Fear Sign. Macfadden, 1961)
Look to the Lady; see The Gyrth Chalice Mystery
The Mind Readers. Morrow, 1965; Macfadden, 1967
Mr. Campion and Others. Doubleday, Doran, 1939; Heinemann, 1939, 1967; Penguin
Mr. Campion: Criminologist. Doubleday, Doran, 1937; Macfadden, 1964
More Work for the Undertaker. Heinemann, 1948; Doubleday, 1949; Penguin, 1961; Macfadden, 1962
The Mysterious Mr. Campion: An Allingham Omnibus. Chatto, 1963
Mystery Mile. Doubleday, Doran, 1929; Jarrolds, 1929; Macfadden, 1960; Penguin
No Love Lost. Doubleday, 1954; Macfadden, 1962; Penguin
Pearls Before Swine. Doubleday, Doran, 1945; Macfadden, 1963 (English title: Coroner's Pidgin. Heinemann, 1945; Penguin, 1950)
Police at the Funeral. Heinemann, 1931; Doubleday, Doran, 1932; Penguin, 1960; Macfadden, 1963
Six Against Scotland Yard, by Margery Allingham et al. Doubleday, Doran, 1936 (English title: Six Against the Yard. Selwyn, 1936)
Six Against the Yard; see Six Against Scotland Yard
Sweet Danger; see The Kingdom of Death
Take Two at Bedtime; see Deadly Duo
Ten Were Missing; see Tether's End
Tether's End. Doubleday, 1958 (English Title: Hide My Eyes. Chatto, 1958. Also published as: Ten Were Missing. Dell, 1961; Avon)
Three Cases for Mr. Campion. Doubleday, 1961
The Tiger in the Smoke. Chatto, 1952; Doubleday, 1952; Avon, 1961
Traitor's Purse. Doubleday, Doran, 1941; Penguin, 1941
Who Killed Chloe?; see Dancers in Mourning
The White Castle Mystery. Jarrolds, 1928

ALLISON, WILLIAM (M) (Pseudonym: "Blinkhoalie")
Alias Richard Power. Doubleday, Page, 1921
Blairmount. International Horse Agency & Exchange Ltd., 1909
A Secret of the Sea. Doubleday, Page, 1920
Turnstile of Night. Doubleday, Page, 1920

ALLSOP, KENNETH (M)
The Leopard-Paw Orchid. McClelland, 1954; Quality, 1954

ALNER, JAMES Z. C. (M)
The Capital Murder. Knopf, 1932; Hurst, 1933

ALROY, LIONEL (S)
Shut Out the Sun. Green, 1955; Longmans, 1955

ALTER, ROBERT EDMUND (M)
Carny Kill. GM, 1966
The Dark Keep. Putnam, 1962
Red Fathom. Avon, 1967
Swamp Sister. GM, 1961

AMBLER, ERIC (S) (Joint pseudonym with Charles Rodda: Eliot Reed)
Ability to Kill and Other Pieces. Bodley Head, 1963
Background to Danger. Knopf, 1937; Triangle, 1943; PB, 1945 (English title: Uncommon Danger. Hodder, 1937; Pan, 1949)
Cause for Alarm. Hodder, 1938; Knopf, 1939; Sun Dial, 1940; Bantam, 1964
Charter to Danger, by Eliot Reed. Sun Dial, 1940; Collins, 1954
A Coffin for Dimitrios. Knopf, 1939; Sun Dial, 1940 (English title: Mask for Dimitrios. Hodder, 1939; Dell, 1964)
Dark Frontier. Hodder, 1936
Dirty Story. Atheneum, 1967
Double Decker: Two Complete Spy Novels. Ryerson, 1945; World Pub., 1945
Epitaph for a Spy. Hodder, 1938; Pan, 1949; Knopf, 1952
Intrigue: Four Great Spy Novels. Knopf, 1943, 1960
The Intriguers: A Second Omnibus. Knopf, 1965
Journey into Fear. Knopf, 1940; PB, 1942; Dell, 1964; Hodder
Judgment on Deltchev. Hodder, 1951; Knopf, 1952; Bantam, 1964; PB
A Kind of Anger. Atheneum, 1964; Bodley Head, 1964; Bantam
The Light of Day. Heinemann, 1962; Knopf, 1963; Bantam, 1964
The Maras Affair, by Eliot Reed. Doubleday, 1953; Permabooks, 1955
Mask for Dimitrios; see A Coffin for Dimitrios
The Night Comers; see State of Siege
A Passage of Arms. Heinemann, 1959; Knopf, 1959; Bantam, 1961
Passport to Panic, by Eliot Reed. Collins, 1957
The Schirmer Inheritance. Heinemann, 1953; Knopf, 1953

Skytip, by Eliot Reed. Doubleday, 1950
State of Siege. Knopf, 1956; Bantam (English title: The Night Comers. Heinemann, 1956)
Tender to Danger, by Eliot Reed. Doubleday, 1951 (English title: Tender to Moonlight. Hodder, 1952)
Tender to Moonlight; see Tender to Danger
Three Great Spy Novels. Random, 1942
To Catch a Spy. Bodley Head, 1964; Atheneum, 1965
Uncommon Danger; see Background to Danger

AMES, CLYDE (S)
Gorgonzola, Won't You Please Come Home? Lancer, 1967

AMES, DELANO L. (M-D)
The Body on Page One. Hodder, 1951; Rinehart, 1951
A Coffin for Christopher. Washburn, 1954 (Also published as: Crime Out of Mind. Washburn, 1956. English title: Crime, Gentleman, Please. Hodder, 1954)
Corpse Diplomatique. Hodder, 1950; Rinehart, 1951
Crime, Gentleman, Please; see A Coffin for Christopher
Crime Out of Mind; see A Coffin for Christopher
Death of a Fellow Traveller. Hodder, 1950; Rinehart, 1950
Doubled Bed on Olympus. Hodder, 1936; Grayson, 1938
For Old Crime's Sake. Lippincott, 1959 (English title: Lucky Jane. Hodder, 1959)
He Found Himself Murdered. Swan, G. G., 1947
Landscape with Corpse. Hodder, 1955; Washburn, 1955
Lucky Jane; see For Old Crime's Sake
The Man in the Tricorn Hat. Methuen, 1960; Regnery, 1966
Man with Three Chins. Methuen, 1965
Man with the Three Jaguars. Methuen, 1961; Regnery, 1967
Murder Begins at Home. Hodder, 1949; Rinehart, 1950
Murder, Maestro, Please. Hodder, 1952; Rinehart, 1952
No Mourning for the Matador. Hodder, 1953; Washburn, 1953
No Traveller Returns. Nicholson, 1934
She Shall Have Murder. Hodder, 1948; Rinehart, 1949
She Wouldn't Say Who. Hodder, 1957; Washburn, 1958
They Journey by Night. Hodder, 1932
Uneasily to Bed. Grayson, 1934

AMES, JENNIFER, pseud; see GREIG, MAYSIE

AMES, LESLIE (S)
Bride of Donnybrook. Arcadia, 1966
The Hidden Chapel. Arcadia, 1967

AMHERST, FRANCES; see WOODWARD, HELEN

AMIS, KINGSLEY (M)
The Anti-Death League. Gollancz, 1966; Harcourt, 1966; Ballantine, 1967

AMOS, ALAN, pseud; see KNIGHT, KATHLEEN MOORE

AMOS, RUSSELL BOOTH (M)
Perhaps I Look Simple. Longmans, 1960
Wasp in the Web. Longmans, 1961

AMY, WILLIAM LACEY (M-D) (Pseudonym: Luke Allan)
Beyond the Locked Door. Jenkins, 1938
The Black Opal. Arrowsmith, 1935
Blue Pete: Detective. Jenkins, 1928
Case of the Open Drawer. Arrowsmith, 1936
The Dark Spot. Arrowsmith, 1932
Five for One. Arrowsmith, 1934
The Fourth Dagger. Arrowsmith, 1932
The Ghost Murder. Jenkins, 1937
The Jungle Crime. Arrowsmith, 1932
The Man on the Twenty-fourth Floor. Jenkins, 1937
The Masked Stranger. Arrowsmith, 1930
Murder at Midnight. Arrowsmith, 1931
Murder at the Club. Arrowsmith, 1933
Scotland Yard Takes a Holiday. Arrowsmith, 1934

ANDERS, T. J. (S)
Behind the Door. Philosophical Lib., 1966

ANDERSCH, ALFRED (S)
Flight to Afar. Coward, 1958; Gollancz, 1958; Pantheon, 1958
The Redhead. Heinemann, 1961; Pantheon, 1961; Popular Lib., 1962

ANDERSON, BETTY (D) (Pseudonym: Claudia Canyon)
The Junior League Murders. Arcadia, 1954

ANDERSON, EDWARD (S)
Thieves Like Us. Lippincott, 1937; Bantam

ANDERSON, FREDERICK IRVING (D)
Adventures of the Infallible Godahl. Crowell, 1914
The Book of Murder. Dutton, 1930
The Notorious Sophie Lang. Heinemann, 1925

ANDERSON, JAN (S-Gothic)
Storm Castle. Pyramid, 1967

ANDERSON, OLIVER (D)
Random All Round. Barker, 1960
Random at Random. Barker, 1959
Random Mating. Barker, 1956
Random Rapture. Barker, 1958
Random Rendezvous. Barker, 1955
Ripe for the Plucking. Barker, 1961
Smiling Tigers. Barker, 1953
Thorn in the Flesh. Barker, 1954

ANDERSON, POUL WILLIAM (M)
(Pseudonym: Winston P. Sanders)
Murder Bound. Macmillan, 1962
Murder in Black Letters. Macmillan, 1960
Perish by the Sword. Macmillan, 1959

ANDERSON, WALTER WADSLEY (M)
Kill One, Kill Two. McClelland, 1940; Morrow, 1940

ANDOVER, HENRY (D)
Death on the Pack Road. Eyre, 1931

ANDREAS, FRED (M)
Death at Heel. Holt, H., 1933
In Court; see The Trial of Gregor Kaska
Theatre Crime. Bles, 1932
The Trial of Gregor Kaska. Holt, H., 1931 (English title: In Court. Bles, 1931; Mellifont, 1938)

ANDREWS, CHARLTON (D)
The Affair of the Malacca Stick. Washburn, 1937
The Affair of the Syrian Dagger. Washburn, 1937
The Butterfly Murders. Sears, 1932

ANDREZEL, PIERRE, pseud; see BLIXEN-FINECKE, BARONESS KAREN CHRISTINE

ANGELLOTTI, MARION POLK (M)
Three Black Bags. Century, 1922

ANGUS, DOUGLAS (M)
Death on Jerusalem Road. Random, 1963
The Green and the Burning. Hale, R., 1958
The Ivy Trap. Bobbs, 1959; Crest, 1961
The Lions Fed the Tigers. Allen, T., 1958; Houghton, 1958

ANKER, JENS, pseud; see HANSON, ROBERT

ANNESLEY, MICHAEL (S)
An Agent Intervenes. Paul, S., 1944
Fenton of the Foreign Office; see Room 14
The Lights That Did Not Fail. Paul, S., 1949
The Missing Agent: A Secret Service Story. Harrap, 1938
Room 14. Harrap, 1935 (Also published as: Fenton of the Foreign Office. Speller, 1937)
Spies Abounding. Paul, S., 1945
Spies Against the Reich. Harrap, 1940
Spies in Action. Harrap, 1937
Spies in the Web. Harrap, 1936
The Spy Corner. Paul, S., 1948
Spy-Counter Spy. Paul, S., 1948
Spy Island. Paul, S., 1950
Suicide Spies. Paul, S., 1944
They Won't Lie Down. Paul, S., 1947
The Unknown Agent. Harrap, 1940
The Vanished Vice-Consul. Harrap, 1939

ANONYMOUS (M)
Kinks; Meaning Love, Money. Mystery House, 1927

———. (M)
Manuscript in the Red Box. Lane, 1903

———. (D)
The Smiling Corpse. Farrar & Rinehart, 1935

ANSLE, DOROTHY PHOEBE (Mrs. Francis I. Keogh) (S) (Pseudonym: Vicky Lancaster)
Royal Deputy. Hale, R., 1957

ANSON, LINDSAY (D)
Even Doctors Die; see Such Natural Deaths
Hung by an Eyelash. Collins, 1939
I Don't Like Cats. Doubleday, Doran, 1940; Collins, 1941
Such Natural Deaths. Collins, 1938 (U.S. title: Even Doctors Die. Doubleday, Doran, 1939)

ANSTEY, EDGAR CARNEGIE (M)
The Mystery of the Blue Inns. Longmans, 1938
The Vanishing Yacht. Longmans, 1937

ANSTEY, F., pseud; see GUTHRIE, THOMAS ANSTEY

ANTHONY, ELIZABETH (M)
Dramatic Murder. Hodder, 1948
Made for Murder. Hodder, 1950; Musson, 1950

ANTHONY, WILDER (M)
Deep Valley. Dorrance, 1940
Hidden Gold. Macaulay, 1922
Men of Mystery. Collins, 1925; Macaulay, 1926
Star of the Hills. Collins, 1926; Macaulay, 1927

ANTILL, ELIZABETH (M)
Death on the Barrier Reef. Hammond, 1952
Murder in Mid-Atlantic. Hammond, 1950

ANTONY, PETER, pseud; see SHAFFER, ANTHONY

APPEL, BENJAMIN (S)
Brain Guy. Knopf, 1934; Constable, 1937
Four Roads to Danger. Knopf, 1935
Life and Death of a Tough Guy. Avon, 1955 (Also published as: Teen-age Mobster. Avon, 1957)
Runaround. Dutton, 1937
Teen-age Mobster; see Life and Death of a Tough Guy

APPLE, A. E. (M)
Mr. Chang's Crime Ray. Chelsea House, 1928
Mr. Chang of Scotland Yard. Chelsea House, 1926

APPLEBY, JOHN (S)
Aphrodite Means Death. Laurie, 1951
The Arms of Venus. Coward, 1951
The Bad Summer. Hodder, 1958; Washburn, 1958
Barbary Hoard. Coward, 1952; Dell
Captive City. Hodder, 1955
The Secret Mountains. Hodder, 1955; Washburn, 1957
Stars in the Water. Laurie, 1952; Coward, 1953
Venice Preserve Me. Hodder, 1954

APPLETON, GEORGE WEBB (M)
The Down Express. Long, 1908
François the Valet. Pearson, 1899
The Ingenious Captain. Long, 1906
The Mysterious Miss Cass. Long, 1904
The Silent Passenger. Long, 1906

APPLIN, ARTHUR (M)
The Actress. Hurst, 1927
The Black Nail. Hurst, 1932
The Death Mask. Hurst, 1928; Duffield, 1930
The Final Payment. Hurst, 1930
The Gold Trap. Hurst, 1930
She Asked for Adventure. Hurst, 1939
Sweeter Than Honey. Hurst, 1936; Green Circle, 1937

ARCHER, A. A., pseud; see JOSCELYN, ARCHIE

ARCHER, FRANK, pseud; see O'CONNOR, RICHARD

ARCHER, MARGARET (M)
Gentle Rain. Jarrolds, 1953

ARCHER, MARY (M)
Body on the Line. Blackfriars Press, 1947
What-No Witnesses? Locker, 1947

ARCHER, ROBERT (M)
The Case of the Vanishing Women. Howell, Soskin, 1942; Swan, G. G., 1950
Death on the Waterfront. Doubleday, Doran, 1941; Swann, G. G., 1948

ARCTANDER, JOHN W. (M)
Guilty. Cochrane, 1910

ARD, WILLIAM (S) (Pseudonyms: Ben Kerr, Thomas Wills)
All I Can Get. Monarch, 1959
And So to Bed. Monarch, 1962
As Bad as I Am. Rinehart, 1959; Boardman, T. V., 1960 (Also published as: Wanted: Danny Fontaine. Dell, 1960)
The Blonde and Johnny Malloy. Pop. Lib., 1959
Club 17, by Ben Kerr. Popular Lib., 1957
Cry Scandal. Rinehart, 1956
The Diary. Rinehart, 1952; Hammond, 1954
Don't Come Crying to Me. Rinehart, 1954
Down I Go, by Ben Kerr. Popular Lib., 1955
Give Me This Woman. Monarch, 1962
Hell Is a City. Rinehart, 1955
I Fear You Not, by Ben Kerr. Popular Lib., 1956
Like Ice She Was. Monarch, 1960
Make Mine Mavis. Monarch, 1961
Mine to Avenge, by Thomas Wills. Fawcett, 1955
Mr. Trouble. Rinehart, 1954
No Angels for Me. Popular Lib., 1954
The Perfect Frame. Mill, 1951; Hammond, 1953
A Private Party. Rinehart, 1953 (English title: Rogue's Murder. Hammond, 1955)
Rogue's Murder; see A Private Party
The Root of His Evil. Rinehart, 1957; Boardman, T. V., 1958
Shakedown, by Ben Kerr. Holt, 1952
.38. Rinehart, 1952 (English title: This Is Murder. Hammond, 1954; also published as When She Was Bad. Dell, 1960)
This Is Murder; see .38
Wanted: Danny Fontaine; see As Bad as I Am
When She Was Bad; see .38

ARDEN, BARBI (M)
Remembered Island. Holt, 1956 (Also published as: Mystery at Indigo. Berkley Pub., 1960)

ARENT, ARTHUR (S)
The Gravedigger's Funeral. Grossman, 1967

ARESBY'S, THE, pseud; see BAMBERGER, MRS. HELEN R.

ARKWRIGHT, RICHARD (M)
Queen Anne's Gate. White, 1889

ARLEN, MICHAEL (Name originally: Dikran Kuyumjian) (M)
Crooked Coronet. Heinemann, 1937
Hell, Said the Duchess. Doubleday, Doran, 1934; Heinemann, 1935
Mayfair. Collins, 1925

ARLEY, CATHERINE, pseud; see D'ARLEY, CATHERINE

ARMAT, MRS. MARY (M)
River House. Dorrance, 1958

ARMITAGE, FLORA (M)
The Five Deceivers. Dodd, 1963

ARMSTRONG, ANTHONY, pseud; see WILLIS, GEORGE ANTHONY ARMSTRONG

ARMSTRONG, CHARLOTTE (M-S) (Pseudonym: Jo Valentine)
The Albatross. Coward, 1957; Davies, 1958 (Also published as: Mask of Evil. Crest, 1958)
Alibi for Murder. PB, 1956
Better to Eat You. Coward, 1954; Davies, 1954 (with Mischief. Ace, 1963)
Black Eyed Stranger. Coward, 1951; Davies, 1954 (with One-faced Girl. Ace, 1963)
The Case of the Weird Sisters. Coward, 1943; Gifford, 1943
Catch-as-Catch Can. Coward, 1952; Davies, 1954 (with Then Came Two Women. Ace, 1962)
Chocolate Cobweb. Coward, 1948; Davies, 1952; Berkley Pub., 1967 (with Who's Been Sitting in My Chair? Ace, 1963)
Death Filled the Glass. Withy Grove, 1945
A Dram of Poison. Coward, 1956; Davies, 1956; Crest, 1964
Dream of Fair Woman. Coward, 1966; Berkley Pub., 1967
Dream-Walker. Coward, 1955 (with The Mark of the Hand. Ace, 1963)
Duo. Coward, 1959; Davies, 1960 (Contains: Incident at a Corner and The Girl with a Secret)
The Gift Shop. Coward, 1966
Girl with a Secret. Crest, 1961. See also Duo
Incident at a Corner. Ace, 1962 (with The Unsuspected). See also Duo
The Innocent Flower. Coward, 1945; Collier
Lay On, McDuff. Coward, 1942; Glifford, 1943
Lemon in the Basket. Coward, 1967
A Little Less Than Kind. Ace, 1963; Coward, 1963; Collins, 1964
Mark of the Hand. Ace, 1963 (with The Dream-Walker)
Mask of Evil; see The Albatross
Mischief. Coward, 1950; Davies, 1951; Penguin, 1957; Ace, 1963 (with Better to Eat You)
The One-faced Girl. Ace, 1963 (with Black Eyed Stranger)
Something Blue. Ace, 1962
Then Came Two Women. Ace, 1962 (with Catch-as-Catch Can)
The Turret Room. Collins, 1965; Coward, 1965; Crest, 1968
The Unsuspected. Coward, 1946; Harrap, 1947; PB (with Incident at a Corner. Ace, 1962)
Who's Been Sitting in My Chair. Ace, 1963 (with Chocolate Cobweb)
Witch's House. Coward, 1962, 1963; Crest, 1966; Collins, 1964

ARMSTRONG, MARGARET NEILSON (M)
The Blue Santo Murder Mystery. Random, 1941; Hale, R., 1943
The Man with No Face. Random, 1940; Hale, R., 1941
Murder in Stained Glass. Hale, R., 1939; Random, 1939

ARMSTRONG, RAYMOND, pseud; see LEE, NORMAN

ARNAUD, GEORGES, pseud; see GIRARD, HENRI GEORGES

ARNIM, MARY ANNETTE BEAUCHAMP GRAFIN VON (Countess Russell) (M) (Pseudonym: "Elizabeth")
Vera. Doubleday, Page, 1921

ARNOLD, ADELAIDE VICTORIA (M)
The Clue. Arnold, E., 1927
The Merlewood Mystery. Nelson, T., 1928

ARNOLD, ALLEN (D)
Branded; or, The Detective Terror. Detective Lib., No. 42, 1883

ARNOLD, SIR EDWIN (M)
Queen's Justice. Burleigh, T., 1899

ARNOLD, MRS. J. O. (M)
Merlewood Mystery. Nelson, 1930

ARNOLD, JOHN (M)
The London Bridge Mystery. Jenkins, 1932
Murder! Jenkins, 1926; Small, 1927
The Murders in Surrey Wood. Dutton, 1928 (English title: The Surrey Wood Mystery. Jenkins, 1928)
The Surrey Wood Mystery; see The Murders in Surrey Wood
Tumult in San Benito. Jenkins, 1934
What Happened at Andals? Jenkins, 1929; Dutton

ARNOLD, RALPH (M)
Death of a Sinner. Heinemann, 1933
Fish and Company. Heinemann, 1951; Macmillan, 1951
Hands Across the Water. Constable, 1946; Macmillan, 1947
Jenkins Green. Heinemann, 1953
On Secret Service. Blackie & Son, 1935
Skeltons and Cupboards. Macmillan, 1951; Heinemann, 1952

ARRE, HELEN, pseud; see ROSS, ZOLA HELEN

ARTHUR, BUDD (S)
Big Squeeze. Bouregy, 1956; Ryerson, 1956

ARTHUR, FRANK (M)
Another Mystery in Suva. Heinemann, 1956
Murder in the Tropic Night. Jenkins, 1961
Suva Harbour Mystery; see Who Killed Netta Maul?
The Throbbing Dark. Jenkins, 1963
Who Killed Netta Maul? Gollancz, 1940 (Also published as: Suva Harbour Mystery. Penguin, 1948)

ARTHUR, HARRY, pseud; see BATES, HARRY ARTHUR

ARTHUR, PHYLLIS (M)
The Paying Guest. Curl, 1944

ARVONEN, HELEN (S)
Circle of Death. Ace, 1967
The Summer of Evil. Ace, 1965

ASBURY, HERBERT (M)
Devil of Pei-Ling. Macy-Masius, 1927
The Tick of the Clock. Macy-Masius, 1928; Burt, 1929

ASCHER, EUGENE (M)
There Were No Asper Ladies. Mitre, 1944

ASHBROOK, HARRIETTE CORA (M)
(Pseudonym: Susannah Shane)
Baby in the Ash Can, by Susannah Shane. Dodd, 1944; Nicholson, 1947
Diamonds in the Dumplings, by Susannah Shane. Doubleday, 1946
He Killed a Thousand Men; see A Most Immoral Murder
Lady in a Million, by Susannah Shane. Dodd, 1943
Lady in a Wedding Dress, by Susannah Shane. Dodd, 1943
Lady in Danger, by Susannah Shane. Dodd, 1942
Lady in Lilac, by Susannah Shane. Dodd, 1941
A Most Immoral Murder. Coward, 1935 (Also published as: He Killed a Thousand Men. Eyre, 1938)
Murder Comes Back. Coward, 1940; Eyre, 1942 (Published in Liberty Magazine as: "Who Killed This Woman")
Murder Makes Murder. Coward, 1937
The Murder of Cecily Thane. Coward, 1930; Eyre, 1931
The Murder of Sigurd Sharon. Coward, 1933; Eldon, 1934
The Murder of Steven Kester. Coward, 1931; Eyre, 1933
The Purple Onion Mystery. Coward, 1941; Eyre, 1950
"Who Killed This Woman?"; see Murder Come Back

ASHBY, RUBIE CONSTANCE (M)
Death on Tiptoe. Hodder, 1930
He Arrived at Dusk. Hodder, 1933; Macmillan, 1933
Out Went the Taper. Hodder, 1934; Macmillan, 1934
Plot Against a Widow. Hodder, 1932

ASHDOWN, CLIFFORD, pseud; see FREEMAN, DR. RICHARD AUSTIN

ASHE, DOUGLAS (S)
A Shroud for Grandma. Scribner, 1951

ASHE, GORDON, pseud; see JOHN CREASEY

ASHE, NICHOLAS (M)
Danger Aft. Low, 1935
A Preface to a Killing. Marston, 1920; Macaulay, 1937 (Also published as: Prelude to a Killing. Low, 1936)
Prelude to a Killing; see A Preface to a Killing

ASHE, SAXON (M)
I Am Saxon Ashe. Alliance, 1941

ASHENHURST, JOHN M. (M)
The World's Fair Murders. Houghton, 1933

ASHFORD, JEFFREY, pseud; see JEFFRIES, RODERIC

ASHLEY, ARTHUR ERNEST (M)
(Pseudonym: Francis Vivian)
Arrow of Death. Jenkins, 1938
Black Alibi. Jenkins, 1938
Dark Moon. Jenkins, 1939
Darkling Death. Jenkins, 1956; Roy Pubs., 1957
Dead Opposite the Church. Jenkins, 1959
Death at the Salutation. Jenkins, 1937
Death of Mr. Lomas. Jenkins, 1941
The Elusive Bowman. Hodder, 1951
The Frog Was Yellow. Jenkins, 1940
Ladies of Locksley. Jenkins, 1953; Roy Pubs., 1957
Laughing Dog. Hodder, 1949
Murder in Angel Yard. Picadilly Novels, 1946
Ninth Enemy. Hodder, 1948
Sable Messenger. Jenkins, 1947
Singing Masons. Hodder 1950
Sleeping Islands. Hodder, 1951
Three Short Men. Jenkins, 1939
Threefold Cord. Jenkins, 1947

ASHLEY, KATE (M)
The Cinnabar Shroud. Long, 1956

ASHLEY, KENNETH H. (M)
Death of a Curate. Lane, 1932

ASHTON, CHARLES (M)
Dance for a Dead Uncle. Museum Press, 1948
Death for Two. Hale, R., 1940
Death Greets a Guest. Nicolson, 1936
Fate Strikes Twice. Withy Grove, 1944
Here's Murder Done. Hale, R., 1943; Withy Grove, 1947
Murder at Melton Peveril. Hale, R., 1946
Murder in Make-up. Nicholson, 1934
Stone Dead. Hale, R., 1939
Tragedy After Tea. Nicholson, 1935

ASHTON, WARREN T. (M)
Hatchie, the Guardian Slave; or, the Heiress of Bellevue. Mussey, 1853

ASHTON, WINIFRED and HELEN DE GUERRY SIMPSON (D) (Pseudonym: Clemence Dane)
Author Unknown. Cosmopolitan, 1930
Enter Sir John. Cosmopolitan, 1928
Re-enter Sir John. Farrar & Rinehart, 1932; Hodder, 1932

ASIMOV, ISAAC (M)
The Caves of Steel. Boardman, T. V., 1954; Doubleday, 1954; Pyramid, 1962
Death Dealers. Avon, 1958 (Also published as: A Whiff of Death. Walker & Co., 1968)
Naked Sun. Doubleday, 1957; Lancer, 1964
A Whiff of Death; see Death Dealers

ASKEW, ALICE; see ASKEW, CLAUDE

ASKEW, CLAUDE and ALICE ASKEW (M)
The Lost Idol. Ward, Lock, 1917

ASPINWALL, MARGUERITE; see JANIS, ELSIE

ASQUITH, LADY CYNTHIA MARY EVELYN CHARTERIS (M)
Black Cap's New Stories of Murder and Mystery. Scribner, 1928; Hutchinson, 1929

ASQUITH, HERBERT (M)
Wind's End. Hutchinson, 1924; Scribner, 1924

ASTERLEY, HUGH CECIL (M)
Mortmain. Sears, 1932 (English title: Tale of Two Murders. Jarrolds, 1932)

ASWELL, MARY LOUISE WHITE (S)
Far to Go. Ambassador, 1957; Farrar, Straus, 1957
S. S. Murder, with Q. Patrick. Cassell, 1933; Farrar & Rinehart, 1933

ATHERTON, GERTRUDE FRANKLIN HORNE (M)
Avalanche. Stokes, 1919
The Bell in the Fog. Harper, 1905
Mrs. Balfame. Stokes, 1916

ATIYAH, EDWARD (M-S)
Black Vanguard. Davies, 1952
The Crime of Julian Masters. Hale, R., 1958
The Cruel Fire; see Donkey from the Mountains
Donkey from the Mountains. Hale, R., 1961 (U.S. title: The Cruel Fire. Doubleday, 1962)
Murder, My Love; see The Thin Line
The Thin Line. Harper, 1951; Davies, 1952 (Also published as: Murder, My Love. Avon, 1957)

ATKEY, BERTRAM (M)
The Amazing Mr. Bunn. Newnes, 1912, 1934; MacDonald & Co., 1949
Arsenic and Gold. Jenkins, 1939; Penn, 1939
Crooks' Castle. Newnes, 1935
The Escapes of Mr. Honey. MacDonald & Co., 1944
The House of Clystevill. Jenkins, 1940
The House of Strange Victims. Appleton, D., 1930

The Man with Yellow Eyes. Newnes, 1923; MacVeagh, 1927
The Midnight Mystery. Appleton-Century, 1928
The Mystery of the Glass Bullet. Appleton, D., 1931
The Smiler Bunn Brigade. Hodder, 1916
Smiler Bunn, Byewayman. Hodder, 1916
Smiler Bunn, Crook. Newnes, 1929
Smiler Bunn, Gentleman-Adventurer. Dial, 1926
Smiler Bunn-Gentleman Crook. Newnes, 1925

ATKEY, PHILIP (M)
The Blue Water Murder. Cassell, 1935
Heirs of Merlin. Cassell, 1945
Juniper Rock. Cassell, 1953

ATKINSON, ALEX (M)
Exit Charlie. Davies, 1955; Knopf, 1956; Penguin, 1957

ATKINSON, HUGH (M)
The Pink and the Brown. Gollancz, 1957
The Reckoning. Bodley Head, 1965

ATLEE, BENGE (M)
Black Feather. Scribner, 1939

ATLEE, PHILIP, pseud; see PHILIPS, JAMES ATLEE

ATWATER, MRS. MARY MEIGS (M)
Crime in Corn Weather. Houghton, 1935 (English title: Murder in Midsummer. Gollancz, 1935)

AUBREY, FRANK (M)
Devil-tree of El Dorado. New Amsterdam, 1897
The Studio Mystery. Jarrolds, 1897

AUBREY-FLETCHER, HENRY LANCELOT (M) (Pseudonym: Henry Wade)
Be Kind to the Killer. Constable, 1952
Bury Him Darkly. Constable, 1936
Constable, Guard Thyself. Constable, 1934; Houghton, 1935
Diplomat's Folly. Constable, 1951; Macmillan, 1952
Duke of York's Steps. Constable, 1929; Grosset, 1930; Harrap, 1932
The Dying Alderman. Constable, 1930; Harcourt, 1930
A Dying Fall. Constable, 1955; MacDonald & Co., 1955
Gold Was Our Grave. Constable, 1954; MacDonald & Co., 1954
The Hanging Captain. Constable, 1932; Harcourt, 1933
Heir Presumptive. Constable, 1953; Macmillan, 1953
Here Comes the Copper. Constable, 1938
The High Sheriff. Constable, 1937
The Litmore Snatch. Constable, 1957; MacDonald & Co., 1957
Lonely Magdalen. Constable, 1940
The Missing Partners. Harcourt, 1928; Constable, 1930
Mist on the Saltings. Constable, 1933
New Graves at Great Norne. Constable, 1947
No Friendly Drop. Constable, 1932; Harcourt, 1932
Policeman's Lot. Constable, 1933
Released for Death. Constable, 1938
Storm. MacDonald & Co., 1954
Too Soon to Die. Constable, 1953; MacDonald & Co., 1953
The Verdict of You All. Constable, 1926; Grosset, 1929; Harrap, 1932

AUDEMARS, PIERRE (D) (Pseudonym: Peter Hodemart)
Confession of Hercule. Low, 1947
The Crown of Night. Harper, 1962; Long, 1962
The Dream and the Dead. Long, 1964
Fair Maids Missing. Doubleday, 1965
The Fire and the Clay. Long, 1959
Hercule and the Gods. Pilot, 1944
Night Without Darkness. Selwyn, 1936
The Obligations of Hercule. Low, 1936
Streets of Grass. Harper, 1963
The Temptations of Hercule. Pilot, 1945
Thieves of Enchantment. Chambers, 1956
Time of Temptation. Doubleday, 1966
The Turns of Time. Harper, 1961; Long, 1961
Two Imposters. Long, 1958
When the Gods Laughed. Foster, W., 1946
The Wings of Darkness. Long, 1963
A Woven Web. Doubleday, 1965

AUDOUARD, YVAN (M)
Little Pig-Allee. Ace, 1961

AUFRICHT-RUDA, HANS (M)
Case for the Defendant. Allen, G., 1929; Little, 1929

AUGUST, JOHN, pseud; see DeVOTO, BERNARD

AULLEN, GILBERT (M)
Mysterious Courier. Putnam, 1953

AUMONIER, STACY (M)
Baby Grand and Other Stories. Heinemann, 1926; Holt, H., 1927
Miss Bracegirdle and Others. Doubleday, Page, 1923; Hutchinson, 1923

AUSTIN, ANNE (M)
Avenging Parrot. Greenberg, 1930; Grosset, 1931; Skeffington, 1931
Black Pigeon. Greenberg, 1929; Grosset, 1930; Skeffington, 1932
Girl Alone. White House, 1930
Murder at Bridge. MacDonald & Co., 1931; Skeffington, 1931
Murder Backstairs. MacDonald & Co., 1930; Skeffington, 1930
Murdered But Not Dead. Macmillan, 1939
One Drop of Blood. Macmillan, 1932; Skeffington, 1932
Wicked Woman. MacDonald & Co., 1933; Hurst, 1934

AUSTIN, BENJAMIN FISH (M) (Pseudonym: Benjamin Nitsua)
The Mystery of Ashton Hall. Austin, 1910

AUSTIN, FREDERICK BRITTEN (M)
On the Borderland. Hurst, 1922; Doubleday, Page, 1923
Told in the Marketplace. Butterworth, T., 1937

AUSTIN, HUGH, pseud; see EVANS, HUGH AUSTIN

AUSTIN, LILIAN EDNA (S)
Shudders. Meador, 1931

AUSTWICK, JOHN, pseud; see LEE, AUSTIN

AUTHEVILLE, FRANÇOIS GEORGES HENRI D' (S)
Checkmate to Destiny. Harvill, 1953; Ryerson, 1953

AVALLONE, MICHAEL ANGELO, JR. (M-S-D) (Pseudonyms: Mark Dane, Nick Carter, Priscilla Dalton, Dorothea Nile, Edwina Noone, Sidney Stuart)
The Alarming Clock. Allen, W. H., 1962
Assassins Don't Die in Bed
The Award Gothic Reader. Award
The Bedroom Bolero. Belmont, 1963; Brown, Watson, 1964
Birds of a Feather Affair. Signet, 1966 (The Girl from U.N.C.L.E. series #1)
The Blazing Affair. Signet, 1966 (The Girl from U.N.C.L.E. series #2)
The Brutal Kook. Belmont, 1964; Brown, Watson, 1966
The Case of the Bouncing Betty. Ace, 1957; Allen, W. H., 1960
The Case of the Violent Virgin. Ace, 1957; Allen, W. H., 1960
China Doll, by Nick Carter. Award, 1964
Corridor of Whispers, by Edwina Noone. Ace, 1965
Crazy Mixed-up Corpse. GM, 1957
The Crimson Fire, by Edwina Noone. Lancer
Dark Cypress, by Edwina Noone. Ace, 1965
The Darkening Willows, by Priscilla Dalton. Paperback Lib., 1965
Daughter of Darkness, by Edwina Noone. Signet, 1966
Dead Game. Allen, W. H., 1954; Holt, 1954
Edwina Noone's Gothic Sampler, by Edwina Noone. Award, 1967
The Evil That Men Do, by Dorothea Nile
The Fat Death. Allen, W. H., 1966
The February Doll Murders. Allen, W. H., 1966; Signet, 1967
Felicia, by Mark Dane. Belmont, 1964; Ballantine, 1966
Felony Squad. Popular Lib., 1967
Fraulein. Ward, Lock, 1964
The Girl from U.N.C.L.E.; see Birds of a Feather Affair and Blazing Affair
Heirloom of Tragedy, by Edwina Noone. Lancer, 1965
The Horrible Man
The Incident
Kaleidescope. Popular Lib., 1966
The Living Bomb. Allen, W. H., 1963
Lust Is No Lady. Belmont, 1964; Ballantine, 1965
Madame X. Popular Lib., 1966
The Man from U.N.C.L.E.; see The Thousand Coffins Affair
The Marble Staircase, by Dorothea Nile. Tower
Meanwhile Back at the Morgue. GM, 1961; Muller, 1964
The Mistress of Farrondale, by Dorothea Nile
The Night Walker. Award
90 Gramercy Park, by Priscilla Dalton. Paperback Lib., 1965
Run, Spy, Run, by Nick Carter. Award
Saigon, by Nick Carter (collaboration). Award, 1964
The Second Secret, by Edwina Noone. Belmont, 1966
Shock Corridor. Belmont, 1963
The Silent Silken Shadows, by Priscilla Dalton. Paperback Lib., 1965
The Spitting Image. Holt, H., 1953; Barker, 1957
Station Six-Sahara. Popular Lib., 1964
Tales of the Frightened. Belmont, 1963
The Tall Dolores. Holt, H., 1953; Barker, 1956
Terror at Deepcliff, by Dorothea Nile
There Is Something About a Dame. Belmont, 1963
The Thousand Coffins Affair. Ace, 1965 (Also published as: The Man from U.N.C.L.E. Ace, 1965)

The Victorian Crown, by Edwina Noone. Belmont, 1966
Violence in Velvet. Signet, 1956; Allen, W. H., 1958
Voodoo Murders. GM, 1957; Muller, 1959
Young Dillinger, by Sidney Stuart. Belmont, 1965 (Novelization of the screenplay)

AVELINE, CLAUDE (M)
Double Death of Frederick Belot. Holt, H., 1940; Dobson, 1949
The Fountains at Marlieux. Dobson, 1954; Roy Pubs., 1954
Prisoner Born. Hutchinson, 1950

AVERY, A. A. (M)
Anything for a Quiet Life. Farrar & Rinehart, 1942; Bantam, 1946

AVERY, ROBERT (M)
The Corpse in Company K. Swift, J., 1942
A Murder a Day! Mystery House, 1940
Murder on the Downbeat. Mystery House, 1943

AVRACH, JOSEPH (M)
Murder in Oil. Westhouse, 1948

AXELROD, GEORGE (S)
Blackmailer. GM, 1952

AYALA, FRANCISCO (M)
Death as a Way of Life. Macmillan, 1964

AYER, FREDERICK (M)
The Man in the Mirror. Gollancz, 1965; Regency, 1965; Signet, 1966

AYERS, PAUL, pseud; see AARONS, EDWARD SIDNEY

AYLING, KAYE (S)
Who Was Ellen Smith? Lancer, 1967

AYMÉ, MARCEL (M)
Secret Stream. Harper, 1953

AYRTON, ELISABETH (S)
Silence in Crete. Morrow, 1964 (English title: The Cretan. Hodder, 1963)

BABCOCK, DWIGHT V. (D)
The Gorgeous Ghoul. Knopf, 1941 (Also published as: The Gorgeous Ghoul Murder Case. Avon, 1943)
The Gorgeous Ghoul Murder Case; see The Gorgeous Ghoul
Hannah Says Foul Play. Avon, 1946
A Homicide for Hannah. Knopf, 1941; Avon, 1943 (English title: Murder for Hannah. Hale, R., 1941)
Murder for Hannah; see A Homicide for Hannah

BABER, DOUGLAS (S) (Pseudonym: John Ritson)
Beneath the Precipice, by John Ritson. Boardman, T. V., 1962
Death of a Mind, by John Ritson. Boardman, T. V., 1962
Desperate Venture. Boardman, T. V., 1963

BACHELLER, IRVING A. (M)
The House of the Three Ganders. Bobbs, 1928; Hutchinson, 1928

BACHMANN, LAWRENCE PAUL (M)
Death in the Doll's House, with Hannah Lees. Random, 1943
Kiss of Death. Knopf, 1946
The Phoenix. Collins, 1955

BACKHOUSE, ELIZABETH (D)
Death Came Uninvited. Hale, R., 1957
Death Climbs a Hill. Hale, R., 1963
Death of a Clown. Hale, R., 1962
Mists Came Down. Hale, R., 1959
Night Has Eyes. Hale, R., 1961
Web of Shadows. Hale, R., 1960

BACON, J. D., pseud; see DODGE, MRS. JOSEPHINE DASKAM

BACON, PEGGY (Full name: Margaret Frances Bacon) (S)
The Inward Eye. Scribner, 1952

BAGBY, GEORGE, pseud; see STEIN, AARON MARC

BAGGALEY, JAMES (S)
Shadow of the Eagle. Harrap, 1956
Spare Men. Harper, 1958; Harrap, 1958

BAGLEY, DESMOND (S)
The Golden Keel. Collins, 1963; Doubleday, 1964; PB, 1965
The High Citadel. Collins, 1965; Doubleday, 1965
Landslide. Collins, 1947; Doubleday, 1967; Berkley Pub., 1968

BAILEY, ELLIOT (M)
The Compden Hill Mystery. Bles, 1926
The Metcalfe Mystery. Bles, 1928

BAILEY, HENRY CHRISTOPHER (D)
Apprehensive Dog; see No Murder
Best of Mr. Fortune Stories. PB, 1942
The Bishop's Crime. Gollancz, 1940; Doubleday, Doran, 1941
Black Land, White Land. Doubleday, Doran, 1937; Gollancz, 1937; Sun Dial, 1938
Call Mr. Fortune. Methuen, 1920; Dutton, 1921; McKinlay
Case for Mr. Fortune. Doubleday, Doran, 1932; Ward, Lock, 1932

Cat's Whiskers; see Dead Men's Effects
Clue for Mr. Fortune. Doubleday, Page, 1926; Gollancz, 1936
Clunk's Claimant. Gollancz, 1937 (U.S. title: Twittering Bird. Doubleday, Doran, 1937; Sun Dial, 1938)
Dead Man's Effects. MacDonald & Co., 1945 (Also published as: The Cat's Whiskers. McClelland, 1944; Doubleday, Doran, 1944)
Dead Man's Shoes. Gollancz, 1942 (U.S. title: Nobody's Vineyard. Doubleday, Doran, 1942)
The Garston Murder Case. Doubleday, Doran, 1930 (English title: Garston's)
Garston's; see The Garston Murder Case
The Great Game. Doubleday, Doran, 1939; Gollancz, 1939
Honor Among Thieves. Doubleday, 1947; McClelland, 1947; MacDonald & Co., 1947
Life Sentence. Doubleday, 1946; MacDonald & Co., 1946
Little Captain. Gollancz, 1941 (U.S. title: Orphan Ann. Doubleday, Doran, 1941)
Man in the Cape. Benn, 1933
Meet Mr. Fortune. Doubleday, Doran, 1942 (Contains: The Bishop's Crime and 12 short stories)
Mr. Clunk's Text; see Veron Mystery
Mr. Fortune Explains. Ward, Lock, 1930; Dutton, 1931
Mr. Fortune Finds a Pig. Doubleday, Doran, 1943; Gollancz, 1943
Mr. Fortune Here. Gollancz, 1940; Doubleday, Doran, 1940; Sun Dial, 1941
Mr. Fortune Is on the Case; see Mr. Fortune Wonders
Mr. Fortune Objects. Doubleday, Doran, 1935; Gollancz, 1935
Mr. Fortune, Please. Methuen, 1927; Dutton, 1928
Mr. Fortune's Practice. Methuen, 1923; Dutton, 1924
Mr. Fortune Speaking. Ward, Lock, 1929; Dutton, 1931
Mr. Fortune's Trials. Methuen, 1925; Dutton, 1926; McKinlay
Mr. Fortune Wonders. Doubleday, Doran, 1933; Pony Books, 1933; Ward, Lock, 1933 (Serial title: Mr. Fortune Is on the Case)
No Murder. Gollancz, 1942 (U.S. title: Apprehensive Dog. Doubleday, Doran, 1942)
Nobody's Vineyard; see Dean Man's Shoes
Orphan Ann; see Little Captain
The Plot. Methuen, 1922
The Queen of Spades. Doubleday, Doran, 1944
The Red Castle Mystery. Doubleday, Doran, 1932; Ward, Lock, 1932
Save a Rope. Doubleday, 1948; MacDonald & Co., 1948
Shadow on the Wall. Doubleday, Doran, 1934; Gollancz, 1934; Ryerson, 1934; Grosset, 1935
Shrouded Death. MacDonald & Co., 1950
Slippery Ann. Gollancz, 1944
The Sullen Sky Mystery. Doubleday, Doran, 1935; Gollancz, 1935; Ryerson, 1935
This Is Mr. Fortune. Doubleday, Doran, 1938; Gollancz, 1938
Twittering Bird; see Clunk's Claimant
Veron Mystery. Gollancz, 1939 (U.S. title: Mr. Clunk's Text. Doubleday, Doran, 1939)
The Wrong Man. Doubleday, Doran, 1945; MacDonald & Co., 1946

BAILEY, HILEA, pseud; see MARTING, RUTH LENORE

BAILEY, PAUL DAYTON (S)
Deliver Me from Eva. Murray & Gee, 1946

BAIN, GRAHAM WARD (S)
Round Robin. Harrap, 1937; Lippincott, 1937

BAIR, PATRICK (S)
Faster, Faster! Eyre, 1950
Gargantua Falls. Eyre, 1951
Gypsum Flower. Eyre, 1959

BAIRD, EDWIN (M)
Paul Pry's Poison Pen. Grafton, 1945

BAKER, ASA, pseud; see DRESSER, DAVIS

BAKER, CHARLOTTE (M)
House of the Roses. Dutton, 1942
A Sombrero for Miss Brown. Dutton, 1941

BAKER, HOWELL NORTH; see BAKER, NORTH

BAKER, HUGH, pseud. (D)
Cartwright Is Dead, Sir! Houghton, 1934

BAKER, MARC (M)
The Hilltop Murders. Bouregy, 1965

BAKER, MARCEIL GENÉE KOLSTAD (M) (Pseudonym: Marc Miller)
Death at the Easel. Arcadia, 1956
Death Is a Liar. Arcadia, 1959
Plaid Shroud. Arcadia, 1957

BAKER, NORTH and WILLIAM BOLTON (M)
Dead to the World. Doubleday, Doran, 1944

BAKER, RICHARD MERRIAM (D)
Death Stops the Bells. Scribner, 1938
Death Stops the Manuscript. Scribner, 1936
Death Stops the Rehearsal. Cassell, 1937; Scribner, 1937

BAKER, SAMM SINCLAIR (M)
Murder Very Dry. Graphic, 1956
One Touch of Blood. Graphic, 1955

BAKER, SIDNEY J. (M)
Time Is an Enemy. Mystery House, 1958

BAKER, W. HOWARD (D-M)
Brussels Dossier. Lancer
Departure Deferred. Macfadden, 1965
The Dirty Game. Lancer, 1967
Every Man an Enemy. Macfadden, 1966 (Sexton Blake series #2)
The Hero Game. Lancer, 1965, 1967
Night of the Wolf. Lancer, 1966
Rape of Berlin. Lancer
Storm over Rockall. Macfadden, 1965
Traitor! Lancer, 1967

BALCHIN, NIGEL MARLIN (S)
Fall of the Sparrow. Collins, 1959
In the Absence of Mrs. Peterson. S & S, 1966
Mine Own Executioner. Collins, 1945; Houghton, 1946
A Sort of Traitor. Collins, 1956

BALFOUR, EVE and BERYL HERNDEN (Pseudonym: Hearnden Balfour)
Anything Might Happen. Hodder, 1931 (U.S. title: Murder and the Red-Haired Girl. Houghton, 1933)
The Enterprising Burglar. Houghton, 1928; McKinlay
The Gentleman from Texas; see The Paper Chase
Murder and the Red-Haired Girl; see Anything Might Happen
The Paper Chase. Hodder, 1927 (U.S. title: The Gentleman from Texas. Houghton, 1927)

BALFOUR, HEARNDEN, pseud; see BALFOUR, EVE

BALL, DORIS BELL COLLIER (D) (Pseudonym: Josephine Bell)
Adventure with Crime. Hodder, 1962
The Alien. Bles, 1964
All in Vanity. Longman, 1940
Backing Winds. Methuen, 1951
Bones in the Barrow. Methuen, 1953; Macmillan, 1955; Ballantine, 1963
The Bottom of the Well. Longmans, 1940
Cage-birds. Methuen, 1955
The Catalyst. Hodder, 1966; Macmillan, 1967
The China Roundabout. Hodder, 1956 (U.S. title: Murder on the Merry-go-round. Ballantine, 1965)
The Convalescent. Bles, 1960
Crime in Our Time. Abelard, 1952
Curtain Call for a Corpse. Macmillan, 1965
Death at Half Term. Longmans, 1939
Death at the Medical Board. Longmans, 1944; Ballantine, 1964
Death in Clairvoyance. Longmans, 1949
Death in Retirement. Macmillan, 1956; Methuen, 1956
Death on the Borough Council. Longmans, 1937
Death on the Reserve. Hodder, 1966; Macmillan, 1966
Double Doom. Hodder, 1957; Macmillan, 1958
Easy Prey. Hodder, 1959; Macmillan, 1959
Fall over Cliff. Macmillan, 1956; Ballantine, 1963
Fiasco in Fulham; see Flat Tyre in Fulham
Fires at Fairlawn. Methuen, 1954
Flat Tyre in Fulham. Hodder, 1963 (U.S. titles: Fiasco in Fulham. Macmillan, 1963 and Room for a Body. Ballantine, 1964)
Hell's Pavement. Methuen, 1955
The House Above the River. Hodder, 1959
The Hunter and the Trapped. Hodder, 1963
Murder in Hospital. Longmans, 1937
Murder on the Merry-go-round; see The China Roundabout
New People at the Hollies. Gollancz, 1961; Macmillan, 1961
No Escape. Macmillan, 1966
The Port of London Murders. Macmillan, 1958
Room for a Body; see Fiasco in Fulham
Safety First. Bles, 1962
The Seeing Eye. Hodder, 1958
Stranger on a Cliff; see To Let—Furnished
The Summer School Mystery. Methuen, 1950
To Let—Furnished. Methuen, 1952 (Also published as: Stranger on a Cliff. Ace, 1964)
The Upfold Witch. Macmillan, 1964; Ballantine, 1966
A Well-Known Face. Hodder, 1960; Washburn, 1960
Whirlpool. Methuen, 1949

BALL, EUSTACE HALE (S)
The Scarlet Fox. Grosset, 1927

Traffic in Souls. Dillingham, G. W., 1914
The Voice on the Wire. Hearst's International Lib., 1915

BALL, JOHN DUDLEY (D)
The Cool Cottontail. Harper & Row, 1966; Bantam, 1967; Joseph, M., 1967
In the Heat of the Night. Harper & Row, 1965; Joseph, M., 1966; Bantam, 1967

BALLARD, ERIC ALLEN, pseud; see ALLEN, ERIC

BALLARD, HELEN MABRY (D)
To the Tune of Murder. Mill, 1952

BALLARD, K. G, pseud; see ROTH, HOLLY

BALLARD, WILLIS TODHUNTER (M-D) (Pseudonyms: Harrison Hunt, Neil MacNeil, John Shepherd)
Dealing Out Death. McKay, 1947
The Death Ride, by Neil MacNeil. GM, 1959
Death Takes an Operation, by Neil MacNeil. GM, 1958
Hot Dam, by Neil MacNeil. GM, 1960
Lights, Camera, Murder, by John Shepherd. Belmont, 1961
Mexican Slay Ride, by Neil MacNeil. GM, 1960
Murder Can't Stop. Putnam, 1942; McKay, 1947
Murder, Las Vegas Style. Tower, 1967
Murder Picks the Jury, by Harrison Hunt. Mystery House, 1948; Curl, 1949
Pretty Miss Murder. PB, 1963
Say Yes to Murder. Putnam, 1943
The Seven Sisters. PB, 1963
The Spy Catchers, by Neil MacNeil. GM, 1966
Third on a Seesaw, by Neil MacNeil. GM, 1959
Three for the Money. PB, 1964
Two Guns for Hire, by Neil MacNeil. GM, 1959
Walk in Fear. GM, 1952

BALLEN, CARMEN; see EDINGTON, ARLO CHANNING

BALLINGER, W. A. (D)
I, the Hangman. Macfadden, 1965, 1967
Starlet for a Penny. Mayflower, 1966 (Sexton Blake series)
The Witches of Nottingham Hill. Macfadden, 1965

BALLINGER, WILLIAM (BILL) SANBORN (D) (Pseudonyms: Frederic Freyer, B. X. Sanborn)
Beacon in the Night. Harper, 1958; Boardman, T. V., 1960; Signet, 1960
The Black, Black Hearse, by Frederic Freyer. St. Martin's, 1955 (Also published as: The Case of the Black, Black Hearse. Avon)
The Body Beautiful. Harper, 1949; Signet, 1964
Body in the Bed. Harper, 1948; Signet, 1964
The Case of the Black, Black Hearse; see The Black, Black Hearse
The Chinese Mask. Signet, 1965
The Darkening Door. Harper, 1952
The Doom-Maker, by B. X. Sanborn. Boardman, T. V., 1959; Dutton, 1959
Formula for Murder. Signet, 1958
The Fourth of Forever. Harper & Row, 1963
The Heir Hunters. Harper & Row, 1966
The Longest Second. Harper, 1957; Corigi, 1960
My Husband Was a Redhead; see The Wife of the Red-Haired Man
Not I, Said the Vixen. GM, 1965
Portrait in Smoke. Harper, 1950; Reinhardt & Evans, 1951; Signet, 1965
Rafferty. Harper, 1953; Reinhardt, 1953
Spy at Angkor Wat. Signet, 1965
The Spy in the Java Sea. Signet, 1966
The Spy in the Jungle. Signet, 1965
The Tooth and the Nail. Harper, 1955; Reinhardt, 1955; Corigi, 1957
The Wife of the Red-haired Man. Harper, 1957; Reinhardt, 1957; Corigi, 1959; Signet, 1965 (Serial title: My Husband Was a Redhead)

BALMER, EDWIN (D-M)
The Achievements of Luther Trant, with William MacHarg. Small, 1910
Blind Man's Eyes, with William MacHarg. Little, 1916
Breath of Scandal. Grosset, 1924
Five Fatal Words, with Philip Wylie. Smith, R. R., 1932; Paul, S., 1933
Flying Death. Dodd, 1927
The Golden Hoard, with Philip Wylie. Stokes, 1934
The Indian Drum, with William McHarg. Grosset, 1917
Keeban. Little, 1923
The Shield of Silence, with Philip Wylie. Stokes, 1936
That Royle Girl. Dodd, 1925
The Torn Letter. Dodd, 1941

BAMBERGER, MRS. HELEN R. and RAYMOND S. BAMBERGER (D) (Pseudonym: The Aresbys)
Mark of the Dead. Washburn, 1929; Skeffington, 1930
Murder at Red Pass. Washburn, 1930
Who Killed Coralie. Washburn, 1927

BAMBERGER, RAYMOND S.; see BAMBERGER, MRS. HELEN R.

BAMBURG, LILIAN (M)
Beads of Silence. Selwyn, 1926; Dutton, 1927
Rays of Darkness. Selwyn, 1927
The Riddle of the Dead, with Charles Platt. Gardner, 1930

BAMFORD, FRANCIS (M)
A Question of Taste. Longmans, 1949
Return to Cottington. Longmans, 1946
This Chequered Floor. Longmans, 1941
Vicious Circle, with Viola Bankes. Parrish, 1965
What Strange Cause? Longmans, 1944

BANCROFT, JOHN, pseud; see JENKINS, ALAN C.

BANDOLIER, STEPHEN (M)
Murder Manana. Duell, 1941

BANGS, JOHN KENDRICK (M)
Mrs. Raffles. Harper, 1905
P. Holmes & Co. Harper, 1906

BANKES, VIOLA; see BAMFORD, FRANCIS

BANKOFF, GEORGE ALEXIS (M)
(Pseudonym: George Braddon)
The Dog It Was That Died. Garnett, 1948
Judgment Deferred. Trelawney, 1948
Murdered Sleep. Garnett, 1949
Time Off for Death. Jenkins, 1952; Roy Pubs., 1958

BANKS, RAYMOND E. (D)
The Computer Kill. Popular Lib., 1961
Meet Me in Darkness. Popular Lib., 1961

BANNER, MICHAEL
Q 39. Knopf, 1937

BANNISTER, WILLIAM (M)
Portrait of Death. Lancer, 1966

BANNON, PETER, pseud; see DURST, PAUL

BANZIE, ERIC DE; see RESSICK JOHN

BARBER, ALEX (M)
Room with No Escape. Hutchinson, 1932

BARBER, WILLETTA ANN and RUDOLPH FREDERICK SCHABELITZ (M)
The Deed Is Drawn. Scribner, 1949
Drawback to Murder. Scribner, 1947
Drawn Conclusion. Doubleday, Doran, 1942
Murder Draws a Line. Doubleday, Doran, 1940
Murder Enters the Picture. Doubleday, Doran, 1942
The Noose Is Drawn. Scribner, 1945
Pencil Points to Murder. Doubleday, Doran, 1945

BARBETTE, JAY, pseud; see SPICER, BART

BARBOUR, ANNA MAYNARD (M)
At the Time Appointed. Lippincott, 1903
Breakers Ahead. Lippincott, 1906
That Mainwaring Affair. Lippincott, 1901, 1908; Ward, Lock, 1901

BARBOUR, RALPH HENRY (D)
Death in the Virgins. Appleton-Century, 1940

BARCLAY, JOHN (D)
The Gilchrist Case. Methuen, 1930

BARCLAY, WILSON (M)
The Seventh Man. Ward, Lock, 1933; Dial, 1935

BARDIN, JOHN FRANKLIN (M)
Burning Glass. Gollancz, 1950
Christmas Comes But Once a Year. Davies, 1955
The Deadly Percheron. Dodd, 1946; Gollancz, 1947; Macfadden, 1968
The Devil Take the Blue Tail Fly. Gollancz, 1948; Macfadden, 1967
The Last of Philip Banter. Dodd, 1947; Gollancz, 1947

BARDON, MINNA (D)
Blood Red Death. Phoenix, 1947
The Case of the Advertised Murder. Hillman-Curl, 1939
The Case of the Dead Grandmother. Phoenix, 1937
Murder Does Light Housekeeping. Phoenix, 1941

BARGONE, FREDERIC CHARLES EDOUARD (M) (Pseudonym: Claude Farrere)
The House of the Secret. Dutton, 1923
The Man Who Killed. Brentano, 1917

BARK, CONRAD VOSS; see VOSS BARK, CONRAD

BARKER, CLARENCE HEDLEY (M-S)
(Pseudonyms: "Seafarer," Frank Hedley)
Blue Water. Cassell, 1933
Bold Buccaneer, by "Seafarer." Ward, Lock, 1953
Captain Firebrace. Ward, Lock, 1958
Case of the Secret Plans. Lloyds, 1921
Cavalier of Crime, by Frank Hedley. Lippincott, 1937
Crooks' Cruise, by "Seafarer." Ward, Lock, 1962

Dark Road of Danger. Withy Grove, 1943
Devil's Brood. Cassell, 1941
Eight Went Cruising. Hale, 1946
Firebrace and Father Kelly, by "Seafarer." Ward, Lock, 1960
Firebrace and the Java Queen, by "Seafarer." 1958
Hallan Moor Mystery. Withy Grove, 1944
Hangman's Honeymoon. Hale, 1943
The Haunted Ship, by "Seafarer." Ward, Lock, 1958
Sailor and the Widow, by "Seafarer," Ward, Lock, 1957
Santa Maria, by "Seafarer." Ward, Lock, 1955
Smuggler's Pay for Firebrace, by "Seafarer." Ward, Lock, 1961
They Stole a Ship. Hale, 1945
Voyage into Peril, by "Seafarer." Ward, Lock, 1956
Wayward Nymph. Cassell, 1933

BARKER, MRS. ELSA (D)
C.I.D. of Dexter Drake. Sears, 1929; Hamilton, 1931
The Cobra Candlestick. Sears, 1928; Grosset, 1929; Hamilton, 1930
The Redman Cave Murder. Sears, 1930

BARKER, LEONARD NOEL (M) (Pseudonym: L. Noel)
Mystery Street. Paul, S., 1930

BARKER, RONALD (D) (Pseudonym: E. B. Ronald)
The Cat and Fiddle Murders, by E. B. Ronald. Gollancz, 1954; Rinehart, 1954
Clue for Murder. Abelard, 1962
The Days Are Long. Cassell, 1959
Death by Proxy. Boardman, T. V., 1956
A Sort of Madness, by E. B. Ronald. Boardman, T. V., 1958; Abelard, 1959
Tendency to Corrupt. Cassell, 1957

BARLING, CHARLES, pseud; see BARLING, MURIEL VERE MANT

BARLING, MURIEL VERE MANT (M) (Pseudonyms: Charles Barling, P. V. Barrington, Pamela Barrington)
Account Rendered, by Pamela Barrington. Barker, 1953
Afternoon of Violence, by Charles Barling. Hale, R., 1963
Among Those Present, by Pamela Barrington. Barker, 1953
Appointment with Death, by Charles Barling. Hale, R., 1964
By Some Person Unknown, by Pamela Barrington. Hammond, 1960
Final Judgment, by Pamela Barrington. Hale, R., 1964
Forty-three Candles for Mr. Beamish, by Pamela Barrington. Evans, 1950
The Fourth Victim, by Pamela Barrington. Barker, 1958
The Gentle Killer, by Pamela Barrington. Hammond, 1961
Mr. Headley's Private Hell, by Pamela Barrington. Long, 1949
The Mortimer Story, by Pamela Barrington. Barker, 1952
Motive for Murder, by Charles Barling. Hale, R., 1963
Night of Violence, by P. V. Barrington. Hammond, 1959
The Rest Is Silence, by Pamela Barrington. Evans, 1951
Saga of a Scoundrel, by Pamela Barrington. Long, 1947
Space of Heaven, by Pamela Barrington. Long, 1936
Time to Kill, by Charles Barling. Hale, R., 1965
The Triangle Has Four Sides, by Pamela Barrington. Evans, 1950
White Pierrot, by Pamela Barrington. Long, 1947

BARLOW, JAMES (S)
The Hour of Maximum Danger. Hamilton, H., 1962; S & S, 1963
The Man with Good Intentions. Cassell, 1958
One Half of the World. Cassell, 1957; Harper, 1957
The Patriots. Hamilton, H., 1960; Harper, 1960
The Protagonists. Cassell, 1956; Harper, 1956; Pan, 1959
Term of Trial. Hamilton, H., 1961; S & S, 1962; Bantam, 1963
This Side of the Sky. S & S, 1964

BARNARD, ALLAN (M)
Harlot Killer. Dodd, 1953; Dell

BARNES, RONALD GORELL; see GORELL, RONALD

BARNETT, GLYN (M)
Call-box Murder. Low, 1935
Death Calls Three Times. Low, 1936
Find the Lady. Low, 1936
I Knew Mrs. Lang. Low, 1937
Murder on Monday. Low, 1937
Silent Street. Barker, 1958
There's Money in Murder. Chapman, 1939

BARNS, GLEN MILLER (M)
Deadly Summer. Lippincott, 1957; Permabooks, 1958; Hale, R., 1959
Lawyers Don't Hang. Arcadia, 1953
Masquerade in Blue. Ace, 1956
Murder Is a Gamble. Ambassador, 1952; Phoenix, 1952; Foulsham, 1954
Murder Is Insane. Lippincott, 1956; Foulsham, 1958

Murder Walks the Stairs. Arcadia, 1954; Foulsham, 1955
Murderous Suspense. Foulsham, 1960

BARON, ALEXANDER (S)
The Lowlife. Collins, 1963; Yoseloff, 1964

BARON, F. (M)
The Flodden Rubies. Swan, G. G., 1947

BARON, PETER, pseud; see CLYDE, LEONARD WORSWICK

BARON, STANLEY WADE
End of the Line. Penguin, 1956

BARR, DENNIS (S)
The Crimson Quest. Sears, 1928
A Dock Brief. Cape, 1928
A Rope Broke. Jarrolds, 1932

BARR, ROBERT (D) (Pseudonym: Luke Sharp)
Strange Happenings. Dunkerley, 1883
Sunshine Johnson, Murderer. Isbister, 1893 (Included in Tavistock Tales, ed. by G. Parker)
The Triumph of Eugene Valmont. Appleton, D., 1906; Hurst, 1906

BARRETT, ALFRED WILSON (M)
The French Master. Ward, Lock, 1903
The Silver Pin. Ward, Lock, 1905
The Town Hill Mystery. Ward, Lock, 1912

BARRETT, FRANK (M)
Found Guilty, Ward & Downey, 1887
Woman of the Iron Bracelets. Chatto, 1893

BARRETT, GRADY (M)
The Barker Case. Vantage, 1966

BARRETT, MARIANNE; see EDINGTON, ARLO CHANNING

BARRETT, MARY ELLIN (S)
Castle Ugly. Dutton, 1966

BARRETT, MICHAEL (S)
Appointment in Zahrein. Joseph, M., 1960 (U.S. title: Escape from Zahrein. GM, 1960)
Escape from Zahrein; see Appointment in Zahrein
The Last Flowers. Longmans, 1956; Farrar, 1957 (Also published as: Rebellion)
Man on the Spike. Joseph, M., 1961
Rebellion; see The Last Flowers
Return of the Cornish Soldier. Joseph, M., 1962
The Reward. Corigi, 1957
Stranger in Galah. Longmans, 1958
Task of Destruction. Joseph, M., 1963
Ten Against Nura. Hale, 1965
Traitor at Twenty Fathoms. Collins, 1960

BARRETT, MONTE (D)
Knotted Silk. Paul, S., 1932
Murder at Belle Camille. Bobbs, 1943; Boardman, T. V., 1946
The Pelham Murder Case. White House, 1930
The Wedding March Murder. Bobbs, 1933; Paul, S., 1933

BARRIE, JAMES MATH (M)
Better Dead. Sonnenschein, 1888; Lovell, Coryell, 1892

BARRINGTON, HOWARD (M) (Pseudonym: Simon Stone)
The Bookmaker's Body. Hutchinson, 1947
Demi-Paradise Regained. Hutchinson, 1945
Knight Missing. Hutchinson, 1944; Macmillan, 1945
Murder Gone Mad. Hutchinson, 1951

BARRINGTON, JOHN H., pseud; see HARVEY, JOHN HENRY

BARRINGTON, MAURICE, pseud; see BROGAN, D. W.

BARRINGTON, P. V., pseud; see BARLING, MURIEL VERE MANT

BARRINGTON, PAMELA, pseud; see BARLING, MURIEL VERE MANT

BARRON, ANN (S)
Gentle Kiss of Murder; see Murder Is a Gentle Kiss
Maybe It's Murder; see Murder Is a Gentle Kiss
Murder Is a Gentle Kiss. Bouregy, 1960 (Also published as: Gentle Kiss of Murder. Tower, 1966 and Maybe It's Murder. Bouregy, 1960; Hammond, 1964)
Spin a Dark Web. Bouregy, 1961; Paperback Lib., 1965

BARRON, DONALD G. (S)
The Zilov Bombs. Deutsch, 1962; Norton, 1963

BARRY, CHARLES, pseud; see BRYSON, CHARLES

BARRY, JEROME (M)
Extreme License. Doubleday, 1959; Boardman, T. V., 1959 (Also published as: Murder Is No Accident. Dell, 1960)

Fall Guy. Doubleday, 1960
Lady of Night. Doubleday, Doran, 1944; Boardman, T. V., 1945
Leopard Cats Cradle. Doubleday, Doran, 1942; Boardman, T. V., 1943
The Malignant Stars. Doubleday, 1960
Murder Is No Accident; see Extreme License
Murder with Your Malted. Boardman, T. V., 1942
Strange Relations. Doubleday, 1962; Boardman, T. V., 1963

BARRY, MRS. JO HANNOLD (M)
Murder Mansion. Exposition, 1959

BARRY, JOE, pseud; see LAKE, JOE BARRY

BARRY, JOHN EVARTS (D-M)
The Skeleton in Concrete. Gifford, 1952
The Uranium Murders. Long, 1951

BARTER, JOHN P. (M)
Sword of Somerled. Hodder, 1953

BARTLETT, VERNON; see JACOBSEN, PER

BARTON, DONALD RICHMOND (S)
Once in Aleppo. Scribner, 1955; Museum Press, 1957

BARTON, GEORGE (M)
Mystery of the Red Flame. Page, 1918
The Pembroke Mason Affair. Page, 1920
Strange Adventures of Bromley Barnes. Page, 1918

BASHFORD, HENRY HOWARTH (M)
Behind the Fog. Heinemann, 1926; Harper, 1927

BASIL, DON (D)
Cat and Feather. Earle, P., 1931; Holt, H., 1931

BASINGER, DONALD (M)
The Devil Within Us. Dobson, 1963; British Book Centre, 1964

BASINSKY, EARLE (S)
The Big Steal. Dutton, 1955; Boardman, T. V., 1956
Death Is a Cold Keen Edge. New Amer. Lib., 1956

BASS, CHARLES BECK (M)
Head Held High. Vantage, 1958

BATCHELOR, DENZIL (M)
Everything Happens to Hector. Heinemann, 1958
The Man Who Loved Chocolates. Heinemann, 1961
The Taste of Blood. Heinemann, 1958

BATES, HARRY ARTHUR (M) (Pseudonym: Harry Arthur)
Summer Showers. Pageant Press, 1953

BATES, HERBERT E. (S)
Dear Life. Joseph, M., 1950

BATESON, DAVID (S)
The Big Tomorrow. Hale, R., 1956
I'll Do Anything. Hale, R., 1960
I'll Go Anywhere. Hale, R., 1959
It's Murder, Senorita. Hale, R., 1954
The Man from the Rock. Hale, R., 1955
The Night Is for Violence. Hale, R., 1958
The Soho Jungle. Hale, R., 1957
This Side of Terror, Hale, R., 1959

BATTYE, GLADYS STARKEY (M) (Pseudonym: Margaret Lynn)
A Light in the Window. Doubleday, 1968
Mrs. Maitland's Affair. Doubleday, 1963; Avon, 1964
To See a Stranger. Doubleday, 1963
Whisper of Darkness. Paperback Lib., 1966

BAULSIR, EDITH (S)
Within Four Walls. Century, 1921

BAWDEN, NINA, pseud; see KARK, NINA MARY

BAX, ROGER, pseud; see WINTERTON, PAUL

BAXT, GEORGE (M)
A Parade of Cockeyed Creatures, or Did Someone Murder Our Wandering Boy? Random, 1967
A Queer Kind of Death. S & S, 1966; Cape, 1967; Signet, 1967
Swing Low, Sweet Harriet. S & S, 1967

BAXTER, GREGOY, pseud; see RESSICK, JOHN SELLAR MATHESON

BAYARD, FRED, pseud; see CAMPBELL, MARGARET ELIZABETH BAIRD

BAYER, ELEANOR and LEO BAYER (M) (Pseudonym: Oliver Weld Bayer)
Brutal Question. Doubleday, 1947
An Eye for an Eye. Doubleday, Doran, 1947
No Little Enemy. Doubleday, Doran, 1944; Hutchinson, 1945
The Paper Chase. Doubleday, Doran, 1943

BAYER, LEO; see BAYER, ELEANOR

BAYER, OLIVER WELD, pseud; see BAYER, ELEANOR

BAYLEY, A. ERIC (M)
The House of Strange Secrets. Sands, 1899
The Secret of Scotland Yard. Sands, 1900

BAYNE, ISABELLA (M)
Cruel as the Grave. Jarrolds, 1956
Death and Benedict. Laurie, 1952

BAYNE, SPENCER, pseud. (D)
Agent Extraordinary. Dutton, 1942
Murder Recalls Van Kill. Harper, 1929; Musson, 1939
The Turning Sword. Harper, 1941; Musson, 1941

BAYNE-POWELL, ISABELLA (M)
Death Enters the Ward. Barmerlea, 1947; Murray, 1947

BAYNE-POWELL, MRS. ROSAMOND (M)
Crime at Cloysters. Murray, J., 1947
Crime at Porches Hill. MacDonald & Co., 1950

BAYNES, JACK (M)
Hand of the Mafia. GM
Meet Morocco Jones. Crest, 1956
Meet Morocco Jones in the Case of the Syndicate Hoods. Crest, 1957
Morocco Jones and the Case of the Golden Angel. Crest, 1959
The Peeping Tom Murders. Crest, 1958

BAZAN, EMILIA PARDO (M)
The Mystery of the Lost Dauphin. Funk, 1906

BEALS, CARLETON (S)
Dawn over the Amazon. Duell, 1950

BEAM, MAURICE and SUMNER BRITTON (D)
Murder in a Shell. Messner, 1939

BEATTY, ELIZABETH (D)
The Jupiter Missile Mystery. Bouregy, 1960; Airmont, 1964
Murder at Auction. Bouregy, 1961

BECHDOLT, FREDERICK RITCHE (M)
The Tree of Death. Doubleday, Doran, 1937

BECHDOLT, JOHN ERNEST (M)
Mystery at Hurricane Hill. Dutton, 1951

BECK, HENRY CHARLTON (D)
Cakes to Kill. Dutton, 1932
Death by Clue. Dutton, 1933
Murder in the News Room. Dutton, 1931
Murder in the Newspaper Guild. Dutton, 1937
Society Editor. Dutton, 1932

BECKE, GEORGE LOUIS (M)
Mystery of the Laughlin Islands. Unwin, 1896

BECKER, STEPHEN DAVID (S) (Pseudonym: Steve Dodge)
A Covenant with Death. Atheneum, 1965; Hamilton, H., 1965; Dell, 1966
Juice. Dell, 1965
Season of the Stranger. Dell
Shanghai Incident, by Steve Dodge. GM, 1955

BEDFORD-JONES, HENRY JAMES O'BRIEN (M)
Mardi Gras Mystery. Doubleday, Page, 1921
The Shadow. Fiction League, 1930
The Trail of the Shadow. Hurst, 1924

BEEDING, FRANCIS, pseud; see PALMER, JOHN LESLIE

BEGBIE, GARSTIN (M)
Murder Mask. Jenkins, 1934
Sudden Death at Scotland Yard. Jenkins, 1933
Trailing Death: A Romance of the Secret Service. Jenkins, 1932

BEHN, NOEL (S)
The Kremlin Letter. S & S, 1966; Dell, 1967

BEHREND, ARTHUR F. (S)
Unlucky for Some. Eyre, 1955

BEKESSY, JEAN (S) (Pseudonym: Hans Habe)
The Devil's Agent. Fell, 1958; Avon, 1966 (English title: Agent of the Devil. Harrap, 1958)

BELL, ABBAN (M)
Out of Circulation. Popular Lib., 1965

BELL, ERIC TEMPLE (M) (Pseudonym: John Taine)
Green Fire. Dutton, 1928
The Iron Star. Dutton, 1930
The Purple Sapphire. Dutton, 1924
The Quayles Invention. Dutton, 1927

BELL, J. J. (M)
Till the Clock Stops. Hodder, 1912; Duffield, 1917

BELL, JOSEPHINE, pseud; see BALL, DORIS BELL COLLIER

BELL, LESLIE (M)
Laughing Fish. Meridian, 1952
Ring the Bell, Sister. Laurie, 1956

BELL, NEIL, pseud; see SOUTHWOLD, STEPHEN

BELL, VICARS WALKER (M)
Death and the Night Watches. Faber, 1955; British Book Centre, 1962
Death Darkens Council. Faber, 1952
Death Has Two Doors. Faber, 1950
Death Under the Stars. Faber, 1959
Death Walks by the River. Faber, 1959
Two by Day and One by Night. Faber, 1950

BELL, WYATT (D)
The Magnolia Murder. GM, 1961

BELLAH, JAMES WARNER (S)
The Bones of Napoleon. Appleton-Century, 1940
The Brass Gong Tree. Appleton-Century, 1936
Seven Must Die. Appleton-Century, 1938

BELLAIRS, GEORGE, pseud; see BLUNDELL, HAROLD

BELLAMANN, HENRY (S)
The Gray Man Walks. Doubleday, Doran, 1936
Victoria Grandolet. Ace, 1964

BELLEM, ROBERT LESLIE (M)
Blue Murder. Phoenix, 1938

BELLOC, HILAIRE (Full name: Joseph Hilaire Pierre Belloc) (M) (Pseudonym: Hilaire Belloc)
But Soft-We Are Observed. Arrowsmith, 1928
Emerald of Catherine the Great. Arrowsmith, 1926; Harper, 1926
Haunted House. Arrowsmith, 1928; Harper, 1928
The Missing Masterpiece. Arrowsmith, 1929

BELMAR, CHARLES (M)
Finnegan's Dilemma. Vantage, 1950

BENCHLEY, NATHANIEL (S)
Catch a Falling Spy. McGraw, 1963
The Off-Islanders. McGraw, 1961; Hutchinson, 1962
Sail a Crooked Ship. Crest, 1960; McGraw, 1960; Hutchinson, 1961

BENDER, W., JR. (S)
Tokyo Intrigue. Brown, Watson

BENEDICT, GERALD (M)
The Case of the Deadly Drops. Phoenix, 1941

BENÉT, JAMES (D)
The Knife Behind You. Harper, 1950
A Private Killing. Harper, 1949

BENÉT, STEPHEN VINCENT (M)
The Last Circle. Farrar, Straus, 1946

BENÉT, WILLIAM ROSE (M)
The First Person Singular. Doran, 1922

BENJAMIN, EDLA (D)
Murder Without Makeup. Random, 1940
A Well-Born Corpse. Random, 1939; Tower, 1943

BENNETT, A. G. (M)
Forest of Fear. Macaulay, 1924

BENNETT, ARNOLD (S)
Grand Babylon Hotel. Doran, 1902; Chatto, 1903; Penguin, 1939
Night Visitors and Other Stories. Cassell, 1931; Doran, 1931

BENNETT, DOROTHEA (S)
The Dry Taste of Fear. Barker, 1960
Under the Skin. Barker, 1961; Mill, 1962; Crest, 1965

BENNETT, DOROTHY (S)
Carrion Crows. Hutchinson, 1950
The Curious Were Killed. Hutchinson, 1947

BENNETT, DOROTHY (D)
How Strange a Thing. Caxton, 1935 (First detective novel in verse)
Murder Unleashed. Doubleday, Doran, 1935; Burt, 1936

BENNETT, EDWIN; see DANNETT, SYLVIA G. L.

BENNETT, ERIC (M)
Murder at the Admiralty. Hutchinson, 1941; Penguin, 1945

BENNETT, F. E. (D)
The Mormon Detective. Ogilvie

BENNETT, GEOFFREY MARTIN (M) (Pseudonym: "Sea-lion")
Cargo for Crooks. Collins, 1948
Damn Desmond Drake. Hutchinson, 1953; McGraw, 1953
Death in Russian Habit. Long, 1958
Phantom Fleet. Collins, 1946
Sink Me a Ship. Collins, 1947
When Danger Threatens. Collins, 1949

BENNETT, JACK (S)
Ocean Road. Joseph, M., 1966; Little, 1966

BENNETT, JAMES WILLIAM (M)
Spinach Jade. Skeffington, 1939

BENNETT, JAY (D)
The Catacombs. Abelard, 1959
Death Is a Silent Room. Abelard, 1965

BENNETT, KEM (S)
Dangerous Knowledge. Collins, 1957
Devil's Current. Doubleday, 1953; Collins, 1956
Passport for a Renegade. Doubleday, 1955

BENNETT, MARGOT (M)
Away Went the Little Fish. Nicholson, 1946; Doubleday, 1947
Farewell Crown and Goodbye King. Walker & Co., 1961; Collier
The Man Who Didn't Fly. Harper, 1956
Someone from the Past. Dutton, 1958; Eyre, 1958; Crest
That Summer's Earthquake. Eyre, 1964
Time to Change Hats. Nicholson, 1945; Doubleday, 1946
The Widow of Bath. Doubleday, 1952; Eyre, 1952

BENNETT, RICHARD LAURENCE (M)
Whispering Money. Heinemann, 1953

BENNETT, ROLF (S)
The Web. Hodder, 1917

BENOIT, PIERRE (S)
The Secret Spring. Dodd, 1920 (English title: Count Philip. Hutchinson, 1920)

BENSON, BEN (D)
Affair of the Exotic Dancer. Mill, 1958
Alibi at Dusk. Mill, 1951
Beware the Pale Horse. Mill, 1951; Bantam
The Black Mirror. Mill, 1957; Collins, 1958; Bantam
The Blonde in Black. Mill, 1958; Collins, 1959; Bantam
The Broken Shield. Mill, 1955
The Burning Fuse. Mill, 1954; Collins, 1956
End of Violence. Collins, 1959; Mill, 1959; Bantam, 1960
The Frightened Ladies. Mill, 1960; Bantam, 1962 (Also published as: Lady With a Past. Bantam, 1960)
The Girl in the Cage. Mill, 1954; Bantam
The Huntress Is Dead. Mill, 1960
Lady with a Past; see The Frightened Ladies
Lily in Her Coffin. Mill, 1952; Boardman, T. V., 1954; Bantam
The Ninth Hour. Mill, 1956
The Running Man. Mill, 1957; Collins, 1958
Seven Steps East. Mill, 1959; Bantam, 1961
The Silver Cobweb. Mill, 1955; Collins, 1959
Stamped for Murder. Mill, 1952
Target in Taffeta. Mill, 1953; Collins, 1955; Bantam
The Venus Death. Mill, 1953

BENSON, EDWARD FREDERIC (M)
The Blotting Book. Doubleday, Page, 1908; Heinemann, 1908
Visible and Invisible. Doran, 1924

BENSON, GODFREY R. (Lord Charnwood) (D)
Tracks in the Snow. Longmans, 1906; Benn, 1927

BENSON, O. G. (S)
Cain's Woman. Dell, 1960

BENSON, THEODORA (M)
Rehearsal for Death. Gollancz, 1954

BENSON, THÉRÈSE, pseud; see KNIPE, EMILIE

BENTLEY, EDMUND CLERIHEW (D)
The Chill; see Elephant's Work: An Enigma
Elephant's Work: An Enigma. Hodder, 1950; Knopf, 1950 (Also published as: The Chill. Dell)
Trent Intervenes. Knopf, 1938; Nelson, 1938
Trent's Case Book. Knopf, 1953
Trent's Last Case, with H. W. Allen. Nelson, 1913 (U.S. title: The Woman in Black. Century, 1913; PB, 1944; Ballantine, 1963)
Trent's Own Case, with H. W. Allen. Constable, 1936; Knopf, 1936
The Woman in Black; see Trent's Last Case

BENTLEY, JOHN (D)
The Berg Case. Eldon, 1934 (Also published as: The Eyes of Death. Doubleday, Doran, 1934)
The Call of the Corpse. Hutchinson
Dangerous Waters. Hutchinson, 1940
The Eyes of Death; see The Berg Case
The Fairbairn Case. Chapman, 1936
The Front Page Murder; see Mr. Marlow Stops for Brandy
The Griffith Case. Eldon, 1935
The Hartland Case. Chapman, 1939
Kill Me Again. Dodd, 1947
The Landor Case. Chapman, 1937
L'Estrange Case. Eldon, 1935
Mr. Marlow Chooses Wine. Houghton, 1941
Mr. Marlow Stops for Brandy. Houghton, 1940 (English title: The Front Page Murder. Hutchinson, 1940)
Mr. Marlow Takes to Rye. Houghton, 1942
Pattern for Perfidy. Hutchinson, 1946
Prelude to Trouble. Hutchinson, 1946

The Radcliffe Case. Chapman, 1938
Rendezvous with Death. Hutchinson, 1941
The Whitney Case. Chapman, 1937

BENTLEY, NICHOLAS CLERIHEW (D)
The Floating Dutchman. Joseph, M., 1950; Duell, 1951
Gammon and Espionage. Cresset, 1938
Third Party Risk. Joseph, M., 1948; Collins
The Tongue-Tied Canary. Joseph, M., 1948; Duell, 1949

BENTLEY, PHYLLIS ELEANOR (S)
The House of Moreys. Gollancz, 1953; Ace, 1964

BENTLEY, STEVE (S)
Angel Eyes. Dell, 1961

BENTON, JOHN (D)
Duane and the Art Murders. Cassell, 1939
Duane and the G-Men. Cassell, 1938

BERCKMAN, EVELYN (M)
The Beckoning Dream. Dodd, 1955 (Also published as: Worse Than Murder. PB, 1957)
Blind Girl's Buff. Dodd, 1962
The Blind Villain. Dodd, 1957; Eyre, 1957 (Also published as: House of Terror. Dell, 1960)
Do You Know This Voice? Dodd, 1960; Eyre, 1961
The Evil of Time. Dodd, 1954; Eyre, 1955; Pyramid, 1967
The Heir of Starvelings. Doubleday, 1967
House of Terror; see The Blind Villain
The Hovering Darkness. Dodd, 1958; Eyre, 1958; Ace, 1963
Jewel of Death; see The Strange Bedfellow
Keys from a Window. Eyre, 1966
Lament for Four Brides. Dodd, 1959
No Known Grave. Dodd, 1960
A Simple Case of Ill-Will. Eyre, 1964; Dodd, 1965
Stalemate. Doubleday, 1966
The Strange Bedfellow. Dodd, 1956; Eyre, 1957 (Also published as: Jewel of Death. Pyramid, 1968)
A Thing That Happens to You. Dodd, 1964
Worse Than Murder; see The Beckoning Dream

BERESFORD, JOHN DAVYS (M)
An Innocent Criminal. Collins, 1931; Dutton, 1931
Instrument of Destiny. Bobbs, 1928; Collins, 1928
The Monkey-Puzzle. Collins, 1925
Nineteen Impressions. Sedgwick, 1918
The Prisoners of Hartling. Collins, 1922

BERESFORD, LESLIE (D)
Murder Can Be Such Fun. Long, 1947
Murder in the Basement

BERESFORD, MARCUS (S) (Pseudonym: Marc Brandel)
Time of the Fire. Random, 1954

BERGER, THOMAS (S)
Killing Time. Dial, 1967

BERGES, M. L. (S)
Woman of Shanghai. Brown, Watson, 1959

BERGMAN, LEE (D)
Walk Softly, Walk Deadly. Belmont, 1963

BERGQUIST, LILLIAN and IRVING MOORE (D)
Your Shot, Darling! Morrow, 1948

BERGSON, LEO and ROBERT McMAHON (M)
The Windowmaster. GM, 1967

BERKELEY, ANTHONY, pseud; see COX, ANTHONY BERKELEY

BERNANOS, GEORGES (D)
A Crime. Dutton, 1936; Hale, R., 1936; Museum Press, 1936

BERNARD, ROBERT, pseud; see MARTIN, ROBERT BERNARD

BERNERS, LORD (M)
The Camel. Constable, 1936

BERRIDGE, ELIZABETH (D)
Across the Common. Lancer, 1966
It Won't Be Flowers. S & S, 1949

BERROW, NORMAN (M)
Bishop's Sword. Ward, Lock, 1948
Claws of the Cougar. Ward, Lock, 1957
Don't Go Out After Dark. Ward, Lock, 1950
Don't Jump, Mr. Boland. Ward, Lock, 1954
Eleventh Plague. Ward, Lock, 1953
Fingers for Ransom. Ward, Lock, 1939
Footprints of Satan. Ward, Lock, 1950
Ghost House. Ward, Lock, 1940
It Howls at Night. Ward, Lock, 1937
Lady's in Danger. Ward, Lock, 1955
Murder in the Melody. Ward, Lock, 1940
Oil Under the Window. Ward, Lock, 1936

One Thrilling Night. Ward, Lock, 1937
Secret Dancer. Ward, Lock, 1936
Singing Room. Ward, Lock, 1948
Smokers of Nashih. Eldon, 1934
Spaniards Thumb. Ward, Lock, 1949
Terror in the Fog. Ward, Lock. 1938
Three Tiers of Fantasy. Ward, Lock, 1947
Words Have Wings. Ward, Lock, 1946

BERRY, J. L. (D)
A Close Call. Ogilvie, 1888

BERRY, JOHN (S)
Don't Betray Me. Signet, 1963
Flight of White Crows. Gollancz, 1962
Krishna Fluting. Gollancz, 1960

BERTON, GUY, pseud; see LA COSTE, GUY ROBERT

BESSELL, J. PERCIVAL (M)
Paid Out. Macaulay, 1919

BESSIE, ALVAH CECIL (M)
Bread and Stone. Swan, G. G., 1932

BEST, HERBERT (M)
Mystery of the Flaming Hut. Cassell, 1932; Harper, 1932
The Twenty-Fifth Hour. Random, 1940

BESTE, RAYMOND VERNON (S)
Faith Has No Country; see The Moonbeams
The Moonbeams. Harper, 1961; Lancer, 1966 (English title: Faith Has No Country. Hodder, 1961)
Repeat the Instructions. Harper & Row, 1967
Seeds of Destruction. Hodder, 1964

BESTER, ALFRED (S)
The Demolished Man. Shasta, 1953; Sidgwick, 1953; New Amer. Lib., 1954 (Science Fiction murder)

BESTER, GEORGE CLINTON (D)
The Corpse Came Calling. Phoenix, 1941
The Postage Stamp Murder. Dial, 1935; Low, 1936
Prelude to Murder. Dial, 1936; Low, 1936

BETHUNE, J. G. (M)
The "F" Cipher. Price, McGill, 1892

BETTANY, GEORGE (M)
Murder at Benfleet. Skeffington, 1946
Secret of the Swamp. Skeffington, 1931

BETTERIDGE, DON, pseud; see NEWMAN, BERNARD CHARLES

BEYER, WILLIAM GRAY (D)
Death of a Puppeteer. Curl, 1946
Murder by Arrangement. Partridge, 1948

BEYERS, CHARLES ALMA (D)
The Inverness Murders. Dial, 1935

BEYNON, JANE (S) (Pseudonym: Lange Lewis)
Birthday Murder. Bodley Head, 1951
Cypress Man. Bobbs, 1944
Death Among Friends; see Murder Among Friends
Juliet Dies Twice. Bobbs, 1943
Meat for Murder. Bobbs, 1943; Bodley Head, 1950
Murder Among Friends. Bobbs, 1942 (English title: Death Among Friends. Bodley Head, 1950)
Passionate Victims, by Lange Lewis. Bobbs, 1952; Lane, 1953

BENYON, JOHN, pseud; see HARRIS, JOHN BEYNON

BICKEL, MARY (M)
Brassbound. Coward, 1934
Trial of Linda Stuart. Hamilton, H., 1935

BICKERTON, DEREK (S)
Payroll. Eyre, 1959

BIDMEAD, CHARLES (M)
Man in the Shadows. Rich, 1954
The Silent Man. Rich, 1955

BIDWELL, MARGARET
Death and His Brother. Hurst, 1940
Death on the Agenda. Hurst, 1939

BIDWELL, MARJORY ELIZABETH SARAH (S) (Pseudonym: Mary Anne Gibbs)
The House of Ravensbourne. Pyramid, 1964 (English title: The Amateur Governess. Hurst, 1964)

BIERCE, AMBROSE (M)
Collected Works of Ambrose Bierce. Neale, 1909-1912
Ghost and Horror Stories. Dover, 1964

BIER, JESSE (S)
Trial at Bannock. Harcourt, 1963; Avon, 1964

BIERSTADT, EDWARD HALE (D)
Enter Murderers. Doubleday, Doran, 1934
Satan Was a Man. Doubleday, Doran, 1935

BIGELOW, JOHN MASON (D)
Death Is an Early Riser. Scribner, 1940

BIGGERS, EARL DERR (M)
The Agony Column. Bobbs, 1916; Grosset
Behind That Curtain. Bobbs, 1928; Harrap, 1928; Paperback Lib., 1964
Black Camel. Bobbs, 1929; Cassell, 1930; Paperback Lib., 1964
Celebrated Cases of Charlie Chan. Bobbs, 1933; Cassell, 1933
Charlie Chan's Caravan. Grosset, 1927
Charlie Chan Carries On. Bobbs, 1930; Cassell, 1931; Paperback Lib., 1964
Charlie Chan Omnibus: The House Without a Key, Behind That Curtain, and Keeper of the Keys. Grosset, 1932
The Chinese Parrot. Bobbs, 1926; Harrap, 1927; Paperback Lib., 1963
Fifty Candles. Bobbs, 1926
The House Without a Key. Bobbs, 1925; Grosset, 1926; Harrap, 1926; Paperback Lib., 1964
Inside the Lines, with Robert Wells Ritchie. Bobbs, 1915
Keeper of the Keys. Bobbs, 1932; Cassell, 1932; Grosset, 1933; Paperback Lib., 1963
Love Insurance. Bobbs, 1914; Grosset, 1916; Collier
Second Floor Mystery. Grosset, 1930
Seven Keys to Baldpate. Bobbs, 1913; Mills & Boon, 1914; Popular Lib.

BIGGLE, LLOYD, JR. (S)
Watchers of the Dark. Doubleday, 1966

BILLANY, DAN (M)
The Opera House Murders. Faber, 1940 (U.S. title: It Takes a Thief. Harper, 1941)

BILLETT, MRS. MABEL BROUGHTON (D)
Calamity House. Hutchinson, 1927
The Robot Detective. Hutchinson, 1932; Macmillan, 1932
The Shadow on the Steppe. Hutchinson, 1930
Smooth Silence. Ryerson, 1936

BINDER, OTTO (S)
The Avengers Battle the Earth-Wrecker. Bantam, 1967

BINDLOSS, HAROLD (M)
Carmen's Messenger. Stokes, 1917
Lone Hand. Stokes, 1928

BINGHAM, EADFRID A; see LA COSTE, GUY ROBERT

BINGHAM, CARSON (S)
The Gang Girls. Monarch, 1963

BINGHAM, JOHN MICHAEL WARD (Baron Clanmorris) (M-D)
Case of Libel. Gollancz, 1963
The Double Agent. Gollancz, 1966; Dutton, 1967
Five Roundabouts to Heaven. Gollancz, 1953 (U.S. title: The Tender Poisoner. Dodd, 1953)
A Fragment of Fear. Gollancz, 1965; Dutton, 1967
Inspector Morgan's Dilemma; see Paton Street Case
Marion. Gollancz, 1958
Murder Off the Record. Dodd, 1957
Murder Plan Six. Gollancz, 1958; Dodd, 1959
My Name Is Michael Sibley. Dodd, 1952; Penguin
Night's Black Agent. Dodd, 1961; Penguin, 1965
Paton Street Case. Gollancz, 1955; Penguin, 1964 (U.S. title: Inspector Morgan's Dilemma. Dodd, 1955)
Story of a Crime. Gollancz, 1954 (U.S. title: The Third Skin. Dodd, 1954)
The Tender Poisoner; see Five Roundabouts to Heaven
The Third Skin; see Story of a Crime

BINNS, OTTWELL (M) (Pseudonym: Ben Bolt)
Flaming Crescent. Ward, Lock, 1931
The Lady of North Star. Knopf, 1922
Lavenham Mystery. Ward, Lock, 1933
Snapshot Mystery. Ward, Lock, 1933
Subway Mystery. Ward, Lock, 1930

BIRCH, BRUCE (S)
Subway in the Sky. Four Square, 1959

BIRCH, VERA BENEDICTA (M)
Game for One Player. Cresset, 1947; Scribner, 1947

BIRD, BRANDON, pseud; see EVANS, GEORGE

BIRKLEY, DOLAN, pseud; see HITCHENS, DOLORES BIRK OLSON

BIRMINGHAM, GEORGE A., pseud; see HANNAY, JAMES OWEN

BIRMINGHAM, STEPHEN (S)
The Towers of Love. Signet, 1966

BIRNEY, HOFFMAN (M) (Pseudonym: David Kent)
Jason Burr's First Case. Random, 1941
A Knife Is Silent. Random, 1947

BISHOP, MOLDEN GRANGE (M)
Scylla. Ace, 1954

BISHOP, MORRIS GILBERT (D) (Pseudonym: W. Bolingbroke Johnson)
The Widening Stain. Knopf, 1942; Lane, 1942

BISS, GERALD (S)
Door of the Unreal. Putnam, 1920

BITTLE, CAMILLA R. (M)
The Boy in the Pool. Lippincott, 1962

BJERKE, ANDRE (D) (Pseudonym: Bernhard Borge)
Death in the Blue Lake. MacDonald & Co., 1961

BLACK, ELIZABETH BEST (D)
The Crime of the Chromium Bowl. Loring & Mussey, 1934
The Ravenelle Riddle. Loring & Mussey, 1933

BLACK, GAVIN, pseud; see WYND, OSWALD

BLACK, IAN STUART (S)
Passionate City. Viking, 1958

BLACK, LADBROKE LIONEL DAY (D)
Killer at Large. Paul, S., 1938
Mr. Preed Investigates. Nelson, 1938
Mr. Preed's Gangster. Nelson, 1939

BLACK, LIONEL (S)
Two Ladies in Verona. Cassell, 1967 (Also published as: The Lady Is a Spy. Paperback Lib., 1968)

BLACK, MANSELL, pseud; see TREVOR, ELLESTON

BLACK, P. (D)
Which of Them? Benn, 1932

BLACK, ROBERT JERE (D)
The Killing of the Golden Goose. Loring & Mussey, 1934

BLACK, THOMAS (D)
Four Dead Mice. Rinehart, 1954
The Pinball Murders. Reynal, 1947
Three-Thirteen Murders. Reynal, 1946
The Whitebird Murders. Reynal, 1946

BLACKBURN, BARBARA
City of Forever. Hale, R., 1963

*BLACKBURN, JOHN, see MOTT, J. MOLDON

BLACKER, IRWIN R. (S)
The Kilroy Gambit. World Pub., 1960; Signet
Search and Destroy. Random, 1966; Dell, 1967

BLACKLEDGE, LEONARD (M)
Behind the Evidence. Hutchinson, 1935

BLACKMON, ANITA (Mrs. Harry Pugh Smith) (D)
Hotel Richelieu; see Murder à la Richelieu
Murder à la Richelieu. Doubleday, Doran, 1937 (English title: Hotel Richelieu. Heinemann. 1939)
Riddle of the Dead Cats. Butterworth, T., 1940
There Is No Return. Doubleday, Doran, 1938

BLACKSTOCK, CHARITY, pseud; see TORDAY, URSULA

BLACKSTOCK, LEE, pseud; see TORDAY, URSULA

BLACKWOOD, ALGERNON (S)
The Dance of Death and Other Tales. MacVeagh, 1928
The Doll and One Other. Arkham House, 1946
The Empty House and Other Ghost Stories. Nash, 1906, 1915
Incredible Adventures. Macmillan, 1914
John Silence. Nash, 1908
The Listener and Other Stories, Nash, 1907
The Lost Valley and Other Stories. Clay & Sons, 1914; Nash, 1914; Vaughan & Gomme, 1914
Shocks. Grayson, 1935; Dutton, 1936
Tales of Algernon Blackwood. Dutton, 1938
Tales of Terror and the Unknown. Dutton, 1965

BLADES, J. K. (M)
The Norwood Mystery. Stockwell, 1933

BLAIR, CHARLES F., JR. and A. J. WALLIS (S)
Thunder Above. Holt, 1956

BLAIR, DOROTHY and EVELYN PAGE (D) (Pseudonym: Roger Scarlett)
Back Bay Murders. Doubleday, Doran, 1930
Beacon Hill Murders. Doubleday, Doran, 1930
The Cat's Paw. Doubleday, Doran, 1931
In the First Degree. Doubleday, Doran, 1933
Murder Among the Angels. Doubleday, Doran, 1932

BLAIR, E. P.; see BLAIR, H. L.

BLAIR, H. L. and E. P. BLAIR (D)
Three Saw the Murder. Spiller, 1938

BLAISDELL, ANNE, pseud; see LININGTON, ELIZABETH

BLAKE, ELEANOR, pseud; see PRATT, MRS. ELEANOR BLAKE ATKINSON

BLAKE, GLADYS (M)
At Bow View. Appleton, D., 1926

**Titles are erroneously listed under MOTT, J. MOLDON. Correction: Author's name is JOHN BLACKBURN.*

The Mysterious Tutor. Appleton, D., 1926
Scratches on the Glass. Appleton, D., 1927

BLAKE, NICHOLAS, pseud; see DAY-LEWIS, CECIL

BLAKER, RICHARD (M)
The Jefferson Secrets. Doubleday, Doran, 1929
Night Shift. Appleton-Century, 1934; Heinemann, 1934

BLAKESTON, OSWELL (M) (Joint pseudonym with Roger d'Este Burford: "Simon")
Cat with the Mustache, by "Simon." Wishart, 1935
Murder Among Friends, by "Simon." Wishart, 1933
Pink Ribbon, As Told to the Police. Quality, 1950

BLANC, SUZANNE (D)
The Green Stone. Harper, 1961; Cassell, 1962; Lancer, 1966
The Rose Window. Doubleday, 1967
The Yellow Villa. Doubleday, 1964; Cassell, 1965

BLANCO, L. W. (S)
Spykill. Lancer, 1966

BLANE, FERGUS, pseud. (M)
Money-Lender in Gloves. Newnes, 1939

BLANEY, C. E.; see HALL, H.

BLANKFORT, MICHAEL (S)
Behold the Fire. New Amer. Lib., 1965
Goodbye, I Guess. S & S, 1962; Signet
Passage to the Place Vendome. Allen, W. H., 1962
The Widow Makers. S & S, 1946

BLASINGAME, WYATT (M)
John Smith Hears Death Walking. Bart, 1944

BLATTY, WILLIAM PETER
Twinkle, Twinkle, "Killer Kane." Doubleday, 1967

BLAU, ERNEST E. (M)
The Queen's Falcon. McKay, 1947

BLAYN, HUGO (S)
Five Matchboxes. Paul, S., 1948
Flashpoint. Paul, S., 1950
What Happened to Hammond? Paul, S., 1951

BLAYNE, SEBASTIEN (S)
Terror in the Night. GM, 1953; Muller, 1954

BLEACKLEY, HORACE WILLIAMS (M)
Night of Peril. Lane, 1931

BLEECH, WEBB (S)
Article 92; Murder-Rape. GM, 1964

"BLINKHOALIE," pseud; see ALLISON, WILLIAM

BLISS, ADAM, pseud; see BURKHARDT, ROBERT

BLISS, TIP (M)
Broadway Murders. Greenberg, 1930

BLIXEN-FINECKE, BARONESS KAREN CHRISTINE (S) (Pseudonyms: Pierre Andrezel, Isak Dinesen)
The Angelic Avengers, by Pierre Andrezel. Putnam, 1946; Random, 1947
Seven Gothic Tales, by Isak Dinesen. Smith, H., 1934
Winter's Tales, by Isak Dinesen. Putnam, 1934

BLIZARD, MARIE (M)
Conspiracy of Silence. Mill, 1954; Hammond, 1957
The Dark Corner. Mill, 1950; Hammond, 1956
The Late, Lamented Lady. Mystery House, 1946
The Men in Her Death. Mystery House, 1947
The Watch Sinister. Mill, 1951; Hammond, 1956

BLOCH, MRS. BLANCHE (D)
The Bach Festival Murders. Harper, 1942; Musson, 1942

BLOCH, ROBERT (S)
Atoms and Evil. GM, 1962
Blood Runs Cold. Hale, R., 1961; S & S, 1961; Popular Lib., 1962
Bogey Men. Pyramid, 1963
Chamber of Horrors. Award, 1966
The Couch. GM, 1962
Dead Beat. S & S, 1960; Hale, R., 1961; Popular Lib., 1961
Even More Nightmares. Belmont
Firebug. Regenry, 1961; GM
Horror-7: Tales of Shock and Terror. Belmont, 1963
House of the Hatchet. Tandem, 1965
Kidnapper. Lion, 1954
Kill for Kali. Belmont, 1961
More Nightmares. Belmont, 1962
Nightmares. Belmont, 1961
Opener of the Way. Arkham House, 1945
Pleasant Dreams-Nightmares. Arkham House, 1959

Psycho. S & S, 1959; Hale, R., 1960; Crest, 1963
The Scarf. Dial, 1947; GM, 1966
Shooting Star. Ace, 1958
The Skull of the Marquis de Sade. Pyramid, 1961
Spiderweb. Ace, 1954
Terror. Belmont, 1962
Terror in the Night. Ace, 1958
Will to Kill. Ace, 1954
Yours Truly, Jack the Ripper. Belmont, 1962

BLOCHMAN, LAWRENCE G. (D)
Appointment in India; see Wives to Burn
Bengal Fire. Collins, 1937; Dell, 1937;
Blowdown. Harcourt, 1939; Collins; 1940 (Serial title: The Resounding Skies)
Bombay Mail. Collins, 1934; Little, 1934; Dell
Clues for Dr. Coffee: a Second Casebook. Lippincott, 1964
Death Walks in Marble Halls. American Magazine, Sept., 1942; Dell, 1945
Diagnosis: Homicide. The Case-book of Dr. Coffee. Lippincott, 1947, 1950
The Lorelei. Doubleday, 1959
Midnight Sailing. Harcourt, 1938 (English title: Sunset Voyage. Collins, 1939)
Pursuit. Quinn Handibooks, 1951
Rather Cool for Mayhem. Lippincott, 1951; Cassell, 1952
Recipe for Homicide. Lippincott, 1952; Hammond, 1954
Red Snow at Darjeeling. Saint Mystery Lib., 1935; Collins, 1938
The Resounding Skies; see Blowdown
See You at the Morgue. Duell, 1941; Cassell, 1946; Collier, 1962
Sunset Voyage; see Midnight Sailing
Wives to Burn. Collins, 1940; Harcourt, 1940 (Also published as: Appointment in India)

BLOCK, LAWRENCE (S)
The Canceled Czech. GM, 1967
Deadly Honeymoon. Macmillan, 1967
Death Pulls a Double Cross. GM, 1961
Girl with the Long Green Heart. Fawcett, 1965; Muller, 1967
Mona. GM, 1961
The Thief Who Couldn't Sleep. GM, 1966

BLOCK, LIBBIE (S)
Bedeviled. Doubleday, 1947

BLOM, ERIC WALTER (M) (Pseudonym: Sebastian Farr)
Death on the Down Beat. Dent, 1941

BLOOD, ADELE and TAM MARRIOTT (S)
The Jade Rabbit. Diamond Press, 1926; Dial, 1927

BLOOD, M. (S)
The Avenger. GM

BLOOM, ROLFE; see ULLMAN, ALLAN

BLOOMFIELD, ROBERT, pseud; see EDGLEY, LESLIE

BLOW, LYNTON (D)
The "Moth" Murder. Holt, H., 1932

BLUNDELL, HAROLD (D) (Pseudonym: George Bellairs)
Body in the Dumb River. Gifford, 1961
Bones in the Wilderness. Gifford, 1959
Calamity at Harwood. Macmillan, 1945
Case of the Demented Spiv. Gifford, 1949; Macmillan, 1950
Case of the Famished Parson. Gifford, 1949; Macmillan, 1949
Case of the Headless Jesuit. Gifford, 1950
Case of the Scared Rabbit. Gifford, 1946
Case of the Seven Whistles. Gifford, 1948; Macmillan, 1948
The Corpse at the Carnival. Gifford, 1958; Penguin, 1964
Corpses in Enderby. Gifford, 1954
Crime at Halfpenny Bridge. Gifford, 1946
Crime in Leper's Hollow. Gifford, 1952
Cursing Stones Murder. Gifford, 1954
Dead March for Penelope Blow. Gifford, 1951; Macmillan, 1951
The Dead Shall Be Raised. Gifford, 1942 (Also published as: Murder Will Speak. Macmillan, 1943)
Death at Half-term
Death Brings in the New Year. Macmillan, 1951
Death Drops the Pilot. Gifford, 1956
Death in Dark Glasses. Gifford, 1952; Macmillan, 1952
Death in Despair. Gifford, 1960
Death in High Provence. Gifford, 1957; Penguin, 1963
Death in Room 5. Gifford, 1955
Death in the Fearful Night. Gifford, 1960
Death in the Night Watches. Gifford, 1945; Macmillan, 1946
Death in the Wasteland. Gifford, 1963
Death of a Busybody. Gifford, 1942; Macmillan, 1943
Death of a Shadow. Gifford, 1964
Death of a Tin God. Gifford, 1961
Death on the Last Train. Gifford, 1948; Macmillan, 1949
Death Sends for the Doctor. Gifford, 1957
Death Stops the Frolic. Macmillan, 1944
Death Treads Softly. Gifford, 1956

Four Unfaithful Servants. Thriller Book Club, 1942
Half-mast for the Deemster. Gifford, 1953
He'd Rather Be Dead. Gifford, 1945
A Knife for Harry Dodd
Littlejohn on Leave. Gifford, 1941
Murder Makes Mistakes. Gifford, 1958
Murder of a Quack. Gifford, 1943; Macmillan, 1944
Murder Will Speak; see Dead Shall Be Raised
Outrage on Gallow's Hill. Gifford, 1949
Toll the Bell for Murder. Gifford, 1959
The Tormentors. Gifford, 1962
Turmoil in Zion. Gifford, 1943

BLUNT, DON (S)
Dead Giveaway. Bouregy, 1963

BOARDMAN, NEIL S. (S)
The Wine of Violence. S & S, 1964; Ballantine, 1965

BOCCA, AL, pseud; see WINTER, BEVIS

BODINGTON, NANCY HERMIONE (S)
(Pseudonym: Shelley Smith)
An Afternoon to Kill. Collins, 1953; Harper, 1954
Background for Murder. Swan, G. G., 1942, 1948
The Ballad of the Running Man. Hamilton, H., 1961; Harper, 1962; Popular Lib., 1963
The Cellar at No. 5; see Party at No. 5
Come and Be Killed. Collins, 1946; Doubleday, 1946
The Crooked Man; see Man Alone
Death Stalks a Lady. Swan, G. G., 1945
He Died of Murder. Collins, 1947; Harper, 1948
Lord Have Mercy. Hamilton, H., 1956; Harper, 1957
Man Alone. Collins, 1951 (U.S. title: The Crooked Man. Harper, 1952)
Man with a Calico Face. Harper, 1950; Collins, 1951
The Party at No. 5. Collins, 1954 (U.S. title: Cellar at No. 5. Doubleday, 1955)
Rachel Weeping. Hamilton, H., 1957
This Is the House. Collins, 1945
Woman in the Sea. Collins, 1948; Harper, 1948

BODKIN, M. McDONNELL (D)
Capture of Paul Beck. Unwin, 1909; Little, 1911
Dora Myrl, the Lady Detective. Chatto, 1900
Paul Beck, Detective. Pearson, 1898; Talbot, 1929
Pigeon Blood Rubies. Nash, 1915
The Quests of Paul Beck. Unwin, 1908

BOETZEL, ERIC and HERBERT CLOCK (S)
Light in the Sky. Coward, 1929

BOGART, WILLIAM (D)
Hell on Friday. Swift, J., 1941
Murder Is Forgetful. Mystery House, 1944
Queen City Murder Case. Mystery House, 1946
Sands Street. Swift, J., 1942

BOGGS, WINIFRED (M)
Murder on the Underground. Jenkins, 1929

BOGUE, HOGAN (M)
Dog and Duck Mystery. Jarrolds, 1931

BOHLE, EDGAR (M)
Man Who Disappeared. Random, 1958; Dell, 1960
The Wife Who Died Twice. Boardman, T. V., 1962; Random, 1962

BOILEAU, PIERRE and THOMAS NARCEJAC (S)
Choice Cuts. Dutton, 1966
The Evil Eye. Hutchinson, 1959
The Living and the Dead. Hutchinson, 1956; Washburn, 1957
The Prisoner. Hutchinson, 1957
Sleeping Beauty. Hutchinson, 1959
Spells of Evil. Hamilton, H., 1961; Mystic, 1966
The Woman Who Was No More. Rinehart, 1954

BOISSIERE, ALBERT (M)
The Man Without a Face. Dillingham, G. W., 1910-11
The Missing Finger. Dodd, 1911

BOK, CURTIS (S)
Star Wormwood. Knopf, 1959; Berkley Pub., 1960

BOLAND, BERTRAM JOHN; see BOLAND, JOHN

BOLAND, JOHN (Full name: Bertram John Boland) (S)
Bitter Fortune. Boardman, T. V., 1959
The Catch. Harrap, 1964; Holt, 1964
Counterpol. Harrap, 1963; Walker & Co., 1965
Counterpol in Paris. Harrap, 1964; Walker & Co., 1965
Fatal Error. Boardman, T. V., 1962
The Gentlemen at Large. Boardman, T. V., 1962
The Gentlemen Reform. Boardman, T. V., 1961; Macmillan, 1964
The Golden Fleece. Boardman, T. V., 1961
Inside Job. Boardman, T. V., 1961

The League of Gentlemen. Boardman, T. V., 1958
The Midas Touch. Boardman, T. V., 1960
The Mysterious Way. Boardman, T. V., 1959
Negative Value. Boardman, T. V., 1960
No Refuge. Joseph, M., 1956
Operation Red Carpet. Boardman, T. V., 1959
Queer Fish. Boardman, T. V., 1958
Vendetta. Boardman, T. V., 1961
White August. Joseph, M., 1955

BOLT, BEN, pseud; see BINNS, OTTWELL

BOLTON, GEORGE, C. (D)
A Specialist in Crime. Richards, 1904

BOLTON, ISABEL, pseud; see MILLER, MARY BRITTON

BOLTON, JOHN (M)
The Air Sleuth. Wright & Brown, 1936; Mellifont, 1939 (Abridged edition)
The Air Smugglers. Wright & Brown, 1938
The Desert Flyer. Wright & Brown, 1936; Mellifont, 1937
The Island Mystery. Wright & Brown, 1938; Mellifont, 1939 (Abridged edition)
The Mystery Plane. Wright & Brown, 1935; Mellifont, 1937 (Abridged edition)
Perils in Persia. Wright & Brown, 1938; Mellifont, 1940 (Abridged edition)
The Spy Hunters. Wright & Brown, 1940
The Swimming Pool Murder. Wright & Brown, 1940

BOLTON, MAISIE SHARMAN (M) (Pseudonym: Stratford Davis)
Death in Seven Hours. Melrose, 1952
His Father's Ghost. Abelard, 1963
No Tears Are Shed. Melrose, 1952
One Man's Secret. Boardman, T. V., 1957
The Troubled Mind. Melrose, 1953

BOLTON, WILLIAM; see BAKER, NORTH

BOMBAL, MARIA-LUISA (M)
The House of Mist. Farrar, Straus, 1947; Belmont, 1964
The Shrouded Woman. Farrar, Straus, 1948; Cassell, 1950

BOMMART, JEAN (M)
The Chinese Fish. Longmans, 1935

BOND, EVELYN (S-Gothic)
Evil in the House. Lancer
Heritage of Fear. Belmont, 1966
House of Distant Voices. Belmont, 1966
House of Shadows. Lancer, 1965
Lady in Darkness. Lancer
Lady of Storm House. Lancer, 1965
The Venetian Secret. Lancer, 1967
Widow in White. Lancer, 1967

BOND, MRS. FLORENCE DEMAREST FOOS (D) (Pseudonym: Anne Demarest)
Murder on Every Floor. Hillman-Curl, 1939

BOND, J. HARVEY (M)
Bye-Bye, Baby! Ace, 1958
If Wishes Were Hearses. Ace, 1961
Murder Isn't Funny. Ace, 1958

BOND, NOREEN (S)
Hide Away. Hodder, 1936
Take Care. Hodder, 1938

BONETT, EMERY, pseud; see COULSON, MRS. FELICITY

BONETT, JOHN, pseud; see COULSON, MRS. FELICITY

BONHAM, FRANK (M)
By Her Own Hand. Monarch, 1963
One for Sleep. GM, 1960
Skin Game. GM, 1962

BONHAM, MARGARET (S)
The House Across the River. Macmillan, 1951

BONIFACE, MARJORIE (M)
Murder as an Ornament. Doubleday, Doran, 1940
Venom in Eden. Doubleday, Doran, 1942
Wings of Death. McBride, 1946

BONNAMY, FRANCIS, pseud; see WALZ, MRS. AUDREY

BONNELL, JAMES FRANCIS (D)
Death Flies West. Scribner, 1941
Death over Sunday. Scribner, 1940

BONNER, GERALDINE (S)
Black Eagle Mystery. Appleton, D., 1916
The Castlecourt Diamond Case. Funk, 1906
The Girl at Central. Appleton, D., 1915
The Leading Lady. Bobbs, 1926
Miss Maitland, Private Secretary. Appleton, D., 1919

BONNER, MARGERIE (S)
The Last Twist of the Knife. Scribner, 1946
The Shapes That Creep. Scribner, 1945

BONNEY, JOSEPH L. (S)
Death by Dynamite. Garrick & Evans, 1940
Murder Without Clues. Garrick & Evans, 1940 (Also published as: No Man's Hand. Heinemann, 1940)
No Man's Hand; see Murder Without Clues

BOORE, WALTER HUGH (M)
Cry on the Wind. Collins, 1967
The Valley and the Shadow. Heinemann, 1963

BOOTH, CHARLES GORDON (M)
The Cat and the Clock. Doubleday, Doran, 1935; Cassell, 1938
The General Died at Dawn. Bell, G., 1937
Gold Bullets. Hodder, 1929; Morrow, 1929
Kings Die Hard. Hammond, 1948
Mr. Angel Goes Aboard. Doubleday, Doran, 1944
Murder at High Tide. Morrow, 1930 (Original title: Seven Were Suspect)
Seven Were Suspect; see Murder at High Tide
Sinister House. Morrow, 1926
Those Seven Alibis. Morrow, 1932

BOOTH, CHRISTOPHER (M)
The Braddigan Murder, with Isabel Ostrander. Hutchinson, 1933
The Deceiver's Door. Chelsea House, 1929
The House of Rogues. Chelsea House, 1924
The Kidnapping Syndicate. Chelsea House, 1925
Killing Jazz. Chelsea House, 1928
The Seaside Mystery. Chelsea House, 1925
The Sleeping Cat, with Isabel E. Ostrander. Chelsea House, 1927
The Telltale Print. Chelsea House, 1927
Ten Thousand Dollar Reward. Chelsea House, 1926

BOOTH, EDWIN (S)
The Broken Window, Arcadia, 1960
Death on a Summer Day. Arcadia, 1960

BOOTH, LOUIS (M)
The Bank Vault Mystery. Dodd, 1933
Broker's End. Dodd, 1935

BOOTHBY, GUY (D)
Beautiful White Devil. Ward, Lock, 1896; Appleton, D., 1897
A Bid for Fortune, or Dr. Nikola's Vendetta. Ward, Lock, 1895
A Cabinet Search. Lippincott, 1901; White, 1901
Curse of the Snake. White, 1902
Doctor Nikola. Appleton, D., 1896; Ward, Lock, 1896
Doctor Nikola's Experiment. Appleton, D., 1899; Hodder, 1899
Farewell Nikola. Lippincott, 1901; Ward, Lock, 1901
The Kidnapped President. Munro, 1902; Ward, Lock, 1902
The League of Twelve. White, 1903
My Strangest Case. Page, 1902; Ward, Lock, 1902
The Mystery of the Clasped Hands. Newnes, 1904
Pharos, the Egyptian. Ward, Lock, 1899
Two-fold Inheritance. Ward, Lock, 1903
The Viceroy's Protégé. New Amsterdam, 1903
The Woman of Death. Pearson, 1900

BOOTON, KAGE (M)
Andrew's Wife. Doubleday, 1964
The Place of Shadows. Dodd, 1959; Gollancz, 1960; Paperback Lib., 1965
Runaway Home! Doubleday, 1967
The Troubled House. Dodd, 1958; Gollancz, 1959

BORDEAUX, HENRY (M)
Murder Party. Dial, 1931; Gollancz, 1931

BORDEN, LOWELL MASON (M)
The Counterfeit Bridegroom. Longmans, 1952; Vanguard, 1956

BORDEN, MARY (M)
You the Jury. Longmans, 1952; Popular Lib., 1964 (Also published as: Martin Merridew. Heinemann, 1952)

BORGE, BERNHARD, pseud; see BJERKE, ANDRE

BORGENICHT, MIRIAM (S)
Corpse in Diplomacy. Mill, 1949; Hamilton, H., 1956
Don't Look Back. Doubleday, 1956; Hale, R., 1958
Extreme Remedies. Doubleday, 1967
Ring and Walk In. Harper, 1952; Hamilton, H., 1956
To Borrow Trouble. Doubleday, 1965; Hale, R., 1966

BORGES, JORGE LUIS (M)
Ficciones. Grove, 1962
Labyrinths. New Directions, 1962

BORNEMAN, ERNEST WILHELM JULIUS (D) (Pseudonym: Cameron McCabe)
Face on the Cutting Room Floor, by Cameron McCabe. Gollancz, 1937
Face the Music
Tremolo. Harper, 1948

BORTH, WILLAN, G., pseud; see BOSWORTH, WILLIAM G.

BORTNER, NORMAN STANLEY (D)
Bond Grayson Murdered. Macrae Smith, 1936
Death of a Merchant of Death. Macrae Smith, 1937

BOSTON, CHARLES K., pseud; see GRUBER, FRANK

BOSWELL, JOHN (S)
Blue Pheasant. Collins, 1958
Lost Girl. Collins, 1959

BOSWORTH, ALLAN R. (M)
Full Crash Dive. Duell, 1942 (Argosy title: "Murder Goes to Sea")

BOSWORTH, WILLIAM G. (M) (Pseudonym: Willan G. Borth)
Monk's Bridge Mystery. Selwyn, 1929

BOTEM, BERNARD (M)
The Prosecuter. S & S, 1956

BOTTOME, PHYLLIS (M)
Murder in the Bud. Faber, 1939

BOUCHER, ANTHONY (William Anthony Parker White) (D) (Pseudonym: H. H. Holmes)
Case of the Baker Street Irregulars. S & S, 1940; Collier, 1962
Case of the Crumpled Knave. S & S, 1939; Pyramid, 1967
Case of the Seven of Calvary. S & S, 1937; Macmillan, 1954
Case of the Seven Sneezes. S & S, 1942; Pyramid, 1966
Case of the Solid Key. S & S, 1941
Nine Times Nine, by H. H. Holmes. Duell, 1940; Collier, 1962
Rocket to the Morgue, by H. H. Holmes. Duell, 1942; Pyramid, 1967

BOUCICAULT, DION and CHARLES READE (M)
Foul Play. Ticknor & Fields, 1868

BOULLE, PIERRE (S)
The Executioner. Vanguard, 1961
A Noble Profession. Vanguard, 1960

BOURNE, HESTER (M)
In the Event of My Death. Doubleday, 1964; Hurst, 1964; Pyramid, 1967
The Spanish House. Hurst, 1962; Pyramid, 1965

BOURNE, PETER, pseud; see JEFFRIES, GRAHAM MONTAGUE

BOUTELL, MRS. ANITA (D)
Cradled in Fear. Putnam, 1942
Death Brings A Storke. Putnam, 1938
Death Has a Past. Joseph, M., 1939; Putnam, 1939
Tell Death to Wait. Joseph, M., 1938; Putnam, 1939

BOVE, EMMANUEL (D)
Murder of Suzy Pommier. Little, 1934

BOWEN, JOSEPH (M)
The Man Without a Head. Covici, 1936; Butterworth, T., 1938

BOWEN, MARJORIE, pseud; see LONG, GABRIELLE MARGARET

BOWEN, ROBERT SIDNEY (D)
Make Mine Murder. Crown, 1946
Murder Gets Around. Crown, 1947

BOWEN-JUDD, SARA HUTTON (S) (Pseudonym: Sara Woods)
Bloody Instructions. Collins, 1962; Harper, 1962
The Case Is Altered. Collins, 1967
Enter Certain Murderers. Collins, 1966; Harper & Row, 1966
Let's Choose Executors. Collins, 1966; Harper & Row, 1966
Malice Domestic. Cassell, 1963
Taste of Fears. Collins, 1963
The Third Encounter. Harper & Row, 1963
This Little Measure, Collins, 1964
Though I Know She Lies. Collins, 1965
Trusted Like the Fox, Cassell, 1964; Harper & Row, 1965
Windy Side of the Law. Cassell, 1965; Harper & Row, 1965

BOWER, B. M., pseud; see SINCLAIR, MRS. BERTHA MUZZY

BOWER, MARIAN and M. LEON LION (M)
The Chinese Puzzle. Holt, H., 1919

BOWERS, DOROTHY (M)
Bells of Old Bailey. Doubleday, 1947; Hodder, 1947
Dead Without a Name. Doubleday, Doran, 1940; Hodder, 1940
Fear and Miss Betony; see Fear for Miss Betony
Fear for Miss Betony. Hodder, 1941 (U.S. title: Fear and Miss Betony. Doubleday, Doran, 1942)
Postscript to Poison. Hodder, 1938
The Shadows Before. Hodder, 1939; Doubleday, Doran, 1940

BOWMAN, GERALD (S)
The Quick and the Wed. Laurie, 1950
The Sawdust Angel. Laurie, 1949

BOX, EDGAR, pseud; see VIDAL, GORE

BOX, MURIEL; see BOX, SYDNEY

BOX, SYDNEY and MURIEL BOX (S)
Forbidden Cargo. Heinemann, 1957

BOYD, AUDREY (S)
No Man's Woman. Dutton, 1930

BOYD, CATHERINE BRADSHAW (M)
Revenge in a Convent. Exposition, 1955

BOYD, EUNICE MAYS (D)
Doom in the Midnight Sun. Farrar, Straus, 1944
Murder Breaks Trail. Farrar, Straus, 1943
Murder Wears Mukuluks. Farrar, Straus, 1945; Murray Hill, 1955; Dell

BOYD, FRANK, pseud; see KANE, FRANK

BOYD, HAMISH (D)
One Night of Murder. Mystery House, 1958; Ward, Lock, 1960

BOYD, JANE (D)
Murder in the King's Road. Harvill, 1953; British Book Centre, 1954

BOYD, MARION M. (D)
Murder in the Stacks. Lothrop, 1934

BOYD, PETER (S)
Slip Sees Red. Melrose, 1950

BOYD, R. S.; see KRASLOW, DAVID

BOYD, RAYMOND (D)
Murder Is a Furtive Thing. Hammond, 1950

BOYERS, AUDREY; see BOYERS, BETTINA

BOYERS, BETTINA (D)
Murder by Proxy. Doubleday, Doran, 1945
The White Mazurka, with Audrey Boyers. Doubleday, 1946

BOYLE, CONSTANCE ANTONINA (M)
Anna's. Allen & Unwin, 1925; Seltzer, T., 1925
Fate Unlamented. Paul, S., 1931
What Became of Mr. Desmond? Allen & Unwin, 1922; Seltzer, T., 1922

BOYLE, DENIS (M)
Strange Corpse on Murder Mile. Hale, R., 1960

BOYLE, JACK (M)
Boston Blackie. Fly, 1919

BOYLE, KAY (M)
A Frenchman Must Die. S & S, 1946
Monday Night. Harcourt, 1938

BRACE, TIMOTHY, pseud; see PRATT, THEODORE

BRACKEEN, STEVEN (S)
Baby Moll. Crest, 1958
Body on the Beach. Bouregy, 1957
Delfina. Fawcett, 1962
The Guardians. Holt, 1964

BRACKETT, LEIGH, pseud; see HAMILTON, MRS. EDMOND

BRADBURY, RAY (S)
The Autumn People. Ballantine, 1966
The Illustrated Man. Doubleday, 1951; Bantam, 1952

BRADDON, GEORGE, pseud; see BANKOFF, GEORGE

BRADDON, MARY ELIZABETH; see MAXWELL, MARY ELIZABETH

BRADDON, RUSSELL (S)
Gabriel Comes to 24. Hutchinson, 1958

BRADFORD, JOHN (M)
Roger Whatmough's Will. (2 Vols) T. Cautley Newby, 1864

BRADLEY, MARION ZIMMER (S)
Castle Terror. Lancer, 1966

BRADLEY, MARY HASTINGS (M)
A Hanging Matter. Appleton-Century, 1937
Murder in Room 700. Appleton, D., 1931
Murder in the Family. Longmans, 1951
Nice People Murder. Longmans, 1952
Nice People Poison. Longmans, 1952
Unconfessed. Appleton-Century, 1934

BRADLEY, MURIEL D. (M)
Affair at Ritos Bay. Doubleday, 1947
Death for My Neighbor. Doubleday, 1951; Hammond, 1954
Devil in the Sky. Doubleday, 1948; Hammond, 1955
Murder in Montana. Doubleday, 1950
Murder Twice Removed. Doubleday, 1951; Hammond, 1954

BRADSHAW, MRS. ALBERT S. (D)
Murder at the Boarding House. Allen, W. H., 1936

BRADSHAW, ANNIE (M)
A Crimson Stain. Cassell, 1885

BRADSHAW, GEORGE (S)
Practice to Deceive. Harcourt, 1963

BRADSHAW-JONES, MALCOLM HENRY (M) (Pseudonym: Bradshaw Jones)
The Crooked Phoenix. Long, 1963

Death Deals in Diamonds. Long, 1965; Walker & Co., 1966
Death on a Pale Horse. Long, 1964
The Embers of Hate. Long, 1966
The Hamlet Problem. Long, 1962
Murder Has No Friends. Long, 1966
Private Vendetta. Long, 1964
Tiger from the Shadows. Long, 1963

BRADY, NICHOLAS, pseud; see TURNER, JOHN VICTOR

BRAHAM, HAL (S) (Pseudonyms: Mel Colton, Merrill Trask)
The Big Fix, by Mel Colton. Ace, 1952
Big Woman, by Mel Colton. Magazine Productions, 1953
Call Me Deadly, by Mel Colton. Graphic, 1957
Double Take, by Mel Colton. Ace, 1953
Murder in Brief, by Merrill Trask. Bouregy, 1956
Never Kill a Cop, by Mel Colton. Ace, 1953

BRAHMS, CARYL, pseud; see ABRAHAMS, DORIS CAROLINE

BRAINERD, MRS. EDITH RATHBONE JACOBS and J. CHAUNCEY BRAINERD (M) (Pseudonym: E. J. Rath)
Too Many Crooks. Watt, 1918

BRAINERD, J. CHAUNCEY; see BRAINERD, MRS. EDITH RATHBONE JACOBS

BRALY, MALCOLM (S)
Felony Tank. GM, 1961
It's Cold Out There. GM, 1966
Shake Him Till He Rattles. GM, 1963

BRAMAH, ERNEST, pseud; see SMITH, ERNEST BRAMAH

BRAMHALL, MARIAN (D)
Button, Button. Doubleday, Doran, 1944
Murder Is an Evil Business. Doubleday, 1948
Murder Is Contagious. Doubleday, 1949
Murder Solves a Problem. Doubleday, Doran, 1944
Tragedy in Blue. Doubleday, Doran, 1945

BRAMLETT, JOHN (M)
The Devil in Broad Daylight. GM, 1967

BRAMLETTE, PAULA; see YATES, MARGARET POLK

BRAMWELL, JAMES GUY (M) (Pseudonym: James Byrom)
Or Be He Dead. Chatto, 1958; Penguin, 1965
Take Only as Directed. Chatto, 1959; Penguin, 1964

BRANCH, PAMELA JEAN (M)
Lion in the Cellar. Hale, R., 1951
Murder Every Monday. Hale, R., 1954
Murder's Little Sister. Hale, R., 1958; Penguin, 1963
Wooden Overcoat. Hale, R., 1951; Penguin

BRAND, CHARLES NEVILLE; see BRAND, NEVILLE

BRAND, CHRISTIANNA, pseud; see LEWIS, MRS. MARY CHRISTIANNA

BRAND, MAX, pseud; see FAUST, FREDERICK

BRAND, NEVILLE (Full name: Charles Neville Brand) (D)
Death in the Forest. Kendall, 1933
The Winning Trick. Putnam, 1931; Lane, 1932

BRANDE, DOROTHEA (S)
The Most Beautiful Lady. Farrar, 1935

BRANDEL, MARC, pseud; see BERESFORD, MARCUS

BRANDON, JOHN GORDON (D)
The Big City. Brentano, 1930; Methuen, 1931
The Black Joss. Methuen, 1931
The Blue-print Murders. Wright & Brown, 1942
The Bond Street Murder. Wright & Brown, 1937
Bonus for Murder. Wright & Brown, 1938
The Call-Girl Murders. Wright & Brown, 1954
Candidate for a Coffin. Wright & Brown, 1946
The Case of the Withered Hand. Wright & Brown, 1936
The Case of the Would-be Widow. Wright & Brown, 1950
The Cork Street Crime. Wright & Brown, 1938
The Corpse from the City. Wright & Brown, 1958
The Corpse Rode On. Wright & Brown, 1951
The Crooked Five. Wright & Brown, 1939
Death in D Division. Wright & Brown, 1943
Death in Downing Street. Wright & Brown, 1937
Death in Duplicate. Wright & Brown, 1945
Death in Jermyn Street. Wright & Brown, 1942
Death in the Dutch. Wright & Brown, 1940
Death in the Quarry. Wright & Brown, 1941

Death of a Greek. Wright & Brown, 1955
Death of a Socialite. Wright & Brown, 1957
Death on Delivery. Wright & Brown, 1939
Death Stalks in Soho. Wright & Brown, 1959
Death Tolls the Gong. Wright & Brown, 1936
The Dragnet. Wright & Brown, 1936
The Fifty Pound Marriage Case. Wright & Brown, 1938
Here Comes the Corpse. Wright & Brown, 1949
Homicidal Holiday. Wright & Brown, 1954
M for Murder. Wright & Brown, 1949
A Mild Case of Murder. Wright & Brown, 1951
Murder in Maytime. Wright & Brown, 1950
Murder in Pimlico. Wright & Brown, 1958
Murder on the Beam. Wright & Brown, 1958
Murderer's Stand-In. Wright & Brown, 1953
Nighthawk. Methuen, 1929
One-Minute Murder. Methuen, 1934; Dial, 1935
The Pawnshop Murder. Methuen, 1936
Red Altars. Cassell, 1958
The Riverside Mystery. Methuen, 1935
The Secret Brotherhood. Dial, 1928
The Silent House. Dial, 1928
A Swell Night for Murder. Wright & Brown, 1947
West End. Methuen, 1933

BRANDON, WILLIAM (D)
The Dangerous Dead. Dodd, 1943

BRANDT, TOM, pseud; see DEWEY, THOMAS B.

BRANSON, HENRY C. (M)
Beggars Choice. S & S, 1953
The Case of the Giant Killer. S & S, 1944
Fearful Passage. S & S, 1945; Lane, 1950
I'll Eat You Last. Musson, 1941; S & S, 1941
Last Year's Blood. S & S, 1947
The Leaden Bubble. S & S, 1949
The Pricking Thumb. S & S, 1942; Lane, 1949

BRAUN, LILLIAN JACKSON (M)
The Cat Who Ate Danish Modern. Dutton, 1967
Cat Who Could Read Backwards. Dutton, 1966

BRAUN, M. G. (S)
Apostles of Violence. Berkley Pub., 1962
Operation Atlantis. Berkley Pub., 1964
Operation Jealousy. Berkley Pub., 1966
That Girl from Istanbul. Berkley Pub., 1966

BRAUN, REINHARD A. (D)
Four Marked for Murder. Wright & Brown, 1957
Murder Four Miles High. Arcadia, 1954; Wright & Brown, 1956

BRAXTON, MRS. HARRY; see SHORE, VIOLA BROTHERS

BRAY, ARTHUR (D)
The Clue of the Postage Stamp. Thom, 1913

BREAN, HERBERT (S)
Clock Strikes Thirteen. Morrow, 1952
Collar for the Killer; see A Matter of Fact
The Darker the Night. Morrow, 1949; Heinemann, 1950
Dead Sure; see A Matter of Fact
Hardly a Man Is Now Alive. Morrow, 1950; Heinemann, 1952; Collier, 1962
A Matter of Fact. Morrow, 1956 (Also published as: Dead Sure. Dell, 1958. English title: Collar for the Killer. Heinemann, 1957)
The Traces of Brillhart. Harper, 1960; Heinemann, 1961; Collier, 1965
Wilders Walk Away. Morrow, 1948; Collier, 1962

BREBNER, PERCY JAMES (D)
The Black Card. Lawrence, 1899
Brown Mask. Cassell, 1911
Christopher Quarles, College Professor and Master Detective. Dutton, 1914
Crucible of Circumstance. Warne, 1906
The Ivory Disc. Duffield, 1920
A London Cobweb. Trischler & Co., 1892
The Master Detective. Dutton, 1916
The Mystery of Ladyplace. Warne, 1900
The Silver Medallion. Mills & Boon, 1912
Suspicion. Ward & Downey, 1889

BREMNER, MARJORIE (D)
Murder Amid Proofs. Hodder, 1955
Murder Most Familiar. Hodder, 1953

BRENN, GEORGE J. (M)
Voices. Century, 1923

BRENNAN, ALICE (S)
The Brooding House. Lancer, 1965

BRENNAN, FREDERICK HAZLITT (S)
Memo to a Firing Squad. Knopf, 1943
One of Our H-Bombs Is Missing. GM, 1955

BRENNAN, JOHN (S) (Pseudonym: John Welcome)
Beware of Midnight. Knopf, 1961
Hard to Handle. Faber, 1964
Run for Cover. Knopf, 1959; Penguin
Stop at Nothing. Knopf, 1960
Wanted for Killing. Holt, 1967

BRENNAN, JOSEPH PAYNE (S)
Nine Horrors and a Dream. Ballantine, 1962
Scream at Midnight. Macabre House, 1963

BRENNAN, LOUIS A. (D)
Death at Flood Tide. Dell, 1958
More Than Flesh. Dell, 1957

BRENNAN, ROBERT (M)
The Man Who Walked Like a Dancer. Rich, 1951

BRENNING, L. H., pseud; see HUNTER, JOHN

BRENT, LORING, pseud; see WORTS, GEORGE F.

BRENT, NIGEL, pseud; see WIMHURST, CECIL GORDON

BRENTER, JAY G. (M)
Blood on the Shrine. Brandon, 1967

BRESLIN, HOWARD (S) (Pseudonym: Michael Niall)
Bad Day at Black Rock, by Michael Niall. Fawcett, 1954
Run Like a Thief. Mill, 1962; Boardman, T. V., 1963; Monarch, 1964

BRETT, MARTIN, pseud; see SANDERSON, DOUGLAS

BRETT, MICHAEL, pseud; see TRIPP, NILES

BREWER, GIL (S)
And the Girl Screamed. Crest, 1956
Angel. Avon, 1960
The Angry Dream. Mystery House, 1957
The Brat. GM, 1957
The Hungry One. GM, 1966
Play It Hard. Monarch, 1964
The Red Scarf. Mystery House, 1958; Crest, 1959
77 Rue Paradis. GM, 1955
Sin For Me. Banner, 1967
Taste of Sin. Berkley Pub., 1961
The Tease. Banner, 1967
Three Way Split. GM, 1960
Vengeful Virgin. Crest, 1958
Wild. GM, 1958, 1964
Wild to Possess. Monarch, 1963

BREWSTER, EUGENE VALENTINE (D)
Surprise Party Murder. Greenberg, 1936

BRICE, MONICA (M)
Green Wood Burns Slow. Lothrop, 1938

BRICKHILL, PAUL CHESTER JEROME (S)
War of Nerves. Morrow, 1963 (English title: The Deadline. Collins, 1963)

BRIDGE, ANN, pseud; see O'MALLEY, LADY MARY DOLLING SAUNDERS

BRIDGES, VICTOR GEORGE DE FREYNE (D)
Accidents Will Happen. MacDonald & Co., 1948
All Very Irregular. MacDonald & Co., 1953
Another Man's Shoes. Doran, 1913; Hodder, 1913
Blue Silver. Hodder, 1936
The Creaking Gate. MacDonald & Co., 1958
The Cruise of the Scandal and Other Stories. Putnam, 1920
Dusky Night. Hodder, 1940
Exit Mr. Marlowe. MacDonald & Co., 1957
The Girl from Belfast. MacDonald & Co., 1961
The Girl in Black. Mills & Boon, 1926; Lippincott, 1927; Grosset, 1929
Greensea Island. Mills & Boon, 1922; Putnam, 1922; Hodder, 1929
The Gulls Fly Low. Hodder, 1943
The Happy Murderer. Hodder, 1933
The House on the Saltings. Hodder, 1941
I Did Not Kill Osborne. Penn, 1934; Grosset, 1935 (Also published as: Three Blind Mice. Hodder, 1933)
It Happened in Essex. Hodder, 1938
It Never Rains. MacDonald & Co., 1944
Jetsam. Mills & Boon, 1914
The King Comes Back. Hodder, 1930
The Lady from Long Acre. Mills & Boon, 1918; Putnam, 1919
The Man from Nowhere. Mills & Boon, 1913; Newnes, 1916; MacDonald & Co., 1952
The Man Who Butted In. Hodder, 1942
The Man Who Limped. MacDonald & Co., 1947
The Man Who Vanished. MacDonald & Co., 1954
Mr. Lyndon at Liberty. Mills & Boon, 1915; Hodder, 1930

Peter in Peril. Hodder, 1935; Penn, 1935
Quite Like Old Days. MacDonald & Co., 1949
The Red Lodge. Doubleday, Page, 1924; Mills & Boon, 1924; Hodder, 1931
Rogue by Compulsion. Putnam, 1915
Secrecy Essential. MacDonald & Co., 1959
The Secret of the Creek. Houghton, 1930; Hodder, 1931
The Secret of the Saltings. MacDonald & Co., 1955
The Seven Stars. Hodder, 1939
The Tenth Commandment. MacDonald & Co., 1951
Three Blind Mice; see I Did Not Kill Osborne
Trouble on the Thames. MacDonald & Co., 1945
We Don't Want to Lose You. MacDonald & Co., 1952
What the Doctor Ordered. MacDonald & Co., 1956

BRIDGMONT, LESLIE (S)
Unbriefed Mission. Falcon Press, 1953

BRIGHOUSE, HAROLD (M)
The Wrong Shadow. McBride, 1923

BRILLIANT, J. MAURICE
Vision of Murder. Comet, 1954

BRINTON, HENRY (D) (Pseudonym: Alex Fraser)
An Apple a Day. Washburn, 1957
Apprentice to Fear. Macmillan, 1961 (English title: An Ordinary Day)
Bury Their Day, by Alex Fraser. Bles, 1959; Roy Pubs., 1960
Can Death Be Sleep? Hutchinson, 1965
Constables Don't Count, by Alex Fraser. Bles, 1957
Coppers and Gold. Macmillan, 1955; Hutchinson, 1958
The Dark Places, by Alex Fraser. Bles, 1961
Death Is So Final, by Alex Fraser. Bles, 1958; Roy Pubs., 1958
Death to Windward. Hutchinson, 1952
Drug of the Market. Hutchinson, 1954; Macmillan, 1954
High Tension, by Alex Fraser. Bles, 1960
Ill Will. Hutchinson, 1956
Now Like to Die. Hutchinson, 1954
One Down and Two to Slay. Hutchinson, 1953
An Ordinary Day; see Apprentice to Fear
Purple Six. Avon, 1962; Walker & Co., 1962
Rude Awakening. Hutchinson, 1960
Three Wives, by Alex Fraser. Bles, 1956; Roy Pubs., 1957

BRISTOW, GWEN and BRUCE MANNING (M)
Gutenberg Murders. Mystery League, 1931
The Invisible Host. Mystery League, 1930
Mardi Gras Murders. Mystery League, 1932
Two and Two Make Twenty-Two. Mystery League, 1932

BRITTON, SUMNER; see BEAM, MAURICE

BROAD, PETER (D)
Death on the Beach. Cassell, 1959

BROCK, ALAN FRANCIS CLUTTON-; see CLUTTON-BROCK, ALAN FRANCIS

BROCK, ALAN ST. HILL (M) (Pseudonym: Peter Dewdney)
Arising from an Accident, by Peter Dewdney. Wright & Brown, 1939
Browns of the Yard. Harrap, 1952
A Casebook of Crime. Rockliff, 1948
Fingerprints, with Douglas Gordon. Browne. Dutton, 1954
Inquiries by the Yard. Harrap, 1950
On Appeal, by Peter Dewdney. Wright & Brown, 1938
Miss Hamblett's Ghost. MacDonald & Co., 1946

BROCK, LYNN, pseud; see McALLISTER, ALISTER

BROCK, STUART, pseud; see TRIMBLE, LOUIS

BRODERICK, GERRY P.; see NISTLER, ERWIN N.

BRODIE, JULIAN PAUL; see GREEN, ALAN BAER

BRODIE-INNES, JOHN WILLIAMS (M)
The Golden Rope. Lane, 1919
The Tragedy of an Indiscretion. Lane, 1916

BROEMEL, ROSE (D) (Pseudonym: Rose d'Evelyn)
The Elusive Criminal. Murray & Co., 1930

BROGAN, COLM (M)
The Ghost Walks. Skeffington, 1932

BROGAN, D. W. (M) (Pseudonym: Maurice Barrington)
Stop on the Green Light. Harper, 1942

BROGAN, JAMES, pseud; see HODDER-WILLIAMS, CHRISTOPHER

BRONSON, FRANCIS WOOLSEY (M)
The Bulldog Has a Key. Farrar, Straus, 1949
Nice People Don't Kill. Farrar & Rinehart, 1940
Uncas Island Murder. Farrar & Rinehart, 1942

BROOK, BARNABY, pseud; see BROOKS, COLLIN

BROOKER, BERTRAM (D) (Pseudonym: Huxley Herne)
The Tangled Miracle. Nelson, 1936

BROOKER, CLAIRE (S)
Dark Mosaic. Acadia, 1957

BROOKS, COLLIN (M) (Pseudonym: Barnaby Brook)
Account Paid. Hutchinson, 1930
The Body Snatchers. Hutchinson, 1924
Found Dead. Hutchinson, 1930
The Ghost Hunters. Sears, 1928; Hutchinson, 1932
Mad-doctor Merciful. Hutchinson, 1932
Mr. Daddy-Detective. Hutchinson, 1933
O Sweet McTavish. Hutchinson, 1930
Three Yards of Cord. Hutchinson, 1931

BROOKS, EDWY SEARLES (D) (Pseudonym: Berkeley Gray)
Alias Norman Conquest. Collins, 1945
The Big Brain. Collins, 1959
Blonde for Danger. Collins, 1943
Calamity Conquest. Collins, 1965
Call Conquest for Danger. Collins, 1961; New English Lib., 1963
Castle Conquest. Collins, 1964
Cavalier Conquest. Collins, 1944, 1963
Conquest After Midnight. Collins, 1957
Conquest Goes Home. Collins, 1957
Conquest Goes West. Collins, 1954
Conquest in California. Collins, 1958
Conquest in Command. Collins, 1956
Conquest in Scotland. Collins, 1951
Conquest in the Underworld. Collins, 1962
Conquest Marches On. Collins, 1939
Conquest on the Run. New English Lib., 1963
Conquest Overboard. Collins, 1964
The Conquest Touch. Collins, 1948; Fontana, 1961
Convict 1066. Collins, 1940
Count-Down for Conquest. Collins, 1963
Dare-Devil Conquest. Collins, 1950
Death on the Hit Parade. Collins, 1958
Duel Murder. Collins, 1949
Follow the Lady. Collins, 1954
The Gay Desperado. Collins, 1944
Get Ready to Die. Collins, 1961
The Half-Open Door. Collins, 1953
The House of the Lost. Collins, 1956
Killer Conquest. Collins, 1947
The Lady Is Poison. Collins, 1952
Leave It to Conquest. Collins, 1939
Meet the Don. Collins, 1939
Miss Dynamite. Collins, 1939
Mr. Ball of Fire. Collins, 1946
Murder and Co. Collins, 1959
Nightmare House. Collins, 1960
Operation Conquest. Collins, 1951
Seven Dawns to Death. Collins, 1950
Six Feet of Dynamite. Collins, 1941
The Spot Marked "X." Collins, 1948
Target for Conquest. Collins, 1953; Fontana, 1961
Thank You, Mr. Conquest. Collins, 1941
Turn Left for Danger. Collins, 1955
Vultures, Ltd. Collins, 1938

BROOKS, VIVIAN COLLIN (Pseudonym: Osmington Mills)
At One Fell Swoop. Bles, 1963
Case of the Flying Fifteen. Bles, 1962
Death Enters the Lists. Roy Pubs., 1967
Enemies of the Bride. Roy Pubs., 1967
Headlines Make Murder. Bles, 1962
No Match for the Law. Bles, 1957
Stairway to Murder, by Osmington Mills et al. Bles, 1959
Traitor Betrayed. Roy Pubs., 1964
Trial by Ordeal. Bles, 1961; Roy Pubs., 1962
Unlucky Break. Roy Pubs., 1957; Bles

BROOME, ADAM, pseud; see JAMES, GODFREY WARDEN

BROPHY, JOHN (M)
The Day They Robbed the Bank of England. Chatto, 1959
Front Door Key. Heinemann, 1960

BROTHERS, WILLIAM P. (M)
Morocco Episode. Hillman-Curl, 1957

BROUN, DANIEL (S)
Counter Weight. Rinehart, 1962
Egypt's Choice. Holt, 1963; Gollancz, 1964
From 9 O'Clock to Jamaica Bay. Holt, 1964
The Subject of Harry Egypt. Gollancz, 1963; Holt, 1963; Tower

BROWN, ALICE (M)
Mysteries of Ann. Macmillan, 1925

BROWN, ALEC JOHN CHARLES (M)
The Bandit; see Time to Kill
Green Lake: or Murder at Moat Farm. Cape, 1930
Hollow Mountain. Macmillan, 1939
Time to Kill, Two Stories. Cape, 1930 (Includes: The Bandit)

BROWN, ANDREW CASSELS (M)
Birds of Prey. Methuen, 1929
Dr. Glazebrooke's Revenge. Dodd, 1928; Mills & Boon, 1928
Josselin Takes a Hand. Dodd, 1927; Mills & Boon, 1927

BROWN, CARNABY (M)
Small Change. Boardman, T. V., 1958; Roy Pubs., 1958

BROWN, CARTER, pseud; see YATES, ALAN GEOFFREY

BROWN, CLINTON GIDDINGS (M)
You May Take the Witness. Univ. of Tex. Press, 1955

BROWN, DOROTHY FOSTER (D)
Grimm Death. Smith & Durrell, 1946

BROWN, E. A. (M)
That Affair at St. Peter's. Lothrop, 1920

BROWN, ELWOOD S. (M)
Elephant Murders. Vantage, 1956

BROWN, FREDRIC (M)
The Bloody Moonlight. Dutton, 1949 (English title: Murder in the Moonlight. Boardman, T. V., 1950)
Compliments of a Fiend. Dutton, 1950; Boardman, T. V., 1951
Dead Ringer. Dutton, 1948
Death Has Many Doors. Dutton, 1951; Boardman, T. V., 1952
Deep End. Dutton, 1952; Boardman, T. V., 1953
The Fabulous Clipjoint. Dutton, 1947
The Far Cry. Dutton, 1951; Boardman, T. V., 1952
The Five-Day Nightmare. Dutton, 1962; Boardman, T. V., 1963; Tower, 1965
Here Comes a Candle. Boardman, T. V., 1950; Dutton, 1950
His Name Was Death. Dutton, 1954; Boardman, T. V., 1955
Knock Three-One-Two. Dutton, 1959; Boardman, T. V., 1960
The Late Lamented. Boardman, T. V., 1959; Dutton, 1959
The Lenient Beast. Dutton, 1956; Boardman, T. V., 1957; Bantam
Mostly Murder. Dutton, 1953; Boardman, T. V., 1954
Mrs. Murphy's Underpants. Dutton, 1963; Boardman, T. V., 1964
Murder Can Be Fun. Dutton, 1948; Boardman, T. V., 1957
Murder in the Moonlight; see The Bloody Moonlight
The Murderers. Dutton, 1961; Boardman, T. V., 1962; Bantam, 1963
The Night of the Jabberwock. Dutton, 1950; Boardman, T. V., 1951
One for the Road. Dutton, 1958; Boardman, T. V., 1959
The Screaming Mimi. Dutton, 1949; Boardman, T. V., 1950
The Shaggy Dog and Other Murders. Dutton, 1963 (English title: The Shaggy Dog and Other Stories. Boardman, T. V., 1964)
The Shaggy Dog and Other Stories; see The Shaggy Dog and Other Murders
We All Killed Grandma. Dutton, 1952; Boardman, T. V., 1953
The Wench Is Dead. Dutton, 1955

BROWN, GEORGE (S)
Sibyl Sue Blue. Doubleday, 1966

BROWN, GERALD (D)
Murder in Plain Sight. Phoenix, 1945
Murder on Beacon Hill. Phoenix, 1941

BROWN, MORNA DAVIS MacTAGGART (D) (Pseudonyms: Elizabeth Ferrars, E. X. Ferrars)
Alibi for a Witch, by E. X. Ferrars. Doubleday, 1952
Always Say Die, by E. X. Ferrars. Collins, 1956
The Busy Body, by Elizabeth Ferrars. Collins, 1962
Cheat the Hangman, by E. X. Ferrars. Doubleday, 1946
The Clock That Wouldn't Stop, by E. X. Ferrars. Doubleday, 1952; Collins, 1954
Count the Cost, by E. X. Ferrars. Doubleday, 1957
The Decayed Gentlewoman, by E. X. Ferrars. Doubleday, 1963
Depart This Life, by E. X. Ferrars. Doubleday, 1958; Popular Lib., 1964
The Doubly Dead, by E. X. Ferrars. Collins, 1963; Doubleday, 1963
Enough to Kill a Horse, by E. X. Ferrars. Doubleday, 1955
Fear the Light, by E. X. Ferrars. Collins, 1960; Doubleday, 1960
Furnished for Murder, by Elizabeth Ferrars. Doubleday, 1951; Collins, 1957
Give the Corpse a Bad Name, by Elizabeth Ferrars. Hodder, 1940
Hunt the Tortoise, by E. X. Ferrars. Doubleday, 1950
I, Said the Fly, by E. X. Ferrars. Doubleday, 1946
Kill or Cure, by E. X. Ferrars. Doubleday, 1956
Legal Fiction, by Elizabeth Ferrars. Collins, 1964
Lying Voices, by Elizabeth Ferrars. Collins, 1954

The March Hare Murders, by E. X. Ferrars. Collins, 1949; Doubleday, 1949
The Milk of Human Kindness, by Elizabeth Ferrars. Collins, 1950
Murder in Time, by Elizabeth Ferrars. Collins, 1953
Murder Moves In, by Elizabeth Ferrars. Collins, 1956
Murder of a Suicide, by E. X. Ferrars. Doubleday, Doran, 1941
Neck in a Noose; see Your Neck in a Noose
The Ninth Life, by Elizabeth Ferrars. Collins, 1965
No Peace for the Wicked, by E. X. Ferrars. Harper & Row, 1966
No Rehearsals for Murder; see Remove the Bodies
Remove the Bodies, by E. X. Ferrars. Hodder, 1940 (U.S. title: No Rehearsals for Murder. Doubleday, Doran, 1941)
Seeing Double, by E. X. Ferrars. Doubleday, 1962
The Shape of a Stain, by E. X. Ferrars. Doubleday, Doran, 1942
Sleeping Dogs, by E. X. Ferrars. Doubleday, 1950
A Tale of Two Murders, by Elizabeth Ferrars. Collins, 1959; Doubleday, 1959
Unreasonable Doubt, by Elizabeth Ferrars. Collins, 1958
The Wandering Widows, by E. X. Ferrars. Doubleday, 1962
We Haven't Seen Her Lately, by E. X. Ferrars. Doubleday, 1956
With Murder in Mind, by Elizabeth Ferrars. Collins, 1948
Your Neck in a Noose, by E. X. Ferrars. Hodder, 1942 (U.S. title: Neck in a Noose)

BROWN, ROBERT CARLTON (M)
The Remarkable Adventures of Christopher Poe. Browne & Howell, 1913

BROWN, ROYAL (M)
Escape. Dutton, 1938

BROWN, WALTER C. (D)
Laughing Death. Lippincott, 1932
Murder at Mocking House. Lippincott, 1933; Burt, 1935
Second Guess. Lippincott, 1929

BROWN, WENZELL (S)
An Act of Passion. Monarch, 1962
The Big Rumble. Popular Lib., 1956
Cry Kill. GM, 1959
Hoods Ride In. Pyramid, 1959
The Kept Man. Lancer
The Kept Woman. Lancer
Murder Kick. GM, 1960
Murder Seeks an Agent. Arcadia, 1947; Curzon, 1947
Naked Hours. Popular Lib., 1956
Prison Girl. Pyramid, 1958
Run, Chico, Run. GM, 1953

BROWN, MRS. ZENITH JONES (D)
(Pseudonyms: Leslie Ford, David Frome)
All for the Love of a Lady, by Leslie Ford. Scribner, 1944; Popular Lib., 1967 (English title: Crack of Dawn. Collins, 1948)
Arsenic in Richmond; see Mr. Pinkerton Goes to Scotland Yard
The Bahamas Murder Case, by Leslie Ford. Scribner, 1952; Popular Lib., 1965
The Black Envelope: Mr. Pinkerton Again, by David Frome. Farrar & Rinehart, 1937 (English title: Mr. Pinkerton's Adventure at Brighton. Longmans, 1939)
The Body in Bedford Square; see Mr. Pinkerton Grows a Beard
Body in the Turl; see Mr. Pinkerton Finds a Body
Burn Forever, by Leslie Ford. Farrar & Rinehart, 1935 (English title: Mountain Madness. Hutchinson, 1935)
By-Pass Murder, by Leslie Ford. Longmans, 1935
By the Watchman's Clock, by Leslie Ford. Farrar & Rinehart, 1932; Popular Lib., 1966
The Capital Crime; see Murder of a Fifth Columnist
Clue of the Judas Tree, by Leslie Ford. Farrar & Rinehart, 1933; Popular Lib., 1961
Crack of Dawn; see All for the Love of a Lady
Date with Death, by Leslie Ford. Scribner, 1949; Popular Lib., 1963 (English title: Shot in the Dark. Collins, 1949)
The Devil's Stronghold, by Leslie Ford. Scribner, 1948; Popular Lib., 1967
Eel Pie Murders, by David Frome. Farrar & Rinehart, 1933 (English title: Eel Pie Mystery. Collins, 1936)
Eel Pie Mystery; see Eel Pie Murders
False to Any Man, by Leslie Ford. Scribner, 1939; Popular Lib., 1963 (English title: Show-White Murder. Collins, 1940)
Footsteps on the Stairs; see The Sound of Footsteps
The Girl from the Mimosa Club, by Leslie Ford. Scribner, 1957
The Hammersmith Murders, by David Frome. Doubleday, Doran, 1930; Dell (English title: Mr. Pinkerton Returns. Methuen, 1930)

Homicide House, by David Frome. Rinehart, 1950
The Honolulu Murder Story; see The Honolulu Story
Honolulu Murders; see The Honolulu Story
The Honolulu Story, by Leslie Ford. Scribner, 1946 (Also published as: Honolulu Murders. Popular Lib., 1967. English title: The Honolulu Murder Story. Collins, 1947)
Ill Met by Moonlight, by Leslie Ford. Farrar & Rinehart, 1937
In at the Death, by David Frome. Longmans, 1930
Invitation to Murder, by Leslie Ford. Scribner, 1954; Popular Lib., 1966
The Lying Jade; see Washington Whispered Murder
The Man from Scotland Yard, by David Frome. Farrar & Rinehart, 1932; Grosset, 1933; PB, 1942
Mr. Cromwell Is Dead; see Reno Rendezvous
Mr. Pinkerton: An Omnibus. Farrar & Rinehart, 1935
Mr. Pinkerton and Inspector Bull, by David Frome. Farrar & Rinehart, 1934
Mr. Pinkerton at the Old Angel, by David Frome. Farrar & Rinehart, 1939
Mr. Pinkerton Finds a Body, by David Frome. Farrar & Rinehart, 1935; Popular Lib., 1967 (English title: Body in the Turl. Longmans, 1936)
Mr. Pinkerton Goes to Scotland Yard, by David Frome. Farrar & Rinehart, 1934 (English title: Arsenic in Richmond. Longmans, 1935)
Mr. Pinkerton Grows a Beard, by David Frome. Farrar & Rinehart, 1935; Popular Lib., 1967 (English title: The Body in Bedford Square. Longmans, 1935)
Mr. Pinkerton Has the Clue, by David Frome. Farrar & Rinehart, 1936
Mr. Pinkerton Returns; see The Hammersmith Murders
Mr. Pinkerton's Adventure at Brighton; see The Black Envelope: Mr. Pinkerton Again
Mountain Madness; see Burn Forever
Murder Comes to Eden, by Leslie Ford. Scribner, 1955; Popular Lib., 1966
Murder Down South; see Murder with Southern Hospitality
Murder in Maryland, by Leslie Ford. Farrar & Rinehart, 1932; Popular Lib., 1966
Murder in the O.P.M., by Leslie Ford. Scribner, 1942 (English title: The Priority Murder. Collins, 1943)
Murder Is the Payoff, by Leslie Ford. Scribner, 1951
Murder of a Fifth Columnist, by Leslie Ford. Scribner, 1941 (English title: The Capital Crime. Collins, 1941)
Murder of an Old Man, by Leslie Ford. Methuen, 1929
Murder on the 6th Hole; see The Strange Death of Martin Green
Murder with Southern Hospitality, by Leslie Ford. Scribner, 1942 (English title: Murder Down South. Collins, 1943)
Old Lover's Ghost, by Leslie Ford. Scribner, 1940; Popular Lib., 1963
The Philadelphia Murder Story, by Leslie Ford. Scribner, 1945; Popular Lib., 1965
The Priority Murder; see Murder in the O.P.M.
Reno Rendezvous, by Leslie Ford. Farrar & Rinehart, 1939; Popular Lib., 1966 (English title: Mr. Cromwell Is Dead. Collins, 1940)
The Road to Folly, by Leslie Ford. Scribner, 1940
Scotland Yard Can Wait, by David Frome. Farrar & Rinehart, 1933 (English title: That's Your Man, Inspector. Longmans, 1936)
Shot in the Dark; see Date with Death
The Simple Way of Poison, by Leslie Ford. Farrar & Rinehart, 1937; Grosset, 1939; PB, 1941; Popular Lib., 1964
Siren in the Night. Popular Lib., 1964
Snow-White Murder; see False to Any Man
The Sound of Footsteps, by Leslie Ford. Doubleday, Doran, 1931 (English title: Footsteps on the Stairs. Gollancz, 1931)
The Strange Death of Martin Green, by David Frome. Doubleday, Doran, 1931 (English title: Murder on the 6th Hole. Methuen, 1931)
The Strangled Witness, by Leslie Ford. Farrar & Rinehart, 1934; Popular Lib.
That's Your Man, Inspector; see Scotland Yard Can Wait
Three Bright Pebbles, by Leslie Ford. Farrar & Rinehart, 1938; Popular Lib., 1965
The Town Cried Murder, by Leslie Ford. Scribner, 1939; Popular Lib., 1963
Trial by Ambush, by Leslie Ford. Scribner, 1962; Popular Lib., 1963 (English title: Trial from Ambush. Collins, 1962)
Trial from Ambush; see Trial by Ambush
Two Against Scotland Yard, by David Frome. Farrar & Rinehart, 1931; Popular Lib., 1967

Washington Whispered Murder, by Leslie Ford. Scribner, 1953; Popular Lib., 1965 (English title: The Lying Jade. Collins, 1953)
The Woman in Black, by Leslie Ford. Scribner, 1947; Popular Lib., 1963

BROWNE, BARUM, pseud.
The Devil and X.Y.Z. Doubleday, Doran, 1931; Gollancz, 1931

BROWNE, DOUGLAS GORDON (D)
The Cotfold Conundrums. Methuen, 1933
The Dead Don't Bite. Methuen, 1933
Death in Perpetuity. Macmillan, 1950
Death in Seven Volumes. MacDonald & Co., 1958
Death Wears a Mask. Hutchinson, 1940; Macmillan, 1954
Fingerprints, with Alan Brock. Dutton, 1954
The Looking-glass Murders. Methuen, 1935
The May-Week Murders. Longmans, 1937
Plan XVI. Doubleday, Doran, 1934; Methuen, 1934
Sergeant Death. Macmillan, 1955
The Stolen Boat-Train. Methuen, 1935
Too Many Cousins. Macmillan, 1953
What Beckoning Ghost. MacDonald & Co., 1947

BROWNE, ELEANORE (D)
Murder by Appointment. Macaulay, 1934

BROWNE, HOWARD (S) (Pseudonym: John Evans)
Halo for Satan. Bobbs, 1948; Boardman, T. V., 1949
Halo in Blood. Bobbs, 1946
Halo in Brass. Bobbs, 1949; Foulsham, 1951
If You Have Tears. Mystery House, 1947
The Taste of Ashes. S & S, 1957; Gollancz, 1958
Thin Air. S & S, 1954; Gollancz, 1955

BROWNING, STERRY (S)
The Crime at Cape Folly. Clerke, 1951
Sex Marks the Spot. Long, 1954

BRUCE, GEORGE (M)
The Corpse Without Flesh. Jenkins, 1939

BRUCE, JEAN (M)
The Last Quarter Hour. Crest, 1955
Trouble in Tokyo. Crest, 1958

BRUCE, KENNEDY (M)
The Poisoned Fang. Jenkins. 1930

BRUCE, LEO, pseud; see CROFT-COOKE, RUPERT

BRUCKER, MARGARETTA (M)
Poison Party. Phoenix, 1938

BRUNE, AIDAN DE (D)
Shadow Crook. Angus, 1930

BRUNNER, JOHN (M)
Wear the Butcher's Medal. PB, 1965

BRUSSEL, JAMES A. (M)
Just Murder, Darling. Scribner, 1959

BRUTON, ERIC (M)
Death in Ten Point Bold. Jenkins, 1957
Die, Darling, Die. Boardman, T. V., 1959
The Finsbury Mob. Boardman, T. V., 1964
The Firebug. Boardman, T. V., 1966
The Wicked Saint: a City of London Police Novel. Boardman, T. V., 1965

BRYAN, FRANK (S)
The Long Shadow. Comet, 1955

BRYAN, JOHN, pseud; see DELVES-BROUGHTON, JOSEPHINE

BRYAN, MICHAEL (D)
Intent to Kill. Dell, 1956; Eyre, 1956
Murder in Majorca. Dell, 1957; Eyre, 1958

BRYANT, MARGUERITE (M)
Mrs. Fuller. Duffield, 1925

BRYANT, MATT (S)
Cue for Murder. Vanguard, 1955; Barker, 1956

BRYSON, CHARLES (D) (Pseudonym: Charles Barry)
The Avenging Ikon. Dutton, 1930; Methuen, 1930
The Boat Train Mystery. Hurst, 1938
Case Dead and Buried. Hurst, 1938
The Case for Tressider. Dutton, 1929; Hodder, 1937
The Clue of the Clot. Hutchinson, 1928; Allan, P., 1936
The Corpse on the Bridge. Methuen, 1927; Dutton, 1928
The Dead Have No Mouths. Hurst, 1940
Death in Darkness. Hurst, 1933
Death of a First Mate. Hurst, 1927; Dutton, 1935
Death Overseas. Hurst, 1937
Detective's Holiday. Dutton, 1926; Methuen, 1926
Ghost of a Clue. Methuen, 1931
The Mouls House Mystery. Methuen, 1926; Dutton, 1927

Murder on Monday. Dutton, 1932; Eyre, 1932
Nicholas Lattermale's Case. Hurst, 1939
Poison in Public. Hurst, 1936
The Red Star Mystery. Mellifont, 1933
Secrecy at Sandhurst. Hurst, 1951
Shot from the Door. Hurst, 1934; Dutton, 1935
The Smaller Penny. Hodder, 1925; Dutton, 1928
The Thirteenth House. Mellifont, 1935
The Witness at the Window. Dutton, 1927; Methuen, 1927
The Wrong Murder Mystery. Dutton, 1933

BRYSON, LEIGH, pseud; see RUTLEDGE, NANCY

BUCHAN, JOHN (Baron John Buchan Tweedsmuir) (S)
The Adventures of Richard Hannay. Houghton, 1939
The Blanket of the Dark. Hodder, 1931
The Courts of the Morning. Houghton, 1926; Hodder, 1929
The Dancing Floor. Hodder, 1926; Houghton, 1926
Four Tales: The 39 Steps, Powerhouse, Watcher by the Threshold, and the Moon Endureth. Blackwood, 1952
Greenmantle. Doran, 1915; Hodder, 1916; PB
The House of the Four Winds. Hodder, 1934
Huntingtower. Doran, 1922; Hodder, 1922
Island of Sheep. Hodder, 1936
John Macnab. Houghton, 1925
The Man from the Norlands. Houghton, 1936
Mr. Standfast. Doran, 1919; Hodder, 1919
Mountain Meadow. Houghton, 1941
The Power-House. Blackwood, 1916; Doran, 1916
The Runagates Club. Hodder, 1928; Houghton, 1928
The Thirty-nine Steps. Blackwood, 1915; Doran, 1915; Popular Lib., 1963
The Three Hostages. Hodder, 1924; Houghton, 1924

BUCHAN, WILLIAM
Helen All Alone. Morrow, 1961; Lancer, 1966

BUCHANAN, B. J. (M) (Pseudonym: Joan Shepherd)
Girl on the Left Bank. Washburn, 1953
Tender Is the Knife. Washburn, 1956

BUCHANAN, CARL (M)
Black Cloak Murders. Pearson, 1936
Night of Horror. Mellifont, 1939
Red Scorpion. Mellifont, 1939

BUCHANAN, MRS. MADELEINE SHARPS (D)
The Black Pearl Murders. McClurg, 1930
The Crimson Blade. Chelsea House, 1926
Haunted Bells. Chelsea House, 1929; Skeffington, 1931
Poison Eye. Chelsea House, 1929; Skeffington, 1929
Powdered Proof. Chelsea House, 1927
The Subway Murder. McClurg, 1930; Grosset, 1931

BUCK, CHARLES NEVILLE (M)
Alias Red Ryan. Doubleday, Page, 1923
A Gentleman in Pajamas. Century, 1924
Marked Men. Doubleday, Page, 1925
The Portuguese Silver. Century, 1925
The Rogue's Badge. Doubleday, Page, 1924

BUCK, PEARL (M)
Death in the Castle. Day, 1965; Methuen, 1966; PB, 1967

BUCKINGHAM, BRUCE, pseud; see LILLEY, PETER

BUCKINGHAM, DAVID (S)
The Wind Tunnel. MacDonald & Co., 1959

BUCKINGHAM, NANCY (S)
Cloud over Malverton. Ace, 1967

BUCKLEY, CHRISTOPHER (M)
Rain Before Seven. Hodder, 1947

BUDD, JACKSON, pseud; see BUDD, WILLIAM JOHN

BUDD, WILLIAM JOHN (D) (Pseudonyms: Jackson Budd, Wallace Jackson)
The Diamonds of Death. Hopkins & Son, 1937; Low, 1937
The Extraordinary Case of Mr. Bell, by Wallace Jackson. Hopkins & Son, 1936
The Gallows Wait, by Budd Jackson. Putnam, 1932 (Also published as: I Stood in the Shadow of the Black Cap. Low, 1932)
I Stood in the Shadow of the Black Cap; see The Gallows Wait.
The Princely Quartet, by Jackson Budd. Marston, 1932
The Sinister Madonna, by Wallace Jackson. Hopkins & Son, 1937; Low, 1937
Two Knocks for Death, by Wallace Jackson. Marston, 1934; Hopkins & Son, 1935

BUDE, JOHN (D)
Another Man's Shadow. MacDonald & Co., 1957
The Cheltenham Square Murder. Skeffington, 1937
The Constable and the Lady. MacDonald & Co., 1951
The Cornish Coast Murder. Skeffington, 1935
Dangerous Sunlight. MacDonald & Co., 1948
Death Deals a Double. Cassell, 1943
Death in White Pajamas. Cassell, 1944
Death Knows No Calendar. Cassell, 1942
Death of a Cad. Hale, 1940
Death on Paper. Hale, 1940
Death on the Riviera. MacDonald & Co., 1952
Death Steals the Show. MacDonald & Co., 1950
A Glut of Red Herring. MacDonald & Co., 1949
Hand on the Alibi. Skeffington, 1939
The Lake District Murder. Skeffington, 1935
The Loss of a Head. Skeffington, 1938
Murder in Montparnasse. Brown, Watson, 1949
The Night the Fog Came Down. Washburn, 1958
A Shift of Guilt. MacDonald & Co., 1956
Slow Vengeance. Hale, 1941
So Much in the Dark. MacDonald & Co., 1954
The Sussex Downs Murder. Skeffington, 1936
Telegram from Le Touquet. MacDonald & Co., 1958
Trouble Abrewing. MacDonald & Co., 1945
Twice Dead. MacDonald & Co., 1953
A Twist of the Rope. MacDonald & Co., 1958
Two Ends to a Town. MacDonald & Co., 1955
When the Case was Opened. MacDonald & Co., 1952

BUDGETT, MRS. SIDNEY; see DEJEANS, ELIZABETH

BUELL, JOHN (M)
Four Days. Farrar, 1962
The Pyx. Crest, 1960

BUHET, GIL (S)
The Grand Catch. Cape, 1957
The Honey Siege. Cape, 1953
The Story Teller. Cape, 1955

BULL, LOIS (D)
The Granville Crypt Murders. Macaulay, 1936
The Yellow Robe Murders. Macaulay, 1935

BULLETT, GERALD WILLIAM (S)
(Pseudonym: Sebastian Fox)
The Jury. Dent, 1935; Knopf, 1935
Odd Woman Out, by Sebastian Fox. Dent, 1939
One Man's Poison, by Sebastian Fox. Chatto, 1956
Trouble at Number 7. Joseph, M., 1952; Pan, 1955
When the Cat's Away. Knopf, 1941

BULLIVANT, CECIL HENRY (D)
Garnett Bell, Detective. Odhams, 1920

BULWER-LYTTON, EDWARD (D)
Eugene Aram. 1832
Pelham: or The Adventures of a Gentleman. 1828

BUMPUS, DORIS MARJORIE (M)
(Pseudonym: Marjorie Alan)
Dark Legacy. Hale, R., 1953
Dark Prophecy; see Masked Murder
The Ivory Locket. Hale, R., 1951
Masked Murder. Hale, R., 1945 (U.S. title: Dark Prophecy. Mill, 1945)
Murder at Puck's Cottage. Hale, R., 1951
Murder in a Maze. Hale, R., 1956
Murder in November. Hale, R., 1946 (U.S. title: Rue the Day. Mill, 1956)
Murder Looks Back. Hale, R., 1955
Murder Next Door. Hale, R., 1950
Pattern in Beads. Hale, R., 1944
Rue the Day; see Murder in November

BUNCE, FRANK (D)
Rehearsal for Murder. Abelard, 1956; Collier, 1962
So Young a Body. S & S, 1950

BUNCE, RICHARD (D)
Here Lies the Body. Putnam, 1942

BUNCE, SYDNEY (M)
Take This Life. Angus, 1960

BUNKER, JANE (M)
Diamond Cut Diamond. Bobbs, 1913

BURANELLI, PROSPER (D)
Big Nick. Doubleday, Doran, 1931
The News Reel Murder. Funk, W., 1940

BURBRIDGE, EDITH JOAN (M) (Pseudonym: Joan Cockin)
Curiousity Killed the Cat. Hodder, 1947
Deadly Earnest. Hodder, 1952
Villainy at Vespers. Hodder, 1949

BURFORD, ROGER d'ESTE (D) (Pseudonym: Roger East. Joint pseud. with Oswell Blakeston: "Simon")
The Bell Is Answered. Collins, 1934
Candidate for Lilies, by Roger East. Collins, 1934; Knopf, 1934

Cat with the Mustache, by "Simon." Wishart, 1935
Detectives in Gum Boots, by Roger East. Collins, 1936
Murder Among Friends, by "Simon." Wishart, 1933
Murder Rehearsal, by Roger East. Collins, 1933; Knopf, 1933
The Mystery of the Monkey-Gland Cocktail, by Roger East. Putnam, 1932
The Pearl Choker, by Roger East. Collins, 1954
Twenty-Five Sanitary Inspectors, by Roger East. Collins, 1935

BURGE, MILWARD RODON KENNEDY (M) (Pseudonym: Milward Kennedy)
The Bleston Mystery. Doubleday, Doran, 1929; Gollancz, 1929
Bull's Eye, by Milward Kennedy. Gollancz, 1933; Kinsey, 1933
Corpse Guard Parade. Gollancz, 1929; Doubleday, Doran, 1930
Corpse in Cold Storage. Gollancz, 1934; Kinsey, 1934
Corpse on the Mat. Gollancz, 1929
Death in a Deck-Chair. Gollancz, 1930; Doubleday, Doran, 1931
Death to the Rescue. Gollancz, 1931
Escape to Quebec. Gollancz, 1946; Pan, 1951
Half-Mast Murder. Doubleday, Doran, 1930; Gollancz, 1930
I'll Be Judge, I'll Be Jury. Gollancz, 1937
The Man Who Rang the Bell. Doubleday, Doran, 1929
The Murderer of Sleep. Gollancz, 1932; Kinsey, 1933
Pleston Mystery. Gollancz, 1929
Poison in the Parish. Gollancz, 1935
The Scornful Corpse; see Sic Transit Gloria
Sic Transit Gloria. Gollancz, 1936 (U.S. title: The Scornful Corpse. Dodd, 1936)

BURGESS, ANTHONY, pseud; see WILSON, JOHN ANTHONY BURGESS

BURGESS, ERIC ALEXANDER (M)
Accident to Adeline. Joseph, M., 1952
Deadly Deceit. Hale, R., 1963
Divided We Fall. Collins, 1959
A Killing Frost. Collins, 1961
Knife for Celeste. Joseph, M., 1949
Malice of Monday. Joseph, M., 1950
United We Stand. Collins. 1959

BURGESS, GELETT, pseud; see STURGIS, JUSTIN

BURGESS, HELEN STEERS; see STEERS, HELEN

BURGESS, TREVOR, pseud; see TREVOR, ELLESTON

BURGESS, WILLIAM WATSON (M)
Life Sentence; or, Duty in Dealing with Crime. Badger, 1905

BURKE, JOHN FREDERICK (M) (Pseudonym: Jonathan Burke)
The Angry Silence. Hodder, 1961
Another Chorus. Laurie, 1949
Chastity House. Laurie, 1952
Deadly Downbeat, by Jonathan Burke. Long, 1962
Echo of Barbara, by Jonathan Burke. Long, 1959
Echo of Treason. Dodd, 1966
Fear by Installments, by Jonathan Burke. Long, 1960
The Outward Walls. Laurie, 1951
The Poison Cupboard. Secker & Warburg, 1956
Teach Yourself Treachery, by Jonathan Burke. Long, 1962
These Haunted Streets. Laurie, 1950
The Weekend Girls, by Jonathan Burke. Long, 1966; Doubleday, 1967
Twisted Tongues, by Jonathan Burke. Long, 1964

BURKE, JONATHAN, pseud; see BURKE, JOHN FREDERICK

BURKE, LEDA, pseud; see GARNETT, DAVID

BURKE, MARGARET ISABEL (S)
When Duty Calls. Dorrance, 1966

BURKE, NOEL, pseud; see HITCHENS, DOLORES BIRK OLSON

BURKE, RICHARD (M)
Barbary Freight. Putnam, 1943
Chinese Red. Putnam, 1942
The Dead Take No Bows. Houghton, 1941
Fourth Star. Mystery House, 1946
The Frightened Pigeon, Putnam, 1944
Here Lies the Body. Putnam, 1942
Murder on High Heels. Gateway, 1940
The Red Gate. Ziff-Davis, 1947
Sinister Street. Ziff-Davis, 1948

BURKE, THOMAS (M)
The Bloomsbury Wonder. Mandrake, 1929
East of Mansion House. Doran, 1926
Limehouse Nights. Richards, G., 1916; McBride, 1917, 1926
More Limehouse Nights. Doran, 1921 (Also published as: Whispering Windows. Richards, G., 1921)
Murder at Elstree. Longmans, 1936
Night Pieces: 18 Tales. Constable, 1935; Appleton-Century, 1936

Pleasantries of Old Quong. Constable, 1931 (Also published as: Tea Shop in Limehouse. Little, 1931)
Tea Shop in Limehouse; see Pleasantries of Old Quong
Whispering Windows; see More Limehouse Nights

BURKHARDT, EVE; see BURKHARDT, ROBERT

BURKHARDT, ROBERT and EVE BURKHARDT (M) (Pseudonyms: Adam Bliss, Rex Jardin)
The Camden Ruby Murder, by Adam Bliss. Barse & Co., 1931
The Devil's Mansion, by Rex Jardin. Fiction League, 1931
Four Times a Widower, by Adam Bliss. Macrae Smith, 1936
Murder Upstairs, by Adam Bliss. Macrae Smith, 1936

BURKS, ALLISON L. (M)
Tight Rope. Duell, 1945

BURLEIGH, DONALD QUIMBY (M)
The Kristiana Killers. Dutton, 1937

BURLEIGH, HILARY (D)
Murder at Maison Manche. Hurst, 1948

BURNABY, NIGEL, pseud; see ELLETT, HAROLD PINCTON

BURNE, GLEN, pseud; see GREEN, ALAN BAER

BURNETT, HALLIE (S)
Watch on the Wall. Morrow, 1965; Pyramid, 1966

BURNETT, WILLIAM RILEY (S)
The Asphalt Jungle. Knopf, 1949
Conant. Popular Lib., 1961
Dark Hazard. Harper, 1933
The Giant Swing. Harper, 1932
High Sierra. Knopf, 1940
Little Caesar. Cape, 1929; Dial, 1929; Avon, 1966
Nobody Lives Forever. Heinemann, 1944
The Quick Brown Fox. Knopf, 1942
Romelle. Knopf, 1946
Round the Clock at Volari's. GM, 1961
Tomorrow's Another Day. Heinemann, 1946
Underdog. Knopf, 1957; Bantam
Vanity Row. Macmillan, 1953; Bantam

BURNHAM, MRS. CLARA LOUISE (D)
Tobey's First Case. Houghton, 1926

BURNHAM, DAVID (M)
Last Act in Bermuda. Scribner, 1940

BURNHAM, HELEN (M)
Murder of Lalla Lee. McBride, 1931; Arrowsmith, 1932
The Telltale Telegram. McBride, 1932

BURNING, MICHAEL and ALTHEN GREY (M)
Dusty Death. Jenkins, 1949

BURNS, ALLIS L. (S)
Tight Rope. Duell, 1945

BURNS, MARY LOVELAND (D)
Murder at Crawford Notch. Humphries, 1944

BURR, MRS. ANNA ROBESON BROWN (M)
Great House in the Park. Duffield, 1924
Palludia. Duffield, 1928
West of the Moon. Duffield, 1926
The Wrong Move. Macmillan, 1923

BURROUGHS, EDGAR RICE (M)
Tarzan and the Castaways. Canaveral, 1965 (Includes: "Tarzan and the Jungle Murders")

BURROWS, PETER E. (M)
Crime of Ruby Rochfort. Neely, 1899

BURT, KATHERINE NEWLIN (M)
The Red Lady. Houghton, 1920
The Safe Road. Macrae Smith, 1938
Scotland's Burning. Little, 1953
Still Water. Macrae Smith, 1948

BURT, MICHAEL (D)
The Case of the Angels' Trumpets. Ward, Lock, 1947
The Case of the Fast Young Lady. Ward, Lock, 1942
The Case of the Laughing Jesuit. Ward, Lock, 1948
The House of Sleep. Ward, Lock, 1945

BURTON, CARL D. (S)
The Long Goodnight. Morrow, 1961

BURTON, J. B. (M)
Mystery of St. James Park. Westbrook

BURTON, MILES (D)
Accidents Do Happen; see The Early Morning Murders
Beware Your Neighbor. Collins, 1951
Bones in the Brickfield. Collins, 1958
The Cat Jumps. Collins, 1946
Charabanc Mystery. Collins, 1934
Chinese Puzzle. Collins, 1957
Clue of the Fourteen Keys; see Death at the Club
Clue of the Silver Brush; see The Milk Churn Murders
Clue of the Silver Cellar; see Where Is Barbara Prentice?

A Crime in Time. Collins, 1955
Dark Is the Tunnel; see Death in the Tunnel
Dead Stop. Collins, 1943
Death at Low Tide. Collins, 1938
Death at Ash House; see This Undesirable Residence
Death at the Club. Collins, 1937 (U.S. title: Clue of the Fourteen Keys. Doubleday, Doran, 1937)
Death at the Crossroads. Collins, 1933
Death in a Duffle Coat. Collins, 1956
Death in Shallow Water. Collins, 1948
Death in the Tunnel. Collins, 1936 (U.S. title: Dark Is the Tunnel. Doubleday, Doran, 1936)
Death Leaves No Card. Collins, 1939
Death of Mr. Gantley. Collins, 1932
Death of Two Brothers. Collins, 1941
Death Takes a Detour. Collins, 1958
Death Takes a Flat. Collins, 1940 (U.S. title: Vacancy with a Corpse. Doubleday, Doran, 1941)
Death Takes the Living. Collins, 1949 (U.S. title: The Disappearing Parson. Doubleday, 1949)
Death Visits Downspring. Doubleday, Doran, 1941
Devereaux Court Mystery. Collins, 1935
Devil's Reckoning. Collins, 1948; Doubleday, 1949
The Disappearing Parson; see Death Takes the Living
The Early Morning Murder. Collins, 1945 (U.S. title: Accidents Do Happen. Doubleday, 1946)
Fate at the Fair. Collins, 1933
Found Drowned. Collins, 1956
Four-Ply Yarn. Collins, 1933 (U.S. title: The Shadow on the Cliff. Doubleday, Doran, 1944)
Ground for Suspicion. Collins, 1950
The Hardway Diamonds Mystery. Collins, 1930; Mystery League, 1930
Heir to Lucifer. Collins, 1947
Legacy of Death. Collins, 1960
Look Alive. Collins, 1949; Doubleday, 1950
The Man with the Tattooed Face; see Murder in Crown Passage
Menace on the Downs. Collins, 1931
The Milk Churn Murders. Collins, 1935 (U.S. title: Clue of the Silver Brush. Doubleday, Doran, 1936)
Mr. Babbacombe Dies. Collins, 1939
Mr. Westerby Missing. Collins, 1940; Doubleday, Doran, 1940
Moth-watch Murder. Collins, 1957
Murder at the Moorings. Collins, 1932; Sears, 1934
Murder in Absence. Collins, 1954
Murder in Crown Passage. Collins, 1937 (U.S. title: The Man with the Tattooed Face. Doubleday, Doran, 1937)
Murder in the Coalhole. Collins, 1940 (U.S. title: Written in Dust. Doubleday, Doran, 1940)
Murder M.D. Collins, 1943 (U.S. title: Who Killed the Doctor? Doubleday, Doran, 1944)
Murder of a Chemist. Collins, 1936
Murder on Duty. Collins, 1952
Murder out of School. Collins, 1951
Murder Unrecognized. Collins, 1955
Not a Leg to Stand On. Collins, 1945; Doubleday, Doran, 1945
The Platinum Cat. Collins, 1938; Doubleday, Doran, 1938
The Secret of High Eldersham. Collins, 1930; Mystery League, 1931
The Shadow on the Cliff; see Four-Ply Yarn
Situation Vacant. Collins, 1946
A Smell of Smoke. Collins, 1959
Something to Hide. Collins, 1953
This Undesirable Residence. Collins, 1942 (U.S. title: Death at Ash House. Doubleday, Doran, 1942)
The Three Corpse Trick. Collins, 1944
The Three Crimes. Collins, 1931
To Catch a Thief. Collins, 1934
Tragedy at the Thirteenth Hole. Collins, 1933
Unwanted Corpse. Collins, 1954
Vacancy with a Corpse; see Death Takes a Flat
Village Afraid. Collins, 1950
Where Is Barbara Prentice? Collins, 1936 (U.S. title: The Clue of the Silver Cellar. Doubleday, Doran, 1937)
Who Killed the Doctor; see Murder M.D.
Will in the Way. Collins, 1947; Doubleday, 1947
Written in the Dust. Doubleday, Doran, 1940

BURTON, THOMAS, pseud; see LONGSTREET, STEPHEN

BUSH, CHRISTOPHER (M) (Pseudonym: Michael Home)
Auber File. Methuen, 1953
The Body in the Bonfire; see Case of the Bonfire Body
Case of the Amateur Actor. MacDonald & Co., 1955; Macmillan, 1956
Case of the April Fools. Cassell, 1933; Morrow, 1953
Case of the Benevolent Bookie. MacDonald & Co., 1955; Macmillan, 1955
Case of the Bonfire Body. Cassell, 1936 (U.S. title: The Body in the Bonfire. Holt, H., 1936)
Case of the Burnt Bohemian. MacDonald & Co., 1953; Macmillan, 1954
Case of the Careless Thief. MacDonald & Co., 1959; Macmillan, 1960
Case of the Chinese Gong. Cassell, 1935; Holt, H., 1935

Case of the Climbing Rat. Cassell, 1940
Case of the Corner Cottage. MacDonald & Co., 1951; Macmillan, 1952
Case of the Corporal's Leave. Cassell, 1945
Case of the Counterfeit Colonel. MacDonald & Co., 1952; Macmillan, 1953
Case of the Curious Client. MacDonald & Co., 1947
Case of the Dead Man Gone. MacDonald & Co., 1961; Macmillan, 1962
Case of the Dead Shepherd. Cassell, 1934
Case of the Deadly Diamonds. MacDonald & Co., 1967
Case of the Extra Grave. MacDonald & Co., 1961; Macmillan, 1962
Case of the Extra Man. MacDonald & Co., 1956; Macmillan, 1957
Case of the Fighting Soldier. Cassell, 1942
Case of the Flowery Corpse. MacDonald & Co., 1956; Macmillan, 1957
The Case of the Flying Ass. Cassell, 1939
Case of the Fourth Detective. MacDonald & Co., 1951
Case of the Frightened Mannequin; see Case of the Happy Warrior
Case of the Good Employer. MacDonald & Co., 1966; Macmillan, 1967
Case of the Grand Alliance. MacDonald & Co., 1964; Macmillan, 1965
Case of the Green Felt Hat. Cassell, 1933; Holt, H., 1939
Case of the Hanging Rope. Cassell, 1937 (U.S. title: Wedding Night Murder. Holt, H., 1937)
Case of the Happy Medium. MacDonald & Co., 1952
Case of the Happy Warrior. MacDonald & Co., 1950 (U.S. title: Case of the Frightened Mannequin. Macmillan, 1951)
Case of the Haven Hotel. MacDonald & Co., 1948
Case of the Heavenly Twin, MacDonald & Co., 1963; Macmillan, 1964
Case of the Housekeeper's Hair. MacDonald & Co., 1948; Macmillan, 1949
Case of the 100% Alibis. Cassell, 1934
Case of the Jumbo Sandwich. MacDonald & Co., 1965; Macmillan, 1966
Case of the Kidnapped Colonel. Cassell, 1942
Case of the Leaning Man. Cassell, 1936 (U.S. title: The Leaning Man. Holt, H., 1938)
Case of the Magic Mirror. Cassell, 1943
Case of the Missing Men. MacDonald & Co., 1946; Macmillan, 1947
Case of the Missing Minutes. Cassell, 1937 (U.S. title: Eight O'Clock Alibi. Holt, H., 1937)
Case of the Monday Murders. Cassell, 1936 (U.S. title: Murder on Mondays. Holt, H., 1936)
Case of the Murdered Major. Cassell, 1941
Case of the Platinum Blonde. Cassell, 1944
Case of the Purloined Picture. MacDonald & Co., 1949; Macmillan, 1955
Case of the Red Brunette. MacDonald & Co., 1954; Macmillan, 1955
Case of the Running Man. MacDonald & Co., 1958; Macmillan, 1959
Case of the Running Mouse. Cassell, 1944
Case of the Russian Cross. MacDonald & Co., 1957; Macmillan, 1958
Case of the Second Chance. MacDonald & Co., 1946
Case of the Sapphire Brooch. MacDonald & Co., 1960; Macmillan, 1961
Case of the Seven Bells. MacDonald & Co., 1949; Macmillan, 1950
Case of the Silken Petticoat. MacDonald & Co., 1953; Macmillan, 1954
Case of the Three Lost Letters. MacDonald & Co., 1954; Macmillan, 1955
Case of the Three-Ring Puzzle. MacDonald & Co., 1962; Macmillan, 1962
Case of the Three Strange Faces. Cassell, 1933
Case of the Treble Twist. MacDonald & Co., 1958 (U.S. title: Case of the Triple Twist. Macmillan, 1958)
Case of the Triple Twist; see Case of the Treble Twist
Case of the Tudor Queen. Cassell, 1938; Holt, H., 1938; Penguin, 1953
Case of the Unfortunate Village. Cassell, 1932; Morrow, 1932
Crank in the Corner. Heinemann, 1932; Morrow, 1933
Cut Throat. Heinemann, 1932; Morrow, 1932
Dancing Death. Doubleday, Doran, 1931; Heinemann, 1932
Dead Man Twice. Doubleday, Doran, 1930; Heinemann, 1930
Dead Man's Music. Doubleday, Doran, 1932; Heinemann, 1932
Death of Cosmo Revere. Doubleday, Doran, 1930; Heinemann, 1930
Eight O'Clock Alibi; see Case of the Missing Minutes
The Kitchen Cake Murder. Morrow, 1934
The Leaning Man; see Case of the Leaning Man
Murder at Fenwold. Heinemann, 1931
Murder on Mondays; see Case of the Monday Murders
Perfect Murder Case. Doubleday, Doran, 1929; Heinemann, 1929
Plumley Inheritance. Jarrolds, 1926
The Tea Tray. Morrow, 1934
Wedding Night Murder; see Case of the Hanging Rope

BUSH-FEKETE, MARY (M) (Pseudonym: M. Fagyas)
The Fifth Woman. Doubleday, 1963; Popular Lib., 1964
The Widowmakers. Doubleday, 1966; Cassell, 1967

BUTCHER, MARGARET (M)
Comet's Hair. Skeffington, 1939
Destiny on Demand. Skeffington, 1938
Hogdown Farm Mystery. Skeffington, 1950
Vacant Possession. Skeffington, 1940

BUTLER, ELLIS PARKER (D)
The Cunning Mulatto, with Fletcher Pratt. Smith, H., 1935
Philo Grubb, Correspondence-School Detective. Houghton, 1918

BUTLER, GEORGE, F.M.D. (D)
Exploit of a Physician Detective. Clinic, 1908

BUTLER, GERALD (S)
Blow Hot, Blow Cold. Rinehart, 1951
Kiss the Blood Off My Hands. Nicolson, 1940; Rinehart, 1946
Mad with Much Heart. Jarrolds, 1946; Rinehart, 1946

BUTLER, GWENDOLINE WILLIAMS (D)
Coffin for Baby. Bles, 1963; Walker & Co., 1963
Coffin in Malta. Bles, 1964; Walker & Co., 1965
Coffin in Oxford. Bles, 1961
Coffin Waiting. Bles, 1964; Walker & Co., 1965
Dead in a Row. Bles, 1957
Death Lives Next Door. Bles, 1960 (U.S. title: Dine and Be Dead. Macmillan, 1960)
Dine and Be Dead; see Death Lives Next Door
The Dull Dead. Bles, 1958; Walker & Co., 1958
The Interloper. Bles, 1959
Make Me a Murderer. Bles, 1961
The Murdering Kind. Bles, 1958; Roy Pubs., 1964
A Nameless Coffin. Bles, 1966; Walker & Co., 1967
Receipt for Murder. Bles, 1956

BUTLER, K. R. (S)
A Desert of Salt. Mill, 1964

BUTLER, LESLIE
Recover or Kill. Hale, 1965

BUTLER, WALTER C., pseud; see FAUST, FREDERICK

BUTLER, WILLIAM (S)
Mr. Three. Putnam, 1964, 1966

BUTOR, MICHAEL (M)
Passing Time. S & S, 1960

BUTTENSHAW, DIANA
Violence in Paradise. Hodder, 1957

BUTTERWORTH, MICHAEL (D)
The Soundless Scream. Doubleday, 1967

BUTTS, ANNE (M)
The Death of Felicity Taverner. Wishart, 1932

BUXTON, ANNE (S-Gothic) (Pseudonym: Anne Maybury)
The Brides of Bellenmore. Ace, 1964
Enchanter's Nightshade; see Winds of Night
The Falcon's Shadow. Ace, 1967
Green Fire. Ace, 1966
The House of Fand. Ace, 1966
I Am Gabriella. Ace, 1966
The Night My Enemy. Ace
The Pavilion at Monkshood. Ace, 1965
Shadow of a Stranger. Ace, 1966
Someone Waiting. Ace, 1961
Stay Until Tomorrow. Ace, 1967
Whisper in the Dark. Ace, 1961
Winds of Night. Ace, 1967 (Original title: Enchanter's Nightshade)

BYRME, MARY (M)
Murder at the "Signal." Long, 1936

BYROM, JAMES, pseud; see BRAMWELL, JAMES GUY

BUZZATI, DINO (M)
Larger Than Life. Walker & Co., 1967

CABOT, ISABEL (M)
Murder Is a House Guest. Bouregy, 1961

CADE, COULSON T. (M)
The Cornish Penny. Stokes, 1922

CADE, PAUL (D)
Death Slams the Door. Modern Age, 1937

CADELL, ELIZABETH (S)
Canary Yellow. Morrow, 1965; Bantam
Shadows on the Water. Morrow, 1958
The Yellow Brick Road. Morrow, 1960

CADMAN, J. (D)
With Dead Bodies. Stockwell, 1957

CAGNEY, PETER, pseud; see WINTER, BEVIS

CAIDIN, MARTIN (S)
Devil Take All. Dutton, 1966

CAILLOU, ALAN, pseud; see LYLE-SMYTHE, ALLAN

CAIN, JAMES MALLAHAN (S)
The Butterfly. Knopf, 1947; Dell, 1946
Career in C Major; see Three of a Kind
Double Indemnity. Avon, 1943
The Embezzler; see Three of a Kind
Galatea. Knopf, 1953; Hale, R., 1954
Jealous Woman. Hale, R., 1955
Love's Lovely Counterfeit. Knopf, 1942
The Magician's Wife. Dial, 1965; Dell, 1966
Mignon. Dial, 1962; Bantam, 1963; Hale, R., 1963
Mildred Pierce. Knopf, 1941; Dial, 1942; Hale, R., 1943
The Moth. Knopf, 1948; Hale, R., 1950; New Amer. Lib., 1950
Past All Dishonor. Knopf, 1946; Dell, 1963
The Postman Always Rings Twice. Knopf, 1934; Cape, 1943; PB
The Root of His Evil. Hale, R., 1954
Serenade. Knopf, 1937; Cape, 1938
Sinful Woman. Avon, 1947; World Pub., 1948
Three Novels. World Pub., 1946 (Contains: The Postman Always Rings Twice, Serenade, and Mildred Pierce)
Three of a Kind. Knopf, 1944; Hale, R., 1945 (Contains: Career in C Major, The Embezzler, and Double Indemnity)

CAIN, PAUL (D) (Pseudonym: Peter Ruric)
Fast One. Doubleday, Doran, 1933; Avon, 1948
Seven Slayers. Saint Enterprises, 1946

CAINE, HALL (M)
Shadow of a Crime. Chatto, 1885

CAIRD, CATHERINE (M)
The Religious Body. Doubleday, 1966

CAIRD, JANET (D-M)
In a Glass Darkly; see Murder Reflected
Murder Reflected. Bles, 1965 (U.S. title: In a Glass Darkly. Morrow, 1966)
Murder Scholastic. Bles, 1966
Perturbing Spirit. Bles, 1966; Doubleday, 1967

CAIRNS, CICELY (D)
Murder Goes to Press. Constable, 1950; MacDonald & Co., 1951

CALDER-MARSHALL, ARTHUR (D)
The Scarlet Boy. Harper, 1961

CALDWELL, ALFRED BETTS (D)
Death Rattle. Doubleday, Doran, 1940
No Tears Shed. Doubleday, Doran, 1937
Turquoise Hazard. Doubleday, Doran, 1936

CALDWELL, JANE MIRIAM TAYLOR HOLLAND (Mrs. Marcus Reback) (M)
The Late Clara Beam. Doubleday, 1963; Collins, 1964; Crest, 1964
Wicked Angel. Crest, 1965

CALEF, NOEL (S)
Frantic. GM, 1961

CALIN, ANNE (S)
Multitude of Shadows. Lancer

CALIN, HAL JASON (D)
Rocks and Ruin. Vanguard, 1954

CALL, WILLIAM TIMOTHY (S)
Blackmail. Call, W. T., 1915

CALLANS, DEV, pseud; see WINCHELL, PRENTICE

CALLAS, THEO, pseud; see McCARTHY, SHAWN

CALLAWAY, SLOANE (M)
The Crime of the Conquistador. Phoenix, 1938

CALVIN, HENRY, pseud; see HANLEY, CLIFFORD

CAMERON, COURTNEY OWEN; see CAMERON, OWEN

CAMERON, DONALD CLOUGH (D)
And So He Had to Die. Holt, H., 1941
Death at Her Elbow. Holt, H., 1940
Dig Another Grave. Mystery House, 1946
Grave Without Grass. Holt, H., 1940
Murder's Coming. Holt, H., 1939
White for a Shroud. Curl, 1947; Broadman, T. V., 1953

CAMERON, EVELYN (D)
Dead Man's Shoes. Doubleday, Doran 1939
Malice Domestic. Doubleday, Doran, 1940

CAMERON, JOHN, pseud; see MACDONELL, ARCHIBALD GORDON

CAMERON, LOU (D)
Angel's Flight. GM, 1960
The Big Red Ball. GM, 1961
The Sky Divers. GM, 1962

CAMERON, MONTGOMERY F. (S)
The Ugly Woman. Vantage, 1966

CAMERON, OWEN (Full name: Courtney Owen Cameron) (M)
Butcher's Wife. S & S, 1954; Hammond, 1955
Catch a Tiger. S & S, 1952; Transworld, 1955
The Demon Stirs; see Fire Trap
Fire Trap. S & S, 1957; Hammond, 1958 (Also published as: The Demon Stirs. Dell, 1958)
Man Hunt. Hammond, 1961
Mountains Have No Shadow. Harper, 1952
The Owl and the Pussycat. Harper, 1949
The Silent One. Random, 1958

CAMERON, WILLIAM ERNEST (D) (Pseudonym: Mark Allerton)
The Case of Richard Eden. Hodder, 1918
Let Justice Be Done. Hurst, 1912

CAMP, CHARLES WADSWORTH (D)
The Abandoned Room. Caldwell, 1917; Doubleday, Page, 1917
The Communicating Door. Doubleday, Page, 1923
The Gray Mask. Doubleday, Page, 1920
The Guarded Heights. Doubleday, Page, 1921
The Hidden Road. Doubleday, Page, 1922
The House of Fear. Doubleday, Page, 1916
Sinister Island. Dodd, 1915

CAMPBELL, MRS. ALICE ORMOND (D) (Pseudonym: Martin Ingram)
Bloodstained Toy. Collins, 1948
The Borrowed Cottage; see No Murder of Mine
Child's Play. Collins, 1947
Click of the Gate. Farrar & Rinehart, 1931; Collins, 1932
Cockroach Sings. Collins, 1946
Corpse Had Red Hair. Collins, 1950
Death Framed in Silver. Collins, 1937
Desire to Kill. Collins, 1934; Farrar & Rinehart, 1934; Grosset, 1935
A Door Closed Softly. Collins, 1939
Flying Blind. Collins, 1938
Juggernaut. Doubleday, Doran, 1928; Hodder, 1928
Keep Away from Water. Farrar & Rinehart, 1935
Murder in Paris. Farrar & Rinehart, 1930 (English title: Spider Web. Hodder, 1930; Penguin, 1940)
Murder of Caroline Bundy. Farrar & Rinehart, 1932; Collins, 1933
No Light Came On. Collins, 1942; Scribner, 1945
No Murder of Mine. Scribner, 1941; Collins, 1943 (Also published as: The Borrowed Cottage)
Ringed with Fire. Random, 1942; Collins, 1943
Spider Web; see Murder in Paris
They Hunted a Fox. Collins, 1940; Scribner, 1940
Traveling Butcher. Collins, 1944
Veiled Murder. Random, 1949
Water Weed. Farrar & Rinehart, 1929; Grosset, 1931
With Bated Breath. Random, 1945; Paperback Lib., 1968

CAMPBELL, ARTHUR (M)
The Mystery of Martha Warne. Robinson, C., 1888

CAMPBELL, DONALD F. and BURTON S. KEIRSTEAD (D)
The Brownsville Murders. Macmillan, 1933

CAMPBELL, LADY HARRIETTE RUSSELL (D)
Crime in Crystal. Harper, 1946
Magic Makes Murder. Harper, 1943
Moor Fires Mystery. Heinemann, 1938; Harper, 1939
Murder Set to Music. Harper, 1941
Mystery of Saint's Island. Harper, 1927
The Porcelain Fish. Heinemann, 1937; Knopf, 1937
The String Glove Mystery. Heinemann, 1936; Knopf, 1936
Three Lost Ladies. Heinemann, 1949
Three Names for Murder. Collins, 1940; Harper, 1940

CAMPBELL, HAZEL (M)
The Burqa. Long, 1930
The Makra Mystery; see The Makra Secret
The Makra Secret. Long, 1931 (Also published as: The Makra Mystery)
The Secret Brotherhood. Long, 1929

CAMPBELL, J. RAMSEY (S)
The Inhabitant of the Lake and Less Welcome Tenants. Arkham House, 1964

CAMPBELL, KEITH, pseud; see WEST-WATSON, KEITH CAMPBELL

CAMPBELL, SIR MALCOLM (S)
Salute to the Gods. Cassell, 1934; Putnam, 1935

CAMPBELL, MARGARET ELIZABETH BAIRD and JOHANNA FREDERIKA JANSEN (M) (Pseudonym: Fred Bayard)
Death and Lilacs. Phoenix, 1948

CAMPBELL, MARY ELIZABETH (M)
Scandal Has Two Faces. Doubleday, Doran, 1943
The White Hand Mystery. Renaissance, 1936

CAMPBELL, R. T. (D)
Apollo Wore a Wig. Westhouse
Bodies in a Bookshop. Westhouse, 1946
Death Cap. Westhouse
Death for Madame. Westhouse
Death Is Our Physician. Westhouse
No Man Lives Forever. Westhouse
Swing Low, Sweet Death. Westhouse
Take Thee a Sharp Knife. Westhouse, 1946
Unholy Dying. Westhouse, 1945

CAMPBELL, REGINALD WILFRID (M)
The Abominable Twilight. Cassell, 1948
The Admiralty Regrets. Cassell, 1937
The Bangkok Murders. Cassell, 1939
Brainstorm. Cassell, 1950
Coffin for a Murderer. Cassell, 1947
Cruiser in Adion. Cassell, 1940
Death by Apparition. Cassell, 1949
Death in Tiger Valley. Hodder, 1931
A Dog's Death, with Peter Motte. Cassell, 1953
Fear in the Forest. Hodder, 1932
The Haunting of Kathleen Saunders. Cassell, 1938
Married into Murder. Cassell, 1951
Murder of My Wife. Cassell, 1952
Murder She Says, with Peter Motte. Cassell, 1953

CAMPBELL, RONALD (M)
Marked for Murder. Hammond, 1958

CAMPBELL, SCOTT, pseud; see DAVIS, FREDERICK WILLIAM

CAMPBELL, WALTER STANLEY (D) (Pseudonym: Stanley Vestal)
Wine Room Murder. Little, 1935

CAMPBELL, WILLIAM EDWARD MARCH (S) (Pseudonym: William March)
The Bad Seed. Rinehart, 1954; Dell, 1967

CAMPION, PETER (D)
Diamonds Worth a Death or Two. Arco Publications, 1955
Model for Murder. Arco Publications, 1955

CANADAY, JOHN EDWIN (D) (Pseudonym: Matthew Head)
The Accomplice. S & S, 1947; Avon, 1965
Another Man's Life. S & S, 1954
Cabinda Affair. S & S, 1949
Congo Venus. S & S, 1950; Avon, 1965
The Devil in the Bush. S & S, 1945; Avon, 1964
Murder at the Flea Club. S & S, 1955; Heinemann, 1957
The Smell of Money. S & S, 1943; Avon 1964

CANDY, EDWARD, pseud; see NEVILLE, ALLISON BARBARA

CANNAN, JOANNA, pseud; see PULLEIN-THOMPSON, MRS. H. J.

CANNING, VICTOR (M-S)
Bird of Prey. Mill, 1951; Berkley Pub., 1963 (English title: Venetian Bird. Hodder, 1951)
Black Flamingo. Hodder, 1962; Sloane, 1963; Berkley Pub., 1965
Burden of Proof. Sloane, 1956; Berkley Pub., 1964 (English title: Hidden Face. Hodder, 1956)
The Burning Eye. Sloane, 1960; Crest, 1961
Castle Minerva; see A Handful of Silver
The Chasm. Hodder, 1947; Mill, 1947; Berkley Pub., 1963
A Delivery of Furies. Sloane, 1961; Berkley Pub., 1964
Doubled in Diamonds. Heinemann, 1966; Morrow, 1967
The Dragon Tree. Hodder, 1958; New English Lib., 1963
Fly Away. Hodder, 1936; Reynal, 1936; Berkley Pub., 1963; Sloane, 1964
A Forest of Eyes. Hodder, 1950; Mill, 1950; Berkley Pub., 1963
Fountain Inn. Hodder, 1939
The Girl from the Turkish Slave. Berkley Pub., 1963
The Golden Salamander. Hodder, 1949; Morrow, 1949; Berkley Pub., 1963
Green Battlefield. Hodder, 1943
A Handful of Silver. Sloane, 1954 (Also published as: Castle Minerva. Berkley Pub., 1964)
Hidden Face; see Burden of Proof
His Bones Are Coral; see Twist of the Knife
House of Fear; see The House of Seven Flies
The House of Seven Flies. Hodder, 1952; Mill, 1952; Berkley Pub., 1963 (Serial title: House of Fear)
The Limbo Line. Berkley Pub., 1963; Heinemann, 1963; Sloane, 1964
The Man from the Turkish Slave. Sloane, 1954; Berkley Pub., 1963
Matthew Silverman. Hodder, 1937
Monasco Road. Hodder, 1957; Sloane, 1957
Oasis Nine; see Young Man on a Bicycle and Other Stories
Panther's Moon. Hodder, 1948; Mill, 1948; Berkley Pub., 1963
Polycarp's Progress. Hodder, 1935
The Python Project. Heinemann, 1967
The Scorpio Letters. Sloane, 1964
Twist of the Knife. Sloane, 1955 (English title: His Bones Are Coral. Hodder, 1955)
Venetian Bird; see Bird of Prey

The Whip Hand. Heinemann, 1965; Sloane, 1965; Signet, 1966
Young Man on a Bicycle and Other Stories. Hodder, 1958 (U.S. title: Oasis Nine. Sloane, 1959)

CANNON, CURT, pseud; see HUNTER, EVAN

CANYON, CLAUDIA, pseud; see ANDERSON, BETTY

CAPEK, KAREL (M)
The Macropoulos Secret. Luce, J. W., 1925
Tales from Two Pockets. Faber, 1932

CAPES, BERNARD EDWARD JOSEPH (D)
Gilead Balm, Knight Errant. Unwin, 1911
The Great Skene Mystery. Methuen, 1907
The Mill of Silence. Rand, 1896
The Skeleton Key. Collins, 1919; Doran, 1920
Why Did He Do It? Methuen, 1910
Will and the Way. Murray, J., 1910

CAPETO, ISABEL (D)
Few Drops of Murder. Arcadia, 1955

CAPIT, ELINE (D)
Run from the Sheep. Arcadia, 1955

CAPON, PAUL (D)
Battered Caravanserai. Heinemann, 1942
Dead Man's Chest. Nicholson, 1947
Death at Shinglestrand. Ward, Lock, 1951
Death on a Wet Sunday. Ward, Lock, 1952
Delay of Doom. Ward, Lock, 1952
Image of a Murder. Boardman, T. V., 1949
Malice Domestic. Ward, Lock, 1954
Margin of Terror. Ward, Lock, 1955
Murder of Jacob Canansey. Heinemann, 1947
No Time for Death. Ward, Lock, 1951
The Seventh Passenger. Ward, Lock, 1953
Thirty Days Hath September. Ward, Lock, 1953
Wonderbolt. Ward, Lock, 1955

"CAPSTAN," pseud; see HARDINGE, REX

CARDEN, PERCY T.; see DICKENS, CHARLES

CARDIN, MARTIN (S)
Devil Take All. Dell, 1967

CAREY, BASIL (D)
Dead Man's Shadow. Constable, 1931
Secret Enterprise. Jarrolds, 1932

CAREY, BERNICE (D)
The Beautiful Stranger. Doubleday, 1951
Body on the Sidewalk. Doubleday, 1950
Fatal Picnic. Doubleday, 1955
Man Who Got Away with It. Doubleday, 1950
The Missing Heiress. Doubleday, 1952
Reluctant Murderer. Doubleday, 1949
Their Nearest and Dearest. Doubleday, 1953
Three Widows. Doubleday, 1952

CAREY, CHARLES, pseud; see WADDEL, CHARLES CAREY

CAREY, DOUGLAS (S)
The Raven's Feathers. Graphic, 1930
The Scorpion. Graphic, 1931

CAREY, ELIZABETH and MARION AUSTIN MAGOON (M) (Joint pseudonym: Carey Magoon)
I Smell the Devil. Farrar & Rinehart, 1943

CAREY, MICHAEL, pseud. (S)
Vice Net. Avon, 1958
Vice Squad Cop. Avon, 1957

CAREY, WYMOND (M)
"No 101." Putnam, 1906

CARGILL, LESLIE (D)
Death Goes by Bus. Jenkins, 1936
Death Sets the Pace. Jenkins, 1950
Death Walks in Scarlet. Jenkins, 1941
Fortune's Apprentice. Jenkins, 1946
Gestapo Gauntlet. Jenkins, 1939
Heads You Lose. Jenkins, 1938
It Might Have Meant Murder. Jenkins, 1940
Lady Was Elusive. Jenkins, 1952
Man from the Rhine. Jenkins, 1943
Man Who Wasn't Himself. Jenkins, 1947
Matrimony Most Murderous. Jenkins, 1949; Roy Pubs., 1958
Missing Background. Jenkins, 1942
Motley Menace. Jenkins, 1949
Murder in the Procession. Jenkins, 1937
Next Door to Murder. Jenkins, 1948
Surprising Sanctuary. Jenkins, 1945
Was It Montelli? Jenkins, 1947
Yellow Phantom. Fiction House, 1935

CARLE, C. E. and DEAN M. DORN (M) (Pseudonym: Michael Morgan)
Nine More Lives. Random, 1947

CARLETON, BARBEE OLIVER (S)
The Witches' Bridge. Holt, 1967

CARLETON, MARJORIE CHALMERS (D-M)
The Bride Regrets. Morrow, 1950
Cry Wolf. Morrow, 1945
Dread the Sunset. Morrow, 1962; Joseph, M., 1963 (Also published as: Shadows on the Hill. Pyramid, 1966)
"The Dreadful Strangers;" see Swan Sang Once
Night of the Good Children. Morrow, 1957; Joseph, M., 1958 (Also published as: One Night of Terror. Berkley Pub., 1960)
One Night of Terror; see Night of the Good Children
Shadows on the Hill; see Dread the Sunset
Swan Sang Once. Morrow, 1947. (Published in American Magazine as: "The Dreadful Strangers")
Their Dusty Hands. Brimmer, 1924
Vanished. Morrow, 1955; Pyramid, 1966

CARLETON, S., pseud; see JONES, SUSAN CARLETON

CARLIN, FRANCIS (D)
Reminiscences of an Ex-Detective. Hutchinson

CARLING, JOHN R. (S)
Viking's Skull. Little, 1906
Weird Picture. Little, 1905

CARLISLE, HELEN GRACE (M)
The Tiger Sniffs the Rose. Doubleday, 1958

CARLON, PATRICIA B. (M)
Circle of Fear. Ward, Lock, 1961
Crime of Silence. Hodder, 1965
Danger in the Dark. Ward, Lock, 1962
The Price of an Orphan. Hodder, 1964
Who Are You, Linda Condrick? Ward, Lock, 1962

CARLSON, NATALIE E. (M)
Old Murders Never Die. Arcadia, 1960

CARLYLE, A. (M)
Children of Chance. Houghton, 1923; Mills & Boon, 1923
Fugitive Millionaire. Houghton, 1922 (English title: The Tavern and the Arrows. Mills & Boon, 1922)
The Tavern and the Arrows; see Fugitive Millions

CARMACK, JESSE (M)
The Tell-Tale Clock Mystery. Stokes, 1937

CARMICHAEL, HARRY, pseud; see OGNALL, LEOPOLD BRUCE

CARNAC, CAROL, pseud; see RIVETT, EDITH CAROLINE

CARNAHAN, WALTER H. (S)
Hoffman's Row. Bobbs, 1963

CARNEY, OTIS (S)
The Paper Bullet. Morrow, 1966

CARPENTER, HELEN ALDEN KNIPE (M)
Whistling in the Dark. Dodd, 1932

CARPENTER, MARGARET (S)
Experiment Perilous. Little, 1943; Pyramid, 1963

CARR, ANTHONY (M)
Candles in the Night. Cassell, 1956
Comedy of Terrors. Cassell, 1955
Girl in Green. Cassell, 1959
The Man in Room 3. Cassell, 1958
A Strange Harmony. Earl, 1948

CARR, GLYN, pseud; see STYLES, FRANK SHOWALL

CARR, JOHN DICKSON (M-D) (Pseudonym: Carter Dickson)
And So to Murder, by Carter Dickson. Morrow, 1940; Heinemann, 1941
The Arabian Nights Murder. Hamilton, H., 1936; Harper, 1936; Collier, 1965
Behind the Crimson Blind, by Carter Dickson. Morrow, 1952 (English title: Tangier. Heinemann, 1952)
Below Suspicion. Harper, 1949; Hamilton, H., 1950; Bantam, 1960
The Black Spectacles; see The Problem of the Green Capsule
Blind Barber. Harper, 1934; Collier, 1962
Bowstring Murders, by Carter Dickson. Morrow, 1933; Heinemann, 1934
Bride of Newgate. Hamilton, H., 1950; Harper, 1950; Avon
The Burning Court. Hamilton, H., 1937; Harper, 1937; Bantam, 1963
Captain Cut-Throat. Hamilton, H., 1955; Harper, 1955
Case of the Constant Suicides. Hamilton, H., 1941; Harper, 1941; Collier, 1963 (Also published as: Case of the Ten Teacups)
Case of the Ten Teacups; see Case of the Constant Suicides
Castle Skull. Harper, 1931; Berkley Pub., 1964
Cavalier's Cup, by Carter Dickson. Morrow, 1953; Heinemann, 1954

The Corpse in the Waxworks. Harper, 1932; Berkley Pub., 1958; Collier, 1965
Crooked Hinge. Hamilton, H., 1938; Harper, 1938; Dell, 1955
The Crossbow Murder; see The Judas Window
The Curse of the Bronze Lamp, by Carter Dickson. Morrow, 1945
Dark of the Moon. Harper & Row, 1967
Dead Man's Knock. Harper, 1958; Bantam, 1960
Death in Five Boxes, by Carter Dickson. Heinemann, 1938; Morrow, 1938; Berkley Pub., 1964
Death Turns the Table. Harper, 1941; Berkley Pub., 1964
Death Watch. Hamilton, H., 1935; Harper, 1935; Collier, 1963; Penguin
The Demoniacs. Harper, 1962; Bantam, 1964
Department of Queer Complaints, by Carter Dickson. Heinemann, 1940; Morrow, 1940 (Also published as: Scotland Yard: Department of Queer Complaints. Dell)
The Devil in Velvet. Hamilton, H., 1951; Harper, 1951; Penguin
Dr. Fell, Detective
Dr. Fell Omnibus. Hamilton, H., 1959
Drop to His Death; see Fatal Descent
The Eight of Swords. Harper, 1934; Hamilton, H., 1936; Collier, 1962
The Emperor's Snuff Box. Harper, 1942; Hamilton, H., 1943; Berkley Pub., 1964
The Exploits of Sherlock Holmes, with Adrian Conan Doyle. Random, 1954; Ace
Fatal Descent, by Carter Dickson and John Rhode. Dodd, 1939 (English title: Drop to His Death. Heinemann, 1939)
Fear Is the Same, by Carter Dickson. Morrow, 1956
Fire, Burn. Hamilton, H., 1957; Harper, 1957; Penguin
Four False Weapons. Harper, 1937; Hamilton, H., 1938; Collier, 1962
The Gilded Man, by Carter Dickson. Heinemann, 1942; Morrow, 1942; Berkley Pub., 1966
Graveyard to Let, by Carter Dickson. Morrow, 1949; Heinemann, 1950
Hag's Nook. Hamilton, H., 1933; Harper, 1946; Collier, 1963; Dell
He Who Whispers. Hamilton, H., 1946; Harper, 1946; Penguin
He Wouldn't Kill Patience, by Carter Dickson. Heinemann, 1944; Morrow, 1944; Berkley Pub., 1966 (Also published as: Murder at the Zoo)
The Hollow Man. Hamilton, H., 1935; Penguin
House at Satan's Elbow. Harper & Row, 1965; Signet, 1967
In Spite of Thunder. Harper, 1960; Penguin
It Walks by Night. Harper, 1930; Avon, 1963
John Dickson Carr Trio: Three Coffins, Crooked Hinge, The Call of the Constant Suicides. Harper, 1957
The Judas Window, by Carter Dickson. Heinemann, 1938; Morrow, 1938 (Also published as: The Crossbow Murder. Berkley Pub., 1964)
Lord of the Sorcerers, by Carter Dickson. Heinemann, 1946
The Lost Gallows. Harper, 1931; Berkley Pub., 1965
The Mad Hatter Mystery. Hamilton, H., 1933; Harper, 1933; Penguin, 1947; Collier, 1965
The Magic Lantern Murders, by Carter Dickson. Heinemann, 1936
The Man Who Could Not Shudder. Hamilton, H., 1940; Harper, 1940; Bantam, 1964
The Man Who Explained Miracles. Harper & Row, 1963; Hamilton, H., 1964; Pyramid, 1964
More Exploits of Sherlock Holmes, with Adrian Conan Doyle. 1964
Most Secret. Harper & Row, 1964
Murder at the Zoo; see He Wouldn't Kill Patience
Murder in the Submarine Zone; see Nine and Death Makes Ten
My Late Wives, by Carter Dickson. Morrow, 1946; Heinemann, 1947; Berkley Pub., 1967
New Exploits of Sherlock Holmes, with Adrian Conan Doyle. Random, 1954
Night at the Mocking Widow, by Carter Dickson. Morrow, 1950; Heinemann, 1951
Nine and Death Makes Ten, by Carter Dickson. Morrow, 1940; Grosset, 1942; PB, 1945; Berkley Pub., 1966 (English title: Murder in the Submarine Zone. Heinemann, 1940)
Nine Wrong Answers. Harper, 1952; Bantam, 1955
Panic in Box C. Harper & Row, 1966
Patrick Butler for the Defense. Harper, 1956; Penguin
Peacock Feather Murder, by Carter Dickson. Morrow, 1937; Berkley Pub., 1963 (English title: Ten Teacups. Heinemann, 1937)
Plague Court Murders, by Carter Dickson. Morrow, 1934; Heinemann, 1935
Poison in Jest. Hamilton, H., 1932; Harper, 1932; Collier, 1965
The Problem of the Green Capsule. Harper, 1939; Bantam, 1964 (English title: The Black Spectacles. Hamilton, H., 1939)

Problem of the Wire Cage. Harper, 1939; Hamilton, H., 1940
The Punch and Judy Murders, by Carter Dickson. Heinemann, 1939; Morrow, 1939; Berkley Pub., 1964
Reader Is Warned, by Carter Dickson. Heinemann, 1939; Morrow, 1939; Berkley Pub., 1964
The Red Widow Murders, by Carter Dickson. Heinemann, 1935, 1967; Morrow, 1935; Grosset, 1936; PB, 1940; Berkley Pub., 1963
Scandal at High Chimneys. Harper, 1959; Bantam, 1960 (English title: The Seat of the Scornful. Hamilton, H., 1942)
Scotland Yard: Department of Queer Complaints; see Department of Queer Complaints
Seat of the Scornful; see Scandal at High Chimneys
Seeing Is Believing, by Carter Dickson. Morrow, 1941; Heinemann, 1942; Berkley Pub., 1966
She Died a Lady. Heinemann, 1943; Morrow, 1943; Berkley Pub., 1966
The Skeleton in the Clock, by Carter Dickson. Morrow, 1948; Heinemann, 1949; Berkley Pub., 1967; Dell
Sleeping Sphinx. Hamilton, H., 1947; Harper, 1947
Tangier; see Behind the Crimson Blind
Ten Teacups; see Peacock Feather Murder
The Third Bullet and Other Stories. Hodder, 1937; Harper, 1954; Bantam, 1965
The Three Coffins. Harper, 1935; Dell, 1965
Three Detective Novels: Arabian Nights Murder, Burning Court, and The Wire Cage. Harper, 1959
Till Death Do Us Part. Hamilton, H., 1944; Harper, 1944; Bantam, 1950
To Wake the Dead. Hamilton, H., 1937; Harper, 1938; Collier, 1967; Dell
Trio. Harper, 1957
The Unicorn Murders, by Carter Dickson. Morrow, 1935; Heinemann, 1936; Berkley Pub., 1964
Waxworks Murder. Hamilton, H., 1952
The White Priory Murders, by Carter Dickson. Morrow, 1934; Heinemann, 1935, 1966; Berkley Pub., 1963
Witch of the Low Tide. Hamilton, H., 1961; Holt, 1961; Penguin

CARR, JOLYON (M)
Freedom for Two. Jenkins, 1939
Masters of the Parachute. Jenkins, 1940
Murders in the Dispensary. Jenkins, 1938

CARR, JOSEPH BAKER (D)
Death Whispers. Viking, 1933
Man with Bated Breath. Viking, 1934

CARR, WILLIAM H. A. (S)
Medical Examiner. Lancer, 1963

CARREL, MARK, pseud; see PAINE, LAURAN

CARRIER, WARREN (S)
Bay of the Damned. Day, 1957
The Hunt. New Directions, 1952; Owen, P., 1952

CARRINGTON, ELAINE STERNE (M)
The Crimson Goddess. Appleton-Century, 1936

CARROLL, THOMAS D. (M)
Grounds for Murder. Lancer, 1966

CARS, GUY DES (S)
The Brute. Greenberg, 1952

CARSON, BART (D)
Bread for the Dead. Hamilton & Co., 1954
Cuban Heel. Hamilton & Co., 1953
The Late Demented. Hamilton & Co., 1953
Murder Matinee. Hamilton & Co., 1953
She Died Downtown. Hamilton & Co., 1953
There Could Be Trouble. Hamilton & Co., 1954
Torment Was a Woman. Hamilton & Co., 1953

CARSON, ROBERT (S)
Legal Bride. Hale, 1955
"Aloha Means Goodbye." Saturday Evening Post, June 28, 1941

CARSTAIRS, HENRY (D)
Black Burying. Ward, Lock, 1945
Blackdrop Hall. Ward, Lock, 1950
Blood, M'Lord. Ward, Lock, 1948
Cruel Dart. Ward, Lock, 1947
Death's Duet. Ward, Lock, 1954
Drifting Death. Ward, Lock, 1944
Harpinger's Hunch. Ward, Lock, 1943
Lying Down Below. Ward, Lock, 1951
Oh, No, You Don't. Ward, Lock, 1952
Secretary of State for Death. Ward, Lock, 1946
When Three Makes Two. Ward, Lock, 1953
Who Lies Bleeding. Ward, Lock, 1949
Winton Street Mystery. Ward, Lock, 1955

CARSTAIRS, JOHN PADDY (S)
The Concrete Kimono. Walker & Co., 1965
Gardenias Bruise Easily. British Book Centre, 1959
No Wooden Overcoat. Allen, W. H., 1959
Pardon My Gun. Allen, W. H., 1962

CARTER, FELICITY WINIFRED, pseud; see COULSON, FELICITY WINIFRED

CARTER, HERBERT (M)
Never Look Back. Vantage, 1966

CARTER, JOHN FRANKLIN. (D)
(Pseudonym: "Diplomat")
Brain Trust Murder, by "Diplomat." Coward, 1935
Corpse on the White House Lawn. Covici, 1932; Hurst, 1933
Death in the Senate, by "Diplomat." Covici, 1933
Murder in the Embassy, by "Diplomat.' Cape, 1930; Harrap, 1932
Murder in the State Department, by "Diplomat." Cape, 1930
Scandal in the Chancery, by "Diplomat.' Cape, 1931
Slow Death at Geneva, by "Diplomat." Coward, 1934

CARTER, NICK, pseud. (D) (This series is authored by many different writers)
A Bullet for Fidel. Award, 1965
A Checkmate in Rio. Award, 1964
The China Doll, by Michael Avallone. Award, 1964
Danger Key. Award, 1966
Dragon Flame. Award
The Eyes of the Tiger. Award, 1965
Fiction's Most Celebrated Detective: Six Astonishing Adventures. Dell, 1963
Fraulein Spy. Award
Hanoi. Award, 1966
Istanbul. Award, 1965
The Mind Poisoners. Award, 1966
Nick Carter, Detective. Macmillan, 1963
Operation Starvation. Award, 1966
Run, Spy, Run, by Michael Avallone. Award
Safari for Spies. Award, 1964
Saigon, partly by Michael Avallone. Award, 1964
Spy Castle. Award
The Terrible Ones. Award
The Thirteenth Spy. Award, 1965
A Web of Spies. Award

CARTER, P. YOUNGMAN; see ALLINGHAM, MARGERY

CARTER, MRS. P. YOUNGMAN; see ALLINGHAM, MARGERY

CARTLIDGE, ALICE (D)
Murder at Moreby. Stockwell, 1935

CARUSO, JOSEPH (S)
The Priest. MacDonald & Co., 1956

CARVER, STEWART (D)
Died o' Wednesday. Melrose, 1953
Sneeze on Monday. Melrose, 1951
Trouble on Tuesday. Melrose, 1952

CARY, F. L.; see THOMSON, A. A.

CASEY, ROBERT JOSEPH (S)
Cambodian Quest. Bobbs, 1931; Mathews, 1932
Hot Ice. Bobbs, 1933; Mathews, 1933
Newsreel; see Secret of the Dark Room
Secret of the Bungalow. Bobbs, 1930; Mathews, 1931
Secret of the Dark Room. Mathews, 1932 (U.S. title: Newsreel. Bobbs, 1932)
Secret of Thirty-Seven Hardy Street. Bobbs, 1929; Mathews, 1930
The Third Owl. Bobbs, 1934; Nicholson, 1934
The Voice of the Lobster. Bobbs, 1930

CASPARY, VERA (S)
Bedelia. Eyre, 1945; Houghton, 1945; Sun Dial, 1946; Dell, 1960
A Chosen Sparrow. Allen, W. H., 1964; Putnam, 1964; Dell, 1965
Death Wish. Eyre, 1951
Evvie. Harper, 1960; Dell, 1961
False Face. Allen, W. H., 1954
The Husband. Harper, 1958
Laura. Houghton, 1943; Eyre, 1944; Dell, 1961
The Man Who Loved His Wife. Putnam, 1966; Dell, 1967
Stranger Than Truth. Random, 1946; Eyre, 1947
The Weeping and the Laughter. Little, 1950

CASSELLS, JOHN, pseud; see DUNCAN, WILLIAM MURDOCH

CASSERA, NORA (M)
Blue Flower Mystery. Heath, 1930

CASSIDAY, BRUCE (D)
The Floater. Abelard, 1960
Operation Goldkill—Code Name: Jericho. Award, 1967

CASSILIS, INA L. (M)
Between Midnight and Dawn. Vizetelley, 1885

CASSILL, RONALD VERLIN (M)
Brass Shroud. Ace, 1958
Corpse in the Picture Window. Ace, 1961
Dormitory Women. Lion, 1954
Hungering Shame. Avon, 1956
While Murder Waits. Graphic, 1957

CASSON, STANLEY (D)
Murder by Burial. Hamilton, H., 1938; Harper, 1938

CASTANG, VIOLA (M)
Invisible Cord. Allen, W. H., 1958

CASTLE, DENNIS (S)
The Fourth Gambler. Muller, 1965

CASTLE, FRANK (S) (Pseudonym: Steve Thurman)
Dead and Kicking. GM, 1956
Hawaiian Eye. Dell, 1962
Lovely and Lethal. GM, 1957
"Mad Dog" Coll, by Steve Thurman. Monarch, 1961
Move Along, Stranger. GM, 1954
Murder in Red. GM, 1957
Night After Night, by Steve Thurman. Monarch, 1961
The Violent Hours. GM, 1956; Jenkins, 1966

CASTLE, HELEN B. (M)
Emergency Ward Nurse. Paperback Lib., 1963

CASTLE, JOHN, pseud; see GARROD, JOHN

CATALAN, HENRI, pseud; see DUPUY-MAZUEL, HENRY

CATTO, MAX, pseud; see FINKEL, MAX

CAUNTER, CYRIL F. (M)
Madness Opens the Door. Butterworth, T., 1932

CAUSEY, JAMES O. (D)
The Baby Doll Murders. GM, 1957
Frenzy. Crest, 1960
Killer Take All. Graphic, 1957; Hale, R., 1960

CAVANAGH, ARTHUR (M)
The Children Are Gone. S & S, 1966

CAVE, HUGH B. (S)
The Cross on the Drum. Doubleday, 1959
Drums of Revolt. Hale, R., 1957

CAVENDISH, CHARLES (S)
The Lure. Collins, 1935

CAVERHILL, WILLIAM MELVILLE (M) (Pseudonym: Alan Melville)
Death of Anton. Skeffington, 1936
Quick Curtain. Skeffington, 1934
The Vicar in Hell. Skeffington, 1935
Weekend at Thrackley. Skeffington, 1934

CAYWOOD, MARK, pseud. (S)
Rainbow Island. Viking, 1927

CECIL, ALLAN (D)
Turquoise Clues. Rich, 1949

CECIL, HENRY, pseud; see LEON, HENRY CECIL

CECIL, OLIVE (M)
Behold the Body. Long, 1932
Four Women Went. Long, 1931

CELIERE, PAUL (D)
The Startling Exploits of Dr. J. B. Quies. Harper, 1886

CERVUS, G. I. (M)
White Feathers. Lippincott, 1884

CHABER, M. E., pseud; see CROSSEN, KENDALL FOSTER

CHADWICK, CHARLES (M)
The Cactus. Crowell, 1925
Moving House of Foscaldo. Cassell, 1926

CHALMERS, STEPHEN (D)
The Affair of the Gallows Tree. Doubleday, Doran, 1930; Selwyn, 1931
Blood on the Heather. Doubleday, Doran, 1932; World's Work, 1935
The Crime in Car 13. Doubleday, Doran, 1930
The House of Two Green Eyes. Doubleday, Doran, 1928; Grosset, 1929
The Vanishing Smuggler. Clode, 1909; Mills & Boon, 1910
The Whispering Ghost. Doubleday, Doran, 1932

CHAMBERLAIN, ANNE (S)
The Tall, Dark Man. Bobbs, 1955; Dell, 1963

CHAMBERLAIN, ELINOR (D)
Appointment in Manila. Dodd, 1945; Eyre, 1949
Manila Hemp. Dodd, 1947
Snare for Witches. Dodd, 1948; Gollancz, 1949

CHAMBERLAIN, GEORGE AGNEW (D)
The Great Van Suttart Mystery. Putnam, 1925
In Defense of Mrs. Maxon. Bobbs, 1938
Night at Lost End. Brewer, 1931; Grosset, 1932 (Serial title: That Looks on Tempests)
The Red House. Bobbs, 1945; Popular Lib.
The Silver Cord. Putnam, 1927
That Looks on Tempests; see Night at Lost End

CHAMBERLAIN, LUCIA (S)
The Other Side of the Door. Bobbs, 1909

CHAMBERS, DANA, pseud; see LEFFINGWELL, ALBERT

CHAMBERS, MARY; see CHAMBERS, WHITMAN ELWYN

CHAMBERS, PETER, pseud; see PHILLIPS, DENNIS JOHN ANDREW

CHAMBERS, ROBERT WILLIAM (M)
The Barbarians. Appleton, D., 1917
The Danger Mark. Appleton, D., 1909, 1919
The Dark Star. Appleton, D., 1917; Burt, 1919
In Secret. Doran, 1919
Laughing Girl. Appleton, D., 1918
The Man They Hanged. Appleton, D., 1926
Moonlit Way. Appleton, D., 1919
The Mystery Lady. Grosset, 1925
Mystery of Choice. Appleton, D., 1897
Secret Service Operator 13. Appleton-Century, 1934
Slayer of Souls. Doran, 1920
Tracer of Lost Persons, N.Y. Appleton, D., 1906
Who Goes There? Appleton, D., 1915

CHAMBERS, WHITMAN ELWYN (M)
Action at World's End. Dutton, 1945
The Affair at the Green Lantern; see Murder for a Wanton
Amigo. Howell, Soskin, 1942
Bright Star of Danger. Doubleday, Doran, 1940
Bring Me Another Murder. Dutton, 1942
The Campanile Murders. Appleton-Century, 1933
Coast of Intrigue. Henkle, 1928; International Fiction Lib., 1930
Contraband Coast. Nelson, 1928
Dangerous Water. Doubleday, Doran, 1941
Dead Men Leave No Fingerprints. Cassell, 1935; Doubleday, Doran, 1935; Sun Dial, 1937
Dog Eat Dog. Doubleday, Doran, 1938
Dry Tortugas. Doubleday, Doran, 1940
In Savage Surrender. Monarch, 1959
Murder for a Wanton. Doubleday, Doran, 1934; Caxton Printers, 1939 (Also published as: The Affair at the Green Lantern. Melrose, 1936)
Murder in the Mist. Cassell, 1938
Murder Lady. Cassell, 1938 (U.S. title: Once Too Often. Doubleday, Doran, 1938)
The Navy Murders, with Mary Chambers. Hutchinson, 1931 (U.S. edition by W. Chambers only. Dodd, 1932)
Once Too Often; see Murder Lady
Thirteen Steps. Doubleday, Doran, 1935
You Can't Get Away by Running. Cassell, 1939; Doubleday, Doran, 1939

CHAMIER, JOHN (S)
Cannonball. Cassell, 1966

CHAMPION, JESSIE (S)
Jimmy's Wife. Lane, 1917

CHAMPION, JOAN (M)
Incidental Murder. MacDonald & Co., 1946

CHAMPLIN, VIRGINIA (D)
Shadowed by a Detective; or, the Woman in Wax. Ogilvie, 1885

CHANCE, JOHN NEWTON (D)
Affair with a Rich Girl. Hale, R., 1958
Alarm at Black Brake. Hale, R., 1960
Aunt Miranda's Murder. Dodd, 1951; MacDonald & Co., 1951
The Black Highway. MacDonald & Co., 1947
Brandy Pole. MacDonald & Co., 1949
Bunst and the Brown Voice. Oxford, 1950
Bunst and the Flying Eye. Oxford, 1953
Bunst and the Secret Six. Oxford, 1951
Bunst the Bold. Oxford, 1950
Commission for Disaster. Hale, R., 1964
Coven Gibbet. MacDonald & Co., 1948
Dead Man's Knock. Hale, R., 1957
Death of an Innocent. Gollancz, 1938
Death Stalks the Cobbled Square. McBride, 1946 (English title: Screaming Fog. MacDonald & Co., 1944)
Death Under Desolate. Hale, R., 1964
The Devil Drives. Gollancz, 1936
The Devil in Greenlands. Gollancz, 1939
The Double Death. Hale, R., 1966
Eye in Darkness. MacDonald & Co., 1946
Fatal Fascination. Hale, R., 1959
Forest Affair. Hale, R., 1963
The Ghost of Truth. Gollancz, 1939
Import of Evil. Hale, R., 1961
The Jason Affair. MacDonald & Co., 1954
Jason and the Sleep Game. MacDonald & Co., 1954
Jason Goes West. MacDonald & Co., 1955
The Jason Murders. MacDonald & Co., 1954
The Knight and the Castle. MacDonald & Co., 1946
Lady in a Frame. Hale, R., 1960
The Last Seven Hours. MacDonald & Co., 1956
Little Crime. Hale, R., 1961

Maiden Possessed. Gollancz, 1937
The Man Behind Me. Hale, R., 1963
The Man in My Shoes. MacDonald & Co., 1952
The Man with No Face. Hale, R., 1959
The Man with Three Witches. Hale, R., 1958
Murder in Oils. Gollancz, 1935
The Night of the Full Moon. MacDonald & Co., 1950
The Night of the Settlement. Hale, R., 1961
The Randy Inheritance. MacDonald & Co., 1953
The Red Knight. MacDonald, 1945; Macmillan, 1945
Rhapsody in Fear. Gollancz, 1937
The Screaming Fog; see Death Stalks the Cobbled Square
The Shadow Called Janet. MacDonald & Co., 1956
Triangle of Fear. Hale, R., 1962
The Twopenny Box. Macmillan, 1952
Wheels in the Forest. Gollancz, 1935
Yellow Belly. Hale, R., 1962

CHANCE, R. (M)
Be Absolute for Death. Davies, 1964

CHANCELLOR, JOHN, pseud; see RIDEAUX, CHARLES DE B.

CHANDLER, DAVID (M)
The Ramsden Case. S & S, 1967

CHANDLER, RAYMOND (D)
The Big Sleep. Hamilton, H., 1939; Knopf, 1939; Penguin, 1950
Farewell, My Lovely. Hamilton, H., 1940; Knopf, 1940; PB, 1945; Penguin, 1956
Finger Man: Three Novelettes. Avon, 1946; Harborough, 1960
Five Murderers. Avon, 1944
Five Sinister Characters. Avon, 1945
The High Window. Knopf, 1942; Hamilton, H., 1943; PB, 1945; Penguin, 1951
Killer in the Rain. Houghton, 1964; PB, 1965
The Lady in the Lake. Hamilton, H., 1943; Knopf, 1943; Penguin, 1946
The Little Sister. Hamilton, H., 1949; Houghton, 1949; PB, 1950; Penguin, 1951
The Long Goodbye. Hamilton, H., 1953; Houghton, 1954; Penguin, 1959; PB, 1964
Pearls Are a Nuisance. Hamilton, H., 1953; Penguin
Pickup on Noon Street. PB, 1952; Harborough, 1960
Playback. Hamilton, H., 1958; Houghton, 1958; PB, 1960
The Raymond Chandler Omnibus. Hamilton, H., 1953; Knopf, 1964
Red Wind. Tower, 1946; World Pub., 1946
The Second Raymond Chandler Omnibus. Hamilton, H., 1962; Knopf, 1964
The Simple Art of Murder. Houghton, 1950 (Also published as: Trouble Is My Business: A Collection of Four Short Stories. PB, 1953)
Smart-Aleck Kill. Hamilton, H., 1953; Penguin
Spanish Blood. World Pub., 1946
Trouble Is My Business; see The Simple Art of Murder

CHANNING, MARK (M)
King Cobra. Hutchinson, 1933
Nine Lives. Harrap, 1937
Poisoned Mountain. Hutchinson, 1935
White Python. Hutchinson, 1934

CHANNON, ETHEL MARY (D)
The Chimney Murder. Benn, 1929; Little, 1929
Gilt-Edge Mystery. Benn, 1932
Golden Glory. Benn, 1931
House with No Address. Benn, 1932

CHANSLOR, ROY (S)
Lowdown. Farrar & Rinehart, 1931

CHANSLOR, TORREY (D)
Our First Murder. Stokes, 1940
Our Second Murder. Stokes, 1941

CHAPIN, CARL M. (D)
Three Died Beside the Marble Pool. Doubleday, Doran, 1936; World's Work, 1937

CHAPMAN, A. EDWARDS (S)
The Ready Blade. Appleton-Century, 1934

CHAPMAN, RAYMOND (M) (Pseudonym: Simon Nash)
Dead Woman's Ditch. Roy Pubs., 1966
Killed by Scandal. Roy Pubs., 1964
Unhallowed Murder. Roy Pubs., 1967

CHAPMAN, ROBERT ALEX MARK (D)
Behind the Headlines. Laurie, 1955
Crime on My Hands. Laurie, 1952
Deep Secret. Rich, 1939
The Downward Path. Hale, 1959
Frozen Stiff. Laurie, 1956
Killed by Scandal. Bles, 1962; Roy Pubs., 1964
Murder for the Million. Laurie, 1953
One Jump Ahead. Laurie, 1951
Seven Sisters. Crowther, 1945
Winter Wears a Shroud. Laurie, 1953
Wish You Were Dead. Hale, 1960

CHARBONNEAU, LOUIS (M)
Night of Violence. Dodd, 1959 (English title: The Trapped Ones. Barker, 1960)
Not All Your Tears. Dodd, 1959
The Trapped Ones; see Night of Violence

CHARLES, FRANKLIN, pseud; see ADAMS, CLEVE FRANKLIN

CHARLES, ROBERT, pseud; see SMITH, ROBERT CHARLES

CHARNWOOD, BARON GODFREY RATHBONE BENSON; see BENSON, GODFREY R.

CHARTERIS, LESLIE
The Ace of Knaves. Doubleday, Doran, 1937; Hodder, 1937; Ace, 1947 (U.S. title: The Saint in Action. Sun Dial, 1938. Also published as: The Saint and the Ace of Knaves. Avon, 1937)
Alias the Saint. Hodder, 1931
Angels of Doom; see She Was a Lady
Arrest the Saint; See First Saint Omnibus
The Avenging Saint; see Knight Templar
The Bandit. Ward, Lock, 1929; Doubleday, Doran, 1930
Boodle, Stories of the Saint. Hodder, 1934; Macfadden, 1966 (U.S. title: The Saint Intervenes. Doubleday, Doran, 1934; Avon, 1944)
Brighter Buccaneer. Doubleday, Doran, 1933; Hodder, 1933 (Also published as: The Saint: The Brighter Buccaneer. Avon)
Call for the Saint. Doubleday, 1948; Hodder, 1948; Avon, 1948
Daredevil. Doubleday, Doran, 1929; Ward, Lock, 1929
Enter the Saint. Musson, 1930; Doubleday, Doran, 1936; Hodder, 1938
Featuring the Saint. Avon, 1931; Doubleday, Doran, 1931; Hodder, 1931
First Saint Omnibus. Hodder, 1934; Doubleday, Doran, 1939; Sun Dial, 1941 (Also published as: Arrest the Saint. Permabooks, 1951)
Follow the Saint. Doubleday, Doran, 1938; Hodder, 1939; Sun Dial, 1939
Getaway. Hodder, 1932 (Also published as: Saint's Getaway. Sun Dial, 1943)
Happy Highwayman. Avon, 1939; Doubleday, Doran, 1939; Hodder, 1939; Triangle, 1941
The Holy Terror. Hodder, 1932 (U.S. title: Saint vs. Scotland Yard. Doubleday, Doran, 1932)
Knight Templar. Hodder, 1930 (U.S. title: The Avenging Saint. Doubleday, Doran, 1931)
The Last Hero. Doubleday, Doran, 1930; Hodder, 1931 (Also published as: The Saint Closes the Case. Sun Dial, 1941)
Meet the Tiger. Doubleday, Doran, 1928; Ward, Lock, 1928 (Also published as: The Saint Meets the Tiger. Sun Dial, 1940)
The Misfourtunes of Mr. Teal. Doubleday, Doran, 1934; Hodder, 1934 (U.S. titles: The Saint in London. Sun Dial, 1941; The Saint in England. Avon)
Once More the Saint. Hodder, 1933 (U.S. title: Saint and Mr. Teal. Avon, 1933; Doubleday, Doran, 1933)
The Pirate Saint; see The Saint Overboard
Prelude for War. Doubleday, Doran, 1938; Hodder, 1938 (Also published as: Saint Plays with Fire. Triangle, 1942)
Saint and Mr. Teal; see Once More the Saint
The Saint and the Ace of Knaves; see The Ace of Knaves
The Saint and the Last Hero. Hodder, 1930
Saint and the Sizzling Saboteur. Avon (From The Saint on Guard)
The Saint Around the World. Doubleday, 1956; Hodder, 1957; Permabooks, 1958; Macfadden, 1966
The Saint at Large. Sun Dial, 1943; Triangle
Saint at the Thieves' Picnic; see Thieves' Picnic
The Saint Bids Diamonds. Triangle, 1942
The Saint Cleans Up. Avon (Stories from: Brighter Buccaneer, Happy Highwayman, and Saint on the Spanish Main)
The Saint Closes the Case; see Last Hero
Saint Errant. Avon, 1948; Doubleday, 1948; Macfadden, 1966
The Saint Goes On. Hodder, 1934; Doubleday, Doran, 1935; Triangle, 1940; Avon, 1943
The Saint Goes West. Doubleday, Doran, 1942; Sun Dial, 1943; Macfadden, 1966
The Saint in Action; see The Ace of Knaves
The Saint in England; see The Misfortunes of Mr. Teal
The Saint in Europe. Avon, 1953; Doubleday, 1953
The Saint in London; see The Misfortunes of Mr. Teal
The Saint in Miami. Doubleday, Doran, 1940; Hodder, 1945; Triangle, 1945
The Saint in New York. Doubleday, Doran, 1935; Burt, 1936; Sun Dial, 1938; Avon, 1951

The Saint Intervenes; see Boodle, Stories of the Saint
The Saint in the Sun. Doubleday, 1963; Hodder, 1964; Macfadden
Saint Meets His Match. Hodder, 1950
The Saint Meets the Tiger; see Meet the Tiger
The Saint on Guard. Doubleday, Doran, 1944; Hodder, 1945; Avon
Saint on the Spanish Main. Doubleday, 1955; Hodder, 1958; Macfadden, 1966
The Saint Overboard. Doubleday, Doran, 1936; Hodder, 1936; Sun Dial, 1936 (Also published as: The Pirate Saint. Triangle, 1941)
Saint Plays with Fire; see Prelude for War
The Saint Sees It Through. Doubleday, 1946; Hodder, 1947
The Saint Steps In. Doubleday, Doran, 1943; Hodder, 1947
The Saint: The Brighter Buccaneer; see Brighter Buccaneer
The Saint to the Rescue. Doubleday, 1959; Permabooks, 1961
Saint: Two in One. Sun Dial, 1942
Saint vs. Scotland Yard; see Holy Terror
The Saint-Wanted for Murder; see Wanted for Murder
Saint's Choice of Humorous Crime. Shaw Press, 1945
Saint's Choice of Hollywood Crime. Saint Enterprises, 1946
Saint's Getaway; see Getaway
Second Saint Omnibus. Doubleday, 1951
Senor Saint. Doubleday, 1958; PB, 1960
She Was a Lady. Hodder, 1931 (U.S. title: Angels of Doom. Doubleday, Doran, 1932, 1936; Sun Dial, 1941)
Thanks to the Saint. Doubleday, 1957; Hodder, 1958
Thieves' Picnic. Doubleday, Doran, 1937; Sun Dial, 1939 (Also published as: The Saint Bids Diamonds. Triangle, 1942 and Saint at the Thieves' Picnic. Avon)
Trust the Saint. Doubleday, 1962; Macfadden, 1966; MacDonald & Co.
Vendetta for the Saint. Doubleday, 1964; Hodder, 1965; PB, 1966
Wanted for Murder. Doubleday, Doran, 1931; Hodder, 1931 (Also published as: The Saint—Wanted for Murder. Sun Dial, 1943; Triangle, 1943 and Featuring the Saint. Avon)
The White Rider. Doubleday, Doran, 1930
X Esquire. Ward, Lock, 1932

CHASE, ALAN LOUIS (S)
The Kidneyed Caper. S & S, 1960

CHASE, ALLAN (S)
The Five Arrows. Random, 1944

CHASE, ARTHUR M. (M)
Danger in the Dark. Dodd, 1933; Eldon, 1934
Murder of a Missing Man. Dodd, 1934
No Outlet. Dodd, 1940
The Party at the Penthouse. Dodd, 1932
Peril at the Spy Nest. Dodd, 1945
Twenty Minutes to Kill. Dodd, 1936

CHASE, JAMES HADLEY, pseud; see RAYMOND, RENÉ

CHASE, JOSEPHINE (M)
Green Jade Necklace. Penn, 1931
Mark of the Red Diamond. Penn, 1929

CHASE, KIP (D)
Killer Be Killed. Hammond, 1963
Murder Most Ingenious. Hammond, 1962
Where There's a Will. Hammond, 1961

CHAVIS, ROBERT (S)
The Terror Package. Ace, 1957

CHAZE, ELLIOT (S)
Black Wings Has My Angel. GM, 1953 (Also published as: One for My Money. Berkley Pub., 1962)
One for My Money; see Black Wings Has My Angel
Stainless Steel Kimono. Macfadden, 1965
Tiger in the Honeysuckle. Bantam

CHEKOV, ANTON PAVLOVICH (M)
Cook's Wedding and Other Stories. Macmillan, 1922 (Also published as: Swedish Match, Detective Story)
The Shooting Party. McKay, 1927

CHELTON, JOHN (S)
My Deadly Angel. Ace, 1955

CHERRILL, FRED (D)
Fingerprints Never Lie. MacDonald & Co., 1954

CHESHIRE, GIFF (M)
Edge of the Desert. Berkley Pub., 1958

CHESNEY, WEATHERBY (D)
Adventures of a Solicitor. Bowden, 1898
Mystery of a Bungalow. Methuen, 1904
Tragedy of the Great Emerald. Methuen, 1904

CHESSMAN, CARYL (S)
The Kid Was a Killer. GM, 1960

CHESTER, ANN (S)
Slightly Imperfect. Arcadia, 1956

CHESTER, GEORGE RANDOLPH (S)
Get-Rich-Quick Wallingford. Altemus, 1908; Richards, 1908
Son of Wallingford. Small, 1921
Wallingford and Blackie Daw. Bobbs, 1913
Wallingford in His Prime. Bobbs, 1913
Young Wallingford. Bobbs, 1910

CHESTER, GILBERT (D)
Death Walks In. Wright & Brown, 1938
Riddle of the Night Garage. Amalgamated Press, 1949

CHESTER, PETER, pseud; see PHILLIPS, DENIS J. A.

CHESTERTON, GILBERT KEITH (D)
Club of Queer Trades. Harper, 1905; Hodder, 1912
Father Brown Omnibus. Dodd, 1951
Father Brown Selected Stories. Oxford, 1955
Father Brown Stories. Cassell, 1929
Four Faultless Felons. Cassell, 1930; Dodd, 1930; Dufour, 1962
Incredulity of Father Brown. Cassell, 1926; Dodd, 1926; Penguin
Man Alive. Nelson, 1912
Man Who Knew Too Much. Cassell, 1922; Harper, 1922; Burt, 1930; Dufour, 1963
Man Who Was Thursday. Arrowsmith, 1908; Putnam, 1960
Paradoxes of Mr. Pond. Cassell, 1937; Dodd, 1937; Dufour, 1963
Pocketbook of Father Brown, PB, 1943
Poet and the Lunatics. Cassell, 1929; Dodd, 1929; Dufour, 1963
Scandal of Father Brown. Cassell, 1935; Dodd, 1935
Secret of Father Brown. Cassell, 1927; Harper, 1927
Ten Adventures of Father Brown. Dell, 1961
Wisdom of Father Brown. Cassell, 1914; Dodd, 1915

CHETWYND, BRIDGET (D)
Death Has Ten Thousand Doors. Hutchinson, 1951
Rubies, Emeralds and Diamonds. Hutchinson, 1952

CHEVALIER, HAAKON MAURICE (M)
For Us the Living. Secker & Warburg, 1949

CHEYNEY, PETER (Full name: Reginald Evelyn Peter Southouse Cheyney) (D)
Account Rendered. Vallancey, 1944
Adventures of Alonzo MacTavish. Todd, 1943
The Adventures of Julie. Poynings Press, 1945; Todd, 1954
Alonzo MacTavish Again. Todd, 1943
Another Little Drink. Collins, 1940
Best Stories of Peter Cheyney. Faber, 1954
Calling Mr. Callaghan. Todd, 1953; Transworld, 1955
Can Ladies Kill? Collins, 1938
Case of the Dark Hero; see Dark Hero
Cocktail for Cupid. Bantam, 1948
Counterspy Murders; see Dark Duet
Curiousity of Etienne MacGregor. Locke, 1947; Todd, 1952
Dames Don't Care. Collins, 1937; Coward, 1938; Dodd, 1953
Dance Without Music. Vallancey, 1945; Collins, 1948; Dodd, 1948
Dangerous Curves. Collins, 1939; Penguin, 1949
Dark Bahama. Collins, 1950; Dodd, 1951 (Also published as: I'll Bring Her Back. Eton)
Dark Duet. Collins, 1942; Dodd, 1943; Penguin, 1949 (Also published as: Counterspy Murders. Avon, 1956)
Dark Hero. Collins, 1946; Dodd, 1946 (Also published as: The Case of the Dark Hero. Avon)
Dark Interlude. Collins, 1947; Dodd, 1947 (Also published as: The Terrible Night. Avon)
Dark Omnibus. Dodd, 1952
The Dark Street. Collins, 1944; Dodd, 1944; Grosset, 1946
Dark Wanton. Black, 1948; Collins, 1948
Date After Dark. Polybooks, 1946
Don't Get Me Wrong. Collins, 1939
Dressed to Kill. Todd, 1954 (Also published as: Night Club. Transworld, 1955; Poynings Press)
Escape for Sandra. Poynings Press, 1945; Todd, 1948
Farewell to the Admiral. Dodd, 1943
Fast Work. Bantam, 1948
G Men at the Yard. Todd, 1953
He Walked in Her Sleep and Other Stories. Polybooks, 1946; Todd, 1954
I'll Bring Her Back; see Dark Bahama
I'll Say She Does. Collins, 1945; Dodd, 1946
Information Received. Bantam, 1948
It Couldn't Matter Less. Collins, 1941
Knave Takes a Queen. Collins, 1939
Ladies Won't Wait. Collins, 1951; Dodd, 1951
Lady, Behave! Collins, 1950
Lady Beware. Dodd, 1950
Lady in Green. Bantam, 1947
Lady in Tears. Bantam, 1948
Lemmy Caution Omnibus. Collins, 1952
The London Spy Murders; see The Stars Are Dark
Love with a Gun. Todd, 1943; Polybooks, 1945
Man Nobody Saw. Dodd, 1949

The Man with the Red Beard. Todd, 1943; Vallancey, 1944 (from You Can't Hit a Woman)
Man with Two Wives. Polybooks, 1946
Meet Mr. Callaghan. Collins, 1953
A Matter of Luck. Bantam, 1947
Mister Caution—Mister Callaghan. S & S
The Mystery Blues. Todd, 1954
Never a Dull Moment. Collins, 1942
Night Club; see Dressed to Kill
No Ordinary Cheyney. Faber, 1948; S & S
One of Those Things. Collins, 1949; Dodd, 1950
Peter Cheyney Omnibus Volume. Collins, 1939
Peter Cheyney's Dark Omnibus. Dodd, 1952
Poison Ivy. Collins, 1937; Penguin, 1949
Sinister Errand. Collins, 1945; Dodd, 1945
Sorry You've Been Troubled. Collins, 1942; Pan, 1950
Spot of Murder. Polybooks, 1946
The Stars Are Dark. Collins, 1943; Dodd, 1943; Pan, 1948 (Also published as: The London Spy Murders. Avon)
The Terrible Night; see Dark Interlude
They Never Say When. Collins, 1944; Dodd, 1945
This Man Is Dangerous. Collins, 1936; Dodd, 1938, 1953
A Time for Caution. Foster, W., 1946
A Tough Spot for Cupid. Vallancey, 1945
A Trap for Bellamy. Dodd, 1941
Try Anything Twice. Collins, 1948; Dodd, 1948
Uneasy Terms. Collins, 1946; Dodd, 1947
Unhappy Lady. Bantam, 1948
Urgent Hangman. Collins, 1938; Coward, 1938; Penguin, 1949; Dodd, 1952
Velvet Johnnie. Collins, 1952
Vengeance with a Twist. Vallancey, 1946
You Can Always Duck. Collins, 1943
You Can Call It a Day. Collins, 1949
You Can't Hit a Woman. Collins, 1937
You Can't Keep the Change. Collins, 1940; Dodd, 1944; Pan, 1951
You'd Be Surprised. Collins, 1940
Your Deal, My Lovely. Collins, 1941

CHICHESTER, JOHN JAY (M)
The Bigamist. Chelsea House, 1925; Burt, 1927; Hutchinson, 1927
House of the Moving Room. Chelsea House, 1926; Hutchinson, 1926
King of Diamonds. Chelsea House, 1930; Hutchinson, 1931
Porcelain Mask. Chelsea House, 1924; Jenkins, 1925; Burt, 1926
Rogues of Fortune. Chelsea House, 1929; Hutchinson, 1930
Sanderson: Master Rogue. Chelsea House, 1929; Hutchinson, 1930
Sanderson's Diamond Lost. Chelsea House, 1935; Hutchinson, 1935
Silent Cracksman. Chelsea House, 1929; Hutchinson, 1929

CHIDSEY, DONALD BARR (M)
Nobody Heard the Shot. Bantam, 1941

CHILD, NELLISE (D)
Diamond Ransom Murders. Knopf, 1935
Murder Comes Home. Knopf, 1933
Wolf on the Fold. Doubleday, Doran, 1941

CHILD, RICHARD WASHBURN (M)
Fresh Waters. Dutton, 1924
The Vanishing Men. Dutton, 1920
The Velvet Black. Dutton, 1921

CHILDERNESS, GEORGE (D)
Murder in False Faces. Phoenix, 1943
Too Many Murderers. Ambassador, 1946; Phoenix, 1946

CHILDERS, ERSKINE (S)
The Riddle of the Sands. Smith, Elder, 1903, 1913; Nelson, 1913; Dodd, 1940; PB, 1940

CHILDERS, JAMES SAXON (M)
The Bookshop Mystery. Appleton, D., 1930

CHILDS, MARQUIS (S)
Taint of Innocence. Harper & Row, 1967

CHIPPERFIELD, ROBERT ORR, pseud; see OSTRANDER, ISABEL EGENTON

CHITTENDEN, FRANK ALBERT (M)
Darkness over Hycroft. Gifford, 1947
Four Cornered Story. Boardman, T. V., 1951
Strange Welcome. Boardman, T. V., 1949; Coward, 1951
The Uninvited. Boardman, T. V., 1954
Widow in White. Gifford, 1949

CHITTY, SIR THOMAS WILLES (M-S)
(Pseudonym: Thomas Hinde)
Games of Chance. Vanguard, 1967 (Contains two novelettes: The Interviewer and The Investigator)
Mr. Nicholas. MacGibbon, 1952

CHOLMONDELEY, MARY (M)
The Danvers Jewels. Bentley, 1887, 1898; Harper, 1900
Red Pottage. Arnold, E., 1899; Harper, 1899

CHRISTIAN, KIT (D)
Death and Bitters. Dutton, 1943

CHRISTIE, AGATHA MARY CLARISSA (Full name: Mrs. Max Edgar Lucien Mallowan) (M-D-S)
The A. B. C. Murders: a Poirot Mystery. Collins, 1935; Dodd, 1936 (Also published as: The Alphabet Murders. PB. Also appears in Surprise Endings. Dodd, 1956)
The Adventure of the Christmas Pudding: Poirot Short Stories. Collins, 1963; Fontana (Published in England only)
After the Funeral: a Poirot Mystery. Collins, 1953 (Also published as: Murder at the Gallop. Fontana. U.S. title: Funerals Are Fatal. Dodd, 1953; PB, 1961)
The Alphabet Murders; see The A. B. C. Murders
And Then There Were None; see Ten Little Niggers
Appointment with Death: a Poirot Mystery. Collins, 1938; Dodd, 1938 (Also in Make Mine Murder. Dodd, 1962; Dell, 1963)
At Bertram's Hotel: a Miss Marple Mystery. Collins, 1965; Dodd, 1965; PB, 1967
The Big Four: a Poirot Mystery. Collins, 1927; Dodd, 1927; Dell, 1965
Blood Will Tell; see Mrs. McGinty's Dead
The Body in the Library: a Miss Marple Mystery. Collins, 1942; Dodd, 1942; PB, 1964 (Also in Murder in Our Midst. Dodd, 1967)
The Boomerang Clue; see Why Didn't They Ask Evans?
Cards on the Table: a Poirot Mystery. Collins, 1936; Dodd, 1937; Dell, 1962 (Also in Surprise Endings. Dodd, 1956)
A Caribbean Mystery: a Miss Marple Mystery. Collins, 1964; Dodd, 1965; PB
Cat Among the Pigeons: a Poirot Mystery. Collins, 1959; Dodd, 1959; PB, 1961
Christie Classics. Dodd, 1957
The Clocks: a Poirot Mystery. Collins, 1963; Dodd, 1964; PB, 1965
Come and Be Hanged; see Towards Zero
The Crime in Cabin 66. Vallancey, 1941 (U.S. title: The Mystery of the Crime in Cabin 66. Bantam, 1943)
Crooked House. Collins, 1949; Dodd, 1949; PB, 1964
Dead Man's Folly: a Poirot Mystery. Collins, 1956; Dodd, 1956; PB, 1957
Dead Man's Mirror. Dodd, 1937; Dell (Published in U.S. only)
Death Comes as the End. Dodd, 1944; Collins, 1945; PB, 1947
Death in the Air; see Death in the Clouds
Death in the Clouds: a Poirot Mystery. Collins, 1935; Pan (U.S. title: Death in the Air. Dodd, 1935; Popular Lib., 1961)
Death on the Nile: a Poirot Mystery. Collins, 1937; Dodd, 1938; Avon, 1960 (Also in The Perilous Journeys of Hercule Poirot. Dodd, 1954)
Destination Unknown. Collins, 1954 (U.S. title: So Many Steps to Death. Dodd, 1955; PB)
Double Sin and Other Stories. Dodd, 1961; Dell, 1964 (Published in U.S. only)
The Dumb Witness: a Poirot Mystery. Collins, 1937 (U.S. title: Poirot Loses a Client. Dodd, 1937; Avon, 1963. Also published as: Murder at Littlegreen House and Mystery at Littlegreen House)
Easy to Kill; see Murder Is Easy
Evil Under the Sun: a Poirot Mystery. Collins, 1941; Dodd, 1941; PB, 1941
Five Little Pigs: a Poirot Mystery. Collins, 1942 (U.S. title: Murder in Retrospect. Dodd, 1942; Dell, 1961. Also in Murder Preferred. Dodd, 1960)
4:50 from Paddington: a Miss Marple Mystery. Collins, 1957 (U.S. title: What Mrs. McGillicuddy Saw! Dodd, 1957. Also published as: Murder She Said. PB, 1962 and "Eyewitness to Murder")
Funerals Are Fatal; see After the Funeral
Hercule Poirot, Master Detective. Dodd, 1936 (Contains: The Murder of Roger Ackroyd, Murder in the Calais Coach, and Thirteen at Dinner)
Hercule Poirot's Christmas: a Poirot Mystery. Collins, 1938 (U.S. titles: Murder for Christmas. Dodd, 1939 and A Holiday for Murder. Bantam, 1962)
Hickory Dickory Death; see Hickory Dickory Dock
Hickory Dickory Dock: A Poirot Mystery. Collins, 1955 (U.S. title: Hickory Dickory Death. Dodd, 1955; PB, 1957)
The Hollow: a Poirot Mystery. Collins, 1946 (U.S. title: Murder After Hours. Dodd, 1946; Dell)
Holiday for Murder; see Hercule Poirot's Christmas
The Hound of Death. Odhams, 1933; Fontana (Published in England only)
The Labours of Hercules: Poirot Short Stories. Collins, 1947; Dodd, 1947; Dell, 1964
The Listerdale Mystery. Collins, 1934; Fontana (Published in England only)

Lord Edgeware Dies: a Poirot Mystery. Collins, 1933; Fontana (U.S. title: Thirteen at Dinner. Dodd, 1933; Dell, 1961. Also in Hercule Poirot, Master Detective. Dodd, 1936)
Make Mine Murder. Dodd, 1962 (Contains: Appointment with Death, Peril at End House, Sad Cypress)
The Man in the Brown Suit. Collins, 1924; Dodd, 1924; Dell, 1962
The Mirror Crack'd from Side to Side: a Miss Marple Mystery. Collins, 1962 (U.S. title: The Mirror Cracked. Dodd, 1963)
The Mirror Cracked; see The Mirror Crack'd from Side to Side
Mr. Parker Pyne, Detective; see Parker Pyne Investigates
The Mousetrap and Other Stories; see Three Blind Mice
The Moving Finger: a Miss Marple Mystery. Dodd, 1942; Collins, 1943; Dell, 1964 (Also in Murder in Our Midst. Dodd, 1967)
Mrs. McGinty's Dead. Dodd, 1952 (Also published as: Blood Will Tell. Black, 1951)
Murder After Hours; see The Hollow
Murder at Hazelmoor; see The Sittaford Mystery
Murder at Littlegreen House; see The Dumb Witness
Murder at the Gallop; see After the Funeral
Murder at the Vicarage: a Miss Marple Mystery. Collins, 1930; Dodd, 1930; Dell, 1961; Fontana (Also in Murder in Our Midst. Dodd, 1937)
Murder for Christmas; see Hercule Poirot's Christmas
Murder in Mesopotamia: a Poirot Mystery. Collins, 1936; Dodd, 1936; Dell, 1961 (Also in The Perilous Journeys of Hercule Poirot. Dodd, 1954. Also in Spies Among Us. Dodd, 1968)
Murder in Our Midst. Dodd, 1967 (Contains: The Body in the Library, Murder at the Vicarage, The Moving Finger)
Murder in Retrospect; see Five Little Pigs
Murder in the Calais Coach; see Murder on the Orient Express
Murder in the Mews: Poirot Short Stories. Collins, 1937; Fontana (Except for one story, this book appeared in the U.S. as: Dead Man's Mirror. Dodd, 1937; Dell)
Murder in Three Acts; see Three-Act Tragedy
A Murder Is Announced: A Miss Marple Mystery. Collins, 1950; Dodd, 1950; PB, 1951 (Also in Murder Preferred. Dodd, 1960)
Murder Is Easy. Collins, 1939 (U.S. title: Easy to Kill. Dodd, 1939; PB, 1960)
The Murder of Roger Ackroyd: a Poirot Mystery. Collins, 1926; Dodd, 1926; PB, 1954 (Also in Hercule Poirot, Master Detective. Dodd, 1936)
Murder on the Links: a Poirot Mystery. Collins, 1923; Dodd, 1923; Dell, 1964
Murder on the Orient Express: a Poirot Mystery. Collins, 1934; Fontana (U.S. title: Murder in the Calais Coach. Dodd, 1934; PB, 1940. Also in Hercule Poirot, Master Detective. Dodd, 1936)
Murder Preferred. Dodd, 1960 (Contains: The Patriotic Murders, Murder Is Announced, Murder in Retrospect)
Murder She Said; see 4:50 from Paddington
Murder With Mirrors; see They Do It with Mirrors
The Mysterious Affair at Styles: a Poirot Mystery. Lane, 1920; Dodd, 1930; Bantam, 1961
The Mysterious Mr. Quin. Collins, 1930; Dodd, 1930 (Also published as The Passing of Mr. Quin. Dell)
Mystery at Littlegreen House; see The Dumb Witness
The Mystery of the Baghdad Chest. Bantam, 1943
The Mystery of the Blue Train. Collins, 1928; Dodd, 1928; PB, 1940 (Also in The Perilous Journeys of Hercule Poirot. Dodd, 1954)
The Mystery of the Crime in Cabin 66; see Crime in Cabin 66
N or M?: a Tommy and Tuppence Beresford Mystery. Collins, 1941; Dodd, 1941; Dell (Also in Spies Among Us. Dodd, 1968)
The Nursery Rhyme Murders; see Ten Little Niggers
One, Two, Buckle My Shoe: a Poirot Mystery. Collins, 1940 (U.S. titles: The Patriotic Murders. Dodd, 1941 and Overdose of Death. Dell, 1964. Also in Murder Preferred. Dodd, 1960)
Ordeal by Innocence. Collins, 1958; Dodd, 1958; PB, 1964
Overdose of Death; see One, Two, Buckle My Shoe
The Pale Horse. Collins, 1961; Dodd, 1962
Parker Pyne Investigates. Collins, 1934; Fontana (U.S. title: Mr. Parker Pyne, Detective. Dodd, 1934; Dell, 1962)
Partners in Crime: a Tommy and Tuppence Beresford Mystery. Collins, 1929; Dodd, 1929; Dell, 1963
The Passing of Mr. Quin; see The Mysterious Mr. Quin

The Patriotic Murders; see One, Two, Buckle My Shoe
The Peril at End House: a Poirot Mystery. Collins, 1932; Dodd, 1932; Dell (Also in Make Mine Murder. Dodd, 1962)
The Perilous Journeys of Hercule Poirot. Dodd, 1954 (Contains: Mystery of the Blue Train, Death on the Nile, Murder in Mesopotamia)
A Pocket Full of Rye: A Miss Marple Mystery. Collins, 1953; Dodd, 1953
Poirot and the Regatta Mystery; see The Regatta Mystery
Poirot Investigates: Poirot Short Stories. Collins, 1924; Dodd, 1925; Avon; Bantam
Poirot Knows the Murderer. Polybooks, 1946 (Published in England only)
Poirot Lends a Hand. Polybooks, 1946 (Published in England only)
Poirot Loses a Client; see The Dumb Witness
Poirot on Holiday: The Regatta Mystery and The Crime in Cabin 66. Polybooks, 1943 (Published in England only)
The Problem at Pollensa Bay and Christmas Adventures. Polybooks, 1943 (Published in England only)
The Regatta Mystery. Dodd, 1939; Dell, 1964 (Also published as: Poirot and the Regatta Mystery. Bantam, 1943)
Remembered Death; see Sparkling Cyanide
Sad Cypress: a Poirot Mystery. Collins, 1940; Dodd, 1940; Dell, 1963; Bantam (Also in Make Mine Murder. Dodd, 1962)
The Secret Adversary: a Tommy and Tuppence Beresford Mystery. Dodd, 1922; Lane, 1922; Pan
The Secret of Chimneys. Collins, 1925; Dodd, 1925; Dell, 1964
The Seven Dials Mystery. Collins, 1929; Dodd, 1929; Bantam, 1964
The Sittaford Mystery. Collins, 1931 (U.S. title: Murder at Hazelmoor. Dodd, 1931; Dell, 1957)
So Many Steps to Death; see Destination Unknown
Sparkling Cyanide. Collins, 1945 (U.S. title: Remembered Death. Dodd, 1945; PB, 1947)
Spies Among Us. Dodd, 1968 (Contains: Murder in Mesopotamia, N or M?, and They Came to Baghdad)
Surprise Endings. Dodd, 1956 (Contains: The A. B. C. Murders, Murder in Three Acts, Cards on the Table)
Surprise! Surprise! Dodd, 1965 (Published in U.S. only)
Taken at the Flood: a Poirot Mystery. Collins, 1948 (U.S. title: There Is a Tide. Dodd, 1948; Dell, 1961
Ten Little Indians; see Ten Little Niggers
Ten Little Niggers. Collins, 1939 (U.S. titles: And Then There Were None. Dodd, 1940; PB, 1944; Ten Little Indians. PB; and The Nursery Rhyme Murders)
There Is a Tide; see Taken at the Flood
They Came to Baghdad. Collins, 1951; Dodd, 1951; PB, 1960; Dell (Also in Spies Among Us. Dodd, 1968)
They Do It with Mirrors: A Miss Marple Mystery. Collins, 1952; Fontana (U.S. title: Murder with Mirrors. Dodd, 1952; PB, 1954)
The Third Girl: a Poirot Mystery. Collins, 1966; Dodd, 1967
Thirteen at Dinner; see Lord Edgeware Dies
13 Clues for Miss Marple. Dell, 1967 (Published in U.S. only)
13 for Luck. Dodd, 1961 (Published in U.S. only)
The 13 Problems. Collins, 1932. (U.S. title: The Tuesday Club Murders. Dodd, 1933)
Three-Act Tragedy: a Poirot Mystery. Collins, 1935 (U.S. title: Murder in Three Acts. Dodd, 1934; Popular Lib., 1961. Also in Surprise Endings. Dodd, 1956)
Three Blind Mice. Dodd, 1948; Dell, 1950 (Also published as: The Mousetrap and Other Stories. Dell)
Towards Zero. Collins, 1944 (U.S. title: Come and Be Hanged and Other Stories. Dodd, 1944; PB)
Triple Threat: Hercule Poirot Exploits. Dodd, 1943
The Tuesday Club Murders; see The 13 Problems
Two Thrillers; see Why Didn't They Ask Evans?
Underdog and Other Stories. Dodd, 1951; Dell, 1955 (Published in U.S. only)
The Veiled Lady and The Mystery of the Baghdad Chest. Polybooks, 1944
Why Didn't They Ask Evans? Collins, 1934 (U.S. title: The Bommerang Clue. Dodd, 1935. Also in Two Thrillers. Daily Express Lib., 1936)
Witness for the Prosecution and Other Stories. Dodd, 1948; Dell, 1948 (Published in U.S. only)
What Mrs. McGillicuddy Saw!; see 4:50 from Paddington

CHRISTOPHER, JOHN (S)
Caves of Night. Crest, 1958
The Little People. S & S, 1967
The Possessors. S & S, 1965

A Scent of White Poppies. Avon, 1959; S & S, 1959
Sweeney's Island. S & S, 1964; Crest, 1967

CHRISTOPHER, MATTHEW F. (D)
Look for the Body. Phoenix, 1952

CHURCH, GRANVILLE, pseud; see PEOPLE, GRANVILLE CHURCH

CHUTE, MARY G. (D)
Sheriff Olson. Appleton-Century, 1942

CHUTE, VERNE (D)
Blackmail. Museum Press, 1949
Flight of an Angel. Morrow, 1945; Museum Press, 1950
Sweet and Deadly. Popular Lib., 1952
Wayward Angel. Knopf, 1948

CICELLIS, KAY (S)
The Day the Fish Came Out. Bantam, 1967

CLAD, NOEL (S)
The Savage. S & S, 1958; Permabooks, 1959
A Taste for Brilliants. Random, 1964

CLAIRE, MARVIN (S)
Drowning Wire. Ace, 1954

CLANCY, EUGENE A. (M)
Fast Money. Chelsea House, 1926

CLANDON, HENRIETTA, pseud; see VAHEY, JOHN GEORGE HASLETTE

CLANMORRIS, JOHN MICHAEL WARD BINGHAM; see BINGHAM, JOHN MICHAEL WARD

CLARE, MARGUERITE, pseud; see HEPPELL, MARY

CLARK, ALFRED ALEXANDER GORDON (M) (Pseudonym: Cyril Hare)
The Best Detective Stories of Cyril Hare. Faber, 1959; Walker & Co., 1961
Death Is No Sportsman. Faber, 1938
Death Walks the Woods. Little, 1954 (Also published as: That Yew Tree's Shade)
An English Murder. Faber, 1951; Little, 1951; Doubleday, 1962
He Should Have Died Hereafter; see Untimely Death
Suicide Excepted. MacDonald & Co., 1954
Tenant for Death. Dodd, 1937; Faber, 1937
That Yew Tree's Shade; see Death Walks the Woods
Tragedy at Law. Faber, 1942; Harcourt, 1943
Untimely Death. MacDonald & Co., 1958; Avon (Also published as: He Should Have Died Hereafter. Faber, 1958)
When the Wind Blows. Faber, 1953
The Wind Blows Death. Little, 1950
With a Bare Bodkin. Faber, 1946

CLARK, DALE, pseud; see KAYSER, RONAL

CLARK, DOROTHY PARK (D)
Just for the Bride. Doubleday, 1950
Poison Speaks Softly. Doubleday, 1947
Roll Jordon Roll. Doubleday, 1947

CLARK, ELLERY H. (M)
Carleton Case. Bobbs, 1910
Loaded Dice. Bobbs, 1909

CLARK, FRANCES BETTY (M)
Darken the Moon. Blackwood, 1953
Drummer's Den. Heinemann, 1964
Pearls of Marguerite. Heinemann, 1963

CLARK, PHILIP (S)
The Dark River. S & S, 1949
Flight into Darkness. S & S, 1948

CLARK, WALTER VAN TILBURG (S)
The Oxbow Incident. Random, 1940; Signet, 1960

CLARK, WESLEY C. (D)
Murder Goes to Bank Night. Hale, 1940

CLARK, WINIFRED (M) (Pseudonym: Scott Finley)
The Case of the Black Sheep. Phoenix, 1950

CLARKE, DONALD HENDERSON (S)
Confidential. Laurie, 1937
Louis Beretti. Knopf, 1930
Murderer's Holiday. Vanguard, 1940; Laurie, 1941

CLARKE, IDA CLYDE (D)
Record No. 33. Appleton, D., 1915

CLARKE, J. CALVITT (M) (Pseudonym: Richard Grant)
The Case of the Baronet's Memoirs. Long, 1960
The Circle of Death. Paul, S., 1952
Death Light. Long, 1959
Doom Candle. Paul, S., 1943
Five Ways to Die. Paul, S., 1947
Formula for Crime. Paul, S., 1956
Legacy of Danger. Paul, S., 1954
Lives in a Box. Paul, S., 1951
Men in Knots. Paul, S., 1945
The Serpent Stirs. Paul, S., 1942

Shoot Your Enemies. Paul, S., 1948
The Silky Ones Sting. Paul, S., 1947
The Slaves of Ishtar. Paul, S., 1951
Spider Murders. Long, 1958
The Storm Gang. Paul, S., 1952
This Is Dynamite. Paul, S., 1955
The Threat of the Cloven Hand. Paul, S., 1950
Who Strikes by Night. Paul, S., 1944

CLARKE, LAURENCE (S)
Bernard Treve's Boots. Hodder, 1920

CLARKE, MARIAN B. (D)
The Model Corpse. Hale, 1942

CLASON, CLYDE B. (D)
Blind Drifts. Doubleday, Doran, 1937
The Death Angel. Doubleday, Doran, 1936; Sun Dial, 1937
Dragons Cave. Doubleday, Doran, 1939
The Fifth Tumbler. Doubleday, Doran, 1936
Green Shiver. Doubleday, Doran, 1941
The Man from Tibet. Doubleday, Doran, 1938; Sun Dial, 1939
Murder Gone Minoan. Doubleday, Doran, 1939
Poison Jasmine. Doubleday, Doran, 1940
The Purple Parrot. Doubleday, Doran, 1937; Sun Dial, 1938
The Whispering Earl. Doubleday, Doran, 1938

CLAUDIA, SUSAN (S)
Madness at the Castle. Signet, 1966
The Searching Spectre. Signet, 1967
The Silent Voice. Signet, 1967

CLAUSEN, CARL (D)
The Gloyne Murder. Dodd, 1930
Jaws of Circumstance. Dodd, 1931; Lane, 1931

CLAY, ROBERT KEATING (M)
By Night. Blackwood, 1927; Lippincott, 1927

CLAYDON, STELLA (D)
Season in Murder. Long, 1960

CLAYMORE, TOD, pseud; see CLEVELY, HUGH DESMOND

CLAYTON, RICHARD HENRY MICHAEL (S) (Pseudonym: William Haggard)
The Antagonists. Cassell, 1964; Washburn, 1964; Signet, 1965
The Arena. Washburn, 1961; Penguin, 1963
Closed Circuit. Washburn, 1960; Penguin, 1963
The Conspirators. Walker & Co., 1968
The Hard Sell. Washburn, 1966; Signet, 1967
The High Wire. Cassell, 1963; Washburn, 1963
The Powder Barrel. Washburn, 1965; Signet, 1966
The Power House. Washburn, 1967
Slow Burner. Little, 1958; Signet, 1965
The Telemann Touch. Little, 1958; Signet, 1963
The Unquiet Sleep. Washburn, 1962; Avon, 1964
Venetian Blind. Cassell, 1959; Washburn, 1959; Signet, 1963

CLEARY, JON (M)
The Fall of an Eagle. Morrow, 1964
The High Commissioner. Morrow, 1966
The Long Pursuit. Morrow, 1967
The Pulse of Danger. Collins, 1966; Avon, 1967

CLEATON, IRENE (S)
The Outsider. Little, 1944

CLEAVER, KAY, pseud; see STRAHAN, MRS. KAY CLEAVER

CLEEVE, BRIAN TALBOT (M)
Assignment to Vengeance. Hammond, 1961
Counterspy; see Vote X for Treason
Dark Blood, Dark Terror. Hammond, 1966; Random, 1966; Lancer, 1967
Death of a Painted Lady. Hammond, 1962; Random, 1963; Avon, 1964
Death of a Wicked Servant. Hammond, 1963, 1966; Random, 1964
The Judas Goat. Random, 1965
Vice Isn't Private. Random, 1966; Lancer, 1967
Violent Death of a Bitter Englishman. Random, 1967
Vote X for Treason. Collins, 1964 (Also published as: Counterspy. Lancer, 1966)

CLEFT-ADDAMS, J. (M)
The Secret Deed. McBride, 1926

CLEM, EMERSON S. (D)
Which- Innocent or Guilty? Comet, 1955

CLEMENS, NANCY; see RANDOLPH, VANCE

CLEMENS, SAMUEL L. (D) (Pseudonym: Mark Twain)
Tom Sawyer, Detective and Other Stories. Harper, 1896

CLEMENT, FRANK A. (M)
Picture Him Dead. Longmans, 1935

CLEMENTS, COLIN CAMPBELL and FLORENCE RYERSON (Mrs. C. C. Clements) (M)

Blind Man's Buff. Long & Smith, 1933 (Also published as: Sleep No More. Grayson, 1933)
The Borgia Blade. Appleton-Century, 1937
Fear of Fear. Appleton, D., 1931; Skeffington, 1931
Shadows. Appleton-Century, 1934
Sleep No More; see Blind Man's Buff

CLEMENTS, EILEEN HELEN (S)
Back in Daylight. Hodder, 1957
Berry Green. Hodder, 1945
Bright Intervals. Hodder, 1940; Dutton, 1941
Chair-Lift. Hodder, 1954
Cherry Harvest. Hodder, 1943
Discord in the Air. Hodder, 1955
High Tension. Hodder, 1959
Honey for the Marshal. Hodder, 1960
Let Him Die. Hodder, 1939; Dutton, 1940
Let or Hindrance. Hale, R., 1963
Make Fame a Monster. Hodder, 1940
Note of Enchantment. Hodder, 1961
The Other Island. Hodder, 1956
Over and Done With. Hodder, 1952
Parcel of Fortune. Hodder, 1954
Perhaps a Little Danger. Dutton, 1942; Hodder, 1942
Rain Every Day. Dutton, 1941; Hodder, 1941
Sea-Change. Hodder, 1951
Uncommon Cold. Hodder, 1958
Weathercock. Hodder, 1949

CLERI, MARIO (S)
Six Graves to Munich. Banner, 1967

CLEVELAND, JOHN (D)
Minus One Corpse. Arcadia, 1954

CLEVELY, HUGH DESMOND (D)
(Pseudonym: Tod Claymore)
The Amateur Crook. Hutchinson, 1936
Appointment in New Orleans, by Tod Claymore. Cassell, 1950; Penguin, 1955
Archer Plus Twenty. Cassell, 1938
Blood and Thunder. Cassell, 1951
Call the Yard! Doubleday, Doran, 1931
Dark Eyes and Danger. Hutchinson, 1934
Dead Man's Secret. Amalgamated Press, 1935
Dead Men Don't Answer, by Tod Claymore. Cassell, 1954
Death's Counterfeit. Hutchinson, 1929, 1937
Flare Path!; see Ships with Wings
Fraser Butts In. Hutchinson, 1929; Clode, 1930
Further Outlook Unsettled. Hutchinson, 1932
Gang Law. Hutchinson, 1931
The Gang-Smasher. Hutchinson, 1928; Clode, 1930
The Gang-Smasher Again. Cassell, 1938; Mellifont, 1954
Garland of Valour. Cassell, 1963
Hell to Pay! Hutchinson, 1930, 1948
The Man with the Amber Eyes, with Edgar A. Jepson. Jenkins, 1930
Mister Munt Carries On. Hutchinson, 1934
More Trouble for Archer. Cassell, 1949
Nest of Vipers, by Tod Claymore. Cassell, 1948; Penguin, 1955
No Peace for Archer. Cassell, 1947
Not Nice People. Cassell, 1950
Public Enemy. Cassell, 1953; Penguin
Rendezvous on an Island, by Tod Claymore. Cassell, 1957
Reunion in Florida, by Tod Claymore. Cassell, 1952; Penguin, 1955
Ships with Wings, by Tod Claymore. Cassell, 1942 (U.S. title: Flare Path. Morrow, 1942)
Somebody Killed Kelvin. Cassell, 1953
Speedwell, by Tod Claymore. Cassell, 1946
This Is What Happened; see You Remember the Case
Three Wooden Overcoats. Cassell, 1939; Withy Grove, 1947
Turning Point; see Wolf That Follows
What Else Could I Do, by Tod Claymore. Cassell, 1948
The Wind Was Cold. Cassell, 1955
The Wolf That Follows. Cassell, 1955 (U.S. title: Turning Point. Morrow, 1955)
The Wrong Murderer. Hutchinson, 1935
You Remember the Case. Nelson, 1939 (U.S. title: This Is What Happened. S & S, 1939)
Zero the 14th. Cassell, 1937; Mellifont, 1953

CLEWES, HOWARD
The Libertines. Doubleday, 1964
Long Memory. Doubleday, 1952

CLEWES, WINSTON
Troy and the Maypole. Joseph, M., 1941

CLIFFORD, CHARLES L. (M)
Parade Ground; see Too Many Boats
Too Many Boats. Little, 1934 (Also published as: Parade Ground)
When the Bells Ring. Doubleday, Doran, 1941

CLIFFORD, FRANCIS, pseud; see THOMPSON, ARTHUR LEONARD BELL

CLIFT, DENISON HALLEY (S)
Spy in the Room. Mystery House, 1944

CLIFTON, BUD (S)
Let Him Go Hang. Ace, 1961

CLINE, LEONARD (S)
Dark Chamber. Viking, 1927

CLINTON, DOROTHY RANDLE (M)
The Maddening Scar. Christopher, 1962

CLIVE, MRS. ARCHER (D)
Why Paul Ferroll Killed His Wife. Saunders, Otley, 1860

CLOCK, HERBERT; see BOETZEL, ERIC

CLOUSTON, JOSEPH STORER (S)
After the Deed. Blackwood, 1931
Carrington's Cases. Blackwood, 1920
Lunatic at Large. Blackwood, 1899
Lunatic Still at Large. Nash & Grayson, 1923; Dutton, 1924
Man from the Clouds Omnibus: Lunatic at Large, Spy in Black, Man from the Clouds, and Simon. Blackwood, 1948
Simon. Blackwood, 1919
The Spy in Black. Blackwood, 1917

CLUGSTON, KATHERINE (D)
A Murderer in the House. Wyn, 1947

CLURMAN, ROBERT (D)
Nick Carter, Detective. Macmillan, 1964

CLUTTON-BROCK, ALAN FRANCIS (D)
Murder at Liberty Hall. Lane, 1941; Macmillan, 1941

CLYDE, LEONARD WORSWICK (D)
(Pseudonym: Peter Baron)
Murder in Wax. Macaulay, 1931
The Opium Murders. Macaulay, 1930
The Round Table Murders. Macaulay, 1931

COATES, JOHN (D)
Time for Tea. MacDonald & Co., 1950

COATES, ROBERT M. (M)
The Man Just Ahead of You. Sloane, 1964
Wisteria Cottage. Harcourt, 1948; Popular Lib., 1948

COBB, BELTON, pseud; see COBB, GEOFFREY BELTON

COBB, CLAYTON W. (D) (Pseudonym: J. Patten)
Mountaineer Detective. 1889

COBB, GEOFFREY BELTON (D)
(Pseudonym: Belton Cobb)
Corpse at Casablanca. Allen, W. H., 1956
Corpse in the Cargo. Allen, W. H., 1961
Corpse Incognito. Methuen, 1953
Dead Girl's Shoes. Allen, W. H., 1964
Death Defies the Doctor. Longmans, 1939
Death in the 13th Dose. Longmans, 1946
Death of a Peeping Tom. Allen, W. H., 1963
Death with a Difference. Allen, W.H., 1960
Detective in Distress. Methuen, 1953
Don't Lie to the Police. Allen, W. H., 1959
Double Detection. Longmans, 1945
Doubly Dead. Allen, W. H., 1957
Drink Alone and Die. Allen, W. H., 1956
Early Morning Poison. Longmans, 1947
Fatal Dose. Longmans, 1937
The Fatal Holiday. Longmans, 1938
The Framing of Carol Woan. Longmans, 1948
Home Guard Mystery. Longmans, 1941
I Never Miss Twice. Allen, W. H., 1965
Inspector Burmann's Black-out. Longmans, 1941
Inspector Burmann's Busiest Day. Longmans, 1939
Like a Guilty Thing. Longmans, 1938; British Book Centre, 1959
The Lunatic, the Lover. Methuen, 1950
Missing Scapegoat. Allen, W. H., 1958
Murder: Men Only. Allen, W. H., 1962
Need a Body Tell? Allen, W. H., 1954
Next-Door to Death. Methuen, 1952
No Alibi. Longmans, 1936
No Charge for the Poison. Methuen, 1950
No Last Words. Longmans, 1949
No Mercy for Margaret. Methuen, 1952
No Shame for the Devil. Allen, W. H., 1964
Poisoner's Base. Allen, W. H., 1957; British Book Centre, 1958
Poisoner's Mistake. Longmans, 1936
Quickly Dead. Longmans, 1937
Search for Sgt. Baxter. Allen, W. H., 1961
Secret of Superintendent Manning. Longmans, 1948
Sergeant Ross in Disguise. Longmans, 1940
Stolen Strychnine. Longmans, 1949
The Willing Witness. Allen, W. H., 1955
With Intent to Kill. Allen, W. H., 1958; British Book Centre, 1958

COBB, IRWIN S. (D)
Alias Ben Alibi. Doran, 1925

Back Home. Doran, 1912
Escape of Mr. Trimm. Hodder, 1913
Faith, Hope and Charity. Bobbs, 1934
Judge Priest Turns Detective. Bobbs, 1937
Murder Day by Day. Bobbs, 1933
Old Judge Priest. Doran, 1916

COBB, IVO GEIKIE (M) (Pseudonym: Anthony Weymouth)
Cornish Crime. Hodder, 1937; Withy Grove, 1949
The Doctors Are Doubtful. Barker, 1935; Withy Grove, 1940
Frozen Death. Barker, 1934; Withy Grove, 1940
Hard Liver. Barker, 1936; Withy Grove, 1941
Inspector Treadgold Investigates. Rich, 1941
No, Sir Jeremy. Barker, 1935; News of the World, 1951

COBB, THOMAS (M)
The Busy Whisper. Chapman, 1915
Chichester Intrigue. Lane, 1908
Crime at Keeper's. Benn, 1932
Crime Without a Clue. Benn, 1929
Death on the Cliff. Benn, 1932
Disappearance of Mr. Derwent. Ward, Lock, 1894; Neely, 1896
House by the Common. Ward, Lock, 1891
Inspector Bedison and the Sunderland Case. Benn, 1932
Inspector Bedison Risks It. Benn, 1931
Sark Street Chapel Murder. Benn, 1931
The Silver Bag. Lane, 1919
Wedderburn's Will. Lever Bros., 1892; Ward, Lock, 1892
Who Closed the Casement? Benn, 1932
Who Opened the Door? Benn, 1930

COBBLESTONE, BENNETT (M)
Last of the Grenvilles. Dutton, 1919

COBDEN, GUY (M)
I Saw Murder. Hale, R., 1962
Murder for Her Birthday. Hale, R., 1960
Murder for His Money. Hale, R., 1959
Murder Inherited. Hale, R., 1961
Murder Was My Neighbor. Rich, 1955
Murder Was Their Medicine. Jarrolds, 1957
My Guess Was Murder. Rich, 1958

COBNOR, JOHN (M)
Four Answers. Cape, 1931

COBURN, MRS. ELEANOR HALLOWELL ABBOTT; see ABBOTT, ELEANOR HALLOWELL

COCCIOLI, CARLO (M)
The White Stone. S & S, 1961

COCKBURN, CLAUD (M) (Pseudonym: James Helvick)
Beat the Devil. Lippincott, 1951
The Horses. Walker & Co., 1964

COCKIN, JOAN, pseud; see BURBRIDGE, EDITH JOAN

COCKRELL, FRANK; see COCKRELL, MARIAN BROWN

COCKRELL, MARIAN BROWN and FRANK COCKRELL (S)
Dark Waters. World Pub., 1944

CODY, C. S., pseud; see WALLER, LESLIE

COE, CHARLES FRANCIS (S)
About 2 A.M. Cosmopolitan, 1931
Ashes. Random, 1952
G-Man. Hutchinson, 1937; Lippincott, 1952
Gunman. Gollancz, 1930
Hooch. Doubleday, Doran, 1929; Grosset, 1930
Knockout. Lippincott, 1936; Hutchinson, 1938
Me—Gangster. Putnam, 1927; Grosset, 1928
The Other Half. Cosmopolitan, 1930; Grosset, 1931
Pressure. Random, 1951; Allen, W. H., 1952; Signet, 1952
Ransom. Lippincott, 1934; Hutchinson, 1937
The River Pirate. Putnam, 1928; Grosset, 1928; Reader's Lib., 1929
Swag. Putnam, 1928; Grosset, 1930
Triumph: The Undoing of Rafferty, Ward Heeler. Sears, 1929; Grosset, 1930

COE, TUCKER, pseud; see WESTLAKE, DONALD

COFFIN, CARLYN (M)
Dogwatch. Farrar & Rinehart, 1944
Mare's Nest. Farrar & Rinehart, 1941

COFFIN, GEOFFREY, pseud; see MASON, FRANCIS VAN WYCK

COFFIN, PETER, pseud. (M)
The Search for My Great Uncle's Head. Doubleday, Doran, 1937

COFFMAN, VIRGINIA (S-M)
The Beckoning. Ace, 1965
The Castle at Witch's Coven. Lancer, 1966
The Chinese Door. Lancer, 1967
The Curse of the Island Pool. Lancer, 1965
The Demon Tower. Signet, 1966
The Devil Vicar. Ace, 1966

The High Terrace. Lancer, 1966
Hounds. Belmont, 1967
Moura. Ace, 1959
The Secret of Shower Tree. Lancer, 1966
The Shadow Box. Lancer, 1966

COFYN, CORNELIUS (M)
The Death Riders. Gollancz, 1935; Knopf, 1935

COGGIN, JOAN (M)
Dancing with Death. Hurst, 1949
The Mystery of Orchard House. Hurst, 1947
Who Killed the Curate? Hurst, 1947
Why Did She Die? Hurst, 1947

COGHLAN, LIDA LAVINIA (M)
The House of Mystery. Herder, 1926

COHEN, OCTAVUS ROY (D-S)
The Backstage Mystery. Appleton, D., 1930 (Also published as: Curtain at Eight. Grosset, 1933)
Bullet for My Love. Macmillan, 1950
Child of Evil. Appleton-Century, 1936
The Corpse That Walked. GM, 1951
The Crimson Alibi. Dodd, 1919, 1929
Curtain at Eight; see The Backstage Mystery
Danger in Paradise. Macmillan, 1945; Hale, R., 1950
Dangerous Lady. Macmillan, 1946; Barker, 1948
Don't Ever Love Me. Macmillan, 1947; Barker, 1948
East of Broadway. Appleton-Century, 1938
Florian Slappey Goes Abroad. Little, 1928
Gray Dusk. Dodd, 1920
I Love You Again. Appleton-Century, 1927
The Iron Chalice. Little, 1925
Jim Hanvey, Detective. Dodd, 1923; Grosset, 1925
Lady in Armour. Appleton-Century, 1941
Love Can Be Dangerous. Macmillan, 1955
Love Has No Alibi. Macmillan, 1946; Hale, R., 1952
The May Day Mystery. Appleton, D., 1929; Grosset, 1931
Midnight. Dodd, 1922
More Beautiful Than Murder. Macmillan, 1948; Barker, 1950
Murder in Season; see Romance in Crimson
Murder Mistress. Ace, 1959
My Love Wears Black. Macmillan, 1948; Barker, 1949
The Outer Gate. Grosset, 1926
Romance in Crimson. Appleton-Century, 1940 (Also published as: Murder in Season. Popular Lib.)
Romance in the First Degree. Macmillan, 1944; Hale, R., 1951
Scrambled Yeggs. Appleton-Century, 1934
Six Seconds of Darkness. Grosset, 1925
The Sound of Revelry. Macmillan, 1943; Hale, R., 1945
Star of Earth. Appleton, D., 1932
Star Trap. GM, 1960
Strange Honeymoon. Appleton-Century, 1939
The Townsend Murder Mystery. Appleton-Century, 1933
Transient Lady. Appleton-Century, 1934

COLBRON, GRACE ISABEL (D)
Club Car Mystery. Macaulay, 1928
The Crippled Hand, with Augusta Groner.

COLBY, ROBERT (S)
Beautiful But Bad. Monarch, 1962
Deadly Desire. GM, 1959
The Faster She Runs. Monarch, 1963
In a Vanishing Room. Ace, 1961
Kill Me a Fortune. Ace, 1961
Kim. Monarch, 1962
Lament for Julie. Monarch, 1964

COLE, DIANE (M)
Murder at the White Tulip. Arcadia, 1960

COLE, GEORGE DOUGLAS HOWARD and M. I. COLE (D)
The Affair at Aliquid. Collins, 1935
The Berkshire Mystery. Brewer, 1930; Payson & Clarke, 1930
Big Business Murder. Doubleday, 1935; Collins, 1935; Burt, 1936
The Blatchington Tangle. Collins, 1926; Macmillan, 1926; Burt, 1928
Bone of the Dinosaur. Vallancey, 1945
The Brooklyn Murders. Collins, 1923; Boni, 1924
The Brothers Sackville. Collins, 1936; Macmillan, 1937
Burglars in Bucks. Collins, 1930
The Corpse in Canonicals; see The Corpse in the Constable's Garden
The Corpse in the Constable's Garden. Morrow, 1931 (Also published as: The Corpse in Canonicals. Collins, 1930)
The Counterfeit Murder. Macmillan, 1941
The Counterpoint Murder. Collins, 1940; Macmillan, 1941
Dead Man's Watch. Collins, 1931; Doubleday, Doran, 1932

Death in the Quarry. Collins, 1934; Doubleday, Doran, 1934
Death in the Sun. Vallancey, 1945
Death in the Tankard. Vallancey, 1945
Death of a Bride. Vallancey, 1945 (Part of Mrs. Warrender's Profession)
Death of a Millionaire. Collins, 1925; Macmillan, 1925
Death of a Star. Collins, 1932; Doubleday, Doran, 1933
Dr. Tancred Begins. Doubleday, Doran, 1935; Collins, 1937
Double Blackmail. Collins, 1939; Macmillan, 1939
End of an Ancient Mariner. Collins, 1933; Doubleday, Doran, 1934
Fatal Beauty. Harrap, 1948
The Great Southern Mystery. Collins, 1931 (U.S. title: Walking Corpse. Morrow, 1931)
Greek Tragedy. Macmillan, 1940
In Peril of His Life. Harrap, 1948
Knife in the Dark. Macmillan, 1942
Last Will and Testament. Doubleday, Doran, 1936; Collins, 1937
A Lesson in Crime. Collins, 1933
Man from the River. Collins, 1928; Macmillan, 1928
The Missing Aunt. Collins, 1937; Macmillan, 1938
The Missing Baronet: Short Stories. Polybooks, 1947
Mrs. Warrender's Profession. Collins, 1938; Macmillan, 1939
Murder at Crome House. Macmillan, 1927
Murder at the Munitions Works. Macmillan, 1940
Murder in Broad Daylight. Bell, 1937
Murder in Four Parts. Collins, 1934
Off with Her Head. Macmillan, 1939
Poison in a Garden Suburb. Collins, 1929; Harcourt, 1929; Payson & Clarke, 1929
Scandal at School. Collins, 1935 (U.S. title: The Sleeping Death. Doubleday, Doran, 1936)
The Sleeping Death; see Scandal at School
Strychnine Tonic; Short Stories. Polybooks, 1947
Superintendent Wakely's Mistake. Vallancey, 1944
Superintendent Wilson's Cases. Collins, 1933
Superintendent Wilson's Holiday. Collins, 1929; Harcourt, 1929
Toper's End. Collins, 1942; Macmillan, 1942
Toys of Death. Harrap, 1948
Walking Corpse; see Great Southern Mystery
Wilson and Some Others. Collins, 1940
Wilson Calling. Vallancey, 1944

COLE, KATHARINE S. (M)
I'm Afraid I'll Live. Houghton, 1936

COLE, LOIS DWIGHT (Pseudonym: Anne Elliot)
Return to Aylforth. Meredith, 1967

COLE, SONIA (M)
Counterfeit. Murrary, J., 1955

COLEMAN, CLARA (S-Gothic)
A Scent of Sandalwood. Lancer, 1966

COLES, CYRIL HENRY and ADELAIDE MANNING (D) (Pseudonym: Manning Coles)
Alias Uncle Hugo. Doubleday, 1952; Hodder, 1953
All That Glitters. Doubleday, 1954 (English title: Not for Export. Hodder, 1954. Also published as: The Mystery of the Stolen Plans. Berkley Pub., 1960)
Among Those Absent. Doubleday, 1948; Hodder, 1948
The Basle Express. Doubleday, 1956; Hodder, 1956; Berkley Pub., 1964
Birdwatcher's Quarry. Doubleday, 1956
Brief Candles. Doubleday, 1954; Hodder, 1954
Brother for Hugh; see With Intent to Deceive
Come and Go. Doubleday, 1954; Hodder, 1958
Concrete Crime. Ballantine, 1962; Doubleday, 1960 (English title: Crime in Concrete. Hodder, 1960)
Crime in Concrete; see Concrete Crime
Dangerous by Nature. Doubleday, 1950; Berkley Pub., 1965
Death of an Ambassador. Doubleday, 1957; Hodder, 1957
Diamonds to Amsterdam. Doubleday, 1949; Hodder, 1950
Drink to Yesterday. Hodder, 1940; Knopf, 1941; Berkley Pub., 1964
Duty Free. Doubleday, 1959; Hodder, 1959
The Exploits of Tommy Hambleton: An Omnibus. Doubleday, 1959
Family Matter; see Happy Returns
The Far Traveler. Doubleday, 1956; Hodder, 1957
The Fifth Man. Doubleday, 1946; Hodder, 1946; Berkley Pub., 1964
Green Hazard. Doubleday, 1945; Hodder, 1945
Happy Returns. Doubleday, 1955 (English title: Family Matter. Hodder, 1956)
House at Pluck's Gutter. Hodder, 1963; Pyramid, 1968
A Knife for the Juggler. Hodder, 1953; Doubleday, 1964 (Also published as: Vengeance Man. Pyramid, 1967)

Let the Tiger Die. Doubleday, 1947; Hodder, 1948
The Man in the Green Hat. Doubleday, 1955; Hodder, 1955
The Mystery of the Stolen Plans; see All That Glitters
Night Train to Paris. Doubleday, 1952; Hodder, 1952; Pyramid, 1963
No Entry. Doubleday, 1958; Hodder, 1958
Not for Export; see All That Glitters
Not Negotiable. Doubleday, 1949; Hodder, 1949; Berkley Pub., 1964
Nothing to Declare. Doubleday, 1960
Now or Never. Doubleday, 1951; Hodder, 1951
Pray Silence. Hodder, 1940 (U.S. title: A Toast for Tomorrow. Doubleday, Doran, 1941; Berkley Pub., 1964)
Search for a Sultan. Doubleday, 1961
They Tell No Tales. Hodder, 1941; Doubleday, Doran, 1942; Berkley Pub., 1964
This Fortress. Hodder, 1941; Doubleday, Doran, 1942; Berkley Pub., 1964
Three Beans. Hodder, 1957
A Toast to Tomorrow; see Pray Silence
Vengeance Man; see A Knife for the Juggler
With Intent to Deceive. Doubleday, 1947; Berkley Pub., 1964 (English title: Brother for Hugh. Hodder, 1947)
Without Lawful Authority. Doubleday, Doran, 1943; Hodder, 1943

COLES, MANNING, pseud; see COLES, CYRIL HENRY

COLIN, AUBREY (D)
Hands of Death. Hammond, 1963

COLIZZI, GUISEPPE (M)
Night Has Another Voice. Abelard, 1963

COLLABORATION (M)
Double Death. Gollancz, 1939

———.
The President's Mystery. Farrar & Rinehart, 1935 (By various writers from an idea suggested by President Franklin D. Roosevelt)

COLLANS, DEV, pseud; see WINCHELL, PRENTICE

COLLIER, JOHN (S)
Devil and All. Nonesuch, 1934
Fancies and Goodnight. Doubleday, 1951; Bantam, 1961
Green Thoughts and Other Strange Tales: A Collection Taken from Two Volumes.
Presenting Moonshine. Viking, 1941
Touch of Nutmeg and More Unlikely Stories. Heritage, 1943; Readers' Club, 1943

COLLIER, RICHARD (S)
The Lovely and the Damned. Pilot, 1949
Pay-off in Calcutta. Pilot, 1948
Solitary Witness. Pellegrini, 1948

COLLINS, CHARLES ALLSTON (M)
At the Bar. Chapman, 1866

COLLINS, COLIN (M)
Human Male. Greening, 1909

COLLINS, DALE (M)
The Fifth Victim. Harrap, 1930

COLLINS, ERROLL (M)
Star of Korania. Lutterworth Press, 1948

COLLINS, GILBERT (M)
The Channel Million. Bles, 1932
Chinese Red; see Red Death
The Dead Walk. Bles, 1933
Death Meets the King's Messenger. Bles, 1934; Doubleday, Doran, 1934
Horror Comes to Thripplands. Bles, 1930
Murder at Brambles. Holt, H., 1932
The Phantom Tower. Bles, 1931
Poison Pool. Bles, 1935
Post-Mortem. Bles, 1930
Red Death. Holt, H., 1932 (English title: Chinese Red. Bles, 1932)
The Starkenden Quest. McBride, 1925
Valley of Eyes Unseen. Duckworth, 1923

COLLINS, HUNT, pseud; see HUNTER, EVAN

COLLINS, MARY G. (D)
Dead Center. Scribner, 1942; Bantam, 1946
Death Warmed Over. Scribner, 1947
Dog Eat Dog. Scribner, 1949
The Fog Comes. Scribner, 1941; Bantam, 1946
Only the Good. Scribner, 1942
The Sister of Cain. Scribner, 1943

COLLINS, MICHAEL, pseud; see LYNDS, DENNIS

COLLINS, NORMAN (M)
The Bat That Flits. Little, 1952
Flames Coming Out of the Top. Gollancz, 1937

COLLINS, WILLIAM WILKIE (M-D)
After Dark. Smith & Elder, 1856
Armadale. Smith & Elder, 1866; Harper, 1873

Dead Secret. Bradbury, 1857; Low, 1861
Hide and Seek. Low, 1861
Lady of Glenwith Grange. Paperback Lib., 1966
The Law and the Lady. Chatto, 1875
Mr. Wray's Cash Box; or, the Mask and the Mystery. Bentley, 1852
The Moonstone. Tinsley, 1868; Smith & Elder, 1871; Oxford, 1928; Dent, 1957; Harper; Penguin, 1960; Pyramid, 1961
No Name. Low, 1862
Queen of Hearts. Hurst, 1859; Low, 1862; Harper, 1874
Woman in White. Harper, 1860; Low, 1861; Dutton, 1950; Doubleday, 1961

COLLIS, E. T. (M)
Murder by Warrant. Glen, 1898

COLLISON, WILSON (M)
Begins with Murder; see Save a Lady
Diary of Death. McBride, 1930; Tudor, 1932
Last Witness. Arrowsmith, 1931
Murder in the Brownstone. McBride, 1929
Murder in the Rain. McBride, 1930
Red-Haired Alibi. McBride, 1932
Save a Lady. Kendall, 1935 (Also published as: Begins with Murder. Long, 1936)
A Woman in Purple Pajamas. McBride, 1931

COLOMBO, PAT (S)
Throw Back the Little Ones. Avon, 1963

COLSON, PERCY; see HOARE, DOUGLAS

COLTER, ELI (D)
Cheer for the Dead. Mill, 1947
The Gulf Cove Murders. Mill, 1944
Rehearsal for the Funeral. Arcadia, 1953

COLTON, A. J. (M)
The Coatine Case. Hale, R., 1953

COLTON, MEL, pseud; see BRAHAM, HAL

COLVER, ANNE (Full Name: Polly Anne Colver Harris) (M) (Pseudonym: Colver Harris)
Going to St. Ives. Macrae Smith, 1936
Hide and Go Seek. Minton, 1933
Murder in Amber. Hillman-Curl, 1938

COLWALL, JAMES (M)
The Coombsberrow Mystery. Cassell, 1890

COMFORT, WILL LEVINGTON (S)
Fate Knocks at the Door. Lippincott, 1912

COMLEY, GERTRUDE (D)
Mansel Disappearance Mystery. Rivers, 1930
Who Murdered Westaway? Rivers, 1932

COMPTON, GUY (D)
Dead on Cue. Long, 1964
Disguise for a Dead Gentleman. Long, 1965
Medium for Murder. Long, 1963
Too Many Murderers. Long, 1962

COMPTON, HERBERT (M)
To Defeat the Ends of Justice. Chatto, 1906

COMPTON-RICKETT, ARTHUR; see LEYTON, PATRICK and SHORT, ERNEST HENRY

COMSTOCK, CAROLINE (M)
Bandar-log Murder. Barker, 1956

CONANT, PAUL (S)
Dr. Gatskill's Blue Shoes. Wyn, 1952

CONDON, RICHARD (S)
The Happy Thieves; see The Oldest Confession
An Infinity of Mirrors. Crest, 1965; McGraw, 1965
The Manchurian Candidate. McGraw, 1959; Joseph, M., 1960; Signet, 1962
The Oldest Confession. Appleton, 1958; Signet, 1967 (Also published as: The Happy Thieves. Bantam, 1962)
Some Angry Angel. McGraw, 1960; Crest, 1961
Talent for Loving. McGraw, 1961; Crest, 1962
The Two-Headed Reader: The Oldest Confession and The Manchurian Candidate. Random, 1966

CONNELL, EDWIN (M)
I Had to Kill Her. Ballantine, 1966

CONNELL, RICHARD E. (D)
Murder at Sea. Jarrolds, 1929; Minton, 1929
Variety. Minton, 1925

CONNELL, VIVIAN (S)
Monte Carlo Mission. GM, 1954

CONNINGTON, J. J., pseud; see STEWART, ALFRED WALTER

CONNOR, KEVIN (S)
New Departure. Jefferson House, 1962

CONNOLLY, PAUL (S)
Get Out of Town. Muller, 1949
So Fair, So Evil. GM, 1955

CONRAD, CLIVE, pseud; see KING, FRANK

CONRAD, JOSEPH (S)
Nature of a Crime, with Ford Madox Ford. Doubleday, Page, 1925
The Secret Agent. Harper, 1907; Methuen, 1908; Doubleday, Page, 1915
A Set of Six. Doubleday, Page, 1908

CONROY, ALBERT (S)
The Mob Says Murder. Muller, 1959; GM
The Murder in Room 13. GM, 1958
Nice Guys Finish Dead. Muller, 1958; GM
The Road's End. Muller, 1958; GM

CONSTINER, MERLE (M)
Hearse of a Different Color. Phoenix, 1952

CONTE, MANFRED (S)
Jeopardy. Sloane, 1955 (Also published as: Cassia)

CONVERSE, FLORENCE (M)
Into the Void. Little, 1926
The Sphinx. Dutton, 1931

CONVERSE, FRANK H. (M)
Mystery of a Diamond. Lovell, 1890

CONVERSE, JANE (M)
Masquerade Nurse. Signet, 1963

CONWAY, JOHN (M)
A Sin in Time. Monarch, 1961

CONYN, CORNELIUS and JON C. MARTIN (M)
The Bali Ballet Murder. Harrap, 1961

COOK, ELLA BOOKER (S)
The Ghost of Windy Hill. Vantage, 1964

COOK, KENNETH (M)
Chain of Darkness. Joseph, M., 1962
Wake in Fright. Joseph, M., 1961; St. Martin's, 1962

COOKE, DAVID C. (M-S)
c/o American Embassy. Dodd, 1967
The 14th Agent. Dodd, 1967

COOKE, G. WALTER (D)
Death Can Wait. Bles, 1957
Death Takes a Dive. Bles, 1962

COOKE, GRACE MacGOWEN (S)
Man Behind the Mask. Stokes, 1927

COOKE, JOHN ESTEN (M)
Doctor Vandyke. Appleton, D., 1872
Out of the Foam. Carleton, G., 1871

COOKE, JOSEPH COLTIN (D)
Vera Gerard Case. Manthorne, 1937

COOKE, M. B. (M)
Clutch of Circumstance. Doran, 1918

COOKE, M. E., pseud; see CREASEY, JOHN

COOKE, RACHEL E. (M)
Four Mad Monarchs. Vantage, 1954

COOKE, RUPERT CROFT-; see CROFT-COOKE, RUPERT

COOKSON, CATHERINE McMULLEN (M)
(Pseudonym: Catherine Marchant)
Evil at Roger's Cross. Lancer, 1965
The Fen Tiger. MacDonald & Co., 1963 (Also published as: The House on the Fens. Lancer, 1965)
Heritage of Folly. MacDonald & Co., 1962
House of Men. MacDonald & Co., 1964
The House on the Fens; see The Fen Tiger

COOLIDGE-RASK, MARIE (D)
London After Midnight. Grosset, 1928

COOMBS, MURDO (M)
A Moment of Need. Dutton, 1947

COONEY, MICHAEL (S)
Doomsday England. Walker & Co., 1968

COOPER, BRIAN (M)
Maria. Vanguard, 1956
A Mission for Betty Smith. Heinemann, 1966, 1967
Murder of Mary Steers. Vanguard, 1966
A Time to Retreat. Vanguard, 1963
A Touch of Thunder. Vanguard, 1962
Van Langeren Girl. Vanguard, 1960; Pyramid, 1961

COOPER, COURTNEY RYLEY (M)
Action in Diamonds. Penn, 1942

COOPER, JAMES FENIMORE (S)
The Ways of the Hour. Putnam, 1850

COOPER, JOIIN C. (M)
Body Was of No Account. Boardman, T. V., 1957

Death in Aberration. Boardman, T. V 1958
Haunted Strangler. Ace, 1959

COOPER, JOHN MURRAY (M) (Pseudonym: William Sutherland)
Behind the Head-lines. Arrowsmith, 1933
Death Rides the Air Lines. Arrowsmith, 1934; Boardman, T. V., 1940
The Proverbial Murder Case. Arrowsmith, 1935

COOPER, MONTE (M)
Death Near the River. Holt, H., 1928

COOPER, MORTON (S)
The Innocent and Willing. GM, 1956 (Also published as: No Angel. Paperback Lib., 1963)

COPE, HARLEY (D)
Death Stalks the Fleet. Lymanhouse, 1940

COPP, A. E., see STUTLEY, S. J.

COPP, DeWITT (S)
Pursuit of Agent M. Mill, 1961; Popular Lib., 1962
Radius of Action. Popular Lib., 1961

COPPEL, ALEC (S)
Mr. Denning Drives North. Harrap, 1950; Dutton, 1951
Over the Line. Doubleday, 1947

COPPLESTONE, BENNETT, pseud; see KITCHIN, FREDERICK HARCOURT

CORBETT, JAMES (M)
Agent No. 5. Jenkins, 1945
Carteret Hotel Mystery. Jenkins, 1948; Roy Pubs., 1957
Dancing with Death. Jenkins, 1950
Death by Appointment. Jenkins, 1945
Death Is My Shadow. Jenkins, 1947
Death Makes a Date. Jenkins, 1949
Gallows Wait. Jenkins, 1946
Her Private Murder. Jenkins, 1932
Hounds of Death. Jenkins, 1944
Merrivale Mystery. Jenkins, 1929; Mystery League, 1931
Murder at Red Grange. Jenkins, 1931
Murder Begets Murder. Jenkins, 1951
Murder Minus Motive. Jenkins, 1943
Rendezvous with Danger. Jenkins, 1939
Somerville Case. Jenkins, 1949
Vampire of the Skies. Jenkins, 1932
White Angel. Jenkins, 1932
Winterton Hotel Mystery. Jenkins, 1932
Who Was the Killer? Jenkins, 1940

CORBY, JANE (M)
As Deadly Does. Bouregy, 1967
Girl in the Tower. Arcadia, 1967

CORDER, R. E. (M)
Tales Told to the Magistrate. Melrose, 1925

CORELLI, MARIE (M)
The Sorrows of Satan. Methuen, 1895

CORES, LUCY (M)
Corpse de Ballet. Duell, 1944; Collier, 1965
Let's Kill George. Duell, 1946
The Misty Curtain. Harper, 1964
Painted for the Kill. Duell, 1943

COREY, FRANK (M)
By Blood Alone. Berkley Pub., 1961

COREY, HERBERT (M)
Crime at Cobb's House. Appleton-Century, 1934

CORKILL, LOUIS (D)
Fish Lane. Bobbs, 1951

CORLE, EDWIN (S)
Burro Alley. Macmillan, 1938; Pennant, 1938; Random, 1938

CORLISS, ALLENE (S)
Error in Judgment. Bouregy, 1964
Unwelcome Visitor. Bouregy, 1962

CORNE, MOLLY E. (M)
Death at a Masquerade. Mill, 1938
Death at the Manor. Mill, 1938
A Magnet for Murder. Mill, 1939

CORNELL, LOUIS (D)
Murder Case Number 38. Coward, 1932
Poison Case Number 10. Coward, 1931; Tudor, 1933

CORNISH, CONSTANCE (S)
Dead of Winter. S & S, 1959

CORNWELL, DAVID JOHN MOORE (S) (Pseudonym: John Le Carré)
Call for the Dead. Gollancz, 1961; Walker & Co., 1962; Signet, 1964
The Incongruous Spy. Walker & Co., 1964 (English title: The Le Carré Omnibus. Gollancz, 1964)
The Le Carré Omnibus; see The Incongruous Spy
The Looking Glass War. Coward, 1965; Heinemann, 1965; Dell, 1966
A Murder of Quality. Gollancz, 1962; Walker & Co., 1963; Penguin, 1964; New Amer. Lib.
The Spy Who Came in from the Cold. Gollancz, 1963; Coward, 1964; Dell, 1964; Watts, F., 1966 (Large print edition)

CORRELL, A. BOYD; see MacDONALD, PHILIP

CORRIGAN, MARK, pseud; see LEE, NORMAN

CORSON, GEOFFREY, pseud; see SHOLL, ANNA McCLURE

CORTAZAR, JULIO (S)
The Winners. Pantheon, 1965

CORY, DESMOND, pseud; see Mc-CARTHY, SHAUN

CORY, RAY (M)
The Valley of Death. Bouregy, 1966

COSTELLO, PAUL (M)
The Blue Diamond. Cassell, 1962
Cat and the Fiddle. Cassell, 1961
Long Silence. Hale, R., 1957
Mortgage for Murder. Cassell, 1960
Red Beard. Hale, R., 1958

COSTIGAN, LEE (D)
Never Kill a Cop. PB, 1960
The New Breed. GM, 1962; Muller, 1963

COTLER, GORDON (S) (Pseudonym: Alex Gordon)
The Bottletop Affair. S & S, 1959; Dell, 1961
The Cipher. S & S, 1961; Boardman, T. V., 1962; Grove, 1962; Pyramid, 1966
Mission in Black. Random, 1967

COTTERELL, BRIAN, pseud; see DINGLE, AYLWARD EDWARD

COTTON, WILL (D)
Night Was Made for Murder. Avon, 1959

COUCH, SIR ARTHUR T. QUILLER-; see QUILLER-COUCH, SIR ARTHUR T.

COUFFER, JACK (S)
The Farther Shore. Constable, 1959 (U.S. title: Swim, Rat, Swim. Lippincott, 1960)

COULSON, MRS. FELICITY CARTER (D) (Pseudonym: Emery Bonett. Joint pseud. with John Hubert Coulson: Emery and John Bonett)
A Banner for Pegasus; see Not in the Script
Better Dead; see Better Off Dead
Better Off Dead, by Emery and John Bonett. Doubleday, 1964 (English title: Better Dead. Joseph, M., 1964)
Dead Lion, by Emery and John Bonett. Doubleday, 1949; Joseph M., 1949
High Pavement; see Old Mrs. Camelot
No Grave for a Lady, by Emery and John Bonett. Doubleday, 1959
Not in the Script, by Emery and John Bonett. Doubleday, 1951 (English title: A Banner for Pegasus. Joseph, M., 1951)
Old Mrs. Camelot, by Emery Bonett. Lippincott, 1944 (English title: High Pavement. Blakiston, 1944)
The Private Face of Murder, by Emery and John Bonett. Doubleday, 1966

COULSON, JOHN HUBERT; see COULSON, MRS. FELICITY CARTER

COULTER, STEPHEN (S) (Pseudonym: James Mayo)
Hammerhead. Morrow, 1964; Dell, 1965
Let Sleeping Girls Lie, by James Mayo. Morrow, 1966; Avon, 1964
Off-Shore. Morrow, 1966
Threshold. Morrow, 1964; Avon, 1967
Rebound, by James Mayo. Heinemann, 1961
Season of Shame, by James Mayo. Heinemann, 1962
Shamelady, by James Mayo. Morrow, 1966; Avon, 1968

COURAGE, JOHN, pseud; see GOYNE, RICHARD

COURNOS, JOHN (D) (Pseudonyms: John Courtney, Mark Gault)
The Face of Death, by Mark Gault. Methuen, 1934
Grandmother Martin Is Murdered, by John Courtney. Farrar & Rinehart, 1930; Skeffington, 1931

COURTHS, MRS. HEDWIG MAHLER (M)
String of Pearls. Lippincott, 1929

COURTIER, SIDNEY HOBSON (M)
Come Back to Murder. Hammond, 1964
A Corpse Won't Sing. Hammond, 1964
Death in Dream Time. Hammond, 1959
Gently Dust the Corpse. Hammond, 1960
A Glass Spear. Wyn, 1950
Mimic a Murderer. Hammond, 1964
Now Seek My Bones. Hammond, 1957
One Cried Murder. Rinehart, 1954; Hammond, 1956
Shroud for Unlac. Hammond, 1958
Who Dies for Me. Hammond, 1962

COURTNEY, JOHN, pseud; see COURNOS, JOHN

COUSINS, EDMUND GEORGE (D)
Death by Marriage. Gifford, 1959
Death by Treble Chance. Gifford, 1959
Untimely Frost. Benn, 1953; Panther, 1959
Weekend with Maxwell. Gifford, 1961

COUSSEAU, JACQUES (D)
Death of Miss Cunningham. Faber, 1962

COVERACK, GILBERT, pseud; see WARREN, JAMES

COVERDALE, HARRY (M)
Seventh Shot. Burt, 1926

COWAN, SADA (S)
Bitter Justice. Doubleday, Doran, 1943

COWDROY, JOAN A. (D)
Death Has No Tongue. Hutchinson, 1938
Disappearance. Hutchinson, 1934
Flying Dagger Murder. McBride, 1932
Framing Evidence. Hutchinson, 1936
The Mask. Hutchinson, 1928
Murder of Lydia. Hutchinson, 1933
Murder Out of Court. Hutchinson, 1944
Murder Unsuspected. Hutchinson, 1930
Mystery of Sett. Hutchinson, 1930
Nine Green Bottles. Hutchinson, 1939
Watch Mr. Moh. Hutchinson, 1931

COX, ANTHONY BERKLEY (D) (Pseudonyms: Anthony Berkeley, Francis Iles)
Amateur Crime, by Anthony Berkeley. Doubleday, Doran, 1928
As for the Woman.
Ask a Policeman, by Anthony Berkeley et al. Morrow, 1933
Before the Fact, by Francis Iles. Doubleday, Doran, 1932; Dell, 1958 (English title: Murder Story for Ladies. Gollancz, 1932)
Dead Mrs. Stratton, by Anthony Berkeley. Doubleday, Doran, 1933 (English title: Jumping Jenny. Hodder, 1934)
Death in the House. Doubleday, Doran, 1939; Hodder, 1939
Jumping Jenny; see Dead Mrs. Stratton
Layton Court Mystery, by Anthony Berkeley. Jenkins, 1926; Doubleday, Doran, 1929
Malice Aforethought, by Francis Iles. Gollancz, 1931; PB, 1947
Mr. Pidgeon's Island, by Anthony Berkeley. Doubleday, Doran, 1934 (English title: Panic Party. Hodder, 1934)
Mr. Priestley's Problem, by Anthony Berkeley. Collins, 1927; Penguin, 1948
Murder in the Basement, by Anthony Berkeley. Doubleday, Doran, 1932; Hodder, 1932
Murder Story for Ladies; see Before the Fact
Mystery at Lover's Cave, by Anthony Berkeley. S & S, 1927 (English title: Roger Sheringham and the Vane Mystery. Collins, 1927)
Not to Be Taken; see Puzzle in Poison
Panic Party; see Mr. Pidgeon's Island
Piccadilly Murder, by Anthony Berkeley. Collins, 1929; Doubleday, Doran, 1930
The Poisoned Chocolates Case, by Anthony Berkeley. Collins, 1929; Doubleday, Doran, 1929; PB, 1951
A Puzzle in Poison, by Anthony Berkeley. Doubleday, Doran, 1938, 1964; Dolphin, 1964 (English title: Not to Be Taken. Hodder, 1938)
Roger Sheringham and the Vane Mystery; see Mystery at Lover's Cave
The Second Shot, by Anthony Berkeley. Doubleday, Doran, 1931; Hodder, 1931
Silk Stocking Murders, by Anthony Berkeley. Collins, 1928; Doubleday, Doran, 1928
Six Against Scotland Yard, by Anthony Berkeley et al. Doubleday, Doran, 1936 (English title: Six Against the Yard. Selwyn, 1936)
Six Against the Yard; see Six Against Scotland Yard
Top Story Murder, by Anthony Berkeley. Doubleday, Doran, 1931; Hodder, 1931
Trial and Error, by Anthony Berkeley. Doubleday, Doran, 1937; Hodder, 1937; Dell, 1967; PB
The Wychford Poisoning Case, by Anthony Berkeley. Collins, 1926; Doubleday, Doran, 1930

COX, IRVING E., JR. (D)
Murder Among Friends. Abelard, 1957; Nelson, Foster & Scott, 1957

COX, WILLIAM R. (D)
Death Comes Early Dell, 1961
Death on Location. Signet, 1962
Hell to Pay. Signet, 1958
Make My Coffin Strong. GM, 1958
Murder in Vegas. Signet, 1960
Way to Go, Doll Baby! Banner, 1967

COXE, GEORGE HARMON (D)
Alias the Dead. Knopf, 1943
Assignment in Guiana. Knopf, 1942
The Barotique Mystery. Knopf, 1936
The Big Gamble. Knopf, 1958; Hammond, 1960; Pyramid, 1967
The Camera Clue. Knopf, 1937
The Candid Imposter. Knopf, 1967
The Charred Witness. Knopf, 1942
The Crimson Clue. Knopf, 1953; Hammond, 1955
Dangerous Legacy. Knopf, 1946
Deadly Image. Knopf, 1964; Pyramid, 1966 (Magazine title: "Girl in the Melody Lounge")
Death at the Isthmus. Knopf, 1954; Hammond, 1956

Error of Judgment. Knopf, 1961; Hammond, 1962
Eye Witness. Knopf, 1950; Hammond, 1953
Fashioned for Murder. Knopf, 1947
The Fifth Key. Knopf, 1947
Flash Casey, Detective. Avon
Focus on Murder. Knopf, 1954; Hammond, 1956
Four Frightened Women. Knopf, 1939
Frightened Financee. Knopf, 1950; Hammond, 1953
"The Girl in the Melody Lounge"; see Deadly Image
The Glass Triangle. Knopf, 1939; Dell
The Groom Lay Dead. Knopf, 1944; Triangle
The Hidden Key. Knopf, 1963; Hammond, 1964
The Hollow Needle. Knopf, 1948; Dell
The Impetuous Mistress. Knopf, 1958; Hammond, 1959; Dell, 1961; Pyramid, 1965
Inland Passage. Knopf, 1949
The Jade Venus. Knopf, 1945
The Lady Is Afraid. Knopf, 1940
Lady Killer. Knopf, 1949; Hammond, 1952
The Last Commandment. Knopf, 1960; Pyramid, 1967
Man on a Rope. Knopf, 1956; Hammond, 1958
The Man Who Died Too Soon. Knopf, 1962; Hammond, 1963
The Man Who Died Twice. Knopf, 1951;
Hammond, 1954
Mission of Fear. Knopf, 1962; Hammond, 1963; Pyramid, 1965
Moment of Violence. Knopf, 1961; Hammond, 1962
Mrs. Murdock Takes a Case. Knopf, 1941
Murder for the Asking. Knopf, 1939
Murder for Two. Knopf, 1943
Murder in Havana. Knopf, 1943
Murder on Their Minds. Knopf, 1957; Hammond, 1958; Dell, 1959
Murder with Pictures. Knopf, 1935
Never Bet Your Life. Knopf, 1952; Hammond, 1955
No Time to Kill. Knopf, 1941
Nobody Wants Julia; see Uninvited Guest
One Hour to Kill. Knopf, 1963; Hammond, 1964; Pyramid, 1965
One Minute Past Eight. Knopf, 1957; Hammond, 1959
One Murder Too Many. Pyramid, 1967
One Way Out. Knopf, 1960; Hammond, 1966; Pyramid, 1967
The Reluctant Heiress. Knopf, 1965
The Ring of Truth. Knopf, 1966
Silent Are the Dead. Knopf, 1942
Slack Tide. Knopf, 1959; Hammond, 1960
Suddenly a Widow. Knopf, 1956; Hammond, 1957
Top Assignment. Knopf, 1955; Hammond, 1957
Triple Exposure: The Glass Triangle, The Jade Venus, and The Fifth Key. Knopf, 1959
Uninvited Guest. Knopf, 1953; Hammond, 1956 (Serial title: Nobody Wants Julia)
Venturous Lady. Knopf, 1948
The Widow Had a Gun. Knopf, 1951; Hammond, 1954
With Intent to Kill. Knopf, 1965; Hammond, 1966; Pyramid, 1967
Woman at Bay. Knopf, 1945

COXE, KATHLEEN BUDDINGTON, pseud; see LONG, AMELIA REYNOLDS

COZZENS, JAMES GOULD (S)
The Just and the Unjust. Harcourt, 1942

CRABB, ARTHUR, pseud. (D)
Ghosts. Century, 1921
Samuel Lyle, Criminologist. Century, 1920

CRAGG, E. H. (D)
Almack the Detective. Literary Society, 1887

CRAIG, JONATHAN (D) (Pseud. of Frank E. Smith)
Alley Girl. Lion, 1954
Case of the Beautiful Body. GM, 1957
Case of the Brazen Beauty. GM, 1966
Case of the Cold Coquette. GM, 1957
Case of the Laughing Virgin. GM, 1961
Case of the Nervous Nude. GM
Case of the Petticoat Murder. Fawcett, 1958; GM
Case of the Silent Stranger. Fawcett, 1964
Case of the Village Tramp. GM, 1959
Come Night, Come Evil. GM, 1957
The Dead Darling. GM, 1956
Morgue for Venus. GM, 1956
So Young, So Wicked. GM, 1957

CRAM, MILDRED (S)
Stranger Things. Dodd, 1924

CRANDALL, EDWARD (S)
White Violets. Little, 1953; Paperback Lib., 1965

CRANE, MRS. FRANCES KIRKWOOD (D)
Amber Eyes. Random, 1963
The Amethyst Spectacles. Random, 1944; Bantam
The Applegreen Cat. Lippincott, 1943
Black Cypress. Random, 1948
Buttercup Case. Hammond, 1958; Random, 1959

The Cinnamon Murder. Random, 1946
Coral Princess Murders. Random, 1954; Hammond, 1955
The Daffodil Blonde. Hammond, 1951
Death in Lilac Time. Random, 1955; Hammond, 1960
Death in the Blue Hour, see Murder in Blue Street
Death Wish Green. Hammond, 1960; Random, 1960
The Flying Red Horse. Random, 1949
The Golden Box. Hammond, 1944
The Gray Stranger; see Man in Gray
Horror on the Ruby X. Hammond, 1956; Random, 1956
The Indigo Necklace. Random, 1945
Man in Gray. Random, 1958 (English title: The Gray Stranger. Hammond, 1958)
Murder in Blue Street. Random, 1951 (English title: Death in the Blue Hour. Hammond, 1952)
Murder in Bright Red. Random, 1953; Hammond, 1959
Murder on the Purple Water. Random, 1947; Bantam
Pink Umbrella. Lippincott, 1943
The Polkadot Murder. Random, 1951
The Reluctant Sleuth. Hammond, 1961
The Shocking Pink Hat. Random, 1946; Hammond, 1948
Thirteen White Tulips. Random, 1953
Three Days in Hong Kong. Hammond, 1965
The Turquoise Shop. Lippincott, 1941; Hammond, 1943
The Ultraviolet Widow. Random, 1956; Hammond, 1957
A Very Quiet Murder. Hammond, 1966
Thirteen White Tulips. Hammond, 1953; Random, 1953
The Yellow Violet. Lippincott, 1943; Hammond, 1944

CRANE, ROBERT (S)
Operation Vengeance. Pyramid, 1965
Paradise Trap. Pyramid, 1967
Strikeback. Pyramid, 1965
Tongue of Treason. Pyramid, 1967

CRANSTON, CLAUDIA (D)
Murder Maritime. Lippincott, 1935
The Murder on Fifth Avenue. Lippincott, 1934

CRANSTON, MAURICE (S)
Philosopher's Hemlock. Westhouse, 1946
Tomorrow We'll Be Sober. Westhouse, 1946

CRAUFORD, WILLIAM HENRY LANE (M)
Almost a Lady. Ward, Lock, 1939
And Then a Boy. Ward, Lock, 1936
And Then There Were Nine. Ward, Lock, 1945
Another Woman's Poison. Ward, Lock, 1945
An Apple a Day. Ward, Lock, 1939
The Bride Wears Black. Ward, Lock, 1948
Cat Dies First. Ward, Lock, 1955
Clothes and the Man. Ward, Lock, 1947
Crimson Mask. Ward, Lock, 1932
A Date with Death. Ward, Lock, 1947
The Dearly Beloved Wives. Ward, Lock, 1953
Dogs in Clover. Ward, Lock, 1933
Drakmere Must Die. Ward, Lock, 1950
Elementary, My Dear Freddie. Ward, Lock, 1950
Final Curtain. Ward, Lock, 1933
Fly Away, Peter. Ward, Lock, 1937
Follow the Lady. Ward, Lock, 1932
Gentlemen, the Queen. Ward, Lock, 1942
Goodbye, George. Ward, Lock, 1940
Hawkmoor Mystery. Ward, Lock, 1932
Imperfect Gentlemen. Ward, Lock, 1935
The Ivory Goddess. Ward, Lock, 1954
Joseph Proctor's Money. Ward, Lock, 1948
Missing Ace. Ward, Lock, 1931
Money for Jam. Ward, Lock, 1946
Murder of a Dead Man. Ward, Lock, 1952
Murder to Music. Ward, Lock, 1936
One Man's Meat. Ward, Lock, 1952
Ravencraft Mystery. Ward, Lock, 1934
Smooth Killing. Ward, Lock, 1949
Till Murder Do Us Part. Ward, Lock, 1949
Where Is Jenny Willet? Ward, Lock, 1953

CRAWFORD, F. MARION (S)
Mr. Issacs. Macmillan, 1882
Uncanny Tales. Unwin, 1957
Upper Berth. Putnam, 1894

CRAWFORD, JACK RANDALL (D)
The Philosopher's Murder Case. Sears, 1931; Long, 1932

CRAWFORD, OSWALD (D) (Pseudonym: George Ira Brett)
League of the White Hand. Chapman, 1909
Revelations of Inspector Morgan. Chapman, 1906; Dodd, 1907

CRAWFORD, STANLEY (S)
Gascoyne. Putnam, 1966

CRAWLEY, J. COOPER (M)
Investment in Crime. Boardman, T. V., 1957
My Rubies Are Blood Red. Boardman, T. V., 1957

CRAWLEY, RAYBURN (S)
The Chattering Gods. Harper, 1931
The Valley of Creeping Men. Harper, 1930

CREASEY, JOHN (M-D-S) (Pseudonyms: Gordon Ashe, M. E. Cooke, Norman Deane, Robert Caine Frazer, Patrick Gill, Michael Halliday, Charles Hogarth, Brian Hope, Colin Hughes, Kyle Hunt, Abel Mann, Peter Manton, J. J. Marric, Richard Martin, Anthony Morton, Jeremy York)
Accident for Inspector West. Hodder, 1957 (U.S. title: Hit and Run. Scribner, 1959)
Accuse the Toff. Long, 1943
Affair for the Baron, by Anthony Morton. Hodder, 1967; Walker & Co., 1968
Alias Blue Mask; see Alias the Baron
Alias the Baron, by Anthony Morton. Low, 1939 (U.S. title: Alias Blue Mask. Lippincott, 1939)
Attack the Baron, by Anthony Morton. Low, 1951
Bad for the Baron, by Anthony Morton. Hodder, 1962 (U.S. title: The Baron and the Stolen Legacy. Scribner,1967)
The Baron Again, by Anthony Morton. Low, 1938 (U.S. title: Salute Blue Mask. Lippincott, 1938)
The Baron and the Beggar, by Anthony Morton. Low, 1947; Duell, 1950
The Baron and the Chinese Puzzle, by Anthony Morton. Hodder, 1965; Scribner, 1965; Avon, 1967
The Baron and the Missing Old Masters, by Anthony Morton. Hodder, 1967
The Baron and the Mogul Swords; see A Sword for the Baron
The Baron and the Stolen Legacy; see Bad for the Baron
The Baron at Bay; see Blue Mask at Bay
The Baron at Large, by Anthony Morton. Low, 1939 (U.S. title: Challenge Blue Mask. Lippincott, 1939)
The Baron Branches Out; see A Branch for the Baron
The Baron Comes Back, by Anthony Morton. Long, 1943
The Baron Goes East, by Anthony Morton. Low, 1953
The Baron Goes Fast, by Anthony Morton. Hodder, 1954
The Baron in France, by Anthony Morton. Hodder, 1953
The Baron on Board, by Anthony Morton. Hodder, 1964; Walker & Co., 1968
The Baron Returns; see The Return of Blue Mask
A Battle for Inspector West. Paul, S., 1948
The Battle for the Cup, by Patrick Gill. Mellifont, 1938
A Beauty for Inspector West. Hodder, 1954; Musson, 1954 (U.S. titles: The Beauty Queen Killer. Harper, 1954; Berkley Pub., 1965 and So Young, So Cold, So Fair. Dell, 1958)
The Beauty Queen Killer; see A Beauty for Inspector West
The Big Call, by Gordon Ashe. Long, 1964
Black for the Baron, by Anthony Morton. Hodder, 1959 (U.S. title: If Anything Happens to Hester. Doubleday, 1962; Avon, 1966)
The Black Heart. Gramol
The Black Spiders. Hodder, 1957
Blame the Baron, by Anthony Morton. Low, 1949; Duell, 1951
The Blight. Hodder, 1968; Walker & Co., 1968
The Blind Spot; see Inspector West at Bay
Blood Red; see Red Eye for the Baron
Blue Mask at Bay, by Anthony Morton. Lippincott, 1938; Scribner, 1967 (English title: The Baron at Bay. Low, 1939)
Blue Mask Strikes Again; see Versus the Baron
Blue Mask Victorious; see Call for the Baron
Books for the Baron, by Anthony Morton. Low, 1949; Duell, 1952
A Branch for the Baron, by Anthony Morton. Hodder, 1961 (U.S. title: The Baron Branches Out. Scribner, 1967)
A Bundle for the Toff. Hodder, 1967; Walker & Co., 1968
By Persons Unknown, by Jeremy York. Bles, 1942
Call for the Baron, by Anthony Morton. Low, 1940 (U.S. title: Blue Mask Victorious. Lippincott, 1940)
Call the Toff. Hodder, 1953
Career for the Baron, by Anthony Morton. Low, 1946; Duell, 1950
Carriers of Death. Melrose, 1937
The Case Against Paul Raeburn; see Triumph for Inspector West
A Case for Inspector West. Evans, 1951 (U.S. title: The Figure in the Dusk. Harper, 1953)
A Case for the Baron, by Anthony Morton. Low, 1945; Duell, 1949
The Case of the Acid Throwers; see Inspector West at Bay
The Case of the Innocent Victims. Hodder, 1960; Scribner, 1966; Berkley Pub., 1967
The Case of the Mad Inventor. Amalgamated Press (Sexton Blake series)
The Case of the Murdered Financier. Amalgamated Press (Sexton Blake series)
Cat and Mouse, by Michael Halliday. Hodder, 1955 (U.S. title: Hilda, Take Heed, by Jeremy York. Scribner, 1957)

Challenge Blue Mask; see The Baron at Large
The Charity Murders, by Peter Manton. Wright & Brown, 1954
The Children of Despair; see The Children of Hate
The Children of Hate. Evans, 1952 (Also published as: The Children of Despair. Jay)
The Cinema Crimes. Pemberton, 1945
The Circle of Justice, by Peter Manton. Wright & Brown, 1931
Close the Door on Murder, by Jeremy York. Melrose, 1948
A Clutch of Coppers, by Gordon Ashe. Long, 1967
Come Here and Die; see Death of a Stranger
Come Home to Crime, by Norman Deane. Hurst, 1945
Come Home to Death, by Gordon Ashe. Long, 1958 (U.S. title: Pack of Lies. Doubleday, 1959)
The Creepers; see Inspector West Cries Wolf
The Crime Haters, by Gordon Ashe. Doubleday, 1960; Long, 1961
The Crime Syndicate, by Peter Manton. Wright & Brown, 1939
The Crime with Many Voices, by Michael Halliday. Paul, S., 1945
The Crooked Killer, by Peter Manton. Wright & Brown, 1954
Cruel as a Cat, by Michael Halliday. Hodder, 1968)
Cry for the Baron, by Anthony Morton. Low, 1950
Cunning as a Fox, by Michael Halliday. Paul, S., 1945 (U.S. edition by Kyle Hunt, Macmillan, 1965)
Danger for the Baron, by Anthony Morton. Hodder, 1953
Danger Woman, by Abel Mann. PB, 1964
Dangerous Journey, by Norman Deane. Hurst, 1939
The Dangerous Quest. Long, 1944
The Dark Circle, by Gordon Ashe. Evans, 1950
Dark Harvest. Long, 1947
Dark Mystery, by Gordon Ashe. Long, 1948
Dark Peril. Paul, S., 1944
Dawn of Darkness. Long, 1949
Day of Fear, by Gordon Ashe. Long, 1956
The Day of Disaster. Long, 1942
Days of Danger. Melrose, 1937
Dead or Alive. Evans, 1951
Deaf, Dumb and Blonde; see Nest Egg for the Baron
Death by Night. Long, 1940
The Death Drive, by M. E. Cooke. Mellifont, 1936
Death from Below, by Gordon Ashe. Long, 1963; Holt, 1968
Death in a Hurry, by Gordon Ashe. Evans, 1952
Death in Cold Print. Hodder, 1961; Scribner, 1962; Berkley Pub., 1965
Death in Diamonds, by Gordon Ashe. Evans, 1951
Death in Flames, by Gordon Ashe. Long, 1943
Death in High Places, by Gordon Ashe. Long, 1942
Death in the Rising Sun. Long, 1945
Death in the Spanish Sun, by Norman Deane. Hurst, 1954; Dell, 1968 (1968 edition by Michael Halliday)
Death in the Trees, by Gordon Ashe. Long, 1954 (Also published as: You've Bet Your Life. Ace, 1957)
Death Looks On, by Peter Manton. Wright & Brown, 1939
The Death Miser. Melrose, 1932
Death of a Postman; see Parcels for Inspector West
Death of a Racehorse. Hodder, 1959; Scribner, 1962; Berkley Pub., 1963
Death of a Stranger, by Michael Halliday. Hodder, 1957 (U.S. title: Come Here and Die, by Jeremy York. Scribner, 1959)
Death of an Assassin; see A Prince for Inspector West
Death on Demand, by Gordon Ashe. Long, 1939
Death on the Move, by Gordon Ashe. Long, 1945
Death out of Darkness, by Michael Halliday. Hodder, 1954; Musson, 1954
Death Round the Corner. Melrose, 1935
Death Stands By. Long, 1938
Death to My Killer, by Jeremy York. Melrose, 1952; Macmillan, 1966
The Department of Death. Evans, 1949
The Depths. Hodder, 1963; Walker & Co., 1966
Dine with Murder, by Michael Halliday. Evans, 1950
The Dissemblers; see A Puzzle for Inspector West
Documents of Death. Mellifont, 1939
A Doll for the Toff. Hodder, 1963; Walker & Co., 1965
Don't Let Him Kill, by Gordon Ashe. Long, 1960 (U.S. title: The Man Who Laughed at Murder. Doubleday, 1960)
Doorway to Death; see Find Inspector West
Double for Death, by Gordon Ashe. Long, 1954
Double for Murder, by Norman Deane. Hurst, 1951
Double for the Toff. Hodder, 1959; Pyramid, 1965; Walker & Co., 1965
The Double Frame; see Frame the Baron
Drop Dead; see The Long Search

The Drought. Hodder, 1959; Walker & Co., 1967 (Also published as: Dry Spell. Four Square, 1967)
Dry Spell; see The Drought
The Dying Witnesses, by Michael Halliday. Evans, 1949
The Edge of Terror, by Michael Halliday. Hodder, 1961 (U.S. edition by Jeremy York. Macmillan, 1963)
Elope to Death, by Gordon Ashe. Long, 1959
The Enemy Within. Evans, 1950
Engagement with Death, by Gordon Ashe. Long, 1948
The Executioners. Hodder, 1967; Scribner, 1967
The Famine. Hodder, 1967; Walker & Co., 1968
Feathers for the Toff. Long, 1945
The Figure in the Dusk; see A Case for Inspector West
Find Inspector West. Hodder, 1957 (U.S. titles: The Trouble at Saxby's. Harper, 1959 and Doorway to Death. Berkley Pub., 1961)
Find the Body, by Jeremy York. Melrose, 1945; Macmillan, 1967
Fire of Death, by M. E. Cooke. Fiction House, 1936
First a Murder, by Michael Halliday. Paul, S., 1948
First Came a Murder. Melrose, 1934
Five to Kill, by Michael Halliday. Paul, S., 1943
The Flood. Hodder, 1956
Follow the Toff. Hodder, 1961; Walker & Co., 1967
Fool the Toff; see Foul Play Suspected
The Foothills of Fear. Hodder, 1961
Foul Play Suspected, by Michael Halliday. Paul, S., 1942 (Also published as: Fool the Toff. Evans, 1950; Walker & Co., 1966)
Four Find Danger, by Michael Halliday. Cassell, 1937
Four Motives for Murder, by Brian Hope. Newnes, 1938
Four of the Best. Hodder, 1955
Frame the Baron, by Anthony Morton. Hodder, 1957 (U S. title: The Double Frame. Doubleday, 1961; Avon, 1966)
The Gallows Are Waiting, by Jeremy York. Melrose, 1949
The Gateway to Escape, by Norman Deane. Hurst, 1944
The Gelignite Gang; see Inspector West Makes Haste
The Gideon Omnibus, by J. J. Marric. Hodder, 1964 (Contains: Gideon's Day, Gideon's Night and Gideon's Week)
Gideon's Badge, by J. J. Marric. Harper & Row, 1966; Hodder, 1966
Gideon's Day, by J. J. Marric. Harper, 1955; Hodder, 1955; Berkley Pub., 1964
Gideon's Fire, by J. J. Marric. Harper, 1961; Hodder, 1961; Signet, 1967
Gideon's Lot, by J. J. Marric. Harper & Row, 1965; Hodder, 1965; Berkley Pub., 1966
Gideon's March, by J. J. Marric. Harper, 1962; Hodder, 1962; Berkley Pub., 1963
Gideon's Month, by J. J. Marric. Harper, 1958; Hodder, 1958; Berkley Pub., 1965
Gideon's Night, by J. J. Marric. Harper, 1957; Hodder, 1957; Berkley Pub., 1965
Gideon's Ride, by J. J. Marric. Harper & Row, 1963; Hodder, 1963; Berkley Pub., 1964
Gideon's Risk, by J. J. Marric. Harper, 1960; Hodder, 1960; Signet, 1967
Gideon's River, by J. J. Marric. Harper & Row, 1968; Hodder, 1968
Gideon's Staff, by J. J. Marric. Harper, 1959; Hodder, 1959
Gideon's Vote, by J. J. Marric. Harper & Row, 1964; Hodder, 1964
Gideon's Week, by J. J. Marric. Harper, 1956; Hodder, 1956; Pyramid, 1963 (Also published as: Seven Days to Death)
Gideon's Wrath, by J. J. Marric. Harper & Row, 1967; Hodder, 1967
The Girl with the Leopard-Skin Bag; see How Many to Kill?
Give a Man a Gun; see A Gun for Inspector West
Give Me Murder, by Gordon Ashe. Long, 1947
Go Ahead with Murder, by Michael Halliday. Hodder, 1960 (U.S. title: Two for the Money, by Jeremy York. Doubleday, 1962)
Go Away, Death. Long, 1941
Golden Death, by Norman Deane. Hurst, 1952
The Great Air Swindle. Amalgamated Press (Sexton Blake series)
The Greyvale School Mystery, by Peter Manton. Low, 1937
A Gun for Inspector West. Hodder, 1953 (U.S. title: Give a Man a Gun. Harper, 1954; Berkley Pub., 1963)
A Hammer in His Hand. Black, 1960
Hammer the Toff. Long, 1947
Hang the Little Man. Hodder, 1963; Scribner, 1964; Berkley Pub., 1966
Hate to Kill, by Michael Halliday. Hodder, 1962 (Also by Jeremy York)
Heir to Murder, by Michael Halliday. Paul, S., 1940
Help from the Baron, by Anthony Morton. Hodder, 1955

Here Comes the Toff. Long, 1940; Walker & Co., 1967
Here Is Danger, by Gordon Ashe. Long, 1946
The Hidden Hoard. Mellifont
Hide and Kill, by Jeremy York. Long, 1959; Scribner, 1960
Hide the Baron, by Anthony Morton. Hodder, 1956
Hilda, Take Heed; see Cat and Mouse
Hit and Run; see Accident for Inspector West
Holiday for Inspector West. Paul, S., 1946
Hollywood Hoax, by Robert Caine Frazer. PB, 1961
The Hounds of Vengeance. Long, 1945
The House of the Bears. Long, 1947
How Many to Kill?, by Michael Halliday. Hodder, 1960 (U.S. title: The Girl with the Leopard-Skin Bag, by Jeremy York. Scribner, 1961)
Hunt the Toff. Evans, 1952
The Hypnotic Demon, by M. E. Cooke. Fiction House, 1932
I Am the Withered Man, by Norman Deane. Hurst, 1941
If Anything Happens to Hester; see Black for the Baron
Incense of Death, by Norman Deane. Hurst, 1954
The Inferno. Hodder, 1965; Walker & Co., 1966
Inspector West Alone. Evans, 1950
Inspector West at Bay. Evans, 1952 (U.S. titles: The Blind Spot. Harper, 1954; Berkley Pub., 1965 and The Case of the Acid Throwers. Avon, 1960)
Inspector West at Home. Paul, S., 1944; Long, 1949
Inspector West Cries Wolf. Evans, 1950 (U.S. title: The Creepers. Harper, 1952)
Inspector West Kicks Off. Paul, S., 1949
Inspector West Leaves Town. Paul, S., 1943
Inspector West Makes Haste. Hodder, 1955 (U.S. titles: The Gelignite Gang. Harper, 1956 and Night of the Watchman. Berkley Pub.)
Inspector West Regrets. Paul, S., 1945
Inspector West Takes Charge. Paul, S., 1942
Intent to Murder, by Norman Deane. Hurst, 1948
Introducing Mr. Brandon, by Anthony Morton. Low, 1944
Introducing the Toff. Long, 1938
Invitation to Adventure, by Gordon Ashe. Long, 1945
The Island Flight Mystery. Long, 1940
The Island of Peril. Long, 1940
The Jungle Flight Mystery. Low, 1936
Keys to Crime, by Richard Martin. Earl, 1947
The Kidnapped Child, by Gordon Ashe. Long, 1958 (Also published as: The Snatch. Corgi, 1965)
Kill a Wicked Man, by Kyle Hunt. S & S, 1957; Barker, 1958
Kill My Love, by Kyle Hunt. S & S, 1958; Boardman, T. V., 1959
Kill Once, Kill Twice, by Kyle Hunt. S & S, 1956; Barker, 1957
Kill or Be Killed, by Gordon Ashe. Evans, 1950
Kill the Toff. Evans, 1950; Walker & Co., 1966
The Killing Strike; see Strike for Death
A Kind of Prisoner. Hodder, 1954
A Knife for the Toff. Evans, 1951; Pyramid, 1964
The Lame Dog Murder, by Michael Halliday. Evans, 1952
The League of Dark Men. Paul, S., 1947
The League of Light. Evans, 1949
Leave It to the Toff. Hodder, 1963; Pyramid, 1965
The Legion of the Lost. Long, 1943
Lend a Hand to Murder, by Michael Halliday. Paul, S., 1947
Let's Kill Uncle Lionel, by Jeremy York. Melrose, 1947
The Long Search, by Gordon Ashe. Long, 1953 (Also published as: Drop Dead. Ace, 1954)
Look at Murder, by Norman Deane. Hurst, 1952
Look Three Ways at Murder. Hodder, 1964; Scribner, 1965; Berkley Pub., 1966
Make-up for the Toff. Hodder, 1956; Walker & Co., 1967
The Man from Fleet Street. Amalgamated Press (Sexton Blake series)
The Man I Didn't Kill, by Norman Deane. Hurst, 1950; Dell, 1965 (1965 edition by Michael Halliday)
The Man I Killed, by Michael Halliday. Hodder, 1961 (U.S. edition by Jeremy York. Macmillan, 1963)
The Man in the Blue Mask; see Meet the Baron
Man on the Run, by Michael Halliday. Hodder, 1953
The Man Who Laughed at Murder; see Don't Let Him Kill
The Man Who Shook the World. Evans, 1950
The Man Who Stayed Alive, by Gordon Ashe. Long, 1955
Mark Kilby and the Miami Mob, by Robert Caine Frazer. PB, 1960 (Also published as: The Miami Mob. Collins, 1965)

Mark Kilby and the Secret Syndicate, by Robert Caine Frazer. PB, 1960 (Also published as: The Secret Syndicate. Collins, 1963)
Mark Kilby Solves a Murder, by Robert Caine Frazer. PB, 1959 (Also published as: R.I.S.C. Collins, 1962)
Mark Kilby Stands Alone, by Robert Caine Frazer. PB, 1962; Collins, 1965 (with The Miami Mob)
Mark Kilby Takes a Risk, by Robert Caine Frazer. PB, 1962
The Mark of the Crescent. Melrose, 1935
A Mask for the Toff; see The Toff Goes Gay
The Masked Gunman; see Who Was the Jester?
Meet the Baron, by Anthony Morton. Harrap, 1937 (U.S. title: The Man in the Blue Mask. Lippincott, 1937)
Men, Maids and Murder. Melrose, 1933
The Menace. Long, 1938
The Miami Mob; see Mark Kilby and the Miami Mob
Missing; see Missing from Home
Missing from Home. Hodder, 1959 (U.S. edition by Jeremy York. Scribner, 1960)
Missing or Dead, by Gordon Ashe. Evans, 1952
Mr. Quentin Investigates, by Anthony Morton. Low, 1943
The Mists of Fear. Hodder, 1955
Model for the Toff. Hodder, 1957; Pyramid, 1957
The Mountain of the Blind. Hodder, 1960
The Mountain Terror, by M. E. Cooke. Mellifont, 1937
The Moving Eye, by M. E. Cooke. Mellifont, 1934
Murder Ahead, by Norman Deane. Hurst, 1953
Murder Assured, by Michael Halliday. Hodder, 1958
Murder at End House, by Michael Halliday. Hodder, 1955
Murder at King's Kitchen, by Michael Halliday. Paul, S., 1943
Murder by the Way, by Michael Halliday. Paul, S., 1941
Murder Came Late, by Jeremy York. Melrose, 1946
Murder Comes Home, by Michael Halliday. Paul, S., 1940
Murder in the Family, by Jeremy York. Melrose, 1944
Murder in the Highlands, by Peter Manton. Wirght & Brown, 1939
Murder in the Stars, by Michael Halliday. Hodder, 1953
Murder-London-Australia. Hodder, 1965; Scribner, 1965; Berkley Pub., 1967
Murder-London-New York. Hodder, 1958; Scribner, 1961
Murder-London-South Africa. Hodder, 1966; Scribner, 1966; Berkley Pub., 1967
Murder Makes Murder, by Michael Halliday. Paul, S., 1946
Murder Manor, by Peter Manton. Wright & Brown, 1937
Murder Most Foul, by Gordon Ashe. Long, 1942
Murder Must Wait. Long, 1939
Murder on Largo Island, by Charles Hogarth. Selwyn, 1943
Murder on the Line. Hodder, 1960; Scribner, 1963; Berkley Pub., 1965
Murder 1, 2, 3; see Two for Inspector West
Murder Tips the Scales; see Two for Inspector West
Murder Too Late, by Gordon Ashe. Long, 1947
Murder Unseen, by Jeremy York. Bles, 1943
Murder Week-End, by Michael Halliday. Evans, 1950
Murder with Mushrooms, by Gordon Ashe. Evans, 1950
My Brother's Killer, by Jeremy York. Long, 1958; Scribner, 1959
The Mysterious Mr. Rocco. Mellifont, 1937
Mystery Centre Forward, by M. E. Cooke. Mellifont, 1939
Mystery Flight. Low, 1937
Mystery Motive, by Michael Halliday. Paul, S., 1947
Mystery of Blackmoor Prison. Mellifont, 1939
The Mystery Plane. Low, 1936
Nest Egg for the Baron, by Anthony Morton. Hodder, 1954 (U.S. title: Deaf, Dumb and Blonde. Doubleday, 1961; Avon, 1966)
Night of the Watchman; see Inspector West Makes Haste
No Alibi, by Jeremy York. Melrose, 1943
No Crime More Cruel, by Michael Halliday. Paul, S., 1944
No Darker Crime. Paul, S., 1943
No End to Danger, by Michael Halliday. Paul, S., 1948
No Escape from Murder, by Peter Manton. Wright & Brown, 1952
No Hurry to Kill, by Norman Deane. Hurst, 1950
No Need to Die, by Gordon Ashe. Long, 1956
No One's Last Crime, by M. E. Cooke. Fiction House, 1936

Out of the Shadows, by Michael Halliday. Hodder, 1954
Pack of Lies; see Come Home to Death
Panic! Long, 1939
Parcels for Inspector West. Hodder, 1956 (U.S. title: Death of a Postman. Harper, 1957; Berkley Pub., 1965)
Peril Ahead. Paul, S., 1946
The Perilous Country; see The Valley of Fear
Plague of Silence. British Book Centre, 1958; Hodder, 1958; Walker & Co., 1968
Play for Murder, by Norman Deane. Hurst, 1946
Poison for the Toff; see The Toff on Ice
The Poison Gas Robberies. Mellifont, 1940
Policeman's Dread. Hodder, 1962; Scribner, 1964; Berkley Pub., 1966
Policeman's Triumph, by Peter Manton. Wright & Brown, 1949
Prepare for Action. Paul, S., 1942
A Prince for Inspector West. Hodder, 1956 (U.S. title: Death of an Assassin. Scribner, 1960)
Private Carter's Crime. Amalgamated Press (Sexton Blake series)
A Promise of Diamonds, by Gordon Ashe. Dodd, 1964; Long, 1965
Prophet of Fire. Evans, 1951
A Puzzle for Inspector West. Evans, 1951 (Also published as: The Dissemblers. Scribner, 1967)
A Puzzle in Pearls, by Gordon Ashe. Long, 1949
Quarrel with Murder, by Michael Halliday. Evans, 1951
Quiet Fear, by Michael Halliday. Hodder, 1963 (U.S. edition by Jeremy York. Macmillan, 1968)
Quilt of Innocence, by Michael Halliday. Hodder, 1964
The Raven, by M. E. Chaber. Mellifont, 1936
Red-Eye for the Baron, by Anthony Morton. Hodder, 1958 (U.S. title: Blood Red. Doubleday, 1960)
Redhead. Hurst, 1934
The Return of Blue Mask, by Anthony Morton. Lippincott, 1937 (English title: The Baron Returns. Harrap, 1938)
Return to Adventure, by Norman Deane. Hurst, 1943
Reward for the Baron, by Anthony Morton. Low, 1945
A Rocket for the Toff. Hodder, 1960; British Book Centre, 1961; Pyramid, 1964
Rogues Rampant, by Gordon Ashe. Long, 1944
Rogues' Ransom, by Gordon Ashe. Doubleday, 1961; Long, 1962
A Rope for the Baron, by Anthony Morton. Low, 1948; Duell, 1949
Run Away to Murder, by Jeremy York. Melrose, 1947
Runaway, by Michael Halliday. Hodder, 1957
Sabotage. Long, 1941
Safari with Fear, by Jeremy York. Melrose, 1953
Salute Blue Mask; see The Baron Again
Salute for the Baron, by Anthony Morton. Hodder, 1960
Salute the Toff. Long, 1941
The Scene of the Crime. Hodder, 1961; Scribner, 1963; Berkley Pub., 1966
The Secret Aeroplane Mystery. Low, 1937
The Secret Errand, by Norman Deane. Hurst, 1939
The Secret Fortune, by M. E. Cooke. Fiction House, 1935
The Secret Murder, by Gordon Ashe. Long, 1940
The Secret Syndicate; see Mark Kilby and the Secret Syndicate
The Secret Supercharger, by Patrick Gill. Mellifont, 1940
Seeds of Murder, by Jeremy York. Paul, S., 1956; Scribner, 1958
Send Inspector West, with Jean Creasey. Hodder, 1953 (Also published as: Send Superintendent West. Pan, 1965)
Send Superintendent West; see Send Inspector West
Sentence of Death, by Jeremy York. Melrose, 1950; Macmillan, 1964
Seven Days to Death; see Gideon's Week
Seven Times Seven. Melrose, 1932
A Shadow of Death, by Gordon Ashe. Long, 1968
Shadow of Doom. Long, 1946
Shadow the Baron, by Anthony Morton. Low, 1951
The Sight of Death, by Jeremy York. Hodder, 1956; Scribner, 1956
The Silent House, by Norman Deane. Hurst, 1947
A Six for the Toff. Hodder, 1955
The Sleep. Hodder, 1964; Walker & Co., 1968
Sleepy Death, by Gordon Ashe. Long, 1953
Sly as the Serpent, by Michael Halliday. Hodder, 1967 (U.S. edition by Kyle Hunt. Macmillan, 1967)
The Snatch; see The Kidnapped Child
So Soon to Die, by Jeremy York. Scribner, 1958
So Young, So Cold, So Fair; see A Beauty for Inspector West
So Young to Burn. Hodder, 1968; Scribner, 1968
Sons of Satan. Long, 1948
The Speaker, by Gordon Ashe. Long, 1939

Sport for the Baron, by Anthony Morton. Hodder, 1966
Stand by for Danger, by Peter Manton. Wright & Brown, 1937
Stars for the Toff. Hodder, 1968; Walker & Co., 1968
The Stolen Formula Mystery, by M. E. Cooke. Mellifont, 1934
Strike for Death. Hodder, 1958 (U.S. title: The Killing Strike. Scribner, 1961)
Successful Alibi, by M. E. Cooke. Mellifont, 1936
A Sword for the Baron, by Anthony Morton. Hodder, 1963 (U.S. title: The Baron and the Mogul Swords. Scribner, 1966)
Take a Body, by Michael Halliday. Evans, 1951
A Taste of Treasure, by Gordon Ashe. Holt, 1966; Long, 1966
£10,000 Motor Rally Mystery, by Patrick Gill. Mellifont, 1939
The Terror: The Return of Dr. Palfrey. Hodder, 1962; Walker & Co., 1966
Terror by Day, by Gordon Ashe. Long, 1940
Terror for the Toff; see The Toff on the Farm
The Terror Trap. Melrose, 1936
There Goes Death, by Gordon Ashe. Long, 1942
Thicker Than Water, by Michael Halliday. Hodder, 1959 (U.S. edition by Jeremy York. Doubleday, 1962)
Thief in the Night, by Peter Manton. Wright & Brown, 1950
Three Days' Terror, by Peter Manton. Wright & Brown, 1938
Three for Adventure, by Michael Halliday. Cassell, 1937
Thunder in Europe. Melrose, 1936
To Kill a Killer, by Kyle Hunt. Boardman, T. V., 1960; Random, 1960
To Kill or Die; see To Kill or to Die
To Kill or to Die, by Jeremy York. Long, 1960; Melrose, 1964; Macmillan, 1966 (Also published as: To Kill or Die. Panther, 1965)
The Toff Among the Millions. Long, 1943; Hamilton, 1964
The Toff and the Curate. Long, 1944
The Toff and the Deep Blue Sea. Hodder, 1955; Walker & Co., 1967
The Toff and the Great Illusion. Long, 1944; Walker & Co., 1967
The Toff and the Kidnapped Child. Hodder, 1960; Walker & Co., 1965
The Toff and the Lady. Long, 1946
The Toff and Old Harry. Long, 1948
The Toff and the Runaway Bride. Hodder, 1959; Walker & Co., 1964; Pyramid, 1965
The Toff and the Spider. Hodder, 1965; Walker & Co., 1966
The Toff and the Stolen Tresses. Hodder, 1958; Pyramid, 1965; Walker & Co., 1965
The Toff and the Teds. Hodder, 1962 (U.S. title: The Toff and the Toughs. Walker & Co., 1968)
The Toff and the Toughs; see The Toff and the Teds
The Toff at Butlins. Hodder, 1954
The Toff at the Fair. Hodder, 1954
The Toff Breaks In. Long, 1940, 1955
The Toff Down Under. Hodder, 1953
The Toff Goes Gay. Evans, 1951 (U.S. title: A Mask for the Toff. Walker & Co., 1966; Pyramid, 1967)
The Toff Goes On. Long, 1939, 1955
The Toff Goes to Market. Long, 1942; Walker & Co., 1967
The Toff in New York. Hodder, 1956; Pyramid, 1964
The Toff in Town. Long, 1948
The Toff in Wax. Hodder, 1966; Walker & Co., 1966
The Toff Is Back. Long, 1942
The Toff on Board. Evans, 1949
The Toff on Fire. Hodder, 1957; Walker & Co., 1966
The Toff on Ice. Long, 1947 (U.S. title: Poison for the Toff. Pyramid, 1965)
The Toff on the Farm. Hodder, 1958; Walker & Co., 1964 (Also published as: Terror for the Toff. Pyramid, 1964)
The Toff Proceeds. Long, 1941; Walker & Co., 1968
The Toff Steps Out. Long, 1939
The Toff Takes Shares. Long, 1948
The Touch of Death. Hodder, 1954
Traitor's Doom. Long, 1943
Trap the Baron, by Anthony Morton. Low, 1950
Treasure Flight. Low, 1936
Triple Murder, by Colin Hughes. Newnes, 1940 (Also published as: What Dark Motive)
Triumph for Inspector West. Paul, S., 1948 (U.S. title: The Case Against Paul Raeburn. Harper, 1958)
The Trouble at Saxby's; see Find Inspector West
Two for Inspector West. Hodder, 1955 (U.S. titles: Murder 1, 2, 3. Scribner, 1960 and Murder Tips the Scales. Berkley Pub., 1962)
Two for the Money; see Go Ahead with Murder
Two Meet Trouble, by Michael Halliday. Cassell, 1938
Two Men Missing, by Gordon Ashe. Long, 1943
The Unknown Mission, by Norman Deane. Hurst, 1940
The Valley of Fear, with John Lock. Long, 1943 (Also published as: The Perilous Country. Long, 1949)

The Verrall Street Affair, by M. E. Cooke. Newnes, 1940
Versus Blue Mask; see Versus the Baron
Versus the Baron, by Anthony Morton. Low, 1940 (U.S. titles: Versus Blue Mask and Blue Mask Strikes Again. Lippincott, 1940)
Vote for Murder, by Richard Martin. Earl, 1948
Voyage with Murder, by Jeremy York. Melrose, 1952
Wait for Death, by Gordon Ashe. Long, 1957
'Ware Danger, by Gordon Ashe. Long, 1941
Warn the Baron, by Anthony Morton. Low, 1952
What Dark Motive; see Triple Murder
Where Is the Withered Man?, by Norman Deane. Hurst, 1942
Who Died at the Grange?, by Michael Halliday. Paul, S., 1942
Who Killed Rebecca?, by Michael Halliday. Paul, S., 1949
Who Said Murder?, by Michael Halliday. Paul, S., 1944
Who Saw Him Die?, by Michael Halliday. Paul, S., 1941
Who Was the Jester, by Gordon Ashe. Newnes, 1940 (Also published as: The Masked Gunman)
Why Murder?, by Norman Deane. Hurst, 1948
Wicked as the Devil, by Michael Halliday. Hodder, 1966 (U.S. edition by Kyle Hunt. Macmillan, 1966)
Wings of Peace. Long, 1948
The Withered Man, by Norman Deane. Hurst, 1940
Yesterday's Murder, by Jeremy York. Melrose, 1945
You've Bet Your Life; see Death in the Trees

CREED, SIBYL (M)
The Shot. Chatto, 1924; Doran, 1924

CREIGHTON, JOHN (M)
The Blond Cried Murder. Ace, 1961
A Half Interest in Murder. Ace, 1960
Not So Evil as Eve. Ace, 1957
Wayward Blonde. Ace, 1958

CRISP, FRANK ROBSON (S)
The Devil Diver. Coward, 1955
Fazackerley's Millions. Paul, S., 1957
Giant of Jembu Gulf. Hodder, 1959
The Golden Quest. Coward, 1954
The Haunted Reef. Coward, 1952
The Java Wreckmen. Coward, 1957
Manila Stranger. Long, 1957
The Sea Ape. Coward, 1960
Sea Robber. Coward, 1953
Treasure of Barby Swim. Coward, 1956

CRISPIN, EDMUND, pseud; see MONTGOMERY, ROBERT BRUCE

CROCKETT, ANTHONY (M)
Perimeter Fence. Hale, R., 1957
Toys of Desperation. Hale, R., 1960

CROCKETT, JAMES (D)
Lullaby with Lugers. Crown, 1946

CROFT, DESMOND WARRICK (M)
Frederick Lonton. Longmans, 1926

CROFT-COOKE, RUPERT (D) (Pseudonym: Leo Bruce)
At Death's Door, by Leo Bruce. Hamilton, H., 1955; British Book Centre, 1962
Barbary Night. Eyre, 1958
Bone and a Hank of Hair, by Leo Bruce. Davies, 1961; British Book Centre, 1962
Case for Sergeant Beef, by Leo Bruce. Nicholson, 1947
Case for Three Detectives, by Leo Bruce. Bles, 1935; Stokes, 1937
Case with Four Clowns, by Leo Bruce. Davies, 1939; Stokes, 1940
Case with No Conclusion, by Leo Bruce. Bles, 1939
Case with Ropes and Rings, by Leo Bruce. Nicholson, 1940
Case Without a Corpse, by Leo Bruce. Bles, 1937; Stokes, 1937
Cold Blood, by Leo Bruce. Gollancz, 1952
Crack of Doom, by Leo Bruce. Davies, 1963 (Also published as: Such Is Death. London House, 1963)
Dead for a Ducat, by Leo Bruce. Davies, 1956
Dead Man's Shoes, by Leo Bruce. Davies, 1958
Death at Hollow's End, by Leo Bruce. British Book Centre, 1966
Death at St. Asprey's School, by Leo Bruce. Allen, W. H., 1967
Death in Albert Park, by Leo Bruce. Allen, W. H., 1964
Death of Cold, by Leo Bruce. Davies, 1956
Die All, Die Merrily, by Leo Bruce. British Book Centre, 1961; Davies, 1961
Furious Old Women, by Leo Bruce. Davies, 1960
Jack on the Gallows Tree, by Leo Bruce. Davies, 1960
Louse for a Hangman, by Leo Bruce. Davies, 1959
Neck and Neck, by Leo Bruce. Gollancz, 1951
Nothing Like Blood, by Leo Bruce. Davies, 1962

Our Jubilee Is Death, by Leo Bruce. Davies, 1958
Seven Thunders. St. Martin's, 1955
Such Is Death; see Crack of Doom
Thief. Eyre, 1960; Doubleday, 1961

CROFTS, FREEMAN WILLS (D)
Affair at Little Wokeham. Hodder, 1943 (U.S. title: Double Tragedy. Dodd, 1943)
Antidote to Venom. Hodder, 1938; Dodd, 1939
Anything to Declare? Hodder, 1957
Box Office Murders. Collins, 1929
The Cask. Collins, 1920; Dodd, 1920; Penguin, 1946; Allen, W. H., 1967
The Cheyne Mystery; see Inspector French and the Cheyne Mystery
Circumstantial Evidence; see James Tarrant, Adventurer
The Crime at Guildford. Collins, 1935; Penguin, 1965 (U.S. title: The Crime at Nornes. Dodd, 1935)
The Crime at Nornes; see The Crime at Guildford
Crime on the Solent; see Mystery on Southampton Waters
Dark Journey; see French Strikes Oil
Death of a Train. Dodd, 1946; Penguin, 1965
Death on the Way. Doubleday, Doran, 1932
Double Tragedy; see Affair at Little Wokeham
Doubled Death. Harper, 1932
The End of Andrew Harrison. Hodder, 1938 (U.S. title: Futile Alibi. Dodd, 1938)
Enemy Unseen. Dodd, 1945; Hodder, 1945
Fatal Venture. Hodder, 1939; Penguin
Fear Comes to Chalfont. Dodd, 1942; Hodder, 1942
Found Floating. Dodd, 1937; Hodder, 1937
French Strikes Oil. Hodder, 1952 (U.S. title: Dark Journey. Dodd, 1951)
Future Alibi; see The End of Andrew Harrison
Golden Ashes. Dodd, 1940; Hodder, 1940; Penguin, 1965
Groote Park Murder. Collins, 1923; Seltzer, 1925; Burt, 1930
Hog's Back Mystery. Hodder, 1933 (U.S. title: The Strange Case of Dr. Earle. Dodd, 1933)
Inspector French and the Cheyne Mystery. Collins, 1926; Penguin, 1965 (U.S. title: The Cheyne Mystery. Burt, 1926)
Inspector French and the Starvel Hollow Tragedy. Collins, 1927; Penguin, 1946 (U.S. title: The Starvel Hollow Tragedy. Harper, 1927)
Inspector French's Greatest Case. Collins, 1924; Penguin, 1965
James Tarrant, Adventurer. Hodder, 1941 (U.S. title: Circumstancial Evidence. Dodd, 1941)
A Losing Game. Collins, 1941; Dodd, 1941; Popular Lib.
The Loss of the Jane Vosper. Collins, 1936; Dodd, 1936; Penguin, 1965
Man Overboard. Collins, 1936; Dodd, 1936
Many a Slip. Hodder, 1955
Mr. Hefton Murders. Vallancey, 1944
Murderers Make Mistakes. Hodder, 1947
Mystery in the Channel. Collins, 1931 (U.S. title: Mystery in the English Channel. Harper, 1931)
Mystery in the English Channel; see Mystery in the Channel
The Mystery of the Sleeping Car Express. Hodder, 1956
Mystery on Southampton Waters. Hodder, 1934 (U.S. title: Crime on the Solent. Dodd, 1934)
Omnibus. Collins, 1932
The Pit-Prop Syndicate. Collins, 1922; Seltzer, 1925; Penguin, 1965
The Ponson Case. Collins, 1921; Boni, 1927; Dodd, 1927
Purple Sickle Murders. Harper, 1929; Penguin
The Sea Mystery. Collins, 1928; Harper, 1928; Grosset, 1931; Penguin, 1965
Silence for the Murderer. Dodd, 1948; Hodder, 1949
Sir John Magill's Last Journey. Collins, 1930; Harper, 1930; Penguin, 1965
The Starvel Hollow Tragedy; see Inspector French and the Starvel Hollow Tragedy
The Strange Case of Dr. Earle; see Hog's Back Mystery
Sudden Death. Collins, 1932; Doubleday, Doran, 1932; Grosset, 1934
Tragedy in the Hollows. Dodd, 1939; Popular Lib.
Twelve-Thirty from Croydon. Hodder, 1934; Penguin, 1965 (U.S. title: Willful and Premeditated. Dodd, 1934)
Willful and Premeditated; see Twelve-Thirty from Croydon

CROMARTY, NOEL (S)
Blind Side. Hodder, 1951
Epitaph for Meredith. Hodder, 1953
Neither Had I Rest. Hodder, 1949

CROMBIE, MICHAEL (D)
The Frightened Girl. Arcadia, 1941

CRONIN, A. J. (S)
Beyond This Place. Gollancz, 1953; Bantam, 1964

CRONIN, BERNARD (M) (Pseudonyms: Dennis Adair, Eric North)
Chip on My Shoulder, by Eric North. Roy Pubs., 1956
Death Rides the Desert, by Dennis Adair. Hutchinson, 1940
Name Is Smith, by Eric North. Roy Pubs., 1957
Nobody Stops Me, by Eric North. Roy Pubs., 1960

CRONIN, BRENDAN LEO (S) (Pseudonyms: Michael Cronin, David Miles)
Ask for Trouble, by Michael Cronin. Hale, R., 1963
Begin with a Gun, by Michael Cronin. Walker & Co., 1960
Climb the Wall, by Michael Cronin. Museum Press, 1956; Washburn, 1957
Curtain Call, by Michael Cronin. Hale, R., 1961
The Dangerous Lady, by Michael Cronin. Hale, R., 1962
Dead, and Done With, by Michael Cronin. Hale, R., 1959
The Elusive Lady, by Michael Cronin. Hale, R., 1957
The Fast Exit, by Michael Cronin. Hale, R., 1962
I Can Cope, by Michael Cronin. Museum Press, 1955
The Last Indictment, by Michael Cronin. Hale, R., 1964
Leave It to Me, by Michael Cronin. Museum Press, 1953
The Loose End, by Michael Cronin. Hale, R., 1961
Loser Takes Nothing, Michael Cronin. Museum Press, 1955
Man at Large, by Michael Cronin. Hale, R., 1962
Murder Mislaid, by Michael Cronin. Hale, R., 1963
Night of the Party, by Michael Cronin. Hale, R., 1957; Washburn, 1958
No Sale, by Michael Cronin. Ward, Lock, 1950
Over the Edge, by David Miles. Hale, R., 1964
Pacific Pearl, by Michael Cronin. Museum Press, 1954
Paid in Full, by Michael Cronin. Museum Press, 1953
Pattern of Chalk, by David Miles. New Authors, 1966
The Second Bounce, by Michael Cronin. Hale, R., 1959
The Spanish Lady, by Michael Cronin. Hale, R., 1960
Strictly Legitimate, by Michael Cronin. Ward, Lock, 1951
Sweet Water, by Michael Cronin. Museum Press, 1957; Washburn, 1957
The Unquiet Night, by Michael Cronin. Hale, R., 1958
You Never Learn, by Michael Cronin. Museum Press, 1952
You Pay Your Money, by Michael Cronin. Museum Press, 1954

CRONIN, MICHAEL, pseud; see CRONIN, BRENDAN LEO

CROOKER, HERBERT (D)
Crime in Washington Mews. Macaulay, 1931
The Hollywood Murder Mystery. Macaulay, 1930

CROSBY, KINGSLAND (D)
The Strange Case of Eleanor Cuyler. Dodd, 1910

CROSBY, LEE, pseud; see TORREY, WARE

CROSS, AMANDA, pseud. (D)
In the Last Analysis. Gollancz, 1964; Macmillan, 1964; Avon, 1966
The James Joyce Murder. Macmillan, 1967

CROSS, BEVERLY (M)
The Nightwalkers. Little, 1957

CROSS, JAMES, pseud; see PARRY, HUGH JONES

CROSS, JOHN KEIR (S)
The Other Passenger. Westhouse, 1944; Ballantine, 1946

CROSS, MARK, pseud; see PECHEY, ARCHIBALD THOMAS

CROSSEN, KENDALL FOSTER (M-D) (Pseudonyms: Bennett Barlay, M. E. Chaber, Richard Foster, Christopher Monig, Clay Richards)
Abra-cadaver, by Christopher Monig. Boardman, T. V., 1958; Dutton, 1958; Dell, 1965
The Acid Nightmare, by M. E. Chaber. Holt, 1967
As Old as Cain, by M. E. Chaber. Holt, H., 1954
Bier for a Chaser, by Richard Foster. GM, 1958
The Big Dive. Dutton, 1958; Eyre, 1958
Blonde and Beautiful, by Richard Foster. Popular Lib., 1953
The Burned Man, by Christopher Monig. Dutton, 1957
The Case of the Curious Heel. 1944-1946
The Case of the Phantom Fingerprints. 1944-1946
The Day It Rained Diamonds, by M. E. Chaber. Holt, 1966

Death of an Angel, by Clay Richards. Bobbs, 1963
Gallows Garden, by M. E. Chaber. Rinehart, 1958 (Also published as: The Lady Came to Kill. PB)
The Gentle Assassin, by Clay Richards. Bobbs, 1964
The Girl from Easy Street, by Richard Foster. Popular Lib., 1952
Hangman's Harvest, by M. E. Chaber. Holt, H., 1951
A Hearse of Another Color, by M. E. Chaber. Boardman, T. V., 1959; PB, 1959; Rinehart, 1959
The Invisible Man Murders, by Richard Foster. 1944-1946
Jade for a Lady, by M. E. Chaber. Boardman, T. V., 1962; Holt, 1962
The Lady Came to Kill; see Gallows Garden
The Laughing Buddha Murders, by Richard Foster. 1944-1946
Lonely Graves, by Christopher Monig. Dutton, 1960
A Lonely Walk, by M. E. Chaber. Boardman, T. V., 1957; Rinehart, 1957
The Man in the Middle, by M. E. Chaber. Holt, 1967
The Man Inside, by M. E. Chaber. Holt, H., 1954
The Marble Jungle, by Clay Richards. Obolensky, 1961; Cassell, 1963
No Grave for March, by M. E. Chaber. Holt, H., 1952; Eyre, 1954
Once Upon a Crime, by Christopher Monig. Dutton, 1959
The Rest Must Die, by Richard Foster. GM, 1960
Satan Came Across, by Bennett Barlay. 1944-1946
Six Who Ran, by M. E. Chaber. Holt, 1964
So Dead the Rose, by M. E. Chaber. Rinehart, 1960
Softly in the Night, by M. E. Chaber. Boardman, T. V., 1963; Holt, 1963
The Splintered Man, by M. E. Chaber. Holt, H., 1955
Too Late for Mourning, by Richard Foster. GM, 1959
The Tortured Path. Dutton, 1957
Uneasy Lies the Dead, by M. E. Chaber. Boardman, T. V., 1964; Holt, 1964
Wanted: Dead Men, by M. E. Chaber. Holt, 1965
Who Steals My Name, by Clay Richards. Bobbs, 1964

CROWE, CECILY (S)
The Tower of Kilrayen. Holt, 1965; Signet, 1966

CRUMP, LOUISE ESKRIGGE (M)
The Face of Fear. Longmans, 1954

CRUNDEN, ALLEN B. and R. M. CRUNDEN (M)
Chicago Winter's Tale. Vantage, 1960

CRUNDEN, R. M.; see CRUNDEN, ALLEN B.

CULLEN, CARTER (S)
The Deadly Chase. Muller, 1958
Don't Get Caught. Muller, 1959

CULLINGFORD, GUY, pseud; see TAYLOR, CONSTANCE LINDSAY

CULLUM, RIDGWELL (M)
The Mystery of the Barren Lands. Cassell, 1928

CULPAN, MAURICE (D)
The Minister of Injustice. Walker & Co., 1966

CUMBERLAND, GERALD (S)
The Poisoner. Richards, 1921

CUMBERLAND, MARTEN (D) (Pseudonym: Kevin O'Hara)
Always Tell the Sleuth, by Kevin O'Hara. Hurst, 1954
And Here Is the Noose, by Kevin O'Hara. Long, 1959
And Then Came Fear. Doubleday, 1948; Hurst, 1949
And Worms Have Eaten Them; see Hate Will Find a Way
Attention Saturnin Dax. Hutchinson, 1962
Booked for Death; see Grave Consequences
The Charge Is Murder. Hurst, 1955
Confetti Can Be Red; see House in the Forest
The Crime School. Eldon, 1949
Customer's Always Wrong, by Kevin O'Hara. Hurst, 1951
Danger: Women at Work, by Kevin O'Hara. Long, 1958
The Dark House. Gramol, 1935
The Devil's Snare. Gramol, 1935
Dilemma for Dax. Doubleday, 1946 (English title: Hearsed in Death. Hurst, 1947)
Don't Neglect the Body, by Kevin O'Hara. Long, 1966
Don't Tell the Police, by Kevin O'Hara. Long, 1963
Etched in Violence. Hurst, 1955; McGraw, 1955
Everything He Touched. MacDonald & Co., 1945
Exit and Curtain, by Kevin O'Hara. Hurst, 1952
Fade Out the Stars. Doubleday, 1952
Far Better Dead. Hutchinson, 1957
The Frightened Brides. Hurst, 1955

Grave Consequences. Doubleday, 1952 (English title: Booked for Death. Hurst, 1947)
Hate Finds a Way. Hutchinson, 1964; Nelson, Foster & Scott, 1964
Hate for Sale. British Book Centre, 1957; Hutchinson, 1957
Hate Will Find a Way. Doubleday, 1947 (English title: And Worms Have Eaten Them. Hurst, 1948)
Hearsed in Death; see Dilemma for Dax
House in the Forest. Doubleday, 1950 (English title: Confetti Can Be Red. Hurst, 1951)
If Anything Should Happen, by Kevin O'Hara. Hurst, 1956
Imposter. Gramol, 1935
It Leaves Them Cold, by Kevin O'Hara. Hurst, 1956
Keep Your Fingers Crossed, by Kevin O'Hara. Hurst, 1955
The Knife Will Fall. Doubleday, Doran, 1944
A Lovely Corpse. Hurst, 1947
Lying at Death's Door. Hurst, 1956
The Man Who Covered Mirrors. Doubleday, 1949; Hurst, 1951
Murmurs in the Rue Morgue. British Book Centre, 1959; Hutchinson, 1959
No Sentiment for Murder. Hutchinson, 1966
Nobody Is Safe. Doubleday, 1953 (English title: Which of Us Is Safe? Hurst, 1954)
Not Expected to Live. Hurst, 1945
On the Danger List. Hurst, 1950
One Foot in the Grave. Hurst, 1952
Out of This World. Hutchinson, 1958
Pace That Kills, by Kevin O'Hara. Hurst, 1957
The Perilous Way. Jarrolds, 1926
Policeman's Nightmare. Doubleday, 1949
Postscript to a Death. Hutchinson, 1963
Questionable Shape. Hurst, 1941
Quislings over Paris. Hurst, 1942
Remains to Be Seen. Hutchinson, 1960
Shadowed. Mellifont, 1936
Sing, Clubman, Sing, by Kevin O'Hara. Hurst, 1952
Someone Must Die. Hurst, 1940
Steps in the Dark. Doubleday, Doran, 1945
Taking Life Easy, by Kevin O'Hara. Long, 1961
There Must Be Victims. Hutchinson, 1961
Unto Death Utterly. McGraw, 1955; Hurst, 1956
Well, I'll Be Hanged, by Kevin O'Hara. Long, 1960
Which of Us Is Safe?; see Nobody Is Safe
Women Like to Know, by Kevin O'Hara. Jarrolds, 1957

CUNNINGHAM, ALBERT BENJAMIN (M) (Pseudonym: Estil Dale)
The Affair at the Boat Landing. Dutton, 1943
The Bancock Murder Case. Dutton, 1942
The Cane Patch Mystery. Dutton, 1944
Death at "The Bottoms." Dutton, 1942
Death Haunts the Dark Lane. Dutton, 1948
Death of a Bullionaire. Dutton, 1947; Dell
Death of a Worldly Woman. Dutton, 1948
Death Rides a Sorrel Horse. Dutton, 1946
Death Visits the Apple Hole. Dutton, 1945
The Great Yant Mystery. Dutton, 1943; Swan, G. G., 1959
The Hunter Is the Hunted. Dutton, 1950
The Killer Watches the Manhunt. Dutton, 1950
The Last Survivor, by Estil Dale. Dutton, 1952
Murder at Deer Lick. Dutton, 1939
Murder at the Schoolhouse. Dutton, 1940
Murder Before Midnight. Dutton, 1945
Murder Without Weapons. Dutton, 1949
One Man Must Die. Dutton, 1946
The Skeleton in the Closet. Dutton, 1951
The Strange Death of Manny Square. Dutton, 1941
Strange Return. Dutton, 1952
Who Killed Pretty Becky Low? Dutton, 1951

CUNNINGHAM, E. V., pseud; see FAST, HOWARD

CUNNINGHAM, LOUIS ARTHUR (S)
Sign of the Burning Ship. Penn, 1940

CURLEY, THOMAS (M)
It's a Wise Child. Putnam, 1961 (Also published as: The Crooked Road. Avon, 1962)

CURRIE, BARTON and AUGUSTIN MCHUGH (M)
Officer 666. Fly, 1912; Burt, 1913

CURRIER, JAY L., pseud; see HENDERSON, JAMES LEAL

CURRY, AVON (M)
Derry Down Death. Allen, W. H., 1960

CURTIS, GEORGE and JOSEPHINE DENVER CURTIS (S)
Chivalry and the Gibbet. Devin-Adair, 1926

CURTIS, JEAN L. (M)
Lucifer's Dream. Lehmann, 1952

CURTIS, JOSEPHINE DENVER; see CURTIS, GEORGE

CURTIS, PETER, pseud; see LOFTS, NORA

CURTIS, ROBERT J.; see WALLACE, EDGAR

CURTIS, THOMAS, pseud; see PENDOWER, JACQUES

CURTIS, WARDON ALLAN (M)
Strange Adventures of Mr. Middleton. Stone, H. S., 1903

CURTISS, MRS. ELIZABETH MANGAM (D)
Dead Dogs Bite. S & S, 1939
Dead Man's Bite. S & S, 1939
Nine Doctors and a Madman. S & S, 1937

CURTISS, PHILIP EVERETT (S)
Gay Conspirators. Harper, 1924
Wanted: A Fool. Harper, 1920

CURTISS, URSULA (S)
Catch a Killer; see The Noonday Devil
Danger: Hospital Zone. Dodd, 1966
The Deadly Climate. Dodd, 1954; Ace, 1965
Face of the Tiger. Dodd, 1959; Eyre, 1960; Ace, 1962
The Forbidden Garden. Dodd, 1962; Ace, 1963; Eyre, 1963
Hours to Kill. Dodd, 1961; Ace, 1963 (Also published as: Stranger at the Wedding)
The Iron Cobweb. Dodd, 1953; Eyre, 1954; Ace, 1964
Looking for a Man; see The Noonday Devil
The Noonday Devil. Dodd, 1951; Eyre, 1957 (Also published as: Catch a Killer and Looking for a Man. PB)
Out of the Dark. Dodd, 1963; Ace, 1965
Second Sickle. Dodd, 1950
So Dies the Dreamer. Dodd, 1960; Eyre, 1961
The Stairway. Dodd, 1957; Eyre, 1958; Ace, 1962
Stranger at the Wedding; see Hours to Kill
Voice out of the Darkness. Dodd, 1948
The Wasp. Dodd, 1963; Eyre, 1964; Ace, 1965
Widow's Web. Dodd, 1956; Ace, 1965

CURZON, COLIN (D)
Body in the Barrage Ballroom. Macmillan, 1942
The Case of the Eighteenth Ostrich. Macmillan, 1944
Out of the Dark. Dodd, 1964

CURZON, SAM, pseud; see KRASNEY, SAMUEL A.

CUSHING, E. LOUISE (D)
Blood on My Rug. Arcadia, 1956
Murder Without Regret. Arcadia, 1954
Murder's No Picnic. Arcadia, 1953
Unexpected Corpse. Arcadia, 1957

CUSHMAN, CLARISSA FAIRCHILD (D)
I Wanted to Murder. Farrar & Rinehart, 1940
The Fatal Step. Little, 1953

CUSHMAN, DAN (S)
Jewel of the Java Sea. GM, 1951
Naked Ebony. GM, 1951
Opium Flower. Bantam, 1963
Port Orient. GM, 1955
Savage Interlude. Ace, 1954

DaCRUZ, DANIEL (S)
Vulcan's Hammer. New Amer. Lib., 1967

DAHL, ROALD (M)
Kiss, Kiss. Knopf, 1960; Dell, 1965
Someone Like You. Knopf, 1953; Dell, 1961

DAIGER, KATHERINE S. (D)
The Fourth Degree. Macrae Smith, 1931; Harrap, 1932
Murder on Ghost Tree Island. Macrae Smith, 1934

DAINGERFIELD, FOXHALL (M)
Ghost House. Appleton, D., 1926
House Across the Way. Appleton, D., 1928; Burt, 1930
Linden Walk Tragedy. Appleton, D., 1929
Silver Urn. Appleton, D., 1927
That Gay Nineties Murder. Doubleday, Doran, 1928
Wilderness House. Appleton, D., 1928

DALE, CELIA (S)
A Helping Hand. Walker & Co., 1966
A Spring of Love. Walker & Co., 1967

DALE, ESTIL, pseud; see CUNNINGHAM, ALBERT BENJAMIN

DALE, VIRGINIA (D)
They Waited for the Night. Doubleday, Doran, 1939

DALE, WILLIAM (D)
John Doe—Murderer. Gateway, 1942

Outside the Law. Dodge, 1938
Terror of the Headless Corpse. Gateway, 1939

DALL, JACK (M)
Death of a Revolutionist. Gateway, 1940

DALMAN, MAX (S)
The Elusive Nephew. Ward, Lock, 1948

DALMAS, HERBERT (M)
Exit Screaming. Walker & Co., 1966
The Fowler Formula. Doubleday, 1967

DALTON, MORAY (S)
Belfrey Murder. Low, 1933
Belgrave Manor Crime. Low, 1935; Ryerson, 1935
Black Death. Low, 1934
The Black Wings. Jarrolds, 1927
The Body in the Road. Harper, 1930; Burt, 1932; Collier
Case of Alan Copeland. Low, 1937
Death in the Cup. Low, 1932
Death in the Dark. Low, 1938
Death in the Forest. Low, 1939
Edge of Doom. Low, 1934
Harvest of Tares. Low, 1933
The Mystery of the Kneeling Woman. Low, 1936
The Night of Fear. Harper, 1931; Low, 1932; Burt, 1933
One by One They Disappeared. Harper, 1929; Jarrolds, 1929; Burt, 1933
The Price of Silence. Low, 1940
The Strange Case of Harriet Hall. Low, 1936
The Stretton Darkness Mystery. Jarrolds, 1927
The Wife of Baal. Low, 1932

DALTON, PRISCILLA, pseud; see AVALLONE, MICHAEL

DALY, CARROLL JOHN (D)
The Amateur Murderer. Washburn, 1933
The Emperor of Evil. Stokes, 1937
The Hidden Hand. Clode, 1929; Grosset, 1930; Hutchinson, 1930
The Man in the Shadows. Clode, 1928; Hutchinson, 1928
Mr. Strange. Stokes, 1936
Murder at Our House. Museum Press, 1950
Murder from the East. Stokes, 1935
Murder Won't Wait. Washburn, 1933
The Mystery of the Smoking Gun. Stokes, 1936
Ready to Burn. Museum Press, 1951
The Snarl of the Beast. Clode, 1927
The Tag Murders. Clode, 1930; Hutchinson, 1932
Tainted Power. Clode, 1931; Hutchinson, 1931
The Third Murderer. Farrar & Rinehart, 1931; Hutchinson, 1932
The White Circle. Clode, 1926

DALY, ELIZABETH (D)
And Dangerous to Know. Hammond, 1952
Any Shape or Form. Farrar & Rinehart, 1945; Hammond, 1949; Berkley Pub., 1964
Arrow Pointing Nowhere. Farrar & Rinehart, 1944; Hammond, 1946; Berkley Pub., 1962
The Book of the Crime. Rinehart, 1951; Hammond, 1954; Berkley Pub., 1964
The Book of the Dead. Farrar & Rinehart, 1944; Hammond, 1946; Berkley Pub., 1962
The Book of the Lion. Rinehart, 1948; Hammond, 1951; Berkley Pub., 1962
Deadly Nightshade. Farrar & Rinehart, 1940; Hammond, 1948; Berkley Pub., 1963
Death and Letters. Rinehart, 1950; Hammond, 1953; Berkley Pub., 1963
Evidence of Things Seen. Farrar & Rinehart, 1943; Hammond, 1946; Berkley Pub., 1962
The House Without the Door. Farrar & Rinehart, 1942; Hammond, 1945
Murders in Volume Two. Farrar & Rinehart, 1941; Eyre, 1943; Berkley Pub., 1962
Mystery Omnibus. Rinehart, 1960
Night Walk. Rinehart, 1947; Hammond, 1950; Berkley Pub., 1963
Nothing Can Rescue Me. Farrar & Rinehart, 1943; Hammond, 1945; Berkley Pub., 1963
Somewhere in the House. Rinehart, 1946; Hammond, 1949; Berkley Pub., 1963
The Street Has Changed. Farrar & Rinehart, 1941
Unexpected Night. Farrar & Rinehart, 1940; Gollancz, 1940; Berkley Pub., 1964
The Wrong Way Down. Rinehart, 1946; Hammond, 1950; Berkley Pub., 1963

DALY, MAUREEN (Mrs. William Peter McGivern) (M)
My Favorite Mystery Stories. Dodd, 1966

DAMER, ANNE and JOHN DENTON SCOTT (M)
Too Lively to Live. Doubleday, Doran, 1945

DANA, DOROTHY (D)
Murder's Web. Harper, 1950

DANA, FREEMAN (D)
Murder at the New York World's Fair. Random, 1938

DANA, MARVIN (M)
The Lake Mystery. McClurg, 1923
Master Mind. Fly, 1913; Grosset
The Mystery of the Third Parrot. McClurg, 1924

DANA, ROSE (S)
Nurse Freda. Macfadden, 1966

DANBY, FRANK, pseud; see FRANKAU, JULIA DAVIS

DANE, CLEMENCE, pseud; see ASHTON, WINIFRED

DANE, JOEL Y., pseud; see DELANY, JOSEPH FRANCIS

DANE, MARK, pseud; see AVALLONE, MICHAEL ANGELO, JR.

DANE, MARY, pseud; see MORLAND, NIGEL

DANIEL, GLYN E. (D) (Pseudonym: Dilwyn Rees)
The Cambridge Murders, by Dilwyn Rees. Gollancz, 1948; Penguin, 1954
Welcome Death. Gollancz, 1954; Dodd, 1955; Penn

DANIEL, ROBIN (M)
Death by Drowning. Gollancz, 1960; Walker & Co., 1961; Collier, 1963

DANIEL, ROLAND (D)
Again the Remover. Wright & Brown, 1939
Amber Eyes. Wright & Brown, 1935
Ann Turns Detective. Wright & Brown, 1932
The Arch-Criminal. Wright & Brown, 1933
Arrested for Murder. Wright & Brown, 1950
The Arrow of Death. Wright & Brown, 1951
At the Silver Butterfly. Wright & Brown, 1938
The Big Racket. Wright & Brown, 1955
The Big Squeal. Wright & Brown, 1940
The Black Eagle. Wright & Brown, 1950
The Black Market. Wright & Brown, 1943
The Black Raven. Wright & Brown, 1939
The Blackmailer. Wright & Brown, 1934
The Blonde Murder Case. Wright & Brown, 1939
The Brown Murder Case. Shaylor, 1930
Brunettes Are Dangerous. Wright & Brown, 1960
The Buddha's Secret. Wright & Brown, 1937
A Bunch of Crooks. Wright & Brown, 1946
The Case of the Blackmailed King. Mellifont, 1955
The Case of the King of Montavia. Wright & Brown, 1953
The Crackswoman. Wright & Brown, 1932
The Crawshay Jewel Mystery. Wright & Brown, 1941
The Crimson Shadow. Wright & Brown, 1935
Dangerous Moment. Wright & Brown, 1957
A Dead Man Sings. Wright & Brown, 1949
Dead Man's Corner. Wright & Brown, 1932
Dead Man's Vengeance. Shaylor, 1931
The Death House. Wright & Brown, 1941
The Desert Crime. Wright & Brown, 1946
The Doublecrosser. Wright & Brown, 1942
Double-Crossing Traitor. Wright & Brown, 1959
The Dragon's Claw. Wright & Brown, 1934
Evil Eyes. Wright & Brown, 1942
Evil Shadows. Wright & Brown, 1944
Frightened Eyes. Wright & Brown, 1956
The Gangster. Wright & Brown, 1932
The Gangster's Last Shot. Wright & Brown, 1939
The Girl by the Roadside. Wright & Brown, 1942
The Girl in the Dark. Wright & Brown, 1945
The Green Jade God. Wright & Brown, 1932
The Haughton Diamond Robbery. Wright & Brown, 1947
Human Vulture. Wright & Brown, 1939
The Hunchback of Soho. Wright & Brown, 1943
Husky Voice. Wright & Brown, 1932
It Happened at Night. Wright & Brown, 1952
The Jail-breakers. Wright & Brown, 1934
The Kenya Tragedy. Wright & Brown, 1948
The Killer. Wright & Brown, 1935
Killers Must Die. Wright & Brown, 1955
The Lady in Scarlet. Wright & Brown, 1947
The Langley Murder Case. Wright & Brown, 1938
The Little Old Lady. Wright & Brown, 1950

The 'Lo Sweeny Gang. Wright & Brown, 1935
Man from Paris. Wright & Brown, 1935
The Man from Prison. Wright & Brown, 1949
The Man Who Sold Secrets. Wright & Brown, 1948
The Man Who Sought Trouble. Wright & Brown, 1935
The Man with the Magnetic Eyes. Wright & Brown, 1938
The Millionaire Crook. Wright & Brown, 1944
The Missing Heiress. Wright & Brown, 1942
The Missing Lady. Wright & Brown, 1937
Mrs. Graystone-Murdered. Wright & Brown, 1947
Murder at a Cottage. Wright & Brown, 1949
Murder at Little Malling. Wright & Brown, 1946
The Murder Gang. Wright & Brown, 1954
Murder Goes Free. Wright & Brown, 1954
Murder in Dawson City. Wright & Brown, 1957
Murder in Piccadilly. Wright & Brown, 1950
Murder of a Bookmaker. Wright & Brown, 1953
Murder of Guy Thorpe. Wright & Brown, 1956
The Murphy Gang. Wright & Brown, 1934
The Mystery of Mary Hamilton. Wright & Brown, 1932
On the Run. Wright & Brown, 1955
The Professor. Wright & Brown, 1944
Quicksilver. Wright & Brown, 1953
Red Murchison. Wright & Brown, 1936
The Remover. Wright & Brown, 1933
The Remover Returns. Wright & Brown, 1935
The Return of Wu Fang. Wright & Brown, 1937
The River Gang. Wright & Brown, 1938
The Rosario Murder Case. Brentano, 1930
Ruby of a Thousand Dreams. Wright & Brown, 1933
Sally of the Underworld. Wright & Brown, 1934
Scarthroat. Wright & Brown, 1934
The Secret Hand. Wright & Brown, 1936
Shattered Hopes. Wright & Brown, 1941
The Shooting of Sergius Leroy. Wright & Brown, 1932
The Signal. Wright & Brown, 1932
Singapore Kate. Wright & Brown, 1943
Slant Eye. Wright & Brown, 1940
The Slayer. Wright & Brown, 1936
Slick-fingered Kate. Wright & Brown, 1936
Snake Face. Wright & Brown, 1936
The Snide Man. Wright & Brown, 1937
The Society of the Spiders. Brentano, 1928
The Son of Wu Fang. Wright & Brown, 1935
Spencer Blair, G-Man. Wright & Brown, 1949
The Spider's Web. Wright & Brown, 1943
The Stedman Gang. Wright & Brown, 1936
The Stolen Necklace. Wright & Brown, 1954
The Stool Pigeon. Wright & Brown, 1936
The Stop-at-Nothing-Man. Wright & Brown, 1950
Suicide Can Be Murder. Wright & Brown, 1956
This Woman Is Wanted. Wright & Brown, 1940
Three Sundays to Live. Wright & Brown, 1952
The Tipster. Wright & Brown, 1937
Trouble at the Inn. Wright & Brown, 1953
The Twenty-Two Windows. Wright & Brown, 1942
The Undercover Girl. Wright & Brown, 1951
White Eagle. Wright & Brown, 1933
Wu Fang. Brentano, 1929
Wu Fang's Revenge. Wright & Brown, 1934
The Yellow Devil. Wright & Brown, 1932
The "Z" Case. Wright & Brown, 1947

DANIELS, DOROTHY (M-Gothics)
Cliffside Castle. Lancer, 1965
Dance in Darkness. Lancer, 1965
Dark Villa. Lancer, 1966
Darkhaven. Paperback Lib., 1965
Knight in Red Armor. Lancer, 1966
The Lily Pond. Paperback Lib., 1965
Mansion of Lost Memories. Lancer, 1967
The Marble Leaf. Lancer, 1966
Marriott Hall. Paperback Lib., 1965
Midday Noon. Lancer, 1966
The Mistress of Falcon Hall. Pyramid, 1965
Mostly by Moonlight. Lancer
Nurse at Danger Mansion. Lancer, 1966
Shadow Glen. Paperback Lib., 1965
The Templeton Memoirs. Lancer
This Ancient Evil. Lancer
The Tower Room. Lancer
The Unguarded. Lancer, 1965

DANIELS, HAROLD R. (S-M)
The Accused. Dell, 1958; Deutsch, 1961
For the Asking. GM, 1963; Muller, 1963
The Girl in 304. Dell, 1956
The House on Greenapple Road. Random, 1966; Deutsch, 1967
In His Blood. Dell, 1955
The Snatch. Deutsch, 1960

DANIELS, NORMAN (S)
Arrest and Trial: The Missing Witness. Lancer, 1963
Baron of Hong Kong. Lancer, 1967
The Captive. Avon, 1960
The Deadly Game. Avon, 1959
The Hunt Club. Pyramid, 1964
The Mausoleum Key. Arcadia, 1960
The Missing Witness. Lancer, 1964
Operation "K." Pyramid, 1965
Operation "N." Pyramid, 1966
Operation "T." Pyramid, 1967 (The Man from A.P.E. series #7)
Operation "VC." Pyramid, 1967
Overkill. Pyramid, 1964
The Secret War. Pyramid, 1964
Some Die Running. Avon, 1960
Something Burning. GM, 1963
Spy Ghost. Pyramid, 1965
Spy Hunt. Pyramid, 1961
Suddenly by Shotgun. GM, 1961

DANNAY, FREDERIC and MANFRED LEE (D) (Pseudonyms: Ellery Queen, Barnaby Ross)
Adventure Omnibus. Grosset, 1941
The Adventures of Ellery Queen: Problems in Detection. Stokes, 1934; Gollancz, 1936; Grosset, 1940; Triangle, 1940; World Pub., 1947; Penguin, 1963
The American Gun Mystery: Death at the Rodeo, by Ellery Queen. Stokes, 1933; Gollancz, 1937; Blue Ribbon Books, 1940; Avon
And on the Eighth Day, by Ellery Queen. Gollancz, 1964; PB, 1964; Random, 1964
Beware the Young Stranger, by Ellery Queen. PB, 1965
The Bizarre Murders, by Ellery Queen. Lippincott, 1962 (Contains: The Siamese Twin Mystery, The Chinese Orange Mystery, and The Spanish Cape Mystery)
Blow Hot, Blow Cold, by Ellery Queen. PB, 1964
Calamity Town, by Ellery Queen. Gollancz, 1942; Little, 1942; Blakiston, 1947; Pan, 1960
Calendar of Crime, by Ellery Queen. Gollancz, 1952; Little, 1952 (Contains 12 stories)
The Case Book of Ellery Queen. Little, 1945; Gollancz, 1949 (Contains: The Adventures of Ellery Queen and The New Adventures of Ellery Queen)
Cat of Many Tails, by Ellery Queen. Gollancz, 1949; Little, 1949; PB, 1951
The Chinese Orange Mystery, by Ellery Queen. Stokes, 1934; Gollancz, 1935; PB, 1939; Blue Ribbon Books, 1941
The Copper Frame, by Ellery Queen. PB, 1965
Dead Man's Tale, by Ellery Queen. PB, 1961
Death Spins the Platter, by Ellery Queen. PB, 1962
The Devil to Pay, by Ellery Queen. Stokes, 1938; Gollancz, 1939; Blue Ribbon Books, 1941
The Devil's Cook, by Ellery Queen. PB, 1966
The Door Between, by Ellery Queen. Gollancz, 1937; Stokes, 1937; Blue Ribbon Books, 1941
Double, Double, by Ellery Queen. Gollancz, 1950; Little, 1950; Penguin, 1958; PB, 1965
The Dragon's Teeth, by Ellery Queen. Gollancz, 1939; Stokes, 1939; Grosset, 1941
Drury Lane's Last Case, by Barnaby Ross. Cassell, 1933; Viking, 1933; Little, 1946; Popular Lib., 1965 (1946 and 1965 editions by Ellery Queen)
The Dutch Shoe Mystery, by Ellery Queen. Gollancz, 1931; Stokes, 1931; Blue Ribbon Books, 1940
The Egyptian Cross Mystery, by Ellery Queen. Gollancz, 1932; Stokes, 1932; Blue Ribbon Books, 1940; PB, 1943; Penguin, 1962
Ellery Queen, Master Detective. Grosset, 1941 (Based on the film Ellery Queen, Master Detective)
Ellery Queen's Big Book. Grosset, 1938 (Contains: The Siamese Twin Mystery and The Greek Coffin Mystery)
Ellery Queen's International Case Book. Dell, 1964
Ellery Queen's Lethal Black Book. Dell, 1965
Ellery Queen's Mystery Parade. World Pub., 1944
Ellery Queen's Omnibus. Gollancz, 1934 (Contains: The French Powder Mystery, The Dutch Shoe Mystery, and The Greek Coffin Mystery)
Ellery Queen's Poetic Justice. Signet, 1967
Face to Face, by Ellery Queen. Gollancz, 1967; New Amer. Lib., 1967
The Finishing Stroke, by Ellery Queen. Gollancz, 1958; S & S, 1958; PB, 1959, 1963; New Amer. Lib., 1967
The Four Johns, by Ellery Queen. PB, 1964

The Four of Hearts, by Ellery Queen. Stokes, 1938; Gollancz, 1939; Grosset, 1940, 1943; American Mercury, 1941; Blue Ribbon Books, 1941; Triangle, 1941; PB, 1944
The Fourth Side of the Triangle, by Ellery Queen. Random, 1965; Gollancz, 1966
The French Powder Mystery, by Ellery Queen. Gollancz, 1930; Little, 1930, 1954; Grosset, 1932; Blue Ribbon Books, 1941; PB, 1964
The Glass Village, by Ellery Queen. Little, 1954; PB, 1963
The Golden Goose, by Ellery Queen. PB, 1964 (Cover Title: Who Killed the Golden Goose)
The Greek Coffin Mystery, by Ellery Queen. Stokes, 1932; PB, 1960
Guess Who's Going to Kill You?, by Ellery Queen. Lancer, 1968
Halfway House, by Ellery Queen. Stokes, 1936; PB, 1944, 1962
Hollywood Murders: An Omnibus. Lippincott, 1957
House of Brass, by Ellery Queen. New Amer. Lib., 1968
How Goes the Murder? by Ellery Queen. Popular Lib., 1967
Inspector Queen's Own Case: November Song. Gollancz, 1956; S & S, 1956; PB, 1957
Kill as Directed, by Ellery Queen. PB, 1963
The Killer Touch, by Ellery Queen. PB, 1965
The King Is Dead, by Ellery Queen. Gollancz, 1952; Little, 1952; Penguin, 1960
"The Lamp of God"; see The New Adventures of Ellery Queen
The Last Score, by Ellery Queen. PB, 1964
Losers, Weepers, by Ellery Queen. Dell, 1966
The Madman Theory, by Ellery Queen. PB, 1966
Murder with a Past, by Ellery Queen. PB, 1963
The Murderer Is a Fox, by Ellery Queen. Gollancz, 1945; Little, 1945; Pan, 1960; Dell, 1966
The New Adventures of Ellery Queen. Gollancz, 1940; Stokes, 1940; PB, 1940; Grosset, 1941; Blue Ribbon Books, 1947; World Pub., 1947 (Includes: "The Lamp of God")
New York Murders: An Omnibus. Little, 1958
The Origin of Evil, by Ellery Queen. Little, 1951; Gollancz, 1953
The Penthouse Mystery, by Ellery Queen. Grosset, 1941
The Perfect Crime, by Ellery Queen. Grosset, 1942
The Player on the Other Side, by Ellery Queen. Gollancz, 1963; Random, 1963; PB, 1965
QBI: Queen's Bureau of Investigation. Little, 1955; PB, 1956
Queens Full. Random, 1954; Gollancz, 1966; Signet, 1966 ("Three novelettes and a pair of short shorts")
The Roman Hat Mystery, by Ellery Queen. Gollancz, 1929; Stokes, 1929; Grosset, 1931; PB, 1962
A Room to Die In, by Ellery Queen. PB, 1965
The Scarlet Letters, by Ellery Queen. Gollancz, 1953; Little, 1953
Sherlock Holmes vs. Jack the Ripper; see A Study in Terror
Shoot the Scene, by Ellery Queen. Dell, 1966
The Siamese Twin Mystery, by Ellery Queen. Stokes, 1933; Gollancz, 1934; Grosset, 1935; Triangle, 1940; PB, 1941, 1962
The Spanish Cape Mystery, by Ellery Queen. Stokes, 1935; Gollancz, 1936; PB, 1962
A Study in Terror, by Ellery Queen. Lancer, 1966 (English title: Sherlock Holmes vs. Jack the Ripper. Gollancz, 1967)
Ten Days' Wonder, by Ellery Queen. Gollancz, 1948; Little, 1948
There Was an Old Woman, by Ellery Queen. Little, 1943; Gollancz, 1944; Grosset, 1944; Sun Dial, 1946
The Tragedy of X, by Barnaby Ross. Cassell, 1932; Viking, 1932; Stokes, 1940; Avon, 1966 (1940 edition by Ellery Queen)
The Tragedy of Y, by Barnaby Ross. Cassell, 1932; Viking, 1932; Stokes, 1941; Avon, 1966 (1941 edition by Ellery Queen)
The Tragedy of Z, by Barnaby Ross. Cassell, 1933; Viking, 1933; Stokes, 1942; Avon, 1961 (1942 and 1961 editions by Ellery Queen)
What's in the Dark?, by Ellery Queen. Popular Lib., 1968
Where Is Bianca? by Ellery Queen. Popular Lib., 1966
Which Way to Die, by Ellery Queen. Popular Lib., 1967
Who Killed the Golden Goose?; see The Golden Goose
Who Spies, Who Kills?, by Ellery Queen. Popular Lib., 1966
Why So Dead?, by Ellery Queen. Popular Lib., 1966
Wife or Death, by Ellery Queen. PB, 1963
The Wrightsville Murders: An Ellery Queen Omnibus. Little, 1956
The XYZ Murders, by Ellery Queen. Lippincott, 1961 (Contains: The Tragedy of X, The Tragedy of Y, and The Tragedy of Z)

DANNETT, SYLVIA G. L. (M)
Defy the Tempest, with Edwin Bennett. Messner, 1944
The Door to the Tower. Lancer, 1966
Nor Iron Bars, with Edwin Bennett. Fortuny, 1940

DANNING, MELROD, pseud; see GLUCK, SINCLAIR

DANVERS, MILTON (M)
A Desperate Dilemma: a Detective Story. Diprose, 1892
Detective's Honeymoon: a Detective Story. Diprose, 1894
The Doctor's Crime; or, Simply Horrible! Diprose, 1891
The Fatal Finger Mark: Rose Courtenay's First Case. Diprose, 1895
Grantham Mystery: a Detective Story. Diprose, 1893
The 'Lone Cross Manor' Mystery; or, Hugh Daniel's Confession. Diprose, 1896
The Mysterious Disappearance of a Bride; or, Who Was She? Diprose, 1895
The Squire's Fatal Will; or, Twenty Years of Plot and Crime. Diprose, 1897

D'APERY, H. (M)
Chinatown Trunk Mystery. Ogilvie

DARBY, J. N., pseud; see GOVAN, CHRISTINE NOBLE

DARBY, RUTH (D)
Beauty Sleep. Doubleday, Doran, 1942
Death Boards the Lazy Lady. Doubleday, Doran, 1939
Death Conducts a Tour. Doubleday, Doran, 1940
If This Be Murder. Doubleday, Doran, 1941
Murder with Orange Blossoms. Doubleday, Doran, 1943

DARE, MICHAEL (D)
Murder Incognito. Muller, 1947

DARK, JAMES (S)
Assignment—Hong Kong. Signet, 1966 (Also published as: Hong Kong Incident. Signet, 1966)
Assignment—Tokyo. Signet, 1966 (Also published as: Operation Miss-Sat. Signet, 1966)
The Bamboo Bomb. Signet, 1965
Come Die with Me. Signet, 1965
Hong Kong Incident; see Assignment—Hong Kong
Operation MissSat; see Assignment—Tokyo
Operation Scuba. Signet, 1967
The Sword of Genghis Khan. Signet, 1967
Throne of Satan. Signet, 1967

DARK, REX (M)
The Channing Affair. Wright & Brown, 1937; Mellifont, 1946
Dead Men Tell. Wright & Brown, 1937; Mellifont, 1939
The Invisible Hand. Wright & Brown, 1937; Mellifont, 1948
The Ming Vase Mystery. Wright & Brown, 1936; Mellifont, 1937
Murder in Berkeley Square. Wright & Brown, 1938; Mellifont, 1945
The Prison Murder. Wright & Brown, 1939; Mellifont, 1943
Spy 222. Wright & Brown, 1940
The Tremlow Murder Case. Wright & Brown, 1938; Mellifont, 1940
The Uranian Jewel Case. Wright & Brown, 1939; Mellifont, 1946
The Wardour Street Mystery. Wright & Brown, 1936; Mellifont, 1938

D'ARLEY, CATHERINE (S) (Pseudonym: Catherine Arley)
Dead Man's Bay. Collins, 1959
Ready Revenge. Random, 1960
Woman of Straw. Collins, 1957; Random, 1958; Bantam, 1964

DARWENT, GEORGE (M)
Mystery in the Snow. Rich, 1935

d'AUTHEVILLE, FRANÇOIS GEORGES HENRI; see AUTHEVILLE, FRANÇOIS GEORGES HENRI d'

DAVEY, JOCELYN, pseud; see RAPHAEL, CHAIM

DAVIDSON, LIONEL (S)
The Menorah Men. Harper & Row, 1966; Dell, 1967
The Night of Wencelas. Gollancz, 1960; Harper, 1960; Avon, 1962; Penguin
The Rose of Tibet. Gollancz, 1962; Harper, 1962; Avon, 1963

DAVIDSON, T. L. (D)
Murder in the Laboratory. Dutton, 1929; Methuen, 1929

DAVIES, ARTHUR CHARLES FOX-; see FOX-DAVIES, ARTHUR CHARLES

DAVIES, BETTY EVELYN (M) (Pseudonym: Pauline Warwick)
Death of a Sinner. Cassell, 1944

DAVIES, ERNEST (M)
Widow's Necklace. Devin-Adair, 1913

DAVIES, HUGH SYKES (M)
The Papers of Andrew Melmoth. Morrow, 1961

DAVIES, JOHN (M)
See Naples and Die. Collins, 1961

DAVIES, LESLIE PURNELL (S)
The Artificial Man. Doubleday, 1967
The Lampton Dreamers. Jenkins, 1966; Doubleday, 1967
The Paper Dolls. Jenkins, 1965; Doubleday, 1966; Signet, 1966
The Reluctant Medium. Doubleday, 1967
Who Is Lewis Pinder? Doubleday, 1966

DAVIES, N. E. (M)
Doctor Cockaigne. Methuen, 1930

DAVIOT, GORDON, pseud; see MACKINTOSH, ELIZABETH

DAVIS, BURTON and CLARE OGDEN DAVIS (D) (Pseudonym: Lawrence Saunders)
The Columnist Murder. Farrar & Rinehart, 1931
Devil's Den. Covici, 1933
Smoke Screen. Sears, 1930

DAVIS, CHARLES (D)
Two Weeks to Find a Killer. Carlton, 1966

DAVIS, CLARE OGDEN; see DAVIS, BURTON

DAVIS, DOROTHY SALISBURY (M)
Black Sheep, White Lamb. Scribner, 1963; Boardman, T. V., 1964; Dell, 1967
Choice of Murders. Scribner, 1958
The Clay Hand. Scribner, 1950; Collier, 1963
Death of an Old Sinner. Scribner, 1957; Secker & Warburg, 1958
Enemy and Brother. Scribner, 1967
A Gentle Murderer. Scribner, 1951
A Gentleman Called. Scribner, 1958; Secker & Warburg, 1960; Dell, 1962
The Judas Cat. Scribner, 1949; Collier, 1962
Old Sinners Never Die. Scribner, 1959; Secker & Warburg, 1960
The Pale Betrayers. Scribner, 1965; Hodder, 1967
A Town of Masks. Scribner, 1952; Collier, 1962

DAVIS, FRANKLIN M. (M-S)
Kiss the Tiger. Pyramid, 1961
The Naked and the Lost. Lion, 1954
Secret: Hong Kong. Pyramid, 1962

DAVIS, FREDERICK CLYDE (D)
(Pseudonym: Stephen Ransome)
Alias His Wife, by Stephen Ransome. Dodd, 1965
Another Morgue Heard From. Doubleday, 1954
Coffins for Three. Doubleday, Doran, 1938
Deadly Bedfellows. Gollancz, 1955
The Deadly Miss Ashley. Doubleday, 1950; Gollancz, 1950
Death Checks In, by Stephen Ransome. Doubleday, Doran, 1939
Deep Lay the Dead. Doubleday, Doran, 1942
Detour to Oblivion. Doubleday, 1947
Drag the Dark. Doubleday, 1953; Ace, 1954; Gollancz, 1954
False Bounty, by Stephen Ransome. Doubleday, 1948
The Frazier Acquittal, by Stephen Ransome. Doubleday, 1955; Popular Lib., 1965
Gone Tomorrow. Doubleday, 1948; Gollancz, 1949
The Graveyard Never Closes. Doubleday, Doran, 1940
He Wouldn't Stay Dead. Doubleday, Doran, 1939; Heinemann, 1939
Hear No Evil. Doubleday, 1953; Gollancz, 1954
Hearses Don't Hurry, by Stephen Ransome. Doubleday, Doran, 1941
The Hidden Hour, by Stephen Ransome. Dodd, 1966; Gollancz, 1966
High Heel Homicide. Ace, 1961
I'll Die for You, by Stephen Ransome. Doubleday, 1959; Gollancz, 1959
Let the Skeletons Rattle. Doubleday, Doran, 1944
Lilies in Her Garden Grew. Doubleday, 1951; Gollancz, 1951
Meet in Darkness, by Stephen Ransome. Dodd, 1964; Gollancz, 1964
The Men in Her Death. Doubleday, 1956; Gollancz, 1957
Murder Doesn't Always Out. Heinemann, 1939
Night Drop. Doubleday, 1955
The Night, the Woman, by Stephen Ransome. Dodd, 1963; Gollancz, 1963
One Man Jury, by Stephen Ransome. Dodd, 1964
One Murder Too Many. Heinemann, 1938
Poor, Poor Yorick. Doubleday, Doran, 1939
A Shroud for Shylock, by Stephen Ransome. Doubleday, Doran, 1939
The Shroud off Her Back, by Stephen Ransome. Doubleday, 1953; Gollancz, 1953
The Sin File, by Stephen Ransome. Dodd, 1965
So Deadly, My Love, by Stephen Ransome. Doubleday, 1957

Some Must Watch. Doubleday, 1961; Gollancz, 1961; PB, 1963
Thursday's Blade. Doubleday, 1947
Tread Lightly, Angel. Doubleday, 1952; Gollancz, 1952
The Unspeakable. Doubleday, 1960; Gollancz, 1961
The Warning Bell, by Stephen Ransome. Doubleday, 1960; Gollancz, 1960
Whose Corpse? Davies, 1939
Without a Trace, by Stephen Ransome. Doubleday, 1962; Gollancz, 1962

DAVIS, FREDERICK WILLIAM (S)
(Pseudonym: Scott Campbell)
Below the Deadline. Dillingham, G. W., 1906

DAVIS, GEORGE (M)
Roag's Syndicate. Chapman, 1960

DAVIS, GORDON, pseud; see DIETRICH, ROBERT

DAVIS, HARRY (S)
My Brother's Wife. Greenberg, 1956
Portrait of Rene. Greenberg, 1956

DAVIS, HOWARD CHARLES (M)
The Big Heist. Long, 1964
The Child Witness. Jarrolds, 1957
Dead Man's Cross. Long, 1965
Death of Laura. Hale, R., 1963
The Man Who Wasn't Murdered. Jarrolds, 1955
Murder out of Class. Ward, Lock, 1961
The Night of the Funeral. Long, 1958
Perhaps to Kill. Hale, R., 1963
Pistol for Miss Preedy. Jarrolds, 1956
The Renegade from Russia. Long, 1959
The Third Assassin. Long, 1959
The Tortured Boy. Ward, Lock, 1961
Trouble in the Bank. Ward, Lock, 1960
Waxworks Spies. Ward, Lock, 1962

DAVIS, JAMES FRANCIS (S)
The Chinese Label. Little, 1920

DAVIS, LAVINIA RIKER (D)
Barren Heritage. Doubleday, 1946
Evidence Unseen. Doubleday, Doran, 1945
Janey's Fortune. Doubleday, 1957
Plow Penny Mystery. Collins, 1942; Doubleday, 1942
Reference to Death. Doubleday, 1950, 1951
The Skyscraper Mystery. Scribner, 1937
Taste of Vengeance. Doubleday, 1947
Threat of Dragons. Doubleday, 1948

DAVIS, MARTHA WIRT (M) (Pseudonym: Wirt Van Arsdale)
The Professor Knits a Shroud. Doubleday, 1951

DAVIS, MARVIN (M)
Lake Mystery. Burt, 1925

DAVIS, MEANS (D)
The Chess Murders. Random, 1937
The Hospital Murders. Smith, H., 1934
Murder Without Weapon. Smith, H., 1934

DAVIS, MELTON S. (M)
All Rome Trembled. Award

DAVIS, MILDRED B. (M)
The Dark Place. S & S, 1955; Ace, 1964
The Room Upstairs. S & S, 1948; PB, 1949; Avon, 1967
The Sound of Insects. Doubleday, 1966; Hodder, 1967; Macfadden, 1967
Strange Corner. Doubleday, 1967
They Buried a Man. S & S, 1953; Ace, 1964
The Voice on the Telephone. Random, 1964; Macfadden, 1965
Walk into Yesterday. Doubleday, 1968

DAVIS, NORBERT (S)
The Mouse in the Mountain. Morrow, 1943
Sally's in the Alley. Morrow, 1943

DAVIS, OLIVE BELL (M)
Exodus: 20. Pageant Press, 1959

DAVIS, R. H. (M)
In the Fog. Harper, 1901

DAVIS, REGINALD (M)
The Crowing Hen. Doubleday, Doran, 1936
Nine Day's Panic. Bles, 1937; Doubleday, Doran, 1938

DAVIS, ROBERT (M)
Goodbye, Bates McGee. Macfadden, 1967

DAVIS, STRATFORD, pseud; see BOLTON, MAISIE SHARMAN

DAVIS, TECH (D)
Full Fare for a Corpse. Doubleday, Doran, 1937
Murder on Alternate Tuesdays. Doubleday, Doran, 1938
Terror at Compass Lake. Doubleday, Doran, 1935

DAVIS, YORKE, pseud. (M)
The Green Cloak. Sidgwick, 1910

DAVIS, ZEKE (M)
Invited. Pageant Press, 1959

DAVISON, GILDEROY (D-M)
Death in the A.R.P. Jenkins, 1939

The Devil's Apprentice. Jenkins, 1933
The Devil's Diamonds; or, Beauty and the Beast. Jenkins, 1938
A Dog Fight with Death. Jenkins, 1940
Exit Mr. Brent. Jenkins, 1936
Jewel of Destiny. Jenkins, 1938
A Killer at Scotland Yard. Jenkins, 1933
The Lily-Pond Mystery. Jenkins, 1937
The Man with Half a Face. Jenkins, 1936
The Man with the Twisted Face. Jenkins, 1931
Murder in a Muffler; or, Dead Man's Farm. Jenkins, 1937
Mysterious Air Ace. Jenkins, 1941
The Mysterious Mr. Brent. Jenkins, 1935
Mystery of the Red-Haired Valet. Jenkins, 1934
The Prince of Spies. Jenkins, 1932
Robin Hoodwinker. Jenkins, 1944
Satan's Satellite. Jenkins, 1945
A Traitor Unmasked. Jenkins, 1932
Twisted Face, the Avenger. Jenkins, 1935
Twisted Face Defends His Title. Jenkins, 1940
Twisted Face Strikes Again. Jenkins, 1939

DAWE, WILLIAM CARLTON LANYON (D)
The Knightsbridge Affair. Ward, Lock, 1928
The Missing Clue. Ward, Lock, 1930
Sign of the Glove. Ward, Lock, 1932

DAWSON, CAROLYN BIRD (S)
The Lady Wept Alone. Doubleday, Doran, 1940
Remind Me to Forget. Doubleday, Doran, 1942

DAWSON, CONINGSBY WILLIAM (M)
The Vanishing Point. Cosmopolitan, 1922

DAWSON, FRANCIS WARRINGTON (M-S)
Adventure in the Night. Doubleday, Page, 1924; Unwin, 1924
Crimson Pall. Bernard Pub., 1927

DAWSON, HELEN (M)
House in Haven Street. Dent, 1960

DAWSON, JAMES (M)
Hell Gate. McKay, 1967

DAWSON, WILLIAM JAMES (M)
The Borrowdale Tragedy. Lane, 1920

DAX, ANTHONY, pseud; see HUNTER, JOHN

DAY, JULIAN (M)
Design for Death. Hale, R., 1958

DAY, LILLIAN and NORBERT LEDERER (D)
Death Comes on Friday. Cassell, 1937; Dutton, 1937
Murder in Time. Cassell, 1935; Furman, 1936

DAY-LEWIS, CECIL (D) (Pseudonym: Nicholas Blake)
The Beast Must Die. Collins, 1938; Harper, 1938; Dell, 1958; Berkley Pub., 1964
The Case of the Abominable Snowman. Collins, 1941 (U.S. title: The Corpse in the Snowman. Harper, 1941)
The Corpse in the Snowman; see The Case of the Abominable Snowman
The Deadly Joker. Collins, 1963
Death and Daisy Bland; see A Tangled Web
Dreadful Hollow. Collins, 1953; Harper, 1953; Collier, 1962
End of Chapter. Collins, 1957; Harper, 1957
Head of a Traveler. Collins, 1949; Harper, 1949; Berkley Pub., 1964
Malice in Wonderland. Collins, 1940 (U.S. titles: The Summer Camp Mystery. Harper, 1953 and Malice with Murder. Pyramid, 1960)
Malice with Murder; see Malice in Wonderland
Minute for Murder. Collins, 1947; Harper, 1947
The Morning After Death. Collins, 1966; Harper & Row, 1966
A Penknife in My Heart. Collins, 1958; Harper, 1959
A Question of Proof. Collins, 1935; Harper, 1935
The Sad Variety. Collins, 1964; Harper & Row, 1964
Shell of Death; see Thou Shell of Death
The Smiler with the Knife. Collins, 1939; Harper, 1939; Berkley Pub., 1964
The Starting Point. Cape, 1937; Harper, 1938
The Summer Camp Mystery; see Malice in Wonderland
The Tangled Web. Collins, 1956; Harper, 1956 (Also published as: Death and Daisy Bland. Dell, 1960)
There's Trouble Brewing. Collins, 1937; Harper, 1937
Thou Shell of Death. Collins, 1936 (U.S. title: Shell of Death. Harper, 1936; Berkley Pub., 1964)
The Whisper in the Gloom. Collins, 1954; Harper, 1954; Pan, 1959
The Widow's Cruise. Collins, 1959; Harper, 1959; Dell, 1963
The Worm of Death. Collins, 1961; Harper, 1961

DEAKIN, HILDA L. (M)
The Secret of the Cove. Methuen, 1930
The Shot That Killed Graeme Andrewe. Nelson, 1931
The Square Mark, with Grace M. White. Methuen, 1929; Dutton, 1930; Newnes, 1930

DEAL, BABS HODGES (S)
Fancy's Knell. Doubleday, 1966; Gollancz, 1967

DEAL, BORDEN (D)
Killer in the House. Signet, 1957
A Long Way to Go. Doubleday, 1965

DEAN, AMBER, pseud; see GETZIN, AMBER DEAN

DEAN, DENNIS (D)
The Emerald Murder Case. Phoenix, 1939

DEAN, DUDLEY (S)
Lila, My Lovely. GM, 1960

DEAN, ELIZABETH (D)
Murder a Mile High. Doubleday, Doran, 1944
Murder Is a Collector's Item. Doubleday, Doran, 1939
Murder Is a Serious Business. Doubleday, Doran, 1940

DEAN, GREGORY, pseud; see POSNER, JACOB D.

DEAN, NELL MARR (S)
The Trials of Dr. Carol. Belmont, 1964

DEAN, ROBERT GEORGE (D) (Pseudonym: George Griswold)
The Affair at Lover's Leap. Doubleday, 1953
The Body Was Quite Cold. Dutton, 1951
The Case of Joshua Locke. Dutton, 1951
A Checkmate by the Colonel, by George Griswold. Dutton, 1952
A Gambit for Mr. Groode, by George Griswold. Dutton, 1952
Layoff. Scribner, 1942
Murder by Marriage. Scribner, 1940
Murder in Mink. Scribner, 1941
Murder Makes a Merry Widow. Doubleday, Doran, 1938
Murder Most Opportune. Doubleday, Doran, 1939
Murder of Convenience. Doubleday, Doran, 1938
Murder on Margin. Doubleday, Doran, 1937
Murder Through the Looking Glass. Doubleday, Doran, 1940
On Ice. Scribner, 1942
The Pinned Man, by George Griswold. Little, 1942
Red Pawns, by George Griswold. Dutton, 1954
The Sutton Place Murders. Doubleday, Doran, 1936
Three Lights Went Out. Doubleday, Doran, 1937
What Gentleman Strangles a Lady? Doubleday, Doran, 1936

DEAN, SPENCER, pseud; see WINCHELL, PRENTICE

DEANE, DONALD (M)
The Fifth Tulip. Hamilton, 1930
Hidden Clues. Hamilton, 1932
Luck of Luce. Hamilton, 1931

DEANE, NORMAN, pseud; see CREASEY, JOHN

DEASY, MARY (M)
The Corioli Affair. Heinemann, 1955; Popular Lib., 1965

DE BANZIE, ERIC; see RESSICK, JOHN

DEBEKKER, JAY, pseud; see WINCHELL, PRENTICE

DE BRA, LEMUEL (S)
Ways That Are Wary. Butterworth, T., 1924

DEBRETT, HAL, pseud; see DRESSER, DAVIS

DE CAIRE, EDWIN (D)
Death Among the Writers. Hodder, 1952
Umgasi Diamonds. Hodder, 1954

DECOIN, DIDIER (M)
The Case Against Love. New Amer. Lib., 1967

DECREST, JACQUES, pseud; see FAURE-BIGUET, JACQUES NAPOLEON

DE HAMEL, HERBERT (D)
Many Thanks, Ben Hassett. Simpkin, 1915

DEIGHTON, LEN (S)
The Billion Dollar Brain. Putnam, 1966; Dell, 1967
An Expensive Place to Die. Putnam, 1967; Dell, 1968
Funeral in Berlin. Cape, 1964; Dell, 1965; Putnam, 1965; Watts, 1966 (Large type edition)
Horse Under Water. Cape, 1963; Putnam, 1968
The Ipcress File. S & S, 1963; Crest, 1965

DE JEAN, LOUIS LEON (S)
The Girl in Black Velvet. Macaulay, 1937

DEJEANS, ELIZABETH (Mrs. Sidney Budgett) (M)
The Double House. Doubleday, Page, 1924
The House of Thane. Lippincott, 1913
Mansions of Unrest. Doubleday, Page, 1926
The Moreton Mystery. Bobbs, 1920
The Romance of a Million Dollars. Bobbs, 1922
Tiger's Coat. Bobbs, 1917

DeJONG, DOLA (M)
The Whirligig of Time. Doubleday, 1964

DEKOBRA, MAURICE, pseud; see TESSIER, ERNEST MAURICE

DE LAGUNA, FREDERICA (D)
Arrow Points to Murder. Doubleday, Doran, 1937
Fog on the Mountain. Doubleday, Doran, 1938

DE LA MARE, WALTER (M)
The Riddle and Other Stories. Selwyn, 1923

DELANCEY, ROGER (M)
Murder Below Wall Street. Appleton-Century, 1934

DELANEY, DENNIS, pseud; see GREEN, PETER

DELANNOY, H. BURFORD (D)
Beaten at the Post. Digby, 1907; Aldine, 1920
Between the Lines. Ward, Lock, 1901
Dead Man's Rooms. Ward, Lock, 1905
The Flat Beneath. Rivers, 1931
In Mid-Atlantic. Ward, Lock, 1904
The Margate Murder Mystery. Ward, Lock, 1902
The Midnight Special. Milne, 1902; Newnes, 1911
The Missing Cyclist, and Other Stories. Simpkin, 1898
The Money Lender. Ward, Lock, 1907
Nineteen Thousand Pounds. Ward, Lock, 1901
The Pound of Flesh. Digby, 1911
Prince Charlie. Ward, Lock, 1906
The Scales of Justice. Digby, 1908
A Studio Model. Digby, 1909

DELANY, JOSEPH FRANCIS (D) (Pseudonym: Joel Y. Dane)
The Cabana Murders. Doubleday, Doran, 1937
The Christmas Tree Murders. Doubleday, Doran, 1938
Grasp at Straws. Doubleday, Doran, 1938
Murder Cum Laude. Smith, H., 1935

DE LA TORRE, LILLIAN, pseud; see McCUE, LILLIAN BUENO

DELL, AMEN (M)
Johnny on the Spot. Arcadia, 1953

DELLBRIDGE, JOHN (D)
The Lady in the Wood. Hurst, 1950
The Moles of Death. Diamond Press, 1927
Searchlight on Hambledon. Hurst, 1947
Unfit to Plead. Hurst, 1949

DELVES-BROUGHTON, JOSEPHINE (M) (Pseudonym: John Bryan)
Contessa Came Too. Faber, 1957
The Difference to Me. Faber, 1957; British Book Centre, 1960
Man Who Came Back. London House, 1959

DELVING, MICHAEL, pseud. (M)
Smiling the Boy Fell Dead. Scribner, 1967

DEMAREST, ANNE, pseud; see BOND, MRS. FLORENCE DEMAREST FOOS

DEMARIS, OVID, pseud; see DESMARAIS, OVIDE E.

DEMBO, SAMUEL (M)
Kalahari Kill. Mill, 1964 (Also published as: The Sands of Lilliput. Redman, 1963)

DEMING, RICHARD (D) (Pseudonym: Max Franklin)
All That Swagger, by Max Franklin. Angus, 1957
Anything But Saintly. PB, 1963
Body for Sale. PB, 1962
The Careful Man. Allen, W. H., 1962
The Case of the Courteous Killer. PB, 1958 (Also published as: Dragnet: The Case of the Courteous Killer)
The Case of the Crime King. PB, 1959
Death of a Pusher. PB, 1964
Dragnet: The Case of the Courteous Killer; see The Case of the Courteous Killer
Edge of the Law. Berkley Pub., 1960
Fall Girl. Zenith, 1959
The Gallows in My Garden. Rinehart, 1952; Boardman, T. V., 1953
Hell Street, by Max Franklin. Rinehart, 1954

Hit and Run. PB, 1960
Justice Has No Sword, by Max Franklin. Rinehart, 1953; Boardman, T. V., 1954
Juvenile Delinquent. Boardman, T. V., 1958
Kiss and Kill. Zenith, 1960
She'll Hate Me Tomorrow. Monarch, 1963
This Game of Murder. Monarch, 1964
This Is My Night. Monarch, 1961
Tweak the Devil's Nose. Rinehart, 1953; Boardman, T. V., 1953
Walk a Crooked Mile. Boardman, T. V., 1959
Vice Cop. Belmont, 1961
Whistle Past the Graveyard. Rinehart, 1954; Boardman, T. V., 1955

DeMORGAN, WILLIAM FREND (M)
The Old Madhouse. Holt, H., 1919

DeMOTT, BENJAMIN (M)
The Body's Cage. Little, 1959

DENBIE, ROGER, pseud; see GREEN, ALAN BAER

DENEVI, MARCO (M)
Rosa at Ten O'Clock. Holt, 1964

DENNISTON, ELEANORE (D-M) (Pseudonyms: Dennis Allan, Rae Foley)
Back Door to Death, by Rae Foley. Dodd, 1963; Hammond, 1964
Born to Be Murdered, by Dennis Allan. Mill, 1945; Hammond, 1952
Brandon Is Missing, by Dennis Allan. Hamilton, 1938; Mill, 1940
Call It Accident, by Rae Foley. Dodd, 1965
The Case of the Headless Corpse, by Dennis Allan. Mill, 1945
Dangerous to Me, by Rae Foley. Hammond, 1960
Dead to Rights, by Dennis Allan. Mill, 1946; Hammond, 1953
Death and Mr. Potter, by Rae Foley. Dodd, 1955
Fatal Lady, by Rae Foley. Dodd, 1964; Hammond, 1964
Fear of a Stranger, by Rae Foley. Dodd, 1967
The House of Treason, by Dennis Allan. Greystone, 1936
It's Murder, Mr. Potter, by Rae Foley. Dodd, 1961; Hammond, 1963
The Last Gamble, by Rae Foley. Dodd, 1956; Boardman, T. V., 1957
Man in the Shadows, by Rae Foley. Dodd, 1953
Repent at Leisure, by Rae Foley. Dodd, 1962
Run for Your Life, by Rae Foley. Dodd, 1957; Boardman, T. V., 1958
Scared to Death, by Rae Foley. Dodd, 1966
The Shelton Conspiracy, by Rae Foley. Dodd, 1967
Suffer a Witch, by Rae Foley. Dodd, 1965
Where Is Mary Bostwick?, by Rae Foley. Boardman, T. V., 1958; Dodd, 1958
Wild Night, by Rae Foley. Dodd, 1966; Hale, R., 1967

DENT, LESTER (S)
Dead at the Take-Off. Cassell, 1946; Doubleday, 1946
Lady Afraid. Doubleday, 1948; Cassell, 1950
Lady So Silent. Doubleday, 1946; Cassell, 1951
Lady to Kill. Doubleday, 1946; Cassell, 1950

DENT, WALTER REDVERS (D)
Show Me Death. Macmillan, 1930

DENTON, RALPH (M)
Charlie Finds a Corpse. Yates Pub., 1940

DE PUE, E. SPENCE; see DE PUY, EDWARD SPENCE

DE PUY, EDWARD SPENCE (M)
Hospital Homicides. Phoenix, 1937
The Long Knife. Doubleday, Doran, 1936

DERBY, MARK, pseud; see WILCOX, HARRY

D'ERIGNY, SIMONE (M)
The Mysterious Madame S. Lippincott, 1934

DERING, JOAN (M)
Louise. Washburn, 1957

DERLETH, AUGUST (D-M) (Pseudonym: Stephen Grendon)
The Adventures of Solar Pons. Mycroft & Moran, 1945
The Casebook of Solar Pons. Arkham, 1965
Colonel Markesan and Less Pleasant People. Arkham, 1966
Dark Mind, Dark Heart. Arkham, 1962
Death by Design. Arcadia, 1953
Death Stalks the Wakely Family; see Murder Stalks the Wakely Family
Fell Purpose. Arcadia, 1953
The Man on All Fours. Mussey, 1934
The Memoirs of Solar Pons. Mycroft & Moran, 1951
Mischief in the Lane. Scribner, 1944; Muller, 1948

Mr. George and Other Odd Persons, by Stephen Grendon. Arkham, 1963; Belmont, 1964
Murder Stalks the Wakely Family. Mussey, 1934 (English title: Death Stalks the Wakely Family. Newnes, 1937)
The Narracong Riddle. Scribner, 1940
No Future for Luana. Scribner, 1945; Muller, 1948
The Praed Street Papers. Candlelight Press
The Reminiscences of Solar Pons. Mycroft & Moran, 1961
The Return of Solar Pons. Mycroft & Moran, 1958
Sentence Deferred. Scribner, 1940
The Seven Who Waited. Scribner, 1943; Muller, 1945
The Sign of Fear. Mussey, 1935
Someone in the Dark. Arkham, 1941
Three Problems for Solar Pons. Mycroft & Moran, 1953
Three Who Died. Mussey, 1935
Travellers by Night. Arkham, 1967

DERRY, JUSTIN (M)
The Massingham Affair. Doubleday, 1963

DES CARS, GUY (S)
The Brute. Wingate, 1952

DES LIGNERIS, FRANÇOISE (M)
Bijoux. Avon, 1963

DESMARAIS, OVIDE E. (Pseudonym: Ovid Demaris)
The Enforcer. GM, 1960
The Extortioners. GM, 1960
The Gold-Plated Sewer. Avon, 1960
The Hoods Take Over. GM, 1957
The Lusting Drive. GM, 1958
Ride the Gold Mare. GM, 1957
The Slasher. GM, 1959

DESMOND HUGH (M)
Appointment at Eight. Wright & Brown, 1957
Blood Cries for Vengeance. Wright & Brown, 1948
Bluebeard's Wife. Wright & Brown, 1947; Albatross, 1950
Bodies in the Cupboard. Wright & Brown, 1963
Breath of Suspicion. Wright & Brown, 1954
Calling Alan Fraser. Wright & Brown, 1951
The Case of the Blue Orchid. Wright & Brown, 1961
A Clear Case of Murder. Wright & Brown, 1950
Condemned. Wright & Brown, 1964
Crime Without a Flaw. Grayson, 1954
Dark Deeds. Wright & Brown, 1952
Dark Shadow. Wright & Brown, 1965
Death by Candlelight. Albatross, 1950
Death in the Shingle. Wright & Brown, 1948; Albatross, 1950
Death Let Loose. Wright & Brown, 1957
The Death Parade. Wright & Brown, 1954
Death Strikes at Dawn. Wright & Brown, 1943
Death Walks in Scarlet. Wright & Brown, 1948; Albatross, 1950
Deliver Us from Evil. Wright & Brown, 1953
A Desperate Gamble. Wright & Brown, 1946
Destination—Death. Wright & Brown, 1955
Doorway to Death. Wright & Brown, 1959
The Edge of Horror. Wright & Brown, 1950
Fanfare for Murder. Wright & Brown, 1961
Fear Rides the Air. Wright & Brown, 1953
Fear Walks the Island. Wright & Brown, 1951
The Fuehrer Dies. Wright & Brown, 1944
Gallow's Fruit. Wright & Brown, 1949
The Hand of Vengeance. Wright & Brown, 1945
The Hangman Waits. Wright & Brown, 1955
Highways of Death. Wright & Brown, 1940
His Reverence the Rogue. Wright & Brown, 1946
In Fear of the Night. Wright & Brown, 1960
Intent to Kill. Hale, R., 1942
The Jacaranda Murders. Wright & Brown, 1951
Lady in Peril. Wright & Brown, 1946
Lady, Where Are You? Wright & Brown, 1957
Look Upon the Prisoner. Wright & Brown, 1958
Misty Pathway. Wright & Brown, 1940
Murder at Midnight. Wright & Brown, 1962
Murder Is Justified. Wright & Brown, 1951
Murder Run Wild. Hale, R., 1941
Murder Strikes at Dawn. Wright & Brown, 1965
Murderer's Bride. Wright & Brown, 1954
The Mystery Killer. Wright & Brown, 1943
Night of Terror. Wright & Brown, 1953
The Night of the Crime. Wright & Brown, 1953
No Reprieve. Wright & Brown, 1957

Not Guilty, My Lord. Wright & Brown, 1965
Overture to Death. Wright & Brown, 1947
A Pact with the Devil. Wright & Brown, 1952
Poison Pen. Wright & Brown, 1958
Put Out the Light. Wright & Brown, 1962
Reign of Terror. Wright & Brown, 1952
Scream in the Night. Wright & Brown, 1959
The Secret of the Moat. Wright & Brown, 1940
The Secret Voice. Wright & Brown, 1942
She Met Murder
The Slasher. Wright & Brown, 1939
Stranger Than Fiction. Wright & Brown, 1961
The Strangler. Wright & Brown, 1947; Albatross, 1950
Strong Dose of Poison. Wright & Brown, 1959
Suicide Fleet. Wright & Brown, 1959
The Terrible Awakening. Wright & Brown, 1949
Terror Walks by Night. Wright & Brown, 1944
They Lived with Death. Wright & Brown, 1945
Turn Back from Death. Wright & Brown, 1960
The Viper's Sting. Wright & Brown, 1946; Albatross, 1950
The Wicked Shall Flourish. Wright & Brown, 1959
A Wife in the Dark. Wright & Brown, 1948

DESPARD, LESLIE, pseud; see HOWITT, JOHN LESLIE DESPARD

DESSART, GINA (M)
Cry for the Loot. Harper, 1959
The Last House. Hodder, 1951
A Man Died Here. Harper, 1947; Hodder, 1948

DE STEIGUER, WALTER (D)
Jewels for a Shroud. Morrow, 1950

DETZER, KARL W. (M)
The Broken Three. Bobbs, 1929

DEVINE, DAVID McDONALD (M)
Devil at Your Elbow. Collins, 1966; Walker & Co., 1967
Doctors Also Die. Collins, 1962; Dodd, 1963
The Fifth Cord. Collins, 1967; Walker & Co., 1967
His Own Appointed Day. Walker & Co., 1966
My Brother's Killer. Collins, 1961; Dodd, 1962
The Royston Affair. Collins, 1964; Dodd, 1965

DEVINE, STEWART (D)
Even in Death. Doubleday, 1950
Listen for a Stranger. Doubleday, 1951

DEVLIN, BARRY, pseud. (S)
Madam Big. Vixen Press, 1953

DeVOTO, BERNARD (S) (Pseudonym: John August)
Advance Agent. Little, 1941; Selwyn, 1943
Rain Before Seven. Little, 1940
Troubled Star. Little, 1939 (English title: The Woman in the Picture. Selwyn, 1939)
The Woman in the Picture; see Troubled Star

DEWDNEY, PETER, pseud; see BROCK, ALAN ST. HILL

DEWES, SIMON, pseud; see MURIEL, JOHN SAINT CLAIR

DEWEY, THOMAS BLANCHARD (D-S) (Pseudonym: Tom Brandt)
And Where She Stops. Popular Lib., 1957
As Good as Dead. Jefferson House, 1946; Dakers, 1952
Brave Bad Girls. S & S, 1956; Boardman, T. V., 1957
Can a Mermaid Kill? Tower, 1965
The Case of the Chased and the Unchaste. Random, 1959; Boardman, T. V., 1960; Crest
Deadline. S & S, 1966; PB, 1968
Death and Taxes. Putnam, 1967; Berkley Pub., 1968
Don't Cry for Long. S & S, 1964; PB, 1966
Draw the Curtain Close. Jefferson House, 1947
Every Bet's a Sure Thing. S & S, 1953
The Girl in the Punchbowl. Dell, 1964
The Girl Who Wasn't There. Boardman, T. V., 1960; S & S, 1960
The Girl with the Sweet Plump Knees. Boardman, T. V., 1963; Dell, 1963; PB, 1963
Go, Honeylou. Boardman, T. V., 1962; Dell, 1962
Go to Sleep, Jeannie. Popular Lib., 1959; Boardman, T. V., 1960
The Golden Hooligan. Dell, 1961
Handle with Fear. Mill, 1951; Dakers, 1955
How Hard to Kill. S & S, 1962; Boardman, T. V., 1963; PB, 1963
Hue and Cry. Morrow, 1944

Hunter at Large. S & S, 1961; Boardman, T. V., 1962; PB, 1963
I. O. U. Murder. Boardman, T. V., 1958
Kiss Me Hard, by Tom Brandt. Popular Lib., 1954
The Mean Streets. S & S, 1955
Mexican Slay Ride. Boardman, T. V., 1961
Mourning After. Mill, 1950; Dakers, 1953
The Murder of Marion Mason. Dakers, 1951
My Love Is Violent. Popular Lib., 1956
Nude in Nevada. Dell, 1965
Only on Tuesdays. Dell, 1963
Portrait of a Dead Heiress. S & S, 1965; PB, 1967
Prey for Me. S & S, 1954; Boardman, T. V., 1955
Sad Song for Singing. S & S, 1963; Boardman, T. V., 1964
A Season for Violence. GM, 1966
Too Hot for Hawaii. Popular Lib., 1960; Boardman, T. V., 1963
You've Got Him Cold. S & S, 1958; Boardman, T. V., 1959

DeWITT, JACK (D)
Murder on Shark Island. Boni, 1941

DEXTER, BRUCE (S)
I'll Sing You the Death of Bill Brown. McGraw, 1963

DEY, FREDERIC VAN RENSSELAER (M) (Pseudonym: Varick Vanardy)
The Girl by the Roadside. Jarrolds, 1923
The Lady of the Night Wind. Skeffington, 1926
The Two-Faced Man. Jarrolds, 1920, 1923

DIAMOND, FRANK (D)
Murder in Five Columns. Bouregy, 1944
Murder Rides a Rocket. Curl, 1946; Natl. Mag., 1947
Widow Maker. Ace, 1962

DIBNER, MARTIN (S)
A God for Tomorrow. Doubleday, 1961; Lancer, 1963

DICK, ALEXANDRA, pseud; see ERIKSON, MRS. SIBYL ALEXANDRA DICK

DICK, PHILIP K. (M)
Time Out of Joint. Lippincott, 1959

DICKENS, CHARLES (M)
Bleak House. Bradbury, 1853
Hunted Down. New York Ledger, 1859
The Mystery of Edwin Drood. Chapman, 1870 (Completed by Percy T. Carden and published as: Murder of Edwin Drood. Palmer, C., 1920)

DICKENS, MONICA (S)
The Room Upstairs. Doubleday, 1966; Ace, 1967

DICKENSON, FRED (D)
Kill 'em with Kindness. Bell, 1950

DICKINSON, WEED (D)
Dead Man Talks Too Much. Lippincott, 1937

DICKSON, CARTER, pseud; see CARR, JOHN DICKSON

DICKSON, GRIERSON (M-S)
Design for Treason. Hutchinson, 1937
The Devil's Torch. Hutchinson, 1936
Seven Screens. Hutchinson, 1950
Soho Racket. Hutchinson, 1935
Traitor's Market. Hutchinson, 1936

DIDELOT, ROGER FRANCIS (D)
Death of the Deputy. Lippincott, 1935
The Many Ways of Death. MacDonald & Co., 1955; Belmont, 1966
Murder in the Bath. Lippincott, 1933
The Seventh Juror. MacDonald & Co., 1961; Belmont, 1963
Warrant for Arrest. MacDonald & Co., 1963

DIDEON, JOAN (S)
Run River. Obolensky, 1963; Bantam, 1964

DIETRICH, ROBERT (D) (Pseudonyms: Gordon Davis, Howard Hunt)
Angel Eyes. Dell, 1961
Be My Victim. Dell, 1957
Counterfeit Kill, by Gordon Davis. GM, 1963
Curtains for a Lover. Lancer, 1962
End of a Stripper. Dell, 1959
House Dick, by Gordon Davis. Fawcett, 1961
The House on Q Street. Dell, 1958
I Came to Kill, by Gordon Davis. Fawcett, 1954
Lovers Are Losers, by Howard Hunt. GM, 1953
Mistress to Murder. Dell, 1960
Murder on Her Mind. Dell, 1960
Murder on the Rocks. Dell, 1957; Ward, Lock, 1958
My Body. Lancer, 1963
Ring Around Rosy, by Gordon Davis. GM, 1964
Steve Bentley's Calypso Caper. Dell, 1961

The Violent Ones, by Howard Hunt. GM, 1958
Where Murder Waits, by Gordon Davis. GM, 1965

DIGNAM, C. B. (M)
Sons of Seven. Hamilton, 1932

DILKE, CHRISTOPHER WENTWORTH (S)
The Guardian. Hale, R., 1953

DILLON, EILIS, pseud; see O'CUILLEANIAN, MRS. CORMAC

DILLON, JACK (S)
A Great Day for Dying. GM, 1967

DILNOT, GEORGE (D) (Pseudonym: Frank Froest)
The Black Ace. Bles, 1929; Houghton, 1929
Counter-Spy. Bles, 1942
The Crook's Castle. Houghton, 1934
The Crook's Game. Bles, 1927; Houghton, 1927
The Fighting Fool. Bles, 1939
The Great Mail Racket. Bles, 1936
The Grell Mystery, by Frank Froest. Clode, 1914
The Inside Track. Bles, 1935
The Lazy Detective. Bles, 1926
The Maelstrom, by Frank Froest. Clode, 1916
Murder at Scotland Yard. Bles, 1937
Murder Masquerade. Bles, 1935
Secret Service Man. Nash, 1916
Sister Satan. Bles, 1933; Houghton, 1933
The Suspected. Clode, 1920
The Thousandth Case. Houghton, 1933; Bles, 1939
Tiger Lily. Bles, 1939

DIMENT, ADAM (S)
The Dolly, Dolly Spy. Dutton, 1967; Bantam, 1968

DINEEN, JOSEPH FRANCIS (M)
Alternate Case: A Documentary Novel. Little, 1958
The Anatomy of a Crime. Scribner, 1954

DINESEN, ISAK, pseud; see BLIXEN-FINECKE, BARONESS KAREN CHRISTINE

DINGLE, AYLWARD EDWARD (S) (Pseudonyms: Brian Cotterell, "Sinbad")
Black Joker, by "Sinbad." Hale, R., 1946
The Bomb Ship, by "Sinbad." Hale, R., 1942
Calamity Jock, by "Sinbad." Hale, R., 1943
Cave of Stars, by "Sinbad." Hale, R., 1950
The Corpse Came Back, by "Sinbad." Hale, R., 1948
Magnolia Island, by "Sinbad." Hale, R., 1952
Reckless Tide, by "Sinbad." Hale, R., 1947
Sargasso Sam, by "Sinbad." Hale, R., 1952
Sinister Eden, by Brian Cotterell. Harrap, 1934

DINGWALL, PETER, pseud; see FORSYTHE, ROBIN

"DIPLOMAT," pseud; see CARTER, JOHN FRANKLIN

DISNEY, DORIS MILES (M-S)
Appointment at Nine. Doubleday, 1947
At Some Forgotten Door. Doubleday, 1966; Macfadden, 1966, 1967
Blackmail. Doubleday, 1958; Foulsham, 1960; Ace, 1962
The Case of the Strawman; see Strawman
A Compound for Death. Doubleday, 1943
Count the Ways. Doubleday, 1949
Dark Lady. Doubleday, 1960; Popular Lib., 1964 (Also published as: Sinister Lady. Hale, R., 1962)
Dark Road. Doubleday, 1946; Popular Lib., 1965
Dead Stop. Dell, 1957
The Departure of Mr. Gaudette. Doubleday, 1964
Did She Fall or Was She Pushed? Doubleday, 1959; Ace, 1962; Hale, R., 1962
Do Unto Others. Doubleday, 1953
Driven to Kill; see The Last Straw
Enduring Old Charms. Doubleday, 1947
Family Skeleton. Doubleday, 1949
Find the Woman. Doubleday, 1962; Popular Lib., 1964; Hale, R., 1964
Fire at Will. Doubleday, 1950
Halloween Murder; see Method in Madness
Heavy, Heavy Hangs. Doubleday, 1952
Here Lies. Doubleday, 1963; Hale, R., 1964; Macfadden, 1967
The Hospitality of the House. Doubleday, 1964
The Last Straw. Doubleday, 1954; Popular Lib., 1965 (English title: Driven to Kill. Foulsham, 1957)
Look Back on Murder. Doubleday, 1951
The Magic Grandfather. Doubleday, 1966
Method in Madness. Doubleday, 1957 (Also published as: Halloween Murder. Foulsham, 1957 and Too Innocent to Kill. Avon, 1957)

Murder on a Tangent. Doubleday, Doran, 1945
Mrs. Meeker's Money. Ace, 1961; Doubleday, 1961; Hale, R., 1963
My Neighbor's Wife. Doubleday, 1957; Foulsham, 1958
Night of Clear Choice. Doubleday, 1967
No Next of Kin. Doubleday, 1959; Foulsham, 1961; Dell, 1963
The Post Office Case; see Unappointed Rounds
Prescription Murder. Doubleday, 1953
Quiet Violence. Foulsham, 1959
Room for Murder. Doubleday, 1955; Foulsham, 1959
Shadow of a Man. Doubleday, 1965; Hale, R., 1966
Should Auld Acquaintance. Doubleday, 1962; Hale, R., 1963; Macfadden, 1967
Sinister Lady; see Dark Lady
Sow the Wind; see Who Rides a Tiger
Strawman. Doubleday, 1951 (English title: The Case of the Strawman. Foulsham, 1958)
Testimony of Silence. Doubleday, 1948
That Which Is Crooked. Doubleday, 1948
Too Innocent to Kill; see Method in Madness
Trick or Treat. Doubleday, 1955
Unappointed Rounds. Doubleday, 1956; Ace, 1961 (English title: The Post Office Case. Foulsham, 1957)
Who Rides a Tiger. Doubleday, 1946; Ace, 1964 (Also published as: Sow the Wind. Hay & Mitchell, 1948; Low, 1948)

DISNEY, DOROTHY CAMERON (D)
The Balcony. Random, 1940
Crimson Friday. Random, 1943
Death in the Back Seat. Random, 1963; Dell
Explosion. Random, 1948
The Golden Swan Murder. Random, 1939
The Hangman's Tree. Random, 1949; Ace, 1964
No Next of Kin. Doubleday, 1959
The Seventeenth Letter. Random, 1945
Strawstack. Random, 1939
Thirty Days Hath September, with George Sessions Perry. Random, 1942

DIVINE, ARTHUR DUNHAM (S) (Pseudonym: David Divine)
Atom at Spithead. Hale, R., 1953; Macmillan, 1953
Boy on a Dolphin. Macmillan, 1953

DIVINE, DAVID, pseud; see DIVINE, ARTHUR DUNHAM

DIX, MAURICE BUXTON (D)
Beacons of Death. Ward, Lock, 1937
The Dartmoor Mystery. Ward, Lock, 1935
Emily Coulton Dies. Ward, Lock, 1936
The Fixer. Ward, Lock, 1936
The Flame of the Khan. Ward, Lock, 1934
The Fleetwood Mansions Mystery. Ward, Lock, 1934
The Golden Fluid. Ward, Lock, 1935
The Kidnapped Scientist. Ward, Lock, 1937
Lady Richly Left. Staples Press, 1951
The Masinglee Murders. Hale, R., 1947
Murder at Grassmere Abbey. Ward, Lock, 1933
Murder Strikes Twice. Ward, Lock, 1939
Night Assassin. Hale, R., 1941
Prologue to Murder. Ward, Lock, 1938
This Is My Murder. Ward, Lock, 1938
Treasure of Scarland. Ward, Lock, 1936
Twisted Evidence. Ward, Lock, 1933

DIXON, CHARLES (D)
A Fortune for the Taking. Hale, R., 1963
A Hand in Murder. Hale, R., 1962
Ministry Murder. Hale, R., 1961
Red Murder File. Hale, R., 1964

DIXON, H. VERNOR (S)
Cry Blood. GM, 1956
Killer in Silk. GM, 1957
Too Rich to Die. GM, 1953

DOBBINS, PAUL H. (D)
Death in the Dunes. Phoenix, 1950

DOCHERTY, JAMES, pseud; see RAYMOND, RENÉ

DODERER, HEIMITO VON (D)
Every Man a Murderer. Knopf, 1964

DODGE, ALICE M. (M)
The Eye of the Peacock. Bouregy, 1966

DODGE, CONSTANCE WOODBURY (S)
The Unrelenting. Doubleday, 1950

DODGE, DAVID (D)
Angel's Ransom. Random, 1956; Dell
Bullets for the Bridegroom. Macmillan, 1944; Joseph, M., 1948
Carambola. Little, 1961
Death and Taxes. Macmillan, 1941
It Ain't Hay. S & S, 1947
The Lights of Skaro. Random, 1954
The Long Escape. Random, 1948
Plunder of the Sun. Random, 1949
Ransom of the Angel. Penguin

The Red Tassel. Random, 1950
Shear the Black Sheep. Macmillan, 1942
To Catch a Thief. Random, 1952

DODGE, MRS. JOSEPHINE DASKAM (M) (Pseudonym: J. D. Bacon)
The Girl at the Window. Appleton-Century, 1934
Medusa's Head. Appleton, D., 1926

DODGE, LANGDON, pseud; see WOLFSON, VICTOR

DODGE, LOUIS (S)
Whispers. Scribner, 1920

DODGE, STEVE, pseud; see BECKER, STEPHEN DAVID

DODSON, DANIEL B. (S)
The Man Who Ran Away. Dutton, 1961

DOE, JOHN, pseud; see THAYER, TIFFANY

DOHERTY, EDWARD J. (D)
The Broadway Murders. Doubleday, Doran, 1929
The Corpse Who Wouldn't Die. Mystery House, 1945

DOLBEY, ETHEL M. and GEOFFREY MAY (D) (Pseudonym: E. M. D. Hawthorne)
Quietly She Lies. Harper, 1953

DOLINER, ROY (M)
Sandra Rifkin's Jewels. New Amer. Lib., 1966

DOLINSKY, MEYER (S)
There Is No Silence. Allen, T., 1959; Hale, R., 1959

DOLLAND, JOHN (S)
A Gentleman Hangs. Macmillan, 1941

DOLPH, JACK (D)
Dead Angel. Doubleday, 1953; Boardman, T. V., 1954
Hot Tip. Doubleday, 1951
Murder Is Mutuel. Morrow, 1948
Murder Makes the Mare Go. Doubleday, 1948
Odds on Murder. Morrow, 1948; Boardman, T. V., 1953

DONAHUE, JACKSON (S)
The Confessor. Barker, 1963; New Amer. Lib., 1964
Erase My Name. Barker, 1964

DONALD, WINIFRED (M)
Linda in Cambridge. Hutchinson, 1955

DONATI, SERGIO (M)
The Paper Tombs. Collins, 1958

DONAVAN, JOHN, pseud; see MORLAND, NIGEL

DONNEL, C. PHILIP (D)
Murder-Go-Round. McKay, 1945

DONOVAN, DICK, pseud; see MUDDOCK, JOYCE EMERSON PRESTON

DORN, DEAN M.; see CARLE, C. E.

DORRINGTON, ALBERT (D)
The Radium Terrors. Munsey, 1910; Doubleday, Page, 1912; Nash, 1912

DORY, JOHN, pseud. (M)
Grip Finds the Lady. Benn, 1932

DOUBLEDAY, ROMAN, pseud; see LONG, LILY AUGUSTA

DOUBTFIRE, DIANNE (S)
Kick a Tin Can. Davies, 1964
Lust for Innocence. Morrow, 1960
Reason for Violence. Davies, 1961

DOUGALL, BERNARD (D)
I Don't Scare Easy. Dodd, 1941
The Singing Corpse. Dodd, 1943

DOUGALL, LILY (M)
The Summit House Mystery. Funk, W., 1905

DOUGLAS, DONALD McNUTT (M)
The Falcon's Flight. Doubleday, Doran, 1929
Grand Inquisitor. Boni & Liveright, 1925
Haunted Harbor
Many Brave Hearts. Harper, 1958; Eyre, 1959
Rebecca's Pride. Harper, 1956
Saba's Treasure. Harper, 1961; Eyre, 1963

DOUGLAS, GAVIN (S)
Captain Samson, A. B. Putnam, 1937
The Obstinate Captain Samson. Putnam, 1937
The Tall Man. Putnam, 1936

DOUGLAS, GEORGE (M)
The Case of the Greedy Rainmaker. Bouregy, 1963

DOUGLAS, MALCOLM, pseud; see SANDERSON, DOUGLAS

DOUGLAS, ROY (M)
Who Is Nemo? Lippincott, 1937

DOW, JOHN (D)
The Little Boy Laughed. Arcadia, 1945

DOWNES, DONALD (S)
The Eastern Dinner. Rinehart, 1960; PB, 1961
Orders to Kill. Rinehart, 1958
Red Rose for Maria. Rinehart, 1959
The Scarlet Thread. Rinehart, 1953
With Gusto and Relish. Deutsch, 1957

DOWNES, QUENTIN, pseud; see HARRISON, MICHAEL

DOWNING, GEORGE TODD (D)
The Case of the Unconquered Sisters. Doubleday, Doran, 1936; Methuen, 1937
The Cat Screams. Doubleday, Doran, 1934; Methuen, 1935
Death Under the Moonflower. Doubleday, Doran, 1938
The Last Trumpet. Doubleday, Doran, 1937; Methuen, 1938
The Lazy Laurence Murders. Doubleday, Doran, 1941
Murder on the Tropic. Doubleday, Doran, 1935; Methuen, 1936; Sun Dial, 1936
Murder on Tour. Doubleday, Doran, 1933
Night over Mexico. Doubleday, Doran, 1937; Methuen, 1938
Vultures in the Sky. Doubleday, Doran, 1935; Methuen, 1936

DOYLE, ADRIAN CONAN (D)
The New Exploits of Sherlock Holmes, with John Dickson Carr. Murray, J., 1954; Random, 1954

DOYLE, SIR ARTHUR CONAN (D)
The Adventures of Sherlock Holmes. Harper, 1892; Newnes, 1892; Berkley Pub., 1963
The Case Book of Sherlock Holmes. Doran, 1927; Murray, J., 1927; Berkley Pub., 1964
The Complete Long Stories: Sherlock Holmes. Murray, J., 1929
The Complete Sherlock Holmes. Doubleday, Doran, 1936, 1960
The Complete Short Stories: Sherlock Holmes. Murray, J., 1929
The First Book of Sherlock Holmes Stories
The Heritage Sherlock Holmes. Heritage, 1957
His Last Bow. Doran, 1917; Murray, J., 1917; Berkley Pub., 1964
Hound of the Baskervilles. Newnes, 1902; McClure, Philips, 1902; Berkley Pub., 1963
The Memoirs of Sherlock Holmes. Edinburgh, 1886; Harper, 1894; Newnes, 1894; Atheneum, 1934; Berkley Pub., 1963
The Return of Sherlock Holmes. Newnes, 1905; McClure, Philips, 1906
A Scandal in Bohemia. Lovell, Coryell, 1891 (Also published in Strand Magazine, April 6, 1891)
The Second Book of Sherlock Holmes
Sign of Four. Lippincott, 1890; Collier, P., 1891
A Study in Scarlet. Ward, Lock, 1888; Lippincott, 1890 (Originally published in Beeton's Christmas Annual. Ward, Lock, 1887)
The Third Book of Sherlock Holmes Stories
The Valley of Fear. Doran, 1915; Smith, Elder, 1915; Berkley Pub., 1964

DRACHMAN, THEODORE SOLOMAN (S)
Addicted to Murder; see Something for the Birds
Cry Plague. Ace, 1953
Something for the Birds. Crown, 1958 (Also published as: Addicted to Murder. Avon, 1958)

DRACO, F., pseud. (M)
Cruise with Death. Rinehart, 1952
The Devil's Church. Rinehart, 1951

DRAGO, HARRY SINCLAIR
The Leather Burners. Doubleday, Doran, 1940

DRAKE, DREXEL (M)
The Falcon Cuts In. Lippincott, 1937
The Falcon Meets a Lady. Lippincott, 1938
The Falcon's Prey. Lippincott, 1936

DRAKE, HENRY BURGESS (M)
Cursed Be the Treasure. Lane, 1926; Macy-Masius, 1928
The Shadowy Thing. Macy-Masius, 1928

DRAKE, MAURICE (D)
The Doom Window. Dutton, 1925
The Ocean Sleuth. Dutton, 1916
WO_2. Dutton, 1913

DRATLER, JAY J. (S)
Ducks in Thunder. Reynal, 1940
The Judas Kiss. Holt, H., 1955

DRAX, PETER, pseud; see ADDIS, ERIC ELRINGTON

DRENNEN, RAYMOND (D)
Murder Beat. Bouregy, 1956

DRESSER, DAVIS (D) (Pseudonyms: Asa Baker, Don Davis, Brett Halliday. Joint pseudonym with Kathleen Rollins: Hal Debrett)

Armed . . .Dangerous, by Brett Halliday. Dell, 1967
Before I Wake, by Hal Debrett. Dodd, 1949
The Blonde Cried Murder, by Brett Halliday. Dodd, 1956; Jarrolds, 1957; Dell, 1963
Blood on Biscayne Bay, by Brett Halliday. Dell, 1966
Blood on the Stars, by Brett Halliday. Dodd, 1948; Dell, 1962
Bodies Are Where You Find Them, by Brett Halliday. Holt, H., 1941; Dell, 1959
The Body Came Back, by Brett Halliday. Dodd, 1963; Dell, 1964
Call for Michael Shayne, by Brett Halliday. Dodd, 1949; Dell, 1959
The Careless Corpse, by Brett Halliday. Dodd, 1961
The Corpse Came Calling, by Brett Halliday. Dodd, 1942; Dell, 1964
The Corpse That Never Was, by Brett Halliday. Dodd, 1963; Dell, 1964
Counterfeit Wife, by Brett Halliday. Ziff-Davis, 1947; Dell
Dangerous Dames, by Brett Halliday. Dell, 1965
Date with a Dead Man, by Brett Halliday. Dodd, 1959; Long, 1960; Dell, 1967
Dead Man's Diary and Dinner at Dupre's, by Brett Halliday. Dell, 1945 (published with A Taste of Cognac. Dell, 1964)
Death Has Three Lines, by Brett Halliday. Dodd, 1955; Dell, 1961
Death on Treasure Trail, by Don Davis. Morrow, 1941
Diamonds for a Lady; see Fit To Kill
Die Like a Dog, by Brett Halliday. Dodd, 1959; Dell, 1967
Dinner at Dupre's; see Dead Man's Diary
Dividend on Death, by Brett Halliday. Holt, H., 1939; Dell, 1959
Dolls Are Deadly, by Brett Halliday. Dodd, 1960; Dell, 1961
Fit to Kill, by Brett Halliday. Dodd, 1958; Dell, 1966 (Also published as: Diamonds for a Lady. Long, 1959)
Framed in Blood, by Brett Halliday. Dodd, 1951; Jarrolds, 1953; Dell, 1967
Guilty as Hell, by Brett Halliday. Dell, 1967
Heads You Lose, by Brett Halliday. Dell, 1965; Dodd, 1956
The Homicidal Virgin, by Brett Halliday. Dodd, 1960; Dell, 1961
In a Deadly Vein, by Brett Halliday. Dodd, 1943; Dell, 1962
Killers from the Keys, by Brett Halliday. Dodd, 1961; Dell, 1962
The Kissed Corpse, by Asa Baker. Carlyle, 1939
A Lonely Way to Die, by Hal Debrett. Dodd, 1950; Jarrolds, 1954
Marked for Murder, by Brett Halliday. Dell, 1963
Mermaid on the Rocks, by Brett Halliday. Dell, 1967
Michael Shayne Investigates, by Brett Halliday. Jarrolds, 1943
Michael Shayne Takes a Hand; see Murder Wears a Mummers Mask
Michael Shayne Takes Over, by Brett Halliday. Holt, H., 1942 (Contains: Dividend on Death, The Private Practice of Michael Shayne, and Bodies Are Where You Find Them)
Michael Shayne's Fiftieth Case, by Brett Halliday. Dodd, 1964; Dell, 1965
Michael Shayne's Long Chance, by Brett Halliday. Dell, 1944
Michael Shayne's Torrid Twelve, by Brett Halliday. Dell, 1961
Michael Shayne's Triple Mystery, by Brett Halliday. Ziff-Davis, 1948
Mum's the Word for Murder, by Asa Baker. Dodd, 1938; Dell, 1964 (1964 edition by Brett Halliday)
Murder and the Married Virgin, by Brett Halliday. Dell, 1963
Murder and the Wanton Bride, by Brett Halliday. Dodd, 1958; Long, 1959; Dell, 1965
Murder by Proxy, by Brett Halliday. Dodd, 1962; Dell, 1963
Murder in Haste, by Brett Halliday. Dodd, 1961; Dell, 1962
Murder Is My Business, by Brett Halliday. Dell, 1963
Murder Spins the Wheel, by Brett Halliday. Dell, 1966
Murder Takes No Holiday, by Brett Halliday. Dodd, 1960; Dell, 1961
Murder Wears a Mummers Mask, by Brett Halliday. Dodd, 1943 (English title: Michael Shayne Takes a Hand. Jarrolds, 1944)
Never Kill a Client, by Brett Halliday. Dodd, 1962; Dell, 1963
Nice Fillies Finish Last, by Brett Halliday. Dell, 1966
One Night with Nora, by Brett Halliday. Dodd, 1953
Pay-off in Blood, by Brett Halliday. Dodd, 1962; Dell, 1963
The Private Practice of Michael Shayne, by Brett Halliday. Holt, H., 1964; Dell
A Redhead for Mike Shayne, by Brett Halliday. Dodd, 1964; Dell, 1965
She Woke to Darkness, by Brett Halliday. Dodd, 1954; Jarrolds, 1955; Dell, 1962
Shoot the Works, by Brett Halliday. Dodd, 1957; Long, 1958; Dell, 1965
Shoot to Kill, by Brett Halliday. Dodd, 1964; Dell, 1965

Stranger in Town, by Brett Halliday. Dodd, 1955; Jarrolds, 1958
Target: Mike Shayne, by Brett Halliday. Dodd, 1959; Dell, 1966
A Taste for Violence, by Brett Halliday. Dodd, 1949; Dell, 1962
A Taste of Cognac; see Dead Man's Diary
This Is It, Michael Shayne, by Brett Halliday. Dodd, 1950; Jarrolds, 1952; Dell, 1962
Tickets for Death, by Brett Halliday. Holt, 1960; Dell, 1965
Too Friendly, Too Dead, by Brett Halliday. Dodd, 1963; Dell, 1964
The Uncomplaining Corpses, by Brett Halliday. Holt, H., 1940; Dell, 1963
The Violent World of Mike Shayne, by Brett Halliday. Dell, 1965
Weep for a Blonde, by Brett Halliday. Dodd, 1957; Long, 1958; Dell, 1964
What Really Happened, by Brett Halliday. Dodd, 1952; Dell, 1963
When Dorinda Dances, by Brett Halliday. Dodd, 1951; Jarrolds, 1953; Dell, 1963

DREWE, MARCUS (M)
The Barber of Littlewick. Jenkins, 1930

DREWRY, EDITH S. (M)
Death Ring. Moor, 1881; Maxwell, J. & R., 1887

DRUMMOND, ANTHONY, pseud; see HUNTER, JOHN

DRUMMOND, JUNE (M)
The Black Unicorn. Gollancz, 1959
Cable Car. Holt, 1967
Welcome, Proud Lady. Gollancz, 1964

DRUMMOND, WILLIAM (S)
Gaslight. Paperback Lib., 1966 (Adapted from the play Angel Street by Patrick Hamilton)
Night Must Fall. Signet, 1964 (Adapted from the play by Emlyn Williams)

DRYER, BERNARD VICTOR (S)
Port Afrique. Harper, 1949; Hamilton & Co., 1956; Bantam, 1964

DuBOIS, THEODORA (M-D)
Armed with a New Terror. Houghton, 1936
The Body Goes Round and Round. Houghton, 1942
The Case of the Perfumed Mouse. Doubleday, Doran, 1945
The Cavalier's Corpse. Doubleday, 1952; Boardman, T. V., 1953
Death Comes to Tea. Houghton, 1940
Death Dines Out. Houghton, 1939
Death Is Late to Lunch. Houghton, 1941
Death Sails in the High Wind. Doubleday, Doran, 1945
Death Tears a Comic Strip. Houghton, 1939
Death Wears a White Coat. Houghton, 1938
The Devil and Destiny. Doubleday, 1948
The Devil's Spoon. Stokes, 1930
The Face of Hate. Doubleday, 1948
The Footsteps. Doubleday, 1947
Fowl Play. Doubleday, 1951
High Tension. Doubleday, 1950
It's Raining Violence. Doubleday, 1949
The Late Bride. Washburn, 1964
The Listener. Doubleday, 1953; Ace, 1965
Murder Strikes an Atomic Unit. Doubleday, 1946
Rogue's Coat. Doubleday, 1949
Seeing Red. Doubleday, 1954; Collins, 1955
Shannon Terror. Washburn, 1964; Ace, 1965
The Wild Duck Murders. Doubleday, Doran, 1943
The Wild Man Murders. Doubleday, Doran, 1943

Du BOIS, WILLIAM (D)
The Case of the Deadly Diary. Little, 1940
The Case of the Frightened Fish. Little, 1940
The Case of the Haunted Brides. Little, 1941

DU BOISGOBEY, FORTUNÉ HIPPOLYTE AUGUSTE (D)
The Blue Veil; or, The Crime of the Tower. Lovell, J. W., 1887; Laird, 1889
The Cat's-Eye Ring; A Secret of Paris Life. Routledge, 1888
The Closed Door. Munro, 1886 (Also published as: The Condemned Door; or, The Secret of Trigabon Castle. Lovell, J. W., 1887)
The Crime of the Opera House. Munro, 1881
The Day of Reckoning. Vizetelly, 1885
The Detective's Eye. Lovell, J. W., 1888 (Also published as: Piédouche, a French Detective. Munro, 1884 and Parisian Detective. Ivers, 1887)
The Golden Tress. Claxton, 1876
The Matapan Affair. Munro, 1882; Lovell, J. W., 1888
The Mystery of an Omnibus. Munro, 1882
Parisian Detective; see The Detective's Eye
Piédouche, a French Detective; see The Detective's Eye
Was It Murder; or, Who Is the Heir? Rand, 1883

DU CANN, CHARLES GARFIELD LOTT (D)
The Secret Hand. Methuen, 1929

DUDLEY, DOROTHY; see SHERIDAN, JUANITA

DUDLEY, ERNEST (D-M)
The Adventures of Jimmy Strange. Long, 1945
Alibi and Dr. Morelle. Hale, R., 1959
The Blind Beak. Hale, R., 1965
Callers for Dr. Morelle. Hale, R., 1957
Confess to Dr. Morelle. Hale, R., 1959
The Confessions of a Special Agent, with Jack Evans. Hale, R., 1957 (U.S. title: The Face of Death. Morrow, 1958)
The Crooked Inn. Hodder, 1953
The Crooked Straight. Hodder, 1948
The Dark Bureau. Hodder, 1950
Dr. Morelle and Destiny. Hale, R., 1958
Dr. Morelle and the Doll. Hale, R., 1960
Dr. Morelle and the Drummer Girl. Hodder, 1950
Dr. Morelle at Midnight. Hale, R., 1959
Dr. Morelle Meets Murder and Other New Adventures. Findon, 1948
Dr. Morelle Takes a Bow, with Jack Evans. Hale, R., 1957
The Face of Death; see The Confessions of a Special Agent
The Harassed Hero. Hodder, 1951
Leatherface. Hale, R., 1958
Look Out for Lucifer. Long, 1952
Meet Dr. Morelle. Long, 1944
Meet Dr. Morelle Again. Long, 1947
Menace for Dr. Morelle. Long, 1947
The Mind of Dr. Morelle. Hale, R., 1958
Mr. Walker Wants to Know. Wright & Brown, 1940
Nightmare for Dr. Morelle. Hale, R., 1960
Picaroon. Hale, R., 1952; Bobbs, 1953
The Private Eye. Long, 1950
The Scarlet Widow. Muller, 1960
To Love and to Perish. Hale, R., 1962
Two Face. Long, 1951
The Whistling Sands. Hodder, 1956

DUDLEY, FRANK, pseud; see GREENE, WARD

DUDLEY-SMITH, TREVOR; see TREVOR, ELLESTON

DUFF, BELDON (D)
Ask No Questions. Doubleday, Doran, 1930
The Central Park Murder. Doubleday, Doran, 1929

DUFF, DAVID (D)
Traitor's Pass. Roy Pubs., 1955

DUFF, JAMES (D)
Dangerous to Know. Ace, 1959
Run from Death. Bouregy, 1957
Some Die Young. Graphic, 1956
Who Dies There? Graphic, 1956

DUHART, WILLIAM H. (D)
The Deadly Pay-off. GM, 1958

DUKE, WILL (S)
Fair Prey. Graphic, 1956

DUKE, WINIFRED (M)
Bastard Verdict. Jarrolds, 1931
Skin for Skin. Little, 1935
Unjust Jury. Jarrolds, 1944

DU MAURIER, DAPHNE (S)
My Cousin Rachel. Doubleday, 1952
Rebecca. Doubleday, Doran, 1938; PB, 1964
The Scapegoat. Doubleday, 1957
Treveryan. Paperback Lib., 1962

DUN, MARIE DE NERVAUD (M)
Point of Death. Hammond, 1954

DUNCAN, ACTEA (M) (Pseudonym: Carolyn Thomas)
The Cactus Shroud. Boardman, T. V., 1957; Lippincott, 1957
The Hearse Horse Snickered. Lippincott, 1954; Boardman, T. V., 1955
Narrow Gauge to Murder. Lippincott, 1952; Boardman, T. V., 1956
Prominent Among the Mourners. Lippincott, 1946

DUNCAN, ALLAN (M)
An Official Secret. Crowell, 1937

DUNCAN, DAVID (M)
Beyond Eden. Ballantine, 1955
The Bramble Bush. Macmillan, 1948; Low, 1949
Dark Dominion. Ballantine, 1954; Heinemann, 1955
The Madrone Tree. Macmillan, 1949; Gollancz, 1950
Remember the Shadows. McBride, 1944
The Serpent's Egg. Macmillan, 1949; Gollancz, 1950
The Shade of Time. Random, 1946; Grey Walls, 1949

DUNCAN, FRANCIS (M)
Behold a Fair Woman. Long, 1954
Dangerous Mr. X. Jenkins, 1939; Withy Grove, 1947
Fear Holds the Key. Jenkins, 1945
The Hand of Justice. Jenkins, 1945
In at the Death. Long, 1952
Justice Limited. Jenkins, 1941

Justice Returns. Jenkins, 1940
The League of Justice. Jenkins, 1937
Ministers Too Are Mortal. Long, 1951
Murder But Gently. Long, 1953
Murder for Christmas. Long, 1949
Murder Has a Motive. Long, 1948
Murder in Man. Jenkins, 1940
Murderer's Bluff. Jenkins, 1938
Night Without End. Jenkins, 1943
Question of Time. Hale, R., 1959
So Pretty a Problem. Long, 1950
The Sword of Justice. Jenkins, 1937
They'll Never Find Out. Jenkins, 1944
Tigers Fight Alone. Jenkins, 1938

DUNCAN, LOIS (M)
Point of Violence. Doubleday, 1966

DUNCAN, PETER (S)
The Tell-Tale Tart. GM, 1961

DUNCAN, WILLIAM MURDOCK (M-D)
(Pseudonyms: John Cassells, Neill Graham, Martin Locke, Peter Malloch, Lovat Marshall)
Again Inspector Flagg, by John Cassells. Muller, 1956
Again Mr. Sandyman, by Neill Graham. Jarrolds, 1952
Again the Dreamer. Long, 1965
The Amazing Mr. Sandyman, by Neill Graham. Jarrolds, 1952
Anchor Island, by Peter Malloch. Long, 1962
The Avenging Picaroon, by John Cassells. Muller, 1956
The Bastion of the Damned, by John Cassells. Melrose, 1947
The Benevolent Picaroon, by John Cassells. Long, 1964
Beware the Picaroon, by John Cassells. Muller, 1956
The Black Mitre. Melrose, 1951
The Blackbird Sings of Murder. Melrose, 1948
Blood Money, by Peter Malloch. Long, 1962
The Blood Red Leaf. Melrose, 1952
Blue Mask, by John Cassells. Hutchinson, 1964
Break Through, by Peter Malloch. Long, 1963
The Brothers of Benevolence, by John Cassells. Long, 1962
The Brothers of Judgment. Melrose, 1950
Case for Inspector Flagg, by John Cassells. Muller, 1954
Case 29, by John Cassells. Long, 1958
Castle of Sin, by John Cassells. Melrose, 1949
Challenge for the Picaroon, by John Cassells. Long, 1964
The Circle of Dust, by John Cassells. Melrose, 1952
The Clue of the Purple Asters, by John Cassells. Melrose, 1952
The Company of Sinners. Melrose, 1951
Cop Lover, by Peter Malloch. Long, 1964
Council of the Rat, by John Cassells. Long, 1963
The Crime Master. Long, 1963
The Cult of the Queer People. Melrose, 1949
Death Beckons Quietly. Melrose, 1946
Death Comes to Lady's Step. Melrose, 1952
Death Stands Round the Corner. Rich, 1955
Death Treads Softly, by Peter Malloch. Rich, 1957
Death Wears a Silk Stocking. Melrose, 1945
Deathmaster. Hutchinson, 1954
The Doctor Deals with Murder. Melrose, 1944
Eleven-Twenty Glasgow Central, by Peter Malloch. Rich, 1955
The Engaging Picaroon, by John Cassells. Long, 1958
Enter Superintendent Flagg, by John Cassells. Long, 1959
Enter the Picaroon, by John Cassells. Muller, 1954
The Enterprising Picaroon, by John Cassells. Long, 1959
Exit Mr. Shane, by Peter Malloch. Long, 1958
Fly Away, Death, by Peter Malloch. Long, 1958
Fugitive Road, by Peter Malloch. Long, 1963
Graft Town, by Neill Graham. Long, 1963
The Green Knight. Long, 1964
The Grey Ghost, by John Cassells. Melrose, 1951
Greyface, by John Cassells. Long, 1965
Hardiman's Landing, by Peter Malloch. Long, 1960
Hit Me Hard, by Neill Graham. Long, 1958
The Hooded Man. Long, 1960
The Hour of the Bishop. Long, 1964
The House in Spite Street. Long, 1961
The House of Wailing Winds. Long, 1965
Inspector Flagg and the Scarlet Skeleton, by John Cassells. Muller, 1955
The Joker Deals with Death. Long, 1958
Killer Keep. Melrose, 1946
Killers Are on Velvet, by Neill Graham. Long, 1960
Knife in the Night. Rich, 1955
Label It Murder, by Neill Graham. Long, 1963
Ladies Can Be Dangerous, by Lovat Marshall. Hale, 1964
Make Mine Murder, by Neill Graham. Long, 1962

The Mark of the Leech, by John Cassells. Melrose, 1950
The Master of the Dark, by John Cassells. Melrose, 1948
Meet the Dreamer. Long, 1963
Meet the Picaroon, by John Cassells. Long, 1957
Money for Murder. Long, 1966
Murder at Marks Caris. Melrose, 1945
Murder Calls the Tune. Long, 1957
Murder Comes to Rothesay, by John Cassells. Melrose, 1949
Murder in Triplicate, by Lovat Marshall. Hale, R., 1963
Murder Is My Weakness, by Neill Graham. Long, 1961
Murder Is the Reason, by Lovat Marshall. Hale, R., 1964
Murder Made Easy, by Neill Graham. Long, 1964
Murder Makes a Date, by Neill Graham. Jarrolds, 1955; Roy Pubs., 1955
Murder Makes It Certain, by Neill Graham. Long, 1963
The Murder Man. Long, 1959
Murder of a Black Cat, by Neill Graham. Long, 1964
Murder of the Man Next Door, by Peter Malloch. Long, 1966
Murder on My Hands, by Neill Graham. Long, 1965
Murder on the Duchess, by Neill Graham. Long, 1961
Murder Rings the Bell. Long, 1959
Murder Walks on Tiptoe, by Neill Graham. Melrose, 1952
Mystery on the Clyde. Melrose, 1945
The Nicholas Snatch, by Peter Malloch. Long, 1964
The Nighthawk. Long, 1962
Passport to Murder, by Neill Graham. Melrose, 1949
Pennies for His Eyes. Rich, 1955
The Picaroon Goes West, by John Cassells. Long, 1962
Presenting Inspector Flagg, by John Cassells. Muller, 1957
Prey for the Picaroon, by John Cassells. Long, 1963
Problem for Superintendent Flagg, by John Cassells. Long, 1961
The Puppets of Father Bouvard. Melrose, 1948
The Quest of Mr. Sandyman, by Neill Graham. Jarrolds, 1951
The Rattler, by John Cassells. Melrose, 1952
Redfingers. Long, 1962
Salute Inspector Flagg, by John Cassells. Muller, 1953
Salute Mr. Sandyman, by Neill Graham. Jarrolds, 1955
Salute the Picaroon, by John Cassells. Long, 1960
Salute to Murder, by Neill Graham. Long, 1958
Say It with Murder, by Neill Graham. Jarrolds, 1956
Score for Superintendent Flagg, by John Cassells. Long, 1960
The Second Mrs. Locke, by John Cassells. Melrose, 1952
The Sniper, by Peter Malloch. Long, 1965
The Sons of the Morning, by John Cassells. Melrose, 1946
Straight Ahead for Danger. Melrose, 1946
Sugar Cuts the Corners, by Lovat Marshall. Hurst, 1957
Sugar for the Lady, by Lovat Marshall. Hurst, 1955
Sugar on the Carpet, by Lovat Marshall. Hurst, 1956
Sugar on the Cuff, by Lovat Marshall. Hale, R., 1960
Sugar on the Kill, by Lovat Marshall. Hale, R., 1961
Sugar on the Loose, by Lovat Marshall. Hale, R., 1962
Sugar on the Prowl, by Lovat Marshall. Hale, R., 1962
Sugar on the Target, by Lovat Marshall. Hurst, 1958
Sweet Lady Death, by Peter Malloch. Rich, 1956
Symbol of the Cat, by Neill Graham. Melrose, 1952
The Temple of Slumber, by Neill Graham. Melrose, 1950
The Tiled House Mystery. Melrose, 1947
The Vengeance of Mortimer Daly, by Martin Locke. Ward, Lock, 1962
Walk in Death, by Peter Malloch. Rich, 1958
The Waters of Sadness, by John Cassells. Melrose, 1952
The Whispering Man. Long, 1960

DUNCOMBE, FRANCES (D)
Death of a Spinster. Scribner, 1958; Secker & Warburg, 1959

DUNDAS, LAWRENCE (D)
He Liked Them Murderous. Hammond, 1964
Spider at the Elivra. Hammond, 1943

DUNDEE, ROBERT (M)
Pandora's Box. Signet, 1962

DUNLOP, AGNES MARY ROBERTSON (Pseudonym: Elizabeth Kyle)
Mally Lee. Doubleday, 1947
The Other Miss Evans, by Elizabeth Kyle. Davies, 1958
The Regent's Candlesticks. Davies, 1954

DUNN, DOROTHY (D)
Murder's Web. Harper, 1950

DUNN, IRMA LARAWAY (M)
A Slightly Disjointed Affair. Vantage, 1963

DUPREE, MORRISON, pseud. (M)
A Tap on the Shoulder. Doubleday, 1929

DUPUY-MAZUEL, HENRI (D) (Pseudonym: Henry Catalan)
Soeur Angele and the Bell Ringer's Niece. Sheed, 1957
Soeur Angele and the Embarrassed Ladies. Sheed, 1955; Dell, 1962
Soeur Angele and the Ghosts of Chambord. Sheed, 1956

DURAND, MORTIMER HENRY MARION (M)
Sincerité. Long, 1924

DURAND, ROBERT (S)
Lady in a Cage. Popular Lib., 1964

DURBRIDGE, FRANCIS (D) (Joint pseudonym with Douglas Rutherford McConnell: Paul Temple)
Another Woman's Shoes. Hodder, 1965
Back Room Girl. Long, 1950
Beware of Johnny Washington. Long, 1951
The Case of the Twisted Scarf; see The Scarf
Design for Murder. Long, 1951
East of Algiers, by Paul Temple. Hodder, 1959
My Friend Charles. Hodder, 1963
News of Paul Temple. Long, 1940
Other Man. Hodder, 1958
Paul Temple and the Front Page Men. Long, 1939
Paul Temple Intervenes. Long, 1944
Portrait of Alison. Dodd, 1962; Hodder, 1962
The Scarf. Hodder, 1960 (U.S. title: The Case of the Twisted Scarf. Dodd, 1961)
Send for Paul Temple. Long, 1938
Send for Paul Temple Again. Long, 1948
Tim Frazer Again. Hodder, 1964
A Time of Day. Hodder, 1959
Tyler Mystery, by Paul Temple. Hodder, 1957
The World of Tim Frazer. Dodd, 1962; Hodder, 1962

DURHAM, DAVID (D)
Against the Law. Jenkins, 1939
The Exploits of Fidelity Dove. Hodder, 1924
The Forgotten Honeymoon. Jenkins, 1938
The Girl Who Dared. Jenkins, 1938
Hounded Down. Hodder, 1923; Collins, 1931
The Pearl-Headed Pin. Hodder, 1925
The Woman Accused. Hodder, 1923

DURHAM, MARY (D)
Castle Mandragora. Gifford, 1950
The Cornish Mystery. Crowther, 1946
Corpse Errant. Skeffington, 1949
Crime Insoluble. Crowther, 1947
The Devil Was Sick. Gifford, 1952
Forked Lightning. Gifford, 1951
Hate Is My Livery. Gifford, 1945
Keeps Death His Court. Crowther, 1946
Murder by Multiplication. Skeffington, 1948
Murder Hath Charms. Skeffington, 1948
Why Pick on Pickles? Crowther, 1946

DURRANT, THEO, pseud. (M)
The Marble Forest. Knopf, 1951

DURRELL, LAWRENCE
White Eagles over Serbia. Faber, 1957

DÜRRENMATT, FRIEDRICH (S)
A Dangerous Game. Cape, 1960 (U.S. title: Traps. Knopf, 1960)
The Judge and His Hangman. Harper, 1955; Jenkins, 1956; Doubleday, 1963
The Pledge. Cape, 1959; Knopf, 1959; Avon, 1967
Traps; see A Dangerous Game

DURST, PAUL (D) (Pseudonym: Peter Bannon)
If I Should Die. Jenkins, 1958
They Want Me Dead. Jenkins, 1958
Whisper Murder Softly. Jenkins, 1963

DURSTON, P. E. H. (S)
Mortissimo. Random, 1967

DU SEE, ROBERT (S)
The Devil Thumbs a Ride. McBride, 1938

DUSTON, MERLE (S)
The Wind in Our Hands. Harlo, 1966

DUTTON, CHARLES JUDSON (D)
Black Fog. Dodd, 1934
The Circle of Death. Dodd, 1933
The Clutching Hand. Dodd, 1928; Burt, 1929
The Crooked Cross. Dodd, 1926
Flying Clues. Dodd, 1927; Burt, 1928
The House by the Road. Dodd, 1924; Lane, 1931
Murder in a Library. Dodd, 1931; Hurst, 1931; Burt, 1932
Murder in the Dark. Shaylor, 1929
Out of the Darkness. Dodd, 1922

Poison Unknown. Dodd, 1932
The Second Bullet. Dodd, 1925
The Shadow of Evil. Dodd, 1930; Hurst, 1930; Burt, 1931
The Shadow on the Glass. Dodd, 1923
Streaked with Crimson. Dodd, 1929
The Underwood Mystery. Dodd, 1921
The Vanishing Murderer. Hurst, 1932

DUTTON, PAUL TOWNSEND (M)
Man on the Edge of the Rope. Dutton, 1961

DWIGHT, OLIVIA, pseud; see HAZZARD, MARY

DYE, WILLIAM H. (M)
Devil's Cameo. Exposition, 1956

DYER, GEORGE (D)
Adriana. Scribner, 1939 (English title: Mystery of Martha's Vineyard. Heinemann, 1939)
The Catalyst Club. Scribner, 1936
Five Fragments. Houghton, 1932; Skeffington, 1933
The Long Death. Scribner, 1937
Mystery of Martha's Vineyard; see Adriana
People Ask Death. Scribner, 1940
A Storm Is Rising. Houghton, 1934
Three-cornered Wound. Houghton, 1931; Skeffington, 1932

EADES, MRS. MAUDE L. (M)
The Torrington Square Mystery. Jenkins, 1932

EADIE, ARLTON (D)
The Crimson Query. Jarrolds, 1929

EADIE, CHARLES (S)
The Tigers Are Hungry. Morrow, 1967

EAST, MICHAEL, pseud; see WEST, MORRIS LANGLO

EAST, ROGER, pseud; see BURFORD, ROGER D'ESTE

EASTMAN, ELIZABETH (M)
The Mouse with Red Eyes. Farrar, Straus, 1948; Heinemann, 1950

EASTON, M. G. (M)
The House by the Bridge. Lane, 1906

EASTON, NAT (D-S)
Always the Wolf. Boardman, T. V., 1957
A Bill for Damages. Roy Pubs., 1959
A Book for Banning. Boardman, T. V., 1959; Roy Pubs., 1959
Frangipani. Boardman, T. V., 1958
Mistake Me Not. Roy Pubs., 1959
Nothing for Nothing. Boardman, T. V., 1958
One Good Turn. Boardman, T. V., 1957
Quick Tempo. Boardman, T. V., 1960
Right for Trouble. Boardman, T. V., 1960

EASTWOOD, JAMES (M)
The Chinese Visitor. Cassell, 1965; Coward, 1965; Dell, 1967
Little Dragon from Peking. Coward, 1967

EBERHARD, FREDERICK GEORGE (M)
The Microbe Murders. Macaulay, 1935
The Secret of the Morgue. Macaulay, 1932
The Skeleton Talks. Macaulay, 1933
Super-Gangster. Macaulay, 1932
The Thirteenth Murder. Macaulay, 1931

EBERHARDT, WALTER F. (D)
Dagger in the Dark. Morrow, 1932

EBERHART, MIGNON GOOD (D)
Another Man's Murder. Random, 1927; Collins, 1958; Popular Lib., 1967
Another Woman's House. Random, 1947; Collins, 1948; Popular Lib., 1963
Brief Return. Collins, 1939
Burn Forever. Popular Lib., 1967
Call After Midnight. Random, 1964; Popular Lib., 1966
The Cases of Susan Dare. Doubleday, Doran, 1934; Lane, 1935; Penguin, 1947
The Chiffon Scarf. Doubleday, Doran, 1939; Collins, 1940; Popular Lib., 1966
The Crimson Paw. Hammond, 1959
The Cup, the Blade or the Gun. Random, 1961; Popular Lib., 1962
Danger in the Dark. Doubleday, Doran, 1936; Macfadden, 1963
The Dark Garden. Doubleday, Doran, 1933; Macfadden, 1962 (English title: Death in the Fog. Lane, 1934)
Dead Man's Plans. Random, 1952; Collins, 1953; Popular Lib., 1963
Deadly Is the Diamond. Random, 1958; Popular Lib.
Death in the Fog; see The Dark Garden
Enemy in the House. Random, 1962; Collins, 1963; Popular Lib., 1963
Escape the Night. Random, 1943; Collins, 1945; Popular Lib., 1965
Fair Warning. Collins, 1936; Doubleday, Doran, 1936; Popular Lib., 1966
Five of My Best. Hammond, 1949
Five Passengers from Lisbon. Collins, 1946; Random, 1946; Popular Lib., 1965

From This Dark Stairway. Doubleday, Doran, 1931; Heinemann, 1932
The Glass Slipper. Collins, 1938; Doubleday, Doran, 1938
Hand in Glove. Collins, 1937
Hangman's Whip. Doubleday, Doran, 1940; Collins, 1941; Popular Lib., 1967
Hasty Wedding. Doubleday, Doran, 1938; Collins, 1939
House of Storm. Collins, 1949; Random, 1949; Popular Lib., 1964
House on the Roof. Collins, 1935; Doubleday, Doran, 1935
Hunt with the Hounds. Random, 1950; Collins, 1951; Popular Lib., 1963
Jury of One. Random, 1960; Popular Lib., 1961
Man Missing. Collins, 1954; Random, 1954; Popular Lib., 1964
The Man Next Door. Random, 1943; Collins, 1944; Popular Lib., 1966
Melora. Random, 1959 (Also published as: Promise of Murder. Dell, 1961)
Murder by an Aristocrat. Doubleday, Doran, 1932 (English title: Murder of My Patient. Lane, 1934; Penguin, 1941)
Murder of My Patient; see Murder by an Aristocrat
The Mystery of Hunting's End. Doubleday, Doran, 1930; Heinemann, 1931; Bodley Head, 1952
Never Look Back. Random, 1951; Collins, 1951; Popular Lib, 1962
The Patient in Room 18. Doubleday, Doran, 1929; Heinemann, 1929
The Pattern. Collins, 1937; Doubleday, Doran, 1937
Postmark Murder. Collins, 1956; Random, 1956; Popular Lib., 1964
Promise of Murder; see Melora
R.S.V.P. Murder. Random, 1965; Popular Lib., 1967
Run Scared. Random, 1963; Collins, 1964; Popular Lib., 1964
Speak No Evil. Collins, 1941; Random, 1941; Penguin, 1955; Popular Lib.
Unidentified Woman. Random, 1943; Collins, 1945; Popular Lib., 1965
The Unknown Quantity. Collins, 1953; Random, 1953; Popular Lib., 1963
While the Patient Slept. Doubleday, Doran, 1930; Heinemann, 1930; Macfadden, 1963
The White Cockatoo. Doubleday, Doran, 1933; Falcon Press, 1933; Penguin, 1939
The White Dress. Random, 1946; Collins, 1947; Popular Lib., 1965
Wings of Fear. Random, 1945; Collins, 1946; Popular Lib., 1965
With This Ring. Random, 1941; Collins, 1942; Popular Lib., 1966
Witness at Large. Random, 1966
Wolf in Man's Clothing. Random, 1942; Collins, 1943; Popular Lib., 1964
The Woman on the Roof. Random, 1968

EBERT, ARTHUR FRANK (M) (Pseudonym: Frank Arthur)
The Abandoned Woman. Heinemann, 1964

EBY, LOIS CHRISTINE and JOHN C. FLEMING (M)
Blood Runs Cold. Dutton, 1946
The Case of the Malevolent Twins. Dutton, 1946
Death Begs the Question. Abelard, 1952
Hell Hath No Fury. Dutton, 1947
Velvet Fleece. Dutton, 1952

ECHARD, MARGARET (M)
Before I Wake. Doubleday, Doran, 1943
Dark Fantastic. Doubleday, 1947
I Met Murder on the Way. Doubleday, 1965
If This Be Treason. Doubleday, Doran, 1944
A Man Without Friends. Doubleday, Doran, 1940
Stand-in for Death. Doubleday, Doran, 1940

EDELSTEIN, MORTIMER S.; see SANDERS, MARIAN K.

EDEN, DOROTHY (S-Gothic) (Pseudonym: Mary Paradise)
Afternoon for Lizards. MacDonald & Co., 1961 (Also published as: Bridge of Fear. Ace, 1961)
Bride by Candlelight. MacDonald & Co., 1961
Bridge of Fear; see Afternoon for Lizards
The Brooding Lake; see Lamb to the Slaughter
Cat's Prey. MacDonald & Co., 1952; Ace, 1967
Crow Hollow. MacDonald & Co., 1950; Ace, 1967
Dark Water. Coward, 1963; Crest, 1966
Darling Clementine. MacDonald & Co., 1955 (Also published as: Night of the Letter. Ace, 1967)
The Deadly Travelers. MacDonald & Co., 1959; Ace, 1966
Death Is a Red Rose. MacDonald & Co., 1956
Face of an Angel, by Mary Paradise. Ace, 1966
Lady of Mallow; see Samantha
Lamb to the Slaughter. MacDonald & Co., 1953 (Also published as: The Brooding Lake. Ace, 1966)
The Laughing Ghost. MacDonald & Co., 1943
Listen to Danger. MacDonald & Co., 1958; Ace, 1967

The Marriage Chest, by Mary Paradise. Coward, 1966
Night of the Letter; see Darling Clementine
Pretty Ones. Macmillan, 1957; Ace, 1966
Ravenscroft. Coward, 1964; Crest
Samantha. Hodder, 1962 (Also published As: Lady of Mallow. Coward, 1962; Ace, 1963)
The Schoolmaster's Daughter. MacDonald & Co., 1948
Shadow of a Witch, by Mary Paradise. Ace, 1966
Singing Shadows. Paul, S., 1940
Sleep in the Woods. Hodder, 1960; Coward, 1961
The Sleeping Bride. Ace, 1959; MacDonald & Co., 1959
Summer Sunday. MacDonald & Co., 1946
Voice of the Dolls. MacDonald & Co., 1950
Walk into My Parlor. MacDonald & Co., 1947
We Are for the Dark. MacDonald & Co., 1944
Whistle for the Crows. Ace, 1964
Winterwood. Coward, 1967; Crest, 1968

EDGLEY, LESLIE (M) (Pseudonym: Robert Bloomfield. Joint pseudonym with Mary Edgley: Brook Hastings)
The Angry Heart. Doubleday, 1947; Barker, 1949
The Demon Within, by Brook Hastings. Doubleday, 1953
Diamonds Spell Death. Barker, 1954 (U.S. title: Runaway Pigeon. Doubleday, 1953)
False Face. S & S, 1947; Barker, 1948
Fear No More. S & S, 1946; Barker, 1948
From This Death Forward, by Robert Bloomfield, Doubleday, 1952
Judas Goat. Doubleday, 1952; Barker, 1953
Kill with Kindness, by Robert Bloomfield. Boardman, T. V., 1962; Doubleday, 1962
Runaway Pigeon; see Diamonds Spell Death
Russian Roulette, by Robert Bloomfield. Harcourt, 1955
Shadow of Guilt, by Robert Bloomfield. Doubleday, 1947
Stranger in Town, by Robert Bloomfield. Doubleday, 1953; Boardman, T. V., 1954
Vengeance Street, by Robert Bloomfield. Doubleday, 1952
When Strangers Meet, by Robert Bloomfield. Doubleday, 1956; Boardman, T. V., 1957

EDGLEY, MARY; see EDGLEY, LESLIE

EDINGTON, ARLO CHANNING and CARMEN BALLEN EDINGTON (M)
Drum Madness, with Marianne Barrett. Cassell, 1934
The House of the Vanishing Goblets. Century, 1930
The Monk's Head Murders. Collins, 1931; Cosmopolitan, 1931
Murder Mystery. Collins, 1929
Murder to Music. Collins, 1930
Studio Murder Mystery. Reilly & Lee, 1929; Collins, 1930

EDINGTON, CARMEN BALLEN; see EDINGTON, ARLO CHANNING

EDMISTON, HELEN JEAN MARY (M-S) (Pseudonym: Helen Robertson)
The Chinese Goose; see Swan Song
The Crystal-Gazers. MacDonald & Co., 1957; Doubleday, 1958
The Shakeup. MacDonald & Co., 1962
Swan Song. Doubleday, 1960 (Also published as: Chinese Goose. MacDonald & Co., 1960)
Venice of the Black Sea. MacDonald & Co., 1956
The Winged Witnesses, by Helen Robertson. MacDonald & Co., 1955

EDMONDS, HARRY MORETON (M)
The East Coast Mystery. Ward, Lock, 1934; Withy Grove, 1942 (Abridged edition)
The North Sea Mystery. Ward, Lock, 1930
The Riddle of the Straits. Ward, Lock, 1931

EDMUNDS, BRENT (M)
Beware the Crimson Cord. Laurie, 1956
Gun in My Back. Laurie, 1955
Ride a Dead Horse. Laurie, 1955
Spiders in the Night. Laurie, 1956

EDQVIST, DAGMAR INGEBORG (M)
Black Sister. Doubleday, 1963; Joseph, M., 1963

EDWARD, MARIE ELAINE (S-Gothic)
Amberleigh. Paperback Lib., 1967

EDWARDS, CHARMAN, pseud; see EDWARDS, FREDERICK ANTHONY

EDWARDS, FREDERICK ANTHONY (M-D) (Pseudonym: Charman Edwards)
The Blue Macaw. Ward, Lock, 1935
Confetti for a Killing. Ward, Lock, 1937
Derision. Ward, Lock, 1926
Dolly's Walk. Ward, Lock, 1950
Drama of Mr. Dilly. Hale, R., 1939

Drink No Deeper. Ward, Lock, 1933
Fear Haunts the Roses. Ward, Lock, 1936
The Yellow Wagon. Ward, Lock, 1932

EDWARDS, HARRY STILLWELL (M)
Marbeau Cousins. Burke, 1921

EDWARDS, HUGH (M)
All Night at Mr. Stanyhursts. Macmillan, 1963

EDWARDS, JAMES G., pseud; see MacQUEEN, JAMES WILLIAMS

EDWARDS, JANE (M)
The Houseboat Mystery. Bouregy, 1964

EDWARDS, STAFFORD (M)
Money Order Murder. Vantage, 1963; Avalon, 1965

EDWIN, MARIBEL THOMSON (M)
Sound Alibi. Ward, Lock, 1935

EGAN, LESLEY, pseud; see LININGTON, ELIZABETH

EGERTON, DENISE (S)
Design for an Accident. Washburn, 1958
Hour of Truth. Washburn, 1960
No Thoroughfare. Hodder, 1954; Coward, 1955

EGGLESTON, EDWARD (M)
Mystery of Metropolisville. Judd, 1873; Routledge, 1873

EHRLICH, JACK (Full name: John Gunther Ehrlich) (S)
Court Martial. Pyramid, 1958
Cry, Baby. Dell, 1962
The Girl Cage. Dell, 1967
Parole. Dell, 1959
Revenge. Dell, 1957
Slow Burn. Dell, 1961

EHRLICH, JOHN GUNTHER; see EHRLICH, JACK

EHRLICH, MAX SIMON (S)
The Big Eye. Doubleday, 1947; Boardman, T. V., 1951
Dead Letter; see The First Train to Babylon
Deep Is the Blue. Doubleday, 1963; Gollancz, 1964
The First Train to Babylon. Harper, 1955 (Also published as: Dead Letter. Gollancz, 1955; Bantam)
Spin the Glass Web. Harper, 1951
The Takers. Gollancz, 1961; Harper, 1961; Bantam, 1962

EICHLER, ALFRED (M)
Bury in Haste. Arcadia, 1957
Death at the Mike. Lantern Press, 1946; Hammond, 1954
Death of an Ad Man. Abelard, 1952
Death of an Artist. Hammond, 1955
Election by Murder. Lantern Press, 1947
Hearse for the Boss. Hammond, 1956
Moment for Murder. Arco, 1956; Hammond, 1957
Murder in the Radio Department. Hammond, 1953
Murder Off Stage. Hammond, 1962

EINSTEIN, CHARLES (S)
The Bloody Spur. Dell, 1953
Wiretap. Dell, 1955

EISINGER, JO (M)
The Walls Came Tumbling Down. Coward, 1943; Jarrolds, 1945

ELDER, EVELYN (D)
Angel in the Case. Methuen, 1932
Murder in Black and White. Methuen, 1931

ELDER, MICHAEL (M)
Phantom in the Wings. Murray, J., 1957; Transatlantic, 1958

ELDRIDGE, GEORGE DYRE (M)
The Millbank Case. Holt, H., 1905; Nash, 1907

ELDRIDGE, GILBERT (M)
Death for the Surgeon. Phoenix, 1939

ELEGANT, ROBERT SAMPSON (S)
A Kind of Treason. Holt, 1966

ELGIN, MARY (M-S)
Highland Masquerade. Mill, 1966; Bantam, 1967 (English title: Return to Glenshael. Hodder, 1965)

ELIAS, DAVID (M)
The Cause of the Screaming. Hammond, 1953
Dress Up and Die. Hammond, 1955
The Gory Details. Hammond, 1954

ELIOT, ANNE, pseud; see COLE, LOIS DWIGHT

ELIOT, ETHEL AUGUSTA (M)
Vanishing Comrade. Doubleday, Page, 1924

ELIOT, HENRY WARE (D)
The Rumble Murders. Houghton, 1932

"ELIZABETH," pseud; see ARNIM, MARY ANNETTE BEAUCHAMP GRAFIN VON

ELLETT, HAROLD PINCTON (M)
(Pseudonym: Nigel Burnaby)
The Clue of the Green-Eyed Girl. Ward, Lock, 1935
The Forest Mystery. Ward, Lock, 1934
The Secret of Matchams. Ward, Lock, 1934
Two Deaths in a Penny. Ward, Lock, 1935

ELLIN, STANLEY (S)
The Big Night; see Dreadful Summit
The Blessington Method. Random, 1964; Signet, 1966
Dreadful Summit. S & S, 1948; Boardman, T. V., 1958 (Also published as: The Big Night. New Amer. Lib., 1966)
The Eighth Circle. Random, 1958; Dell, 1964
The House of Cards. Random, 1967
The Key to Nicholas Street. S & S, 1951; Boardman, T. V., 1953; Signet, 1966
Mystery Stories. S & S, 1956; Boardman, T. V., 1957 (Also published as: Quiet Horror. Signet, 1965)
Quiet Horror; see Mystery Stories

ELLINGER, GEOFFREY (D)
The Lyddon House Mystery. Jenkins, 1929

ELLINGTON, RICHARD (M-S)
Exit for a Dame. Morrow, 1951; Boardman, T. V., 1954
It's a Crime. Morrow, 1948; Cassell, 1956
Just Killing Time. Morrow, 1953; Boardman, T. V., 1954
Shoot the Works. Morrow, 1948; Cassell, 1950
Stone Cold Dead. Morrow, 1950; Cassell, 1952

ELLIOTT, PEERS (M)
The Mystery of the Black Dagger. Hale, R., 1952
The Payout. Hale, R., 1940
Silent Bullet. Hale, R., 1941
Trust the Police. Hale, R., 1939

ELLIOTT, WILLIAM JAMES (M)
Bren Hardy Again. Swan, G. G., 1945
Bren Hardy, Tough Dame. Swan, G. G., 1942
Gunning in England. Swan, G. G., 1946
Kissed Corpse. Swan, G. G., 1941
Mystery of Me. Swan, G. G., 1944
One Million Pounds. Swan, G. G., 1949
The Running Killer. Swan, G. G., 1946
The Silver Panther. Gramol, 1934
The Suicide Circle. Gramol, 1934
The Wolf of Corsica. Mellifont, 1932
The Yellow Fiend. Mellifont, 1932

ELLIS, J. C. (M)
Black Fame. Hutchinson, 1926
Blackmailers & Co. Selwyn, 1929
Night of Mystery. Selwyn, 1929

ELLIS, JOHN BRECKENRIDGE (M)
The Mysterious Dr. Oliver. Macaulay, 1929

ELLIS, N. A. TEMPLE-, pseud; see HOLDAWAY, NEVILLE ALDRIDGE

ELLISON, HARLAN (S)
The Deadly Streets. Ace, 1958
Gentleman Junkie. Regency, 1961
The Juvies. Ace, 1961
The Man with Nine Lives. Ace, 1960
Memos from Purgatory. Regency, 1961
Rumble. Pyramid, 1958
Tomboy. Bantam, 1960
A Touch of Infinity. Ace, 1960

ELLSON, HAL (S)
Games. Ace, 1967
Nightmare Street. Ballantine, 1964

ELLSWORTH, ELMER, JR., pseud; see THAYER, TIFFANY

ELLSWORTH, PAUL, pseud; see TRIEM, PAUL ELLSWORTH

ELSNER, DON VON (S)
Ace of Spies. Award, 1967
Jack of Diamonds. Award, 1967

ELSWORTHY, ALEXANDER LOCKHART (M)
Death Glides In. Hutchinson, 1935

ELVESTAD, SVEN CHRISTOPHER SVENDSEN (M)
The Case of Robert Robertson. Knopf, 1930; Lane, 1930
The Man Who Plundered the City. McBride, 1924
The Mystery of the Abbe Montrose. Jarrolds, 1924

ELVIN, HAROLD (M-S)
Avenue to the Door of Death. Blond, A., 1962
Cockney in Moscow. Cresset, 1959
Fandango for a Crown of Thorns. Garnett, 1951
The Ride to Chandigarh. Macmillan, 1954
Story at Canons. Garnett, 1949
To Heaven with the Devil. Nevill, 1954
When She Cried on Friday. Southern Cross Press, 1960

ELWIN, MALCOLM (S)
Little Hangman. MacDonald & Co., 1953

ELY, DAVID, pseud; see LILIENTHAL, DAVID, JR.

EMERICK, LUCILLE (S)
The City Beyond. Holt, H., 1952
Web of Evil. Doubleday, 1948; Paperback Lib., 1968
You'll Hang, My Love, with Francis I. Swann. Lancer, 1967

EMERY, J. INMAN (M)
The Tiger of Barangunga. Putnam, 1925

EMERY, RUSSELL GUY (M)
Front for Murder. Macrae Smith, 1947; Boardman, T. V., 1948

EMERY, SAMUEL M. (M)
The House That Whispered. Dutton, 1929; Paul, S., 1929
Mantle of Masquerade. Dutton, 1926

ENDORE, GUY (M-S)
Detour at Night; see Detour Through Devon
Detour Through Devon. Gollancz, 1959 (U.S. title: Detour at Night. S & S, 1959; Award, 1965)
The Man from Limbo. Gollancz, 1931
Methinks the Lady. Duell, 1945; Cresset, 1947
The Werewolf of Paris. Farrar & Rinehart, 1933; Grosset, 1935; Avon, 1951; Ace, 1962

ENEFER, DOUGLAS STALLARD (S)
The Last Door. World Distributors, 1959

ENGLAND, GEORGE ALLAN (M)
The Alibi. Small, 1916
The Cursed. Small, 1919
The Greater Crime. Cassell, 1907

ENGLISH, RICHARD (S)
The Sugarplum Staircase. S & S, 1947

ENGSTRAND, STUART (M)
More Deaths Than One. Messner, 1955

ENRIGHT, RICHARD (M)
The Borrowed Shield. Burt, 1927
Vultures of the Dark. Brentano, 1924

ENSOR, DAVID (M)
Verdict Afterwards. Jenkins, 1960

EPPLEY, LOUISE and REBECCA GAYTON (M)
Murder in the Cellar. Morrow, 1931; Grayson, 1932

ERICSON, WALTER, pseud; see FAST, HOWARD

ERIKSON, MRS. SIBYL ALEXANDRA DICK (M) (Pseudonyms: Alexandra Dick, Frances Hay)
The Comet's Tail, by Alexandra Dick. Hodder, 1938
The Crime in the Close, by Alexandra Dick. Hale, R., 1955
Cross Purposes, by Alexandra Dick. Hurst, 1950
The Curate's Crime, by Alexandra Dick. Hurst, 1945; Bouregy, 1946
Death at the Golden Crown, by Alexandra Dick. Hale, R., 1956
The Innocence of Rosamond Prior, by Alexandra Dick. Hale, R., 1953
MacAlastair Looks On, by Alexandra Dick. Hurst, 1947
A Pack of Cards, by Alexandra Dick. Hodder, 1940
There Was No Moon, by Frances Hay. Jenkins, 1957

ERNST, PAUL (M)
The Bronze Mermaid. Mill, 1952; Cassell, 1954
Hangman's Hat. Mill, 1951; Muller, 1952
Lady, Get Your Gun. Mill, 1955
Rose from the Dead. Cassell, 1956
Short Murder. Bouregy, 1959

ERSKINE, FIRTH (M)
Naked Murder. Macaulay, 1933

ERSKINE, MARGARET, pseud; see WILLIAMS, MARGARET WETHERBY

ERVIN, MARI (M)
Death in the Yew Alley. Phoenix, 1937

ESHLEMAN, JOHN M. (M)
The Long Chase. Washburn, 1954
The Long Window. Washburn, 1953

ESMOND, SIDNEY (M-S)
The Dead Look Down. Hutchinson, 1945
The Evil Cross. Hutchinson, 1944
Peacock's Feather. Hutchinson, 1947
Sacrament of Death. Redman, 1950
The Secret Cargo. Hutchinson, 1945
Verboten. Hutchinson, 1940

ESSEX, RICHARD, pseud; see STARR, RICHARD

ESTES, CARROLL COX (M)
Eavesdropping on Death. Arcadia, 1952
Moon Gate. Barker, 1954; Doubleday, 1954
Unhappy New Year. Doubleday, 1953

ESTEVEN, JOHN, pseud; see SHELLABARGER, SAMUEL

ESTRIDGE, ROBIN (M) (Pseudonym: Philip Loraine)
And to My Beloved Husband. Mill, 1950 (English title: White Lie the Dead. Hodder, 1950)
The Angel of Death. Hodder, 1961; Macmillan, 1961
The Break in the Circle. Hodder, 1951; Mill, 1951
Day of the Arrow. Mill, 1964 (Also published as: Thirteen. Lancer, 1966)
The Dublin Nightmare; see Nightmare in Dublin
Exit with Intent. Hodder, 1950
Nightmare in Dublin. Mill, 1952 (English title: The Dublin Nightmare. Hodder, 1952)
Thirteen; see Day of the Arrow
White Lie the Dead; see And to My Beloved Husband
W.I.L. One to Curtis. Random, 1967

ETHAN, JOHN B. (D)
Black Gold Murders. PB, 1960
Call Girls for Murder. PB, 1960
Murder on Wall Street. Mill, 1960; PB, 1962

ETHERIDGE, A. I. (M)
The Elvin Court Mystery. Stockwell, 1929

ETON, ROBERT, pseud; see MEYNELL, LAURENCE WALTER

EUSTACE, ROBERT, pseud; see RAWLINS, EUSTACE

EUSTIS, HELEN (S)
The Fool Killer. Doubleday, 1954; Popular Lib., 1964
The Horizontal Man. Harper, 1946; Hamilton, H., 1947; PB, 1948

EVANS, ALFRED JOHN (M)
All's Fair on Lake Gerda. Hodder, 1958
V2 Expert. Hodder, 1956

EVANS, DEAN (M)
No Slightest Whisper. Abelard, 1955

EVANS, GEORGE and KAY EVANS (M) (Pseudonyms: Brandon Bird, Harris Evans)
Death in Four Colors, by Brandon Bird. Dodd, 1950; Constable, 1951; Dell
Downbeat for a Dirge, by Brandon Bird. Dodd, 1952
Hawk Watch, by Brandon Bird. Dodd, 1954; Boardman, T. V., 1955
Never Wake a Dead Man, by Brandon Bird. Dodd, 1950; Constable, 1952
The Pink Carrara, by Harris Evans. Dodd, 1960

EVANS, GWYN (M-S)
Bluebeard's Keys. Wright & Brown, 1937
The Case of the Climbing Corpse. Wright & Brown, 1939
Castle Sinister. Wright & Brown, 1936
The Clue of the Missing Link. Wright & Brown, 1938
Coffins for Two. Wright & Brown, 1939
Crook of Fleet Street. Wright & Brown, 1939
Death Speaking. Wright & Brown, 1934
The Hanging Judge. Wright & Brown, 1936
Hercules, Esq.; see Mr. Hercules
His Majesty—the Crook. Wright & Brown, 1935
The Homicide Club. Shaylor, 1931; MacVeagh, 1932
Iron Mask. Wright & Brown, 1938
The Man with the Scarlet Skull. Wright & Brown, 1935
Mr. Hercules. MacVeagh, 1931 (Also published as: Hercules, Esq. Shaylor, 1931)
Murderers Meet. Wright & Brown, 1934
Mysterious Miss Death. Wright & Brown, 1937
The Return of Hercules, Esq. Wright & Brown, 1937
Satan Ltd. Wright & Brown, 1935
The Sign of the Saracen. Wright & Brown, 1936
Triangle of Terror. Wright & Brown, 1938

EVANS, HARRIS, pseud; see EVANS, GEORGE

EVANS, HOWEL (M)
Actor's Knife. Jarrolds, 1930
Crabtree House. Richards, 1919
Girl Alone. Richards, 1917; Putnam, 1918
Murder Club. Jarrolds, 1924; Putnam, 1925
Murder Trap. Richards, 1929; Cayme Press, 1930
The Sixth Commandment. Jarrolds, 1925
Who Killed George Dunn? Pearson, 1935

EVANS, HUGH AUSTIN (M) (Pseudonym: Hugh Austin)
Cock's Tail Murder. Doubleday, Doran, 1938
Death Has Seven Faces. Scribner, 1949
Drink the Green Water. Scribner, 1948
It Couldn't Be Murder. Doubleday, Doran, 1935; Heinemann, 1936
Lilies for Madame. Doubleday, Doran, 1938; Heinemann, 1938
The Milkmaid's Millions. Scribner, 1948

Murder in Triplicate. Doubleday, Doran, 1935; Heinemann, 1936
Murder of a Matriarch. Doubleday, Doran, 1936; Heinemann, 1937
Upside Down Murder. Doubleday, Doran, 1937; Heinemann, 1938

EVANS, JACK; see DUDLEY, ERNEST

EVANS, JOHN, pseud; see BROWNE, HOWARD

EVANS, JULIA RENDEL (M) (Pseudonym: Polly Hobson)
Brought Up in Bloomsbury. Constable, 1959
Murder Won't Out. Jenkins. 1964
The Mystery House. Benn, 1963

EVANS, KAY; see EVANS, GEORGE

EVANS, MARGUERITE F. H. (D) (Pseudonym: Oliver Sandys)
Dot on the Spot. Hurst, 1949

EVARTS, HAL G. (S)
The Turncoat. GM, 1961

EVELYN, ROSE d', pseud; see BROEMEL, ROSE

EVELYN, JOHN MICHAEL (M) (Pseudonym: Michael Underwood)
Adam's Case. Doubleday, 1961
The Anxious Conspirators. Doubleday, 1966
The Arm of the Law. Hammond, 1959
The Case Against Philip Quest. MacDonald & Co., 1962
Cause of Death. Hammond, 1960
The Crime of Colin Wise. Doubleday, 1964; MacDonald & Co., 1964
Death by Misadventure. Hammond, 1960
Death on Remand. Hammond, 1956
False Witness. Hammond, 1957; Walker & Co., 1961
Girl Found Dead. MacDonald & Co., 1963
Lawful Pursuit. Doubleday, 1958
Murder Made Absolute. Hammond, 1955; Washburn, 1957
Murder on Trial. Hammond, 1954; Washburn, 1958
The Unprofessional Spy. Doubleday, 1964

EVENING STANDARD, (M)
Did It Happen? British Book Service, 1956; Daily Express Book Dept., 1956

EVERETT, PETER (S)
Negatives. S & S, 1965

EVERMAY, MARCH, pseud. (M)
They Talked of Poison. Macmillan, 1938; Jarrolds, 1939
This Death Was Murder. Jarrolds, 1940; Macmillan, 1940

EVERTON, FRANCIS, pseud; see STOKES, FRANCIS WILLIAMS

EWERS, HANNS HEINZ (S)
Vampire. Day, 1934 (Also published as: Vampire's Prey. Jarrolds, 1935)

EYRE, KATE (M)
Step in the Dark. Cassell, 1894

EYRE, KATHERINE WIGMORE (S)
The Chinese Box. Popular Lib., 1966
The Lute and the Glove. Ace, 1963
Monk's Court. Meredith, 1966

F, INSPECTOR, pseud; see RUSSELL, WILLIAM

FADIMAN, EDWIN, JR. (S)
An Act of Violence. Signet, 1957

FAGAN, NORBERT (S)
The Crooked Mile. GM, 1953
One Against the Odds. GM, 1954

FAGYAS, M., pseud; see BUSH-FEKETE, MARY

FAHERTY, ROBERT (D)
Better Than Dying. Doubleday, Doran, 1935

FAIR, A. A., pseud; see GARDNER, ERLE STANLEY

FAIRFAX, DENNIS (M)
The Masked Ball Murder. Jenkins, 1934

FAIRLIE, GERARD T. (D) (Pseudonym: "Sapper," after H. C. McNeile)
Birds of Prey. Hodder, 1932
Bulldog Drummond Attacks, by "Sapper." Hodder, 1939; Gateway, 1940
Bulldog Drummond on Dartmoor, by "Sapper." Hillman-Curl, 1939; Hodder, 1939
Bulldog Drummond Stands Fast, by "Sapper." Hodder, 1947
Calling Bulldog Drummond, by "Sapper." Hodder, 1951; British Book Centre, 1953
Captain Bulldog Drummond, by "Sapper." Hodder, 1945; Musson, 1945
Copper at Sea. Hodder, 1934
Deadline for MaCall. Mill, 1946
Double the Bluff. Hodder, 1957
Hands Off Bulldog Drummond, by "Sapper." Hodder, 1949
MaCall Gets Curious. Hodder, 1959
The Man Who Laughed. Hodder, 1928; Little, 1928; Burt, 1929
The Man with Talent. Musson, 1930; Hodder, 1931

Men for Counters. Hodder, 1933
Mr. Malcolm Presents. Hodder, 1932
Muster of the Vultures. Hodder, 1929; Little, 1930
No Sleep for MaCall. Hodder, 1955
The Pianist Shoots First. Hodder, 1938
Please Kill My Cousin. Hodder, 1961
The Reaper. Little, 1929
The Return of the Black Gang, by "Sapper." Hodder, 1954
The Rope Which Hangs. Hodder, 1932
Scissors Cut Paper. Hodder, 1927; Little, 1928; Burt, 1929
Shot in the Dark. Doubleday, Doran, 1932; Hodder, 1932; Burt, 1933
Stone Blunts Scissors. Hodder, 1929; Little, 1929
Suspect. Doubleday, Doran, 1930; Hodder, 1930
That Man Returns. Hodder, 1934
The Treasure Nets. Hodder, 1933
Unfair Lady. Hodder, 1931
Winner Take All. Dodd, 1953; Hodder, 1953
Yellow Munro. Little, 1929

FAIRMAN, PAUL W. (M)
Search for a Dead Nympho. Lancer, 1967

FAIRWAY, SIDNEY (S)
The Long Tunnel. Doubleday, Doran, 1936

FALKNER, JOHN MEADE (M)
The Lost Stradivarius. Blackwood, 1895
The Nebuly Coat. Arnold, E., 1903

FALKNER, LEONARD (D)
M, a Detective Novel. Holt, H., 1931
Murder off Broadway, Holt, H., 1930

FALLON, MARTIN, pseud; see PATTERSON, HENRY

FALSTEIN, LOUIS (S)
Sole Survivor. Dell, 1954

FAMOUS, WILLIAM N. (D)
Colonel Crook Stories. Excelsior, 1909

FANE, ANTHONY (D)
Wycliffe-Pepin Case. Poe Pub., 1931

FANGER, HORST (D)
A Life for a Life. Ballantine, 1954

FARINGTON, JOSEPH (S)
The Hand. Jenkins, 1961

FARJEON, BENJAMIN LEOPOLD (D)
Devlin the Barber. Ward, 1888
Death Trance.
The Great Porter Square: A Mystery. Ward & Downey, 1884; Harper, 1885
Joshua Marvel. Tinsley Bros., 1871
March of Fate. White, 1893
The Mesmerists. Hutchinson, 1900
The Mystery of M. Felix. Lovell, J. W., 1890; White, 1890
The Mystery of the Royal Mail. Hutchinson, 1902
The Nine of Hearts. Ward, Lock, 1886
119 Great Porter Square. Munro, 1881
The Sacred Nugget. Ward & Downey, 1885
Samuel Boyd of Catchpole Square. Hutchinson, 1899
Secret Inheritance. Ward & Downey, 1887
Shadows on the Snow. Hay, W., 1865; Munro, 1878
Something Occurred. Routledge, 1893
Three Times Tried. 1886

FARJEON, JOSEPH JEFFERSON (M)
(Pseudonym: Anthony Swift)
Adventure at Eighty. MacDonald & Co., 1948
Adventure for Nine. MacDonald & Co., 1951
Adventure of Edward. Wright & Brown, 1936
Appointed Date. Dial, 1930; Burt, 1932
At the Green Dragon. Harrap, 1927
Aunt Sunday Sees It Through. Collins, 1940 (U.S. title: Aunt Sunday Takes Command. Bobbs, 1940)
Aunt Sunday Takes Command; see Aunt Sunday Sees It Through
Back to Victoria. MacDonald & Co., 1947
Ben on the Job. Collins, 1952
Ben Sees It Through. Collins, 1932; Dial, 1933
Black Castle. Collins, 1944
Bob Hits the Headlines. Bodley Head, 1954
The Caravan Adventure. MacDonald & Co., 1955
The Castle of Fear. Collins, 1954
Cause Unknown. Collins, 1950
Change with Me. MacDonald & Co., 1950
Confusing Friendship. Brentano, 1924
The Crook's Shadow. Dial, 1927; Harrap, 1927
Dangerous Beauty. Collins, 1936
Dark Lady. Collins, 1938
Dead Man's Heath. Collins, 1933 (U.S. title: Mystery of Dead Man's Heath. Dodd, 1934; Burt, 1935)
Death in Fancy Dress. Bobbs, 1939
Death in the Inkwell; see End of an Author
Death of a World. Collins, 1948
Detective Ben. Collins, 1936
The Disappearance of Uncle David. Collins, 1949
Double Crime. Collins, 1953
End of an Author. Collins, 1939 (U.S. title: Death in the Inkwell. Bobbs, 1942)

Exit John Horton. Collins, 1939 (U.S. title: Friday the 13th. Bobbs, 1940)
Facing Death. Quality
The Fancy Dress Ball. Collins, 1934
5:18 Mystery. Collins, 1929; Dial, 1929
Following Footsteps. Dial, 1930
Friday the 13th; see Exit John Horton
The Golden Singer. Wright & Brown, 1935
The Green Dragon. Dial, 1926
Greenmask. Bobbs, 1944; Collins, 1944
His Lady Secretary. Wright & Brown, 1935
Holiday at Half Mast. Collins, 1937
The Holiday Express. Collins, 1935
The House of Disappearance. Dial, 1927; Harrap, 1928
The House of Shadows. Collins, 1943; Doubleday, Doran, 1943
The House on the Marsh; see Mystery of the Creek
The House Opposite. Collins, 1931; Dial, 1931
The House over the Tunnel. Collins, 1951
The Impossible Guest. MacDonald & Co., 1949
Interrupted Honeymoon, by Anthony Swift. Hale, R., 1944
The Invisible Companion and Other Stories. Polybooks, 1943
The Judge Sums Up. Collins, 1942
Little God Ben. Collins, 1935
Little Things That Happen. Methuen, 1925
Llewellyn Jewel Mystery. Collins, 1948
The Lone House Mystery. Collins, 1949
The Master Criminal. Brentano, 1924; Burt, 1925
Midnight Adventure. Polybooks, 1946
Money Walks. MacDonald & Co., 1953
More Little Happenings. Methuen, 1928
Mother Goes Gay. Macmillan, 1950
Mountain Mystery. Collins, 1925
Murder at a Police Station, by Anthony Swift. Hale, R., 1942
Murderer's Trail. Collins, 1931
Mystery in White. Collins, 1937; Bobbs, 1938
Mystery of Dead Man's Heath; see Dead Man's Heath
Mystery of the Creek. Collins, 1933 (U.S. title: The House on the Marsh. Dial, 1933)
Mystery of the Map. Collins, 1953
Mystery on the Moor. Collins, 1930
Mystery on Wheels. Collins, 1952
Mystery Underground. Collins, 1928, 1932 (U.S. title: Underground. Burt, 1928; MacVeagh, 1928)
November 9th at Kersea, by Anthony Swift. Hale, R., 1944; Lothian, 1945
Number Nineteen. Collins, 1952
Number 17. Dial, 1926; Hodder, 1926; Penguin, 1939
Old Man Mystery. Collins, 1933
The Oval Table. Collins, 1946
Peril in the Pyrenees. Collins, 1946
A Person Called Z. Dial, 1929; Collins, 1930
Phantom Fingers. MacVeagh, 1931
Prelude to Crime. Collins, 1948; Doubleday, 1948
Rona Runs Away. MacDonald & Co., 1945
Room Number 6. Collins, 1941
Seven Dead. Bobbs, 1939; Collins, 1939
Shadow of Thirteen. Collins, 1949
Shadows by the Sea. Dial, 1928; Harrap, 1929
Sinister Inn. Collins, 1934; Dodd, 1934
The Third Victim. Collins, 1941
Thirteen Guests. Collins, 1936; Bobbs, 1938
Trunk Call. Collins, 1932 (U.S. title: Trunk Call Mystery. Dial, 1932)
Trunk Call Mystery; see Trunk Call
Underground; see Mystery Underground
Uninvited Guests. Brentano, 1925; Dial, 1925
Waiting for the Police. Todd, 1943
The Windmill Mystery. Collins, 1934
The Yellow Devil. Collins, 1937
Z Murders. Collins, 1932; MacVeagh, 1932

FARMER, BERNARD JAMES (D)
Death at the Cascades. Heinemann, 1953
Death of a Bookseller. Heinemann, 1956
Murder Next Year. Heinemann, 1959
Once, and Then the Funeral. Heinemann, 1958

FARNDALE, JOHN, pseud; see HARVEY, JOHN WILFRED

FARNOL, JOHN JEFFERY (M)
The Amateur Gentleman. Low
The Loring Mystery. Little, 1925; Burt, 1927; Low, 1930
Murder by Nail; see The Valley of Night
The Valley of Night. Doubleday, Doran, 1942 (English title: Murder by Nail. Low, 1942)

FARR, CAROLINE (S)
A Castle in Spain; see Web of Horror
Granite Folly. Signet, 1967
The House of Tombs. Signet, 1966
The Mansion of Evil. Signet, 1966
The Secret of the Chateau. Signet, 1967
Web of Horror. Signet, 1966 (Also published as: A Castle in Spain. Signet, 1967)
Witch's Hammer. Signet, 1967

FARR, FINIS (S)
The Elephant Valley. Arlington, 1967

FARR, JOHN, pseud; see WEBB, JACK

FARR, SEBASTIAN, pseud; see BLOM, ERIC W.

FARRAR, HELEN (D)
Murder Goes to School. Ziff-Davis, 1948

FARRAR, STEWART (M)
Death in the Wrong Bed. Walker & Co., 1964
The Snake on 99. Washburn, 1959; Collins, 1960
Zero in the Gate. Walker & Co., 1961

FARRELL, HENRY (D-S)
Death on the Sixth Day. Holt, 1961; Avon, 1963
The Hostage. Avon, 1963
How Awful About Allan. Holt, 1963; Avon, 1965
Such a Gorgeous Kid Like Me. Dell, 1967
Whatever Happened to Baby Jane? Avon, 1960; Rinehart, 1960; Eyre, 1961

FARRELL, KATHLEEN
Mistletoe Malice. Hart, 1951

FARRER, KATHERINE DOROTHY NEWTON (M)
The Cretan Counterfeit. Collins, 1954
Gownsman's Gallows. Hodder, 1957
The Missing Link. Collins, 1952; Penguin, 1955

FARRERE, CLAUDE, pseud; see BARGONE, FREDERIC CHARLES EDOUARD

FARRIS, JOHN (D)
The Corpse Next Door. Graphic, 1956
When Michael Calls. Trident, 1967

FAST, HOWARD (S) (Pseudonyms: E. V. Cunningham, Walter Ericson)
Alice, by E. V. Cunningham. Doubleday, 1963; Ballantine, 1965
Fallen Angel, by Walter Ericson, Little, 1952; McClelland, 1952 (Also published as: Mirage. Crest, 1965; PB)
Lydia: An Entertainment, by E. V. Cunningham. Doubleday, 1964
Helen, by E. V. Cunningham. Doubleday, 1966
Mirage; see Fallen Angel
Penelope: An Entertainment, by E. V. Cunningham. Doubleday, 1965; PB, 1966
Phyllis, by E. V. Cunningham. Doubleday, 1962; Crest, 1963
Sally, by E. V. Cunningham. Morrow, 1967
Samantha, by E. V. Cunningham. Morrow, 1967
Shirley: An Entertainment, by E. V. Cunningham. Doubleday, 1964
Sylvia, by E. V. Cunningham. Doubleday, 1960; Crest, 1965
The Winston Affair. Crown, 1959; Bantam, 1960

FAST, JULIUS (M)
Down Through the Night; see Walk in Shadow
Model for Murder. Rinehart, 1956; Hale, R., 1957
Street of Fear. Rinehart, 1958
Walk in Shadow. Rinehart, 1947 (Also published as: Down Through the Night. Crest, 1956)
Watchful at Night. Farrar, Straus, 1945

FAULEY, WILBUR FINLEY (M)
Fires of Fate. Metropolitan Book Service, 1923
The Shuddering Castle. Green Circle, 1936

FAULKNER, WILLIAM (M)
Knight's Gambit. Random, 1949; Signet, 1956

FAUR, MICHAEL P., JR. (S)
A Friendly Place to Die. Signet, 1966

FAURE-BIGUET, JACQUES NAPOLEON (D) (Pseudonym: Jacques Decrest)
Body on the Beach. Hammond, 1953
Meet a Body. Hammond, 1953

FAUST, FREDERICK (D) (Pseudonyms: Max Brand, Walter C. Butler, Frederick Frost)
The Bamboo Whistle, by Frederick Frost. Macrae Smith, 1937 (Sequel to Secret Agent Number One and Spy Meets Spy)
Calling Dr. Kildare, by Max Brand. Dodd, 1940
Cross over Nine, by Walter C. Butler. Macaulay, 1935
"The Dark Peril"; see The Night Flower
"The Downfall"; see Spy Meets Spy
"The Gilded Box"; see Spy Meets Spy
The Night Flower, by Walter C. Butler. Macaulay, 1936 (Published in Detective Fiction Weekly as "The Dark Peril")
Secret Agent Number One, by Frederick Frost. Macrae Smith, 1936 (Published in Detective Fiction Weekly as four novelettes)
Spy Meets Spy, by Frederick Frost. Macrae Smith, 1937 (Sequel to Secret Agent Number One. Published in Detective Fiction Weekly as four novel-

ettes: "Treason Against a King," "The Gilded Box," "Wings over Moscow," and "The Downfall.")
"Treason Against a King"; see Spy Meets Spy
"Wings over Moscow"; see Spy Meets Spy

FAY, DOROTHY, pseud; see LINDHOLM, ANNA CHANDLER

FEAGLES, ANITA MacRAE (D) (Pseudonym: Travis Macrae)
Death in View. Holt, 1960; Hale, R., 1961
Multiple Murder. Hammond, 1961
Trial by Slander. Rinehart, 1960
Twenty Per Cent. Holt, 1961

FEARING, KENNETH (M)
The Big Clock. Harcourt, 1946; Ballantine, 1962
Clark Gifford's Body. Random, 1942
Dagger of the Mind. Lane, 1941; Macmillan, 1941; Random, 1941; Ballantine, 1962
Generous Heart. Harcourt, 1954
The Loneliest Girl in the World. Harcourt, 1951; Bodley Head, 1952

FEARNLY, JOHN BLAKEWAY (D)
Corpse to Bury. Jarrolds, 1956
Murder by Degrees. Hale, R., 1940

FEARON, DIANA (M)
Death Before Breakfast. Hale, R., 1959
Murder-on-Thames. Hale, R., 1960
Nairobi Nightcap. Hale, R., 1958

FEIN, HARRY H. (S)
The Flying Chinaman. Knopf, 1938

FEKETE, MARY BUSH-; see BUSH-FEKETE, MARY

FELDER, LOUIS (D)
Rocky Libido in San Francisco. Angel Island Publications, 1963

FELIX, CHARLES (M)
The Notting Hill Mystery. Saunders, Otley, 1865
Velvet Lawn. Saunders, Otley, 1864

FELTNER, BERT, JR. (D)
Death Comes Easy. Carlton, 1964

FENISONG, RUTH (D)
Bite the Hand. Doubleday, 1956
Blackmailer. Foulsham, 1958
But Not Forgotten. Ace, 1960; Doubleday, 1960
The Butler Died in Brooklyn. Doubleday, Doran, 1943
The Case of the Gloating Landlord. Foulsham, 1958
Dead Weight. Doubleday, 1962; Hale, R., 1964
Dead Yesterday. Doubleday, 1951
Deadlock. Doubleday, 1952; Collier, 1966
Death of the Party. Doubleday, 1958
Desperate Cure. Doubleday, 1946
Grim Rehearsal. Doubleday, 1950
Ill Wind. Doubleday, 1950
Jenny Kissed Me. Doubleday, Doran, 1944; Collier, 1965
The Lost Caesar. Doubleday, Doran, 1945
Miscast for Murder. Doubleday, 1954
Murder Needs a Face. Doubleday, Doran, 1942
Murder Needs a Name. Doubleday, Doran, 1942
Murder Runs a Fever. Doubleday, Doran, 1943
The Schemers. Ace, 1957; Doubleday, 1957
Sinister Assignment. Foulsham, 1960
Villainous Company. Doubleday, 1967
The Wench Is Dead. Doubleday, 1953
Widow's Blackmail. Foulsham, 1957
Widow's Plight. Doubleday, 1955

FENN, CAROLINE K.; see McGREW, JULIA

FENN, GEORGE MANVILLE (M)
Bag of Diamonds. Appleton, D., 1887; Lovell, F. F., 1887; Ward & Downey, 1887
Black Blood. Lovell, F. F., 1888; Lovell, J. W., 1888
Dark House. Appleton, D., 1885; Harper, 1885; Marquis, 1885; Donohue, 1896
Double Cunning. Appleton, D., 1886; U.S. Book, 1891
Mynns' Mystery. Chapman, 1886; Munro, 1886; Lovell, F. F., 1889; Warne, 1890
Witness to the Deed. Cassell, 1893

FENN, LOUIS ANDERSON (M)
The Killing Bottle Murder. Methuen, 1936

FENWICK, ELIZABETH P. (M)
A Friend of Mary Rose. Harper, 1961
The Inconvenient Corpse. Farrar & Rinehart, 1944
Long Way Down. Gollancz, 1959; Harper, 1959
The Make-Believe Man. Harper, 1963; Avon, 1964
Murder in Haste. Farrar & Rinehart, 1944
A Night Run. Gollancz, 1961
The Passenger. Atheneum, 1967
Poor Harriet. Harper, 1957
The Silent Cousin. Atheneum, 1966
Two Names for Death. Farrar & Rinehart, 1945; Gardner, 1949

FERENNCZY, ARPAD (S)
Ants of Timothy Thummel. Harcourt, 1924

FERGUSON, JOHN ALEXANDER (M)
The Dark Geraldine. Lane, 1921
Death Comes to Perigord. Dodd, 1931; Collins, 1932
Death of Mr. Dodsley. Collins, 1937
The Grouse Moor Murder. Collins, 1934; Dodd, 1934
The Man in the Dark. Dodd, 1928; Lane, 1928
Murder on the Marsh. Dodd, 1930; Lane, 1930
Night in Glengyle. Dodd, 1933
The Secret Road. Dodd, 1925; Lane, 1925
Stealthy Terror. Lane, 1918; Penguin, 1939
Terror on the Island. Vanguard, 1942

FERGUSON, MARGARET (S)
Sign of the Ram. Blakiston, 1945; Bantam, 1948

FERGUSON, WILLIAM BLAIR MORTON (D) (Pseudonym: William Morton)
The Black Company. Chelsea House, 1924; Jenkins, 1929
The Case of Casper Gault, by William Morton. Hurst, 1932
Lightnin' Calvert. McBride, 1930; Long, 1931
Little Lost Lady, by William Morton. Hurst, 1931
Masquerade. Nelson, 1930
The Murder of Christine Wilmerding. Liveright, 1932; Mason, 1932
The Murderer, by William Morton. Hurst, 1932
The Mystery of the Human Bookcase, by William Morton. Mason, 1931; Hurst, 1932
The Pilditch Puzzle. Liveright, 1932
The Riddle of the Rose. McBride, 1929; Jenkins, 1930
The Singing Snake. Long, 1932
The Vanishing Men. Long, 1932

FERGUSSON, BERNARD E. (S)
The Rare Adventure. Rinehart, 1955

FERGUSSON, ERNA (M)
Murder and Mystery in New Mexico. Merle, 1948

FERNANDES, J. R. (S)
Yokohama Hood. Vantage, 1967

FERNEE, HERBERT (M)
They Wetted His Head. Faber, 1943

FERRARS, E. X., pseud; see BROWN, MORNA DAVIS MacTAGGART

FERRARS, ELIZABETH, pseud; see BROWN, MORNA DAVIS MacTAGGART

FESSIER, MICHAEL (M)
Fully Dressed and in His Right Mind. Gollancz, 1935; Knopf, 1935

FETHALAND, JOHN (M)
Murder at Charters. Gollancz, 1939

FETTA, EMMA LOU (D)
Dressed to Kill. Doubleday, Doran, 1941
Murder in Style. Doubleday, Doran, 1939
Murder on the Face of It. Doubleday, Doran, 1940

FETTER, ELIZABETH HEAD (M) (Pseudonym: Hannah Lees)
The Dark Device. Harper, 1946
Death in a Doll's House, with Lawrence Paul Bachmann. Random, 1943; Murray, J., 1944
RX: Prescription for Murder. Random, 1941

FICKLING, G. G., pseud; see FICKLING, SKIP FORREST

FICKLING, SKIP FORREST (D) (Pseudonym: G. G. Fickling)
Blood and Honey. Pyramid, 1961
Bombshell. Pyramid, 1964
The Case of the Radioactive Redhead. Belmont, 1963
Crazy Mixed-up Nude. Ballantine
Dig a Dead Doll. Pyramid, 1961
Girl on the Loose. Pyramid, 1958
Girl on the Prowl. Pyramid, 1958
A Gun for Honey. Pyramid, 1958
Honey in the Flesh. Pyramid, 1959
Honey West. Pyramid, 1961
Hurricane Honey. Pyramid, 1964
Kiss for a Killer. Pyramid, 1960
Naughty But Dead. Belmont, 1962
This Girl for Hire. Pyramid, 1957

FIDLER, HENRY J. (M)
Chronicles of Dennis Chetwynd. Hutchinson, 1927

FIELD, HERBERT (D)
The Marsh Gang. Jarrolds, 1929
Needle. Jarrolds, 1929

FIELD, MEDORA (D) (Full name: Medora Field Perkerson)
Blood on Her Shoe. Macmillan, 1942; Jarrolds, 1943
Who Killed Aunt Maggie? Macmillan, 1939; Jarrolds, 1940; Popular Lib.

FIELD, MOIRA (M)
Foreign Body. Bles, 1950; Macmillan, 1951

FIELD, RACHEL (M)
All This and Heaven Too. Macmillan, 1938

FIELD, TEMPLE (S)
Five. Farrar & Rinehart, 1931
Killer's Carnival. Farrar & Rinehart, 1932

FIELDING, ARCHIBALD E. (D) (Pseudonym: Dorothy Fielding)
Black Cats Are Lucky. Collins, 1937; Kinsey, 1938
The Case of the Missing Diary. Collins, 1935; Kinsey, 1936
The Case of the Two Pearl Necklaces. Collins, 1936; Kinsey, 1936
The Cautley Conundrum; see The Cautley Mystery
The Cautley Mystery. Kinsey, 1934 (English title: The Cautley Conundrum. Collins, 1934)
The Charteris Mystery. Collins, 1925; Knopf, 1925
The Clifford Affair. Collins, 1927; Knopf, 1927; Burt, 1929
The Cluny Problem. Collins, 1928; Knopf, 1929; Burt, 1931
The Craig Poisoning Mystery. Collins, 1930; Cosmopolitan, 1930
The Death of John Tait. Collins, 1932; Kinsey, 1932
Deep Currents. Collins, 1924
The Eames-Erskine Case. Collins, 1924; Knopf, 1925
The Footsteps That Stopped. Collins, 1926; Knopf, 1926
In the Night
Murder at the Nook. Knopf, 1930; Collins, 1932
Murder in Suffolk. Collins, 1938; Kinsey, 1938
The Mysterious Partner. Collins, 1929; Knopf, 1929
The Mystery at the Rectory. Collins, 1936; Kinsey, 1937
The Net Around Joan Ingilby. Collins, 1928; Knopf, 1928; Burt, 1930
The Paper Chase Mystery. Collins, 1934; Kinsey, 1935
Scarecrow. Collins, 1937; Kinsey, 1937
The Tall House Mystery. Collins, 1933; Kinsey, 1933
The Tragedy at Beechcroft. Collins, 1935; Kinsey, 1935
The Upfold Farm Mystery. Collins, 1931; Kinsey, 1932
The Wedding-Chest Mystery. Collins, 1930; Kinsey, 1932
The Westwood Mystery. Collins, 1932; Kinsey, 1933

FIELDING, DOROTHY, pseud; see FIELDING, ARCHIBALD E.

FIELDING, HOWARD, pseud; see HOOKE, CHARLES W.

FIELDING, PETER (D)
Text for Murder. Evans, 1951

FILER, TOM (S)
The Man on Watch. Harper, 1961

FINDLEY, FERGUSON, pseud; see FREY, CHARLES W.

FINDLEY, TIMOTHY (S)
The Last of the Crazy People. Meredith, 1967

FINECKE, BARONESS KAREN CHRISTINE BLIXEN-; see BLIXEN-FINECKE, BARONESS KAREN CHRISTINE

FINKEL, MAX (M-S) (Pseudonyms: Maxwell Jeffrey Catto, Simon Kent)
Charlie Gallagher, My Love, by Simon Kent. Hutchinson, 1960
D-Day in Paradise, by Max Catto. Heineman, 1963; Morrow, 1964
The Devil at Four O'clock, by Max Catto. Heinemann, 1958; Morrow, 1959; Popular Lib., 1961
Ferry to Hong Kong, by Simon Kent. Hutchinson, 1957
Fire Down Below, by Simon Kent. Hutchinson, 1954
Gold in the Sky, by Max Catto. Heinemann, 1957; Morrow, 1958
The Killing Frost, by Max Catto. Heinemann, 1950 (Also published as: Trapeze. Four Square, 1959)
Lions at the Kill, by Simon Kent. Hutchinson, 1959
Melody of Sex, by Max Catto. Heinemann, 1959; Morrow, 1960; Popular Lib., 1962
Mister Moses, by Max Catto. Heinemann, 1961; Morrow, 1961; Popular Lib., 1963
Prize of Gold, by Max Catto. Heinemann, 1953
The Tiger in the Bed, by Max Catto. Heinemann, 1963; Morrow, 1963; Lancer, 1964
Trapeze; see The Killing Frost

FINLEY, GLENNA (M)
Death Strikes Out. Arcadia, 1957

FINLEY, SCOTT, pseud; see CLARK, WINIFRED

FINNEGAN, ROBERT, pseud; see RYAN, PAUL WILLIAM

FINNEY, JACK (S)
Assault on a Queen. S & S, 1959; Eyre, 1960; Dell, 1960

The Body Snatchers. Eyre, 1955; Odhams, 1957; Dell, 1961
Five Against the House. Doubleday, 1954; Eyre, 1954
House of Numbers. Dell, 1957; Eyre, 1957

FIRTH, ANTHONY (S)
Tall, Balding and Thirty-five. Harper & Row, 1966

FISCHER, BURNO (M)
Angels Fell. Dodd, 1950; Boardman, T. V., 1951
The Bleeding Scissors. Ambassador, 1948; Ziff-Davis, 1948; Signet, 1955; Collier, 1962 (Also published as: Scarlet Scissors. Foulsham, 1950)
Croaked the Raven; see Quoth the Raven
Dead Men Grin. McKay, 1945; Musson, 1945; Quality, 1945
Flesh Was Gold
Girl Between. GM, 1961
The Hornet's Nest. McClelland, 1944; Morrow, 1944; Quality, 1944
Kill to Fit. Quality, 1949
Knee-deep in Death. GM, 1956
More Deaths Than One. Ambassador, 1947; Ziff-Davis, 1947; Foulsham, 1950; Collier, 1961
Murder in the Raw. GM, 1957
The Paper Circle. Dodd, 1951; Boardman, T. V., 1952 (Also published as: Stripped for Murder. Dell)
The Pigskin Bag. Ambassador, 1946; Ziff-Davis, 1946; Foulsham, 1951; Collier, 1961
Quoth the Raven. Doubleday, Doran, 1944; McClelland, 1944 (Also published as: Croaked the Raven. Quality, 1948)
The Restless Hands. Dodd, 1949; Foulsham, 1950; Dell
Run for Your Life. GM, 1953
Scarlet Scissors; see The Bleeding Scissors
Second-hand Nude. GM, 1959
Silent Dust. Dodd, 1950; Boardman, T. V., 1951
So Much Blood. Greystone, 1939
So Wicked My Love. GM, 1954
The Spider Lily. McKay, 1946; Musson, 1946; Benn, 1953
Stripped for Murder; see The Paper Circle

FISH, ROBERT L. (D) (Pseudonym: Robert Pike)
Always Kill a Stranger. Longmans, 1967; Putnam, 1967
Assassination Bureau, by Robert Pike. McGraw, 1963 (Completed Jack London Story)
Brazilian Sleigh Ride. S & S, 1965; Berkley Pub., 1967
The Brinkmanship of Galahad Treepwood. S & S, 1965
The Diamond Bubble. S & S, 1965; Berkley Pub., 1966
The Fugitive. S & S, 1962; Boardman, T. V., 1963; Avon
The Hochmann Miniatures. New Amer. Lib., 1967
The Incredible Schlock Homes. S & S, 1966
Isle of the Snakes. S & S, 1963; Avon, 1964; Boardman, T. V., 1964 (Completed from notes of Jack London)
Mute Witness, by Robert Pike. Avon, 1963; Doubleday, 1963
Police Blotter, by Robert Pike. Doubleday, 1965; Deutsch, 1966; Berkley Pub., 1967
The Quarry, by Robert Pike. Doubleday, 1964; Berkley Pub., 1967
The Shrunken Head, by Robert Pike. S & S, 1963; Boardman, T. V., 1965; Avon, 1966
Trials of O'Brien. Signet, 1965

FISHER, DOUGLAS (D)
Corpse in Community. Hodder, 1953
Death at Pyford Hall. Hodder, 1952
Poison-Pen at Pyford. Hodder, 1951
What's Wrong at Pyford? Hodder, 1950

FISHER, GERARD (D)
Hospitality for Murder. Hale, R., 1959; Washburn, 1959
It's Your Turn to Die. Hale, R., 1960

FISHER, LAINE, pseud; see HOWARD, JAMES ARCH

FISHER, LAWRENCE (D)
Death by the Day. Berkley Pub., 1961

FISHER, LAWRENCE V. (D)
Die a Little Everyday. Boardman, T. V., 1963; Random, 1963

FISHER, RUDOLPH (M)
Conjure Man Dies. Covici, 1932

FISHER, STEPHEN GOULD (M) (Pseudonyms: Stephen Gould, Grant Lane)
Destination Tokyo. Appleton-Century, 1943
Homicide Johnny, by Stephen Gould. Mystery House, 1940
I Wake Up Screaming. Dodd, 1941; Bantam, 1961
Image of Hell. Dutton, 1961
Murder of the Admiral, by Stephen Gould. Macaulay, 1936
Murder of the Pigboat Skipper. Hillman-Curl, 1937
Night Before Murder. Hillman-Curl, 1939

No House Limit. Dutton, 1958; Bantam, 1961
Satan's Angel. Macaulay, 1935
Spend the Night, by Grant Lane. Phoenix, 1935
Take All You Can Get. Random, 1955
Winter Kill. Dodd, 1946

FISHTER, JACOB FRANTZ (M)
The Ambassador of Death. Macaulay, 1937

FITT, MARY, pseud; see FREEMAN, MRS. KATHLEEN

FITTS, JAMES FRANKLIN (M)
Sharp Night's Work. Laird, 1888

FITZGERALD, KEVIN (M)
Dangerous to Lean Out. Heinemann, 1960; Macmillan, 1961
It's Different in July. Heinemann, 1955
It's Safe in England. Heinemann, 1949
Quiet Under the Sun. Heinemann, 1953; Little, 1954
Throne of Bayonets. Heinemann, 1952

FITZGERALD, NIGEL (M)
Black Welcome. Doubleday, 1961; Macmillan, 1962
Candles Are All Out. Collins, 1957; Macmillan, 1960
The Day of the Adder. Collins, 1963; Doubleday, 1963 (Also published as: Echo Answers Murder. Macmillan, 1965)
Echo Answers Murder; see The Day of the Adder
The House Is Falling. Collins, 1955
Imagine a Man. Collins, 1956
Midsummer Malice. Collins, 1953; Macmillan, 1959
The Rosy Pastor. Collins, 1954
Student Body. Collins, 1958
Suffer a Witch. Collins, 1958
This Won't Hurt You. Collins, 1959; Macmillan, 1960

FITZSIMMONS, CORTLAND (D)
The Bainbridge Murder. Grosset, 1930; McBride, 1930; Eyre, 1931
Crimson Ice. McClelland, 1935; Stokes, 1935
Death on the Diamond. McClelland, 1934; Stokes, 1934; Grosset, 1936
Death Rings a Bell. Lippincott, 1942; Longmans, 1942
The Evil Men Do. McClelland, 1941; Stokes, 1941
The Girl in the Cage, with John Mulholland. Stokes, 1939
The Manville Murders. McBride, 1930; Grosset, 1933 (Also published as: The Scarlet Thread Mystery)
The Moving Finger. Stokes, 1937
The Mystery at Hidden Harbor. Stokes, 1938; Lane, 1939
No Witness. Stokes, 1932; Hutchinson, 1933; Grosset, 1934
One Man's Poison. Stokes, 1940
Red Rhapsody. Stokes, 1933; Grosset, 1935
The Scarlet Thread Mystery; see The Manville Murders
Seventy Thousand Witnesses. McBride, 1931; Grosset, 1932
The Sudden Silence; the Case of the Murdered Bandleader. Stokes, 1938; Lane, 1939; McClelland, 1939
This - Is Murder!, with Gerald Adams. Stokes, 1941
Tied for Murder. Lippincott, 1943
The Whispering Window. McClelland, 1936; Stokes, 1936; Grosset, 1938

FLAGG, JOHN (D) (Pseudonym: John Gearon)
Dear Deadly Beloved. GM, 1954
Death and the Naked Lady. Muller, 1953; GM
Death's Lovely Mask, GM, 1958
The Paradise Gun. GM, 1961

FLAVIN, MARTIN (S)
Cameron Hill. Harper, 1957

FLEISCHMAN, A. S. (S)
Counterspy Express. Ace, 1954
Look Behind You, Lady. Fawcett, 1963
Malay Woman. GM, 1954
Murder's No Accident. Phoenix, 1949
Shanghai Flame. GM, 1951, 1955
The Straw Donkey Case. Phoenix, 1948
The Venetian Blonde. GM, 1963

FLEMING, BRANDON (D)
The Crime Maker. White, 1923
The Crooked House. Clode, 1921

FLEMING, IAN (M-S)
"Berlin Escape"; see Octopussy
Bonded Fleming: a James Bond Omnibus. Viking, 1965
Casino Royale. Cape, 1950; Macmillan, 1953; Signet, 1960
The Complete Ian Fleming. Signet, 1965 (Boxed set)
Diamonds Are Forever. Macmillan, 1956; Permabooks, 1957; Signet, 1961
Doctor No. Macmillan, 1958; Signet, 1963
For Your Eyes Only. Viking, 1960; Signet, 1961
From Russia, with Love. Cape, 1957; Macmillan, 1957; Signet, 1957
Gilt-Edge Bonds: Casino Royale, From Russia, with Love, Doctor No. Macmillan, 1961
The Golden Gun. Cape, 1965 (U.S. title: The Man with the Golden Gun. New Amer. Lib., 1965)

Goldfinger. Macmillan, 1959; Signet, 1960
Live and Let Die. Cape, 1954; Macmillan, 1954; Permabooks, 1956; Signet
The Man with the Golden Gun; see The Golden Gun
Moonraker. Cape, 1955; Macmillan, 1955; Signet, 1960 (Also published as: Too Hot to Handle. Cape, 1957)
More Gilt-Edge Bonds: Live and Let Die, Moonraker, Diamonds Are Forever. Macmillan, 1965
Octopussy. New Amer. Lib., 1966; Signet, 1967 (Also includes: "The Living Daylights" and "Property of a Lady." "Octopussy" originally appeared in Playboy, March-April, 1966; and "The Living Daylights" in Argosy, 1962, under the title "Berlin Escape")
On Her Majesty's Secret Service. Cape, 1963; Signet, 1964
"Property of a Lady." Playboy, January, 1965
The Spy Who Loved Me. Viking, 1962; Signet, 1963
Thunderball. Cape, 1961; Signet, 1962
Too Hot to Handle; see Moonraker
You Only Live Twice. Cape, 1964; New Amer. Lib., 1964; Signet, 1965

FLEMING, JOAN MARGARET (D)
The Chill and the Kill. Collins, 1964; Washburn, 1964; Ballantine, 1967
Death of a Sardine. Collins, 1963; Washburn, 1964; Ballantine, 1967
The Deeds of Dr. Deadcert. Hutchinson, 1955; Washburn, 1957; Lancer, 1956
The Good and the Bad. Doubleday, 1953; Hutchinson, 1955
He Ought to Be Shot. Doubleday, 1955
In the Red. Collins, 1961; Washburn, 1961; Lancer, 1964
Maiden's Prayer. Collins, 1957; Washburn, 1958; Ballantine, 1968
Malice Matrimonial. Washburn, 1959; Collins, 1964; Ballantine, 1967
The Man from Nowhere. Collins, 1960; Washburn, 1961; Lancer, 1964
The Man Who Looked Back. Hutchinson, 1953
The Midnight Hag. Washburn, 1966
Miss Bones. Collins, 1959; Washburn, 1960
No Bones About It. Collins, 1967; Washburn, 1967; Ballantine, 1968
Nothing Is the Number When You Die. Collins, 1965; Washburn, 1965
When I Grow Rich. Washburn, 1962; Collier, 1965
You Can't Believe Your Eyes. Collins, 1957; Washburn, 1957

FLEMING, JOHN C.; see EBY, LOIS CHRISTINE

FLEMING, OLIVER, pseud; see MacDONALD, PHILIP

FLEMING, PETER (M)
The Sixth Column. Hart-Davis, 1951; Scribner, 1951; Avon, 1966

FLEMING, ROBERT (D)
The Night Freight Murders. Smith & Durrell, 1942

FLEMING, RUDD (M)
Cradled in Murder. Hamilton, H., 1938; S & S, 1938

FLEMING, THOMAS J. (D)
A Cry of Whiteness. Morrow, 1967

FLETCHER, DOROTHY (S)
House of Hate. Lancer, 1967

FLETCHER, HARRY LUFT VERNE (M-D) (Pseudonym: John Garden)
All on a Summer's Day. Joseph, M., 1949
Day of Reckoning. Lippincott, 1951
Miss Agatha Doubles for Death. Messner, 1947; Bantam, 1948

FLETCHER, HENRY LANCELOT AUBREY-; see AUBREY-FLETCHER, HENRY LANCELOT

FLETCHER, JOSEPH SMITH (D)
The Adventures of Archer Dawe, Sleuth-Hound. Digby, 1909
The Amaranth Club. Ward, Lock, 1918; Knopf, 1926
The Ambitious Lady. Ward, Lock, 1923
And Sudden Death. Hillman-Curl, 1938
The Annexation Society. Ward, Lock, 1916; Knopf, 1925; Grosset, 1927
The Bartenstein Case. Long, 1914 (U.S. title: The Bartenstein Mystery. MacVeagh, 1927; Burt, 1929)
The Bartenstein Mystery; see The Bartenstein Case
The Bedford Row Mystery. Hodder, 1925
Behind the Monocle and Other Stories. Jarrolds, 1928; Doubleday, Doran, 1930; Grosset, 1932
Behind the Panel; see In the Mayor's Parlour
Black Money; see The Charing Cross Mystery
The Borgia Cabinet. Knopf, 1930; Grosset, 1931; Jenkins, 1932; Mellifont, 1942
The Borough Treasurer. Ward, Lock, 1919; Knopf, 1921; Grosset, 1923
The Box Hill Murder. Knopf, 1929; Jenkins, 1931

The Burma Ruby. Benn, 1932; MacVeagh, 1933
The Canterbury Mystery. Collins, 1933 (Also published as: The Ravenswood Mystery)
The Carrismore Ruby. Jarrolds, 1935
The Cartwright Gardens Murder. Collins, 1924; Knopf, 1926
The Charing Cross Mystery. Grosset, 1923; Putnam, 1923 (English title: Black Money. Jenkins, 1923)
The Chestermarke Instinct. Allen & Unwin, 1918; Knopf, 1921; Grosset, 1923
The Clue of the Artificial Eye. Hillman-Curl, 1939
The Cobweb Castle. Jenkins, 1928; Knopf, 1928
The Contents of the Coffin. London Book, 1928
The Copper Box. Doran, 1923; Hodder, 1923; Grosset, 1923
Dead Men's Money. Grosset, 1920; Knopf, 1920 (English title: Droonin' Water. Allen & Unwin, 1919, 1928)
The Death That Lurks Unseen. Ward, Lock, 1899
The Diamond Murders. Dodd, 1929; Burt, 1930 (Also published as: The Diamonds. Digby, 1904; Collins, 1924)
The Diamonds; see The Diamond Murders
The Double Chance. Dodd, 1928; Grayson, 1928
The Dressing Room Murder. Knopf, 1931; Jenkins, 1932
Droonin' Water; see Dead Men's Money
The Ebony Box. Butterworth, T., 1934; Knopf, 1934; Ryerson, 1934
The Eleventh Hour. Butterworth, T., 1935; Knopf, 1935; Macmillan, 1935
Exterior to the Evidence. Hodder, 1920; Knopf, 1923
False Scent. Jenkins, 1924; Knopf, 1925
Fear of the Night and Other Stories. Routledge, 1903; Selwyn, 1931
Find This Woman. Collins, 1933
The Flamstock Mystery; see The Malachite Jar
The Fletcher Omnibus. Collins, 1932; Knopf, 1933
The Golden Spur. Long, 1923; MacVeagh, 1928
The Great Brighton Mystery. Hodder, 1925; Knopf, 1926
Green Ink; see Green Ink and Other Stories
Green Ink and Other Stories. Jenkins, 1926; Small, 1926 (Also published as: Green Ink. Grosset, 1927)
The Green Rope. Jenkins, 1927; Knopf, 1927; Grosset, 1929
The Guarded Room. Clode, 1931; Long, 1931
Hardican's Hollow. Everett, 1910; Doran, 1927
Harvest Moon. Nash, 1908; Doran, 1927
The Heaven-Kissed Hill. Doran, 1924; Grosset, 1924
Heaven-Sent Witness and Other Stories. Doubleday, Doran, 1930
The Herapath Property. Ward, Lock, 1920; Knopf, 1921
The House in Tuesday Market. Knopf, 1929; Jenkins, 1930
In the Mayor's Parlour. Lane, 1922 (Also published as: Behind the Panel. Collins, 1931)
The Investigators. Long, 1902; Clode, 1930; Burt, 1931
The Ivory God. Murray, J., 1927
The Kang-He Vase. Collins, 1924; Knopf, 1926; Grosset, 1928
The King Versus Wargrave. Ward, Lock, 1915; Knopf, 1924
The Lost Mr. Linthwaite. Hodder, 1920; Knopf, 1923
The Malachite Jar and Other Stories. Collins, 1930 (Also published as: The Flamstock Mystery. Collins, 1932 and The Manor House Mystery. Collins, 1933)
The Man in Number Three. Collins, 1931
The Man in the Fur Coat and Other Stories. Collins, 1932
The Manor House Mystery; see The Malachite Jar
Many Engagements. Long, 1923
The Markenmore Mystery. Jenkins, 1922; Knopf, 1923; Grosset, 1925
Marrendom Mystery and Other Stories. Collins, 1931
The Massingham Butterfly and Other Stories. Small, 1926
The Matheson Formula. Knopf, 1929; Jenkins, 1930; Grosset, 1931
The Mazaroff Murder. Jenkins, 1923; Knopf, 1924
The Middle of Things. Knopf, 1922; Ward, Lock, 1922
The Middle Temple Murders. Knopf, 1919; Ward, Lock, 1919
The Mill House Murder. Knopf, 1937 (Also published as: Todmanhawe Grange. Butterworth, T., 1937)
The Missing Chancellor. Knopf, 1927; Grosset
Mr. Spivey's Clerk. Ward & Downey, 1890; Jarrolds, 1932
The Mortover Grange Affair. Jenkins, 1926; Knopf, 1927
The Murder at Wrides Park. Harrap, 1931; Knopf, 1931
Murder in Four Degrees. Harrap, 1931; Knopf, 1931
The Murder in Medora Mansions. Collins, 1933
The Murder in the Pallant. Jenkins, 1927; Knopf, 1928

Murder in the Squire's Pew. Harrap, 1932; Knopf, 1933
Murder of a Banker; see Mystery of the London Banker
Murder of the Lawyer's Clerk. Knopf, 1933 (Also published as: Who Killed Alfred Snowe? Harrap, 1933)
Murder of the Ninth Baronet. Harrap, 1932; Knopf, 1932
Murder of the Only Witness. Harrap, 1933; Knopf, 1933
Murder of the Secret Agent. Harrap, 1934; Knopf, 1934
The Mysterious Chinaman. Jenkins, 1923
The Mystery of Lynne Court. Norman, 1923; Grosset, 1924
The Mystery of the London Banker. Harrap, 1933 (U.S. title: Murder of a Banker. Knopf, 1933)
Old Lattimer's Legacy. Jarrolds, 1892; Clode, 1929
The Orange-Yellow Diamond. Knopf, 1921; Newnes, 1921; Grosset, 1922
Paradise Court. Unwin, 1908; Doubleday, Doran, 1929
The Paradise Mystery. Knopf, 1920; Grosset
The Passenger to Folkstone. Jenkins, 1927; Knopf, 1927
Paul Campenhaye, Specialist in Criminology. Ward, Lock, 1918
The Perilous Crossways. Ward, Lock, 1917; Hillman-Curl, 1938; McLeod, 1938
The Pinfold. Everett, 1911; Doubleday, Doran, 1928
The Ransom for London. Long, 1914; MacVeagh, 1929
Ravensdene Court. Knopf, 1922; Ward, Lock, 1922; Grosset, 1925
The Ravenswood Mystery; see The Canterbury Mystery
The Rayner-Slade Amalgamation. Allen & Unwin, 1917; Knopf, 1922; Grosset, 1925
The Rippling Ruby. Putnam, 1923; Grosset, 1925
The Root of All Evil. Hodder, 1921; Doran
The Safety Pin. Grosset, 1924; Jenkins, 1924; Putnam, 1924
Scarhaven Keep. Ward, Lock, 1920; Knopf, 1922; Grosset, 1924
Sea Fog. Jenkins, 1925; Knopf, 1926
The Secret of Secrets. Clode, 1929
The Secret of the Barbicans and Other Stories. Hodder, 1924; Doran, 1925
The Secret Way. Digby, 1903; Small, 1925
Seven Days' Secret. Jarrolds, 1919; Clode, 1930
The Shadow of Ravenscliffe. Digby, 1914; Clode, 1928
The Solution of a Mystery. Doubleday, Doran, 1932; Harrap, 1932
The South Foreland Murder. Knopf, 1930; Jenkins, 1931
The Stolen Budget. Hodder, 1926
The Strange Case of Mr. Henry Marchmont. Knopf, 1927
The Talleyrand Maxim. Ward, Lock, 1919; Knopf, 1920
Three Days' Terror. Long, 1901; Clode, 1927
The Time-Worn Town. Knopf, 1924; Collins, 1929
Todmanhawe Grange; see Mill House Murder
The Town of Crooked Ways. Estes, 1912; Nash, 1912
The Valley of Headstrong Men. Hodder, 1921; Doran, 1924; Grosset, 1926
Who Killed Alfred Snow?; see Murder of the Lawyer's Clerk
The Wild Oat. Jarrolds, 1928; Doubleday, Doran, 1929
The Wolves and the Lamb. Ward, Lock, 1914; Knopf, 1928
The Wrist Mark. Knopf, 1928; Jenkins, 1929
The Wrychester Paradise. Ward, Lock, 1921
The Yorkshire Moorland Murder. Jenkins, 1930; Knopf, 1930

FLETCHER, LUCILLE (S)
And Presumed Dead. Eyre, 1963; Random, 1963; Bantam, 1964
Blindfold. Eyre, 1960; Random, 1960; Bantam, 1961
The Daughters of Jasper Clay. Holt, H., 1958
Night Man, with Allan Ullman. Random, 1951
Sorry, Wrong Number, with Allan Ullman. Random, 1948
The Strange Blue Yawl. Random, 1964

FLORA, FLETCHER (D-M)
The Hot Shot. Avon, 1956
Irrepressible Peccadillo. Macmillan, 1962; Boardman, T. V., 1963
Killing Cousins. Macmillan, 1960
Let Me Kill You, Sweetheart. Avon, 1958
Skulldoggery. Belmont, 1967
Wake Up with a Stranger. New Amer. Lib., 1959

FLOWER, ELLIOTT (D)
Policeman Flynn. Copp, 1902

FLOWER, PAT (M)
Goodbye, Sweet William. Angus, 1959; Ryerson, 1959
Hell for Heather. Hale, R., 1962
One Rose Less. Angus, 1961
Term of Terror. Hale, R., 1963
Wax Flowers for Gloria. Angus, 1958
Wreath of Water Lilies. Angus, 1960; Ryerson, 1960

FLOWERDEU, HERBERT
Villa Mystery. Paul, S., 1912

FLOYD, LOUISE McKNIGHT (D)
The Commencement Day Murders. Vantage, 1955

FLYNN, BRIAN (M)
And Cauldron Bubble. Long, 1951
The Billiard Room Mystery. Hamilton, H., 1927; Macrae Smith, 1929
The Black Agent. Long, 1950
Black Edged. Macrae Smith, 1929; Long, 1939
The Case of Elymas the Sorcerer. Long, 1945
The Case of the Black Twenty-two. Hamilton, H., 1928; Macrae Smith, 1929; Grosset, 1930
The Case of the Faithful Heart. Long, 1939
The Case of the Purple Calf. Long, 1934 (Also published as: The Ladder of Death. Macrae Smith, 1935; Grosset, 1936)
Cold Evil. Long, 1938
Conspiracy at Angel. Long, 1947
The Creeping Jenny Mystery. Long, 1930 (Also published as: The Crime at the Crossways. Macrae Smith, 1932; Grosset, 1933)
The Crime at the Crossways; see The Creeping Jenny Mystery
The Dice Are Dark. Long, 1956
The Doll's Done Dancing. Long, 1954
The Ebony Stag. Long, 1938
The Edge of Terror. Long, 1932
Exit Sir John. Long, 1949
Fear and Trembling. Long, 1936; Ryerson, 1936 (Also published as: The Somerset Murder Case. Mill, 1937)
The Feet of Death. Long, 1954
The Five Red Fingers. Mill, 1938; Long, 1959
The Fortescue Candle. Long, 1936
The Grim Maiden. Long, 1944
The Hands of Justice. Long, 1957
The Invisible Death. Hamilton, H., 1929
The Ladder of Death; see The Case of the Purple Calf
The League of Matthias. Long, 1934
Men for Pieces. Long, 1949
The Mirador Collection. Long, 1957
Murder En Route. Long, 1930; Macrae Smith, 1932; Grosset, 1934
Murders Near Mapleton. Hamilton, H., 1929; Macrae Smith, 1930
The Mystery of the Peacock's Eye. Hamilton, H., 1928; Macrae Smith, 1930; Grosset, 1932
The Nine Cuts. Long, 1959
The Orange Axe. Long, 1931
Out of the Dusk. Long, 1953
The Padded Door. Long, 1932
Reverse the Charges. Long, 1932
Ring of Innocent. Long, 1952
Running Nun. Long, 1952
The Saints Are Sinister. Long, 1960
The Seventh Sign. Long, 1952
The Shaking Spear. Long, 1955
The Sharp Guillet. Long, 1947
The Somerset Murder Case; see Fear and Trembling
The Spiked Lion. Long, 1933; Macrae Smith, 1934; Grosset, 1935
Such Bright Disguises. Long, 1941
The Sussex Cockoo. Long, 1935
The Swinging Death. Long, 1949
They Never Came Back. Long, 1940
The Toy Lamb. Long, 1957
Tragedy at Trinket. Nelson, 1934
Tread Softly. Long, 1937; Mill, 1938
The Triple Bite. Long, 1931
Where There Was Smoke. Long, 1951
The Wife Who Disappeared. Long, 1957

FLYNN, J. M. (M-S)
Deadly Boodle. Ace, 1958
Deep-Six. Ace, 1962
Drink with the Dead. Ace, 1959
The Girl from Las Vegas. Ace, 1961
One for the Death House. Ace, 1961 (Double novel. Includes: Drop Dead, Please by Bob McKnight)
Surf Side 6. Dell, 1962
Terror Tournament. Bouregy, 1959; Ace (Abridged edition)

FLYNN, JAY (M)
The Action Man. Avon, 1961
A Body for McHugh. Avon, 1960
It's Murder, McHugh. Avon, 1960
McHugh. Avon, 1959

FLYNN, THOMAS THEODORE (D)
It's Murder. Kelly, 1950
Murder Caravan. Kelly, 1950

FLYNN, WILLIAM JAMES (M)
The Barrel Mystery. McCann, 1919

FOLEY, PEARL (M)
The Octagon Crystal. Brentano, 1929; Carrier & Isles, 1929
The Yellow Circle. Lippincott, 1937

FOLEY, RAE, pseud; see DENNISTON, ELEANORE

FONSECA, ESTHER HAVEN (D)
The Affair at the Grotto. Doubleday, Doran, 1939
The Death Below the Dam. Doubleday, Doran, 1936
The Thirteenth Bed in the Ballroom. Doubleday, Doran, 1937

FOOTMAN, DAVID J. (M)
The Mine in the Desert. Long, 1930

FOOTNER, HULBERT (D)
Almost Perfect Murder. Lippincott, 1937
Anybody's Pearls. Doubleday, Doran, 1930; Hodder, 1930
Cap'n Sue. Doubleday, Doran, 1928; Hodder, 1928
The Casual Murderer; see The Casual Murderer and Other Stories
The Casual Murderer and Other Stories. Collins, 1932 (Also published as: The Casual Murderer. Lippincott, 1937)
Dangerous Cargo. Collins, 1934; Harper, 1934
The Dark Ships. Harper, 1937
Dead Man's Hat. Collins, 1932; Harper, 1932
Death of a Celebrity. Harper, 1938
Death of a Saboteur. Harper, 1943; Musson, 1943; Collins, 1944; Penguin
The Deaves Affair. Doran, 1922; Collins, 1931
The Doctor Who Held Hands. Doubleday, Doran, 1929; Collins, 1930
Easy to Kill. Harper, 1931; Collins, 1932
The Folded Paper Mystery; see The Mystery of the Folded Paper
The Four-Toed Track; see The Whip-poor-will Mystery
The House with the Blue Door. Harper, 1942
The Island of Fear. Cassell, 1936; Harper, 1936
Kidnapping of Madame Storey and Other Stories. Collins, 1936
Madame Storey. Doran, 1926
Murder of a Bad Man. Harper, 1936
Murder Runs in the Family. Harper, 1934
The Murder That Had Everything. Harper, 1939
Murderer's Vanity. Harper, 1940
The Mystery of the Folded Paper. Harper, 1930 (English title: The Folded Paper Mystery. Collins, 1932)
The Nation's Missing Guest. Harper, 1939
The New Made Grave. Collins, 1935
The Obeah Murders. Harper, 1937
Officer! Collins, 1924; Doran, 1924
Orchids to Murder. Collins, 1945; Harper, 1945
The Owl Taxi. Doran, 1921
The Queen of Clubs. Doran, 1928; Collins, 1929
Ramshackle House. Doran, 1922; Collins, 1932
The Ring of Eyes. Collins, 1933; Harper, 1933
Scarred Jungle. Cassell, 1935; Harper, 1935 (Also published as: The Sink of Iniquity)
Self-Made Thief. Collins, 1929; Doubleday, Doran, 1929
Sinfully Rich. Harper, 1940
The Sink of Iniquity; see Scarred Jungle
Substitute Millionaire. Doran, 1919; Collins, 1931
Thieves' Wit. Doran, 1918
Trial by Water. Hodder, 1930; Farrar & Rinehart, 1931
Under Dogs. Doran, 1925
Unneutral Murder. Collins, 1944; Harper, 1944
Velvet Hand: New Madame Storey Mysteries. Doubleday, Doran, 1928; Collins, 1930
The Viper. Collins, 1930
The Whip-poor-will Mystery. Harper, 1935 (Serial title: The Four-Toed Track)
Who Killed the Husband? Harper, 1941

FORBES, DeLORIS STANTON (D-M)
(Pseudonyms: Stanton Forbes, Tobias Wells. Joint pseudonym with Helen Rydell: Forbes Rydell)
Annalisa, by Forbes Rydell. Dodd, 1959; Gollancz, 1960
A Business of Bodies, by Stanton Forbes. Doubleday, 1966; Hale, R., 1967
Dead by the Light of the Moon, by Tobias Wells. Doubleday, 1967
Encounter Darkness, by Stanton Forbes. Doubleday, 1967; Hale, R., 1968
Grieve for the Past, by Stanton Forbes. Doubleday, 1963; Gollancz, 1964; Avon, 1966
If She Should Die, by Forbes Rydell. Doubleday, 1961; Popular Lib., 1964
The Long Hate; see The Terrors of the Earth
A Matter of Love and Death, by Tobias Wells. Doubleday, 1966; Gollancz, 1966
Melody of Terror; see The Terrors of the Earth
No Questions Asked, by Forbes Rydell. Doubleday, 1963; Gollancz, 1963
Relative to Death, by Stanton Forbes. Doubleday, 1965; Hale, R., 1966
Terror Touches Me, by Stanton Forbes. Doubleday, 1966; Hale, R., 1967
The Terrors of the Earth, by Stanton Forbes. Doubleday, 1964 (Also published as: Melody of Terror. Pyramid, 1967. English title: The Long Hate. Hale, R., 1966)
They're Not Home Yet, by Forbes Rydell. Doubleday, 1962
What Should You Know of Dying?, by Tobias Wells. Doubleday, 1967

FORBES, DONALD (M)
The Eleventh Hour. Roy Pubs., 1955

FORBES, STANTON, pseud; see FORBES, DeLORIS STANTON

FORD, BRYANT (M)
Show Business. Dodd, 1939

FORD, COREY (D) (Pseudonym: John Riddel)
The John Ridell Murder Case: A Philo Vance Parody. Scribner, 1930

FORD, ELBUR, pseud; see HIBBERT, ELEANOR BURFORD

FORD, ELIZABETH (M)
A Country Holiday. Hurst, 1966 (U.S. title: Dangerous Holiday. Ace, 1967)

FORD, FLORENCE (S)
Shadow on the House. Morrow, 1954

FORD, JEREMY (D)
Murder Laughs Last. Bouregy, 1956; Ward, Lock, 1959

FORD, LESLIE, pseud; see BROWN, MRS. ZENITH JONES

FORD, MARY FORKER (M)
Murder Country Style. Bouregy, 1964
Shadow of Murder. Bouregy, 1965
The Silent Witness. Bouregy, 1964

FORES, JOHN (S)
Forgotten Places. Coward, 1956

FORESTER, C. S. (M)
Payment Deferred. Lane, 1930; Little, 1942; Popular Lib., 1965
The Peacemaker. Little, 1934
Plain Murder. Dell, 1934

FORGIONE, LOUIS (M)
The Men of Silence. Dent, 1928; Dutton, 1928

FORMAN, HENRY JAMES (D)
Guilt. Boni & Liveright, 1924
The Rembrandt Murder. Paul, S., 1931; Smith, R. R., 1931

FORREST, ALFRED EDGAR (M)
Silent Guests. Covici, 1927

FORREST, NORMAN, pseud; see MORLAND, NIGEL

FORREST, WILLIAMS (S)
The Huntress. GM, 1964

FORRESTER, ANDREW (D)
The Female Detective. London, 1864
The Private Detective. London, 1868
The Revelations of a Private Detective. Ward, Lock, 1863
Secret Service, or Recollections of a City Detective. Ward, Lock, 1864
Tales of a Female Detective. London, 1868

FORRESTER, IZOLA LOUISE (M)
The Dangerous Inheritance; or, The Mystery of the Tittani Rubies. Houghton, 1920
The Secret of the Blue Macaw. Macrae Smith, 1936

FORRESTER, LARRY (S)
A Girl Called Fathom. GM, 1967

FORSYTH, PHIL (M)
The Man Who Feared. Jarrolds, 1927

FORSYTHE, CHARLES (D)
Diplomatic Death. British Book Service, 1961; Cassell, 1961; Morrow, 1961
Dive into Danger. Morrow, 1962 (Also published as: Diving Death. Cassell, 1962)
Diving Death; see Dive into Danger

FORSYTHE, ROBIN (D-M) (Pseudonym: Peter Dingwall)
Ginger Cat Mystery; see Murder at Marston Moor
Hounds of Justice. Lane, 1931
Missing or Murdered? Lane, 1929
Murder at Marston Moor. Appleton-Century, 1935 (Also published as: Ginger Cat Mystery. Lane, 1935)
Murder on Paradise Island. World's Work, 1937
Pleasure Cruise Mystery. Appleton-Century, 1934; Lane, 1934; Ryerson, 1934
The Poison Duel, by Peter Dingwall. Methuen, 1934
Polo Ground Mystery. Lane, 1932
Spirit Murder Mystery. Lane, 1936

FOSBURGH, HUGH (S)
The Drowning Stone. Cape, 1959

FOSTER, JAN (M)
Echo My Tears. Dial, 1948

FOSTER, JOHN (S)
Dark Heritage. GM, 1955

FOSTER, JOHN (S)
The Searchers. Doran, 1920

FOSTER, MAXIMILLIAN (S)
Humdrum House? Appleton, D., 1924

FOSTER, REGINALD FRANCIS (M)
Anthony Ravenhill, Crime Merchant. Jarrolds, 1929
Dark Night. Grayson, 1932
The Moat House Mystery. Macaulay, 1928; Nash & Grayson, 1928
Murder from Beyond. Nash, 1930; Macaulay, 1931
The Music Gallery Murder. Unwin, 1927; Benn, 1929

The Mystery of Chillery. Fiction League, 1931 (English title: Something Wrong at Chillery. Grayson, 1931)
Something Wrong at Chillery; see The Mystery of Chillery

FOSTER, RICHARD, pseud; see CROSSEN, KENDALL FOSTER

FOSTER, W. BERT (M)
From Six to Six. Clode, 1927

FOURNIER, PIERRE (S) (Pseudonym: Pierre Gascar)
Lambs of Fire. Braziller, 1965

FOURTON, ALAIN REYNAUD-; see REYNAUD-FOURTON, ALAIN

FOUTS, EDWARD LEE (D) (Pseudonym: Edward Lee)
A Fish for Murder. Doubleday, Doran, 1944; Hurst, 1947
The Needle's Eye. Doubleday, Doran, 1944

FOWLER, HELEN M.
Hold a Bright Mirror. Angus, 1959
The Intruder; see Shades Will Not Vanish
Shades Will Not Vanish. Landsbrough, 1959 (Also published as: The Intruder)

FOWLER, MARIE LOUIS (M)
The Toll. Field, 1938

FOWLER, SYDNEY, pseud; see WRIGHT, SYDNEY FOWLER

FOWLES, JOHN (S)
The Collector. Little, 1963; Dell, 1964

FOX, DAVID, pseud; see OSTRANDER, ISABEL EGENTON

FOX, GEORGE R. (M)
The Fangs of the Serpent. Minton, 1924

FOX, JAMES M., pseud; see KNIPSCHEER, JAMES M. W.

FOX, MARION (M)
The Mystery Keepers. Lane, 1919

FOX, SEBASTIAN, pseud; see BULLETT, GERALD WILLIAM

FOX-DAVIES, ARTHUR CHARLES (D)
The Duplicate Death. Long, 1910
The Mauleverer Murders. Lane, 1907

FOXE, ALISON (S)
Heirs to Kildrennan. Melrose, 1951
Winged Danger. Melrose, 1952

FRANCIS, BASIL (D)
Death in Act IV. Jenkins, 1956

FRANCIS, C. (M)
Ask the River. Hale, R., 1964

FRANCIS, C. D. E., pseud; see HOWARTH, PATRICK

FRANCIS, DICK (D)
Blood Sport. Harper & Row, 1968
Dead Cert. Holt, 1962; Joseph, M., 1962; Avon, 1965
Flying Finish. Joseph, M., 1966; Harper & Row, 1967
For Kicks. Harper & Row, 1965; Joseph, M., 1965; Berkley Pub., 1968
Nerve. Harper & Row, 1964; Joseph, M., 1965; Signet, 1965
Odds Against. Berkley Pub., 1965; Harper & Row, 1965; Joseph, M., 1965; Longmans, 1965; Pan, 1966

FRANCIS, STEPHEN (S) (Pseudonym: Hank Janson)
Angel, Shoot to Kill. Frances, S. D., 1949
Baby, Don't Dare Squeal. Frances, S.D., 1951
Blonde on the Spot. Gaywood Press, 1949
The Bride Wore Weeds. Gaywood Press, 1950
Broads Don't Scare Easy. New Fiction Press, 1951
Conflict. New Fiction Press, 1952
Contraband. Moring, 1955
Deadly Mission. Moring, 1955
Death Wore a Petticoat. Frances, S. D., 1951
Desert Fury. New Fiction Press, 1953
Don't Dare Me, Sugar. Gaywood Press, 1950
Don't Mourn Me, Toots. Frances, S. D., 1951
The Filly Wore a Rod. New Fiction Press, 1952
48 Hours. Moring, 1955
Frails Can Be Tough So Tough. New Fiction Press, 1951
Framed. Moring, 1955
Gun Moll for Hire. Frances, S. D., 1948
Gunsmoke in Her Eyes. Frances, S. D., 1949
Honey, Take My Gun. Frances, S. D., 1949
Hotsy, You'll Be Chilled. Frances, S. D., 1951
It's Always Eve That Weeps. Frances, S. D., 1951
The Jane with Green Eyes. Gaywood Press, 1950
Kill Her If You Can. New Fiction Press, 1952
The Lady Has a Scar. Gaywood Press, 1950

Lady, Mind That Corpse. Frances, S. D., 1948
Lady Toll the Bell. Gaywood Press, 1950
Lilies for My Lovely. Frances, S. D., 1949
Lola Brought Her Wreath. Gaywood Press, 1950
Menace. Moring, 1955
Milady Took the Rap. New Fiction Press, 1951
Murder. New Fiction Press, 1951
One Man in His Time. New Fiction Press, 1953
Sadie, Don't Cry Now. New Fiction Press, 1952
Sister, Don't Hate Me. Frances, S. D., 1951
Skirts Bring Me Sorrow. New Fiction Press, 1952
Slay-ride for Cutie. Frances, S. D., 1949
Smart Girls Don't Talk. Frances, S. D., 1949
Some Look Better Dead. Frances, S. D., 1950
Sweetheart, Here's Your Grave! Frances, S. D., 1949
Sweetie, Hold Me Tight. Frances, S. D., 1952
Tension. New Fiction Press, 1952
This Dame Dies Soon. Frances, S. D., 1951
This Woman Is Death. Frances, S. D., 1948
Tomorrow and a Day. Moring, 1955
Torment for Trixy. Gaywood Press, 1950
When Dames Get Tough. Ward & Hitchon, 1946
Whiplash. New Fiction Press, 1952
Women Hate Till Death. New Fiction Press, 1951

FRANCIS, WILLIAM, pseud; see URELL, WILLIAM FRANCIS

FRANK, PAT H. H. (S)
An Affair of State. Lippincott, 1948; Longmans, 1948
Mr. Adam. Lippincott, 1946; Longmans, 1946; Gollancz, 1947
Seven Days to Never. Constable, 1957

FRANK, THEODORE, pseud; see GARDINER, DOROTHEA FRANCES

FRANK, WALDO DAVID (M)
Chalk Face. Boni & Liveright, 1924

FRANK, WALTER I. (M)
Diner on the Other Track. Vantage, 1956
Good for One More Ride. Vantage, 1956

FRANKAU, GILBERT (D)
Air Ministry, Room 28. Dutton, 1942 (English title: Winter of Discontent)
Experiments in Crime and Other Stories. Dutton, 1937; Hutchinson, 1937
The Lonely Man. Hutchinson, 1932; Dutton, 1933
Winter of Discontent; see Air Ministry, Room 28

FRANKAU, MRS. JULIA DAVIS (M)
(Pseudonym: Frank Danby)
The Story Behind the Verdict. Cassell, 1915; Dodd, 1915

FRANKAU, PAMELA (M)
A Democrat Dies. Heinemann, 1939 (U.S. title: Appointment with Death)

FRANKISH, H. (D)
Dr. Cunliffe—Investigator. Heath, 1913

FRANKLAND, EDWARD (D)
Murders at Crossby. Dent, 1955

FRANKLIN, CHARLES, pseud; see USHER, FRANK HUGH

FRANKLIN, MAX, pseud; see DEMING, RICHARD

FRASER, ALEC, pseud; see BRINTON, HENRY

FRASER, FERRIN L. (M)
The Screaming Portrait. Sears, 1928; Grosset, 1929

FRASER, HERMIA (D)
One Touch of Murder. Arcadia, 1953

FRASER-SIMSON, MRS. CICELY DEVENISH (M)
Count the Hours. Hutchinson, 1940
Danger Follows. Heinemann, 1929
Footsteps in the Night. Methuen, 1926; Dutton, 1927; Burt, 1929
The Swinging Shutter. Heinemann, 1927; Dutton, 1928

FRAWLEY, WILBUR (S)
The Shuddering Castle. Green Circle, 1936

FRAY, AL (D)
And Kill Once More. Graphic, 1955
Built for Trouble. Dell, 1959; Hale, R., 1960
Come Back for More. Dell, 1958; Hale, R., 1960
The Dame's the Game. Popular Lib., 1960
The Dice Spelled Murder. Dell, 1957

FRAYN, MICHAEL (S)
The Russian Interpreter. Viking, 1966; Lancer, 1967

FRAZEE, STEVE (S)
The Running Target. GM, 1957
The Sky Block. Rinehart, 1953; Clarke, Irwin, 1953; Lane, 1955; Lion

FRAZER, ANDREW, pseud; see MARLOWE, STEPHEN

FRAZER, DIANE (S)
Date with Danger. PB, 1966

FRAZER, MARTIN (M)
Dangerous Waters. Wright & Brown, 1951
Secret in Seven Fathoms. Wright & Brown, 1946

FRAZER, ROBERT CAINE, pseud; see CREASEY, JOHN

FREDERICKS, ARNOLD, pseud; see KUMMER, FREDERICK ARNOLD

FREDERICKS, ERNEST JASON (M)
Lost Friday. Hale, R., 1959
Murder Matrix. Ward, Lock, 1960
Shakedown Hotel. Ace, 1958

FREDERICS, JOCKO (M)
Everybody's Ready to Die. Holt, 1966

FREEDGOOD, MORTON (M) (Pseudonym: John Godey)
The Man in Question. Doubleday, 1951; Boardman, T. V., 1953
This Year's Death. Boardman, T. V., 1953; Doubleday, 1953
A Thrill A Minute with Jack Albany. S & S, 1967
The Wall-to-Wall Trap. S & S, 1957; Jarrolds, 1958; Macfadden, 1964

FREELING, NICHOLAS (D)
Because of the Cats. Gollancz, 1963; Harper & Row, 1964; Ballantine, 1965
Criminal Conversation. Gollancz, 1965; Harper & Row, 1966; Ballantine, 1967
Death in Amsterdam. Gollancz, 1962; Ballantine, 1964 (U.S. title: Love in Amsterdam. Harper & Row, 1962)
Double-Barrel. Gollancz, 1964; Harper & Row, 1964; Ballantine, 1966
Dresden Green. Harper & Row, 1967; Ballantine, 1968
Guns Before Butter. Gollancz, 1963; Penguin
The King of the Rainy Country. Harper & Row, 1965; Ballantine, 1968
Love in Amsterdam; see Death in Amsterdam
A Question of Loyalty. Gollancz, 1963; Harper & Row, 1964; Ballantine, 1965
Strike Out Where Not Applicable. Gollancz, 1967

FREEMAN, MRS. KATHLEEN (D) (Pseudonym: Mary Fitt)
Aftermath of Murder; see Death and Mary Dazill
The Banquet Ceases. MacDonald & Co., 1949
Bulls Like Death. Nicholson, 1937
Case for the Defense. British Book Centre, 1958; MacDonald & Co., 1958
Clues to Christabel. Doubleday, Doran, 1944; Joseph, M., 1944
Death and Mary Dazill. Joseph, M., 1941; Penguin, 1948 (Also published as: Aftermath of Murder. Doubleday, Doran, 1941)
Death and the Bright Day. MacDonald & Co., 1948
Death and the Pleasant Voices. Joseph, M., 1946; Putnam, 1947
Death and the Shortest Day. MacDonald & Co., 1952
Death at Dancing Stones. Nicholson, 1939; Saunders, S. J. R., 1939; Gardner, 1949
Death Finds a Target; see Death on Herons' Mere
Death on Herons' Mere. Joseph, M., 1941; Ryerson, 1941; Penguin, 1948 (Also published as: Death Finds a Target. Doubleday, Doran, 1942)
Death Starts a Rumor. Nicholson, 1940; Saunders, S. J. R., 1940
Expected Death. Nicholson, 1938; Saunders, S. J. R., 1938; Gardner, 1948
A Fine and Private Place. MacDonald & Co., 1947; Putnam, 1947; Gardner, 1949
Ill Wind. MacDonald & Co., 1951
Island Castle. Nelson, 1953
The Late Uncle Max. MacDonald & Co., 1957; British Book Centre, 1958
Love from Elizabeth. MacDonald & Co., 1954
The Man Who Shot Birds and Other Tales. MacDonald & Co., 1954
Mizmaze. British Book Centre, 1959; Collins, 1959; Joseph, M., 1959; Penguin
Murder Mars the Tour. Nicholson, 1936
Murder of a Mouse. Nicholson, 1939; Saunders, S. J. R., 1939; Gardner, 1951
Night-Watchman's Friend. MacDonald & Co., 1951
Pity for Pamela. MacDonald & Co., 1950; Harper, 1951; Collier, 1962
Pomeroy's Postscript. Nelson, 1955

Requiem for Robert. Joseph, M., 1942; Ryerson, 1942; Penguin, 1948
Sky-rocket. Nicholson, 1938; Saunders, S. J. R., 1938
Sweet Poison. MacDonald & Co., 1956
There Are More Ways of Killing. British Book Centre, 1960; Joseph, M., 1960
The Three Hunting Horns. Nicholson, 1937; Penguin, 1940; Lothian, 1946
Three Sisters Flew Home. Doubleday, Doran, 1936; Nicholson, 1936; Penguin, 1953

FREEMAN, MARTIN JOSEPH (D-M)
The Case of the Blind Mouse. Dutton, 1935
Murder by Magic. Dutton, 1932
Murder of a Midget. Dutton, 1931; Eldon, 1934
The Scarf on the Scarecrow. Dutton, 1938

FREEMAN, MARY ELEANOR WILKINS (D)
The Long Arm and Other Detective Stories. Chapman, 1895

FREEMAN, DR. RICHARD AUSTIN (D)
(Joint pseudonym with John James Pitcairn: Clifford Ashdown)
Adventures of Dr. Thorndyke. Popular Lib.
Adventures of Romney Pringle, by Clifford Ashdown. Ward, Lock, 1902
As a Thief in the Night. Dodd, 1928; Burt, 1929; Hodder, 1930
The Blue Scarab; see Dr. Thorndyke's Case Book
Cat's Eye. Hodder, 1923; Dodd, 1927; Burt, 1928
A Certain Dr. Thorndyke. Hodder, 1927; Dodd, 1928; Burt, 1929
The D'Arblay Mystery. Hodder, 1926; Dodd, 1927; Burt, 1928
Death at the Inn. Dodd, 1937 (English title: Felo de Se? Hodder, 1929)
Debut of Dr. Thorndyke; see The Red Thumb Mark
Dr. Thorndyke Intervenes. Dodd, 1933; Hodder, 1933
Dr. Thorndyke Investigates. Hodder, 1931
Dr. Thorndyke Omnibus. Hodder, 1929; Dodd, 1932
Dr. Thorndyke's Case Book. Hodder, 1923 (U.S. title: The Blue Scarab. Dodd, 1924; Burt, 1925)
Dr. Thorndyke's Cases; see John Thorndyke's Cases
Dr. Thorndyke's Crime File. Dodd, 1941
Dr. Thorndyke's Discovery; see When Rogues Fall Out
The Exploits of Danby Croker. Duckworth, 1916
Eye of Osiris. Hodder, 1911; Scribner, 1928; Dodd, 1929; Burt, 1930 (Also published as: The Vanishing Man. Dodd, 1911; Collier)
Famous Cases of Dr. Thorndyke. Hodder, 1929; Musson, 1930
Felo de Se?; see Death at the Inn
Flighty Phyllis. Hodder, 1928
For the Defense: Dr. Thorndyke. Dodd, 1934; Hodder, 1934
The Great Portrait Mystery. Hodder, 1918
Helen Vardon's Confession. Hodder, 1922
The Jacob Street Mystery; see Unconscious Witness
John Thorndyke's Cases. Chatto, 1909; Hodder, 1930 (U.S. title: Dr. Thorndyke's Cases. Dodd, 1931; Burt, 1932)
The Magic Casket. Dodd, 1927; Hodder, 1927; Burt, 1928
Mr. Polton Explains. Dodd, 1940; Popular Lib.
Mr. Pottermack's Oversight. Dodd, 1930; Hodder, 1930; Burt, 1931; Collier, 1962
The Mystery of Angelina Frood. Hodder, 1924; Dodd, 1925; Burt, 1926
The Mystery of 31 New Inn. Winston, 1913; Dodd, 1930
The Penrose Mystery. Dodd, 1936; Hodder, 1936
Pontifex, Son & Thorndyke. Dodd, 1931; Hodder, 1931
Puzzle Lock. Hodder, 1925; Dodd, 1926; Burt, 1927
The Red Thumb Mark. Collingwood, 1907; Hodder, 1911; Newton, D. W., 1911; Dodd, 1924; Burt, 1926 (Also published as: Debut of Dr. Thorndyke)
The Savant's Vendetta. Pearson, 1920 (Also published as: The Uttermost Farthing)
The Shadow of the Wolf. Dodd, 1925; Burt, 1926; Hodder, 1930
A Silent Witness. Hodder, 1914; Winston, 1915; Dodd, 1929; Burt, 1930; PB, 1942
The Singing Bone. Hodder, 1918; Dodd, 1923; Burt, 1925; Norton, 1965
The Stoneware Monkey. Hodder, 1938; Dodd, 1939
The Surprising Experiences of Mr. Shuttlebury Cobb. Hodder, 1927
The Unconscious Witness. Avon, 1942; Dodd, 1942 (Also published as: Jacob Street Mystery. Hodder, 1942; Musson, 1942)
The Unwilling Adventurer. Hodder, 1913
The Uttermost Farthing; see The Savant's Vendetta
The Vanishing Man; see Eye of Osiris
When Rogues Fall Out. Hodder, 1932 (U.S. title: Dr. Thorndyke's Discovery. Dodd, 1932; Avon)

FREESTONE, BASIL (S)
The Golden Drum. Quality, 1954

FREMLIN, CELIA, pseud; see GOLLER, MRS. CELIA MARGARET

FRENCH, ALLEN (S)
The Hiding Places. Scribner, 1917

FRENCH, E. T. (S)
Never Smile at Children. Pyramid, 1959

FREUND, PHILIP (S)
The Spymaster. Allen, W. H., 1965; Washburn, 1966

FREY, CHARLES W. (M) (Pseudonym: Ferguson Findley)
A Handful of Murder. Reinhardt, 1955
The Man in the Middle. Duell, 1952
My Old Man's Badge. Duell, 1950; Reinhardt & Evans, 1950
Remember That Face. Reinhardt & Evans, 1951
Waterfront. Duell, 1951

FREYER, FREDERIC, pseud; see BALLINGER, WILLIAM SANBORN

FRIEDMAN, STUART (D)
Free Are the Dead. Abelard, 1954
Gray Eyes. Abelard, 1955

FRIEND, OSCAR JEROME (D) (Pseudonym: Owen Fox Jerome)
Bloody Ground. McClurg, 1928
The Corpse Awaits, by Owen Fox Jerome. Mystery House, 1946
Domes of Silence. Paul, S., 1929
The Golf Club Murder, by Owen Fox Jerome. Clode, 1929
Five Assassins, by Owen Fox Jerome. Mystery House, 1958
The Hand of Horror, by Owen Fox Jerome. Clode, 1927; Skeffington, 1930
Mississippi Hawk. Hammond, 1950
The Murder at Avalon Arms, by Owen Fox Jerome. Hutchinson, 1930; Clode, 1931
The Red Kite Clue, by Owen Fox Jerome. Clode, 1928; Skeffington, 1930

FROEST, FRANK, pseud; see DILNOT, GEORGE

FROME, DAVID, pseud; see BROWN, MRS. ZENITH JONES

FROST, BARBARA (D)
The Corpse Died Twice. Coward, 1952
The Corpse Said No. Coward, 1949
The Innocent Bystander. Coward, 1955
The Unwelcome Corpse. Coward, 1947

FROST, FREDERICK, pseud; see FAUST, FREDERICK

FROST, LESLEY (M)
Murder at Large. Coward, 1932

FROST, WALTER ARCHER (M)
The Marworth Mystery. Long, 1930

FRY, PAMELA (D)
Harsh Evidence. Wingate, 1953; Roy Pubs., 1956

FRY, PETE, pseud; see KING, JAMES CLIFFORD

FULLER, ANNE; see ALLEN, MARCUS

FULLER, BLAIR (S)
A Far Place. Harper, 1957

FULLER, LESTER, pseud; see ROLFE, EDWIN

FULLER, ROGER, pseud; see TRACY, DONALD FISKE

FULLER, ROY BROODBENT (S)
Fantasy and Fugue. Verschoyle, 1954; Macmillan, 1956
The Second Curtain. Verschoyle, 1953; Macmillan, 1956
With My Little Eyes. Macmillan, 1957

FULLER, S. M. (S)
The Dark Page. Duell, 1944

FULLER, TIMOTHY (D)
Harvard Has a Homicide. Little, 1936
Keep Cool, Mr. Jones. Little, 1950
Reunion with Murder, Little, 1941
This Is Murder, Mr. Jones. Little, 1943
Three-Thirds of a Ghost. Little, 1941; Popular Lib.

FULLER, VINCENT, pseud. (D)
The Long Green Gaze. Viking, 1925

FULLER, WILLIAM (S)
Brad Dolan's Blond Cargo. Dell, 1957
The Girl in the Frame. Dell, 1957
Goat Island. Dell, 1954
The Pace That Kills. Dell, 1956

FULLERTON, ALEXANDER
Bury the Past. Davies, 1954

FURBER, DOUGLAS, pseud; see LEWIN, MICHAEL SULTAN

FURNESS, AUDREY (S)
Letter to a Ghost. Mills & Boon, 1963 (Also published as: House of Menace. Paperback Lib., 1966)

FÜRST, VIKTOR (Pseudonym: Victor Trefus)
But No Man Seen. Methuen, 1955

FUTRELLE, JACQUES (D)
The Chase of the Golden Plate. Dodd, 1906; Burt, 1911 (First appearance of The Thinking Machine)
The Diamond Master. Bobbs, 1909
Elusive Isabel. Bobbs, 1909
The High Hand. Bobbs, 1911; Grosset, 1912
My Lady's Garter. Rand, 1912; Hodder, 1931
The Problem of Cell 13; see The Thinking Machine
The Simple Case of Susan. Appleton, D., 1908
The Thinking Machine. Dodd, 1907 (Also published as: The Problem of Cell 13. Dodd, 1917)
The Thinking Machine on the Case. Appleton, D., 1908

GABORIAU, EMILE (D)
Baron Trigault's Vengeance. Scribner, 1913 (Sequel to The Count's Millions)
Beautiful Scourge. Tousey, 1883
The Blackmailers. Brentano, 1922
Captain Contanceau; or, The Volunteers of 1792. Munro, 1889; Ogilvie
Caught in the Net. Street, 1891; Scribner, 1913
Castastrophe. Butterworth, R., c. 1890
Champdoce Mystery. Ward & Lock, 1889; Street, 1891; Scribner, 1913 (Sequel to Caught in the Net)
The Clique of Gold. Estes & Lauriat, 1874; Street, 1891; Scribner, 1913
The Count's Millions. Vizetelly, 1885; Lovell, J. W., 1888; Scribner, 1913
Crime At Orcival; see The Mystery of Orcival
The Detective's Dilemma. Street, 1891 (Part I of Monsieur Lecoq)
The Detective's Triumph. Street, 1891 (Part II of Monsieur Lecoq)
File No. 114. Laird, 1887 (Sequel to File No. 113)
File No. 113. Lovell, F. F., 1883; Osgood, 1875; Brown, 1889; Scribner, 1900, 1916, 1923
Honor of the Name. Estes & Lauriat, 1880, 1904
In Peril of His Life. Vizetelly, 1882; Lovell, F. F., 1883; Munro, 1888; Crowell, 1902
Lerouge Case; see The Widow Lerouge
Little Old Man of the Batignolles; A Chapter from a Detective's Memoirs. Munro, 1880, 1888
The Men of the Bureau. Munro, 1880
Monsieur Lecoq. Estes & Lauriat, 1880; Lovell, F. F., 1887; Scribner, 1900, 1904, 1910 (See also The Detective's Dilemma and The Detective's Triumph)
The Mystery of Orcival. Estes & Lauriat, 1871; Scribner, 1900
Other People's Money. Estes & Lauriat, 1874; Osgood, 1875; Lovell, F. F., 1883; Scribner, 1900
The Slaves of Paris. Estes & Lauriat, 1882; Lovell, J. W., 1888; Munro, 1888
The Thirteen Hussars. Ogilvie
The Widow Lerouge. Estes & Lauriat, 1873; Osgood, 1873; Vizetelly, 1885; Street, 1891; Scribner, 1900 (Also published as: Lerouge Case. U.S. Book, 1892)
Within an Inch of His Life. Estes & Lauriat, 1873; Osgood, 1874; Scribner, 1913

GAINES, AUDREY (M)
The Old Must Die. Crowell, 1939
Omit Flowers, Please. Messner, 1946
The Voodoo's Goat. Crowell, 1942
While the Wind Howled. Crowell, 1940

GAINES, ROBERT (M)
Against the Public Interest. MacDonald & Co., 1959; Walker & Co., 1964
The Cruel Deadline. MacDonald & Co., 1960
The Invisible Evil. Walker & Co.. 1963

GAINHAM, SARAH (S)
Appointment in Vienna. Dutton, 1958; Lancer, 1967 (English title: The Mythmaker. Barker, 1957)
The Cold Dark Night. Barker, 1957; British Book Centre, 1958; Walker & Co., 1961; Award, 1967
The Mythmaker; see Appointment in Vienna
The Silent Hostage. Dutton, 1960; Lancer, 1968
The Stone Roses. Dutton, 1959; Eyre, 1959
Time Right Deadly. Barker, 1956; Walker & Co., 1961; Collier, 1965

GAIR, MALCOLM (D)
Bad Dream. Collins, 1960
Burning of Troy. Doubleday, 1958
A Long Hard Look. Collins, 1958; Pan, 1961
Sapphires on Wednesday. Collins, 1957; Doubleday, 1957
Schultz Money. Collins, 1960; Doubleday, 1960
Snow Job. Collins, 1962; Doubleday, 1962

GALE, ADELA (S)
Goddess of Terror. Signet, 1967

GALE, JOHN, pseud; see GAZE, RICHARD

GALLAGHER, GALE, pseud; see OURSLER, WILLIAM CHARLES

GALLAGHER, PATRICIA (S)
The Fires of Brimstone. Avon, 1966

GALLICO, PAUL WILLIAM (S)
The Adventures of Hiram Holliday. Knopf, 1939
The Hand of Mary Constable. Doubleday, 1964
Too Many Ghosts. Doubleday, 1959; Joseph, M., 1961; PB, 1961
Trial by Terror. Dell, 1952; Joseph, M., 1952; Knopf, 1952

GALLIE, MENNA (S)
Strike for a Kingdom. Gollancz, 1959; Harper, 1959

GALLIMORE, F. A. (M)
The Ebony Mirror. Methuen, 1933

GALWAY, ROBERT CONINGTON (S)
Assignment London. Hale, R., 1963
Assignment New York. Hale, R., 1963

GALWEY, GEOFFREY VALENTINE (M)
The Lift and the Drop. Bodley Head, 1948
Murder on Leave. Lane, 1947

GAMBIER, KENYON, pseud; see LATHROP, LORIN ANDREWS

GAMMON, DAVID J. (S)
The Getaway Gang. Archer, 1946
The Gobi Secret. Warne, 1950
Meet the Falcon. Archer, 1947
The Mystery of Monster Lake. Little, 1962
The Secret of the Sacred Lake. Lutterworth Press, 1947

GANACHILLY, ALFRED (M)
The Whispering Dead. Methuen, 1919; Knopf, 1920

GANN, ERNEST (S)
Of Good and Evil. S & S, 1963; Crest, 1964
Soldier of Fortune. Popular Lib., 1954; Sloane, 1954

GANNET, JAMES (D)
Murder After Dark. Muller, 1956

"GANPAT," pseud; see GOMPERTZ, MARTIN LOUIS ALAN

GANT, MATHEW, pseud. (S)
Queen Street. Regency, 1963

GARD, OLIVER (S)
The Seventh Chasm. Dodd, 1953

GARDEN, JOHN, pseud; see FLETCHER, HARRY LUFT VERNE

GARDENSHIRE, SAMUEL MAJOR (D)
The Long Arm. Harper, 1906

GARDINER, DOROTHEA FRANCES (M)
(Pseudonym: Theodore Frank)
The Lifted Latch. Butterworth, T., 1929

GARDINER, MRS. DOROTHY KEMPE (D)
Beer for Psyche. Doubleday, Doran, 1936; Hurst, 1948
The Case of the Hula Clock. Hammond, 1947
A Drink for Mr. Cherry. Doubleday, Doran, 1934 (English title: Mr. Watson Intervenes. Hurst, 1936)
Lion in Wait. Doubleday, 1963 (English title: Lion? or Murder? Hammond, 1964)
Lion? or Murder?; see Lion in Wait
Mr. Watson Intervenes; see A Drink for Mr. Cherry
The Seventh Mourner. Doubleday, 1958; Hammond, 1960; Popular Lib., 1964
The Transatlantic Ghost. Doubleday, Doran, 1933; Harrap, 1933; Popular Lib., 1964
What Crime Is It? Doubleday, 1956

GARDINER, GORDON (M)
At the House of Dree. Houghton, 1928

GARDINER, HEATHER (D)
Money on Murder. Hutchinson, 1951
Murder in Haste. Hutchinson, 1954; Roy Pubs., 1954

GARDINER, STEPHEN (D)
Death Is an Artist. Barker, 1958; Washburn, 1959

GARDNER, ALAN HAROLD (S)
Assignment Tahiti. Muller, 1965
Six Day Week. Coward, 1966; Muller, 1966; Berkley Pub., 1967

GARDNER, CURTISS T. (M)
Bones Don't Lie. McLeod, 1946; Mill, 1946

GARDNER, ERLE STANLEY (D)
(Pseudonyms: A. A. Fair, Carleton Kendrake, Charles J. Kenny)
Axe to Grind; see Give 'Em the Axe
Bachelors Get Lonely, by A. A. Fair. Morrow, 1961; Heinemann, 1962; PB, 1962
Bats Fly at Dusk, by A. A. Fair. Hale, R., 1952; Morrow, 1962; Dell, 1963

Bedrooms Have Windows, by A. A. Fair. Morrow, 1942; Collins, 1949; Heinemann, 1956; Dell, 1963, 1966
Beware the Curves, by A. A. Fair. Morrow, 1956; Heinemann, 1957; PB, 1960
Big Mystery Book. Grosset, 1941 (Contains: The Case of the Shoplifter's Shoe and The D. A. Calls It Murder)
The Bigger They Come, by A. A. Fair. Morrow, 1939; PB, 1963
The Case of the Amorous Aunt. Morrow, 1963; PB, 1965
The Case of the Angry Mourner. Morrow, 1951; PB, 1956; Heinemann, 1958
The Case of the Backward Mule. Morrow, 1946; Heinemann, 1955; PB, 1961
The Case of the Baited Hook. Morrow, 1940; Cassell, 1941
The Case of the Beautiful Beggar. Morrow, 1965; PB, 1966
The Case of the Bigamous Spouse. Morrow, 1961; PB, 1963; Heinemann, 1967
The Case of the Black-eyed Blonde. Morrow, 1944; Cassell, 1948; Penguin
The Case of the Blonde Bonanza. Morrow, 1962; PB, 1964
The Case of the Borrowed Brunette. Morrow, 1946; Cassell, 1951; PB, 1960
The Case of the Buried Clock. Morrow, 1943; Cassell, 1946; PB, 1950
The Case of the Calendar Girl. Morrow, 1958; Heinemann, 1964; PB, 1964
The Case of the Careless Kitten. Morrow, 1942; Cassell, 1945; Penguin
The Case of the Caretaker's Cat. Morrow, 1935; Penguin
The Case of the Cautious Coquette. Morrow, 1949; PB, 1954; Heinemann, 1955
The Case of the Counterfeit Eye. Morrow, 1933; PB, 1942; Penguin
The Case of the Crooked Candle. Morrow, 1944, Cassell, 1947; Penguin
The Case of the Curious Bride. Morrow, 1934; Penguin
The Case of the Dangerous Dowager. Morrow, 1937; Cassell, 1939; PB, 1961; Penguin
The Case of the Daring Decoy. Morrow, 1957; Heinemann, 1963; PB, 1963
The Case of the Daring Divorcee. Morrow, 1964; PB, 1965
The Case of the Dead Man's Daughter; see The Case of the Long-legged Models
The Case of the Deadly Toy. Morrow, 1959; Heinemann, 1964 (Also published as: The Case of the Greedy Grandpa)
The Case of the Demure Defendant. Morrow, 1956; Heinemann, 1962; PB, 1963 (Also published as: The Case of the Missing Poison)
The Case of the Drowning Duck. Morrow, 1942; Cassell, 1944; Penguin
The Case of the Drowsy Mosquito. Morrow, 1943; Cassell, 1947; Penguin
The Case of the Dubious Bridegroom. Morrow, 1949; Heinemann, 1954; PB, 1959
The Case of the Duplicate Daughter. Morrow, 1960; PB, 1962
The Case of the Empty Tin. Morrow, 1941; Cassell, 1943; PB, 1949; Penguin
The Case of the Fan-Dancer's Horse. Morrow, 1947; Heinemann, 1952; PB, 1960
The Case of the Fiery Fingers. Morrow, 1951; Heinemann, 1957; PB, 1961
The Case of the Footloose Doll. Morrow, 1958; PB, 1960; Heinemann, 1964
The Case of the Fugitive Nurse. Morrow, 1954; Heinemann, 1959
The Case of the Gilded Lily. Morrow, 1956; PB, 1959, 1962; Heinemann, 1962
The Case of the Glamorous Ghost. Morrow, 1955; Heinemann, 1962; PB, 1963
The Case of the Gold-Digger's Purse. Cassell, 1945; Morrow, 1945; Penguin
The Case of the Greedy Grandpa; see The Case of the Deadly Toy
The Case of the Green-Eyed Sister. Morrow, 1953; Heinemann, 1959
The Case of the Grinning Gorilla. Morrow, 1952; Heinemann, 1958
The Case of the Half-Wakened Wife. Mill, 1945; Penguin
The Case of the Haunted Husband. Morrow, 1941; Cassell, 1942; PB, 1963
The Case of the Hesitant Hostess. Morrow, 1953; Heinemann, 1959
The Case of the Horrified Heirs. Morrow, 1964; PB
The Case of the Howling Dog. Morrow, 1934; Penguin
The Case of the Ice-Cold Hands. Morrow, 1962; PB, 1964
The Case of the Lame Canary. Morrow, 1937; Cassell, 1939; Penguin
The Case of the Lazy Lover. Morrow, 1947; PB, 1952; Heinemann, 1954
The Case of the Lonely Heiress. Morrow, 1948; Heinemann, 1953; PB, 1964
The Case of the Long-Legged Models. Morrow, 1958; Heinemann, 1963; PB, 1964 (Also Published as: The Case of the Dead Man's Daughter)
The Case of the Lucky Legs. Morrow, 1934; PB, 1959
The Case of the Lucky Losers. Morrow, 1957; Heinemann, 1962; PB
The Case of the Mischievous Doll. Morrow, 1963
The Case of the Missing Poison; see The Case of the Demure Defendant
The Case of the Moth-Eaten Mink. Morrow, 1952; Heinemann, 1958

The Case of the Musical Cow. Morrow, 1950; Heinemann, 1957
The Case of the Mythical Monkeys. Morrow, 1959; PB, 1964
The Case of the Negligent Nymph. Morrow, 1950; Heinemann, 1956
The Case of the Nervous Accomplice. Morrow, 1955; Heinemann, 1961
The Case of the One-Eyed Witness. Morrow, 1950; Heinemann, 1956
The Case of the Perjured Parrot. Cassell, 1939; Morrow, 1939; PB, 1960; Penguin
The Case of the Phantom Fortune. Morrow, 1964; PB, 1965
The Case of the Queenly Contestant. Morrow, 1967
The Case of the Reluctant Model. Morrow, 1962
The Case of the Restless Redhead. Morrow, 1954; Heinemann, 1960
The Case of the Rolling Bones. Morrow, 1939; Cassell, 1940; Penguin
The Case of the Runaway Corpse. Morrow, 1954; Heinemann, 1960; PB, 1963
The Case of the Screaming Woman. Morrow, 1957; Heinemann, 1963
The Case of the Shapely Shadow. Morrow, 1960; PB, 1962
The Case of the Shoplifter's Shoe. Morrow, 1938; Cassell, 1941; Penguin
The Case of the Silent Partner. Cassell, 1940; Morrow, 1940; Penguin; PB
The Case of the Singing Skirt. Morrow, 1959
The Case of the Sleepwalker's Niece. Morrow, 1936; Cassell, 1938; Penguin
The Case of the Smoking Chimney. Morrow, 1943; Cassell, 1945; Penguin
The Case of the Spurious Spinster. Morrow, 1961; PB, 1963; Heinemann, 1966
The Case of the Stepdaughter's Secret. Morrow, 1963; PB, 1965
The Case of the Stuttering Bishop. Morrow, 1936; Cassell, 1940; Penguin
The Case of the Substitute Face. Morrow, 1938; PB, 1960; Penguin
The Case of the Sulky Girl. Morrow, 1933
The Case of the Sun Bather's Diary. Morrow, 1955; PB, 1963
The Case of the Talking Mule
The Case of the Terrified Typist. Morrow, 1956; Heinemann, 1961; PB, 1962
The Case of the Troubled Trustee. Morrow, 1965; PB, 1967
The Case of the Turning Tide. Morrow, 1941; Cassell, 1942; Penguin
The Case of the Vagabond Virgin. Morrow, 1948; PB, 1959
The Case of the Velvet Claws. Morrow, 1933; PB, 1963
The Case of the Waylaid Wolf. Morrow, 1959; PB, 1962
The Case of the Worried Waitress. Morrow, 1966
Cats Prowl at Night, by A. A. Fair. Morrow, 1943; Hale, R., 1950; Dell, 1963
The Count of Nine, by A. A. Fair. Morrow, 1958; Heinemann, 1959
Crows Can't Count, by A. A. Fair. Morrow, 1946; Heinemann, 1953; Dell, 1966
Cut Thin to Win, by A. A. Fair. Morrow, 1965; PB, 1966
The D. A. Breaks a Seal. Morrow, 1946; Cassell, 1950
The D. A. Breaks an Egg. Morrow, 1949; Heinemann, 1957
The D. A. Calls a Turn. Books, 1944; Cassell, 1947
The D. A. Calls It Murder. Morrow, 1937; Cassell, 1938; PB
The D. A. Cooks a Goose. Morrow, 1942; Cassell, 1943
The D. A. Draws a Circle. Morrow, 1939; Cassell, 1940
The D. A. Goes to Trial. Morrow, 1940; Cassell, 1941
The D. A. Holds a Candle. Morrow, 1938; Cassell, 1941
The D. A. Takes a Chance. Morrow, 1948; Heinemann, 1956
Double or Quits, by A. A. Fair. Morrow, 1941; Hale, R., 1949; Dell, 1963
Fish or Cut Bait, by A. A. Fair. Morrow, 1963; Heinemann, 1964
Fools Die on Friday, by A. A. Fair. Morrow, 1947; Heinemann, 1955; Dell, 1963
Give 'em the Axe, by A. A. Fair. Morrow, 1944; Dell, 1962 (English title: Axe to Grind. Heinemann, 1951)
Gold Comes in Bricks, by A. A. Fair. Morrow, 1940; Dell, 1963
Kept Women Can't Quit, by A. A. Fair. Morrow, 1960; PB, 1963
Lam to the Slaughter, by A. A. Fair.
Murder Up My Sleeve. Morrow, 1937; Cassell, 1939; PB, 1962
Owls Don't Blink, by A. A. Fair. Morrow, 1942; Hale, R., 1951; Dell, 1963
Pass the Gravy, by A. A. Fair. Morrow, 1959; Heinemann, 1960; PB, 1964
Perry Mason Case Book. PB, 1946
Perry Mason Omnibus. World Pub., 1945
Shills Can't Cash Chips, by A. A. Fair. Morrow, 1961
Some Slips Don't Show, by A. A. Fair. Morrow, 1957; PB, 1964
Some Women Won't Wait, by A. A. Fair. Morrow, 1953; Heinemann, 1958; Dell, 1966
Spill the Jackpot, by A. A. Fair. Morrow, 1941
Stop at the Red Light, by A. A. Fair. Heinemann, 1962

This Is Murder, by Charles J. Kenny. Morrow, 1935; PB, 1963
Top of the Heap, by A. A. Fair. Morrow, 1952; Heinemann, 1957; Dell, 1963, 1966
Traps Need Fresh Bait. Morrow, 1967
Triple Decker. Grosset, 1949
Try Anything Once, by A. A. Fair. Morrow, 1962; Heinemann, 1963; PB, 1964
Turn on the Heat, by A. A. Fair. Morrow, 1940; Dell, 1962
Two Clues. Morrow, 1947; Penguin (Contains: The Clue of the Runaway Blonde and The Clue of the Hungry Horse)
Up for Grabs, by A. A. Fair. Morrow, 1964
You Can Die Laughing, by A. A. Fair. Morrow, 1957; Heinemann, 1958; PB, 1964
Widows Wear Weeds, by A. A. Fair. Morrow, 1966; Dell, 1967

GARDNER, JOHN (S)
Amber Nine. Viking, 1966
The Liquidator. Muller, 1964; Viking, 1964; Crest
Understrike. Muller, 1965; Viking, 1965; Crest, 1968

GARFIELD, BRIAN (M) (Pseudonym: Frank O'Brian)
The Rimfire Murders. Bouregy, 1962

GARFORTH, JOHN (S)
The Floating Game. Berkley Pub., 1967 (Avengers series, #1)
Heil Harris! Berkley Pub., 1967 (Avengers series, #4)
The Laugh Was on Lazarus. Berkley Pub., 1967 (Avengers series, #2)
The Passing of Gloria Munday. Berkley Pub., 1967 (Avengers series, #3)

GARLAND, ISABEL (D) (Joint pseudonym with Mindret Lord; Garland Lord)
Abandon Hope, by Garland Lord. Arcadia, 1941
Murder, Plain and Fancy. Doubleday, Doran, 1943
Murder with Love, by Garland Lord. Morrow, 1943
Murder's Little Helper, by Garland Lord. Doubleday, Doran, 1942
She Never Grew Old, by Garland Lord. Doubleday, Doran, 1942

GARLAND, RODNEY (S)
The Troubled Midnight. Coward, 1955; Lion, 1956

GARNER, WILLIAM (S)
Overkill. New Amer. Lib., 1966

GARNETT, DAVID (S) (Pseudonym: Leda Burke)
Dope-Darling, by Leda Burke. Laurie, 1919
Lady into Fox. Knopf, 1923; Chatto, 1929; Norton, 1966

GARNETT, ROGER, pseud; see MORLAND, NIGEL

GARRATT, MARIE (S)
And Then Look Down. Ace, 1964 (Also published as: Dangerous Enchantment. Ace, 1966)
Dangerous Enchantment; see And Then Look Down
Festival of Darkness; see Where No Fire Burns
Where No Fire Burns. Ace, 1963 (Also published as: Festival of Darkness. Ace, 1966)

GARRETT, TRUMAN, pseud; see JUDD, HARRISON

GARRETT, WILLIAM A. (M)
Dr. Ricardo. Appleton, D., 1925; Hutchinson, 1925
Friday to Monday. Appleton, D., 1923
From Dusk to Dawn. Appleton, D., 1929; Lane, 1931
Treasure Royal. Appleton, D., 1926

"GARRITY," pseud; see GARRITY, DAVID JAMES

GARRITY, DAVID JAMES (S) (Pseudonym: "Garrity")
Cry Me a Killer, by "Garrity." GM, 1961
Dragon Hunt. Signet, 1967
Kiss Off the Dead, by "Garrity." GM, 1960

GARROD, JOHN and RONALD PAYNE (S) (Pseudonym: John Castle)
Flight into Danger, with Arthur Hailey. Souvenir, 1958; Doubleday, 1959 (Also published as: Runaway Zero-Eight. Bantam, 1960)
Password Is Courage. Ballantine, 1957
Runaway Zero-Eight; see Flight into Danger
The Seventh Fury. Walker & Co., 1961

GARTH, DAVID (M)
Challenge for Three. Putnam, 1938; Hale, R., 1940; Popular Lib.
Three Roads to a Star. Putnam, 1955
Thunderbird. Kinsey, 1942; Paul, S., 1943
The Tortured Angel. Putnam, 1948

GARTH, WILL, pseud; see KUTTNER, HENRY

GARTHWAITE, M. H. (M)
The Mystery of Skull Cap Island. Doubleday, 1959

GARTLAND, HANNAH (D)
The Globe Hollow Mystery. Dodd, 1923
The House of Cards. Dodd, 1922

GARVE, ANDREW, pseud; see WINTERTON, PAUL

GASCAR, PIERRE, pseud; see FOURNIER, PIERRE

GASK, ARTHUR (D)
Beachy Head Murder. Jenkins, 1942
Crime upon Crime. Jenkins, 1952; Roy Pubs., 1957
The Dark Highway. Jenkins, 1928
The Dark Mill Stream. Jenkins, 1947
The Fall of a Dictator. Jenkins, 1939
Gentlemen of Crime. Jenkins, 1932; Macaulay, 1933
The Gravedigger of Monks Arden. Jenkins, 1938
The Hangman's Knot. Jenkins, 1936
The Hidden Door. Jenkins, 1934; Macaulay, 1935
His Prey Was Man. Jenkins, 1942
The House on the Fens. Jenkins, 1940
The House on the Island. Jenkins, 1932
The House on the High Wall. Jenkins, 1948
Jest of Life. Jenkins. 1936
The Judgment of Larose. Macaulay, 1935; Jenkins, 1936
The Lonely House. Jenkins, 1929; Macaulay, 1931
Man of Death. Jenkins, 1946
Marauders by Night. Jenkins, 1951
The Master Spy. Jenkins, 1937; Macaulay, 1937
Murder in the Night. Macaulay, 1932
The Mystery of Fell Castle. Jenkins, 1944
Night and Fog. Jenkins, 1951
The Night of the Storm. Jenkins, 1939
Poisoned Goblet. Jenkins, 1935
The Secret of the Sandhills. Jenkins, 1930
The Shadow of Larose. Jenkins, 1935
The Silent Dead. Jenkins, 1950
The Storm Breaks. Jenkins, 1949
The Tragedy of the Silver Moon. Jenkins, 1940
Unfolding Years. Jenkins, 1947
The Vaults of Blackarden Castle. Jenkins, 1950
The Vengeance of Larose. Jenkins, 1939

GASKIN, CATHERINE (D)
The File on Devlin. Doubleday, 1965; Crest, 1966
The Tilsit Inheritance. Collins, 1963; Doubleday, 1963; Dell, 1964

GASTON, W. J. (M)
Deep Green Death. Hammond, 1963
Drifting Death. Hammond, 1964

GATENBY, ROSEMARY (S)
Evil Is as Evil Does. Mill, 1967

GATES, HENRY LEYFORD (M)
The House of Murder. Fiction League, 1930
The Laughing Peril. Macaulay, 1933
Murder in the Fog. Macaulay, 1932 (Also published as: Murder in the Mist. Hurst, 1933)
Murder in the Mist; see Murder in the Fog
The Scarlet Fan. Macaulay, 1932

GATES, NATALIE (S)
Hush Hush Johnson. Holt, 1967

GAUL, AVERY (M)
Five Nights at the Five Pines. Century, 1922

GAULT, MARK, pseud; see COURNOS, JOHN

GAULT, WILLIAM CAMPBELL (M-S)
Blood on the Boards. Dutton, 1953; Boardman, T. V., 1954
The Bloodstained Bokhara; see The Bloody Bokhara
The Bloody Bokhara. Dutton, 1952 (Also published as: The Bloodstained Bokhara. Boardman, T. V., 1953)
The Canvas Coffin. Boardman, T. V., 1953; Dutton, 1953
The Checkered Flag. Dutton, 1964
Come Die with Me. Boardman, T. V., 1941; Random, 1959
The Convertible Hearse. Random, 1957; Boardman, T. V., 1958
County Kill. S & S, 1952; Boardman, T. V., 1963
The Day of the Ram. Random, 1956; Boardman, T. V., 1958
Dead Hero. Dutton, 1963; Boardman, T. V., 1964
Death out of Focus. Boardman, T. V., 1959; Random, 1959; Dell, 1960
Don't Call Tonight. Boardman, T. V., 1960
Don't Cry for Me. Boardman, T. V., 1952; Dutton, 1952
End of a Call Girl. Crest, 1958
The Hundred Dollar Girl. Dutton, 1961; Boardman, T. V., 1963; Signet, 1964
Million Dollar Tramp. Crest, 1960; Boardman, T. V., 1962
Night Lady. Crest, 1959; Boardman, T. V., 1962
Ring Around Rosa. Boardman, T. V., 1955; Dutton, 1955
Run, Killer, Run. Dutton, 1954; Boardman, 1955; Collier, 1962

Square in the Middle. Random, 1956; Boardman, T. V., 1957
Sweet Wild Wench. Crest, 1959; Boardman, T. V., 1961
Vein of Violence. S & S, 1961; Boardman, T. V., 1962; Award, 1965
The Wayward Widow. Crest, 1959; Boardman, T. V., 1960

GAUNT, M. B., pseud; see HORSFIELD, RICHARD HENRY

GAUTIER, JEAN-JACQUES (D)
Triple Mirror. Roy Pubs., 1954; Barker, 1951

GAVIN, MARIAN (S)
Jailer, My Jailer. Doubleday, 1964

GAYE, PHOEBE FENWICK (Mrs. F. L. S. Pickard) (S)
Treen and Wild Horses. Cassell, 1958

GAYLE, ETHEL (D)
Murder Buys a Rug. Farrar, Straus, 1944

GAYLE, NEWTON, pseud; see GUINESS, MAURICE C.

GAYTON, CATHERINE (S)
Adeliza. Murray, J., 1952

GAYTON, REBECCA; see EPPLEY, LOUISE

GAZE, RICHARD (M) (Pseudonym: John Gale)
Death by Chalk Face. Long, 1962
Death for Short; see The Short Reaction
The Short Reaction. Long, 1960 (Also published as: Death for Short. Macmillan, 1962)
Spare Time for Murder. Long, 1960; Macmillan, 1961

GEARON, JOHN, pseud; see FLAGG, JOHN

GEHMAN, RICHARD (D)
The Jury Is Still Out. Harper, 1959
A Murder in Paradise. Rinehart, 1954; Davies, 1955; Signet, 1956
Slander of Witches. Rinehart, 1955

GEIS, RICHARD E. (S)
Eye at the Window. Brandon, 1967

GELBER, JACK (M)
On Ice. Macmillan, 1964

GELLER, ELI (M)
Window Episode. Mystery House, 1958

GELLER, STEPHEN (M)
She Let Him Continue. Ballantine, 1967

GEOHEGEN, LAURENCE (D)
The Breckenridge Enigma. Methuen, 1929

GEORGE, PETER (M) (Pseudonym: Bryan Peters)
The Big H, by Bryan Peters. Boardman, T. V., 1961; Holt, 1963
Come Blonde, Came Murder. Boardman, T. V., 1952
Cool Murder. Boardman, T. V., 1958
The Final Steal. Dell, 1965
Hong Kong Kill, by Bryan Peters. Boardman, T. V., 1958; Washburn, 1959
Pattern of Death. Boardman, T. V., 1954

"GEORGIUS," pseud; see GUIEBOURG, GEORGES

GÉRARD, FRANCIS (S)
The Concrete Castle Murders. Holt, H., 1936
The Bare Bodkin. MacDonald & Co., 1951
Fatal Friday. Holt, H., 1937
Flight with Fear. MacDonald & Co., 1948
Golden Guilt. Dutton, 1940
The Mark of the Moon. MacDonald & Co., 1952
The One-Two-Three Murders. Holt, H., 1937
Prince of Paradise. Dutton, 1941
The Promise of the Sphinx. MacDonald, & Co., 1950
The Red Rope. Dutton, 1939
Return of Sanders of the River. Dutton, 1939
The Secret Sceptre. Dutton, 1939
Sinister Secret. MacDonald & Co., 1952
The Sorcerer's Shaft. MacDonald & Co., 1947
Transparent Traitor. MacDonald & Co., 1950

GERARD, LOUISE (M)
The Golden Centipede. Dutton, 1927
The Strange Young Man. Macaulay, 1931

GEROULD, GORDON HALL (M)
The Midsummer Mystery. Appleton, D., 1925

GERRARE, WIRT, pseud; see GREENER, WILLIAM OLIVER

GERSON, NOEL BERTRAM (S) (Pseudonym: Leon Phillips)
The Split Bamboo. Doubleday, 1966

GIBBON, CHARLES (D)
A Hard Knot. Chatto, 1885

GIBBONS, CROMWELL (D)
Murder in Hollywood. Kemp, 1936

GIBBONS, STELLA (S)
Cold Comfort Farm. Dell, 1965

GIBBS, ANGELICA (M)
Murder Between Drinks. Morrow, 1932

GIBBS, GEORGE FORT (M)
The Castle Rock Mystery. Appleton, D., 1927
The Golden Bough. Appleton, D., 1918

GIBBS, HENRY (S) (Pseudonym: Simon Harvester)
Arrival in Suspicion. Jarrolds, 1953
The Bamboo Screen. Jarrolds, 1955
Battle Road. Jarrolds, 1967; Walker & Co., 1967
A Breastplate for Aaron. Rich, 1949
Cat's Cradle. Jarrolds, 1952
The Chinese Hammer. Jarrolds, 1960; Walker & Co., 1961
The Copper Butterfly. Jarrolds, 1957; Walker & Co., 1962
Delay in Danger. Jarrolds, 1954
Dragon Road. Jarrolds, 1956
Epitaph for Lemmings. Rich, 1943
Flight in Darkness. Rich, 1946; Walker & Co., 1965
The Flying Horse. Walker & Co., 1964
The Golden Fear. Jarrolds, 1957
An Hour Before Zero. Jarrolds, 1959
A Lantern for Diogenes. Rich, 1946
Let Them Prey. Rich, 1942
Lucifer at Sunset. Jarrolds, 1959
Maybe a Trumpet. Rich, 1945
Moonstone Jungle. Jarrolds, 1961
Obols for Charon. Jarrolds, 1951
The Paradise Men. Jarrolds, 1956
Red Road. Jarrolds, 1963; Macfadden, 1967
Sheep May Safely Graze. Rich, 1950
Silk Road. Walker & Co., 1963
Spider's Web. Jarrolds, 1953
Tiger in the North. Jarrolds, 1955; Walker & Co., 1963
Traitor's Gate. Jarrolds, 1952
Treacherous Road. Jarrolds, 1966; Macfadden, 1967; Walker & Co., 1967
Troika. Jarrolds, 1962
The Unsung Road. Jarrolds, 1960; Walker & Co., 1961
The Vessel May Carry Explosives. Jarrolds, 1951
Whatsoever Things Are True. Rich, 1947
Witch Hunt. Jarrolds, 1951
The Yesterday Walkers. Jarrolds, 1958

GIBBS, MARY ANNE, pseud; see BIDWELL, MARJORY ELIZABETH SARAH

GIBBS-SMITH, CHARLES HARVARD (M)
The Caroline Affair. Viking, 1954 (Also published as: Operation Caroline. Heinemann, 1955)

GIBERSON, DOROTHY DODDS (S)
The Echoing Wave. Coward, 1960; Avon, 1964

GIBSON, WALTER D. (M) (Pseudonym: Maxwell Grant)
Cry Shadow. Belmont
Mark of the Shadow. Belmont, 1966
The Night of the Shadow. Belmont, 1966
The Return of the Shadow. Belmont, 1962
Shadow Beware. Belmont
The Shadow: Destination Moon. Belmont, 1967
Shadow-Go Mad! Belmont, 1966
The Shadow Strikes. Belmont, 1964
The Shadow's Revenge. Belmont, 1965
The Weird Adventures of the Shadow. Grosset, 1966

GIELGUD, VAL HENRY (D)
The Broken Men. Constable, 1933; Houghton, 1933; Rich, 1941
Death as an Extra, with Holt Marvell. Rich, 1935
Death at Broadcasting House, with Holt Marvell. Rich, 1934 (U.S. title: London Calling. Doubleday, Doran, 1934)
Death in Budapest, with Holt Marvell. Rich, 1939
Fall of a Sparrow. Collins, 1949 (U.S. title: Stalking Horse. Morrow, 1950)
The First Television Murder, with Holt Marvell. Hutchinson, 1941
The Goggle-box Affair. Cassell, 1963 (U.S. title: Through a Glass Darkly. Scribner, 1964)
London Calling; see Death at Broadcasting House
The Ruse of the Vanished Women. Doubleday, Doran, 1934
Special Delivery. Collins, 1934, 1950
Stalking Horse; see Fall of a Sparrow
Through a Glass Darkly; see The Goggle-box Affair
Under London, with Holt Marvell. Rich, 1933

GIFFORD, LEE (S)
Pieces of the Game. GM, 1960

GILBERT, ANTHONY, pseud; see MALLESON, LUCY BEATRICE

GILBERT, ELLIOTT (S)
Don't Push Me Around. Popular Lib., 1955
Vice Trap. Avon, 1958

GILBERT, MICHAEL FRANCIS (D)
After the Fine Weather. Harper & Row, 1963; Lancer, 1964
The Bargain. Constable, 1961
Be Shot for Sixpence. Hodder, 1956; Harper, 1957; Doubleday, 1961
Blood and Judgment. Harper, 1959; Hodder, 1959; Doubleday, 1961
Claimant. Constable, 1957
Close Quarters. Walker & Co., 1963
Country-House Burglar. Harper, 1955 (Also published as: Sky-high. Hodder, 1955; Musson, 1955; Lancer, 1964)
The Crack in the Teacup. Harper & Row, 1966
Danger Within. Harper, 1952 (English title: Death in Captivity. Hodder, 1952)
Death Has Deep Roots. Harper, 1952; Lancer, 1964 (Also published as: The Trial of Victoria Lamartine)
Death in Captivity; see Danger Within
The Doors Open. Walker & Co., 1962
Fear to Tread. Harper, 1953; Lancer, 1964
Game Without Rules. Harper & Row, 1967
He Didn't Mind Danger. Harper, 1948 (English title: They Never Looked Inside. Hodder, 1948)
Overdrive. Harper & Row, 1967
Sky High; see Country-House Burglar
Smallbone Deceased. Harper, 1950; Hodder, 1950; Lancer, 1964
They Never Looked Inside; see He Didn't Mind Danger
The Trial of Victoria Lamartine; see Death Has Deep Roots

GILES, GUY ELWYN (D)
Target for Murder. Morrow, 1942
Three Died Variously. Reynal, 1941

GILES, KENNETH (M)
Death in Diamonds. Gollancz, 1967
A Provenance of Death. Gollancz, 1966; S & S, 1967

GILES, KRIS, pseud; see NIELSON, HELEN

GILL, ELIZABETH (M)
Crime Coast. Doubleday, Doran, 1931 (English title: Strange Holiday. Cassell, 1931)
Crime de Luxe. Doubleday, Doran, 1933; Cassell, 1935
Strange Holiday; see Crime Coast
What Dread Hand? Cassell, 1932; Doubleday, Doran, 1932

GILL, HERBERT J. (M)
The Second Knife. Houghton, 1935

GILL, JOSEPHINE ECKERT (M)
Dead of Summer. Doubleday, 1959; MacDonald & Co., 1960; Popular Lib., 1964
The House That Died. Doubleday, 1955; Collins, 1956

GILL, PATRICK, pseud; see CREASEY, JOHN

GILLA, ESKER N. (M)
Cap and Gown for a Shroud. Vantage, 1960

GILLES, DANIEL (M) (Pseudonym: Marigold Johnson)
The Anthill. Vanguard, 1963

GILLETTE, WILLIAM HOOKER (D)
The Astounding Crime on Torrington Road. Harper, 1927

GILLIAN, MICHAEL (M)
Warrant for a Wanton. Mill, 1952

GILLMORE, RUFUS HAMILTON (M)
The Alster Case. Appleton, D., 1914
The Ebony Bed Murder. Mystery League, 1932
The Mystery of the Second Shot. Appleton, D., 1912
The Opal Pin. Appleton, D., 1914

GILMAN, DOROTHY (S)
Uncertain Voyage. Doubleday, 1967
The Unexpected Mrs. Pollifax. Doubleday, 1966; Hale, R., 1967

GILMAN, WILLIAM (S)
The Spy Trap. Bart, 1944

GILRUTH, SUSAN (D)
Corpse for Charybdis. Hodder, 1956
Death in Ambush. Hale, R., 1952
Drown Her Remembrance. Hodder, 1961
Postscript for Penelope. Hale, R., 1954
The Snake Is Living Yet. Hodder, 1963
Sweet Revenge. Hale, R., 1951
To This Favour. Hodder, 1957

GIPSON, HENRY CLAY; see MASON, FRANCIS VAN WYCK

GIRARD, HENRI GEORGES (S) (Pseudonym: Georges Arnaud)
Wages of Fear. Bodley Head, 1952

GIVENS, CHARLES G. (D)
All Cats Are Grey. Bobbs, 1937
Jig-Time Murders. Bobbs, 1936
The Rose-Petal Murders. Bobbs, 1935

GLAISTER, JOHN (M)
The Power of Poison. Morrow, 1955

GLANVILLE, ALEC, pseud; see GRIEVE, ALEXANDER HAIG GLANVILLE

GLANVILLE, BRIAN (S)
After Rome, Africa. Secker & Warburg, 1959

GLASKIN, GERALD M. (S)
The Man Who Didn't Count. Dell, 1967

GLEN, ELSA (M)
The Secret of Villa Vanesta. Collins, 1935

GLEW, DORIS MURIEL (M)
The Fourth Murder. Melrose, 1927

GLICK, CARL (D)
Death Sits In. Washburn, 1954
The Laughing Buddha. Bell, G., 1937; Lothrop, 1937

GLIDDEN, FREDERICK DILLEY (M) (Pseudonym: Luke Short)
The Barren Land Murders. GM, 1940

GLOAG, JULIAN (S)
Our Mother's House. S & S, 1963; Secker, 1963; PB, 1964

GLOVER, ROBERT (D-M)
Lace in the Mews. Elek, 1956
Murderer's Maze. Elek, 1951
Things Happen. Eyre, 1941

GLUCK, SINCLAIR (M) (Pseudonym: Melrod Danning)
The Blind Fury. Mills & Boon, 1929; Dodd, 1930
Death Comes to Dinner. Mills & Boon, 1931
The Deeper Scar. Dodd, 1927; Mills & Boon, 1929
A Delicate Case of Murder. Macmillan, 1937; Mills & Boon, 1937
The Dragon in Harness. Dodd, 1932
The Four Winds. Dodd, 1926; Mills & Boon, 1930
The Great London Mystery. Mills & Boon, 1936
The Green Blot. Dodd, 1925; Burt, 1926
The House of the Missing. Dodd, 1922; Burt, 1926
The Last Trap. Dodd, 1928; Mills & Boon, 1928
The Majesty of the Law, by Melrod Danning. Hodder, 1916
The Man Who Never Blundered. Dodd, 1929
Red Emeralds. Mills & Boon, 1932
The Shadow in the House. Mills & Boon, 1928; Dodd, 1929
Theives' Honor. Dodd, 1925
The White Streak. Clode, 1924; Grosset, 1926
Wildcat. Mills & Boon, 1931; Dodd, 1932

GOBLE, NEIL (S)
Condition Green: Tokyo. Tuttle, 1967

GODEY, JOHN, pseud; see FREEDGOOD, MORTON

GODFREY, LIONEL ROBERT HOLCOMBE (M) (Pseudonym: Scott Mitchell)
Deadly Persuasion. Hammond, 1964
Sables Spell Trouble. Hammond, 1963
Some Dames Play Rough. Hammond, 1963

GODFREY, PETER (D)
Death Under the Table. Scientific Pub., 1954
Wanton Murder.

GODLEY, ROBERT (D) (Pseudonym: Franklin James)
The Killer in the Kitchen. Lantern Press, 1947

GODWIN, JOHN (M)
Killers in Paradise. Hart, 1966
Killers Unknown. Jenkins, 1960; Collier, 1962
Requiem for a Rat. Jenkins, 1963

GOLD, G. (D) (Pseudonym: Hank Janson)
The Brazen Seductress. New Inter. Lib.; Gold Star (#3 of series)
Hell's Angels. New Inter. Lib. (#6 of series)
Her Weapon Is Passion. New Inter. Lib. (#9 of series)
Hot House. New Inter. Lib. (#7 of series)
It's Bedtime, Baby! (#5 of series)
Kill Her with Passion. New Inter. Lib. (#1 of series)
Lover. New Inter. Lib. (#2 of series)
A Nice Way to Die. New Inter. Lib. (#4 of series)
A Nympho Named Sylvia. New Inter. Lib., 1965

GOLDBERG, HARRY (S) (Pseudonym: Harry Grey)
Call Me Duke. Crown, 1955
The Hoods. Crown, 1952 (Also published as: The Hoods Are Coming)
The Hoods Are Coming; see The Hoods

GOLDIE, BERTHA BARRE (M)
Whispering Galleries. Ward, Lock, 1940

GOLDIE, VALENTINE FRANCIS TAUBMAN-; see TAUBMAN-GOLDIE, VALENTINE FRANCIS

GOLDING, LOUIS (S)
The Pursuer. Farrar & Rinehart, 1936; Gollancz, 1936

GOLDMAN, LAWRENCE (M)
Dangerous Design. Arcadia, 1952
Fall Guy for Murder. Dutton, 1943; Gifford, 1946
Tiger by the Tail. McKay, 1946

GOLDMAN, RAYMOND LESLIE (M)
Death Plays Solitaire. Coward, 1939
The Hartwell Case. Skeffington, 1930
Judge Robinson Murdered. Coward, 1936; Grosset, 1938; Methuen, 1940
Murder Behind the Mike. Coward, 1942; Longmans, 1942
Murder of Harvey Blake. Skeffington, 1931
Murder Without Motive. Coward, 1938
Out on Bail. Coward, 1937; Longmans, 1940
Purple Shells. Ziff-Davis, 1947
The Snatch. Coward, 1940; Longmans, 1940

GOLDMAN, WILLIAM (M) (Pseudonym: Harry Longbaugh)
No Way to Treat a Lady. GM, 1964; Harcourt, 1968

GOLDSMITH, FREDERIC (M)
Murder in Mayfair. Allen, W. H., 1954
The Smugglers. Allen, W. H., 1954

GOLDSMITH, GENE (D)
Layout for a Corpse. Mill, 1949; Boardman, T. V., 1950
Murder on His Mind. Mill, 1947; Quality, 1954

GOLDSMITH, LOUIS C. (S)
Streamlined Dragon. World's Work, 1948

GOLDSMITH, MARTIN M. (M)
Detour. Macaulay, 1939; Hurst, 1940
Double Jeopardy. Macaulay, 1938; Hurst, 1940
Shadows at Noon. Ziff-Davis, 1943

GOLDSMITH, NORMAN (M)
Atlantic City Murder Mystery. Macaulay, 1936; McLeod, 1936

GOLDSTONE, LAWRENCE ARTHUR; see TREAT, LAWRENCE

GOLDTHWAITE, EATON KENNETH (S)
Cat and Mouse. Duell, 1946 (English title: Cat and Mouse Murder. Jarrolds, 1950)
Cat and Mouse Murder; see Cat and Mouse
Cut for Partners. Duell, 1951
Don't Mention My Name. Duell, 1942
Root of Evil. Duell, 1948
Scarecrow. Duell, 1945; Jarrolds, 1948
The Sixpenny Dame. Dodd, 1953
You Did It. Duell, 1943; Jarrolds, 1945

GOLLER, MRS. CELIA MARGARET (S) (Pseudonym: Celia Fremlin)
The Hours Before Dawn. Gollancz, 1958; Lippincott, 1959
The Jealous One. Lippincott, 1965; Avon, 1966
Poisoner's Base. Lippincott, 1967
The Trouble Makers. Gollancz, 1963; Lippincott, 1963; Avon, 1967
Seven Lean Years; see Wait for the Wedding
Uncle Paul. Gollancz, 1959; Lippincott, 1960; Collier, 1962
Wait for the Wedding. Harper, 1961; Avon, 1967 (English title: Seven Lean Years. Gollancz, 1961)

GOLLOMB, JOSEPH (S)
The Curtain of Storm. Macmillan, 1933; Grosset, 1936
The Girl in the Fog. Boni, 1923
The Portrait Invisible. Macmillan, 1928
The Subtle Trail. Macmillan, 1929; Heinemann, 1931
The Unquiet. Dodd, 1935; Lane, 1936

GOMPERTZ, MARTIN LOUIS ALAN (Pseudonym: "Ganpat")
Mirror of Dreams. Doubleday Doran, 1928; Hodder, 1928
Speakers in Silence. Hodder, 1929
The Three R's. Musson, 1930; Doubleday, Doran, 1931
Walls Have Eyes. Hodder, 1930

GONZALES, JOHN (M)
Death for Mr. Big. GM
Follow That Hearse. GM, 1961

GOODCHILD, GEORGE (M) (Pseudonym: Jesse Templeton)
Ace High. Hodder, 1927; Newnes, 1934
Again, McLean. Hodder, 1939
The Barton Mystery. Jarrolds, 1916, 1922; Newnes, 1937
Behind That Door. Ward, Lock, 1943
The Black Orchid. Hodder, 1926
Call McLean. Hodder, 1937
Captain Crash. Collins, 1930
Captain Sinister. Hodder, 1933
Cauldron Bubble. MacDonald & Co., 1946
Chief Inspector McLean. Hodder, 1932
The Clock Struck Seven. Hale, R., 1932
The Crimson Domino, by Jesse Templeton. Simpkin, 1919
Dandy McLean Library. Thomson, D. C., 1933

Danger Below. Hodder, 1937
Dead or Alive, by Jesse Templeton. Ward, Lock, 1937
Dear Conspirator. Ward, Lock, 1948
The Dear Old Gentleman, with C. E. Bechhofer Roberts. Jarrolds, 1935
Death on the Centre Court. Hodder, 1935; Furman, 1936
Doctor Zil's Experiment. Ward, Lock, 1953
Double Acrostic. Rich, 1955
East of Singapore. Mellifont, 1946
The Efford Tangle. Rich, 1950
Final Score. Ward, Lock, 1950
Find the Lady! Rich, 1955
For Reasons Unknown. Hodder, 1932
Hail McLean! Hodder, 1945
Having No Hearts. Hodder, 1937
How Now, McLean? Hodder, 1931
Inch of the C. I. D., by Jesse Templeton. Ward, Lock, 1936
The Infamous Gentleman. Hale, R., 1938
Inspector McLean's Casebook. Rich, 1949
Inspector McLean's Holiday; see McLean Takes a Holiday
Jack O'Lantern. Hodder, 1929; Mystery League, 1930; Newnes, 1936
The Jury Disagrees, with C. E. Bechhofer Roberts. Jarrolds, 1934
Last Redoubt. Rich, 1954
Lead On, McLean. Hodder, 1936
Last Secret. Rich, 1956
McLean at the Golden Owl. Musson, 1930; Hodder, 1931
McLean Carries On. Rich, 1950
McLean Deduces. Hodder, 1940
McLean Excels. Hodder, 1939
McLean Finds a Way. Hodder, 1936
McLean Incomparable. Hodder, 1938
McLean Intervenes. Hodder, 1939
McLean Investigates. Hodder, 1930
McLean Keeps Going. Hodder, 1941
McLean Knows Best. Ward, Lock, 1935
McLean: Non-Stop. Hodder, 1941
McLean of Scotland Yard. Hodder, 1929, 1934
McLean Plays a Hand. Ward, Lock, 1934
McLean Predominant. Rich, 1951
McLean Prevails. Ward, Lock, 1935
McLean Remembers. Hodder, 1936
McLean Sees It Through. Hodder, 1939
McLean Steps In. Rich, 1952
McLean Takes a Holiday. Hodder, 1942 (Also published as: Inspector McLean's Holiday. Pan, 1951)
McLean Takes Charge. Hodder, 1937
McLean the Magnificent. Hodder, 1940
McLean to the Dark Tower Came. Rich, 1951
The Man Who Wasn't. Jenkins, 1923
The Monster of Grammont. Hodder, 1927; Mystery League, 1930
A Murder Will Be Committed. Hale, R., 1937
No Exit. Newnes, 1936
Operator No. 19. Ward, Lock, 1937
Q33. Odhams, 1933
Q33-Spy Catcher. Newnes, 1937
The Quest of Nigel Rix. Ward, Lock, 1934
The Spanish Steps. Ward, Lock, 1951
The Splendid Crime. Houghton, 1930; Grosset, 1931; Hodder, 1931
This Woman Is Wanted. Newnes, 1936
The Triumph of McLean. Hodder, 1933
Trust McLean. Rich, 1954
Uncle Oscar's Niece. Hodder, 1944
Up, McLean! Hodder, 1940
Watch McLean. Rich, 1955
Well Caught, McLean! Rich, 1953
The Woman Accused, by Jesse Templeton. Mellifont, 1934
Yes, Inspector McLean. Hodder, 1934

GOODE, BILL, pseud; see GOODYKOONTZ, WILLIAM F.

GOODE, GEORGE (D)
King Dan, the Factory Detective. Ogilvie

GOODIS, DAVID (S)
Black Friday. Lion, 1954
Dark Passage. Messner, 1946
Fire in the Flesh. GM, 1957
Night Squad. GM, 1961
Of Missing Persons. Morrow, 1950
Somebody's Done for. Banner, 1967

GOODMAN, GEORGE and WINTHROP KNOWLTON (D)
A Killing in the Market. Doubleday, 1958

GOODSPEED, EDGAR JOHNSON (M)
The Curse in the Colophon. Willett, 1935

GOODWIN, JOHN, pseud; see GOWING, SIDNEY FLOYD

GOODYKOONTZ, WILLIAM F. (M)
(Pseudonym: Bill Goode)
The Senator's Nude. Ziff-Davis, 1947

GORDON, ALEX, pseud; see COTLER, GORDON

GORDON, DONALD (M)
The Flight of the Bat. Hodder, 1963; Morrow, 1964

GORDON, FRITZ (S)
Flight of the Bamboo Saucer. Award, 1967

GORDON, GORDON; see GORDON, MILDRED NIXON

GORDON, IAN (D)
The Burden of Guilt. S & S, 1951

GORDON, JAN (M) (Pseudonym: William Gore)
Death in the Wheelbarrow. Harrap, 1936; Bouregy, 1940
Murder Most Artistic. Harrap, 1938 (U.S. title: The Mystery of the Painted Nude. Doubleday, Doran, 1938)
The Mystery of the Painted Nude; see Murder Most Artistic

GORDON, MRS. MILDRED NIXON and GORDON GORDON (D-S) (Pseudonym: The Gordons)
The Big Frame. Doubleday, 1957; MacDonald & Co., 1957
Campaign Train. Doubleday, 1952 (Also published as: Murder Rides the Campaign Train. Popular Lib., 1964)
Captive. Doubleday, 1957; MacDonald & Co., 1958
Case File: FBI. Doubleday, 1953; Bantam, 1963
The Case of the Talking Bug. Doubleday, 1955 (Also published as: Playback. MacDonald & Co., 1955)
Experiment in Terror; see Operation Terror
The FBI Story. Doubleday, 1950
Journey with a Stranger; see The Menace
The Little Man Who Wasn't There, by Mildred Gordon. Doubleday, 1946
Make Haste to Live. Doubleday, 1950
The Menace. Doubleday, 1962 (Also published as: Journey with a Stranger. MacDonald & Co., 1963)
Murder Rides the Campaign Train; see Campaign Train
Operation Terror. Doubleday, 1961; McDonald & Co., 1961 (Also published as: Experiment in Terror. Bantam, 1962)
Playback; see The Case of the Talking Bug
Tiger on My Back. Doubleday, 1960; MacDonald & Co., 1960
Undercover Cat. Doubleday, 1963; MacDonald & Co., 1964
Undercover Cat Prowls Again. Doubleday, 1966; Bantam, 1967; MacDonald & Co., 1967

GORDON, NEIL, pseud; see MACDONNELL, ARCHIBALD GORDON

GORDON, RUSSELL (M)
Dead Level. Morrow, 1948
She Posed for Death. Avon

GORDONS, THE, pseud; see GORDON, MILDRED NIXON

GORE, WILLIAM, pseud; see GORDON, JAN

GORE-BROWNE, ROBERT (M)
By Way of Confession. Doubleday, Doran, 1930; Grosset, 1931
Death on Delivery. Collins, 1932
In Search of a Villain. Doubleday, Doran, 1928; Grosset, 1929
Murder of an M. P. Collins, 1931

GORELL, BARON RONALD GORELL BARNES (D)
The Devil's Drum. Murray, J., 1929
The Devouring Fire. Murray, J., 1928
Earl's End. Ward, Lock, 1951
In the Night. Longmans, 1917
Murder at Manor House. Ward, Lock, 1954
Murder at Mavering. Murray, J., 1943

GORMAN, HERBERT S. (S)
A Place Called Dagon. Doran, 1927

GOSLING, JOHN (S)
The Ghost Squad. Doubleday, 1959

GOUDGE, ELIZABETH (S)
The Castle on the Hill. Popular Lib., 1966

GOUGH, BARBARA WORSLEY-; see WORSLEY-GOUGH, BARBARA

GOULART, RON (M)
The Hardboiled Dicks. Sherbourne, 1965; Boardman, T. V., 1967; PB, 1967

GOULD, STEPHEN, pseud; see FISHER, STEPHEN GOULD

GOUZE, ROGER (S)
A Quiet Game of Bambu. Doubleday, 1964

GOVAN, CHRISTINE NOBLE (D) (Pseudonyms: Mary Allerton, J. N. Darby)
Murder in the House with the Blue Eyes, by J. N. Darby. Bobbs, 1939
Murder on the Mountain, by Mary Allerton. Houghton, 1938
The Plantation Murder, by Mary Allerton. Houghton, 1938
The Shadow and the Web, by Mary Allerton. Bobbs, 1940

GOVER, ROBERT (S)
The Maniac Responsible. Grove, 1963; MacGibbon, 1963

GOWING, SIDNEY FLOYD (D) (Pseudonym: John Goodwin)
The Avenger. Putnam, 1926

Blackmail. Jenkins, 1932
Blood Money. Jenkins, 1932; Putnam, 1932
Dead Man's Treasure. Putnam, 1929; Wright & Brown, 1937
King's Elm Mystery. Jenkins, 1934
Let It Lie. Putnam, 1929
The Man with the Brooding Eyes. Putnam, 1921
Sealed Orders. Putnam, 1929
The Shadow Man. Putnam, 1932; Wright & Brown, 1936
The Sign of the Serpent. Putnam, 1923
When Dead Men Tell Tales. Putnam, 1928
Without Mercy. Putnam, 1920; Jenkins, 1931

GOYDER, MARGOT and NEVILLE GOYDER JOSKE (M) (Pseudonym: Margot Neville)
Come and See Me Die. Bles, 1963
Come, Thick Night. Bles, 1951
Confession of Murder. Bles, 1960
Divining Rod for Murder. Doubleday, 1952
Drop Dead. Bles, 1962
Flame of Murder. Bles, 1958
Hateful Voyage. Bles, 1956; Collins, 1956
Ladies in the Dark. Bles, 1965
Lena Hates Men. Arcadia, 1943
Murder and Gardenias. Bles, 1946
Murder and Poor Jenny. Bles, 1954
Murder Before Marriage. Bles, 1951; Doubleday, 1951
Murder Beyond the Pale. Bles, 1961
Murder in a Blue Moon. Bles, 1948; Doubleday, 1949
Murder in Rockwater. Bles, 1944, 1949
Murder of a Nymph. Bles, 1949; Doubleday, 1950
Murder of Olympia. Bles, 1958
Murder of the Well-Beloved. Bles, 1953; Doubleday, 1953
Murder to Welcome Her. Bles, 1957
My Bad Boy. Bles, 1964
The Seagull Said Murder. Bles, 1952
Sweet Night for Murder. Bles, 1959

GOYNE, RICHARD (D) (Pseudonym: John Courage)
The Affair Ravel. Paul, S., 1948
The Clock. Paul, S., 1951
Corpse for Charlie. Paul, S., 1957
The Courtway Case. Paul, S., 1951
Crime Philosopher. Paul, S., 1945
Danger in Suburbia. Paul, S., 1939
Dark Mind. Macaulay, 1937; Paul, S., 1948
The Darkened Room. Paul, S., 1952
Death by Desire. Paul, S., 1936
Death Goes to the Fair. Paul, S., 1937
Death in Harbour. Paul, S., 1937
Death of a Gentleman. Paul, S., 1951
Death of a Village. Paul, S., 1954
Death on Tour. Paul, S., 1937
Destination Unknown. Paul, S., 1945
Dread Cave. Paul, S., 1952
Fear Haunts the Fells. Paul, S., 1944
Five Roads Inn. Paul, S., 1944
Four Doors to Death. Paul, S., 1936
The Fugitive Men. Paul, S., 1956
The Gravel Patch; see Harvest of Hate
Hanged I'll Be. Paul, S., 1937
Harvest of Hate. Paul, S., 1952 (Also published as: The Gravel Patch. Paul, S., 1955)
House with a Past. Paul, S., 1955
International Commando. Paul, S., 1944
Introducing the Super. Paul, S., 1957
Invisible Verdict. Paul, S., 1952
Lakeland Tragedy. Paul, S., 1947
The Lipstick Clue. Paul, S., 1954
Made to Murder. Long, 1957
Man in the Trilby Hat. Paul, S., 1946
Merrylees Mystery. Paul, S., 1940
Missing Minx. Paul, S., 1958
Murder at the Inn. Paul, S., 1935
Murder Made Easy. Paul, S., 1944
Murder Run Riot. Paul, S., 1940
Murderer's Moon, Paul, S., 1949
My Wife's Lover. Paul, S., 1953
Nightingales Never Sing. Paul, S., 1950
No Moon Tonight. Paul, S., 1950
Obliging Corpse. Paul, S., 1954
Overnight. Paul, S., 1953
The Parker Case. Paul, S., 1958
Perhaps the Prodigal. Paul, S., 1953
Produce the Body. Paul, S., 1935
Savarin's Shadow. Paul, S., 1947
Seven Were Suspect. Paul, S., 1939
Spooks Sometime Sing. Paul, S., 1946
Strange Motives, Paul, S., 1934
Suicide Squad. Paul, S., 1942
They All Come Back. Paul, S., 1945
Traitors Tide. Paul, S., 1948
We, the Unworthy. Paul, S., 1944
Who Killed My Wife? Paul, S., 1940
Who Screamed? Paul, S., 1939
Why Murder Mrs. Hope? Paul, S., 1940
You Can't Kill Shadows. Paul, S., 1954

GRAAF, PETER (D)
Daughter Fair. Joseph, M., 1958; Washburn, 1959
Dust and the Curious Boy; see Give the Devil His Due
Give the Devil His Due. Mill, 1957 (Also published as: Dust and the Curious Boy. Joseph, M., 1957)
The Sapphire Conference. Joseph, M., 1959; Washburn, 1959

GRABO, CARL; see YARDLEY, HERBERT O.

GRACE, ALICIA (S-Gothic)
Hawksboll Manor. Lancer, 1967

GRADY, FRANK P. (D)
Sergeant Death. Mussey, 1936

GRAEME, BRUCE, pseud; see JEFFRIES, GRAHAM MONTAGUE

GRAEME, DAVID, pseud; see JEFFRIES, GRAEME MONTAGUE

GRAEME, RODERIC, pseud; see JEFFRIES, RODERIC

GRAEME-HOLDER, W. (M)
Decker. Lane, 1931

GRAFFY, JOSEPH (M)
The Man Who Was Not Himself. Hodder, 1958

GRAFTON, CORNELIUS WARREN (D)
Beyond a Reasonable Doubt. Farrar & Rinehart, 1940; Heinemann, 1951
The Rat Began to Gnaw the Rope. Farrar & Rinehart, 1943; Gollancz, 1944
The Rope Began to Hang the Butcher. Farrar & Rinehart, 1944; Gollancz, 1945

GRAHAM, ANTHONY (D)
Act of Silence. Boardman, T. V., 1955
Minus a Shamus. Boardman, T. V., 1955
No Sale for Haloes. Boardman, T. V., 1954

GRAHAM, NANCY (M)
Black Swan. British Book Service, 1958; Cassell, 1958
The Purple Jacaranda. Cassell, 1958

GRAHAM, NEILL, pseud; see DUNCAN, WILLIAM MURDOCK

GRAHAM, PETER (M)
Tiger Mark. Hamilton, 1930

GRAHAM, ROSS (D)
Death on a Smoke Boat. Hurst, 1947

GRAHAM, STEPHEN (S)
Surfeit of Sun. Doubleday, 1966

GRAHAM, WINSTON (S)
After the Act. Doubleday, 1966
Fortune Is a Woman. Doubleday, 1952
Greek Fire. Doubleday, 1958
The Little Walls. Doubleday, 1955; Hodder, 1955
Marnie. Doubleday, 1961; Crest, 1964
Night Journey. Doubleday, 1968
Night Without Stars. Doubleday, 1950; Hodder, 1950
The Sleeping Partner. Doubleday, 1956
Take My Life. Bodley Head, 1965; Doubleday, 1967
The Walking Stick. Doubleday, 1967
The Wreck of the Grey Cat. Doubleday, 1958

GRAHAME, ARTHUR W. (M)
Rabbitfoot. Dorrance, 1967

GRAINGER, FRANCIS EDWARD (D)
(Pseudonym: Headon Hill)
Clues from a Detective's Camera. Simpkin, 1893
The Duke Decides. Cassell, 1903; Wessels, 1903
The Epson Mystery: A Race with Ruin. Fenno, 1908
Millions of Mischief. Saalfield, 1905; Ward, Lock, 1905
The Monksglade Mystery. Fenno, 1910
One Who Saw. Cassell, 1905; Victoria Press, 1905; Stitt Pub., 1906; Dodge, 1908
Spriggs the Cracksman. Ogilvie, 1912
Unmasked at Last. Fenno, 1909
Zambra, the Detective. Chatto, 1894

GRANBY, GEORGE (M)
The Secret of Musterton House. Dutton, 1929; Mills & Boon, 1929

GRANGER, HENRY FRANCIS (M)
The Gray Gull. Garden City Pub., 1924

GRANT, ALAN, pseud; see KENNINGTON, ALAN

GRANT, AMBROSE, pseud; see RAYMOND, RENÉ

GRANT, DOUGLAS, pseud; see OSTRANDER, ISABEL EGENTON

GRANT, HILDA KAY (S) (Pseudonym: Jan Hilliard)
Morgan's Castle. Abelard, 1964

GRANT, JAMES EDWARD (M)
The Green Shadow. Hartney, 1935

GRANT, JOAN (S)
The Laird and the Lady. Methuen, 1949 (Also published as: Castle Cloud. Ace, 1966)

GRANT, MAXWELL, pseud; see GIBSON, WALTER

GRANT, RICHARD, pseud; see CLARKE, J. CALVITT

GRANTLAND, KEITH (S)
Run from the Hunter. GM, 1957

GRAY, BERKELEY, pseud; see BROOKS, EDWY SEARLES

GRAY, CHARLES EDWARD (M)
Murder Defies the Roman Emperor. Humphries, 1958

GRAY, CURME (M)
Murder in Millennium VI. Shasta, 1952 (A Science-fiction murder)

GRAY, DULCIE (D-M)
Baby Face. Barker, 1959
The Devil Wore Scarlet. MacDonald & Co., 1964
Epitaph for a Dead Actor. Barker, 1960
Murder in Melbourne. Barker, 1958
Murder in Mind. MacDonald & Co., 1963
Murder on a Saturday. Barker, 1961
Murder on the Stairs. Barker, 1957; British Book Centre, 1958
No Quarter for a Star. MacDonald & Co., 1965

GRAY, HARRIET, pseud; see ROBINS, DENISE

GRAY, HILARY (M)
Frightened to Death. Hurst, 1950
Weekend with Death. Hurst, 1951

GRAY, JONATHAN, pseud; see ADAMS, HERBERT

GRAY, OSCAR (M)
The Bagshot Mystery. Macaulay, 1929; Selwyn, 1929
Three Shots. Selwyn

GRAYSON, RICHARD, pseud; see GRINDAL, RICHARD

GREEN, ALAN BAER (D) (Joint pseudonym with Gladys Elizabeth Green: Glen Burne; with Julian Paul Brodie: Roger Denbie)
Death Cruises South, by Roger Denbie. Morrow, 1934; Nicholson, 1937
Death on the Limited, by Roger Denbie. Morrow, 1933; Burt, 1935 (English title: Timetable Murder. Nicholson, 1936)
Murder to Music, by Glen Burne. Dodd, 1934
They Died Laughing. S & S, 1952; Collier, 1963
Timetable Murder; see Death on the Limited
What a Body! S & S, 1949; Redman, 1950

GREEN, ANNE KATHERINE (Mrs. Anna Katherine Rohlfs) (D)
Agatha Webb. Putnam, 1899, 1903
The Amethyst Box. Bobbs, 1905
Behind Closed Doors. Putnam, 1888
The Chief Legatee. Authors & Newspapers Assn., 1906; Dodd, 1916
The Circular Study. McClure, Phillips, 1900
Cynthia Wakeman's Money. Putnam, 1907
Dark Hollow. Dodd, 1914; Burt, 1919
The Doctor, His Wife and the Clock. Unwin, 1895
Doctor Izard. Putnam, 1895
The Filigree Ball. Bobbs, 1903
Forsaken Inn. Grosset, 1910
The Golden Slipper. Putnam, 1915; Burt, 1917
Hand and Ring. Putnam, 1883
House in the Mist. Bobbs, 1905
The House of the Whispering Pines. Nash, 1910; Putnam, 1910; Burt, 1912
Initials Only. Dodd, 1911; Street
The Leavenworth Case. Putnam, 1878; Strahan, 1884
Lost Man's Lane. Putnam, 1898
Marked "Personal." Putnam, 1893
Masterpieces of Mysteries. Dodd, 1913 (Also published as: Room Number Three and Other Detective Stories. Dodd, 1919)
A Matter of Millions. Bonner, 1890; Routledge, 1890
The Mayor's Wife. Bobbs, 1907
The Mill Mystery. Putnam, 1886, 1916
Millionaire Baby. Bobbs, 1905
Miss Hurd: an Enigma. Putnam, 1894
The Mystery of the Hasty Arrow. Dodd, 1917
The Old House. Putnam, 1891
One of My Sons. Putnam, 1901
Room Number 3; see Masterpieces of Mystery
Scarlet and Black; see To the Minute
Seven to Twelve: A Detective Story. Putnam, 1887
The Step on the Stair. Dodd, 1923
A Strange Disappearance. Putnam, 1880; Burt, 1916
Sword of Damocles. Putnam
That Affair Next Door. Putnam, 1897; Burt, 1915
Three Thousand Dollars. Badger, R. G., 1910
To the Minute, and Scarlet and Black. Putnam, 1916
The Woman in the Alcove. Bobbs, 1906
XYZ. Putnam, 1883

GREEN, CHALMERS (M)
The Scarlet Venus. Muller, 1959

GREEN, DANIEL DAVID (M)
Hangman's Noose. Stockwell, 1954

GREEN, EVELYN EVERETT (M)
The Secret of Wold Hall. McClurg, 1906

GREEN, FRANCIS NIMMO (M)
The Devil to Pay. Scribner, 1918

GREEN, FREDERICK LAWRENCE (M)
Ambush for the Hunter. Joseph, M., 1952; Random, 1952
Clouds in the Wind. Joseph, M., 1950
A Flask for the Journey. Joseph, M., 1946; Reynal, 1948
A Fragment of Glass. Joseph, M., 1947
Give Us the World. Joseph, M., 1941
The Magician. Coward, 1951; Joseph, M., 1951
Mist on the Waters. Joseph, M., 1948; Harcourt, 1949
Music in the Park. Joseph, M., 1942
Odd Man Out. Joseph, M., 1945; Reynal, 1947
On the Edge of the Sea. Joseph, M., 1944
On the Night of the Fire. Joseph, M., 1939; Macmillan, 1939
Song for the Angels. Joseph, M., 1943
Sound of Winter. Joseph, M., 1940

GREEN, MRS. GLADYS ELIZABETH BLUM; see GREEN, ALAN BAER

GREEN, GLINT, pseud; see PETERSON, MARGARET

GREEN, HELEN (M)
Mr. Jackson. Dodge, B. W., 1909

GREEN, JANET; see GRIBBLE, LEONARD REGINALD

GREEN, PETER (S) (Pseudonym: Denis Delaney)
Cat in Gloves, by Denis Delaney. Gryphon, 1956
Habeas Corpus. World Pub., 1961; Signet, 1962

GREENE, ELIZABETH PLUNKET; see GREENE, RICHARD

GREENE, GRAHAM (S)
Brighton Rock. Heinemann, 1938; Viking, 1938
The Confidential Agent. Viking, 1938; Heinemann, 1939
Gun for Sale; see This Gun for Hire
The Ministry of Fear. Heinemann, 1934; Bantam, 1963
Nineteen Stories. Viking, 1949; Lion
The Orient Express. Doubleday, Doran, 1933; Bantam, 1935 (English title: Stamboul Train. Heinemann)
Our Man In Havana. Viking, 1958; Bantam, 1960
Stamboul Train; see The Orient Express
Ten Stories; see Twenty-one Stories
The Third Man. Bantam, 1950; Viking, 1950
This Gun for Hire. Doubleday, Doran, 1936; Bantam (English title: Gun for Sale. Heinemann, 1938)
Three by Graham Greene. Viking, 1952
Twenty-one Stories. Viking, 1962 (A re-revision of Ten Stories. Viking, 1949. Four deal with crime.)

GREENE, JOSIAH E. (D)
The Laughing Loon. Morrow, 1939
Madmen Die Alone. Morrow, 1938

GREENE, L. PATRICK; see MASTERMAN, WALTER S.

GREENE, RICHARD and ELIZABETH PLUNKET GREENE (D)
Eleven Thirty Till Twelve. Secker, 1934
Where Ignorance Is Bliss. Murray, J., 1932

GREENE, WARD (D) (Pseudonym: Frank Dudley)
Death in the Deep South. Stackpole Sons, 1936; Cassell, 1937
The Havana Hotel Murders, by Frank Dudley. Houghton, 1936; Bell, G., 1937
King Cobra, by Frank Dudley. Carrick, 1940
Ride the Nightmare, by Frank Dudley. Cape, 1930; Smith, H., 1930
Route 28, by Frank Dudley. Doubleday, Doran, 1940

GREENER, WILLIAM OLIVER (S) (Pseudonym: Wirt Gerrare)
The Exploits of Jo Salis, A British Spy. Hurst, 1905
A Secret Agent in Port Arthur. Constable, 1905

GREENFIELD, GEORGE
At Bay. Cassell, 1955

GREENLEAVES, WINIFRED (M)
The Trout Inn Mystery. Dial, 1929 (English title: The Trout Inn Tragedy. Collins, 1929)

GREENWALL, HARRY I. (M)
They Were Murdered in France. Jarrolds, 1957

GREENWOOD, EDWIN (M)
The Deadly Dowager. Doubleday, Doran, 1935 (English title: Skin and Bone. Skeffington, 1934)
Fair Devil. Doubleday, Doran, 1935 (English title: Pins and Needles. Skeffington, 1935)
French Farce. Doubleday, Doran, 1936; Skeffington, 1936
Miracle in the Drawing Room. Skeffington, 1935; Doubleday, Doran, 1936
Old Goat; see Under the Fig Leaf
Pins and Needles; see Fair Devil

Skin and Bone; see The Deadly Dowager
Under the Fig Leaf. Doubleday, Doran, 1937 (English title: Old Goat. Heinemann, 1937)

GREGG, CECIL FREEMAN (D)
Accidental Murder. Methuen, 1952
Airtight Alibi. Methuen, 1956
The Body Behind the Bar. Methuen, 1932
The Body in the Safe. Dial, 1930
The Brazen Confession. Hutchinson, 1930 (U.S. title: I Have Killed a Man. Dial, 1931)
The Chief Constable. Methuen, 1955
Danger at Cliff House. Methuen, 1935; Dial, 1936
Danger in the Dark. Methuen, 1939
Dead on Time. Methuen, 1956
Double Solution. Hutchinson, 1931; Dial, 1932
Duke's Last Trick. Methuen, 1933
Execution of Diamond Deutsch. Methuen, 1934 (U.S. title: Murder in the Park. Dial, 1935)
Exit Harlequin. Methuen, 1946
Expert Evidence. Methuen, 1938
Fatal Error. Methuen, 1940
Finlay of the Sentinel. Methuen, 1957
From Information Received. Methuen, 1950
Henry Prince in Action. Methuen, 1936
I Have Killed a Man; see The Brazen Confession
Inspector Higgins Goes Fishing. Methuen, 1951
Inspector Higgins Hurries. Dial, 1931; Hutchinson, 1931
Inspector Higgins Sees It Through. Appleton-Century, 1934; Methuen, 1934
Justice. Methuen, 1941
The Man with a Monocle. Methuen, 1948
Melander's Millions. Methuen, 1944
Murder at Midnight. Methuen, 1947
Murder in the Park; see Execution of Diamond Deutsch.
Murder of Estelle Cantor; see Ten Black Pearls
Murder on the Bus. Dial, 1930; Hutchinson, 1930
Murdered Manservant. Hutchinson, 1928
The Mystery at Moor Street. Methuen, 1938
Night Flight to Zurich. Methuen, 1954
Obvious Solution. Methuen, 1958
The Old Manor. Methuen, 1945; McNaughton, 1946
Professional Jealousy. Methuen, 1960
The Return of Henry Prince. Methuen, 1943
The Rutland Mystery. Dial, 1931; Hutchinson, 1931
Sufficient Rope. Methuen, 1953
Ten Black Pearls. Methuen, 1935 (U.S. title: The Murder of Estelle Cantor. Dial, 1936)
Three Daggers. Dial, 1929; Hutchinson, 1929; Burt, 1931
Tragedy at Wembley. Dial, 1936; Methuen, 1936
Two Died at Three. Methuen, 1943; Arcadia, 1944
The Ugly Customer. Methuen, 1949
The Vandor Mystery. Methuen, 1942
Who Dialed 999? Methuen, 1939
The Wrong House. Methuen, 1937

GREGOR, PAUL (S)
Jump into the Sun. Berkley Pub., 1961

GREGORY, FRANKLIN LONG (M)
Cipher of Death. Harper, 1934
Murder at Four Dot Ranch. World's Work, 1936

GREGORY, HARRY (S)
The Man from M.O.T.H.E.R. PB, 1967

GREGORY, JACKSON (D)
A Case for Mr. Paul Savoy. Scribner, 1933 (English title: The Second Case of Mr. Paul Savoy. Hodder, 1933)
The Emerald Murder Trap. Scribner, 1934 (English title: The Third Case of Mr. Paul Savoy. Hodder, 1936)
The First Case of Mr. Paul Savoy; see House of the Opal
House of the Opal. Grosset, 1934 (English title: The First Case of Mr. Paul Savoy. Hodder, 1933)
The Mystery at Spanish Hacienda. Dodd, 1929
The Second Case of Mr. Paul Savoy; see A Case for Mr. Paul Savoy
The Third Case of Mr. Paul Savoy; see The Emerald Murder Trap

GREGORY, MASON (D)
If Two of Them Are Dead. Arcadia, 1953

GREGORY, SACHA, pseud. (M)
Yellowleaf. Heinemann, 1919

GREIG, IAN BAXTER (M)
Baxter's Second Death. Benn, 1932; Kinsey, 1933
False Scent. Benn, 1933
King's Club Murder; see Silver King Mystery
Murder at Lintercombe. Benn, 1931
Silver King Mystery. Holt, H., 1930 (English title: King's Club Murder. Benn, 1930)
Tragedy of the Chinese Mine. Benn, 1930; Holt, H., 1931

GREIG, MAYSIE (M) (Pseudonym: Jennifer Ames)
Danger in Eden; see Danger Wakes the Heart
Danger Wakes the Heart. Collins, 1949 (U.S. title: Danger in Eden. Bouregy, 1950)
Dark Carnival. Random, 1950; Collins, 1951
Date with Danger; see Frightened Heart
Fear Kissed My Lips. Collins, 1947
Frightened Heart. Collins, 1952 (U.S. title: Date with Danger. Random, 1952)
Journey in the Dark. Collins, 1945
Lovers in the Dark. Collins, 1945
This Fearful Paradise. Random, 1953

GRENDON, STEPHEN, pseud; see DERLETH, AUGUST

GRENVIL, WILLIAM, pseud; see MARTYN WYNDAM

GRESHAM, ELIZABETH F. (M) (Pseudonym: Robin Grey)
Puzzle in Pewter. Duell, 1947
Puzzle in Porcelain. Duell, 1945

GREW, WILLIAM, pseud; see O'FARRELL, WILLIAM

GREX, LEO, pseud; see GRIBBLE, LEONARD REGINALD

GREY, A. F., pseud; see NEAL, ADELINE PHYLLIS

GREY, ALTHEN; see BURNING, MICHAEL

GREY, DONALD, pseud; see THOMAS, EUGENE

GREY, DOUGLAS (M)
Tracking of K. K. Chelsea House, 1925

GREY, HARRY, pseud; see GOLDBERG, HARRY

GREY, ROBIN, pseud; see GRESHAM, ELIZABETH F.

GRIBBEN, JAMES (M) (Pseudonym: Vincent James)
Island of the Pit. Benn, 1955; Messner, 1956
Red Sky. Quality, 1953

GRIBBLE, LEONARD REGINALD (D) (Pseudonyms: Leo Grex, Louis Grey, Dexter Muir)
The Ace of Danger, by Leo Grex. Hutchinson, 1952
The Arsenal Stadium Mystery, by Leo Grex. Harrap, 1939; Jenkins, 1950
The Atomic Murder. Harrap, 1947; Ziff-Davis, 1947
The Brass Knuckles, by Leo Grex. Long, 1964
The Carlent Manor Crime. Hutchinson, 1939
The Case-Book of Anthony Slade. Quality, 1937
The Case of the Malverne Diamonds. Harrap, 1936; Greenberg, 1937
The Case of the Marsden Rubies. Harrap, 1929; Doubleday, Doran, 1930
Clues That Spelled Guilty. Long, 1961
The Crooked Sixpence, by Leo Grex. Harrap, 1940
Crooner's Swan Song, by Leo Grex. Hutchinson, 1935
Death Chime. Harrap, 1934
Death Pays the Piper. Jenkins, 1956; Roy Pubs., 1958
Don't Argue with Death. Roy Pubs., 1959
The Frightened Chameleon. Jenkins, 1951
The Gillespie Suicide Mystery. Harrap, 1929 (Also published as: The Terrace Suicide Mystery. Doubleday, Doran, 1929)
The Glass Alibi. Jenkins, 1952; Roy Pubs., 1956
The Grand Modena Murder. Harrap, 1930; Doubleday, Doran, 1931
Hangman's Moon, by Leo Grex. Allen, W. H., 1950
Heads You Die. Jenkins, 1964
The Inverted Crime, by Leo Grex. Jenkins, 1954
Is This Revenge? Harrap, 1933
King Spiv, by Leo Grex. Harrap, 1948
Larceny in Her Heart, by Leo Grex. Long, 1959
The Lonely Inn Mystery, by Leo Grex. Hutchinson, 1933
Madison Murder, by Leo Grex. Hutchinson, 1933
The Man from Manhattan, by Leo Grex. Doubleday, Doran, 1935; Hutchinson, 1935
Murder in the Sanctuary, by Leo Grex. Hutchinson, 1934
Murder Mistaken, with Janet Green. Allen & Unwin, 1953
Murder Out of Season, by Leo Grex. Jenkins, 1952
Mystery at Tudor Arches. Harrap, 1935
Mystery Manor. Mark Goulden, 1951
The Neighbors, by Leo Grex. Hutchinson, 1931
Nightborn. Hutchinson, 1931
Pilgrims Meet Murder, by Dexter Muir. Jenkins, 1948
The Riddle of the Ravens. Harrap, 1934
Riley of the Special Branch. Harrap, 1936

Rosemary for Death, by Dexter Muir. Jenkins, 1952
Sally of Scotland Yard, with Geraldine Laws. Allen, W. H., 1954
The Secret of Tangles. Harrap, 1933; Lippincott, 1934
The Secret of the Red Mill. Burke Pub., 1948
The Serpentine Murder. Dodd, 1932
She Died Laughing, by Leo Grex. Jenkins, 1953
The Signet of Death, by Louis Grey. Nicholson, 1934; Withy Grove, 1941; Jenkins, 1946
The Speckled Swan, by Dexter Muir. Jenkins, 1949
Stalag-Mites, by Leo Grex. Harrap, 1947
Stand-in for Murder. Roy Pubs., 1958
Stolen Death, by Leo Grex. Hutchinson, 1936
The Stolen Home Secretary. Harrap, 1932 (Also published as: The Stolen Statesman. Dodd, 1932)
The Stolen Statesman; see The Stolen Home Secretary
Superintendent Slade Investigates. Roy Pubs., 1957; Jenkins, 1958
The Terrace Suicide Mystery; see The Gillespie Suicide Mystery
Terror Wears a Smile, by Leo Grex. Long, 1962
Thanks for the Felony, by Leo Grex. Long, 1960
They Kidnapped Stanley Mathews. Jenkins, 1950
Tombstone for Harriet, by Leo Grex.
Tragedy at Draythorpe, by Leo Grex. Hutchinson, 1931
Tragedy in E-Flat, by Leo Grex. Harrap, 1938; Hillman-Curl, 1939
Transatlantic Trouble, by Leo Grex. Hutchinson, 1937
Wantons Die Hard. Jenkins, 1961; Roy Pubs., 1961
Who Killed Oliver Cromwell? Greenberg, 1938; Harrap, 1939
The Yellow Bungalow Mystery. Harrap, 1933
The Velvet Mask. Allen, W. H., 1952

GRIEG, MICHAEL (S)
A Fire in His Hand. Doubleday, 1963

GRIERSON, EDWARD (D-M)
A Crime of One's Own. Putnam, 1967
The Massingham Affair. Doubleday, 1963
Reputation for a Song. Chatto, 1952
The Second Man. Knopf, 1956; Dell, 1964

GRIERSON, FRANCIS DURHAM (M)
The Acrefield Mystery. Butterworth, T., 1938
Blackmail in Red. Hale, R., 1954
The Blind Frog. Hale, R., 1955
The Blue Bucket Mystery. Bles, 1929; Clode, 1930
The Boomerang Murder. Hutchinson, 1951
The Buddha of Fleet Street. Hutchinson, 1949
The Cabaret Crime. Butterworth, T., 1938
The Compleat Crook—in France. Butterworth, T., 1934
A Convenant with Death. Butterworth, T., 1938
The Cowards' Club. Butterworth, T., 1937
The Crimson Cat. Eyre, 1944
Death on Deposit. Butterworth, T., 1935
The Double Thumb. Hodder, 1925
The Empty House. Butterworth, T., 1933; Appleton-Century, 1934
Entertaining Murder. Eyre, 1945
The Green Diamond Mystery. Collins, 1929
He Had It Coming to Him. Eyre, 1948
The Heart in the Box. Butterworth, T., 1936
Heart of the Moon. Rivers, 1928
The Ink Street Murder. Eyre, 1941
The Jackdaw Mystery. Collins, 1931
Judas C.I.D. Hale, R., 1954
Lady of Despair. Collins, 1930
The Limping Man. Hodder, 1924; Grosset, 1927
The Lost Pearl. Hodder, 1924; Grosset, 1928
The Mad Hatter Murder. Eyre, 1941
Madame Shadow. Hutchinson, 1952
The Man from Madagascar. Butterworth, T., 1937
The Monkhurst Murder. Collins, 1933
Murder at Lancaster Gate. Butterworth, T., 1934
Murder at the Wedding. Collins, 1953
Murder in Black. Appleton-Century, 1935; Butterworth, T., 1935
Murder in Mortimer Square. Collins, 1932
Murder in the Garden. Clode, 1927; Grosset, 1928
Mysterious Mademoiselle. Collins, 1930
Mystery in Red. Collins, 1931
The Mystery of the Golden Angel. Collins, 1933
The Mystery of the Two-Faced Man. Butterworth, T., 1939
No Wreaths for the Duchess. Hutchinson, 1948
Out of the Ashes. Eyre, 1946
Pan's Punishment. Laurie, 1917
The Second Man. Knopf, 1956
Secret Judges. Hodder, 1925
Sign of the Nine. Hale, R., 1956

The Smiling Death. Bles, 1927
The Strange Case of Edgar Heriot. Hutchinson, 1950
Thrice Judas. Eyre, 1942
Traitor's Cross. Hutchinson, 1953
The White Camellia. Clode, 1929; Bles, 1930
Yellow Rat. Collins, 1930
The Zoo Murders. Bles, 1930

GRIERSON, LINDEN
The Senorita Penny. Hale, R., 1959
Sunken Garden. Hale, R., 1963

GRIEVE, ALEXANDER HAIG GLANVILLE (M) (Pseudonym: Alec Glanville)
The Body in the Trawl. Harrap, 1938
Death Goes Ashore. Harrap, 1936
Death in Our Wake. Harrap, 1937
Out of the Shadows. Roy Pubs., 1958

GRIFFIN, EDITHA ACEITUNA (M)
The Punt Murder. Low, 1936

GRIFFIN, FRANK (M)
Danger at Midnight. Mellifont, 1948
Death After Dark. Fiction House, 1947
Death Takes a Hand. Bear, 1945
She Deserved to Die. Yates Pub., 1951

GRIFFITH, JASON, pseud; see GRIFFITH, MR. and MRS. E. G.

GRIFFITH, MR. and MRS. E. G. (Pseudonym: Jason Griffith)
The Monkey Wrench. Stratford, 1933

GRIFFITHS, MAJOR ARTHUR (M)
Fast and Loose. Chapman, 1884-85
Locked Up. Blackwood, 1887
The Passenger from Calais. Doubleday, Page, 1906
The Rome Express. Milne, 1896
The Wrong Road. Blackwood, 1888

GRILLET, ALAIN ROBBE-; see ROBBE-GRILLET, ALAIN

GRIMSHAW, BEATRICE ETHEL (M)
The Mystery of Tumbling Reef. Houghton, 1932
The Wreck of Redwing. Hale, R., 1937

GRINDAL, RICHARD (S) (Pseudonym: Richard Grayson)
Cotton Gunston. Dutton, 1936
Dead So Soon. Hammond, 1960
Death in Melting. Hammond, 1959
Death Rides the Forest. Nash, 1931; Dutton, 1938
Gun Cotton - A Romance of the Secret Service. Grayson, 1939
Gun Cotton - Adventurer. Grayson, 1932
Gun Cotton - Secret Airman. Grayson, 1939
Madman's Whispers. Hammond, 1958
Secret Agent in Africa. Dutton, 1939
Spiral Path. Hammond, 1959

GRISEWOOD, HARMON (M)
The Last Cab in the Rank. MacDonald & Co., 1964

GRISWOLD, GEORGE, pseud; see DEAN, ROBERT GEORGE

GRONER, AUGUSTA (M-D)
The Crippled Hand, with Grace I. Colbron.
Joe Muller, Detective. Duffield, 1910
Man with the Black Cord. Chatto, 1911

GROOM, ARTHUR JOHN PELHAM; see GROOM, PELHAM

GROOM, KATHLEEN CLARICE (M)
The Folly of Fear. Hurst, 1947
Phantom Fortune. Hurst, 1948
The Recoil. Hutchinson, 1952

GROOM, PELHAM (M)
Fourth Seal. Jarrolds, 1949
Mohune's Nine Lives. Liveright, 1944 (English title: What Are Your Angels Now? Jarrolds, 1943)
What Are Your Angels Now?; see Mohune's Nine Lives

GROPPER, MILTON HERBERT; see SHERRY, EDNA

GROTE, WILLIAM (S)
Cain's Girl Friend. Ace, 1957

GROVE, WALT (S)
The Man Who Said No. GM, 1950

GRUBB, DAVIS (S)
The Night of the Hunter. Harper, 1943
Twelve Tales of Suspense and the Supernatural. Scribner, 1964
The Watchman. Scribner, 1961; Crest, 1962

GRUBER, FRANK (D) (Pseudonyms: Stephen Acre, Charles K. Boston, John K. Vedder)
The Beagle-Scented Murder. Rinehart, 1947
The Bridge of Sand. Dutton, 1963; Boardman, T. V., 1964
The Brothers of Silence. Boardman, T. V., 1962; Dutton, 1962
The Buffalo Box. Farrar & Rinehart, 1942
The Corpse Moved Upstairs; see The Mighty Blockhead
The Fourth Letter. Rinehart, 1947
The French Key. Farrar & Rinehart, 1940; Hale, R., 1940; Belmont, 1964

The Gift Horse. Farrar & Rinehart, 1942
The Greek Affair. Boardman, T. V., 1965; Dutton, 1965
The Honest Dealer. Rinehart, 1947
The Hungry Dog. Farrar & Rinehart, 1941
The Last Doorbell, by John K. Vedder. Holt, H., 1941
The Laughing Fox. Farrar & Rinehart, 1940; Nicholson, 1942
The Leather Duke. Rinehart, 1949
The Limping Goose. Rinehart, 1954
Little Hercules. Dutton, 1965
The Lock and the Key. Rinehart, 1948 (Also published as: Run Thief, Run. Crest, 1955)
The Lonesome Badger. Rinehart, 1954
The Mighty Blockhead. Grosset, 1943 (Also published as: The Corpse Moved Upstairs. Belmont, 1964)
Murder '97. Rinehart, 1948; Barker, 1956
The Navy Colt. Farrar & Rinehart, 1941
Run, Fool, Run. Dutton, 1966
Run Thief, Run; see The Lock and the Key
The Scarlet Feather. Rinehart, 1948
The Silver Jackass, by Charles K. Boston. Reynal, 1941
The Silver Tombstone. Farrar, Straus, 1945; Signet, 1948
Simon Lash, Detective; see Simon Lash, Private Detective
Simon Lash, Private Detective. Farrar & Rinehart, 1941 (Also published as: Simon Lash, Detective. Nicholson, 1943)
Swing Low, Sweet Dead. Farrar, Straus, 1945; Belmont, 1964
The Talking Clock. Farrar & Rinehart, 1941; Penguin, 1944
Twenty Plus Two. Boardman, T. V., 1961; Bantam, 1961; Dutton, 1961
The Twilight Man. Dutton, 1967
The Whispering Master. Rinehart, 1947
The Yellow Overcoat, by Stephen Acre. Dodd, 1942

GUEST, FRANCIS HAROLD (M) (Pseudonym: James Spenser)
Crime Against Society. Longmans, 1938

GUIEBOURG, GEORGES (D) (Pseudonym: "Georgius")
My Fair Lady. Roy Pubs., 1954

GUIGO, ERNEST PHILIP (M) (Pseudonym: E. Carleton Holt)
Mystery at Arden Court. Stockwell, 1954

GUILDFORD, JOHN, pseud; see HUNTER, BLUEBELL MATILDA

GUINESS, KATHERINE DAVIS
Fisherman's End. MacDonald & Co., 1958

GUINESS, MAURICE C. and MUNA LEE DE MUNOZ MARIN (M) (Pseudonym: Newton Gayle)
Death Follows a Formula. Scribner, 1935; Gollancz, 1936
Death in the Glass. Gollancz, 1937; Scribner, 1937
Murder at 28:10. Scribner, 1936; Collins, 1937
Murder in the Haunted Sentry-box; see The Sentry-box Murder
The Sentry-box Murder. Scribner, 1935 (English title: Murder in the Haunted Sentry-box. Gollancz, 1935)
Sinister Crag. Gollancz, 1938; Scribner, 1939

GUISE, STANLEY (M)
The Falcon Mystery. Long, 1930; Withy Grove, 1941

GULIK, ROBERT HANS VAN (D)
The Chinese Bell Murders. Joseph, M., 1958; Harper, 1959; Avon, 1963
The Chinese Gold Murders. Harper, 1959; Joseph, M., 1965; Avon, 1963
The Chinese Lake Murders. Harper, 1960; Joseph, M., 1960; Avon, 1964
The Chinese Maze Murders. Hoeve, 1956; Lounz, 1957; Joseph, M., 1962
The Chinese Nail Murders. Joseph, M., 1961; Harper, 1962; Avon, 1964
Dee Goong An. Paul, 1949
The Emperor's Pearl. Heinemann, 1963; Scribner, 1964; Penguin
The Haunted Monastery. Heinemann, 1963; Lounz, 1963
Judge Dee at Work. Heinemann, 1967
The Lacquer Screen. Lounz, 1963; Heinemann, 1964
The Monkey and the Tiger. Scribner, 1966
Murder in Canton. Heinemann, 1966; Scribner, 1967
The Phantom of the Temple. Heinemann, 1966; Scribner, 1967
The Red Pavillion. Lounz, 1961; Scribner, 1968
The Willow Pattern. Scribner, 1965

GULL, CYRIL ARTHUR EDWARD RANGER (M) (Pseudonym: Guy Thorne)
Black Honey. Greening, 1913; Aldine, 1925
The Iron Box. Hurst, 1923
The Lost Judge. White, 1914
The Monstrous Enemy. Laurie, 1915
Murder Limited. Laurie, 1913
The Parrot Faced Man. White, 1912

The Ravenscroft Affair; see The Ravenscroft Horror
The Ravenscroft Horror. Laurie, 1917 (Also published as: The Ravenscroft Affair. Clode, 1924; Grosset, 1926)
The Terror by Night. White, 1909

GUNN, JAMES EDWARD (S)
Deadlier Than the Male. Duell, 1942; Tower

GUNN, NEIL MILLER
Lost Chart. Faber, 1949

GUNN, VICTOR (D)
Alias the Hangman. Collins, 1950
All Change for Murder. Collins, 1962
The Body in the Boot. Collins, 1963
The Body Vanishes. Collins, 1952
The Borgia Head Mystery. Collins, 1951
Castle Dangerous. Collins, 1957
The Crippled Canary. Collins, 1954
The Crooked Staircase. Collins, 1954
Dead in a Ditch. Collins, 1959
The Dead Man's Laugh. Collins, 1944
Dead Man's Warning. Collins, 1949
Dead Men's Bells. Collins, 1956
Death at Traitor's Gate. Collins, 1960
Death Comes Laughing. Collins, 1952
Death on Bodmin Moor. Collins, 1960
Death on Shivering Sand. Collins, 1946
Death's Doorway. Collins, 1941
Devil in the Maze. Collins, 1961
Footsteps of Death. Collins, 1939
The Golden Monkey. Collins, 1957
Ironsides' Lone Hand. Collins, 1941
Ironsides of the Yard. Collins, 1940
Ironsides on the Spot. Collins, 1948
Ironsides Sees Red. Collins, 1945
Ironsides Smashes Through. Collins, 1940
Ironsides Smells Blood. Collins, 1946
The Laughing Grave. Collins, 1955
Mad Hatter's Rock. Collins. 1942
Murder at the Hotel. Collins, 1964
Murder on Ice. Collins, 1951
Murder with a Kiss. Collins, 1964
Next One to Die. Collins, 1959
Nice Day for a Murder. Collins, 1945
The Painted Dog. Collins, 1955
Road to Murder. Collins, 1949
Sixty-Four Thousand Murder. Collins, 1958
Sweet Smelling Death. Collins, 1961
Three Dates with Death. Collins, 1947
The Whistling Key. Collins, 1953

GUNTHER, JOHN (D)
Bright Nemesis. Bobbs, 1932; Secker, 1932; Popular Lib., 1963

GUTHRIE, ALFRED BERTRAM (M)
Murders at Moon Dance. Dutton, 1943 (Also published as: Trouble at Moon Dance. Popular Lib., 1951)

GUTHRIE, P. R. (M) (Pseudonym: Barry Pain)
Collected Tales. Secker, 1914; Stokes, 1914
Memoirs of Constantine Dix. Unwin, 1905
The Mystery of Evelin Delorme. Arena, 1894
One Kind and Another. Secker, 1914; Stokes, 1914
Stories and Interludes. Harper, 1892; Henry, 1892
Stories in the Dark. Richards, 1901

GUTHRIE, THOMAS ANSTEY (S) (Pseudonym: F. Anstey)
The Brass Bottle. Smith, Elder, 1900

GWINN, WILLIAM R. (M) (Pseudonym: William Randall)
Deadly the Daring. Bouregy, 1956

HAASE, JOHN (S)
The Noon Balloon to Rangoon. S & S, 1967

HABE, HANS, pseud; see BEKESSY, JEAN

HACKFORTH-JONES, FRANK GILBERT (M)
Crack of Doom. Hodder, 1961
Death of an Admiral. Hodder, 1956
Fish Out of Water. Hodder, 1954
The Questing Hound. Hodder, 1948
Sole Survivor. Hodder, 1953

HADDOW, DENNIS (M)
Hanged by a Thread. Hutchinson, 1947

HADEN, ALLEN (M)
My Enemy-My Wife. Allen, T., 1951; Putnam, 1951

HAEDRICH, MARCEL, pseud. (M)
The Crack in the Mirror. Allen, W. H., 1960; Dell, 1961

HAGEN, MIRIAM-ANN (D)
Dig Me Later. Doubleday, 1949
Murder - but Natch. Doubleday, 1951
Plant Me Now. Doubleday, 1947

HAGERTY, H. T. (M)
The Jasmine Trail. Lothrop, 1936

HAGGARD, PAUL, pseud; see LONG-STREET, STEPHEN

HAGGARD, WILLIAM, pseud; see CLAY-TON, RICHARD HENRY MICHAEL

HAILEY, ARTHUR; see GARROD, JOHN

HALDANE, EMMA (M)
Maluti Murder. Eldon, 1933

HALE, CHRISTOPHER, pseud; see STEVENS, MRS. FRANCES MOYER ROSS

HALE, EDGAR (D)
Blue Murder. Ward, Lock, 1948
Coffee for One. Ward, Lock, 1949
Death Came Back. Ward, Lock, 1948
Death Dealt the Cards. Ward, Lock, 1947
The Devil's Tears. Ward, Lock, 1948
Never Shoot a Lady. Ward, Lock, 1947
So the Lady Died. Ward, Lock, 1949

HALES, JOHN; see MANVELL, ROGER

HALKET, ROBERTSON (M)
Documentary Evidence. Nicholson, 1936

HALL, ADAM, pseud; see TREVOR, ELLESTON

HALL, ANDREW (S)
Frost. Putnam, 1967

HALL, GEOFFREY HOLIDAY (M)
The End Is Known. S & S, 1949; Heinemann, 1950
The Watcher at the Door. Musson, 1954; S & S, 1954

HALL, H. and C. E. BLANEY (D)
The Millionaire Detective. Ogilivie

HALL, HOLWORTHY, pseud; see PORTER, HAROLD EVERETT

HALL, JAY (M)
Evidently Murdered. Dorrance, 1943

HALL, JENNI (M)
Ask Agamemnon. Atheneum, 1964; Cassell; 1964
Mr. Capon. Harcourt, 1965

HALL, L. B. (M)
Sinister House. Houghton, 1919

HALL, OAKLEY MAXWELL (D) (Pseudonym: Jason Manor)
Murder City. Farrar-Straus, 1949; Barker, 1950
The Pawns of Fear, by Jason Manor. Viking, 1955
The Red Jaguar, by Jason Manor. Viking, 1954
Too Dead to Run, by Jason Manor. Viking, 1953
The Tramplers, by Jason Manor. Secker & Warburg, 1956; Viking, 1956

HALL, WARNER (M)
Even Jericho. Macrae Smith, 1944

HALL, WHYTE, pseud; see RAYNER, AUGUSTUS ALFRED

HALLERAN, EUGENE E. (D)
Thirteen Toy Pistols. McKay, 1945; Musson, 1945

HALLIDAY, BRETT, pseud; see DRESSER, DAVIS

HALLIDAY, DAVE (M)
The Triumverate. Doubleday, 1966

HALLIDAY, LEONARD (M)
The Devil's Door. Hammond, 1959
Smiling Spider. Hammond, 1955
Top Secret. Hammond, 1957

HALLIDAY, MICHAEL, pseud; see CREASEY, JOHN

HALLIFAX, CLIFFORD; see MEADE, MRS. L. T.

HALSTEAD, JOHN (M)
Black Nat. Paul, S., 1932

HAMBLEDON, PHYLLIS MacVEAN (D) (Pseudonym: Phillipa Vane)
Death of an Uncle. Hale, R., 1962
I Know a Secret. Laurie, 1951
Here Is the Evidence, by Phillipa Vane. Hammond, 1950
Invitation to Terror. Laurie, 1950
Keys for the Criminal. Hale, R., 1958
Listening Boy. Laurie, 1951
Murder and Miss Ming. Hale, R., 1959
Murder's No Picnic. Hale, R., 1961
Passports to Murder. Hale, R., 1958
Priority for Death, by Phillipa Vane. Hammond, 1947
The Uninvited. Ward, Lock, 1961

HAMILTON, ALEX (D)
Beam of Malice. McKay, 1967 (Short stories)

HAMILTON, ANTHONY WALTER PATRICK; see HAMILTON, PATRICK

HAMILTON, ARTHUR DOUGLAS BRUCE (M) (Pseudonym: Bruce Hamilton)
Dead Reckoning. S & S, 1937 (Also published as: Middle Class Murder. Methuen, 1937)
The Hanging Judge. Harper, 1948
Middle Class Murder; see Dead Reckoning
To be Hanged. Doubleday, Doran, 1930
Too Much Water. Cresset, 1958

HAMILTON, BRUCE, pseud; see HAMILTON, ARTHUR DOUGLAS BRUCE

HAMILTON, DONALD BENGTSSON (D-S)
The Ambushers. GM, 1963, 1967
Assignment: Murder; see Assassins Have Starry Eyes

Assassins Have Starry Eyes. GM, 1946 (Also published as: Assignment: Murder. Dell, 1956)
The Betrayers. GM, 1966
The Black Cross; see Murder Twice Told
Date with Darkness. Dell, 1947; Rinehart, 1947; Wingate, 1951
Deadfall; see Murder Twice Told
Death of a Citizen. GM, 1960
The Devastators. GM, 1966
Line of Fire. GM, 1955; Wingate, 1956
The Menacers. GM, 1967
Murder Twice Told. Rinehart, 1947; GM, 1947; Wingate, 1952 (Contains: Deadfall and The Black Cross)
Murderer's Row. GM, 1962
The Night Walker. Dell, 1954; GM, 1965
The Ravagers. GM, 1964
The Removers. GM, 1961
The Shadowers. GM, 1964, 1967
The Silencers. GM, 1962
The Steel Mirror. GM, 1948; Rinehart, 1948; Wingate, 1950
The Wrecking Crew. GM, 1960

HAMILTON, E. W. (D)
Four Tragedies of Memworth. Gollancz, 1929

HAMILTON, MRS. EDMOND (S) (Pseudonym: Leigh Brackett)
An Eye for an Eye. Doubleday, 1957; Boardman, T. V., 1958
No Good from a Corpse. Coward, 1944; Collier, 1964
The Tiger Among Us. Doubleday, 1957; Boardman, T. V., 1958

HAMILTON, ELAINE (M)
The Westminister Mystery. Century, 1931

HAMILTON, LORD FREDERIC SPENCER (D)
The Beginnings of Mr. P. J. Davenant. Hodder, 1917
The Education of Mr. P.J. Davenant. Nash, 1916
More About the Secret Service Boy. Nelson, 1923
Nine Holiday Adventures of Mr. P.J. Davenant in the Year 1915. Newnes, 1916
Some Further Adventures of Mr. P.J. Davenant. Nash, 1915

HAMILTON, HENRIETTA (M)
Answer in the Negative. Hodder, 1959
At Night to Die. Hodder, 1959
Death at One Blow. Hodder, 1957
The Two Hundred Ghost. Hodder, 1956

HAMILTON, IAN (M)
The Creeping Vicar. Lippincott, 1967 (English title: The Man with the Brown Paper Face. Constable, 1967)
The Man with the Brown Paper Face; see The Creeping Vicar
The Persecutor. Constable, 1965; Lippincott, 1965

HAMILTON, MRS. MARY AGNES ADAMSON (Pseudonym: "Iconoclast")
Murder in the House of Commons. Hamilton, H., 1931

HAMILTON, MOLLIE, pseud; see KAYE, M. M.

HAMILTON, PATRICK (Full name: Anthony Walter Patrick Hamilton) (M)
Hangover Square. Random, 1942; World Pub., 1944

HAMMETT, DASHIELL (D)
The Adventures of Sam Spade and Other Stories. Mercury Mystery, 1944; World Pub., 1945 (Also published as: A Man Called Spade and Other Stories. Dell, 1954 and They Can Only Hang You Once and Other Stories. Mercury Mystery, 1949)
The Big Knockover; see $106,000 Blood Money
Blood Money; see $106,000 Blood Money
The Complete Dashiell Hammett. Knopf, 1942 (English title: The Dashiell Hammett Omnibus. Cassell, 1950)
The Continental Op. Bestseller Mystery, 1943; Dell, 1946
The Continental Op: More Stories from the Big Knockover. Dell, 1967
The Creeping Siamese. Jonathan Press, 1950; Dell
Creeps by Night. Day, 1931; World Pub., 1943 (English title: Modern Tales of Horror. Gollancz, 1932)
The Dain Curse. Knopf, 1929, 1946; Grosset, 1943; PB, 1961; Dell, 1968
The Dashiell Hammett Omnibus. Knopf, 1935; Cassell, 1950
The Dashiell Hammett Omnibus; see The Complete Dashiell Hammett
The Dashiell Hammett Story Omnibus. Cassell, 1966
Dead Yellow Women. Jonathan Press, 1947; Dell
The Glass Key. Cassell, 1931; Knopf, 1931, 1945; Permabooks, 1961; Dell, 1966; Penguin
Hammett Homicides. Bestseller Mystery, 1946; Dell
The Maltese Falcon. Knopf, 1929; Cassell, 1931; Modern Lib., 1934; Grosset, 1943; Dell, 1966

The Maltese Falcon and The Thin Man. Random, 1964
A Man Called Spade; see The Adventures of Sam Spade and Other Stories
A Man Named Thin and Other Stories. Mercury Press, 1962
Modern Tales of Horror; see Creeps by Night
$106,000 Blood Money. Bestseller Mystery, 1943; Jonathan Press, 1948 (Also published as: The Big Knockover. Dell, 1966; Random, 1966 and Blood Money. World Pub., 1943; Dell, 1951)
Mystery Omnibus. McClelland, 1944; World Pub., 1944 (Contains: The Glass Key and The Maltese Falcon)
Nightmare Town. Mercury Mystery, 1948; Dell, 1950
Novels of Dashiell Hammett. Knopf, 1965
The Red Brain and Other Thrillers. Four Square, 1967
Red Harvest. Knopf, 1929; Grosset, 1941; PB, 1943
The Return of the Continental Op. Jonathan Press, 1945; Dell, 1947
They Can Only Hang You Once; see The Adventures of Sam Spade and Other Stories
The Thin Man. Knopf, 1934, 1946; Penguin, 1935; Heinemann, 1940; PB, 1943; Dell, 1966
Woman in the Dark. Jonathan Press, 1952

HAMMOCK, CLAUDE STUART (D)
Why Murder the Judge? Macmillan, 1931

HAMMOND-INNES, RALPH (S) (Pseudonyms: Ralph Hammond, Hammond Innes)
Air Bridge, by Hammond Innes. Collins, 1951; Knopf, 1951
Air Disaster, by Hammond Innes. Jenkins, 1938
All Roads Lead to Friday, by Hammond Innes. Jenkins, 1939
The Angry Mountain, by Hammond Innes. Collins, 1950; Harper, 1950; Avon, 1967; Ballantine, 1962
Atlantic Fury, by Hammond Innes. Knopf, 1962; Dell, 1963
Attack Alarm, by Hammond Innes. Collins, 1941; Macmillan, 1942
Berlin Air Bridge. Knopf, 1952
Black Gold on the Double Diamond, by Ralph Hammond. Collins, 1953
Blue Ice, by Hammond Innes. Collins, 1948; Harper, 1948; Ballantine, 1962
Campbell's Kingdom, by Hammond Innes. Collins, 1952; Knopf, 1952; Ballantine, 1963
Cocos Gold, by Ralph Hammond. Collins, 1950; Harper, 1950
Cruise of Danger, by Ralph Hammond. Westminster, 1952 (Also published as: Saracens Tower. Collins, 1952)
Dead and Alive, by Hammond Innes. Collins, 1946
The Doomed Oasis, by Hammond Innes. Knopf, 1960; Dell, 1963
Doppelganger, by Hammond Innes. Jenkins, 1938
Fire in the Snow, by Hammond Innes. Harper, 1947; Collier, 1962 (English title: The Lonely Skier. Collins, 1947)
Gale Warning, by Hammond Innes. Collins, 1948; Ballantine, 1962 (Also published as: Maddon's Rock. Collins, 1948)
Island of Peril; see Isle of Strangers
Isle of Strangers, by Ralph Hammond. Collins, 1951 (Also published as: Island of Peril. Westminster, 1952)
The Killer Mine, by Hammond Innes. Collins, 1947; Harper, 1947; Ballantine, 1962; Avon, 1968 (Also published as: Run by Night. Bantam, 1947)
The Land God Gave to Cain, by Hammond Innes. Collins, 1958; Knopf, 1958; Dell, 1964
The Lonely Skier; see Fire in the Snow
Mary Deare; see The Wreck of the Mary Deare
Maddon's Rock; see Gale Warning
The Naked Land, by Hammond Innes. Knopf, 1954; Ballantine, 1963 (English title: Strange Land. Collins, 1954)
Run by Night; see Killer Mine
Sabotage Broadcast, by Hammond Innes. Jenkins, 1938
Saracens Tower; see Cruise of Danger
Strange Land; see Naked Land
The Survivors, by Hammond Innes. Harper, 1949; Collier, 1962 (English title: The White South. Collins, 1949)
Trapped, by Hammond Innes. Putnam, 1940 (English title: Wreckers Must Breathe. Collins, 1956)
The Trojan Horse, by Hammond Innes. Collins, 1940
The White South; see The Survivors
The Wreck of the Mary Deare, by Hammond Innes. Knopf, 1956 (English title: Mary Deare. Collins, 1956)
Wreckers Must Breathe; see Trapped

HANCOCK, H. I. (D)
Detective Johnson of New Orleans. Ogilvie
His Evil Eye. Ogilvie
Inspector Henderson, the Central Office Detective. Ogilvie

HANDLEY, ALAN (M)
Kiss Your Elbow. McKay, 1948

HANKINS, ARTHUR PRESTON (D)
Judy the Torch. Chelsea House, 1928
Tong Men and a Million. Chelsea House, 1928

HANLEY, CLIFFORD (M) (Pseudonym: Henry Calvin)
The Italian Gadget. Hutchinson, 1966
It's Different Abroad. Harper & Row, 1963; Hutchinson, 1963; Avon, 1965
The System. Hutchinson, 1962

HANNA, MRS. FRANCES NICHOLS (M) (Pseudonym: Fan Nichols)
Be Silent, Love. S & S, 1956
The Loner. S & S, 1956; Boardman, T. V., 1957

HANNAY, JAMES FREDERICK WYNNE (M)
Flight of an Angel. Methuen, 1932
Gin and Ginger. Methuen, 1931
Murder of Me. Hutchinson, 1937
Rebels' Triumph. Methuen, 1933
The Thirteenth Floor. Methuen, 1931
Three Alibis. Hutchinson, 1938
When the Wicked Man. Methuen, 1934

HANNAY, JAMES OWEN (M) (Pseudonym: George A. Birmingham)
The Hymn Tune Mystery. Bobbs, 1931; Methuen, 1931
Wild Justice. Bobbs, 1930; Methuen, 1930

HANSEN, ROBERT POWELL (D)
Back to the Wall. Mill, 1957; Boardman, T. V., 1958
Dead Pigeon, Mill, 1951; Barker, 1953
Deadly Purpose. Mill, 1958; Boardman, T. V., 1959
Mark Three for Murder. Boardman, T. V., 1957; Mill, 1957
Murder Is Where You Find It. Mill, 1956; Boardman, T. V., 1957
There's Always a Payoff. Mill, 1959; Boardman, T. V., 1960
Trouble Comes Double. Mill, 1954; Barker, 1955
Walk a Wicked Mile. Boardman, T. V., 1955; Mill, 1955

HANSHEW, HAZEL PHILLIPS HANSHEW
Murder in the Hotel. Long, 1932
The Riddle of the Winged Death. Long, 1931

HANSHEW, MARY; see HANSHEW, THOMAS W.

HANSHEW, THOMAS W. (D)
The Amber Junk, with Mary Hanshew. Doubleday, Page, 1924; Hutchinson, 1924
Beautiful, But Dangerous; or, The Heir of Shadowdene. Street, 1891
Cleek of Scotland Yard. Cassell, 1914; Doubleday, Page, 1914; Burt, 1936
Cleek, the Man of Forty Faces. Burt, 1920; Cassell, 1930
Cleek, the Master Detective. Doubleday, Page, 1918
Cleek's Government Cases. Doubleday, Page, 1917
Cleek's Greatest Riddles, with Mary Hanshew. Simpkin, 1916
The Frozen Flames, with Mary Hanshew. Doubleday, Doran, 1928 (Also published as: The Riddle of the Frozen Flame)
The Great Ruby. Ward, Lock, 1902
The House of Discord, with Mary Hanshew. Hutchinson, 1922
The House of the Seven Keys, with Mary Hanshew. Hutchinson, 1925
The Mallison Mystery. Ward, Lock, 1903
The Man of the Forty Faces. Cassell, 1910
The Riddle of the Amber Ship, with Mary Hanshew. Doubleday, Page, 1924
The Riddle of the Frozen Flames; see The Frozen Flames
The Riddle of the Mysterious Light, with Mary Hanshew. Doubleday, Page, 1921
The Riddle of the Night. Doubleday, Page, 1915
The Riddle of the Purple Emperor, with Mary Hanshew. Doubleday, Page, 1919
The Riddle of the Spinning Wheel, with Mary Hanshew. Doubleday, Page, 1922
The Shadow of a Dead Man. Ward, Lock, 1906

HANSOM, MARK (M)
The Beasts of Brahm. Wright & Brown, 1937; Mellifont, 1940
The Ghost of Gaston Revere. Wright & Brown, 1935; Mellifont, 1944
The Madman. Wright & Brown, 1938; Mellifont, 1940
Master of Souls. Wright & Brown, 1937; Mellifont, 1951
The Shadow on the House. Wright & Brown, 1934; Mellifont, 1945
Sorcerer's Chessman. Mellifont, 1939; Wright & Brown, 1939
The Wizard of Berner's Abbey. Wright & Brown, 1935; Mellifont, 1944

HANSON, PER (S)
The Greatest Gamble. Norton, 1967

HANSON, ROBERT (M) (Pseudonym: Jens Anker)
Two Dead Men. Knopf, 1922

HANSON, VIRGINIA (D)
Casual Slaughters. Doubleday, Doran, 1939
Death Walks the Post. Doubleday, Doran, 1938
Mystery for Mary. Doubleday, Doran, 1942

HARBAGE, ALFRED BENNETT (M)
(Pseudonym: Thomas Kyd)
Blood Is a Beggar. Lippincott, 1946
Blood of Vintage. Lippincott, 1947
Blood on the Bosom Divine. Lippincott, 1948
Cover His Face. Lippincott, 1949

HARBOU, THEA von
Spies. Putnam, 1929

HARDIE, D. W. F. (M)
The Case of the Praying Evangelist. Nicholson, 1950
The Riddle of the Cambrian Venus. Nicholson, 1949

HARDIN, PETER, pseud; see VACZEK, LOUIS C.

HARDING, ALBERT (M)
Death on Raven's Scar. Staples Press, 1953

HARDINGE, GEORGE (D) (Pseudonym: George Milner)
Case Against Marcella. Hodder, 1963 (Also published as: Crime Against Marcella. 1963)
Crime Against Marcella; see Case Against Marcella
A Leavetaking. Dodd, 1966, 1967; Hodder, 1966
Scarlet Fountains. Collins, 1956
Shark Among Herrings. Collins, 1954
Stately Homicide. Collins, 1954
Your Money and Your Life. Collins, 1957

HARDINGE, REX (S) (Pseudonym: "Capstan")
Black Magic. Wright & Brown, 1941
The Broadcast Murder. Mellifont, 1939
Cap't Luke, Filibuster. Wright & Brown, 1937
Carver of the Swamp. Wright & Brown, 1938
The Chinese Cabinet. Mellifont, 1941
Forbidden Territory. Wright & Brown, 1949
Hole in the Mountain. Wright & Brown, 1939
Inkosi Carver Investigates. Wright & Brown, 1943
Murder on the Veld. Wright & Brown, 1956
Night Coach. Mellifont, 1938
Polite Pirate. Wright & Brown, 1938
Secret of the Sheba. Wright & Brown, 1957

HARDWICK, RICHARD (M-S)
Hawk. Belmont, 1966
The Plotters. Doubleday, 1966; Hale, R., 1967
The Season to Be Deadly. Doubleday, 1966; Hale, R., 1967

HARDY, ARTHUR S. (M)
No. 13, Rue du Bon Diable. Houghton, 1917

HARDY, JOCELYN LEE (S)
Recoil. Collins, 1936; Doubleday, Doran, 1936

HARDY, LINDSAY (M)
The Faceless Ones. Hale, R., 1956
The Nightshade Ring. Appleton, 1954; Signet, 1965
Requiem for a Redhead. Appleton, 1953; Signet, 1965

HARDY, ROBERT (M)
Winter's Tale. Chatto, 1959

HARDY, WILLIAM MARION (M)
The Case of the Missing Co-ed; see A Little Sin
Lady Killer. Dodd, 1957; Penguin; Dell
A Little Sin. Dodd, 1958; Hamilton, H., 1959 (Also published as: The Case of the Missing Co-ed. Dell, 1960)
Submarine Wolfpack; see Wolfpack
A Time of Killing. Dodd, 1962; Dell, 1963; Hamilton, H., 1963
Wolfpack. Hamilton, H., 1960 (U.S. title: Submarine Wolfpack. Dodd, 1961)

HARE, ARNOLD (S)
The Man Who Never Laughed. Norton, 1963

HARE, CYRIL, pseud; see CLARK, ALFRED ALEXANDER GORDON

HARE, ROBERT, pseud; see HUTCHINSON, ROBERT HARE

HARKNETT, TERRY (M)
The Benevolent Blackmailer. Hale, R., 1962
Dead Little Rich Girl. Hale, R., 1963
The Evil Money. Hale, R., 1964
Invitation to a Funeral. Hale, R., 1963
The Man Who Did Not Die. Hale, R., 1964
Scratch on Surface. Hale, R., 1962

HARLING, ROBERT (S)
The Endless Colonnade. Chatto, 1958; Putnam, 1960; Pan, 1961

The Enormous Shadow. Chatto, 1955; Harper, 1956; Pan, 1958; Collier, 1962
The Paper Palace. Chatto, 1951; Harper, 1951; Pan, 1958

HARMAN, NEAL (M)
The Case of the Wounded Mastiff. Barker, 1947
Death and the Archdeacon. Barker, 1947
Peace and Pete Lamont. Barker, 1950
Yours Truly, Angus MacIvor. Barker, 1952

HARNAN, TERRY (S)
Signal for Danger. Doubleday, 1946

HARRINGTON, JOSEPH (D)
The Blind Spot. Lippincott, 1966
The Last Known Address. Lippincott, 1965; Hale, R., 1966

HARRIS, CHARLES (M)
Death of a Barrow Boy. Phoenix, 1952

HARRIS, COLVER, pseud; see COLVER, ANNE

HARRIS, HERBERT (M)
Who Kill to Live. Jenkins, 1962

HARRIS, JOHN (S)
Light Cavalry Action. Hutchinson, 1967; Morrow, 1967
The Old Trade of Killing. Hutchinson, 1966; Sloane, 1966

HARRIS, JOHN BEYNON (M) (Pseudonyms: John Beynon, John Wyndham)
Foul Play Suspected, by John Beynon. Newnes, 1935
The Midwich Cuckoos, by John Wyndham. Joseph, M., 1957

HARRIS, JOHN NORMAN (S)
The Weird World of Wes Beattie. Harper & Row, 1963; Faber, 1964; Popular Lib., 1968

HARRIS, LARRY M., pseud; see JANIFER, LAURENCE M.

HARRIS, PETER (S)
Letters of Discredit. Long, 1965

HARRIS, POLLY ANNE COLVER; see COLVER, ANNE

HARRIS, VIVIAN BEYNON (M)
The Confusion at Campden Trig. Museum Press, 1948

HARRIS-BURLAND, JOHN (M)
The Shadow of Malreward. Knopf, 1919

HARRISON, B. (D)
A-100. Dutton, 1930

HARRISON, MICHAEL (M) (Pseudonym: Quentin Downes)
Heads I Win. Roy Pubs., 1956
No Smoke, No Flame. Roy Pubs., 1956
They Hadn't a Clue. Arco, 1956

HARRISON, RICHARD MOTTE (D) (Pseudonym: Peter Motte)
Aftermath of Murder. Jarrolds, 1942
Black Widow. Jarrolds, 1946
Bootlaces for Bastion. Jarrolds, 1949
Brickbats for Bastion. Jarrolds, 1948
C.I.D. and F.B.I. Muller, 1956
The Circle of Van Boden. Jarrolds, 1944
The Criminal Calendar. Jarrolds, 1952
The Dog It Was. Jarrolds, 1940
A Dog's Death, by Peter Motte and Reginald W. Campbell. Cassell, 1953
Fall of the Curtain, by Peter Motte. Cassell, 1958
Fell Clutch, by Peter Motte. Cassell, 1956
Foul Deed Will Rise. Long, 1958
House at Hog's Corner, by Peter Motte. Cassell, 1958
Murder-on-Sea. Jarrolds, 1949
Murder She Says!, by Peter Motte and Reginald W. Campbell. Cassell, 1953
Our Doom Is Gone. Jarrolds, 1951
Phoenix from the Gutter, by Peter Motte. Cassell, 1956
Rope over Jezebel. Jarrolds, 1950
The Shuttle of Hate. Jarrolds, 1942
Suburban Saraband. Jarrolds, 1952
The Utmost Ebb. Jarrolds, 1944
The Village Called Death, by Peter Motte. Cassell, 1955

HART, MRS. FRANCES NEWBOLD NOYES (M)
The Bellamy Trial. Doubleday, Doran, 1928; Heinemann, 1928; Dell, 1958
The Crooked Lane. Doubleday, Doran, 1934; Heinemann, 1936
Hide in the Dark. Doubleday, Doran, 1929; Heinemann, 1929

HART, INNES RUTH GRAY (M)
Dead Hand. Benn, 1931
Double Image. Benn, 1930
Facets. Benn, 1930
Forests of the Night. Benn, 1939
Frontier of Fear. Benn, 1929
Torture Island. S & S, 1928

HARTER, WALTER L. (S)
Nice Young Man. Holt, 1962

HARTLEY, LESLIE POLES (M)
The Killing Battle. Putnam, 1932
Night Fears and Other Stories. Putnam, 1924

HARTLEY, O. (M)
The Malaret Mystery. Small, 1926

HARTMAN, LEE FOSTER (M)
The White Sapphire. Harper, 1914

HARTMANN, HELMUT (M) (Pseudonym: H. Seymour)
Appointment with Murder. Gifford, 1962
The Bristol Affair. Gifford, 1960
Intrigue in Tangier. Gifford, 1958
The Paperchase Murder. Gifford, 1961
Run for Your Money. Gifford, 1959

HARTOG, JAN DE
The Inspector. Atheneum, 1960; Hamilton, H., 1960

HARVESTER, SIMON, pseud; see GIBBS, HENRY

HARVEY, ANNIE JANE TENNANT (M) (Pseudonym: Andrée Hope)
The Secret of Wardale Court and Other Stories. Wilsons & Milne, 1894
The Vyvyans; or, the Murder in the Rue Bellechasses. Chapman, 1893

HARVEY, JACK; see RAISON, MILTON M.

HARVEY, JOHN HENRY (D) (Pseudonym: John H. Barrington)
The Moving Finger. Langdon, 1947
Murder in White Pit. Langdon, 1947

HARVEY, JOHN WILFRED (M) (Pseudonym: John Farndale)
The Nine Nicks. Methuen, 1930

HARVEY, MARION (M)
Alias the Eagle. Shaylor, 1928
The Clue of the Clock. Clode, 1929
The Dragon of Lung Wang. Clode, 1928
The House of Seclusion. Small, 1925
The Mystery of the Hidden Room. Clode, 1922
The Vengeance of the Ivory Skull. Clode, 1923

HARVEY, WILLIAM CLUNIE (M)
Death's Treasure Hunt. Eldon, 1933
Murder Abroad. Eldon, 1933

HARVEY, WILLIAM FRYER (M)
The Arm of Mrs. Eagan. Dutton, 1952
The Beast with Five Fingers. Dutton, 1928; Dent, 1932
The Midnight House and Other Tales. Dent, 1910

HASLETTE, JOHN, pseud; see VAHEY, JOHN GEORGE HASLETTE

HASTINGS, BROOK, pseud; see EDGLEY, LESLIE

HASTINGS, DOROTHY GRACE (D)
Death at the Depot. Harper, 1944

HASTINGS, GRAHAM (M)
Twice Checked. Hale, R., 1959

HASTINGS, MacDONALD (D)
Cork and the Serpent. Joseph, M., 1955; Penguin, 1959
Cork in Bottle. Joseph, M., 1953; Knopf, 1953; Penguin, 1957
Cork in the Doghouse. Joseph, M., 1957; Knopf, 1958; Penguin, 1961
Cork on Location; see Cork on the Telly
Cork on the Telly. Joseph, M., 1966 (U.S. title: Cork on Location. Walker & Co., 1967)
Cork on the Water. Joseph, M., 1951; Random, 1951; Penguin, 1956

HASTINGS, MICHAEL (D)
Coast of No Return. Methuen, 1953
Death in Deep Green. Methuen, 1952
Digger of the Pit. Methuen, 1955
Man Who Came Back. MacDonald & Co., 1957
They Killed a Spy. Harrap, 1940
Twelve on Endurance. MacDonald & Co., 1958

HASTINGS, ROSLYN S. (M)
Dead Wrong. Bouregy, 1963
Mind over Murder. Bouregy, 1960
Plain Unvarnished Murder, with Kate Klein. Arcadia, 1959
Where There's a Will. Bouregy, 1960

HASTINGS, W. S. (M)
The Professor's Mystery. Bobbs, 1911

HASTY, JOHN EUGENE (M)
Angel with Dirty Wings. GM, 1961
The Man Without a Face. Dodd, 1958; Long, 1960
Some Mischief Still. GM, 1963

HATCH, ERIC (M)
The Delinquent Ghost. Bart

HATCH, MARY R. PLATT (M)
The Berkeley Street Mystery. Page, 1928

HAUCK, MRS. LOUISE PLATT (M) (Pseudonym: Louise Landon)
Green Light. Penn, 1931
The Mystery of Tumult Rock. Burton Pub., 1920

HAWK, JOHN, pseud. (M)
The House of Sudden Sleep. Mystery League, 1930; Skeffington, 1930
It Was Locked. Farrar & Rinehart, 1930 (English title: Locked Door. Skeffington, 1930)

Locked Door; see It Was Locked
The Lone Lodge Mystery. Doran, 1926; Grosset, 1928; Skeffington, 1930
The Mid-Ocean Tragedy. Doran, 1927; Hodder, 1927; Grosset, 1929
The Murder at Arondale Farm. Farrar, 1932; Skeffington, 1932
The Murder of the Mystery Writer. Doubleday, Doran, 1929; Skeffington, 1930
The Serpent-Headed Stick. Doran, 1927; Hodder, 1927; Grosset, 1929
The Titanic Hotel Mystery. Doubleday, Doran, 1928; Skeffington, 1928

HAWKINS, SIR ANTHONY HOPE (M)
(Pseudonym: Anthony Hope)
The Secret of the Tower. Appleton, D., 1919 (English title: Beaumaroy Home from the Wars)

HAWKINS, DEAN (M)
Headsman's Holiday. Bouregy, 1946
In Memory of Murder. Doubleday, Doran, 1936
Skull Mountain. Doubleday, Doran, 1941
Walls of Silence. Doubleday, Doran, 1943

HAWKINS, JOHN and WARD HAWKINS (M)
Death Watch. Dodd, 1958; Eyre, 1959
Floods of Fear. Dodd, 1956; Eyre, 1957
The Missing Witness. Dodd, 1958; Eyre, 1959
Violent City. Dodd, 1957; Eyre, 1958
We Will Meet Again. Dial, 1940

HAWKINS, WARD; see HAWKINS, JOHN

HAWKINS, WILLARD E. (M)
The Cowled Menace. Sears, 1930

HAWTHORN, E. M. D., pseud; see DOLBY, ETHEL M.

HAWTON, HECTOR (M)
Case of the Crazy Atom. Ward, Lock, 1948
Deadly Nightcap. Ward, Lock, 1949
Death of a Witch. Ward, Lock, 1952
Green Scorpion. Ward, Lock. 1957
Murder at Headquarters. Ward, Lock, 1945
Murder by Mathematics. Ward, Lock, 1948
Murder Most Foul. Ward, Lock, 1946
Nine Singing Apes. Ward, Lock, 1949
Operation Superman. Ward, Lock, 1951
Rope for the Judge. Ward, Lock, 1954
The Skeleton in the Cupboard. Ward, Lock, 1955
Tower of Darkness. Hodder, 1950; Roy Pubs., 1951
Unnatural Causes. Ward, Lock, 1947

HAY, FRANCES, pseud; see ERIKSON, MRS. SIBYL ALEXANDRA DICK

HAY, JAMES, JR. (M)
The Bellamy Case. Dodd, 1925
The Hidden Woman. Dodd, 1929; Grosset, 1930
The Man Who Forgot. Little, 1915
The Melwood Mystery. Dodd, 1920
Mrs. Marden's Ordeal. Little, 1918
No Clue. Dodd, 1920
That Washington Affair. Dodd, 1926
The Unlighted House. Dodd, 1921
The Winning Clue. Dodd, 1919

HAY, MARIE (M)
The Evil Vineyard. Putnam, 1924

HAY, MAVIS DORIEL (M)
Death on the Cherwell. Skeffington, 1935
Murder Underground. Skeffington, 1934
Santa Klaus Murder. Skeffington, 1936

HAY, WILLIAM LAING (M)
Who Cut the Colonel's Throat? Longmans, 1931

HAYES, JOSEPH ARNOLD (S)
The Deep End. Viking, 1967
The Desperate Hours. Deutsch, 1954; Random, 1954
The Hours After Midnight. Random, 1958; Deutsch, 1959
The Third Day. Allen, W. H., 1964; McGraw, 1964

HAYES, MILTON (M)
Cling of the Clay. Adelphi, 1926; Hodder, 1926

HAYES, RALPH E. (S)
Nurse in Hong Kong. Bouregy, 1967

HAYES, WILLIAM EDWARD (D)
Before the Cock Crowed. Doubleday, Doran, 1937
Black Chronicle. Doubleday, Doran, 1938
The Black Doll. Doubleday, Doran, 1936

HAYLES, KENNETH (M)
The Death Masque. Roy Pubs., 1963
The Purple Sheba. Hale, R., 1959
The Volcano. Hale, R., 1958

HAYNES, ANNIE (M)
The Abbey Court Murder. Lane, 1930
The Crime at Caltenham Corner. Lane, 1930
The Crow's Inn Tragedy. Dodd, 1927; Grosset, 1928
The Crystal Beads Murder. Lane, 1930
The Secret of Greylands. Watt, 1925; Lane, 1931
Who Killed Charmian Karslake? Dodd, 1930

HAYS, HOFFMAN REYNOLDS (S)
Lie Down in Darkness. Reynal, 1944

HAYS, PETER (M) (Pseudonym: Ian Jefferies)
It Wasn't Me. Cape, 1961
Thirteen Days. Cape, 1959

HAYS, MRS. SUE BROWN (D)
Go Down, Death. Scribner, 1946

HAZARD, FORRESTER (D)
The Hex Murder. Lippincott, 1935

HAZARD, LAURENCE (M)
The Andean Murders. Barker, 1960

HAZZARD, MARY (M) (Pseudonym: Olivia Dwight)
Close His Eyes. Harper, 1961

HEAD, ANN, pseud; see MORSE, ANNE CHRISTENSON

HEAD, HELEN SMITH (D)
Death Below Zero. Comet, 1954

HEAD, MATTHEW, pseud; see CANADAY, JOHN EDWIN

HEALEY, BEN (D-M)
The Terrible Pictures. Harper & Row, 1967
Waiting for the Tiger. Harper & Row, 1965, 1967; Lancer, 1966

HEALEY, E. (M)
Let X Equal Murder. Long, 1961

HEALY, EUGENE P. (D)
Craine's First Case. Holt, H., 1938; Hale, R., 1939
Mr. Sandeman Loses His Life. Holt, H., 1940

HEARD, GERALD (Full name: Henry FitzGerald Heard) (M-D)
Black Fox. Harper, 1951
The Great Fog: Weird Tales of Terror and Detection. Vanguard, 1944
Murder by Reflection. Vanguard, 1942
The Notched Hairpin. Vanguard, 1949
Reply Paid. Vanguard, 1942; Lancer, 1964
A Taste for Honey. Vanguard, 1941; Cassell, 1942; Lancer, 1964; PB (Also published as: A Taste for Murder. Avon)
A Taste for Murder; see A Taste for Honey

HEARD, HENRY FITZGERALD; see HEARD, GERALD

HEARN, J. VAN (M)
Don't Betray Me. Belmont, 1962

HEATH, ELIZABETH ALDEN (M)
Affair at Tideways. Crowell, 1932

HEATH, ERIC (D)
Death Takes a Dive. Hillman-Curl, 1938
Murder in the Museum. Hillman-Curl, 1939
Murder of a Mystery Writer. Arcadia, 1955
The Murder Pool. Arcadia, 1954

HEATH, MONICA (S-Gothic)
Dunleary. Signet, 1967
Falconlough. Signet, 1966
Secrets Can Be Fatal. Signet, 1967

HEATH, SHARON (S)
Nurse at Shadow Manor. Ace, 1966

HEATH, WILLIAM L. (M)
Ill Wind. Hamilton, H., 1957
Violent Saturday. Harper, 1955

HEATTER, BASIL (S)
Act of Violence. Lion, 1954
Any Man's Girl. GM, 1961
The Mutilators. GM, 1962

HEBDEN, MARK, pseud. (M)
The Eye Witness. Harcourt, 1966

HEBERDEN, MARY VIOLET (D) (Pseudonym: Charles Leonard)
Aces, Eights, and Murder. Doubleday, Doran, 1941
The Case of the Eight Brothers. Doubleday, 1948
Deadline for Destruction, by Charles Leonard. Doubleday, Doran, 1942
Death on the Doormat. Doubleday, Doran, 1939
Drinks on the Victim. Doubleday, 1948
Engaged to Murder. Doubleday, 1949
Exit This Way. Doubleday, 1950
Expert on Murder, by Charles Leonard. Doubleday, Doran, 1945
Fanatic of Fez, by Charles Leonard. Doubleday, Doran, 1943
The Fourth Funeral, by Charles Leonard. Doubleday, 1947; Museum Press, 1951
Fugitive from Murder. Doubleday, Doran, 1940
Ghosts Can't Kill; see That's the Spirit
The Lobster Pick Murder. Doubleday, Doran, 1941
Murder Cancels All Debts. Doubleday, 1946
Murder Follows Desmond Shannon. Doubleday, Doran, 1942
Murder Goes Astray. Doubleday, Doran, 1943
Murder Makes a Racket. Doubleday, Doran, 1942

Murder of a Stuffed Shirt. Doubleday, Doran, 1944
Murder Unlimited. Doubleday, 1953
Pursuit in Peru. Doubleday, 1946; Museum Press, 1948
Search for a Scientist, by Charles Leonard. Doubleday, 1947; Museum Press, 1950
The Secret of the Spa, by Charles Leonard. Doubleday, 1946
Secrets for Sale, by Charles Leonard. Doubleday, 1950
Sinister Shelter. Doubleday, 1950; Museum Press, 1951
Sleeping Witness. Doubleday, 1951
The Stolen Squadron, by Charles Leonard. Doubleday, Doran, 1942
Subscription to Murder. Doubleday, Doran, 1940
That's the Spirit. Doubleday, 1950 (English title: Ghosts Can't Kill. Clerke, 1951)
They Can't All Be Guilty. Doubleday, 1947
To What Dread End. Doubleday, Doran, 1943
Tragic Target. Doubleday, 1952
Treachery in Trieste, by Charles Leonard. Doubleday, 1951
Vicious Pattern. Doubleday, Doran, 1945

HECHT, BEN (M)
Actors Blood. Covici, 1936
The Florentine Dagger. Boni, 1923; World Pub., 1942
The Hollywood Mystery; see I Hate Actors.
I Hate Actors. Crown, 1944 (Also published as: The Hollywood Mystery. Bart)
The Mystery of the Fabulous Laundryman

HECKSTALL-SMITH, ANTHONY (M)
The Man with Yellow Shoes. Roy Pubs., 1958
Murder on the Brain. Roy Pubs., 1958; Wingate, 1958
Where There Are Vultures. Roy Pubs., 1959

HEDGES, S. G. (D)
The Channel Tunnel Mystery. Jenkins, 1931
The Malta Mystery. Jenkins, 1932
The Weird Boyd Mystery. Jenkins, 1931

HEDLEY, FRANK, pseud; see BARKER, CLARENCE HEDLEY

HEED, RUFUS (M)
Ghosts Never Die. Vantage, 1954

HEFFERNAN, DEAN (M)
Murder at Sunset Gables. Duffield, 1932

HEITNER, IRIS (M) (Pseudonym: Robert James)
Board Stiff. Doubleday, 1955
Death Wears Pink Shoes. Doubleday, 1952

HELD, PETER (M)
Take My Face. Bouregy, 1957

HELLER, FRANK, pseud; see SERNER, GUNNAR

HELLER, LARRY (M)
Body of Crime. Pyramid, 1962
I Get What I Want. Popular Lib., 1956

HELLER, LORENZ (M)
Murder Is Makeup. Messner, 1937

HELLER, MIKE (M)
So I'm a Heel. GM, 1957

HELM, JEANETTE (M)
Without Clues. Boni, 1923

HELM, PETER (D)
Dead Man's Fingers; see Walk into Murder
Death Has a Thousand Entrances. Long, 1962
Walk into Murder. Scribner, 1960 (English title: Dead Man's Fingers. Long, 1960)

HELMORE, THOMAS (M)
The Affair at Quala. Cape, 1965; Tower, 1965; S & S, 1964

HELSETH, HENRY E. (S)
The Brothers Brannigan. Signet, 1961
The Chair for Martin Rome. Dodd, 1947
This Man Dawson. Signet, 1962
Yellow Angels. Harper, 1940

HELVICK, JAMES, pseud; see COCKBURN, CLAUD

HELY, ELIZABETH; see YOUNGER, ELIZABETH HELY

HEMINGWAY, KENNETH (M)
Murder Flight. Quality, 1954

HENDERSON, DONALD LANDEL (D) (Pseudonym: D. H. Landels)
Announcer, by D. H. Landels. Hurst, 1944 (U.S. title: A Voice Like Velvet. Random, 1946)
Mr. Bowling Buys a Newspaper. Random, 1944
Murder at Large. Paul, S., 1936
Procession to Prison. Paul, S., 1936
A Voice Like Velvet; see Announcer

HENDERSON, JAMES LEAL (M) (Pseudonym: Jay L. Currier)
Cargo of Fear. Messner, 1947

HENDERSON, WILLIAM (D)
Clues; or, Leaves from a Chief Constable's Note Book. Oliphant & Co., 1889
Detective Stories. Heywood, 1891

HENDRYX, JAMES B. (M)
Courage of the North. Hammond, 1954
Murder in the Outlands. Doubleday, 1949
Murder on Halfaday Creek. Doubleday, 1951

HENRY, CHARLES, pseud. (S)
Devils Burn Too. Boardman, T. V., 1963
Hostage. Random, 1959

HENRY, JACK (M)
Flannelfoot, Phantom Crook. Hutchinson, 1949
Lucifer and Partner. Nod, 1950

HENRY, O., pseud; see PORTER, WILLIAM SIDNEY

HENRY, VERA (M)
Mystery of Cedar Valley. Bouregy, 1964

HENSHAW, MRS. NANCY ELY (M)
Worse and More of It. Vantage, 1959

HENSLEY, JOE L. (S)
The Color of Hate. Ace, 1958

HEPPELL, MARY (M) (Pseudonym: Marguerite Clare)
Candle in the Night. Wright & Brown, 1963
The Cintra Story. Wright & Brown, 1960
Deadline for Loren. Wright & Brown, 1962
Fear Treads Soft Shod. Wright & Brown, 1956
The Mask of Danger. Wright & Brown, 1952
Pierce the Gloom. Wright & Brown, 1958
Pillar of Fire. Hale, R., 1964
Spin a Dark Web. Wright & Brown, 1961
The Wild Secret. Wright & Brown, 1961

HERBER, WILLIAM (M)
Almost Dead. Lippincott, 1957; Foulsham, 1958
Death Paints a Portrait. Foulsham, 1958; Lippincott, 1958
King-Sized Murder. Lippincott, 1954; Foulsham, 1955
Live Bait for Murder. Lippincott, 1955; Foulsham, 1956

HERING, HENRY A. (M)
The Burglars' Club. Cassell, 1906

HERITAGE, MARTIN, pseud; see HORLER, SIDNEY

HERMAN, LOUIS; see TARG, WILLIAM

HERMAN, WALTER (S)
Operation Intrigue. Avon, 1956

HERNDEN, BERYL; see BALFOUR, EVE

HERNE, HUXLEY, pseud; see BROOKER, BERTRAM

HERRIES, NORMAN (M)
Death Has Two Faces. Ace, 1955
My Private Hanging. Ace, 1956

HERRING, PAUL (D)
Midnight Murder. Lippincott, 1932
Sir Toby and the Regent. Lippincott, 1929

HERRINGTON, LEE (D)
Carry My Coffin Slowly. S & S, 1951

HERSHATTER, RICHARD L. (S)
The Spy Who Hated Licorice. Signet, 1966

HERSHMAN, MORRIS (M-S)
Guilty Witness. Belmont, 1964
Target for Terror. Belmont, 1967

HERVEY, HARRY (M)
The Black Parrot. Century, 1923
Caravans at Night. Century, 1922

HERVEY, MAURICE A. (M)
Dead Man's Court. Mellifont, 1936

HESKY, OLGA (S)
The Serpent's Smile. Dodd, 1967
Time for Treason. Doubleday, 1968

HEWENS, FRANK E. (M)
The Murder of the Dainty-Footed Model. Macmillan, 1968

HEWETT, JOAN (S)
Women Are Dynamite. Jenkins, 1951

HEWITT, KATHLEEN DOUGLAS (M) (Pseudonym: Dorothea Martin)
The Mice Are Not Amused. Jarrolds, 1943

HEWLETT, WILLIAM (M)
The Crimson Claw. Allan, P., 1936

HEXT, HARRINGTON, pseud; see PHILLPOTTS, EDEN

HEYER, GEORGETTE (D-M) (Pseudonym: Stella Martin)
Behold, Here's Poison. Doubleday, Doran, 1936; Hodder, 1936
A Blunt Instrument. Doubleday, Doran, 1938; Heinemann, 1938; Bantam, 1966
Death in the Stocks; see Merely Murder
Detection Unlimited. Heinemann, 1952
Devil's Cub. Heinemann, 1932
Duplicate Death. Heinemann, 1951
Envious Casca. Doubleday, Doran, 1941; Heinemann, 1941
Footsteps in the Dark. Longmans, 1932
Merely Murder. Doubleday, Doran, 1935 (English title: Death in the Stocks. Longmans, 1935)
No Wind of Blame. Doubleday, Doran, 1939; Hodder, 1939
Penhallow. Doubleday, Doran, 1943
Pistols for Two. Dutton, 1964
Powder and Patch. Heinemann, 1923
Simon the Coldheard. Heinemann, 1925
These Old Shades. Heinemann, 1926; Small, 1926
They Found Him Dead. Doubleday, Doran, 1937; Hodder, 1937; Sun Dial, 1938
The Transformation of Philip Jettan, by Stella Martin. Mills & Boon, 1923
The Unfinished Clue. Longmans, 1934; Doubleday, Doran, 1937
Why Shoot a Butler? Longmans, 1933; Doubleday, Doran, 1936

HEYES, DOUGLAS (M)
The Kiss-off. S & S, 1951
The Twelfth of Never. Random, 1963; Boardman, T. V., 1964

HEYMAN, EVAN LEE (M)
Cain's Hundred. Popular Lib., 1961
Dead Heat on a Merry-Go-Round. Avon, 1966 (Original story and screenplay by Bernard Girard)
Miami Undercover. Popular Lib., 1961

HEYWARD, DOROTHY HARTZELL (D)
The Pulitzer Prize Murders. Farrar & Rinehart, 1932

HIBBERT, ELEANOR BURFORD (S) (Pseudonyms: Elbur Ford, Victoria Holt, Kathleen Kellow)
Bed Disturbed, by Elbur Ford. Laurie, 1952
Bitter Business, by Elbur Ford. Heinemann, 1953 (U.S. title: Evil in the House. Morrow, 1954)
Bride of Pendorric, by Victoria Holt. Doubleday, 1963; Crest, 1964
Danse Macabre, by Kathleen Kellow. Hale, R., 1952
Evil in the House; see Bitter Business
Flesh and the Devil, by Elbur Ford. Laurie, 1950
The King of the Castle, by Victoria Holt. Doubleday, 1967
Kirkland Revels, by Victoria Holt. Doubleday, 1962; Crest, 1963
The Legend of the Seventh Virgin, by Victoria Holt. Doubleday, 1965; Crest, 1966
Menfreya in the Morning, by Victoria Holt. Doubleday, 1966; Crest, 1967
Mistress of Mellyn, by Victoria Holt. Doubleday, 1960; Crest, 1963
Poison in Pimlico, by Elbur Ford. Laurie, 1950

HICHENS, ROBERT SMYTHE (M)
The Paradine Case. Benn, 1933; Doubleday, Doran, 1933; Penguin, 1938; Convoy, 1948

HICKOK, FRANCES (M)
An Eye for an Eye. Hale, 1929; Paul, S., 1930

HIGGINSON, HAROLD WYNYARD (M)
Murder by the Arch. Crowell, 1931

HIGHET, MRS. HELEN MacINNES; see MacINNES, HELEN

HIGHSMITH, PATRICIA (D)
The Blunderer. Coward, 1954
The Cry of the Owl. Harper, 1952
Deep Water. Harper, 1957; Bantam, 1967 (English title: Mask of Innocence. Heinemann, 1958)
A Game for the Living. Harper, 1958; Heinemann, 1959
The Glass Cell. Doubleday, 1964; Heinemann, 1965; Macfadden, 1968
Mask of Innocence; see Deep Water
The Story-Teller. Doubleday, 1965
Strangers on a Train. Harper, 1949
The Talented Mr. Ripley. Coward, 1955; Longmans, 1955; Dell
This Sweet Sickness. Harper, 1960; Heinemann, 1960
Those Who Walk Away. Doubleday, 1967; Macfadden, 1968
The Two Faces of January. Doubleday, 1964; Heinemann, 1964

HILL, AMY HOSKIN (M)
Murder on the Mountain. Arcadia, 1961

HILL, BRIAN (D) (Pseudonym: Marcus Magill)
Death-in-the-Box. Lippincott, 1930
Hide and I'll Find You! Hutchinson, 1933
I Like a Good Murder. Lippincott, 1930; Hutchinson, 1933
Murder in Full Flight. Hutchinson, 1932; Lippincott, 1933

Murder Out of Tune. Hutchinson, 1931; Lippincott, 1931
Who Shall Hang? Knopf, 1929; Lippincott, 1929

HILL, FREDERICK TREVOR (M)
The Accomplice. Harper, 1905

HILL, H. HAVERSTOCK, pseud; see WALSH, JAMES MORGAN

HILL, HEADON, pseud; see GRAINGER, FRANCIS EDWARD

HILL, J. (D)
Dope Ring. Methuen, 1931

HILL, KATE F., pseud. (M)
The Mysterious Case; or, Tracing a Crime. Ward, Lock, 1890

HILL, KATHERINE (D)
A Case for Equity. Dutton, 1945
Dear Dead Mother-in-Law. Dutton, 1944

HILL, LAURENCE (M)
The Corpse Without Boots. Collins, 1940
Dagger Drawn. Collins, 1939

HILL, NEWTON (M)
The Body Drank Coffee. Hale, R., 1951

HILL, SAM (S)
The Nodding Towers. Vantage, 1966

HILL, VINCENT (M)
Amber to Red. Hodder, 1952
Cunning Enemy. Hodder, 1957
The Lady from Hamburg. Hodder, 1954
Soft Guy. Hodder, 1953

HILL, W. (M)
The Crystal Skull. Jarrolds, 1930

HILL, WELDON, pseud. (S)
A Man Could Get Killed That Way. McKay, 1967

HILLGARTH, ALAN HUGH (M)
What Price Paradise? Lippincott, 1929

HILLIARD, ALEC ROWLEY (M)
Justice Be Damned. Farrar & Rinehart, 1941
Outlaw Island. Farrar & Rinehart, 1942

HILLIARD, JAN, pseud; see GRANT, HILDA KAY

HILTON, JAMES (M) (Pseudonym: Glen Trevor)
Was It Murder? Harper, 1933; Bantam, 1946 (English title: Murder at School. Benn, 1931)

HIMES, CHESTER (D)
All Shot Up. Berkley Pub., 1966
The Big Gold Dream. Avon, 1960; Berkley Pub., 1966
Cotton Comes to Harlem. Putnam, 1964; Muller, 1965; Dell, 1966
The Crazy Kill. Avon, 1959; Berkley Pub., 1966
The Heat's On. Muller, 1966; Putnam, 1966; Dell, 1967
The Real Cool Killers. Avon, 1959; Berkley Pub., 1966
Run, Man, Run. Putnam, 1966; Dell, 1967

HIMMEL, RICHARD (D)
The Chinese Keyhole. GM
The Cry of the Flesh. GM, 1955
I Have Gloria Kirby. GM
It's Murder, Maguire. Jenkins, 1963
The Name's Maguire. Jenkins, 1963
The Rich and the Damned. GM, 1958

HINDE, THOMAS, pseud; see CHITTY, SIR THOMAS W.

HINDS, ROY W. (D)
The Treasure of Caricar. Long, 1930
Tunnel to Doom. Chelsea House, 1927

HIRAI, TARŌ (M) (Pseudonym: Edogawa Rampo)
Japanese Tales of Mystery and Imagination. Tuttle, 1956

HIRD, F. (M)
The Bannantyne Sapphire. Paul, S., 1930
Clipped Hedges. Paul, S., 1932

HIRSCH, LEE, pseud; see HIRSCH, LEON DAVID

HIRSCH, LEON DAVID (M) (Pseudonym: Lee Hirsch)
Murder Steals the Show. Fell, 1946

HIRSCHBERG, CORNELIUS (M)
Florentine Finish. Harper & Row, 1963; Avon, 1964; Gollancz, 1964

HISCOCK, LESLIE (S) (Pseudonym: Patrick Marsh)
Breakdown. Longmans, 1952

HISCOCK, ROBIN (M)
The Killer Wind. Barker, 1958
Last Run South. Longmans, 1956; Knopf, 1958
Send-off. Heinemann, 1957

HITCHENS, BERT; see HITCHENS, DOLORES BIRK OLSEN

HITCHENS, DOLORES BIRK OLSEN (D-S) (Pseudonyms: Dolan Birkley, Noel Burke, D. B. Olsen)

The Abductor. Boardman, T. V., 1962; S & S, 1962; Popular Lib., 1963
The Alarm of the Black Cat, by D. B. Olsen. Doubleday, Doran, 1942
The Bank with the Bamboo Door. S & S, 1965; Lancer, 1966
Beat Back the Tide. Doubleday, 1954
The Blue Geranium, by Dolan Birkley. Musson, 1941; S & S, 1941
Bring the Bride a Shroud, by D. B. Olsen. Doubleday, Doran, 1945
Cat and Capricorn, by D. B. Olsen. Doubleday, 1951
The Cat Saw Murder, by D. B. Olsen. Doubleday, Doran, 1939
The Cat Walks, by D. B. Olsen. Doubleday, 1953
The Cat Wears a Mask, by D. B. Olsen. Doubleday, 1949
The Cat Wears a Noose, by D. B. Olsen. Doubleday, Doran, 1944
The Cat's Claw, by D. B. Olsen. Doubleday, Doran, 1943
Cats Don't Need Coffins, by D. B. Olsen. Doubleday, 1946
Cats Don't Smile, by D. B. Olsen. Doubleday, Doran, 1945
Cats Have Tall Shadows, by D. B. Olsen. Ziff-Davis, 1948
Clue in the Clay, by D. B. Olsen. Phoenix, 1938
Death Cuts a Silhouette, by D. B. Olsen. Doubleday, Doran, 1939
Death Walks on Cat Feet, by D. B. Olsen. Doubleday, 1956; Popular Lib., 1966
Devious Design, by D. B. Olsen. Doubleday, 1948
The End of the Line, with Bert Hitchens. Doubleday, 1957; Boardman, T. V., 1958
Enrollment Cancelled, by D. B. Olsen. Doubleday, 1952
F.O.B. Murder, with Bert Hitchens. Doubleday, 1955; Boardman, T. V., 1957
Fool's Gold. Doubleday, 1958
Footsteps in the Night. Boardman, T. V., 1961; Doubleday, 1961; Permabooks, 1962
Gallows for the Groom, by D. B. Olsen. Doubleday, 1947
The Grudge, with Bert Hitchens. Boardman, T. V., 1963; Doubleday, 1963; Popular Lib., 1965
Love Me in Death, by D. B. Olsen. Doubleday, 1951
The Man Who Cried All the Way Home. S & S, 1946
The Man Who Followed Women, with Bert Hitchens. Doubleday, 1959; Boardman, T. V., 1960; PB, 1961
Nets to Catch the Wind. Doubleday, 1952
One Way Ticket, with Bert Hitchens. Doubleday, 1956; Boardman, T. V., 1958
Postscript to Nightmare. Putnam, 1967
The Shivering Bough, by Noel Burke. Dutton, 1942
Sleep with Slander. Doubleday, 1960; Boardman, T. V., 1961
Sleep with Strangers. Doubleday, 1955; Berkley Pub., 1968
Something About Midnight. Doubleday, 1950
Stairway to an Empty Room. Doubleday, 1951; Popular Lib., 1965
Terror Lurks in Darkness. Doubleday, 1953
The Ticking Hearty, by D. B. Olsen. Doubleday, 1953
The Unloved, by Dolan Birkley. Doubleday, 1965; Hale, R., 1967
The Watcher. Doubleday, 1959; Permabooks, 1961
Widows Ought to Weep, by D. B. Olsen. Ziff-Davis, 1947

HITCHENS, HUBERT (BERT); see HITCHENS, DOLORES BIRK OLSEN

HITCHENS, ROBERT S. (M)
The Paradine Case. Doubleday, Doran, 1933

HITTLEMAN, CARL K. (S)
Thirty-Six Hours. Popular Lib., 1965

HIVELY, MILDRED ENGLISH (M)
The Moday Mystery. Vantage, 1966

HOARE, DOUGLAS and PERCY COLSON (M)
Murder to Music. Gifford, 1945

HOBART, DONALD BAYNE (D)
The Cell Murder Mystery. Fiction League, 1931
Double Shuffle. Clode, 1928
Homicide Honeymoon. Arcadia, 1959

HOBART, ROBERTSON, pseud; see LEE, NORMAN

HOBBS, ROE RAYMOND (M)
Gates of Flame. Neale, 1908

HOBHOUSE, DANNY (D)
The Hangover Murders. Knopf, 1935

HOBSON, FRANCIS (D)
Death on a Back Bench. Eyre, 1959; Harper, 1959; Doubleday, 1963

HOBSON, HANK (D) (Pseudonym: Hank Janson)
The Big Twist. Cassell, 1959
Death Makes a Claim. Cassell, 1958
The Gallant Affair. Cassell, 1957
The Mission House Murder. Cassell, 1957; British Book Centre, 1959

HOBSON, POLLY, pseud; see EVANS, JULIA RENDEL

HOCKABY, STEPHEN, pseud; see MITCHELL, GLADYS

HOCKING, ANNE, pseud; see MESSER, MRS. MONA NAOMI ANNE

HOCKING, MARY (S)
Ask No Questions. Morrow, 1967

HODDER, ALFRED (M) (Pseudonym: Francis Walton)
A Woman. Farrar & Rinehart, 1931

HODDER-WILLIAMS, CHRISTOPHER (M) (Pseudonym: James Brogan)
Chain Reaction. Doubleday, 1959
The Cummings Report, by James Brogan. Hodder, 1958
Final Approach. Doubleday, 1960
The Main Experiment. Hodder, 1964; Ballantine, 1966
Turbulence. Hodder, 1961

HODEMART, PETER, pseud; see AUDEMARS, PIERRE

HODGE, JANE AIKEN (S)
Here Comes the Candle. Doubleday, 1967
Maulever Hall. Doubleday, 1964; Pyramid, 1965
Watch the Wall, My Darling. Doubleday, 1966

HODGES, A. NOEL (D)
Bancaster Mystery. Eyre, 1932

HODGES, ARTHUR (M)
Along the Road. Butterworth, T., 1936
The Body in the Car. Butterworth, T., 1932
Embassy Murder. Butterworth, T., 1931
Glittering Hour. Hurst, 1933
Man of Substance. Hurst, 1931

HODGES, CARL G. (D)
Crime on My Hands. Phantom Books, 1953
Murder by the Pack. Ace, 1953
Naked Villainy. Suspense Books, 1951

HODGIN, M. R. (D)
Dead Indeed. Macmillan, 1956
Student Body. Scribner, 1949

HODGSON, WILLIAM HOPE (M)
Captain Gault. McBride, 1918
Carnacke, the Ghost Finder. Mycroft & Moran, 1913; Arkham, 1948
Deep Waters. Arkham, 1967

HOFFENBERG, JACK (S)
A Thunder at Dawn. Avon, 1965

HOFFMAN, E. T. A. (M)
Eight Tales of Hoffman. Bodley Head, 1951 (Edited and translated by John Michael Cohen)
Weird Tales. Scribner, 1923

HOFFMAN, LEE (M)
Bred to Kill. Ballantine, 1967

HOFFMAN, RICHARD (M)
The Prodigal Duke. Farrar & Rinehart, 1933

HOGARTH, CHARLES, pseud; see CREASEY, JOHN

HOGARTH, EMMETT, pseud; see WILLSON, MITCHELL A.

HOGARTH, GRACE ALLEN; see NORTON, ALICE MARY

HOGG, DANIEL (M)
Murder at the Microphone. Quality, 1949

HOGUE, WILBUR OWINGS (Pseudonym: Carl Shannon)
Fatal Footsteps. Boardman, T. V., 1951
Lady, That's My Skull. Boardman, T. V., 1948
Murder Me Never. Boardman, T. V., 1951

HOLBROOK, MARION (M)
Crime Wind. Dodd, 1945
Suitable for Framing. Dodd, 1941
Wanted: a Murderess. Dodd, 1943

HOLDAWAY, NEVILLE ALDRIDGE (D) (Pseudonym: N. A. Temple-Ellis)
Death of a Decent Fellow. Hodder, 1941
A Case in Hand. Hodder, 1933
The Cauldron Bubbles. Methuen, 1930
Dead in No Time. Hodder, 1935
Hollow Land. Hodder, 1934
The Inconsistent Villains. Dutton, 1929; Methuen, 1929
The Man Who Was There. Dutton, 1930; Methuen, 1930
Murder in the Ruins. Dial, 1936
Quest. Methuen, 1931
Six Lines. Hodder, 1932
Three Went In. Hodder, 1934

HOLDEN, GENEVIEVE, pseud; see POU, GENEVIEVE LONG

HOLDEN, J. RAILTON (M)
Death Flies High. Newnes, 1935

HOLDEN, JOANNE (S-Gothic)
Dangerous Legacy. Lancer, 1967
Nurse at the Castle. Lancer, 1965

HOLDEN, LARRY, pseud; see LORENZ, FREDERICK

HOLDEN, RAYMOND P. (D)
Death on the Border. Holt, H., 1937
Murder in Strange Houses. Minton, 1929
The Penthouse Murders. Doubleday, Doran, 1931

HOLDER, W. GRAEME-; see GRAEME-HOLDER, W.

HOLDER, WILLIAM (D)
The Case of the Dead Divorcee. Signet, 1958

HOLDING, ELIZABETH SANXAY (D)
The Blank Wall. S & S, 1947; Ace, 1962 (with The Girl Who Had to Die)
Dark Power. Vanguard, 1930
The Death Wish. Dodd, 1934
The Girl Who Had to Die. Dodd, 1940; Ace, 1962 (with The Blank Wall)
The Innocent Mrs. Duff. S & S, 1946; Ace, 1962 (with The Virgin Huntress)
Kill Joy. Collins, 1942; Duell, 1942; Ace, 1964 (with Speak of the Devil)
Lady Killer. Duell, 1942; Ace, 1964
Miasma. Dutton, 1929
Net of Cobwebs. S & S, 1945; Ace, 1963 (with The Unfinished Crime)
The Obstinate Murderer. Dodd, 1938; Ace, 1963 (with The Old Battle Axe)
The Old Battle Axe. Doubleday, Doran, 1943; Ace, 1963 (with The Obstinate Murderer)
Speak of the Devil. Duell, 1941; Ace, 1964 (with Kill Joy)
The Strange Crime in Bermuda. Dodd, 1937
Too Many Battles. S & S, 1951
The Unfinished Crime. Dodd, 1935; Ace, 1963 (with Net of Cobwebs)
The Virgin Huntress. S & S, 1951; Ace, 1962 (with The Innocent Mrs. Duff)
Who's Afraid? Duell, 1940; Ace, 1963 (with Widow's Mite)
Widow's Mite. S & S, 1953; Ace, 1963 (with Who's Afraid. Serial title: I'll Never Leave You)

HOLLAND, MARTY (S)
Fallen Angel. Dutton, 1945
Glass Heart. Messner, 1946

HOLLAND, R. S. (M)
Mystery of the Opal. Macrae Smith, 1924
Peter Cotterell's Treasure. Lippincott, 1922

HOLLINGWORTH, LEONARD (D)
Body on the Bus. Murray, 1930
Dead Man's Alibi. Murray, J., 1933
Death Leaves Us Naked. Murray, J., 1931

HOLLIS, JIM, pseud; see SUMMERS, HOLLIS SPURGEON

HOLLOWAY, ELIZABETH HUGHES (M)
Cobweb House. Dutton, 1931

HOLLY, J. HUNTER, pseud; see HOLLY, JOAN CAROL

HOLLY, JOAN CAROL (S) (Pseudonym: J. Hunter Holly)
The Assasination Affair. Ace, 1967 (The Man from U.N.C.L.E. series, #10)
Encounter. Bouregy, 1959
The Running Man. Monarch, 1963

HOLMAN, HUGH (M)
Another Man's Poison. Mill, 1947
Death Like Thunder. Phoenix, 1942
Slay the Murderer. Mill, 1946
Trout in the Milk, Mill, 1945
Up This Crooked Way. Mill, 1946

HOLMES, DARRELL FORSYTHE, JR. (M)
Implied Immunity. Vantage, 1963

HOLMES, DAVID CHARLES (M)
The Velvet Ape. Bouregy, 1957

HOLMES, GORDON, pseud; see TRACY, LOUIS

HOLMES, GRANT, pseud; see KNIP-SCHEER, JAMES M.

HOLMES, H. H., pseud; see BOUCHER, ANTHONY

HOLMES, PAUL A. (M)
Murders Buttoned Up. Dutton, 1948

HOLMES, RICK (M)
Child Woman. Monarch, 1966

HOLMGREN, FLORENCE DEPPE (M)
The Mystery of Bent Cove. Bouregy, 1966

HOLT, ALLISON (M)
Bier for a Hussy. Phoenix, 1943

HOLT, BARRY (M)
The Mowbray Mystery. Stockwell, 1933

HOLT, DEBEN (M)
Circle of Shadows. Gifford, 1957
Sinner Takes All. Gifford, 1958

HOLT, E. CARLETON, pseud; see GUIGO, ERNEST PHILIP

HOLT, GAVIN, pseud; see RODDA, CHARLES

HOLT, HARRISON JEWELL (D)
Midnight at Mears House. Simpkin, 1916

HOLT, HENRY (D) (Pseudonym: Stanley Hopkins)
The Ace of Spades. Dial, 1930; Harrap, 1930
Call Out the Flying Squad; see Gallows Grange
Calling All Cars. Collins, 1934 (U.S. title: The Sinister Shadow. Doubleday, Doran, 1934)
Calling Scotland Yard. Hale, R., 1944
Don't Shoot, Darling. Hale, R., 1961; Roy Pubs., 1963
The Flying Squad. Doubleday, Doran, 1933
Gallows Grange. Harrap, 1933 (U.S. title: Call Out the Flying Squad. Doubleday, Doran, 1933)
The Man Who Forgot. Hale, R., 1943
The Mayfair Murder; see The Mayfair Mystery
The Mayfair Mystery. Harrap, 1929 (U.S. title: The Mayfair Murder. Dial, 1929)
The Midnight Mail. Doubleday, Doran, 1931; Harrap, 1931
Minks and Murder. Hale, R., 1958
Motley and Murder. Hale, R., 1945
Murder at the Bookstall. Collins, 1934
Murder by Inches, by Stanley Hopkins. Harcourt, 1943
Murder, My Sweet. Museum Press, 1950
Murder of a Film Star. Collins, 1940
Murderer's Luck. Doubleday, Doran, 1932; Harrap, 1932
Mystery of the Smiling Doll, by Stanley Hopkins. Collins, 1939
The Necklace of Death. Doubleday, Doran, 1931; Harrap, 1931
No Lilies. Hale, R., 1947
No Medals for Murder. Museum Press, 1954
The Parchment Key, by Stanley Hopkins. Harcourt, 1944
The Scarlet Messenger. Collins, 1933; Doubleday, Doran, 1933
The Sinister Shadow; see Calling All Cars
There Has Been A Murder. Collins, 1936
The Tiger of Mayfair. Collins, 1935; Mellifont, 1948
The Unknown Terror. Collins, 1935
The Vultures. Bles, 1945
Wanted for Murder. Collins, 1938
The Whispering Man. Collins, 1938; Mellifont, 1955
The Wolf; see The Wolf's Claw
The Wolf's Claw. Harrap, 1932 (U.S. title: The Wolf. Doubleday, Doran, 1932)
Wreath for a Lady. Hale, R., 1959

HOLT, VICTORIA, pseud; see HIBBERT, ELEANOR BURFORD

HOLTON, LEONARD, pseud; see WIBBERLY, LEONARD

HOME, GEOFFREY, pseud; see MAINWARING, DANIEL

HOME, MICHAEL, pseud; see BUSH, CHRISTOPHER

HOMERSHAM, BASIL HENRY (M) (Pseudonym: Basil Manningham)
Arsenic on the Menu. Paul, S., 1936
Motive for Murder, by Basil Manningham. Hale, R., 1939
Murder of an M.P. Paul, S., 1935

HOOD, MARGARET PAGE (D)
The Bell on Lonely. Coward, 1959
Drown the Wind. Coward, 1961
In the Dark Night. Coward, 1957; Longmans, 1957 (Also published as: The Murders on Fox Island. Dell, 1960)
The Murders on Fox Island; see In the Dark Night
The Scarlet Thread. Coward, 1956
Silent Women. Coward, 1953
The Sin Mark. Coward, 1963; Longmans, 1963
Tequila. Coward, 1952; Melrose, 1952

HOOKE, CHARLES W. (D) (Pseudonym: Howard Fielding)
Hidden Out. Chelsea House, 1927
Straight Crooks. Chelsea House, 1927

HOOKE, NINA WARNER (M)
Deadly Record. Hale, R., 1958

HOPE, ANDRÉE, pseud; see HARVEY, ANNIE JANE

HOPE, ANTHONY, pseud; see HAWKINS, SIR ANTHONY HOPE

HOPE, BRIAN, pseud; see CREASEY, JOHN

HOPE, COLIN (M)
Death in the Fens. Hamilton, 1935
A Ghost from the Past. Fiction House, 1938
The Horne Grange Mystery. Mellifont, 1935

The Mystery at Crowstone. Hamilton, 1936
The Phantom Killer. Fiction House, 1935

HOPE, ESSEX (M) (Pseudonym: Essex Smith)
The Wye Valley Mystery. Hutchinson, 1929

HOPE, FIELDING (M)
Marie Arnaud, Spy. Belmont, 1964
The Mystery of the House of Commons. Dial, 1930; Selwyn, 1930

HOPKINS, A. T., pseud; see TURNGREN, ANNETTE

HOPKINS, LINTON C. (M)
The Candle. Joseph, M., 1936

HOPKINS, KENNETH (D)
Body Blow. Holt, 1962; MacDonald & Co., 1962
Campus Corpse. MacDonald & Co., 1963
Dead Against My Principles. MacDonald & Co., 1960; Holt, 1963
The Forty-first Passenger. MacDonald & Co., 1958
The Girl Who Died. MacDonald & Co., 1955
Pierce with a Pin. Holt, 1961; MacDonald & Co., 1961
She Died Because. MacDonald & Co., 1957; Holt, 1964

HOPKINS, NEVIL MONROE (D)
The Racoon Lake Mystery. Lippincott, 1917
The Strange Cases of Mason Brant. Lippincott, 1916

HOPKINS, STANLEY, pseud; see HOLT, HENRY

HOPLEY, GEORGE, pseud; see HOPLEY-WOOLRICH, CORNELL GEORGE

HOPLEY-WOOLRICH, CORNELL GEORGE (Pseudonyms: George Hopley, William Irish, Cornell Woolrich)
After Dinner Story, by William Irish. Lippincott, 1943; Hutchinson, 1947 (Also published as: Six Times Death. Popular Lib., 1948)
And So to Death; see I Wouldn't Be in Your Shoes
The Best of William Irish. Lippincott, 1960
Beyond the Night, by Cornell Woolrich. Avon, 1959
Black Alibi, by Cornell Woolrich. S & S, 1942; Collier, 1965
The Black Angel, by Cornell Woolrich. Doubleday, Doran, 1943
The Black Curtain, by Cornell Woolrich. S & S, 1941; Collier, 1963
The Black Path of Fear, by Cornell Woolrich. Doubleday, Doran, 1944
The Blue Ribbon, by William Irish. Lippincott, 1949 (Also published as: Dilemma of the Dead Lady. Graphic, 1950)
Borrowed Crime and Other Stories, by William Irish. Avon, 1946
The Bride Wore Black, by Cornell Woolrich. S & S, 1940; Grosset, 1942; PB, 1944; Collier, 1964
A Collection of Short Stories, by Cornell Woolrich. Boardman, T. V., 1966
The Dancing Detective, by William Irish. Lippincott, 1946; Popular Lib., 1951 (Title story in Haycraft's and Beecroft's Ten Great Mysteries. Doubleday, 1959)
The Dark Side of Love, by Cornell Woolrich. Walker & Co., 1965
Dead Man Blues, by William Irish. Lippincott, 1947
Deadline at Dawn, by William Irish. Lippincott, 1944
Deadly Night Call; see Somebody on the Phone
Death Is My Dancing Partner, by Cornell Woolrich. Pyramid, 1959
Dilemma of the Dead Lady; see The Blue Ribbon
The Doom Stone, by Cornell Woolrich. Avon, 1961
Eyes That Watch You, by William Irish. Rinehart, 1952
Fright, by George Hopley. Rinehart, 1950
I Married a Dead Man, by William Irish. Lippincott, 1948
I Wouldn't Be in Your Shoes, by William Irish. Lippincott, 1943 (Also published as: And So to Death. Jonathan Press, 1947)
If I Should Die Before I Wake, by William Irish. Avon, 1945
The Night Has a Thousand Eyes, by George Hopley. Farrar & Rinehart, 1945; Paperback Lib., 1967
Night I Died; see Somebody on the Phone
Nightmare, by Cornell Woolrich. Dodd, 1938; Dell, 1964
The Phantom Lady, by William Irish. Lippincott, 1942
Rendezvous in Black, by Cornell Woolrich. Rinehart, 1948; Ace, 1968
Savage Bride, by Cornell Woolrich. Fawcett, 1950
Six Nights of Mystery. Popular Lib., 1950
Six Times Death; see After Dinner Story
Somebody on the Phone: A Book of Short Stories, by William Irish. Lippincott, 1950 (Also published as: Deadly Night

Call. PB. English title: Night I Died. Hutchinson, 1951)
Strangler's Serenade, by William Irish. Rinehart, 1951
The Ten Faces of Cornell Woolrich. S & S, 1965
Violence, by Cornell Woolrich. Dodd, 1958
Waltz into Darkness, by William Irish. Lippincott, 1947

HOPWOOD, AVERY; see RINEHART, MARY ROBERTS

HORLER, SIDNEY (M-D) (Pseudonym: Martin Heritage)
Adventure Calling. Hodder, 1931
The Ball of Fortune. Collins, 1938
The Beacon Light. Jenkins, 1949
Beauty and the Policeman and Other Stories. Hutchinson, 1933
The Black Heart. Hodder, 1927
Black Souls. Jarrolds, 1931
The Blade Is Bright. Eyre, 1952
The Blanco Case. Quality, 1950; Transworld, 1953
Breed of the Beverleys. Odhams, 1921; Aldine, 1925; Allied Newspapers, 1937
A Bullet for the Countess. Quality, 1945; Brown, Watson, 1950
The Cage. Hale, R., 1953
Cavalier of Chance. Hodder, 1931
The Charlatan; see Formula
Checkmate. Hodder, 1930
Chipstead of the Lone Hand. Hodder, 1928; Nelson, 1947
The Closed Door. Pilot, 1948
Corridors of Fear. Quality, 1947; Brown, Watson, 1950
The Curse of Doone. Hodder, 1928; Mystery League, 1930; Paperback Lib., 1966
Danger Preferred. Hodder, 1942
Danger's Bright Eyes. Hodder, 1930; Nelson, 1948
Dark Danger. Arcadia, 1945
The Dark Hostess. Eyre, 1955
Dark Journey. Hodder, 1938
The Dark Night. Hodder, 1953
Death at Court Lady. Collins, 1936; Eyre, 1955
Death of a Spy. Museum Press, 1953
The Destroyer. Hodder, 1938
The Devil and the Deep. Crowther, 1946
Devil Comes to Bolobyn. Marshall, P., 1951
Doctor Cupid. Jenkins, 1941
Dying to Live and Other Stories. Hutchinson, 1935
The Enemy Within the Gates. Hodder, 1940, 1953
Enter the Ace. Hodder, 1941
The Evil Chateau. Hodder, 1930; Knopf, 1931
The Evil Messenger. Hodder, 1938, 1949
Exit the Disguiser. Hodder, 1948, 1954
The Exploits of Peter. Collins, 1930
The Face of Stone. Barker, 1952
False Face. Doran, 1926; Hodder, 1926; Nelson, 1948
False Purple. Mystery League, 1932
Fear Walked Behind. Hale, R., 1942
The Fellow Hagan! Cassell, 1927
Formula. Long, 1933 (U.S. title: The Charlatan. Little, 1934)
Gentleman for the Gallows. Hillman-Curl, 1938; Hodder, 1938
Gentleman-in-Waiting. Benn, 1932
Great Adventure and Out of a Dark Sky. Hale, R., 1946
The Grim Game. Little, 1935; Collins, 1936; Withy Grove, 1942; Eyre, 1948
Haloes for Hire. Jenkins, 1949
Harlequin for Death. Little, 1933; Long, 1933
Heart Cut Diamond. Hodder, 1938
Hell's Brew. Hodder, 1952
Here Is an SOS. Hodder, 1939, 1942
The Hidden Hand. Collins, 1937; Eyre, 1955
The High Game. Redman, 1950
High Hazard. Hodder, 1943
High Pressure. Jenkins, 1946
High Stakes. Collins, 1932; Little, 1935
Horror's Head. Hodder, 1932
The Hostage. Quality, 1943
Hour with Light. Hodder, 1948
House Divided; see The House of Wingate
The House in Greek Street. Hodder, 1935
The House of Jackals. Hodder, 1951
The House of Secrets. Hodder, 1926, 1938; Doran, 1927; Nelson, 1947
The House of the Uneasy Dead. Barker, 1950
The House of Wingate, by Martin Heritage. Hurst, 1928 (U.S. title: House Divided. Macaulay, 1929)
The House with the Light. Hodder, 1948
The Huntress of Death. Hodder, 1933
In the Dark. Hodder, 1927
Instruments of Darkness. Hodder, 1937
Knaves and Company. Collins, 1938
Knight at Arms. Crowther, 1946
Lady of the Night. Hodder, 1929; Knopf, 1930; Crowther, 1946
The Lady with a Limp. Hodder, 1944
The Lessing Murder Case. Collins, 1935; Crowther, 1945
Life for Sale. Doubleday, Doran, 1928
The Lord of Terror. Collins, 1935; Hillman-Curl, 1937
Love, the Sportsman. Hodder, 1923 (Also published as: The Man with Two Faces. Collins, 1934; Mellifont, 1951)
Man Alive. Jenkins, 1948
The Man from Scotland Yard. Hutchinson, 1934

The Man in the Cloak. Eyre, 1951
The Man in the Hood. Redman, 1955
The Man in the Shadows. Hale, R., 1955
The Man in White. Staples, 1942
A Man of Affairs. Pilot, 1949
A Man of Evil. Barker, 1951
The Man Who Did Not Hang. Quality, 1948; Transworld, 1953
The Man Who Died Twice. Hodder, 1939; Musson, 1959
The Man Who Loved Spiders. Barker, 1949
The Man Who Preferred Cocktails. Crowther, 1943
The Man Who Saved the Club. Aldine, 1926
The Man Who Used Perfume. Hodder, 1941; Wingate, 1952
The Man Who Walked with Death. Knopf, 1931; Hodder, 1941
The Man with Dry Hands. Eyre, 1944
The Man with Three Wives. Jenkins, 1947
The Man with Two Faces; see Love, the Sportsman
The Master of Venom. Hodder, 1949
The Menace. Collins, 1933; Little, 1933
Miss Mystery. Hodder, 1928; Little, 1935
The Mocking Face of Murder. Hale, R., 1952
Murder for Sale. Vallancey, 1945
Murder Is So Simple. Eyre, 1943; Transworld, 1954
The Murder Mask. Readers' Lib., 1930; Chevron, 1938
Murderer at Large. Hodder, 1952
My Lady Dangerous. Collins, 1932; Harper, 1933
The Mystery Mission. Hodder, 1931
The Mystery of Mr. X. Foulsham, 1951
The Mystery of Number One. Hodder, 1925
The Mystery of the Seven Cafes. Hodder, 1935; Crowther, 1944
Nap On, Nighthawk. Hodder, 1950
Night of Reckoning. Eyre, 1942
Nighthawk Mops Up. Hodder, 1944
Nighthawk Strikes to Kill. Hodder, 1941
Nighthawk Swears Vengeance. Hodder, 1954
Now Let Us Hate. Quality, 1942
Order of the Octopus. Doran, 1926
Peril. Mystery League, 1930
The Prince of Plunder. Hodder, 1934; Little, 1934
Princess After Dark. Hodder, 1931
Queer Things at Queechy. Educ. Pub, 1942
The Red-Haired Death. Hodder, 1938
The Return of Nighthawk. Hodder, 1940
Ring Up Nighthawk. Hodder, 1947
Scarlett Gets the Kidnapper. Foulsham, 1951
Scarlett - Special Branch. Foulsham, 1950
The Screaming Skull and Other Stories. Hodder, 1930
Secret Agent. Collins, 1934; Little, 1934
The Secret Hand. Barker, 1954
The Secret Service Man. Knopf, 1930; Crowther, 1946
Sidney Horler Omnibus of Excitement. Hodder, 1936
Sinister Street. Vallancey, 1944
S.O.S. Hutchinson, 1934; Readers' Lib., 1946
Song of the Scrum. Hutchinson, 1934
Springtime Comes to William. Jenkins, 1943
The Spy. Hodder, 1931
The Stroke Sinister and Other Stories. Hutchinson, 1935
The Temptation of Mary Gordon. Newnes, 1931
Terror Comes to Twelvetrees. Eyre, 1945
Terror on Tiptoe. Hodder, 1939
These Men and Women. Museum Press, 1951
They Called Him Nighthawk. Hodder, 1937
They Thought He Was Dead. Hodder, 1949, 1954
The Thirteenth Hour. Readers' Lib., 1928; Queensway, 1935
Tiger Standish. Doubleday, Doran, 1932; Long, 1932
Tiger Standish Comes Back. Hutchinson, 1934
Tiger Standish Does His Stuff. Hodder, 1941
Tiger Standish Has a Party. Todd, 1943; Vallancey, 1944
Tiger Standish on the Warpath
Tiger Standish Steps on It. Hodder, 1940
Tiger Standish Takes the Field. Hodder, 1939
The Traitor. Collins, 1936; Little, 1936; Eyre, 1948
The Vampire. Hutchinson, 1935
Virus X. Quality, 1946; Archer Press, 1950
Vivanti. Hodder, 1927; Crowther, 1946
Vivanti Returns. Crowther, 1946
The Web. Redman, 1951
Wolves of the Night. Readers' Lib., 1931
The Worst Man in the World. Hodder, 1929

HORN, HOLLOWAY (M)
Murder at Linpara. Collins, 1931

HORN, R. S.
The Twin Serpents. Macmillan, 1965

HORNBLOW, ARTHUR (M)
The Argyle Case. Harper, 1913

HORNE, GEOFFREY (M) (Pseudonym: Gil North)
Beware of the Dog. Morrow, 1939
The Methods of Sergeant Cluff. Chapman, 1961
Sergeant Cluff Goes Fishing. Chapman, 1961

HORNUNG, ERNEST WILLIAM (D)
The Amateur Cracksman. Scribner, 1899
The Camera Fiend. Scribner, 1911
Crime Doctor. Bobbs, 1914
Dead Men Tell No Tales. Scribner, 1889
Denis Dent. Stokes, 1904
Mr. Justice Raffles. Scribner, 1909
Raffles. Scribner, 1901
Raffles: More Adventures of the Amateur Cracksman. Scribner, 1908
The Shadow of the Rope. Scribner, 1902; Lancer, 1966
Stingaree. Scribner, 1905
A Thief in the Night. Scribner, 1905

HORSFIELD, RICHARD HENRY (M) (Pseudonym: M. B. Gaunt)
The Leases of Death. Long, 1937

HORTON, GEORGE (M)
The Monk's Treasure. Bobbs, 1905

HOSKEN, CLIFFORD JAMES WHEELER (D) (Pseudonym: Richard Keverne)
Artifex Intervenes. Constable, 1934
At the Blue Gates. Constable, 1932; Doubleday, Doran, 1932
The Black Cripple. Collins, 1941
Carteret's Cure. Constable, 1926; Houghton, 1926; Harrap, 1932
Coroner's Verdict: Accident; see Lady in No. 4
Crook Stuff. Constable, 1935
Fleet Hall Inheritance. Harper, 1931; Constable, 1933
The Havering Plot. Harper, 1929; Constable, 1930; Burt, 1931
He Laughed at Murder. Constable, 1934; Holt, H., 1935; Lothian, 1945
Lady in No. 4. Collins, 1944 (U.S. title: Coroner's Verdict: Accident. McKay, 1945)
The Man in the Red Hat. Constable, 1930; Harper, 1930; Burt, 1932
The Menace. Constable, 1933
Missing from His Home. Putnam, 1932
The Pretender. Harrap, 1930
The Sanfield Scandal. Constable, 1929; Harper, 1929; Lothian, 1945
Shadow Syndicate. Dial, 1930; Harrap, 1930
The Strange Case of William Cooke; see William Cooke, Antique Dealer
White Gas. Constable, 1937
William Cooke, Antique Dealer. Constable, 1928 (U.S. title: The Strange Case of William Cooke. Harper, 1928)

HOSTER, GRACE (M)
Goodbye, Dear Elizabeth. Farrar & Rinehart, 1943
Trial by Murder. Farrar & Rinehart, 1944

HOSTOVSKÝ, EGON (S)
Midnight Patient. Appleton, 1954; Heinemann, 1955
Missing. Viking, 1951; Bantam
The Plot. Doubleday, 1961

HOTCHNER, A. E. (S)
The Dangerous American. Random, 1958; Weidenfeld, 1959

HOUGH, STANLEY BENNETT (M) (Pseudonym: Bennett Stanley)
The Alscott Experiment, by Bennett Stanley. Hodder, 1954
Beyond the Eleventh Hour. Hodder, 1961
The Bronze Perseus. Walker & Co., 1959 (U.S. title: The Tender Killer. Avon, 1961)
Dear Daughter Dead. Walker & Co., 1966
Government Contract, by Bennett Stanley. Hodder, 1955
Mission in Guemo. Hodder, 1953; Walker & Co., 1964; Award, 1967
Moment of Decision. Hodder, 1952
Sea to Eden, by Bennett Stanley. Hodder, 1954
The Seas South. Hodder, 1953
The Tender Killer; see The Bronze Perseus

HOUGHTON, CLAUDE, pseud; see OLDFIELD, CLAUDE HOUGHTON

HOUGRON, JEAN (S)
A Question of Character. Farrar, Straus, 1958 (Also published as: Trapped. Dell, 1959)

HOULT, NORAH (M)
A Death Occurred. Hutchinson, 1954
Scene for Death. Heinemann, 1943

HOUSEHOLD, GEOFFREY (S)
Arabesque. Little, 1948; Pyramid, 1964
Brides of Solomon; see Fellow Passenger
The Courtesy of Death. Little, 1967; Bantam, 1968
Fellow Passenger. Little, 1955 (Also published as: Brides of Solomon. Pyramid, 1963)
Olura. Little, 1965

Rogue Male. Little, 1939; Pyramid, 1963
A Rough Shoot. Little, 1951; Pyramid, 1964
Sabres on the Sand. Little, 1966
A Time to Kill. Little, 1951; Joseph, M., 1952; Pyramid, 1964
Watcher in the Shadows. Little, 1951

HOVICK, ROSE LOUISE (M) (Pseudonym: Gypsy Rose Lee)
The G-String Murders. S & S, 1941 (Also published as: The Striptease Murders. Paperback Lib., 1963)
Mother Finds a Body. S & S, 1942; Paperback Lib., 1963
The Striptease Murders; see The G-String Murders

HOWARD, HARTLEY, pseud; see OGNALL, LEOPOLD BRUCE

HOWARD, HERBERT EDMUND (M) (Pseudonym: R. Philmore)
Death in Arms. Collins, 1939
Journey Downstairs. Doubleday, Doran, 1934
No Mourning in the Family. Collins, 1937
Procession of Two. Collins, 1940
Short List. Collins, 1938

HOWARD, JAMES ARCH (M) (Pseudonym: Laine Fisher)
Blow Out My Torch. Popular Lib., 1956
Bullet Proof Martyr. Dutton, 1961; Ace, 1962
Die on Easy Street. Popular Lib., 1957
Fare Prey. Ace, 1959
I Like It Tough. Popular Lib., 1955
I'll Get You Yet. Popular Lib., 1956
Murder in Mind, by Laine Fisher. Dutton, 1959
Murder Takes a Wife. Dutton, 1958

HOWARD, LEIGH (M)
Blind Date. Longmans, 1955; S & S, 1955

HOWARD, ROBERT ERWIN (S)
The Dark Man and Others. Arkham, 1963

HOWARD, VECHEL, pseud; see RIGSBY, HOWARD

HOWARTH, CAROLINE M. (M)
Eyes in the Night. Pageant Press, 1953

HOWARTH, DAVID (M)
Across to Norway. Sloane, 1952
Thieves' Hole. Rinehart, 1954

HOWARTH, PATRICK (M) (Pseudonym: C. D. E. Francis)
Portrait of a Killer. Hammond, 1960

HOWATCH, SUSAN (M-S)
Call in the Night. Ace, 1967
The Dark Shore. Ace, 1965
The Waiting Sands. Ace, 1966

HOWE, GEORGE (S)
Call It Treason. Hart-Davis, 1950; Pyramid, 1966; Viking, 1966

HOWE, MURIEL (S)
Affair at Falconers. MacDonald & Co., 1957
Pendragon. MacDonald & Co., 1958

HOWE, RUSSELL WARREN
Behold the City. Secker & Warburg, 1953

HOWES, ROYCE (D)
The Callao Clue. Appleton-Century, 1936
The Case of the Copy-Book Killing. Dutton, 1945
Death Dupes a Lady. Doubleday, Doran, 1937
Death on the Bridge. Doubleday, Doran, 1935
Death Rides a Hobby. Doubleday, Doran, 1939
Murder at Maneuvers. Doubleday, Doran, 1938
The Nasty Name Murders. Doubleday, Doran, 1939
The Night of the Garter Murders. Doubleday, Doran, 1937

HOWIE, EDITH (D)
The Band Played Murder. Mill, 1946
Cry Murder. Mill, 1944
Murder at Stone House. Farrar & Rinehart, 1942
Murder for Christmas. Farrar & Rinehart, 1941
Murder's So Permanent. Farrar & Rinehart, 1942
No Face to Murder. Mill, 1945

HOWITT, JOHN LESLIE DESPARD (M) (Pseudonym: Leslie Despard)
The Crime Without a Flaw. Nash & Grayson, 1931
The Mystery of the Tower Room. Hodder, 1925

HOYT, EDWIN PALMER, JR. (M)
A Matter of Conscience. Duell, 1966

HUBBARD, GEORGE; see THOMPSON, LILIAN BENNET

HUBBARD, MARGARET ANN; see PRILEY, MARGARET ANN HUBBARD

HUBBARD, PHILIP MAITLAND (M-S)
Flush as May. Atheneum, 1963; Joseph, M., 1963; Ballantine, 1964

A Hive of Glass. Atheneum, 1965; Joseph, M., 1965
The Holm Oaks. Joseph, M., 1965; Atheneum, 1966
Picture of Millie; see Portrait of Millie
Portrait of Millie. Atheneum, 1964 (English title: Picture of Millie. British Book Centre, 1965)
The Tower. Atheneum, 1967

HUBER, BERTRAND (M)
Death and the Dowager. Appleton-Century, 1934 (English title: Murder with Gloves. Hale, R., 1936)

HUBLER, RICHARD G. (S)
The Chase. Coward, 1952

HUCH, RICARDA OCTAVIA (M)
The Deruga Trial. Macaulay, 1929

HUDIBURGS, EDWARD (M)
Killer's Game. Lion, 1957

HUDSON, WILLIAM CADWALADER (M)
(Pseudonym: Barclay North)
The Diamond Button: Whose Was It?, by Barclay North. Cassell, 1890
Jack Gordon, Knight Errant, Gotham, by Barclay North. Cassell, 1890
The Man with a Thumb. Cassell, 1891

HUESTON, ETHEL (M)
Idle Island. Bobbs, 1927

HUGGINS, ROY (D)
The Double Take. Morrow, 1946; PB, 1948
Lovely Lady, Pity Me. Duell, 1949
Seventy-Seven, Sunset Strip. Dell, 1958
Too Late for Tears. Morrow, 1947

HUGHES, B. (D)
Murder in the Zoo. Appleton, D., 1932
Mystery of St. Martin's Corpse. Heath, 1929

HUGHES, COLIN, pseud; see CREASEY, JOHN

HUGHES, DOROTHY BELLE FLANAGAN (D)
The Bamboo Blonde. Duell, 1941
The Blackbirder. Duell, 1943
The Candy Kid. Duell, 1950
The Cross-eyed Bear. Duell, 1940
The Davidian Report. Duell, 1952; Pyramid, 1964
The Delicate Ape. Duell, 1944
Dread Journey. Duell, 1945
The Expendable Man. Random, 1963; Avon, 1964; Deutsch, 1964
The Fallen Sparrow. Duell, 1942 (Serial title: The Wobblefoot)
In a Lonely Place. Duell, 1947
Johnnie. Duell, 1944; World Pub., 1946
The Omnibus of Terror. Duell, 1943
Ride the Pink Horse. Duell, 1946; Dell
The So Blue Marble. Duell, 1950; Pyramid, 1965

HUGHES, JOHN CLEDWYN (S)
He Dared Not Look Behind. Wyn, 1947 (English title: The Inn Closes for Christmas. Pilot, 1947)

HULL, ERIC TRAVIS (D)
Murder Lays a Golden Egg. Doubleday, 1961

HULL, HELEN ROSE (M)
Close Her Pale Blue Eyes. Dodd, 1963
A Tapping on the Wall. Dodd, 1960; Popular Lib., 1962

HULL, RICHARD, pseud; see SAMPSON, RICHARD HENRY

HULTMAN, HELEN JOAN (M)
Death at Windward Hill. Fiction League, 1931
Find the Woman. Doubleday, Doran, 1929
Murder in the French Room. Mystery League, 1931
Murder on Route Forty. Phoenix, 1940
Ready for Death. Phoenix, 1939

HUME, DAVID, pseud; see TURNER, JOHN VICTOR

HUME, DORIS (M)
Dark Purpose. Popular Lib., 1960

HUME, FERGUS (M)
The Blue Talisman. Clode, 1925
Crimson Cryptogram. Buckles, 1905
Lone Inn. Ogilvie, 1900
Lost Parchment. Dillingham, G. W., 1914
The Man Who Vanished. Ogilvie
The Mandarin's Fan. Dillingham, G. W., 1905
The Mystery of the Hansom Cab. Melbourne, 1887; Ivers, 1888; Lovell, F. F., 1888; Munroe, 1888
Mystery Queen. Dillingham, G. W., 1912
Peacock of Jewels. Dillingham, G. W., 1910
Red Money. Dillingham, G. W., 1911
Red Skull. Dodge, B. W., 1912
Secret Passage. Dillingham, G. W., 1905
Steel Crown, Dillingham, G. W., 1912
The Third Volume. Cassell, 1894
Whispering Lane. Small, 1925

HUMPHREYS, ROY (M)
Hunch. Mussey, 1934

HUMPHRIES, MRS. ADELAIDE (M)
A Case for Nurse Marian. Bouregy, 1957

HUNT, CHARLOTTE (S)
Gilded Sarcophagus. Ace, 1967

HUNT, CLARENCE (D)
Small Town Corpse. Phoenix, 1951

HUNT, HARRISON, pseud; see BALLARD, WILLIS TODHUNTER

HUNT, HOWARD, pseud; see DIETRICH, ROBERT

HUNT, KATHERINE CHANDLER (M)
(Pseudonym: Chandler Nash)
Murder Is My Shadow. Macmillan, 1959; Hale, R., 1960

HUNT, KYLE, pseud; see CREASEY, JOHN

HUNT, MARY VINCENT (M)
Mystery of Daria Kane. Bouregy, 1960

HUNT, PETER, pseud; see YATES, GEORGE WORTHING

HUNT, VIOLET (S)
More Tales of the Uneasy. Heinemann, 1925

HUNTER, ALAN JAMES HERBERT (D)
Gently by the Shore. Cassell, 1956; Rinehart, 1956
Gently Does It. Rinehart, 1955
Gently Down the Stream. Cassell, 1957; Roy Pubs., 1960
Gently Floating. Cassell, 1963; Berkley Pub., 1964; Pan, 1965
Gently Go Man. Cassell, 1961; Pan, 1963; Berkley Pub., 1964
Gently in an Omnibus. Cassell, 1966
Gently in the Sun. Cassell, 1959; Berkley Pub., 1964
Gently North-West. Cassell, 1967
Gently Sahib. Cassell, 1964
Gently Through the Mill. Cassell, 1958
Gently to the Summit. Cassell, 1961; Berkley Pub., 1965
Gently Where the Roads Go. Cassell, 1962; Pan, 1964
Gently with the Painters. Cassell, 1960; Pan, 1963
Landed Gently. Cassell, 1957; Roy Pubs., 1960

HUNTER, BLUEBELL MATILDA (M)
(Pseudonym: John Guildford)
Big Ben Looks On! Grayson, 1933
Death Dams the Tide. Grayson, 1932

HUNTER, EVAN (M-D) (Pseudonyms: Curt Cannon, Hunt Collins, Ed McBain, Richard Marsten)
The April Robin Murders, with Craig Rice. Random, 1958; Hammond, 1959; Dell, 1965
Ax. S & S, 1964; PB, 1965
Buddwing. S & S, 1964; PB, 1965
Con Man. Permabooks, 1957; S & S, 1957; Boardman, T. V., 1960
Cop Hater. Permabooks, 1956; S & S, 1956; Boardman, T. V., 1958
Cut Me In, by Hunt Collins. Abelard, 1954; Boardman, T. V., 1960
Death of a Nurse. PB, 1964
Doll, by Ed McBain. Delacorte, 1965; Dell, 1966
Don't Crowd Me. Popular Lib., 1964
Eighty Million Eyes. Dell, 1957; Delacorte, 1966
Eighty-Seventh Precinct, by Ed McBain. S & S, 1959
Eighty-Seventh Squad, by Ed McBain. S & S, 1960
The Empty Hours, by Ed McBain. S & S, 1962; PB, 1963 (Same with subtitle: Three 87th Precinct Novelettes. Boardman, T. V., 1963)
Give the Boys a Great Big Hand, by Ed McBain. Boardman, T. V., 1960; S & S, 1960
Happy New Year, Herbie and Other Stories. S & S, 1963; PB, 1964
He Who Hesitates, by Ed McBain. Delacorte, 1965; Dell, 1966
The Heckler. S & S, 1960; Permabooks, 1961
I Like 'Em Tough, by Curt Cannon. GM, 1958
I'm Cannon—for Hire, by Curt Cannon. GM
Killer's Choice. S & S, 1957; Boardman, T. V., 1960; Permabooks, 1962
Killer's Payoff, by Ed McBain. Permabooks, 1958; S & S, 1958; Boardman, T. V., 1960
Killer's Wedge, by Ed McBain. S & S, 1959; Dell, 1967
King's Ransom, by Ed McBain. S & S, 1959; PB, 1960; Penguin
Lady Killer, by Ed McBain. Permabooks, 1958; S & S, 1958; Dell, 1967
Lady, Lady, I Did It, by Ed McBain. S & S, 1961; Boardman, T. V., 1963
The Last Spin. Constable, 1960; S & S, 1962
Like Love, by Ed McBain. S & S, 1962; PB, 1963; Hamilton, H., 1964
A Matter of Conviction. Constable, 1959; S & S, 1959; PB, 1961
The Mugger, by Ed McBain. S & S, 1956; Boardman, T. V, 1959
Murder in the Navy, by Richard Marsten. GM, 1953

The Pusher, by Ed McBain. Permabooks, 1956; S & S, 1956; Boardman, T. V., 1959
Runaway Black, by Richard Marsten. GM, 1954
See Them Die. S & S, 1960; Boardman, T. V., 1963
The Sentries, by Ed McBain. S & S, 1965; Dell, 1966
The Spiked Heel, by Richard Marsten. Holt, H., 1956; Constable, 1957; Crest, 1963
Squad Room, by Ed McBain. S & S, 1961 (Contains: Killer's Payoff and Lady Killer)
Ten Plus One, by Ed McBain. S & S, 1963; Hamilton, H., 1964; PB, 1964
'Till Death, by Ed McBain. S & S, 1959; PB, 1960; Penguin
Vanishing Ladies, by Richard Marsten. Boardman, T. V., 1961

HUNTER, JACK D. (S)
The Expendable Spy. Dutton, 1965; Muller, 1966; Bantam
One of Us Works for Them. Clarke, Irwin, 1967; Dutton, 1967; Bantam, 1968

HUNTER, JOHN (M) (Pseudonyms: John Addiscombe, L. H. Brenning, Anthony Dax, Anthony Drummond)
Blood Money, by Anthony Drummond. Gramol, 1935
Boulevard, by L. H. Brenning. Cassell, 1931
Dead Man's Gate. Cassell, 1931
The Death Plot, by L. H. Brenning. Cassell, 1931
Desperado. Cassell, 1932
Devil's Laughter, by L. H. Brenning. Cassell, 1929
Devil's Signpost, by Anthony Drummond. Gramol, 1935
Drums of Death, by John Addiscombe. Hurst, 1929
The Island of Dangerous Men, by Anthony Drummond. Gramol, 1937
The Man Behind, by Anthony Dax. World's Work, 1937; Dutton, 1938
Parisian Adventure, by L. H. Brenning. Cassell, 1934
Parisian Love, by L. H. Brenning. Cassell, 1926
The Scented Death, by Anthony Drummond. Unwin, 1924
Three Die at Midnight. Dutton, 1937
When the Gunmen Came. Cassell, 1930
The White Phantom. Cassell, 1934

HUNTINGDON, JOHN, pseud; see PHILLIPS, GERALD WILLIAMS

HUNTSBERRY, WILLIAM EMERY (M)
Dangerous Harbour; see Harbor of the Little Boats
Harbor of the Little Boats. Rinehart, 1958 (English title: Dangerous Harbor. Hammond, 1960)
Oscar Mooney's Head. Holt, 1961

HURD, FLORENCE (S-Gothic)
The Secret of Canfield House. GM, 1966
Wade House. Signet, 1967

HURLEY, GENE (D)
Have You Seen This Man? Bobbs, 1944

HURST, IDA (M)
African Heart-Beat. Long, 1947
I've Been Around. Long, 1946

HURT, FREDA MARY E. (M)
Body at Bowman's Hollow. MacDonald & Co., 1959
Death and the Bridegroom. Hale, R., 1963
Death by Bequest. MacDonald & Co., 1960
Sweet Death. MacDonald & Co., 1961

HUSTON, HOWARD CHAUNCEY (M)
The Blind Saw Murder. Macmillan, 1954
With Murder for Some. Macmillan, 1953

HUTCHINSON, HORATIO GORDON (D)
The Mystery of the Summerhouse. Doran, 1919

HUTCHINSON, ROBERT HARE (M) (Pseudonym: Robert Hare)
The Doctor's First Murder, by Robert Hare. Hurst, 1933; Longmans, 1933
The Fourth Challenge. Hurst, 1932
The Hand of the Chimpanzee, by Robert Hare. Hurst, 1934; Longmans, 1934
Spectral Evidence, by Robert Hare. Hurst, 1932

HUTCHINSON, VERE (M)
Sea Wreck. Century, 1923

HUTCHISON, GRAHAM SETON (M) (Pseudonym: Graham Seton)
Blood Money. Hutchinson, 1934
Eye for an Eye. Farrar & Rinehart, 1933
The K Code Plan. Rich, 1938
The W Plan. Butterworth, T., 1929; Cosmopolitan, 1930; Penguin, 1938

HUTTEN zum STOLZENBERGER, BETTINA von (M)
Cowardly Custard; see Gentleman's Agreement
Die She Must. Dutton, 1936
Gentleman's Agreement. Dutton, 1936 (English title: Cowardly Custard. Hutchinson, 1937)

HUTTON, JOY FERRIS (D)
Too Good to Be True. S & S, 1948

HUXLEY, ALDOUS LEONARD (M)
Mortal Coils. Doran, 1922

HUXLEY, ELSPETH JOSCELIN GRANT (D)
The African Poison Murder; see Death of an Aryan
Death of an Aryan. Methuen, 1939 (U.S. title: The African Poison Murders. Harper, 1940; Grosset, 1943)
The Incident at the Merry Hippo. Chatto, 1963; Morrow, 1964; Penguin
A Man from Nowhere. Morrow, 1965
Murder at Government House. Harper, 1937; Methuen, 1937
Murder on Safari. Harper, 1938; Methuen, 1938
Red Strangers. Harper, 1939

HYATT, BETTY HALE (M)
The Vesper Bells. Arcadia, 1967

HYATT, STANLEY PORTAL
Markham Affair. Grosset, 1928

HYDE, THEODORE, pseud. (M)
After the Execution. Eyre, 1934
Murder in Whitehall. Murray, J., 1942

HYLAND, HENRY STANLEY (M)
Green Grow the Tresses-o. Gollancz, 1959; Bobbs, 1967
Who Goes Hang? Gollancz, 1958; Dodd, 1959

HYND, ALAN
Betrayal from the East. McBride, 1943

HYTHE, GABRIEL, pseud. (D)
Death of a Goblin. MacDonald & Co., 1960
Death of a Puppet. MacDonald & Co., 1959

IAMS, JACK (D)
The Body Missed the Boat. Morrow, 1947; Triangle, 1948
A Corpse of the Old School. Gollancz, 1955
Death Draws the Line. Morrow, 1947
Do Not Murder Before Christmas. Morrow, 1949; Dell
Girl Meets Body. Morrow, 1947
Into Thin Air. Morrow, 1952
Prematurely Gay. Morrow, 1948
A Shot of Murder. Morrow, 1950
What Rhymes with Murder. Morrow, 1950

"Iconoclast," pseud; see HAMILTON, MRS. MARY AGNES

IGGULDEN, JOHN (S)
Dark Stranger. McGraw, 1965

ILES, BERT, pseud; see ROSS, ZOLA HELEN

ILES, FRANCIS, pseud; see COX, ANTHONY BERKELEY

IMBERT-TERRY, H. (M)
Acid. Skeffington, 1929
Doom. Skeffington, 1930

INCHBALD, RALPH MORDAUNT ELLIOT (M)
Colonel Paternoster. Hodder, 1951
Five Inns. Hodder, 1953
September Story. Hodder, 1953

INGHAM, H. LLOYD (M)
Bury Me Deep. Hammond, 1963

INGRAM, ELEANOR MARIE (M)
The Thing from the Lake. Lippincott, 1921

INGRAM, KENNETH (D)
Death Comes at Night. Sears, 1933
The Steep Steps. Allen, 1931

INGRAM, MARTIN, pseud; see CAMPBELL, MRS. ALICE ORMOND

INNES, HAMMOND, pseud; see HAMMOND-INNES, RALPH

INNES, JOHN WILLIAMS BRODIE-; see BRODIE-INNES, JOHN WILLIAMS

INNES, MICHAEL, pseud; see STEWART, JOHN INNES MACKINTOSH

INNES, MURRAY (D)
Cosgrove: Detective. Stockwell, 1938

IRISH, WILLIAM, pseud; see HOPLEY-WOOLRICH, CORNELL GEORGE

IRONSIDE, JOHN, pseud; see TAIT, EUPHEMIA MARGARET

IRVINE, HELEN DOUGLAS (S)
77 Willow Road. Doubleday, Doran, 1945

IRVING, ALEXANDER (M-S)
Bitter Ending. Dodd, 1946
Deadline. Dodd, 1947
Symphony in Two Time. Dodd, 1948

IRVING, CLIFFORD MICHAEL (S)
The Losers. Coward, 1957

IRVING, PETER (S)
An Italian Called Mario. Evans, 1954

The Lady and the Unicorn. Evans, 1953
One Way Street. Hurst, 1948

IRWIN, INEZ HAYNES (M)
A Body Rolled Downstairs. Random, 1938
Many Murders. Random, 1941
Murder in Fancy Dress; see Murder Masquerade
Murder Masquerade. Smith, H., 1935 (Also published as: Murder in Fancy Dress. Heinemann, 1935)
The Poison Cross Mystery. Smith, H., 1936
Women Swore Revenge. Random, 1946

IRWIN, JUDY (D)
Murderous Welcome. Roy Pubs., 1967

IRWIN, WALLACE (M)
The Julius Caesar Murder Mystery. Appleton-Century, 1935

IRWIN, WILLIAM HENRY (M)
House of Mystery. Century, 1910

ISRAEL, CHARLES (S)
The Hostages. Popular Lib., 1967

JACKSON, CHARLES ROSS (D)
Quintus Oakes. Unwin, 1904
The Third Degree. Unwin, 1903

JACKSON, FELIX (S)
So Help Me, God. Viking, 1955; Bantam

JACKSON, GILES, pseud; see LEFFINGWELL, ALBERT

JACKSON, MARR (M)
A Dram of Poison. Bell, G., 1938
Escape into Murder. Cassell, 1939

JACKSON, RALPH (S)
Violent Night. Ace, 1956

JACKSON, SHIRLEY (Mrs. Stanley Edgar Hyman) (S)
Hangsaman. Farrar, Straus, 1951; Gollancz, 1951; Ace, 1964
The Haunting of Hill House. Viking, 1959; Joseph, M., 1960; Popular Lib., 1963
The Lottery. Farrar, Straus, 1949; Gollancz, 1950; Lion, 1950; Avon
The Road Through the Wall. Farrar & Rinehart, 1940; Lion, 1950
We Have Always Lived in the Castle. Viking, 1958; Popular Lib., 1963

JACKSON, WALLACE, pseud; see BUDD, WILLIAM JOHN

JACKSON, WILLIAM SCARBOROUGH (M)
Nine Points of the Law. Lane, 1903

JACOBI, CARL (S)
Portraits in Moonlight. Arkham, 1964

JACOBS, T. C. H., pseud; see PENDOWER, JACQUES

JACOBS, THOMAS CURTIS HICKS, pseud; see PENDOWER, JACQUES

JACOBS, WILLIAM WYMARK (M)
The Interruption. World Pub., 1943 (In Cuppy, William Jacob. World's Greatest Mystery Stories)
The Lady of the Barge. Harper, 1902

JACOBSSON, PER and VERNON BARTLETT (D) (Pseudonym: Peter Oldfeld)
The Alchemy Murder. Washburn, 1929; Constable, 1933
The Death of a Diplomat. Constable, 1928; Washburn, 1928

JAEDIKER, KERMIT (M)
Here's Lust. Lion, 1953
Tall, Dark & Deadly. Mystery House, 1947

JAKES, JOHN W. (D)
The Devil Has Four Faces. Mystery House, 1958
The Imposter. Macmillan, 1959
Johnny Havoc and the Doll Who Had "IT." Belmont, 1963
Johnny Havoc Meets Zelda. Belmont, 1962
Night for Treason. Bouregy, 1956

JAMES, BARBARA (S)
Beauty That Must Die. Ace, 1967
Bright, Deadly Summer. Ace, 1966

JAMES, BRENI (M)
Night of the Kill. S & S, 1961; Hammond, 1963
The Shakeup. S & S, 1964

JAMES, FLORENCE ALICE PRICE (M) (Pseudonym: Florence Warden)
Abbot's Moat. White, 1913
The Adventures of a Pretty Woman. Paul, S., 1909; Jarrolds, 1919
The Bad Lord Lockington. Long, 1912
The Baronet's Wife. Unwin, 1908
Beatrice Foyle's Crime. Pearson, 1903, 1934
The Case for the Lady. Greening, 1910
The Case of Sir Geoffrey. Long, 1908
The Colonel's Past. Ward, Lock, 1910
Cross Fires. Cassell, 1915
A Devil's Bargain. Long, 1908
The Disappearance of Nigel Blair. Ward, Lock, 1911
The Face in the Flashlight. Long, 1905
A Fight to the Finish. Chatto, 1901

The Harlingham Case. Ward, Lock, 1918
Law Not Justice. Hurst, 1906
The Mill House Mystery. Jarrolds, 1911
Miss Ferriby's Clients. Laurie, 1910
The Mystery of Dudley Horne. White, 1897; Long, 1916
A Mystery of the Thames. Ward, Lock, 1913
A Night Surprise. Ward, Lock, 1919
No. 3, The Square. Long, 1903
Nurse Revel's Mistake. Simpkin, 1889
The Old House at the Corner. Chatto, 1906
A Sensational Case. Ward, Lock, 1898
Serles' Secret. Everett, 1909
Sir Julian's Crime. Ward, Lock, 1921
The Veiled Lady. Long, 1909
Who Was Lady Thurne? Long, 1905

JAMES, FRANKLIN, pseud; see GODLEY, ROBERT

JAMES, GODFREY WARDEN (M) (Pseudonym: Adam Broome)
The Black Mamba. Bles, 1936
The Cambridge Murders. Bles, 1936
The Crocodile Club. Bles, 1935
Crowner's Quest. Benn, 1930
Dream Murder. MacDonald & Co., 1946
The Island of Death. Bles, 1932
The Oxford Murders. Bles, 1929; Readers' Lib., 1939
Porro Palaver. Bles, 1929
The Queen's Hall Murder. Bles, 1933
The Red Queen Club. Bles, 1939

JAMES, HENRY (M)
The Ghostly Tales of Henry James. Grosset, 1963
Two Magics: The Turn of the Screw and Covering End. Macmillan, 1924

JAMES, HENRY COLBERT (M)
The Girl from Taiping. Jarrolds, 1954
The Green Opal. Jarrolds, 1953
The Madness of Charlie Pierce. Jarrolds, 1952

JAMES, LEIGH (S)
The Chameleon File. Dutton, 1967; Weybright & Talley, 1967; Berkley Pub., 1968

JAMES, P. D. (M)
Cover Her Face. Faber, 1962; Scribner, 1962
A Mind to Murder. British Book Centre, 1963; Faber, 1963; Scribner, 1967
Unnatural Causes. Scribner, 1967

JAMES, ROBERT, pseud; see HEITNER, JAMES

JAMES, SELWYN (M)
The Hungry Spider. Doubleday, 1950

JAMES, STUART (M)
Jack the Ripper. Fell, 1960

JAMES, VINCENT, pseud; see GRIBBEN, JAMES

JAMESON, (MARGARET) STORM (M)
Before the Crossing. Macmillan, 1947

JANIFER, LAURENCE M. (D-S) (Pseudonym: Larry M. Harris)
Final Affair. Belmont, 1967
The Picked Poodles, by Larry M. Harris. Random, 1960; Boardman, T. V., 1961 (A continuation of the Craig Rice characters)
The Protector, by Larry M. Harris. Boardman, T. V., 1960; Random, 1960
You Can't Escape. Lancer, 1967

JANIS, ELSIE and MARGUERITE ASPINWALL (M)
Counter Currents. Putnam, 1926

JANSEN, JOHANNA FREDERIKA; see CAMPBELL, MARGARET ELIZABETH

JANSEN, LAURA MAE (S-Gothic)
Bride of the Shadows. Lancer, 1967

JANSON, HANK, pseud; see FRANCIS, STEPHEN

JANSON, HANK, pseud; see GOLD, G.

JANSON, HANK, pseud; see HOBSON, HANK

JAPRISOT, SEBASTIEN (D-M)
Lady in the Car with Glass and a Gun. S & S, 1967
The 10:30 from Marseilles. Doubleday, 1963; PB, 1964
A Trap for Cinderella. S & S, 1964; PB, 1965

JARDIN, REX, pseud; see BURKHARDT, ROBERT

JARRETT, CORA (M-S) (Pseudonym; Farraday Keene)
The Ginkgo Tree. Farrar & Rinehart, 1935; Barker, 1936
Night over Fitch's Pond. Barker, 1933; Houghton, 1933
Pattern in Black and Red, by Farraday Keene. Barker, 1934; Houghton, 1934
Strange Houses. Farrar & Rinehart, 1936; Heinemann, 1937

JARVIE, CLODAGH GIBSON (M)
He Would Provoke Death. Boardman, T. V., 1959; Roy Pubs., 1959

Variations on a Theme of Murder. Thanet Press, 1936
Vicious Circuit. Boardman, T. V., 1957

JARVIS, HENRY WOOD (M)
House of Silence. Muller, 1959

JAY, CHARLOTTE, pseud; see JAY, GERALDINE

JAY, GERALDINE (M) (Pseudonym: Charlotte Jay)
Arms for Adonis. Collins, 1960; Harper, 1960; Collier, 1962
Beat Not the Bones. Collins, 1952; Harper, 1953; Avon
The Brink of Silence; see The Feast of the Dead
The Feast of the Dead. Hale, R., 1956 (U.S. title: The Brink of Silence. Harper, 1957; Collier, 1962)
The Fugitive Eye. Collins, 1953; Harper, 1954
A Hank of Hair. Harper & Row, 1964; Heinemann, 1964; Macfadden, 1966
A Knife Is Feminine. Collins, 1951
The Man Who Walked Away. Collins, 1958 (U.S. title: Stepfather. Harper, 1959)
Stepfather; see The Man Who Walked Away
The Yellow Turban. Collins, 1955; Harper, 1955; Paperback Lib., 1963

JAY, SIMON, pseud; see ALEXANDER, COLIN JAMES

JAY, WILLA (S)
Fear in Borzano. Lancer, 1967

JEFFERIS, BARBARA (S)
One Black Summer. Morrow, 1967
Undercurrent. Sloane, 1953

JEFFERSON, BEATRICE W. (M)
Small Town Murder. Dutton, 1941

JEFFRIES, IAN, pseud; see HAYS, PETER

JEFFRIES, BRUCE GRAHAM MONTAGUE (D) (Pseudonyms: Peter Bourne, Bruce Graeme, David Graeme)
Accidental Clue, by Bruce Graeme. Hutchinson, 1958
Adventures of Blackshirt; see Blackshirt Again
Alias Blackshirt, by Bruce Graeme. Harrap, 1932
Almost Without Murder, by Bruce Graeme. Hutchinson, 1963
Black Gold, by Peter Bourne. Hutchinson, 1964
Blackshirt Again, by Bruce Graeme. Hutchinson, 1929 (U.S. title: Adventures of Blackshirt. Dodd, 1929)
Blackshirt, Counter-Spy, by Bruce Graeme. Hutchinson, 1938
Blackshirt Interferes, by Bruce Graeme. Hutchinson, 1939
Blackshirt Strikes Back, by Bruce Graeme. Hutchinson, 1940
Blackshirt Takes a Hand, by Bruce Graeme. Hutchinson, 1937
Blackshirt the Adventurer, by Bruce Graeme. Hutchinson, 1936
Blackshirt the Audacious, by Bruce Graeme. Hutchinson, 1935
Body Unknown, by Bruce Graeme. Hutchinson, 1939
Boomerang, by Bruce Graeme. Hutchinson, 1959
A Brief for O'Leary, by Bruce Graeme. Hutchinson, 1947
Calling Lord Blackshirt, by Bruce Graeme. Hutchinson, 1943
Cardyce for the Defence, by Bruce Graeme. Hutchinson, 1936
The Coming of Carew, by Bruce Graeme. Hutchinson, 1945
The Corporal Died in Bed, by Bruce Graeme. Hutchinson, 1940
Dead Pigs at Hungry Farm, by Bruce Graeme. Hutchinson, 1951
Disappearance of Roger Tremayne, by Bruce Graeme. Hutchinson, 1937
The Drums Beat Red, by Bruce Graeme. Hutchinson, 1963
Encore Allain!, by Bruce Graeme. Hutchinson, 1941
Epilogue, by Bruce Graeme. Hutchinson, 1933 (A modern continuation of "The Mystery of Edwin Drood")
Fog for a Killer, by Bruce Graeme. Hutchinson, 1960
Gigins Court, by Bruce Graeme. Hutchinson, 1932
Hate Ship, by Bruce Graeme. Hutchinson, 1928
The House with the Crooked Walls, by Bruce Graeme. Hutchinson, 1942
Impeached!, by Bruce Graeme. Hutchinson, 1933
The Imperfect Crime, by Bruce Graeme. Hutchinson, 1932
The Inn of Thirteen Swords, by David Graeme. Harrap, 1938
An International Affair, by Bruce Graeme. Hutchinson, 1934
John Jenkin, Public Enemy; see Public Enemy Number One
Just an Ordinary Case, by Bruce Graeme. Hutchinson, 1957
Lady in Black, by Bruce Graeme. Hutchinson, 1952
Long Night, by Bruce Graeme. Hutchinson, 1959

Lord Blackshirt, by Bruce Graeme. Hutchinson, 1942
Madame Spy, by Bruce Graeme. Allan, P., 1935
The Man from Michigan, by Bruce Graeme. Hutchinson, 1938 (U.S. title: Mystery of Stolen Hats. Lippincott, 1939)
Monsieur Blackshirt, by David Graeme. Harrap, 1933
Mr. Whimset Buys a Gun, by Bruce Graeme. Hutchinson, 1953
A Murder of Some Importance, by Bruce Graeme. Hutchinson, 1931
Mystery of the Stolen Hats; see The Man from Michigan
Mystery on the Queen Mary, by Bruce Graeme. Hutchinson, 1937
No Clues for Dexter, by Bruce Graeme. Hutchinson, 1948
Not Proven, by Bruce Graeme. Hutchinson, 1935
Passion, Murder and Mystery, by Bruce Graeme. Hutchinson, 1928
The Penance of Brother Alaric, by Bruce Graeme. Hutchinson, 1930
Poisoned Sleep, by Bruce Graeme. Hutchinson, 1939
Public Enemy - Number One, by Bruce Graeme. Hutchinson, 1934 (U.S. title: John Jenkin, Public Enemy. Lippincott, 1935)
Racing Yacht Mystery, by Bruce Graeme. Hutchinson, 1938
The Return of Blackshirt, by Bruce Graeme. Unwin, 1927
Satan's Mistress, by Bruce Graeme. Hutchinson, 1935
Seven Clues in Search of a Crime, by Bruce Graeme. Hutchinson, 1941
So Sharp the Razor, by Bruce Graeme. Hutchinson, 1955
Soldiers of Fortune, by Peter Bourne. Hutchinson, 1962; Putnam, 1963
Son of Blackshirt, by Bruce Graeme. Hutchinson, 1941
Suspense, by Bruce Graeme. Hutchinson, 1953
The Sword of Monsieur Blackshirt, by David Graeme. Harrap, 1934
Ten Trails to Tyburn, by Bruce Graeme. Hutchinson, 1944
Thirteen in a Fog, by Bruce Graeme. Hutchinson, 1940
Through the Eyes of a Judge, by Bruce Graeme. Hutchinson, 1930
Tigers Have Claws, by Bruce Graeme. Hutchinson, 1949
Trouble!, by Bruce Graeme. Harrap, 1929
The Undetective, by Bruce Graeme. London House, 1963
Unsolved, by Bruce Graeme. Hutchinson, 1931
The Vengeance of Monsieur Blackshirt, by David Graeme. Harrap, 1934
The Way Out, by Bruce Graeme. Hutchinson, 1954
Without Malice, by Bruce Graeme. Hutchinson, 1946
Work for the Hangman, by Bruce Graeme. Hutchinson, 1944

JEFFRIES, RODERIC (D) (Pseudonyms: Jeffrey Ashford, Roderic Graeme)
The Amazing Mr. Blackshirt, by Roderic Graeme. Hutchinson, 1955
The Benefits of Death. Collins, 1963; Dodd, 1964
Blackshirt Finds Trouble, by Roderic Graeme. Long, 1961
Blackshirt Helps Himself, by Roderic Graeme. Long, 1951
Blackshirt Meets the Lady, by Roderic Graeme. Hutchinson, 1956
Blackshirt on the Spot, by Roderic Graeme. Long, 1963
Blackshirt Passes By, by Roderic Graeme. Hutchinson, 1953
Blackshirt Saves the Day, by Roderic Graeme. Long, 1964
Blackshirt Sees It Through, by Roderic Graeme. Long, 1960
Blackshirt Sets the Pace, by Roderic Graeme. Long, 1959
Blackshirt Takes the Trail, by Roderic Graeme. Long, 1962
Blackshirt Wins the Trick, by Roderic Graeme. Hutchinson, 1953
The Burden of Proof, by Jeffrey Ashford. Harper, 1962
Call for Blackshirt, by Roderic Graeme. Long, 1963
Concerning Blackshirt, by Roderic Graeme. Hutchinson, 1952
Consider the Evidence. Walker & Co., 1966
Counsel for the Defense, by Jeffrey Ashford. Harper, 1961; Collier, 1965
Dead Against the Lawyers. Cassell, 1965; Dodd, 1966
The D.I.; see The Investigations Are Proceeding
Double for Blackshirt, by Roderic Graeme. Long, 1958
An Embarrassing Death. Collins, 1964; Doubleday, 1964
Enquiries Are Continuing, by Jeffrey Ashford. Long, 1964
Evidence of the Accused. Collins, 1961; London House, 1963
Forget What You Saw, by Jeffrey Ashford. Long, 1967
The Hands of Innocence, by Jeffrey Ashford. Walker & Co., 1966
The Investigations Are Proceeding, by Jeffrey Ashford. Long, 1961 (U.S. title: The D.I. Harper, 1962)
Paging Blackshirt, by Roderic Graeme. Long, 1957
Salute to Blackshirt, by Roderic Graeme. Hutchinson, 1954

Superintendent's Room, by Jeffrey Ashford. Harper & Row, 1965
Will Anyone Who Saw the Accident . . ., by Jeffrey Ashford. Long, 1963; Harper & Row, 1964

JELLETT, DR. HENRY; see MARSH, NGAIO

JENKINS, ALAN C. (S) (Pseudonym: John Bancroft)
The Borodin Affair. Epworth, 1966

JENKINS, CECIL (M)
Message from Sirius. Dodd, 1961; Bantam, 1963

JENKINS, ELIZABETH (M)
Harriet. Doubleday, Doran, 1934; Gollancz, 1934; Bantam, 1946

JENKINS, GEOFFREY (S)
The Disappearing Island; see A Grue of Ice
A Grue of Ice. Collins, 1962; Viking, 1962 (Also published as: The Disappearing Island. Avon, 1964)
Hunter, Killer. Putnam, 1967; Berkley Pub., 1968
A River of Diamonds. Collins, 1964; Viking, 1964; Avon, 1966
A Twist of Sand. Viking, 1959; Avon, 1965

JENKINS, HERBERT (D)
The Adventures of Bindle. Jenkins, 1919
Malcom Sage, Detective. Jenkins, 1921; Roy Pubs., 1957

JENKINS, WILLIAM FITZGERALD (M) (Pseudonym: Murray Leinster)
The Man Who Feared. Gateway, 1942
Murder in the Family. Hamilton, 1935
Murder Madness, by Murray Leinster. Brewer, 1931
The Murder of the U.S.A. Crown, 1946
Murder Will Out, by Murray Leinster. Hamilton, 1932
No Clues. Wright & Brown, 1938
Scalps, by Murray Leinster. Brewer, 1930

JENKS, GEORGE R.; see MOORE, CARLYLE

JEPSON, EDGAR ALFRED (D)
Arsène Lupin, with Maurice Leblanc. Doubleday, Page, 1909
The Barradine Detective. Jenkins, 1937
Buried Rubies. Jenkins, 1925
Cuirass of Diamonds. Jenkins, 1929; Vanguard, 1929
The Dangerous Twins. Jenkins, 1935
Emerald Tiger. Macy-Masius, 1928
The Four Philanthropists. Unwin, 1907
The Garden at No. 19. Wessels, 1910
The House on the Mall. Dillingham, G. W., 1911
The Loudwater Mystery. Knopf, 1920; Harrap, 1928
The Man with the Amber Eyes, with Hugh D. Clevely. Jenkins, 1930
The Murder in Romney Marsh. Jenkins, 1929
The Pocket Hercules. Jenkins, 1938

JEPSON, SELWYN (M)
The Assassin. Lippincott, 1957
The Black Italian. Collins, 1954; Doubleday, 1955
Death Gong. Harrap, 1927; Watt, G. H., 1927; Grosset, 1929
Fear in the Wind. Allen, W. H., 1964
The Golden Dart. Doubleday, 1949; MacDonald & Co., 1949
Golden Eyes. Harrap, 1924
The Hungry Spider. Doubleday, 1950; MacDonald & Co., 1951
I Met Murder. Harper, 1930; Hodder, 1930
Keep Murder Quiet. Joseph, M., 1940; Doubleday, Doran, 1941
Love - and Helen. Watt, G. H., 1928
Man Dead. Collins, 1951; Doubleday, 1951
Man Running. MacDonald & Co., 1948
The Mystery of the Rabbit's Paw. Harper, 1932 (English title: Rabbit's Paw. Hodder, 1932)
Noise in the Night. Davies, 1957; Lippincott, 1957
Outrun the Constable. Doubleday, 1948
Rabbit's Paw; see The Mystery of the Rabbit's Paw
Rogues and Diamonds. Dial, 1929; Harrap, 1929
The Sutton Papers. MacVeagh, 1924
Tiger Dawn. Hodder, 1929
Verdict in Question. Doubleday, 1960

JEROME, JEROME K. (M)
Novel Notes. Holt, H., 1893

JEROME, JUDSON (S)
The Fell of Dark. Houghton, 1966

JEROME, OWEN FOX, pseud; see FRIEND, OSCAR JEROME

JESSE, F. TENNYSON (M)
A Pin to See the Peepshow. Doubleday, Doran, 1934; Heinemann, 1934
Solange Stories. Heinemann, 1931

JESSUP, RICHARD (S)
The Cincinnati Kid. Little, 1963; Gollancz, 1964; Dell, 1965; Pan, 1965
Cry Passion. Dell, 1956
Deadly Duo. Dell, 1959; Boardman, T. V., 1961

Lowdown. Secker & Warburg, 1958; Dell, 1960
Man in Charge. Secker & Warburg, 1957; GM, 1962
Night Boat to Paris. Dell, 1956
Port Angelique. GM, 1961
Wolf Cop. GM, 1961; Muller, 1963

JOCELYN, DAVEY, pseud; see RAPHAEL, CHAIM

JOHN, OWEN (S)
Thirty Days Hath September. Dutton, 1967; Joseph, M., 1967

JOHNS, FOSTER, pseud; see SELDES, GILBERT VIVIAN

JOHNS, RICHARD (M)
Fleshy Shadow. Cassell, 1941
Man with a Background of Flames. Roy Pubs., 1954

JOHNS, VERONICA PARKER (D)
Hush, Gabriel. Dell, 1940
Murder by the Day. Doubleday, 1953; Collier, 1962
Servant's Problem. Doubleday, 1958; Collier, 1963
Shady Doings, Duell, 1941
The Singing Widow. Duell, 1941

JOHNS, WILLIAM EARL (M)
Man Who Lost His Way. Macmillan, 1960
The Murder at Castle Deeping. Hamilton, 1940
Murder by Air. Newnes, 1937
Steeley Flies Again. Newnes, 1936

JOHNSON, EVELYN DAVIES and GRETTA PALMER (M)
Murder. Covici, 1928
Murder and Mystery. Cayme Press, 1930

JOHNSON, GEORGE CLAYTON (S)
Ocean's Eleven. PB, 1960

JOHNSON, GLAYS ETTA (M)
Moon Country. Penn, 1924
The Wind Along the Waste. Century, 1921

JOHNSON, MRS. GRACE CECILIA and HAROLD NELS JOHNSON (M)
The Broken Rosary. Bruce Pub., 1959
The Roman Collar Detective. Bruce Pub., 1953

JOHNSON, HAMMEL (M)
Prydehurt. Appleton, D., 1926

JOHNSON, HAROLD NELS; see JOHNSON, MRS. GRACE CECILIA

JOHNSON, JAMES L. (S)
Code Name Sebastian. Lippincott, 1967

JOHNSON, LEE, pseud; see JOHNSON, LILIAN BEATRICE

JOHNSON, LILIAN BEATRICE (M)
(Pseudonym: Lee Johnson)
The Medallion. Gifford, 1962
Murder Began Yesterday. Gifford, 1966

JOHNSON, MARIGOLD, pseud; see GILLES, DANIEL

JOHNSON, MAURICE C. (M)
The Damning Trifles. Knopf, 1932

JOHNSON, PAMELA HANSFORD and NEIL STEWART (M) (Pseudonym: Nap Lombard)
The Grinning Pig; see Murder's a Swine
Murder's a Swine. Hutchinson, 1943 (U.S. title: The Grinning Pig. S & S, 1943)
Tidy Death. Cassell, 1940

JOHNSON, T. M.; see PHILIPS, JUDSON PENTECOST

JOHNSON, W. BOLINGBROKE, pseud; see BISHOP, MORRIS GILBERT

JOHNSON, ZOË (M)
Mourning After. Bles, 1939

JOHNSTON, FRANK (M)
The Prince of Turf Crooks. Long, 1954
Turf Crook. Long, 1938

JOHNSTON, GEORGE H. (M)
Death Takes Small Bites. Dodd, 1948; Penguin

JOHNSTON, MADELAINE (M)
Comets Have Long Tails. Doubleday, Doran, 1938; Eyre, 1939
Death Casts a Lure. Doubleday, Doran, 1938

JOHNSTON, RONALD (M)
Collision Ahead. Doubleday, 1965; Signet, 1966
Danger at Bravo Key. Doubleday, 1965 (English title: Red Sky in the Morning. Collins, 1965)
Red Sky in the Morning; see Danger at Bravo Key
The Stowaway. Harcourt, 1966; Collins, 1967

JOHNSTON, VELDA (M)
Along a Dark Path. Dell, 1967; Dodd, 1967

JOHNSTON, WILLIAM (D)
And Loving It. Grosset, 1967 (Get Smart series, #6)
Get Smart! Grosset, 1965 (Get Smart series, #1)
Get Smart Once Again. Grosset, 1966 (Get Smart series, #3)
Max Smart and the Perilous Pellets. Grosset, 1966 (Get Smart series, #4)
Missed It by That Much. Grosset, 1966 (Get Smart series, #5)
Sorry, Chief. Grosset, 1966 (Get Smart series, #2)

JOHNSTON, WILLIAM ANDREW (M)
Accidental Accomplice. Doubleday, Doran, 1928; Burt, 1929
The Affair in Duplex 9B. Doran, 1927; Burt, 1928
The Apartment Next Door. Little, 1919
The House of Whispers. Little, 1918; Grosset
The Marriage Cage. Stuart, L., 1960
The Mystery in the Ritsmore. Little, 1920; Grosset
The Tragedy at the Beach Club. Little, 1922
The Waddington Cipher. Doubleday, Page, 1923; Burt, 1926

JONES, ARTHUR E. (M)
It Makes You Think. Long, 1958
Too Dead to Talk. Hutchinson, 1957
You Know the Way It Is. Hutchinson, 1956

JONES, BRADSHAW, pseud; see BRADSHAW-JONES, MALCOM HENRY

JONES, CHARLES REED (M)
The King Murders. Dutton, 1929
The Rum Row Murders. Macaulay, 1931
The Torch Murder. Dutton, 1930
The Van Norton Murders. Macaulay, 1931

JONES, EUGENE (M)
The Last Clue. Selwyn, 1931
Who Killed Gregory? Stokes, 1928

JONES, G. WAYMAN (M)
Alias Mr. Death. Fiction League, 1932

JONES, GREGORY (M)
Prowl Cop. Ace, 1956

JONES, HENRY JAMES O'BRIEN BEDFORD; see BEDFORD-JONES, HENRY JAMES O'BRIEN

JONES, INIGO, pseud. (M)
The Albatross Murders. Arcadia, 1942
The Clue of the Hungry Corpse. Arcadia, 1939

JONES, JENNIFER (M)
Dirge for a Dog. Doubleday, Doran, 1939
Murder Al Fresco. Doubleday, Doran, 1939
Murder-on-Hudson. Crowell, 1937

JONES, MALCOLM HENRY BRADSHAW-; see BRADSHAW-JONES, MALCOLM HENRY

JONES, MAYNARD BENEDICT (M) (Pseudonym: Nard Jones)
The Case of the Hanging Lady. Dodd, 1938

JONES, NARD; pseud; see JONES, MAYNARD BENEDICT

JONES, PHILIP (S)
Johnny Lost, Holt, 1965
The Month of the Pearl. Heinemann, 1964; Holt, 1964; Avon, 1966

JONES, ROBERT PAGE (M)
The Heisters. Monarch, 1963 (Manhunt magazine title: "The Big Haul")

JONES, SUSAN CARLETON (M) (Pseudonym: S. Carleton)
The LaChance Mine Mystery. Little, 1920

JORDAN, ELIZABETH GARVER (M)
After the Verdict. Appleton-Century, 1939
The Blue Circle. Century, 1922
The Devil and the Deep Sea. Century, 1929
Faith Desmond's Last Stand. Extension Press, 1924
Herself. Appleton-Century, 1943
The Lady of Pentlands. Century, 1924
The Life of the Party. Appleton-Century, 1936
Miss Blake's Husband. Century, 1926
The Night Club Mystery. Century, 1930
Page Mr. Pomeroy. Appleton-Century, 1934
Red Riding Hood. Century, 1925
The Trap. Appleton-Century, 1937

JORGENSON, GEORGE ELLINGTON; see JORGENSON, NORA

JORGENSON, H. RAYMOND (D)
The Red Lacquer Case. World Pub., 1933

JORGENSON, IVAR (S)
Rest in Agony. Monarch, 1963

JORGENSON, NORA and GEORGE ELLINGTON JORGENSON (M)
Circle of Vengeance. Appleton, D., 1930

JOSCELYN, ARCHIE (D) (Pseudonym: A. A. Archer)
Eric Hearle, Detective; see The Golden Bowl
The Golden Bowl. International Fiction Lib., 1931 (Also published as: Eric Hearle, Detective. World Pub., 1934)
Three Men Murdered, by A. A. Archer. Phoenix, 1936
The Week-end Murders, by A. A. Archer. Phoenix, 1938

JOSEPH, GEORGE (M)
Before I Die. Boardman, T. V., 1959
The Curtain Has Lace Fringes. Muller, 1954
The Insider. Boardman, T. V., 1963
Lie Fallow My Acre. Jenkins, 1957
Murder in Paradise. Boardman, T. V., 1958
Needle in the Haystack. Boardman, T. V., 1957
Swan Song for a Thrush. Boardman, T. V., 1957
This Is for Keeps. Popular Lib., 1958
Three Strangers. Boardman, T. V., 1956
Venom in the Cup. Boardman, T. V., 1958

JOSKE, NEVILLE GOYDER; see GOYDER, MARGOT

JUDD, HARRISON (M) (Pseudonym: Truman Garrett)
Murder - First Edition. Arcadia, 1956
Shadow of Doubt. GM, 1961; Muller, 1962

JUDD, MARGARET (M)
Gospel of Death. Arcadia, 1960
Husband of the Corpse. Arcadia, 1958
Murder Is a Best Seller. Arcadia, 1959
Murder Makes Its Mark. Arcadia, 1961

JUDD, SARA HULTON BOWEN-; see BOWEN-JUDD, SARA HULTON

JUDSON, JEANNE (M)
Treasure of Wycliffe House. Avalon, 1967

KADES, HANS (M)
House of Crystal. Angus, 1957

KAGEY, RUDOLPH (Full name: Rudolph Hornaday Steel) (M) (Pseudonym: Kurt Steel)
Ambush House. Harcourt, 1943
Crooked Shadow. Little, 1939
Dead of Night. Little, 1940
The Imposter. Harcourt, 1942
Judas Incorporated. Little, 1939
Madman's Buff. Little, 1941
Murder for What? Bobbs, 1936
Murder Goes to College. Bobbs, 1936
Murder in G-Sharp. Bobbs, 1937
Murder of a Dead Man. Bobbs, 1935

KAMPF, HAROLD (M) (Pseudonyms: H. B. Kaye, Harold B. Kaye)
Death Is a Black Camel, by H. B. Kaye. Hammond, 1952
Grave Can Wait, by Harold B. Kaye. Gifford, 1950
Hungry Heart, by Harold B. Kaye. Gifford, 1950
Man in My Chair, by Harold B. Kaye. Gifford, 1949
My Brother, O My Brother, by Harold B. Kaye. Chapman, 1953
Red Rafferty, by Harold B. Kaye. Gifford, 1948
This Man Is a Stranger, by Harold B. Kaye. Gifford, 1950
Touch of the Sun, by Harold B. Kaye. Quality, 1952
When He Shall Appear. Little, 1954
You Only Die Once, by Harold B. Kaye. Gifford, 1950

KANE, FRANK (D-S) (Pseudonym: Frank Boyd)
About Face. Mystery House, 1947
Bare Trap. Washburn, 1952; Dell, 1965
Barely Seen. Dell, 1963
Bullet Proof. Washburn, 1951; Dell, 1961
The Conspirators. Dell, 1962
Dead Weight. Washburn, 1951; Dell, 1962
Due or Die. Dell, 1961
Esprit de Corpse. Dell, 1965
Fatal Undertaking. Dell, 1964
Final Curtain. Dell, 1964
The Flesh Peddlers, by Frank Boyd. Monarch, 1959
Frank Kane's Stacked Deck. Dell, 1961
Grave Danger. Washburn, 1954; Dell, 1960
Grave Matter. Dell, 1963
Green Light for Death. Washburn, 1949
The Guilt Edged Frame. Dell, 1964
Hang by Your Neck. S & S, 1959
Hearse Class Male. Dell, 1963
Johnny Come Lately. Dell, 1963
Johnny Liddell's Morgue. Dell, 1959
Johnny Staccato, by Frank Boyd. GM, 1960
Juke Box King. Dell, 1959
Key Witness. Dell, 1956
The Lineup. Dell, 1959
The Living End. Dell, 1957
Liz. Beacon, 1958
Maid in Paris. Dell, 1966
Margin for Terror. Dell, 1967
The Mourning After. Dell, 1961

Poisons Unknown. Washburn, 1953; Dell, 1960
A Real Gone Guy. Rinehart, 1956; Boardman, T. V., 1957
Red Hot Ice. Washburn, 1955; Boardman, T. V., 1956; Dell, 1967
Ring-a-ding-ding. Dell, 1963
A Short Bier. Dell, 1960, 1964
Slay Ride. Washburn, 1960
Stacked Desk. Dell, 1962
Syndicate Girl. Dell, 1950
Time to Prey. Dell, 1960
Trigger Mortis. Rinehart, 1958
Two to Tangle. Dell, 1965
Violent Ends. Melrose, 1953

KANE, HENRY (S-D) (Pseudonym: Anthony McCall)
Armchair in Hell. S & S, 1948; Boardman, T. V., 1949
The Case of the Murdered Madame. Avon, 1955; Signet, 1965
Conceal and Disguise. Boardman, T. V., 1966; Macmillan, 1966
A Corpse for Christmas. Boardman, T. V., 1952; Lippincott, 1955 (Also published as: Homicide at Yuletide. Signet, 1966)
The Crumpled Cup. Boardman, T. V., 1961; Signet, 1963
Dangling Man. Boardman, T. V., 1959
Dead in Bed. Boardman, T. V., 1963
Deadly Finger. Popular Lib., 1957
Death for Sale. Dell, 1957
Death Is the Last Lover. Avon, 1959; Signet, 1966
Death of a Dastard. Boardman, T. V., 1962
Death of a Flack. Boardman, T. V., 1961; Signet, 1961
Death of a Hooker. Boardman, T. V., 1961; Avon, 1963
Death on the Double. Boardman, T. V., 1958; Signet, 1965
The Devil to Pay. Boardman, T. V., 1966
Dirty Gertie. Boardman, T. V., 1963; Belmont, 1965
Edge of Panic. S & S, 1950; Boardman, T. V., 1951
Finger. Boardman, T. V., 1957
A Fistful of Death. Avon, 1958; Signet, 1965
Frenzy of Evil. Boardman, T. V., 1963; Dell, 1966
Halo for Nobody. S & S, 1947; Boardman, T. V., 1949 (Also published as: Martinis and Murder. Avon, 1960)
Hang by Your Neck. Boardman, T. V., 1950; Belmont
Holocaust, by Anthony McCall. Trident, 1967
Homicide at Yuletide; see A Corpse for Christmas
Killer's Kiss. Boardman, T. V., 1962
Kisses of Death. Belmont, 1962
Laughter Came Screaming. Boardman, T. V., 1953 (Also published as: A Mask for Murder. Avon, 1954)
A Mask for Murder; see Laughter Came Screaming
Martinis and Murder; see A Halo for Nobody
Midnight Man; see Other Sins Only Speak
Murder for the Millions. Boardman, T. V., 1964
Murder of the Park Avenue Playgirl
My Business Is Murder. Signet, 1965
My Darlin' Evangeline. Dell, 1961
The Name Is Chambers. Pyramid, 1957
Narrowing Lust. Boardman, T. V., 1956
Nirvana Can Also Mean Death. Boardman, T. V., 1959
Nobody Loves a Loser. Belmont, 1963; Boardman, T. V., 1964
Operation Delta, by Anthony McCall. Trident, 1966
Other Sins Only Speak. Boardman, T. V., 1965 (Also published as: Midnight Man. Macmillan, 1966)
The Perfect Crime. Boardman, T. V., 1961; Belmont, 1967
Peter Gunn. Dell, 1960
Prey by Dawn. Boardman, T. V., 1965
Private Eyeful. Pyramid, 1959; Boardman, T. V., 1960
Report for a Corpse. S & S, 1948; Boardman, T. V., 1950
Run for Doom. Boardman, T. V., 1960; Signet, 1962
Sleep Without Dreams. Boardman, T. V., 1958
Snatch an Eye. Boardman, T. V., 1964; PB, 1964
Sweet Charlie. Boardman, T. V., 1957
Too French and Too Deadly. Avon, 1955
Two Must Die. Tower, 1963
Trilogy in Jeopardy. Boardman, T. V., 1955
Trinity in Violence. Boardman, T. V., 1954; Avon, 1955; Signet, 1964
Triple Terror. Boardman, T. V., 1958
Unholy Trio. PB, 1967
Until You're Dead. S & S, 1951; Boardman, T. V., 1952
Who Killed Sweet Sue? Avon, 1956; Signet, 1965

KANE, WILLIAM R.; see WRIGHT, MASON

KANTOR, McKINLEY (S)
It's About Crime. Signet, 1960
Signal Thirty-Two. Random, 1950; Bantam

KARIG, WALTER (M) (Pseudonym: Keats Patrick)
Death Is a Tory. Bobbs, 1935; Melrose, 1936

KARK, NINA MARY (Pseudonym: Nina Bawden)
Devil by the Sea. Lippincott, 1957
Odd Flamingo. Collins, 1954
Solitary Child. Collins, 1956; Lancer, 1966

KARLOVA, IRINA (S)
Dreadful Hollow. Vanguard, 1942; Paperback Lib., 1965

KARP, DAVID (D)
Cry Flesh. (Also published as: Girl on Crown Street. Banner, 1967)

KASTLE, HERBERT D. (M)
Countdown to Murder. Crest, 1961
Hot Prowl. GM, 1965

KATAEV, VALENTINE
The Embezzlers. MacVeagh, 1929

KATCHER, LEO (M)
The Blind Cave. Viking, 1966; Avon, 1968

KATHRENS, WILLIAM HAROLD VAUGHAN (S)
Benny Went First. Melrose, 1952
Hit and Run. Melrose, 1953
The Lady Makes News. Melrose, 1954
Violent End. Melrose, 1955

KAUFFMAN, FRANK (S)
The Coconut Wireless. Macmillan, 1948

KAUFFMAN, REGINALD WRIGHT (D)
Beg Pardon, Sir! Penn, 1929
Blind Man. Duffield, 1927
Miss Francis Baird - Detective. Page, 1906

KAUFFMANN, LANE (S)
The Perfectionist. Lippincott, 1954; Avon, 1965
Waldo: A Novel About Murder. Lippincott, 1960; Gollancz, 1962

KAUFFMANN, STANLEY (S)
The Tightrope. S & S, 1952; Avon

KAUFMAN, LOUIS (M) (Pseudonym: Dan Keller)
One Way Street. Hale, R., 1960

KAUFMAN, MAXINE (M)
I Am Adam. Knopf, 1956

KAUFMAN, WOLFE (M)
I Hate Blondes. S & S, 1946

KAVANAUGH, CYNTHIA (S)
Bride of Lenore. Pyramid, 1966
The Deception. Pyramid, 1966

KAY, CAMERON (M)
Thieves Fall Out. GM, 1953

KAY, KENNETH (M)
Trouble in the Air. Eyre, 1959

KAYE, H. B., pseud; see KAMPF, HAROLD

KAYE, HAROLD B., pseud; see KAMPF, HAROLD

KAYE, MARY MARGARET (S) (Pseudonym: Mollie Hamilton)
Death Walked in Berlin. Staples Press, 1955
Death Walked in Cyprus. Staples Press, 1956
Death Walked in Kashmir. Staples Press, 1953
The House of Shade. Coward, 1959
Later Than You Think, by Mollie Hamilton. Coward, 1958; Longmans, 1958
Night on the Island, by Mollie Hamilton. Longmans, 1960
Shadow of the Moon. Popular Lib.
Trade Wind. Longmans, 1963

KAYSER, RONAL (M) (Pseudonym: Dale Clark)
Country Coffins. Bouregy, 1961
Death Wore Fins. Bouregy, 1959
Focus on Murder. Lippincott, 1943
Narrow Cell. Lippincott, 1944
Red Rods. Messner, 1946

KEATE, EDITH MURRAY (D)
Wildcat Scheme. Rivers, 1929

KEATING, HENRY RAYMOND FITZWALTER (D)
Death and the Visiting Fireman. Doubleday, 1959; Gollancz, 1959; Penguin, 1962
Death of a Fat God. Gollancz, 1962; Collins, 1963; Dutton, 1963
The Dog It Was That Died. Doubleday, 1962; Gollancz, 1962
Inspector Ghote Caught in the Meshes. Collins, 1967; Dutton, 1968
Inspector Ghote's Good Crusade. Collins, 1966; Dutton, 1966
Is Skin Deep, Is Fatal. Collins, 1965; Dutton, 1965; Signet, 1967
The Perfect Murder. Collins, 1964; Dutton, 1965; Signet, 1966
A Rush on the Ultimate. Doubleday, 1961; Gollancz, 1961
Zen There Was Murder. Doubleday, 1960; Gollancz, 1960; Penguin, 1963

KEATOR, MAUDE (M)
The Eyes Through the Trees. Appleton, D., 1930

KECK, MAUD and OLIVE ORBISON (M)
(Pseudonym: Keck Orbison)
Behind the Devil Screen. Washburn, 1928; Long, 1929
The Crested Key; see The Key to the Casa
The Key to the Casa. Washburn, 1929 (Also published as: The Crested Key. Long, 1929)
Thursday Island. Washburn, 1932

KEELER, HARRY STEPHEN (M-D)
The Ace of Spades Murder; see The Case of the Jeweled Ragpicker
The Amazing Web. Ward, Lock, 1929; Dutton, 1930
Behind That Mask. Ward, Lock, 1933; Dutton, 1938
The Barking Clock, with Hazel Goodwin Keeler. Ward, Lock, 1951
The Black Satchel. Ward, Lock, 1931
The Blue Spectacles; see The Spectacles of Mr. Cagliostro
The Book with the Orange Leaves. Dutton, 1942; Ward, Lock, 1943
The Bottle with the Green Wax Seal. Dutton, 1942
The Box from Japan. Dutton, 1932; Ward, Lock, 1933
By Third Degree. Ward, Lock, 1948
The Case of the Canny Killer. Phoenix, 1946 (English title: Murder in the Mills. Ward, Lock, 1946)
The Case of the Ivory Arrow. Phoenix, 1945
The Case of the Jeweled Ragpicker. Phoenix, 1948 (English title: Ace of Spades Murder. Ward, Lock, 1949)
The Case of the Mysterious Moll. Phoenix, 1945
The Case of the Sixteen Beans. Phoenix, 1944 (English title: The Sixteen Beans. Ward, Lock, 1945)
The Case of the Transposed Legs, with Hazel Goodwin Keeler. Ward, Lock, 1951
The Case of the Two Strange Ladies. Phoenix, 1943 (English title: Two Strange Ladies. Ward, Lock, 1945)
The Chameleon. Dutton, 1939
Cheung, Detective. Ward, Lock, 1938 (U.S. title: Y. Cheung, Business Detective. Dutton, 1939)
Cleopatra's Tears. Dutton, 1940; Ward, Lock, 1940
The Crilly Court Mystery. Ward, Lock, 1933
The Crimson Box. Ward, Lock, 1940 (U.S. title: The Man with the Crimson Box. Dutton, 1940)
The Defrauded Yeggman. Dutton, 1937
The Face of the Man from Saturn. Dutton, 1933
The Fiddling Cracksman. Ward, Lock, 1934 (U.S. title: The Mystery of the Fiddling Cracksman. Dutton, 1934)
Find Actor Hart. Ward, Lock, 1939 (U.S. title: The Portrait of Jirjohn Cobb. Dutton, 1940)
Find the Clock. Hutchinson, 1925; Dutton, 1927; Ward, Lock, 1931
Finger! Finger! Dutton, 1938
The Five Silver Buddhas. Dutton, 1935; Ward, Lock, 1935
The Fourth King. Ward, Lock, 1929; Dutton, 1930
The Green Jade Hand. Dutton, 1930; Ward, Lock, 1930
The Iron Ring. Ward, Lock, 1944
The Lavender Gripsack. Ward, Lock, 1941 (U.S. title: The Case of the Lavender Gripsack. Phoenix, 1944)
The Magic Eardrums. Ward, Lock, 1939 (U.S. title: The Man with the Magic Eardrums. Dutton, 1939)
The Man With the Crimson Box; see The Crimson Box
The Man with the Magic Eardrums; see The Magic Eardrums
The Man with the Wooden Spectacles. Dutton, 1941 (English title: Wooden Spectacles. Ward, Lock, 1941)
The Marceau Case. Dutton, 1936; Ward, Lock, 1936
The Matilda Hunter Murder. Dutton, 1931
The Monocled Monster. Ward, Lock, 1947
Murder in the Mills; see The Case of the Canny Killer
The Murder of London Lew. Ward, Lock, 1952
The Murdered Mathematician. Ward, Lock, 1949
The Mysterious Mr. I. Ward, Lock, 1937; Dutton, 1938
The Mystery of the Fiddling Cracksman; see The Fiddling Cracksman
The Peacock Fan. Dutton, 1941; Ward, Lock, 1942
The Portrait of Jirjohn Cobb; see Find Actor Hart
The Riddle of the Traveling Skull; see The Traveling Skull
The Riddle of the Yellow Zuri. Dutton, 1931
The Search for X-Y-Z. Ward, Lock, 1943
The Sharkskin Book. Dutton, 1941
Sing Sing Nights. Hutchinson, 1927; Dutton, 1928; Ward, Lock, 1932
The Sixteen Beans; see The Case of the Sixteen Beans
The Skull of the Waltzing Clown. Dutton, 1935
The Spectacles of Mr. Cagliostro. Hutchinson, 1926; Dutton, 1929 (Also published as: The Blue Spectacles. Ward, Lock, 1931)
Stand By - London Calling, with Hazel Goodwin Keeler. Ward, Lock, 1953
The Steeltown Strangler. Ward, Lock, 1950

The Strange Will, with Hazel Goodwin Keeler. Ward, Lock, 1949
Ten Hours. Ward, Lock, 1934; Dutton, 1937
Thieves' Nights. Dutton, 1929; Ward, Lock, 1930
The Tiger Snake. Ward, Lock, 1931
The Traveling Skull. Ward, Lock, 1934 (U.S. title: The Riddle of the Traveling Skull. Dutton, 1934)
Two Strange Ladies; see The Case of the Two Strange Ladies
Under Twelve Stars. Ward, Lock, 1933
The Vanishing Gold Truck. Dutton, 1941; Ward, Lock, 1942
The Voice of the Seven Sparrows. Hutchinson, 1924; Dutton, 1928; Ward, Lock, 1932
The Washington Square Enigma. Dutton, 1933
When Thief Meets Thief. Ward, Lock, 1938
The Wonderful Scheme; see The Wonderful Scheme of Christopher Thorne
The Wonderful Scheme of Christopher Thorne. Dutton, 1936 (English title: The Wonderful Scheme. Ward, Lock, 1937)
The Wooden Spectacles; see The Man with the Wooden Spectacles
X Jones. Ward, Lock, 1936 (U.S. title: X Jones of Scotland Yard. Dutton, 1936)
X Jones of Scotland Yard; see X Jones
Y. Cheung: Business Detective; see Cheung, Detective.

KEELER, HAZEL GOODWIN; see KEELER, HARRY STEPHEN

KEEN, GREGORY (M)
Show No Mercy. Popular Lib., 1955

KEENE, DAY (M-S)
The Brimstone Bed. Avon, 1960
Bring Him Back Dead. GM, 1956; Lancer, 1963
Bye, Baby Bunting. Allen, W. H., 1963; Holt, 1963
Carnival of Death. Macfadden, 1965
Chicago 11. Dell, 1966
Dead Dolls Don't Talk. Crest, 1959; Muller, 1963
Death House Doll. Ace, 1954
Evidence Most Blind; see Framed in Guilt
Framed in Guilt. Mill, 1949; Macfadden (Also published as: Evidence Most Blind. Locke, 1950)
Joy House. Lion, 1954
Love Me and Die. Paperback Lib., 1962
Miami 59. Dell, 1959
Mrs. Homicide. Macfadden, 1966
Murder on the Side. GM, 1958
Naked Fury. Berkley Pub., 1959
Passage to Samoa. GM, 1959
Payola. Pyramid, 1960
Sleep with the Devil. Lion, 1954
So Dead, My Lovely. Pyramid, 1959
Take a Step to Murder. GM, 1959
There Was a Crooked Man. Lancer, 1963
To Kiss or Kill. Jenkins, 1962
Too Hot to Hold. GM, 1959; Jenkins, 1967
Who Has Wilma Lathrop? GM, 1955
World Without Women. GM, 1965

KEENE, FARRADAY, pseud; see JARRETT, CORA

KEIRSTEAD, BURTON SEELY; see CAMPBELL, DONALD FREDERICK

KEITH, CARLETON, pseud; see ROBERTSON, KEITH

KEITH, DAVID, pseud; see STEEGMÜLLER, FRANCIS

KELLAND, CLARENCE BUDINGTON (D-M)
Arson Incorporated; see Where There's Smoke
The Artless Heiress. Dodd, 1942, 1962
The Cardiff Giant Affair; see The Lady and the Giant
The Case of the Nameless Corpse. Harper, 1956; Hale, R., 1958 (Serial title: The Secret of Shinning Brook)
Contraband. Hodder, 1928
The Counterfeit Cavalier; see The Counterfeit Gentleman
The Counterfeit Gentleman. Dodd, 1960 (English title: The Counterfeit Cavalier. Hale, R., 1961)
Dangerous Angel. Harper, 1953; Hale, R., 1955
Death Keeps a Secret. Harper, 1953 (Also published as: Spy and Counterspy)
The Great Mail Robbery. Harper, 1951; Museum Press, 1954
The Key Man. Harper, 1952; Hale, R., 1954
The Lady and the Giant. Dodd, 1959 (Also published as: The Cardiff Giant Affair)
The Land of the Torreones. Harper, 1945; Musson, 1945
Mark of Treachery. Dodd, 1961
Murder for a Million. World's Work, 1947
Murder Makes an Entrance. Harper, 1955
No Escape. Museum Press, 1951
The Secret of Shinning Brook; see The Case of the Nameless Corpse
The Sinister Strangers. Dodd, 1961

Spy and Counterspy; see Death Keeps a Secret
Stolen Goods. Harper, 1950; Museum Press, 1951
Where There's Smoke. Harper, 1959 (English title: Arson Incorporated. Hale, R., 1960)

KELLER, DAN, pseud; see KAUFMAN, LOUIS

KELLER, HARRY A. (D)
Death Sits In. Coward, 1932

KELLEY, AUDREY; see ROOS, AUDREY KELLEY

KELLEY, MARTHA MOTT; see WEBB, RICHARD WILSON

KELLIER, ELIZABETH (S)
Matravers Hall; see The Return of Nurse Maine
Nurse Missing; see Nurse to a Stranger
Nurse to a Stranger. Hale, R., 1961 (U.S. title: Nurse Missing. Ace, 1967)
The Patient at Tonesburry Manor. Ace, 1966
The Return of Nurse Maine. Hale, R., 1962 (U.S. title: Matravers Hall. Ace, 1967)

KELLIHER, DAN T. and W. G. SECRIST (M) (Pseudonym: Kelliher Secrist)
Murder Makes By-lines. Mystery House, 1941
Murder Melody. Phoenix, 1939

KELLOW, KATHLEEN, pseud; see HIBBERT, ELEANOR BURFORD

KELLY, F. J. (D)
The Gates of Brass. Monarch, 1963

KELLY, GEORGE C. (M) (Pseudonym: Père Absinthe)
The Red Bandana. Darling, 1880

KELLY, MARY COOLICAN (M)
The Christmas Egg. Secker & Warburg, 1958; Holt, 1966
A Cold Coming. Secker & Warburg, 1956
Dead Corse. Joseph, M., 1966; Holt, 1967
Dead Man's Riddle. Secker & Warburg, 1957; British Book Centre, 1958; Walker & Co., 1967
The Dead of Summer; see Due to a Death
Due to a Death. Joseph, M., 1962 (U.S. title: The Dead of Summer. Morrow, 1963)
March to the Gallows. Joseph, M., 1964; Holt, 1965
The Spoilt Kill. British Book Centre, 1962; Joseph, M., 1962; Penguin, 1964; Walker & Co., 1967

KELLY, VINCE (S)
The Greedy Ones. Angus, 1958

KELLY, WILLIAM PATRICK (M)
The Harrington Street Mystery. Simpkin, 1915

KELSEY, VERA (M)
The Bride Dined Alone. Doubleday, Doran, 1943
Fear Came First. Doubleday, Doran, 1945
The Owl Sang Three Times. Doubleday, Doran, 1941
Satan Has Six Fingers. Doubleday, Doran, 1943
Whisper Murder. Doubleday, 1946

KELSTON, ROBERT H. (M)
Kill One, Kill Two. Ace, 1958
Murder's End. Graphic, 1956

KEMELMAN, HARRY (D)
Friday, the Rabbi Slept Late. Crown, 1964; Crest, 1965, Hutchinson, 1965
The Nine Mile Walk. Putnam, 1967
Saturday, the Rabbi Went Hungry. Crown, 1966; Crest, 1967; Hutchinson, 1967

KEMP, HAROLD CURRY (M)
As the Devil Burned. Hammond, 1949
Dead Snake's Venom. Hammond, 1949
Death of a Dwarf. Bles, 1957
Heat Not a Furnace. Hammond, 1958
Mark of a Witch. Bles, 1959
Murder Humane. Hammond, 1947
Red for Murder. Bles, 1957

KEMP, RONALD (M)
No Time to Die. Staples, 1954

KENDALL, CAROL (M)
The Baby Snatcher. Lane, 1952; Bodley Head, 1953
The Black Seven. Harper, 1946; Musson, 1950

KENDALL, KATHRYA (M)
Black Terrace. Arcadia, 1955
Death Rides the Storm. Arcadia, 1958
You Die Today. Morrow, 1952 (English title: You Diet Today. Hale, R., 1957)
You Diet Today; see You Die Today

KENDRAKE, CARLETON, pseud; see Gardner, Erle Stanley

KENDRICK, BAYNARD HARDWICK (D)
The Aluminum Turtle. Dodd, 1960

Blind Allies. Morrow, 1954
Blind Man's Bluff. Little, 1943; Methuen, 1944
Blood on Lake Louise. Greenberg, 1934; Methuen, 1937; Triangle, 1943; Penguin
Bright Victory; see Lights Out
Clear and Present Danger. Doubleday, 1958
Death Beyond the Go-Thru. Doubleday, Doran, 1938
Death Knell. Morrow, 1945; Grosset, 1946; Methuen, 1946
Eleven of Diamonds. Greenberg, 1936; Methuen, 1937; Penguin
Flight from a Firing Wall. S & S, 1966
Frankincense and Murder. Dodd, 1961; Hale, R., 1962
Hot Red Money. Dodd, 1959; Avon, 1963
The Iron Spiders. Greenberg, 1936; Methuen, 1938; World Pub., 1944
The Last Express. Doubleday, Doran, 1937; Methuen, 1938
Lights Out. Morrow, 1945; Allen, W. H., 1948 (Also published as: Bright Victory. Transworld, 1953)
Make Mine Maclain. Morrow, 1947
Murder Made in Moscow, by Baynard Kendrick et al. Saint Mystery Lib., 1959
The Odor of Violets. Little, 1941; Methuen, 1941
Out-of-Control. Methuen, 1947; Morrow, 1945
Reservations for Death. Hale, R., 1957; Morrow, 1957
The Spear Gun Murders. Hale, R., 1961
The Tunnel. Scribner, 1949
The Whistling Hangman. Doubleday, Doran, 1937; Hale, R., 1959

KENEALLY, THOMAS
The Place at Whitton. Cassell, 1964

KENNEDY, HARVEY J. (M)
Murder and the Shocking Miss Williams. Vantage

KENNEDY, HOWARD ANGUS (M)
The Unsought Adventure. Carrier, 1929

KENNEDY, JOHN (M)
The Paper Chase. Abelard, 1956

KENNEDY, JOHN DE NAVARRE (M)
Crime in Reverse. Nelson, 1939
In the Shadow of the Cheka. Nelson, 1935
The Rain of Death. Nelson, 1945

KENNEDY, MILWARD, pseud; see BURGE, MILWARD

KENNEDY, STETSON (S)
Passage to Violence. Lion, 1955

KENNINGTON, ALAN (Full name: Gilbert Alan Kennington) (M) (Pseudonym: Alan Grant)
All Fall Down; see Young Man with a Scythe
A Bagful of Bones. Jarrolds, 1942
Blood Velvet. Jarrolds, 1956
Death of a Shrew. Jarrolds, 1937
The Golden Horse. Hale, R., 1958
It Walks the Woods, by Alan Grant. Nicholson, 1936; Mellifont, 1944
The Lost One. Jarrolds, 1957
Murder M.A. Jarrolds, 1941; Readers' Lib., 1944 (Abridged edition)
The Night Has Eyes. Jarrolds, 1939; Readers' Lib., 1946
See How They Run. Dickson, 1934
She Died Young. Jarrolds, 1938
Since There's No Help. Jarrolds, 1948
Young Man with a Scythe. Macmillan, 1951 (Also published as: All Fall Down. Jarrolds, 1952)

KENNINGTON, GILBERT ALAN; see KENNINGTON, ALAN

KENNY, CHARLES J., pseud; see GARDNER, ERLE STANLEY

KENT, ARTHUR (S)
Corpse to Cuba. Macfadden, 1967
Plant Poppies on My Grave. Avon, 1967

KENT, DAVID, pseud; see BIRNEY, HOFFMAN

KENT, ELIZABETH (M)
Who? Putnam, 1912

KENT, MARY and MICHAEL KENT (M)
The Armitage Case. Crowther, 1943

KENT, MICHAEL; see KENT, MARY

KENT, SIMON, pseud; see FINKEL, MAX

KENYON, LARRY (S)
Challenge at Le Mans. Avon, 1967
Countdown at Monaco. Avon, 1967
Devil's Ring. Avon, 1967
Revenge at Indy. Avon, 1967

KENYON, MICHAEL (S)
May You Die in Ireland. Morrow, 1965
The Trouble with Series Three. Morrow, 1967 (English title: Whole Hog. Collins, 1967)
Whole Hog; see The Trouble with Series Three

KEOGH, MRS. FRANCIS I.; see ANSLE, DOROTHY PHOEBE

KEOGH, THEODORA (D)
The Case of the Muckrakers. Macfadden, 1967 (Sexton Blake series, #4)

KERKOW, HERBERT (M)
Fateful Star Murder. Mohawk, 1931

KERNER, BEN and TOM VAN DYKE (M)
Not with My Neck. Messner, 1947

KERR, BEN, pseud; see ARD, WILLIAM

KERR, GEOFFREY (M)
Under the Influence. Joseph, M., 1953; Lippincott, 1954

KERR, SOPHIE (M)
The Blue Envelope. Doubleday, Page, 1917
The Man Who Knew the Date. Rinehart, 1951; Allen, W. H., 1952

KERRUISH, JESSE DOUGLAS (M)
The Undying Monster. Macmillan, 1936

KERSH, GERALD
The Secret Murders. Ballantine, 1953 (English title: The Great Wash. Heinemann, 1953)

KESSEL, JOSEPH (S)
The Bernan Affair. St. Martin's, 1965

KETCHUM, PHILIP (M) (Pseudonym: Carl McK. Saunders)
Death in the Library. Crowell, 1937
Death in the Night. Phoenix, 1939
The Stalkers. Berkley Pub., 1961

KEVERNE, RICHARD, pseud; see HOSKEN, CLIFFORD JAMES WHEELER

KEYES, MRS. FRANCES PARKINGTON WHEELER (S)
Dinner at Antoine's. Messner, 1948
Gold Slippers; see Victorine
Letter from Spain; see Station Wagon in Spain
The Royal Box. Messner, 1954; Crest, 1963
Station Wagon in Spain. Farrar, Straus, 1959; Avon, 1961 (English title: Letter from Spain. Eyre, 1959)
Victorine. Messner, 1958; Crest, 1959 (English title: Gold Slippers. Eyre, 1958)

KEYES, MICHAEL (M)
The Dead Parrot. Doubleday, Doran, 1933

KEYSTONE, OLIVER, pseud; see MANTINBAND, JAMES

KIDDY, MAURICE GEORGE (M)
The Devil's Dagger. Hutchinson, 1928
The Jade Hatpin. Hutchinson, 1933
Killing No Murder. Hutchinson, 1931
The Orange Ray. Hutchinson, 1934
Stonewall Stevens Investigates. Hutchinson, 1933
The Watcher in the Wood. Hutchinson, 1929

KIELLAND, ALEX (S)
Dangerous Honeymoon. Little, 1946
Live Dangerously; see The Shape of Danger
The Shape of Danger. Little, 1945 (English title: Live Dangerously. Collins, 1944)

KIERAN, JAMES
Come Murder Me. GM, 1952

KILPATRICK, MRS. FLORENCE ANTOINETTE WHARTON (D)
Elizabeth Finds the Body. Jenkins, 1949
Elizabeth the Sleuth. Jenkins, 1946
Motive for Murder. Thacker

KILVINGTON, E. (D)
Mystery in Glass. Houghton, 1931

KIMBERLEY, HUGH (M)
Wreath for a Dead Angel. Clerke, 1952

KIMMINS, ANTHONY MARTIN (M)
Lugs O'Leary. Heinemann, 1960

KINDON, THOMAS (M)
Black Beret. Roy Pubs., 1959
The Murder in the Moor. Dutton, 1929

KING, CHARLES DALY (D)
The Arrogant Alibi. Collins, 1938; Appleton-Century, 1939
Bermuda Burial. Collins, 1940; Funk, 1941
The Careless Corpse. Collins, 1937
The Curious Mr. Tarrant. Collins, 1935
The Obelists at Sea. Heritage, J., 1932; Knopf, 1933
The Obelists en Route. Collins, 1934
The Obelists Fly High. Collins, 1935

KING, FRANCIS
Dividing Stream. Longmans, 1951; Morrow, 1951

KING, FRANK (D) (Pseudonym: Clive Conrad)
The Big Blackmail. Hale, R., 1954
The Big Book of Mystery Stories. Grosset, 1933
Candidates for Murder. Hale, R., 1945
The Case of the Frightened Brother. Hale, R., 1959
The Case of the Painted Girl. Jarrolds, 1931
The Case of the Strange Beauties. Hale, R., 1952

The Case of the Vanishing Artist. Hale, R., 1956
The Catastrophe Club. Hale, R., 1947, 1949
The Crime of His Life, by Clive Conrad. Museum Press, 1951
Crooks' Caravan. Hale, R., 1955
Crooks' Cross. Hale, R., 1953
Death Changes His Mind. Hale, R., 1953
Death Has a Double. Hale, R., 1955
Death of a Cloven Hoof. Hale, R., 1951
Death of a Halo. Hale, R., 1950
Dictator of Death. Jarrolds, 1935
The Dormouse Has Nine Lives. Hale, R., 1938
Dormouse - Peacemaker. Hale, R., 1938
Dormouse - Undertaker. Hale, R., 1937
Dough for the Dormouse. Hale, R., 1939
The Empty Flat. Hale, R., 1957
Enter the Dormouse. Hale, R., 1936
Gestapo Dormouse. Hale, R., 1944
The Ghoul. Bles, 1928; Watt, G. H., 1929
Green Gold. Jarrolds, 1936
Greenface. Jarrolds, 1929; Low, 1949
The House of Sleep. Jarrolds, 1934
The Midnight Sleep. Hale, R., 1941
Mr. Balkram's Band
Molly on the Spot. Hale, R., 1940
Money's Worth of Murder, by Clive Conrad
Night at Krumlin Castle. Jarrolds, 1932; Hale, R., 1938
Only Half the Doctor Died. Hale, R., 1954
Operation Halter. Hale, R., 1948
Operation Honeymoon. Hale, R., 1950
The Owl. Jarrolds, 1930
Sinister Light. Hale, R., 1946
The Smiling Mask. Jarrolds, 1935
Terror at Staups House. Bles, 1927
That Charming Crook. Hale, R., 1958
There Was a Little Man, by Clive Conrad. Museum Press, 1948
They Vanish at Night. Hale, R., 1941, 1952
This Doll Is Dangerous. Hale, R., 1941
Two Who Talked. Hale, R., 1958
What Price Doubloons? Hale, R., 1942, 1952

KING, JAMES CLIFFORD (D) (Pseudonym: Pete Fry)
Barcelona with Love. Allen, G., 1959
The Black Beret, by Pete Fry. Boardman, T. V., 1959; Roy Pubs., 1959
The Bright Green Waistcoat, by Pete Fry. Roy Pubs., 1967
The Grey Sombrero, by Pete Fry. Boardman, T. V., 1959; Roy Pubs., 1959
The Paint-Stained Flannels, by Pete Fry. Roy Pubs., 1966
A Place to Hide. Hart-Davies, 1951; Icon Books, 1963
The Purple Dressing Gown. Boardman, T. V., 1960
The Red Stockings, by Pete Fry. Roy Pubs., 1962
The Scarlet Cloak. Boardman, T. V., 1958
The Thick Blue Sweater, by Pete Fry. Roy Pubs., 1964
Two Shadows Pass. Hart-Davis, 1952
The Yellow Trousers. Roy Pubs., 1963

KING, LOUIS (S)
Cornered. Ace, 1958

KING, LOUISE W. (S)
The Rochemer Hag. Doubleday, 1967

KING, O. B. (M)
Five Million in Cash. Doubleday, Doran, 1932; Jarrolds, 1933

KING, RAYMOND SHERWOOD (M)
(Pseudonym: Sherwood King)
Between Murders. Appleton-Century, 1935
Death Carries a Cane. Withy Grove, 1941
If I Die Before I Wake. World's Work, 1930; S & S, 1938 (Also published as: The Lady from Shanghai. World's Work, 1947)
The Lady from Shanghai; see If I Die Before I Wake

KING, RUFUS (D)
The Case of the Constant God. Doubleday, Doran, 1936; Methuen, 1938
The Case of the Dowager's Etchings. Doubleday, Doran, 1944; Methuen, 1946
The Case of the Redoubled Cross. Doubleday, 1949
Crime of Violence. Doubleday, Doran, 1937; Methuen, 1938
Deadly Dove. Doubleday, Doran, 1945
Design in Evil. Doubleday, Doran, 1942
Diagnosis: Murder. Doubleday, Doran, 1941; Methuen, 1942
Duenna to a Murder. Doubleday, 1951; Methuen, 1951
The Faces of Danger. Doubleday, Doran, 1928
The Fatal Kiss Mystery. Doubleday, Doran, 1928
Holiday Homicide. Doubleday, Doran, 1940; Methuen, 1941
The Lesser Antilles Case. Doubleday, Doran, 1934 (Also published as: Murder Challenges Valcour in the Lesser Antilles Case. Dell, 1929)
Lethal Lady. Doubleday, 1947
Lieutenant Valcour's Mammoth Mysteries. Burt, 1936

Malice in Wonderland. Doubleday, 1958
Murder by Latitude. Doubleday, Doran, 1930; Heinemann, 1931
Murder by the Clock. Doubleday, Doran, 1929; Chapman, 1929
Murder Challenges Valcour in the Lesser Antilles Case; see The Lesser Antilles Case
Murder De Luxe; see Mystery De Luxe
Murder Masks Miami. Doubleday, Doran, 1939; Methuen, 1939
Murder in the Willett Family. Collier, 1931; Doubleday, Doran, 1931
Murder on the Yacht. Doubleday, Doran, 1932; Hamilton, H., 1932
Museum Piece No. 13. Doubleday, Doran, 1946
Mystery De Luxe. Doubleday, Doran, 1927 (Also published as: Murder De Luxe. Parsons, 1927; Burt, 1929)
Profile of a Murder. Harcourt, 1935
Somewhere in This House. Doubleday, Doran, 1930
Stairway to Murder, by Rufus King et al. Bles, 1959
Steps to Murder. Doubleday, 1960
Valcour Meets Murder. Doubleday, Doran, 1932
A Variety of Weapons. Doubleday, Doran, 1943
A Woman Is Dead. Chapman, 1929

KING, SHERRY, pseud; see KING, RAYMOND SHERWOOD

KING, SHERWOOD, see KING, RAYMOND SHERWOOD

KING, TERRY JOHNSON (M)
The Neutron Beam Murder. Abelard, 1965

KINGSLEY, MICHAEL (S)
Shadows over Elveron. Random, 1963 (Also published as: Branches of Evil. Macfadden, 1964)

KINGSTON, CHARLES, pseud; see O'MAHONY, CHARLES KINGSTON

KINLAY, ALVIN (M)
Killers Cannot Live. Mitcham, 1961

KINNEL, GALWAY (S)
Black Light. Houghton, 1966

KINNEY, THOMAS (M)
The Devil Take the Foremost. Doubleday, 1947

KIPLEY, JOSEPH (M)
The Ice Pond Mystery. Ogilvie

KIPLING, RUDYARD (M)
Phantoms and Fantasies. Doubleday, 1965

KIPPAX, PETER (D)
Goring's First Case. Joseph, M., 1936

KIRK, LAURENCE, pseud; see SIMSON, ERIC ARTHUR

KIRK, RUSSELL (M)
Lost Lake; see The Surly Sullen Bell
The Old House of Fear. Fleet Pub., 1961; Avon, 1962; Gollancz, 1962
The Surly Sullen Bell. Paperback Lib., 1964 (Also published as: Lost Lake. Paperback Lib., 1966)

KIRST, HANS HELMUT (M)
Brothers in Arms. Collins, 1966; Harper & Row, 1967
The Last Card. Pyramid, 1967
The Night of the Generals. Harper & Row, 1964; Bantam, 1966; Collins, 1966
The Officer Factory. Doubleday, 1963; Pyramid, 1964

KITCHIN, CLIFFORD HENRY BENN (M)
Crime at Christmas. Harcourt, 1935
Death of His Uncle. Constable, 1939
Death of My Aunt. Harcourt, 1930; World Pub., 1960

KITCHIN, FREDERICK HARCOURT (M)
(Pseudonym: Bennett Copplestone)
Diversion of Dawson. Murray, J., 1923; Dutton, 1924
The Lost Naval Papers. Murray, J., 1917

KLEIN, ALEXANDER (S)
The Counterfeit Traitor. Holt, H., 1958

KLEIN, ERNST (M)
The Blackmailer. Avon, 1952

KLEIN, KATE; see HASTINGS, ROSALYN

KLEIN, NORMAN (M)
The Destroying Angel. Farrar & Rinehart, 1933
No! No! the Woman! Farrar & Rinehart, 1932
Terror by Night. Farrar & Rinehart, 1935

KLINGER, HENRY (D)
The Essence of Murder. Permabooks, 1963
Lust for Murder. Trident, 1966
Murder Off-Broadway. Permabooks, 1962
Wanton for Murder. Permabooks, 1961

KLINGSBERG, HARRY (M)
Doowinkle, D.A. Dial, 1940

KNAPP, GEORGE LEONARD (M)
The Scales of Justice. Lippincott, 1910

KNEBEL, FLETCHER (S)
Vanished. Doubleday, 1968

KNEVELS, GERTRUDE (M)
By Candlelight. Appleton, D., 1926
Death on the Clock. Doubleday, Doran, 1940
The Diamond Rose Mystery. Appleton, D., 1928
Octagon House. Appleton, D., 1925
Out of the Dark. Penn, 1932

KNIGHT, ADAM, pseud; see LARIAR, LAWRENCE

KNIGHT, CLIFFORD (M-D)
The Affair at Palm Springs. Dodd, 1938
The Affair in Death Valley. Dodd, 1940
The Affair of the Black Sombrero. Dodd, 1939; Grosset, 1940
The Affair of the Circus Queen. Dodd, 1940; Grosset, 1941
The Affair of the Corpse Escort. McKay, 1946
The Affair of the Crimson Gull. Dodd, 1941
The Affair of the Dead Stranger. Dodd, 1944
The Affair of the Fainting Butler. Dodd, 1943
The Affair of the Ginger Lei. Dodd, 1938
The Affair of the Golden Buzzard. McKay, 1947
The Affair of the Heavenly Voice. Dodd, 1937; Grosset, 1939
The Affair of the Jade Monkey. Dodd, 1943
The Affair of the Limping Sailor. Dodd, 1942
The Affair of the Scarlet Crab. Dodd, 1937
The Affair of the Sixth Button. McKay, 1947
The Affair of the Skiing Clown. Dodd, 1941
The Affair of the Splintered Heart. Dodd, 1942
The Affair on the Painted Desert. Dodd, 1939; Grosset, 1941
Dark Abyss. Dutton, 1949
The Dark Road. Dutton, 1951
Death and the Little Brother. Dutton, 1952
Death of a Big Shot. Dutton, 1951
Hangman's Choice. Dutton, 1949
The Yellow Cat. Dutton, 1950

KNIGHT, DAVID, pseud; see PRATHER, RICHARD SCOTT

KNIGHT, DORIS (S-Gothic)
Nurse on Terror Island. Belmont, 1967

KNIGHT, KATHLEEN MOORE (M)
(Pseudonym: Alan Amos)
Acts of Black Night. Doubleday, Doran, 1938
Akin to Murder. Doubleday, 1953; Hammond, 1955
Bait for Murder. Doubleday, 1948; Hammond, 1951
The Bass Derby Murder. Doubleday, 1949; Hammond, 1953
Beauty Is a Beast. Doubleday, 1959; Hammond, 1960
Bells for the Dead. Doubleday, Doran, 1942; Withy Grove, 1943
Birds of Ill Omen. Doubleday, Doran, 1948; Hammond, 1951
The Blue Horse of Taxco. Doubleday, 1947; Hammond, 1950
Borderline Murder, by Alan Amos. Doubleday, 1947
The Clue of the Poor Man's Shilling. Doubleday, Doran, 1936 (English title: The Poor Man's Shilling. Hammond, 1947)
Cry in the Jungle. Hammond, 1958
Death Blew Out the Match. Doubleday, Doran, 1935; Heinemann, 1935
Death Came Dancing. Doubleday, Doran, 1940; Withy Grove, 1946
Death Goes to a Reunion. Doubleday, Doran, 1940; Hammond, 1954
Design in Diamonds. Hammond, 1945; Doubleday, 1955
The Dying Echo. Hammond, 1945; Doubleday, 1949
Exit a Star. Doubleday, Doran, 1941; Withy Grove, 1943
Fatal Harvest, by Alan Amos. Doubleday, 1957; Hammond, 1958
Footbridge to Death. Doubleday, 1947; Hammond, 1949
High Rendezvous. Doubleday, 1954; Hammond, 1960
Intrigue for Empire. Doubleday, Doran, 1944; Hammond, 1946
Invitation to Vengeance. Doubleday, 1960; Hammond, 1961; PB, 1962
Panic in Paradise. Doubleday, 1951
The Poor Man's Shilling; see The Clue of the Poor Man's Shilling
The Port of Seven Strangers. Doubleday, Doran, 1945; Hammond, 1948
Pray for a Miracle. Duell, 1941
Rendezvous with the Past. Doubleday, Doran, 1940; Withy Grove, 1941
The Robineau Look. Doubleday, 1955; Pyramid, 1965 (English title: The Robineau Murders. Hammond, 1956)
The Robineau Murders; see The Robineau Look
Seven Were Suspect; see Seven Were Veiled
Seven Were Veiled. Doubleday, Doran, 1937 (Also published as: Seven Were Suspect. Withy Grove, 1942)

The Silent Partner. Doubleday, 1950; Hammond, 1953
Stream Sinister. Doubleday, Doran, 1945; Hammond, 1948
The Tainted Token. Doubleday, Doran, 1938; Withy Grove, 1942
Terror by Twilight. Doubleday, Doran, 1943; Withy Grove, 1943
They're Going to Kill Me. Doubleday, 1955; Heinemann, 1957
Three of Diamonds. Doubleday, 1953; Hammond, 1955
The Trademark of a Traitor. Doubleday, Doran, 1943; Hammond, 1945
The Trouble at Turkey Hill. Doubleday, 1946; Hammond, 1949
Valse Macabre. Doubleday, 1952; Hammond, 1954
The Wheel That Turned. Doubleday, Doran, 1936

KNIGHT, LEONARD ALFRED (M)
The Astounding Dr. Yell. Low, 1950
The Brazen Head. Low, 1948
Close the Frontier. Low, 1939
Conqueror's Road. Low, 1945
Contraband. Low, 1949
The Creaking Tree Mystery. Low, 1931
The Creeping Death. Low, 1933
The Dancing Stones. Low, 1946
Dangerous Knowledge. Low, 1950
Deadman's Bay. Low, 1930
Death Stands Near. Low, 1936
High Treason. Gryphon, 1954
Judgment Rock. Low, 1947
Man Hunt. Low, 1930
Murder by Experiment. Low, 1935
The Night Express Murder. Low, 1936
One Way Only. Gryphon, 1956
The Pawn. Low, 1931
The Paying Guest. Low, 1951
Redbeard. Low, 1935
The Riddle of Nap's Hollow. Low, 1932
Rider in the Sky. Gryphon, 1953
The S.S. Mystery. Low, 1938
The Solander Box Mystery. Low, 1940
Spanish Cove. Low, 1945
Spring Cruise. Low, 1934
The Super-Cinema Murder. Low, 1937
The Valley of Green Shadows. Gryphon, 1955
The Viking Feast Mystery. Low, 1951

KNIGHT, MALLORY T. (D)
Dirty Rotten Depriving Ray. Award, 1967
The Man from T.O.M.C.A.T. The Dozen Deadly Dragons of New York. Award, 1967
The Terrible Ten. Award, 1967

KNIPE, EMILIE (M) (Pseudonym: Thérèse Benson)
Death Wears a Mask. Harper, 1935
Fool's Gold. Dodd, 1932
The Fourth Lovely Lady. Bobbs, 1932
Gallant Adventuress. Dodd, 1932
The Go-Between. Dodd, 1930
Strictly Private. Dodd, 1931
The Unknown Daughter. Dodd, 1929

KNIPSCHEER, JAMES M. W. (M)
(Pseudonym: James M. Fox)
The Aleutian Blue Mink. Little, 1951; Williams & Norgate, 1952
Bright Serpent. Little, 1953; Hammond, 1956
Cheese from a Mousetrap. Davies, 1944
Code Three. Little, 1953; Hammond, 1956
Dark Crusade. Little, 1954; Cassell, 1955
Death Commits Bigamy. Coward, 1947; Williams & Norgate, 1950
Don't Try Anything Funny. Davies, 1943
Free Ride. Popular Lib., 1957
The Gentle Hangman. Little, 1950; Williams & Norgate, 1952
Hell on the Way. Davies, 1943
The Inconvenient Bride. Coward, 1948; Williams & Norgate, 1951
The Iron Virgin. Little, 1951; Hammond, 1954
The Lady Regrets. Coward, 1947; Davies, 1947
Scarlet Slippers. Little, 1952; Hammond, 1955
A Shroud for Mr. Bundy. Little, 1952; Hammond, 1955
The Wheel Is Fixed. Little, 1951; Williams & Norgate, 1952

KNOBLOCK, KENNETH THOMAS (M)
Murder in the Mind. Harper, 1932
Take up the Bodies. Harper, 1933
There's Been Murder Done. Harper, 1931; Selwyn, 1931
Winter in Mallorca. Harper, 1934

KNOTTS, RAYMOND, pseud; see VOLK, GORDON

KNOWLAND, HELEN DAVIS (M)
Madame Baltimore. Dodd, 1949

KNOWLER, JOHN (S)
The Trap. Cape, 1964; Knopf, 1965; Avon, 1966

KNOWLTON, EDWARD ROGERS (S)
(Pseudonym: Kerk Rogers)
With Intent to Destroy. Hammond, 1946

KNOWLTON, ROBERT (S)
Court of Crows. Gollancz, 1961; Harper, 1961; Paperback Lib., 1963

KNOWLTON, WINTHROP; see GOODMAN, GEORGE

KNOX, BILL (S) (Pseudonym: Robert MacLeod)
Blacklight. Doubleday, 1967; Long, 1967
Cave of Bats, by Robert MacLeod. Holt, 1964
The Cockatoo Crime. Long, 1958
Deadline for a Dream. Long, 1959
Death Calls the Shots. Long, 1961
Death Department. Long, 1960
Devilweed. Doubleday, 1966; Long, 1966
Die for Big Betsy. Long, 1961
Drum of Power, by Robert MacLeod. Long, 1964
The Drum of Ungara. Doubleday, 1963
The Ghost Car. Doubleday, 1966
The Grey Sentinels. Doubleday, 1963
In at the Kill. Doubleday, 1961
Justice on the Rocks. Doubleday, 1967; Long, 1967
The Killing Game. Doubleday, 1963
Leave It to the Hangman. Doubleday, 1960; Long, 1960
Little Drops of Blood. Doubleday, 1962; Long, 1962
The Man in the Battle. Long, 1963
Murder on Vacation, by Robert MacLeod. Bouregy, 1962
Sanctuary Isle. Long, 1962
The Scavengers. Doubleday, 1964; Long, 1964
The Taste of Proof. Doubleday, 1965; Long, 1966

KNOX, RONALD ARBUTHNOTT (D)
Double Cross Purposes; see Settled Out of Court
Footsteps at the Lock. Methuen, 1928; Penguin
Settled Out of Court. Dutton, 1934 (Also published as: Double Cross Purposes. Hodder, 1937)
Still Dead. Dutton, 1934; Hodder, 1934
Three Taps. S & S, 1927; Penguin
The Viaduct Murder. S & S, 1925; Methuen, 1926

KNOX, TIMOTHY (M)
Death in the State House. Houghton, 1934

KNOX, WINIFRED; see PECK, WINIFRED

KNYE, CASSANDRA (S-Gothic)
Castle and the Key. Paperback Lib., 1967
The House That Fear Built. Paperback Lib., 1966

KOEHLER, ROBERT PORTNER (M)
The Blue Parakeet Murders. Phoenix, 1948
The Case of the Dead Cadet. Phoenix, 1938
Corpse in the Wind. Phoenix, 1944
The Doctor's Murder Case. Phoenix, 1939
The Hooded Vulture Murders. Phoenix, 1947
The Murder Expert. Phoenix, 1945
Murder in the Green Sedan. Phoenix, 1942
Puppets of Chance. Sears, 1933
The Road House Murders. Phoenix, 1946
Salute to Murder. Phoenix, 1944
Sing a Song of Murder. Phoenix, 1941
Some Try Murder. Ryerson, 1943
Steps to Murder. Phoenix, 1943
Tread Gently, Death. Phoenix, 1945

KOONCE, CHARLES (M)
The Weeping Willow Murders. Burton Pub., 1934

KOOTZ, SAMUEL MELVIN (M)
Puzzle in Paint. Crown, 1943
Puzzle in Petticoats. Crown, 1944

KORNBLUTH, CYRIL M. (Pseudonym: Jordon Park)
A Man of Cold Rages. Pyramid, 1959

KRAMER, KARL (S)
Kiss Me Quick. Monarch, 1964

KRASLOW, DAVID and R. S. BOYD
A Certain Evil. Little, 1965; Barker, 1966

KRASNER, WILLIAM
Stag Party. Harper, 1957
Walk the Dark Streets. Harper, 1949

KRASNEY, SAMUEL A. (D) (Pseudonym: Sam Curzon)
Death Cries in the Street. Rinehart, 1957
Design for Dying. Ace, 1960
Homicide Call. Morrow, 1962
Homicide West. Morrow, 1961; Allen, W. H., 1962; PB, 1963
Mania for Blondes. Ace, 1961
The Morals Squad. Ace, 1959
The Rapist. Ace, 1960

KREPPS, ROBERT W. (S)
Gamble My Last Game. Macmillan, 1958
Tell It on the Drums. Hale, 1957

KROLL, HENRY HARRISON (M)
The Ghosts of the Slave Drivers Bend. Bobbs, 1937

KRUGER, PAUL (M)
A Bullet for a Blonde. Dell, 1958
Dig Her a Grave. Ace, 1960

Message from Marise. GM, 1963; Muller, 1964
Weave a Wicked Web. S & S, 1967
Weep for Willow Green. S & S, 1966

KRUGER, RAYNE (M)
Ferguson. Appleton-Century, 1957
My Name Is Celia. Macmillan, 1955
The Spectacle. Macmillan, 1954

KRULL, FELIX, pseud; see WHITE, JAMES DILLON

KRUMGOLD, JOSEPH (M)
Thanks to Murder. Vanguard, 1935

KUMMER, FREDERICK ARNOLD (M) (Pseudonym: Arnold Fredericks)
Blue Lights. Watt, 1915; Grosset, 1916; Garden City Pub., 1926
Death at Eight Bells. Lothrop, 1937
Design for Murder. Lothrop, 1936
Film of Fear. Hayes, 1921
The Ivory Snuff-box. Watt, 1912; Simpkin, 1917; Garden City Pub., 1926
The Little Fortune. Watt, 1915; Simpkin, 1917
The Mark of the Rat. Paul, S., 1930; Sears, 1930
One Million Francs. Nash, 1920
The Road to Fortune. Doran, 1925; Hodder, 1926
The Scarecrow Murders. Dodd, 1938
The Spanish Lady. Sears, 1933
The Web. Century, 1919

KURNITZ, HARRY (M) (Pseudonym: Marco Page)
Fast Company. Dodd, 1937; Heinemann, 1938; Paperback Lib., 1963
Invasion of Privacy. Random, 1955; Paperback Lib., 1964
Reclining Figure, by Marco Page. Eyre, 1952; Random, 1952; Paperback Lib., 1963
The Shadowy Third. Dodd, 1946; Paperback Lib., 1964 (Also published as: Suspects All. Withy Grove, 1948)
Suspects All; see The Shadowy Third

KUTAK, ROSEMARY (M)
Darkness of Slumber. Lippincott, 1944; PB, 1946
I Am the Cat. Farrar, Straus, 1948; Collier, 1964

KUTTNER, HENRY (M) (Pseudonyms: Will Garth, Lewis Padgett)
The Brass Ring, by Lewis Padgett. Duell, 1946
The Day He Died, by Lewis Padgett. Duell, 1947
Dr. Cyclops, by Will Garth. Phoenix, 1940
A Man Drowning. Harper, 1952
Murder of a Mistress. Permabooks, 1957
Murder of a Wife. Permabooks, 1958
The Murder of Ann Avery. PB, 1956
Murder of Eleanor Pope. Permabooks, 1956

KYD, THOMAS, pseud; see HARBAGE, ALFRED BENNETT

KYLE, ELIZABETH, pseud; see DUNLOP, AGNES MARY ROBERTSON

KYLE, ELLA JANE (M)
Old Gumber's Mill. Ben Hur Press, 1928

KYLE, ROBERT (S)
Ben Gates Is Hot. Dell, 1964
Blackmail, Inc. Dell, 1958
The Crooked City. Dell, 1954
The Golden Urge. GM, 1963; Muller, 1964
Model for Murder. Dell, 1959
Nice Guys Finish Last. Dell, 1955
Some Like It Cool. Dell, 1962

KYLE, SEFTON
Bloomsbury Treasure. Jenkins, 1932
Guilty, But - ? Jenkins, 1930
Hawk. Jenkins, 1932
Vengeance of Mrs. Danvers. Jenkins, 1932

LA BERN, ARTHUR (M)
Goodbye Piccadilly, Farewell Leicester Square. Stein & Day, 1967

LABORDE, JEAN (M)
A Fair Trial. Doubleday, 1962
A Privileged Character. Doubleday, 1963

LA COSTE, GUY ROBERT and EADFRID A. BINGHAM (M) (Pseudonym: Guy Berton)
Art Thou the Man? Dodd, 1905

LACY, ED, pseud; see ZINBERG, LEN

LADLINE, ROBERT (M)
A Devil in Downing St. Jenkins, 1937
If the Shoe Fits. Jenkins, 1936
The Man Who Made a King. Jenkins, 1936
Quest of the Vanishing Star. Jenkins, 1932
Sinister Craft. Jenkins, 1939

LADY, FREDERICK (M)
Master of Money. Jarrolds, 1931
Million Pounds Reward. Jarrolds, 1929

LAFFEATY, CHRISTINA (S-Gothic)
Mistress of Tara. Paperback Lib., 1967 (Also published as: Reluctant Bride)

LAFFIN, JOHN (S) (Pseudonym: Mark Napier)
Doorways to Danger. Abelard, 1966
A Very Special Agent. Funk, 1967

LAFLIN, JACK (S)
The Reluctant Spy. Belmont, 1966
The Spy in White Gloves. Belmont, 1965
The Spy Who Didn't. Belmont, 1966
The Spy Who Loved America. Belmont, 1964

LA FORCE, BEATRICE (M)
The Sound of Hasty Footsteps. Bouregy, 1963

LA FRANCE, MARSTEN (D)
Miami Murder-Go-Round. World Pub., 1951

LA GARDE, HENRY (S)
Tide Waits for No Man. Forbes Robertson, 1952

LAING, ALEXANDER KINNAN (D)
The Cadaver of Gideon Wyck. Farrar & Rinehart, 1934; Macmillan, 1960 (Abridged edition); Collier, 1962
Dr. Scarlett. Farrar & Rinehart, 1936
The Methods of Dr. Scarlett, with T. Painter. Farrar & Rinehart, 1937
The Motives of Nicholas Holtz, with T. Painter. Farrar & Rinehart, 1936

LAING, JANET (M)
Villa Jane. Century, 1929; Hodder, 1929

LAING, KENNETH (M)
The Malignant Snowman. Jenkins, 1950
The Midnight Walkers. Jenkins, 1951
No Man's Laughter. Jenkins, 1950
Shadow People. Jenkins, 1952; Roy Pubs., 1956

LAING, PATRICK, pseud; see LONG, AMELIA REYNOLDS

LAKE, JOE BARRY (D) (Pseudonym: Joe Barry)
The Clean Up. Arcadia, 1947
The Fall Guy. Mystery House, 1945
The Pay-Off. Arcadia, 1943
Third Degree. Mystery House, 1943
The Triple Cross. Mystery House, 1946

LAKIN, RICHARD (S)
The Body Fell on Berlin. Putnam, 1943

LA MASTER, SLATER (M)
The Phantom in the Rainbow. McClurg, 1929; Hamilton, H., 1931

LAMB, ANTONIO (S)
The Greenhouse. Pyramid, 1966

LAMBERT, CHRISTINE, pseud; see LOEWENGARD, HEIDI HUBERTA FREYBE

LAMBERT, DUDLEY; see LAMBERT, ROSA

LAMBERT, ELISABETH (D)
The Sleeping House Party. Coward, 1951

LAMBERT, ERIC (S)
Hiroshima Reef. Norton, 1967

LAMBERT, GERARD BARNES (D)
Murder in Newport. Scribner, 1938

LAMBERT, ROSA and DUDLEY LAMBERT (M)
Crime in Quarantine. Nelson, 1938
The Mediterranean Murder. Wishart, 1930; Nelson, 1933
Monsieur Faux-Pas. Wishart, 1928; Nelson, 1933
The Mystery of the Golden Wings. Nelson, 1935

LANCASTER, BRUCE (S)
The Secret Road. Little, 1952; Permabooks, 1955

LANCASTER, PAUL (D)
Disappearance of Norman Langdale. Paul, S., 1929
Executioner's Axe. Paul, S., 1930
Jolly Roger Mystery. Paul, S., 1929

LANCASTER, VICKY, pseud; see ANSLE, DOROTHY PHOEBE

LANCE, LESLIE (S-Gothic)
Bride of Emersham. Pyramid, 1967

LAND, MYRICK (M)
Search the Dark Woods. Funk, 1955

LANDELS, D. H., pseud; see HENDERSON, DONALD LANDELS

LANDON, CHRISTOPHER GUY (M)
Dead Man Rise Up Never. Heinemann, 1963; Sloane, 1963
Flag in the City. Macmillan, 1954
Hornet's Nest. Heinemann, 1956
Ice Cold in Alex. Heinemann, 1957; Sloane, 1957
Mirror Room. Heinemann, 1960; Pan, 1962
Shadow of Time; see Unseen Enemy

Stone Cold Dead in the Market. Heinemann, 1955
Unseen Enemy. Doubleday, 1957 (English title: Shadow of Time. Heinemann, 1957)

LANDON, HERMAN (M)
The Back Seat Murder. Liveright, 1931
Buy My Silence. Cassell, 1931
Death on the Air. Liveright, 1929
Elusive Picaroon. Cassell, 1932
The Forbidden Door. MacVeagh, 1927; Burt, 1928
Gray Magic. Watt, G. H., 1925
Gray Phantom. Watt, G. H., 1921; Burt, 1924
Gray Phantom's Return. Burt, 1924
Gray Terror. Watt, G. H., 1923; Burt, 1925
The Green Shadow. MacVeagh, 1928
Hands Unseen. Watt, G. H., 1924; Burt, 1925
Haunting Fingers. Jarrolds, 1930
Murder Mansion. Liveright, 1928
Mystery Mansion. Cassell, 1930
The Owl's Warning. Liveright, 1932
Picaroon Does Justice. Cassell, 1929
Picaroon in Pursuit. Cassell, 1932
Picaroon Resumes Practice. Cassell, 1931
The Room Under the Stairs. Watt, G. H., 1923; Burt, 1925
Silver Chest. Jarrolds, 1932
Three Brass Elephants. Liveright, 1930 (Also published as: Whispering Shadows. Jarrolds, 1930)
Trailing Picaroon. Cassell, 1930
Voice in the Closet. Liveright, 1930
Whispering Shadows; see Three Brass Elephants

LANDON, LOUISE, pseud; see HAUCK, MRS. LOUISE PLATT

LANE, GRANT, pseud; see FISHER, STEPHEN GOULD

LANE, GRET (D)
Cancelled Score Mystery. Jenkins, 1930
Curlew Coombe Mystery. Jenkins, 1931
Lantern House Affair. Jenkins, 1932

LANE, JEREMY (M)
Murder Menagerie. Phoenix, 1946
Murder Spoils Everything. Phoenix, 1949

LANE, KENDALL (S)
Gambit. GM, 1966

LANE, KENNETH WESTMACOTT (S) (Pseudonym: Keith West)
Hanging Waters. Putnam, 1933

LANG, ANDREW (S)
The Disentanglers. Longmans, 1903

LANG, ANTHONY, pseud; see VAHEY, JOHN GEORGE HASLETTE

LANG, HARRY (M)
The Corpse on the Hearth. Macrae Smith, 1946

LANG, THEO (Name originally: Theo Langbehn) (M) (Pseudonym: Peter Piper)
The Corpse That Came Back. Random, 1954
Death Came in Straw. Hurst, 1945
Death in Canongate. Hodder, 1952
Margot Leck. Hurst, 1947
Murder After the Blitz. Hurst, 1942
Woman Delia. Hodder, 1957

LANGBEHN, THEO; see LANG, THEO

LANGDON, JOHN (S)
Vicious Circuit. Macmillan, 1963

LANGE, JOHN (S)
Odds On. Signet, 1966
Scratch One. Signet, 1967

LANGHAM, JAMES R. (D)
Pocket Full of Clues. S & S, 1941
Sing a Song of Homicide. S & S, 1940

LANGLEY, LEE (D)
Osiris Died in Autumn. Doubleday, 1964

LANGLEY, NOEL (M)
Tales of Mystery and Revenge. Barker, 1950

LANGMAID, KENNETH (M)
The Mystery Cruise. Hale, R., 1958

LANGSLOW, JANE; see LARMINIE, MARGARET R.

LANGTON, JANE (D)
Transcendental Murder. Harper & Row, 1964

LANHAM, EDWIN MOULTRIE (D)
Case of the Missing Corpse; see Death of a Corinthian
Death in the Wind. Harcourt, 1956; Boardman, T. V., 1957
Death of a Corinthian. Harcourt, 1953 (Serial title: The Case of the Missing Corpse)
Double Jeopardy. Gollancz, 1959; Harcourt, 1959; PB, 1961
It Shouldn't Happen to a Dog. Boardman, T. V., 1949

Monkey on a Chain. Harcourt, 1963; Gollancz, 1964
Murder on My Street. Gollancz, 1958; Harcourt, 1958; PB, 1961; Penguin
No Hiding Place. Harcourt, 1962; Gollancz, 1963
One Murder Too Many. Harcourt, 1952
Passage to Danger. Gollancz, 1962; Harcourt, 1962; Longmans, 1962
Politics Is Murder. Harcourt, 1947
Six Black Camels. Gollancz, 1961; Harcourt, 1961; PB, 1963
Slug It Slay. Harcourt, 1946

LANNING, GEORGE (S)
The Pedestal. Harper & Row, 1966; Joseph, M., 1966

LARBALESTIER, PHILIP GEORGE (M)
Black Shrouds the Bride. Gifford, 1951
Darling, Don't Be Dumb. Gifford, 1950
Death Casts No Shadow. Gifford, 1951
The Singing Sword. Gifford, 1954
The Yellow Card Mystery. Gifford, 1953

LARIAR, LAWRENCE (D) (Pseudonyms: Adam Knight, Michael Stark)
The Day I Died. Appleton, 1952
Death Paints the Picture. Phoenix, 1943
Friday for Death. Crown, 1949; Boardman, T. V., 1950
The Girl with the Frightened Eyes. Dodd, 1945; Cassell, 1950
Girl Running, by Adam Knight. New Amer. Lib., 1956
He Died Laughing. Phoenix, 1943; Boardman, T. V., 1951
I'll Kill You Next, by Adam Knight. Appleton, 1954; Signet, 1965
Kill-Box; see Run for Your Life
Kiss and Kill, by Adam Knight. Crown, 1953; Boardman, T. V., 1954
Knife at My Back, by Adam Knight. Crown, 1952
The Man with the Lumpy Nose. Dodd, 1944
Murder for Madame, by Adam Knight. Crown, 1951
Run for Your Life, by Michael Stark. Crown, 1946 (Also published as: Kill-Box. Ace, 1954)
Stone Cold Blonde, by Adam Knight. Crown, 1951; Boardman, T. V., 1952
The Sunburned Corpse, by Adam Knight. Crown, 1952
Win, Place and Die! Appleton, 1953
You Can't Catch Me, by Adam Knight. Crown, 1951

LARKIN, MARGARET (S)
Seven Shares in a Gold Mine. S & S, 1959

LARMINIE, MARGARET RIVERS and JANE LANGSLOW (M)
Gory Knight. Longmans, 1937

LA ROCHE, K. ALLISON (D)
Dear Dead Professor. Phoenix, 1944

LARSON, RUSSELL W. (D)
Death Stalks a Marriage. Bellevue, 1956

LA SPINA, GREYE (S)
Shadows of Evil. Paperback Lib., 1966

LATHAM, ALISON and ESTHER LATHAM (M) (Pseudonym: Murray Latham)
Enjoy Such Liberty. Hutchinson, 1943
Even from the Law. Hutchinson, 1946
Flight Without Wings. Hutchinson, 1950
River in the Dark. Hutchinson, 1945
Some Names Are Dangerous. Hutchinson, 1948

LATHAM, EDYTHE (M)
The Seasons of God. Doubleday, 1963

LATHAM, ESTHER; see LATHAM, ALISON

LATHAM, MURRAY, pseud; see LATHAM, ALISON

LATHEN, EMMA, pseud. (D)
Accounting for Murder. Macmillan, 1964; Gollancz, 1965; Avon, 1966
Banking on Death. Macmillan, 1961; Gollancz, 1962; Avon, 1964
Death Shall Overcome. Macmillan, 1966; Gollancz, 1967
Murder Against the Grain. Macmillan, 1967
Murder Makes the Wheels Go Round. Gollancz, 1966; Macmillan, 1966
A Place for Murder. Macmillan, 1963; Gollancz, 1964; Avon, 1966

LATHROP, LORIN ANDREWS (M) (Pseudonym: Kenyon Gambier)
Princess of Paradise Island. Doran, 1925
The White Horse and the Red-Haired Girl. Doran, 1919

LATIMER, JONATHAN (D)
Black Is the Fashion for Dying. Random, 1959; PB, 1961
The Dead Don't Care. Doubleday, Doran, 1938; Macfadden, 1964
Headed for a Hearse. Doubleday, Doran, 1935; Dell, 1957; Macfadden, 1964
The Lady in the Morgue. Doubleday, Doran, 1936, 1953; Sun Dial, 1937; PB, 1944; Methuen, 1957

The Mink-lined Coffin. Methuen, 1960
Red Gardenias. Doubleday, Doran, 1939
Sinners and Shrouds. S & S, 1955; Methuen, 1956
Solomon's Vineyard. Pan, 1961

LATIMER, RUPERT, pseud; see MILLS, ALGERNON VICTOR

LATTA, GORDON
Arnholt Makes His Bow. Benn, 1932
Re-enter Arnholt. Benn, 1932
Toni Diamonds. Dial, 1931

LAUFERTY, LILIAN (M)
The Crimson Thread. S & S, 1942
The Hungry House. S & S, 1943; World Pub., 1945

LAUNAY, ANDREW JOSEPH (D)
A Corpse in Camera. Boardman, T. V., 1963
Death and Still Life. Boardman, T. V., 1964
The New Shining White Murder. Boardman, T. V., 1962
She Modelled Her Coffin. Boardman, T. V., 1961

LAURENCE, JOHN (D)
Honeymoon Mystery. Long, 1929
Secret of Sheen. International Fiction Lib., 1929

LAURENCE, ROBERT JACKSON (M)
Murder in Mayfair. Comet, 1958

LAURENSON, R. M. (D)
Better Off Dead. Arcadia, 1955
The Case of the Six Bullets. Foulsham, 1950
The Railroad Murder Case. Phoenix, 1948

LAURENT, CECIL SAINT (M)
The Cautious Maiden. Crown, 1955

LAURISTON, VICTOR (M)
The Twenty-first Burr. Doran, 1922

LAWRENCE, DAVID (D)
Dead Orchid. Ward, Lock, 1958
Death Has Two Hands. Ward, Lock, 1960

LAWRENCE, GIL (S)
Fury Without Legs. Pyramid, 1958

LAWRENCE, H. L. (S)
The Sparta Medallion. MacDonald & Co., 1961

LAWRENCE, HILDA (D)
Blood Upon the Snow. S & S, 1944
Composition for Four Hands; see Duet for Death
Death of a Doll. S & S, 1947; PB
Duet of Death. S & S, 1947 (Also published as: Composition for Four Hands. Ace, 1947)
The Pavilion. S & S, 1946; Dell, 1965
A Time to Die. S & S, 1945

LAWRENCE, MARYJANE (S)
Intruder. Mitcham, 1961

LAWS, GERALDINE; see GRIBBLE, LEONARD REGINALD

LAYHEW, MRS. JANE (D)
R_x for Murder. Lippincott, 1946

LEA, HUGH (M)
The Ghosts of Perranprah. Hodder, 1937
The Mine of Ill Omen. Hodder, 1939

LEACROFT, ERIC, pseud; see YOUNG, ERIC BRETT

LEADERMAN, GEORGE, pseud; see ROBINSON, RICHARD BLUNDELL

LEAMAN, ADELE (M)
The Green Bag. Skeffington, 1932

LEASOR, JAMES (S)
Passport to Oblivion. Heinemann, 1964; Lippincott, 1965 (Also published as: Where the Spies Are. Signet)
Passport to Peril; see Spylight
Spylight. Lippincott, 1966; Signet, 1967 (English title: Passport to Peril. Heinemann, 1966)
Where the Spies Are; see Passport to Oblivion
The Yang Meridian. Putnam, 1967

LEBHERZ, RICHARD
Altars of the Heart. Grove, 1958

LeBLANC, MAURICE (D)
The Arrest of Arsène Lupin. Nash, 1911
Arsène Lupin, with Edgar Jepson. Doubleday, Page, 1909
Arsène Lupin: Gentleman Burglar. Donahue, M. A.; Ogilvie
Arsène Lupin: Gentleman-Cambriolur. Ginn, 1938
Arsène Lupin Intervenes. Macaulay, 1929
Arsène Lupin, Super Sleuth. Macaulay, 1927
Arsène Lupin versus Holmlock Shears. Richards, 1909
The Blonde Lady. Doubleday, Page, 1910
The Confessions of Arsène Lupin. Newnes, 1913; Walker & Co., 1967
The Crystal Stopper. Macaulay, 1913
The Eight Strokes of the Clock. Macaulay, 1925

The Exploits of Arsène Lupin. Harper, 1907; Dufour, 1962 (Also published as: The Seven of Hearts and The Extraordinary Adventures of Arsène Lupin, Gentleman Burglar. Cassell, 1908)
The Extraordinary Adventures of Arsène Lupin; see The Exploits of Arsène Lupin
The Fair-Haired Lady. Richards, 1909
The Golden Triangle. Macaulay, 1917
The Hollow Needle. Macaulay, 1929; Dufour, 1962
Man of Miracles. Macaulay, 1931
The Melamore Mystery. Macaulay, 1930
The Memoirs of Arsène Lupin. Macaulay, 1925
The Return of Arsène Lupin. Macaulay
The Secret of Sarek. Burt, 1920
The Seven Hearts; see The Exploits of Arsène Lupin
The Teeth of the Tiger. Doubleday, Page, 1914; Grosset, 1916
Three Eyes. Macaulay, 1921
Woman of Mystery. Macaulay, 1916
Woman with Two Smiles. Macaulay, 1933

LeBRETON, AUGUSTE (S)
The Law of the Streets. Collins, 1957, 1960

LeCARRÉ, JOHN, pseud; see CORNWELL, DAVID JOHN MOORE

LEDERER, NORBERT; see DAY, LILLIAN

LEDIG, A. K.; see MALAN, ERNESTINE

LEE, AUSTIN (D) (Pseudonym: John Austwick)
Call in Miss Hogg. Cape, 1956
The County Library Murders, by John Austwick. Hale, R., 1962
Highland Homicide, by John Austwick. Hale, R., 1957
Hubberthwaite Horror, by John Austwick. Hale, R., 1958
Miss Hogg and the Brontë Murders. Cape, 1957
Miss Hogg and the Covent Garden Murders. Cape, 1960
Miss Hogg and the Dead Dean. Cape, 1958
Miss Hogg and the Missing Sisters. Cape, 1961
Miss Hogg and the Squash Club Murder. Cape, 1957
Miss Hogg Flies High. Cape, 1958
Miss Hogg's Last Case. Cape, 1963
The Mobile Library Murders, by John Austwick. Hale, R., 1964
Murder in the Borough Library, by John Austwick. Hale, R., 1959

LEE, BABS, pseud; see LEE, MARION VAN DER VEER

LEE, DORIAN (S)
Cut the Cards, Lady! Long, 1952

LEE, EDWARD, pseud; see FOUTS, EDWARD LEE

LEE, ELSIE (M-Gothic)
Clouds over Vellanti. Lancer, 1965
The Curse of Carranca. Lancer, 1966
Dark Moon, Lost Lady. Lancer, 1965
Mansion of the Golden Windows. Lancer, 1966
Spy at Villa Miranda. Lancer, 1967
Sinister Abbey. Lancer, 1967

LEE, GERALD (M)
Murder and Music. Talbot, 1943

LEE, GYPSY ROSE, pseud; see HOVICK, ROSE LOUISE

LEE, JEANETTE BARBOUR PERRY (M)
The Green Jacket. Scribner, 1917
The Mysterious Office. Scribner, 1922

LEE, LEONARD (M)
The Twisted Mirror. Ziff-Davis, 1947

LEE, MANFRED; see DANNAY, FREDERIC

LEE, MARION VAN DER VEER (M) (Pseudonym: Babs Lee)
Measured for Murder, with Clare Castler Saunders. Scribner, 1944
A Model Is Murdered. Scribner, 1942
Passport to Oblivion. Scribner, 1945

LEE, NOEL (S)
Danger in Numbers. Wright & Brown, 1944
Fear Without End. Wright & Brown, 1949
Papers Mean Peril. Wright & Brown, 1942

LEE, NORMA (D)
Beautiful Gunner. Laurier, 1953

LEE, NORMAN (M) (Pseudonyms: Raymond Armstrong, Mark Corrigan, Robertson Hobart)
Australian Adventure, by Mark Corrigan. Allen, T., 1960; Hale, R., 1960
Big Boys Don't Cry, by Mark Corrigan. Angus, 1956
The Big Squeeze, by Mark Corrigan. Angus, 1955
Blood on the Lake, by Robertson Hobart. Hale, R., 1961
Bullets and Brown Eyes, by Mark Corrigan. Laurie, 1948

The Case of the Shaven Blonde, by Robertson Hobart. Allen, T., 1959; Hale, R., 1959
Cavalier of the Night, by Raymond Armstrong. Long, 1956
Cruel Lady, by Mark Corrigan. Angus, 1957
Dangerous Cargoes, by Robertson Hobart. Allen, T., 1960; Hale, R., 1960
Dangerous Limelight, by Raymond Armstrong. Long, 1947
Danger's Green Eyes, by Mark Corrigan. Angus, 1962
Death of a Love, by Robertson Hobart. Hale, R., 1961
Dumb as They Come, by Mark Corrigan. Angus, 1957
The Girl from Moscow, by Mark Corrigan. Angus, 1959
The Golden Angel, by Mark Corrigan. Laurie, 1950
Honolulu Snatch, by Mark Corrigan. Angus, 1958
I Like Danger, by Mark Corrigan. Laurie, 1954
The Lady from Tokyo, by Mark Corrigan. Angus, 1961; Consul, 1962
The Lady of China Street, by Mark Corrigan. Laurie, 1952
Madame Sly, by Mark Corrigan. Laurie, 1951
Menace in Siam, by Mark Corrigan. Angus, 1959; Hamilton & Co., 1960
The Midnight Cavalier, by Raymond Armstrong. Long, 1954
Murder of a Marriage, by Raymond Armstrong. Long, 1960
The Naked Lady, by Mark Corrigan. Brown, Watson, 1960
The Riddle of Double Island, by Mark Corrigan. Angus, 1962
The Riddle of the Spanish Circus, by Mark Corrigan. Angus, 1964
The Shanghai Jezebel, by Mark Corrigan. Laurie, 1951
The Sin of Hong Kong, by Mark Corrigan. Angus, 1957; Consul, 1963
Singapore Downbeat, by Mark Corrigan. Angus, 1959; Consul, 1963
The Sinister Playhouse, by Raymond Armstrong. Long, 1949
The Sinister Widow, by Raymond Armstrong. Long, 1951
The Sinister Widow Again, by Raymond Armstrong. Long, 1952
The Sinister Widow at Sea, by Raymond Armstrong. Long, 1959
The Sinister Widow Comes Back, by Raymond Armstrong. Long, 1957
The Sinister Widow Down Under, by Raymond Armstrong. Long, 1958
The Sinister Widow Returns, by Raymond Armstrong. Long, 1953
Sinner Takes All, by Mark Corrigan. Laurie, 1949
Sweet and Deadly, by Mark Corrigan. Laurie, 1953
Sydney for Sin, by Mark Corrigan. Angus, 1956
They Couldn't Go Wrong, by Raymond Armstrong. Long, 1951
The Wayward Blonde, by Mark Corrigan. Laurie, 1950
Why Do Women?, by Mark Corrigan. Angus, 1963
The Widow and the Cavalier, by Raymond Armstrong. Long, 1956

LEE, THORNE (M)
Monster of Lazy Hook. Duell, 1949
Summer Shock. Abelard, 1956

LEE DE MUNOZ MARIN, MUNA; see GUINESS, MAURICE C.

LEES, HANNAH, pseud; see FETTER, ELIZABETH HEAD

LE FANU, JOSEPH SHERIDAN (M)
Carmilla
Checkmate. Hurst, 1871
The Dragon Volant. Newnes, 1907 (Also published as: The Flying Dragon. Collins, 1930)
The Flying Dragon; see The Dragon Volant
House by the Churchyard. Chapman, 1863, 1870; Warne, 1881; Macmillan, 1899
In a Glass Darkly. Bentley, 1872; Davies, 1929; Lehmann, 1947
The Room at the Dragon Inn. Avon (Also published as: The Room in the Dragon Volant)
The Room in the Dragon Volant; see The Room at the Dragon Inn
Uncle Silas. Bentley, 1864; Chapman, 1870; Oxford, 1926; Penguin, 1940; Cresset, 1948, 1964; Dufour, 1964; Dover, 1966

LEFEBURE, MOLLY (M)
Evidence for the Crown. Lippincott, 1955

LEFEVRE, EDWIN (S)
The Plunderers. Harper, 1916

LEFFINGWELL, ALBERT (D) (Pseudonyms: Dana Chambers, Giles Jackson)
Blonde Died First, by Dana Chambers. Dial, 1941; Hale, R., 1943
Case of Caroline Animus, by Dana Chambers. Dial, 1946; Hale, R., 1951
Court of Shadows, by Giles Jackson. Museum Press, 1944
Darling, This Is Death, by Dana Chambers. Dial, 1945; Hale, R., 1951
Death Against Venus, by Dana Chambers. Dial, 1946; Hale, R., 1953

The Frightened Man, by Dana Chambers. Hale, R., 1945
The Last Secret, by Dana Chambers. Dial, 1944; Hale, R., 1949
Rope for an Ape, by Dana Chambers. Dial, 1947; Hale, R., 1952
She'll Be Dead by Morning, by Dana Chambers. Dial, 1940; Hale, R., 1941
Someday I'll Kill You, by Dana Chambers. Dial, 1939; Hale, R., 1939
Too Like the Lightning, by Dana Chambers. Dial, 1939; Hale, R., 1940
Witch's Moon, by Giles Jackson. Museum Press, 1943

LEIGH, HILARY (S)
Greystones. Pyramid, 1966

LEIGHTON, FLORENCE; see PFALZGRAF, FLORENCE LEIGHTON

LEIGHTON, WING (M)
Whistle Me over the Water. Hurst, 1944

LEINSTER, MURRAY, pseud; see JENKINS, WILLIAM FITZGERALD

LEITE GEORGE THURSTON and JODY SCOTT (D) (Pseudonym: Thurston Scott)
Cure It with Honey. Harper, 1957

LEITFRED, ROBERT H. (D)
The Corpse That Spoke. Green Circle, 1936
The Man Who Was Murdered Twice. Furman, 1937

LEJEUNE, ANTHONY, pseud; see THOMPSON, EDWARD ANTHONY

LeMAY, ALAN (M)
One of Us Is a Murderer. Doubleday, Doran, 1930

LEMIEUX, KENNETH (S)
Night Without Darkness. Coward, 1966

LEMMON, LAURA LEE (S) (Pseudonym: Lee Wilson)
This Deadly Dark. Dodd, 1946

LENEHAN, CHRISTOPHER (M)
Boston Belle Meets Murder. Jenkins, 1935
Carnival of Death. Jenkins, 1934
Deadly Decree. Jenkins, 1936
Death Dances Thrice. Jenkins, 1933
Driven to Death. Jenkins, 1955
Guilty But Not Insane. Jenkins, 1938
The Joyful Jays. Jenkins, 1938
The Mansfield Mystery. Jenkins, 1932
The Marked Pistol. Jenkins, 1929
The Masked Blackmailer. Jenkins, 1933
One Murder Too Many. Jenkins, 1943
The Silecroft Case. Jenkins, 1931
The Tunnel Mystery. Jenkins, 1929

LENNOX, JOHN (S)
Paper Doll. Quality, 1950

LEON, HENRY CECIL (M) (Pseudonym: Henry Cecil)
According to the Evidence. Chapman, 1954; Harper, 1954
Alibi for a Judge. Joseph, M., 1960; Penguin, 1964
The Asking Price. Harper & Row, 1966
Brothers-in-Law. Joseph, M., 1955; Collier, 1962
Child Divided. Harper & Row, 1966
Daughters-in-Law. Harper, 1961; Penguin, 1964
The Long Arm. Harper, 1957
Natural Causes. Chapman, 1953
No Bail for the Judge. Harper, 1959; Joseph, M., 1959
Portrait of a Judge. Joseph, M., 1964; Harper & Row, 1965
Settled Out of Court. Harper, 1959; Joseph, M., 1959
Ways and Means. Harper, 1952; Penguin, 1964
A Woman Named Anne. Harper & Row, 1967

LEONARD, A. B., pseud; see ALDRICH, EARL AUGUSTUS

LEONARD, CHARLES, pseud; see HEBERDEN, MARY VIOLET

LeQUEUX, WILLIAM TUFNELL (M-D-S)
The Amazing Count. Ward, Lock, 1929
As We Forgive Them. White, 1904
Behind the Bronze Door. Macaulay, 1923
Behind the German Lines. London Mail, 1917 (Sequel to Hushed Up at German Headquarters)
Behind the Throne. Wright & Brown, 1932
The Black Owl. Ward, Lock, 1926
Blackmailed. Nash & Grayson, 1927; Mellifont, 1942 (Abridged edition)
Bleke, the Butler: Being the Exciting Adventures of Robert Bleke. Jarrolds, 1924
The Blue Bungalow. Hurst, 1925
The Bomb-Makers. Jarrolds, 1917
The Bond of Black. Dillingham, G. W., 1899; White, 1899
The Breath of Suspicion. Long, 1917
The Broadcast Mystery. Holden, 1925
The Broken Thread. Ward, Lock, 1916
The Bronze Face. Ward, Lock, 1923

The Catspaw. Lloyds, 1918; Jenkins, 1929; Mellifont, 1942 (Abridged edition)
The Chameleon. Hodder, 1927 (U.S. title: Poison Shadows. Macaulay, 1928)
Cinders of Harley Street. Ward, Lock, 1916
Cipher Six. Hodder, 1919; Odhams, 1921 (Abridged edition)
The Closed Book. Methuen, 1904; Smart Set, 1904; Daily Mail Sixpenny Novels, 1910
Concerning This Woman. Newnes, 1928
Confessions of a Ladies' Man. Being the Adventures of Cuthbert Croom of His Majesty's Diplomatic Service. Hutchinson, 1905
The Count's Chauffeur. Nash, 1907; Daily Mail Sixpenny Novels, 1911; Mellifont, 1940
The Court of Honour. White, 1901
The Crime Code; see Double Nought
The Crimes Club. Nash & Grayson, 1927
The Crinkled Crown. Macaulay, 1929 (Abridged edition); Ward, Lock, 1929
The Crooked Way. Methuen, 1908
The Crystal Claw. Hodder, 1924; Macaulay, 1924
The Czar's Spy. Hodder, 1905; Smart Set, 1905
The Dangerous Game; see The Hidden Hands
The Day of Temptation. Dillingham, G. W., 1899
The Death-Doctor. Hurst, 1912; Pearson, 1935
The Devil's Carnival. Hurst, 1917
The Devil's Dice. White, 1896; Rand, 1897; Mellifont, 1944 (Abridged edition)
The Doctor of Pimlico. Cassell, 1919; Macaulay, 1920; Burt, 1922
Donovan of Whitehall. Pearson, 1917
Double Nought. Hodder, 1927, 1935 (U.S. title: The Crime Code. Macaulay, 1928)
The Double Shadow. Hodder, 1915
England's Peril. White, 1899; Newnes, 1900
An Eye for an Eye. White, 1900; Ward, Lock, 1931
The Eye of Istar. Stokes, 1897; White, 1897; Long, 1921
The Factotum and Other Stories. Ward, Lock, 1931
The Fatal Face. Hurst, 1926
Fatal Fingers. Cassell, 1912
Fatal Thirteen. Being the Unpublished Manuscript of Charles Cayler. Paul, S., 1909; Mascot Novels, 1913
The Fifth Finger. Paul, S., 1921
Fine Feathers. Paul, S., 1924; Mellifont, 1939 (Abridged edition)
The Forbidden Word. Odhams, 1919; Hodder, 1929
The Four Faces. Brentano, 1914; Paul, S., 1914; Pearson, 1917
The Gamblers. Hutchinson, 1901
The Gay Traingle. Jarrolds, 1923
The German Spy. Newnes, 1914
The Golden Face. Cassell, 1922; Macaulay, 1922
The Golden Three. Ward, Lock, 1930; Fiction League, 1931
The Great Court Scandal. White, 1906; Hodder, 1913
The Great God Gold. Badger, R. G., 1910
The Great Plot. Hodder, 1907; Skeffington, 1918
The Great White Queen. White, 1896
The Green Ray; see The Mystery of the Green Ray
Guilty Bonds. Routledge, G., 1891; Fenno, 1895
The Hand of Allah. Cassell, 1914
Hidden Hands. Hodder, 1926 (U.S. title: The Dangerous Game. Macaulay, 1926)
The Hotel X. Ward, Lock, 1919
The House of Evil. Ward, Lock, 1927, 1936
The House of the Wicked. Hurst, 1906
The House of Whispers. Brentano, 1910; Methuen, 1913
The Hunchback of Westminster. Methuen, 1904
Hushed Up! Nash, 1911
Hushed Up at German Headquarters. London Mail, 1917
The Idol of the Town. White, 1903
In Secret. Odhams, 1921; Hodder, 1929
The Intriguers. Hodder, 1920; Macaulay, 1921; Mellifont, 1934 (Abridged edition)
The Lady in the Car. Lippincott, 1908; Methuen, 1914
The Lawless Hand. Hurst, 1927; Macaulay, 1928
The Letter E. Cassell, 1926 (U.S. title: The Tattoo Mystery. Macaulay, 1927)
The Luck of the Secret Service. Pearson, 1914
Mademoiselle of Monte Carlo. Cassell, 1921; Macaulay, 1921
The Man About Town. A Story of Society and Blackmail. Long, 1916
The Man from Downing Street. Hurst, 1904
The Man with the Fatal Finger
The Marked Man. Ward, Lock, 1925
The Mask. Long, 1905
The Money-spider. Badger, R. G., 1911; Cassell, 1911
More Mysteries of a Great City. Mellifont, 1934
Mysteries. Ward, Lock, 1913

Mysteries of a Great City. Hodder, 1920; Mellifont, 1934 (Abridged edition)
The Mysterious Mr. Miller. Hodder, 1906; Skeffington, 1918
The Mysterious Three. Ward, Lock, 1915
The Mystery of a Motor-Car. Hodder, 1906
The Mystery of Mademoiselle. Hodder, 1926
The Mystery of Nine. Nash, 1912; Newnes, 1917
The Mystery of the Green Ray. Hodder, 1915 (U.S. title: The Green Ray. Mellifont, 1934)
No. 7, Saville Square. Ward, Lock, 1920
No. 70, Berlin. Hodder, 1916; Mellifont, 1938
Of Royal Blood. Hutchinson, 1900
The Office Secret. Ward, Lock, 1927
The Open Verdict. Hodder, 1921
The Pauper of Park Lane. Cassell, 1908; Cupples & Leon, 1908
The Peril of Helen Marklove and Other Stories. Jarrolds, 1928
The Place of Dragons. Ward, Lock, 1916
Poison Shadows; see The Chameleon
The Rainbow Mystery. Hodder, 1917
The Rat Trap. Ward, Lock, 1928; Macaulay, 1930
The Red Hat. Daily Mail, 1904
The Red Room. Little, 1911; Cassell, 1912
The Red Widow; or, The Death-Dealers of London. Cassell, 1920
Revelations of the Secret Service. Newnes, 1907
The Riddle of the Ring. Federation Press, 1927
The Room of Secrets. Ward, Lock, 1913; Newnes, 1916
Sant of the Secret Service. Odhams, 1918; Hodder, 1930
The Scandal-Monger. Ward, Lock, 1917
The Scarlet Sign. Ward, Lock, 1926
The Secret Formula. Ward, Lock, 1928
The Secret of the Square. White, 1907; London Book, 1928
The Secret Telephone. Jarrolds, 1921; McCann, 1922; Cassell, 1924
Secrets of Monte Carlo. White, 1899; Dillingham, G. W., 1900; Newnes, 1903
Secrets of the Foreign Office, Describing the Doings of Duckworth Drew of the Secret Service. Hutchinson, 1903
The Seven Secrets. Hutchinson, 1903; Universal Lib., 1930
The Sign of Silence. Ward, Lock, 1915
Sins of the City. White, 1905
Sons of Satan. White, 1914; Newnes, 1916
The Spider's Eye. Cassell, 1905
The Spy Hunter. Pearson, 1916
The Sting. Hodder, 1928; Macaulay, 1928
The Stolen Statesman. Skeffington, 1918
The Stretton Street Affair. Macaulay, 1922; Cassell, 1924
The Tattoo Mystery; see The Letter E
The Terror of the Air. Lloyds, 1920
Three Knots. Ward, Lock, 1922
The Tickencote Treasure. Newnes, 1903
Tracked by Wireless. Moffat, Yard, 1922; Paul, S., 1922
Treasure of Israel. Nash, 1910
Twice Tried. Hurst, 1928; Mellifont, 1940
Two in a Tangle. Hodder, 1917
The Under-Secretary. Hutchinson, 1906
The Valrose Mystery. Ward, Lock, 1925
The Voice from the Void. Cassell, 1922; Macaulay, 1923
The White Glove. Nash, 1915; Newnes, 1918
The White Lie. Ward, Lock, 1914
Without Trace. Nash, 1912
The Woman at Kensington. Cassell, 1906
The Woman in the Way. Newnes, 1910
The Yellow Ribbon. Hodder, 1918

LEROUX, GASTON (M-D)
The Amazing Adventures of Carolus Herbert. Mills & Boon, 1922
The Burgled Heart. Long, 1925 (U.S. title: The New Terror. Macaulay, 1926)
Cheri-Bibi and Cecily. Laurie, 1923 (U.S. title: Missing Men, the Return of Cheri-Bibi. Macaulay, 1923)
Cheri-Bibi, Mystery Man. Long, 1924
The Dancing Girl. Long, 1925 (U.S. title: Nomads of the Night. Macaulay, 1925)
The Dark Road. Macaulay, 1924
The Double Life. Kearney, 1909
The Floating Prison. Laurie, 1922; Readers' Lib., 1930 (U.S. title: Wolves of the Sea. Macaulay, 1923. Original English title: The Prison Ship)
The Haunted Chair. Dutton, 1931
The Kiss That Killed. Macaulay, 1934
Lady Helena; or, The Mysterious Lady. Dutton, 1931; Laurie, 1931
The Machine to Kill. Macaulay, 1935
The Man of a Hundred Faces; see The Man of a Hundred Masks
The Man of a Hundred Masks. Cassell, 1930 (U.S. title: The Man of a Hundred Faces. Macaulay, 1930)
The Man Who Came Back from the Dead. Nash, 1916
The Man with the Black Feather. Hurst, 1912; Small, 1912; Macaulay, 1930

The Masked Man. Long, 1927; Macaulay, 1929
The Midnight Lady. Long, 1930
The Missing Archduke. Long, 1931
Missing Men, the Return of Cheri-Bibi; see Cheri-Bibi and Cecily
The Mystery of the Yellow Room. Arnold, E., 1909; Mills & Boon, 1920; Scribner, 1928; Readers' Lib., 1938
The New Idol. Long, 1938
The New Terror; see The Burgled Heart
Nomads of the Night; see The Dancing Girl
The Octopus of Paris; see The Sleuth Hound
The Perfume of the Lady in Black. Brentano, 1909; Nash, 1911
The Phantom Clue; see The Slave Bangle
The Phantom of the Opera. Bobbs, 1911; Mills & Boon, 1911; Hutchinson, 1925
The Prison Ship; see The Floating Ship
The Secret of the Night. Macaulay, 1914; Nash, 1914
The Slave Bangle. Long, 1925 (U.S. title: The Phantom Clue. Macaulay, 1926)
The Sleuth Hound. Long, 1926 (U.S. title: The Octopus of Paris. Macaulay, 1927
The Son of Three Fathers. Long, 1927; Macaulay, 1928
The Veiled Prisoner. Mills & Boon, 1923
Wolves of the Sea; see The Floating Prison

LESLIE, DESMOND (D)
Hold Back the Night. Owen, P., 1956

LESLIE, FRANCIS (M)
Second Stroke. Hurst, 1951
Who Keeps the Keys? Hurst, 1949

LESLIE, JEAN (M)
The Darling Sin. Doubleday, 1951; Hodder, 1952
Hair of the Dog. Doubleday, 1947
Intimate Journal of Warren Winslow. Doubleday, 1952
The Man Who Held Five Aces. Doubleday, 1949; Hodder, 1950
One Cried Murder. Doubleday, Doran, 1945; Edwards, W., 1946
Shoes for My Love. Doubleday, 1948
Three-Cornered Murder. Doubleday, 1947; Hodder, 1948
Two Faced Murder. Doubleday, 1946; Edwards, W., 1946

LESLIE, NORMAN (D)
Death Comes to Kenya. Ward, Lock, 1948
The Man with the Glass Eye. Ward, Lock, 1948
Prelude to Murder. Barker, 1954
Widows Can Be Dangerous. Barker, 1958

LESLIE, O. H., pseud; see SLESAR, HENRY

LESLIE, PETER (S)
The Diving Dames Affair. Ace, 1967 (The Man from U.N.C.L.E. series, #9)
The Gay Deceiver. Stein & Day, 1967
Hell for Tomorrow. Macfadden, 1965
The Radioactive Camel Affair. Ace, 1966 (The Man from U.N.C.L.E. series, #7)

LESSER, MILTON; see MARLOWE, STEPHEN

LESTER, EDWARD CASTELLAIN (M)
The Guy Fawkes Murder. Long, 1936
The Murder of Martin Fotherill. Long, 1937

LESTER, FRANK, pseud; see USHER, FRANK HUGH

LESTER, VINCENT (M)
Crook's Crossing. Butterworth, T., 1935
Justice by Accident. Butterworth, T., 1936

LETHBRIDGE, OLIVE (M)
The Black Parrot. Hurst, 1931

LETHERBY, JACK (M)
Murder Lays the Odds. Ward, Lock, 1935
The Outsider. Ward, Lock, 1953

LETT, GORDON (M)
The Many-Headed Monster. Hodder, 1957

LETTON, JEANETTE (M)
Cragsmoor. Macrae Smith, 1966; Macfadden, 1968
Incident at Hendon. Macrae Smith, 1967
Jenny and I. Macrae Smith, 1963

LEVEL, MAURICE (M)
The Grip of Fear. Richards, 1909
Tales of Mystery and Horror. McBride, 1920
Those Who Return. McBride, 1923

LEVENE, PHILIP (D)
Ambrose in London. Hale, R., 1959
Ambrose in Paris. Hale, R., 1960

LEVERAGE, HENRY (M)
Phantom Alibi. Chelsea House, 1926

The Purple Limited. Chelsea House, 1927
Where Dead Men Walk. Moffat, 1920
Whispering Wires. Moffat, 1918; Grosset, 1922
The White Cipher. Moffat, 1919

LEVEY, ROBERT A. (D)
Murder in Lima. Avon, 1957

LEVIN, IRA (S)
A Kiss Before Dying. S & S, 1953; Joseph, M., 1954; Pyramid, 1964; Penguin
Rosemary's Baby. Joseph, M., 1967; Random, 1967; Dell, 1968

LEVIN, MEYER (S)
Compulsion. S & S, 1956; Muller, 1957

LEVINE, WILLIAM (D) (Pseudonym: Will Levinrew)
Death Points a Finger. Mystery League, 1933
For Sale-Murder. Mystery League, 1932
Murder from the Grave. McBride, 1930; Tudor, 1932
Murder on the Palisades. Gollancz, 1930; McBride, 1930
Poison Plague. McBride, 1929; Cassell, 1930
The Wheelchair Corpse. Bart

LEVINREW, WILL, pseud; see LEVINE, WILLIAM

LEVISON, ERIC (M)
Ashes of Evidence. Bobbs, 1921
Eye Witness. Bobbs, 1921
Hidden Eyes. Bobbs, 1920

LEVON, FRED (D)
Much Ado About Murder. Dodd, 1955; Boardman, T. V., 1957

LEWIN, ALBERT (S)
The Unaltered Cat. Scribner, 1967

LEWIN, MICHAEL SULTAN (M) (Pseudonym: Douglas Furber)
Just Another Murder. Dakers, 1950

LEWIS, CECIL DAY-; see DAY-LEWIS, CECIL

LEWIS, FLORENCE JAY (Mrs. Edmund Speare) (S)
The Climax. Books, 1944

LEWIS, GITA; see MARTIN, HENRIETTA

LEWIS, HILDA (D)
The Case of the Little Doctor. Random, 1949
Strange Story. Random, 1947

LEWIS, JANET (M)
The Trial of Soren Qvist. Doubleday, 1947

LEWIS, KEN (S)
Look Out Behind You. Ace, 1957

LEWIS, LANGE, pseud; see BEYNON, JANE

LEWIS, MARY CHRISTIANNA (D) (Pseudonym: Christianna Brand)
Cat and Mouse. Knopf, 1950; Joseph, M., 1950
The Crooked Wreath. Dodd, 1946
Death in High Heels. Lane, 1941; Dodd, 1944
Death of Jezebel. Dodd, 1948; Bodley Head, 1949; Transworld, 1953
Fog of Doubt. Scribner, 1953
Green for Danger. Dodd, 1944; Lane, 1945; Pan, 1948; Bantam; Penguin
Heads You Lose. Dodd, 1941; Lane, 1941
Heaven Knows Who. Scribner, 1960
Suddenly at His Residence. Bodley Head, 1947; Penguin, 1951
Three-Cornered Halo. Joseph, M., 1957; Scribner, 1957
Tour de Force. Joseph, M., 1955; Scribner, 1955

LEWIS, MICHAEL ARTHUR (M)
Roman Gold. Allen & Unwin, 1927; Houghton, 1928
The Three Amateurs. Allen & Unwin, 1929; Houghton, 1929

LEWIS, NORMAN (S)
Day of the Fox. Cape, 1955; Rinehart, 1955
Small War Made to Order. Harcourt, 1966

LEWIS, PHYLLIS (M)
The Death-Dealing Doctor. Collins, 1930

LEYFORD, HENRY, pseud. (D)
Murder Moon. Macaulay, 1933

LEYLAND, ERIC (D)
Challenge. Hutchinson, 1952
The Counterfeit Mystery. Museum Press, 1951

LEYTON, PATRICK (M)
The Barronwell Mystery. Paul, S., 1929
By Foul Means. Paul, S., 1928; International Fiction Lib., 1929
The Crime at Grandison Hall. Paul, S., 1929
The Crime with Ten Solutions. Jenkins, 1935

The Dalmayne Mystery. Jenkins, 1938
Exit Silas Danvers. Jenkins, 1932
Foul Play at Lentwood. Jenkins, 1935
Gentlemen of the Jury, with Arthur Compton-Rickett. Jenkins, 1927
Grim Inheritance. Jenkins, 1941
Harvest of Hate. Jenkins, 1948
The Haunted Abbey. Jenkins, 1926
The Inevitable Crime. Jenkins, 1926
The Island of Atonement. Selwyn, 1928
The Man Who Knew. Jenkins, 1925; Small, 1926
Murder Will Out. Jenkins, 1930
The Ordeal of Mark Bannister, with Arthur Compton-Rickett. Jenkins, 1927
Outside the Law. Jenkins, 1927
Silent Death. Jenkins, 1940
Treasure at Grayladies. Jenkins, 1934
Within Twenty-four Hours. Jenkins, 1931

LIDDON, ELOISE S. (Mrs. George Albert Soper) (M)
Between Four and Five; see The Riddle of the Russian Princess
The Riddle of the Florentine Folio. Doubleday, Doran, 1935
The Riddle of the Russian Princess. Doubleday, Doran, 1934 (Serial title: Between Four and Five)

LIEBLER, JEAN MAYER (S) (Pseudonym: Virginia Mather)
You, the Jury. Farrar, Straus, 1941

LILIENTHAL, DAVID, JR. (S) (Pseudonym: David Ely)
Seconds. Pantheon, 1963
The Tour. Delacorte, 1967; Dell, 1968
Trot. Pantheon, 1963; Signet, 1964

LILLEY, PETER and ANTHONY STANSFELD (M) (Pseudonym: Bruce Buckingham)
Boiled Alive. Joseph, M., 1957
Three Bad Nights. Joseph, M., 1956; Penguin, 1961

LILLY, JEAN (D)
Death in B-Minor. Dutton, 1934; Cassell, 1935
Death Thumbs a Ride. Dutton, 1940
False Face. Dutton, 1929
Seven Sisters. Dutton, 1928; Dent, 1929

LIMNELIUS, GEORGE, pseud; see ROBINSON, LEWIS GEORGE

LINCOLN, JOSEPH C. (M)
Blair's Attic. Coward, 1929

LINCOLN, NATALIE SUMMER (M)
The Blue Car Mystery. Appleton, D., 1926; Burt, 1928
The Cat's Paw. Appleton, D., 1922
The Dancing Silhouette. Appleton, D., 1927; Burt, 1929
The Fifth Latchkey. Appleton, D., 1929; Burt, 1931
I Spy. Appleton, D., 1916
The Lost Despatch. Appleton, D., 1913
The Man Inside. Appleton, D., 1914
Marked Cancelled. Appleton, D., 1930; Burt, 1932
The Meredith Mystery. Appleton, D., 1923
The Missing Initial. Appleton, D., 1925
The Moving Finger. Appleton, D., 1918
The Nameless Man. Appleton, D., 1917
P.P.C. Appleton, D., 1927; Burt, 1929
The Official Chaperone. Appleton, D., 1915; Macaulay, 1915
The Red Seal. Appleton, D., 1920
The Secret of Mohawk Pond. Appleton, D., 1928
Thirteen, Thirteenth Street. Appleton, D., 1932
The Thirteenth Letter. Appleton, D., 1924
The Three Strings. Appleton, D., 1918
The Trevor Case. Appleton, D., 1912
The Unseen Ear. Appleton, D., 1921

LINCOLN, VICTORIA (D)
The Swan Island Murders. Farrar & Rinehart, 1930; Cassell, 1931

LINDHOLM, ANNA CHANDLER (M) (Pseudonym: Dorothy Fay)
The Black Pearl of Passion. Galleon, 1936

LINDOP, AUDREY ERSKINE (S)
Two Start Counting. Doubleday, 1966

LINDSAY, DAVID T. (M-D)
Air Bandits. Hamilton, 1937
Another Case for Inspector Jackson. Hamilton, 1937
The Black Fetish. Hamilton, 1937
The Flying Armada. Hamilton, 1938
The Flying Crusader. Hamilton, 1937
The Green Ray. Hamilton, 1937
Inspector Jackson Goes North. Hamilton, 1939
Inspector Jackson Investigates. Hamilton, 1936
The Man Nobody Knew. Hamilton, 1938
Masked Judgement. Hamilton, 1937
Mystery of the Tumbling V. Hamilton, 1940
The Ninth Plague. Hamilton, 1936
Stranglehold. Hamilton, 1939
The Temple of the Flaming God. Hamilton, 1938
The Two Red Capsules. Hamilton, 1936
Vengance Rides North. Hamilton, 1939
Wings over Africa. Hamilton, 1936
Wings over the Amazon. Hamilton, 1937

LINDSAY, KATHLEEN
Mystery at Greystones. Jenkins, 1932

LINDSAY, ROBERT HOWARD (D)
Fowl Murder. Little, 1941

LINGO, ADA E. (D)
Murder in Texas. Houghton, 1935

LININGTON, ELIZABETH (D) (Pseudonyms: Anne Blaisdell, Lesley Egan, Dell Shannon)
Ace of Spades, by Dell Shannon. Morrow, 1961; Oldbourne, 1963
Against the Evidence, by Lesley Egan. Harper, 1962; Gollancz, 1963
Borrowed Alibi, by Lesley Egan. Harper, 1962
Case for Appeal, by Lesley Egan. Harper, 1961
Case Pending, by Dell Shannon. Gollancz, 1960; Harper, 1960; Dell, 1964
Chance to Kill, by Dell Shannon. Morrow, 1967
Coffin Corner, by Dell Shannon. Gollancz, 1966; Morrow, 1966
Date with Death. Harper & Row, 1966
The Death Bringers, by Dell Shannon. Morrow, 1965; Gollancz, 1966
Death by Inches, by Dell Shannon. Morrow, 1965; Gollancz, 1967
Death of a Busybody, by Dell Shannon. Morrow, 1963; Oldbourne, 1963
Detective's Due, by Leslie Egan. Harper & Row, 1965
Double Bluff, by Dell Shannon. Morrow, 1963; Oldbourne, 1965
Extra Kill, by Dell Shannon. Morrow, 1962
Greenmask. Harper & Row, 1964
Knave of Hearts, by Dell Shannon. Morrow, 1962
Mark of Murder, by Dell Shannon. Morrow, 1964
My Name Is Death, by Lesley Egan. Gollancz, 1964; Harper & Row, 1964
The Nameless Ones, by Lesley Egan. Harper & Row, 1967
Nightmare, by Anne Blaisdell. Harper, 1961
No Evil Angel. Longmans, 1964; Harper & Row, 1965
Rain with Violence, by Dell Shannon. Morrow, 1967
Root of All Evil, by Dell Shannon. Harper & Row, 1963; Gollancz, 1964
Run to Evil, by Lesley Egan. Harper & Row, 1963; Gollancz, 1964
Some Avenger, Rise! by Lesley Egan. Harper & Row, 1966; Gollancz, 1967
Something Wrong? Harper & Row, 1967
With a Vengeance, by Dell Shannon. Morrow, 1966

LINKLATER, J. LANE, pseud; see WATKINS, ALEX

LINKS, J. C.; see WHEATLEY, DENNIS

LINN, KAY (D)
Laughing Mountain. Dutton, 1936

LINNELL, GERTRUDE (M)
Black Ghost of the Highway. Longmans, 1931

LINSINGEN, FREDERICK WILLIAM BERRY VON (D)
Pressure Gauge Murder. Dutton, 1930

LION, LEON M.; see BOWER, MARIAN

LIPMAN, CLAYRE and MICHEL LIPMAN (S)
House of Evil. Lion, 1955

LIPMAN, MICHEL; see LIPMAN, CLAYRE

LIPPINCOTT, NORMAN (D)
Murder at Glen Athol. Doubleday, Doran, 1935; World's Work, 1935

LIPPMAN, JULIE MATHILDE (M)
Mannequin. Duffield, 1917

LIPSKY, ELEAZAR (S)
Kiss of Death. Penguin, 1947; Dell, 1961
Murder One. Doubleday, 1948
People Against O'Hara. Doubleday, 1950

LIPTON, MRS. LAWRENCE; see RICE, CRAIG

LISPECTOR, CLARICE (S)
The Apple in the Dark. Knopf, 1967

LISTER, STEPHEN, pseud. (M)
Delorme in Deep Water. Davies, 1958

LITSEY, EDWIN CARLISLE (M)
Beast. Bouregy, 1959

LITTLE, CONSTANCE and GWENYTH LITTLE (D)
The Black Coat. Doubleday, 1948; Collins, 1949
Black Corridors. Doubleday, Doran, 1940; Collins, 1941
The Black Curl. Doubleday, 1953
Black Dream. Doubleday, 1952; Collins, 1953
Black Express. Collins, 1945
Black Eye. Doubleday, Doran, 1945; Collins, 1946
The Black Gloves. Doubleday, Doran, 1939; Collins, 1940

The Black Goatee. Collins, 1947; Doubleday, Doran, 1947
The Black-Headed Pins. Doubleday, Doran, 1938; Davies, 1939; Popular Lib.
The Black Honeymoon. Collins, 1944; Doubleday, Doran, 1944
The Black House. Collins, 1950; Doubleday, 1950
The Black Iris. Collins, 1953; Doubleday, 1953
The Black Lady. Collins, 1944
The Blackout. Doubleday, 1951; Collins, 1952
The Black Paw. Collins, 1941; Doubleday, Doran, 1941
The Black Piano. Collins, 1948; Doubleday, 1948
The Black Rustle. Doubleday, Doran, 1943
The Black Shrouds. Doubleday, Doran, 1941; Collins, 1942
The Black Smith. Doubleday, 1950; Collins, 1951
The Black Stockings. Doubleday, 1946; Collins, 1947
The Black Thumb. Collins, 1943; Doubleday, 1947
The Great Black Kamba. Doubleday, Doran, 1945
The Grey Mist Murders. Doubleday, Doran, 1938

LITTLE, GWENYTH; see LITTLE, CONSTANCE

LITTLEFIELD, ANNE (M)
Which Mrs. Bennett? Doubleday, 1959; Popular Lib., 1964

LITVINOVA, IVY (M)
The Moscow Mystery. Coward, 1943

LIVINGSTON, ARMSTRONG (M)
The Doublecross. Skeffington, 1929
The Guilty Accuser. Jarrolds, 1928
In Cold Blood. Bobbs, 1931; Skeffington, 1932
The JuJu Man. Paul, S., 1924
Light Fingered Ladies. Jarrolds, 1928
Magic for Murder. Skeffington, 1936
The Monster in the Pool. Bobbs, 1929
Murder Is Easy. Skeffington, 1933
The Murder Trap. Bobbs, 1931; Skeffington, 1932
The Mystery of the Twin Rubies. Paul, S., 1923
Night of Crime. Sovereign House, 1938
On the Right Wrists. Jarrolds, 1927
Trackless Death. Bobbs, 1930; Skeffington, 1930

LIVINGSTON, KENNETH, pseud; see STEWART, KENNETH LIVINGSTON

LIVINGSTON, WALTER (M)
The Mystery of Burnleigh Manor. Mystery League, 1930
The Mystery of Villa Sinister. Mystery League, 1931

LLOYD, JACK BATES (M)
Key Without a Lock. Vantage, 1964

LLOYD, LAVENDER
Linton Memorial. Longmans, 1957

LLOYD, STANLEY (D)
Jam Sauce. Paul, S., 1949
Thick Treacle. Paul, S., 1951

LLOYD, STEPHANIE (S)
Graveswood. Paperback Lib., 1966

LOBAN, ETHEL H. (M)
The Calloused Eye. Collier, 1931; Doubleday, Doran, 1931
Signed in Yellow. Doubleday, Doran, 1930

LOBAUGH, MRS. ELMA K. (M) (Pseudonym: Kenneth Lowe)
Catalyst, by Kenneth Lowe. Doubleday, 1958; Boardman, T. V., 1959
The Haze of Evil, by Kenneth Lowe. Doubleday, 1953
I Am Afraid. Doubleday, 1949
No Tears for Shirley Minton, by Kenneth Lowe. Doubleday, 1955; Boardman, T. V., 1957
Shadows in Succession. Doubleday, 1946
She Never Reached the Top. Doubleday, Doran, 1945

LOBELL, GRISELDA G. and NATHAN DAVID LOBELL (D)
The Shadow and the Blot. Harper, 1949

LOBELL, NATHAN DAVID; see LOBELL, GRISELDA G.

LOCKE, GLADYS EDSON (M)
The Fenwood Murders. Long, 1931
The Golden Lotus. Page, 1927
The House on the Downs. Page, 1925
The Ravensdale Mystery. Page, 1935
The Red Cavalier. Page, 1922; Burt, 1927
Redmaynes. Page, 1928
The Scarlet Macaw. Page, 1923
That Affair at Portstead Manor. Sherman, French, 1914

LOCKE, MARTIN, pseud; see DUNCAN, WILLIAM MURDOCK

LOCKE, WILLIAM J. (D)
The Joyous Adventures of Aristede Pujol. Dodd, 1912

LOCKHART, JOHN GILBERT (M)
East All the Way. Appleton, D., 1928

LOCKRIDGE, MRS. FRANCES LOUISE DAVIS and RICHARD LOCKRIDGE (D)
(Pseudonym: Francis Richards)
Accent on Murder, by Francis Richards. Lippincott, 1958; Long, 1960
And Left for Dead. Hutchinson, 1962; Lippincott, 1962
Burnt Offerings, by Francis Richards. Lippincott, 1955; Hutchinson, 1959
Call in Coincidence, by Francis Richards. Long, 1962
Catch as Catch Can. Lippincott, 1958; Long, 1960
Client Is Canceled. Lippincott, 1951; Hutchinson, 1955
Curtain for a Jester. Lippincott, 1953
Dead as a Dinosaur. Lippincott, 1952; Hutchinson, 1956
Death and the Gentle Bull. Lippincott, 1954; Hutchinson, 1957
Death by Association. Lippincott, 1952; Hutchinson, 1957
Death Has a Small Voice. Lippincott, 1953; Hutchinson, 1954
Death of a Tall Man. Lippincott, 1946; Hutchinson, 1949
Death of an Angel. Lippincott, 1955; Hutchinson, 1957
Death on the Aisle. Lippincott, 1942; Hutchinson, 1949
Death Takes a Bow. Lippincott, 1943; Hutchinson, 1945
The Devious Ones. Lippincott, 1964
Dishonest Murderer. Lippincott, 1949; Hutchinson, 1951
The Distant Clue. Lippincott, 1963; Long, 1964
Drill Is Death. Lippincott, 1961; Long, 1963
The Empty Day, by Richard Lockridge. Lippincott, 1965
Encounter in Key West, by Richard Lockridge. Lippincott, 1966
Faceless Adversary. Lippincott, 1956
First Come, First Kill. Lippincott, 1962; Long, 1963; Pyramid, 1964
Foggy, Foggy Death. Lippincott, 1950; Hutchinson, 1953
Four Hours to Fear, by Francis Richards. Long, 1965
Golden Man. Lippincott, 1960; Hutchinson, 1961
Hanged for a Sheep. Lippincott, 1942; Hutchinson, 1944
I Want to Go Home. Lippincott, 1948
The Innocent House, by Francis Richards. Lippincott, 1959; Long, 1961
Judge Is Reversed. Lippincott, 1960; Hutchinson, 1961
Key to Death. Lippincott, 1954
Killing the Goose. Lippincott, 1944; Hutchinson, 1947
Let Dead Enough Alone, by Francis Richards. Lippincott, 1955
The Long Skeleton. Lippincott, 1958; Longmans, 1958; Pyramid, 1963
Murder and Blueberry Pie. Lippincott, 1959
Murder by the Book. Lippincott, 1963; Hutchinson, 1964
Murder Can't Wait, by Richard Lockridge. Lippincott, 1964; Long, 1965 (English edition by Francis Richards)
Murder Comes First. Lippincott, 1951
Murder for Art's Sake, by Richard Lockridge. Lippincott, 1967
Murder Has Its Points. Lippincott, 1961; Hutchinson, 1962
Murder in a Hurry. Lippincott, 1950; Hutchinson, 1952
Murder Is Served. Lippincott, 1948; Hutchinson, 1950
Murder Is Suggested. Lippincott, 1959; Hutchinson, 1961
Murder, Murder, Murder! Lippincott, 1957
Murder Out of Town. Joseph, M., 1941; Stokes, 1941
Murder Roundabout, by Richard Lockridge. Lippincott, 1966
Murder Within Murder. Lippincott, 1946; Pyramid, 1965
Night of Shadows. Lippincott, 1962; Long, 1964
No Dignity in Death, by Francis Richards. Long, 1962
The Norths Meet Murder. Joseph, M., 1940; Stokes, 1940
Payoff for the Banker. Lippincott, 1945; Hutchinson, 1948
A Pinch of Poison. Stokes, 1941; Grosset, 1944; PB, 1945; Hutchinson, 1948
Practice to Deceive. Lippincott, 1957; Hutchinson, 1959
Quest of the Bogeyman. Lippincott, 1964
Show Red for Danger. Lippincott, 1960; Long, 1961 (English edition by Francis Richards)
Spin Your Web, Lady. Lippincott, 1949; Hutchinson, 1952
Squire of Death, by Richard Lockridge. Lippincott, 1965; Long, 1966 (English edition by Francis Richards)
Stand Up and Die. Lippincott, 1953; Hutchinson, 1955
Tangled Cord. Lippincott, 1957; Longmans, 1957
Think of Death. Lippincott, 1947
Ticking Clock. Lippincott, 1962; Hutchinson, 1963
Untidy Murder. Lippincott, 1947
Voyage into Violence. Lippincott, 1956; Hutchinson, 1960; Pyramid, 1963
With One Stone. Lippincott, 1961
With Option to Die, by Richard Lockridge. Lippincott, 1967

LOCKRIDGE, RICHARD; see LOCKRIDGE, FRANCES LOUISE DAVIS

LOCKWOOD, DAVID (D)
Death Has Scarlet Candles. Hodder, 1949
Night and Green Ginger. Hodder, 1951

LOCKWOOD SARAH (S)
The Man from Masabi. Doubleday, Page, 1925

LODER, VERNON, pseud; see VAHEY, JOHN GEORGE HASLETTE

LODWICK, JOHN (M)
Brother Death. Duell, 1951
Love Bade Me Welcome. Roy Pubs., 1954

LOEWENGARD, HEIDI HUBERTA FREYBE (Pseudonyms: Martha Albrand, Christine Lambert)
After Midnight, by Martha Albrand. Chatto, 1949; Random, 1948; Ace, 1965; Dell
A Call from Austria, by Martha Albrand. Hodder, 1963; Random, 1963; Pyramid
A Day in Monte Carlo, by Martha Albrand. Hodder, 1959; Random, 1959; Ace, 1965
Desperate Moment, by Martha Albrand. Chatto, 1951; Random, 1951
The Door Fell Shut, by Martha Albrand. New Amer. Lib., 1966
Endure No Longer, by Martha Albrand. Random, 1944; Chatto, 1945
The Hunted Woman, by Martha Albrand. Random, 1952; Hodder, 1953
The Linden Affair, by Martha Albrand. Random, 1956; Berkley Pub., 1960; Pyramid, 1966
The Mask of Alexander, by Martha Albrand. Random, 1955; Pyramid
Meet Me Tonight, by Martha Albrand. Random, 1960; Hodder, 1961 (Also published as: Return to Terror. Ace, 1964)
Nightmare in Copenhagen, by Martha Albrand. Hodder, 1954; Random, 1954; Pyramid
No Surrender, by Martha Albrand. Chatto, 1943; Popular Lib., 1965
None Shall Know, by Martha Albrand. Chatto, 1946; Award, 1967
The Obsession of Emmet Booth, by Martha Albrand. Gollancz, 1957; Random, 1957
Remembered Anger, by Martha Albrand. Random, 1946
Return to Terror; see Meet Me Tonight
The Story That Cannot Be Told, by Martha Albrand. Hodder, 1956
A Sudden Woman, by Christine Lambert. Atheneum, 1964
Wait for the Dawn, by Martha Albrand. Chatto, 1950; Random, 1950
Whispering Hill, by Martha Albrand. Random, 1947; Chatto, 1948
Without Orders, by Martha Albrand. Chatto, 1943; Little, 1943; Award, 1967

LOFTS, NORAH ROBINSON (D)
(Pseudonym: Peter Curtis)
Dead March in Three Keys. Davies, 1940
The Devil's Own. Doubleday, 1960; MacDonald & Co., 1960; Pyramid, 1966 (English title: The Witches. Pan, 1966)
No Question of Murder. Doubleday, 1959
The Witches; see The Devil's Own
You're Best Alone. MacDonald & Co.

LOGAN, CAROLYNNE CHITWOOD and MALCOLM LOGAN (D)
One of These Seven. Bouregy, 1946

LOGAN, MALCOLM; see LOGAN, CAROLYNNE CHITWOOD

LOMAS, JOHN E. W. (M)
The Man with the Scar. Houghton, 1926

LOMBARD, NAP, pseud; see JOHNSON, PAMELA HANSFORD

LOMBARDI, CYNTHIA (M)
Lighting Seven Candles. Appleton, D., 1926

LONDON, JACK (M)
The Assassination Bureau. McGraw, 1963 (Completed by Robert L. Fish)

LONG, AMELIA REYNOLDS (D)
(Pseudonyms: Patrick Laing, Adrian Reynolds, Peter Reynolds. Joint pseudonym with Edna McHugh: Kathleen Buddington Coxe)
Behind the Evidence, by Peter Reynolds. Visionary Pub., 1936
A Brief Case of Murder, by Patrick Laing. Phoenix, 1949
Carter Kidnapping Case. Pemberton, 1944
Corpse at the Quill Club. Phoenix, 1940
Corpse Came Back. Phoenix, 1947
Death Has a Will. Phoenix, 1944
Death Looks Down. Ziff-Davis, 1945
Death Wears a Scarab. Phoenix, 1943
Formula for Murder, by Adrian Reynolds. Phoenix, 1947
Four Feet in the Grave. Phoenix, 1941; Ryerson, 1941

The House with Green Shutters. Phoenix, 1950
If I Should Murder, by Patrick Laing. Phoenix, 1945
Invitation to Death. Phoenix, 1940
The Lady Is Dead, by Patrick Laing. Phoenix, 1951
The Lady Saw Red. Phoenix, 1952
The Leprechaun Murders, by Adrian Reynolds. Phoenix, 1950
Murder by Magic. Mystery House, 1947
Murder by Scripture. Phoenix, 1942
Murder by Treason. Phoenix, 1944
Murder from the Mind, by Patrick Laing. Phoenix, 1946
Murder Goes South. Phoenix, 1942
Murder Most Foul, by Kathleen Buddington Coxe. Phoenix, 1946
Murder Times Three. Phoenix, 1940
Murder to Type. Phoenix, 1943
Once Acquitted. Phoenix, 1946
The Round Table Murders, by Adrian Reynolds. Arcadia, 1952
The Shadow of Murder, by Patrick Laing. Phoenix, 1947
The Shakespeare Murders. Phoenix, 1939
Stone Dead, by Patrick Laing. Phoenix, 1945
Symphony in Murder. Ziff-Davis, 1944
The Triple Cross Murder. Ziff-Davis, 1944

LONG, ERNEST LAURIE (S)
The Blindness of Flynn. Ward, Lock, 1959
Captain Flynn Ret'd. Ward, Lock, 1949
Captain Flynn, Sheriff. Ward, Lock, 1962
Coolie Tramp. Ward, Lock, 1956
Crime Cruise. Ward, Lock, 1957
Cumsha Cruise. Ward, Lock, 1941
The Curtailed Voyage. Ward, Lock, 1957
Dope Ship. Ward, Lock, 1955
Flynn's Sampler. Ward, Lock, 1948
Four in a Fairlead. Ward, Lock, 1950
The Gabbart Destiny. Ward, Lock, 1956
High Noon to High Noon. Ward, Lock, 1959
Hunslett's Yard. Ward, Lock, 1962
In-Full Commission. Ward, Lock, 1963
Lieutenant Flynn, R. N. Ward, Lock, 1948
Loot Curran, R. N. Ward, Lock, 1963
Lugger Audace. Ward, Lock, 1957
Lumber Ship. Ward, Lock, 1949
Madam Captain. Ward, Lock, 1958
Masters of Kaolina. Ward, Lock, 1961
Open Roadsteads. Ward, Lock, 1963
River Passage. Ward, Lock, 1956
The Sailor and the Widow. Ward, Lock, 1957
The Strong Room of the Sutro. Ward, Lock, 1948
Surgeons Adrift. Ward, Lock, 1960
Trawl Adrift. Ward, Lock, 1958
The Vengeance of Flynn. Ward, Lock, 1942

LONG, FRANK BELKNAP (S)
The Horror from the Hills. Arkham, 1963
So Dark a Heritage. Lancer, 1966

LONG, MRS. GABRIELLE MARGARET VERE CAMPBELL (M) (Pseudonyms: Marjorie Bowen, George Preedy, Joseph Shearing)
The Abode of Love, by Joseph Shearing. Hutchinson, 1945; Berkley Pub., 1966
Airing in a Closed Carriage, by Joseph Shearing. Harper, 1943; Collier, 1962
Album Leaf, by Joseph Shearing. Heinemann, 1933 (U.S. title: The Spider in the Cup. Smith, H., 1934; Doubleday, 1963; Berkley Pub., 1965)
Aunt Beardie, by Joseph Shearing. Harrison-Hilton, 1940; Berkley Pub., 1965
Blanche Fury, by Joseph Shearing. Harrison-Hilton, 1939; Berkley Pub., 1965
The Crime of Laura Sarelle; see Laura Sarelle
The Devil Snard, by George Preedy. Benn, 1932
The Fetch; see The Spectral Bride
For Her to See, by Joseph Shearing. Hutchinson, 1947 (U.S. title: So Evil, My Love. Harper, 1947; Collier, 1962)
Forget-me-not, by Joseph Shearing. Heinemann, 1932 (U.S. titles: Lucille Cléry; A Woman of Intrigue. Harper, 1932 and The Strange Case of Lucille Cléry. World Pub., 1944; Berkley, 1966)
Golden Violet, by Joseph Shearing. Berkley Pub., 1965
The Heiress of Frascati; see Within the Bubble
The Lady and the Arsenic, by Joseph Shearing. Smith & Durrell, 1944
Laura Sarelle, by Joseph Shearing. Hutchinson, 1940 (U.S. title: The Crime of Laura Sarelle. Smith & Durrell, 1941; New Amer. Lib., 1965)
Lucille Cléry; A Woman of Intrigue; see Forget-me-not
Mignonette, by Joseph Shearing. Harper, 1948; Heinemann, 1949; Collier, 1962
Moss Rose, by Joseph Shearing. Smith, H., 1935; New Amer. Lib., 1965
Orange Blossoms, by Joseph Shearing. Heinemann, 1938
So Evil, My Love; see For Her to See
The Spectral Bride, by Joseph Shearing. Smith & Durrell, 1942; Berkley Pub., 1965

The Spider in the Cup; see Album Leaf
The Strange Case of Lucille Cléry; see Forget-me-not
To Bed at Noon, by Joseph Shearing. Heinemann, 1951; Berkley Pub., 1965
Within the Bubble, by Joseph Shearing. Heinemann, 1950 (U.S. title: The Heiress of Frascati. Berkley Pub., 1966)

LONG, HARMAN (M)
A Corpse Can't Walk. Rich, 1950
The Golden Cat. Rich, 1947
The Master of Evil. Rich, 1946
Seven to Die. Rich, 1946
Silverface. Rich, 1948
Silverface Surrenders. Rich, 1951

LONG, JULIUS (D)
Keep the Coffins Coming. Messner, 1947

LONG, LILY AUGUSTA (M) (Pseudonym: Roman Doubleday)
The Green Tree Mystery. Appleton, D., 1917
The Hemlock Avenue Mystery. Little, 1908
Red House on Rowan Street. Little, 1910
The Saintsbury Affair. Little, 1912

LONG, MANNING (D)
Bury the Hatchet. Duell, 1944; Hammond, 1949
Dull Thud. Duell, 1947; Hammond, 1950
False Alarm. Duell, 1943
Here's Blood in Your Eye. Duell, 1941; Hammond, 1946
The Savage Breast. Duell, 1948; Hammond, 1951
Short Shrift. Duell, 1945; Hammond, 1949
Vicious Circle. Duell, 1942; Hammond, 1946

LONG, MAX FREEDOM (M)
Death Goes Native. Lippincott, 1941
The Lava Flow Murders. Lippincott, 1940
Murder Between Dark and Dark. Lippincott, 1939; Hutchinson, 1940

LONGBAUGH, HARRY, pseud; see GOLDMAN, WILLIAM

LONGMAN, M. B., pseud. (S)
One Night at Bourbon Annie's. Dell, 1963

LONGMAN, M. E. (M)
I Was Murdered. Wright & Brown, 1936; Mellifont, 1937
The Phantom Millionaire. Wright & Brown, 1935
Terror Island. Wright & Brown, 1934

LONGMATE, NORMAN RICHARD (D)
Death in Office. Hale, R., 1961
Death Won't Wash. Cassell, 1957
A Head for Death. Cassell, 1958
Strip Death Naked. Cassell, 1959
Vote for Death. Cassell, 1960

LONGSTREET, STEPHEN (M) (Pseudonyms: Thomas Burton, Paul Haggard, Henri Weiner)
Bloodbird, by Thomas Burton. Smith & Durrell, 1941
The Case of the Severed Skull. Mystery Book of the Month, 1941
The Crime. S & S, 1959; Crest, 1961
Crime on the Cuff, by Henri Weiner. Morrow, 1936
Dead Is the Doornail, by Paul Haggard. Lippincott, 1937
Death Talks Shop, by Paul Haggard. Hillman-Curl, 1938
Death Walks on Cat Feet, by Paul Haggard. Hillman-Curl, 1938
Poison from a Wealthy Widow, by Paul Haggard. Hillman-Curl, 1938

LONGSTRETH, T. MORRIS (S)
Dangerline. Macmillan, 1955
Murder at Belly Butte, with H. Vernon. Century, 1931

LOOKABEE, EMMITT, pseud. (M)
Twist of Yarn. Pageant Press, 1956

LORAC, E. C. R., pseud; see RIVETT, EDITH CAROLINE

LORAINE, PHILIP, pseud; see ESTRIDGE, ROBIN

LORD, GARLAND, pseud; see GARLAND, ISABEL

LORD, GARLAND, pseud; see GARLAND, ISABEL

LORD, JEREMY, pseud; see REDMAN, BEN RAY

LORD, MINDRET; see GARLAND, ISABEL

LORENZ, FREDERIC (S) (Pseudonym: Larry Holden)
Dead Wrong. Pyramid, 1957
Hot. Lion, 1957
A Party Every Night. Lion, 1956
Ruby. Lion, 1956
The Savage Chase. Lion, 1954

LORING, EMILIE BAKER (M)
Bright Skies. Bantam, 1965
Follow Your Heart. Little, 1963

LORRAINE, JOHN, pseud. (S)
Men of Career. Crown, 1961

LOTT, STANLEY MAKEPEACE (S)
The Judge Will Call It Murder. Rich, 1951
Twopence for a Rat's Tail. Rich, 1947

LOVECRAFT, HOWARD PHILLIPS (S)
The Case of Charles Dexter Ward. Belmont, 1965
Dagon. Arkham, 1965
The Dunwich Horror and Others. Arkham, 1963

LOW, GARDNER, pseud; see RODDA, CHARLES PERCIVAL

LOWE, F. J. (M)
Blood Money. Stockwell, 1957
Killer from the Grave. Stockwell, 1959

LOWE, KENNETH, pseud; see LOBAUGH, MRS. ELMA K.

LOWE, MARJORIE (S)
The Sudden Lady. Putnam, 1961; Paperback Lib., 1965

LOWELL, B. E. (S)
And Incidentally Murder. Bouregy, 1952

LOWIS, CECIL CHAMPAIN (S)
The District Bungalow. Cape, 1927; Doubleday, Doran, 1928
Green Sandals. Cape, 1926
The Green Tunnel. Dickson, 1935
The Huntress. Cape, 1929

LOWNDES, MARIE ADELAIDE BELLOC (M)
Afterwards. Doubleday, Page, 1925; Grosset, 1927
And Call It Accident. Longmans, 1936
Another Man's Wife. Longmans, 1934
The Chianti Flask. Longmans, 1934
The Chink in the Armor. Scribner, 1912; Heinemann, 1931; Eyre, 1934
The Christine Diamond. Longmans, 1940
The End of Her Honeymoon. Scribner, 1913; Grosset, 1925
Letty Lynton. Cape, 1931
The Lodger. Scribner, 1911; Methuen, 1950; Dell, 1964
The Lonely House. Cape, 1931
Love and Hatred. Chapman, 1917; Doran, 1917
Murder Omnibus. Grosset, 1936
Novels of Mystery. Longmans, 1933
One of Those Ways. Knopf, 1929
Reckless Angel. Longmans, 1939
The Second Key. Longmans, 1936
The Story of Ivy. Heinemann, 1927; Doubleday, Doran, 1928
Studies in Love and Terror. Scribner, 1913
The Terriford Mystery. Doubleday, Page, 1924
Thou Shalt Not Kill. Eyre, 1933
The Vanderlyn Adventure. Cape, 1931
What Really Happened. Doubleday, Page, 1926; Hutchinson, 1926
What Timmy Did. Hutchinson, 1921; Doran, 1922
Who Rides on a Tiger. Longmans, 1935
Why It Happened. Longmans, 1938

LUARD, NICHOLAS (S)
The Warm and Golden War. Pantheon, 1967

LUCAS, CARY (M)
Unfinished Business. S & S, 1947

LUCAS, NORMAN (M)
Corner in Crime. Jenkins, 1952; Roy Pubs., 1957
Red Dice. Jenkins, 1952
Situations Vacant. Jenkins, 1956
Testament of Death. Jenkins, 1953

LUCK, PETER (M)
Crime Legitimate. Jenkins, 1937
Infallible Witness. Jenkins, 1932
The Killing of Ezra Burgoyne. Jenkins, 1929
Terror by Night. Jenkins, 1934
The Transome Murder Mystery. Jenkins, 1930
Two Shots. Jenkins, 1931
Under the Fourth-? Jenkins, 1927
Who Killed Robin Cockland? Jenkins, 1933
The Wingrave Case. Jenkins, 1935
The Wrong Number. Jenkins, 1926

LUDDECKE, WERNER I. (S)
Thursday at Dawn. Doubleday, 1965; Allen, W. H., 1966

LUDLOW, GEOFFREY; see MEYNELL, LAURENCE WALTER

LUEHRMANN, ADELE (M)
The Curious Case of Marie Dupont. Century, 1916
The Other Brown. Century, 1917
The Triple Mystery. Dodd, 1920

LUHRS, VICTOR (M)
The Longbow Murder. Norton, 1941

LUKENS, JOHN (S)
Adders Abounding. Hodder, 1954

LUPTON, LEONARD (D)
Murder Without Tears. Graphic, 1957

LUSTGARTEN, EDGAR M. (M)
Blondie Iscariot. Scribner, 1948
Game for Three Losers. Scribner, 1952
One More Unfortunate. Dell, 1959; Scribner, 1962
Verdict in Dispute. Scribner, 1950

LUTHUR, MARK LEE and LILLIAN C. FORD (D)
Card 13. Bobbs, 1930
The Saranoff Murder. Bobbs, 1930

LUTHUR, RAY (S)
Intermind. Banner, 1967

LYALL, GAVIN (S)
Midnight Plus One. Hodder, 1965; Scribner, 1965; Dell, 1966
The Most Dangerous Game. Scribner, 1963; Hodder, 1964; Macfadden, 1964
Shooting Script. Hodder, 1966; Scribner, 1966; Avon, 1967
The Wrong Side of the Sky. Scribner, 1961; Macfadden, 1963

LYELL, WILLIAM DARLING (M)
The House in Queen Anne's Square. Putnam, 1921

LYLE-SMYTHE, ALLAN (M) (Pseudonym: Alan Caillou)
Alien Virus. Davies, 1957
Journey to Orassia. Allen, W. H., 1966; Avon, 1967
Marseilles. PB, 1964
The Mindinao Pearl. Davies, 1959
The Plotter. Davies, 1960; Harper, 1960
Rogue's Gambit. Davies, 1955
Who'll Buy My Evil. PB, 1966

LYNCH, DAN (S)
Four-Time Loser. GM, 1962

LYNCH, LAWRENCE, pseud; see VAN DEVENTER, EMMA MURDOCH

LYNCH, MIRIAM (S-Gothic)
Amber Twilight. Belmont, 1967
Blacktower. Paperback Lib., 1966
Crime for Christmas. Arcadia, 1959
Gateway to the Grave. Arcadia, 1958
Graymists. Paperback Lib., 1967
Grow Cold Along with Me. Arcadia, 1958
A Heritage of Danger. Bouregy, 1964
Meeting with Murder. Arcadia, 1956
The Night of the Moonrose. Paperback Lib., 1966
Pale Hand of Danger. Bouregy, 1962
Poor Roger Is Dead. Arcadia, 1957
Road to Midnight. Paperback Lib., 1966
Secret of Lucifer's Island. Paperback Lib., 1967
The Silken Web. Bouregy, 1961
A Summer for Witches. Bouregy, 1962
Your Casket Awaits, Madame. Arcadia, 1957

LYNDE, FRANCIS (M)
Blind Man's Buff. Scribner, 1928

LYNDS, DENNIS (D) (Pseudonym: Michael Collins)
Act of Fear. Dodd, 1967

LYNN, MARGARET, pseud; see BATTYE, GLADYS STARKEY

LYON, DANA (S)
The Frightened Child. Ace, 1948; Harper, 1948 (Also published as: The House on Telegraph Hill)
The House on Telegraph Hill; see The Frightened Child
It's My Own Funeral. Farrar & Rinehart, 1941; Hammond, 1948
The Lost One. Ace, 1958; Harper, 1958
Spin the Web Tight. Ace, 1963
The Tentacles. Harper, 1950; Ace, 1963
The Trusting Victim. Ace, 1964

LYON, WINSTON (M)
Criminal Court. PB, 1966

LYONS, AUGUSTA WALLACE (S)
Season of Desire. Signet, 1961

LYONS, DELPHINE (S-Gothic)
The Depths of Yesterday. Lancer, 1966
The House of Four Windows. Lancer, 1967

LYTLE, ANDREW (S)
The Long Night. Bobbs, 1936; Eyre, 1937
A Name for Evil. Bobbs, 1947

LYTTON, EDWARD BULWER-; see BULWER-LYTTON, EDWARD

MAASS, JOACHIM (M)
Gouffe Case. Harper, 1960; Dell, 1966

McALLISTER, ALISTER (D) (Pseudonyms: Lynn Brock, Anthony Wharton)
Colonel Gore's Second Case. Collins, 1925; Harper, 1926
Colonel Gore's Third Case. Collins, 1925 (U.S. title: The Kink. Harper, 1927)
Dagwort Coombie Murder. Collins, 1930
Deductions of Colonel Gore. Collins, 1924; Harper, 1925
Four Fingers, by Lynn Brock. Collins, 1940
The Kink; see Colonel Gore's Third Case
The Mendip Mystery. Collins, 1929
Murder at the Inn. Harper, 1929
Murder on the Bridge. Harper, 1930
Nightmare. Collins, 1932
Q. E. D. Collins, 1930
Riddle of the Roost, by Lynn Brock. Collins, 1939

Silver Sickle Case, by Lynn Brock. Collins, 1939
The Slip Carriage Mystery. Collins, 1928; Harper, 1928
Stoat, by Lynn Brock. Collins, 1940
Stoke Silver Case. Harper, 1929
Two of Diamonds. Collins, 1930

MACARDLE, DOROTHY
Dark Enchanted. Doubleday, 1953; Bantam, 1966
Uneasy Freehold. Davies, 1942 (U.S. title: The Uninvited. Doubleday, Doran, 1942)
The Uninvited; see Uneasy Freehold

MacARTHUR, DAVID WILSON (M)
Death at Slack Water. Ward, Lock, 1962

MACAULAY, ROSE (M)
Mystery at Geneva. Collins, 1922; Boni & Liveright, 1923

McAULIFFE, FRANK (M)
Of All the Bloody Cheek. Ballantine, 1965

McBAIN, ED, pseud; see HUNTER, EVAN

McCABE, CAMERON, pseud; see BORNEMAN, ERNST WILHELM JULIUS

McCAGUE, JAMES
To Be a Hero. Crown, 1962

McCALL, ANTHONY, pseud; see KANE, HENRY

McCALL, VINCENT, pseud; see MORLAND, NIGEL

McCARTHY, DAVID (D)
The Killing at the Big Tree. Doubleday, 1960

McCARTHY, JAMES REMINGTON (S)
Special Agent. Bobbs, 1938

McCARTHY, SHAUN (S) (Pseudonyms: Theo Callas, Desmond Cory)
Begin, Murderer, by Desmond Cory. Muller, 1951
City of Kites, by Theo Callas. Muller, 1955; Walker & Co., 1964
Deadfall, by Desmond Cory. Walker & Co., 1965
Dead Man Falling, by Desmond Cory. Muller, 1953
Feramontov. Walker & Co., 1956; Award, 1968
Hammerhead, by Desmond Cory. Muller, 1963 (Also published as: Shockwave. Walker & Co., 1964; Signet, 1965)
Head, by Desmond Cory. Muller, 1960
The Height of Day, by Desmond Cory. Muller, 1955
High Requiem, by Desmond Cory. Muller, 1956
Intrigue, by Desmond Cory. Muller, 1954
Johnny Goes East, by Desmond Cory. Muller, 1958
Johnny Goes North, by Desmond Cory. Muller, 1956
Johnny Goes South, by Desmond Cory. Muller, 1959; Walker & Co., 1964; Signet, 1966
Johnny Goes West, by Desmond Cory. Muller, 1959; Walker & Co., 1967; Award, 1968
Johnny on the Belgrade Express, by Desmond Cory. Muller, 1960
Lady Lost, by Desmond Cory. Muller, 1953
The Name of the Game Is Death. Muller, 1964
The Phoenix Sings, by Desmond Cory. Muller, 1955
Pilgrim at the Gate, by Desmond Cory. Washburn, 1958
Pilgrim on the Island, by Desmond Cory. Walker & Co., 1961
Secret Ministry, by Desmond Cory. Muller, 1951
The Shaken Leaf, by Desmond Cory. Muller, 1955
Shockwave; see Hammerhead
Stranglehold, by Desmond Cory. Muller, 1961
This Is Jezebel, by Desmond Cory. Muller, 1952
This Traitor, Death, by Desmond Cory. Muller, 1952
Timelock, by Desmond Cory. Muller, 1967; Walker & Co., 1967
Undertow, by Desmond Cory. Muller, 1962; Walker & Co., 1962; Signet, 1965

McCHESNEY, MARY F. (D) (Pseudonym: Joe Rayter)
Asking for Trouble. Mill, 1955; Ward, Lock, 1957
Stab in the Dark. Mill, 1954; Ward, Lock, 1958
The Victim Was Important. Scribner, 1954

McCLOY, HELEN (D)
Alias Basil Willing. Random, 1951
Before I Die. Dodd, 1963; Gollancz, 1963; Dell, 1967
Cue for Murder. Bantam, 1942; Morrow, 1942
Dance of Death. Morrow, 1938
The Deadly Truth. Morrow, 1941
Do Not Disturb. Morrow, 1943
The Further Side of Fear. Dodd, 1967
Goblin Market. Collier, 1943

He Never Came Back. Random, 1954 (Also published as: Unfinished Business)
The Long Body. Random, 1955; Ace, 1965
The Man in the Moonlight. Morrow, 1940
The One That Got Away. Gollancz, 1945; Morrow, 1945
Panic. Morrow, 1944
She Walks Alone. Random, 1948
The Singing Diamonds. Dodd, 1965
The Slayer and the Slain. Random, 1957; Gollancz, 1958
Through a Glass Darkly. Random, 1950; Collier, 1965
Two Thirds of a Ghost. Random, 1956; Gollancz, 1957; Dell, 1958
Unfinished Business; see He Never Came Back
Unfinished Crime. Random, 1954
Who's Calling? Morrow, 1942

McCLURE, VICTOR (D)
Boost of the Golden Snail. Harrap, 1936
Clue of the Dead Goldfish. Harrap, 1933; Lippincott, 1934
Counterfeit Murders. Harrap, 1932
Crying Pig Murder. Morrow, 1930
Death Behind the Door. Houghton, 1933
Death on the Set. Harrap, 1934; Lippincott, 1935
Diva's Emeralds. Harrap, 1937
Hi-Spy-Kick-the-Can. Harrap, 1936
She Stands Accused. Lippincott, 1935

McCOMB, KATHERINE (M)
A Day for Murder. Bouregy, 1963
Death in a Downpour. Arcadia, 1960

McCOMBS, R. L. F. (D)
Clue in Two Flats. Eldon, 1942

McCONNAUGHEY, JAMES (M)
Three for the Money. Sloane, 1954

McCONNELL, JAMES DOUGLAS RUTHERFORD (M) (Pseudonym: Douglas Rutherford. Joint pseudonym with Francis Durbridge: Paul Temple)
The Black Leather Murders, by Douglas Rutherford. Collins, 1966; Walker & Co., 1966
Comes the Blind Fury, by Douglas Rutherford. Faber, 1950
The Creeping Flesh, by Douglas Rutherford. Collins, 1963; Walker & Co., 1965
East of Algiers, by Paul Temple. Hodder, 1959
Flight into Peril, by Douglas Rutherford. Dodd, 1952 (English title: Telling of Murder. Faber, 1952)
The Grand Prix Murders, by Douglas Rutherford. Collins, 1955
The Long Echo, by Douglas Rutherford. Collins, 1957; Abelard, 1958
Meet a Body, by Douglas Rutherford. Faber, 1951
Murder Is Incidental, by Douglas Rutherford. Collins, 1961
The Perilous Sky, by Douglas Rutherford. Collins, 1955
Skriek of Tyres, by Douglas Rutherford. Collins, 1958
Telling of Murder; see Flight into Peril
Tyler Mystery, by Paul Temple. Hodder, 1957

McCONNOR, VINCENT (S)
The French Doll. Hill & Wang, 1965; Avon, 1966

MacCORMACK, PAT (S)
The Grave Gives Up. Exposition, 1964

McCOY, TRENT (D)
Quinton Clyde, Private Investigator. Baker, 1952
Wake Not the Sleeping Wolf. Hamilton, 1952

McCRACKEN, MIKE (M)
Black Death. Hamilton & Co., 1952
Black Hammer. Hamilton & Co., 1952
Killer in Canvas Jeans. Hamilton & Co., 1952

McCRAE, ELIZABETH (S)
House of the Whispering Winds. Signet, 1966
The Intrusion. Signet, 1967

McCREADY, JACK, pseud; see POWELL, TALMADGE

McCUE, LILLIAN BUENO (D) (Pseudonym: Lillian De La Torre)
The Detections of Dr. Sam: Johnson. Doubleday, 1960
Dr. Sam: Johnson, Detector. Knopf, 1946
Elizabeth Is Missing. Knopf, 1945
The Heir of Douglas. Knopf, 1952

McCULLEY, JOHNSTON (M)
Avenging Twins. Chelsea House, 1927
Crimson Clown. Chelsea House, 1929
Crimson Clown Again. Cassell, 1930
The Demon. Chelsea House, 1925
Spider's Debt. Chelsea House, 1930
Thunderbolt's Jest. Chelsea House, 1927

McCULLY, WALBRIDGE (D)
Blood on Nassau's Moon. Doubleday, Doran, 1945
Death Rides Tandem. Doubleday, Doran, 1942
Doctor's Beware. Doubleday, Doran, 1943

McCUTCHAN, PHILIP DONALD (S)
Bluebolt One. Harrap, 1962; Berkley Pub., 1965
Bowering's Breakwater. Harrap, 1964
The Dead Line. Berkley Pub., 1966; Harrap, 1966
Gibraltar Road. Harrap, 1960; Berkley Pub., 1965
Hopkinson and the Devil of Hate. Harrap, 1961
Kid. Harrap, 1958
Leave the Dead Behind Us. Harrap, 1962
The Man from Moscow. Harrap, 1963; Day, 1965; Berkley Pub., 1966
Moscow Coach. Harrap, 1963; Day, 1964; Berkley Pub., 1967
On Course for Danger. St. Martin's, 1959
Red Cap. Harrap, 1961; Berkley Pub., 1965
Skyprobe. Day, 1967; Berkley Pub., 1968
Sladd's Evil. Harrap, 1965; Day, 1967
Storm South. Harrap, 1959
Warmaster. Harrap, 1963; Day, 1964; Berkley Pub., 1965
Whistle and I'll Come. Harrap, 1957

McCUTCHEON, GEORGE BARR (D)
Anderson Crow, Detective. Dodd, 1920
The Daughter of Anderson Crow. Dodd, 1907
Green Fancy. Dodd, 1917
Sherry. Dodd, 1919

McCUTCHEON, HUGH DAVIE MARTIN (D)
And the Moon Was Full; see Killer's Moon
The Angel of Light. Rich, 1951 (U.S. title: Murder at the Angel. Dutton, 1952)
The Black Attendant. Long, 1966
Comes the Blind Fury. Long, 1961
Cover Her Face. Rich, 1955
The Deadly One. Long, 1962
Killer's Moon. Long, 1966 (U.S. title: And the Moon Was Full. Doubleday, 1967)
The Long Night Through. Rich, 1956
Murder at the Angel; see The Angel of Light
None Shall Sleep Tonight. Dutton, 1953; Rich, 1954
Prey for the Nightingale. Rich, 1953
Suddenly in Vienna. Long, 1963
To Dusty Death. Long, 1960
Treasure of the Sun. Long, 1964
Yet She Must Die. Doubleday, 1962; Long, 1962

McDANIEL, DAVID (S)
The Dagger Affair. Ace, 1966 (The Man from U.N.C.L.E. series, #4)
The Monster Wheel Affair. Ace, 1967 (The Man from U.N.C.L.E. series, #8)
The Rainbow Affair. Ace, 1967 (The Man from U.N.C.L.E. series, #13)
The Vampire Affair. Ace, 1966 (The Man from U.N.C.L.E. series, #6)

McDERMID, FINLAY (M)
Ghost Wanted. S & S, 1943
See No Evil. S & S, 1959

McDONALD, HAZEL CHRISTIE (D)
Death Walks Softly. Phoenix, 1951

MacDONALD, JOHN, pseud; see MILLAR, KENNETH

MacDONALD, JOHN DANN (M-S)
All These Condemned. GM, 1954, 1965
April Evil. Dell, 1956; GM, 1965
Area of Suspicion. Dell, 1954; Fawcett, 1961; GM, 1967
Ballroom of the Skies. Greenberg, 1952
The Beach Girls. GM, 1959, 1965; Muller, 1964
The Blood Game. Doubleday, 1965
Border Town Girl. Popular Lib., 1956
The Brass Cupcake. GM, 1950, 1965
Bright Orange for the Shroud. GM, 1965
A Bullet for Cinderella. Dell, 1955; GM, 1966 (Also published as: On the Make. Dell, 1960; Pan, 1963)
Cancel All Our Vows. Appleton, 1953; Hale, R., 1955; Pyramid, 1965
Cape Fear; see The Executioners
Clemmie. GM, 1958, 1966
Contrary Pleasure. Appleton, 1954; Hale, R., 1955
The Crossroads. S & S, 1959; Crest, 1960
Cry Hard, Cry Fast. GM, 1955; Popular Lib., 1966
The Damned. GM, 1952; Muller, 1964
Darker Than Amber. GM, 1966
Dead Low Tide. GM, 1953, 1966
A Deadly Shade of Gold. GM, 1965
Deadly Welcome. Dell, 1959; Pan, 1964
Death Trap. Dell, 1957; GM, 1965; Pan, 1964
The Deceivers. Dell, 1958; GM, 1965
The Deep Blue Good-Bye. GM, 1964
The Drowner. GM, 1963, 1965; Hale, R., 1964
The Empty Trap. Popular Lib., 1957
The End of Night. S & S, 1960; GM, 1966
The End of the Tiger and Other Stories. GM, 1966
The Executioners. S & S, 1958 (Also published as: Cape Fear. Pan, 1961; Crest, 1965)

A Flash of Green. S & S, 1962; Crest, 1963
The Girl, the Gold Watch & Everything. GM, 1962, 1965
The House Guests. Doubleday, 1965
Judge Me Not. GM, 1951, 1965; Muller, 1964
A Key to the Suite. GM, 1962, 1966
The Last One Left. Doubleday, 1967; Crest, 1968
A Man of Affairs. Dell, 1957; GM, 1965
Murder for the Bride. GM, 1951
Murder in the Wind. Dell, 1956; GM, 1965
The Neon Jungle. GM, 1953, 1966; Hale, R., 1962
Nightmare in Pink. GM, 1964
On the Make; see A Bullet for Cinderella
On the Run. GM, 1963, 1965
One Fearful Yellow Eye. GM, 1966
One Monday We Killed Them All. GM, 1961; Hale, R., 1963
The Only Girl in the Game. GM, 1960; Hale, R., 1962
Please Write for Details. S & S, 1959; GM, 1966
The Price of Murder. Dell, 1957; GM, 1965
A Purple Place for Dying. GM, 1964
The Quick Red Fox. GM, 1964
Slam the Big Door. GM, 1960, 1965; Hale, R., 1961
Soft Touch. Dell, 1958; GM, 1966
Three for McGee. Doubleday, 1967
Weep for Me. GM, 1951; Muller, 1964
Where Is Janice Gantry? GM, 1961; Hale, R., 1963
Wine of the Dreamers. Greenberg, 1951
You Only Live Once. Popular Lib., 1955 (Also published as: You Kill Me. Popular Lib., 1961)
You Kill Me; see You Only Live Once

MacDONALD, JOHN ROSS, pseud; see MILLAR, KENNETH

MacDONALD, PHILIP (D) (Pseudonym: Martin Porlock. Joint pseudonym with Ronald MacDonald: Oliver Fleming)
Ambrotox and Limping Dick, by Oliver Fleming. Ward, Lock, 1920
The Choice. Collins, 1931
Crime Conductor. Doubleday, Doran, 1931; Collins, 1932
Dark Wheel, with A. Boyd Correll. Morrow, 1948
Death and Chicanery: A Collection of Tales. Doubleday, 1962; Jenkins, 1963; Popular Lib., 1964
Death on My Left. Collins, 1933; Doubleday, Doran, 1933
Escape. Doubleday, Doran, 1932
Fingers of Fear and Other Stories. Collins, 1953
Guest in the House. Doubleday, 1955; Penguin, 1964; Pyramid, 1966
The Link. Collins, 1930; Doubleday, Doran, 1930
The List of Adrian Messenger. Doubleday, 1959; Jenkins, 1960; Bantam, 1963; Penguin, 1963
Man Out of the Rain and Other Stories. Doubleday, 1955; Jenkins, 1955
The Maze. Collins, 1932
The Menace. Doubleday, Doran, 1933
Murder Gone Mad. Collins, 1931; Doubleday, Doran, 1931; Avon, 1965
Mystery at Friar's Pardon, by Martin Porlock. Collins, 1931
Mystery in Kensington Gore, by Martin Porlock. Collins, 1932, 1960
Mystery of the Dead Police. Doubleday, Doran, 1933; Macfadden, 1965
The Noose. Collins, 1930; Dial, 1930
The Nursemaid Who Disappeared. Collins, 1932
Omnibus. Collins, 1931 (Contains: The Rasp, The White Cow, The Link, and Murder Gone Mad)
Persons Unknown. Doubleday, Doran, 1930
Polferry Mystery; see Polferry Riddle
Polferry Riddle. Doubleday, Doran, 1931 (English title: Polferry Mystery. Collins, 1932)
Queen's Mate. Collins, 1930
The Rasp. Doubleday, Doran, 1925; Collins, 1933; Avon, 1965
R. I. P. Collins, 1933
Rope to Spare. Collins, 1932; Doubleday, Doran, 1932
Rynox Murder. Doubleday, Doran, 1931; Avon, 1965 (English title: Rynox Mystery. Collins, 1930)
Rynox Mystery; see Rynox Murder
Something to Hide: A Collection of Four Short Stories and Two Novelettes. Doubleday, 1952
Spandan Quid, by Oliver Fleming. Palmer, C., 1923
Three for Midnight. Doubleday, 1963 (Contains: The Rasp, Murder Gone Mad, and The Rynox Murder)
Triple Jeopardy. Doubleday, 1962
Warrant for X. Doubleday, Doran, 1938; Dell, 1962
The White Crow. Collins, 1928; MacVeagh, 1929
The Wraith. Doubleday, Doran, 1931
X vs. Rex, by Martin Porlock. Collins, 1933

MacDONALD, RONALD; see MacDONALD, PHILIP

MacDONALD, ROSS, pseud; see MILLAR, KENNETH

MacDONALD, WILLIAM COIT (M)
The Gloved Saskia. Bouregy, 1964
The Devil's Drum. Hodder, 1962

MACDONELL, ARCHIBALD GORDON (D)
(Pseudonyms: John Cameron, Neil Gordon)
Big Ben Alibi. Lane, 1930
Body Found Stabbed. Methuen, 1932
Crew of the Anaconda. Macmillan, 1940
Factory on the Cliff. Longmans, 1938
Flight from a Lady. Macmillan, 1939
Murder in Earl's Court. Lane, 1931
The New Gun Runners. Harcourt, 1928
The Professor's Poison. Harcourt, 1927; Longmans, 1928
Seven Stabs. Doubleday, Doran, 1930; Gollancz, 1931
The Shakespeare Murders. Barker, 1933; Holt, H., 1933
The Silent Murder. Doubleday, Doran, 1930; Longmans, 1930

McDONELL, GORDON (M)
The Burning Secret. Hart-Davis, 1959
Intruder from the Sea. Harrap, 1953; Little, 1953
Jump for Glory. Harrap, 1936
My Sister Goodnight. Little, 1948
The Reprieve of Roger Maine. Prentice-Hall, 1961; Chatto, 1962
Silver Bugle. Harrap, 1938
They Won't Believe Me. Harrap, 1947
Wind Without Rain. Chatto, 1963

McDONELL, MARGARET (M)
Althea. Doubleday, 1951

McDOUGALD, ROMAN (D)
Blushing Monkey. S & S, 1953
Deaths of Lora Karen. S & S, 1944; Bart, 1945
Lady Without Mercy. S & S, 1948
Purgatory Street. S & S, 1946
The Whistling Legs. S & S, 1945
Woman Under the Mountains. S & S, 1950

McDOUGALL, MURDOCH CHRISTIE (S)
Chase the Snowman. Boardman, T. V., 1957
Soft as Silk. Boardman, T. V., 1957

McDOWELL, EMMETT (S)
Bloodline to Murder. Ace, 1960
In at the Kill. Ace, 1960
Stamped for Death. Ace, 1958
Switcheroo. Ace, 1954

MacDOWELL, ROBERT (M)
The Hound's Tooth. Mill, 1965; Cassell, 1967

MacDUFF, DAVID (D)
Murder Strikes Three. Modern Age, 1937

MACE, HELEN (D)
House of Hate. Hammond, 1958
Murder Among Those Present. Hammond, 1957

MACE, MERLDA (M)
Blondes Don't Cry. Messner, 1945
Headlong for Murder. Messner, 1943
Motto for Murder. Messner, 1943

McELFRESH, ADELINE (S)
Keep Back the Dark. Phoenix, 1951

McELROY, HUGH FRANCIS (M)
The Curtain of the Dark. Chapman, 1944
The House of Malory. Chapman, 1948
The Silver Venus. Chapman, 1942
Unkindly Cup. Chapman, 1946

MacELWAIN, MIRANDA (D)
Penguin Island Murders. Quality, 1954

McFADDEN, GERTRUDE VIOLET (M)
The Honest Lawyer. Lane, 1916

MacFADYEN, VIRGINIA (M)
The Bittern Point. Boni, 1926; Grosset, 1927

McFARLANE, ARTHUR EMERSON (M)
Behind the Bolted Door. Dodd, 1916

McFARLANE, LESLIE (M)
The Murder Tree. Dutton, 1931; Paul, S., 1932
Streets of Shadow. Dutton, 1930; Paul, S., 1931

MacFARLANE, PETER CLARK (D)
The Crack in the Bell. Doubleday, Page, 1918

McGERR, PATRICIA (D-M)
Catch Me If You Can. Doubleday, 1948; Collins, 1949
Death in a Million Living Rooms. Doubleday, 1951
Die Laughing. Collins, 1952
Fatal in My Fashion. Doubleday, 1954; Collins, 1955
Follow as the Night. Doubleday, 1950; Macfadden, 1968
Is There a Traitor in the House? Doubleday, 1964; Avon, 1966
The Missing Years. Doubleday, 1953; Allen, W. H., 1954
Murder Is Absurd. Doubleday, 1967
Pick Your Victim. Doubleday, 1946; Collins, 1947
Save the Witness. Doubleday, 1949; Collins, 1950
Seven Deadly Sisters. Doubleday, 1947; Collins, 1948; Dell
Your Loving Victim. Collins, 1951

McGHEE, BILL (S)
Cut and Run. Hammond, 1962

McGIBENY, DONALD (M)
.32 Caliber. Bobbs, 1920

McGIVERN, WILLIAM PETER (S)
(Pseudonym: Bill Peters)
The Big Heat. Dodd, 1953; Hamilton, H., 1953
Blondes Die Young, by Bill Peters. Dodd, 1952
But Death Runs Faster. Boardman, T. V., 1945; Dodd, 1945
The Caper of the Golden Bulls. Dodd, 1966; Collins, 1967; PB, 1967
A Choice of Assassins. Dodd, 1963; Bantam, 1964; Collins, 1964
Crooked Frame. Dodd, 1952
The Darkest Hour. Dodd, 1955
Killer on the Turnpike and Other Stories. PB, 1961
Lie Down, I Want to Talk to You. Dodd, 1967
Margin of Terror. Dodd, 1953; Collins, 1955
Night Extra. Dodd, 1957; Collins, 1958
Odds Against Tomorrow. Dodd, 1957
Police Special. Dodd, 1962 (Contains: The Seven File, The Darkest Hour, and Rogue Cop)
Rogue Cop. Dodd, 1954; Collins, 1955
Savage Streets. Dodd, 1959; Collins, 1960; PB, 1961
Seven File. Dodd, 1956
Seven Lies South. Dodd, 1960; Collins, 1961; Crest, 1962
Shield for Murder. Dodd, 1951
Very Cold for May. Dodd, 1951

McGIVERN, MRS. WILLIAM PETER; see DALY, MAUREEN

McGLOIN, JOSEPH THADDEUS (M)
(Pseudonym: Thaddeus O'Finn)
Happy Holiday. Rinehart, 1950
I'll Die Laughing. Bruce Pub., 1955

McGOVAN, JAMES (D)
Brought to Bay; or, Experiences of a City Detective. Edinburgh Pub., 1878; Menzies, 1890
Hunted Down; or, Recollections of a City Detective. Edinburgh Pub., 1897
The Invisible Pickpocket; or, Records of a City Detective. Jenkins, 1922
Solved Mysteries; or, Revelations of a City Detective. Menzies, 1888
Strange Clues; or, Chronicles of a City Detective. Edinburgh Pub., 1881
Traced and Tracked; or, Memoirs of a City Detective. Menzies, 1884

MacGOVERN, JAMES (S)
The Berlin Couriers. Abelard, 1960; Pyramid, 1961

MacGOWAN, ALICE and PERRY NEWBERRY (M)
The Million Dollar Suitcase. Hutchinson, 1922; Stokes, 1922
The Mystery Woman. Hutchinson, 1924; Stokes, 1924
The Seventh Passenger. Stokes, 1926; Hutchinson, 1928
Shaken Down. Hutchinson, 1925; Stokes, 1925
Who Is This Man? Hutchinson, 1927; Stokes, 1927

MacGRATH, HAROLD (M)
The Blue Rajah Murder. Doubleday, Doran, 1930; Long, 1931
The Green Complex. Doubleday, Doran, 1930; Grosset, 1932
The Green Stone. Doubleday, Page, 1924; Grosset, 1926
Man with Three Names. Doubleday, Doran, 1920; Hutchinson, 1920
The Million Dollar Mystery. Grosset, 1915
The Other Passport. Doubleday, Doran, 1931
Private Wire to Washington. Harper, 1919
The Voice in the Fog. Bobbs, 1915
The World Outside. Long, 1924
Yellow Typhoon. Harper, 1919

McGREW, FENN, pseud; see McGREW, JULIA

McGREW, JULIA and CAROLINE K. FENN (D) (Pseudonym: Fenn McGrew)
Made for Murder. Rinehart, 1954
Murder by Mail. Rinehart, 1951
Taste of Death. Rinehart, 1953

McGUIRE, ATHA (S)
Homicide Hussy. GM, 1955

MacGUIRE, NICHOLAS, pseud; see MELIDES, NICHOLAS

McGUIRE, PATRICK O. (M)
Fiesta for Murder. Hammond, 1962
A Time for Murder. Hammond, 1955

MacGUIRE, PAUL (D)
The Black Rose Murder. Coward, 1932
Born to Be Hanged. Skeffington, 1935
Burial Service. Heinemann, 1938 (U.S. title: Funeral in Eden. Morrow, 1938)
Cry Aloud for Murder. Heinemann, 1937
Daylight Murder. Skeffington, 1934 (U.S. title: Murder at High Noon. Doubleday, Doran, 1935)
Death Fugue. Skeffington, 1934 (U.S. title: Death Tolls the Bell. Coward, 1933)
Death Tolls the Bell; see Death Fugue

Enter Three Witches; see The Spanish Steps
Funeral in Eden; see Burial Service
Murder at High Noon; see Daylight Murder
Murder by the Law. Skeffington, 1932 (Also published as: Tower Mystery. Heinemann, 1932)
Murder in Bostall. Skeffington, 1931
Murder in Haste. Skeffington, 1934
Prologue to the Gallows. Skeffington, 1936
Seven-thirty Victoria. Skeffington, 1935
The Spanish Steps. Heinemann, 1940 (U.S. title: Enter Three Witches. Morrow, 1940)
There Sits Death. Skeffington, 1933
Three Dead Men. Skeffington, 1931
Threepence to Marble Arch. Skeffington, 1936
Tower Mystery; see Murder by Law
W. 1. Heinemann, 1937

McGURK, SLATER (D)
The Copenhagen Affair; see The Denmark Bus
The Denmark Bus. Walker & Co., 1966 (Also published as: The Copenhagen Affair. Lancer, 1966)
The Grand Central Murders. Macmillan, 1964

MACHARD, ALFRED (S)
The Wolf Man. Clode, 1925 (Also published as: The Were-wolf)

MacHARG, WILLIAM; see BALMER, EDWIN

MACHEN, ARTHUR (S)
Classics of Mystery. Vol. 6
Great God Pan and Other Weird Stories. Knopf, 1922
The Terror. McBride, 1917; Norton, 1965
The Three Imposters. Knopf, 1924; Baker, J., 1965

McHUGH, AUGUSTIN; see CURRIE, BARTON

McHUGH, EDNA; see LONG, AMELIA REYNOLDS

McHUGH, FRANCES Y. (M)
The China Shepherdess. Arcadia, 1966

MacINNES, HELEN (Mrs. Gilbert Highet) (S)
Above Suspicion. Harcourt, 1941; Harrap, 1941; Dell, 1962
Assignment in Brittany. Harcourt, 1942; Harrap, 1942; Dell, 1963
Assignment: Suspense. Harcourt, 1961 (Contains: Above Suspicion, Horizon, and Assignment in Brittany)
Decision at Delphi. Harcourt, 1960; Crest, 1963
The Double Image. Crest, 1967
Friends and Lovers. Harcourt, 1947; Harrap, 1948
Horizon. Harcourt, 1945; Harrap, 1945; Dell, 1964
I and My True Love. Harcourt, 1952; Collins, 1953; Crest, 1965
Neither Five Nor Three. Collins, 1951; Harcourt, 1951; Crest, 1966
North From Rome. Harcourt, 1958; Crest, 1959, 1962
Pray for a Brave Heart. Collins, 1955; Harcourt, 1955; Dell, 1965
Rest and Be Thankful. Harcourt, 1949; Harrap, 1949; Crest, 1967
The Venetian Affair. Harcourt, 1963; Collins, 1964; Crest, 1964
While Still We Live. Harcourt, 1944; Crest, 1964

McINTIRE, WEBB KYLE (M)
Cider Row. Exposition, 1961

McINTOSH, KIM HAMILTON (S)
(Pseudonym: Catherine Aird)
A Most Contagious Game. Doubleday, 1967
The Religious Body. Doubleday, 1966

MacINTYRE, JOHN THOMAS (D)
(Pseudonym: Kerry O'Neil)
Ashton-Kirk: Criminologist. Robinson & Birch, 1921
Ashton-Kirk: Investigator. Robinson & Birch, 1921
Ashton-Kirk: Secret Agent. Palmer, C., 1916
Death at Dakar, by Kerry O'Neil. Doubleday, Doran, 1943
Death Strikes at Heron House, by Kerry O'Neil. Farrar & Rinehart, 1943
Mooney Moves Around, by Kerry O'Neil. Reynal, 1939
The Museum Murder. Doubleday, Doran, 1929; Bles, 1930
Ninth Floor: Middle City Tower, by Kerry O'Neil. Farrar & Rinehart, 1943
Secret Agent: Ashton-Kirk. Robinson & Birch, 1921
Special Detective: Ashton-Kirk. Robinson & Birch, 1922

MacISAAC, FRED (M)
The Dealer of Death. Methuen, 1938
Death Rides the Deep. Methuen, 1938
Don't Let Him Burn. Methuen, 1938
False-Face. Sovereign Books, 1939
Hot Gold. Sovereign Books, 1938
The Mental Marvel. McClurg, 1930
Millions for Murder. Methuen, 1938
The Murder Special. Methuen, 1938
The Vanishing Professor. Sovereign Books, 1939

The Wild Man of Cape Cod. Methuen, 1938
The Winged Murderer. Sovereign Books, 1939
The Yellow Shop. Hurst, 1928

MacKAIL, DENIS GEORGE (M)
The Majestic Mystery. Houghton, 1923; Heinemann, 1924

McKAY, KELVIN (D)
Murder at Barclay House. Phoenix, 1936

McKECHNIE, NEIL KENNETH (M)
The Saddleroom Murder. Penn, 1937

McKELWAY, ST. CLAIR
The Edinburgh Caper. Holt, 1963

MacKENNA, MARTHE (S)
Arms and the Spy. Jarrolds, 1942
Double Spy. Jarrolds, 1938
Drums Never Beat. Jarrolds, 1936
Hunt the Spy. Jarrolds, 1939
Lancer Spy. Jarrolds, 1937
Nightfighter Spy. Jarrolds, 1943
Set a Spy. Jarrolds, 1937
The Spy in Khaki. Jarrolds, 1941
A Spy Was Born. Jarrolds, 1935
Spying Blind. Jarrolds, 1939
Three Spies for Glory. Jarrolds, 1950

MacKENZIE, ANDREW CARR (M)
Always Fight Back. Boardman, T. V., 1955
Grave Is Waiting. Boardman, T. V., 1957
House at the Estuary. Ward, Lock, 1948
The Man from the Past. Boardman, T. V., 1958
The Man Who Wanted to Die. Ward, Lock, 1951
Missile. Boardman, T. V., 1959
Point of a Gun. Ward, Lock, 1951
Reaching Hand. Boardman, T. V., 1957
Search in the Dark. Ward, Lock, 1948
Shadow of a Spy. Boardman, T. V., 1958
Shadows on the River. Ward, Lock, 1949 (Also published as: Splash of Red. Ward, Lock, 1955)
Splash of Red; see Shadows on the River
Three Hours to Hang. Boardman, T. V., 1955
Voice from the Cell. Hale, R., 1961
Week of Suspense. Hale, R., 1962
Whisper If You Dare. Ward, Lock, 1950

MacKENZIE, DONALD (S)
Cool Sleeps Balaban. Collins, 1964; Houghton, 1964; Avon, 1966
Dangerous Silence. Berkley Pub., 1960; Collins, 1960; Houghton, 1960
Death Is a Friend. Houghton, 1967
Double Exposure. Cassell, 1963; Houghton, 1963 (Also published as: I Spy. Avon, 1964)
The Genial Stranger. Collins, 1962; Houghton, 1962; Pan, 1964
I Spy; see Double Exposure
The Juryman. Elek, 1957
The Knife Edge. Houghton, 1961
The Lonely Side of the River. Hodder, 1964; Houghton, 1964
Manhunt. Houghton, 1957
Moment of Danger; see Scent of Danger
Nowhere to Go. Elek, 1957
Occupation: Thief. Bobbs, 1956
Salute from a Dead Man. Houghton, 1966
Scent of Danger. Houghton, 1958 (Also published as: Moment of Danger. Dell, 1959)

MacKENZIE, JEANNE (M)
The Deadly Game. Hutchinson, 1939

MacKENZIE, KENNETH (M) (Pseudonym: Seaforth Mackenzie)
Dead Men Rising. Cape, 1951; Harper, 1951

MACKENZIE, NIGEL (D)
Bandit's Moon. Wright & Brown, 1952
Consider Your Verdict. Wright & Brown, 1952
Could It Be Murder? Wright & Brown, 1948
The Dark Night. Wright & Brown, 1950
Day of Judgment. Wright & Brown, 1959
Death for a Traitor. Wright & Brown, 1948
Footprints of Death. Wright & Brown, 1957
The Ghost Walks. Wright & Brown, 1949
The Horror in the Dark. Wright & Brown, 1962
House of Horror. Wright & Brown, 1959
In Great Danger. Wright & Brown, 1959
Murder for Two. Wright & Brown, 1951
Murder in Cardigan Square. Wright & Brown, 1954
Murder in the Rain Forrest. Wright & Brown, 1952
Murder over Karnak. Wright & Brown, 1949
Pyramid of Death. Wright & Brown, 1953
Race Toward Death. Wright & Brown, 1963
Red Light. Wright & Brown, 1950
Seven Days to Death. Wright & Brown 1959

MACKENZIE, SCOBIE (M)
Doctor Fram. Dutton, 1933

MACKENZIE, SEAFORTH, pseud; see MACKENZIE, KENNETH

MACKEY, COL. LEWIS HUGH (Pseudonym: Hugh Matheson)
The Third Force. Washburn, 1960

McKIMMEY, JAMES (S)
Blue Mascara Tears. Ballantine, 1965
Cornered. Dell, 1960; Boardman, T. V., 1965
The Long Ride. Dell, 1961; Boardman, T. V., 1963
The Perfect Victim. Dell, 1958
Run If You're Guilty. Lippincott, 1963; Boardman, T. V., 1964
Squeeze Play. Dell, 1962
Twenty-four Hours to Kill. Dell, 1961; Boardman, T. V., 1963
Winner Take All. Boardman, T. V., 1963
The Wrong Ones. Dell, 1961; Boardman, T. V., 1964

McKINLEY, FRANCES BURKS (D)
Death Sails the Nile. Stratford, 1933

MacKINNON, ALLAN (S)
Assignment in Iraq. Collins, 1960; Doubleday, 1960
Cormorant's Isle. Doubleday, 1960; Long, 1962
Danger by My Side. Collins, 1950
Dead on Departure. Long, 1964
House of Darkness. Collins, 1947; Doubleday, 1947; Dell
Man Overboard. Doubleday, 1965
Map of Mistrust. Collins, 1948; Doubleday, 1948
Money on the Black; see Nine Days' Murder
Murder, Repeat, Murder. Doubleday, 1952
Nine Days' Murder. Collins, 1945, 1952 (U.S. title: Money on the Black. Doubleday, 1946)
No Wreath for Manuela. Long, 1965
The Red-winged Angel. Collins, 1958
Report from Argyll. Doubleday, 1964
Summons from Baghdad. Doubleday, 1958

MACKINNON, CLARK
Flame Lily. Dakers, 1954

MACKINTOSH, ELIZABETH (D)
(Pseudonyms: Gordon Daviot, Josephine Tey)
Brat Farrar, by Josephine Tey. Davies, 1949; Macmillan, 1950; Berkley Pub., 1960
The Daughter of Time, by Josephine Tey. Davies, 1951; Macmillan, 1952; Berkley Pub., 1962; Dell, 1964; Watt, F., 1966
Four, Five, and Six by Tey: Singing Sands, A Shilling for Candles, and Daughter of Time. Macmillan, 1958
The Franchise Affair, by Josephine Tey. Davies, 1948; Macmillan, 1948; Berkley Pub., 1961; Dell, 1965
The Man in the Queue, by Gordon Daviot. Macmillan, 1927; Dutton, 1929 (Reissued in 1953 under the pseudonym Josephine Tey); Berkley Pub., 1962
Miss Pym Disposes, by Josephine Tey. Davies, 1946; Macmillan, 1948; Dell, 1964
A Shilling for Candles, by Josephine Tey. Methuen, 1936; Macmillan, 1954; Berkley Pub., 1960; Dell, 1964
The Singing Sands, by Josephine Tey. Davies, 1952; Macmillan, 1953; Dell, 1965
Three by Tey: Miss Pym Disposes, Franchise Affair, Brat Farrar. Macmillan, 1954
To Love and Be Wise, by Josephine Tey. Davies, 1950; Macmillan, 1951; Berkley Pub., 1960; Dell, 1965

McKNIGHT, BOB (D)
Bikini Bombshell. Ace
Downwind. Ace
Drop Dead, Please. Ace, 1961 (Double Novel. Includes: One for the Death House, by J. M. Flynn)
Flying Eye. Ace
Homicide Handicap. Ace, 1963 (Double Novel. Includes: The Dead and the Deadly, by Louis Trimble)
Kiss the Babe Goodbye. Ace
Murder Mutual. Ace, 1958
Slice of Death. Ace
Stone Around Her Neck. Ace
Swamp Sanctuary. Ace, 1959

MacKNUTT, M. G. (D)
Death on the Cuff. Phoenix, 1951

MACKWORTH, JOHN DOLBEN (D)
The Axe Is Laid. Longmans, 1925
Broadcast. Longmans, 1925

MACLAREN-ROSS, JULIAN (M)
The Doomsday Book. Hamilton, H., 1961; Obolensky, 1961
Until the Day She Dies. Hamilton, H., 1960

McLARTY, NANCY (D)
Chain of Death. Doubleday, 1962

MacLEAN, ALISTAIR (S) (Pseudonym: Ian Stuart)
The Black Strike, by Ian Stuart. Scribner, 1961; Popular Lib., 1963
Fear Is the Key. Doubleday, 1961; PB, 1963
The Golden Rendezvous. Collins, 1962; Doubleday, 1962; Popular Lib., 1963
The Guns of Navarone. Collins, 1964
Ice Station Zebra. Doubleday, 1963; Crest, 1967
Last Frontier; see Secret Ways
Night Without End. GM, 1967
The Satan Bug. Scribner, 1962; Collins, 1964
Secret Ways. Doubleday, 1959 (English title: Last Frontier. Collins, 1959)
When Eight Bells Toll. Doubleday, 1967
Where Eagles Dare. Doubleday, 1967

McLEAN, ALLAN CAMPBELL (D)
The Carpet-Slipper Murder. Ward, Lock, 1956; Washburn, 1957
Deadly Honeymoon. Ward, Lock, 1960
Death on All-Hallows. Ward, Lock, 1958; Washburn, 1959
Murder by Invitation. Ward, Lock, 1959
The Snow on the Ben. Ward, Lock, 1961
Stand in for Murder. Ward, Lock, 1960

MacLEOD, ADAM GORDON (D)
The Case of Matthew Crake. Harrap, 1932; Dial, 1933
Death Stalked the Fells. Harrap, 1937
The Cathra Mystery. Dial, 1926; Harrap, 1931
Marloe Mansions Murder. Dial, 1928; Harrap, 1931

MacLEOD, ANGUS (S)
Blessed Above Women. Roy Pubs., 1967
The Eighth Seal. Dobson, 1962; Roy Pubs., 1962
The Tough and the Tender. Dobson, 1960; Roy Pubs., 1960

MacLEOD, CHARLOTTE (M)
Mystery of the White Knight. Bouregy, 1964
Next Door to Danger. Bouregy, 1965

MacLEOD, ROBERT, pseud; see KNOX, BILL

McMAHON, ROBERT; see BERGSON, LEO

McMANUS, CHRIS (M)
Whiskey Johnny. Harrap, 1956

MacMILLAN, GEORGETTE (M)
The Woman in Mauve. Chelsea House, 1925

McMORROW, THOMAS (M)
The Sandalwood Fan. Sears, 1928
Sinister History of Ambrose Hinkle. Sears, 1929

McMULLEN, MARY (M)
The Death of Miss X. Collins, 1952
Strangle-Hold. Harper, 1951

McNAMARA, ED (S)
Once over Deadly. Abelard, 1958

McNAMARA, LENA RANDOLPH BROOKS (D)
Death Among the Sands. Arcadia, 1957
Murder in Miniature. Arcadia, 1959
The Penance Was Death. Bruce Pub., 1964
Pilgrim's End. Ace, 1967

MACNAUGHTAN, RICHARD (M)
The Preparatory School Murder. Fenland, 1934

MacNEIL, NEIL, pseud; see BALLARD, WILLIS TODHUNTER

McNEILE, HERMAN CYRIL (M) (Pseudonym: "Sapper")
Ask for Ronald Standish. Hodder, 1936; Musson, 1936
The Black Gang. Hodder, 1922
Bulldog Drummond. Doran, 1920; Hodder, 1920; Grosset, 1935
Bulldog Drummond at Bay. Doubleday, Doran, 1935; Hodder, 1935
Bulldog Drummond Double Header. Garden City Pub., 1937
Bulldog Drummond Returns. Doubleday, 1953; Garden City Pub., 1932 (English title: Return of Bulldog Drummond. Hodder, 1934)
Bulldog Drummond Strikes Back. Doubleday, Doran, 1933 (English title: Knockout. Hodder, 1934)
Bulldog Drummond's Third Round. Grosset, 1925
The Challenge. Doubleday, Doran, 1937; Hodder, 1937
The Death Scratch
The Dinner Club. Hodder, 1923; Doran, 1924
The Female of the Species. Doubleday, Doran, 1928
Fifty-One Stories. Hodder, 1934; Musson, 1935
The Final Count. Hodder, 1926
Finger of Fate. Doubleday, Doran, 1931; Hodder, 1931
Four Rounds of Bulldog Drummond. Hodder, 1930; Musson, 1930
Guardians of the Treasure. Doubleday, Doran, 1930
Island of Terror. Hodder, 1932
Jim Brent. Hodder, 1932
Jim Maitland. Hodder, 1932

Knockout; see Bulldog Drummond Strikes Back
The Man in Rat Catcher. Doran, 1919; Hodder, 1921
Out of the Blue. Doran, 1921
Return of Bulldog Drummond; see Bulldog Drummond Returns
Ronald Standish. Hodder, 1933
The Saving Clause. Hodder, 1927
Shorty Bill. Hodder, 1935
Temple Tower. Doubleday, Doran, 1929; Hodder, 1929
The Third Round. Doubleday, Doran, 1924; Hodder, 1924
Tiny Carteret. Doubleday, Doran, 1930; Hodder, 1930
When Carruthers Laughed. Hodder, 1934
Word of Honor. Hodder, 1926; Doran, 1926

McNEILLY, WILFRED (M-S)
The Case of the Muckrakers. Macfadden, 1967
No Way Out. Macfadden, 1966

MACOMBER, DARIA, pseud; see STEVENSON, FERDINAN

MACONECHY, JOANNA (M)
Four Extra Daughters. Chatto, 1932
James Ballingray, Murderer. Collins, 1925
The Secret Journal of Charles Dunbar. Collins, 1923
Vanishing Shadows. Chatto, 1930

McPARTLAND, JOHN (S)
Affair in Tokyo. GM, 1954 (Also published as: Tokyo Doll. GM, 1954)
Danger for Breakfast. GM, 1956
The Face of Evil. GM, 1955
I'll See You in Hell. GM, 1956
Kingdom of Johnny Cool. GM, 1959
Love Me Now. Muller, 1957
Ripe Fruit. GM, 1958
Tokyo Doll; see Affair in Tokyo
The Wild Party. GM, 1956

MacQUADE, MIKE (M)
Who's for Dying. Hale, R., 1961

MacQUEEN, JAMES WILLIAM (D)
(Pseudonym: James G. Edwards)
But the Patient Died. Doubleday, 1948
Death Among Doctors. Doubleday, Doran, 1942
Death Elects a Mayor. Doubleday, Doran, 1938
F Corridor. Doubleday, Doran, 1936
Murder at Leisure. Doubleday, Doran, 1937
Murder in the Surgery. Doubleday, Doran, 1935
The Odor of Bitter Almonds. Doubleday, Doran, 1938
The Private Pavillion. Doubleday, Doran, 1935

MACRAE, TRAVIS, pseud; see FEAGLES, ANITA MacRAE

McROYD, ALLAN (D)
Death in Costume. Greystone, 1940
The Double Shadow Murders. Greystone, 1939
Golden Goose Murders. Greystone, 1938

McSHANE, MARK (S)
The Crimson Madness of Little Doom. Doubleday, 1966; Hale, R., 1967
The Girl Nobody Knows. Doubleday, 1965; Hale, R., 1966
Night's Evil. Doubleday, 1966; Hale, R., 1966
The Passing of Evil. Cassell, 1961
Séance on a Wet Afternoon. Cassell, 1961; Doubleday, 1962; Crest, 1965
Untimely Ripped. Cassell, 1962; Doubleday, 1963; Crest, 1965
The Way to Nowhere. Hale, R., 1967

MacSWAN, NORMAN (M)
Inn with the Wooden Door. Cassell, 1958

MacTYRE, PAUL (D)
Bar Sinister. Hodder, 1964
Fish on a Hook. Hodder, 1963

MacVEIGH, SUE, pseud. (D)
The Corpse and the Three Ex-Husbands. Houghton, 1941
The Grand Central Murder. Houghton, 1939
Murder Under Construction. Houghton, 1939
Streamlined Murder. Houghton, 1940

MacVICAR, ANGUS (D)
The Cavern. Paul, S., 1936
Crime's Masquerader. Paul, S., 1939
The Crooked Finger. Paul, S., 1936
The Crouching Spy. Paul, S., 1941
The Dancing Horse. Long, 1961
Death by the Mistletoe. Paul, S., 1934
Death on the Machar. Paul, S., 1946
Eleven for Danger. Paul, S., 1939
Escort to Adventure. Paul, S., 1952
Flowering Death. Paul, S., 1937
Fugitive's Road. Paul, S., 1949
The Grey Shepherds. Long, 1964
Greybreek. Paul, S., 1947
The Hammers of Fingal. Long, 1963
The Killing of Kersivay. Long, 1962
The Purple Rock. Paul, S., 1939
The Screaming Gull. Paul, S., 1935
The Singing Spider. Paul, S., 1939

Strangers from the Sea. Paul, S., 1939
The Temple Falls. Paul, S., 1935
The Ten Green Brothers. Paul, S., 1936

MADDEN, EDWARD STANISLAUS (M)
Craig's Spur. Heinemann, 1961; Vanguard, 1963

MADDOCK, L. (M)
Fantine Avenal. Cornhill

MADDOCK, STEPHEN (M)
Close Shave. Collins, 1952
Conspirators at Large. Collins, 1937
Conspirators in Capri. Collins, 1935
Conspirators Three. Collins, 1936
Danger After Dark. Collins, 1934
Date with a Spy. Collins, 1941
Doorway to Danger. Collins, 1938
Drums Beat at Dusk. Collins, 1943
East of Piccadilly. Collins, 1948
Exit Only. Collins, 1947
The Eye at the Keyhole. Collins, 1935
Forbidden Frontiers. Collins, 1936
Gentlemen of the Night. Collins, 1934
I'll Never Like Friday Again. Collins, 1945
Keep Your Fingers Crossed. Collins, 1949
Lamp Post 592. Collins, 1938
Overture to Trouble. Collins, 1946
Private Line. Collins, 1950
Public Mischief. Collins, 1951
Something on the Stairs. Collins, 1944
Spades at Midnight. Collins, 1940
Spies Along the Severn. Collins, 1939
Step Aside to Death. Collins, 1942
The White Siren. Collins, 1934

MADELEY, JOAN (M)
The Shining Head. Hale, R., 1955

MAGARSHACK, DAVID (D)
Big Ben Strikes Eleven. Constable, 1934; Macmillan, 1935
Death Cuts a Caper. Constable, 1935; Holt, H., 1935

MAGILL, MARCUS, pseud; see HILL, BRIAN

MAGOON, CAREY, pseud; see CAREY, ELIZABETH

MAGOON, MARIAN AUSTIN; see CAREY, ELIZABETH

MAGUIRE, P. P. (M)
Certain Dr. Mellor. Browne & Nolan, 1946

MAHANNAH, FLOYD (D)
Broken Angel. Macrae Smith, 1958
Golden Goose. Duell, 1951
The Golden Widow. Macrae Smith, 1956; Boardman, T. V., 1957; Permabooks, 1957 (Mercury Mystery Book magazine title: "Ivy")
"Ivy"; see The Golden Widow
Stopover for Murder. Macrae Smith, 1953; Boardman, T. V., 1954
Yellow Hearse. Duell, 1950; Boardman, T. V., 1952

MAINWARING, DANIEL (D) (Pseudonym: Geoffrey Homes)
Build My Gallows High. Morrow, 1946
The Doctor Died at Dusk. Morrow, 1936
Finders Keepers. Morrow, 1940
Forty Whacks. Morrow, 1941
Hill of the Terrified Monk. Morrow, 1943
The Man Who Didn't Exist. Morrow, 1937; Eyre, 1939
The Man Who Murdered Goliath. Morrow, 1938; Eyre, 1940
The Man Who Murdered Himself. Lane, 1936; Morrow, 1936
No Hands on the Clock. Morrow, 1939
Six Silver Handles. Morrow, 1944
The Street of the Crying Women. Morrow, 1942
Then There Were Three. Morrow, 1938; Withy Grove, 1945

MAINWARING, MARION (D)
Murder at Midyears. Macmillan, 1953; Gollancz, 1954
Murder in Pastiche. Macmillan, 1954; Gollancz, 1955; Collier, 1962

MAIR, GEORGE BROWN (D)
Death's Foot Footward. Jarrolds, 1963; Random, 1963; Macfadden, 1964
Kisses from Satan. Jarrolds, 1965
Miss Turquoise. Jarrolds, 1964; Random, 1964

MAIR, JOHN (S)
Never Come Back. Gollancz, 1941; Little, 1941

MAKEPEACE, ANN (M)
Mistaken Marriage. Hale, R., 1958
Thunderstorm. Hale, R., 1957

MAKIN, WILLIAM J. (M)
Gipsy in Evening Dress. Eldon, 1935
Murder at Covent Garden. Jarrolds, 1930
Queer Mr. Quell. McBride, 1938

MALAN, ERNESTINE and A. K. LEDIG (D)
Cobwebs and Clues. Dorrance, 1944

MALCOLM, JEAN (S)
Discourse with Shadows. Doubleday, 1958

MALCOLM-SMITH, GEORGE (S)
Come Out, Come Out. Doubleday, 1965
If a Body Meet a Body. Doubleday, 1959; Hale, R., 1960
The Lady Finger. Doubleday, 1962
The Trouble with Fidelity. Doubleday, 1957; Hale, R., 1959

MALIM, BARBARA (D)
Death by Misadventure. Macmillan, 1934; Murray, J., 1934
Murder on Holiday. Murray, J., 1937

MALINA, FRED (S)
Some Like 'Em Shot. Mill, 1949

MALLESON, LUCY BEATRICE (D)
(Pseudonyms: Anthony Gilbert, Anne Meredith)
After the Verdict, by Anthony Gilbert. Random, 1961; Pyramid, 1964
And Death Came Too, by Anthony Gilbert. Random, 1956; Pyramid, 1964
Bell of Death, by Anthony Gilbert. Collins, 1940
Black Death; see Footsteps Behind Me
Black Stage, by Anthony Gilbert. Collins, 1945; Barnes, A. S., 1946
The Body on the Beam, by Anthony Gilbert. Collins, 1932; Dodd, 1932
By Hook or by Crook; see Spinster's Secret
The Case Against Andrew Fane, by Anthony Gilbert. Collins, 1931; Dodd, 1931
A Case for Mr. Crook; see Miss Pinnegar Disappears
Case of the Tea-Cosy's Aunt, by Anthony Gilbert. Collins, 1942 (U.S. title: Death in the Blackout. Smith & Durrell, 1943; Bantam)
Clock in the Hat Box, by Anthony Gilbert. Collins, 1940; Arcadia, 1943
Courtier to Death, by Anthony Gilbert. Collins, 1938
Dark Death; see Footsteps Behind Me
Dear Dead Woman, by Anthony Gilbert. Mystery House, 1942
Death Against the Clock, by Anthony Gilbert. Collins, 1958; Random, 1958
Death at Four Corners. Collins, 1929; Dial, 1929
Death at the Door; see He Came by Night
Death Casts a Long Shadow, by Anthony Gilbert. Random, 1959; Pyramid, 1966
Death in Fancy Dress, by Anthony Gilbert. Collins, 1933
Death in the Blackout; see Case of the Tea-Cosy's Aunt
Death in the Wrong Room, by Anthony Gilbert. Barnes, A. S., 1947; Collins, 1947
Death Knocks Three Times, by Anthony Gilbert. Black, 1949; Collins, 1949; Random, 1949
Death Lifts the Latch; see Don't Open the Door
Death Takes a Wife, by Anthony Gilbert. Collins, 1959
Die in the Dark, by Anthony Gilbert. Collins, 1947 (U.S. title: Missing Widow. Barnes, A. S., 1948)
Don't Open the Door, by Anthony Gilbert. Collins, 1945 (U.S. title: Death Lifts the Latch. Barnes, A. S., 1946; Bantam, 1950)
Dover Train Mystery, by Anthony Gilbert. Dial, 1936
The Fingerprint, by Anthony Gilbert. Collins, 1964
First Mr. Crook Book
Footsteps Behind Me, by Anthony Gilbert. Collins, 1953 (U.S. titles: Black Death. Random, 1953 and Dark Death. Pyramid, 1963)
Give Death a Name. Collins, 1957
He Came by Night, by Anthony Gilbert. Collins, 1944 (U.S. title: Death at the Door. Barnes, A. S., 1945)
The Innocent Bottle; see Lift Up the Lid
Is She Dead Too? Collins, 1955
Lady-Killer, by Anthony Gilbert. Collins, 1951
Lift Up the Lid, by Anthony Gilbert. Collins, 1948 (U.S. title: The Innocent Bottle. Barnes, A. S., 1949)
Long Shadow, by Anthony Gilbert. Collins, 1932
The Looking Glass Murder. Collins, 1966; Random, 1967
Man in the Button Boots, by Anthony Gilbert. Collins, 1934; Holt, H., 1935
Man in the Family, by Anne Meredith. Hodder, 1959
Man Who Was Too Clever, by Anthony Gilbert. Collins, 1935
Man Who Wasn't There, by Anthony Gilbert. Collins, 1937
Miss Pinnegar Disappears, by Anthony Gilbert. Collins, 1952 (U.S. title: A Case for Mr. Crook. Random, 1952; Pyramid, 1964)
Missing Widow; see Die in the Dark
Mouse Who Wouldn't Play Ball, by Anthony Gilbert. Collins, 1943 (U.S. title: Thirty Days to Live. Barnes, A. S., 1944)
Murder by Experts, by Anthony Gilbert. Dial, 1937
Murder Comes Home, by Anthony Gilbert. Collins, 1950; Random, 1951; Pyramid, 1965
Murder Has No Tongue, by Anthony Gilbert. Collins, 1938
The Murder of Mrs. Davenport, by Anthony Gilbert. Collins, 1928; Dial, 1928

Musical Comedy Crime, by Anthony Gilbert. Collins, 1933
The Mystery in the Woodshed; see Something Nasty in the Woodshed
The Mystery of the Open Window, by Anthony Gilbert. Dodd, 1930; Gollancz, 1930
Nice Cup of Tea, by Anthony Gilbert. Collins, 1950 (U.S. title: The Wrong Body. Random, 1951)
Night of the Fog, by Anthony Gilbert. Dodd, 1930; Gollancz, 1930
No Dust in the Attic, by Anthony Gilbert. Collins, 1962; Random, 1963
Old Lady Dies, by Anthony Gilbert. Collins, 1934
Out for the Kill, by Anthony Gilbert. Collins, 1960; Random, 1960
Passenger to Nowhere, by Anthony Gilbert. Random, 1966
Portrait of a Murderer, by Anne Meredith. Reynal, 1934
Prelude to Murder; see Third Crime Lucky
A Question of Murder, by Anthony Gilbert. Collins, 1955; Random, 1955
Riddle of a Lady, by Anthony Gilbert. Collins, 1956; Random, 1956
Ring for a Noose, by Anthony Gilbert. Collins, 1963; Random, 1964
The Scarlet Button, by Anthony Gilbert. Collins, 1944; Smith & Durrell, 1945
She Shall Die, by Anthony Gilbert. Collins, 1961
She Vanished in the Dawn; see Vanishing Corpse
Snake in the Grass, by Anthony Gilbert. Collins, 1954
Something Nasty in the Woodshed, by Anthony Gilbert. Collins, 1942 (U.S. title: The Mystery in the Woodshed. Smith & Durrell, 1942)
Spinster's Secret, by Anthony Gilbert. Collins, 1946 (U.S. title: By Hook or by Crook. Barnes, A. S., 1947)
Spy for Mr. Crook, by Anthony Gilbert. Barnes, A. S., 1944
Third Crime Lucky, by Anthony Gilbert. Collins, 1959 (U.S. title: Prelude to Murder. Random, 1959)
Thirty Days to Live; see Mouse Who Wouldn't Play Ball
Tragedy at Freyne, by Anthony Gilbert. Collins, 1927
Treason in My Breast, by Anthony Gilbert. Collins, 1938
Uncertain Death, by Anthony Gilbert. Collins, 1961; Random, 1963
Vanishing Corpse, by Anthony Gilbert. Collins, 1941 (U.S. title: She Vanished in the Dawn. Arcadia, 1941)
The Visitors, by Anthony Gilbert. Random, 1967
The Voice, by Anthony Gilbert. Collins, 1964; Random, 1965
Wise Child, by Anne Meredith. Hodder, 1960
The Woman in Red, by Anthony Gilbert. Collins, 1941; Smith & Durrell, 1943
The Wrong Body; see Nice Cup of Tea

MALLOCH, PETER, pseud; see DUNCAN, WILLIAM MURDOCH

MALLORY, ARTHUR (D)
Apperson's Folly. Chelsea, 1930
Black Valley Murders. Chelsea, 1930
Doctor Krook. Chelsea, 1929
The Fiery Serpent. Chelsea, 1929
The House of Carson. Chelsea, 1927

MALLOWAN, MRS. MAX EDGAR LUCIEN; see CHRISTIE, AGATHA

MALM, DOROTHEA (S)
Clair. Bantam, 1966
On a Fated Night. Doubleday, 1965; Lancer, 1966
To the Castle. Davies, 1955; Ace, 1957, 1963

MALMAR, McKNIGHT (M)
Fog Is a Shroud. Hurst, 1950
Never Say Die. Coward, 1943; Hurst, 1944
The Past Won't Die. Hurst, 1948

MALO, VINCENT GASPARD (M)
And Why Not? Barker, 1958; Abelard, 1959
Murder on the Mistral. Abelard, 1958; Crest, 1959

MANCERON, GENEVIEVE (S)
The Deadlier Sex. Dell, 1961

MANCHESTER, WILLIAM (S)
Beard the Lion. Mill, 1958 (Also published as: Cairo Intrigue. PB, 1959)

MANCHIP, JACK (S)
The Mercenaries. Long, 1958

MANGIONE, JERRE GERLANDO (S)
Night Search. Crown, 1966

MANKIEWICZ, DON M. (S)
Trial. Dell, 1955, 1966

MANN, ABLE (S)
Danger Woman. PB, 1966

MANN, ERNEST L. (M)
The Chislehurst Mystery. Eyre, 1938

MANN, JACK (D)
Coulson Alone. Wright & Brown, 1936
Coulson Goes South. Wright & Brown, 1933

The Dead Man's Chest. Wright & Brown, 1934
Detective Coulson. Wright & Brown, 1936
Egyptian Nights. Wright & Brown, 1934
Gee's First Case. Wright & Brown, 1936
The Glass Too Many. Wright & Brown, 1940
Gray Shapes. Wright & Brown, 1937
The Kleinert Case. Wright & Brown, 1938
Maker of Shadows. Wright & Brown, 1938
Nightmare Farm. Wright & Brown, 1937
The Ninth Life. Wright & Brown, 1939
Reckless Coulson. Wright & Brown, 1933

MANN, LEONARD (D)
A Murder in Sydney. Cape, 1937; Doubleday, Doran, 1937

MANNERS, DAVID X. (D)
Dead to the World. McKay, 1947
Memory of a Scream. Curl, 1946

MANNERS, GORDON (D)
Murders at the Crab Apple Cafe. Jenkins, 1933

MANNING, ADELAIDE FRANCIS OKE; see COLES, CYRIL HENRY

MANNING, BRUCE; see BRISTOW, GWEN

MANNING, PADRAIC, pseud; see O'BRINE, MANNING

MANNINGHAM, BASIL, pseud; see HOMERSHAM, BASIL HENRY

MANNON, M. M., pseud; see MANNON, MARTHA

MANNON, MARTHA and MARY ELLEN MANNON (D) (Pseudonym: M. M. Mannon)
Here Lies Blood. Bobbs, 1942
Murder on the Program. Bobbs, 1944

MANNON, MARY ELLEN; see MANNON, MARTHA

MANOR, JASON, pseud; see HALL, OAKLEY MAXWELL

MANSFIELD, PAUL H. (M)
Final Exposure. Collins, 1957; Macmillan, 1958

MANSON, WILL (S)
The Chinese Conundrum. Caravelle, 1967

MANTINBAND, JAMES (M) (Pseudonym: Oliver Keystone)
Arsenic for the Teacher. Phoenix, 1951
Deep as a Grave. Phoenix, 1950

MANTLE, BEATRICE (M)
In the House of Another. Century, 1920

MANTON, PETER, pseud; see CREASEY, JOHN

MANVELL, ROGER and JOHN HALES (S)
The Dreamers. S & S, 1958; Bantam, 1963

MANVILLE, G. (M)
The Dark House. 1885

MARA, BERNARD (M)
Bullet for My Lady. GM, 1955
French for Murder. GM, 1954

MARBLE, DANA (M)
Sail into Silence. Mystery House, 1958

MARBLE, MARGARET SHARP (S)
Die by Night. Rinehart, 1947; Barker, 1948
Everybody Makes Mistakes. Rinehart, 1946; Barker, 1947
The Lady Forgot. Harper, 1947

MARCH, JERMYN, pseud; see WEBB, DOROTHY ANNA

MARCH, MAXWELL (M)
The Man of Dangerous Secrets. Doubleday, Doran, 1933 (English title: Other Man's Danger. Collins, 1933)
Other Man's Danger; see The Man of Dangerous Secrets
Rogue's Holiday. Collins, 1935; Doubleday, Doran, 1935
The Shadow in the House. Collins, 1936; Doubleday, Doran, 1936

MARCH, WILLIAM, pseud; see CAMPBELL, WILLIAM EDWARD MARCH

MARCHANT, CATHERINE, pseud; see COOKSON, CATHERINE McMULLEN

MARCHMONT, ARTHUR WILLIAMS (M)
The Old Mill Mystery. Ogilvie

MARCUS, ARTHUR A. (D)
Make Way for Murder. Graphic, 1955
Widow Gay. McKay, 1948

MARFIELD, DWIGHT (M)
The Ghost on the Balcony. Dutton, 1939
The Man with the Paper Skull. Dutton, 1932
The Mandarin's Sapphire. Dutton, 1938
The Mystery of the King Cobra. Dutton, 1933

MARINO, NICK, pseud. (S)
City Limits. Pyramid, 1958
One Way Street. Holt, H., 1952

MARIO, C.
Six Graves to Munich. Banner, 1967

MARIO, QUEENA (D)
Death Drops Delilah. Dutton, 1944
Death in View. Holt, 1960
Murder in the Opera House. Dutton, 1934
Murder Meets Mephisto. Dutton, 1942; Bart
Twenty Per Cent. Holt, 1961

MARION, ELIZABETH (S)
The Keys to the House. Crowell, 1944; Hale, 1948

MARK, TED (S-Satire)
Dr. Nyet. Lancer, 1966
The Girl from Pussycat. Lancer, 1965
A Hard Day's Knight. Lancer, 1966
The Man from O.R.G.Y. Lancer, 1965
My Son, the Double Agent. Lancer, 1966
The Nine-Month Caper. Lancer, 1966
The Nude Wore Black. Lancer, 1967
Pussycat, Pussycat. Lancer, 1966
The Real Gone Girls. Lancer, 1966
The Ted Mark Reader. Lancer, 1966
The Unhatched Egghead. Lancer, 1966

MARKHAM, VIRGIL (D)
Black Door. Knopf, 1930
The Dead Are Prowling. Collins, 1934
The Deadly Jest. Collins, 1935
Death in the Dusk. Knopf, 1928
The Devil Drives. Bart, 1932; Collins, 1933
Inspector Rusby's Finale. Collins, 1933; Farrar & Rinehart, 1933
Red Warning. Farrar & Rinehart, 1933
Snatch. Collins, 1936
Song of Doom. Collins, 1932

MARKO, ZEKIAL (M)
Scratch a Thief. 1961 (Also published as: Once a Thief. GM, 1965)

MARKS, PERCY (D)
A Dead Man Dies. Century, 1929
Knave of Diamonds. Reynal, 1943

MARKSON, DAVID (S)
Epitaph for a Dead Beat. Dell, 1961
Epitaph for a Tramp. Dell, 1959
Miss Doll, Go Home. Dell, 1965

MARLETT, MRS. MELBA BALMAT GRIMES (D)
Another Day Toward Dying. Doubleday, Doran, 1943
Death Has a Thousand Doors. Doubleday, Doran, 1941; Popular Lib.
Death Is in the Garden. Doubleday, 1951; Popular Lib., 1965
The Devil Builds a Chapel. Doubleday, Doran, 1942
Escape While I Can. Doubleday, Doran, 1944; Ace, 1966
The Frightened Ones. Doubleday, 1956
Witness in Peril. Withy Grove, 1948

MARLOWE, DAN JAMES (S)
Backfire. Berkley Pub., 1961
Death Deep Down. GM, 1965
Doom Service. Avon, 1960
Doorway to Death. Avon, 1959
The Fatal Frails. Avon, 1960
Four for the Money. GM, 1966
Killer with a Key. Avon, 1959
The Name of the Game Is Death. GM, 1962
Never Live Twice. GM, 1964
The Raven Is a Blood Red Bird, with William Odel. GM, 1967
Route of the Red Gold. GM, 1967
Shake a Crooked Town. Avon, 1961
The Vengeance Man. GM, 1966

MARLOWE, DEREK (S)
A Dandy in Aspic. Putnam, 1966; Dell, 1967

MARLOWE, FRANCIS (M)
Adventure Mysterious. Gray, 1934
Crooked Business. Gramol, 1933
Crooked Company. Gramol, 1933
The Hatton Garden Mystery. Gray, 1934; Gramol, 1935
In Pursuit of a Million. Gray, 1936
The Man Who Lost an Hour. Aldine, 1926
The Secret of the Sandhills. Low, 1907
Seven Red-headed Men. Gramol, 1934
So the Wheel Spins. Gramol, 1936
The Son-in-law Syndicate. Gramol, 1934

MARLOWE, HUGH, pseud; see PATTERSON, HENRY

MARLOWE, PIERS (D)
The Dead Don't Scare. Gifford, 1963
Demon in the Blood. McGraw, 1955; Paul, S., 1955
The Double Thirteen. Low, 1947
Loaded Dice. Low, 1949
The Men in Her Death. Gifford, 1964

MARLOWE, STEPHEN (Milton Lesser) (D-S) (Pseudonyms: Andrew Frazer, Jason Ridgway, C. H. Thames)
Adam's Fall, by Jason Ridgway. PB, 1960
Catch the Brass Ring, by Stephen Marlowe. Ace, 1952
Danger Is My Line, by Stephen Marlowe. GM, 1960
Dead on Arrival, by Stephen Marlowe. GM, 1954
Death Is My Comrade, by Stephen Marlowe. GM, 1961

Double Trouble, by Stephen Marlowe and Richard Prather. GM, 1960
Drum Beat - Berlin, by Stephen Marlowe. GM, 1964
Drum Beat - Dominque, by Stephen Marlowe. GM, 1965
Drum Beat - Erica, by Stephen Marlowe. GM, 1967
Drum Beat - Madrid, by Stephen Marlowe. GM, 1966
The Fall of Manny Moon, by Andrew Frazer. Avon, 1961
Find Ellen Hardin, by Andrew Frazer. Avon, 1960
Francesca, by Stephen Marlowe. GM, 1963
Hardly a Man Is Now Alive, by Jason Ridgway. PB, 1961
Homicide Is My Game, by Stephen Marlowe. GM, 1959
Jeopardy Is My Job, by Stephen Marlowe. GM, 1961
Killers Are My Meat, by Stephen Marlowe. GM, 1957
Manhunt Is My Mission, by Stephen Marlowe. GM, 1963
Mecca for Murder, by Stephen Marlowe. GM, 1956
Model for Murder, by Stephen Marlowe. Graphic, 1954; Berkley Pub., 1960
Murder Is My Dish, by Stephen Marlowe. GM, 1957
Passport to Peril, by Stephen Marlowe. Crest, 1961
People in Glass Houses, by Jason Ridgway. PB, 1961
Peril Is My Pay, by Stephen Marlowe. GM, 1960
The Search for Bruno Heidler, by Stephen Marlowe. Macmillan, 1966
The Second Longest Night, by Stephen Marlowe, GM, 1955
Terror Is My Trade, by Stephen Marlowe. GM, 1958
The Treasure of the Cosa Nostra, by Jason Ridgway. PB
Trouble Is My Name, by Stephen Marlowe. GM, 1956
Turn Left for Murder, by Stephen Marlowe. Ace, 1955
Violence Is Golden, by C. H. Thames. Bouregy, 1956
Violence Is My Business, by Stephen Marlowe. GM, 1958

MARQUAND, ALIX DE (S)
So Many Midnights. Lancer

MARQUAND, JOHN PHILLIPS (D)
The Black Cargo. Hodder, 1925; Scribner, 1925
It's Loaded, Mr. Bauer. Hale, R., 1949
Last Laugh, Mr. Moto. Little, 1942; Hale, R., 1943; Berkley Pub,, 1963
The Last of Mr. Moto; see Stopover Tokyo
Ming Yellow. Dickson, 1935; Pyramid, 1960
Mr. Moto Is So Sorry. Little, 1938; Hale, R., 1939; Berkley Pub., 1963
Mr. Moto Takes a Hand. Hale, R., 1940
Mr. Moto's Three Aces. Little, 1956
No Hero. Little, 1935; Grosset, 1937 (Also published as: Your Turn, Mr. Moto. Berkley Pub., 1963)
Stopover Tokyo. Little, 1957 (Also published as: The Last of Mr. Moto. Berkley Pub., 1963)
Thank You, Mr. Moto. Little, 1936; Jenkins, 1937; Berkley Pub., 1963
Think Fast, Mr. Moto. Little, 1937; Hale, R., 1938; Berkley Pub., 1963
Warning Hill. Little, 1930; Hale, R., 1939; Pyramid, 1964
Your Turn, Mr. Moto; see No Hero

MARQUIS, DON, pseud; see PERRY, ROBERT

MARRAH, DERMET (M)
The Mummy Case Mystery. Harper, 1933

MARRIC, J. J., pseud; see CREASEY, JOHN

MARRIOT, TAM; see BLOOD, ADELE

MARS, ALASTAIR
Atomic Submarine. Elek, 1957 (Also published as: Fire in Anger. Mill, 1958)

MARSDEN, ANTHONY, pseud; see SUTTON, GRAHAM

MARSH, JEAN (D)
Death Among the Stars. Long, 1955
Death at Peak Hour. Long, 1954
Death Stalks the Bride. Long, 1945
Death Visits the Circus. Long, 1953
Identity Unwanted. Long, 1951
Murder Next Door. Long, 1933
The Pattern Is Murder. Long, 1954
The Reluctant Executioner. Hale, 1959
Shore House Mystery. Hamilton, 1931

MARSH, JOHN
Brain of Paul Menoloff. Robertson, 1953
Hidden Answer. Gifford, 1956
Reluctant Executioner. Hale, R., 1959

MARSH, NGAIO (D)
Another Three Act Special. Little, 1962 (Contains: False Scent, Scales of Justice, and Singing in the Shrouds)
Artists in Crime. Bles, 1938; Furman, 1938; Berkley Pub., 1963

Colour Scheme. Collins, 1943; Little, 1943; Berkley Pub., 1961; Fontana, 1964
Dead Water. Little, 1963; Bantam, 1964; Collins, 1964
Death and the Dancing Footman. Little, 1941; Berkley Pub., 1961
Death at the Bar. Collins, 1940; Little, 1940; Berkley Pub., 1962
Death in a White Tie. Bles, 1938; Furman, 1938; Berkley Pub., 1962
Death in Ecstacy. Bles, 1936; Sheridan, 1941; Berkley Pub., 1962
Death of a Fool. Little, 1956; Berkley Pub., 1963 (English title: Off with His Head. Collins, 1957)
Death of a Peer. Little, 1940; Berkley Pub., 1961
Died in the Wool. Collins, 1945; Little, 1945; Berkley Pub., 1961
Enter a Murderer. Bles, 1935; PB, 1941; Sheridan, 1942; Berkley Pub., 1963
False Scent. Little, 1959; Collins, 1960; Crest, 1961; Berkley Pub., 1967
Final Curtain. Collins, 1947; Little, 1947; Berkley Pub., 1967
Hand in Glove. Collins, 1947; Little, 1962; Berkley Pub., 1963
Killer Dolphin. Little, 1966; Berkley Pub., 1967; Collins, 1967
A Man Lay Dead. Bles, 1934; Sheridan, 1942; Berkley Pub., 1962
Night at the Vulcan. Little, 1951; Berkley Pub., 1963 (English title: Opening Night. Collins, 1951)
The Nursing-Home Murders, with Dr. Henry Jellett. Sheridan, 1941; Berkley Pub., 1962
Off with His Head; see Death of a Fool
Opening Night; see Night at the Vulcan
Overture to Death. Berkley Pub., 1963
Scales of Justice. Collins, 1955; Little, 1955; Berkley Pub., 1964
Singing in the Shrouds. Little, 1958; Collins, 1959; Berkley Pub., 1964
Spinsters in Jeopardy. Little, 1953; Collins, 1954; Berkley Pub., 1965
Surfeit of Lampreys. Collins, 1941
Swing, Brother, Swing; see A Wreath for Rivera
Three Act Special. Little, 1960 (Contains: A Wreath for Rivera, Spinsters in Jeopardy, and Night at the Vulcan)
Vintage Murder. Bles, 1937; Sheridan, 1940; Berkley Pub., 1966
A Wreath for Rivera. Little, 1949; Berkley Pub., 1962 (English title: Swing, Brother, Swing. Collins, 1949)

MARSH, PATRICK, pseud; see HISCOCK, LESLIE

MARSH, RICHARD (M)
The Beetle. Skeffington, 1897; Putnam, 1917
The Crime and the Criminal. Ward, Lock, 1897
The Datchet Diamonds. Ward, Lock, 1898
The Death Whistle. Treherne, 1903
The Garden of Mystery. Long, 1911
Marvels and Mysteries. Methuen, 1900
A Master of Deception. Methuen, 1913

MARSHALL, ARCHIBALD (Full name: Arthur Hammond Marshall) (M)
The Mote House Mystery, with H. A. Vachell. Dodd, 1926
The Mystery of Redmarsh Farm. Paul, S., 1911; Dodd, 1925

MARSHALL, ARTHUR CALDER-; see CALDER-MARSHALL, ARTHUR

MARSHALL, ARTHUR HAMMOND; see MARSHALL, ARCHIBALD

MARSHALL, BRUCE (M)
The Month of the Falling Leaves. Doubleday, 1963

MARSHALL, CHARLES HUNT; see YATES, GEORGE WORTHING

MARSHALL, HURST (D)
Enter Two Murderers. Longmans, 1937

MARSHALL, IAN (M)
The Strange Case of Vintrix Polbarton. Nelson, 1929
The Vengeance of Kali. Nelson, 1930

MARSHALL, JOSEPH R. (D)
Murder in an Artist's Colony

MARSHALL, LOVAT, pseud; see DUNCAN, WILLIAM MURDOCK

MARSHALL, MARGUERITE MOOERS (M)
Murder Without Morals. Lewis, C., 1947

MARSHALL, RAYMOND, pseud; see RAYMOND, RENÉ

MARSHALL, SIDNEY (M)
Some Like It Hot. Morrow, 1941

MARSTEN, RICHARD, pseud; see HUNTER, EVAN

MARTENS, PAUL, pseud; see SOUTHWOLD, STEPHEN

MARTIN, A. RICHARD (D)
The Cassiodore Case. Methuen, 1927; McBride, 1928
Death of a Claimant. McBride, 1929; Methuen, 1929

MARTIN, ABSALOM (M)
Kastle Krags. Duffield, 1922

MARTIN, ARCHIBALD EDWARD (D)
The Bridal Bed Murders. S & S, 1954
The Chinese Bed Mysteries. Reinhardt, 1955
The Curious Crime. Doubleday, 1952; Muller, 1953
Death in the Limelight. S & S, 1946
The Outsiders. S & S, 1945
Sinners Never Die. S & S, 1944

MARTIN, DESMOND (D)
No Hero. Boardman, T. V., 1957
Wine, Women, and Murder. Boardman, T. V., 1955

MARTIN, DOROTHEA, pseud; see HEWITT, KATHLEEN DOUGLAS

MARTIN, HECTOR P. (M)
Time for Murder. Skeffington, 1938

MARTIN, HELEN R. (M)
The House on the Marsh. Dodd, 1936

MARTIN, HENRIETTA and GITA LEWIS (M)
The Naked Eye. Greenberg, 1950

MARTIN, RICHARD, pseud; see CREASEY, JOHN

MARTIN, ROBERT BERNARD (M)
(Pseudonym: Robert Bernard)
Death Takes a Sabbatical. Norton, 1967
To Have and To Kill. Dodd, 1960

MARTIN, ROBERT LEE (D) (Pseudonym: Lee Roberts)
The Case of the Missing Lovers, by Lee Roberts. Dodd, 1956; Foulsham, 1957
Catch a Killer. Dodd, 1956; Hale, R., 1958
A Coffin for Two. Hale, R., 1962
Dark Dream. Dodd, 1951; Muller, 1954
Death of a Ladies Man, by Lee Roberts. GM, 1959
The Echoing Shore. Dodd, 1955
Handpicked for Murder. Dodd, 1957
If the Shoe Fits, by Lee Roberts. Dodd, 1958; Crest, 1960; Hale, R., 1960
The Judas Journey. Dodd, 1956
Just a Corpse at Twilight. Dodd, 1955
Key to the Morgue. Dodd, 1959
Killer Among Us. Dodd, 1958; Hale, R., 1959
Little Sister, by Lee Roberts. GM, 1952
The Mahogany Murder, by Lee Roberts. Foulsham, 1957
Once a Widow, by Lee Roberts. Dodd, 1957; Hale, R., 1957
The Pale Door, by Lee Roberts. Dodd, 1954
Sleep, My Love. Dodd, 1952; Muller, 1955
She, Me, and Murder. Hale, R., 1962
Suspicion, by Lee Roberts. Hale, R., 1964
Tears for the Bride. Dodd, 1953; Muller, 1955
The Widow and the Web. Dodd, 1954

MARTIN, SHANE (M)
The Man Made of Tin. Collins, 1958
Mourner's Voyage. Collins, 1962; Doubleday, 1963
The Myth Is Murder; see The Third Statue
The Saracen Shadow. Collins, 1957
The Third Statue. Morrow, 1959 (English title: The Myth Is Murder. Collins, 1959)
Twelve Girls in the Garden. Collins, 1957; Morrow, 1957
A Wake for Mourning. Collins, 1962

MARTIN, STELLA, pseud; see HEYER, GEORGETTE

MARTIN, STUART (M)
Capital Punishment. Hutchinson, 1930
Fifteen Cells. Harper, 1927; Selwyn, 1927
The Green Ghost. Selwyn, 1929
Hangman's Guests. Harper, 1931; Hutchinson, 1931
Only Seven Were Hanged. Harper, 1929
The Trial of Scotland Yard. Harper, 1930; Hutchinson, 1930

MARTINEK, FRANK VICTOR (D)
Don Winslow, U.S.N. in Ceylon. Rosenow, 1934

MARTING, RUTH LENORE (D) (Pseudonym: Hilea Bailey)
Breathe No More, My Lady. Doubleday, 1946
Give Thanks to Death. Doubleday, Doran, 1940
The Smiling Corpse. Doubleday, Doran, 1941
What Night Will Bring. Doubleday, Doran, 1939; Davies, 1940

MARTYN, OLIVER, pseud; see WHITE, HERBERT OLIVER

MARTYN, WYNDHAM (D) (Pseudonym: William Grenvil)
Anthony Trent: Avenger. Jenkins, 1928
Anthony Trent, Master Criminal. Moffat, 1919; Jenkins, 1931; Mellifont, 1942; Grosset
The Bathhurst Complex. Jenkins, 1924
Blue Ridge Crime. Jenkins, 1937

Cairo Crisis. Jenkins, 1945
Capture. Jenkins, 1940
Christopher Bond, Adventurer. Jenkins, 1932
The Chromium Cat. Jenkins, 1952
Criminals All. Jenkins, 1934
Death by the Lake. Jenkins, 1934
Death Fear. McBride, 1929; Jenkins, 1930
The Denmede Mystery. Jenkins, 1936
Ghost City Killings. Jenkins, 1940
The Great Ling Plot. Jenkins, 1933
Headland House Affair. Jenkins, 1941
The House of Secrets. Jenkins, 1936
The Last Scourge. Jenkins, 1946
Manhunt in Murder. Jenkins, 1950; Roy Pubs., 1958
The Marrowby Myth. Jenkins, 1938
Men Without Faces. Jenkins, 1943
Murder in Beacon Street. McBride, 1930
Murder Island. McBride, 1928; Jenkins, 1930
Murder Walks the Deck. Jenkins, 1938
The Mysterious Mr. Garland. Jenkins, 1923
Nightmare Castle. Jenkins, 1937
Noonday Devils. Jenkins, 1923
Old Manor Crime. Jenkins, 1937
Recluse of 5th Avenue. McBride, 1929
The Return of Anthony Trent. Barse & Hopkins, 1925; Grosset, 1925; Jenkins, 1936
The Scarlett Murder. Jenkins, 1931
Secret of the Silver Car. Jenkins, 1932
Shadow Agent. Jenkins, 1941
Social Stroming. Jenkins, 1931
Spies of Peace. Jenkins, 1934
Trent Fights Again. Jenkins, 1939
Trent of the Lone Hand. Jenkins, 1927
The Trent Trial. Jenkins, 1930

MARVELL, HOLT (Pseudonym of Eric Maschwitz); see GIELGUD, VAL HENRY

MASCHWITZ, ERIC (Pseudonym: Holt Marvell); see GIELGUD, VAL HENRY

MASKE, JOHN (M)
The Cherbourg Mystery. Rich, 1934
The Dinard Mystery. Rich, 1933
Ghost of a Cardinal. Rich, 1935
The Saint-Malo Mystery. Rich, 1933

MASON, ALFRED EDWARD WOODLEY (D)
The Affair at the Semiramis Hotel. Scribner, 1917
At the Villa Rose. Hodder, 1910; Scribner, 1910; Penguin, 1962
Dean's Elbow. Hodder, 1930; Doubleday, Doran, 1931
Dilemmas. Doubleday, Doran, 1935; Hodder, 1936
Four Corners of the World. Hodder, 1917; Scribner, 1917
The Four Feathers. Macmillan, 1902; Smith, Elder, 1902
Hanaud Omnibus. Musson, 1935
The House in Lordship Lane. Dodd, 1946; Hodder, 1946
The House of the Arrow. Doran, 1924; Hodder, 1924; Penguin
Inspector Hanaud's Investigations. Hodder, 1931
No Other Tiger. Doran, 1927; Hodder, 1931; Pan, 1948
The Prisoner in the Opal. Doubleday, Doran, 1928; Hodder, 1933
Sapphire. Doubleday, Doran, 1933; Hodder, 1933
The Secret Fear. Doubleday, Doran, 1940
They Wouldn't Be Chessmen. Doubleday, Doran, 1935; Hodder, 1935
The Winding Stair. Doran, 1923; Hodder, 1923
Witness for the Defense. Hodder, 1913; Scribner, 1914

MASON, ARTHUR CHARLES
The Man With the Big Head. Gardner, 1930

MASON, CHARLES (M) (Pseudonym: S. C. Mason)
Bloody Murder. Bell, G., 1937
The Gold of Gabria. Warne, 1950
The Man on the Spot. Bles, 1938; Mellifont, 1953
Murder at Bador. Bell, G., 1938
Murder on Maneuvers. Bell, G., 1937

MASON, FRANCIS VAN WYCK (D) (Pseudonyms: Geoffrey Coffin, Ward Weaver)
The Branded Spy Murders. Doubleday, Doran, 1932; Eldon, 1936
The Bucharest Ballerina Murders. Stokes, 1940; Jarrolds, 1941
The Budapest Parade Murders. Doubleday, Doran, 1935; Eldon, 1936
The Cairo Garter Murders. Doubleday, Doran, 1938; Jarrolds, 1938
Captain North's Three Biggest Cases. Grosset, 1936 (Contains: The Vesper Service Murders, The Branded Spy Murders, and The Yellow Arrow Murders)
The Castle Island Case, by Henry Clay Gipson and Geoffrey Coffin. Reynal, 1937; Jarrolds, 1938
Dardanelles Derelict. Barker, 1950
The Forgotten Fleet Mystery. Dodge, 1936; Jarrolds, 1943
The Fort Terror Murders. Doubleday, Doran, 1931; Eldon, 1936
The Gracious Lily Affair. Doubleday, 1957; Hale, R., 1958

Hang My Wreath, by Ward Weaver. Funk, 1941; Jarrolds, 1942
Himalayan Assignment. Doubleday, 1950
The Hong Kong Airbase Murders. Doubleday, Doran, 1937; Jarrolds, 1940 (Contains: The Yellow Arrow Murders, The Cairo Garter Murders, and The Rio Casino Intrigue)
The Man From G-2. Reynal, 1943
Maracaibo Mission. Doubleday, 1965; PB, 1967
Military Intelligence -8. Stokes, 1941 (Contains: The Washington Legation Murders, The Hong Kong Airbase Murders, and The Singapore Exile Murders)
The Multi-million Dollar Murders. PB, 1960
Murder in the Senate, by Geoffrey Coffin. Dodge, 1935; Hurst, 1937
Oriental Division G-2. Reynal, 1942 (Contains: The Sulu Sea Murders, The Fort Terror Murders, and The Shanghai Bund Murders)
Rio Casino Intrigue. Reynal, 1941; Jarrolds, 1942
Saigon Singer. Doubleday, 1946; Barker, 1948
Secret Mission to Bangkok. Doubleday, 1960
Seeds of Murder. Doubleday, Doran, 1930; Eldon, 1937
Seven Seas Murder. Doubleday, Doran, 1936; Eldon, 1937
The Shanghai Bund Murders. Doubleday, Doran, 1933; Eldon, 1937
The Singapore Exile Murders. Doubleday, Doran, 1939; Jarrolds, 1939
Spider House. Mystery League, 1932; Hale, R., 1959
The Sulu Sea Murders. Doubleday, Doran, 1933; Eldon, 1936
Trouble in Burma. Doubleday, 1962; PB, 1963
Two Tickets for Tangier. Doubleday, 1955
The Vesper Service Murders. Doubleday, Doran, 1931; Eldon, 1937
The Washington Legation Murders. Doubleday, Doran, 1935; Eldon, 1937
The Yellow Arrow Murders. Doubleday, Doran, 1932; Eldon, 1936
Zanzibar Intrigue. Doubleday, 1963; Hale, R., 1964; PB, 1965

MASON, HOWARD, pseud; see RAMAGE, JENNIFER

MASON, JOHN WILLIAM (M)
Hot Blood-Cold Blood. Hale, R., 1958
Jail Bait. Hale, R., 1959
The Saboteurs. Muller, 1955
The Tiger's Back. Hale, R., 1957; Viking, 1957

MASON, S. C., pseud; see MASON, CHARLES

MASON, RAYMOND (M)
Someone and Felicia Warwick. GM, 1962

MASON, SARAH ELIZABETH (M)
Crimson Feathers. Doubleday, Doran, 1945
The House That Hate Built. Doubleday, Doran, 1944
Murder Rents a Room. Doubleday, Doran, 1943
The Whip. Morrow, 1948; Transworld, 1952

MASSEY, MORRELL (D)
Left Hand Left. Hutchinson, 1932; Penn, 1932

MASSEY, RUTH (Full name: Ruth Massey Tovell) (D)
Death in the Wind. Nelson, 1932 (Aslo published as: Crime in the Boulevard Raspail. Nelson, 1932)

MASSIE, CHRIS (M)
Death Goes Hunting. Faber, 1953
Farewell, Pretty Ladies. Random, 1942
The Green Circle. Random, 1943

MASSON, RENE
Landru. Doubleday, 1965

MASTERMAN, JOHN CECIL
The Case of the Four Friends. Hodder, 1957; British Book Centre, 1959
The Oxford Tragedy. Gollancz, 1933; Penguin, 1956

MASTERMAN, MARGARET (Mrs. Richard B. Braithwaite) (M)
Death of a Friend. Nicholson, 1938

MASTERMAN, WALTER S. (M)
The Avenger Strikes. Dutton, 1937; Jarrolds, 1937
Back from the Grave. Jarrolds, 1940
The Baddington Horror. Dutton, 1934; Jarrolds, 1934
Blood on the Floor. Newnes, 1935
Bloodhounds Bay. Dutton, 1930; Jarrolds, 1937
Borderline. Dutton, 1937; Jarrolds, 1937
Crime of the Reckaviles; see The Curse of Reckaviles
The Curse of Cantire. Grosset, 1928; Jarrolds, 1939
The Curse of Reckaviles. Dutton, 1927 (English title: Crime of the Reckaviles. Methuen, 1934)

Death Coins. Jarrolds, 1940
Death Turns Traitor. Dutton, 1936; Methuen, 1936
The Flying Beast. Dutton, 1932; Jarrolds, 1932
The Green Toad. Dutton, 1929; Gollancz, 1929
The Hooded Monster. Jarrolds, 1939
The Hunted Man. Dutton, 1938; Jarrolds, 1940
The Man Without a Head. Jarrolds, 1942
Murder Beacon, with L. Patrick Greene. Low, 1932; Mellifont, 1949
The Mystery of Fifty-Two. Dutton, 1931; Jarrolds, 1931
The Nameless Crime. Dutton, 1932; Jarrolds, 1932
The Perjured Alibi. Dutton, 1935; Methuen, 1935
Rose of Death. Methuen, 1935; Dutton, 1936
The Secret of the Downs. Dutton, 1939; Jarrolds, 1939
The Silver Leopard. Jarrolds, 1941
Tangle. Jarrolds, 1931
2. L.O. Dutton, 1928
The Wrong Letter. Dutton, 1926; Jarrolds, 1938
The Wrong Verdict. Dutton, 1938; Jarrolds, 1937
The Yellow Mistletoe, with L. Patrick Greene. Dutton, 1930; Jarrolds, 1930

MASTERS, JOHN (S)
The Breaking Strain. Dell, 1967

MASTERS, W. W. (D)
Murder in the Mirror. Longmans, 1932

MASTERSON, WHIT, pseud; see MILLER, BILL

MASUR, HAROLD Q. (D)
The Big Money. S & S, 1954; Boardman, T. V., 1955; Avon, 1964
Bury Me Deep. S & S, 1947; Boardman, T. V., 1961
The Last Breath. Boardman, T. V., 1958
The Last Gamble. S & S, 1958 (Also published as: Murder on Broadway. Avon, 1965)
The Legacy Lenders. Random, 1967; Bantam, 1968
Make a Killing. Random, 1964; Avon, 1965
Murder on Broadway; see The Last Gamble
The Name Is Jordon. Pyramid, 1962
Send Another Hearse. Boardman, T. V., 1960; Random, 1960; Dell, 1965
So Rich, So Lovely, So Dead. S & S, 1952; Boardman, T. V., 1953; Dell, 1961
Suddenly a Corpse. S & S, 1949; Boardman, T. V., 1950
Tall, Dark and Deadly. S & S, 1956; Boardman, T. V., 1957; Avon, 1964
You Can't Live Forever. S & S, 1950; Boardman, T. V., 1951; Dell, 1959

MATCH, JACK (M)
Ask for Lois. Monarch, 1962
Gambler's Girl. Athena, 1961
Prowler in the Night. GM, 1959

MATHER, BERKLEY, pseud. (M)
The Achilles Affair. Scribner, 1959; Collins, 1961
The Gold of Malabar. Collins, 1966; Scribner, 1967
The Pass Beyond Kashmir. Scribner, 1960; Collins, 1964; Popular Lib., 1966

MATHER, VIRGINIA, pseud; see LIEBLER, JEAN MAYER

MATHERS, HELEN B. (M)
The Land o' the Leal. Munro, 1878 (Includes: "As He Comes Up the Stair" and "Stephen Halton")

MATHESON, HUGH, pseud; see MACKEY, COL. LEWIS HUGH

MATHESON, JEAN (M)
The Dire Departed. Hodder, 1958
So Difficult to Die. Collins, 1957

MATHESON, RICHARD (S)
Fury on Sunday. Lion, 1954
I Am Legend. Transworld, 1960; Bantam, 1964
Ride the Nightmare. Ballantine, 1962
Shock. Thirteen Tales to Thrill and Terrify. Dell, 1961; Transworld, 1962
Shock II. Dell, 1964
Shock III. Dell, 1966
Someone Is Bleeding. Lion, 1953
A Stir of Echoes. Cassell, 1958; Lippincott, 1958
The Third Force. Washburn, 1960

MATHEWS, DONNA L. (M)
The Fatal Amateur. Rinehart, 1959; Jenkins, 1960
The Late Unlamented. Jenkins, 1961
Reach of Fear. Rinehart, 1958; Jenkins, 1961
A Very Welcome Death. Holt, 1961

MATHEWS, MRS. FRANCES H. SHORTT; see SHORTT, VERE DAWSON

MATHEWS, NIEVES M. (M)
The Jade Ring. Oxford, 1931
She Died Without Light. Hodder, 1956

MATHIESON, THEODORE (D)
The Devil and Ben Franklin. S & S, 1961; Popular Lib., 1962
The Great Detectives. S & S, 1960

MATSCHAT, CECILE (M)
Murder at the Black Crook. Farrar & Rinehart, 1943; Cassell, 1945
Murder in Okefenokee. Farrar & Rinehart, 1941

MAUGHAM, ROBERT CECIL (M)
The Man with Two Shadows. Harper, 1959

MAUGHAM, WILLIAM SOMERSET (S)
Ashenden; or, The British Agent. Doubleday, Page, 1927; Heinemann, 1928; Avon, 1964

MAURICE, ARTHUR BARTLETT (M)
The Riddle of the Rovers. Dodd, 1942

MAURICE, MICHAEL, pseud; see SKINNER, CONRAD ARTHUR

MAVITY, NANCY BARR (Mrs. Arthur Benton Mavity) (D)
The Body on the Floor. Doubleday, Doran, 1929; Collins, 1933
The Case of the Missing Sandals. Collins, 1934
The Fate of Jane McKenzie. Collins, 1933
He Didn't Mind Hanging. Collins, 1933 (U.S. title: The Man Who Didn't Mind Hanging. Grosset, 1934)
The Man Who Didn't Mind Hanging; see He Didn't Mind Hanging
The Other Bullet. Doubleday, Doran, 1930; Collins, 1934
The State vs. Elna Jepson. Doubleday, Doran, 1937
The Tule Marsh Murder. Collins, 1933

MAXFIELD, HENRY S. (S)
Legacy of a Spy. Harper, 1958; Avon, 1965

MAXON, P. B. (D)
Waltz of Death. Mystery House, 1941; Bart

MAXWELL, BRIGID (D)
The Case of the Six Mistresses. Harrap, 1955

MAXWELL, MARY ELIZABETH BRADDON (M)
Captain of the Vulture. Ward, Lock, 1862
Just as I Am. Harper, 1880
Lady Audley's Secret. Tinsley, 1862 (3 Vols.); Dick & Fitzgerald, 1877; Lovell, J. W., 1883
Like and Unlike. Blackett, S., 1887 (3 Vols.); Munro, 1887
Run to Earth. Ward, Lock, 1868 (3 Vols.)
A Strange World. Harper, 1875

MAXWELL, WILLIAM BABINGTON (M)
The Case of Bevan Yorke. Benn, 1927

MAY, GEOFFREY; see DOLBY, ETHEL M.

MAY, HENRY BAK (M)
The Doctor Didn't Prescribe Murder. Exposition, 1957

MAYBURY, ANNE, pseud; see BUXTON, ANNE

MAYLON, B. J. (D)
The Corpse with Knee Action. Phoenix, 1940

MAYNE, ETHEL COLBURN (M)
Come In. Chapman, 1917

MAYO, JAMES, pseud; see COULTER, STEPHEN

MAYOR, DOROTHY (M)
It's an Ill Will. Mill, 1947
Last Call for Lissa. Mill, 1948

MAYSE, ARTHUR (M)
Desperate Search. Morrow, 1952; Harrap, 1953
Perilous Passage. Morrow, 1949; Harrap, 1952

"MAZ," pseud; see MAZURE, ALFRED LEONARDUS

MAZURE, ALFRED LEONARDUS (M) (Pseudonym: "Maz")
Cash on Destruction. Spearman, N., 1962

MEADE, DOROTHY COLE (M)
Death over Her Shoulder. Scribner, 1939
Fatal Shadows. Long & Smith, 1933

MEADE, MRS. LILLIE THOMAS and CLIFFORD HALIFAX (M)
The Sanctuary Club. Ward, Lock, 1906
The Sorceress of the Strand, with Robert Eustace. Ward, Lock, 1903
Stories from the Diary of a Doctor. Newnes, 1894

MEADOWS, CATHERINE (M)
Doctor Moon. Putnam, 1935
Friday Market. Gollancz, 1938; Macmillan, 1938

MEAKER, MARIJANE (S) (Pseudonym: Vin Packer)
The Evil Friendship. GM, 1963
Girl on the Best Seller List. GM, 1960
Intimate Victims. GM, 1962; Muller, 1963
Something in the Shadows. GM, 1961; Muller, 1962

MEANS, MARY and THEODORE SAUNDERS (M) (Pseudonym: Denis Scott)
Beckoning Shadow. Bobbs, 1946; Hammond, 1956
Murder Makes A Villain. Bobbs, 1944; Hammond, 1955

MEARSON, LYON (M)
Footsteps in the Dark. Macaulay, 1927; Hutchinson, 1928
Phantom Fingers. Hutchinson, 1929
Whisper on the Stair. Hutchinson, 1924; Macaulay, 1924

MECHEM, KIRKE (D)
Frame for Murder. Doubleday, Doran, 1936

MECHEM, PHILIP (M)
And Not for Love. Duell, 1942
The Columbine Cabin Murders. Scribner, 1932

MEGAW, ARTHUR STANLEY (M) (Pseudonym: Arthur Stanley)
The Monkhurst Case. MacDonald & Co., 1946

MEIK, VIVIAN (M)
The Curse of the Red Shiva. Hillman-Curl, 1938

MELIDES, NICHOLAS (M) (Pseudonym: Nicholas MacGuire)
Buns from the Gutter. Paladin Press, 1951

MELVILLE, ALAN, pseud; see CAVERHILL, WILLIAM MELVILLE

MELVILLE, JENNIE (M)
Burning Is a Substitute for Loving. Joseph, M., 1963; London House, 1964
Come Home and Be Killed. Joseph, M., 1962; London House, 1964
A Different Kind of Summer. Hodder, 1967
Murderers' Houses. Joseph, M., 1964

MERCER, CECIL WILLIAM (M) (Pseudonym: Dornford Yates)
Adele & Co. Minton, 1931
The Blind Corner. Hodder, 1927; Minton, 1927
An Eye for a Tooth. Putnam, 1944
Gale Warning. Putnam, 1940
The House That Berry Built. Ward, Lock, 1945
The Ne'er Do Well. Ward, Lock, 1954
She Painted Her Face. Putnam, 1937
Shoal Water. Putnam, 1941
The Stolen March. Minton, 1933
Storm Music. Minton, 1934
Were Death Denied. Putnam, 1941

MERCER, IAN (M)
Curs in Clover. Earl, 1948
The Green Windmill. Crowther, 1945
A Man Gets His Tomb. Earl, 1948
A Mission to Majorca. Boardman, T. V., 1958

MEREDITH, ANNE, pseud; see MALLESON, LUCY BEATRICE

MEREDITH, DAVID WILLIAMS, pseud; see MIERS, EARL SCHENK

MEREDITH, PETER, pseud; see WORTHINGTON-STUART, BRIAN ARTHUR

MERGENDAHL, CHARLES (M)
With Kisses Four. Morrow, 1954

MERRETT, CHARLES H. (D)
Hidden Lives. Long, 1929

MERRICK, GORDON (S)
The Demon of Noon. Messner, 1954 (Also published as: Lovers in Torment. Popular Lib., 1955)

MERRICK, MOLLIE (M)
The Mysterious Mr. Frame. Washburn, 1938
The Upper Case. Washburn, 1936

MERRICK, WILLIAM (D)
The Packard Case. Gollancz, 1961; Random, 1961

MERRILL, P. J., pseud; see ROTH, HOLLY

MERRITT, ABRAHAM (M)
Burn, Witch, Burn. Liveright, 1933; Methuen, 1934
Creep Shadow! Doubleday, Doran, 1934; Methuen, 1935
Seven Footprints to Satan. Liveright, 1928; Richards, 1928; Avon, 1963

MERSEREAU, JOHN (M)
The Corpse Comes Ashore. Lippincott, 1941
Murder Loves Company. Lippincott, 1940

MERTZ, BARBARA (S-Gothic) (Pseudonym: Barbara Michaels)
The Master of Blacktower. Appleton, 1966; Bantam, 1967
Sons of the Wolf. Meredith, 1967

MERWIN, SAMUEL, JR. (D)
A Knife in My Back. Arcadia, 1945
Lady Can Do. Houghton, 1929
A Matter of Policy. Mystery House, 1946
A Message from a Corpse. Mystery House, 1945
Murder in Miniatures. Doubleday, Doran, 1940

MESERVEY, RUSS, pseud. (M)
Masquerade into Madness. GM, 1953

MESSENGER, ELIZABETH MARGERY ESSON (M)
Dive Deep for Death. Hale, R., 1959
Growing Evil. Hale, R., 1964
A Heap of Trouble. Hale, R., 1963
Light on Murder. Hale, R., 1960
Material Witness. Hale, R., 1959
Murder Stalks the Bay. Hale, R., 1958
Publicity for Murder. Hale, R., 1961
The Wrong Way to Die. Hale, R., 1961
You Won't Need a Coat. Hale, R., 1964

MESSER, MRS. MONA NAOMI ANNE (M) (Pseudonym: Anne Hocking)
All my Pretty Chickens; see Death Loves a Shining Mark
And No One Wept. Allen, W. H., 1954
As I Was Going to St. Ives. Paul, S., 1937
At the Cedars. Bles, 1949
The Best Laid Plans. Doubleday, 1950; Bles, 1952
Candidates for Murder. Long, 1961
Cat's Paw. Paul, S., 1933
Deadly Is the Evil Tongue; see Old Mrs. Fitzgerald
Death Among the Tulips. Allen, W. H., 1953
Death at the Wedding. Bles, 1946
Death Duel. Paul, S., 1933
Death Loves a Shining Mark. Doubleday, Doran, 1943 (Also published as: All My Pretty Chickens)
Epitaph for a Nurse. Allen, W. H., 1958 (U.S. title: A Victim Must Be Found. Doubleday, 1959)
The Evil That Men Do. Allen, W. H., 1953
The Finishing Touch; see Prussian Blue
He Had to Die. Long, 1962
The House of En-dor. Paul, S., 1936
The Hunt Is Up. Paul, S., 1934
Ill Deeds Done. Bles, 1938
Killing Kin. Doubleday, 1951
Little Victims Play. Bles, 1938
Mediterranean Murder. Evans, 1951
Miss Milverton. Bles, 1941 (U.S. title: Poison Is a Bitter Brew. Doubleday, Doran, 1942)
Murder at Mid-day. Allen, W. H., 1956
Night's Candles. Bles, 1941
Nile Green. Bles, 1944
Old Mrs. Fitzgerald. Bles, 1939 (U.S. title: Deadly Is the Evil Tongue. Doubleday, Doran, 1940)
One Shall Be Taken. Bles, 1942
Poison in Paradise. Allen, W. H., 1955; Doubleday, 1955
Poison Is a Bitter Brew; see Miss Milverton
The Poisoned Chalice. Long, 1959
Prussian Blue. Bles, 1947 (U.S. title: The Finishing Touch. Doubleday, 1948)
Reason for Murder. Allen, W. H., 1955
Relative Murder. Allen, W. H., 1957
The Simple Way of Poison. Washburn, 1957; Allen, W. H., 1958
Six Green Bottles. Bles, 1943
So Many Doors. Bles, 1939
Stranglehold. Paul, S., 1936
There's Death in the Cup. Evans, 1952
To Cease Upon Midnight. Long, 1959
A Victim Must be Found; see Epitaph for a Nurse
The Vultures Gather. Bles, 1945
Walk into My Parlour. Paul, S., 1935
What a Tangled Web. Paul, S., 1937
The Wicked Flee. Bles, 1940
Without the Option. Paul, S., 1935

METCALFE, JOHN (M)
Smoking Leg and Other Stories. Jarrolds, 1927

METCALFE, WHITAKER (M)
Two Weeks Before Murder. Arcadia, 1959

METHOLD, KENNETH (D-M)
All Suspect. MacDonald & Co., 1960

MEYER, BILL (S)
Ultimatum. Signet, 1966

MEYERS, ALFRED (M)
Murder Ends the Song. Reynal, 1941

MEYNELL, LAURENCE WALTER (D) (Pseudonyms: Robert Eton, Geoffrey Ludlow)
Abandoned Doll. Collins, 1960
And Be a Villain. Nicholson, 1939
Asking for Trouble. Ward, Lock, 1934
Bluefeather. Appleton, D., 1928; Harrap, 1928, 1950
The Breaking Point. Collins, 1957
The Bright Face of Danger. Collins, 1948
The Bus Leaves for the Village. Nicholson, 1936

Camouflage. Harrap, 1930; Hay & Mitchell, 1947; Low, 1947
The Creaking Chair. Collins, 1941
Danger Round the Corner. Collins, 1952
The Dark Square. Collins, 1941
Death's Eye; see The Shadow and the Stone
The Dividing Air. Harrap, 1935
The Door in the Wall. Harper, 1937; Nicholson, 1937
The Echo in the Cave. Collins, 1949
The Evil Hour. Collins, 1947
The Frightened Man. Collins, 1952
The Gentlemen Go By. Lippincott, 1934 (English title: Watch the Wall. Harrap, 1934)
Give Me the Knife. Collins, 1954
His Aunt Came Late. Nicholson, 1939
The House in Marsh Road. Collins, 1960
The House in the Hills. Harper, 1930; Nicholson, 1937
The House on the Cliff. Hutchinson, 1932; Lippincott, 1932
The Hut. Nicholson, 1938
Inside Out! or Mad as a Hatter. Harrap, 1934
The Lady on Platform One. Collins, 1950
The Man No One Knew. Collins, 1951
Mockbeggar. Harrap, 1924
More Deadly Than the Male. Collins, 1964
The Mystery at Newton's Ferry. Lippincott, 1930
Not in Our Stars, by Robert Eton. Nicholson, 1937
Odds on Bluefeather. Harrap, 1935; Lippincott, 1935
On the Night of the 18th. Nicholson, 1936; Harper, 1937
One Step from Murder. Collins, 1958
Paid in Full; see So Many Doors
Palace Pier, by Robert Eton. Nicholson, 1938
A Party of Eight. Collins, 1950
The Pit in the Garden. Collins, 1961
Saturday Out. Collins, 1956; Walker & Co., 1962
The Shadow and the Stone. Appleton, D., 1929 (English title: Death's Eye. Harrap, 1929; Withy Grove, 1955)
Sleep of the Unjust. Collins, 1963
So Many Doors. Lippincott, 1933 (English title: Paid In Full. Harrap, 1935)
Storm Against the Wall. Hutchinson, 1931
Strange Landings. Collins, 1946
Third Time Unlucky. Harrap, 1935
Too Clever by Half. Collins, 1953
Virgin Luck. Collins, 1963; S & S, 1964; Avon, 1966
Watch the Wall; see The Gentlemen Go By
Where Is She Now? Collins, 1955

MEYNELL, MARY (M)
The Broken Arc. Cassell, 1945
The Weekend at Green Trees. Bles, 1955

MEYRICK, GORDON (M)
Body on the Pavement. Eldon, 1942
The Ghost Hunters. Crowther, 1947
The Green Phantom. Eldon, 1941
Pennyworth of Murder. Eldon, 1943

MICHAELS, BARBARA, pseud; see MERTZ, BARBARA

MICHEL, MILTON SCOTT (D)
Murder in the Consulting Room. Hammond, 1954
The Psychiatric Murders. Mystery House, 1946
Sweet Murder. Coward, 1943
The X-Ray Murders. Coward, 1942

MIDDLETON, TED (S)
Operation Tokyo. Avon, 1956

MIERS, EARL SCHENK (D) (Pseudonym: David William Meredith)
The Christmas Card Murders. Knopf, 1951

MILBROOK, JOHN (M)
A Bridgeport Dagger. Lane, 1930

MILES, DAVID, pseud; see CRONIN, BRENDAN LEO

MILES, STELLA (D)
Murder at the Arab Stud. Jenkins, 1951
Murder Knows No Master. Jenkins, 1952
Prescription for Murder. Jenkins, 1954
Saddled with Murder. Jenkins, 1953

MILLAR, KENNETH (D) (Pseudonyms: John MacDonald, John Ross MacDonald, Ross MacDonald)
Archer in Holywood, by Ross MacDonald. Knopf, 1967
The Barbarous Coast, by Ross MacDonald. Knopf, 1956; Cassell, 1957; Bantam, 1966
Black Money, by Ross MacDonald. Knopf, 1966; Bantam, 1967 (Magazine title: "The Demon Lover")
The Blue City. Knopf, 1947; Cassell, 1949
The Chill, by Ross MacDonald. Knopf, 1963; Bantam, 1965
The Dark Tunnel. Dodd, 1944
The Doomsters, by Ross MacDonald. Knopf, 1958; Bantam, 1959

The Drowning Pool, by John Ross MacDonald. Knopf, 1949; Gollancz, 1955; PB, 1966
Experience With Evil; see Meet Me at the Morgue
The Far Side of the Dollar, by Ross MacDonald. Knopf, 1964; Bantam, 1966
The Ferguson Affair, by Ross MacDonald. Knopf, 1960; Collins, 1961; Bantam, 1963; Fontana, 1963
Find A Victim, by John Ross MacDonald. Knopf, 1954; Bantam, 1955; Cassell, 1955
The Galton Case, by Ross MacDonald. Knopf, 1959; Cassell, 1960; Pan, 1962; Bantam, 1966 (English editions by John Ross MacDonald)
Harper; see The Moving Target
The Ivory Grin, by John Ross MacDonald. Knopf, 1952; Cassell, 1953
Meet Me at the Morgue, by John Ross MacDonald. Knopf, 1953; PB, 1967 (English title: Experience with Evil. Cassell, 1955)
The Moving Target, by John MacDonald. Knopf, 1949 (Also published as: Harper. PB, 1966)
The Name Is Archer, by John Ross MacDonald. Bantam, 1955
The Three Roads. Knopf, 1949; Cassell, 1950; Bantam, 1968
Trouble Follows Me. Dodd, 1946
The Way Some People Die, by John Ross MacDonald. Knopf, 1951; Cassell, 1953; PB, 1967
The Wycherly Woman, by Ross MacDonald. Knopf, 1961; Collins, 1962; Bantam, 1968
The Zebra-Striped Hearse, by Ross MacDonald. Knopf, 1962; Collins, 1963; Bantam, 1964

MILLAR, MARGARET STURM (Mrs. Kenneth Millar) (S)
An Air That Kills. Random, 1957; Bantam, 1960
The Beast in View. Gollancz, 1955; Random, 1955; Bantam, 1966
The Cannibal Heart. Random, 1949; Hamilton, H., 1950
The Devil Loves Me. Doubleday, Doran, 1942; Popular Lib., 1966
Do Evil in Return. Random, 1950; Lancer, 1965
Experiment in Springtime. Random, 1947
The Fiend. Gollancz, 1964; Random, 1964; Dell, 1966
Fire Will Freeze. Random, 1944; Signet, 1967
How Like an Angel. Random, 1962; Gollancz, 1963; Dell, 1965
The Invisible Worm. Doubleday, Doran, 1941; Long, 1943
The Iron Gates. Random, 1945; Dell, 1960
The Listening Walls. Random, 1959; Dell, 1964, 1967
Rose's Last Summer. Random, 1952; Lancer, 1965
A Stranger in My Grave. Random, 1960; Transworld, 1962; Dolphin, 1963
Taste of Fear. Hale, R., 1950; Penguin, 1962
Vanish in an Instant. Random, 1952; Lancer, 1965
Wall of Eyes. Random, 1943; Lancer, 1966
The Weak-eyed Bat. Doubleday, Doran, 1942

MILLAR, R. (D)
Half a Corpse. Eyre, 1935; Musson, 1935

MILLARD, JOSEPH JOHN (M)
The Wickedest Man. GM, 1954

MILLER, AGNES (M)
The Colfax Book-plate. Century, 1926

MILLER, BILL and BOB WADE (D)
(Pseudonyms: Whit Masterson, Wade Miller, Dale Wilmer)
All Through the Night, by Whit Masterson. Dodd, 1955
Badge of Evil, by Whit Masterson. Dodd, 1956
Calamity Fair, by Wade Miller. Farrar, Straus, 1950
A Cry in the Night, by Whit Masterson. Dodd, 1955; Bantam, 1956
Dark Fantastic, by Whit Masterson. Dodd, 1959; Avon, 1966
Dead Fall, by Dale Wilmer. Mystery House, 1954
Dead, She Was Beautiful, by Whit Masterson. Allen, W. H., 1955; Black, 1955; Dodd, 1955; Bantam, 1956
Deadly Weapon, by Wade Miller. Farrar, Straus, 1946; Low, 1947; Signet
Devil on Two Sticks, by Wade Miller. Farrar, Straus, 1949 (Also published as: Killers Choice. Signet)
Evil Come, Evil Go, by Whit Masterson. Allen, W. H., 1961; Dodd, 1961; PB, 1962
Fatal Step, by Wade Miller. Farrar, Straus, 1948; Low, 1949; Signet
The Girl from Midnight. GM, 1966
Guilty Bystander, by Wade Miller. Farrar, Straus, 1947; Low, 1948; Signet
Hammer in His Hand, by Whit Masterson. Dodd, 1960; Bantam, 1963; Transworld, 1963

Killer's Choice; see Devil on Two Sticks
Kiss Her Goodbye, by Wade Miller. Lion, 1956; Allen, W. H., 1957
The Man on a Nylon String, by Whit Masterson. Allen, W. H., 1963; Dodd, 1963; Avon, 1964
Memo for Murder, by Dale Wilmer. Graphic, 1951
Murder Charge, by Wade Miller. Farrar, Straus, 1950; Signet
Murder Queen High, by Wade Miller. Allen, W. H., 1958
Nightmare Cruise, by Wade Miller. Ace, 1961
Play Like You're Dead, by Whit Masterson. Dodd, 1967
Pop Goes the Queen, by Wade Miller. Farrar, Straus, 1947
711-Officer Needs Help, by Whit Masterson. Dodd, 1965 (Also published as: The Warning Shot. Popular Lib., 1967)
Shadow in the Wild, by Whit Masterson. Dodd, 1957; Bantam, 1960
Shoot to Kill, by Wade Miller. Farrar, Straus, 1951; Allen, W. H., 1953; Signet
South of the Sun. GM, 1954
Stolen Woman, by Wade Miller
The Stroke of Seven, by Bob Wade. Morrow, 1965
Tiger's Wife, by Wade Miller. GM
The Uneasy Street, by Wade Miller. Farrar, Straus, 1948; Low, 1949; Signet
The Warning Shot; see 711-Officer Needs Help

MILLER, FLOYD C. (S)
The Savage Streets. Popular Lib., 1956

MILLER, JOHN (D)
Murder of a Professor. Hale, 1937; Putnam, 1937

MILLER, MARC, pseud; see BAKER, MARCEIL GENEE

MILLER, MARY BRITTON (S) (Pseudonym: Isabel Bolton)
Many Mansions. Scribner, 1952; Macmillan, 1953

MILLER, MERLE (M)
A Secret Understanding. Viking, 1956; Lancer, 1966

MILLER, SIGMUND (M)
The Snow Leopard. Ward, Lock, 1960; GM, 1961

MILLER, WADE, pseud; see MILLER, BILL

MILLHAUSER, BERTRAM (M)
What Goes Up. Doubleday, Doran, 1945

MILLIN, SARAH GERTRUDE (M)
Three Men Die. Harper, 1934

MILLS, ALGERNON VICTOR (M) (Pseudonym: Rupert Latimer)
Death in Real Life. MacDonald & Co,, 1943
Murder After Christmas. MacDonald & Co., 1944

MILLS, ARTHUR FREDERIC HOBART (M)
Brighton Alibi. Collins, 1936
The Danger Game. Hutchinson, 1926
Don't Touch the Body. Collins, 1947
Escapade. Collins, 1931
Intrigue Island. Collins, 1930
Jewel Thief. Collins, 1939; Mellifont, 1948
The Jockey Died First. Staples Press, 1953
Judgment of Death. Collins, 1932
Last Seen Alive. Evans, 1951
Live Bait. Hutchinson, 1927
The Maliday Mystery. Staples Press, 1954
One Man's Secret. Collins, 1932
Paris Agent. Collins, 1935; Gardner, 1947
Pursued. Collins, 1929
Shroud of Snow. Evans, 1950
The Yellow Dragon. Hutchinson, 1924
Your Number Is Up. Evans, 1952

MILLS, CARLEY (M)
The Nearness of Evil. Coward, 1961

MILLS, HARRY ROLAND WOOSMAN; see MILLS, WOOSMAN

MILLS, HUGH TRAVERS (D) (Pseudonym: Hugh Travers)
In Pursuit of Evil. Lippincott, 1967
Madame Aubrey and the Police. Harper & Row, 1966, 1967
Madame Aubrey Dines with Death. Harper & Row, 1967

MILLS, OSMINGTON, pseud; see BROOKS, VIVIAN COLLIN

MILLS, WOOSNAM (Full Name: Harry Roland Woosman Mills) (M)
Biting Fortune. Nelson, 1939
Blind Reckoning. Hodder, 1951
Dark Encounter. Nelson, 1938
Dusty Coinage. Hodder, 1953
French Hazard. Hodder, 1942
Grim Chancery. Nelson, 1937
Knaves Rampant. Nelson, 1938
Phantom Scarlet. Hodder, 1940
Shadow Crusade. Hodder, 1941
Tarnished Gold. Hodder, 1951

MILLWARD, EDWARD J. (M)
The Aero Club Mystery. Harrap, 1939
The Body Lies. Harrap, 1936
The Copper Bottle. Dutton, 1929; Methuen, 1929; Newnes, 1931
The House of Wraith. Harrap, 1935; Houghton, 1935; Withy Grove, 1941

MILNE, A. A. (D)
Four Days' Wonder. Dutton, 1933; Methuen, 1933
The Red House Mystery. Dutton, 1922; Methuen, 1923; Dell, 1959

MILNE, SHIRLEY (M)
Stiff Silk. Hale, R., 1962

MILNER, GEORGE, pseud; see HARDINGE, GEORGE

MILTON, JOSEPH (S)
Assignment: Assignation. Lancer, 1964
Baron Sinister. Lancer, 1965
The Big Blue Death. Lancer, 1965
The Death-Makers. Lancer, 1966
The Man Who Bombed the World. Lancer, 1966
President's Agent. Lancer, 1967
Worldbreaker. Lancer, 1964

MINTON, PAULA (S-Gothic)
The Dark of Memory. Lancer, 1967
Engraved in Evil. Lancer, 1965
Hand of the Imposter. Lancer, 1965
Orphan of the Shadows. Lancer, 1965
Portrait of Terror. Belmont, 1967
The Secret Melody. Lancer, 1964
Shadow of a Witch. Belmont, 1967
Thunder over the Reefs. Lancer, 1967

MITCHAM, GILROY (M)
Dead Reckoning. Dobson, 1960; Roy Pubs., 1960
The Full Stop. Dobson, 1957; Roy Pubs., 1958
The Man from Bar Harbour. Dobson, 1958; Roy Pubs., 1960
Uncertain Judgement. Dobson, 1961; Roy Pubs., 1962

MITCHELL, GLADYS (D) (Pseudonym: Stephen Hockaby)
Adders on the Heath. British Book Centre, 1963; Joseph, M., 1963
The Brazen Tongues. Joseph, M., 1940
Come Away, Death. Joseph, M., 1937
The Dancing Druids. Joseph, M., 1948
The Dead Man's Morris. Joseph, M., 1936
Death and the Maiden. Joseph, M., 1947
Death at the Opera. Grayson, 1934 (Also published as: Death in the Wet. Macrae Smith, 1934)
Death in the Wet; see Death at the Opera
Death of a Blue Delft. Joseph, M., 1964
The Devil at Saxon Wall. Grayson, 1935
The Devil's Elbow. Joseph, M., 1951
The Echoing Strangers. Joseph, M., 1952
Faintly Speaking. Joseph, M., 1954
Gabriel's Hold, by Stephen Hockaby. Grayson, 1935
Grand Master, by Stephen Hockaby. Joseph, M., 1936
The Groaning Spinney. Joseph, M., 1950
Hangman's Curfew. Joseph, M., 1940
Here Comes a Chopper. Joseph, M., 1946
Laurels Are Poison. Joseph, M., 1942; Penguin, 1961
The Longer Bodies. Gollancz, 1930
The Man Who Grew Tomatoes. British Book Centre, 1959; Joseph, M., 1959
Marsh Hay, by Stephen Hockaby. Grayson, 1933, 1937
Merlin's Furlong. Joseph, M., 1953
My Bones Will Keep. Joseph, M., 1952
My Father Sleeps. Joseph, M., 1944
The Mystery of a Butcher's Shop. Dial, 1930; Gollancz, 1930
The Nodding Canaries. Joseph, M., 1961
Printer's Error. Joseph, M., 1939
The Rising of the Moon. Joseph, M., 1945
St. Peter's Finger. Joseph, M., 1938
The Saltmarsh Murders. Gollancz, 1931; Macrae Smith, 1933
Say It with Flowers. British Book Centre, 1960; Joseph, M., 1960
Seven Stars and Orion, by Stephen Hockaby. Grayson, 1934
Shallow Brown. Joseph, M., 1936
Speedy Death. Dial, 1929; Gollancz, 1929
Spotted Hemlock. British Book Centre, 1958; Joseph, M., 1958
Sunset over Soho. Joseph, M., 1943
Tom Brown's Body. Joseph, M., 1949
Twelve Horses and the Hangman's Noose. Joseph, M., 1956; British Book Centre, 1958
The Twenty-Third Man. Joseph, M., 1957
Watson's Choice. Joseph, M., 1955; Penguin, 1957
When Last I Died. Joseph, M., 1941; Knopf, 1940
The Worsted Viper. Joseph, M., 1942

MITCHELL, HUTTON (M)
The Fourth Man. Selwyn, 1931

MITCHELL, JAMES (M)
Among Arabian Sands. Davies, 1963
Die Rich, Die Happy. Knopf, 1966
The Way Back. Morrow, 1960

MITCHELL, LEBBEUS (M)
The Parachute Murder. Macaulay, 1933

MITCHELL, SCOTT, pseud; see GODFREY, LIONEL R. H.

MITCHELL, WILL (D)
The Goldfish Murders. GM, 1950

MITFORD, C. GUISE (M)
The Dual Identity. Long, 1915
The Hidden Mask. Greening, 1914
The Paxton Plot. Long, 1908

MOCKLER, GRETCHEN (S-Gothic)
Roanleigh. Signet, 1966

MODELL, MIRIAM (S) (Pseudonym: Evelyn Piper)
Bunny Lake Is Missing. Harper, 1957; Secker & Warburg, 1958; Dell, 1965
Hanno's Doll. Atheneum, 1961; Crest, 1964
The Innocent. S & S, 1949; Boardman, T. V., 1951
The Lady and Her Doctor. Doubleday, 1956
The Motive. S & S, 1950; Dell, 1965
The Naked Murderer. Atheneum, 1962
The Nanny. Atheneum, 1964; Crest, 1965
The Plot. S & S, 1951

MOFFETT, CLEVELAND LANGSTON (M)
Master Mind. Appleton, D., 1927
The Seine Mystery. Melrose, 1924; Dodd, 1925
Through the Wall. Appleton, D., 1909

MOLE, WILLIAM, pseud; see YOUNGER, WILLIAM

MOLL, ELICK
Night Without Sleep. Little, 1950; Davies, 1951; Transworld, 1955; Paperback Lib., 1962

MOLNAR, LOUIS; see SAXBY, CHARLES

MOMEY, TEDD (M)
And Dream of Evil. Abelard, 1954

MONAHAN, JOHN (S)
Big Stan. GM, 1954

MONIG, CHRISTOPHER, pseud; see CROSSEN, KENDALL

MONMOUTH, JACK, pseud; see PEMBER WILLIAM LEONARD

MONRO, GAVIN (M)
Who Killed Amanda? Hale, R., 1967

MONROE, ROY, pseud. (M)
The Judge Speaks. Exposition, 1958

MONSARRAT, NICHOLAS (M)
Castle Garac. Pyramid, 1966
Smith & Jones. Cassell, 1963; Sloane, 1963

MONTAYNE, CARLETON STEVENS (M)
The Blue Cross
Moons of Gold. Lippincott, 1936; Harrap, 1938

MONTEILHET, HUBERT (S)
Cupid's Executioners. S & S, 1967
Phoenix from the Ashes; see Return from the Ashes
The Praying Mantises. S & S, 1962; Signet
The Prisoner of Love. S & S, 1965
Return from the Ashes. S & S, 1963; Signet, 1965 (English title: Phoenix from the Ashes. Hamilton, H., 1963)
The Road to Hell. S & S, 1964; Pyramid, 1965

MONTGOMERY, IONE (D)
Death Won a Prize. Doubleday, Doran, 1941; Withy Grove, 1944
The Golden Dress. Doubleday, Doran, 1940; Boardman, T. V., 1944

MONTGOMERY, MARY
Somebody Knew. Arcadia, 1961

MONTGOMERY, ROBERT BRUCE (D) (Pseudonym: Edmund Crispin)
Beware of the Trains. Gollancz, 1953; Walker & Co., 1962
Buried for Pleasure. Lippincott, 1948; Gollancz, 1949; Penguin
The Case of the Gilded Fly. Gollancz, 1944; Penguin, 1954 (U.S. title: Obsequies at Oxford. Lippincott, 1945)
Death and Dumb; see Swan Song
Frequent Hearses. Gollancz, 1950 (U.S. title: Sudden Vengeance. Dodd, 1950)
Holy Disorders. Gollancz, 1945; Lippincott, 1946
The Long Divorce. Dodd, 1951; Gollancz, 1951; Penguin
Love Lies Bleeding. Lippincott, 1948
The Moving Toyshop. Gollancz, 1946; Lippincott, 1946
Obsequies at Oxford; see The Case of the Gilded Fly
Sudden Vengeance; see Frequent Hearses
Swan Song. Gollancz, 1947 (U.S. title: Dead and Dumb. Lippincott, 1947)

MONTROSS, DAVID (S)
Fellow-Travelers. Doubleday, 1965; Paperback Lib., 1967

Traitor's Wife. Doubleday, 1962; Paperback Lib., 1967
Troika. Doubleday, 1963; Gollancz, 1964 (Also published as: Who is Elissa Sheldon? Paperback Lib., 1967)
Who Is Elissa Sheldon?; see Troika

MOODEY, MARTHA LIVINGSTON (M)
The Tragedy of Brinkwater. Cassell, 1888

MOODIE, EDWIN (M)
Great Shakes. Museum Press, 1956

MOODY, LAWRENCE (M)
Some Must Die. Hale, R., 1964

MOON, KENNETH (M)
The Fire Serpent Mystery. Benn, 1963

MOORE, AUSTIN, pseud; see MUIR, AUGUSTUS

MOORE, CARLYLE and GEORGE R. JENKS (M)
Stop Thief. Fly, 1913

MOORE, DONALD (S)
Highway of Fear. Hodder, 1961

MOORE, HARRY F. S. (D)
Death at 7:10. Doubleday, Doran, 1943
Murder Goes Rolling. Doubleday, Doran, 1942
Shed a Bitter Tear. Doubleday, Doran, 1944

MOORE, IRVING, see BERGQUIST, LILLIAN

MOORE, PHILIPS (S)
Once upon a Friday. Tower, 1965

MOORE, MRS. WINNIE FIELDS (M)
Wings of Destiny. Wetzel, 1930 (Contains: "Phantom of the Desert," "The Grey Shadow," "The Hand," and "Hightide")

MOORHOUSE, HERBERT JOSEPH (M) (Pseudonym: Hopkins Moorhouse)
The Gauntlet of Alceste. Musson, 1921; Hodder, 1922
The Golden Scarab. Musson, 1926

MOORHOUSE, HOPKINS, pseud; see MOORHOUSE, HERBERT JOSEPH

MORGAN, BETTY (S)
Pursuit. Houghton, 1966

MORGAN, BRYAN (S)
The Business at Blanche Capel. Hamilton, H., 1953; Little, 1954

MORGAN, GEOFFREY (M)
Murderer's Moon. Jenkins, 1942
No Crest for the Wicked. Forbes Robertson, 1952

MORGAN, LORNA NICHOLL (M)
Another Little Murder. MacDonald & Co., 1947
The Death Box. MacDonald & Co., 1946
Murder in Devil's Hollow. World's Work, 1944
Talking of Murder. Harrap, 1945

MORGAN, MICHAEL, pseud; see CARLE, C. E.

MORGAN, MURRAY C. (M) (Pseudonym: Cromwell Murray)
Day of the Dead. McKay, 1946
The Viewless Winds. Dutton, 1949

MORGAN, THOMAS CHRISTOPHER (M) (Pseudonym: John Muir)
Creatures of Satan. Hutchinson, 1958
Crook's Turning. Hutchinson, 1958

MORLAND, NIGEL (D) (Pseudonyms: Mary Dane, John Donavan, Norman Forrest, Roger Garnett, Neal Shepherd, Vincent McCall)
The Big Killing. Foster, W., 1946
Blood on the Stars. Low, 1951
Bullet for Midas: A Mrs. Pym Story. Cassell, 1958
Call Him Early for the Murder: A Mrs. Pym Story. Cassell, 1952
The Careless Hangman; see The Clue of the Careless Hangman
The Case of the Beckoning Dead, by John Donavan. Hale, R., 1938; Hillman-Curl, 1938
The Case of the Coloured Wind, by John Donavan. Hodder, 1939 (U.S. title: The Case of the Violet Smoke. Arcadia, 1940)
The Case of the Innocent Wife. Martin & Reid, 1947
The Case of the Plastic Man, by John Donavan. Hodder, 1940 (U.S. title: The Case of the Plastic Mask. Arcadia, 1940)
The Case of the Plastic Mask; see The Case of the Plastic Man
The Case of the Rusted Room, by John Donavan. Hale, R., 1937
The Case of the Talking Dust, by John Donavan. Hale, R., 1940; Arcadia, 1941
The Case of the Violet Smoke; see The Case of the Coloured Wind
The Case Without a Clue. Cassell, 1938; Farrar & Rinehart, 1938
The Clue in the Mirror. Cassell, 1937; Farrar & Rinehart, 1938

The Clue of the Bricklayer's Aunt. Cassell, 1936; Farrar & Rinehart, 1937
The Clue of the Careless Hangman. Cassell, 1940 (U.S. title: The Careless Hangman. Farrar & Rinehart, 1941)
Coffin for the Body. Cassell, 1943
The Concrete Maze. Cassell, 1960
The Corpse in the Circus. Vallancey, 1945
The Corpse in the Circus and Other Stories. Polybooks, 1946
The Corpse on the Flying Trapeeze: A Mrs. Pym Story. Cassell, 1941
The Corpse Was No Lady. Low, 1950
The Croaker, by Roger Garnett. Wright & Brown, 1938
Danger—Death at Work, by Roger Garnett. Wright & Brown, 1941
The Dead Have No Friends, by John Donavan. Home & Van Thal, 1952
The Dear, Dead Girls: A Mrs. Pym Story. British Book Centre, 1961; Cassell, 1961
Death and the Golden Boy: A Mrs. Pym Story. Cassell, 1958
Death Flies Low, by Neal Shepherd. Constable, 1938
Death for Sale. Hale, R., 1957
Death in Piccadilly, by Roger Garnett. Wright & Brown, 1936
Death Rides Swiftly, by Neal Shepherd. Constable, 1939
Death Spoke Sweetly, by Roger Garnett. Wright & Brown, 1946
Death Takes a Star. Todd, 1943; Vallancey, 1944
Death Takes an Editor. Aldus Pub., 1949
Death Took a Greek God, by Norman Forrest. Harrap, 1937; Hillman-Curl, 1939; Withy Grove, 1946 (Abridged edition)
Death Took a Publisher, by Norman Forrest. Harrap, 1936; Hillman-Curl, 1939; Withy Grove, 1946 (Abridged edition)
Death Traps the Killer, by Mary Dane. Wright & Brown, 1938
Death Walks Softly, by Neal Shepherd. Constable, 1938
Death When She Wakes. Evans, 1951
Death's Sweet Music; see Exit to Music
Dressed to Kill: A Mrs. Pym Story. Cassell, 1947
Dusky Death, by Roger Garnett. Wright & Brown, 1948
Eve Finds the Killer, by Roger Garnett. Martin & Reid, 1947
Exit to Music, by Neal Shepherd. Constable, 1940
Exit to Music and Other Stories. Bonde, A., 1947 (Abridged edition published as: Death's Sweet Music. Century Press, 1947)
Fish Are So Trusting. Century Press, 1948
A Girl Died Singing. Evans, 1952
A Gun for God. Cassell, 1940 (U.S. title: Murder in Wardour Street: A Mrs. Pym Story. Farrar & Rinehart, 1940)
The Hatchet Murders. Martin & Reid, 1947
He Hanged His Mother on Monday. Low, 1951
The Killing of Paris Norton, by Roger Garnett. Wright & Brown, 1940
A Knife for the Killer: A Mrs. Pym Story. Cassell, 1939 (U.S. title: Murder at Radio City. Farrar & Rinehart, 1939)
The Laboratory Murder and Other Stories. Polybooks, 1944
The Lady Had a Gun: A Mrs. Pym Story. Cassell, 1951
Look in Any Doorway: A Mrs. Pym Story. Cassell, 1957
A Man Died Talking, by Roger Garnett. Wright & Brown, 1943
The Moon Murders. Cassell, 1935
The Moon Was Made for Murder. Low, 1953
Murder at Radio City; see A Knife for a Killer
Murder in Wardour Street; see A Gun for a God
Murder Runs Wild. Halle, A., 1946
No Coupons for a Shroud. Low, 1949
Pattern of Murder. Elek, 1964
The Phantom Gunman. Cassell, 1935
Rope for the Hanging: A Mrs. Pym Mystery. Cassell, 1938
She Didn't Like Dying. Low, 1948
Sing a Song of Cyanide: A Mrs. Pym Story. Cassell, 1953
Smash and Grab. Martin & Reid, 1942
So Quiet a Death: A Mrs. Pym Story. Cassell, 1960
The "Soopers" Cases. Todd, 1943
Starr Bedford Dies, by Roger Garnett. Wright & Brown, 1937
Strangely She Died. Jenkins, 1946
The Street of the Leopard. Cassell, 1936
That Nice Miss Smith. Muller, 1958
This Friendless Lady. Muller, 1957
Twenty-six Three Minute Thrillers: A Collection of Ingenious Puzzle Yarns. Martin & Reid, 1947
Two Dead Charwomen. Low, 1949

MORLEY, CHRISTOPHER DARLINGTON (M)
The Haunted Bookshop. Doubleday, Page, 1919; Chapman, 1920

MORLEY, FRANK VIGOR (M)
Death in Dwelly Lane. Harper, 1952 (English title: Dwelly Lane. Eyre, 1952)

MORLEY, WILLIAM (M)
My Dead Wife. S & S, 1948

MOROSO, JOHN ANTONIO (D)
The City of Silent Men. Macaulay, 1913 (Also published as: The Quarry. Little, 1913)
The Listening Man. Appleton, D., 1924
The Quarry; see The City of Silent Men

MORRAH, DERMOT MACGREGOR (D)
The Mummy Case Mystery. Harper, 1933; Musson, 1933 (Also published as: The Mummy Case. Faber, 1934)

MORRIS, ANTHONY P. (D)
Cipher Detective. Westbrook

MORRIS, ARTHUR (M)
The Dealer in Death and Other Stories. Cotton Press, 1897

MORRIS, CHARLES (D) (Pseudonym: Hugh Allen)
The Detective's Crime; or, The Van Peltz Diamonds. Rand, 1887

MORRIS, EDWARD (M)
The Five Fowlers. Bles, 1953
The Plume of Smoke. Bles, 1952
The Small Hotel. Bles, 1953

MORRIS, JEAN (M)
Man and Two Gods. Cassell, 1953; Viking, 1954

MORRIS, JOE ALEX (S)
The Bird Watcher. McKay, 1966

MORRIS, SARA, pseud; see BURKE, JOHN FREDERICK

MORRIS, SHAYNE (M)
Golden Hooves. Ward, Lock, 1952
Horse of Many Colours. Ward, Lock, 1954

MORRIS, THOMAS BADEN (D)
The Blind Bargain. Hale, R., 1957
Crash into Murder. Hale, R., 1961
Death Among the Orchids. Hale, R., 1959
Mandrakes in the Cupboard. Hale, R., 1960
Murder on the Loire. Hale, R., 1964
The Papyrus Murder. Hale, R., 1958
Return of a Traitor. Hale, R., 1962
So Many Dangers. Hale, R., 1960

MORRIS, WALTER FREDERICK (M)
The Channel Mystery. Joseph, M., 1939
The Holdup. Bles, 1933

MORRISON, ALEXANDER (M)
The Crookshaven Murder. Houghton, 1927

MORRISON, ARTHUR (D)
The Adventures of Martin Hewitt. Ward, Lock, 1896
The Chronicles of Martin Hewitt. Appleton, D., 1896; Page, 1907
Cunning Murrell. Doubleday, Page, 1900; Methuen, 1900
The Green Diamond. Wessel, 1903; Page, 1904
The Hole in the Wall. McClure, Phillips, 1902; Hodder, 1947
Martin Hewitt, Investigator. Harper, 1894; Ward, Lock, 1894
The Red Triangle. Nash, 1903; Page, 1903

MORRISON, EMMELINE
Tale Untold. Hutchinson, 1956

MORRISON, HUGO (D)
The Low Road. Methuen, 1930

MORRISON, ROBERTA (S-Gothic)
Tree of Evil. Paperback Lib., 1966

MORRISON, THOMAS JAMES (M) (Pseudonym: Alan Muir)
Death Comes on Derby Day. Jarrolds, 1940

MORRISON, WOODS (M)
Road End. Putnam, 1927

MORRISSEY, JAMES LAWRENCE (M)
Design for Blackmail. Hutchinson, 1935
The Double Problem. Burns, 1932; Mellifont, 1940 (Abridged edition)
High Doom. Hutchinson, 1933; Mellifont, 1939
Necktie for Norman. Gifford, 1949
Off with His Head. Gifford, 1947
Poison Is Queen. Gifford, 1949

MORROW, SUSAN (S)
The Insiders. Doubleday, 1967
The Moonlighters. Doubleday, 1966
Murder May Follow. Collins, 1960; Doubleday, 1960
The Rules of the Game. Doubleday, 1964

MORSE, ANNE CHRISTENSON (M) (Pseudonym: Ann Head)
Always in August. Doubleday, 1961; Hurst, 1964
Everybody Adored Cara. Doubleday, 1963; Hurst, 1964

MORSE, FLORENCE VORPE (M)
Black Eagles Are Flying. Doubleday, Doran, 1943

MORTLOCK, BILL, pseud. (M)
A Planned Coincidence. Gollancz, 1963; Macmillan, 1964

MORTON, ANTHONY, pseud; see CREASEY, JOHN

MORTON, GUY EUGENE (D)
Ashes of Murder. Skeffington, 1935; Greenberg, 1936
Black Gold. Small, 1924
The Black Robe. Minton, 1927
The Burleigh Murders. Skeffington, 1936
The Enemy Within. Saulsbury, 1918
The Forbidden Road. Hodder, 1928
King of the World; or, The Pommeray Case. Hodder, 1927
The Mystery at Hardacres. Skeffington, 1936
The Perrin Murder Case. Greenberg, 1930; Skeffington, 1930
The Ragged Robin Murders. Skeffington, 1935; Greenberg, 1937
The Scarlet Thumb Print. Skeffington, 1931
The Silver-voiced Murder. Skeffington, 1933
Zola's Thirteen. Skeffington, 1930

MORTON, PATRICIA (S)
Destiny's Child. Belmont, 1967
Province of Darkness. Banner, 1967

MORTON, WILLIAM, pseud; see FERGUSON, WILLIAM BLAIR MORTON

MOSELEY, DANA (M)
Dead of Summer. Abelard, 1953; Bodley Head, 1955

MOSER, MAURICE and CHARLES RIDEAL (D)
Stories from Scotland Yard. Routledge, 1890

MOSHER, JOHN S. (M)
Liar Dice. S & S, 1939

MOSKOWITZ, SAM; see ELWOOD, ROGER

MOSLER, BLANCHE Y. (S)
Terror Stalks the Night Nurse. Paperback Lib., 1963

MOSLEY, LEONARD O. (M)
So I Killed Her. Joseph, M., 1936; Doubleday, Doran, 1937

MOSLEY, NICHOLAS (S)
The Assassins. Hodder, 1966; Coward, 1967

MOTT, J. MOLDON (M)
JOHN BLACKBURN
Blue Octavo. Cape, 1963 (U.S. title: Bound to Kill. Mill, 1963)
Bound to Kill; see Blue Octavo
Colonel Bogus. Cape, 1964 (U.S. title: Packed for Murder. Mill, 1964)
Dead Man Running. Mill, 1961; Cape, 1961; Lancer, 1966
The Gaunt Woman. Cape, 1962; Morrow, 1962
Murder at Midnight; see The Winds of Midnight
Packed for Murder; see Colonel Bogus
A Ring of Roses. Cape, 1965 (U.S. title: Wreath of Roses. Lancer, 1965; Mill, 1965)
A Scent of New Mown Hay. Mill, 1958; Secker & Warburg, 1958
A Sour Apple Tree. Cape, 1958; Mill, 1959
The Winds of Midnight. Cape, 1964 (U.S. title: Murder at Midnight. Mill, 1964)
Wreath of Roses; see A Ring of Roses

MOTT, MARIE MURPHY (S)
The Cape Jasmine Story. Vantage, 1963

MOTTE, PETER, pseud; see HARRISON, RICHARD MOTTE

MOWBRAY, JOHN, pseud; see VAHEY, JOHN GEORGE HASLETTE

MOWERY, WILLIAM BYRON (S)
Sagas of the Mounted Police. Bouregy, 1953 (Also published as: Tales of the Mounted Police. Airmont, 1962)

MOYES, PATRICIA (D)
Dead Men Don't Ski. Ballantine, 1965; Collins, 1959; Holt, 1959
Death on the Agenda. Collins, 1962; Holt, 1962; Ballantine, 1965
Down Among the Dead Men. Holt, 1961; Ballantine, 1965
Falling Star. Collins, 1963; Holt, 1964; Ballantine, 1966
Johnny Underground. Holt, 1966; Ballantine, 1967
Murder à la Mode. Holt, 1963; Ballantine, 1966
Murder Fantastical. Holt, 1967
Murder by Threes. Holt, 1965 (Omnibus)
Natural Causes. Scribner, 1967
The Sunken Sailor. Collins, 1961

MUAT, PAGAN (M)
Murder's No Picnic. Gifford, 1947

MUDDOCK, JOYCE EMERSON (D)
(Pseudonym: Dick Donovan)
The Adventures of Tyler Tatlock, Private Detective. Chatto, 1900

Caught at Last! Leaves from the Note-Book of a Detective. Chatto, 1889
The Chronicles of Michael Danevitch of the Russian Secret Service. Chatto, 1897
The Crime of the Century. Being the Life Story of Richard Piggott. Long, 1904
Deacon Brodie; or, Behind the Mask. Chatto, 1901
A Detective's Triumphs. Chatto, 1891
Eugene Vidocq: Soldier, Thief, Spy, Detective. Hutchinson, 1895
The Fatal Ring. Hurst, 1905
For Honor or Death. Ward, Lock, 1910
Found and Fettered. Hutchinson, 1894
From Clue to Capture. Hutchinson, 1893
From Information Received. Chatto, 1892
A Gilded Serpent. The Story of a Dark Deed. Ward, Lock, 1908
The Gold-Spinner. White, 1907
The Great Turf Fraud, and Other Notorious Crimes. Mellifont, 1936
"Jim the Penman." The Life Story of One of the Most Astounding Criminals Who Ever Lived. Newnes, 1901
In the Face of Night. Long, 1908
In the Grip of the Law. Chatto, 1892
In the Queen's Service. Long, 1907
A Knight of Evil. White, 1905
The Knutsford Mystery. White, 1906
Link by Link. Chatto, 1893
The Man from Manchester. Chatto, 1890
The Man-Hunter. Stories from the Note-book of a Detective. Chatto, 1888
The Mystery of Jamaica Terrace. Chatto, 1896
The Records of Vincent Trill of the Detective Service. Chatto, 1899
Riddles Read. Chatto, 1896
Suspicion Aroused. Chatto, 1893
Tales of Terror. Chatto, 1899
Tangled Destinies. Laurie, 1908
Thurtell's Crime: The Story of a Strange Tragedy. Laurie, 1906
Tracked and Taken. Chatto, 1890
Tracked to Doom: The Story of a Mystery and Its Unraveling. Chatto, 1892
The Trap. White, 1911
The Triumphs of Fabian Field: Criminologist. White, 1912
The Turning Wheel: A Story of the Charn Hall Inheritance. White, 1912
Wanted! A Detective's Strange Adventures. Chatto, 1892
Who Poisoned Hetty Duncan? and Other Detective Stories. Chatto, 1890

MUGGERIDGE, MALCOLM (M)
Affairs of the Heart. Hamilton, H., 1949; Walker & Co., 1961; Dell, 1965

MUIR, ALAN, pseud; see MORRISON, THOMAS JAMES

MUIR, AUGUSTUS (Name originally: Charles Augustus Muir) (M) (Pseudonym: Austin Moore)
Ace of Danger. Bobbs, 1927 (English title: Black Pavilion. Methuen, 1935)
Beginning the Adventure. Methuen, 1932 (U.S. title: The Dark Adventure. Putnam, 1933)
Birds of the Night, by Austin Moore. Smith, R. R., 1931
Black Pavillion; see Ace of Danger
The Dark Adventure; see Beginning the Adventure
The House of Lies, by Austin Moore. Doubleday, Doran, 1932; Hodder, 1932
The Shadow on the Left. Bobbs, 1928; Methuen, 1929
The Silent Partner. Bobbs, 1930; Methuen, 1930
The Third Warning. Bobbs, 1925; Methuen, 1925

MUIR, CHARLES AUGUSTUS; see MUIR, AUGUSTUS

MUIR, DENNIS (D)
Death Defies the Doctor. Phoenix, 1944

MUIR, DEXTER, pseud; see GRIBBLE, LEONARD

MUIR, JOHN, pseud; see MORGAN, THOMAS CHRISTOPHER

MUIR, P. P. and E. D. H. TOLLEMACHE (M)
Green Wounds. Boardman, T. V., 1947

MUIR, THOMAS (D)
Death Below Zero. Hutchinson, 1950
Death in Reserve. Hutchinson, 1948
Death in the Lock. Hutchinson, 1949
Death in the Soundings. Hutchinson, 1955
Death on the Agenda. Hutchinson, 1953
Death Under Virgo. Hutchinson, 1952
Death Without Question. Hutchinson, 1951
Trouble Abroad. Hutchinson, 1957

MUKERJI, DHAN GOPAL (M)
Secret Listeners of the East. Dutton, 1926

MULHOLLAND, JOHN; see FITZ-SIMMONS, CORTLAND

MULLALLY, FREDERIC (M)
The Assassins. Barker, 1964; Walker & Co., 1966
Danse Macabre. Secker & Warburg, 1959 (Also published as: Marianne. Viking, 1960; Bantam, 1961)

Death Pays a Dividend. Gollancz, 1944
Marianne; see Danse Macabre

MULLEN, CLARENCE (D)
Thereby Hangs a Corpse. Curl, 1946

MULVIHILL, WILLIAM (S)
The Mantrackers. Signet, 1960
Sands of the Kalahari. Crest, 1965

MUNDIS, HESTER JANE (S-Gothic)
Mercy at the Manor Manor. PB, 1967; Scribner, 1967

MUNDY, MAX (M)
Death is a Tiger. Long, 1960
Dig for a Corpse. Long, 1962

MUNDY, TALBOT (D)
Black Light. Bobbs, 1930; Hutchinson, 1930
Caves of Terror. Hutchinson, 1932
C.I.D. Century, 1932; Hutchinson, 1932
The Devil's Guard. Bobbs, 1926
Jimgrim. Century, 1931; Hutchinson, 1932
The Mystery of Khufu's Tomb. Appleton, D., 1935 (Also published as: Khufu's Real Tomb)
Nine Unknown. Bobbs, 1924
Om: The Secret of Ahbor Valley. Bobbs, 1924
Red Flame of Erinpura. Hutchinson, 1934

MUNRO, HUGH M. (D)
A Clue for Clutha. MacDonald & Co., 1960
Clutha Plays a Hunch. MacDonald & Co., 1959; Washburn, 1959
Who Told Clutha? MacDonald & Co., 1958; Washburn, 1958

MUNRO, JAMES (S)
Die Rich, Die Happy. Hammond, 1966; Knopf, 1966
The Man Who Sold Death. Hammond, 1965; Knopf, 1965; Bantam, 1966

MUNSLOW, BRUCE JAMES (M)
Deep Sand. Hodder, 1955
Joker Take Queen. Long, 1965; Holt, 1966
No Safe Road. Long, 1959; Walker & Co., 1962

MURIEL, JOHN SAINT CLAIR (M)
(Pseudonym: Simon Dewes)
Cul-de-sac. Rich, 1941
Death Stalks the Waterway. Rich, 1946
Panic in Pursuit. Rich, 1945

MURPHY, JOHN, pseud. (S)
The Gunrunners. Macmillan, 1966

MURPHY, MARQUERITE (M)
Borrowed Alibi. Bouregy, 1961

MURPHY, ROBERT and HELEN WILLS (D)
Death Serves an Ace. Hutchinson, 1939; Scribner, 1939
Murder in Waiting. Scribner, 1938

MURRAY, AUDREY ALISON (M)
The Blanket. Vanguard, 1957; Belmont, 1960

MURRAY, CROMWELL, pseud; see MORGAN, MURRAY

MURRAY, MAX (D)
Corpse for Breakfast. Washburn, 1956
The Doctor and the Corpse. Farrar, Straus, 1952; Joseph, M., 1953
Good Luck to the Corpse. Farrar, Straus, 1951; Joseph, M., 1953
The King and the Corpse. Joseph, M., 1949; Farrar, Straus, 1952
The Neat Little Corpse. Farrar, Straus, 1950; Joseph, M., 1951
No Duty for the Corpse. Joseph, M., 1950
The Queen and the Corpse. Farrar, Straus, 1949
The Right Honorable Corpse. Farrar, Straus, 1951; Joseph, M., 1952; Collier, 1965
Royal Bed for a Corpse. Joseph, M., 1955; Washburn, 1955
The Sunshine Corpse. Joseph, M., 1954
The Voice of the Corpse. Farrar, Straus, 1947; Joseph, M., 1948
Wait for a Corpse. Joseph, M., 1957; Washburn, 1957

MURRAY, PAUL (M)
The Free Agent. Holt, H., 1952; Bles, 1953

MURRAY, WILLIAM HUTCHINSON (M)
Appointment in Tibet. Putnam, 1959
Dark Rose the Phoenix. McKay, 1965; Secker & Warburg, 1965
Five Frontiers. Dent, 1959

MYERS, ISABEL BRIGGS (M)
Give Me Death. Stokes, 1934; Gollancz, 1935
Murder Yet Come. Stokes, 1930; Gollancz, 1931

MYERS, PHINEAS BARTON (M)
The Hollywood Murder. Exposition, 1958

NAPIER, MARK, pseud; see LAFFIN, JOHN

NAPIER, N. K. S. (M)
Seaview; or, The Secret Formula. Williams, 1931

NARCEJAC, THOMAS; see BOILEAU, PIERRE

NASH, ANNE (M)
Cabbages and Crime. Doubleday, Doran, 1945; Hammond, 1948
Death by Design. Doubleday, Doran, 1944; Hammond, 1954
Said with Flowers. Doubleday, Doran, 1943; Hammond, 1953
Unhappy Rendezvous. Doubleday, 1946; Hammond, 1951

NASH, CHANDLER, pseud; see HUNT, KATHERINE CHANDLER

NASH, FRANK (M)
The House Cried Murder. Phoenix, 1952

NASH, SIMON, pseud; see CHAPMAN, RAYMOND

NASIELSKI, ADAM (M)
The Ace of Spades. MacDonald & Co., 1943

NASON, LEONARD HASTINGS (M)
Contact Mercury. Doubleday, 1946

NEAL, ADELINE PHYLLIS (M)
(Pseudonym: A. F. Grey)
Momentary Stoppage. Gollancz, 1942

NEBEL, FREDERICK (S)
Fifty Roads to Town. Cape, 1936; Little, 1936
Sleepers East. Little, 1933; Collins, 1934

NEELEY, DETA PETERSON (M)
A Candidate for Hell. Meador, 1939
Through Devil's Gate, with Nathan Glen Neeley. Meador, 1941

NEELEY, NATHAN GLEN; see NEELEY, DETA PETERSON

NEIDIG, WILLIAM JONATHAN (M)
The Fire Fingers. Dodd, 1919

NELMS, HENNING (D) (Pseudonym: Hake Talbot)
Hangman's Handyman. S & S, 1942
Rim of the Pit. S & S, 1944; Bantam, 1965

NELSON, CHOLMONDELEY M. (M)
Barren Harvest. Doubleday, 1949

NELSON, COUTTS (M)
What Old Father Thames Said. Tinsley, S., 1876 (3 Vols.)

NELSON, HUGH LAURENCE (D)
Copper Lady. Rinehart, 1947
Dark Echo. Rinehart, 1949
Dead Giveaway. Rinehart, 1950; Dell
The Fence. Rinehart, 1953
Fountain of Death. Rinehart, 1948
Gold in Every Grave. Rinehart, 1951
Island of Escape. Rinehart, 1948
Kill with Care. Rinehart, 1953
Murder Comes High. Rinehart, 1950
Ring the Bell at Zero. Rinehart, 1949
The Season for Murder. Rinehart, 1952 (Also included in Death and Detection. Benn, 1957; McClelland, 1957)
Sleep Is Deep. Rinehart, 1952
Suspect. Rinehart, 1954
Title Is Murder. Rinehart, 1947

NELSON, MARG (M)
Mystery at Little Squaw River. Berkley Pub., 1966

NESBIT, E. (M)
Something Wrong. Innes, 1893

NEUBAUER, WILLIAM (M)
The Golden Heel. Arcadia, 1965
This Darkling Love. Arcadia, 1966

NEUMANN, ROBERT (M)
The Inquest. Dutton, 1945

NEVILLE, ALLISON BARBARA (D)
(Pseudonym: Edward Candy)
Bones of Contention. Gollancz, 1952
Congo Venus. S & S, 1950
Which Doctor? Gollancz, 1953; Rinehart, 1954

NEVILLE, MARGOT, pseud; see GOYDER, MARGOT

NEW, CLARENCE HERBERT (M)
The Unseen Hand. Doubleday, Page, 1918

NEWBERRY, PERRY; see MacGOWAN, ALICE

NEWBY, PERCY HOWARD (M)
The Loot Runners. Lehmann, 1949

NEWELL, AUDREY (D)
Murder Is Not Mute. Macrae Smith, 1940
Who Killed Cavellotti? Century, 1930

NEWLAND, N. M. (D)
Walk to Your Grave. Phoenix, 1951

NEWMAN, BERNARD CHARLES (D)
(Pseudonym: Don Betteridge)
Balkan Spy, by Don Betteridge. Jenkins, 1942
Case of the Berlin Spy, by Don Betteridge. Hale, R., 1954
Cast Iron Alibi, by Don Betteridge. Jenkins, 1939
Centre Court Murder. Gollancz, 1951
Contact Man, by Don Betteridge. Hale, R., 1960

Cup Final Murder. Gollancz, 1951
Dead Man Murder. Gollancz, 1946
Death at Lord's, by Don Betteridge. Gollancz, 1952
Death of a Harlot, by Don Betteridge. Laurie, 1934
Death to the Fifth Column, by Don Betteridge. Gollancz, 1939
Death to the Spy. Gollancz, 1939
Death Under Gibraltar, by Don Betteridge. Gollancz, 1938
Dictator's Destiny, by Don Betteridge. Jenkins, 1945
Double Menace, by Don Betteridge. Hale, R., 1954
Escape of General Gerard, by Don Betteridge. Jenkins, 1943
German Spy, by Don Betteridge. Gollancz, 1936
Gibraltar Conspiracy, by Don Betteridge. Hale, R., 1955
Lady Doctor—Woman Spy, by Don Betteridge. Hutchinson, 1937
Maginot Line Murder. Gollancz, 1939 (U.S. title: Papa Pontivy and the Maginot Murder. Holt, H., 1940)
Moscow Murder, by Don Betteridge. Gollancz, 1948
Mussolini Murder Plot. Hillman-Curl, 1939
Not Single Spies, by Don Betteridge. Hale, R., 1951
The Otan Plot. Brown, Watson, 1963
The Package Holiday Spy Case, by Don Betteridge. Hale, R., 1962
Papa Pontivy and the Maginot Murder; see Maginot Line Murder
Potsdam Murder Plot, by Don Betteridge. Jenkins, 1947
Scotland Yard Alibi, by Don Betteridge
Secret Servant, by Don Betteridge. Gollancz, 1935
Secret Weapon, by Don Betteridge. Gollancz, 1941
Siegfred Spy, by Don Betteridge. Gollancz, 1940
Spies Left, by Don Betteridge. Hale, R., 1950
The Spies of Peenemünde, by Don Betteridge. Hale, R., 1958
Spy, by Don Betteridge. Appleton-Century, 1935; Gollancz, 1935
The Spy Catchers, by Don Betteridge. Gollancz, 1945
Spy-Counter Spy, by Don Betteridge. Hale, R., 1953
The Spy in the Brown Derby, by Don Betteridge. Gollancz, 1945

NEWMAN, ROBERT (S)
The Enchanter. Paperback Lib., 1967

NEWMAN, RONALD M. (M)
The Man with a Million Pounds. Hutchinson, 1923

NEWMAN, TERRY
Raphael Resurrection. Eyre, 1954

NEWTON, MACDONALD (M)
To Have and To Hold. Boardman, T. V., 1963

NEWTON, WILFRID DOUGLAS (M)
Black Finger. Mellifont, 1940
The Crime Specialist. Mellifont, 1942
Dark Pathway. Cassell, 1938
Double Crossed. Appleton, D., 1922
Falcon of the Foreign Office. Mellifont, 1940
The Golden Cat. Cassell, 1930
Green Ladies. Hurst, 1919
The Jade-Green Garter. Cassell, 1929
Laughing Gangster. Pemberton, T. A. & E., 1948
The Red Judas. Cassell, 1934

NIALL, MICHAEL, pseud; see BRESLIN, HOWARD

NICHOLAI, CHARLES (M)
Murder in the Fine Arts. Hammond, 1964

NICHOLAS, JEROME (M)
The Asbestos Mask. Hodder, 1948

NICHOLAS, ROBERT (M)
The White Shroud. Collins, 1961

NICHOLS, BEVERLY, pseud; see NICHOLS, JOHN BEVERLY

NICHOLS, FAN, pseud; see HANNA, MRS. FRANCES NICHOLS

NICHOLS, JOHN BEVERLY (M)
(Pseudonym: Beverly Nichols)
Death to Slow Music. Dutton, 1956; Hutchinson, 1956
The Moonflower; see The Moonflower Murder
The Moonflower Murder. Dutton, 1955 (English title: The Moonflower. Hutchinson, 1955)
Murder by Request. Dutton, 1960; Hutchinson, 1960
No Man's Street. Dutton, 1954; Hutchinson, 1954
The Rich Die Hard. Dutton, 1957; Hutchinson, 1957

NICHOLS, PETER, pseud. (M)
Patchwork of Death. Holt, 1965

NICHOLSON, JOHN URBAN (M)
Fingers of Fear. Covici, 1937; Paperback Lib., 1966

NICHOLSON, MEREDITH (M)
The House of a Thousand Candles. Bobbs, 1905

The Port of Missing Men. Bobbs, 1907
The Seige of Seven Suitors. Constable, 1910; Houghton, 1910

NICOLE, CHRISTOPHER (S) (Pseudonym: Andrew York)
The Co-ordinator. Lippincott, 1967
The Eliminator. Lippincott, 1966

NICOLET, CHARLES CATHCART (M)
Death of a Bridge Expert. S & S, 1932; Gollancz, 1933

NIELSON, HELEN BERNIECE (D-M) (Pseudonym: Kris Giles)
After Midnight. Morrow, 1966; Gollancz, 1967
Borrow the Night. Morrow, 1956; Gollancz, 1957
The Crime Is Murder. Gollancz, 1957; Morrow, 1957
Dead on the Level; see Gold Coast Nocturne
Detour. Washburn, 1953
False Witness. Washburn, 1958; Ballantine, 1959
The Fifth Caller. Gollancz, 1959; Morrow, 1959
Gold Coast Nocturne. Washburn, 1952 (Also published as: Dead on the Level. Dell)
A Killer in the Streets. Morrow, 1967
The Kind Man. Washburn, 1951
Murder by Proxy. Gollancz, 1952
Obit Delayed. Washburn, 1953
Sing Me a Murder. Morrow, 1960; Gollancz, 1961; Ace, 1962
Stranger in the Dark. Washburn, 1955
Verdict Suspended. Morrow, 1964
Woman Missing and Other Stories. Ace, 1962 (Also includes: Sing Me a Murder)
The Woman on the Roof. Washburn, 1954; Dell

NIELSON, VIRGINIA (S)
Dangerous Dream. Bouregy, 1961

NILE, DOROTHEA, pseud; see AVALLONE, MICHAEL ANGELO, JR.

NISOT, MAVIS ELIZABETH HOCKING (M) (Pseudonym: William Penmare)
Alixe Derring. Paul, S., 1934
Extenuating Circumstances. Paul, S., 1937
False Witness. Paul, S., 1938
Hazardous Holiday. Paul, S., 1936
The Scorpion, by William Penmare. Hodder, 1929
Shortly Before Midnight. Paul, S., 1934
The Sleepless Men. Doubleday, 1959
Twelve to Dine. Paul, S., 1935
Unnatural Deeds. Paul, S., 1939

NISTLER, ERWIN N. and GERRY P. BRODERICK (S)
Roadside Night. Pyramid, 1963

NITSUA, BENJAMIN, pseud; see AUSTIN, BENJAMIN FISH

NOEL L., pseud; see BARKER, LEONARD

NOEL, STERLING (S)
Empire of Evil. Avon, 1961
Few Die Well. Farrar, Straus, 1953; Hale, R., 1954
I Killed Stalin. Farrar, Straus, 1951; Hale, R., 1952
Intrigue in Paris; see Storm over Paris
Run for Your Life. Avon, 1958
Storm over Paris. Farrar, Straus, 1955 (Also published as: Intrigue in Paris. Avon)

NOLAN, JEANETTE COVERT (M)
A Fearful Way to Die. Washburn, 1956; Muller, 1957
Final Appearance. Duell, 1943
I Can't Die Here. Messner, 1945
Profile in Gilt. Funk, 1941
Sudden Squall. Washburn, 1955

NONWEILER, ARVILLE (D)
Murder on the Pike. Phoenix, 1944

NOONE, EDWINA, pseud; see AVALLONE, MICHAEL ANGELO, JR.

NOONE, JOHN (S)
The Man with the Chocolate Egg. Grove, 1966

NORMAN, BRUCE (M)
Black Pawn. Dial, 1927; Arrowsmith, 1930
Thousand Hands. Dial, 1927; Arrowsmith, 1930

NORMAN, CHARLES (D)
The Genteel Murderer. Macmillan, 1956; Collier, 1963

NORMAN, EARL (S)
Kill Me in Atami. Berkley Pub., 1962
Kill Me in Shimbashi. Berkley Pub., 1959, 1961
Kill Me in Shinjuku. Berkley Pub., 1961
Kill Me in Tokyo. Berkley Pub., 1959
Kill Me in Yokahoma. Berkley Pub., 1960
Kill Me in Yoshiwara. Berkley Pub., 1961
Kill Me on the Ginza. Berkley Pub., 1962

NORMAN, JAMES, pseud; see SCHMIDT, JAMES NORMAN

NORRIS, FRANK (M)
Third Circle. Lane, 1909

NORRIS, KATHLEEN (M)
The Black Flemings. Doubleday, Page, 1926 (Also published as: Gabrielle. Paperback Lib., 1965)
Gabrielle; see The Black Flemings
Mystery House. Doubleday, Doran, 1939; Paperback Lib., 1965
The Secrets of Hilliard House. Doubleday, 1947; Paperback Lib., 1965 (English title: Romance at Hillyard House. Murray, J., 1948)
The Secret of the Marshbanks. Doubleday, Doran, 1940; Paperback Lib., 1965

NORRIS, WILLIAM EDWARD (M)
Obstinate Lady. Brentano, 1919; Hutchinson, 1919
Troubled Tranton. Constable, 1915; Brentano, 1916

NORSWORTHY, GEORGE (D)
The Crime at the Villa Gloria. Greenberg, 1936; Low, 1936
House-Party Mystery. Low, 1935
Murder at Mulberry Cottage. Low, 1937
Murder in Sussex. Hutchinson, 1940

NORTH, ANDRÉ, pseud; see NORTON, ALICE MARY

NORTH, BARCLAY, pseud; see HUDSON, WILLIAM C.

NORTH, ERIC, pseud; see CRONIN, BERNARD

NORTH, GIL, pseud; see HORNE, GEOFFREY

NORTH, GILBERT CHARLES (M)
Beware of the Dog. Morrow, 1939

NORTH, WILLIAM (M) (Pseudonym: Ralph Rodd)
The Claverton Case. Mellifont, 1940
Midnight Murder. Collins, 1931
The Secret of the Flames. Collins, 1924; MacVeagh, 1929
Without Judge or Jury. Collins, 1928; Dial, 1929

NORTON, ALICE MARY (Pseudonym: André North. Joint pseudonym with Grace Allen Hogarth: Allen Weston)
At Sword's Point, by André North. Harcourt, 1954
Murders for Sale, by Allen Weston. Hammond, 1951

NORTON, BROWNING (D)
I Prefer Murder. Graphic, 1956

NORWAY, NEVIL SHUTE (M) (Pseudonym: Nevil Shute)
So Disdained. Cassell, 1928 (U.S. title: Mysterious Aviator. Houghton, 1929)

NORWOOD, JOHN, pseud; see STARK, RAYMOND

NOTLEY, JOHN FRANKE (M)
Corruption in Cantock. Jarrolds, 1941
Murder Has an Echo. Arcadia, 1945

NYLAND, GENTRY (M)
Mr. Smith Burned His Mouth. Morrow, 1946
Run for Your Money. Long, 1941

OAKLEY, JOHN; see OAKLEY, NANCY

OAKLEY, NANCY and JOHN OAKLEY (D)
The Clevedon Case. Jenkins, 1928

O'BRIAN, FRANK, pseud; see GARFIELD, BRIAN

O'BRIEN, FITZ JAMES (M)
What Was It? and Other Stories. Ward & Downey, 1889

O'BRIEN, HOWARD VINCENT (D)
Four-and-twenty Blackbirds. Doubleday, Doran, 1928; Hodder, 1928

O'BRINE, PADRAIC MANNING (M)
Corpse to Cairo. Hammond, 1952
Dead as a Dodo; see Dodos Don't Duck
Deadly Interlude. Hammond, 1954
Dodos Don't Duck. Hammond, 1953 (Also published as: Dead as a Dodo)
The Hungry Killer. Hammond, 1956
Killers Must Eat. Hammond, 1951
Passport to Treason. Hammond, 1955

O'CALLAGHAN, DIMITRI (M)
The Scavengers. Paperback Lib.

O'CONNELL, CHARLES CHRISTOPHER (M)
The Vanishing Island. Talbot, 1957; Devin-Adair, 1958

O'CONNOR, JOHN MARSHALL (M)
Anonymous Footsteps. Cheshire, 1932

O'CONNOR, RAMONCITA SAYER (M)
Murder Won't Wait. Arcadia, 1953

O'CONNOR, RICHARD (S) (Pseudonyms: Frank Archer, Patrick Wayland)
Counterstroke, by Patrick Wayland. Doubleday, 1964
Double Defector, by Patrick Wayland. Doubleday, 1964
The Malabang Pearl, by Frank Archer. Doubleday, 1964

Out of the Blue, by Frank Archer. Doubleday, 1964
Turquoise Spike, by Frank Archer. GM, 1967
The Waiting Game, by Patrick Wayland. Doubleday, 1965
The Widow Watchers, by Frank Archer. Doubleday, 1965

O'CUILLEANIAN, MRS. CORMAC O. (M) (Pseudonym: Eilis Dillon)
Bitter Glass. Appleton, 1958; British Book Centre, 1958; Faber, 1958
Death at Crane's Court. Faber, 1953; Walker & Co., 1963
Sent to His Account. Faber, 1954; British Book Centre, 1961

ODELL, WILLIAM; see MARLOWE, DAN J.

ODLUM, JEROME (S)
Each Dawn I Die. Bobbs, 1938; Grosset, 1939
Mirabilis Diamond. Scribner, 1945
The Morgue Is Always Open. Scribner, 1944
Night and No Moon. Allen, T., 1942; Howell, Soskin, 1942
Nine Lives Are Not Enough. Sheridan, 1940; Boardman, T. V., 1944

O'DONNELL, ELLIOTT (M)
Jennie Barlowe, Adventuress. Greening, 1906
Murder at Hide and Seek. Eldon, 1945

O'DONNELL, LILLIAN (M)
Babes in the Woods. Abelard, 1965
Death Blanks the Screen. Arcadia, 1960
Death of a Player. Abelard, 1965
Death on the Grass. Arcadia, 1960
Death Schuss. Abelard, 1963
Murder Under the Sun. Abelard, 1964
The Sleeping Beauty Murders. Abelard, 1967

O'DONNELL, PETER (S)
Modesty Blaise. Doubleday, 1965; Souvernir, 1965; Crest, 1966
I, Lucifer. Doubleday, 1967
Sabre Tooth. Doubleday, 1966; Crest, 1967

O'DONNELL, S.
Great Diamond Robbery. Ogilvie

O'DUFFY, EIMAR ULTAN (D)
The Bird Cage. Bles, 1932; Kinsey, 1933
Head of a Girl. Bles, 1935
Secret Enemy. Bles, 1933

OELLRICHS, INEZ HILDAGARD (M)
And Die She Did. Doubleday, Doran, 1945; Hammond, 1953
Death in a Chilly Corner. Hammond, 1964
Death of a White Witch. Doubleday, 1949; Hammond, 1953
Kettel Mill Mystery. Doubleday, Doran, 1939; Davies, 1940
Man Who Didn't Answer. Davies, 1939; Doubleday, Doran, 1939
Murder Comes at Night. Doubleday, Doran, 1940; Hammond, 1955
Murder Helps. McKay, 1947
Murder Makes Us Gay. Doubleday, Doran, 1941; Hammond, 1956

O'FARRELL, WILLIAM (S) (Pseudonym: William Grew)
Brandy for a Hero. Duell, 1948
Causeway to the Past. Duell, 1950; Transworld, 1954
The Devil His Due. Doubleday, 1955; Hale, R., 1955
Doubles in Death, by William Grew. Doubleday, 1953
Grow Young and Die. Doubleday, 1952; Dakers, 1954
Gypsy, Go Home. GM, 1962
Harpoon of Death; see The Snakes of St. Cyr
Murder Has Many Faces, by William Grew. Graphic, 1955
Repeat Performance. Houghton, 1942; Allen, W. H., 1948
The Secret Fear. Transworld, 1954
The Snakes of St. Cyr. Duell, 1951 (English title: Harpoon of Death. Dakers, 1953)
These Arrows Point to Death. Duell, 1951; Foulsham, 1952
The Thin Edge of Violence. Duell, 1949
The Ugly Woman. Duell, 1948; Collier, 1966
Walk the Dark Bridge. Doubleday, 1953
Wetback. Dell, 1956

OFFORD, LEONORE GLEN (D)
And Turned to Clay. Jarrolds, 1950
Clues to Burn. Duell, 1942; Grayson, 1943
Distinguished Visitors. Eldon, 1943
The Glass Mask. Duell, 1944; Jarrolds, 1946; Dell
Murder Before Breakfast. Jarrolds, 1938
Murder on Russian Hill. Macrae Smith, 1938
My True Love Lies. Duell, 1947
Nine Dark Hours. Duell, 1941; Eldon, 1941
The Skeleton Key. Duell, 1943; Books, 1944; Eldon, 1944
The Smiling Tiger. Jarrolds, 1951
Walking Shadow. S & S, 1959

O'FINN, THADDEUS, pseud; see McGLOIN, JOSEPH THADDEUS

O'FLAHERTY, LIAM (S)
The Informer. Harcourt, 1925

OGBURN, DOROTHY (M)
Death on the Mountain. Little, 1931
Ra-Ta-Plan! Little, 1930; Grayson, 1931; Grosset, 1931
The Will and the Deed. Dodd, 1935

OGNALL, LEOPOLD HORACE (M-D)
(Pseudonyms: Harry Carmichael, Hartley Howard)
Alibi, by Harry Carmichael. Collins, 1961; Macmillan, 1962
The Armitage Secret, by Hartley Howard. Collins, 1959
The Big Snatch, by Hartley Howard. Collins, 1958
Bowman at a Venture, by Hartley Howard. Collins, 1954
Bowman on Broadway, by Hartley Howard. Collins, 1954
Bowman Strikes Again, by Hartley Howard. Collins, 1953
The Bowman Touch, by Hartley Howard. Collins, 1956
Confession, by Harry Carmichael. Collins, 1961
Countdown, by Hartley Howard. Collins, 1962
Dead of the Night, by Harry Carmichael. Collins, 1956
Deadline, by Hartley Howard. Collins, 1959
Deadly Night-Cap, by Harry Carmichael. Collins, 1953
Death Counts Three, by Harry Carmichael. Collins, 1954
Death Leaves a Diary, by Harry Carmichael. Collins, 1952
Death of Cecilia, by Hartley Howard. Collins, 1952
Double Finesse, by Hartley Howard. Collins, 1962
Emergency Exit, by Harry Carmichael. Collins, 1957
Extortion, by Hartley Howard. Collins, 1960
Fall Guy, by Hartley Howard. Collins, 1960
A Hearse for Cinderella, by Hartley Howard. Collins, 1956
I'm No Hero, by Hartley Howard. Collins, 1961
Into Thin Air, by Harry Carmichael. Doubleday, 1957
James Knowland, Deceased, by Harry Carmichael. Collins, 1958
Justice Enough, by Harry Carmichael. Collins, 1956
Key to the Morgue, by Hartley Howard. Collins, 1957
The Last Appointment, by Hartley Howard. Collins, 1957
The Last Deception, by Hartley Howard. Collins, 1952
The Last Vanity, by Hartley Howard. Collins, 1951
The Late Unlamented, by Harry Carmichael. Doubleday, 1961
The Link, by Harry Carmichael. Collins, 1962
The Long Night, by Hartley Howard. Collins, 1957
Marked Man, by Harry Carmichael. Doubleday, 1959
Money for Murder, by Harry Carmichael. Collins, 1955
No Target for Bowman, by Hartley Howard. Collins, 1955
Noose for a Lady, by Harry Carmichael. Collins, 1955
Of Unsound Mind, by Harry Carmichael. Doubleday, 1962
Or Be He Dead, by Harry Carmichael. Doubleday, 1958; Collins, 1959
The Other Side of the Door, by Hartley Howard. Collins, 1953
Post Mortem, by Harry Carmichael. Doubleday, 1966
Put Out That Star, by Harry Carmichael. Collins, 1957
A Question of Time, by Harry Carmichael. Collins, 1958
Requiem for Charles, by Harry Carmichael. Collins, 1960
Safe Secret, by Harry Carmichael. Macmillan, 1964
School for Murder, by Harry Carmichael. Collins, 1953
The Screaming Rabbit, by Harry Carmichael. S & S, 1955
Seeds of Hate, by Harry Carmichael. Collins, 1960
Sleep for the Wicked, by Hartley Howard. Collins, 1955
Sleep My Pretty One, by Hartley Howard. Collins, 1958
Stranglehold, by Harry Carmichael. Collins, 1959
The Stretton Case, by Hartley Howard. Collins, 1963
Time Bomb, by Hartley Howard. Collins, 1961
The Vanishing Trick, by Harry Carmichael. Collins, 1952
Vendetta, by Harry Carmichael. Macmillan, 1963
Why Kill Johnny?, by Harry Carmichael. Collins, 1954

O'GRADY, ROHAN, pseud; see SKINNER, JUNE O'GRADY

O'HANLON, JAMES D. (D)
As Good as Murdered. Random, 1940; Withy Grove, 1941

Murder at Coney Island. Phoenix, 1939
Murder at Horsethief. Boardman, T. V., 1943
Murder at Malibu. Phoenix, 1937
Murder at 300 to 1. Long, 1939

O'HARA, KENNETH (M)
Double Cross Purposes. Cassell, 1962
Sleeping Dogs Lying. Macmillan, 1962
Underhandover. Cassell, 1961; Macmillan, 1963
View to Death. Cassell, 1958

O'HARA, KEVIN, pseud; see CUMBERLAND, MARTEN

O'HIGGINS, HARVEY JERROLD (D)
Adventures of Detective Barney. Century, 1915
Detective Duff Unravels It. Liveright, 1929

OLAY, LIONEL (M)
Dark Corners of the Night. Signet, 1960

OLDFELD, PETER, pseud; see JACOBSSON, PER

OLDFIELD, CLAUDE HOUGHTON (M) (Pseudonym: Claude Houghton)
The Clock Ticks. Hutchinson, 1954
The Enigma of Conrad Stone. Collins, 1952
A Hair Divides. Butterworth, T., 1931; Doubleday, Doran, 1931
I Am Jonathan Scrivener. Butterworth, T., 1930; S & S, 1930

OLESKER, HARRY (M)
Exit Dying. Random, 1959; Dell, 1960
Impact. Random, 1961; Dell, 1965
Now Will You Try for Murder? S & S, 1958; Boardman, T. V., 1959

OLIPHANT, MARGARET (S)
Stories of the Seen and the Unseen. Blackwood, 1881; Roberts, 1889

OLIVER, GAIL, pseud; see SCOTT, MARIAN GALLAGHER

OLIVER, GEORGE (M) (Pseudonym: Oliver Onions)
Case in Camera. Macmillan, 1921

OLIVER, JOHN (D)
Detection in a Topper. Joseph, M., 1936

OLIVER, N. T. (M)
The Whitechapel Mystery. Eagle Pub., 1889

OLMSTED, LORENA ANN (M)
Cover of Darkness. Bouregy, 1961
Death Walked In. Bouregy, 1960
Footsteps of the Cat. Bouregy, 1963
Setup for Murder. Bouregy, 1962
To Love a Stranger. Bouregy, 1964

OLSEN, D. B., pseud; see HITCHENS, DOLORES B.

O'MAHONY, CHARLES KINGSTON (M) (Pseudonym: Charles Kingston)
The Brighton Beach Mystery. Ward, Lock, 1936
The Circle of Guilt. Ward, Lock, 1937
Death Came Back. Paul, S., 1944
The Delacott Mystery. Ward, Lock, 1941
Fear Followed. Paul, S., 1945
The Great London Mystery. Lane, 1931
The Guilty House. Lane, 1928; Withy Grove, 1941
The Highgate Mystery. Lane, 1928; Mellifont, 1936
I Accuse. Mellifont, 1939
The Infallible System. Lane, 1929; Mellifont, 1948
The Law-Breakers. Lane, 1930; Withy Grove, 1938
A Miscarriage of Justice. Paul, S., 1925
Murder in Disguise. Ward, Lock, 1938
Murder in Piccadilly. Ward, Lock, 1936
Murder Tunes In. Ward, Lock, 1942
Mystery in the Mist. Ward, Lock, 1942
Poison in Kensington. Ward, Lock, 1934
The Portland Place Mystery. Paul, S., 1925; Federation Press, 1926
The Rigdale Puzzle. Ward, Lock, 1937
The Secret Barrier. Ward, Lock, 1939
Six Under Suspicion. Ward, Lock, 1940
Slander Villa. Ward, Lock, 1939

O'MALLEY, FRANK, pseud; see O'ROURKE, FRANK

O'MALLEY, LADY MARY DOLLING SAUNDERS (S) (Pseudonym: Ann Bridge)
The Dangerous Islands. McGraw, 1963; Chatto, 1964
The Dark Moment. Macmillan, 1952
Emergency in the Pyrenees. McGraw, 1965; Berkley Pub., 1966
Episode at Toledo. Chatto, 1966; Berkley Pub., 1967; McGraw, 1967
Julia Involved. McGraw, 1962
The Numbered Account. McGraw, 1960
The Portuguese Escape. Chatto, 1958
Singing Waters. Macmillan, 1946
The Tightening String. McGraw, 1962

O'MALLEY, PATRICK (D)
The Affair of the Blue Pig. Morrow, 1965

The Affair of the Bumbling Briton. Mill, 1965
The Affair of Chief Strongheart. Mill, 1964
The Affair of John Donne. McLeod, 1964; Mill, 1964
The Affair of Jolie Madame. Mill, 1963
The Affair of Swan Lake. Mill, 1962
The Affair of the Red Mosaic. Mill, 1961

O'MEARA, WALTER (S)
Minnesota Gothic. Macfadden, 1956 (Also published as: Castle Danger. Macfadden, 1966)

O'NEIL, KERRY, pseud; see MacINTYRE, JOHN THOMAS

O'NEILL, DESMOND (M)
Life Has No Price. Dodd, 1959; Gollancz, 1959

ONIONS, OLIVER, pseud; see OLIVER, GEORGE

"OPERATOR FIVE" (S)
The Army of the Dead. Corinth, 1966
Blood Reign of the Dictator. Corinth, 1966
Hosts of the Flaming Death. Corinth, 1966
Invasion of the Yellow Warlords. Corinth, 1966
Legions of the Dead Master. Corinth, 1966
March of the Flame Marauders. Corinth, 1966
Master of Broken Men. Corinth, 1966

OPPENHEIM, EDWARD PHILLIPS (M-S-D) (Pseudonym: Anthony Partridge)
Aaron Rodd, Diviner. Hodder, 1920; Little, 1927
The Adventures of Mr. Joseph P. Cray. Hodder, 1925; Little, 1927
Advice Limited. Hodder, 1935; Little, 1936
Amazing Judgment. Downey, 1897
The Amazing Partnership. Cassell, 1914
The Amazing Quest of Mr. Ernest Bliss. Hodder, 1921 (U.S. title: The Curious Quest. Little, 1919)
Ambrose Lavendale, Diplomat. Hodder, 1920
The Amiable Charlatan. Little, 1916
And Still I Cheat the Gallows. Hodder, 1939
Anna, the Adventuress. Little, 1904; Ward, Lock, 1904
As a Man Lives. Ward, Lock, 1898; Little, 1908 (Also published as: Yellow House. Doscher, 1908)
Ask Miss Mott. Hodder, 1936; Little, 1937
The Avenger. Little, 1908
The Bank Manager; see The Man Without Nerves
Battle of Basinghall Street. Hodder, 1935; Little, 1935
The Betrayal. Dodd, 1904; Ward, Lock, 1904
The Bird of Paradise; see The Floating Peril
The Black Box. Grosset, 1915; Hodder, 1917
The Black Watcher. Hodder, 1921 (Also published as: Kingdom of Earth, by Anthony Partridge. Little, 1909; Mills & Boon, 1909)
Blackman's Wood. Readers' Lib., 1929 (with Underdog by Agatha Christie)
The Box with Broken Seals. Little, 1919 (English title: The Strange Case of Mr. Jocelyn Thew. Hodder, 1920)
Burglars Must Dine. Todd, 1943; Vallencey, 1945
The Channay Syndicate. Hodder, 1927; Little, 1927
The Chronicles of Melhampton. Hodder, 1928
The Cinema Murder. Little, 1917 (English title: The Other Romilly. Hodder, 1918)
Clowns and Criminals. Little, 1931
The Colossus of Arcadia. Hodder, 1938; Little, 1938
The Conspirators. Ward, Lock, 1907
The Court of St. Simon, by Anthony Partridge. Little, 1912
The Crooks in the Sunshine. Hodder, 1932; Little, 1933
The Curious Happenings to the Rooke Legatees. Hodder, 1937; Little, 1938
The Curious Quest; see The Amazing Quest of Mr. Ernest Bliss
A Daughter of Astrea. Arrowsmith, 1884, 1930; Collier, 1910
A Daughter of the Marionis. Ward & Downey, 1895; Ward, Lock, 1901, 1934; Little, 1920
The Devil's Paw. Little, 1920; Hodder, 1921
The Distributors, by Anthony Partridge. McClure, 1908 (Also published as: Ghosts of Society. Hodder, 1908)
The Double Four. Cassell, 1911 (See also Peter Ruff)
The Double Life of Mr. Alfred Burton. Little, 1913; Methuen, 1914, 1934
The Double Traitor. Little, 1915; Hodder, 1918
The Dumb Gods Speak. Hodder, 1937; Little, 1937
Enoch Stone. Little, 1901 (English title: A Master of Men. Methuen, 1901)
Envoy Extraordinary. Hodder, 1937; Little, 1937

The Evil Shepherd. Little, 1922; Hodder, 1923
Ex-Detective. Hodder, 1933; Little, 1933
The Ex-Duke; see The Interlopers
Exit a Dictator. Hodder, 1939; Little, 1939
Expiation. Maxwell, J & R, 1887; Ward, Lock, 1913
The Exploits of Pudgy Pete & Co. Hodder, 1928
A Falling Star; see The Moving Finger
False Evidence. Ward, Lock, 1896
The Floating Peril. Little, 1936; New York Post, 1936 (English title: The Bird of Paradise. Hodder, 1936)
For the Queen. Ward, Lock, 1912; Little, 1913
The Fortunate Wayfarer. Hodder, 1928; Little, 1928
Gabriel Samara, Peacemaker. Hodder, 1925; Little, 1925
The Gallows of Chance. Hodder, 1934; Little, 1934
The Game of Liberty. Cassell, 1915
General Besserley's Puzzle Box. Hodder, 1935; Little, 1935
General Besserley's Second Puzzle Box. Hodder, 1939; Little, 1940
Ghosts of Society; see The Distributors
The Glenlitten Murder. Hodder, 1929; Little, 1929
The Golden Beast. Hodder, 1926; Little, 1926
The Golden Web, by Anthony Partridge. Little, 1911; Burt, 1913; Lloyds, 1918; Hodder, 1925
The Governors. Ward, Lock, 1908
The Grassleys Mystery. Hodder, 1940; Little, 1940
The Great Awakening. Ward, Lock, 1902 (Also published as: A Sleeping Memory. Dillingham, G. W., 1902)
The Great Impersonation. Hodder, 1920; Little, 1921; Popular Lib., 1964
The Great Prince Shan. Hodder, 1922; Little, 1922
The Great Secret; see The Secret
Harvey Garrard's Crime. Little, 1926; Hodder, 1927
Havoc. Little, 1911; Hodder, 1912
The Hillman. Little, 1917; Methuen, 1917, 1933
The Honorable Algernon Knox, Detective. Hodder, 1920
The Human Chase. Hodder, 1929
The Illustrious Prince. Hodder, 1910; Burt, 1913
The Inevitable Millionaires. Hodder, 1923; Little, 1925
Inspector Dickens Retires. Hodder, 1931
The Interlopers. Little, 1927 (English title: The Ex-Duke. Hodder, 1927)
Jacob's Ladder. Hodder, 1921; Little, 1921
Jeane of the Marshes. Little, 1909; Ward, Lock, 1934
Jennerton & Co. Hodder, 1928
Jeremiah and the Princess. Hodder, 1933
Judy of Bunter's Building; see The Magnificent Hoax
Kingdom of Earth, by Anthony Partridge. Little, 1909; Mills & Boon, 1909 (English title: The Black Watcher. Hodder, 1921)
The Kingdom of the Blind. Little, 1916; Hodder, 1917
The Last Train Out. Little, 1940; Hodder, 1941
The Light Beyond. Hodder, 1928; Little, 1928
The Lighted Way. Hodder, 1912; Little, 1912
The Lion and the Lamb. Hodder, 1930; Little, 1930
The Little Gentleman from Okehampstead. Hodder, 1926
The Long Arm. Ward, Lock, 1909
Long Arm of Mannister. Little, 1908
The Lost Ambassador. Little, 1910 (English title: The Missing Delora. Methuen, 1910)
A Lost Leader. Little, 1906; Ward, Lock, 1906
Madame. Hodder, 1927
Madame and Her Twelve Virgins. Little, 1927
The Magnificent Hoax. Little, 1936 (English title: Judy of Bunter's Building. Hodder, 1936)
A Maker of History. Ward, Lock, 1905; Little, 1906
The Malefactor. Little, 1906 (English title: Mr. Wingrave, Millionaire. Ward, Lock, 1906)
The Man and His Kingdom. Lippincott, 1899; Ward, Lock, 1899, 1936
The Man from Sing Sing. Little, 1932; Burt, 1933 (English title: Moran Chambers Smiled. Hodder, 1932)
The Man Who Changed His Plea. Hodder, 1942; Little, 1942
The Man Who Saved the World; see The Spy Paramount
The Man Who Thought He Was a Pauper. Polybooks, 1943
The Man Without Nerves. Little, 1934 (English title: The Bank Manager. Hodder, 1934)
Many Mysteries. Rich, 1933
The Master Mummer. Ward, Lock, 1905; Little, 1906
The Master of Men; see Enoch Stone
Matorni's Vineyard. Little, 1928; Hodder, 1929
Mayor on Horseback. Little, 1937
Michael's Evil Deeds. Little, 1923; Hodder, 1924
Milan Grill Room. Hodder, 1940; Little, 1941

The Million Pound Deposit. Hodder, 1930; Little, 1930
Millionaire of Yesterday. Ward, Lock, 1900, 1957; Little, 1906
The Mischief-Maker. Hodder, 1913; Little, 1913; Burt, 1915
Miss Brown of X.Y.O. Hodder, 1927; Little, 1927
The Missing Delora; see The Lost Ambassador
The Missioner. Ward, Lock, 1908; Burt, 1913
Mr. Billingham, the Marquis and Madelon. Hodder, 1927
Mr. Grex of Monte Carlo. Little, 1915; Methuen, 1915; Burt, 1920
Mr. Laxworthy's Adventures. Cassell, 1913
Mr. Lessingham Goes Home; see The Zeppelin's Passenger
Mr. Marx's Secret. Simpkin, 1899; Ward, Lock, 1909
Mr. Mirakel. Hodder, 1943
Mr. Wingrave, Millionaire. Ward, Lock, 1906
A Modern Prometheus. Unwin, 1896
A Monk of Cruta. Little, 1894; Ward, Lock, 1894
Moran Chambers Smiled; see The Man from Sing Sing
The Moving Finger. Little, 1911 (English title: A Falling Star. Hodder, 1911)
Murder at Monte Carlo. Hodder, 1933; Little, 1933
The Mysteries of the Riviera. Cassell, 1916
The Mysterious Mr. Sabin. Ward, Lock, 1898; Little, 1905
The Mystery of Mr. Bernard Brown. Bentley, 1896; Ward, Lock, 1901, 1933
The Mystery Road. Little, 1923; Hodder, 1924
The New Tenant. Collier, 1910
Nicholas Goode, Detective. Hodder, 1927; Little, 1929
Nobody's Man. Hodder, 1922; Little, 1922
The Oppenheim Omnibus. Hodder, 1931; Burt, 1934
The Ostrekoff Jewels. Hodder, 1932
The Other Romilly; see The Cinema Murder
Passers By, by Anthony Partridge. Little, 1910; Lloyds, 1918
The Passionate Quest. Hodder, 1924; Little, 1924
The Pawn's Count. Hodder, 1918; Little, 1918
The Peer and the Woman. Ward, Lock, 1895; Ogilvie, 1905; Whitman, 1907; Fenno, 1908
A People's Man. Little, 1914; Methuen, 1915
Peter Ruff. Hodder, 1912; Burt, 1915 (Also published as: Peter Ruff and The Double-Four. Little, 1912)
The Postmaster of Market Deighton. Routledge, 1897; Ward, Lock, 1934
A Prince of Sinners. Ward, Lock, 1903
The Prodigals of Monte Carlo. Hodder, 1926; Little, 1926
The Profiteers. Hodder, 1921; Little, 1921
The Pulpit in the Grill Room. Hodder, 1938; Little, 1939
The Secret. Ward, Lock, 1907 (Also published as: The Great Secret. Little, 1908)
The Secret Service Omnibus. Hodder, 1932
The Seeing Life. Lloyds, 1919
The Seven Conundrums. Little, 1923; Hodder, 1924
Shudders and Thrills: the Second Oppenheim Omnibus. Blue Ribbon Books, 1934
The Shy Plutocrat. Hodder, 1941
Simple Peter Cradd. Hodder, 1931; Burt, 1933
Sinners Beware. Hodder, 1932; Little, 1932
Sir Adam Disappeared. Little, 1939
Slane's Long Shots. Hodder, 1930
A Sleeping Memory; see The Great Awakening
Spies and Intrigues. Little, 1936
The Spy Paramount. Little, 1934; Hodder, 1935 (Serial title: The Man Who Saved the World)
The Spymaster. Hodder, 1938; Little, 1938
Stolen Idols. Hodder, 1925; Little, 1925
The Strange Boarders of Palace Crescent. Little, 1934; Hodder, 1935
The Strange Case of Mr. Jocelyn Thew; see The Box with the Broken Seals
The Stranger's Gate. Little, 1939; Hodder, 1940
The Survivor. Brentano, 1901; Ward, Lock, 1901; Little, 1912
The Tempting of Tavernake. Little, 1912; Hodder, 1913
The Terrible Hobby of Sir Joseph Londebart. Hodder, 1924; Little, 1927
Those Other Days. Ward, Lock, 1912; Little, 1913
The Tragedy of Andrea. Ogilvie, 1906
The Traitors. Ward, Lock, 1902; Little, 1906
The Treasure House of Martin Hews. Little, 1928; Collier, 1929; Hodder, 1929
Up the Ladder of Gold. Hodder, 1931
The Vanished Messenger. Little, 1914; Methuen, 1914; Burt, 1916
The Way of These Women. Methuen, 1914; Little, 1915

What Happened to Forester. Hodder, 1929
The Wicked Marquis. Hodder, 1919; Little, 1919
The Wooing of Fortune. Ward & Downey, 1896
The World's Great Snare. Lippincott, 1896; Ward & Downey, 1896; Little, 1900; Ward, Lock, 1900
The Wrath to Come. Little, 1924; Hodder, 1925
The Yellow Crayon. Dodd, 1903; Ward, Lock, 1903; Little, 1906
The Zeppelin's Passenger. Little, 1918 (English title: Mr. Lessingham Goes Home. Hodder, 1919)

ORAM, JOHN (S)
The Copenhagen Affair. Ace, 1965 (The Man from U.N.C.L.E. series #3)

ORBISON, KECK, pseud; see KECK, MAUD

ORBISON, OLIVE; see KECK, MAUD

ORCZY, BARONESS EMMUSKA (Mrs. Montagu Barstow) (D)
The Case of Miss Elliott. Greening, 1905
The Elusive Pimpernel. Hutchinson, 1908
Lady Molly of Scotland Yard. Cassell, 1910
Links in the Chain of Life. Hutchinson, 1947
The Man in Gray. Cassell, 1918
The Man in the Corner. Pearson, 1902; Dodd, 1909; Norton, 1966 (Also published as: The Old Man in the Corner. Greening, 1909)
The Old Man in the Corner; see The Man in the Corner
The Scarlet Pimpernel. Greening, 1905; Airmont, 1963; Bouregy, 1963; Putnam, 1966 (41st impression)
Sir Percy Hits Back. Doran, 1927
The Skin of My Tooth. Doubleday, Doran, 1928; Hodder, 1928
Unraveled Knots. Hutchinson, 1925
The Way of the Scarlet Pimpernel. Putnam, 1934

ORDE-POWLETT, NIGEL AMYAS (D)
The Cast to Death. Benn, 1932; Houghton, 1932
Driven Death. Benn, 1933

ORDWAY, PETER (M)
Conspiracy of Vipers. Davies, 1961
Face in the Shadows. Wyn, 1952; Permabooks
Night of Reckoning. S & S, 1965; Hale, R., 1967
The Teak Forest. Boardman, T. V., 1958

O'REILLY, MARY BOYLE (S)
The Black Fan. Reilly & Lee, 1928

ORGILL, DOUGLAS (S)
The Cautious Assassin; see Ride a Tiger
Days of Darkness. Davies, 1965 (U.S. title: Man in the Dark. Morrow, 1965)
The Death Bringers. Davies, 1962; Transworld, 1964 (U.S. title: Journey into Violence. Morrow, 1963)
Journey into Violence; see The Death Bringers
Man in the Dark, see Days of Darkness
Ride a Tiger. Davies, 1963 (U.S. title: The Cautious Assassin. Morrow, 1964)

ORIOL, LAWRENCE
Short Circuit. World Pub., 1968

ORNSTEIN, ALFRED (M)
The Secret of the Ashes. Hutchinson, 1926

O'ROURKE, FRANK (S-M) (Pseudonym: Frank O'Malley)
The Best Go First, by Frank O'Malley. Random, 1950; Benn, 1955
High Dive. Random, 1954
Window in the Dark. Morrow, 1960

ORR, CLIFFORD (D)
The Dartmouth Murders. Farrar & Rinehart, 1929; Hamilton, 1931
The Wailing Rock Murders. Farrar & Rinehart, 1932; Cassell, 1933

ORR, MYRON DAVID (M)
White Gold. Capper, 1936

ORVIS, KENNETH (S)
Night Without Darkness. Berkley Pub., 1967

OSBORNE, WILLIAM HAMILTON (M)
The Blue Buckle. McBride, 1914; Hodder, 1915
The Catspaw. Dodd, 1911; Hodder, 1916
The Girl of Lost Island. Hodder, 1916
The Red Mouse. Hodder, 1916; Odhams, 1921

OSBOURNE, LLOYD (M)
Not to Be Opened. Cosmopolitan, 1928
Peril. Heinemann, 1929
The Wrong Box, with Robert Louis Stevenson. Scribner, 1889

OSGOOD, LUCIAN AUSTIN (M)
Murder in the Tomb. Unique Mystery Novels, 1937

O'SHEA, SEAN (M)
Operation Boudoir. Belmont, 1967

OSTRANDER, ISABEL EGENTON (D)
(Pseudonyms: Robert Orr Chipperfield, David Fox, Douglas Grant)
Above Suspicion, by Robert Orr Chipperfield. Hurst, 1923; McBride, 1923
Annihilation. Hurst, 1923; McBride, 1924
Ashes to Ashes. McBride, 1919; Hurst, 1921
At One-Thirty. Watt, 1915; Simpkin, 1916
The Black Joker. McBride, 1925; Hurst, 1926
Booly, by Douglas Grant. Hurst, 1921
The Braddigan Murder, with Christopher Booth. Hutchinson, 1933
Bright Lights, by Robert Orr Chipperfield. Hurst, 1924; McBride, 1924
The Clue in the Air. Skeffington, 1920
The Crimson Blotter. Hurst, 1921; McBride, 1921
The Doom Dealer, by David Fox. McBride, 1923; Hurst, 1925
Dust to Dust. Hurst, 1924; McBride, 1924
Ethel Opens the Door, by David Fox. McBride, 1922; Hurst, 1924
The Fifth Ace, by Douglas Grant. Garden City Pub., 1918, 1928
The Handwriting on the Wall, by Robert Orr Chipperfield. Hurst, 1925
The Heritage of Cain. Watt, 1916; Garden City Pub., 1926
The Island of Intrigue. McBride, 1918
Liberation. McBride, 1924
McCarty, Incog. McBride, 1922
The Man in the Jury Box, by Robert Orr Chipperfield. Hurst, 1921; McBride, 1921
The Man Who Convicted Himself, by David Fox. Hurst, 1923
The Mathematics of Guilt. McBride, 1926
The Neglected Clue. Hurst, 1925; McBride, 1925
The Second Bullet, by Robert Orr Chipperfield. McBride, 1919; Skeffington, 1920
The Single Track, by Douglas Grant. Hurst, 1922
The Sleeping Cat, with Christopher Booth. Hurst, 1926; McBride, 1926
Suspense. Hurst, 1918; McBride, 1918
The Tattooed Arm. McBride, 1922
The Trigger of Conscience, by Robert Orr Chipperfield. McBride, 1921; Hurst, 1922
Twenty-six Clues. Watt, 1919
Two-Gun Sue, by Douglas Grant. McBride, 1922
Unseen Hands, by Robert Orr Chipperfield. McBride, 1920; Hurst, 1921

O'SULLIVAN, JAMES BRENDAN (D)
Backlash. Ward, Lock, 1960
The Casket of Death. Pillar, 1946
The Castle of Death. Grafton, 1945
The Cherry in the Wine-Glass. Grafton, 1945
Death Came Late. Mitre, 1945; Pillar, 1945
Death Card. Mitre, 1945; Pillar, 1945
Death on Ice. Mitre, 1946; Pillar, 1946
Death Stalks the Stadium. Pillar, 1946
Disordered Death. Ward, Lock, 1957
Don't Hang Me Too High. Laurie, 1954; Mill, 1954
I Die Possessed. Laurie, 1953; Mill, 1953
It Could Happen to You. Pillar, 1946
Make My Coffin Big. Ward, Lock, 1964
Nerve Beat. Laurie, 1953
Raid. Ward, Lock, 1958
Someone Walked over My Grave. Laurie, 1954
The Stuffed Man. Laurie, 1955
The Third Horseman. Mellifont, 1946

OTTOLENGUI, RODRIGUES (M)
An Artist in Crime. Putnam, 1892
A Conflict of Evidence. Putnam, 1893; Ward, Lock, 1904
The Crime of the Century. Putnam, 1896 (Sequel to: Final Proof)
Final Proof; or, The Value of Evidence. Putnam, 1898 (Sequel to: An Artist in Crime)

OURSLER, CHARLES FULTON (D)
(Pseudonym: Anthony Abbot)
About the Disappearance of Agatha King. Farrar & Rinehart, 1932
About the Man Afraid of Women. Collins, 1937; Farrar & Rinehart, 1937
About the Murder of a Startled Lady. Farrar & Rinehart, 1935; Collins, 1937
About the Murder of Geraldine Foster. Covici, 1930; Collins, 1931
About the Murder of the Circus Queen. Covici, 1932; Collins, 1935
About the Murder of the Clergyman's Mistress. Covici, 1931 (English title: The Crime of the Century. Collins, 1933)
About the Murder of the Night Club Lady. Covici, 1931
The Bungalow on the Roof, with Alexander N. Romanoff. Mystery League, 1931
The Creeps. Farrar & Rinehart, 1939
The Crime of the Century; see About the Murder of the Clergyman's Mistress
The Shudders. Farrar & Rinehart, 1943
These Are Strange Tales. Winston, 1948
The Trail of the Beast, with Alexander N. Romanoff. McCann, 1919

OURSLER, FULTON; see OURSLER, CHARLES FULTON

OURSLER, GRACE
The Spider. Harper, 1929 (From the play by Fulton Oursler and Lowell Brentano)

OURSLER, WILLIAM CHARLES (Pseudonym: Gale Gallagher)
Chord in Crimson, by Gale Gallagher. Coward, 1949
Departure Delayed. S & S, 1947
Folio on Florence White. S & S, 1942
I Found Him Dead, by Gale Gallagher. Coward, 1947
Murder Memo: To the Commissioner. S & S, 1950
The Trial of Vincent Doon. S & S, 1941; World Pub., 1943

OVALOV, LEV (M)
Comrade Spy. Award, 1965
Secret Weapon. Award, 1965

OWEN, HANS C. (M)
Ways of Death. Furman, 1937

OZAKI, MILTON K. (D) (Pseudonym: Robert O. Saber)
The Case of the Cop's Wife. GM, 1958
The Case of the Deadly Kiss. GM, 1957
The Cuckoo Clock. Ziff-Davis, 1946
A Dame Called Murder, by Robert O. Saber. Graphic, 1955
The Deadly Pickup. Berkley Pub., 1960
A Fiend in Need. Ziff-Davis, 1947
Inquest. GM, 1960
Maid for Murder. Ace, 1956
Murder Doll. Berkley Pub., 1959
Sucker Bait, by Robert O. Saber. Graphic, 1955
Time for Murder, by Robert O. Saber. Graphic, 1956
Wake up and Scream. GM, 1956

PACKARD, FRANK LUCIUS (M)
The Adventures of Jimmy Dale. Copp, 1917; Doran, 1917; Cassell, 1918
The Beloved Traitor. Copp, 1915; Doran, 1916; Hodder, 1916; Burt, 1918
The Big Shot. Copp, 1929; Hodder, 1929
Broken Waters. Copp, 1925; Hodder, 1927
The Devil's Mantle. Doran, 1927; Hodder, 1928
Doors of the Night. Copp, 1922; Doran, 1922; Hodder, 1922
The Dragon's Jaws. Doran, 1937; Hodder, 1937
The Four Stragglers. Copp, 1923; Doran, 1923; Hodder, 1923; Burt, 1925
From Now On. Copp, 1919; Doran, 1919; Burt, 1921
The Further Adventures of Jimmy Dale. Burt, 1919; Hodder, 1926
The Gold Skull Murders. Doran, 1931; Hodder, 1931
Greater Love Hath No Man. Copp, 1913; Doran, 1913; Hodder, 1913; Burt, 1918
The Hidden Door. Doubleday, Doran, 1933; Hodder, 1933
Jimmy Dale and the Blue Envelope Murder. Copp, 1930; Hodder, 1930
Jimmy Dale and the Missing Hour. Doubleday, Doran, 1935; Hodder, 1935
Jimmy Dale and the Phantom Clue. Copp, 1922; Doran, 1922; Hodder, 1923
The Locked Book. Copp, 1924; Doran, 1924; Hodder, 1924
The Miracle Man. Copp, 1914; Doran, 1914; Hodder, 1914
More Knaves Than One. Copp, 1914; Hodder, 1938
The Night Operator. Copp, 1919; Doran, 1919
On the Iron at Big Cloud. Crowell, 1911
Pawned. Copp, 1921; Doran, 1921; Hodder, 1921
The Purple Ball. Doran, 1933; Hodder, 1934
The Red Ledger. Doran, 1926; Hodder, 1926; Burt, 1927
Running Special. Copp, 1925; Doran, 1925; Hodder, 1925
Shanghai Jim. Doubleday, Doran, 1928; Hodder, 1928
The Sin That Was His. Copp, 1917; Doran, 1917; Hodder, 1926
Tiger Claws. Doran, 1928; Hodder, 1929
Two Stolen Idols. Burt, 1927; Doran, 1927
The White Moll. Copp, 1920; Doran, 1920; Hodder, 1920
The Wire Devils. Copp, 1918; Doran, 1918

PACKER, JOY (S)
The Man in the Mews. Dutton, 1965; Ace, 1966

PACKER, VIN, pseud; see MEAKER, MARIJANE

PADDON, WREFORD (M)
A Corpse in the Coupe. Hammond, 1951
Solo for No Voices. Boardman, T. V., 1955

PADGET, MEG (S)
House of Strangers. Lancer, 1965

PADGETT, LEWIS, pseud; see KUTTNER, HENRY

PAGE, EVELYN; see BLAIR, DOROTHY

PAGE, MARCO, pseud; see KURNITZ, HARRY

PAGE, MICHAEL FITZGERALD
Innocent Bystander. Hale, R., 1957
Spare the Vanquished. Hale, R., 1953

PAGE, STANLEY HART (M)
Fool's Gold. Knopf, 1933; Paul, S., 1934
Murder Flies the Atlantic. King, A. H., 1933
Resurrection Murder Case. Knopf, 1932; Paul, S., 1934
Sinister Cargo. Knopf, 1932; Paul, S., 1933
The Tragic Curtain. Dial, 1935

PAHLOW, MRS. GERTRUDE CURTIS BROWN (D)
Murder in the Morning. Clode, 1931

PAIN, BARRY, pseud; see GUTHRIE, P. R.

PAINE, LAURAN (D) (Pseudonym: Mark Carrel)
The Case of the Hollow Man. Foulsham, 1958
The Case of the Innocent Witness. Foulsham, 1959
The Case of the Perfect Alibi. Foulsham, 1960

PAINTER, T.; see LAING, ALEXANDER

PALERMO, ANTHONY J. (M)
Who? Vantage, 1964

PALMER, BRUCE HAMILTON (M)
Blind Man's Mark. S & S, 1959 (Also published as: The Shattered Affair. Avon, 1960)
Flesh and Blood. S & S, 1960
The Shattered Affair; see Blind Man's Mark

PALMER, GRETTA; see JOHNSON, EVELYN DAVIES

PALMER, JOHN LESLIE. (Joint pseudonym with Hilary Aidan St. George Saunders: Francis Beeding)
Big Fish; see Heads Off at Midnight
The Black Arrows, by Francis Beeding. Harper, 1938
Death in Four Letters, by Francis Beeding. Harper, 1935; Hodder, 1936
Death Walks in Eastrepps, by Francis Beeding. Mystery League, 1931; Norton, 1966
Eight Crooked Trenches, by Francis Beeding. Harper, 1936
Eleven Were Brave, by Francis Beeding. Harper, 1941
The Emerald Clasp, by Francis Beeding. Hodder, 1933; Little, 1933
Five Flamboys, by Francis Beeding. Hodder, 1930
The Four Armourers, by Francis Beeding. Little, 1930
He Could Not Have Slipped, by Francis Beeding. Harper, 1939
Heads Off at Midnight, by Francis Beeding. Harper, 1938 (English title: Big Fish. Hodder, 1938)
Hell Let Loose, by Francis Beeding. Harper, 1937
The Hidden Kingdom, by Francis Beeding. Little, 1927
The House of Dr. Edwards, by Francis Beeding. Little, 1928 (Also published as: Spellbound. World Pub., 1945)
The League of Discontent, by Francis Beeding. Little, 1930
The Little White Hag, by Francis Beeding. Little, 1926; Burt, 1928
The Man in the Purple Gown. Dodd, 1939
The Man with Two Names. Dodd, 1940 (English title: Mandragora. Gollancz, 1940)
Mandragora; see The Man with Two Names
Murder Intended, by Francis Beeding. Hodder, 1932; Little, 1932
Murdered: One by One, by Francis Beeding. Harper, 1937; Grosset, 1939 (English title: No Fury. Hodder, 1939)
The Nine Waxed Faces, by Francis Beeding. Harper, 1936; Hodder, 1936
No Fury; see Murdered: One by One
The Norwich Victims, by Francis Beeding. Harper, 1935
Not a Bad Show; see The Secret Weapon
One Sane Man, by Francis Beeding. Little, 1934
Pretty Sinister, by Francis Beeding. Hodder, 1929; Little, 1929
The Secret Weapon, by Francis Beeding. Harper, 1940 (English title: Not a Bad Show. Hodder, 1940)
The Seven Sleepers, by Francis Beeding. Little, 1925
Sit Up with Beeding, by Francis Beeding. Hodder, 1937
The Six Proud Walkers, by Francis Beeding. Hodder, 1928; Little, 1928
Spellbound; see The House of Dr. Edwards
Street of the Serpents, by Francis Beeding. Harper, 1934
Take It Crooked, by Francis Beeding. Little, 1932
The Ten Holy Horrors, by Francis Beeding. Harper, 1939; Hodder, 1941
There Are Thirteen, by Francis Beeding. Harper, 1946; Hodder, 1946
The Three Fishers, by Francis Beeding. Little, 1931; Burt, 1933

The Twelve Disguises, by Francis Beeding. Harper, 1942; Hodder, 1942
Two Undertakers, by Francis Beeding. Hodder, 1933; Little, 1933

PALMER, STUART (D) (Pseudonym: Jay Stewart)
The Ace of Jades. Mohawk, 1931
At One Fell Swoop; see The Green Ace
Before It's Too Late, by Jay Stewart. Mill, 1950
Cold Poison. Black, 1954; Mill, 1954; Pyramid, 1964 (English title: Exit Laughing. Collins, 1954)
Death in Grease Paint; see Unhappy Hooligan
Exit Laughing; see Cold Poison
Four Lost Ladies. Mill, 1949; Collins, 1950
The Green Ace. Mill, 1950; Pyramid, 1964 (English title: At One Fell Swoop. Collins, 1951)
Hear No Evil. Doubleday, 1953
Miss Withers Regrets. Doubleday, 1947; Collins, 1948
The Monkey Murder. Mercury Pub., 1950
Murder Mask; see Unhappy Hooligan
Murder on the Blackboard. Brentano, 1932; Eldon, 1934
Murder on Wheels. Brentano, 1932; Long, 1932
Nipped in the Bud. Mill, 1951; Collins, 1952
No Flowers by Request; see Omit Flowers
Omit Flowers. Doubleday, Doran, 1937 (English title: No Flowers by Request. Collins, 1937)
The Penguin Pool Murder. Brentano, 1931; Long, 1932
The People vs Withers and Malone, with Craig Rice. S & S, 1963; Award, 1965
The Puzzle of the Blue Banderilla. Collins, 1937; Doubleday, Doran, 1937
The Puzzle of the Briar Pipe; see The Puzzle of the Red Stallion
The Puzzle of the Happy Hooligan. Collins, 1941; Doubleday, Doran, 1941
The Puzzle of the Pepper Tree. Doubleday, Doran, 1933; Jarrolds, 1934
The Puzzle of the Red Stallion. Doubleday, Doran, 1936 (English title: The Puzzle of the Briar Pipe. Collins, 1936)
The Puzzle of the Silver Persian. Doubleday, Doran, 1934; Collins, 1935
Unhappy Hooligan. Harper, 1946 (English title: Death in Grease Paint. Collins, 1956. Also published as: Murder Mask)

PANBOURNE, OLIVER, pseud; see ROCKEY, HOWARD

PANCOAST, CHALMERS LOWELL (M)
Cub. Devin-Adair, 1928

PANGBORN, EDGAR (M)
The Trial of Callista Blake. St. Martin's, 1961; Davies, 1962; Dell, 1963

PARADISE, MARY, pseud; see EDEN, DOROTHY

PARADISE, VIOLA (D)
The Girl Died Laughing. Harper, 1934; Heinemann, 1935

PARGETER, EDITH (M) (Pseudonym: Ellis Peters)
Assize of the Dying. Doubleday, 1958; Heinemann, 1958
Black Is the Colour of My True-Love's Heart. Collins, 1967; Morrow, 1967
Death and the Joyful Woman. Collins, 1961; Doubleday, 1961; Avon, 1963
Death Mask. Collins, 1959; Doubleday, 1960; Avon, 1964
Fallen into the Pit. Heinemann, 1951
Flight of a Witch. Collins, 1964
Funeral of Figaro. Collins, 1962; Morrow, 1964
The Piper on the Mountain. Morrow, 1966
Where There's a Will. Doubleday, 1960; Avon, 1966 (English title: The Will and the Deed. Collins, 1960)
Who Lies Here? Morrow, 1965
The Will and the Deed; see Where There's a Will

PARISH, DAVID MONROE (S)
The House of Rhinestad. Pageant, 1965

PARK, JORDON, pseud; see KORNBLUTH, CYRIL M.

PARKE, F. G., pseud. (D)
The First Night Murder. MacVeagh, 1931; Paul, S., 1932

PARKER, MAUDE (D)
Along Came a Spider. Hodder, 1957
Blood Will Tell. Hodder, 1952
Death Makes a Deal. Hodder, 1961
Final Crossroads. Hodder, 1955
The Intriguer. Rinehart, 1952
The Invisible Red. Rinehart, 1953; Hodder, 1954
Murder in Jackson Hole. Rinehart, 1955
Secret Envoy. Bobbs, 1930
Which Mrs. Torr? Rinehart, 1951; Hodder, 1952

PARKER, RICHARD (M)
The Gingerbread Man. Collins, 1953; Scribner, 1954

Harm Intended. Scribner, 1956
Killer. Doubleday, 1954
A Kind of Misfortune. Collins, 1954; Scribner, 1955
Only Some Had Guns. Collins, 1952

PARKER, RICHARD A. (M)
Three Knots. Macaulay, 1924

PARKER, ROBERT B. (S)
Passport to Peril. Rinehart, 1951; Hodder, 1952
Ticket to Oblivion. Rinehart, 1950; Macmillan, 1951

PARKS, MRS. GEORGE RICHMOND; see ROBINS, ELIZABETH

PARMER, CHARLES B. (D)
Murder at the Kentucky Derby. Doubleday, Doran, 1942

PARRISH, RANDALL (D)
The Case and the Girl. Knopf, 1922; Paul, S., 1923
The Mystery of the Silver Dagger. Doran, 1920; Hodder, 1920
The Strange Case of Cavendish. Doran, 1918; Hodder, 1919

PARRY, HUGH JONES (M) (Pseudonym: James Cross)
The Dark Road. Messner, 1959; Crest, 1960; Heinemann, 1960
Grave of Heroes. Heinemann, 1961
Root of Evil. Messner, 1957
To Hell for Half-a-Crown. Random, 1967

PARSONS, ANTHONY (D)
The Case of the Dangra Millions. Amalgamated Press, 1949
Death by the Nile. Wright & Brown, 1955
Death of a Governor. Wright & Brown, 1954
Death on the Mall. Wright & Brown, 1947
The Income-Tax Conspiracy. Amalgamated Press, 1948
The Loot of Pakistan. Amalgamated Press, 1948
The Man Who Backed Out. Amalgamated Press, 1948
The Murder at the Red Cockatoo. Wright & Brown, 1955
The Mystery of the Avenue Road. Amalgamated Press, 1948
The Mystery of the One-Day Alibi. Amalgamated Press, 1948
The Mystery of the Red Cockatoo. Amalgamated Press, 1948
The Mystery of the Whitehall Bomb. Amalgamated Press, 1947
No Alibi for Murder. Wright & Brown, 1951
The Riddle of the Russian Bride. Amalgamated Press, 1948
Terror at Tree Tops. Amalgamated Press, 1948

PARSONS, LUKE
Clough Plays Murder. Jarrolds, 1942

PARTRIDGE, ANTHONY, pseud; see OPPENHEIM, EDWARD PHILLIPS

PATERNOSTER, SIDNEY (M)
Hand of the Spoiler. Hodder, 1908

PATERSON, NEIL (S)
Man on the Tight-Rope. Random, 1953

PATRICK, CHANN (M)
The House of Retrogression. Jacobsen, 1932

PATRICK, KEATS, pseud; see KARIG, WILLIAM

PATRICK, Q., pseud; see WEBB, RICHARD WILSON

PATRICK, VICTOR (D)
Three to Make Murder. Mystery House, 1947

PATTEE, FRED LEWIS (M)
The House of the Black King. Holt, H., 1905

PATTEN, J., pseud; see COBB, CLAYTON W.

PATTERSON, ARTHUR M. (M)
The Heaviest Pipe. Jacobs, 1921

PATTERSON, HARRY, pseud; see PATTERSON, HENRY

PATTERSON, HENRY (M-S) (Pseudonyms: Martin Fallon, Hugh Marlowe, Harry Patterson)
A Candle for the Dead, by Hugh Marlowe. Abelard, 1966
Comes the Dark Stranger, by Harry Patterson. Long, 1962
Cry of the Hunter, by Harry Patterson. Long, 1960; World Distributors, 1963
The Dark Side of the Island, by Harry Patterson. Long, 1963
Graveyard Shift, by Harry Patterson. Long, 1965
Hell Is Too Crowded, by Harry Patterson. Long, 1962
The Iron Tiger, by Harry Patterson. Long, 1966
The Keys of Hell, by Martin Fallon. Abelard, 1965

Midnight Never Comes, by Martin Fallon. Long, 1966
Passage by Night, by Hugh Marlowe. Abelard, 1966; Avon, 1966
Pay the Devil, by Harry Patterson. Barrie & Rockliff, 1963
A Phoenix in the Blood, by Harry Patterson. Barrie & Rockliff, 1964
Sad Wind from the Sea, by Harry Patterson. Long, 1959
Seven Pillars to Hell, by Hugh Marlowe. Abelard, 1963
The Testament of Casper Schultz, by Martin Fallon. Abelard, 1962
The Thousand Faces of Night, by Harry Patterson. Long, 1961
Thunder at Noon, by Harry Patterson. Long, 1964
Wrath of the Lion, by Harry Patterson. Long, 1964
Year of the Tiger, by Martin Fallon. Abelard, 1960

PATTERSON, INNIS (Full name: Isabella Innis Patterson) (D)
The Eppworth Case. Farrar & Rinehart, 1930
The Standish Gaunt Case. Farrar & Rinehart, 1931

PATTERSON, ISABELLA INNIS; see PATTERSON, INNIS

PATTERSON, ROBERT (M)
Gold Is the Color of Blood. Ballantine, 1960

PATTINSON, JAMES
Contact Mr. Delgardo. Harrap, 1959
Mystery of Gregory Kotovsky. Harrap, 1958

PATTON, DAVID KNOX (D)
Murder on the Pacific. Dodd, 1940

PAUL, ELLIOT HAROLD (D) (Pseudonym: Brett Rutledge)
The Black and the Red. Random, 1956
Black Gardenia. Random, 1952
Fracas in the Foothills. Random, 1940
Hugger-Mugger in the Louvre. Random, 1940; Ballantine, 1962
I'll Hate Myself in the Morning and Summer in December. Random, 1945
Mayhem in B-Flat. Random, 1940; Bantam, 1950; Collier, 1962
Murder on the Left Bank. Random, 1951
Mysterious Mickey Finn; or Murder at the Café du Dome. Modern Age, 1939; Penguin, 1952; Collier, 1962; Avon
Summer in December; see I'll Hate Myself in the Morning
Waylaid in Boston. Random, 1953

PAUL, GENE (S)
Naked in the Dark. Lion, 1953

PAUL, HUGO (S)
The Smashers. Lancer, 1965

PAUL, JOHN (M)
Murder by Appointment. Skeffington, 1952
Oil by Murder. Skeffington, 1953

PAUL, PHYLLIS
Echo of Guilt; see Pulled Down
Pulled Down. Heinemann, 1964; Norton, 1965 (Also published as: Echo of Guilt. Lancer, 1966)
A Little Treachery. Heinemann, 1962; Norton, 1962
Twice Lost. Norton, 1960

"PAUL-JAMES" (M)
What Became of Eugene Ridgewood? Carleton, G., 1883

PAYES, RACHEL C. (D)
Curiosity Killed Kitty. Bouregy, 1962
Death Sleeps Lightly. Bouregy, 1960
Forsythia Finds Murder. Bouregy, 1960
Memoirs of Murder. Bouregy, 1964
The Mystery of Echo Caverns. Bouregy, 1966
Shadow of Fear. Bouregy, 1961

PAYN, JAMES (M)
Found Dead. Hall, 1869; Munro, 1878; Harper
Mystery of Mirbridge. Harper, 1888

PAYNE, ALAN (S)
This'll Slay You. Ace, 1958

PAYNE, EVELYN (M)
Held Open for Death. Arcadia, 1958

PAYNE, LAURENCE (S)
The First Body. Avon, 1964
The Nose on My Face. Hodder, 1961; Macmillan, 1961
Too Small for His Shoes. Hodder, 1962; Macmillan, 1963; Penguin

PAYNE, RACHEL ANN (S)
Ghostwind. Paperback Lib., 1966

PAYNE, RONALD; see GARROD, JOHN

PAYNE, WILL (M)
Overlook House. Dodd, 1921
The Scarred Chin. Dodd, 1920

PAYNTER, THOMAS CAMBORNE (M)
They Sailed on a Friday. Longmans, 1928

PEARCE, DICK (M)
The Darby Trial. Lippincott, 1954

PEARL, JACK (S)
Our Man Flint. PB, 1965

PEARSON, D. A. G. (S)
The Golden Stone. Dutton, 1929; Methuen, 1929

PEARSON, DENISE NAOMI O'NEILL; see ROBINS, DENISE

PEARSON, DIANE (D-Gothic)
Bride of Tancred. Bantam, 1967

PEARSON, WILLIAM (S)
The Beautiful Frame. S & S, 1953; Reinhardt, 1954
Hunt the Man Down. S & S, 1956; Ward, Lock, 1957

PECHEY, ARCHIBALD THOMAS (D) (Pseudonyms: Mark Cross, "Valentine")
The Adjusters, by "Valentine." Anglo-Eastern, 1930
The Best-laid Schemes, by Mark Cross. Ward, Lock, 1955
The Black Spider, by Mark Cross. Ward, Lock, 1953
Challenge to the Four, by Mark Cross. Ward, Lock, 1939
The Circle of Freedom, by Mark Cross. Ward, Lock, 1953
Find the Professor, by Mark Cross. Ward, Lock, 1940
Foul Deeds Will Arise, by Mark Cross. Ward, Lock, 1960
The Four at Bay, by Mark Cross. Ward, Lock, 1939
The Four Get Going, by Mark Cross. Ward, Lock, 1938
The Four Make Holiday, by Mark Cross. Ward, Lock, 1938
The Four Strike Home, by Mark Cross. Ward, Lock, 1937
The Green Circle, by Mark Cross. Ward, Lock, 1942
The Grip of the Four, by Mark Cross. Ward, Lock, 1934
The Hand of the Four, by Mark Cross. Ward, Lock, 1935
How Was It Done? by Mark Cross. Ward, Lock, 1941
In the Dead of the Night, by Mark Cross. Ward, Lock, 1955
It Couldn't Be Murder, by Mark Cross. Ward, Lock, 1940
The Jaws of Darkness, by Mark Cross. Ward, Lock, 1952
The Mark of the Four, by Mark Cross. Ward, Lock, 1936
Missing from His Home, by Mark Cross. Ward, Lock, 1949
Murder as Arranged, by Mark Cross. Ward, Lock, 1943
Murder in Black, by Mark Cross. Ward, Lock, 1944
Murder in the Air, by Mark Cross. Ward, Lock, 1943
Murder in the Pool, by Mark Cross. Ward, Lock, 1941
Murder Will Speak, by Mark Cross. Ward, Lock, 1954
The Mystery at Gruden's Gap, by Mark Cross. Ward, Lock, 1942
The Mystery of Joan Marryat, by Mark Cross. Ward, Lock, 1945
Not Long to Live, by Mark Cross. Ward, Lock, 1959
On the Night of the 14th, by Mark Cross. Ward, Lock, 1950
Other Than Natural Causes, by Mark Cross. Ward, Lock, 1949
Over Thin Ice, by Mark Cross. Ward, Lock, 1959
The Secret of the Grange, by Mark Cross. Ward, Lock, 1946
The Shadow of the Four, by Mark Cross. Ward, Lock, 1934
The Strange Affair at Greylands, by Mark Cross. Ward, Lock, 1948
The Strange Case of Pamela Wilson, by Mark Cross. Ward, Lock, 1954
Strange Experiment, by "Valentine." Ward, Lock, 1937
Surprise for the Four, by Mark Cross. Ward, Lock, 1937
Third Time Unlucky, by Mark Cross. Ward, Lock, 1959
The Unseen Hand, by "Valentine." Jarrolds, 1924
Wanted for Questioning, by Mark Cross. Ward, Lock, 1960
The Way of the Four, by Mark Cross. Ward, Lock, 1936
When Danger Threatens, by Mark Cross. Ward, Lock, 1959
Who Killed Henry Wickenston? by Mark Cross. Ward, Lock, 1951

PECK, DAVID WARNER (M)
Decision at Law. Dodd, 1961
The Green Case. S & S, 1955; Penguin, 1963

PECK, WINIFRED (Full name: Lady Winifred Frances Knox Peck) (M)
The Warrielaw Jewel. Dutton, 1933; Faber, 1933

PECKHAM, RICHARD
Murder in Strange Houses. Minton, 1929; Eyre, 1930

PEEL, FREDERICK; see SIDDLE, CHARLES

PEI, MARIO (M)
The Sparrows of Paris. Philosophical Lib., 1958

PELL, FRANKLYN, pseud; see PELLIGRIN, FRANK E.

PELLIGRIN, FRANK E. (M) (Pseudonym: Franklyn Pell)
Hangman's Hill. Dodd, 1946

PEMBER, WILLIAM LEONARD (M) (Pseudonym: Jack Monmouth)
The Donovan Case. Jarrolds, 1955
Lightning over Mayfair. Hale, R., 1958
Lonely, Lovely Lady. Jarrolds, 1956
Not Ready to Die. Hale, R., 1960
Sleepy-Eyed Blonde. Hale, R., 1957

PEMBERTON, SIR MAX (M)
Captain Black. Cassell, 1911
Gentlemen's Gentleman. Harper, 1896
The Iron Pirate. Cassell, 1893
John Dighton: Mystery Millionaire. Cassell, 1931
The Mystery of the Green Heart. Dodd, 1910

PENDEXTER, HUGH (M)
Harry Idaho. Bobbs, 1926; Collins, 1927

PENDOWER, JACQUES (M) (Pseudonyms: T. C. H. Jacobs, Thomas Curtis Hicks Jacobs)
Anxious Lady. Hale, R., 1960
Appointment with the Hangman, by T. C. H. Jacobs. Macaulay, 1936; Paul, S., 1936
Aspects of Murder, by Thomas Curtis Hicks Jacobs. Paul, S., 1956
Betrayed. Paperback Lib., 1967
The Black Box, by T. C. H. Jacobs. Paul, S., 1946
Black Trinity, by Thomas Curtis Hicks Jacobs. Long, 1960
Blood and Sun-Tan, by Thomas Curtis Hicks Jacobs. Paul, S., 1952
Broken Alibi, by Thomas Curtis Hicks Jacobs. Paul, S., 1957; Roy Pubs., 1957
The Broken Knife, by Thomas Curtis Hicks Jacobs. Paul, S., 1941
The Bronkhurst Case, by T. C. H. Jacobs. Paul, S., 1931 (U.S. title: Documents of Murder. Macaulay, 1931)
Brother Spy, by T. C. H. Jacobs. Paul, S., 1940
Cause for Suspicion, by Thomas Curtis Hicks Jacobs. Paul, S., 1956
Cavalcade of Murder, by Thomas Curtis Hicks Jacobs. Paul, S., 1955
The Curse of Khatri, by T. C. H. Jacobs. Paul, S., 1947
Danger Money, by Thomas Curtis Hicks Jacobs. Hale, R., 1963
Dangerous Fortune, by Thomas Curtis Hicks Jacobs. Paul, S., 1951
Dark Avenue. Ward, Lock, 1957
The Deadly Race, by Thomas Curtis Hicks Jacobs. Long, 1958
Death in the Mews, by Thomas Curtis Hicks Jacobs. Paul, S., 1955
Death on the Moor. Hale, R., 1962
Documents of Murder; see The Bronkhurst Case
Double Diamond. Hale, R., 1959
The Elusive Mr. Drago, by Thomas Curtis Hicks Jacobs. Hale, R., 1964
Goodnight, Sailor, by Thomas Curtis Hicks Jacobs. Paul, S., 1955
The Grenson Murder Case, by T. C. H. Jacobs. Paul, S., 1943
Identity Unknown, by T. C. H. Jacobs. Paul, S., 1938
The Kestrel House Mystery, by T. C. H. Jacobs. Paul, S., 1932; Macaulay, 1933
Lady What's Your Game?, by Thomas Curtis Hicks Jacobs. Paul, S., 1952
The Laughing Men, by T. C. H. Jacobs. Hodder, 1937
Let Him Stay Dead, by Thomas Curtis Hicks Jacobs. Hale, R., 1961
Lock the Door, Mademoiselle, by Thomas Curtis Hicks Jacobs. Paul, S., 1951
Long Shadow. Hale, R., 1959
Mademoiselle, by Thomas Curtis Hicks Jacobs. Paul, S., 1951
Mission in Tunis. Hale, R., 1958; Paperback Lib., 1967
Murder Market, by Thomas Curtis Hicks Jacobs. Hale, R., 1962
No Sleep for Elsa, by Thomas Curtis Hicks Jacobs. Paul, S., 1953
Operation Carlo. Hale, R., 1963
Pageant of Murder, by Thomas Curtis Hicks Jacobs. Paul, S., 1957
The Perfect Wife. Hale, R., 1962
The Red Eyes of Kali, by Thomas Curtis Hicks Jacobs. Paul, S., 1952
The Red Net, by Thomas Curtis Hicks Jacobs. Hale, R., 1962
Results of an Accident, by Thomas Curtis Hicks Jacobs. Paul, S., 1955
Reward for Treason, by T. C. H. Jacobs. Paul, S., 1944
The Scorpion's Trail, by T. C. H. Jacobs. Paul, S., 1933; Macaulay, 1934
The Secret Power, by Thomas Curtis Hicks Jacobs. Hale, R., 1963
The Silent Terror, by T. C. H. Jacobs. Paul, S., 1936; Macaulay, 1937
The Sinister Quest, by T. C. H. Jacobs. Macaulay, 1934; Paul, S., 1934
Target for Terror, by Thomas Curtis Hicks Jacobs. Hale, R., 1961
The Tattooed Man, by Thomas Curtis Hicks Jacobs. Hale, R., 1961
The Terror of Torlands, by T. C. H. Jacobs. Paul, S., 1930
The Thirteenth Chime, by T. C. H. Jacobs. Macaulay, 1934; Paul, S., 1935
Traitor Spy, by T. C. H. Jacobs. Paul, S., 1939
The Widow from Spain. Hale, R., 1961

With What Motive?, by T. C. H. Jacobs. Paul, S., 1948
Women Are Like That, by Thomas Curtis Hicks Jacobs. Hale, R., 1960
The Women Who Waited, by Thomas Curtis Hicks Jacobs. Paul, S., 1954

PENFIELD, CORNELIA (D)
After the Deacon Was Murdered. Putnam, 1933
After the Widow Changed Her Mind. Putnam, 1933

PENMARE, WILLIAM, pseud; see NISOT, MAVIS ELIZABETH HOCKING

PENNY, RUPERT (M)
The Sealed-Room Murder. Collins, 1941
The Talkative Policeman. Collins, 1936

PENTECOST, HUGH, pseud; see PHILIPS, JUDSON

PEOPLE, GRANVILLE CHURCH (S) (Pseudonym: Granville Church)
Bombs Burst Once. Mill, 1941 (Also published as: Devil Sprouts Wings)
Devil Sprouts Wings; see Bombs Burst Once
Race with the Sun. McLeod, 1944; Mill, 1944

PERCY, CATHERINE, pseud. (D)
Death Is Skin Deep. Abelard, 1953

PERDUE, VIRGINIA (M)
Alarum and Excursion. Doubleday, Doran, 1944; Jarrolds, 1947
The Case of the Foster Father. Jarrolds, 1946
The Case of the Grieving Monkey. Doubleday, Doran, 1940
He Fell Down Dead. Doubleday, Doran, 1943; Jarrolds, 1944
The Singing Clock. Doubleday, Doran, 1941; Jarrolds, 1945

PERKERSON, MEDORA FIELD; see FIELD, MEDORA

PERKINS, KENNETH (S)
Voodoo'd. Harper, 1931 (English title: The Horror of the Juvenal Manse. Hutchinson, 1931)

PEROWNE, BARRY (D)
All Exits Blocked; see Gibraltar Prisoner
Arrest These Men! Cassell, 1932
Ask No Mercy. Cassell, 1937
Blonde Without Escort. Cassell, 1940
Enemy of Women. Cassell, 1934
Gibraltar Prisoner. Cassell, 1942 (U.S. title: All Exits Blocked. Arcadia, 1942)
The Girl on Zero. Cassell, 1939
I'm No Murderer. Cassell, 1938
Ladies in Retreat. Cassell, 1935
Raffles After Dark. Cassell, 1933 (U.S. title: Return of Raffles. Day, 1933)
Raffles and the Key Man. Lippincott, 1940
Raffles in Pursuit. Cassell, 1934
Raffles Under Sentence: The Amateur Cracksman Escapes. Cassell, 1936
Return of Raffles; see Raffles After Dark
She Married Raffles. Cassell, 1936
Ten Words of Poison; see The Whispering Cracksman
The Tilted Moon. Cassell, 1949
The Whispering Cracksman. Cassell, 1940 (U.S. title: Ten Words of Poison. Arcadia, 1941)

PERRY, FRANK (M)
The Mystery of the Girl in Blue. Dodge, 1938

PERRY, GEORGE S.; see DISNEY, DOROTHY CAMERON

PERRY, JAMES DeWOLFF (M)
Murder Walks the Corridors. Macmillan, 1937 (English title: Corridors of Fear. Constable, 1937)

PERRY, ROBERT (M) (Pseudonym: Don Marquis)
The Cruise on the Jasper B. Appleton, D., 1916

PERRY, TYLINE (D)
The Owner Lies Dead. Covici, 1930; Gollancz, 1930

PERTWEE, RONALD (D)
Death in a Domino. Houghton, 1932
Interference. Cassell, 1927; Houghton, 1927
Men of Affairs. Knopf, 1922
Transactions of Lord Louis Lewis. Murray, J., 1917

PERUTZ, KATHRIN (S)
The Garden. Atheneum, 1962 (Also published as: A House on the Sound. Signet, 1966)

PERUTZ, LEO (S)
From Nine to Nine. Viking, 1926
Master of the Day of Judgment. Boni, 1930; Collier, 1963

PESKETT, S. JOHN (D)
Murders at Turbot Towers. Butterworth, T., 1937

PETERS, ALAN (D)
Who Killed the Doctors? Heath, 1933; Mussey, 1934

PETERS, BILL, pseud; see McGIVERN, WILLIAM PETER

PETERS, BRYAN, pseud; see GEORGE, PETER

PETERS, ELLIS, pseud; see PARGETER, EDITH

PETERS, LUDOVIC (M-S)
Cry Vengeance. Abelard, 1961; Hamilton, 1962
Out by the River. Hodder, 1964; Walker & Co., 1965
Riot '71. Walker & Co., 1967
Snatch of Music. Abelard, 1962
Tarakian. Abelard, 1964
Two After Malic. Hodder, 1966; Walker & Co., 1966
Two Sets to Murder. Hodder, 1963; Coward, 1964

PETERSEN, HERMAN (D)
The D.A's Daughter. Duell, 1943
Murder in the Making. McBride, 1940
Murder R.F.D. Duell, 1942
Old Bones. Duell, 1943

PETERSON, JAN (S)
The Gestapo Trial. Gollancz, 1939

PETERSON, MARGARET (M) (Pseudonym: Glint Green)
Beauty—a Snare, by Glint Green. Hutchinson, 1933
Blind Eyes. Melrose, 1914
Deadly Nightshade. Hurst, 1924
The Death Drum. Hurst, 1919
Death in Goblin Waters. Hutchinson, 1934
Devil Spider, by Glint Green. Hutchinson, 1932
The Eye of Isis. Hutchinson, 1931
Fatal Shadows. Hutchinson, 1931
Fear Shadowed. Hutchinson, 1927
The Feet of Death. Hutchinson, 1927
Green Stones of Evil. Melrose, 1921
Guilty, My Lord. Hutchinson, 1928
Poison Death, by Glint Green. Hutchinson, 1933
Strands of Red...Hair!, by Glint Green. Hutchinson, 1931

PETRIE, RHONA (M)
Death in Deakins Wood. Gollancz, 1963; Dodd, 1964
Murder by Precedent. Doubleday, 1964; Gollancz, 1964
Running Deep. Doubleday, 1965; Gollancz, 1965

PETTEE, FLORENCE MAE (M)
The Palgrave Mummy. Payson & Clarke, 1929; Jacobsen, 1931

PETTIT, PAUL (M)
The Spaniard. Harper, 1953; Musson, 1953

PEVERETT, ALLAN (M)
Death Stalks in Kenya. Stockwell, 1957

PFALZGRAF, FLORENCE LEIGHTON (M) (Pseudonym: Florence Leighton)
As Strange a Maze. Archer, 1935

PHILIPS, JUDSON PENTECOST (D) (Pseudonym: Hugh Pentecost)
The Assassins, by Hugh Pentecost. Dodd, 1955
The Black Glass City. Dodd, 1964; Gollancz, 1965
The Brass Chills, by Hugh Pentecost. Dodd, 1943; Hale, R., 1944
Cancelled in Red, by Hugh Pentecost. Dodd, 1939; Heinemann, 1939
The Cannibal Who Overate, by Hugh Pentecost. Dodd, 1962; Avon, 1963; Boardman, T. V., 1963
Choice of Violence, by Hugh Pentecost. Dodd, 1961; Boardman, T. V., 1962
The Creeping Hours, by Hugh Pentecost. Dodd, 1966
The Dead Can't Love. Dodd, 1963; Gollancz, 1963
A Dead Ending. Dodd, 1962; Gollancz, 1963
Dead Woman of the Year, by Hugh Pentecost. Dodd, 1967
The Deadly Friend. Dodd, 1961; Boardman, T. V., 1962
Death Delivers a Postcard. Washburn, 1939; Hurst, 1940
Death Syndicate. Washburn, 1938; Hurst, 1939
Death Wears a Copper Tie and Other Stories, by Hugh Pentecost. Edwards, W., 1946
The Evil That Men Do, by Hugh Pentecost. Boardman, T. V., 1966; Dodd, 1966; GM, 1967
The Fourteenth Trump. Dodd, 1942; Hale, R., 1951
The Golden Trap, by Hugh Pentecost. Dodd, 1967
Hide Her from Every Eye. Dodd, 1966
I'll Sing at Your Funeral, by Hugh Pentecost. Dodd, 1942; Hale, R., 1945
Killer on the Catwalk. Dodd, 1959; Gollancz, 1960
The Kingdom of Death, by Hugh Pentecost. Dodd, 1960; Bantam, 1961; Boardman, T. V., 1961
The Laughter Trap. Dodd, 1964
Lieutenant Pascal's Tastes in Homicide, by Hugh Pentecost. Dodd, 1954; Boardman, T. V., 1955
The Lonely Target, by Hugh Pentecost. Dodd, 1959; Boardman, T. V., 1960

Memory of Murder, by Hugh Pentecost. Ziff-Davis, 1945
Murder Clear, Track Fast. Dodd, 1961; Gollancz, 1962; PB, 1962
Murder in Marble. Dodd, 1940; Hale, R., 1950
The Obituary Club, by Hugh Pentecost. Dodd, 1958; Boardman, T. V., 1959; Dell, 1960
Odds on the Hot Seat. Dodd, 1941; Hale, R., 1946
Only the Rich Die Young, by Hugh Pentecost. Boardman, T. V., 1964; Dodd, 1964
Red War, with T. M. Johnson. Doubleday, Doran, 1936
Shadow of Madness, by Hugh Pentecost. Dodd, 1950
The Shape of Fear, by Hugh Pentecost. Boardman, T. V., 1964; Dodd, 1964
Sniper, by Hugh Pentecost. Dodd, 1965
The Tarnished Angel, by Hugh Pentecost. Boardman, T. V., 1963; Dodd, 1963; Avon, 1965
Thursday's Folly. Dodd, 1967
The Twenty-fourth Horse, by Hugh Pentecost. Dodd, 1940; Hale, R., 1951
The Twisted People. Dodd, 1965
Where the Snow Was Red, by Hugh Pentecost. Dodd, 1949; Hale, R., 1951
Whisper Town. Dodd, 1960; Gollancz, 1961; Bantam, 1964
The Wings of Madness. Dodd, 1966; Gollancz, 1967

PHILIPS, PAGE; see SCARBOROUGH, GEORGE

PHILLIFENT, JOHN T. (M)
The Mad Scientist Affair. Ace, 1966 (The Man from U.N.C.L.E. series #5)

PHILLIPS, CONRAD (M)
Cry of the Dingo. Barker, 1956
Dolls with Sad Faces. Barker, 1957; Roy Pubs., 1957
The Empty Cot. Barker, 1958
The Unrepentant. Barker, 1958; Roy Pubs., 1958

PHILLIPS, DENNIS JOHN ANDREW (S) (Pseudonyms: Peter Chambers, Peter Chester)
Always Take the Big Ones, by Peter Chambers. Hale, R., 1965
The Big Goodbye, by Peter Chambers. Hale, R., 1962
Blueprint for Larceny, by Peter Chester. Jenkins, 1964
Dames Can Be Deadly, by Peter Chambers. Hale, R., 1963; Abelard, 1964
Don't Bother to Knock. Hale, R., 1966
The Down-Beat Kill, by Peter Chambers. Hale, R., 1963; Abelard, 1964
Killing Comes Easy, by Peter Chester. Jenkins, 1958; Roy Pubs., 1960
Lady, This Is Murder, by Peter Chambers. Hale, R., 1963
Murder Forestalled, by Peter Chester. Jenkins, 1960; Roy Pubs., 1961
Murder Is for Keeps, by Peter Chambers. Hale, R., 1961; Abelard, 1962; Monarch, 1964
No Gold When You Go. Hale, R., 1966
Nobody Lives Forever, by Peter Chambers. Hale, R., 1964
The Pay-Grab Murders, by Peter Chester. Jenkins, 1962
This'll Kill You, by Peter Chambers. Hale, R., 1964
The Traitors, by Peter Chester. Jenkins, 1964
Wreath for a Redhead, by Peter Chambers. Abelard, 1962; Hale, R., 1962
You're Better Off Dead, by Peter Chambers. Hale, R., 1965

PHILLIPS, GERALD WILLIAM (D) (Pseudonym: John Huntingdon)
Seven Black Chessmen. Holt, H., 1928

PHILLIPS, JAMES ATLEE (M) (Pseudonym: Philip Atlee)
The Case of the Shivering Chorus Girls. Coward, 1942; Bodley Head, 1950
The Deadly Mermaid, by Philip Atlee. Dell, 1954
The Death Bird Contract, by Philip Atlee. GM, 1966
The Green Wound, by Philip Atlee. GM, 1963 (Also published as: The Green Wound Contract. GM, 1967)
The Green Wound Contract; see The Green Wound
The Irish Beauty Contract, by Philip Atlee. GM, 1966
Pagoda. Macmillan, 1951; Bodley Head, 1953; Transworld, 1954
The Paper Pistol Contract, by Philip Atlee. GM, 1966
The Silken Baroness, by Philip Atlee. GM, 1966 (Also published as: The Silken Baroness Contract. GM, 1966)
The Silken Baroness Contract; see The Silken Baroness
The Star Ruby Contract, by Philip Atlee. GM, 1967
Suitable for Framing. Macmillan, 1949; Bodley Head, 1952

PHILLIPS, JEAN (S)
Greenwood. Lancer, 1965

PHILLIPS, LEON, pseud; see GERSON, NOEL BERTRAM

PHILLIPS, RUSSELL R. (M)
Death Smiles. Macaulay, 1936

PHILLPOTTS, EDEN (D) (Pseudonym: Harrington Hext)
The Anniversary Murder. Dutton, 1936
Awake Deborah! Methuen, 1940; Macmillan, 1941
Black, White and Brindled. Macmillan, 1923; Richards, 1923
The Captain's Curio. Hutchinson, 1933; Macmillan, 1933
A Close Call. Hutchinson, 1936; Macmillan, 1936
A Clue from the Stars. Hutchinson, 1932; Macmillan, 1932
Deed Without a Name. Hutchinson, 1941
The Farm of the Dagger. Dodd, 1904; Newnes, 1904
Found Drowned. Hutchinson, 1930; Macmillan, 1931
The Grey Room. Hurst, 1921; Macmillan, 1927
The Hidden Hand. Hutchinson, 1952
Jigsaw. Macmillan, 1926; White House, 1929
The Jury. Hutchinson, 1927; Macmillan, 1927
Lycanthrope. Butterworth, T., 1937; Macmillan, 1938
Mr. Digweed and Mr. Lumb. Macmillan, 1934
Monkshood. Macmillan, 1939; Methuen, 1939
The Monster, by Harrington Hext. Macmillan, 1925
Number 87, by Harrington Hext. Butterworth, T., 1922; Macmillan, 1922
Portrait of a Scoundrel. Macmillan, 1938; Murray, J., 1938
The Red Redmaynes. Macmillan, 1922; Hutchinson, 1923
The Thing at Their Heels, by Harrington Hext. Butterworth, T., 1923; Macmillan, 1923
A Voice from the Dark. Hutchinson, 1925; Macmillan, 1925
Who Killed Cock Robin? by Harrington Hext. Macmillan, 1924 (English title: Who Killed Diana? Butterworth, T., 1924)
Who Killed Diana?; see Who Killed Cock Robin?
The Wife of Elias. Hutchinson, 1935; Dutton, 1937

PHILMORE, R., pseud; see HOWARD, HERBERT EDMUND

PICKARD, MRS. F. L. S.; see GAYE, PHOEBE FENWICK

PICKERING, EDITH (M)
Murder of a Headmistress. Longmans, 1937

PICKERING, ROBERT (S)
The Uncommitted Man. Farrar, 1967

PICTON, BERNARD, pseud. (D)
The Lately Deceased. Jenkins, 1963

PIERSON, ELEANOR M. (D)
The Defense Rests. Howell, Soskin, 1942
Good Neighbor Murder. Howell, Soskin, 1941

PIKE, ROBERT, pseud; see FISH, ROBERT L.

PILGRIM, CHAD (D)
The Silent Slain. Abelard, 1958

PIM, SHEILA (D)
Brush with Death. Hodder, 1950
Common or Garden Crime. Hodder, 1945
Creeping Venom. Hodder, 1947
A Hive of Suspects. Hodder, 1952; British Book Centre, 1953

PINCHOT, ANN (S)
The Twisted Cross. Paperback Lib., 1964

PINGET, ROBERT (S)
The Inquisitory. Grove, 1967

PINKERTON, ALLAN (D)
The Bank Robbers and the Detectives. Carleton, G., 1883
Claude Melnotte as a Detective and Other Stories. Keen, 1875
The Detective and the Somnambulist: the Murderer and the Fortune Teller. Keen, 1875
The Expressman and the Detective. Keen, 1874
The Model Town and the Detective: Byron as a Detective. Carleton, G., 1876
The Railroad Forger and the Detectives. Carleton, G., 1881

PINKERTON, FRANK (M)
Jim Cummings: or, the Great Adams Express Robbery. Laird, 1887

PIPER, EVELYN, pseud; see MODELL, MIRIAM

PIPER, H. BEAM (D)
The Murder in the Gunroom. Knopf, 1953

PIPER, PETER, pseud; see LANG, THEO

PIRKIS, CATHERINE LOUISA (D)
The Experiences of Loveday Brooke, Lady Detective. Hutchinson, 1894

PITCAIRN, JOHN JAMES; see FREEMAN, DR. RICHARD AUSTIN FREEMAN

PITMAN, WILLIAM DENT (M)
The Quincunx Case. Turner, 1904

PLAIN, JOSEPHINE (D-M)
The Pazenger Problem. Butterworth, T., 1936
The Secret of the Sandbank. Butterworth, T., 1934
The Secret of the Snows. Butterworth, T., 1935

PLANTZ, DONALD (S)
Marked for Death. Monarch, 1964

PLATT, CHARLES; see BAMBURG, LILIAN

PLATT, ROBERT (M)
The Swaying Corpse. Phoenix, 1941

PLAYER, ROBERT (D)
The Ingenious Mr. Stone. Gollancz, 1945; Rinehart, 1946

PLEASANTS, W. SHEPARD (D)
The Stingaree Murders. Mystery League, 1932

PLEYDELL, GEORGE BANCROFT (M)
The Ware Case. Doran, 1913; Methuen, 1913

PLUM, MARY (D)
The Broken Vase Mystery. Eyre, 1933
Dead Man's Secret. Eyre, 1931; Harper, 1931
The Killing of Judge MacFarlane. Eyre, 1930; Harper, 1930
Murder at the Hunting Club. Harper, 1932; Eyre, 1933
Murder at the World's Fair. Harper, 1933
Murder of a Redhaired Man. Arcadia, 1952
State Department Cat. Doubleday, Doran, 1945
Suzanna, Don't You Cry. Doubleday, 1946

PLUMMER, THOMAS ARTHUR (M)
(Pseudonym: Michael Sarne)
The Ace of Death. Paul, S., 1930
Alias - The Crimson Snake. Paul, S., 1933
The Barush Murder. Paul, S., 1946
The Black Rat. Paul, S., 1955
The Black Ribbon Murders. Paul, S., 1940
Brent - of Bleak House. Paul, S., 1948
The Broken Trust. Thomson, D. C., 1929
Condemned to Live. Paul, S., 1957
Cornered. Long, 1938
The Creaking Gallows. Paul, S., 1934
Crime at Crooked Gables. Paul, S., 1941
Death Haunts the Repertory. Paul, S., 1950
The Death Letter. Paul, S., 1951
Death on Danger Hill. Paul, S., 1931
The Death Symbol. Paul, S., 1937
Death Takes a Hand. Paul, S., 1934
The Devil's Tea-Party. Paul, S., 1942
The Dumb Witness. Paul, S., 1936
Elusive Killer. Long, 1958
Five Were Murdered. Paul, S., 1938
The Fool of the Yard. Paul, S., 1942
Frampton of the Yard. Paul, S., 1935
Frampton Sees Red. Paul, S., 1953
The Girl in a Hurry. Thomson, D.C., 1932
Haunting Lights. Paul, S., 1932
The House in Sinister Lane. Paul, S., 1931
Hunted! Paul, S., 1948
The "J for Jennie" Murders. Paul, S., 1945
Lonely Hollow Mystery. Paul, S., 1933
Lying Lips. Long, 1938
The Man They Feared. Paul, S., 1937
The Man They Put Away. Paul, S., 1938
The Man Who Changed His Face. Paul, S., 1943
The Man with the Crooked Arm. Paul, S., 1945
Melody of Death. Paul, S., 1940
Murder at Lantern Corner. Long, 1959
Murder at Marlinton. Paul, S., 1951
Murder by an Idiot. Paul, S., 1944
The Murder House. Paul, S., 1930
Murder in the Surgery. Paul, S., 1955
Murder in the Village. Paul, S., 1945
Murder in Windy Coppice. Paul, S., 1954
Murder Limps By. Paul, S., 1943
The Murder of Doctor Grey. Paul, S., 1950
Murder Through Room 45. Paul, S., 1952
The Muse Theatre Murder. Paul, S., 1939
The Pierced Ear Murders. Paul, S., 1947
The Scarlet Saint, by Michael Sarne. Paul, S., 1932
A Scream at Midnight. Paul, S., 1954
Shadowed by the C.I.D. Paul, S., 1932
Shot at Night. Paul, S., 1934
The Silent Four. Paul, S., 1947
Simon Takes the Rap. Paul, S., 1944
Staring Eyes! Paul, S., 1935
The Starry Eyed Murder. Paul, S., 1952
The Strangler. Paul, S., 1945

Strychnine for One. Paul, S., 1949
Two Men from the East. Paul, S., 1939
Was the Mayor Murdered? Paul, S., 1936
The Westlade Murders. Paul, S., 1953
Who Fired the Factory? Paul, S., 1947
The Yellow Disc Murders. Paul, S., 1950

POATE, ERNEST M. (M)
Behind Locked Doors. Chelsea House, 1923
Doctor Bentiron: Detective. Chelsea House, 1930
Murder on the Brain. Chelsea House, 1930
Pledged to the Dead. Chelsea House, 1925
Trouble at Pinelands. Chelsea House, 1922; Burt, 1925

POCOCK, DORIS A.
The Mystery of the Marsh. Appleton, D., 1929
The Secret of Hallowdene Farm. Nisbet, 1923; Appleton, D., 1924

POE, EDGAR ALLAN (D)
Eighteen Best Stories. Dell, 1965
The Gold Bug and Other Tales. Humphries, 1965
Tales of Mystery and Imagination. Dent, 1908; Dutton, 1931

POE, EDGAR ALLAN, JR. (M)
The House Party. Lippincott, 1940

POLANSKY, ABRAHAM; see WILLSON, MITCHELL A.

POLLARD, ALFRED OLIVER (M)
Deal in Death. Hutchinson, 1947
Death Game. Hutchinson, 1936
Death Parade. Hutchinson, 1952
The Iron Curtain. Hutchinson, 1947
Red Target. Hutchinson, 1952
Sinister Secret. Hutchinson, 1956
Smugglers Buoy. Hutchinson, 1960
Wrong Verdict. Long, 1960

POLLARD, MADELAINE (M-S)
Minutes of a Murder. Holt, 1967
Thicker Than Water. Holt, 1965; Pyramid, 1966; Hutchinson, 1967

POLLOCK, CHANNING (M)
Synthetic Gentleman. Farrar & Rinehart, 1934

POLSKY, THOMAS (D)
The Cudgel. Dutton, 1950
Curtains for the Copper. Dutton, 1941
Curtains for the Editor. Dutton, 1939
Curtains for the Judge. Dutton, 1939

PONDER, ZITA INEZ
The Bandaged Face. Selwyn, 1927; Macaulay, 1929

POPKIN, ZELDA (D)
Dead Man's Gift. Lippincott, 1941; Hutchinson, 1948
Death Wears a White Gardenia. Lippincott, 1938; Hutchinson, 1939
Murder in the Mist. Lippincott, 1940; Hutchinson, 1941
No Crime for a Lady. Lippincott, 1942
Quiet Street. Lippincott, 1951
So Much Blood. Lippincott, 1944; Hutchinson, 1946
Time Off for Murder. Hutchinson, 1940; Lippincott, 1940

PORCELAIN, SIDNEY E. (D)
The Crimson Cat Murders. Phoenix, 1946
The Purple Pony Murders. Phoenix, 1944; Partridge, 1948

PORLOCK, MARTIN, pseud; see MacDONALD, PHILIP

PORTER, HAROLD EVERETT (M)
(Pseudonym: Holworthy Hall)
What He Least Expected. Bobbs, 1917

PORTER, JOYCE (D)
Dover and the Unkindest Cut of All. Cape, 1967; Scribner, 1967
Dover One. Cape, 1964; Scribner, 1964; Crest, 1966
Dover Three. Cape, 1963; Scribner, 1966
Dover Two. Cape, 1965; Scribner, 1965; Crest, 1968
Sour Cream with Everything. Scribner, 1966

PORTER, MONICA (M)
Mercy of the Court. Norton, 1955

PORTER, REBECCA NEWMAN (M)
The Rest Hollow Mystery. Century, 1922; Long, 1924

PORTER, WILLIAM SYDNEY (Pseudonym: O. Henry)
The Complete Works. Doubleday, Page, 1927
The Gentle Grafter. McClure, 1908

POSNER, JACOB D. (D) (Pseudonym: Gregory Dean)
The Case of Marie Corwin. Covici, 1933; Nicholson, 1935
The Case of the Fifth Key. Covici, 1934; Nicholson, 1936
Murder on Stilts. Hillman-Curl, 1939

POST, MELVILLE DAVISSON (D)
The Bradmoor Murder. Sears, 1929 (Also published as: The Garden in Asia. Brentano, 1929)
The Corrector of Destinies. Clode, 1908
Dwellers in the Hills. Putnam, 1901
The Garden in Asia; see The Bradmoor Murders
The Gilded Chair. Appleton, D., 1910
The Man of Last Resort. Putnam, 1898
Monsieur Jonquelle, Prefect of Police of Paris. Appleton, D., 1923
The Mystery at the Blue Villa. Appleton, D., 1929
The Nameless Thing. Appleton, D., 1912
Randolph Mason: The Clients. Putnam, 1923
Randolph Mason: Corrector of Destinies Putnam, 1923
Revolt of the Birds. Appleton, D., 1927
The Silent Witness. Farrar & Rinehart, 1930
The Sleuth of St. James' Square. Appleton, D., 1920
The Strange Schemes of Randolph Mason. Putnam, 1908
Uncle Abner, Master of Mysteries. Appleton, D., 1918; Collier, 1962
Walker of the Secret Service. Appleton, D., 1924

POST, MORTIMER (M)
Candidate for Murder. Doubleday, Doran, 1936

POSTGATE, JOHN W. (M)
The Mystery of Paul Chadwick. Laird, 1896
Private Detective No. 39. Ogilvie
Woman's Devotion; or, The Mixed Marriage. Rand, 1886

POSTGATE, RAYMOND (M)
The Ledger Is Kept. Joseph, M., 1953
Somebody at the Door. Joseph, M., 1943; Knopf, 1943; Grosset
The Verdict of Twelve. Doubleday, Doran, 1940; PB, 1946; Knopf, 1967; Triangle

POTTER, GEORGE WILLIAM (M) (Pseudonym: E. L. Withers)
The Birthday. Doubleday, 1962
Diminishing Returns. Rinehart, 1960; PB, 1961
Heir Apparent. Doubleday, 1961; Avon, 1962
House on the Beach. Rinehart, 1957
The Salazar Grant. Rinehart, 1957

POTTER, JEREMY (M)
Foul Play. Constable, 1967

POTTS, JEAN (D)
Blood Will Tell. Gollancz, 1959
The Death of a Stray Cat. Scribner, 1955; Berkley Pub., 1961
The Diehard. Scribner, 1956; Dell
The Evil Wish. Scribner, 1962; Ace, 1964
The Footsteps on the Stairs. Scribner, 1966; Gollancz, 1967
Go, Lovely Rose. Scribner, 1954; Gollancz, 1955; Berkley Pub., 1961; Penguin, 1961
Home Is the Prisoner. Scribner, 1960; Berkley Pub., 1961; Gollancz, 1961; Penguin
Lightning Strikes Twice. Scribner, 1959; Dell
The Man with the Cane. Scribner, 1957; Gollancz, 1958; Berkley Pub., 1961; Penguin
The Only Good Secretary. Scribner, 1965; Ace, 1966
The Trash Stealers. Scribner, 1968

POU, GENEVIEVE LONG (D) (Pseudonym: Genevieve Holden)
Deadlier Than the Male. Doubleday, 1961
Don't Go in Alone. Doubleday, 1965; Hale, R., 1966
Killer Loose! Doubleday, 1953
Something's Happened to Kate. Doubleday, 1958; Ace, 1965
Sound an Alarm. Doubleday, 1954
The Velvet Target. Doubleday, 1956; Ace, 1965

POWELL, DAVID H. (D)
Dragnet '68. Popular Lib., 1967

POWELL, FRANCES (M)
The Prisoner of Ornith Farm. Scribner, 1906

POWELL, ISABELLA BAYNE-; see BAYNE-POWELL, ISABELLA

POWELL, LESTER (S)
The Black Casket. Collins, 1955
The Count of Six. Collins, 1948
Shadow Play. Collins, 1949
Spot the Lady. Collins, 1950
The Still of Night. Collins, 1952

POWELL, PERCIVAL HENRY (D)
Death of an Expert Witness. Hale, R., 1957
Fatal Mistake. Hale, R., 1956
Murder Premeditated. Jenkins, 1951; Roy Pubs., 1958
Now Lying Dead. Jenkins, 1953
Only Three Died. Low, 1951
The Police Murders. Hale, R., 1955
Why Kill a Butler? Jenkins, 1952; Roy Pubs., 1957

POWELL, RICHARD PITTS (D)
All Over But the Shooting. S & S, 1944
And Hope to Die. S & S, 1947
Don't Catch Me. S & S, 1943
False Colors. S & S, 1955
Lay That Pistol Down. S & S, 1945
Say It with Bullets. S & S, 1953
Shark River. S & S, 1949
Shell Game. S & S, 1950
Shoot If You Must. S & S, 1946
A Shot in the Dark. S & S, 1952; Award, 1965

POWELL, ROSAMUND BAYNE-; see BAYNE-POWELL, ROSAMUND

POWELL, TALMAGE (D-S) (Pseudonym: Jack McCready)
Bad Girls. Crest, 1958
Corpus Delectable, by Jack McCready. PB
The Girl Who Killed Things. Zenith, 1960
The Girl's Number Doesn't Answer. PB, 1960
The Killer Is Mine, by Jack McCready. PB, 1959
Man Killer. Ace, 1960
Murder in Miami. Dell, 1959 (Anthology)
The Raper, by Jack McCready. Monarch, 1962
The Smasher, by Jack McCready. Macmillan, 1959
Start Screaming Murder. Permabooks, 1962
With a Madman Behind Me, by Jack McCready. Permabooks, 1962

POWLETT, NIGEL AMYAS ORDE-; see ORDE-POWLETT, NIGEL AMYAS

POYNTER, BEULAH (M)
Disappearance of Mary Ambler. Greenberg, 1934
Murder on 47th Street. Doubleday, Doran, 1931
The Murillo Mystery. Altemus, 1927

PRAED, MRS. CAMPBELL (M)
Brother of the Shadow. Routledge, 1886
Mystery Woman. Cassell, 1913

PRATHER, RICHARD SCOTT (D) (Pseudonyms: David Knight, Douglas Ring)
Always Leave 'Em Dying. GM, 1954
Bodies in Bedlam. GM, 1951
The Case of the Vanishing Beauty. GM, 1950, 1966
The Cockeyed Corpse. GM, 1963
The Comfortable Coffin. GM, 1960, 1966
Dagger of Flesh. Falcon, 1952; GM, 1956
Dance with the Dead. GM, 1960, 1964
Darling, It's Death. GM, 1952, 1965
Dead Heat. PB, 1963
Dead Man's Walk. PB, 1965
Dig That Crazy Grave. GM, 1961, 1965; Muller, 1962
Double in Trouble, with Stephen Marlowe. GM, 1959, 1965
Dragnet - Case No. 561, by David Knight. PB, 1956
Everybody Had a Gun. GM, 1951; Muller, 1953
Find This Woman. GM, 1951, 1965
Gat Heat. S & S, 1967; Trident, 1967
Have Gat - Will Travel. GM, 1957
The Joker in the Deck. GM, 1963
Kill Him Twice. PB, 1965
Kill the Clown. GM, 1962
The Kubla Khan Caper. Trident, 1966
Lie Down, Killer. Lion, 1952; GM, 1964
The Meandering Corpse. Trident, 1965; PB, 1966
Over Her Dear Body. GM, 1959, 1965
Pattern for Murder, by David Knight. Graphic, 1952 (Also published as: The Scrambled Yeggs. GM, 1963)
Pattern for Panic. Abelard, 1954; Muller, 1962; GM, 1963
The Peddler, by Douglas Ring. Lion, 1952; GM, 1962; Muller, 1963
Ride a High Horse; see Too Many Crooks
The Scrambled Yeggs; see Pattern for Murder
Shell Scott's Seven Slaughters. GM, 1961
Slab Happy. GM, 1958, 1965
Strip for Murder. GM, 1955
Take a Murder, Darling. GM, 1958
Three's a Shroud. GM, 1957
Too Many Crooks. GM, 1953, 1965 (Also published as: Ride a High Horse. GM, 1953)
The Trojan Horse. PB, 1956
The Wailing Frail. GM, 1956
The Way of a Wanton. GM, 1952, 1965

PRATT, MRS. ELEANOR BLAKE ATKINSON (D) (Pseudonym: Eleanor Blake)
Death Down East. Putnam, 1940

PRATT, FLETCHER; see BUTLER, ELLIS PARKER

PRATT, THEODORE (D) (Pseudonym: Timothy Brace)
Murder Goes Fishing. Dutton, 1936; Selwyn, 1937
Murder Goes in a Trailer. Dutton, 1937
Murder Goes to the Dogs. Dutton, 1938
Murder Goes to the World's Fair. Dutton, 1939

PRAVIEL, ARMAND (M)
The Murder of Monsieur Fualdes. Boni, 1924; Seltzer, 1924

PREEDY, GEORGE, pseud; see LONG, MRS. GABRIELLE MARGARET

PRESCOT, JULIAN (M)
A Case for Hearing. Barker, 1963

PRESCOTT, HILDA FRANCES MARGARET (M)
Dead and Not Buried. Macmillan, 1954; Eyre, 1957; Collier, 1965

PRESNELL, FRANK G. (M)
No Mourners Present. Morrow, 1940; Nicholson, 1943
Send Another Coffin. Heinemann, 1939; Morrow, 1939
Too Hot to Handle. Mill, 1951

PRESS, SYLVIA (M)
Care of Devils. Beacon, 1958

PRESSBURGER, EMERIC (S)
Killing a Mouse on Sunday. Harcourt, 1961 (Also published as: Behold a Pale Horse. Collins, 1961; Bantam, 1964)

PREST, THOMAS (M)
Varnery the Vampire; or, The Feast of Blood. Lloyd, E., 1847

PRICE, FRANK J. (D)
The Mind Wreckers, Limited, and Other Adventures of Barrow—Ace Insurance Detective. Spectator, 1933

PRICE, WESLEY (M)
Death Is a Stowaway. Wright & Brown, 1935

PRICHARD, VERNON HESKETH (D)
November Joe, Detective of the Woods. Hodder, 1913

PRIDHAM, SYLVIA SANDYS (M)
Case of the Poisoned Pup. Arcadia,1961

PRIESTLEY, CLIVE RYLAND (Pseudonym: Clive Ryland)
The Case of the Back Seat Girl. Hutchinson, 1952
The Case of the Brown-eyed Housemaid. Hutchinson, 1951
The Selminster Murders. Hutchinson, 1938
Three Died for Morson. Hutchinson, 1950
Visitors for Venning. Hutchinson, 1948

PRIESTLEY, JOHN BOYNTON (M)
Blackout in Gretley. Harper, 1942; Heinemann, 1942
The Old Dark House. Grosset, 1928
Saturn over The Water. Doubleday, 1961; PB, 1963
The Shapes of Sleep. Doubleday, 1962; Popular Lib., 1963

PRIESTLEY, LEE SHORE (D)
Murder Takes the Baths. Arcadia, 1962

PRILEY, MARGARET ANN HUBBARD (M)
Murder at St. Dennis. Bruce Pub., 1952
Murder Takes the Veil. Bruce Pub., 1950
Sister Simon's Murder Case. Bruce Pub., 1959

PRIOR, ALLAN (S)
The Interrogators. S & S, 1965; Ballantine, 1966
One Away. Eyre, 1961; Pan, 1964
The Operators. S & S, 1967
Z Cars Again. Jenkins, 1964

PROCTER, ARTHUR WYMAN (D)
Murder in Manhattan. Morrow, 1930

PROCTER, MAURICE (D)
A Body to Spare. Harper, 1962; Hutchinson, 1962; Collier, 1965
The Chief Inspector's Statement. Hutchinson, 1949 (U.S. title: The Pennycross Murders. Harper, 1951; Avon)
The Devil in Moonlight. Hutchinson, 1962
The Devil Was Handsome. Harper, 1961; Pyramid, 1965
Devil's Due. Harper, 1960; Collier, 1962
Each Man's Destiny. Longmans, 1947
The End of the Street. Longmans, 1948
Exercise Hoodwink. Harper & Row, 1967
The Graveyard Rolls. Harper & Row, 1964
Hell Is a City. Hutchinson, 1953 (U.S. title: Somehwere in This City. Harper, 1954; Pyramid, 1964)
His Weight in Gold. Harper & Row, 1965
Homicide Blonde. Harper & Row, 1965
Hurry the Darkness. Harper, 1950; Hutchinson, 1952; Dell
I Will Speak Daggers. Hutchinson, 1956 (U.S. title: The Ripper. Harper, 1956)
Killer at Large. Harper, 1958; Hutchinson, 1959; Collier, 1962
Man in Ambush. Hutchinson, 1958; Harper, 1960; Collier, 1962
The Midnight Plumber. Doubleday, 1955; Hutchinson, 1957
Moonlight Flitting. Hutchinson, 1963

No Proud Chivalry. Longmans, 1946
The Pennycross Murders; see The Chief Inspector's Statement
The Pub Crawler. Harper, 1956; Hutchinson, 1958; Pyramid, 1965
Rich Is the Treasure. Hutchinson, 1952
The Ripper; see I Will Speak Daggers
Rogue Running. Harper & Row, 1966
Somewhere in This City; see Hell Is a City
The Spearhead Death. Hutchinson, 1961
Three at the Angel. Harper, 1957; Hutchinson, 1958
Two Men in Twenty. Harper & Row, 1964; Hutchinson, 1964

PROKOSCH, FREDERICK (S)
The Conspirators. Chatto, 1943; Harper, 1943

PROPPER, MILTON (D)
And Then Silence. Faber, 1931
The Boudoir Murder. Harper, 1931
The Case of the Cheating Bride. Harper, 1938; Harrap, 1939
The Divorce Court Murder. Faber, 1934; Harper, 1934
The Election Booth Murder. Harper, 1935 (English title: Murder at the Polls. Harrap, 1936)
The Family Burial Murders. Harrap, 1935
The Great Insurance Murders. Harrap, 1938
Hide the Body. Harper, 1939
Murder at the Polls; see The Election Booth Murder
Murders in Sequence. Jenkins, 1947
Murder of an Initiate; see The Student Fraternity Murder
One Murdered, Two Dead. Harper, 1936; Harrap, 1937
The Station Wagon Murder. Harper, 1940
The Strange Disappearance of Mary Young. Harper, 1929
The Student Fraternity Murder. Bobbs, 1932 (English title: Murder of an Initiate. Faber, 1933)
The Ticker Tape Murder. Collier, 1930; Harper, 1930
You Can't Gag the Dead. Jenkins, 1949

PROSPER, JOHN (M)
The Gold-Killer. Doran, 1922

PROUDFOOT, WALTER, pseud; see VAHEY, JOHN GEORGE HASLETTE

PROUT, GEOFFREY (M)
Mystery Marsh. Lutterworth Press, 1939
The Mystery of the Marshes. Lloyd's Detective Series, 1932

PRUITT, ALAN, pseud; see ROSE, ALVIN E.

PRYCE, RICHARD (M)
The Quiet Mrs. Fleming. Methuen, 1892

PRYDE, ANTHONY, pseud; see WEEKES, AGNES RUSSELL

PULLEIN-THOMPSON, JOSEPHINE (M) (Pseudonym: Joanna Cannan)
And Be a Villain. Gollancz, 1958
Blind Messenger. Gollancz, 1941
Body in the Beck. Gollancz, 1953
Death at the Dog. Gollancz, 1940; Reynal, 1941
Frightened Angels. Harper, 1936
Gin and Murder. Hammond, 1959
The High Table. Benn, 1930; Doubleday, Doran, 1931
Long Shadows. Gollancz, 1955
Murder Included. Gollancz, 1950 (Also published as: They Died in the Spring. Hammond, 1960)
No Walls of Jasper. Benn, 1931; Doubleday, Doran, 1931
Poisonous Relations. Morrow, 1950
They Died in the Spring; see Murder Included
They Rang Up the Police. Gollancz, 1939
Under Proof. Hodder, 1934

PULSFORD, NORMAN GEORGE (M) (Pseudonym: A. C. Trevor)
Death Haunts the Lounge. Harper, 1936; Harrap, 1936

PUNNETT, IVOR; see PUNNETT, MARGARET

PUNNETT, MARGARET and IVOR PUNNETT (M-D) (Pseudonym: Roger Simons)
Arrangement for Murder. Bles, 1961; Roy Pubs., 1963
Bullet for a Beast. Bles, 1964; Roy Pubs., 1965
Dead Reckoning. Bles, 1965
Dolphin Sailed North. Heinemann, 1954
A Frame for Murder. Bles, 1960
A Gamble with Death. Bles, 1961; Roy Pubs., 1963
The Houseboat Killing. Bles, 1959
Island Adventure. Heinemann, 1962
The Killing Chase. Bles, 1962
Murder Joins the Chorus. Bles, 1960
Silver and Death. Bles, 1963
Veil of Death. Bles, 1966; Roy Pubs., 1967

PUNSHON, ERNEST ROBERTSON (M)
The Arrows of Chance. Ward, Lock, 1917
The Attending Truth. Gollancz, 1952
The Bath Mysteries. Gollancz, 1936
The Blue John Diamond. Withy Grove, 1946

Brought to Light. Gollancz, 1954
The Choice. Ward, Lock, 1908
Comes a Stranger. Gollancz, 1938
The Conqueror Inn. Gollancz, 1943
Constance West. Lane, 1905
The Cottage Murder. Benn, 1931, 1952
The Crossword Mystery. Gollancz, 1934; Penguin, 1948
The Dark Garden. Gollancz, 1941
Dark Is the Clue. Gollancz, 1955
Death Among the Sunbathers. Benn, 1934
Death Comes to Cambers. Gollancz, 1935
Death of a Beauty Queen. Gollancz, 1935; Penguin, 1948
Diabolic Candelabra. Gollancz, 1942
Dictator's Way. Gollancz, 1938
Dunslow. Ward, Lock, 1922
The Dusky Hour. Gollancz, 1937
Everybody Always Tells. Gollancz, 1950
Four Strange Women. Gollancz, 1940
Genius in Murder. Benn, 1932, 1952
The Golden Dagger. Gollancz, 1951
Hidden Lives. Ward, Lock, 1913
The House of Godwinsson. Gollancz, 1948
Information Received. Benn, 1933; Penguin, 1955
It Might Lead Anywhere. Gollancz, 1946
Murder Abroad. Gollancz, 1939
Music Tells All. Gollancz, 1948
The Mystery of Lady Isobel. Hurst, 1907, 1947
The Mystery of Mr. Jessop. Gollancz, 1937
Mystery Villa. Gollancz, 1934; Penguin, 1950
Night's Cloak. Gollancz, 1944
Proof, Counter Proof. Benn, 1931
The Secret Search. Gollancz, 1951
Secrets Can't Be Kept. Gollancz, 1944
So Many Doors. Gollancz, 1949
The Solitary House. Ward, Lock, 1919; Thomson, D. C., 1929
The Spin of the Coin. Hurst, 1908, 1947
Strange Ending. Gollancz, 1953
Suspects-Nine. Gollancz, 1939
Ten Star Clues. Gollancz, 1941
There's a Reason for Everything. Gollancz, 1945
Three Cases of Murder. Benn, 1956
Triple Quest. Gollancz, 1955
Truth Came Out. Benn, 1932
Unexpected Legacy. Benn, 1929
The Woman's Footprint. Hodder, 1919

PURDUE, VIRGINIA (D)
The Case of the Grieving Monkey. Doubleday, Doran, 1941
It Fell Down Dead. Doubleday, Doran, 1943
The Singing Clock. Doubleday, Doran, 1941

PURSER, PHILIP (M-S)
Four Days to the Fireworks. Hodder, 1964; Walker & Co., 1965
The Twenty Men. Hodder, 1967; Walker & Co., 1967

PURTELL, JOSEPH (M)
To a Blindfold Lady. Reynal, 1942

PYKE, RIVINGTON (M)
The Fellow Passengers. Greening, 1898

QUARRY, NICK, pseud; see ALBERT, MARVIN H.

QUARTERMAIN, H. J. (D)
Death Before Launching. Hamilton, H., 1964

QUEEN, ELLERY, pseud; see DANNAY, FREDERIC

QUENTIN, PATRICK, pseud; see WEBB, RICHARD WILSON

QUICK, DOROTHY (M)
Cry in the Night. Arcadia, 1957
The Fifth Dagger. Scribner, 1947
Something Evil. Arcadia, 1958
Too Strange a Hand. Arcadia, 1959

QUIGLEY, JOHN (M)
Secret Soldier. New Amer. Lib., 1966

QUILLER-COUCH, SIR ARTHUR T. (M)
Castle Dor. Dent, 1962 (Completed by Daphne Du Maurier)
Dead Man's Rock. Cassell, 1887
I Saw Three Ships. Cassell, 1892
Old Fires and Profitable Ghosts. Scribner, 1900
Poison Island. Smith, Elder, 1907

QUIN, ANN MARIE (S)
Berg. Calder, J., 1964; Scribner, 1965

QUIN, BASIL GODFREY (M)
The Death Box. Hutchinson, 1929
Mistigris. Hutchinson, 1932
The Murder Rehearsal. Hutchinson, 1931; Greenberg, 1932
Mystery of the Black Gate. Hutchinson, 1930
Phantom Murder. Hutchinson, 1932

QUINN, ELEANOR BAKER (M)
Dead Harm No One. Heinemann, 1938
Death Is a Restless Sleeper. Heinemann, 1940
One Man's Muddle. Heinemann, 1936; Macmillan, 1937

QUINN, SEABURY (M)
Phantom-Fighter. Mycroft & Moran, 1966

QUIRK, JOHN (S)
The Bunnies. Avon, 1965
The Survivor. Avon, 1965
The Tournament. Avon, 1965; Signet, 1966

QUIRK, LESLIE and HORATIO WINSLOW (M)
Into Thin Air. Doubleday, Doran, 1929; Gollancz, 1929

RABE, PETER (S)
Agreement to Kill. GM, 1951
Anatomy of a Killer. Abelard, 1960; Berkley Pub., 1961
Benny Muscles In. GM, 1955
Blood on the Desert. GM, 1959
The Box. GM, 1962
Bring Me Another Corpse. GM, 1954
Code Name Gadget. GM, 1967
Dig My Grave Deep. GM, 1957
The Girl in the Big Brass Bed. GM, 1965
A House in Naples. GM, 1956
It's My Funeral. GM, 1957
Journey into Terror. GM, 1964
Kill the Boss Goodbye. GM, 1956
Mission for Vengeance. GM, 1958
Murder Me for Nickels. GM, 1960
My Lovely Executioner. GM, 1960
The Out Is Death. GM, 1957
A Shroud for Jesso. GM, 1955
The Spy Who Was Three Feet Tall. GM, 1966
Stop This Man. GM
Time Enough to Die. GM, 1959

RACE, PHILIP (S)
Johnny Come Deadly. Hillman, 1961
Killer Take All. GM, 1959
Self-made Widow. GM, 1958

RADCLIFFE, GARNETT (M-S) (Pseudonym: Stephen Travers)
Flower Gang. Butterworth, T., 1936
The Forgotten of Allah. Butterworth, T., 1936
Great Orme Terror. Butterworth, T., 1934
In the Grip of the Brute. Butterworth, T., 1937
The Lady from Venus. MacDonald & Co., 1947
The Prisoners in the Wall. Butterworth, T., 1933
The Return of the Ceteosaurus and Other Tales. Davies, 1926
The Sky Wolves. Butterworth, T., 1938
The Straight Road. Butterworth, T., 1935
The Thirteenth Mummy. Butterworth, T., 1936
Top Floor Back. MacDonald & Co., 1943

RADFORD, EDWIN and MONA AUGUSTA RADFORD (D)
A Cozy Little Murder. Allen, T., 1963; Hale, R., 1963
Crime Pays No Dividends: Inspector Manson Again. Melrose, 1945
Death and the Professor. Hale, R., 1961
Death at the Chateau Noir. Allen, T., 1960; Hale, R., 1960
Death of a Frightened Editor. Hale, R., 1959
Death on the Broads. Long, 1957
Death Takes the Wheel. Hale, R., 1962
Death's Inheritance. Hale, R., 1961
From Information Received. Hale, R., 1962
The Heel of Achilles. Melrose, 1950
The Hungry Killer. Allen, T., 1964; Hale, R., 1964
Inspector Manson's Success. Melrose, 1944
It's Murder to Live. Melrose, 1947
John Kyleing Died. Melrose, 1949
Look in at Murder. Long, 1957
Married to Murder. Hale, R., 1959
Murder Isn't Cricket. Melrose, 1944
Murder Jigsaw. Melrose, 1944
Murder of Three Ghosts. Allen, T., 1963; Hale, R., 1963
Murder on My Conscience. Allen, T., 1960; Hale, R., 1960
No Reason For Murder. Hale, R., 1967
Who Killed Dick Whittington? Melrose, 1947

RADFORD, MONA AUGUSTA; see RADFORD, EDWIN

RAE, HUGH C. (S)
Night Pillow. Viking, 1967

RAGG, THOMAS MURRAY (D) (Pseudonym: Murray Thomas)
Buzzards Pick the Bones. Longmans, 1932
Inspector Wilkins Reads the Proofs. Jenkins, 1935
Inspector Wilkins Sees Red. Jenkins, 1934

RAIMOND, C. E., pseud; see ROBINS, ELIZABETH

RAINE, RICHARD, pseud. (S)
The Corder Index. Harcourt, 1967

RAINE, WILLIAM McCLOUD (D)
Cry Murder; see Cry Murder in the Market Place
Cry Murder in the Market Place. Hodder, 1941 (Also published as: Cry Murder. Phoenix, 1947)
Tangled Trails. Hodder, 1921; Houghton, 1921

RAISON, MILTON MICHAEL (M)
The Gay Mortician. Murray & Gee, 1946; Archer, 1947
Murder in a Lighter Vein. Murray & Gee, 1947
No Weeds for the Widow. Archer, 1946; Murray & Gee, 1946
Nobody Loves a Dead Man. Murray & Gee, 1945; Archer, 1946
The Phantom of Forty-Second Street, with Jack Harvey. Macmillan, 1936

RALEIGH, ALAN (M)
The Man in the Car. Long, 1913

RAMAGE, JENNIFER (D) (Pseudonym: Howard Mason)
The Body Below. Joseph, M., 1955
The Proud Adversary. Joseph, M., 1951
The Red Bishop. Mill, 1954

RAMPO, EDOGAWA, pseud; see HIRAI, TARO

RAMSEY, GUY HAYLETT WALKER (D)
Stop Press, Murder. Dakers, 1953

RAND, LOU (D)
The Gay Detective. Paperback Lib., 1965 (Also published as: Rough Trade. Paperback Lib., 1965)

RANDALL, FLORENCE ENGEL (S)
Hedgerow. Harcourt, 1967

RANDALL, RONA, pseud; see SHAMBROOK, RONA GREEN

RANDALL, WILLIAM, pseud; see GWINN, WILLIAM R.

RANDALL, WILLIAM R. (M)
The Crystal Eye. Greenberg, 1935
The Syndicate Murders. Greenberg, 1935

RANDAU, CARL and LEANE ZUGSMITH (S)
The Visitor. Random, 1944; Gollancz, 1945

RANDELL, CHRISTINE (S)
House of Shadows; see Whisper of Fear
Whisper of Fear. Paperback Lib., 1966 (Original title: House of Shadows)
A Woman Possessed. Paperback Lib., 1966

RANDOLPH, ELLEN (S)
The Castle on the Hill. Bouregy, 1964
Rendezvous in Amsterdam. Bouregy, 1965

RANDOLPH, MARION, pseud; see RODELL, MRS. MARIE FRIED

RANDOLPH, VANCE and NANCY CLEMENS (D)
The Camp-Meeting Murders. Vanguard, 1936

RANK, MARY O. (S)
A Dream of Falling. Houghton, 1959; Crest

RANSOME, STEPHEN, pseud; see DAVIS, FREDERICK CLYDE

RAPHAEL, CHAIM (M) (Pseudonym: Jocelyn Davey)
A Capitol Offense. Knopf, 1956 (English title: Undoubted Deed. Chatto, 1956)
Killing in Hats. Chatto, 1965
Naked Villainy. Chatto, 1958; Knopf, 1958
A Touch of Stage Fright. Chatto, 1960
Undoubted Deed; see A Capitol Offense

RAPHAEL, JOHN N. (M)
The Mystery of the Rue de Babylone. Newnes, 1916

RATH, E. J., pseud; see BRAINERD, MRS. EDITH RATHBONE JACOBS

RATH, VIRGINIA ANNE (D)
Anger of the Bells. Doubleday, Doran, 1937
The Dark Cavalier. Doubleday, Doran, 1938
Death at Dayton's Folly. Doubleday, Doran, 1935
Death Breaks the Ring. Doubleday, Doran, 1941
Death of a Lucky Lady. Doubleday, Doran, 1940
A Dirge for Her. Ziff-Davis, 1947
Epitaph for Lydia. Doubleday, Doran, 1942
Excellent Night for a Murder. Doubleday, Doran, 1937
Ferryman, Take Him Across. Doubleday, Doran, 1936
Murder with a Theme Song. Doubleday, Doran, 1939
Posted for Murder. Doubleday, Doran, 1942
A Shroud for Rowena. Ziff-Davis, 1947

RATHBONE, CORNELIA KANE (D)
Darkened Windows. Appleton, D., 1924
Jeremy Takes a Hand. Appleton, D., 1927

RATHBONE, EDWARD (M)
The Brass Knocker. Appleton, D., 1934; Cape, 1934

RATHBONE, JULIAN (S)
Diamonds Bid. Joseph, M., 1966; Walker & Co., 1967

RATHBONE, RICHARD ADAMS (D)
Death in the Drawing Room. Comet, 1954

RATHBONE, ST. GEORGE (D)
The Detective and the Poisoner. Aldine, 1885

RATTRAY, SIMON, pseud; see TREVOR, ELLESTON

RAVEN, SIMON (S)
Brother Cain. S & S, 1960; Panther, 1966; Berkley Pub., 1967
Doctors Wear Scarlet. S & S, 1961; Avon, 1963

RAWLINGS, FRANK (D)
The Lisping Man. Gateway, 1942

RAWLINS, EUSTACE (M) (Pseudonym: Robert Eustace)
The Brotherhood of the Seven Kings. 1899
The Sorceress of the Strand, with Clifford Hallifax and L. T. Meade. 1922

RAWSON, CLAYTON (D) (Pseudonym: Stuart Towne)
The Case of the Deadly Clown; see The Headless Lady
Death from a Top Hat. Putnam, 1938; Grosset, 1939; Collins, 1940; Collier, 1962
Death Out of Thin Air, by Stuart Towne. Coward, 1941; Cassell, 1948 (Also published as: Ghost of the Undead)
The Footprints on the Ceiling. Collins, 1939; Putnam, 1939; Collier, 1962
Ghost of the Undead; see Death Out of Thin Air
The Headless Lady. Putnam, 1940; Collins, 1942; Collier, 1962 (Also published as: The Case of the Deadly Clown and The Headless Mystery)
The Headless Mystery; see The Headless Lady
No Coffin for the Corpse. Little, 1942; Collier, 1963

RAY, JEAN (S)
Ghouls in My Grave. Berkley Pub., 1965

RAY, RÈNE (M)
A Man Named Seraphin. Eyre, 1952
Wraxton Marne. Green, 1946

RAYMOND, CLIFFORD SAMUEL (M)
Four Corners. Doran, 1921
Men on the Dead Man's Chest. Bobbs, 1930
Mystery of Hartley House. Doran, 1917
One of Three. Doran, 1919

RAYMOND, ERNEST (M)
Chorus Ending. Cassell, 1951
The Marsh. Cassell, 1937
We, the Accused. Cassell, 1935

RAYMOND, RENÉ (M-S) (Pseudonyms: James Hadley Chase, James L. Docherty, Ambrose Grant, Raymond Marshall)
The Big Steal; see Safer Dead
The Blondes' Requiem, by Raymond Marshall. Jarrolds, 1945; Crown, 1946
But a Short Time to Live, by Raymond Marshall. Jarrolds, 1945
The Case of the Strangled Starlet, by James Hadley Chase. Signet, 1959
A Coffin from Hong Kong, by James Hadley Chase. Hale, R., 1962
Come Easy—Go Easy, by James Hadley Chase. Hale, R., 1960
The Dead Stay Dumb, by James Hadley Chase. Jarrolds, 1940
The Double Shuffle, by James Hadley Chase. Hale, R., 1952; Dutton, 1953
Eve, by James Hadley Chase. Jarrolds, 1945; Phoenix, 1945
The Fast Buck, by James Hadley Chase. Hale, R., 1952
Figure It Out for Yourself, by James Hadley Chase. Hale, R., 1950; Duell, 1951
The Flesh of the Orchid, by James Hadley Chase. Jarrolds, 1948
The Guilty Are Afraid, by James Hadley Chase. Hale, R., 1957
He Won't Need It Now, by James L. Docherty. Rich, 1939
Hit and Run, by Raymond Marshall. Hale, R., 1958
I Would Rather Stay Poor, by James Hadley Chase. Hale, R., 1962
I'll Bury My Dead, by James Hadley Chase. Hale, R., 1953; Dutton, 1954
I'll Get You for This, by James Hadley Chase. Jarrolds, 1946
In a Vain Shadow, by Raymond Marshall. Jarrolds, 1951
Just Another Sucker, by James Hadley Chase. Hale, R., 1961
Just the Way It Is, by Raymond Marshall. Jarrolds, 1944
Lady, Here's Your Wreath, by Raymond Marshall. Jarrolds, 1940
Lay Her Among the Lilies, by James Hadley Chase. Hale, R., 1950 (U.S. title: Too Dangerous to Be Free. Duell, 1951)
A Lotus for Miss Quon, by James Hadley Chase. Hale, R., 1961
Make the Corpse Walk, by Raymond Marshall. Jarrolds, 1946
Mallory, by Raymond Marshall. Jarrolds, 1950
Miss Callaghan Comes to Grief, by James Hadley Chase. Jarrolds, 1941

Miss Shumway Waves a Wand, by James Hadley Chase. Jarrolds, 1944
Mission to Sienna, by Raymond Marshall. Hale, R., 1955
Mission to Venice, by Raymond Marshall. Hale, R., 1954
More Deadly Than the Male, by Ambrose Grant. Eyre, 1946
No Business of Mine, by Raymond Marshall. Jarrolds, 1947
No Orchids for Miss Blandish, by James Hadley Chase. Jarrolds, 1939; Howell, Soskin, 1942; Avon, 1966
Not Safe to Be Free, by James Hadley Chase. Hale, R., 1958
One Bright Summer Morning, by James Hadley Chase. Hale, R., 1963
The Paw in the Bottle, by Raymond Marshall. Jarrolds, 1947
Safer Dead, by James Hadley Chase. Hale, R., 1956 (Originally announced as: The Big Steal)
Shock Treatment, by James Hadley Chase. Hale, R., 1959
The Soft Centre, by James Hadley Chase. Hale, R., 1953
Strictly for Cash, by James Hadley Chase. Hale, R., 1951
The Sucker Punch, by Raymond Marshall. Jarrolds, 1954
Tell It to the Birds, by James Hadley Chase. Hale, R., 1963
There's Always a Price Tag, by James Hadley Chase. Hale, R., 1956
The Things Men Do, by Raymond Marshall. Jarrolds, 1954
This Is for Real, by James Hadley Chase. Walker & Co., 1967
This Way for a Shroud, by James Hadley Chase. Hale, R., 1953
Tiger by the Tail, by James Hadley Chase. Hale, R., 1954
Too Dangerous to Be Free; see Lay Her Among the Lilies
Trusted Like the Fox, by Raymond Marshall. Jarrolds, 1948
Twelve Chinks and a Woman, by James Hadley Chase. Jarrolds, 1940; Howell, Soskin, 1941
The Wary Transgressor, by Raymond Marshall. Jarrolds, 1952
The Way the Cookie Crumbles, by James Hadley Chase. Hale, R., 1965
What's Better Than Money?, by James Hadley Chase. Hale, R., 1960
Why Pick on Me?, by Raymond Marshall. Jarrolds, 1951
The World in My Pocket, by James Hadley Chase. Hale, R., 1959
You Find Him - I'll Fix Him, by James Hadley Chase. Hale, R., 1956
You Never Know with Women, by James Hadley Chase. Jarrolds, 1949
You're Lonely When You're Dead, by James Hadley Chase. Hale, R., 1949; Duell, 1950
You've Got It Coming, by James Hadley Chase. Jarrolds, 1949

RAYNE, GEOFFREY (M)
Headline—Murder. Hale, R., 1967

RAYNER, AUGUSTUS ALFRED (M) (Pseudonym: Whyte Hall)
Crime and a Clock. Harrap, 1936
Death and the Golden Image. Harrap, 1936
Death of a Doctor's Wife. Quality, 1939

RAYNER, CLAIRE (S-Gothic)
House on the Fen. Bantam, 1967

RAYTER, JOE, pseud; see McCHESNEY, MARY F.

REA, MARGARET LUCILE PAINE (D)
Blackout at Rehearsal. Doubleday, Doran, 1943
Compare These Dead. Doubleday, Doran, 1941
Curtain for Crime. Doubleday, Doran, 1941
Death of an Angel. Doubleday, Doran, 1943
Death Walks the Dry Tortugas. Doubleday, Doran, 1942

REACH, JAMES (M)
Blind Gambit. Coward, 1954; Collier, 1962
The Innocent One. Coward, 1953; Collier, 1962
Late Last Night. Morrow, 1949

READE, CHARLES; see BOUCICAULT, DION

REAGAN, THOMAS B. (S)
Bank Job. Dodd, 1964

REBACK, M.; see CALDWELL, JANET TAYLOR

REDGATE, JOHN (D)
The Killing Season. Trident, 1967

REDGRAVE, MICHAEL (M)
Mountebank's Tale. Harper, 1961

REDMAN, BEN RAY (D) (Pseudonym: Jeremy Lord)
The Bannerman Case. Doubleday, Doran, 1935; Hurst, 1936
Sixty-Nine Diamonds. Doubleday, Doran, 1940; Hurst, 1940

REDMOND, LIAM (D)
Death Is So Kind. Devin-Adair, 1959

REDMOND-HOWARD, LOUIS (D)
The Siege of Scotland Yard. Shaylor, 1929

REED, BLAIR (D) (Pseudonym: Adam Ring)
Killers Play Rough, by Adam Ring. Crown, 1947
Pass Key to Murder. Phoenix, 1948

REED, SIR EDWARD CHARLES (M)
Boothroyd's Mill. Long, 1929
The Dream Murder. Long, 1929
The Pedgate Mystery. Long, 1930
The Strangler. Long, 1929

REED, ELIOT, pseud; see AMBLER, ERIC; also RODDA, CHARLES

REED, HARLAN (D)
The Case of the Crawling Cockroach. Dutton, 1937
Swing Music Murder. Dutton, 1938

REED, WALLACE (D)
Marked for Murder. Phoenix, 1941
Motive for Murder. Arcadia, 1957
No Sign of Murder. Phoenix, 1940
Time to Kill. Phoenix, 1940

REES, ARTHUR JOHN (M)
The Brink; see The Swaying Rock
The Corpse That Traveled. Dodd, 1938
The Cup of Silence. Lane, 1924; Dodd, 1925
Greymarsh. Dodd, 1927; Jarrolds, 1927
The Hampstead Mystery, with John Reay Watson. Lane, 1916
Hand in the Dark. Dodd, 1920; Lane, 1920
Investigations of Calwyn Grey. Jarrolds, 1932
Moon Rock. Dodd, 1922; Lane, 1922
Mystery at Peak House. Dodd, 1933 (English title: Peak House. Jarrolds, 1933)
Mystery of the Downs, with John Reay Watson. Lane, 1918
The Pavilion by the Lake. Dodd, 1930; Lane, 1930
Peak House; see Mystery at Peak House
River Mystery. Dodd, 1932; Jarrolds, 1932
The Shrieking Pit. Lane, 1919
The Swaying Rock. Dodd, 1931 (English title: The Brink. Lane, 1931)
The Threshhold of Fear. Dodd, 1925; Hutchinson, 1925
Tragedy at Twelvetrees. Dodd, 1931; Lane, 1931
Unquenchable Flame. Dodd, 1926

REES, DILWYN, pseud; see DANIEL, GLYN E.

REEVE, ARTHUR BENJAMIN (D)
The Adventuress. Harper, 1917; Collins, 1918, 1930
Atavar. Harper, 1924
The Black Hand; see The Silent Bullet
Boy Scouts' Craig Kennedy. Harper, 1925
Clutching Hand. Reilly & Lee, 1934
Constance Dunlap, Woman Detective. Harper, 1913; Hodder, 1916
Craig Kennedy, Detective. Simpkin, 1916
Craig Kennedy Listens In. Harper, 1923; Hodder, 1924
Craig Kennedy on the Farm. Harper, 1925
The Diamond Queen. Hodder, 1917
Dream Doctor. Hodder, 1916; Harper, 1917
Ear in the Wall. Harper, 1916; Hodder, 1917
Enter Craig Kennedy. Macaulay, 1935
Exploits of Elaine. Harper, 1915; Hodder, 1915
Film Mystery. Harper, 1921; Hodder, 1922
Fourteen Points. Harper, 1927
Gold of the Gods. Harper, 1915; Hodder, 1916
Guy Garrick. Harper, 1914; Hodder, 1916
Kidnap Club. Macaulay, 1932
The Master Mystery. Grosset, 1919
The Mystery Mind. Grosset, 1921
Panama Plot. Harper, 1918; Collins, 1920
Pandora. Harper, 1926
Poisoned Pen. Harper, 1913; Hodder, 1916
The Radio Detective. Grosset, 1926
The Romance of Elaine. Harper, 1916; Hodder, 1916
The Silent Bullet. Harper, 1912 (Also published as: The Black Hand. Nash, 1912; Dodd)
The Social Gangster. Hearst, 1916
The Soul Scar. Harper, 1919
The Stars Scream Murder. Appleton-Century, 1936
Treasure Train. Harper, 1917; Collins, 1920
The Triumph of Elaine. Hodder, 1916
The War Terror. Harper, 1915

REEVE, CHRISTOPHER (M)
The Emerald Kiss. Morrow, 1931; Jarrolds, 1932
The Ginger Cat. Collins, 1929; Morrow, 1931
The House That Waited. Ward, Lock, 1944
The Hunter's Way. Jarrolds, 1934
Lady, Be Careful. Ward, Lock, 1948; Mill, 1950
Murder Steps Out. Ward, Lock, 1942; Mill, 1951
The Toasted Blonde. Collins, 1930; Morrow, 1930

REEVES, H. B. (M)
The Mystery of No. 13. Ogilvie

REEVES, ROBERT, pseud. (D)
Cellini Smith, Detective. Houghton, 1943
Dead and Done For. Knopf, 1939; Cassell, 1940
No Love Lost. Holt, H., 1941

REGESTER, SEELEY, pseud; see VICTOR, META VICTORIA

REGIS, JULIUS (M)
The Copper House. Hodder, 1923; Holt, H., 1923
No. 13, Toroni. Hodder, 1923; Holt, 1922

REID, C. L. (M)
Masque of Mystery. Books for Today, 1947

REILLY, MRS. HELEN KIERNAN (Pseudonym: Kiernan Abbey)
All Concerned Notified. Doubleday, Doran, 1939; Heinemann, 1939; Macfadden, 1964
And Let the Coffin Pass, by Kiernan Abbey. Scribner, 1942
Beyond the Dark, by Kiernan Abbey. Scribner, 1944
The Canvas Dagger. Random, 1956; Hale, R., 1957; Ace, 1963 (Double novel)
Certain Sleep. Random, 1961; Hale, R., 1962; Ace, 1963
Compartment K. Random, 1961; Ace, 1964 (English title: Murder Rides the Express. Hale, R., 1964)
The Day She Died. Random, 1962; Hale, R., 1963; Ace, 1964
The Dead Can Tell. Random, 1940
Dead for a Ducat. Doubleday, Doran, 1939; Heinemann, 1939
Dead Man Control. Doubleday, Doran, 1936; Heinemann, 1937; Macfadden, 1964
Death Demands an Audience. Doubleday, Doran, 1940; Macfadden, 1967
The Diamond Feather. Doubleday, Doran, 1930
Ding Dong Bell. Random, 1958; Hale, R., 1959; Ace, 1963 (Double novel)
The Doll's Trunk Murder. Farrar & Rinehart, 1932; Hutchinson, 1933 (Also published as: The Doll's Trunk Mystery)
The Doll's Trunk Mystery; see The Doll's Trunk Murder
The Double Man. Random, 1952; Museum Press, 1954; Dell
The Farmhouse. Random, 1947; Hammond, 1950; Dell
File on Rufus Ray. Jarrolds, 1937; Morrow, 1937
Follow Me. Random, 1960; Ace, 1962 (Double novel)
Lament for a Bride. Random, 1951; Museum Press, 1954
The Line-up. Doubleday, Doran, 1934; Cassell, 1935; Macfadden, 1967
McKee of Centre Street. Doubleday, Doran, 1934
The Man with the Painted Head. Farrar & Rinehart, 1931
Mr. Smith's Hat. Cassell, 1936; Doubleday, Doran, 1936
Mourned on Sunday. Random, 1941
Murder at Arroways. Random, 1950; Museum Press, 1952
Murder in Shinbone Alley. Doubleday, Doran, 1940; Macfadden, 1964
Murder in the Mews. Doubleday, Doran, 1931; Macfadden, 1966; Collier
Murder on Angler's Island. Random, 1945; Hammond, 1948; Collier
Murder Rides the Express; see Compartment K
Name Your Poison. Random, 1942
Not Me, Inspector. Random, 1959; Hale, R., 1960; Ace, 1963 (Double novel)
The Opening Door. Random, 1960; Ace, 1962 (Double novel)
Run with the Hare, by Kiernan Abbey. Scribner, 1941
The Silver Leopard. Random, 1946; Hammond, 1949
Staircase 4. Random, 1949; Hammond, 1950
Tell Her It's Murder. Random, 1954; Museum Press, 1955
The Thirty-first Bullfinch. Doubleday, Doran, 1930
Three Women in Black. Random, 1941; Dell
The Velvet Hand. Random, 1953; Museum Press, 1955

REISNER, MARY (M-S)
Black Hazard. Belmont, 1966
The Four Witnesses. Dodd, 1947; Hammond, 1948 (Also published as: Web of Fear. Belmont, 1967)
The House of Cobwebs. Dodd, 1944; Methuen, 1948; Belmont, 1965
The Hunted. Belmont, 1967
The Mirror of Delusion. Hammond, 1947; Belmont, 1965
Shadows on the Wall. Belmont, 1965
Twelve Steps at Miramar. Methuen, 1946
Web of Fear; see Four Witnesses

REMENHAM, JOHN, pseud; see VLASTO, JOHN ALEXANDER

REMY, JACQUES (S)
A Race for Life. Lane, 1957

RENARD, MAURICE (M)
Blind Circle, with Jean Albert. Dutton, 1928; Gollancz, 1929
The Hands of Orlac. Dutton, 1929
The Snake of Luvercy. Dutton, 1930

RENAUD, J. JOSEPH (D)
Doctor Mephisto. Hutchinson, 1929

RENAULT, MARY (S)
Return to Night. Longmans, 1947; Morrow, 1947

RENDALL, VERNON (M)
London Nights of Belsize. Lane, 1918

RENDELL, RUTH (M-S)
From Doon with Death. Long, 1964; Doubleday, 1965; Ballantine, 1966
In Sickness and in Health. Doubleday, 1966
A New Lease of Death. Doubleday, 1967
To Fear a Painted Devil. Doubleday, 1965

RESSICK, JOHN and ERIC DE BANZIE (M) (Pseudonym: Gregory Baxter)
The Ainceworth Mystery. Appleton, D., 1930; Benn, 1931
Blue Lighting. Cassell, 1926
Calamity Comes of Age. Macaulay, 1935; Hutchinson, 1936
Climax at the Falls. Benn, 1932
Death Strikes at Six Bells. Benn, 1930
Murder Could Not Kill. Benn, 1932; Macaulay, 1934
The Narrowing Lust. Selwyn, 1928

REVELL, LOUISA (D)
The Bus Station Murders. Macmillan, 1947
The Kindest Use a Knife. Macmillan, 1953
The Men with Three Eyes. Macmillan, 1955
No Pockets in a Shroud. Macmillan, 1948
A Party for the Shooting. Macmillan, 1960; Collier, 1962
See Rome and Die. Macmillan, 1947; Gollancz, 1958
The Silver Spade. Macmillan, 1950

REY, LESTER del (S)
Scheme of Things. Belmont, 1966

REYBURN, WALLACE (M)
Port of Call. Cassell, 1957

REYMOND, HENRY (S)
Deadlier Than the Male. Signet, 1967

REYNAUD-FOURTON, ALAIN (S)
The Reluctant Assassin. Collins, 1964; Coward, 1965; PB, 1966

REYNOLDS, ADRIAN, pseud; see LONG, AMELIA REYNOLDS

REYNOLDS, MRS. BAILLIE; see REYNOLDS, GERTRUDE M. ROBINS

REYNOLDS, BARBARA LEONARD (M)
Alias for Death. Coward, 1951

REYNOLDS, GERTRUDE M. ROBINS (Mrs. Baillie Reynolds) (M)
Accessory After the Fact. Hodder, 1928
The Affair at the Chateau. Doubleday, Doran, 1929; Hodder, 1931
Also Ran. Doran, 1920
Beware of the Dog. Wright & Brown, 1932
Black Light. Hodder, 1937; Doubleday, Doran, 1938
Brother Wolf. Wright & Brown, 1931
Castle to Let. Doran, 1917
Confession Corner. Hurst, 1929
False Position. Hutchinson, 1930
The Gift in the Gauntlet. Doran, 1927
In the Balance. Hurst, 1929
The Innocent Accomplice. Doubleday, Doran, 1928
The Intrusive Tourist. Doubleday, Doran, 1935; Hodder, 1939
It Is Not Safe to Know. Doubleday, Doran, 1939; Hodder, 1939
The King's Widow. Doran, 1919; Cassell, 1931
The Lost Discovery. Doran, 1923; Hodder, 1923
The Man Who Won. Hutchinson, 1931
The Missing Two. Doubleday, Doran, 1932; Hodder, 1932
Notorious Miss Lisle. Hodder, 1916
Open Sesame. Hurst, 1929
Out of the Night. Hodder, 1910
Stranglehold. Doubleday, Doran, 1930
The Trouble at Glaye. Doubleday, Doran, 1936; Hodder, 1936
A Very Private Secretary. Doubleday, Doran, 1933
Whereabouts Unknown. Doubleday, 1931; Hutchinson, 1931

REYNOLDS, LIGGETT, pseud; see SIMON, ROBERT ALFRED

REYNOLDS, MACK (D)
The Case of the Little Green Men. Phoenix, 1951

REYNOLDS, M. J. (M)
The Terror. Macmillan, 1930

REYNOLDS, MINNIE JOSEPHINE (M)
The Crayon Clue. Kennerley, 1915

REYNOLDS, PETER, pseud; see LONG, AMELIA REYNOLDS

REYWALL, JOHN, pseud. (M)
The Trial of Alvin Boaker. Boardman, T. V., 1948; Random, 1948

RHOADES, KNIGHT (M)
She Died on the Stairway. Arcadia, 1947

RHODE, JOHN, pseud; see STREET, CECIL JOHN CHARLES

RHODES, DENYS (M)
Fly Away, Peter. Richards Press, 1952

RHODES, KATHLYN (M)
Crime on a Cruise. Hutchinson, 1935
The Lady Was Warned. Hutchinson, 1936

RICE, CRAIG (Mrs. Lawrence Lipton) (D) (Pseudonyms: Daphne Sanders, Michael Venning)
April Robin Murders, with Ed McBain. Random, 1958; Hammond, 1959; Dell, 1965
The Big Midget Murders. S & S, 1942
But the Doctor Died. Lancer, 1967
The Corpse Steps Out. S & S, 1940
Craig Rice Crime Digest. Anson Bond, 1946
Double Frame; see Knocked for a Loop
Eight Faces at Three. S & S, 1939
The Fourth Postman. Hammond, 1948; S & S, 1948
Having a Wonderful Crime. S & S, 1943
Home, Sweet Homicide. S & S, 1944; World Pub., 1946
Innocent Bystanders. S & S, 1949 (English title: Murder Go Round. Hammond, 1958)
Jethro Hammer, by Michael Venning. Coward, 1944
Knocked for a Loop. S & S, 1957 (English title: Double Frame. Hammond, 1958)
The Lucky Stiff. S & S, 1945
The Man Who Slept All Day, by Michael Venning. Coward, 1942
Murder Go Round; see Innocent Bystanders
Murder Through the Looking Glass, by Michael Venning. Coward, 1943
My Kingdom for a Hearse. S & S, 1957; Hammond, 1959
The Name Is Malone. Hammond, 1960; Pyramid, 1967
The People vs. Withers and Malone, with Stuart Palmer. S & S, 1963; Award, 1965
The Right Murder. S & S, 1941
The Sunday Pigeon Murders. S & S, 1942
Telefair, the House on the Island. Bobbs, 1942
The Thursday Turkey Murders. S & S, 1943
To Catch a Thief, by Daphne Sanders. Dial, 1943
Trial by Fury. S & S, 1941
The Wrong Murder. S & S, 1940

RICE, LAVERNE (D)
Well Dressed for Murder. Doubleday, Doran, 1938

RICE, LOUISE (M)
By Whose Hand. Macaulay, 1930
The Girl Who Walked Without Fear. Sheldon, 1927

RICH, KATHLEEN (S-Gothic)
The Lucifer Mask. Tower, 1967

RICH, WILLARD, pseud. (M)
Brain Waves and Death. Scribner, 1940

RICHARD, SUSAN (S-Gothic)
Ashley Hall. Paperback Lib., 1967
Intruder at Maison Benedict. Paperback Lib., 1967
Secret of Chateau Kendall. Paperback Lib., 1967

RICHARDS, ALLEN, pseud; see ROSENTHAL, RICHARD A.

RICHARDS, CLAY, pseud; see CROSSEN, KENDALL FORREST

RICHARDS, DAVID (S)
Double Game. Brown, Watson, 1958

RICHARDS, FRANCIS, pseud; see LOCKRIDGE, FRANCES LOUISE

RICHARDS, STELLA, pseud; see STARR, RICHARD

RICHARDSON, ANTHONY T. S. C. (S)
Ransom. Constable, 1925

RICHART, MARY (D)
Murder in the Town. Farrar, 1947

RICHMOND, MARY (M-S)
Brides of Doom. Wright & Brown, 1946
Cabin Nineteen. Wright & Brown, 1953
The Clock Strikes Ten. Wright & Brown, 1944
Concealed Identity. Wright & Brown, 1938
Danger Ahead. Wright & Brown, 1937
Dark Horizon. Wright & Brown, 1937
The Devil Laughed. Wright & Brown, 1950
Disciples of Satan. Wright & Brown, 1936
Footprints in the Sand. Wright & Brown, 1939

The Hidden Horror. Wright & Brown, 1937
Hounded! Wright & Brown, 1936
In Fear of the Hangman. Wright & Brown, 1938
In the Grip of the Dragon. Wright & Brown, 1939
Jewels of Death. Wright & Brown, 1938
Judgment of Death. Wright & Brown, 1942
Justice for Julia. Wright & Brown, 1955
Lady in Distress. Wright & Brown, 1936
A Leap in the Dark. Wright & Brown, 1949
Magnet for Danger. Wright & Brown, 1943
The Mark of the Dragon. Wright & Brown, 1935
The Masked Terror. Wright & Brown, 1934
Murder by a Maniac. Wright & Brown, 1937; Mellifont, 1949
No Escape. Wright & Brown, 1952
Passport to Danger. Wright & Brown, 1938
The Pointing Finger. Wright & Brown, 1940
Poison Weed. Wright & Brown, 1940
Red Claws. Wright & Brown, 1940
The Secret Hour. Wright & Brown, 1949; Albatross, 1950
The Secret of the Marshes. Wright & Brown, 1940
The Secret of the Priory. Wright & Brown, 1935
The Seven Bloodhounds. Wright & Brown, 1937
Shadow of the Gallows. Wright & Brown, 1940
Stealthy Death. Wright & Brown, 1935
Strange Cargo. Wright & Brown, 1933
Suspicious Company. Wright & Brown, 1938
Tempest at Dawn. Wright & Brown, 1944
Terror by Night. Wright & Brown, 1939
Terror Stalks Abroad. Wright & Brown, 1939
That Fatal Night. Wright & Brown, 1949
Thin Ice. Wright & Brown, 1950
This Road Is Dangerous. Wright & Brown, 1950
Traitor's Harvest. Wright & Brown, 1942
Troubled Heritage. Wright & Brown, 1942
Unnatural Death. Wright & Brown, 1952
The Valley of Doom. Wright & Brown, 1947
The Valley of the Shadow. Wright & Brown, 1947

RICKARD, JESSIE LOUISA (Mrs. Victor Rickard) (M)
The Baccarat Club. Liveright, 1929
Blindfold. Cape, 1922
The Empty Villa. Hodder, 1929; Liveright, 1929
Murder by Night. Jarrolds, 1936
The Mystery of Vincent Dane. Hodder, 1930
Not Sufficient Evidence. Constable, 1926
Upstairs. Doubleday, Page, 1926

RICKARD, MRS. VICTOR; see RICKARD, JESSIE LOUISA

RICKETT, ARTHUR COMPTON-; see LEYTON, PATRICK

RICKETT, FRANCES (S)
The Prowler. S & S, 1963; Hale, R., 1964; Popular Lib., 1964
Tread Softly. Hale, R., 1964; S & S, 1964; Popular Lib., 1965

RICO, DON (D)
Daisy Dilemma. Lancer, 1967 (The Man from Pansy series, #2)
Last of the Breed. Lancer, 1965
The Man from Pansy. Lancer, 1967 (The Man from Pansy series, #1)
Nightmare of Eyes. Lancer, 1967

RIDDEL, JOHN, pseud; see FORD, COREY

RIDDELL, MRS. J. H. (M)
The Disappearance of Jeremiah Redworth. Routledge, 1879
Fort Minster, M. P.: A Westminster Mystery. Arrowsmith, 1885

RIDEAL, C.; see MOSER, M.

RIDEAUX, CHARLES DE B. (M)
(Pseudonym: John Chancellor)
The Dark God. Hutchinson, 1927; Century, 1928
Murder Syndicate. Eldon, 1949
Mystery at Angel's End. Long, 1930
Mystery of Norman's Court. Hutchinson, 1923
Return of Frass. Hutchinson, 1930
Stolen Gold. Hutchinson, 1932

RIDEOUT, HENRY MILNER (M)
Dulcarnon. Duffield, 1925; Hurst, 1926
The Twisted Foot. Houghton, 1910

RIDER, ANNE (S)
Bad Samaritan. Bodley Head, 1965

RIDER, SARAH (D)
The Misplaced Corpse. Houghton, 1940

RIDGE, W. PETT (M)
Breaker of Laws. Methuen, 1903

RIDGEWAY, JASON, pseud; see MARLOWE, STEPHEN

RIDLEY, ARNOLD; see ALEXANDER, RUTH

RIEFE, ALAN (S)
Tales of Horror. PB, 1965

RIEMAN, TERRY (M)
Vamp Till Ready. Harper, 1954; Gollancz, 1955

RIENITS, REX (S)
Assassin for Hire. Muller, 1952

RIESS, CURT (S)
High Stakes. Putnam, 1942

RIGSBY, HOWARD (D-S) (Pseudonym: Vechel Howard)
As a Man Falls. GM, 1954
Calliope Reef. Dell, 1967; Doubleday, 1967
Clash of Shadows. Lippincott, 1959; Crest, 1960
High Spirits. Nelson, 1941
Kill and Tell. Morrow, 1951; Muller, 1954
Lucinda. GM, 1954; Muller, 1955
Murder for the Holidays. Morrow, 1951; Muller, 1952
Murder on Her Mind, by Vechel Howard. GM, 1959
Murder with Love, by Vechel Howard. GM, 1959
A Time for Passion. Dell, 1960
The Tulip Tree. Doubleday, 1962; Paperback Lib., 1965

RIMEL, DUANE W. (M)
Curse of Cain. McKay, 1945
The Jury Is Out. Withy Grove, 1947
Motive for Murder. Withy Grove, 1945

RIMMER, ROBERT H. (S)
The Zolotov Affair. Sherbourne, 1967

RINEHART, MARY ROBERTS (D-M)
The Afterhouse. Houghton, 1914; Dell, 1960
The Album. Cassell, 1933; Farrar & Rinehart, 1933
Alibi for Isobel. Farrar & Rinehart, 1944; Cassell, 1946; Dell, 1967
Amazing Adventures of Letitia Carberry. Bobbs, 1911; Hodder, 1919
The Bat, with Avery Hopwood. Doran, 1926; Dell, 1965
Best of Tish. Rinehart, 1955
The Breaking Point. Hodder, 1922; Doran, 1923; Dell, 1966
The Case of Elinor Norton; see The State vs. Elinor Norton
Case of Jennie Brice. Bobbs, 1913; Hodder, 1919; Dell, 1960
The Circular Staircase. Bobbs, 1908; Hodder, 1914; Dell, 1963; Grosset
The Confession and Sight Unseen. Doran, 1921; Hodder, 1921; Dell, 1959
Dangerous Days. Hodder, 1919; Dell, 1966
The Door. Farrar & Rinehart, 1930; Hodder, 1930; Dell, 1964
The Double Alibi. Cassell, 1932
The Episode of the Wandering Knife. Holt, 1949; Dell, 1961
The Frightened Wife and Other Murder Stories. Rinehart, 1953; Cassell, 1954; Dell, 1963
The Great Mistake. Rinehart, 1940; Cassell, 1941; Dell, 1964
The Haunted Lady. Rinehart, 1942; Cassell, 1942; Dell, 1967
The Man in Lower Ten. Bobbs, 1909; Cassell, 1909; Hodder, 1919; Dell, 1964
Miss Pinkerton. Farrar & Rinehart, 1932; Rinehart, 1959; Dell, 1964
The Mystery Lamp. Hodder, 1925
The Pool; see The Swimming Pool
The Red Lamp. Doran, 1925; Dell, 1962
The State vs. Elinor Norton. Farrar & Rinehart, 1934; Dell, 1961 (English title: The Case of Elinor Norton. Cassell, 1934)
The Swimming Pool. Rinehart, 1952; Dell, 1962 (English title: The Pool. Cassell, 1953)
This Strange Adventure. Doubleday, Doran, 1929; Hodder, 1929; Dell, 1966
Tish Marches On. Farrar & Rinehart, 1937
Tish Plays the Game. Doran, 1926
Two Flights Up. Doubleday, Doran, 1928; Hodder, 1928
The Wall. Cassell, 1938; Farrar & Rinehart, 1938; Dell, 1963
The Wandering Knife: Three Mystery Tales. Cassell, 1951
Where There's a Will. Bobbs, 1912
The Window at the White Cat. Bobbs, 1910; Nash, 1911; Dell, 1961; Triangle
The Yellow Room. Farrar & Rinehart, 1945; Cassell, 1949; Penguin, 1953; Dell, 1962, 1967

RING, ADAM, pseud; see REED, BLAIR

RING, DOUGLAS, pseud; see PRATHER, RICHARD SCOTT

RIPLEY, CLEMENTS (M)
Murder Walks Alone. Messner, 1935

RISING, LAWRENCE (M)
She Who Was Helena Cass. Doran, 1920; Hodder, 1920

RITCHIE, ROBERT WELLES; see BIGGERS, EARL DERR

RITSON, JOHN, pseud; see BABER, DOUGLAS

RIVER, WALTER LESLIE (D)
Death of a Young Man. S & S, 1927

RIVERS, R. (M)
The Counterfeiters. Ogilvie

RIVETT, EDITH CAROLINE (D)
(Pseudonyms: Carol Carnac, E. C. R. Lorac)
Accident by Design, by E. C. R. Lorac. Collins, 1950; Doubleday, 1951
The Affair at Helen's Court, by Carol Carnac. Doubleday, 1958
The Affair on Thor's Head, by E. C. R. Lorac. Low, 1932
And Then Put Out the Light; see Policeman in the Precinct
Ask a Policeman, by E. C. R. Lorac. Collins, 1955
Bats in the Belfry, by E. C. R. Lorac. Collins, 1937; Macaulay, 1937
Black Beadle, by E. C. R. Lorac. Collins, 1939
Burning Question, by Carol Carnac. Collins, 1957
The Case in the Clinic, by E. C. R. Lorac. Collins, 1941
The Case of Colonel Marchand, by E. C. R. Lorac. Low, 1933; Macaulay, 1933
The Case of the First Class Carriage, by Carol Carnac. Davies, 1939
Checkmate to Murder, by E. C. R. Lorac. Arcadia, 1944; Bart, 1946
The Clue Sinister, by Carol Carnac. MacDonald & Co., 1947
Copy for Crime, by Carol Carnac. MacDonald & Co., 1947
Crime Counter Crime, by E. C. R. Lorac. Collins, 1936; Macaulay, 1937
Crook o'Lune, by E. C. R. Lorac. Collins, 1953 (U.S. title: Shepherd's Crook. Doubleday, 1953)
Crossed Skiis, by Carol Carnac. Collins, 1952
Dangerous Domicile, by E. C. R. Lorac. Collins, 1957
Death at Dyke's Counter, by E. C. R. Lorac. Collins, 1940
Death Before Dinner, by E. C. R. Lorac. Collins, 1948 (U.S. title: Screen for Murder. Doubleday, 1948)
Death Came Softly, by E. C. R. Lorac. Collins, 1943
Death in the Diving Pool, by Carol Carnac. Davies, 1940
Death in Triplicate, by E. C. R. Lorac. Collins, 1958
Death of a Lady, by Carol Carnac. Collins, 1958
Death of an Author, by E. C. R. Lorac. Low, 1935
Death on the Oxford Road, by E. C. R. Lorac. Low, 1933
The Devil and the C.I.D., by E. C. R. Lorac. Collins, 1938
The Dog It Was That Died, by E. C. R. Lorac. Collins, 1952; Doubleday, 1952
Double for Detection, by Carol Carnac. MacDonald & Co., 1945
Double Turn, by Carol Carnac. Collins, 1956
Fell Murder, by E. C. R. Lorac. Collins, 1944
Fire in the Thatch, by E. C. R. Lorac. Collins, 1946
The Greenwell Mystery, by E. C. R. Lorac. Low, 1932; Macaulay, 1934
I Could Murder Her; see Murder of a Martinet
Impact of Evidence, by Carol Carnac. Collins, 1954; Doubleday, 1954
It's Her Own Funeral, by Carol Carnac. Collins, 1951; Doubleday, 1952
John Brown's Body, by E. C. R. Lorac. Collins, 1939
The Last Escape, by E. C. R. Lorac. Doubleday, 1959; Popular Lib., 1964
The Late Miss Trimming, by Carol Carnac. Doubleday, 1957
Let Well Alone, by E. C. R. Lorac. Collins, 1954
The Long Shadows, by Carol Carnac. Collins, 1958
Murder Among Members, by Carol Carnac. Collins, 1955
Murder as a Fine Art, by Carol Carnac. Collins, 1953
The Murder at Mornington, by Carol Carnac. Skeffington, 1937
Murder by Matchlight, by E. C. R. Lorac. Collins, 1945; Mystery House, 1946
Murder in Chelsea, by E. C. R. Lorac. Low, 1934; Macaulay, 1935
Murder in St. John's Wood, by E. C. R. Lorac. Low, 1934; Macaulay, 1934
Murder in the Mill-Race, by E. C. R. Lorac. Collins, 1952 (U.S. title: Speak Justly of the Dead. Doubleday, 1953)
Murder in Vienna, by E. C. R. Lorac. Collins, 1956
Murder of a Martinet, by E. C. R. Lorac. Collins, 1951 (U.S. title: I Could Murder Her. Doubleday, 1951; Popular Lib., 1968)
Murder on a Monument, by E. C. R. Lorac. Collins, 1958

Murder on the Burrows, by E. C. R. Lorac. Low, 1931; Macaulay, 1932
Murderer's Mistake, by E. C. R. Lorac. Low, 1935; Arcadia, 1947 (Also published as: Theft of the Iron Dogs. Collins, 1946)
The Organ Speaks, by E. C. R. Lorac. Low, 1935
Over the Garden Wall, by Carol Carnac. Doubleday, 1949
A Pall for a Painter, by E. C. R. Lorac. Collins, 1936
A Part for a Poisoner, by E. C. R. Lorac. Collins, 1948 (U.S. title: A Place for a Poisoner. Doubleday, 1949)
People Will Talk, by E. C. R. Lorac. Doubleday, 1958
Picture of Death, by E. C. R. Lorac. Collins, 1957
A Place for a Poisoner; see A Part for a Poisoner
Policeman at the Door, by Carol Carnac. Collins, 1953; Doubleday, 1954
Policemen in the Precinct, by E. C. R. Lorac. Collins, 1949 (U.S. title: And Then Put Out the Light. Doubleday, 1950; Bantam, 1968)
Post After Post-Mortem, by E. C. R. Lorac. Collins, 1936
Relative Poison, by E. C. R. Lorac. Collins, 1947; Doubleday, 1948
Rigging the Evidence, by Carol Carnac. Collins, 1955
Rope's End, Rogue's End, by E. C. R. Lorac. Collins, 1942
Screen for Murder; see Death Before Dinner
Shepherd's Crook; see Crook o'Lune
Shroud of Darkness, by E. C. R. Lorac. Collins, 1954; Doubleday, 1954
The Sixteenth Stair, by E. C. R. Lorac. Collins, 1942
The Slippery Staircase, by E. C. R. Lorac. Collins, 1938
Speak Justly of the Dead; see Murder in the Mill-Race
Still Waters, by E. C. R. Lorac. Collins, 1949
The Theft of the Iron Dogs; see Murderer's Mistake
These Names Make Clues, by E. C. R. Lorac. Collins, 1937
Tryst for a Tragedy, by E. C. R. Lorac. Collins, 1940
Upstairs and Downstairs; see Upstairs, Downstairs
Upstairs, Downstairs, by Carol Carnac. MacDonald & Co., 1950 (U.S. title: Upstairs and Downstairs. Doubleday, 1950)

ROBBE-GRILLET, ALAIN (S)
The Erasers. Grove, 1964
Voyeur. Grove, 1958

ROBBINS, CLARENCE AARON (M)
(Pseudonym: Tod Robbins)
In the Shadow. Mathews, 1929
Master of Murder. Allan, P., 1933
The Unholy Three. Lane, 1917

ROBBINS, CLIFTON (D)
The Clay Harrison Omnibus. Benn, 1933
Death Forms Three. Rich, 1940
Death on the Highway. Benn, 1933
The Devil's Beacon. Benn, 1933
Dusty Death. Benn, 1931; Appleton, D., 1932
The Man Without a Face. Benn, 1932
Methylated Murder. Butterworth, T., 1935
Murder by Twenty-five. Butterworth, T., 1936
Six Sign-Post Murder. Rich, 1939
Smash and Grab. Benn, 1934

ROBBINS, TOD, pseud; see ROBBINS, CLARENCE AARON

ROBERTS, CARL ERIC BECHHOFER; see GOODCHILD, GEORGE

ROBERTS, JAMES HALL, pseud. (S)
The February Plan. Morrow, 1967
The Q Document. Morrow, 1964; Cape, 1965; Crest, 1965

ROBERTS, KATHERINE (M)
The Center of the Web. Doubleday, Doran, 1942 (Also published as: The House on Harmony Street)

ROBERTS, LEE, pseud; see MARTIN, ROBERT LEE

ROBERTS, MARION (M)
A Mask for Crime. Eldon, 1935

ROBERTS, MARY CARTER (M)
Little Brother Fate. Farrar, 1957; Gollancz, 1958; Penguin, 1963

ROBERTS, MORLEY (M)
The Grinder's Wheel. Nelson, 1907
Midsummer Madness. Nash, 1909
The Scent of Death. Nash & Grayson, 1931

ROBERTS, RICHARD ELLIS (M)
The Other End. Palmer, C., 1923

ROBERTS, WALTER ADOLPHE (M)
The Haunting Hand. Macaulay, 1926
The Mind Reader. Macaulay, 1929
The Top-Floor Killer. Nicholson, 1935

ROBERTS, WILLO DAVIS (M-Gothic)
The Girl Who Wasn't There. Arcadia, 1957
Nurse at Mystery Villa. Ace, 1967

ROBERTSON, COLIN (M-D)
Alibi in Black. Ward, Lock, 1945
The Amazing Corpse. Ward, Lock, 1942
Calling Peter Gayleigh. Ward, Lock, 1948
Conflict of Shadows. Allen, T., 1963; Hale, R., 1963
Dark Knight. Ward, Lock, 1946
Dark Money. Hale, R., 1962
Dead on Time. Hale, R., 1964
Death Wears Red Shoes. Ward, Lock, 1949
Demon's Moon. Ward, Lock, 1951
Devil or Saint? Ward, Lock, 1936
The Devil's Lady. Ward, Lock, 1949
Double Take. Hale, R., 1967
Dusky Limelight. Ward, Lock, 1950
The Eastlake Affair. Long, 1957
Explosion. Ward, Lock, 1945
The Fake. Ward, Lock, 1937
The Frightened Widow. Hale, R., 1964
Ghost Fingers. Ward, Lock, 1941
The House of Intrigue. Ward, Lock, 1937
Knaves' Castle. Ward, Lock, 1948
Lady, Take Care. Allen, W. H., 1952
The Marble Tomb Mystery. Ward, Lock, 1936
Murder in the Morning. Long, 1957
Murder Sits Pretty. Hale, R., 1961
Night Shadows. Ward, Lock, 1935
No Trial, No Error. Allen, W. H., 1953
North for Danger. Allen, W. H., 1952
Painted Faces. Ward, Lock, 1935
Peter Gayleigh Flies High. Ward, Lock, 1951
Pirate of the Pacific. Bantam, 1967
Sinister Moonlight. Hale, R., 1965
Smugglers' Moon. Ward, Lock, 1954
Soho Spy. Ward, Lock, 1941
Stalking Stranger. Ward, Lock, 1939
Sweet Justice. Ward, Lock, 1949
Temple of Dawn. Ward, Lock, 1940
Threatening Shadows. Hale, R., 1959
The Tiger's Claws. Ward, Lock, 1951
Time to Kill. Hale, R., 1961
The Venetian Mask. Ward, Lock, 1956
The White Menace. Ward, Lock, 1938
Who Rides a Tiger? Long, 1958
Without Music. Pendulum, 1946
The Yellow Strangler. Ward, Lock, 1934
You Can Keep the Corpse. Ward, Lock, 1955
Zero Hour. Ward, Lock, 1942

ROBERTSON, MRS. CONSTANCE NOYES (Pseudonym: Dana Scott)
Five Fatal Letters. Farrar & Rinehart, 1937

ROBERTSON, E. ARNOT (M)
Four Frightened People. Cape, 1931

ROBERTSON, HELEN, pseud; see EDMISTON, HELEN JEAN MARY

ROBERTSON, KEITH CARLTON (M) (Pseudonym: Carleton Keith)
The Crayfish Dinner. Doubleday, 1966, 1967
The Diamond-Studded Typewriter. Macmillan, 1958 (Also published as: A Gem of a Murder. Dell, 1959)
A Gem of a Murder; see The Diamond-Studded Typewriter
The Hiding Place. Doubleday, 1965
Missing, Presumed Dead. Doubleday, 1961
Rich Uncle. Doubleday, 1963

ROBERTSON, L. M. (S)
Frederika and the Convict. Doubleday, 1965

ROBERTSON, WILFRID (M)
Black Meg's. Dent, 1958
The House on the Broads. Quality, 1954
The Missing Legatee. Oxford, 1947
The Mystery at Manthorpe. Dent, 1957

ROBESON, KENNETH (S)
Brand of the Werewolf. Bantam, 1965
Fantastic Island. Bantam
Fear Cry. Bantam
The Land of Always Night. Bantam
The Land of Terror. Bantam, 1965
The Lost Oasis. Bantam
The Man of Bronze. Bantam, 1964
The Meteor Menace. Bantam, 1964
The Monsters. Bantam, 1965
Murder Melody. Bantam, 1963
The Mystic Mullah. Bantam, 1965
The Phantom City. Bantam, 1966
Pirate of the Pacific. Bantam, 1967
The Polar Treasure. Bantam, 1965
The Red Skull. Bantam, 1967
Sargasso Ogre. Bantam, 1967
The Secret in the Sky. Bantam, 1967
The Spook Legion. Bantam, 1963
The Thousand-Headed Man. Bantam, 1964
The Quest of Qui. Bantam

ROBINS, MRS. DENISE (M)
Dance in the Dust. Hale, R., 1959
Gold for the Gay Masters. Rich, 1956

ROBINS, ELIZABETH (Mrs. George Richmond Parks) (M) (Pseudonym: C. E. Raimond)
The Secret That Was Kept. Harper, 1926
Time Is Whispering. Harper, 1923

ROBINS, RAYMOND (D)
Murder at Bayside. Crowell, 1933

ROBINSON, BERTRAM FLETCHER (M)
Chronicles of Addington Peace. Harper, 1905

ROBINSON, DAVID (M)
The Confessions of Alma Quartier. Signet, 1962

ROBINSON, ELIOT HARLOW (M)
Dee Dee. Small, 1925
The Scarred Hand. Page, 1931

ROBINSON, ETHELBERT McKENNON (D)
Death Designs a Dress. Hammond, 1958
The Secret of the Swinging Boom. Hammond, 1957

ROBINSON, LEWIS GEORGE (D) (Pseudonym: George Limnelius)
The General Goes Too Far. Nicholson, 1935; Putnam, 1936
The Manuscript Murder. Barker, 1933
The Medbury Fort Murder. Doubleday, Doran, 1929; Benn, 1931
Tell No Tales. Bles, 1931

ROBINSON, PATRICIA; see STEVENSON, FERDINAN

ROBINSON, PHILIP (S)
The Pakistani Agent. Hart-Davis, 1965

ROBINSON, RICHARD BLUNDELL (M) (Pseudonym: George Leaderman)
Death in Pursuit. Hurst, 1935
The Door Was Violence. Hurst, 1935

ROBINSON, ROBERT HENRY (D)
Landscape with Dead Dons. Gollancz, 1956; Rinehart, 1956; Penguin, 1963

ROBLES, EMMANUEL (M)
Dawn on Our Darkness. Collins, 1954; Messner, 1954
Knives. Collins, 1958

ROBY, MARY LINN (M)
Afraid of the Dark. Dodd, 1965
Still as the Grave. Dodd, 1964; Cassell, 1965

ROCHE, ARTHUR SOMERS (M-S)
Among Those Present. Sears, 1930
The Case Against Mrs. Ames. Dodd, 1934; Archer, 1935
The Eyes of the Blind. Doran, 1919
Find the Woman. Hodder, 1921; Burt, 1922
In the Money. Dodd, 1936
Loot. Bobbs, 1916
The Pleasure Buyers. Macmillan, 1925
Plunder. Bobbs, 1917
Ransom. Doran, 1918
Shadow of Doubt. Dodd, 1935
Slander. Sears, 1933
Star of Midnight. Dodd, 1936
Uneasy Street. Burt, 1921

ROCHE, KAY (M)
The Shuttered House. Hurst, 1950

ROCHE, PETER (M)
The Dean of Clonbury. Wright & Brown, 1957

ROCHESTER, GEORGE ERNEST (S)
The Black Chateau. Amalgamated Press, 1935
The Crimson Threat. Amalgamated Press, 1934
Dead Man's Gold. Amalgamated Press, 1935; Hamilton, 1936

ROCKEY, HOWARD (M) (Pseudonym: Oliver Panbourne)
The Varanoff Tradition. Macrae Smith, 1926

ROCKWOOD, HARRY, pseud; see YOUNG, ERNEST

RODD, RALPH, pseud; see NORTH, WILLIAM

RODDA, CHARLES PERCIVAL (D-M-S) (Pseudonyms: Gavin Holt, Gardner Low. Joint pseudonym with Eric Ambler: Eliot Reed)
Begonia Walk, by Gavin Holt. Hodder, 1946 (U.S. title: Send No Flowers. Howell, Soskin, 1947)
Black Bullets, by Gavin Holt. Hodder, 1935
Charter to Danger, by Eliot Reed. Collins, 1954
Dark Lady, by Gavin Holt. Hodder, 1933
The Dark Street, by Gavin Holt. Hodder, 1942
Death Takes the Stage, by Gavin Holt. Hodder, 1934; Little, 1934
Drum Beat at Night, by Gavin Holt. Hodder, 1932
Dusk at Penarder. Hodder, 1956
The Emerald Spider, by Gavin Holt. Hodder, 1935
Eyes in the Night, by Gavin Holt. Hutchinson, 1927
The Garden of Silent Beasts, by Gavin Holt. Hodder, 1932
Garlands for Sylvia. Hodder, 1958
Give a Man Rope, by Gavin Holt. Hodder, 1942
The Golden Witch, by Gavin Holt. Hodder, 1933
Green for Danger, by Gavin Holt. Gollancz, 1939
Green Talons, by Gavin Holt. Hodder, 1930; Bobbs, 1931
Invitation to Kill, by Gardner Low. Gollancz, 1937; Putnam, 1937
The Ivory Ladies, by Gavin Holt. Hodder, 1937

Ladies in Ermine, by Gavin Holt. Hodder, 1947
Maras Affair, by Eliot Reed. Doubleday, 1953
Mark of the Paw, by Gavin Holt. Hodder, 1933
Murder at Marble Arch, by Gavin Holt. Hodder, 1931
Murder Train, by Gavin Holt. Hodder, 1936
No Curtain for Cora, by Gavin Holt. Hodder, 1950
Passport to Panic, by Eliot Reed. Collins, 1957
Pattern of Guilt, by Gavin Holt. Hodder, 1959; Walker & Co., 1962
The Praying Monkey, by Gavin Holt. MacVeagh, 1930
Red Eagle, by Gavin Holt. Hodder, 1932
Send No Flowers; see Begonia Walk
Six Minutes Past Twelve, by Gavin Holt. Hodder, 1928
Skytip, by Eliot Reed. Doubleday, 1950
Steel Shutters, by Gavin Holt. Hodder, 1936
Storm, by Gavin Holt. Hodder, 1931; Swain, 1933
Swing It, Death, by Gavin Holt. Gollancz, 1940
Take Away the Lady, by Gavin Holt. Hodder, 1954
Tender to Danger, by Eliot Reed. Doubleday, 1951 (English title: Tender to Moonlight. Hodder, 1952)
Tender to Moonlight; see Tender to Death
The Theme Is Murder, by Gavin Holt. Gollancz, 1938; S & S, 1939
Tonight Is for Death, by Gavin Holt. Hodder, 1952
Trafalgar Square, by Gavin Holt. Hodder, 1934
The Trail of the Skull, by Gavin Holt. Hodder, 1931
Valse Caprice, by Gavin Holt. Hodder, 1932
The White-Faced Man, by Gavin Holt. Hodder, 1929

RODELL, MARIE FREID (M) (Pseudonym: Marion Randolph)
Breathe No More. Heinemann, 1940; Holt, H., 1940
Grim Grow the Lilacs. Holt, H., 1941; Museum Press, 1943
This'll Kill You. Holt, H., 1940; Museum Press, 1944

RODELL, VIC (D)
The Free-Lance Murder. Bouregy, 1957

RODEN, HENRY WISDOM (M)
One Angel Less. Morrow, 1945; Hammond, 1949
Too Busy to Die. Morrow, 1944; Hammond, 1947
Wake for a Lady. Morrow, 1946; Hammond, 1950
You Only Hang Once. Morrow, 1944; Hammond, 1946

RODNEY, BRYAN (M)
Owl Flies Home. Wright & Brown, 1952
Owl Meets the Devil. Wright & Brown, 1949

ROE, VINGIE EVE (M)
The Slow White Oxen. Cassell, 1950

ROEBURT, JOHN (M)
The Climate of Hell. Abelard, 1958 (Also published as: The Long Nightmare)
The Hollow Man. S & S, 1954; Jarrolds, 1955
Jigger Moran. Gardner, 1948
The Long Nightmare; see The Climate of Hell
The Lunatic Time. S & S, 1956
The Mobster. Pyramid, 1961
Seneca, USA. Curl, 1947
Sing Out, Sweet Homicide. Dell, 1961
There Are Dead Men in Manhattan. Bouregy, 1946 (Also published as: Triple Cross. Belmont, 1962)
Tough Cop. S & S, 1949; Pyramid, 1959
Triple Cross; see There Are Dead Men in Manhattan

ROFFMAN, JAN, pseud; see SUMMERTON, MARGARET

ROGERS, JOEL TOWNSLEY (D)
Once in a Red Moon. Brentano, 1923
The Red Right Hand. S & S, 1945; Pyramid
The Stopped Clock. S & S, 1958

ROGERS, KERK, pseud; see KNOWLTON, EDWARD ROGERS

ROGERS, SAMUEL GREENE ARNOLD (M)
Don't Look Behind You. Harper, 1944; Musson, 1944; Lancer, 1966
You Leave Me Cold. Harper, 1946; Musson, 1946
You'll Be Sorry. Harper, 1945; Musson, 1945

ROHDE, ROBERT H. (D)
Hunted Down. Chelsea House, 1928
Sucker Money. Chelsea House, 1927

ROHDE, WILLIAM L. (M)
Help Wanted - for Murder. Fawcett, 1953
High Red for Dead. Fawcett, 1953
Uneasy Lies the Dead. Ace, 1957

ROHLFS, MRS. ANNA KATHERINE; see GREEN, ANNE KATHERINE

ROHMER, ELIZABETH SAX (M)
Bianca in Black. Bouregy, 1958

ROHMER, SAX, pseud; see WARD, ARTHUR SARSFIELD

ROLFE, EDWIN (M) (Pseudonym: Lester Fuller)
The Glass Room. Rinehart, 1946; Low, 1948

ROLLINS, KATHLEEN; see DAVIS, DRESSER

ROLLINS, WILLIAM (M) (Pseudonym: O'Connor Stacy)
Midnight Treasure. Coward, 1929
Murder at Cypress Hall. Macaulay, 1933
The Ring and the Lamp. S & S, 1947
The Shadow Before. McBride, 1934

ROLLS, ANTHONY, pseud; see VULLIAMY, COLWYN EDWARD

ROMAN, HOWARD (S)
Pitfall in August. Harper, 1960

ROMANOFF, ALEXANDER NICHOLAYEVITCH (M) (Pseudonym: Achmed Abdullah)
The Bungalow on the Roof, with Charles Fulton Ousler. Mystery League, 1931
The Man on Horseback. McCann, 1919; Burt, 1926
The Trail of the Beast, with Charles Fulton Ousler. McCann, 1919

ROME, ANTHONY, pseud; see ALBERT, MARVIN H.

ROMSEY, PETER (M)
The Lidless Eye. Jenkins, 1957; Roy Pubs., 1957

RONALD, E. B., pseud; see BARKER, RONALD

RONALD, JAMES (M)
The Angry Woman. Hodder, 1948
Counsel for the Defense. Gramol, 1932
Cross Marks the Spot. Hodder, 1933
Death Croons the Blues. Hodder, 1934; Phoenix, 1940
Diamonds of Death. Gramol, 1934
The Green Ghost Murder. Gramol, 1936
Hanging's Too Good. Rich, 1933
Lord Peter Goes a-Wooing. Gramol, 1933
The Man Who Made Monsters. Gramol, 1935
Medal for the General. Hodder, 1943
The Monocled Man. Gramol, 1933
Murder for Cash. Rich, 1938; Withy Grove, 1947
Murder in the Family. Lane, 1936; Lippincott, 1940; Belmont, 1964
She Got What She Asked For. Lippincott, 1941
Six Were to Die. Hodder, 1932; Withy Grove, 1947
The Sparks Fly Upward. Hodder, 1954
The Sundial Drug Mystery. Gramol, 1934
They Can't Hang Me. Doubleday, Doran, 1938; Rich, 1938
This Way Out. Lippincott, 1939; Rich, 1940
The Unholy Trio. Gramol, 1933
Young Quentin. Hodder, 1952

RONNS, EDWARD, pseud; see AARONS, EDWARD SIDNEY

ROOF, KATHERINE METCALF (D)
Murder on the Salem Road. Houghton, 1931

ROONEY, FRANK (M)
Heel of Spring. Vanguard, 1956

ROOS, AUDREY KELLEY and WILLIAM ROOS (D) (Pseudonym: Kelley Roos)
The Blonde Died Dancing. Dodd, 1956 (English title: She Died Dancing. Eyre, 1957)
A Cry in the Night. Dodd, 1966
A Few Days in Madrid. Scribner, 1965
Frightened Stiff. Dodd, 1942; Hale, R., 1951
Ghost of a Chance. Wyn, 1947
Grave Danger. Dodd, 1965; Eyre, 1966
If the Shroud Fits. Dodd, 1941
Made Up for Murder; see Made Up to Kill
Made Up to Kill. Dodd, 1940 (English title: Made Up for Murder. Jarrolds, 1941)
Murder in Any Language. Wyn, 1948
Murder Noon and Night. Eyre, 1959
Necessary Evil. Dodd, 1965
One False Move. Dodd, 1966
Requiem for a Blonde. Dodd, 1958; Dell, 1960
Sailor, Take Warning. Dodd, 1944; Hale, R., 1952
She Died Dancing; see The Blonde Died Dancing
Scent of Mystery. Dell, 1959
There Was a Crooked Man. Dodd, 1945; Hale, R., 1953
Triple Threat. Wyn, 1949
Who Saw Maggie Brown? Dodd, 1967

ROOS, KELLEY, pseud; see ROOS, AUDREY KELLEY

ROOS, WILLIAM; see KELLEY, AUDREY

ROOSEVELT, FRANKLIN D. (M)
The President's Mystery Story. Farrar & Rinehart, 1935; Lane, 1936; Prentice-Hall, 1967

ROOT, PAT (M)
The Devil of the Stairs. S & S, 1956; Lancer
Evil Became Them. S & S, 1952; Lancer

ROSCOE, JOHN and MICHAEL RUSO (M) (Pseudonym: Mike Roscoe)
Death Is a Round Black Ball. Crown, 1952; Foulsham, 1954
The Midnight Eye. Ace, 1958
One Tear for My Grave. Crown, 1955, Foulsham, 1956; Signet, 1964
Riddle Me This. Crown, 1952; Foulsham, 1955
A Slice of Hell. Crown, 1954; Foulsham, 1955; Signet

ROSCOE, MIKE, pseud; see ROSCOE, JOHN

ROSCOE, THEODORE (M)
A Grave Must Be Deep. Harrap, 1937
I'll Grind Their Bones. Dodge, 1936
Murder on the Way. Dodge, 1935
Only in New England. Scribner, 1959

ROSE, ALVIN EMMANUEL (M) (Pseudonym: Alan Pruitt)
The Restless Corpse. Ziff-Davis, 1947

ROSE, FREDERICK HORACE VINCENT (S)
Bride of Kalahari. Duckworth, 1940
Four Kings in the Street of Gold. Duckworth, 1942
The Harp of Life. Duckworth, 1946
Hell's Acre. Duckworth, 1941
Maniac's Dream. Duckworth, 1946
The Prodigal Soldier. Duckworth, 1942

ROSENBERG, ELIZABETH and JOHN ROSENBERG (D)
Fanfare for a Murderer. Hogarth, 1960
Out, Brief Candle. Hogarth, 1959

ROSENBERG, JOHN; see ROSENBERG, ELIZABETH

ROSENHAYN, PAUL (D)
Joe Jenkins Case Book. Heinemann, 1930
Joe Jenkins: Detective. Allan, P., 1929; Heinemann, 1929; Doubleday, Doran, 1930

ROSENKRANTZ, BARON PALLE (D)
The Magistrate's Own Case. Methuen, 1908

ROSENTHAL, RICHARD A. (M) (Pseudonym: Allen Richards)
The Merchandise Murders, by Allen Richards. Hammond, 1964
To Market, To Market. Macmillan, 1961; Collier, 1962

ROSER, VAL (M)
Murder in the Wind. Long, 1947

ROSMANITH, OLGA L. (M)
Signature to a Crime. Cassell, 1930

ROSNY, J. H. (M)
The Giant Cat. McBride, 1924

ROSS, CARLTON (M)
The Black Skull Murders. Swan, G. G., 1942
Racketeers of the Turf. Swan, G. G., 1947

ROSS, CLARISSA, pseud; see ROSS, DAN

ROSS, DAN (S-Gothic) (Pseudonyms: Clarissa Ross, Marilyn Ross)
Assignment: Danger, by Marilyn Ross. Paperback Lib., 1967
Beware, My Love, by Marilyn Ross. Paperback Lib., 1965
Cameron Castle, by Marilyn Ross. Paperback Lib., 1967
The Castle on the Cliff. Avalon, 1967
Cliffhaven, by Marilyn Ross. Avalon, 1966
Dark Legend, by Marilyn Ross. Paperback Lib., 1966
Dark Shadows, by Marilyn Ross. Paperback Lib., 1966
Desperate Heiress, by Marilyn Ross. Paperback Lib., 1966
Durrell Towers, by Clarissa Ross. Pyramid
Fog Island, by Marilyn Ross. Paperback Lib., 1965
A Gathering of Evil, by Marilyn Ross. Paperback Lib., 1966
The Locked Corridor, by Marilyn Ross. Paperback Lib., 1965
Memory of Evil, by Marilyn Ross. Paperback Lib., 1966
Mistress of Ravenswood, by Clarissa Ross. Arcadia, 1966; Paperback Lib., 1967
Murder at City Hall. Bouregy, 1965
Mystery of Fury Castle, by Marilyn Ross. Bouregy, 1965; Paperback Lib., 1967
Phantom Manor, by Marilyn Ross. Paperback Lib., 1966
Satan's Rock, by Marilyn Ross. Paperback Lib., 1966
Secret of Mallet Castle, by Clarissa Ross. Arcadia, 1966
Strangers at Collins House, by Marilyn Ross. Paperback Lib., 1967

Tread Softly, Nurse Scott, by Marilyn Ross. Paperback Lib., 1966
Victoria Winters, by Marilyn Ross. Paperback Lib., 1967

ROSS, HELEN HALYBURTON (D)
The Scarab Clue. Hutchinson, 1935

ROSS, IVAN T., pseud; see ROSSNER, ROBERT

ROSS, JAMES (M)
They Don't Dance Much. Houghton, 1940; Jarrolds, 1940

ROSS, JAMES E. (M)
The Dead Are Mine. McKay, 1935

ROSS, JOHN (S)
The Black Spot. Hodder, 1936
Bless the Wasp. Hodder, 1938
The Drone-Man. Hodder, 1937
Federal Agent. Collins, 1941
The Major. Hodder, 1938
The Major Steps Out. Hodder, 1939
The Man from the Chamber of Horrors. Hodder, 1939
The Moccasin Men. Hodder, 1936
The Tall Man. Collins, 1940

ROSS, JULIAN MacLAREN-; see JULIAN MacLAREN-ROSS

ROSS, LEONARD, pseud; see ROSTEN, LEO

ROSS, MANDER (M)
The Sorting Van Murder. Melrose, 1935

ROSS, MARILYN, pseud; see ROSS, DAN

ROSS, PHYLLIS (S)
Miranda Clair. PB, 1965

ROSS, SAM (S)
The Hustlers. Popular Lib., 1965
He Ran All the Way. Farrar, Straus, 1947; Tower
Ready for the Tiger. Farrar, 1964
The Tight Corner. Farrar, 1950; Tower, 1965

ROSS, ZOLA HELEN (D) (Pseudonyms: Helen Arre, Bert Iles)
Assignment in Ankara, by Helen Arre with Lucile Saunders. MacDonald & Co., 1959; Nelson, T., 1959
The Corpse by the River, by Helen Arre. Arcadia, 1958
The Golden Shroud, by Helen Arre. Arcadia, 1958
Murder by the Book. Arcadia, 1960
Murder in Mink, by Bert Iles. Arcadia, 1956
No Tears for the Funeral, by Helen Arre. Arcadia, 1954
One Corpse Missing. Bobbs, 1948
Overdue for Death. Bobbs, 1947
Three Down Vulnerable. Bobbs, 1946
Write It Murder, by Helen Arre. Arcadia, 1956

ROSSNER, ROBERT (D) (Pseudonym: Ivan T. Ross)
The Man Who Would Do Anything. Doubleday, 1963; Heinemann, 1965
Murder out of School. Heinemann, 1960; S & S, 1960
Old Students Never Die. Doubleday, 1962; Heinemann, 1963
Requiem for a Schoolgirl. S & S, 1961
Teacher's Blood. Doubleday, 1964

ROSTEN, LEO (S) (Pseudonym: Leonard Ross)
Adventure in Washington, by Leonard Ross. Harcourt, 1940
A Most Private Intrigue. Atheneum, 1967

ROTH, HOLLY (D-S) (Pseudonyms: K. G. Ballard, P. J. Merrill)
Bar Sinister, by K. G. Ballard. Doubleday, 1960
Button, Button. Harcourt, 1966; Hamilton, H., 1967
The Coast of Fear, by K. G. Ballard. Doubleday, 1958
The Content Assignment. Hamilton, H., 1954; S & S, 1954 (Also published as: The Girl Who Vanished. Penguin, 1958)
The Crimson in the Purple. Hamilton, H., 1957; S & S, 1957; Penguin, 1962
The Girl Who Vanished; see The Content Assignment
The Mask of Glass. Vanguard, 1954; Hamilton, H., 1955; Penguin, 1957; Berkley Pub., 1963
Operation Doctors. Hamilton, H., 1962 (U.S. title: Too Many Doctors. Random, 1963; Avon, 1964)
Shadow of a Lady. Hamilton, H., 1957; S & S, 1957; Award, 1965
The Sleeper. Hamilton, H., 1955; S & S, 1955; Penguin, 1959
The Slender Thread, by P. J. Merrill. Harcourt, 1959; MacDonald & Co., 1960; Panther, 1963
Too Many Doctors; see Operation Doctors
Trial by Desire, by K. G. Ballard. Boardman, T. V., 1959; Avon, 1964
The Van Dreisen Affair. Random, 1959; Hamilton, H., 1960

ROTHBERG, ABRAHAM (S)
The Heirs of Cain. Putnam, 1966
The Thousand Doors. Holt, 1965; Dell, 1966

ROTHWELL, HENRY TALBOT (S)
Dive Deep for Danger. Roy Pubs., 1966
Duet For Three Spies. Roy Pubs., 1967
Exit a Spy. Hale, R., 1966

ROUDYBUSH, ALEXANDRA (M)
Before the Ball Was Over. Doubleday, 1965
Death of a Moral Person. Doubleday, 1967

ROUECHE, BERTON (S)
Black Weather. Reynal, 1945
The Last Enemy. Dell, 1956; Grove, 1956

ROUGVIE, CAMERON (S)
Medal from Pamplona. Ballantine, 1964; Barker, 1964
Tangier Assignment. Ballantine, 1965; Barker, 1965

ROURKE, JAMES F.; see SUMMERS, HOLLIS SPURGEON

ROWE, ANNE V. (M)
Curiousity Killed a Cat. Morrow, 1941
Deadly Intent. Mill, 1946
Fatal Purchase. Mill, 1945
Little Dog Barked. Mill, 1942
Too Much Poison. Mill, 1944
Turn of a Wheel. Macaulay, 1930
Up to the Hill. Mill, 1945

ROWE, JOHN C. (M)
Death Flash; or, Horror of Monkstone Wood. Modern Pub., 1900 (?)

ROWLAND, HENRY COTTRELL (M)
Duds. Harper, 1920
The Peddler. Harper, 1920

ROWLAND, JOHN HERBERT SHELLEY (M)
Bloodshed in Bayswater. Jenkins, 1935
Calamity in Kent. Jenkins, 1950
The Cornish Riviera Mystery. Jenkins, 1939
The Crooked House. Jenkins, 1940
Dangerous Company. Jenkins, 1937
Death Beneath the River. Jenkins, 1943
The Death of Nevill Norway. Jenkins, 1942
Death on Dartmoor. Jenkins, 1936; Mellifont, 1947
The Devil Came to Devon. Jenkins, 1938
Grim Souvenir. Jenkins, 1950
Gunpowder Alley. Jenkins, 1941
Murder—by Persons Unknown. Mellifont, 1941
Murder in the Museum. Jenkins, 1938
Orange Tree Mystery. Jenkins, 1949
The Professor Dies. Jenkins, 1947
Puzzle in Pyrotechnics. Jenkins, 1947
Sinister Creek. Fiction House, 1946
Slow Poison. Jenkins, 1939
The Spy with the Scar. Jenkins, 1940
Suicide Alibi. Jenkins, 1937; Mellifont, 1946
Time for Killing. Jenkins, 1950

ROYCE, KENNETH (M)
The Angry Island. Cassell, 1963
The Day the Wind Dropped. Cassell, 1964
The Long Corridor. Cassell, 1960
My Turn to Die. Barker, 1958
The Night Seekers. Cassell, 1962
No Paradise. Cassell, 1961
The Soft-footed Moor. Barker, 1959

ROYDE-SMITH, NAOMI GWLADYS (M)
The Altar-piece. Macmillan, 1939
John Fanning's Legacy. Constable, 1927
Madam Julia's Tale and Other Queer Stories. Gollancz, 1932

ROYERS, LOUIS-CHARLES (S)
Redhead from Chicago. Pyramid, 1954

RUBEL, JAMES LYON (D)
No Business for a Lady. GM, 1965

RUBENSTEIN, SOL; see WEAVER, ROBERT G.

RUBENSTEIN, STANLEY (M)
Merry Murder. Jarrolds, 1949

RUCK, BERTA (M)
Pearl Thief. Dodd, 1926

RUD, ANTHONY M. (M)
Devil's Heirloom. Garden City Pub., 1924
House of the Damned. Macaulay, 1934
Rose Bath Riddle. Macaulay, 1934
The Stuffed Men. Macaulay, 1935; Newnes, 1936

RUDA, HANS AUFRICHT-; see AUFRICHT-RUDA, HANS

RUEGG, ALFRED HENRY (D)
Flash: A Moorland Mystery. Daniel, 1929

RUEGG, K. C. (M)
John Clutterbuck. Daniel, 1923

RUMSEY, ADELINE (S)
Crying at the Lock. Hammond, 1945

RUNYON, CHARLES (D-S)
The Black Moth. GM, 1967
The Bloody Jungle. Ace, 1966
Color Him Dead. Fawcett, 1963
The Death Cycle. GM, 1963

RUNYON, POKE (D)
Commando X. Pyramid, 1967

RURIC, PETER, pseud; see CAIN, PAUL

RUSHTON, CHARLES, pseud; see SHORTT, CHARLES RUSHTON

RUSO, MICHAEL; see ROSCOE, JOHN

RUSSELL, CHARLOTTE MURRAY (D)
Bad Neighbor Murder. Doubleday, 1946
Between Us and Evil. Doubleday, 1950
The Careless Mrs. Christian. Doubleday, 1949
The Case of the Topaze Flower. Doubleday, Doran, 1939
The Clue of the Naked Eye. Doubleday, Doran, 1939
Cook Up a Crime. Doubleday, 1951
Death of an Eloquent Man. Doubleday, Doran, 1936
Dreadful Reckoning. Doubleday, Doran, 1941
Hand Me a Crime. Cherry Tree, 1950
I Heard the Death Bell Ring. Doubleday, Doran, 1941
Ill Met in Mexico. Doubleday, 1948
June, Moon, and Murder. Doubleday, 1952
Lament for William. Doubleday, 1947
Market for Murder. Doubleday, 1953
Message of the Mute Dog. Doubleday, Doran, 1942
Murder at the Old Stone House. Doubleday, Doran, 1935
Murder Steps In. Doubleday, Doran, 1942
Night on the Devil's Pathway; see Night on the Pathway
Night on the Pathway. Doubleday, Doran, 1938 (Also published as: Night on the Devil's Pathway. World's Work, 1938)
No Time for Crime. Doubleday, Doran, 1945
The Tiny Diamond. Doubleday, Doran, 1937

RUSSELL, DONN (M)
Difference in Death. Faber, 1957

RUSSELL, FOX (S)
The Phantom Spy. Nelson, 1904

RUSSELL, JOHN (M)
Cops 'n Robbers. Norton, 1930
The Red Mark. Knopf, 1919

RUSSELL, MARTIN JAMES (M)
No Through Road. Collins, 1965; Coward, 1966

RUSSELL, VICTOR (M)
Under Control. Melrose, 1951

RUSSELL, WILLIAM (D) (Pseudonyms: Inspector F, "Waters")
Autobiography of an English Detective, by "Waters." Maxwell, J. (2 vols.)
Experiences of a French Detective Officer, Adapted from the Mss. of Theodore Duhamel, by "Waters." Clarke, C. H., 1861
Experiences of a Real Detective, by Inspector F and edited by "Waters." Ward, Lock, 1862
Mrs. Waldgraves' Will and Other Tales. Ward, Lock
Recollections of a Detective Police Officer, by "Waters." Brown, 1856; Clarke, C. H., 1956; Kent, W., 1859, 2nd series
A Skeleton in Every House, by "Waters." Clarke, C. H., 1860 (Parlour Lib.)
Undiscovered Crimes, by "Waters." Ward, Lock, 1862

RUTHERFORD, ANWORTH (M)
Bottle of Dust. Caxton, 1940
Hidden Island. Little, 1927

RUTHERFORD, CONSTANCE (M)
Door Without a Key. Hale, R., 1948
Double Entry. Heinemann, 1939
The Forgotten Terror. Heinemann, 1938

RUTHERFORD, DOUGLAS, pseud; see McCONNELL, JAMES DOUGLAS RUTHERFORD

RUTLAND, HARRIET (D)
Blue Murder. Skeffington, 1938
Knock, Murderer, Knock. Harrison-Hilton, 1939
Poison Fly Murder. Smith & Durrell, 1940

RUTLEDGE, ARTHUR (S)
Object of Jealousy. Tower, 1965

RUTLEDGE, BRETT, pseud; see PAUL, ELLIOT HAROLD

RUTLEDGE, NANCY (M) (Pseudonym: Leigh Bryson)
Beware the Hoot Owl. Farrar & Rinehart, 1944
Blood on the Cat. Farrar & Rinehart, 1945
Cry Murder. Dutton, 1954
Easy to Murder. Doubleday, 1951
Emily Will Know. Doubleday, 1949
The Frightened Murderer. Random, 1957
Murder for Millions. Harrap, 1950
Murder on the Mountain. Muller, 1956; Random, 1956

The Preying Mantis. Doubleday, 1947
Wanted for Murder. Muller, 1956; Random, 1956

RUTTER, AMANDA (M)
Murder at Eastover. Arcadia, 1958
Murder Is Where You Find It. Arcadia, 1958

RYAN, JESSICA (M)
Exit Harlequin. Doubleday, 1947
The Man Who Asked Why. Doubleday, Doran, 1945

RYAN, MICH (M)
Intent to Kill. Dell, 1956

RYAN, PAUL WILLIAM (M) (Pseudonym: Robert Finnegan)
The Bandaged Nude. S & S, 1947; Boardman, T. V., 1949; Penguin, 1949
The Lying Ladies. S & S, 1946; Bodley Head, 1949
Many a Monster. S & S, 1948; Boardman, T. V., 1950

RYAN, RACHEL (M)
Death of a Sadist. Jenkins, 1937
Devil's Shelter. Jenkins, 1937
Echo of a Curse. Jenkins, 1939
Freak Museum. Jenkins, 1938
No Escape. Jenkins, 1940
The Right to Kill. Jenkins, 1936
The Subjugated Beast. Jenkins, 1938

RYAN, STELLA (D)
Death Never Weeps. Coward, 1946

RYDELL, FORBES, pseud; see FORBES, DeLORIS STANTON

RYDELL, HELEN; see FORBES, DeLORIS STANTON

RYDER, SABIN (S)
Three on the Road. Bouregy, 1963

RYERSON, FLORENCE; see CLEMENTS, COLIN CAMPBELL

RYLAND, CLIVE, pseud; see PRIESTLEY, CLIVE RYLAND

RYLAND, JOHN KNOX (M)
Death Meets the Coroner. Paul, S., 1936
The Easter Guests Mystery. Paul, S., 1935
The Tragedy Near Tring. Paul, S., 1934

S. D. C. L., pseud. (M)
Experience of a Barrister. Brown, 1856

SABATINI, RAFAEL (S)
Turbulent Tales. Hutchinson, 1945

SABER, ROBERT O., pseud; see OZAKI, MILTON K.

SABRE, DIRK (M)
Murder by Bamboo. Hammond, 1958

SACHS, MRS. EMANIE LOUISE NAHM (M)
The Octangle. Cape, 1930; Eyre, 1932

SAGE, DANA (M)
The Moon Was Red. S & S, 1944
The Twenty-Two Brothers. S & S, 1950

SAGER, GORDON (M)
Formula. Lippincott, 1952
The Rape of Europa. Chapman, 1952

ST. CLAIR, DEXTER, pseud; see WINCHELL, PRENTICE

ST. CLAIR, EILEEN ADAMS (M)
Murder Unplanned. Quality, 1949; Brown, Watson, 1952
Murdered Man's Derby. Gramol, 1935

SAINT CLAIR, IAN (M)
Bled White. Stockwell, 1938

ST. DENNIS, MADELON (D)
The Death Kiss. Jacobsen, 1932
Perfumed Lure. Clode, 1932

ST. JOHN, DARBY (M)
The Westgate Mystery. Random, 1941

ST. JOHN, DAVID (S)
Festival for Spies. Signet, 1965
On Hazardous Duty. Signet, 1965
One of Our Agents Is Missing. Signet, 1967
Return from Vorkuta. Signet, 1965
The Towers of Silence. Signet, 1966
The Venus Probe. Signet, 1966

ST. JOHN, GENEVIEVE (S-Gothic)
The Dark Watch. Belmont, 1966
Daughter of Evil. Belmont, 1967
Death in the Desert. Belmont, 1966
Night of Evil. Belmont, 1967
The Secret of Kensington Manor. Belmont, 1965
Shadow on Spanish Swamp. Belmont, 1966
Sinister Voice. Belmont, 1967
Strangers in the Night. Belmont, 1967

ST. JOHN, J. ALLEN (M)
The Face in the Pool. McClurg, 1906

ST. MICHAELS, DONELLA (M)
The Prisoner. Lancer

SALE, RICHARD BERNARD (S)
Benefit Performance. S & S, 1946
Cardinal Rock. Cassell, 1940

Death Looks In. Cassell, 1943
Destination Unknown. World's Work, 1943
Is a Ship Burning? Dodd, 1938
Lazarus #7. S & S, 1942
Not Too Narrow, Not Too Deep. Cassell, 1936; S & S, 1936
Passing Strange. S & S, 1944
Sailor Take Warning. Gardner, 1942

SALMON, GERALDINE GORDON (M)
(Pseudonym: J. G. Sarasin)
Fleur de Lys. Doubleday, Doran, 1929; Hutchinson, 1929

SALTER, ELIZABETH FULTON (M)
Death in a Mist. Bles, 1957; Ace, 1968
Once Upon a Tombstone. Hutchinson, 1965; Ace, 1967
There Was a Witness. Bles, 1960
The Voice of the Peacock. Bles, 1962
The Will to Survive. Bles, 1958

SALTER, MARIAN ARMOUR (M)
The Cat's Paw. Rinehart, 1952

SALTMARSH, MAX (M)
Clouded Moon. Joseph, M., 1937; Knopf, 1938
Highly Inflammable. Little, 1936 (English title: Highly Unsafe. Joseph, M., 1937)
Highly Unsafe; see Highly Inflammable

SALTUS, EDGAR EVERTON (M)
Paliser Case. Boni & Liveright, 1919

SAMAT, JEAN TOUSSAINT-; see TOUSSAINT-SAMAT, JEAN

SAMPSON, RICHARD HENRY (M)
(Pseudonym: Richard Hull)
And Death Came Too, by Richard Hull. Collins, 1939
Beyond Reasonable Doubt, by Richard Hull. Messner, 1941
Excellent Intentions, by Richard Hull. Faber, 1938
The Ghost It Was, by Richard Hull. Faber, 1936; Putnam, 1937
Invitation to an Inquest. Collins, 1950
Keep It Quiet. Faber, 1935; Putnam, 1936
Left-Handed Death. Collins, 1948
A Matter of Nerves. Collins, 1950
Murder Isn't Easy. Faber, 1936; Putnam, 1936
Murder of My Aunt, by Richard Hull. Minton, 1934
The Murderers of Monty. Faber, 1937; Putnam, 1937
My Own Murderer, by Richard Hull. Collins, 1940; Messner, 1940
The Unfortunate Murder, by Richard Hull. Messner, 1942

SAMPSON, VICTOR (M)
The Komani Mystery. Jenkins, 1930
The Murder of Paul Rougier. Jenkins, 1928

SANBORN, B. X., pseud; see BALLINGER, WILLIAM (BILL) SANBORN

SANBORN, RUTH BURR (D)
Murder by Jury. Little, 1932; Jarrolds, 1933
Murder on the Aphrodite. Macmillan, 1935

SANDERS, BRUCE (M)
Blonde Blackmail, Jenkins, 1945
Code of Dishonour. Jenkins, 1964
Deadly Jade. Jenkins, 1957
Kiss for a Killer. Roy Pubs., 1956
Madame Bluebeard. Jenkins, 1951; Roy Pubs., 1957
Midnight Hazard. Jenkins, 1955
Murder Behind the Bright Lights. Jenkins, 1958
Murder in Big Cities. Jenkins, 1962
Murder in Lovely Places. Jenkins, 1960
Pink Silk Alibi. Jenkins, 1946
Secret Dragnet. Jenkins, 1958
Tawny Menace. Jenkins, 1948
To Catch a Spy. Jenkins, 1958; Roy Pubs., 1958

SANDERS, DAPHNE, pseud; see RICE, CRAIG

SANDERS, GEORGE (D)
Crime on My Hands. S & S, 1944
Stranger at Home. S & S, 1946

SANDERS, JOAN (S)
The Nature of Witches. Houghton, 1964

SANDERS, JOHN (S)
A Fireworks for Oliver. Walker & Co., 1965 (Historical mystery)

SANDERS, MARIAN K. and MORTIMER S. EDELSTEIN (M)
The Bride Laughed Once. Farrar & Rinehart, 1943

SANDERS, W. FRANKLIN (S)
The Whip Hand. GM, 1961

SANDERS, WINSTON P., pseud; see ANDERSON, POUL WILLIAM

SANDERSON, DOUGLAS (Full name: Ronald Douglas Sanderson) (M)
(Pseudonyms: Martin Brett, Malcolm Douglas)
Catch a Fallen Starlet. Avon, 1960
Cry Wolfram. Secker & Warburg, 1959
The Darker Traffic, by Martin Brett. Dodd, 1954

A Dum-Dum for the President, by Martin Brett. Hammond, 1961
Exit in Green, by Martin Brett. Dodd, 1953 (English title: Murder Came Tumbling. Hammond, 1959)
Final Run. Secker & Warburg, 1953
Flee from Terror, by Martin Brett. Popular Lib., 1957
Hot Freeze, by Martin Brett. Dodd, 1954
Lam to Slaughter. Hale, R., 1964
Mark It for Murder. Avon, 1959
Murder Came Tumbling; see Exit in Green
Night of the Horns. Secker & Warburg, 1948; Penguin
Prey by Night, by Malcolm Douglas. GM, 1956
Pure Sweet Hell, by Malcolm Douglas. GM, 1957
Rain of Terror, by Malcolm Douglas. 1955

SANDERSON, RONALD DOUGLAS; see SANDERSON, DOUGLAS

SANDFORD, KEN (M)
Dead Reckoning. Hutchinson, 1955
Dead Secret. Hutchinson, 1957

SANDS, LESLIE (D)
Something to Hide. Muller, 1965

SANDYS, JAMES (M)
Darkest Under the Lamp. Paul, S., 1949
Death Echo. Paul, S., 1948
From Laughter to Death. Paul, S., 1945
The Lodestar of Death. Paul, S., 1946
The Lone Commando. Paul, S., 1944
The Man Who Wasn't There. Paul, S., 1953

SANDYS, OLIVER, pseud; see EVANS, MRS. MARGUERITE F. H.

SANGER, JOAN (D)
The Case of the Missing Corpse. Green Circle, 1936

SANGSTER, J. (S)
The Revenge of Frankenstein
The Terror of the Tongs. Brown, Watson, 1962

SANSOM, J. (M)
The Man Who Could Cheat Death

"SAPPER," pseud; see FAIRLIE, G. T.; also McNEILE, H. C.

SARASIN, J. G., pseud; see SALMON, GERALDINE GORDON

"SARBAN," pseud; see WALL, JOHN W.

SARGEANT, A. (M)
The Mill Street Mystery. Westbrook

SARNE, MICHAEL, pseud; see PLUMMER, THOMAS ARTHUR

SARSFIELD, MAUREEN (M)
Dinner for None. Nicholson, 1948
Green December Fills the Graveyard. Pilot, 1945; Coward, 1946
A Party for Lawtry. Coward, 1948

SATCHELL, WILLIAM (M)
The Greenstone Door. Sidgwick, 1914

SATURDAY EVENING POST
Danger. Doubleday, 1967

SAUER, MURIEL S.; see STAFFORD, MURIEL

SAUNDERS, CARL McK., pseud; see KETCHUM, PHILIP

SAUNDERS, CLAIRE CASTLER (M)
A Design for Treachery. Scribner, 1947
Measured for Murder, with Babs Lee. Scribner, 1944

SAUNDERS, HILARY AIDAN ST. GEORGE (See also PALMER, JOHN LESLIE)
The Sleeping Bacchus. Joseph, M., 1952

SAUNDERS, LAWRENCE, pseud; see DAVIS, BURTON

SAUNDERS, MONTAGU (M)
The Mystery in the Drood Family. Camb. Univ. Press, 1914 (Completion of Charles Dickens' The Mystery of Edwin Drood)

SAUNDERS, THEODORE; see MEANS, MARY

SAVAGE, JOHN (M)
A Shady Place to Die. Dell, 1957

SAVAGE, MARY (S)
A Likeness to Voices. Dodd, 1963; Dell, 1965

SAVAGE, RICHARD (D)
The Horrible Hat. Jarrolds, 1948
The Innocents. Washburn, 1959
The Lightning's Eye. Museum Press, 1957
Murder for Fun. Jarrolds, 1947
Murder Goes to School. Jarrolds, 1947
Poison and the Root. Jarrolds, 1950
Stranger's Meeting. Museum Press, 1957

SAWKINS, RAYMOND (D)
Snow in Paradise. Harcourt, 1967; Heinemann, 1967
Snow on High Ground. Heinemann, 1966; Harcourt, 1967

SAXBY, CHARLES (D)
Death Cuts the Film, with Louis Molnar. Dutton, 1939
Death in the Sun. Dutton, 1940
Death Joins the Woman's Club. Dutton, 1940
Death over Hollywood. Dutton, 1937
Death Wears Roses. Dutton, 1942
Even Bishops Die. Dutton, 1942
Murder at the Mike, with Louis Molnar. Dutton, 1938
Out of It All. Dutton, 1941

SAXON, JOHN A. (D)
Half-Past Mortem. Mill, 1947
Liability Limited. Mill, 1947
This Was No Accident. Fousham, 1949

SAXTON, MARK (M)
Danger Road. Farrar & Rinehart, 1939
Year of August. Farrar & Rinehart, 1943

SAYER, W. W. (M)
Mine Sinister Host. Wright & Brown, 1948
The Nemesis Club. Wright & Brown, 1946
Sellers of Death. Wright & Brown, 1940

SAYERS, DOROTHY LEIGH (D)
Busman's Honeymoon. Gollancz, 1937; Harcourt, 1937; Harper, 1960; PB, 1945; Avon, 1968; Penguin
Clouds of Witness, MacVeagh, 1927; Collins, 1931; Gollancz, 1935; Harcourt, 1938; Harper, 1956; Avon, 1966 (The 1939 edition includes The Documents in the Case)
The Dawson Pedigree; see Unnatural Death
The Documents in the Case, with Robert Eustace. Benn, 1930; Brewer, 1930; Harcourt, 1938
The Five Red Herrings. Gollancz, 1931; Harper, 1938, 1958; Avon, 1968 (Also published as: Suspicious Characters. Harcourt, 1931)
Gaudy Night. Gollancz, 1935; Harcourt, 1936; Harper, 1960
Hangman's Holiday. Gollancz, 1933; Harcourt, 1933, 1938; Coward, 1935
Have His Carcase. Brewer, 1932; Gollancz, 1932; Harcourt, 1936; PB, 1942; Avon, 1968
In the Teeth of the Evidence and Other Stories. Gollancz, 1939; Harcourt, 1940; Avon
Learned Adventure of the Dragon's Head. Watkins, 1928
Lord Peter Omnibus. Gollancz, 1964
Lord Peter Views the Body. Brewer, 1929; Gollancz, 1929, 1935; Harcourt, 1938 (1938 edition includes The Dawson Pedigree)
Murder Must Advertise. Gollancz, 1933; Harcourt, 1933, 1938; Harper, 1959; Avon, 1967 (1938 edition includes Hangman's Holiday)
New Sayers Omnibus. Gollancz, 1956 (Contains: Five Red Herrings, Have His Carcase, and Murder Must Advertise)
Nine Tailors. Gollancz, 1934; Harcourt, 1934, 1966
The Omnibus. Harcourt, 1934 (Contains: Whose Body?, Unpleasantness at the Bellona Club, and Suspicious Characters)
Omnibus. Gollancz, 1933 (Contains: Five Red Herrings, Strong Poison, and Lord Peter Views the Body)
Sayers Holiday Book. Gollancz, 1963
Sayers Tandem. Gollancz, 1957 (Contains: Nine Tailors and Busman's Honeymoon)
Strong Meat. Hodder, 1939
Strong Poison. Brewer, 1930; Gollancz, 1930; Harcourt, 1936; Harper & Row, 1963; Watts, 1965 (Large type edition); Avon, 1967 (1936 edition includes Have His Carcase)
Suspicious Characters; see Five Red Herrings
Treasury of Sayers Stories. Gollancz, 1958
Unnatural Death. Benn, 1927; Gollancz, 1927; Avon, 1964 (Also published as: The Dawson Pedigree. MacVeagh, 1928; Harcourt, 1938. The 1938 edition includes: Lord Peter Views the Body)
The Unpleasantness of the Bellona Club. Benn, 1928; Payson & Clarke, 1928; Harper, 1957; Avon, 1963 (Also in Omnibus. Harcourt, 1937)
Whose Body? Boni & Liveright, 1923; Unwin, 1923; Harper, 1956 (Also in Omnibus. Harcourt, 1937)

SCANNELL, VERNON (S)
Shadowed Place. Long, 1961

SCARBOROUGH, GEORGE; see PHILIPS, PAGE

SCARLETT, ROGER, pseud; see BLAIR, DOROTHY

SCHABELITZ, RUDOLPH F.; see BARBER, WILLETTA ANN

SCHERF, MARGARET (M)
Always Murder a Friend. Doubleday, 1948; Low, 1949
The Case of the Kippered Corpse. Putnam, 1941; Books, 1946

The Cautious Overshoes. Doubleday, 1956
Corpse Grows a Beard. Putnam, 1940
Corpse in the Flannel Nightgown. Doubleday, 1965; Hale, R., 1966
Curious Custard Pie. Doubleday, 1950
Dead: Senate Office Building. Doubleday, 1953
Death of the Diplomat. Doubleday, 1963; Hale, R., 1964
The Diplomat and the Gold Piano. Doubleday, 1963; Popular Lib., 1965
The Elk and the Evidence. Doubleday, 1952
Gilbert's Last Toothache. Doubleday, 1949
Glass on the Stairs. Doubleday, 1954; Barker, 1955
Green Plaid Pants. Doubleday, 1951
The Gun in Daniel Webster's Bust. Doubleday, 1949
Judicial Body. Doubleday, 1957
Murder Makes Me Nervous. Doubleday, 1948; Low, 1952
The Mystery of the Velvet Box. Watts, F., 1963
Never Turn Your Back. Doubleday, 1959; Popular Lib., 1964
Owl in the Cellar. Doubleday, Doran, 1945
They Came to Kill. Putnam, 1942
Wedding Train. Doubleday, 1960

SCHISGALL, OSCAR (S)
Baron Ixell, Crime Breaker. Longmans, 1929
The Devil's Daughter. Fiction League, 1932

SCHLEY, STURGES MASON (D)
The Deepening Blue. Doubleday, Doran, 1935
Dr. Roby Finds Murder. Random, 1941
Dream Sinister. Morrow, 1950
Who'd Shoot a Genius? Random, 1940

SCHMALZ, FLORA (M)
The Constable's Stories. Gardner, 1903

SCHMIDT, JAMES NORMAN (M) (Pseudonym: James Norman)
An Inch of Time. Morrow, 1942; Joseph, M., 1945
Murder Chop Chop. Morrow, 1941; Joseph, M., 1943
The Nightwalkers. Ziff-Davis, 1946; Penguin, 1953

SCHOENFELD, HOWARD (M)
Let Them Eat Bullets. GM, 1954

SCHOLEY, ERIC (M)
Answer in the Negative. Ward, Lock, 1952

SCHORER, MARK (M)
Colonel Markesan and Less Pleasant People. Arkham, 1966

SCHURMACHER, EMILE C. (S)
Assignment X: Top Secret. Paperback Lib., 1965

SCHURR, CATHLEEN (M)
Dark Death. Foulsham, 1957
Dark Encounter. Holt, 1955

SCHWARTZ, ALVIN (M)
The Blow-Top. Dial, 1948

SCIASCIA, LEONARDO (S)
The Mafia Vendetta. Cape, 1963; Knopf, 1964

SCOBIE, ALASTAIR (D)
The Cape Town Affair. Cassell, 1952
Murder à la Mozambique. Cassell, 1950

SCOTLAND, JAY (M)
The Seventh Man. Bouregy, 1958

SCOTT, BARBARA MONTAGU (M)
The Road Back. Hutchinson, 1952

SCOTT, DANA, pseud; see ROBERTSON, MRS. CONSTANCE NOYES

SCOTT, DENIS, pseud; see MEANS, MARY

SCOTT, JAMES MAURICE (S)
Seawife. Dutton, 1955 (Also published as: SeaWyf. Crest, 1957)
Seawyf; see Seawife
A Touch of the Nettle. Hodder, 1951

SCOTT, JODY; see LEITE, GEORGE THURSTON

SCOTT, JOHN DENTON; see DAMER, ANNE

SCOTT, JOHN REED (M)
The Cab of the Sleeping Horse. Putnam, 1916
The Man in Evening Clothes. Putnam, 1917
Red Emerald. Lippincott, 1914

SCOTT, LEROY (M)
Folly's Gold. Houghton, 1926
The Living Dead Man. Washburn, 1929
Mary Regan. Houghton, 1918
Partners of the Night. Century, 1916

SCOTT, LILY K. (S)
A House of Women. Pyramid, 1966

SCOTT, MANSFIELD (D)
Behind Red Curtains. Small, 1919; Nash, 1920
The Black Circle. Lane, 1929
The Phantom Passenger. Clode, 1927; Lane, 1930
The Spider's Web. Clode, 1929
The Sportsman-Detective. Clode, 1930

SCOTT, MARIAN GALLAGHER (M)
(Pseudonym: Gail Oliver)
Dead Hands Reaching. Macmillan, 1932
The Moon Saw Murder, by Gail Oliver. Macmillan, 1937; Bels, 1938

SCOTT, MARY CLARKE and JOYCE WEST (M)
The Mangrove Murder. Paul, S., 1963

SCOTT, MARY SEMPLE (D)
Crime Hound. Scribner, 1940

SCOTT, NATALIE ANDERSON (S)
Husband. MacDonald & Co., 1950

SCOTT, REGINALD THOMAS MAITLAND (D)
The Agony Column Murders. Dutton, 1946
Ann's Crime. Dutton, 1926; Heinemann, 1927
Aurelius Smith-Detective. Dutton, 1927; Heinemann, 1928
The Black Magician. Dutton, 1925; Heinemann, 1926
The Mad Monk. Kendall, 1931; Rich, 1933
Murder Stalks the Mayor. Rich, 1935; Dutton, 1936
The Nameless Ones. Dutton, 1947
Secret Service Smith. Dutton, 1923; Hodder, 1924; Triangle

SCOTT, SUTHERLAND (D)
A. R. P. Mystery. Paul, S., 1939
Capitol Punishment. Paul, S., 1949
Crazy Murder Show. Hillman-Curl, 1937; Paul, S., 1937
Diagnosis: Murder. Paul, S., 1954
Doctor Dodd's Experiment. Paul, S., 1956
Escape to Murder. Paul, S., 1946
The Influenza Mystery. Paul, S., 1938
The Mass Radiography Murders. Paul, S., 1947
Murder in the Mobile Unit. Paul, S., 1941
Murder Is Infectious. Paul, S., 1936
Murder Without Mourners. Paul, S., 1936
The Night Air Is Dangerous. Paul, S., 1943
Operation Urgent. Paul, S., 1946
Tincture of Murder. Paul, S., 1951

SCOTT, TARN (M)
Don't Let Her Die. GM, 1957

SCOTT, THURSTON, pseud; see LEITE, GEORGE THURSTON

SCOTT, WARWICK, pseud; see TREVOR, ELLESTON

SCOTT, WILL (D)
The Black Stamp. Macrae Smith, 1926
Disher-Detective. Cassell, 1925
The Mask. Macrae Smith, 1929
Shadows. Cassell, 1928; Macrae Smith, 1928

SEABROOKE, JOHN PAUL (M)
The Eye Witness. Chelsea House, 1925
Four Knocks on the Door. Chelsea House, 1925
The Green Bag. Chelsea House, 1926
The Woman in 919. Chelsea House, 1926

"SEAFARER," pseud; see BARKER, CLARENCE HEDLEY

"SEA-LION," pseud; see BENNETT, GEOFFREY MARTIN

"SEAMARK," pseud; see SMALL, AUSTIN J.

SEATON, STUART (M)
Cage of Fear. Long, 1960
Don't Take It to Heart. Boardman, T. V., 1955
Dust in Your Eyes. Boardman, T. V., 1957

SECRET AGENT X (S)
City of the Living. Corinth, 1966
Curse of the Mandarin's Fan. Corinth, 1966
The Death-Torch Terror. Corinth, 1966
Octopus of Crime. Corinth, 1966
Servants of the Skull. Corinth, 1966
The Sinister Scourge. Corinth, 1966
The Torture Trust. Corinth, 1966

SECRIST, KELLIHER, pseud; see KELLIHER, DAN T.

SECRIST, W. G.; see KELLIHER, DAN T.

SEE, INGRAM (S)
No Scars to See. Bouregy, 1965

SEELEY, CLINTON (S)
Storm Fear. Holt, H., 1954

SEELEY, MABEL HODNEFIELD (D)
The Beckoning Door. Collins, 1950; Doubleday, 1950; Pyramid, 1966

The Chuckling Fingers. Doubleday, Doran, 1941; Collins, 1942
The Crying Sisters. Doubleday, Doran, 1939; Collins, 1940; Pyramid, 1963
Eleven Came Back. Collins, 1943; Doubleday, Doran, 1943; Pyramid, 1968
The Listening House. Doubleday, Doran, 1938; Collins, 1939; Pyramid, 1964
The Stranger Beside Me. Doubleday, 1951; Muller, 1953
The Whispering Cup. Doubleday, Doran, 1940; Collins, 1941; Pyramid, 1966
The Whistling Shadow. Doubleday, 1954; Pyramid, 1964

SEIBERT, ELIZABETH G. (M)
Death Follows the Flower Show. Arcadia, 1958

SEIFERT, ADELE; see SEIFERT, SHIRLEY LOUISE

SEIFERT, ELIZABETH (M)
A Certain Dr. French. Dodd, 1943

SEIFERT, SHIRLEY LOUISE and ADELE SEIFERT (M)
Deeds Ill Done. Mill, 1942
Shadows Tonight. Mill, 1939
Three Blind Mice. Mill, 1942

SEIGNOLLE, CLAUDE (S)
The Accursed. Coward, 1967

SEILAZ, AILEEN (M)
The Veil of Silence. Ace, 1965

SELDES, GILBERT VIVIAN (Pseudonym: Foster Johns)
The Square Emerald. Day, 1928
The Victory Murders. Day, 1927

SELLARS, ELEANORE KELLY (D)
Murder à la Mode. Dodd, 1941; Muller, 1943

SELMAN, ROBERT (M)
Once Upon a Crime. Mill, 1947; Foulsham, 1949

SELMARK, GEORGE, pseud; see TRUSS, SELDON

SELTZER, CHARLES ALDEN (M)
Mystery Range. Doubleday, Doran, 1928; Hodder, 1928
Parade of the Empty Boots. Doubleday, Doran, 1937; Hodder, 1938

SELVER, PAUL (Full name: Percy Paul Selver) (M)
Private Life. Jarrolds, 1929; Harper, 1930

"SELWYN," pseud; see WATSON, SELWYN VICTOR

SEMENOV, JULIAN SEMENOVICH (M)
Petrovka 38. MacGibbon, 1965; Stein & Day, 1965

SENNOCKE, T. J. R. (M)
Inquest on a Lady. Rudkin, 1941
Inquest on a Mistress. Rudkin, 1943
Inquests Betraying. Rudkin, 1943
Inquests by Jury. Rudkin, 1944
Inquests on the Deceased. Rudkin, 1944
What Is Your Verdict? Eyre, 1936 (Problems in detection with their solutions)

SERENY, GITTA
The Medallion. Gollancz, 1951

SERGE, VICTOR (M)
The Case of Comrade Tulayev. Hamilton, H., 1951

SERLING, ROBERT J. (S)
The President's Plane Is Missing. Doubleday, 1967

SERLING, ROD (S)
More Stories from the Twilight Zone. Bantam, 1961
New Stories from the Twilight Zone. Bantam, 1962
The Season to Be Wary. Little, 1967
Stories from the Twilight Zone. Bantam, 1960

SERNER, GUNNAR (M) (Pseudonym: Frank Heller)
The London Adventures of Mr. Collin. Crowell, 1924
Mr. Collin Is Ruined. Crowell, 1925
The Strange Adventures of Mr. Collin. Crowell, 1926
Thousand and Second Night. Crowell, 1925

SERRESTER, LEONARD (D)
The Frog Murders. Dorrance, 1955

SERVICE, ROBERT WILLIAM (M)
The House of Fear. Dodd, 1927
The Master of the Microbes. Barse & Hopkins, 1926
Poisoned Paradise. Dodd, 1922

SETON, GRAHAM, pseud; see HUTCHISON, GRAHAM SETON

SEVERY, MELVIN LINWOOD (M)
Maitland's Master Mystery. Ball, 1912
The Mystery of June 13. Stevens, 1905

SEWARD, JACK (S)
Cave of the Chinese Skeletons. Tuttle, 1964; Tower, 1965

SEWARD, WILLIAM WARD, JR. (M)
Skirts of the Dead Night. Bookman Associates, 1950

SEYMOUR, H., pseud; see HARTMANN, HELMUT

SHAFER, ROBERT (M)
Conquered Place. Putnam, 1954

SHAFFER, ANTHONY and PETER SHAFFER (D) (Pseudonym: Peter Antony)
How Doth the Little Crocodile? Evans, 1952; Macmillan, 1957
Withered Murder. Gollancz, 1955; Macmillan, 1956
Woman in the Wardrobe. Evans, 1951

SHAFFER, PETER; see SHAFFER, ANTHONY

SHALLIT, JOSEPH (M-D)
The Billion Dollar Body. Lippincott, 1947; Hammond, 1952
Kiss the Killer. Lippincott, 1952; Hammond, 1954
Lady, Don't Die on My Doorstep. Lippincott, 1951; Hammond, 1952
Yell, Bloody Murder. Lippincott, 1951 (English title: Yell, Ruddy Murder. Hammond, 1958)
Yell, Ruddy Murder; see Yell, Bloody Murder

SHAMBROOK, RONA GREEN (S) (Pseudonym: Rona Randall)
Leap in the Dark. Ace, 1967
Murmuring Willow; see The Willow Herb
Seven Days from Midnight. Collins, 1965; Ace, 1967
The Willow Herb. Ace, 1964 (Also published as: Murmuring Willow. Ace, 1967)

SHAND, WILLIAM (D)
Man Called Tempest. Jenkins, 1957
Tempest in a Tea-cup. Jenkins, 1958; Roy Pubs., 1959
Tempest Weaves a Shroud. Jenkins, 1957

SHANE, SUSANNAH, pseud; see ASHBROOK, HARRIETTE CORA

SHANKS, EDWARD (M)
Dark Green Circle. Bobbs, 1936
Old King Cole. Macmillan, 1936

SHANNON, BRAD (D)
The Big Snatch. Scion, 1950
The Body Was Lonely. Scion, 1952
Bury the Guy! Scion, 1951
The Lady's for Killing. Scion, 1950
Murder!—So What? Scion, 1951
"Stir" Crazy. Scion, 1950

SHANNON, CARL, pseud; see HOGUE, WILBUR OWINGS

SHANNON, DELL, pseud; see LININGTON, ELIZABETH

SHANNON, JIMMY (D)
The Devil's Passkey. Appleton, 1952

SHAPIRO, LIONEL (S)
The Sealed Verdict. Doubleday, 1947; Jarrolds, 1950
Torch for a Dark Journey. Doubleday, 1950; Jarrolds, 1951

SHAPLEIGH, MARY YALE (M)
Johnny Counterfeit. Hopkins & Son, 1938

SHARKEY, JACK; see SHARKEY, JOHN MICHAEL

SHARKEY, JOHN (JACK) MICHAEL (M)
Death for Auld Lang Syne. Holt, 1962; Joseph, M., 1963
Murder, Maestro, Please. Abelard, 1961

SHARP, DAVID (M)
Code-Letter Mystery. Houghton, 1932
Disputed Quarry. Jenkins, 1938
I, the Criminal. Benn, 1932
Inconvenient Corpse. Benn, 1933
My Particular Murder. Benn, 1931; Houghton, 1931
None of My Business. Benn, 1931

SHARP, LUKE, pseud; see BARR, ROBERT

SHARP, MARGERY (M)
Tigress on the Hearth. Collins, 1955

SHARP, ROBERT GEORGE (D)
Death Comes to Rehearsal. Hutchinson, 1951
Death in the Headlines. Hutchinson, 1950

SHARP, WILLOUGHBY (D)
Murder in Bermuda. Kendall, 1933
Murder of the Honest Broker. Kendall, 1934

SHATTUCK, RICHARD (M)
The Half-Haunted Saloon. S & S, 1945
Said the Spider to the Fly. S & S, 1944
Snark Was a Boojum. Morrow, 1941
The Wedding Guest Sat on a Stove. Morrow, 1940; Collier, 1963

SHAW, CHARLES (Pseudonym: Bant Singer)
Don't Slip, Delaney. Collins, 1954
Have Patience, Delaney. Collins, 1954
Your Move, Delaney. Collins, 1958
You're Wrong, Delaney. Crown, 1953

SHAW, FRANK H. (M)
Atlantic Murder. Matthews, 1932; McBride, 1933

SHAW, JOSEPH T. (M)
Blood on the Curb. Dodge, 1936
It Happened at the Lake. Dodd, 1937

SHAY, FRANK (D)
Charming Murder. Macaulay, 1930
Murder on Cape Cod. Macaulay, 1931

SHAYNE, GORDON, pseud; see WINTER, BEVIS

SHEARING, JOSEPH, pseud; see LONG, MRS. GABRIELLE

SHECKLEY, ROBERT (S)
Calibre 50. Bantam, 1961
Dead Run. Bantam, 1961
The Game of X. Delacorte, 1965; Dell, 1966
The Live Gold. Bantam, 1962
Time Limit. Bantam, 1967
White Death. Bantam, 1963

SHEDD, GEORGE CLIFFORD (M)
The Lady of Mystery House. Gardner, A., 1920

SHEDD, MARGARET (M)
Run. Doubleday, 1956; Gollancz, 1956

SHEEHAN, PERLEY POORE (M)
House with a Bad Name. Boni & Liveright, 1920
Three Sevens. Chelsea House, 1927
Whispering Chorus. Watt, 1927

SHEERS, JAMES C. (S)
Counterfeit Courier. Dell, 1961

SHEFLER, HARRY F. (M)
Devil Take the Hindmost. Exposition, 1955

SHELDON, RICHARD, pseud. (M)
Harsh Evidence. Hutchinson, 1950
Poor Prisoner's Defense. Hutchinson, 1949; S & S, 1950

SHELDON, WALT (S)
The Blue Kimono Kill. GM, 1965
The Man Who Paid His Way. Lippincott, 1955; Bantam

SHELLABARGER, SAMUEL (M-D)
(Pseudonym: John Esteven)
Assurance Double Sure. Hodder, 1939
Blind Man's Night. Hodder, 1938
By Night at Dinsmore. Doubleday, Doran, 1935
Door of Death. Century, 1928; Methuen, 1928
Graveyard Watch. Modern Age, 1938
Voodoo. Methuen, 1928; Doubleday, Doran, 1930
While Murder Waits. Doubleday, Doran, 1937; Harrap, 1938

SHELLEY, JOHN (M)
Hired Gun. Berkley Pub., 1963

SHELLEY, MARY WOLLSTONECRAFT (S)
Frankenstein, or the Modern Prometheus. Routledge, 1882; Dutton, 1901, 1912; Airmont, 1963; Signet, 1965

SHELLEY, SIDNEY (M)
Francine. Belmont, 1963

SHENKIN, ELIZABETH (S)
Brownstone Gothic. Holt, 1961
Midsummer Nightmare. Rinehart, 1960; Ward, Lock, 1961

SHEPHERD, ERIC (M)
More Murder in a Nunnery. Sheed, 1954; All Saints, 1963
Murder in a Nunnery. Sheed, 1940

SHEPHERD, JOAN, pseud; see BUCHANAN, B. J.

SHEPHERD, JOHN, pseud; see BALLARD, WILLIS TODHUNTER

SHEPHERD, NEAL, pseud; see MORLAND, NIGEL

SHER, JACK (S)
Cold Companion. Rinehart, 1948

SHERATON, NEIL
Cairo Ring. Hale, R., 1958

SHERIDAN, JUANITA (D-M)
Chinese Chop. Doubleday, 1949; Barker, 1951
Kahuna Killer. Doubleday, 1951; Heinemann, 1955; Macmillan, 1966
Mamo Murders. Doubleday, 1952
Waikiki Widow. Doubleday, 1953
What Dark Secret, with Dorothy Dudley. Morrow, 1943
While the Coffin Waited. Heinemann, 1953

SHERIDAN, SOLOMON NEILL (M)
The Typhoon's Secret. Doubleday, Page, 1920

SHERMAN, ROBERT (M)
Picture Mommy Dead. Lancer, 1966

SHERRING, ALBERT WILLIAM
Double Exposure. Hale, R., 1965

The Big Haul. Hale, R., 1962
Night of Vengeance. Hale, R., 1960
The Pay-off. Hale, R., 1961
The Tip-off. Hale, R., 1959

SHERRY, EDNA (S)
Backfire. Dodd, 1956; Hodder, 1957
Call the Witness. Dodd, 1961; Hodder, 1962
The Defense Does Not Rest. Dodd, 1959; Hodder, 1960
Girl Missing. Dodd, 1962; Hodder, 1963
No Questions Asked. Dodd, 1949; Hodder, 1950
Is No One Innocent?, with Milton Herbert Gropper. Cosmopolitan, 1930
Strictly a Loser. Dodd, 1965
Sudden Fear. Dodd, 1948; Hodder, 1949
The Survival of the Fittest. Dodd, 1960; Hodder, 1961
Tears for Jessie Hewitt. Dodd, 1958; Hodder, 1959

SHERRY, JOHN (S)
The Loring Affair. PB

SHERWOOD, JOHN (D)
Ambush for Anatol. Doubleday, 1952; Hodder, 1952
The Disappearance of Dr. Bruderstein; see Dr. Bruderstein Vanishes
Dr. Bruderstein Vanishes. Doubleday, 1949 (English title: The Disappearance of Dr. Bruderstein. Hodder, 1949)
Half Hunter. Gollancz, 1961
Mr. Blessington's Imperialistic Plot. Doubleday, 1951, 1964 (English title: Mr. Blessington's Plot. Hodder, 1951)
Mr. Blessington's Plot; see Mr. Blessington's Imperialistic Plot
The Sleuth and the Liar. Doubleday, 1961
Two Died in Singapore. Hodder, 1954
Undiplomatic Exit. Doubleday, 1963
Vote Against Poison. Hodder, 1956

SHIEL, MATTHEW PHIPPS (D)
The Black Box. Vanguard, 1930
Dr. Krasiniski's Secret. Jarrolds, 1929
How the Old Woman Got Home. Collier, 1962
Prince Zaleski. Lane, 1895
The Rajah's Sapphire. Ward, Lock, 1896

SHIEVELLEY, ANGELA (S)
Dread of Night. Paperback Lib., 1966

SHOLL, ANNA McCLURE (D) (Pseudonym: Geoffrey Corson)
Carmichael: Blue Blood and Red. Hodder, 1915

SHORE, JULIAN (M)
Rattle His Bones. Morrow, 1941

SHORE, P. R. (M)
The Bolt. Dutton, 1929; Methuen, 1929
The Death Film. Methuen, 1932

SHORE, VIOLA BROTHERS (Mrs. Harry Braxton) (M)
The Beauty-Mask Murder. Smith, R. R., 1930 (English title: The Beauty Mask Mystery. Hamilton, 1932)
The Beauty-Mask Mystery; see The Beauty Mask Murder
Murder on the Glass Floor. Smith, R. R., 1932; Harrap, 1933

SHORETELL, LESLIE T. (M)
The Hounds Are Restless Tonight. Rich, 1949

SHORT, CHRISTOPHER (Full name: Charles Christopher Dudley Short) (S)
The Big Cat. Chapman, 1962; Dodd, 1965; PB, 1966
The Black Room. Cape, 1964; Dodd, 1966
The Blue-Eyed Boy. Dodd, 1966; PB, 1968
The Dark Lantern. Scribner, 1961; Chapman, 1962

SHORT, ERNEST HENRY and ARTHUR COMPTON-RICKETT (M)
The Hope Strange Mystery. Jenkins, 1927

SHORT, LUKE, pseud; see GLIDDEN, FREDERICK DILLEY

SHORTT, CHARLES RUSHTON (M) (Pseudonym: Charles Rushton)
Another Crime. Jenkins, 1934
Black Destiny. Jenkins, 1929
Bloody with Spurring. Jenkins, 1939
Crime Looks Up. Jenkins, 1947
Danger in the Deed. Jenkins, 1933
Dark Amid the Blaze. Jenkins, 1950
The Dead Men. Jenkins, 1935
Death in the Wood. Jenkins, 1936
Devil's Power. Jenkins, 1952
The Doctor from Devil's Island. Jenkins, 1935; Withy Grove, 1942
Furnace for a Foe. Jenkins, 1951
Madman's Manor. Jenkins, 1932
The Master of Fear. Jenkins, 1930
Murder in Bavaria. Jenkins, 1937
The Murder Market. Jenkins, 1934; Withy Grove, 1939
Murder Out of Tune. Jenkins, 1939
Night of Murder. Jenkins, 1937
No Beast So Fierce. Jenkins, 1950
No Second Stroke. Jenkins, 1938

Terror Tower. Jenkins, 1933; Withy Grove, 1940
The Trail of Blood. Jenkins, 1929

SHORTT, VERE DAWSON and MRS. FRANCES H. SHORTT MATHEWS (M)
The Rod of the Snake. Lane, 1918

SHOUBRIDGE, DONALD (D)
Yard Lengths. Pendulum, 1946

SHRIBER, IONE SANDBERG (D)
As Long as I Live. Rinehart, 1947; Lancer, 1966
A Body for Bill. Farrar & Rinehart, 1942; Nicholson, 1946
The Dark Arbour. Nicholson, 1945
A Family Affair. Farrar & Rinehart, 1941
Head Over Heels in Murder. Farrar & Rinehart, 1940
Invitation to Murder. Rinehart, 1943; Nicholson, 1946
The Last Straw. Rinehart, 1946
Murder Well Done. Farrar & Rinehart, 1941
Never Say Die. Rinehart, 1950
Pattern for Murder. Farrar & Rinehart, 1944
Ready or Not. Rinehart, 1953; Boardman, T. V., 1954

SHUBIN, SEYMOUR (S)
Stranger to Myself. Benn, 1954

SHULMAN, IRVING (S)
The Amboy Dukes. Doubleday, 1947
Cry Tough. Paperback Lib., 1963
The Notorious Landlady. GM, 1962

SHULMAN, MILTON (S)
Kill 3. Random, 1967

SHULMAN, SANDRA (S)
The Menacing Darkness. Paperback Lib., 1966

SHUTE, NEVIL, pseud; see NORWAY, NEVIL SHUTE

SIBLEY, CELESTINE (S)
The Malignant Heart. Doubleday, 1958; Gollancz, 1958

SIBLY, JOHN
Girl on the Run. Cape, 1958

SIBSON, FRANCIS (M)
Unthinkable. Methuen, 1933; Smith, H., 1933

SIDDLE, CHARLES and FREDERICK PEEL (M) (Pseudonym: Rufus Slingsby)
The Murders at Highbridge. Long, 1929
Running to Seed. Jenkins, 1927

SIDGWICK, CHRISTOPHER (S)
Manhunt in Dalmatia. Davies, 1959

SIEGAL, BENJAMIN (S)
A Kind of Justice. Harcourt, 1960; Avon, 1962
The Witch of Salem. GM, 1953

SIEGEL, DORIS (D-M) (Pseudonym: Susan Wells)
Death Is My Name. Scribner, 1942
Footsteps in the Air. S & S, 1940
How Still, My Love. Mill, 1957; Gollancz, 1958
Murder Is Not Enough. S & S, 1939
Witch's Pond. Doubleday, 1947 (Also published as: Witch's Pool. 1947)
Witch's Pool; see Witch's Pond

SIEGEL, JACK (S)
Dawn at Kahlenberg. Pyramid, 1966

SIEVEKING, LANCELOT DE GIBERNE (D)
Stamped. Brentano, 1928
Tomb with a View. Faber, 1950
Ultimate Island. International Pub., 1925

SILBERRAD, UNA L. (M)
The Mystery of Barnard Hanson. Hutchinson, 1915

SILBERSTANG, EDWIN (S)
Rapt in Glory. PB, 1964

SILLER, VAN, pseud; see VAN SILLER, HILDA

SILLIMAN, VERA (M)
Haunted Wood Hollow. Commercial, 1928

SILLIPHANT, STERLING (S)
Maracaibo. Farrar, 1955
The Naked City. Dell, 1959 (Adapted by Charles Einstein)

SILVERMAN, MARGUERITE RUTH (D)
I Had No Alibi; see Nine Had No Alibi
Nine Had No Alibi. Nicholson, 1951 (Also published as: I Had No Alibi)
The Vet It Was That Died. Nicholson, 1945
Who Should Have Died? Nicholson, 1948

SIMENON, GEORGES JOSEPH CHRISTIAN (D)
The Accomplices. Signet, 1965 (See also The Blue Room)
Account Unsettled. Hamilton, H., 1962
Across the Street. Routledge & Paul, 1954
Act of Passion. Prentice-Hall, 1952; Routledge & Paul, 1953; Penguin

Affairs of Destiny. Routledge & Paul, 1942
An American Omnibus. Harcourt, 1967
Aunt Jeanne. Routledge & Paul, 1953
A Battle of Nerves and At the Gai-Moulin. Penguin, 1950
The Bells of Bicêtre; see The Patient
Black Rain. Routledge & Paul, 1949; Penguin
The Blue Room and The Accomplices. Harcourt, 1964; Hamilton, H., 1965; Signet, 1965
The Brothers Rico. Hamilton, H., 1954; Four Square
The Burgomaster of Furnes. Routledge & Paul, 1952
The Burial of Monsieur Bouvet. Berkley Pub.
Chit of a Girl. Routledge & Paul, 1949
The Confessional. Hamilton, H., 1967
The Crime at Lock 14; see The Triumph of Inspector Maigret
Crime in Holland. Penguin, 1952
Crossroad Murders; see Introducing Inspector Maigret
Danger Ahead. Hamilton, H., 1955 (Contains: Red Lights and The Watchmaker of Everton)
Destinations. Doubleday, 1955 (Contains: The Hitchiker and The Burial of M. Bouvet)
Disintegration of J.P.G. Routledge & Paul, 1937
The Door. Hamilton, H., 1964
Escape in Vain. Routledge & Paul, 1943
The Fate of the Malous. Hamilton, H., 1962; Penguin
First-Born; see Magnet of Doom
Five Times Maigret; see Maigret Omnibus
The Hatter's Ghosts. Penguin, 1960
Havoc by Accident. Routledge & Paul, 1943
The House by the Canal. Routledge & Paul, 1952
In Case of Emergency. Doubleday, 1958; Macfadden, 1964; Penguin
In Two Latitudes; see Two Latitudes
Inquest of Bouvet. Hamilton, H., 1958; Penguin
Inspector Maigret and the Burglar's Wife; see Maigret and the Burglar's Wife
Inspector Maigret and the Dead Girl; see Maigret and the Young Girl
Inspector Maigret and the Killers. Doubleday, 1954; Signet, 1964
Inspector Maigret and the Strangled Stripper. Doubleday, 1954; Signet, 1964
Inspector Maigret in New York's Underworld; see Maigret in New York's Underworld
Inspector Maigret Investigates. Hurst, 1933 (U.S. title: Strange Case of Peter the Lett. Covici, 1933. Also published as: Maigret and the Enigmatic Lett. Penguin, 1964)
Introducing Inspector Maigret. Hurst, 1933 (U.S. title: Crossroad Murders. Covici, 1933)
The Iron Staircase. Hamilton, H., 1963; Penguin
The Judge and the Hatter. Hamilton, H., 1958 (Contains: The Witnesses and The Hatter's Ghosts)
Justice. Routledge & Paul, 1949
Little Man from Archangel. Harcourt, 1966; Hamilton, H., 1957; Penguin
Madame Maigret's Friend. Hamilton, H., 1960
Madame Maigret's Own Case. Pyramid, 1963
Magnet of Doom. Routledge & Paul, 1948 (U.S. title: First Born. Reynal, 1947)
Maigret Abroad. Routledge & Paul, 1940
Maigret Afraid. Hamilton, H., 1961; Penguin
Maigret and M. L'Abbé. Routledge & Paul, 1941; Harcourt, 1942
Maigret and the Burglar's Wife. Hamilton, H., 1950; Penguin (U.S. title: Inspector Maigret and the Burglar's Wife. Doubleday, 1956; Dell, 1957)
Maigret and the Enigmatic Lett; see Inspector Maigret Investigates
Maigret and the Headless Corpse. Hamilton, H., 1967
Maigret and the Hundred Gibbets. Penguin, 1963
Maigret and the Lazy Burglar. Hamilton, H., 1963
Maigret and the Nahour Case. Hamilton, H., 1967
Maigret and the Old Lady. Hamilton, H., 1958; Penguin, 1962
Maigret and the Reluctant Witness. Hamilton, H., 1959; Ace, 1962
Maigret and the Saturday Caller. Hamilton, H., 1964
Maigret and the Young Girl. Hamilton, H., 1955 (U.S. title: Inspector Maigret and the Dead Girl. Doubleday, 1955)
Maigret at the Crossroads. Penguin, 1964
Maigret Cinq; see The Second Maigret Omnibus
Maigret Goes Home. Penguin, 1967
Maigret Goes to School. Hamilton, H., 1959; Four Square
Maigret Has Scruples. Ace, 1962; Penguin, 1962
Maigret in Court. Hamilton, H., 1961
Maigret in Montmarte. Penguin, 1958
Maigret in Society. Hamilton, H., 1962
Maigret in New York's Underworld. Doubleday, 1955 (Also published as: Inspector Maigret in New York's Underworld. Signet, 1964)

Maigret Keeps a Rendezvous. Routledge & Paul, 1940
Maigret Loses His Temper. Hamilton, H., 1965
Maigret Meets M'Lord. Penguin, 1963
Maigret Mystified. Penguin
A Maigret Omnibus. Hamilton, H., 1962 (U.S. title: Five Times Maigret. Harcourt, 1964)
Maigret on Holiday. Routledge & Paul, 1950 (U.S. title: No Vacation for Maigret. Doubleday, 1955)
Maigret on the Defensive. Hamilton, H., 1966
Maigret Rents a Room; see Maigret Takes a Room
Maigret Right and Wrong. Hamilton, H., 1954 (Contains: Maigret in Monmartre and Maigret's Mistake)
Maigret Sets a Trap. Hamilton, H., 1965
Maigret Sits It Out. Routledge & Paul, 1941
Maigret Stonewalled. Penguin, 1963
Maigret Takes a Room. Hamilton, H., 1960; Penguin (U.S. title: Maigret Rents a Room. Doubleday, 1961; Popular Lib., 1962)
Maigret to the Rescue. Routledge & Paul, 1940; Hamilton, H., 1960
Maigret Travels South. Routledge & Paul, 1940
Maigret's Dead Man; see Maigret's Special Murder
Maigret's Failure. Hamilton, H., 1962; Penguin
Maigret's First Case. Hamilton, H., 1958
Maigret's Little Joke. Hamilton, H., 1957 (U.S. title: None of Maigret's Business. Doubleday, 1958)
Maigret's Memoirs. Hamilton, H., 1963
Maigret's Mistake. Penguin, 1958
Maigret's Revolver. Hamilton, H., 1956; Penguin
Maigret's Special Murder. Hamilton, H., 1964; Penguin (U.S. title: Maigret's Dead Man. Doubleday, 1964)
The Man Who Watched the Trains Go By. Routledge & Paul, 1942; Reynal, 1946; Penguin, 1964
The Man with the Little Dog. Hamilton, H., 1965
The Methods of Maigret; see My Friend Maigret
Monsieur Monde Vanishes. Hamilton, H., 1967
Mrs. Hires' Engagement. Hutchinson, 1958
The Murder. Penguin, 1958
My Friend Maigret. Hamilton, H., 1956; Penguin (U.S. title: The Methods of Maigret. Doubleday, 1957; Bantam, 1959)
Negro. Hamilton, H., 1959
A New Lease of Life. Hamilton, H., 1963 (U.S. title: A New Lease on Life. Doubleday, 1963)
A New Lease on Life; see A New Lease of Life
No Vacation for Maigret; see Maigret on Holiday
None of Maigret's Business; see Maigret's Little Joke
On the Danger Line. Harcourt, 1944; Penguin, 1952
The Ostenders. Routledge & Paul, 1952
The Patience of Maigret. Routledge & Paul, 1939
The Patient. Hamilton, H., 1963 (U.S. title: The Bells of Bicêtre. Harcourt, 1964; Signet, 1965)
Pedigree. Hamilton, H., 1962
Poisoned Relations. Routledge & Paul, 1950; Penguin
The Premier. Hamilton, H., 1961; Harcourt, 1966
Red Lights; see Danger Ahead
Sacrifice. Hamilton, H., 1958
The Second Maigret Omnibus. Hamilton, H., 1964 (U.S. title: Maigret Cinq. Harcourt, 1965)
A Sense of Guilt. Hamilton, H., 1955
The Shadow Falls. Routledge & Paul, 1945
Shadow in the Courtyard; see The Triumph of Inspector Maigret
The Short Cases of Inspector Maigret. Doubleday, 1959; Ace, 1963
A Simenon Omnibus. Hamilton, H., 1965
The Son. Hamilton, H., 1958; Four Square
The Stain on the Snow. Routledge & Paul, 1953; Penguin, 1964
The Stowaway. Hamilton, H., 1957
Strange Case of Peter the Lett; see Inspector Maigret Investigates
Strange Inheritance. Routledge & Paul, 1950
Strangers in the House. Routledge & Paul, 1951
The Striptease. Hamilton, H., 1959; Penguin
Sunday. Hamilton, H., 1960; Harcourt, 1966
Three Beds in Manhattan. Doubleday, 1964
Ticket of Leave. Routledge & Paul, 1954; Penguin
To Any Lengths. Penguin, 1954
The Train. Hamilton, H., 1964; Harcourt, 1964; Penguin
The Trial of Bébé Donge. Routledge & Paul, 1952
The Triumph of Inspector Maigret. Hurst, 1934 (U.S. title: Shadow in the Courtyard, and The Crime at Lock 14. Covici, 1934)
Tropic Moon. Harcourt, 1943

Two Latitudes. Routledge & Paul, 1942 (Also published as: In Two Latitudes. Penguin, 1952)
Versus Inspector Maigret. Doubleday, 1960
Violent Ends. Hamilton, H., 1954
The Watchmaker of Everton; see Danger Ahead
The Widower. Hamilton, H., 1960; Penguin
Wife at Sea. Routledge & Paul, 1949
Window over the Way. Routledge & Paul, 1951; Penguin, 1966
The Witnesses. Doubleday, 1956

SIMMEL, JOHANNES MARIO (S)
It Can't Always Be Caviar. Doubleday, 1965

SIMMONS, ADDISON (D)
Dead Weight. Phoenix, 1947
Death on the Campus. Crowell, 1935

SIMMONS, D. (M)
Stolen Laces. Ogilvie

"SIMON," pseud; see BURFORD, ROGER d'ESTE

SIMON, ROBERT ALFRED (D) (Pseudonym: Liggett Reynolds)
The Weekend Mystery. Watt, G. H., 1926; Burt, 1927

SIMON, S. J.; see ABRAHAMS, DORIS CAROLINE

SIMONS, ROGER, pseud; see PUNNETT, MARGARET

SIMPSON, HELEN DE GUERRY (M) (See also Ashton, Winifred)
The Prime Minister Is Dead. Doubleday, Doran, 1931

SIMPSON, RONALD (M)
End of a Diplomat. Monarch, 1964
Make Every Kiss Count. Monarch, 1961
The Return of Colonel Pho. Monarch, 1965

SIMPSON, SPENCER (M)
Crooks in Cabaret. Nicholson, 1935
The Four Dead Men. Methuen, 1936

SIMS, DOROTHY RICE; see WILLIAMS, VALENTINE

SIMS, GEORGE R. (S-M)
The Last Best Friend. Gollancz, 1967
Sleep No More. Gollancz, 1966; Harcourt, 1966
The Terrible Door. Bodley Head, 1964; Horizon Press, 1964; PB, 1966

SIMS, GEORGE ROBERT (D)
The Case of George Candlemas. Chatto, 1890
The Death Gamble. Paul, S., 1909
Dorcas Dene, Detective. White, 1897
Dramas of Life. Chatto, 1890
The Mystery of Mary Ann. Chatto, 1907
Tales of Today. Chatto, 1889
Tinkletop's Crime. Chatto, 1891

SIMSON, CICELY DEVENISH FRASER-; see FRASER-SIMSON, CICELY DEVENISH

SIMSON, ERIC ANDREW (M) (Pseudonym: Laurence Kirk)
Whispering Tongues. Doubleday, Doran, 1934

"SINBAD," pseud; see AYLWARD, EDWARD DINGLE

SINCLAIR, MRS. BERTHA MUZZY (M) (Pseudonym: B. M. Bower)
The Haunted Hills. Little, 1934
The Voice at Johnny Water. Little, 1932

SINCLAIR, CLAUDE EDWARD ROBERT (M)
Problem Island. Witherby, 1950

SINCLAIR, FIONA (M)
But the Patient Died; see Death of a Physician
Death of a Physician. Bles, 1961 (U.S. title: But the Patient Died. Doubleday, 1962)
Meddle with the Mafia. Bles, 1963
Scandalize My Name. Bles, 1960
Three Slips to a Noose. Bles, 1964

SINCLAIR, FREDERIC (M)
Drop One, Carry Four. Doubleday, 1947

SINCLAIR, MAY (S)
Uncanny Stories. Hutchinson, 1923

SINCLAIR, ROBERT BRUCE (M)
The Eleventh Hour. Cassell, 1951; Mill, 1951
It Couldn't Be Murder. Mill, 1954; Boardman, T. V., 1955

SINCLAIR, SALLY (M)
Muted Murder. Arcadia, 1953

SINGER, BANT, pseud; see SHAW, CHARLES

SINGLETON, FRANK (M)
Independent Means. Chatto, 1948; Macmillan, 1948

SINSTADT, GERALD (M)
The Fidelio Score. Long, 1965
Ship of Spies. Lancer, 1966

SIODMAK, CURT
Donovan's Brain. Knopf, 1943; Chapman, 1944; Transworld, 1944; Popular Lib., 1961

SJOWALL, MAJ; see WAHLOO, PER

SKALLAND, HARLEY L. (M)
The Wrong Slant of Red. Dorrance, 1967

SKENE, ANTHONY (D)
Five Dead Men. Paul, S., 1932

SKINNER, CONRAD ARTHUR (M) (Pseudonym: Michael Maurice)
Not in Our Stars. Lippincott, 1923
Permanent Eclipse. Frank-Maurice, 1926

SKINNER, JUNE O'GRADY (S) (Pseudonym: Rohan O'Grady)
Let's Kill Uncle. Macmillan, 1963; Ace, 1964; Longmans, 1964
Master of Montrolfe Hall; see Pippin's Journal
Pippin's Journal. Macmillan, 1962 (Also published as: The Master of Montrolfe Hall. Ace, 1965)

SKIRROW, DESMOND (M)
It Won't Get You Anywhere. Bodley Head, 1966; Carlton, 1966; Lippincott, 1967

SKLAR, GEORGE (S)
The Identity of Dr. Frazier. Knopf, 1961; Popular Lib., 1963

SLANEY, GEORGE WILSON (M) (Pseudonym: George Woden)
Dusk for Dreams. Hutchinson, 1941
The Mystery of the Amorous Music Master. Hutchinson, 1951
The Puzzled Policeman. Hutchinson, 1949
The Wrenfield Mystery. Parsons, L., 1923

SLATE, JOHN (D)
Black Maria, M.A. Rich, 1944
Death in Silhouette. Rich, 1950
Framed in Guilt. Rich, 1948
Maria Marches On. Rich, 1945
One Remained Seated. Rich, 1946
Thy Arm Alone. Rich, 1954

SLATER, HUMPHREY (S)
Calypso. Longmans, 1953
The Conspirator. Lehmann, 1948
Three Among Mountains. Wingate, 1958

SLATER, WILL (D)
The Adventures of D'Arcy Dewpond, Detective. Drane, 1927

SLESAR, HENRY (M) (Pseudonym: O. H. Leslie)
A Bouquet of Clean Crimes and Neat Murders. Avon, 1960
The Bridge of Lions. Macmillan, 1963; Gollancz, 1964
A Crime for Mothers and Others. Avon, 1960
Enter Murderers. Random, 1960; Gollancz, 1961
The Gray Flannel Shroud. Random, 1959; Deutsch, 1960

SLIGH, NIGEL (S)
The Beast with Two Backs. Laurie, 1951

SLINGSBY, RUFUS, pseud; see SIDDLE, CHARLES

SLOANE, WILLIAM MILLIGAN (M)
The Edge of Running Water. Dodd, 1939; Methuen, 1940 (Also published as: Unquiet Corpse. Dell, 1955)
To Walk the Night. Farrar & Rinehart, 1937; Barker, 1938
Unquiet Corpse; see The Edge of Running Water

SMALL, AUSTIN J. (D) (Pseudonym: "Seamark")
The Avenging Ray. Doubleday, Doran, 1930; Burt, 1931; Hodder, 1931
The Death Maker. Doran, 1927; Burt, 1929
Down River. Hodder, 1929
The Man They Couldn't Arrest. Doran, 1927; Hodder, 1927; Burt, 1928
The Master Mystery. Doubleday, Doran, 1928; Hodder, 1929; Burt, 1930
Master Vorst. Hodder, 1926
The Mystery Maker. Hodder, 1929; Burt, 1930; Doubleday, Doran, 1930
The Needle's Kiss. Doubleday, Doran, 1929; Burt, 1930
Out of the Dark. Hodder, 1931
The Pearls of Desire. Heinemann, 1924; Houghton, 1925; Grosset, 1927
The Seamark Omnibus of Thrills. Hodder, 1937
The Silent Six. Hodder, 1930
The Vantine Diamonds. Musson, 1930; Doubleday, Doran, 1931; Hodder, 1931; Burt, 1932
The Web of Destiny. Hodder, 1930
The Web of Murder. Doubleday, Doran, 1929; Burt, 1930

SMITH, ALEXANDER CLARK; see SMITH, CLARK

SMITH, ANITA BLACKMON; see BLACKMON, ANITA

SMITH, ANTHONY HECKSTALL-; see HECKSTALL-SMITH, ANTHONY

SMITH, C. I. D. (M)
No Epitaph for Mr. Zarke. Jenkins, 1941
Thy Guilt Is Great. Jenkins, 1939

SMITH, CAESAR, pseud; see TREVOR, ELLESTON

SMITH, CARMICHAEL (S)
Atomsk. Duell, 1949

SMITH, CHESTER ALFRED (M)
Web of Deceit. Comet, 1957

SMITH, CLARK (Full name: Alexander Clark Smith) (S)
The Case of Torches. Penguin, 1964
The Speaking Eye. Hammond, 1955

SMITH, DON (S)
The China Coaster. Holt, H., 1953
Perilous Holiday. Holt, H., 1953

SMITH, LADY ELEANOR FURNEAUX (S)
The Man in Grey. Hutchinson, 1941; Doubleday, Doran, 1942 (Also published as: A Dark and Splendid Passion. Ace, 1965)

SMITH, ERNEST BRAMAH (D) (Pseudonym: Ernest Bramah)
Bravo of London. Cassell, 1934
The Eyes of Max Carrados. S & S, 1923; Doran, 1924
Max Carrados. London, 1914
Max Carrados Mysteries. Hodder, 1927; Penguin, 1964
The Specimen Case. Hodder, 1924; Doran, 1925
The Wallet of Kai-Lung. Doran, 1923

SMITH, ESSEX, pseud; see HOPE, ESSEX

SMITH, FRANK E.; see CRAIG, JONATHAN

SMITH, FRED (M)
The Broadcast Murders. Day, 1931

SMITH, FREDERICK ESCREET (S)
The Dark Cliffs; see The Other Cousin
Lydia Trendennis. Hutchinson, 1957; Paperback Lib., 1964
The Other Cousin. Gresham, 1962; Paperback Lib., 1962 (Also published as: The Dark Cliffs. Paperback Lib., 1965)

SMITH, FREDERIKA SHUMWAY (M)
The House and the Tower. Christopher, 1952

SMITH, GARRET (D)
I Did It! Chelsea House, 1928

SMITH, GEORGE MALCOLM-; see MALCOLM-SMITH, GEORGE

SMITH, GODFREY (S)
The Flaw in the Crystal. Gollancz, 1954; Putnam, 1954; Penguin, 1964

SMITH, MRS. HARRY PUGH; see BLACKMON, ANITA

SMITH, HERBERT MAYNARD (D)
Inspector Frost and Lady Brassingham. Benn, 1931
Inspector Frost and the Waverdale Fire. Benn, 1931
Inspector Frost in Crevenna Cove. Benn, 1933; Putnam, 1933
Inspector Frost in the Background. Faber, 1941
Inspector Frost in the City. Doubleday, Doran, 1930; Benn, 1931
Inspector Frost's Jigsaw. Benn, 1929; Doubleday, Doran, 1930

SMITH, JOHNSON (M)
Murder in the Square. Archer, 1933

SMITH, LAWRENCE DWIGHT (M)
The Corpse with the Listening Ear. Mystery House, 1940
Death Is Thy Neighbor. Lippincott, 1938
Follow This Fair Corpse. Mystery House, 1941
Girl Hunt. Lippincott, 1937

SMITH, NAOMI G. ROYDE-; see ROYDE-SMITH, NAOMI G.

SMITH, RICHARD (M)
Death Be Nimble. Signet, 1967

SMITH, ROBERT CHARLES (Pseudonym: Robert Charles)
Mission of Murder. Hale, R., 1965

SMITH, SHELLEY, pseud; see BODINGTON, NANCY HERMIONE

SMITH, THORNE (M)
Did She Fall? Doubleday, Doran, 1930; Sun Dial, 1937; Barker, 1936

SMITH, WILLARD (D)
The Bowery Murder. Doubleday, Doran, 1929; Collins, 1931

SMITH, YORK (M)
The Banana Murders. MacDonald & Co., 1958
Night of Wrath. MacDonald & Co., 1959

SMITH, Z. Z., pseud; see WESTHEIMER, DAVID

SMITHIES, A. RICHARD (S)
An Academic Question. Horizon Press, 1965 (Also published as: Death Gets an A. Signet, 1968)
Death Gets an A; see An Academic Question
Disposing Mind. Horizon Press, 1966

SMYTH, CLIFFORD (M)
The Gilded Man. Boni, 1918

SMYTHE, ALLAN LYLE-; see LYLE-SMYTHE, ALLAN

SNAITH, JOHN COLLIS (D)
Lord Cobleigh Disappears. Appleton-Century, 1936
Mrs. Fitz. Smith, Elder, 1910
Thus Far. Appleton, D., 1910
The Unforseen. Appleton, D., 1930

SNEDDEN, ROBERT WILLIAM (D)
Monsieur X. Dial, 1929

SNELL, EDMUND (M)
Blue Murder. Lippincott, 1927; Unwin, 1927
Kontrol. Lippincott, 1928; Benn, 1930
Murder in Switzerland. Hillman-Curl, 1938
The White Owl. Hodder, 1930; Lippincott, 1930
The Yu-Chi Stone. Macaulay, 1926; Unwin, 1926
Z-Ray. Lippincott, 1932; Skeffington, 1932

SNOW, CHARLES HORACE (Mysteries with a Western setting)
The Bonanza Murder Case. Wright & Brown, 1934
The Brush Creek Murders. Wright & Brown, 1937
The Buckhorn Murder Case. Wright & Brown, 1952
The Desert Castle Mystery. Wright & Brown, 1936
The Highgrade Murder. Wright & Brown, 1949
The Hollow Stump Mystery. Wright & Brown, 1934
The Lakeside Murder. Wright & Brown, 1933
The Mountain Murder Case. Wright & Brown, 1951
Murder on the Cattle Ranch. Wright & Brown, 1935
The Mysterious Missile. Wright & Brown, 1951
The Mystery of Devil's Canyon. Wright & Brown, 1942
The Sign of the Death Circle. Wright & Brown, 1935
Twice Murdered. Wright & Brown, 1954

SNOW, CHARLES PERCY (M)
Death Under Sail. Doubleday, Doran, 1932; Heinemann, 1932; Penguin

SNOW, JACK (S)
Dark Music and Other Spectral Tales. Herald, 1947

SNOW, WALTER (S)
Golden Nightmare. Austin-Phelps, 1952

SOHL, JERRY (S)
Prelude to Peril. Rinehart, 1957

SOKOLOFF, BORIS (M)
The Crime of Dr. Garine. Covici, 1928

SOMERS, JOHN (S)
The Brethren of the Axe. Dutton, 1927

SOMERS, PAUL, pseud; see WINTERTON, PAUL

SOMERS, SUZANNE (S)
Mists of Morning. Tower, 1966

SONIN, ROY (D)
The Dance Band Mystery. Quality, 1940
The Death Pack. Fenland, 1933
Murder in Print. Jenkins, 1953; Roy Pubs., 1956
Twice Times Murder. Jenkins, 1954
The Mystery of the Tailor's Dummy. Harrap, 1935

SOPER, MRS. GEORGE ALBERT; see LIDDON, ELOISE S.

SOSKIN, HENRY; see RODDA, CHARLES PERCIVAL

SOUTAR, ANDREW (M-D)
Back from the Dead. Hodder, 1920; Thomson, 1930
Back to Eden. Hutchinson, 1927
Battling Barker. Hutchinson, 1923
The Black Spot Mystery. Hutchinson, 1938
Chain Murder. Hutchinson, 1939
Consider Your Verdict. Hutchinson, 1928
Delilah of Mayfair. Hutchinson, 1926
The Devil's Triangle. Hutchinson, 1931
Eight Three Five. Hutchinson, 1935
Facing East. Hutchinson, 1936
The Great Conspiracy. Hutchinson, 1934
Hagar, Called Hannah. Hutchinson, 1933
The Hanging Sword. Hutchinson, 1933
Hornet's Nest. Murray, J., 1922
The House of Corbeen. Hutchinson, 1929
In the Blood. Jarrolds, 1929

Justice Is Done. Hutchinson, 1936
Kharduni. Hutchinson, 1933
The Leopard's Spots. Hutchinson, 1928
The Master Key. Federation Press, 1926
Motive for the Crime. Hutchinson, 1941, 1936
The Museum Mystery. Hutchinson,
Neither Do I Condemn Thee. Hutchinson, 1924
Night of Horror. Hutchinson, 1934
Not Mentioned. Hutchinson, 1930
One Page Missing. Hutchinson, 1938
Opportunity. Hutchinson, 1932
Ostrich Man. Hutchinson, 1937
Other Men's Shoes. Hodder, 1917; Long, 1924
Pagans. Hutchinson, 1928
The Perverted Village. Hutchinson, 1936
The Phantom in the House. Hutchinson, 1928; Readers' Lib., 1930; Mellifont, 1939
Public Ghost Number One. Hutchinson, 1941
Pursuit. Hutchinson, 1927
Robert Harlow's Wife. Hutchinson, 1935
Salome Had a Sister. Hutchinson, 1939
Secret Ways. Hutchinson, 1932
Silence. Hutchinson, 1930
Silent Accuser. Hutchinson, 1938
Silent Thunder. Hutchinson, 1929
Sinister River. Hutchinson, 1936
Some Fell Among Thorns. Hutchinson, 1931
The Stars I'd Give. Hutchinson, 1937
The Story of Peter Trussock. Hutchinson, 1940
Strange Bedfellows. Hutchinson, 1931
The Strange Case of Sir Merton Quest. Hutchinson, 1940
A Stranger Came to Dinner. Hutchinson, 1939
Study in Suspense. Hutchinson, 1941
Thirty Pieces of Silver. Hutchinson, 1931
This Frail Woman. Hutchinson, 1924
Tomorrow Is Yesterday. Hutchinson, 1933
The Wolves and the Lamb. Hutchinson, 1940
Worldly Goods. Hutchinson, 1928

SOUTH, MARSHALL (M)
The Curse of the Sightless Fish. World's Work, 1948

SOUTHWICK, ALBERT P. (M)
The Catherwood Mystery. Taylor, 1892

SOUTHWOLD, STEPHEN (M) (Pseudonyms: Neil Bell, Paul Martens)
Death Rocks the Cradle, by Paul Martens. Collins, 1933
The Disturbing Affair of Noel Blake. Gollancz, 1932
The Endless Chain, by Neil Bell. Redman, 1956
The Precious Porcelain. Gollancz, 1931
What No Woman Knows, by Neil Bell. Eyre, 1957

SOUTHWORTH, MRS. EMMA D. E. (M)
The Mystery of Dark Hollow. Federal, 1875

SOUVESTRE, PIERRE; see ALLAIN, MARCEL

SOUZA, E., pseud; see WINTERTON, PAUL

SPAIN, JOHN, pseud; see ADAMS, CLEVE FRANKLIN

SPAIN, NANCY (M)
Cinderella Goes to the Morgue. Hutchinson, 1950
Death Before Wicket. Hutchinson, 1946
Death Goes on Skiis. Hutchinson, 1949
Kat Strikes. Hutchinson, 1955
Murder, Bless It! Hutchinson, 1951
Not Wanted on Voyage. Hutchinson, 1951; Penguin, 1957
Out, Damned Tot. Hutchinson, 1952
Poison for Teacher. Hutchinson, 1949
Poison in Play. Hutchinson, 1946
R in the Month. Hutchinson, 1950
Thank You, Nelson. Hutchinson, 1945

SPARK, MURIEL (S)
The Comforters. Lippincott, 1957; Macmillan, 1957; Avon, 1964
The Mandelbaum Gate. Fawcett, 1967
Robinson. Lippincott, 1958; Macmillan, 1958; Avon, 1964
Voices at Play. Macmillan, 1961; Lippincott, 1962

SPARROY, MASSICKS, pseud. (M)
The Leper's Bell. Collins, 1921; Putnam, 1921
The Listening Woman. Faber, 1922

SPATZ, H. DONALD (D)
Murder with Long Hair. Phoenix, 1941

SPEARE, MRS. EDMUND; see LEWIS, FLORENCE JAY

SPEIGHT, THOMAS WILKINSON (M)
Crime in the Wood. Long, 1899
Doom of Siva. Chatto, 1899
Heart of a Mystery. Fenno, 1896; Jarrolds, 1896
Under a Cloud. Digby, 1906
Under Lock and Key. Turner Bros., 1896

SPENCER, ERLE (M)
The Death of Captain Shand. Hodder, 1930
The Four Lost Ships. Hodder, 1931
The King of Spain's Daughter. Hodder, 1934
Or Give Me Death! Harrap, 1936
The Piccadilly Ghost. Hodder, 1929; Macmillan, 1930
Stop, Press! Hodder, 1932

SPENCER, JOHN, pseud; see VICKERS, ROY

SPENCER, LEE (M)
The Furtive Men. Jarrolds, 1951

SPENCER, PHILIP (S)
Full Term. Faber, 1961

SPENDER, JEAN MAUDE (M)
The Charge Is Murder. Eyre, 1934
Death Comes in the Night. Eyre, 1938
Death Renders Account. Hale, R., 1960
Full Moon for Murder. Evans, 1948
Murder on the Prowl. Hale, R., 1960
Seven Days for Hanging. Hale, R., 1958

SPENSER, JAMES, pseud; see GUEST, FRANCIS HOWARD

SPERDUTI, DOMINICK ROCKE (M)
For You, I Commit Murder. Christopher, 1956

SPEWACK, SAMUEL (M) (Pseudonym: A. A. Abbott)
Murder in the Gilded Cage. S & S, 1929
Skyscraper Murder. Macaulay, 1928

SPICER, BART (S) (Joint pseudonym with Betty Coe Spicer: Jay Barbette)
Act of Anger. Antheneum, 1962; Bantam, 1963; Barker, 1963
Black Sheep Run. Dodd, 1951; Collins, 1952
Blues for the Prince. Dodd, 1950; Collins, 1952
The Burned Man. Atheneum, 1966; Bantam, 1967
The Dark Light. Dodd, 1949; Collins, 1950
Day of the Dead. Dodd, 1955; Hodder, 1956
The Deadly Doll, by Jay Barbette. Dodd, 1958
Dear Dead Days, by Jay Barbette. Dodd, 1953; Barker, 1954
Exit, Running. Dodd, 1959; Hodder, 1960
Final Copy, by Jay Barbette. Dodd, 1950; Barker, 1952
The Golden Door. Collins, 1951; Dodd, 1951
The Long Green. Dodd, 1952 (English title: Shadow of Fear. Collins, 1953)
Look Behind You, by Jay Barbette. Dodd, 1960
Shadow of Fear; see The Long Green
The Taming of Carney Wilde. Dodd, 1954; Hodder, 1955

SPICER, BETTY COE; see SPICER, BART

SPILLANE, FRANK MORRISON (D)
(Pseudonym: Mickey Spillane)
The Big Kill. Dutton, 1951; Barker, 1952; Signet
Bloody Sunrise. Dutton, 1965; Signet, 1965
The Body Lovers. Dutton, 1967; Signet, 1967
By-Pass Control. Dutton, 1966; Barker, 1967; Signet, 1967
Day of the Guns. Dutton, 1964; Barker, 1965; Signet, 1965
The Death Dealers. Dutton, 1965; Signet, 1965
The Deep. Barker, 1961; Dutton, 1961; Signet, 1962, 1965
The Delta Factor. Dutton, 1967; Signet, 1967
The Flier. Transworld, 1964
The Girl Hunters. Dutton, 1962; Barker, 1963; Signet, 1963
I, the Jury. Dutton, 1947; Barker, 1952; Signet, 1964
Kiss Me Deadly. Dutton, 1952; Barker, 1953; Signet, 1964
The Long Wait. Dutton, 1951; Barker, 1953; Signet, 1964
Me, Hood! Transworld, 1963
My Gun Is Quick. Dutton, 1950; Barker, 1951; Signet, 1964
One Lonely Night. Dutton, 1951; Barker, 1952; Signet, 1964
Return of the Hood. Transworld, 1964
The Snake. Barker, 1964; Dutton, 1964; Signet, 1964
The Twisted Thing. Dutton, 1966; Signet, 1966
Vengeance Is Mine! Dutton, 1950; Barker, 1951; Signet, 1964

SPILLANE, MICKEY, pseud; see SPILLANE, FRANK MORRISON

SPILLER, ANDREW (D)
Alias Mr. Orson. Paul, S., 1951
And Thereby Hangs. Paul, S., 1948
As They Shall Sow. Paul, S., 1952
Birds of a Feather. Paul, S., 1950
Black Cap for Murder. Paul, S., 1957
Brains Trust for Murder. Paul, S., 1956
Brief Candle. Paul, S., 1949
Crooked Highway. Archer, 1947
Curtain Call for Murder. Long, 1957
The Evil That Men Do. Paul, S., 1953
If Murder Interferes with Business. Archer, 1945

It's in the Bag. Paul, S., 1955
Kiss the Book. Paul, S., 1952
The Man Who Caught the 4:15. Paul, S., 1950
Murder Has Three Dimensions. Archer, 1948
Murder Is a Shady Business. Paul, S., 1954
Murder on a Shoestring. Long, 1958
Murder Without Malice. Paul, S., 1954
Phantom Circus. Paul, S., 1950
Queue Up to Listen. Archer, 1946
Ring Twice for Murder. Paul, S., 1955
Rope for Breakfast. Archer, 1945
Sing a Song of Murder. Long, 1959
They Tell No Tales. Paul, S., 1953
What's in a Name? Archer, 1947
When Crook Meets Crook. Archer, 1947
Who Plays with Sin. Paul, S., 1951
Whom Nobody Owns. Archer, 1945
You Can't Get Away with Murder. Archer, 1948

SPINELLI, MARCUS (S)
Assignment Without Glory. Lippincott, 1945; Bantam

SPRAGUE, GRETCHEN (S)
Signpost to Terror. Dodd, 1967

SPRIGG, C. ST. JOHN (D)
The Corpse with the Sunburned Face. Doubleday, Doran, 1935
Crime in Kensington. Eldon, 1933; Withy Grove, 1942
Death of an Airman. Hutchinson, 1934; Doubleday, Doran, 1935
Fatality in Fleet Street. Eldon, 1933
Pass the Body. Dial, 1933
The Perfect Alibi. Doubleday, Doran, 1934; Eldon, 1934
The Six Queer Things. Doubleday, Doran, 1937; Jenkins, 1937

SPRIGGE, ELIZABETH (M)
Old Man Dies. Heinemann, 1933

SPROUL, KATHLEEN (D)
Birthday Murder. Dutton, 1932
Death Among the Professors; see Murder Off Key
Murder Off Key. Dutton, 1934 (English title: Death Among the Professors. Eyre, 1934)
Mystery of the Closed Car. Dutton, 1935

SPROULE, WESLEY (M)
Freeway to Murder. Hale, R., 1967

SPURGEON, DOUGLAS W. (M)
The Appletree Manor Mystery. Ward, Lock, 1925
The Missing Witness. Ward, Lock, 1927
The Wheel of Circumstance. Ward, Lock, 1926

STACKELBERG, GENE (S)
Double Agent. Popular Lib., 1959

STACPOOLE, HENRY DE VERE (M)
Cottage on the Fells. Laurie, 1930 (Also published as: Murder on the Fells. Allied Newspapers, 1940)
The Golden Ballast. Dodd, 1924; Hutchinson, 1930
Murder on the Fells; see Cottage on the Fells
The Mystery of Uncle Ballard. Doubleday, Doran, 1928; Cassell, 1929
Tales of Mynheer Amayat. Newnes, 1930

STACY, O'CONNOR, pseud; see ROLLINS, WILLIAM

STAFFORD, MARJORIE (M)
Death Plays the Gramaphone. Macmillan, 1953

STAFFORD, MURIEL (M) (Pseudonym: Muriel S. Sauer)
X Marks the Dot. Duell, 1943

STAGG, CLINTON HOLLAND (D)
Silver Sandals. Watt, 1916
Thornley Colton, Blind Detective. Watt, G. H., 1923

STAGGE, JONATHAN, pseud; see WEBB, RICHARD WILSON

STANDISH, BURT L. (D)
Dick Merriwell's Detective Work, or The Lure of the Ruby. Street, 1911

STANFORD, ALFRED (S)
The Mission in Sparrow Brush Lane. Morrow, 1966

STANLEY, ARTHUR, pseud; see MEGAW, ARTHUR STANLEY

STANLEY, BENNETT, pseud; see HOUGH, STANLEY BENNETT

STANLEY, FAY GRISSON (M)
Murder Leaves a Ring. Rinehart, 1950

STANLEY, GEORGE (D)
The Adventures of the Black Pilgrim. Metropolitan, 1945
The Blue Light. Blackie & Son, 1935, 1946
The Brotherhood of Death. Mitre,
Case of the Seven Keys. Modern Fiction, 1945

Further Adventures of the Black Pilgrim. Modern Fiction, 1945
Gangsters All. Mitre, 1945
Gansters' Parade. Mitre, 1945
The League of Twelve. Mellifont, 1940
Men of the Mist. Martin & Reid, 1947
The Mission Million. Gifford, 1938
Rubberface. Modern Fiction, 1945
The Secret of the Seven Spiders. Fenland, 1932; Modern Pub., 1950
The Seven Saints. Swam, G. G., 1945
The Seven Shadows. Blackie & Son, 1935; Modern Pub., 1951
The Sign of Seven. Coker, 1950
Sinister Valley. Bear, 1946

STANLEY, JACKSON (M)
The Florentine Ring. Doubleday, 1962

STANLEY, WILLIAM (D)
Mr. Holroyd Takes a Holiday. Abelard, 1966

STANNERS, HAROLD H. (M)
At the Tenth Clue. Eyre, 1937
The Crowning Murder. Eyre, 1938
Murder at Markendon Court. Eyre, 1936

STANSFELD, ANTHONY; see LILLEY, PETER

STAPLETON, D., pseud; see STAPLETON, DOUGLAS

STAPLETON, DOROTHY; see STAPLETON, DOUGLAS

STAPLETON, DOUGLAS and DOROTHY STAPLETON (M) (Pseudonym: D. Stapleton)
Corpse and Robbers. Arcadia, 1955
The Crime, the Place, and the Girl. Arcadia, 1955
Late for the Funeral. Arcadia, 1953

STARK, MICHAEL, pseud; see LARIAR, LAWRENCE

STARK, RAYMOND (M) (Pseudonym: John Norwood)
No Time to Laugh. Ward, Lock, 1958

STARK, RICHARD, pseud; see WESTLAKE, DONALD

STARK, SHELDON (S)
Too Many Sinners. Ace, 1954

STARNES, RICHARD (D-S)
And When She Was Bad, She Was Murdered. Lippincott, 1950; PB, 1951; Muller, 1953
Another Mug for the Bier. Lippincott, 1940; Muller, 1952
The Other Body in Grant's Tomb. Lippincott, 1951; Muller, 1954
Requiem in Utopia. Trident, 1967

STARR, JIMMY (D)
The Corpse Came C.O.D. Murray & Gee, 1944; Coker, 1951
Heads You Lose. Fell, 1950
Three Short Biers. Murray & Gee, 1945; Bart

STARR, JONATHAN (M)
Crook. Cape, 1930
Grapevine. Liveright, 1930

STARR, RICHARD (M-D) (Pseudonyms: Richard Essex, Stella Richards)
All the Tomorrows. Jenkins, 1937
Assisted by Lessinger. Jenkins, 1939
Athalie Takes Her Chance. Low, 1933
Bachelor Girls. Jenkins, 1931
Beautiful Sister. Jenkins, 1938
Belinda Tries Again. Jenkins, 1930
Berrington's Wife. Low, 1939
The Black Skinners. Low, 1936
Blood from a Stranger. Jenkins, 1939
Cabaret Girl. Jenkins, 1935
Daphne, Limited. Jenkins, 1930
The Fifty-Fifty Marriage. Jenkins, 1931
Flaming Dawn, by Stella Richards. Jenkins, 1937
Galloway's Daughter. Low, 1937
Gangster's Girl. Jenkins, 1935
Gypsy Love. Jenkins, 1940
The Hero's Wife. Jenkins, 1934
His Own People. Jenkins, 1937
The Hope of the Corletts. Jenkins, 1934
Jacqueline on Her Own. Jenkins, 1929
Joan and Garry. Low, 1936
Lessinger Comes Back. Jenkins, 1935
Looking After Leatrice. Low, 1933
Lover Abroad. Jenkins, 1939
Marinova of the Secret Service. Jenkins, 1937
Married to a Spy. Hurst, 1915
Mary Elizabeth, Adventuress. Low, 1932
Monica in the Talkies. Low, 1932
Murder in the Bank. Jenkins, 1936
Nobody's Child. Low, 1939
Our Daughters. Low, 1935
Pamela Clicks. Low, 1931
Peggy Leaves Home. Low, 1930
Penelope's Progress. Jenkins, 1934
The Primitive Call. Jenkins, 1940
Purple Patches. Jenkins, 1933
The Return of Yolanda. Low, 1938
Rich Man, Poor Man. Jenkins, 1938
Romantic Inheritance. Jenkins, 1941
Scandal's Child. Low, 1937
Secret Lives. Jenkins, 1936
The Sin of Mary Wilder. Low, 1934
Slade of the Yard, by Richard Essex. Jenkins, 1932

Slade Scores Again, by Richard Essex. Jenkins, 1933
Somebody's Baby. Low, 1938
The Stunt Girl. Low, 1931
Susannah the Dauntless. Low, 1930
Tessa. Jenkins, 1932
The Twain Shall Meet, by Stella Richards. Jenkins, 1938
Wendy's Family. Low, 1935

STARRETT, CHARLES VINCENT EMERSON; see STARRETT, VINCENT

STARRETT, VINCENT (Full name: Charles Vincent Emerson Starrett) (D)
The Blue Door. Doubleday, Doran, 1930
The Case Book of Jimmy Lavender. Gold Label, 1944
Coffin for Two. Covici, 1924
Dead Man Inside. Doubleday, Doran, 1931
The End of Mr. Garment. Doubleday, Doran, 1932
The Great Hotel Murder. Doubleday, Doran, 1935
The Laughing Buddha. Magna, 1937
Midnight and Percy Jones. Covici, 1938
Murder in Peking. Lantern Press, 1946
Murder on "B" Deck. Doubleday, Doran, 1929; Grosset, 1930

STEAD, PHILIP JOHN (M)
In the Street of the Angel. Art & Educ. Pubs., 1947

STEAD, ROBERT JAMES CAMPBELL (D)
The Copper Disc. Doubleday, Doran, 1931

STED, RICHARD (S)
They All Bleed Red. S & S, 1954; Boardman, T. V., 1955

STEEGMÜLLER, FRANCIS (M) (Pseudonym: David Keith)
The Blue Harpischord. Doubleday, 1949
A Matter of Accent. Dodd, 1943
A Matter of Iodine. Dodd, 1940

STEEL, KURT, pseud; see KAGEY, RUDOLPH

STEEL, RUDOLPH HORNADAY; see KAGEY, RUDOLPH

STEELE, CHESTER (D)
The Crime at Red Towers. Clode, 1927
The Diamond Cross Mystery. Sully, 1918; Jenkins, 1919, 1931
The Great Radio Mystery. Chelsea House, 1928
The House of Disappearances. Chelsea House, 1927
The Mansion of Mystery. Cupples, 1911

STEELE, DERWENT (S)
The Avengers. Modern Pub., 1935
The Phantom Slayer. Modern Pub., 1935
The Purple Plague. Modern Pub., 1935

STEELE, WILBUR DANIEL (S)
Full Cargo. Doubleday, 1952
The Man Who Saw Through Heaven. Harper, 1927
The Sound of Rowlocks. Harper, 1938
The Tower of Sand. Harper, 1929
The Way to Gold. Doubleday, 1955

STEEMAN, ANDRE (M)
The Night of the 12th-13th. Lippincott, 1933
Six Dead Men. Farrar & Rinehart, 1932; Hurst, 1933

STEERS, HELEN (Full name: Helen Steers Burgess) (M)
Death Will Find Me. Dodd, 1947

STEEVES, HARRISON ROSS (M)
Good-night, Sheriff. Random, 1941; Rich, 1942

STEIN, AARON MARC (D) (Pseudonyms: George Bagby, Hampton Stone)
And High Water. Doubleday, 1946
The Babe with the Twistable Arm, by Hampton Stone. S & S, 1962; Popular Lib., 1963; Hale, R., 1964
Bachelor's Wife, by George Bagby. Covici, 1932
Bird Walking Weather, by George Bagby. Doubleday, Doran, 1939; Cassell, 1940
Blood on the Stars. Doubleday, 1964; Hale, R., 1965
Blood Will Tell, by George Bagby. Doubleday, 1950
The Body in the Basket, by George Bagby. Doubleday, 1954; MacDonald & Co., 1956
The Case of the Absent-Minded Professor. Doubleday, Doran, 1943
Coffin Corner, by George Bagby. Doubleday, 1949
Cop Killer, by George Bagby. Doubleday, 1956; Boardman, T. V., 1957
Corpse Candle, by George Bagby. Doubleday, 1967; Popular Lib., 1968
The Corpse in the Corner Saloon, by Hampton Stone. S & S, 1948
The Corpse That Refused to Stay Dead, by Hampton Stone. S & S, 1952; Dobson, 1954
The Corpse Who Had Too Many Friends, by Hampton Stone. S & S, 1953; Foulsham, 1954
The Corpse Who Had Too Much to Lose, by George Bagby. Foulsham, 1955; S & S, 1955

The Corpse with Sticky Fingers, by George Bagby. Doubleday, 1952
The Corpse with the Purple Thighs, by George Bagby. Doubleday, Doran, 1939
The Corpse Wore a Wig, by George Bagby. Doubleday, Doran, 1940
The Cradle and the Grave. Doubleday, 1948
Days of Misfortune. Doubleday, 1949; Collier, 1963
Dead Drunk, by George Bagby. Doubleday, 1953; MacDonald & Co., 1954
Dead on Arrival, by George Bagby. Doubleday, 1946
Dead Storage, by George Bagby. Doubleday, 1956; Boardman, T. V., 1959
The Dead Thing in the Pool. Doubleday, 1952
Dead Wrong, by George Bagby. Doubleday, 1957; Boardman, T. V., 1958
Deadly Delight. Doubleday, 1967; Popular Lib., 1968
Death Ain't Commercial, by George Bagby. Doubleday, 1951
Death Meets 400 Rabbits. Doubleday, 1953
Death Takes a Paying Guest. Doubleday, 1947
Dirty Pool, by George Bagby. Doubleday, 1966
A Dirty Way to Die, by George Bagby. Doubleday, 1955; MacDonald & Co., 1956
Drop Dead, by George Bagby. Doubleday, 1949
Evil Genius, by George Bagby. Hammond, 1954; Doubleday, 1961
The Frightened Amazon. Doubleday, 1950
The Funniest Killer in Town, by Hampton Stone. S & S, 1967
The Girl Who Kept Knocking Them Dead, by Hampton Stone. Foulsham, 1957; S & S, 1957
The Girl with the Hole in Her Head, by Hampton Stone. S & S, 1949; Boardman, T. V., 1958
Give the Little Corpse a Great Big Hand, by George Bagby. Doubleday, 1953; MacDonald & Co., 1954
Her Body Speaks. Covici, 1931
Here Comes the Corpse, by George Bagby. Doubleday, Doran, 1941; Long, 1943
Home and Murder. Doubleday, 1962
I Fear the Greeks. Doubleday, 1966
In Cold Blood, by George Bagby. Doubleday, 1948
The Kid Was Last Seen Hanging Ten, by Hampton Stone. S & S, 1966
The Man Who Had Too Much to Lose, by Hampton Stone. Foulsham, 1955; S & S, 1955
The Man Who Looked Death in the Eye, by Hampton Stone. S & S, 1961
The Man Who Was Three Jumps Ahead, by Hampton Stone. S & S, 1959; Boardman, T. V., 1960
A Mask for Murder. Doubleday, 1952
Moonmilk and Murder. Doubleday, 1955
Murder at the Piano, by George Bagby. Covici, 1935; Low, 1936
Murder Calling "50," by George Bagby. Doubleday, Doran, 1942
Murder Half Baked, by George Bagby. Covici, 1937; Cassell, 1938
Murder on the Nose, by George Bagby. Doubleday, Doran, 1938; Cassell, 1939
The Murder That Wouldn't Stay Solved, by Hampton Stone. S & S, 1951
Murder's Little Helper, by George Bagby. Doubleday, 1963; Hammond, 1964
Mysteriouser and Mysteriouser, by George Bagby. Doubleday, 1965 (English title: Mystery in Wonderland. Hammond, 1965)
Mystery in Wonderland; see Mysteriouser and Mysteriouser
The Needle That Wouldn't Hold Still, by Hampton Stone. S & S, 1950; Boardman, T. V., 1958
Never Need an Enemy. Doubleday, 1959
Only the Guilty. Doubleday, Doran, 1942
Original Carcase, by George Bagby. Doubleday, 1946; Aldor, F., 1946
Pistols for Two. Doubleday, 1951
Real Gone Goose, by George Bagby. Doubleday, 1959; Boardman, T. V., 1960
The Real Serendipitious Kill, by Hampton Stone. S & S, 1964
Red Is for Killing, by George Bagby. Doubleday, Doran, 1944; Long, 1944
Ring Around a Murder, by George Bagby. Covici, 1936
Scared to Death, by George Bagby. Doubleday, 1952
The Second Burial. Doubleday, 1949
Shoot Me Dacent. Doubleday, 1951; MacDonald & Co., 1957
Sitting Up Dead. Doubleday, 1958; MacDonald & Co., 1959
Spirals. Covici, 1930
Starting Gun, by George Bagby. Doubleday, 1948
The Strangler; see The Strangler Who Couldn't Let Go
The Strangler Who Couldn't Let Go, by Hampton Stone. S & S, 1956 (English title: The Strangler. Foulsham, 1957)
The Sun Is a Witness. Doubleday, Doran, 1940
Three-Time Losers, by George Bagby. Boardman, T. V., 1958; Doubleday, 1958
Three with Blood. Doubleday, 1950
The Twin Killing, by George Bagby. Doubleday, 1947

Up to No Good. Doubleday, Doran, 1941
We Saw Him Die. Doubleday, 1947

STEIN, GERTRUDE (M)
Blood on the Dining Room Floor. Banyan, 1948

STELLIER, KILSYTH (M)
Taken by Force. Gale, 1891

STEPHENS, DeVERE ASHMORE (M)
Echoes from Castor Hills. Comet, 1959

STEPHENS, ROBERT NEILSON (M)
The Mystery of Murray Davenport. Copp, 1903; Nash, 1903; Page, 1903

STEPHENSON, HUMPHREY MEIGH (M)
Death on the Deep. Doubleday, Doran, 1931
Missing Partner. Hutchinson, 1932

STEPHENSON, RALPH (D)
The Body in My Arms. Gifford, 1963
Darkest Death. Gifford, 1964

STERLING, STEWART, pseud; see WINCHELL, PRENTICE

STERLING, THOMAS (M)
The Evil of the Day. Gollancz, 1955; S & S, 1955; Grove, 1963
The House Without a Door. S & S, 1950; Boardman, T. V., 1951
The Silent Siren. Gollancz, 1958; S & S, 1958
Strangers and Afraid. Boardman, T. V., 1952; S & S, 1952

STERN, GLADYS BRONWYN (S)
The Shortest Night. Heinemann, 1931

STERN, DAVID (M) (Pseudonym: Peter Stirling)
Stop Press—Murder! Phoenix, 1947

STERN, PHILIP VAN DOREN (S) (Pseudonym: Peter Storme)
It's Always Too Late to Mend. Jarrolds, 1952
The Thing in the Brook, by Peter Storme. S & S, 1937

STERN, RICHARD MARTIN (S)
The Bright Road to Fear. Ballantine, 1959; Secker & Warburg, 1959
Cry Havoc. Scribner, 1963; Cassell, 1964
I Hide, We Seek. Scribner, 1965
The Kessler Legacy. Scribner, 1967
The Search for Tabatha Carr. Scribner, 1960; Secker, 1960; Macfadden, 1964
Suspense: Four Short Novels. Ballantine, 1959
These Unholy Deeds. Scribner, 1960

STEVENS, MRS. FRANCES MOYER ROSS (M) (Pseudonym: Christopher Hale)
Dead of Winter. Doubleday, Doran, 1941
Deadly Ditto. Doubleday, 1948; Boardman, T. V., 1949
Exit Screaming. Doubleday, Doran, 1942; Boardman, T. V., 1943
Ghost River. Doubleday, Doran, 1937; Boardman, T. V., 1947
Hangman's Tie. Doubleday, Doran, 1943; Boardman, T. V., 1947
He's Late This Morning. Doubleday, 1949; Boardman, T. V., 1951
Midsummer Nightmare. Doubleday, Doran, 1945; Boardman, T. V., 1948
Murder in Tow. Doubleday, Doran, 1943; Boardman, T. V., 1944
Murder on Display. Doubleday, Doran, 1939; Boardman, T. V., 1947
Rumor Hath It. Doubleday, Doran, 1945; Boardman, T. V., 1947
Smoke Screen. Harcourt, 1935; Boardman, T. V., 1948
Stormy Night. Boardman, T. V., 1937; Doubleday, Doran, 1937
Witchwood. Doubleday, Doran, 1940; Boardman, T. V., 1946

STEVENS, FRANK EDMUND (M)
She Left a Silver Slipper. Mill, 1954

STEVENS, JAMES (M)
In Shadows of Desire. Exposition, 1964

STEVENS, K. M. (M)
Panic in the Solomons. Bles, 1951

STEVENS, LUCILE VERNON (M)
Death Wore Gold Shoes. Bouregy, 1966

STEVENSON, BURTON EGBERT (D)
Affairs of State. Holt, H., 1906; Chatto, 1907
The Gloved Hand. Dodd, 1912
The Holloday Case. Heinemann, 1903; Holt, H., 1903
The Marathon Mystery. Holt, H., 1904
The Mystery of the Boule Cabinet. Dodd, 1912; Nash, 1915; Hodder, 1917
The Mystery of Villa Aurelia. Rich, 1933
The Red Carnation. Dodd, 1939
Storm Center. Dodd, 1924; Hutchinson, 1924

STEVENSON, FERDINAN and PATRICIA ROBINSON (Pseudonym: Daria Macomber)
Hunter, Hunter, Get Your Gun. Hodder, 1966 (U.S. title: Return to Octavia. New Amer. Lib., 1967)

STEVENSON, ROBERT LOUIS (M)
The Body Snatchers. Merriam, 1895
Dr. Jekyll and Mr. Hyde. Longmans, 1886; Scribner, 1886; Arco, 1964
The Dynamiter. Longmans, 1885
The Merry Men and Other Tales. Bles
New Arabian Nights. Chatto, 1882
The Suicide Club. Scribner, 1896; Penguin, 1963
The Wrecker. Cassell, 1892
The Wrong Box, with Lloyd Osbourne. Scribner, 1889

STEWART, ALFRED WALTER (D)
(Pseudonym: J. J. Connington)
The Boathouse Riddle. Little, 1931; Gollancz, 1932
The Brandon Case. Little, 1934 (English title: Ha-Ha Case. Hodder, 1934)
The Case with Nine Solutions. Gollancz, 1929; Little, 1929
The Castleford Conundrum. Hodder, 1932; Little, 1932; Grosset, 1935
Commonsense Is All You Need. Hodder, 1947
The Counsellor. Hodder, 1939; Little, 1939
The Dangerfield Talisman. Benn, 1926; Little, 1927
Death at Swaythling Court. Benn, 1926; Little, 1926; Grosset (Also included in Death and Detection. Benn, 1957; McClelland, 1957)
The Eye in the Museum. Gollancz, 1929; Little, 1930; Grosset, 1933
For Murder Will Speak. Hodder, 1930 (U.S. title: Murder Will Speak. Little, 1938)
Four Defences. Hodder, 1940; Little, 1940
Gold Brick Island. Little, 1933 (English title: Tom Tiddler's Island. Hodder, 1933)
Grim Vengeance. Little, 1929
Ha-Ha Case; see The Brandon Case
In Whose Dim Shadows; see Tau Cross Mystery
Jack in the Box. Hodder, 1944; Little, 1944
A Minor Operation. Hodder, 1937; Little, 1937
Murder in the Maze. Benn, 1927; Little, 1927; Grosset
Murder Will Speak; see For Murder Will Speak
Mystery at Lynden Sands. Gollancz, 1928; Little, 1928
Nemesis at Raynham Parva. Gollancz, 1929
No Past Is Dead. Hodder, 1924; Little, 1942
Nordenholt's Million. Constable, 1923
Sweepstake Murders. Hodder, 1931; Little, 1932
Tau Cross Mystery. Little, 1935 (English title: In Whose Dim Shadow. Hodder, 1935)
Tom Tiddler's Island; see Gold Brick Island
Tragedy at Ravensthorpe. Benn, 1927; Little, 1928; Grosset
Truth Comes Limping. Hodder, 1928; Little, 1938
Twenty-one Clues. Hodder, 1941; Little, 1941
Two Ticket Puzzle. Gollancz, 1930; Little, 1930

STEWART, ANITA MARIE (M)
The Devil's Toy. Dutton, 1935

STEWART, DESMOND STERLING (S)
Leopard in the Grass. Euphorion, 1951

STEWART, JAY, pseud; see PALMER, STUART

STEWART, JOHN INNES MACKINTOSH (D) (Pseudonym: Michael Innes)
Appleby Intervenes. Dodd, 1965
Appleby on Ararat. Dodd, 1941; Gollancz, 1941; Berkley Pub., 1964
Appleby Plays Chicken. Gollancz, 1956 (U.S. title: Death on a Quiet Day. Dodd, 1957; Berkley Pub., 1963)
Appleby Talking. Gollancz, 1954 (U.S. title: Dead Man's Shoes. Dodd, 1954)
Appleby Talks Again. Gollancz, 1956; Dodd, 1957
Appleby's End. Gollancz, 1945; Dodd, 1956; Collier, 1965
The Bloody Wood. Dodd, 1966
The Case of Sonia Wayward. Dodd, 1960 (Also published as: New Sonia Wayward. Gollancz, 1960 and The Last of Sonia Wayward. Collier, 1962)
The Case of the Journeying Boy; see The Journeying Boy
A Change of Heir. Dodd, 1966
Christmas at Candleshoes. Dodd, 1953; Gollancz, 1953
A Comedy of Terrors. Dodd, 1940; Berkley Pub., 1964
The Connoisseur's Case. Penguin
The Crabtree Affair. Dodd, 1962; Berkley Pub., 1963
The Daffodil Affair. Dodd, 1942; Berkley Pub., 1964; Penguin
Dead Man's Shoes; see Appleby Talking
Death at the President's Lodgings. Gollancz, 1936 (U.S. title: Seven Suspects. Dodd, 1937; Berkley Pub., 1965)
Death on a Quiet Day; see Appleby Plays Chicken
From London Far. Gollancz, 1946 (U.S. title: The Unsuspected Chasm. Dodd, 1946)
The Guardians. Gollancz, 1955; Norton, 1957

Hamlet, Revenge! Dodd, 1937; Gollancz, 1937; Collier, 1962; Penguin
Hare Sitting Up. Dodd, 1959; Gollancz, 1959; Berkley Pub., 1964
The Journeying Boy. Gollancz, 1949 (U.S. title: The Case of the Journeying Boy. Dodd, 1949; Berkley Pub., 1963)
Lament for a Maker. Dodd, 1938; Gollancz, 1938
The Last of Sonia Wayward; see The Case of Sonia Wayward
The Long Farewell. Dodd, 1958; Gollancz, 1958; Berkley Pub., 1963
The Man from the Sea. Dodd, 1955; Gollancz, 1955; Avon, 1964
The Man Who Wrote Detective Stories. Gollancz, 1959; Norton, 1959
Mark Lambert's Supper. Gollancz, 1954
Money from Holme. Dodd, 1964
Murder Is an Art. Avon, 1959
New Sonia Wayward; see The Case of Sonia Wayward
A Night of Errors. Dodd, 1947; Gollancz, 1948; Berkley Pub., 1963
Old Hall, New Hall. Gollancz, 1956; Penguin (U.S. title: Question of Queens. Dodd, 1956)
One Man Show; see Private View
Operation Pax. Gollancz, 1951 (U.S. title: The Paper Thunderbolt. Dodd, 1951; Berkley Pub., 1966)
The Paper Thunderbolt; see Operation Pax
Private View. Gollancz, 1952 (U.S. title: One Man Show. Dodd, 1952)
Question of Queens; see Old Hall, New Hall
The Secret Vanguard. Gollancz, 1940; Dodd, 1941; Berkley Pub., 1965
Seven Suspects; see Death in the President's Lodgings
Silence Observed. Dodd, 1961; Gollancz, 1961; Berkley Pub., 1964
The Spider Strikes. Dodd, 1939
Stop Press. Gollancz, 1939
There Came Both Mist and Snow. Gollancz, 1940
The Unsuspected Chasm; see From London Far
The Use of Riches. Gollancz, 1957; Norton, 1957
The Weight of the Evidence. Dodd, 1943; Gollancz, 1944; Berkley Pub., 1964
What Happened at Hazelwood. Dodd, 1946; Gollancz, 1946

STEWART, KENNETH LIVINGSTON (D)
(Pseudonym: Kenneth Livingston)
The Dodd Cases. Doubleday, Doran, 1934

STEWART, MARY (S)
Airs Above the Ground. Mill, 1965; Crest, 1966
The Gabriel Hounds. Mill, 1967; Crest, 1968
The Ivy Tree. Hodder, 1961; Mill, 1962; Crest, 1963
Madame, Will You Talk? Hodder, 1954; Mill, 1955; Crest, 1964
The Moon-spinners. Hodder, 1962; Mill, 1963; Crest, 1964
My Brother Michael. Mill, 1959; Crest, 1960; Hodder, 1960
Nine Coaches Waiting. Crest, 1958; Hodder, 1958
This Rough Magic. Mill, 1963; Crest, 1964; Hodder, 1964
Thunder on the Right. Hodder, 1957; Mill, 1958; Crest, 1963
Wildfire at Midnight. Appleton, 1956; Hodder, 1956; Mill, 1961; Crest, 1965

STEWART, NEIL; see JOHNSON, PAMELA HANSFORD

STICKNEY, F. L.
The Rubber Mask. Chelsea House, 1937

STILSON, CHARLES BILLINGS (M)
Seven Blue Diamonds. Watt, G. H., 1927

STINSON, HUNTER (D)
Fingerprints. Holt, H., 1925

STIRLING, PETER, pseud; see STERN, DAVID

STIVENS, DALLAS (M)
The Wide Arch. Angus, 1959

STOCKWELL, GAIL (M)
The Candy Killings. Greystone, 1940
Death by Invitation. Macmillan, 1937
Embarrassed Murder. Macmillan, 1938

STOKER, ABRAHAM (BRAM) (M)
Dracula. Constable, 1897; Doubleday, 1899, 1917; Dell, 1965
Dracula's Guest. Routledge, 1914
The Garden of Evil; see The Lair of the White Worm
The Jewel of the Seven Stars. Heinemann, 1903; Harper, 1904
The Lady of the Shroud. Heinemann, 1909; Paperback Lib., 1966
The Lair of the White Worm. Rider, W., 1911 (Also published as: The Garden of Evil. Paperback Lib., 1966)
The Mystery of the Sea. Doubleday, Page, 1902; Heinemann, 1902
Snake's Pass. Low, 1891
Under the Sunset. Low, 1881

STOKES, CEDRIC, pseud. (M)
The Staffordshire Assassins. MacDonald & Co., 1945

STOKES, DONALD HUBERT (S)
Appointment with Fear. Coward, 1950; Signet, 1951
Captive in the Night. Coward, 1951

STOKES, FRANCIS WILLIAM (D)
(Pseudonym: Francis Everton)
The Dalehouse Murder. Bobb, 1927
The Hammer of Doom. Collins, 1928; Bobbs, 1929
Insoluble. Collins, 1934
The Murder at Plenders. Collins, 1930 (U.S. title: Murder Through the Window. Morrow, 1930)
Murder May Pass Unpunished. Collins, 1936
Murder Through the Window; see The Murder at Plenders
The Young Vanish. Collins, 1932; Morrow, 1932

STOKES, MANNING LEE (M)
The Case of the Judas Spoon. Arcadia, 1957
The Dying Room. Phoenix, 1947
The Grave's in the Meadow. Dell, 1961
Green for a Grave. Phoenix, 1946
The Lady Lost Her Head. Phoenix, 1950
Murder Can't Wait. Graphic, 1955
Under Cover of Night. Dell, 1958
The Wolf Howls Murder. Phoenix, 1945

STONE, ANDREW L. (S)
Cry Terror. Hamilton, 1958
The Decks Ran Red. Signet, 1958
Julie. Hamilton, 1957

STONE, AUSTIN (M)
Blood Stays Red. Gifford, 1949
Deadly Night-Blade. Gifford, 1950
Death Throws a Party. Gifford, 1949
The Headsman. Eldon, 1936; Mellifont, 1949
Murders in the Mortuary. Eldon, 1935; Putnam, 1936

STONE, CLARA (M)
Death in Cranford. Hutchinson, 1959

STONE, DAVID (S)
The Tired Spy. Putnam, 1961; Tower, 1965

STONE, ELIZABETH (D)
Murder at the Mardi Gras. Sheridan, 1947
Poison, Poker, and Pistols. Sheridan, 1946

STONE, GRACE ZARING (S) (Pseudonym: Ethel Vance)
Escape. Collins, 1939; Little, 1939; Grosset, 1940; Popular Lib., 1964

STONE, HAMPTON, pseud; see STEIN, AARON MARC

STONE, HARRIET (S)
The Heiress of Bayou Vache. Lancer, 1965

STONE, PETER (M)
Charade. GM, 1963

STONE, SIMON, pseud; see BARRINGTON, HOWARD

STONEHAM, CHARLES THURLEY (S)
Kenya Mystery. Museum Press, 1954
The Man in the Pig Mask. Hutchinson, 1929

STORER, MARIA (M)
The Borodino Mystery. Herder, 1916

STORM, JOAN (M)
The Bitter Rubies. Hammond, 1952
The Dark Emerald. Hammond, 1951
The Deadly Diamond. Hammond, 1953

STORM, MICHAEL (M)
China Cane. Bouregy, 1959
Cry, Tiger! Bouregy, 1958
Edge of Danger. Bouregy, 1957

STORME, PETER, pseud; see STERN, PHILIP VAN DOREN

STORY, JACK TREVOR (S)
Mix Me a Person. Allen, W. H., 1959; Macmillan, 1960
Money Goes Round and Round. Redman, 1958
Protection for a Lady. Laurie, 1950
The Trouble With Harry. Macmillan, 1950

STOUT, REX TODHUNTER (D)
All Aces: A Nero Wolfe Omnibus. Viking, 1958 (Contains: Some Buried Caesar, Too Many Women, and Trouble in Triplicate)
Alphabet Hicks. Farrar & Rinehart, 1941 (Also published as: Sound of Murder. Pyramid, 1965)
And Be a Villain. Viking, 1948; Bantam, 1961 (English title: More Deaths Than One. Collins, 1949)
And Four to Go. Viking, 1958
Bad for Business. Murray Hill, 1940; Pyramid, 1965; Dell
Before Midnight. Viking, 1955; Bantam, 1957, 1963
The Black Mountain. Viking, 1954; Bantam, 1964
Black Orchids. Farrar & Rinehart, 1942; Pyramid, 1963 (1942 edition contains Cordially Invited to Meet Death)
Booby Trap; see Not Quite Dead
The Broken Vase. Farrar & Rinehart, 1941; Pyramid, 1965; Dell

Champagne for One. Collins, 1959; Viking, 1959; Bantam, 1960
Cordially Invited to Meet Death; see Black Orchids
Crime and Again. Collins, 1959
Crime on Her Hands; see Hand in the Glove
Curtains for Three. Viking, 1951; Bantam
Dark Revenge; see The Mountain Cat Murders
Death of a Doxy. Viking, 1966; Bantam, 1967; Collins, 1967
The Doorbell Rang. Viking, 1965; Pyramid, 1966
Double for Death. Farrar & Rinehart, 1939; Pyramid, 1964; Dell
Even in the Best Families; see In the Best Families
Fer-de-lance. Farrar & Rinehart, 1934; Dell, 1958; Pyramid, 1964
The Final Deduction. Viking, 1961; Bantam, 1963
Five of a Kind: Third Nero Wolfe Omnibus. Viking, 1961
Full House: A Nero Wolfe Omnibus. Viking, 1955
Gambit. Viking, 1962; Collins, 1963; Bantam, 1967
The Golden Spiders. Viking, 1953; Bantam, 1964
The Hand in the Glove. Farrar & Rinehart, 1937; Pyramid, 1964; Dell (English title: Crime on Her Hands. Collins, 1939)
Homicide Trinity. Viking, 1962; Collins, 1963; Bantam
How Like a God. Pyramid, 1963
If Death Ever Slept. Viking, 1957; Collins, 1958
In the Best Families. Viking, 1950; Bantam, 1962 (English title: Even in the Best Families. Collins, 1951)
The League of Frightened Men. Farrar & Rinehart, 1935; Pyramid, 1963
Might as Well Be Dead. Collins, 1956; Viking, 1956; Bantam
More Deaths Than One; see And Be a Villain
The Mother Hunt. Viking, 1963; Bantam, 1964; Collins, 1964
The Mountain Cat Murders. Farrar & Rinehart, 1939; Dell, 1964 (Original title: Dark Revenge)
Murder by the Book. Viking, 1951; Collins, 1952
Murder in Style. Collins, 1960
Not Quite Dead Enough. Farrar & Rinehart, 1944; Grosset, 1946; Pyramid, 1962; Dell (1944 edition also contains Booby Trap)
Out Goes She; see Prisoner's Base
Over My Dead Body. Farrar & Rinehart, 1940; Pyramid, 1964; Avon
Plot It Yourself. Viking, 1959; Pyramid
The President Vanishes. Farrar & Rinehart, 1934; Grosset, 1935; Pyramid, 1967
Prisoner's Base. Viking, 1952; Bantam, 1955 (English title: Out Goes She. Collins, 1953)
The Red Box. Farrar & Rinehart, 1937; Avon, 1943; Pyramid, 1964
Red Threads. Murray Hill, 1929; Pyramid, 1964; Dell
A Right to Die. Viking, 1964; Bantam, 1965; Cassell, 1965
Royal Flush: The Fourth Nero Wolfe Omnibus. Viking, 1965
The Rubber Band. Farrar & Rinehart, 1936; Cassell, 1938; Pyramid, 1964 (Also published as: To Kill Again. Hillman, 1960)
The Second Confession. Viking, 1949; Collins, 1950; Bantam
The Silent Speaker. Viking, 1946; Bantam, 1948
Some Buried Caesar. Farrar & Rinehart, 1939; Pyramid, 1963
The Sound of Murder; see Alphabet Hicks
Three at Wolfe's Door. Bantam, 1961; Viking, 1961
Three Doors to Death. Collins, 1950; Viking, 1950; Bantam, 1966
Three for the Chair. Viking, 1957; Bantam, 1963
Three Men Out. Bantam, 1964; Viking, 1954
Three Witnesses. Viking, 1956; Bantam, 1957
To Kill Again; see The Rubber Band
Too Many Clients. Doubleday, 1960; Bantam, 1962
Too Many Cooks. Farrar & Rinehart, 1938; Pyramid, 1963; Dell
Too Many Women. Viking, 1947; Bantam, 1967
Trio for Blunt Instruments. Viking, 1964; Bantam, 1967; Banner
Triple Jeopardy. Viking, 1952; Bantam, 1963
Trouble in Triplicate. Viking, 1949; Bantam, 1967
Where There's a Will. Farrar & Rinehart, 1940; Avon, 1941, 1963

STOWELL, WILLIAM AVERILL (M)
The Marston Murder Case. Appleton, D., 1930
The Mystery of the Singing Walls. Appleton, D., 1925

STRACHAN, TONY SIMPSON (M)
Fire Escape. Laurie, 1950
Key Major. Heinemann, 1954
No Law in Illyria. Heinemann, 1957
Short Weekend. Hammond, 1953

STRAHAN, MRS. KAY CLEAVER (M)
(Pseudonym: Kay Cleaver)
Death Traps. Doubleday, Doran, 1930; Gollancz, 1930
Desert Lake Mystery. Bobbs, 1936; Methuen, 1937
Desert Moon Mystery. Doubleday, Doran, 1928; Gollancz, 1929
Footprints. Doubleday, Doran, 1929; Gollancz, 1929
Hobgoblin Murder. Bobbs, 1934; Methuen, 1935
The Meriweather Mystery. Doubleday, Doran, 1933
October House. Doubleday, Doran, 1932; Gollancz, 1932

STRAKER, JOHN FOSTER (M)
Final Witness. Harrap, 1963
Ginger Horse. Harrap, 1956
Goodbye, Aunt Charlotte. Harrap, 1958
Gun to Play With. Harrap, 1956
Pick Up the Pieces. Harrap, 1955
Postman's Knock. Harrap, 1954
Shape of Murder. Harrap, 1964

STRANGE, CARLTON (M)
The Beechcourt Mystery. Newnes, 1894

STRANGE, JOHN STEPHEN, pseud; see TILLET, MRS. DOROTHY STOCKBRIDGE

STRANGE, MARK (M)
Midnight. Faber & Gwyer, 1927

STRATENUS, LOUISA (M)
Suspected. Chapman, 1892

STRATTON, HENRY, pseud. (M)
The Blanket. MacDonald & Co., 1959

STRATTON, ROY OLIN (M)
The Decorated Corpse. Mill, 1962
One Among None. Mill, 1965

STRATTON, THOMAS (S)
The Invisibility Affair. Ace, 1967 (The Man from U.N.C.L.E. series, #11)
The Mind Twister's Affair. Ace, 1967 (The Man from U.N.C.L.E. series, #12)

STRAUS, RALPH (M)
Pengard, Awake. Appleton, D., 1920; Methuen, 1920

STRAUSS, THEODORE (M)
Moonrise. Viking, 1946; Hamilton, H., 1947

STREET, BRADFORD (S)
In Like Flint. Dell, 1967

STREET, CECIL JOHN CHARLES (D)
(Pseudonym: John Rhode)
A.S.F.: The Story of a Great Conspiracy. Bles, 1924
The Affair of the Substitute Doctor; see Dr. Greenwood's Locum
The Alarm. Bles, 1925
An Artist Dies. Bles, 1956 (U.S. title: Death of an Artist. Dodd, 1956)
Blackthorn House. Bles, 1949; Dodd, 1949
The Bloody Tower. Collins, 1938 (U.S. title: The Tower of Evil. Dodd, 1938)
Body Unidentified. Dodd, 1938
Bricklayer's Arms. Collins, 1945 (U.S. title: Shadow of a Crime. Dodd, 1945)
By Registered Post. Bles, 1952 (U.S. title: Mysterious Suspect. Dodd, 1953)
The Case of the Forty Thieves. Dodd, 1954
The Claverton Affair; see The Claverton Mystery
The Claverton Mystery. Collins, 1933 (U.S. title: The Claverton Affair. Dodd, 1933)
The Corpse in the Car. Collins, 1935; Dodd, 1935
The Davidson Case. Bles, 1929 (U.S. title: Murder at Bratton Grange. Dodd, 1929; Burt, 1930)
Dead Men at the Folly. Collins, 1932; Dodd, 1932; Burt, 1933
Dead of the Night; see Night Exercise
Dead on the Track. Collins, 1943; Dodd, 1943
Death at Breakfast. Collins, 1936; Dodd, 1936
Death at the Dance. Bles, 1952; Dodd, 1953
Death at the Helm. Collins, 1941; Dodd, 1941
Death at the Inn. Bles, 1953
Death in Harley Street. Bles, 1946; Dodd, 1946
Death in the Hop Fields. Collins, 1937
Death in Wellington Road. Bles, 1952; Dodd, 1952
Death Invades the Meeting. Collins, 1944; Dodd, 1944
Death of a Bridegroom. Bles, 1957; Dodd, 1958
Death of a Godmother. Bles, 1955 (U.S. title: Delayed Payment. Dodd, 1956)
Death of an Artist; see An Artist Dies
Death of an Author. Bles, 1947; Dodd, 1948
Death on Sunday. Collins, 1939
Death on the Board. Collins, 1937 (U.S. title: Death Sits on the Board. Dodd, 1937)
Death on the Boat Train. Collins, 1940; Dodd, 1940

Death on the Lawn. Bles, 1954; Dodd, 1954
Death Pays a Dividend. Collins, 1939; Dodd, 1939
Death Sits on the Board; see Death on the Board
Death Takes a Partner. Collins, 1958; Dodd, 1959
Delayed Payment; see Death of a Godmother
Dr. Greenwood's Locum. Bles, 1951 (U.S. title: The Affair of the Substitute Doctor. Dodd, 1951)
Dr. Priestley Investigates. Dodd, 1930; Burt, 1931
Dr. Priestley Lays a Trap; see Motor Rally Mystery
Dr. Priestley's Quest. Bles, 1926
Domestic Agency. Bles, 1955 (U.S. title: Grave Matters. Dodd, 1955)
Double Florin. Bles, 1924
Double Identities; see The Two Graphs
The Dovebury Murders. Bles, 1954; Dodd, 1954
Drop to His Death, with Carter Dickson. Heinemann, 1939 (U.S. title: Fatal Descent. Dodd, 1939)
The Eel Pie Murder. Farrar & Rinehart, 1933
The Ellerby Case. Bles, 1927; Dodd, 1927; Burt, 1928
The Elm Tree Murder. Dodd, 1939
Experiment in Crime. Collins, 1947; Dodd, 1947 (Also published as: Nothing But the Truth. Bles, 1947)
Family Affairs. Bles, 1950
Fatal Descent; see Drop to His Death
Fatal Garden; see Up the Garden Path
The Fatal Pool. Dodd, 1961
Fire at Greycombe Farm; see Mystery at Greycombe Farm
The Fourth Bomb. Collins, 1942; Dodd, 1942
Grave Matters; see Domestic Agency
The Hanging Woman. Collins, 1931; Dodd, 1931
The Harvest Murder. Dodd, 1937
Hendon's First Case. Collins, 1935; Dodd, 1936
The House on Tollard Ridge. Bles, 1929; Dodd, 1929; Penguin, 1938
In the Face of the Verdict. Collins, 1936; Dodd, 1940
Invisible Weapons. Collins, 1938; Dodd, 1938
The Lake House. Bles, 1946 (U.S. title: The Secret of the Lake House. Dodd, 1946)
The Last Suspect. Dodd, 1950
Licensed for Murder. Bles, 1959; Dodd, 1959
Links in the Chain. Dodd, 1948
Mademoiselle from Armentieres. Bles, 1927
Men Die at Cyprus Lodge. Collins, 1943; Dodd, 1944
The Motor Rally Mystery. Collins, 1933 (U.S. title: Dr. Priestley Lays a Trap. Dodd, 1933)
Murder at Bratton Grange; see The Davidson Case
Murder at Derivale. Bles, 1958; Dodd, 1958
Murder at Lilac Cottage. Collins, 1940; Dodd, 1940
Murder at the Motor Show; see Mystery at Olympia
Murders in Praed Street. Bles, 1927; Dodd, 1928; Penguin
The Mysterious Suspect; see By Registered Post
Mystery at Greycombe Farm. Collins, 1932 (U.S. title: Fire at Greycombe Farm. Dodd, 1932)
Mystery at Olympia. Collins, 1935 (U.S. title: Murder at the Motor Show. Dodd, 1936)
Night Exercises. Collins, 1942 (U.S. title: Dead of the Night. Dodd, 1942)
Nothing But the Truth; see Experiment in Crime
Open Verdict. Bles, 1956; Dodd, 1957
The Paddington Mystery. Bles, 1925
The Paper Bag. Bles, 1948
The Peril at Cranbury Hall. Bles, 1930; Dodd, 1930
Pinehurst. Bles, 1930
Poison for One. Collins, 1934; Dodd, 1935
Proceed with Caution. Collins, 1937
Robbery with Violence. Bles, 1957; Dodd, 1957
The Robthorne Mystery. Collins, 1934; Dodd, 1934
Secret Meeting. Bles, 1951; Dodd, 1952
Secret of the Lake; see The Lake House
Shadow of a Crime; see Bricklayer's Arms
Shadow of an Alibi; see The Telephone Call
Shot at Dawn. Collins, 1934; Dodd, 1935
Signal for Death; see They Watched by Night
The Telephone Call. Bles, 1948 (U.S. title: Shadow of an Alibi. Dodd, 1948)
They Watched by Night. Collins, 1941 (U.S. title: Signal for Death. Dodd, 1941)
Three Cousins Die. Bles, 1959; Dodd, 1959
Too Many Suspects; see Vegetable Duck
The Tower of Evil; see The Bloody Tower
Tragedy of the Unicorn. Bles, 1928; Burt, 1928
Tragedy on the Line. Collins, 1931; Dodd, 1931
Twice Dead. Bles, 1960; Dodd, 1960
The Two Graphs. Bles, 1950 (U.S. title: Double Identities. Dodd, 1950)

Up the Garden Path. Bles, 1949 (U.S. title: The Fatal Garden. Dodd, 1949)
The Vanishing Diary. Dodd, 1961
Vegetable Duck. Collins, 1944 (U.S. title: Too Many Suspects. Dodd, 1945)
The Venner Crime. Odhams, 1933; Dodd, 1934; Collins, 1938
White Menace. McBride, 1926; White House, 1931

STREVENS, ROBERT (M)
Murder in Manuscript. Rich, 1948

STRIBLING, THOMAS SIGISMUND (D)
Clues of the Caribbees. Doubleday, Doran, 1929; Heinemann, 1931

STRINGER, ARTHUR J. A. (M)
City of Peril. Knopf, 1923
Diamond Thieves. Bobbs, 1924
Door of Dread. Bobbs, 1916
The Ghost Plane. Bobbs, 1940
Hand of Peril. Burt, 1915
The House of Intrigue. Bobbs, 1918
In Bad with Sinbad. Bobbs, 1926
Man Lost. Bobbs, 1934
The Man Who Couldn't Sleep. Bobbs, 1919
Night Hawk. Burt, 1926
Phantom Wires. Little, 1907
Shadow. Century, 1913
Under Grooves. McClure, 1908
Wire Tappers. Little, 1906

STROBEL, MARION (Mrs. James H. Mitchell) (M)
Ice Before Killing. Scribner, 1943
Kiss and Kill. Scribner, 1946

STRONG, BEN, pseud. (M)
The Secret of Gnome Head. Hodder, 1928
The Shadow on the Course. Hamilton, J., 1926
The Studdingly Stables Mystery. Hodder, 1926
The Track of the Slayer. Hodder, 1925

STRONG, HARRINGTON (M)
Brand of Silence. Chelsea House, 1924
The Hooded Stranger. Hutchinson, 1926
Legal Settlement. Lloyds, 1922
The Scarlet Scourge. Hutchinson, 1927
The Spider's Den. Hutchinson, 1926
Who Killed William Drew? Chelsea House, 1925

STRONG, LEONARD A. G. (M)
All Fall Down. Collins, 1944; Doubleday, Doran, 1944
Deliverance. Methuen, 1955
Murder Plays an Ugly Scene. Doubleday, Doran, 1945
Othello's Occupation. Collins, 1945
Slocombe Dies. Collins, 1952
Treason in the Egg. Collins, 1958
Tuesday Afternoon. Gollancz, 1935
Which I Never. Collins, 1950; Macmillan, 1952

STRUTTON, B. (M)
Jury of Angels. Hodder, 1957

STUART, ALAN
Unwilling Angel. Ward, Lock, 1955

STUART, BRIAN, pseud; see WORTHINGTON-STUART, BRIAN ARTHUR

STUART, ELIZABETH (S-Gothic)
Shaking Shadow. Signet, 1967

STUART, ESME (M)
Arrested. White, 1896

STUART, IAN, pseud; see MACLEAN ALISTAIR

STUART, ROBERT (D)
Duncan Ross—Detective-Sergeant. Blackie & Son, 1935

STUART, SIDNEY, pseud; see AVALLONE, MICHAEL

STUART, WILLIAM L. (M)
Dead Lie Still. Farrar, Straus, 1945
Night Cry. Dial, 1948

STURGEON, THEODORE (S)
Some of Your Blood. Ballantine, 1961

STURGIS, JUSTIN (D) (Pseudonym: Gelett Burgess)
Ladies in Boxes. Alliance, 1942
Master of Mysteries. Bobbs, 1912
Two O'Clock Courage. Bobbs, 1934

STURT, E. M. LEADER (D)
A Detective's Memoirs and Other Stories. Drane, 1921

STUTLEY, S. J. and A. E. COPP (M)
The Melbourne Mystery. Lane, 1929
Poisoned Glass. Lane, 1932

STYLES, FRANK SHOWELL (D) (Pseudonym: Glyn Carr)
The Corpse at Camp Two. Bles, 1955
The Corpse in the Crevasse. Bles, 1952
Death of a Weirdy. Bles, 1965
Death on Milestone Buttress. Bles, 1953
Death Under Snowdon. Bles, 1954
The Ice Axe Murders. Bles, 1958
Lewker in Norway. Bles, 1963
Murder on the Matterhorn. Bles, 1951; Dutton, 1953

Murder of an Owl. Bles, 1956
Swing Away, Climber. Washburn, 1960
Traitor's Mountain. Macmillan, 1946
Youth Hostel Murders. Bles, 1952; Dutton, 1953

SUDAK, EUNICE (M-Satire)
Icepick in Ollie Birk. Lancer, 1966

SUE, EUGENE (M)
Mysteries of Paris. Harper, 1843

SULLIVAN, ALAN (Full name: Edward Alan Sullivan) (M)
The Jade God. Bles, 1925; Century, 1925

SULLIVAN, EDWARD ALAN; see SULLIVAN, ALAN

SULLIVAN, VIRGINIA (M)
Permanent Wave. Macrae Smith, 1929

SUMMERS, KEITH (M)
Design for Death. Boardman, T. V., 1957

SUMMERS, HOLLIS SPURGEON and JAMES F. ROURKE (M) (Pseudonym: Jim Hollis)
Teach You a Lesson. Harper, 1955

SUMMERTON, MARGARET (M-S) (Pseudonym: Jan Roffman)
Ashes in an Urn, by Jan Roffman. Doubleday, 1966
Death of a Fox, by Jan Roffman. Doubleday, 1964 (Also published as: Reflection of Evil. Ace, 1965)
Likely to Die, by Jan Roffman. Bles, 1964
A Memory of Darkness. Dutton, 1967
Nightingale at Noon. Dutton, 1963; Hodder, 1963; Ace, 1964
A Penny for the Guy, by Jan Roffman. Bles, 1965; Doubleday, 1965
Quin's Hide. Hodder, 1964; Dutton, 1965; Ace, 1966
Reflection of Evil; see Death of a Fox
Ring of Mischief. Dutton, 1965; Ace, 1966
The Sea House. Holt, 1960
Sunset Hour. Hodder, 1957
Winter of the Fox. Bles, 1964
With Murder in Mind, by Jan Roffman. Doubleday, 1963

SUMNER, CID RICKETTS (M)
Withdraw Thy Foot. Coward, 1964

SUNDERLAND-LEWIS, W. R. (M)
Cubwood. Boni, 1926

SUNMAN, WILLIAM R. (M)
Mystery of Wolverton Grange. Crombie, 1889

SUTHERLAND, NIGEL
The Pawn. Heinemann, 1952

SUTHERLAND, WILLIAM, pseud; see COOPER, JOHN MURRAY

SUTPHEN, WILLIAM GILBERT VAN TASSEL (M)
In Jeopardy. Harper, 1922

SUTTON, GRAHAM (M) (Pseudonym: Anthony Marsden)
Death on the Downs. Jarrolds, 1929
Death Strikes from the Rear. Low, 1934; Readers' Lib., 1939
The Man in the Sandhills. Jarrolds, 1927
The Moonstone Mystery. Jarrolds, 1928
The Mycroft Murder Case. Low, 1935
The Six-Hour Mystery. Jarrolds, 1929
Thieves' Justice. Jarrolds, 1929

SWAIN, VIRGINIA (M)
The Hollow Skin. Farrar & Rinehart, 1938

SWANN, FRANCIS (M-S)
The Brass Key. S & S, 1964; Gollancz, 1965; Lancer, 1968
Royal Street. Lancer, 1966
You'll Hang, My Love, with Lucile Emerick. Lancer, 1967

SWARTOUT, ROBERT EGERTON (M)
The Boat Race Murder. Grayson, 1933

SWAYNE, MARTIN LUTRELL (S)
Blue Germ. Doran, 1918; Hodder, 1918

SWEM, CHARLES LEE (S)
The Werewolf. Doubleday, Doran, 1928; Hutchinson, 1928

SWIFT, ANTHONY, pseud; see FARJEON, JOSEPH JEFFERSON

SWIGGETT, HOWARD (M)
The Corpse in the Derby Hat. Little, 1937 (English title: The Stairs Lead Nowhere. Heinemann, 1937)
The Hidden and the Hunted. Morrow, 1950; Heinemann, 1951
Most Secret, Most Immediate. Houghton, 1944
The Stairs Lead Nowhere; see The Corpse in the Derby Hat
The Strongbox. Houghton, 1955; Permabooks, 1956

SWITZER, ROBERT I. (M)
I Was Going Anyway. Macmillan, 1961

SYDELL, ELEANOR (S)
Diplomatic Immunity. Lancer, 1966

SYKES, WILLIAM STANLEY (M)
Harness of Death. Dodd, 1932; Lane, 1932
The Man Who Was Dead. Dodd, 1931 (English title: Missing Money-Lender. Lane, 1931)
Missing Money-Lender; see The Man Who Was Dead

SYLVESTER, ROBERT (S)
The Big Boodle. Random, 1954 (English title: Night in Havana. Hammond, 1957)

SYMONDS, FRANCIS ADDINGTON (M)
Smile and Murder. Boardman, T. V., 1954

SYMONS, MRS. BERYL (M)
The Divine Court Mystery. Jenkins, 1931
The Leering House. Jenkins, 1929
The Opal Murder Case. Jenkins, 1932

SYMONS, JULIAN (D)
The Belting Inheritance. Cassell, 1965; Harper & Row, 1965; Signet, 1966
Bland Beginning. Collins, 1944; Harper, 1949; Doubleday, 1962
Bogue's Fortune; see Paper Chase
The Broken Penny. Harper, 1953; Doubleday, 1961
The Color of Murder. Collins, 1957; Harper, 1958; Dell, 1967
The End of Solomon Grundy. Collins, 1964; Harper & Row, 1965
The Gigantic Shadow. Collins, 1958 (U.S. title: Pipe Dream. Harper, 1959; Collier, 1962)
Immaterial Murder Case. Macmillan, 1957; Penguin, 1954
The Killing of Francie Lane. Collins, 1962
Lot 41—Dead Auctioneer. Boardman, T. V., 1964
The Man Who Killed Himself. Barker, 1967; Harper & Row, 1967
Murder! Murder! Collins, 1961
The Narrowing Circle. Gollancz, 1954; Harper, 1955; Doubleday, 1961
Paper Chase. Collins, 1956 (U.S. title: Bogue's Fortune. Harper, 1957)
Pattern of Murder. Boardman, T. V., 1962
Pipe Dream; see The Gigantic Shadow
The Plain Man. Collins, 1962; Harper & Row, 1963
Progress of a Crime. Collins, 1960; Harper, 1960; Doubleday, 1962
The Thirty-first of February. Harper, 1951; Bantam, 1953

SYNON, MARY (M)
The Good Red Bricks. Little, 1929

TABER, HARRY P. (M)
The Gordon Elopement. Doubleday, Page, 1904
Mystery Girl. Lippincott, 1922

TABORI, PAUL (S)
The Doomsday Brain. Pyramid, 1967
He Never Came Back. Dutton, 1947
The Invisible Eye. Pyramid, 1967
Perdita's End. Cassell, 1952

TACK, ALFRED (D-M)
Death Kicks a Pebble. Jenkins, 1951
Death Takes a Dive. Jenkins, 1950; Roy Pubs., 1957
Forecast - Murder. Long, 1967
A Murder Is Staged. Jenkins, 1949
The Prospect's Dead. Jenkins, 1948
Selling's Murder. Jenkins, 1949
The Test Match Murder. Jenkins, 1948

TAFT, WILLIAM NELSON (M)
On Secret Service. Harper, 1921

TAINE, JOHN, pseud; see BELL, ERIC TEMPLE

TAIT, EUPHEMIA MARGARET (M)
(Pseudonym: John Ironside)
The Call-Box Mystery. Methuen, 1923 (U.S. title: The Phone Booth Mystery. Holt, H., 1924)
The Marten Mystery. Arrowsmith, 1933
The Phone Booth Mystery; see The Call-Box Mystery
Red Symbol. Little, 1910; Nash, 1911

TALBOT, HAKE, pseud; see NELMS, HENNING

TANNOCK, MALCOLM
Uneasy Money. Ward, Lock, 1951

TARG, WILLIAM and LEWIS HERMAN (D)
The Case of Mr. Cassidy. Phoenix, 1939; World Pub., 1944

TARPEY, JESSE TOLER KINGSLEY (M)
The Bulldog Bungalow Murder. Butterworth, T., 1930

TARRANT, C. A., pseud. (M)
The Cat Climbs. Secker & Warburg, 1936; Lippincott, 1937

TATE, SYLVIA (M)
Never by Chance. Harper, 1949

TAUBES, FRANK (S)
Run, Run . . . Run. Crowell, 1955; Muller, 1955

TAUBMAN-GOLDIE, VALENTINE FRANCIS (M)
The Case of Sir Edward Talbot. Dutton, 1922

TAUNTON, HAROLD ROBY (M)
Death in Diamonds. Hurst, 1936
It Prowls at Dark. Hurst, 1937
The Red Club. Hurst, 1926
The Second Wager. Hurst, 1927
Six Foot of Rope. Hurst, 1938

TAYLOR, A. FRANK (M)
How I Made a Million Dollars. Pageant Press, 1960

TAYLOR, CONSTANCE LINDSAY (M)
(Pseudonym: Guy Cullingford)
Brink of Disaster. Bles, 1964; Roy Pubs., 1966
Conjurer's Coffin. Hammond, 1954; Lippincott, 1954
Framed for Hanging. Lippincott, 1956
If Wishes Were Hearses. Hammond, 1952; Lippincott, 1953
Post Mortem. Hammond, 1953; Lippincott, 1953
Third Party Risk. Bles, 1962
A Touch of Drama. Hammond, 1960
The Whipping Boys. Penguin, 1964

TAYLOR, ELIZABETH TEBBETT-; see TEBBETT-TAYLOR, ELIZABETH

TAYLOR, H. BALDWIN, pseud; see WAUGH, HILLARY BALDWIN

TAYLOR, JUDSON R. (D)
Gipsy Blair, the Western Detective. Ogilvie, 1914
Macon Moore. Ogilvie

TAYLOR, KATHERINE HAVILAND (M)
Barbara of Baltimore. Doran, 1919

TAYLOR, PHILIP NEVILLE WALKER-; see WALKER-TAYLOR, PHILIP NEVILLE

TAYLOR, PHOEBE ATWOOD (D)
(Pseudonym: Alice Tilton)
The Annulet of Gilt. Norton, 1938; Collins, 1939
Asey Mayo Trio. Collins, 1946; Messner, 1946
Banbury Bog. Norton, 1938, 1964; Collins, 1939; Pyramid, 1967
Beginning with a Bash, by Alice Tilton. Collins, 1938
The Cape Cod Mystery. Bobbs, 1931; Pyramid, 1965
Cold Steal, by Alice Tilton. Norton, 1939
Criminal C.O.D. Collins, 1940; Norton, 1940, 1965
The Crimson Patch. Gollancz, 1936; Norton, 1936, 1965
The Cut Direct, by Alice Tilton. Norton, 1938
Dead Ernest, by Alice Tilton. Norton, 1944, 1966
Deadly Sunshade. Norton, 1940, 1967; Collins, 1941
Death Lights a Candle. Bobbs, 1932
Deathblow Hill. Norton, 1935, 1967; Gollancz, 1936
Diplomatic Corpse. Collins, 1951; Little, 1951
Figure Away. Norton, 1937, 1964; Collins, 1938
File for Record, by Alice Tilton. Norton, 1943, 1967
Going, Going, Gone. Blakiston, 1943; Collins, 1944; Norton, 1966
Hollow Chest, by Alice Tilton. Norton, 1941, 1967
Iron Clew, by Alice Tilton. Farrar, Straus, 1947 (English title: Iron Hand. Collins, 1947)
Iron Hand; see Iron Clew
The Left Leg, by Alice Tilton. Norton, 1940
The Mystery of the Cape Cod Players. Norton, 1933; Eyre, 1934
The Mystery of the Cape Cod Tavern. Norton, 1934; Eyre, 1935; Withy Grove, 1942
Octagon House. Norton, 1937, 1964; Collins, 1938; Pyramid, 1964
Out of Order. Norton, 1936, 1965; Gollancz, 1937
The Perennial Boarder. Norton, 1941, 1965; Collins, 1942
The Proof of the Pudding. Collins, 1945; Norton, 1945, 1963; Pyramid, 1963
Punch with Care. Farrar, Straus, 1946; Collins, 1947
Sandbar Sinister. Norton, 1934; Gollancz, 1936
Six Iron Spiders. Norton, 1942, 1966; Collins, 1943
Spring Harrowing. Collins, 1939; Norton, 1939, 1964
Three Plots for Asey Mayo. Norton, 1942
The Tinkling Symbol. Gollancz, 1935; Norton, 1935, 1967

TAYLOR, RAY WARD (S)
Doomsday Square. Dutton, 1966

TAYLOR, SAM S. (D)
No Head for Her Pillow. Dutton, 1952
Sleep No More. Dutton, 1949
So Cold My Bed. Dutton, 1953

TAYLOR, SAMUEL W. (M)
The Grinning Gismo. Wyn, 1951; Hodder, 1952

The Man with My Face. Wyn, 1948; Hodder, 1949; Penguin, 1954; Collier, 1962

TEAGLE, MIKE (D)
Death over San Silvestro. Hillman-Curl, 1936
Murders in Silk. Hillman-Curl, 1938

TEAGUE, RUTH and WALTER DORWIN TEAGUE (M)
You Can't Ignore Murder. Putnam, 1942

TEAGUE, WALTER DORWIN; see TEAGUE, RUTH

TEBBETT-TAYLOR, ELIZABETH (D)
Now I Lay Me Down to Die. Arcadia, 1955

TEILHET, DARWIN L. (D)
The Big Runaround. Coward, 1964 (Also published as: Dangerous Encounter. Paperback Lib., 1967)
The Broken Face Murders, with Hildegarde Teilhet. Doubleday, Doran, 1940; Gollancz, 1940
The Crimson Hair Murders, with Hildegarde Teilhet. Doubleday, Doran, 1936; Gollancz, 1937
Dangerous Encounter; see The Big Runaround
Death Flies High. Long, 1931; Morrow, 1931
Double Agent, with Hildegarde Teilhet. Doubleday, Doran, 1945; Gollancz, 1946
The Fear Makers. Appleton-Century, 1945; Gollancz, 1946
The Feather Cloak Murders, with Hildegarde Teilhet. Doubleday, Doran, 1936
Murder in the Air. Morrow, 1931
Odd Man Pays. Little, 1944
The Rim of Terror, with Hildegarde Teilhet. Coward, 1950
The Talking Sparrow Murders. Morrow, 1934
The Ticking Terror Murders. Doubleday, Doran, 1935

TEILHET, MRS. HILDEGARDE TOLMAN (D) (See also Teilhet, Darwin)
The Assassins. Gollancz, 1947
Hero by Proxy. Little, 1942; Gollancz, 1943
A Private Undertaking. Coward, 1952

TELFAIR, RICHARD (D)
Bloody Medallion. GM, 1959
The Corpse That Talked. 1959
Good Luck, Sucker. GM, 1961
Scream Bloody Murder. GM, 1960
The Slavers. GM, 1961
Target for Tonight. Dell, 1962

TELFER, DANIEL (M)
The Corrupters. S & S, 1964; Dell, 1965

TEMPLE, PAUL, pseud; see DURBRIDGE, FRANCIS

TEMPLE-ELLIS, N. A.; see HOLDAWAY, NEVILLE ALDRIDGE

TEMPLER, JOHN (D)
Jaggers, Air-Detective. Oxford, 1936
Jaggers at Bay. Oxford, 1938
Jaggers Swoops Again. Oxford, 1937

TEMPLETON, JESSE, pseud; see GOODCHILD, GEORGE

TERAMOND, E. C. (M)
The Mystery of Lucien Delorme. Appleton, D., 1915

TERHUNE, ALBERT PAYSON (M)
The Amateur Inn. Doran, 1923; Hodder, 1924
Black Caesar's Clan. Doran, 1923; Hodder, 1924
Black Gold. Doran, 1922; Hodder, 1922
Grudge Mountain. Harper, 1939 (English title: The Mystery of Grudge Mountain. Chapman, 1939)
Letters of Marque. Harper, 1934
Man in the Dark. Dutton, 1921
The Mystery of Grudge Mountain; see Grudge Mountain
The Pest. Dutton, 1923
The Runaway Bag. Doran, 1925
The Secret of Sea-Dream House. Harper, 1929
The Tiger's Claw. Doran, 1924; Hodder, 1925
The Unseen. Harper, 1937

TERRALL, ROBERT (M)
A Killer Is Loose Among Us. Duell, 1948
Madam Is Dead. Duell, 1947
They Deal in Death. S & S, 1943

TESSIER, ERNEST MAURICE (M)
(Pseudonym: Maurice Dekobra)
Chinese Puzzle. Allen, W. H., 1956
Death Requests the Pleasure. Laurie, 1940
Honeymoon in Shanghai. Laurie, 1946 (Also published as: Shanghai Honeymoon. Philosophical Lib., 1946)
Lady Is a Vamp. Allen, W. H., 1960
Madonna of the Sleeping Cars. Payson & Clarke, 1927
The Man Who Died Twice. Allen, W. H., 1954
Operation Magali. Allen, W. H., 1952
Poison at Plessis. Allen, W. H., 1953
Serenade to the Hangman. Laurie, 1929

Shanghai Honeymoon; see Honeymoon in Shanghai
She Wore Pink Gloves. Allen, W. H., 1958
Widow's Might. Allen, W. H., 1957

TEY, JOSEPHINE, pseud; see MACKINTOSH, ELIZABETH

THAMES, C. H., pseud; see MARLOWE, STEPHEN

THAYER, CHARLES WHEELER (S)
Checkpoint. PB, 1965

THAYER, LEE (Mrs. Emma Redington Lee Thayer) (D)
Accessory After the Fact. Dodd, 1943; Hurst, 1944
Accident, Manslaughter or Murder? Dodd, 1945; Hurst, 1946
Alias Dr. Ely. Doubleday, Page, 1927; Hurst, 1927
And One Cried Murder. Dodd, 1961; Long, 1962
Blood on the Knight. Dodd, 1952; Hurst, 1953
Clancy's Secret Mission. Hurst, 1952
A Clue for Clancy; see Pig in a Poke
Counterfeit. Sears, 1933 (English title: Counterfeit Bill. Hurst, 1937)
Counterfeit Bill; see Counterfeit
Dark of the Moon. Dodd, 1936 (English title: Death in the Gorge. Hurst, 1937)
Darkest Spot. Hurst, 1928; Sears, 1928
Dead End Street, No Outlet. Dodd, 1936 (English title: Murder in the Mirror. Hurst, 1936)
Dead Men's Shoes. Hurst, 1929; Sears, 1929
Dead on Arrival. Dodd, 1960; Long, 1962
Dead Reckoning. Dodd, 1954 (English title: Murder on the Pacific. Hurst, 1955)
Dead Storage. Dodd, 1935
Death in the Gorge; see Dark of the Moon
Death Walks in Shadow; see Dusty Death
Death Weed. Hurst, 1935
Death Within the Vault; see Within the Vault
Do Not Disturb. Dodd, 1951
Doctor S.O.S. Doubleday, Page, 1925; Hurst, 1925
Dusty Death. Dodd, 1966 (English title: Death Walks in Shadow. Long, 1966)
Evil Root. Dodd, 1949; Hurst, 1951
Fatal Alibi; see Who Benefits?
Five Bullets. Dodd, 1944; Hurst, 1947
Glass Knife. Hurst, 1932; Sears, 1932
Guilt Edged. Dodd, 1951 (English title: Guilt-Edged Murder. Hurst, 1953)
Guilt-Edged Murder; see Guilt Edged
Guilt Is Where You Find It. Dodd, 1957; Long, 1958
Guilty! Dodd, 1940; Hurst, 1941
Hair's Breath. Dodd, 1946; Hurst, 1947
Halloween Homicide. Dodd, 1941; Hurst, 1942
Hanging's Too Good. Dodd, 1943; Hurst, 1945
Hell-Gate Tides. Hurst, 1933; Sears, 1933
Jaws of Death. Dodd, 1946; Hurst, 1948
The Key. Doubleday, Page, 1924; Hurst, 1924
Last Shot. Hurst, 1931; Sears, 1931
Last Trump. Dodd, 1937; Hurst, 1937
Lightning Strikes Twice. Dodd, 1939; Hurst, 1939
A Man's Enemies. Dodd, 1937
Murder in the Mirror; see Dead End Street, No Outlet
Murder Is Out. Dodd, 1942; Hurst, 1943
Murder on Location. Dodd, 1942; Hurst, 1944
Murder on the Pacific; see Dead Reckoning
Murder Stalks the Circle. Dodd, 1947; Hurst, 1949
Mystery of the 13th Floor. Century, 1919
No Holiday for Death. Dodd, 1954; Hurst, 1955
Out, Brief Candle! Dodd, 1941; Hurst, 1950
Persons Unknown. Dodd, 1941; Hurst, 1942
Pig in a Poke. Dodd, 1947 (English title: Clue for Clancy. Hurst, 1950)
Plain Case of Murder. Dodd, 1944; Hurst, 1945
Poison. Doubleday, Page, 1926; Heinemann, 1926
Prisoner Pleads "Not Guilty." Dodd, 1953; Hurst, 1954
Puzzle. Hurst, 1932
Q.E.D. Doubleday, Page, 1922
The Ransom Racket. Dodd, 1938; Hurst, 1938
Red-handed; see Sudden Death
Scrimshaw Millions. Dodd, 1932; Hurst, 1933
Second Bullet. Dodd, 1934 (English title: Second Shot. Hurst, 1935)
Second Shot; see Second Bullet
Set a Thief. Sears, 1931 (English title: To Catch a Thief. Hurst, 1932)
Sinister Mark. Doubleday, Page, 1923; Hurst, 1923
Stark Murder. Dodd, 1939; Hurst, 1940
Still No Answer. Dodd, 1958 (English title: Web of Hate. Long, 1959)
Strange Sylvester Affair; see That Strange Sylvester Affair
Sudden Death. Dodd, 1935 (English title: Red-handed. Hurst, 1936)

That Affair at The Cedars. Doubleday, Page, 1921; Hurst, 1924
That Strange Sylvester Affair. Dodd, 1938 (English title: Strange Sylvester Affair. Hurst, 1940)
They Tell No Tales. Hurst, 1930; Sears, 1930
This Man's Doom. Hurst, 1938
To Catch a Thief; see Set a Thief
Too Long Endured. Dodd, 1950; Hurst, 1952
Two Ways to Die. Dodd, 1959; Long, 1961
Unlatched Door. Century, 1920
Web of Hate; see Still No Answer
Who Benefits? Dodd, 1955 (English title: Fatal Alibi. Hurst, 1956)
Within the Vault. Dodd, 1950 (English title: Death Within the Vault. Hurst, 1951)
X Marks the Spot. Dodd, 1940; Hurst, 1941

THAYER, TIFFANY (M) (Pseudonyms: John Doe, Elmer Ellsworth, Jr.)
Eye Witness. Hurst, 1931
The Illustrious Corpse. Fiction League, 1930

THIELEN, BERNARD (M)
Charm of Finches. Bouregy, 1959
Open Season. Bouregy, 1958

THIESSEN, VAL
My Brother Cain. Monarch, 1964

THIMBLETHORPE, JUNE SYLVIA (M) (Pseudonym: Sylvia Thorpe)
The Golden Panther. Rich, 1956
Smuggler's Moon. Rich, 1955 (Also published as: Strangers on the Moor. Pyramid, 1966)
Strangers on the Moor; see Smuggler's Moon

THOMAS, ALAN ERNEST WENTWORTH (D)
Daggers Drawn. Brewer, 1930; Benn, 1931
Death of Laurence Vining. Benn, 1929; Lippincott, 1929
Death of the Home Secretary. Benn, 1933
The Fugitives. Gollancz, 1953
The Mask and the Man. Gollancz, 1951
The Stolen Cellini. Benn, 1932; Lippincott, 1932
The Tremayne Case. Lippincott, 1930; Benn, 1931

THOMAS, ALBERT E. (D)
Double Cross. Dodd, 1924; Methuen, 1924

THOMAS, CAROLYN, pseud; see DUNCAN, ACTEA

THOMAS, DYLAN (M)
The Doctor and the Devils. Dent, 1953

THOMAS, EUGENE (M) (Pseudonym: Donald Grey)
Yellow Magic. Dodd, 1934

THOMAS, LESLIE (S)
Orange Wednesday. Dell, 1968

THOMAS, MAUD MAY (M)
Wait Long, Wait Still. Arcadia, 1954

THOMAS, MURRAY, pseud; see RAGG, THOMAS MURRAY

THOMAS, PAUL (S)
Code Name: Rubble. Tower, 1967

THOMAS, ROBERT (S)
Dead Ringer. GM, 1964

THOMAS, RONALD WILLS (M) (Pseudonym: Ronald Wills)
Big Fish. Roy Pubs., 1954
Black Weever. Roy Pubs., 1955
Food for Fishes. Dakers, 1954
Live Bait. Wingate, 1950

THOMAS, ROSS (S)
Cast a Yellow Shadow. Morrow, 1967
The Cold War Swap. Morrow, 1966; Avon, 1967
The Seersucker Whipsaw. Morrow, 1967
The Spy in the Vodka. Hodder, 1967

THOMAS, TAMMY (S)
Wild Is My Heart. Exposition, 1965

THOMEY, TEDD (S)
And Dream of Evil. Abelard, 1954
I Want Out. Ace, 1959

THOMPSON, ARTHUR LEONARD BELL (S) (Pseudonym: Francis Clifford)
Act of Mercy. Collins, 1960; Coward, 1960; Hamilton, H., 1960
All Men Are Lonely Now. Coward, 1967
The Green Fields of Eden. Coward, 1963; Signet, 1966
The Hunting Ground. Coward, 1964; Signet, 1966
The Naked Runner. Coward, 1965; Signet, 1967
Overdue. Dutton, 1957
Spanish Duet. Coward, 1966 (Contains: "Time Is an Ambush" and "The Trembling Earth")
The Third Side of the Coin. Coward, 1964; Signet, 1966
"Time Is an Ambush"; see Spanish Duet
"The Trembling Earth"; see Spanish Duet

THOMPSON, CHINA, pseud. (M)
Starrbelow. Scribner, 1958

THOMPSON, EDWARD ANTHONY (M)
(Pseudonym: Anthony Lejeune)
Crowded and Dangerous. MacDonald & Co., 1959
The Dark Trade. MacDonald & Co., 1965; Doubleday, 1966
Death of a Pornographer. Lancer, 1967
Duel in the Shadows. MacDonald & Co., 1963
Glint of Spears. MacDonald & Co., 1963
News of Murder. MacDonald & Co., 1961

THOMPSON, ESTELLE (M)
The Lawyer and the Carpenter. Hodder, 1963; Washburn, 1964
The Twig Is Bent. Abelard, 1961

THOMPSON, JIM (M)
After Dark, My Sweet. Popular Lib., 1956
The Criminal. Lion, 1954
The Golden Gizmo. Lion, 1954
Hell of a Woman. Lion, 1954
Ironside. Popular Lib., 1967
The Killer Inside Me. GM, 1952, 1965
The Kill-off. Lion, 1957
The Nothing Man. Dell, 1954
Nothing More Than Murder. Harper, 1949
Savage Night. Lion, 1953
A Swell-looking Babe. Lion, 1954
Wild Town. Signet, 1958

THOMPSON, JOSEPHINE PULLEIN-; see PULLEIN-THOMPSON, JOSEPHINE

THOMPSON, KENNETH (S)
Member's Lobby. British Book Centre, 1967

THOMPSON, LEWIS; see BOSWELL, CHARLES

THOMPSON, LILIAN BENNET and GEORGE HUBBARD (M)
Break of Death. Chelsea House, 1929
Death Fire. Chelsea House, 1929
Golden Ball. Chelsea House, 1929

THOMPSON, LLOYD S. (M)
Death Stops the Show. Crown, 1946
Hear Not My Steps. Abelard, 1953

THOMPSON, VANCE C. (M)
Diplomatic Mysteries. Lippincott, 1905
Green Ray. Bobbs, 1924; Hutchinson, 1925
Mr. Guelpa. Bobbs, 1925; Hutchinson, 1925
The Pointed Tower. Bobbs, 1923; Hutchinson, 1923
The Scarlet Iris. Bobbs, 1924

THOMSON, A. A. and F. L. CARY (D)
Murder at the Ministry. Jenkins, 1947

THOMSON, SIR BASIL HOME (M)
The Case of Naomi Clynes. Doubleday, Doran, 1934; Burt (English title: Inspector Richardson C.I.D. Eldon, 1936)
The Case of the Dead Diplomat. Doubleday, 1935; Burt, 1936 (English title: Richardson Goes Abroad. Eldon, 1936)
Court Intrigue. Heinemann, 1896
The Dartmoor Enigma. Doubleday, Doran, 1936 (English title: Richardson Solves a Dartmoor Mystery. Eldon, 1935)
Death in the Bathroom; see Who Killed Stella Pomeroy?
Inspector Richardson C.I.D.; see The Case of Naomi Clynes
Metal Flask. Methuen, 1929
Milliner's Hat; see The Mystery of the French Milliner
Mr. Pepper, Investigator. Castle, 1925
Murder Arranged; see When Thieves Fall Out
The Mystery of the French Milliner. Doubleday, Doran, 1937 (English title: Milliner's Hat. Eldon, 1937)
P. C. Richardson's First Case. Doubleday, Doran, 1933; Eldon, 1933
Richardson Goes Abroad. Eldon, 1935
Richardson Scores Again; see Richardson's Second Case
Richardson Solves a Dartmouth Mystery; see The Dartmoor Enigma
Richardson's Second Case. Doubleday, Doran, 1934 (English title: Richardson Scores Again. Eldon, 1934)
When Thieves Fall Out. Doubleday, Doran, 1937 (English title: Murder Arranged. Eldon, 1937)
Who Killed Stella Pomeroy? Doubleday, Doran, 1937 (English title: Death in the Bathroom. Eldon, 1936)

THOMSON, DAISY HICKS (M)
Prelude to Love. Hale, R., 1963
To Love and Honour. Hale, R., 1964

THORN, ALEX (M)
Blackmail for Free. Boardman, T. V., 1963

THORN, RONALD SCOTT (S)
The Dark Shadow; see Second Opinion
The Twin Serpents. Macmillan, 1965
Second Opinion. Macmillan, 1962
(Also published as: The Dark Shadow. Macfadden, 1964)

THORNBURG, ETHEL (S)
We've Been Waiting for You. Bobbs, 1947

THORNDYKE, ARTHUR RUSSELL (M)
The Courageous Exploits of Dr. Syn. Rich, 1936
The Devil in the Belfry; see Herod's Peal
Doctor Syn. Nelson, 1915
Doctor Syn on the High Seas. Rich, 1936
Doctor Syn Returns. Rich, 1935 (U.S. title: The Scarecrow Rides)
Herod's Peal. Butterworth, T., 1931 (U.S. title: The Devil in the Belfry. Dial, 1932; Dial, 1935)
Master of the Macabre. Rich, 1947
The Scarecrow Rides; see Doctor Syn Rides
The Slype. Holden, 1928; Dial, 1935

THORNE, E. P. (D-S)
Angel Steps In. Wright & Brown, 1960
Assignment Haiti. Wright & Brown, 1963
The Bengal Spider Plan. Wright & Brown, 1961
Black Sadhu. Wright & Brown, 1939
Black Sunset. Wright & Brown, 1963
Chinese Poker. Wright & Brown, 1964
Date with the Departed. Wright & Brown, 1955
The Death Rust. Wright & Brown, 1965
The Devil's Chapel. Wright & Brown, 1957
Die Wearing a Rose. Wright & Brown, 1959
Evil in the Cup. Wright & Brown, 1958
Expect No Mercy. Wright & Brown, 1962
The Face of Inspector Britt. Wright & Brown, 1947
Gallows Inn. Wright & Brown, 1958
Ganges Mud. Wright & Brown, 1936
The House of the Fragrant Lotus. Wright & Brown, 1962
Justice Is Mine. Wright & Brown, 1950
Lady with a Gun. Wright & Brown, 1956
Moon Dance. Wright & Brown, 1953
Operation Dragnet. Wright & Brown, 1966
Red Bamboo. Wright & Brown, 1954
Seven Red Herrings. Wright & Brown, 1956
The Shadow of Dr. Ferrari. Wright & Brown, 1950
Sinister Sanctuary. Wright & Brown, 1949
The Smile of Cheng Su. Wright & Brown, 1946
They Never Come Back. Wright & Brown, 1961
Three Silent Men. Wright & Brown, 1939
The White Arab. Wright & Brown, 1936
Yoga Mist. Wright & Brown, 1938
Zero Minus Nine. Wright & Brown, 1964

THORNE, EMILY (M)
The House on Sixteenth Street. Bouregy, 1966
The Mystery of Knickerbocker Towers. Bouregy, 1960

THORNE, GUY, pseud; see GULL, CYRIL ARTHUR

THORNE, MABEL; see THORNE, PAUL

THORNE, PAUL (M)
Murder in the Fog. Penn, 1929
The Secret Toll, with Mabel Thorne. Dodd, 1922
The Sheridan Road Mystery, with Mabel Thorne. Dodd, 1921
Spiderweb Clues. Penn, 1928
That Evening in Shanghai. Penn, 1931

THORNE, RONALD SCOTT (S)
Second Opinion. Macmillan, 1963 (Also published as: The Dark Shadow. Macfadden, 1964)

THORP, RODERICK (S)
The Detective. Dial, 1966; Avon, 1967; Barker, 1967

THORPE, SYLVIA, pseud; see THIMBLETHORPE, JUNE SYLVIA

THURLEY, NORGROVE (M)
Giants of Darkness. Paul, S., 1957
Murder Strikes North. Paul, S., 1952

THURMAN, STEVE, pseud; see CASTLE, FRANK

THURSTON, ERNEST T. (M)
The Man in a Black Hat. Cassell, 1930; Doubleday, Doran, 1931

THYNNE, MOLLY (M)
The Case of Sir Adam Braid. Nelson, 1930
The Crime at the "Noah's Ark." Nelson, 1931
The Draycott Murder Mystery. Nelson, 1928; Stokes, 1928
He Dies and Makes No Sign. Hutchinson, 1933
The Murder in the Dentist Chair. Covici, 1932; Hutchinson, 1932
Murder on the Enriqueta; see The Strangler
The Red Dwarf. Nelson, 1928
The Strangler. Minton, 1929 (English title: Murder on the Enriqueta. Nelson, 1929)

TICKELL, JERRARD (M)
High Water at Four. Doubleday, 1966
The Hunt for Richard Thorpe; see Whither Do You Wander?
Whither Do You Wander? Hodder, 1959 (U.S. title: The Hunt for Richard Thorpe. Doubleday, 1960)

TIGER, JOHN (D-S)
Countertrap. Popular Lib., 1967 (I Spy series, #5)
Death Hits the Jackpot. Avon, 1954
Doomdate. Popular Lib., 1967
I Spy. Popular Lib., 1965
Masterstroke. Popular Lib., 1966 (I Spy series, #2)
Mission Impossible. Popular Lib., 1967
Superkill. Popular Lib., 1967 (I Spy series, #3)
Wipeout. Popular Lib., 1967

TILLET, MRS. DOROTHY STOCKBRIDGE (M) (Pseudonym: John Stephen Strange)
All Men Are Liars. Doubleday, 1948 (English title: Come to Judgment. Collins, 1949)
The Bell in the Fog. Doubleday, Doran, 1936; Collins, 1937; Dolphin, 1960
Black Hawthorn. Doubleday, Doran, 1933 (English title: Chinese Jar Mystery. Collins, 1934)
Catch the Gold Ring. Doubleday, 1955
Chinese Jar Mystery; see Black Hawthorn
Clue of the Second Murder. Collins, 1929; Doubleday, Doran, 1929
Come to Judgment; see All Men Are Liars
Corpse and the Lady; see Silent Witnesses
Dead End. Collins, 1953
Deadly Beloved. Collins, 1952; Doubleday, 1952
Eye Witness. Doubleday, 1961; Collins, 1962
For the Hangman. Doubleday, Doran, 1934; Collins, 1935
Handful of Silver. Doubleday, Doran, 1941; Collins, 1955
Let the Dead Past. Doubleday, 1953
Look Your Last. Doubleday, Doran, 1943; Collins, 1949
Make My Bed Soon. Collins, 1948; Doubleday, 1948
The Man Who Killed Fortescue. Doubleday, Doran, 1928; Collins, 1929
Murder Game; see Murder on the Ten-Yard Line
Murder Gives a Lovely Light. Doubleday, Doran, 1941; Collins, 1942
Murder on the Ten-Yard Line. Doubleday, 1931; Grosset, 1933 (English title: Murder Game. Collins, 1933)
Night of Reckoning. Doubleday, 1958; Collins, 1959
Picture of the Victim. Collins, 1940; Doubleday, Doran, 1940
Reasonable Doubt. Collins, 1951; Doubleday, 1951
Rope Enough. Doubleday, Doran, 1938; Collins, 1939
Silent Witnesses. Doubleday, Doran, 1938 (English title: Corpse and the Lady. Collins, 1938)
The Strangler Fig. Doubleday, Doran, 1930; Collins, 1931
Uneasy Is the Grave; see Unquiet Grave
Unquiet Grave. Doubleday, 1949 (English title: Uneasy Is the Grave. Collins, 1950)

TILTON, ALICE, pseud; see TAYLOR, PHOEBE ATWOOD

TIMINS, DOUGLAS (M)
Double Quest. Methuen, 1930

TOBIAS, KATHERINE (S)
The Lady in the Lightning. Lancer, 1966

TODD, ROBERT HENRY (M)
Solver of Mysteries and Other Stories. Brampton, Charters, 1930

TOLLEMACHE, E. D. H.; see MUIR, P. P.

TOLMAN, HILDEGARDE; see TEILHET, HILDEGARDE TOLMAN

TOMERLIN, JOHN (S)
Return to Vikki. GM, 1959

TOMPKINS, PETER (S)
Spy in Rome. Avon

TOPOR, ROLAND (M)
The Tenant. Doubleday, 1966; Bantam, 1967

TORDAY, URSULA (M-S) (Pseudonyms: Paula Allardyce, Charity Blackstock, Lee Blackstock)
Adam and Evelina, by Paula Allardyce. Ward, Lock, 1958
All Men Are Murderers, by Lee Blackstock. Doubleday, 1958 (English title: Shadow of Murder. Hodder, 1959)
The Briar Patch; see Young Lucifer
Bitter Conquest, by Charity Blackstock. Hodder, 1959
Death, My Lover, by Paula Allardyce. Ward, Lock, 1959
Dewey Death, by Charity Blackstock. British Book Centre, 1958; Hodder, 1958

The English Wife, by Charity Blackstock. Coward, 1964; Macfadden, 1965
The Exorcism, by Charity Blackstock. Hodder, 1961 (U.S. title: A House Possessed. Lippincott, 1962; Ballantine, 1965)
The Factor's Wife, by Charity Blackstock. Hodder, 1964
Foggy, Foggy Dew. Hodder, 1958
The Gallant, by Charity Blackstock. Hodder, 1962; Ballantine, 1966
The Gentle Highwayman, by Paula Allardyce. Ward, Lock, 1962
A House Possessed; see The Exorcism
Johnny Danger, by Paula Allardyce. Ward, Lock, 1961
The Knock at Midnight, by Charity Blackstock. Coward, 1967; Hodder, 1967
Miss Fenny, by Charity Blackstock. Hodder, 1957
Mr. Christopoulous, by Charity Blackstock. Hodder, 1963; British Book Centre, 1964; Ballantine, 1965
Monkey on a Chain; see When the Sun Goes Down
No Peace for the Wicked, by Charity Blackstock. Nelson, 1937
Octavia, by Paula Allardyce. Hodder, 1965
Party in Dolly Creek; see The Widow
The Respectable Miss Parkington-Smith, by Charity Blackstock. Hodder, 1964
Shadow of Murder; see All Men Are Murderers
When the Sun Goes Down, by Charity Blackstock. Hodder, 1965 (U.S. title: Monkey on a Chain. Coward, 1965; Macfadden, 1966)
The Widow, by Charity Blackstock. Coward, 1967 (English title: Party in Dolly Creek)
Witch's Sabbath, by Paula Allardyce. Hodder, 1961; Macmillan, 1962
Woman in the Woods, by Lee Blackstock. Doubleday, 1958; Ballantine, 1965
Young Lucifer, by Charity Blackstock. Lippincott, 1960 (English title: The Briar Patch. Hodder, 1962)

TORGERSON, EDWIN DIAL (M)
The Murderer Returns. Smith, R. R., 1930; Lane, 1931

TORR, DOMINIC, pseud. (S)
Diplomatic Cover. Harcourt, 1966

TORREY, ROGER
42 Days for Murder. Hillman-Curl, 1938

TORREY, WARE (M) (Pseudonym: Lee Crosby)
Bridge House. Belmont, 1965
Doors to Death. Belmont, 1965
Midsummer's Night Murder. Dutton, 1942
Night Attack. Dutton, 1943
Terror by Night. Dutton, 1938
Too Many Doors. Dutton, 1941

TOUSSAINT-SAMAT, JEAN (D)
Dead Man at the Window. Lippincott, 1934
Ships Aflame. Lippincott, 1935
The Shoes That Walked Twice. Lippincott, 1933

TOVELL, RUTH MASSEY; see MASSEY, RUTH

TOWER, STELLA (M)
Dumb Vengeance. Hutchinson, 1933

TOWNE, STUART, pseud; see RAWSON, CLAYTON

TOWNSEND, PAUL (D)
Died o'Wednesday. Collins, 1959; Walker & Co., 1962
The Man at the End of the Rope. Collins, 1960; Dutton, 1960

TOYE, STANLEY PERCIVAL (D)
The Laughing Cat. Melrose, 1950
The Line Between. Melrose, 1948
Murder in the Lady Chapel. Melrose, 1944
Prelude to Peril. Melrose, 1946
Sinners in Clover. Melrose, 1945

TRACY, DONALD FISKE (D) (Pseudonym: Roger Fuller)
The Big Blackout. PB, 1960
Criss Cross. Vanguard, 1936
Deadly to Bed. PB, 1960
Eve of Judgment. PB, 1965
Fear in a Desert Town. PB, 1964
The Hated One. S & S, 1960; PB, 1964
How Sleeps the Beast. Mill, 1938
Naked She Died. PB, 1962
Ordeal. PB, 1965
Second Try, by Roger Fuller. Westminster, 1954
Who Killed Beau Sparrow? PB, 1964
Who Killed Madcap Millicent? PB, 1964

TRACY, LOUIS (M) (Pseudonym: Gordon Holmes)
The Albert Gate Affair. Ward, Lock, 1904; Fenno, 1914
The Arncliffe Puzzle, by Gordon Holmes. Clode, 1906; Laurie, 1906; Jarrolds, 1932
The Bartlette Mystery. Clode, 1919
The Black Cat. Clode, 1925; Hodder, 1925
By Force of Circumstances, by Gordon Holmes. Mills & Boon, 1910; Jarrolds, 1932

Dangerous Situation. Clode, 1932
Diana of the Moons. Hutchinson, 1930
The Feldishame Mystery, by Gordon Holmes. Amalgamated Press, 1911
The Gleave Mystery. Clode, 1926; Hodder, 1926
The House Around the Corner, by Gordon Holmes. Ward, Lock, 1914
The House of Peril; see One Wonderful Night
A King of Diamonds. Clode, 1904
The Lastingham Murder. Clode, 1929
The Late Tenant, by Gordon Holmes. Cassell, 1907; Jarrolds, 1932
The Law of the Talon. Clode, 1926; Hodder, 1926
The Manning-Burke Murder. Clode, 1930
A Mysterious Disappearance, by Gordon Holmes. Clode, 1927; Hodder, 1927
No Other Way, by Gordon Holmes. Clode, 1912; Ward, Lock, 1913
Number Seventeen. Clode, 1915; Hutchinson, 1930
One Wonderful Night. Clode, 1931 (Contains: The House of Peril and The Black Cat)
The Park Lane Mystery. Hodder, 1924
The Passing of Charles Lanson. Hodder, 1925; Grosset
The Pelham Affair. Clode, 1923; Grosset, 1924
The Pillar of Light. Clode, 1904; Ward, Lock, 1905 (Also published as: Wreck of the Chinook. Clode, 1930)
The Postmaster's Daughter. Cassell, 1917; Hutchinson, 1930
The Revellers. White, 1903
The Sandling Case. Clode, 1931
The Silent House. Nash, 1911; Grayson, 1932
The Stowmarket Mystery. Fenno, 1904
The Strange Case of Mortimer Fenley. Clode, 1919
The Strange Disappearance of Lady Delia. Pearson, 1901
The Token. Clode, 1924; Hodder, 1924
What Would You Have Done? Hodder, 1930
Wheel O' Fortune. Ward, Lock, 1908
The Women in the Case. Clode, 1928; Grosset
The Wreck of the Chinook; see The Pillar of Light

TRACY, VIRGINIA (M)
Moment After. Doubleday, Doran, 1930; Mathews, 1932
The Personal Appearance of a Lioness. Lippincott, 1937
Persons Unknown. Century, 1914

TRAIN, ARTHUR C. (D)
The Adventures of Ephraim Tutt. Scribner, 1937
The Blind Goddess. Scribner, 1926
By Advice of Counsel. Scribner, 1921
The Confessions of Artemas Quibble. Scribner, 1911
The Hermit of Turkey Hollow. Scribner, 1921
McAllister and His Double. Scribner, 1905
Manhattan Murder. Scribner, 1936
Mr. Tutt Comes Home. Scribner, 1941
Mr. Tutt Finds a Way. Scribner, 1945
Mr. Tutt Takes the Stand. Scribner, 1936
Mr. Tutt's Case Book. Scribner, 1936
Old Man Tutt. Scribner, 1938
Page Mr. Tutt. Scribner, 1926
Princess Pro Tem. Scribner, 1932
Tut, Tut! Mr. Tutt. Scribner, 1934
Tutt and Mr. Tutt. Scribner, 1921
Tutt for Tutt. Scribner, 1934
Yankee Lawyer-Autobiography of Ephraim Tutt. Scribner, 1943

TRALINS, ROBERT (D-S)
The Chic Chick Spy. Belmont, 1966
Dragnet '67. Popular Lib., 1967
Miss from S.I.S. Belmont, 1966
Ring-a-Ding UFO's. Belmont, 1967

TRANTER, NIGEL
The Enduring Flame. Hodder, 1957
Man Behind the Curtain. Hodder, 1959
Rio D'Oro. Ward, Lock, 1955
Stone. Hodder, 1958; Putnam, 1959

TRASK, KEITH (D)
Captain Trask Investigates. Butterworth, T., 1932
Dead Men Do Tell. Farrar & Rinehart, 1931
Murder Incidental. Farrar & Rinehart, 1931

TRASK, MERRILL, pseud; see BRAHAM, HAL

TRAUBEL, HELEN (D)
The Metropolitan Opera Murders. S & S, 1951; Avon, 1964

TRAVER, ROBERT, pseud; see VOELKER, JOHN DONALDSON

TRAVERS, HUGH, pseud; see MILLS, HUGH TRAVERS

TRAVERS, STEPHEN, pseud; see RADCLIFFE, GARNETT

TRAVIS, GERRY, pseud; see TRIMBLE, LOUIS

TRAVIS, GRETCHEN (M)
She Fell Among Thieves. Doubleday, 1963

TREASE, GEOFFREY (S)
A Thousand for Sicily. Vanguard, 1966

TREAT, LAWRENCE (Name originally: Lawrence Arthur Goldstone) (D)
B as in Banshee. Duell, 1940
The Big Shot. Harper, 1951; Collier, 1961; Bantam
D as in Dead. Duell, 1941
F as in Flight. Morrow, 1948; Boardman, T. V., 1949
H as in Hangman. Duell, 1942
H as in Hunted. Books, 1945; Duell, 1946; Boardman, T. V., 1950
Lady, Drop Dead. Abelard, 1961
The Leather Man. Duell, 1944; Rich, 1947
Murder in Mind. Dutton, 1967
O as in Omen. Dutton, 1943
Over the Edge. Morrow, 1949; Boardman, T. V., 1958
Step into Quicksand. Morrow, 1949; Boardman, T. V., 1959
T as in Trapped. Morrow, 1947
Trial and Terror. Morrow, 1949; Boardman, T. V., 1958
V as in Victim. Duell, 1945; Rich, 1950; Collier, 1962
Venus Unarmed. Doubleday, 1961
Weep for a Wanton. Ace, 1957; Boardman, T. V., 1957

TREE, GREGORY, pseud. (M)
The Case Against Butterfly. Scribner, 1951
The Case Against Myself. Scribner, 1950; Gollancz, 1951; Transworld, 1953
Shroud for Grandmama. Gollancz, 1951; Transworld, 1953
So Young to Die. Gollancz, 1953; Scribner, 1953

TREFUS, VICTOR, pseud; see FÜRST, VICTOR

TREGASKIS, RICHARD (S)
China Bomb. Washburn, 1967

TREMAINE, F. ORLIN (M)
I'll Kill You Often. 1944

TRENCH, JOHN (S)
Beyond the Atlas. Macmillan, 1963
Dishonored Bones. Macmillan, 1955
Docken Dead. MacDonald & Co., 1953; Macmillan, 1954; Penguin
What Rough Beast. MacDonald & Co., 1957; Macmillan, 1957

TRENT, PAUL (M)
The Craven Mystery. Ward, Lock, 1930

TREVOR, A. C., pseud; see PULSFORD, NORMAN GEORGE

TREVOR, ELLESTON (Name originally: Trevor Dudley-Smith) (M-S) (Pseudonyms: Mansell Black, Trevor Burgess, Adam Hall, Simon Rattray, Warwick Scott, Caesar Smith)
The Berlin Memorandum, by Adam Hall. Collins, 1965 (U.S. title: The Quiller Memorandum. S & S, 1965; Pyramid, 1966)
The Big Pickup. Macmillan, 1955
The Billboard Madonna. Heinemann, 1960; Morrow, 1961
Bishop in Check, by Simon Rattray. Boardman, T. V., 1953; Mill, 1961
A Blaze of Roses. Boardman, T. V., 1951; Harper, 1952
The Burning Shore. Heinemann, 1961; Harper, 1962 (Also published as: The Pasang Run. Avon, 1964)
Chorus of Echoes. Boardman, T. V., 1950
Cockpit; see Image in the Dust
Dead Circuit, by Simon Rattray. Boardman, T. V., 1955
Dead on Course, by Mansell Black. Hodder, 1951
Dead Silence, by Simon Rattray. Boardman, T. V., 1954
Doomsday; see The Doomsday Story
The Doomsday Story, by Warwick Scott. Davies, 1952 (U.S. title: Doomsday. Lion, 1953)
Flight of the Phoenix. Harper & Row, 1964; Heinemann, 1964
The Freebooters. Doubleday, 1967
Gale Force. Heinemann, 1956; Macmillan, 1957; Ballantine, 1965
Heatwave, by Caesar Smith. Wingate, 1957; Ballantine, 1958
Image in the Dust, by Warwick Scott. Davies, 1951 (U.S. title: Cockpit. Lion, 1953)
The Killing Ground. Heinemann, 1956; Macmillan, 1957; Ballantine, 1965
Knight Sinister, by Simon Rattray. Boardman, T. V., 1951
The Naked Canvas, by Warwick Scott. Davies, 1954; Popular Lib., 1955
The Ninth Directive, by Adam Hall. S & S, 1967
The Pasang Run; see The Burning Shore
The Passion and the Pity. Heinemann, 1953
The Pillars of Midnight. Heinemann, 1957; Morrow, 1959; Ballantine, 1963
Queen in Danger, by Simon Rattray. Boardman, T. V., 1952
The Quiller Memorandum; see The Berlin Memorandum
Redfern's Miracle. Boardman, T. V., 1951
The Shoot. Doubleday, 1966; Avon, 1967
Sinister Cargo, by Mansell Black. Hodder, 1952

A Spy at Monk's Court, by Trevor Burgess. Hutchinson, 1949
Squadron Airborne. Heinemann, 1956; Macmillan, 1956
Tiger Street. Boardman, T. V., 1951; Lion, 1953
The V.I.P. Heinemann, 1959; Morrow, 1960
The Volcanoes of San Domingo, by Adam Hall. S & S, 1964; Ballantine, 1965

TREVOR, GLEN, pseud; see HILTON, JAMES

TREVOR, JAMES (S)
Savage Game. Award, 1967

TREVOR, RALPH, pseud; see WILMOT, JAMES REGINALD

TREYNOR, BLAIR (D)
If You Should Ever Need Me.
Silver Doll. Holt, H., 1952
Widow's Pique. Mill, 1956; Ward, Lock, 1958

TRIEM, PAUL ELLSWORTH (M) (Pseudonym: Paul Ellsworth)
Alias John Doe. Chelsea House, 1930; Hamilton, H., 1931

TRIMBLE, LOUIS (D) (Pseudonyms: Stuart Brock, Gerry Travis)
The Big Bite, by Gerry Travis. Mystery House, 1951; Bouregy, 1957
Cargo for the Styx. Ace, 1959
Case of the Blank Cartridge. Phoenix, 1949
A Corpse Without a Country. Ace
Date for Murder. Phoenix, 1942
The Dead and the Deadly. Ace, 1963
Death Is My Lover, by Stuart Brock. Mill, 1948
Design for Dying. Phoenix, 1945
Duchess of Skid Row. Ace, 1960
Fit to Kill. Phoenix, 1941
Girl on a Slay Ride. Avon, 1960
Give Up the Body. Superior Pub., 1946
Just Around the Coroner, by Stuart Brock. Mill, 1948
Killer's Choice, by Stuart Brock. Graphic, 1956
Love Me and Die. Ace, 1961
A Lovely Mask for Murder, by Gerry Travis. Bouregy, 1956; Mystery House, 1956
Murder Trouble. Phoenix, 1945
Orbit Deferred. Ace, 1959
The Smell of Trouble. Ace, 1958
Surfside Caper. Ace, 1961
The Tide Can't Wait. Mystery House, 1957
Till Death Do Us Part. Ace
You Can't Kill a Corpse. Phoenix, 1946
The Virgin Victim. Mercury Mystery Book, 1956

TRINIAN, JOHN (M)
House of Evil. Pyramid, 1962
Scandal on the Sand. GM, 1964
Scratch a Thief. Ace, 1961

TRIPP, MILES (S) (Pseudonym: Michael Brett)
Diecast. Macmillan, 1963; GM, 1964
An Ear for Murder. PB, 1967
The Fifth Point of the Compass. Macmillan, 1967
The Fight of the Stiff. PB, 1967
Kill Him Quickly, It's Raining. PB, 1967
Kilo Forty. Macmillan, 1963; Holt, 1964; Avon, 1966
A Plague of Dragons. Barker, 1965
A Quartet of Three. Macmillan, 1965
The Skin Dealer. Macmillan, 1964; Holt, 1965
Turn Blue, You Murderers. PB, 1967
We the Killers. PB, 1967

TROTT, NICHOLAS (M)
Monkey Boat. Macmillan, 1932

TROTTA, GERALDINE (GERI) (D)
Dead as Diamonds. Boardman, T. V., 1956
Veronica Died Monday. Dodd, 1952

TROY, SIMON, pseud; see WARRINER, THURMAN

TRUAX, RHODA, pseud; see ALDRICH, RHODA TRUAX

TRUESDELL, JUNE (D)
Be Still My Love. Dodd, 1947
Burden of Proof. Boardman, T. V., 1951
The Morgue the Merrier. Dodd, 1945

TRUSS, SELDON (Full name: Leslie Seldon Truss) (D-M) (Pseudonym: George Selmark)
Always Ask a Policeman. Doubleday, 1952; Hodder, 1953
The Barberton Intrigue. Hodder, 1956
The Bride That Got Away, by George Selmark. Doubleday, 1967
The Coroner Presides. Minton, 1932 (English title: Mr. Coroner Presides. Harrap, 1932)
The Crooks' Shepherd. Lothrop, 1936
The Daughters of Belial. Jarrolds, 1934
Deadline for a Diplomat. Merit Books, 1954
Death of No Lady. Doubleday, 1952
The Disappearance of Julie Hintz. Hodder, 1940
The Doctor Was a Dame. Doubleday, 1953
Draw the Blinds. Hodder, 1936
Escort to Danger. Hodder, 1937

The Eyes at the Window, by George Selmark. Doubleday, 1966; Hale, R., 1966
False Face. Doubleday, 1955
Footsteps Behind Them. Hodder, 1937
Foreign Bodies. Hodder, 1938
Gallows Bait. Butterworth, T., 1934
Hidden Men. Hodder, 1959
High Wall; see The Other Side of the Wall
The Hunterstone Outrage. Mystery League, 1931
In Secret Places. Hodder, 1958; Doubleday, 1959
Ladies Always Talk. Hodder, 1950
The Living Alibi. Coward, 1929
The Long Night. Hodder, 1956
Man to Match the Hour. Doubleday, 1959
The Man Who Played Patience. Hodder, 1937
Man Without Pity; see Number Naught
Mr. Coroner Presides; see The Coroner Presides
Murder in Silence, by George Selmark. Doubleday, Doran, 1939
Murder Paves the Way. Hodder, 1937
Never Fight a Lady. Doubleday, 1950
Number Naught. Dodd, 1930 (English title: Man Without Pity. Butterworth, T., 1930)
One Man's Death; see One Man's Enemies
One Man's Enemies. Doubleday, 1960 (English title: One Man's Death. Hale, R., 1960)
The Other Side of the Wall. Doubleday, 1954 (English title: High Wall. Hodder, 1955)
Put Out the Light. Hodder, 1954
Rooksmiths. Hodder, 1936
Seven Year's Dead. Doubleday, 1961
The Stolen Millionaire. Butterworth, T., 1929; Coward, 1929
A Store of Wrath. Doubleday, 1956
Sweeter for His Going. Hodder, 1950
Technique for Treachery. Doubleday, 1963; Hale, R., 1963
They Came by Night. Jarrolds, 1934
A Time to Hate. Doubleday, 1962
The Truth About Claire Veryan. Doubleday, 1957; Hodder, 1957
Turmoil at Brede. Mystery League, 1931; Harrap, 1932
Walk a Crooked Mile. Hale, R., 1964
Where's Mr. Chumley? Doubleday, 1949
Why Slug a Postman? Doubleday, 1950

TUCKER, ARTHUR WILSON (S)
The Chinese Doll. Rinehart, 1946; Cassell, 1948
The Dove. Rinehart, 1948; Cassell, 1950
Hired Target. Ace, 1957
Last Stop. Doubleday, 1963
The Long Loud Silence. Rinehart, 1952; Bodley Head, 1953
A Man in My Grave. Rinehart, 1956; MacDonald & Co., 1958
A Procession of the Damned. Doubleday, 1956; Hale, R., 1967
Red Herring. Rinehart, 1951; Cassell, 1953
The Stalking Man. Rinehart, 1949; Cassell, 1950
To Keep or Kill. Rinehart, 1947; Cassell, 1950
The Warlock. Doubleday, 1967

TUCKER, LAEL; see WERTENBAKER, LAEL TUCKER

TUCKER, WILSON; see TUCKER, ARTHUR WILSON

TUFFNELL, EVERETT SPENCE (M)
Brass Knuckle Shoes. Lovewell, 1955
The Deadly Twist. Wind & Frank, 1963
Flying Fish in Air. Lovewell, 1954
Martinis Without Olives. Ross, 1959
Through a Fine-Toothed Comb Clearly. Wind & Frank, 1955 (Mystery in verse)

TURNBULL, DORA AMY DILLON (D)
(Pseudonym: Patricia Wentworth)
Account Rendered. Lippincott, 1940 (English title: Who Pays the Piper? Hodder, 1940)
The Alington Inheritance. Lippincott, 1958; Pyramid, 1966
The Amazing Chance. Hodder, 1926; Lippincott, 1927
Anna Belinda. Hodder, 1927
Anna, Where Are You? Lippincott, 1951; Hodder, 1953 (Also published as: Death at Deep End. Pyramid, 1963)
The Annam Jewel. Melrose, 1924; Small, 1925; Grosset
The Astonishing Adventures of Jane Smith. Melrose, 1923; Small, 1924
Beggar's Choice. Hodder, 1930; Lippincott, 1931
The Benevent Treasure. Lippincott, 1954; Pyramid, 1966
The Black Cabinet. Hodder, 1925; Small, 1926; Grosset
The Blind Side. Lippincott, 1931; Popular Lib.
Blindfold. Hodder, 1935
The Brading Collection. Lippincott, 1950; Hodder, 1952; Pyramid, 1967
The Case Is Closed. Hodder, 1937; Lippincott, 1937
The Case of William Smith. Lippincott, 1948; Hodder, 1950
The Catharine Wheel. Lippincott, 1949; Pyramid, 1967

The Chinese Shawl. Hodder, 1943; Lippincott, 1943; Pyramid, 1966
The Clock Strikes Twelve. Lippincott, 1944; Hodder, 1945; Popular Lib.
The Coldstone. Hodder, 1930
Danger Calling. Hodder, 1931
Danger Point; see In the Balance
Dead or Alive. Hodder, 1936; Lippincott, 1936
Death at Deep End; see Anna, Where Are You?
Devil-in-the-Dark. Hodder, 1934
Devil's Wind. Melrose, 1912
The Dover House Mystery. Hodder, 1925; Small, 1926
Down Under. Hodder, 1937; Lippincott, 1937
The Eternity Ring. Lippincott, 1948; Hodder, 1950
Fear by Night. Hodder, 1934; Lippincott, 1934
The Fingerprint. Lippincott, 1956; Hodder, 1959; Pyramid, 1963
The Fire Within. Melrose, 1913
Fool Errant. Hodder, 1929; Lippincott, 1929
The Gazebo. Lippincott, 1955 (Also published as: The Summerhouse. Pyramid, 1967; Penguin)
Grey Mask. Hodder, 1928
Hole and Corner. Hodder, 1936
Hue and Cry. Hodder, 1927; Lippincott, 1927; Grosset
In the Balance. Lippincott, 1941 (English title: Danger Point. Hodder, 1942)
The Ivory Dagger. Lippincott, 1951; Hodder, 1953; Pyramid, 1965
The Key. Hodder, 1946
Kingdom Lost. Hodder, 1931
Ladies' Bane. Lippincott, 1952; Hodder, 1954
The Latter End. Lippincott, 1947; Hodder, 1949
The Listening Eye. Lippincott, 1955
Little More Than Kin. Melrose, 1911
Lonesome Road. Hodder, 1939; Lippincott, 1939
Marriage Under the Terror. Melrose, 1910
Miss Silver Comes to Stay. Lippincott, 1949; Hodder, 1951
Miss Silver Deals with Death. Lippincott, 1943 (English title: Miss Silver Intervenes. Hodder, 1944)
Miss Silver Intervenes; see Miss Silver Deals with Death
Mr. Zero. Hodder, 1938; Lippincott, 1938
Nothing Ventured. Cassell, 1932
Out of the Past. Lippincott, 1953; Hodder, 1955
Pilgrim's Rest. Lippincott, 1946; Hodder, 1948
Poison in the Pen. Lippincott, 1955; Pyramid, 1964
Pursuit of a Parcel. Hodder, 1942; Lippincott, 1942; Popular Lib.
Queen Anne Is Dead. Melrose, 1915
Red Danger. Cassell, 1932
The Red Lacquer Case. Melrose, 1924; Small, 1924; Grosset
Red Shadow. Lippincott, 1932
Red Stefan. Hodder, 1935
Rolling Stone. Hodder, 1940; Lippincott, 1940
Run! Hodder, 1938; Lippincott, 1938
Seven Green Stones. Cassell, 1933
She Came Back. Lippincott, 1945; Pyramid, 1966 (English title: The Traveller Returns. Hodder, 1948)
Silence in Court. Hodder, 1947; Pyramid, 1965
The Silent Pool. Lippincott, 1954; Pyramid, 1965
Simon Heriot. Melrose, 1914
The Spotlight; see Wicked Uncle
The Summerhouse; see The Gazebo
Through the Wall. Lippincott, 1950; Hodder, 1952
The Traveller Returns; see She Came Back
Unlawful Occasions; see Weekend with Death
The Vanishing Point. Lippincott, 1953; Hodder, 1955; Penguin
Walk with Care. Lippincott, 1933; Cassell, 1943
Watersplash. Lippincott, 1952; Hodder, 1953
Weekend with Death. Lippincott, 1941 (English title: Unlawful Occasions. Hodder, 1941)
Who Pays the Piper?; see Account Rendered
Wicked Uncle. Lippincott, 1947 (English title: The Spotlight. Hodder, 1949)
Will o' the Wisp. Hodder, 1928

TURNBULL, MARGARET (M)
The Coast Road Murder. Lippincott, 1934
In the Bride's Mirror. Lippincott, 1934
Madame Judas. Jenkins, 1926; Lippincott, 1926
The Return of Jenny Weaver. Lippincott, 1932; Ward, Lock, 1932

TURNER, BILL; see TURNER, WILLIAM PRICE

TURNER, JAMES ERNEST (M)
The Crimson Moth. Cassell, 1962
The Crystal Wave. Cassell, 1957
Dark Index. Cassell, 1959
A Death by the Sea. Cassell, 1955
Deeper Malady. Cassell, 1959
Frontiers of Death. Cassell, 1957; British Book Centre, 1959
The Long Avenues. Cassell, 1964
Mass of Death. Fortune, 1937
Murder at Landrec Hall. Cassell, 1954

Nettle Shade. Cassell, 1963
The Slate Landscape. Cassell, 1964

TURNER, JOHN VICTOR (D) (Pseudonyms: Nicholas Brady, David Hume)
Amos Petrie's Puzzle. Bles, 1933
Below the Belt. Collins, 1934
Below the Clock. Collins, 1936
Bring 'Em Back Dead, by David Hume. Appleton-Century, 1936; Collins, 1939
Bullets Bite Deep. Putnam, 1932
Call in the Yard. Collins, 1935
Carnival Murder; see Fair Murder
Cemetery First Stop! Collins, 1937
Come Back for the Body, by David Hume. Collins, 1945
Corpses Never Argue, by David Hume. Collins, 1938
Coupons for Death, by Nicholas Brady. Hale, R., 1945
Crime Combine. Collins, 1936
Crime Unlimited. Collins, 1933; McBride, 1933
Dangerous Mr. Dell. Appleton-Century, 1935; Collins, 1935
Death Before Honour, by David Hume. Collins, 1939
Death Must Have Laughed. Putnam, 1932 (U.S. title: First Round Murder. Holt, H., 1932)
Dishonour Among Thieves, by David Hume. Collins, 1943
Ebenezer Investigates, by Nicholas Brady. Bles, 1934
Fair Murder, by Nicholas Brady. Bles, 1933 (U.S. title: Carnival Murder. Holt, H., 1933)
First Round Murder; see Death Must Have Laughed
Foursquare Murder. McBride, 1933 (Also published as: Murders Form Fours. Putnam, 1933)
Gaol Gates Are Open. Collins, 1935 (U.S. title: Jail Gates Are Open. Appleton-Century, 1935)
Get Out the Cuffs, by David Hume. Collins, 1943
Heading for a Wreath, by David Hume. Collins, 1946
Heads You Live, by David Hume. Collins, 1939
Homicide Haven. Collins, 1935; Appleton-Century, 1936
The House of Strange Guests. Bles, 1932; Holt, H., 1932
Invitation to the Grave, by David Hume. Collins, 1940
Jail Gates Are Open; see Gaol Gates Are Open
Make Way for the Mourners, by David Hume. Collins, 1939
Meet the Dragon. Collins, 1936
Murder—Nine and Out. Bles, 1934
Murders Form Fours; see Foursquare Murder
Never Say Live, by David Hume. Collins, 1942
Requiem for Rogues, by David Hume. Collins, 1942
They Called Him Death. Collins, 1934; Appleton-Century, 1935
They Never Came Back, by David Hume. Collins, 1945
Toast to a Corpse, by David Hume. Collins, 1944
Too Dangerous to Live. Collins, 1934
You'll Catch Your Death, by David Hume. Collins, 1940
Weekend Murders. Bles, 1933
Who Spoke Last? Holt, H., 1933

TURNER, ROBERT (M)
The Girl in the Cop's Pocket. Ace, 1956
The Night Is for Screaming. Pyramid, 1960
The Tobacco Auction Murder. Ace, 1954

TURNER, RUSSELL (M)
The Short Night. Hillman-Curl, 1957

TURNER, WILLIAM (BILL) PRICE (D)
Bound to Die. Constable, 1967; Walker & Co., 1967

TURNEY, CATHERINE (S)
The Other One. Holt, H., 1952

TURNGREN, ANNETTE (M) (Pseudonym: A. T. Hopkins)
Have a Lovely Funeral. Rinehart, 1954

TUTTLE, WILBUR C. (D)
The Mystery of the JHC Ranch. Houghton, 1932
The Mystery of the Red Triangle. Collins, 1929; Houghton, 1942
The Silver Bar Mystery. Collins, 1932; Houghton, 1933
Thicker Than Water. Houghton, 1927

TWAIN, MARK, pseud; see CLEMENS, SAMUEL L.

TWEEDALE, MRS. VIOLET CHAMBERS (M)
The Beautiful Mrs. Davenant. Stokes, 1920

TYLER, CHARLES W. (M)
Blue Jean Billy. Chelsea House, 1926

TYLER, ESTHER (D)
The Family Skeleton. Bell, G., 1937
Murder on the Bluff. S & S, 1936

TYRE, NEDRA (D)
Death of an Intruder. Knopf, 1953; Collins, 1954

Everyone Suspect. Macmillan, 1964
Hall of Death. S & S, 1960 (Also published as: Reformatory Girls. Ace, 1962)
Journey to Nowhere. Collins, 1954; Knopf, 1954
Mouse in Eternity. Knopf, 1952
Red Wine First. S & S, 1947
Reformatory Girls; see Hall of Death

TYRELL, PATRICK (M)
Robber King. Ogilvie

TYRER, WALTER (M)
The Affair of the Hollywood Contract. Amalgamated Press, 1949
The Case Against Dr. Ripon. Amalgamated Press, 1948
Daughter of the Scafford. Amalgamated Press, 1935
Ellen Morgan. Columbine, 1939
The Hangman's Daughter. Amalgamated Press, 1936; Columbine, 1939
Jane the Ripper. Columbine, 1939
The Motor Coach Mystery. Amalgamated Press, 1948
Myra Grey—Medium. Amalgamated Press, 1949
The Mystery of the Woman Overboard. Amalgamated Press, 1948
Notorious Marie Deeming. Amalgamated Press, 1949
She Sent Her Mother to the Scaffold. Amalgamated Press, 1936
Such Friends Are Dangerous. Staples Press, 1954
Trunk Crime Number Three. Columbine, 1939

TYRRELL, ROSS (D)
Pathway of Adventure. Knopf, 1920

TYSON, JOHN AUBREY (M)
The Barge of Haunted Lives. Macmillan, 1923
The Rhododendron Man. Dutton, 1930; Mills & Boon, 1931
The Scarlet Tanager. Macmillan, 1922

UHNAK, DOROTHY (D)
Rogoff. S & S, 1967

ULLIN, ROBERT (D)
Besides the Wench Is Dead. Doubleday, Doran, 1935

ULLMAN, ALLAN (S)
The Naked Spur, with Rolfe Bloom. Random, 1953; Corgi, 1955
Night Man, with Lucille Fletcher. Gollancz, 1951; Random, 1951
Sorry, Wrong Number, with Lucille Fletcher. Random, 1948; Gollancz, 1952; Macfadden, 1966

ULLMAN, JAMES MICHAEL (M)
Goodnight, Irene. S & S, 1965; PB, 1967
The Neon Hystack. S & S, 1963; Cassell, 1964; PB, 1965
The Venus Trap. S & S, 1966

ULLMAN, RICHARD (M)
A Taste of Poison. Laurie, 1954

ULLYET, KENNETH (M)
Crime Out of Hand. Joseph, M., 1963

UNDERWOOD, MICHAEL, pseud; see EVELYN, JOHN MICHAEL

UNEKIS, RICHARD (S)
The Chase. Gollancz, 1963; Walker & Co., 1963 (Also published as: Pursuit. Signet)

UNTERMEYER, WALTER, JR. (S)
Evil Roots. Lion, 1954

UPFIELD, ARTHUR WILLIAM (D)
An Author Bites the Dust. Angus, 1948; Doubleday, 1948
The Bachelors of Broken Hill. Doubleday, 1950; Heinemann, 1958
The Barakee Mystery. Hutchinson, 1929
Battling Prophet. Heinemann, 1956
The Beach of Atonement. Hutchinson, 1930
The Body at Madman's Bend. Doubleday, 1963
The Bone Is Pointed. Angus, 1938; Hamilton, 1939; Doubleday, 1947
Bony and the Black Virgin. Heinemann, 1959; Collier, 1965
Bony and the Kelly Gang. Heinemann, 1960 (U.S. title: Valley of Smugglers. Doubleday, 1960)
Bony and the Mouse. Heinemann, 1959 (U.S. title: Journey to the Hangman. Doubleday, 1959)
Bony and the White Savage. Heinemann, 1961 (U.S. title: The White Savage. Doubleday, 1961)
Bony Buys a Woman. Doubleday, 1957; Heinemann, 1957 (Also published as: The Bushman Who Came Back. Berkley Pub., 1963)
The Bushman Who Came Back; see Bony Buys a Woman
The Bushranger of the Skies. Angus, 1940; London House, 1963
Cake in the Hatbox. Heinemann, 1955 (U.S. title: Sinister Stones. Doubleday, 1954; Berkley Pub., 1964)
Death of a Lake. Doubleday, 1954; Heinemann, 1954; Berkley Pub., 1963
Death of a Swagman. Doubleday, 1945; Aldor, F., 1946; Angus, 1947; British Book Centre, 1962

The Devil's Steps. Doubleday, 1946; Aldor, F., 1948
Gripped by Drought. Hutchinson, 1932
The House of Cain. Hutchinson, 1928; Dorrance, 1929
Journey to the Hangman; see Bony and the Mouse
The Lure of the Bush. Doubleday, 1965
Man of Two Tribes. Doubleday, 1956; Heinemann, 1956
Mr. Jelly's Business. Angus, 1937; Hamilton, 1938; Doubleday, Doran, 1943; London House, 1964 (Also published as: Murder Down Under. Penguin, 1951)
The Mountains Have a Secret. Doubleday, 1948; Heinemann, 1952
Murder Down Under; see Mr. Jelly's Business
Murder Must Wait. Doubleday, 1953; Heinemann, 1953; Berkley Pub., 1963
The Mystery of Swordfish Reef. Angus, 1939; Doubleday, Doran, 1943; Heinemann, 1960
The New Shoe. Doubleday, 1951; Heinemann, 1952; Berkley Pub., 1964
No Footprints in the Bush. Doubleday, Doran, 1944; Penguin, 1949
A Royal Abduction. Hutchinson, 1932
The Sands of Windee. Hutchinson, 1939; British Book Centre, 1958
Sinister Stones; see Cake in the Hatbox
Valley of Smugglers; see Bony and the Kelly Gang
Venom House. Doubleday, 1952; Heinemann, 1953; Berkley Pub., 1963
The White Savage; see Bony and the White Savage
The Widows of Broome. Doubleday, 1950; Heinemann, 1951
The Will of the Tribe. Doubleday, 1962; Heinemann, 1962; Berkley Pub., 1964
The Winds of Evil. Angus, 1937; Hamilton, 1939; British Book Centre, 1961; Berkley Pub., 1964
The Winged Mystery. Hamilton, 1937
Wings Above the Claypan; see Wings Above the Diamantina
Wings Above the Diamantina. Angus, 1936; Penguin, 1965 (U.S. title: Wings Above the Claypan. Doubleday, Doran, 1943)

UPWARD, ALLEN (M)
The Club of Masks. Lippincott, 1926 (English title: The Domino Club. Faber, 1926)
The Domino Club; see The Club of Masks
The House of Sin. Faber, 1926; Lippincott, 1927
The Venetian Key. Faber, 1927; Lippincott, 1927

URELL, WILLIAM FRANCIS (D) (Pseudonym: William Francis)
Bury Me Not. Morrow, 1943; Boardman, T. V., 1950; McClelland, 1950
The Corrupters. Lion, 1953
Kill or Cure. McClelland, 1942; Morrow, 1942; Boardman, T. V., 1951
Rough on Rats. McClelland, 1942; Morrow, 1942

URIS, LEON (S)
Topaz. McGraw, 1967

URNER, NATHAN D. (D)
Link by Link; or, The Chain of Evidence. Laird & Lee, 1888

URQUHART, MacGREGOR (M)
The Bitter Lemon Mob. Boardman, T. V., 1966
The Bluebottle. Boardman, T. V., 1964
Contact Lens. Boardman, T. V., 1964
Dig the Missing. Boardman, T. V., 1963
Frail on the North Circular. Boardman, T. V., 1962
Girl on the Waterfront. Boardman, T. V., 1962
The Grey Man. Boardman, T. V., 1965
The Open Mouth. Boardman, T. V., 1967

USHER, FRANK HUGH (D) (Pseudonyms: Charles Franklin, Frank Lester)
The Bamboo Girl, by Frank Lester. Hale, R., 1961
The Bath of Acid, by Charles Franklin. Hale, R., 1962
The Body in Velvet, by Charles Franklin. Hale, R., 1963
Breathe No More, by Charles Franklin. Hale, R., 1959
Cocktails with a Stranger, by Charles Franklin. Collins, 1947
The Corpse Wore Rubies, by Frank Lester. Hale, R., 1958
The Dangerous One, by Charles Franklin. Hale, R., 1964
Darling Murderess, by Charles Franklin. Hale, R., 1957
Death and the South Wind, by Frank Lester. Hale, R., 1958
Death in Error. Hale, R., 1959
Death in Sunlight, by Frank Lester. Hale, R., 1965
Death in the East, by Charles Franklin. Hale, R., 1967
Death Is Waiting. Long, 1958
Death of a Frightened Traveler, by Frank Lester. Hale, R., 1959
Death of a Pale Man, by Frank Lester. Hale, R., 1960
Death on My Shoulder, by Charles Franklin. Hale, R., 1958
Die, My Darling. Hale, R., 1960

Escape to Death, by Charles Franklin. Collins, 1951
Exit Without Permit, by Charles Franklin. Collins, 1946
Face the Music, by Charles Franklin. Hale, R., 1957
The Faceless Stranger. Hale, R., 1961
Fall into My Grave. Hale, R., 1962
Fear Runs Softly, by Charles Franklin. Hale, R., 1961
Finch Takes to Crime, by Frank Lester. Hale, R., 1963
First to Kill. Long, 1959
Fly Me a Killer, by Frank Lester. Long, 1962
The Fortieth Victim, by Charles Franklin. Hale, R., 1963
Gallows for a Fool, by Charles Franklin. Collins, 1952
Ghost of a Chance. Long, 1956
The Golden Murder, by Frank Lester. Hale, R., 1959
Guilt for Innocence, by Charles Franklin. Hale, R., 1960
Guilty You Must Be, by Charles Franklin. Hale, R., 1959
Handful of Sinners, by Charles Franklin. Hale, R., 1960
Hide My Body, by Frank Lester. Hale, R., 1961
Lead Me to the Gallows, by Frank Lester. Hale, R., 1962
The Lonely Cage. Long, 1956
Maid for Murder, by Charles Franklin. Collins, 1955
The Man from Moscow. Hale, R., 1965
The Mark of Kane, by Charles Franklin. Collins, 1949
Murder Before Dinner, by Charles Franklin. Hale, R., 1963
No Other Victim, by Charles Franklin. Collins, 1952
On the Day of the Shooting. Hale, R., 1965
One Night to Kill, by Charles Franklin. Collins, 1950
Out of Time, by Charles Franklin. Collins, 1955
Perchance to Kill, by Charles Franklin. Collins, 1954
Play with Death, by Charles Franklin. Collins, 1953
Portrait of Fear. Long, 1957
The Price of Death. Long, 1957
Rope of Sand, by Charles Franklin. Collins, 1948
She'll Love You Dead, by Charles Franklin. Collins, 1950
Shot in the Dark. Hale, R., 1961
Stairway to Murder. Hale, R., 1964
Stop That Man, by Charles Franklin. Collins, 1954
Storm in an Inkpot, by Charles Franklin. Collins, 1949
The Stranger Came Back, by Charles Franklin. Collins, 1953
The Trembling Thread, by Charles Franklin. Collins, 1955
Who Killed Rosa Gray? Hale, R., 1962
The Woman in the Case. Hale, R.

USHER, GRAY (D)
Death Goes Caving. Long, 1959
Death in the Bag. Long, 1960
Death in the Straw. Long, 1955
Death Sped the Plough. Long, 1956
Death Takes a Teacher. Long, 1957
Triggerman. Scion, 1951

USHER, JACK (D)
Brothers and Sisters Have I None. Mill, 1958; Heinemann, 1960 (Also published as: Reason for Murder. PB, 1960)
The Fix. Mill, 1959
The Girl in the White Mercedes. Heinemann, 1960
Reason for Murder; see Brothers and Sisters Have I None

USHER, WILFRED (M)
Creeping Shadows. Paul, S., 1929
The Great Hold-up Mystery. Paul, S., 1928
The Mystery of the Seven. Paul, S., 1930

VACHELL, H. A.; see MARSHALL, A.

VACZEK, LOUIS C. (M) (Pseudonym: Peter Hardin)
The Frightened Dove. Scribner, 1950; Heinemann, 1952
The Golden Calf. Sloane, 1956
The Hidden Grave. Harper, 1953; Muller, 1956

VAHEY, JOHN GEORGE HASLETTE (D) (Pseudonyms: Henrietta Clandon, John Haslette, Anthony Lang, Vernon Loder, John Mowbray, Walter Proudfoot)
Arrest, by Walter Proudfoot. Hutchinson, 1933
Between Twelve and One, by Vernon Loder. Morrow, 1929
Call the Yard, by John Mowbray. Skeffington, 1931
The Case with the Three Threads, by Anthony Lang. Melrose, 1927
Choose Your Weapon, by Vernon Loder. Collins, 1937
The Conspiracy, by Walter Proudfoot. Hutchinson, 1933
The Crime, by Anthony Lang. Melrose, 1927
The Crime in the Arcade, by Walter Proudfoot. Hutchinson, 1931
Death by the Gaff. Skeffington, 1932
Death in the Thicket, by Vernon Loder. Collins, 1932
Death of an Editor, by Vernon Loder. Collins, 1931; Morrow, 1931

The Death Pool, by Vernon Loder. Morrow, 1931
Desmond Rourke, by John Haslette. Appleton, D., 1911
The Essex Murders, by Vernon Loder. Collins, 1930
Evidence. Melrose, 1930
The Ghost Party, by Henrietta Clandon. Bles, 1934
Good by Stealth, by Henrietta Clandon. Bles, 1936
Inquest, by Henrietta Clandon. Bles, 1933
Mr. Nemesis. Ward, Lock, 1930
Murder from Three Angles, by Vernon Loder. Collins, 1934
Mystery at Stowe, by Vernon Loder. Collins, 1928
Mystery at the Inn. Ward, Lock, 1931
Red Stain, by Vernon Loder. Collins, 1928
Rope, by Arrangement, by Henrietta Clandon. Bles, 1935
The Shop Window Murder, by Vernon Loder. Collins, 1930; Morrow, 1930
Spies in Ambush. Eyre, 1934
Trail of the Ruby, by Walter Proudfoot. Hutchinson, 1932
Two Dead, by Vernon Loder. Collins, 1934
The Vase Mystery, by Vernon Loder. Collins, 1929
Whose Hand?, by Vernon Loder. Collins, 1929
Witness in Support. Skeffington, 1932

VAIL, LAURENCE (M)
Murder! Murder! Davies, 1931

VAILE, WILLIAM N. (M)
The Mystery of the Golconda. Doubleday, Page, 1925; Heinemann, 1925

VAIZEY, GEORGE DE HORNE (M)
Inherit the Wind. Harrap, 1952
Into Thin Air. Harrap, 1939

VALBECK, MICHAEL (M)
Headlong from Heaven. Mill, 1947

VALE, G. V. (M)
The Mystery of the Papyrus. Methuen, 1929; Newnes, 1931

"VALENTINE," pseud; see PECHEY, ARCHIBALD THOMAS

VALENTINE, DOUGLAS, pseud; see WILLIAMS, VALENTINE

VALENTINE, JO, pseud; see ARMSTRONG, CHARLOTTE

VANARDY, VARICK, pseud; see DEY, FREDERIC VAN RENSSELEAR

VAN ARSDALE, WIRT, pseud; see DAVIS, MARTHA WIRT

VAN ATTA, WINFRED (M)
The Hatchet Man. Doubleday, 1962; Boardman, T. V., 1964
The Last Calcutta. Doubleday, 1963
Shock Treatment. Doubleday, 1961; Boardman, T. V., 1964; Crest, 1964

VANCE, ETHEL, pseud; see STONE, GRACE ZARING

VANCE, JOHN HOLBROOK (D)
The Fox Valley Murders. Allen, T., 1966; Bobbs, 1966
The Man in the Cage. Boardman, T. V., 1960; Random, 1960
The Pleasant Grove Murder. Bobbs, 1967

VANCE, LOUIS JOSEPH (M-D)
Alias the Lone Wolf. Doubleday, Page, 1921; Hodder, 1921
Baroque: a Mystery. Dutton, 1923; Hodder, 1923 (Published in McCall's as: "Double Doom")
The Black Bag. Bobbs, 1908; Richards, 1908
The Dark Mirror. Doubleday, Page, 1920; Hurst, 1921
The Dark Power. Bles, 1925
The Dead Ride Hard. Lippincott, 1926; Bles, 1927
The Destroying Angel. Copp, 1912; Little, 1912; Richards, 1913; Nelson, 1920
Detective. Lippincott, 1932; Jarrolds, 1933
Encore the Lone Wolf. Lippincott, 1933; Jarrolds, 1934
The False Faces. Doubleday, Page, 1918; Skeffington, 1920; Avon, 1964
The Lone Wolf. Nash, 1915; Skeffington, 1919; Hodder, 1929; Avon, 1964
The Lone Wolf Returns. Dutton, 1923; Hodder, 1924
The Lone Wolf's Last Prowl. Lippincott, 1934; Jarrolds, 1935 (Published in McCall's as: "The Last Prowl")
The Lone Wolf's Son. Lippincott, 1931; Jarrolds, 1932
Red Masquerade; Being the Story of Lone Wolf's Daughter. Doubleday, Page, 1921; Hodder, 1921
The Street of Strange Faces. Jarrolds, 1934; Lippincott, 1934
The Woman in the Shadow. Lippincott, 1930; Jarrolds, 1931

VANCE, WILLIAMS (D)
Homicide Lost. Graphic, 1956

VANDAM, ALBERT DRESDEN (M)
The Mystery of the Patrician Club. Chapman, 1894

VANDEBURG, MILLIE BIRD (M)
The Clean Hand. Cassell, 1928
The Door to the Moor. Dorrance, 1925

VANDERCOOK, JOHN WOMACK (D)
Danger Island. Harper, 1937
Murder in Fiji. Doubleday, Doran, 1936; Heinemann, 1936
Murder in Haiti. Eyre, 1956; Macmillan, 1956
Murder in New Guinea. Macmillan, 1959
Murder in Trinidad. Doubleday, Doran, 1933; Heinemann, 1934; Collier, 1962

VANDERPUIJI, NII AKRAMPAHENE (M)
The Counterfeit Corpse. Comet, 1956

VAN DEUSEN, DELIA (D)
The Garden Club Murders. Bobbs, 1941; Selwyn, 1943
Murder Bicarb. Bobbs, 1940; Selwyn, 1943

VAN DEVENTER, EMMA MURDOCH (D) (Pseudonym: Lawrence Lynch)
Against Odds. Rand, 1894; Ward, Lock, 1894
The Danger Line. Ward, Lock, 1903
Dangerous Ground; or, The Rival Detectives. Routledge, 1887
Dead Man's Step. Rand, 1893; Ward, Lock, 1893
The Diamond Coterie. Donnelly, 1885; Routledge, 1887; Ward, Lock, 1887; Loyd, 1890
High Stakes. Ward, Lock, 1901
The Last Stroke. Ward, Lock, 1896
Lost Witness; or, The Mystery of Leah Paget. Laird, 1890; Ward, Lock, 1890
Man and Master. Ward, Lock, 1909
Moina: A Detective Story. Laird, 1891; Ward, Lock, 1898
Mountain Mystery. Loyd, 1889
No Proof. Ward, Lock, 1895
Out of a Labyrinth. Ward, Lock, 1887
A Sealed Verdict. Long, 1916
Shadowed by Three. Ward, Lock, 1884; Routledge, 1887
A Slender Clue; or, the Mystery of the Mardi Gras. Ward, Lock, 1892
The Unseen Hand. Ward, Lock, 1896
The Woman Who Dared. Ward, Lock, 1902

VAN DINE, S. S., pseud; see WRIGHT, WILLARD HUNTINGTON

VAN DYKE, TOM; see KERNER, BEN

VANE, DEREK (M)
Dancer's End. Eldon, 1937
The Ferrybridge Mystery. Moffat
Five Hundred Pound Reward. Eldon, 1936
Intrigue and Matrimony. Hurst, 1928
The Scar. Clode, 1925
The Sign of the Snake. Hurst, 1927; Macrae Smith, 1928
White Panthers. Macmillan, 1930
Who Goes There? Eldon, 1936

VANE, PHILLIPA, pseud; see HAMBLEDON, PHYLLIS

VAN GULIK, ROBERT HANS; see GULIK, ROBERT HANS VAN

VAN ORDEN, BIANCA (M)
309 East and A Night of Levitation. Harcourt, 1947; Hart-Davis, 1957

VAN RENSBURG, HELEN and LOUWRENS VAN RENSBURG (M)
Death Is a Dark Pool. Joseph, M., 1954
The Man with Two Ties. Joseph, M., 1954

VAN RENSBURG, LOUWRENS; see VAN RENSBURG, HELEN

VAN SILLER, HILDA (D) (Pseudonym: Van Siller)
Bermuda Murder. Hammond, 1956
A Complete Stranger. Doubleday, 1965; Ward, Lock, 1966
The Curtain Between. Doubleday, 1947; Jarrolds, 1950
Echo of a Bomb. Doubleday, Doran, 1943; Jarrolds, 1943
Good Night Ladies. Doubleday, Doran, 1943
The Last Resort. Lippincott, 1952; Hammond, 1954
The Lonely Breeze. Doubleday, 1965
The Mood for Murder. Doubleday, 1966; Ward, Lock, 1967
Murder Is My Business. Hammond, 1958
The Murders at Hibiscus Bay. Hammond, 1965
One Alone. Doubleday, 1946; Jarrolds, 1948
Paul's Apartment. Doubleday, 1948; Hammond, 1953
The Red Geranium. Hammond, 1966
The Road. Hammond, 1960 (Original title: Thy Name Is Woman)
Somber Memory. Jarrolds, 1949
Thy Name Is Woman; see The Road
Under a Cloud. Doubleday, Doran, 1944; Jarrolds, 1947
The Widower. Popular Lib., 1965

VAN URK, MRS. VIRGINIA NELLIS (M)
Grounds for Murder. Arcadia, 1958

VARNADO, DONALD (M)
Washington Woman. Vantage, 1956

VARNAM, JOHN (M)
Beware the Dog. Hodder, 1954
Death Rehearses. Hodder, 1950
Travelling Deadman. Hodder, 1951

VEDDER, JOHN K., pseud; see GRUBER, FRANK

"VEDETTA," pseud; see WILLIAMS, VALENTINE

VEILLER, BAYARD (M)
Bait for a Tiger. Reynal, 1941

VEITCH, JAMES (M)
Live Till Tomorrow. Jenkins, 1956
Unknown Quantity. Jenkins, 1956

VENNING, MICHAEL, pseud; see RICE, CRAIG

VERMANDEL, JANET GREGORY (S)
So Long at the Fair. Dodd, 1968

VERNEDE, R. E. (M)
The Pursuit of Mr. Faviel. Rivers, 1905

VERNER, GERALD (M)
Alias the Ghost. Wright & Brown, 1933
Angel. Wright & Brown, 1939
The Black Hunchback. Wright & Brown, 1933
The Black Skull. Wright & Brown, 1933
The Case of Mr. Budd; see The Cleverness of Mr. Budd
The Cleverness of Mr. Budd. Wright & Brown, 1935 (U.S. title: The Case of Mr. Budd. Macaulay, 1938)
The Clue of the Green Candle. Wright & Brown, 1938
The Con Man. Wright & Brown, 1934
The Coupon Crimes. Mellifont, 1946
Crimson Ramblers. Wright & Brown, 1960
The Crooked Circle. Wright & Brown, 1935; Macaulay, 1937
Dead Secret. Wright & Brown, 1967
Death Play. Wright & Brown, 1933
Death Set in Diamonds. Wright & Brown, 1965
Dene of the Secret Service. Wright & Brown, 1941
The Embankment Murder. Wright & Brown, 1933
The Faceless Ones. Wright & Brown, 1964
The Football Pool Murders. Wright & Brown, 1939
The Frightened Man. Wright & Brown, 1937
Ghost House. Wright & Brown, 1961
The Ghost Man. Macaulay, 1936; Wright & Brown, 1936
The Ghost Squad. Wright & Brown, 1963
The Glass Arrow. Wright & Brown, 1937
Green Mask. Wright & Brown, 1934
Grim Death. Wright & Brown, 1960
The Grim Joker. Wright & Brown, 1936
The Hand of Fear. Wright & Brown, 1936
The Hangman. Wright & Brown, 1934
The Heel of Achilles. Wright & Brown, 1945
The Huntsman. Wright & Brown, 1940
I Am Death. Wright & Brown, 1963
The Jockey. Wright & Brown, 1937
The Lady of Doom. Wright & Brown, 1934
The Last Warning. Wright & Brown, 1962
The Manor House Murders. Wright & Brown, 1964
Mr. Big. Wright & Brown, 1966
Mr. Budd Again. Wright & Brown, 1939
Mr. Budd Investigates. Wright & Brown, 1963
Mr. Midnight. Wright & Brown, 1953
Mr. Whipple Explains. Wright & Brown, 1936
The Moor House Murder. Wright & Brown, 1964
Murder in Manuscript. Wright & Brown, 1963
The Next to Die. Wright & Brown, 1934
The Nightmare Murders. Wright & Brown, 1940
Noose for a Lady. Wright & Brown, 1952
The Nursery Rhyme Murder. Wright & Brown, 1960
Phantom Hollow. Wright & Brown, 1933
The Poisoner. Wright & Brown, 1940
The Q Squad. Wright & Brown, 1935; Macaulay, 1938
Queer Face. Wright & Brown, 1935
The Red Tape Murders. Wright & Brown, 1962
The Return of Mr. Budd. Wright & Brown, 1938
The River House Mystery. Mellifont, 1950
The River Men. Wright & Brown, 1936
The Royal Flush Murders. Wright & Brown, 1948
The Seven Clues. Wright & Brown, 1936
The Seven Lamps. Wright & Brown, 1947
The Shadow Men. Wright & Brown, 1961
The Show Must Go On. Wright & Brown, 1950
The Silver Horseshoe. Wright & Brown, 1938
Sinister House. Wright & Brown, 1934
Six Men Died. Wright & Brown

The Sorcerer's House. Hutchinson, 1956
The Squealer. Wright & Brown, 1934
Terror Tower. Wright & Brown, 1935
They Walk in Darkness. Wright & Brown, 1947
The Third Key. Wright & Brown, 1961
Thirsty Evil. Westhouse
The Three Gnomes. Wright & Brown, 1937
The Tipster. Wright & Brown, 1949
The Token. Wright & Brown, 1937
The Tudor Garden Mystery. Wright & Brown, 1966
The Twelve Apostles. Wright & Brown, 1946
The Vampire Man. Wright & Brown, 1941
The Watcher. Wright & Brown, 1936
Whispering Woman. Wright & Brown, 1949
White Wig. Wright & Brown, 1935
The Witches' Moon. Wright & Brown, 1938

VERNON, H.; see LONGSTRETH, T. MORRIS

VERRON, ROBERT (M)
The Country Club Murder. Wright & Brown, 1958
The Curse at Craig's End. Wright & Brown, 1953
The Day of the Dust. Wright & Brown, 1964
Death Waits Outside. Wright & Brown, 1953
The Fifth Must Die. Wright & Brown, 1949
Murder Calls the Tune. Wright & Brown, 1958
Murder Indicted. Wright & Brown, 1957
Murder Lands the Odds. Wright & Brown, 1963
Murder Lifts the Veil. Wright & Brown, 1955
Murder Most Black. Wright & Brown, 1957
Murder Most Monstrous. Wright & Brown, 1958
Murder of No Consequence. Wright & Brown, 1963
Murder on Demand. Wright & Brown, 1961
Murder Points East. Wright & Brown, 1956
Party to Murder. Wright & Brown, 1963
Point of No Return. Wright & Brown, 1955
Return a Gain for Murder. Wright & Brown, 1961
Right Turn for Murder. Wright & Brown, 1952

VESEY, ARTHUR HENRY (M)
The Clock and the Key. Appleton, D., 1905

VESTAL, STANLEY, pseud; see CAMPBELL, WALTER STANLEY

VEXIN, NOEL (M)
Murder in Montmarte. Dell, 1960

VIALETTE, ALEXANDRE (S)
Fruit of the Congo. Museum Press, 1954

VICARY, JEAN (S)
Saverstall. Ace, 1967

VICKERS, ROY (D) (Pseudonym: John Spencer)
Bardelow's Heir. Jenkins, 1935
Brenda Gets Married. Jenkins, 1941
A Date with Danger. Vanguard, 1944
The Department of Dead Ends. Faber, 1946; Spivak, 1947; Penguin, 1956 (Also published as: Murder Will Out. Faber, 1950)
Double Image and Other Stories. Jenkins, 1955; British Book Centre, 1959
Eight Murders in the Suburbs. Jenkins, 1954; British Book Centre, 1958
The Enemy Within. Jenkins, 1939
The Exploits of Fidelity Dove. Newnes, 1935
Find the Innocent. Jenkins, 1961
Four Past Four. Jenkins, 1925; Jefferson House, 1945
The Girl in the News. Jenkins, 1938
Gold and Wine. Jenkins, 1949; Walker & Co., 1961
Hide These Diamonds. Newnes, 1936
Hounded Down. Newnes, 1935
I'll Never Tell. Jenkins, 1938
Life Between. Jenkins, 1938
Maid to Murder. Mill, 1950 (English title: The Murdering Mr. Velfrage. Faber, 1950)
Murder for a Million
Murder in Two Flats. Mill, 1952
Murder of a Snob. Jenkins, 1951; British Book Centre, 1958
Murder Will Out; see Department of Dead Ends
The Murdering Mr. Velfrage; see Maid to Murder
Playgirl Wanted. Jenkins, 1940
Six Came to Dinner. Jenkins, 1951
Six Murders in the Suburbs. Detective Book Club, 1955
Seven Chose Murder. Faber, 1959
She Walked in Fear. Jenkins, 1940
The Sole Survivor and Kynsard Affair. Gollancz, 1952
The Terror of Tongues. Newnes, 1938

They Can't Hang Caroline. Jenkins, 1950
The War Bride. Jenkins, 1942
Whispering Death. Hodder, 1940; Jefferson House, 1947

VICTOR, META VICTORIA (Pseudonym: Seeley Regester)
Dead Letter. Beadle, 1886

VIDAL, GORE (D) (Pseudonym: Edgar Box)
Death Before Bedtime. Dutton, 1953; Heinemann, 1954; Signet
Death in the Fifth Position. Dutton, 1952; Heinemann, 1954; Signet, 1964
Death Likes It Hot. Dutton, 1954; Heinemann, 1955; Signet, 1964

VIERECK, GEORGE SYLVESTER (M)
All Things Human. Duckworth, 1950

VILLER, FREDERICK (M)
The Black Tortoise. Heinemann, 1901

VINCE, HENRY SCOTT (M)
Two Pardons in Vols. Ward & Downey, 1889

VINCENT, CLAIRE (S)
Spellbound. Tower

VINN, WALTER (M)
Suddenly He Knew. Greenwich, 1958

VINTON, ARTHUR DUDLEY (D)
The Pomfret Mystery. Ogilvie, 1886; Street, 1890
The Unpardonable Crime. Ogilvie, 1889

VIRDEN, KATHERINE (D)
Crooked Eye. Chapman, 1930; Doubleday, Doran, 1930
The Thing in the Night. Doubleday, Doran, 1930

VIVIAN, EVELYN CHARLES (M)
The Barking Dog Murder Case. Hillman-Curl, 1937
The Man in Gray. Hillman-Curl, 1938

VIVIAN, FRANCIS, pseud; see ASHLEY, ARTHUR ERNEST

VLASTO, JOHN ALEXANDER (M) (Pseudonyms: John Alexander, John Remenham)
Arsenic, by John Remenham. Skeffington, 1930
Canal Mystery, by John Remenham. Skeffington, 1933
The Crooked Bough, by John Remenham. MacDonald & Co., 1948
Dump, by John Remenham. Skeffington, 1931
Fog: A Dartmoor Mystery, by John Remenham. Skeffington, 1929
The House of Shayle, by John Alexander. Low, 1934
The Loom, by John Remenham. Skeffington, 1933
The Lurking Shadow, by John Remenham. MacDonald & Co., 1946
Murder at the Eclipse, by John Alexander. Low, 1934
The Peacemaker, by John Remenham. MacDonald & Co., 1947
Righteous Abel, by John Remenham. MacDonald & Co., 1943
Seed of Envy, by John Remenham. MacDonald & Co., 1944
Sea Gold. Skeffington, 1931
Tregar's Treasure, by John Remenham. Skeffington, 1932

VOELKER, JOHN DONALDSON (M) (Pseudonym: Robert Traver)
Anatomy of a Murder. St. Martin's, 1957; Dell, 1959
Hornstein's Boy. St. Martin's, 1960; Dell, 1963
Laughing Whitefish. McGraw, 1965; Dell, 1966

VOLK, GORDON (M) (Pseudonym: Raymond Knotts)
And the Deep Blue Sea. Farrar & Rinehart, 1944
Meeting by Moonlight. Doubleday, Doran, 1945

VON ELSNER, DON BYRON (D)
The Ace of Spies. Award, 1966
Countdown for a Spy. Signet, 1966
Don't Just Stand There, Do Someone. Signet, 1962
How to Succeed at Murder Without Really Trying. Signet, 1963
Jack of Diamonds. Award, 1967
Just Not Making Mayhem Like They Used To. Signet, 1962
Pour a Swindle Through a Loop-hole. Belmont, 1964
Those Who Prey Together, Slay Together. Signet, 1961
Who Says a Corpse Has to Be Dull? Signet, 1964
You Can't Do Business with Murder. Signet, 1962

VON LINSINGEN, FREDERICK WILLIAM BERRY; see LINSINGEN, FREDERICK WILLIAM BERRY VON

VOSS BARK, CONRAD LYDDON (M-S)
Mr. Holmes and the Fair Armenian. MacDonald & Co., 1964
Mr. Holmes and the Love Bank. MacDonald & Co., 1964

Mr. Holmes at Sea. MacDonald & Co., 1962; Macmillan, 1962
Mr. Holmes Goes to Ground. MacDonald & Co., 1963; Macmillan, 1964
Sealed Entrance. Chapman, 1947
The Shepherd File. Gollancz, 1966; Berkley Pub., 1967

VROOMAN, HENRY WELLINGTON (M)
Half a Million Insurance; or, Dr. Lauterback's Strange Patient. Amer. News, 1888

VULLIAMY, COLWYN EDWARD (D)
(Pseudonym: Anthony Rolls)
The Body in the Boudoir. Joseph, M., 1956
Cakes for Your Birthday. British Book Centre, 1959; Joseph, M., 1959
Clerical Error, by Anthony Rolls. Little, 1932
Don Among the Dead Men. Joseph, M., 1952

WADDEL, CHARLES CAREY (M)
(Pseudonym: Charles Carey)
Girl of the Guard Line. Moffat, 1915
Juror No. 17. King, A. H., 1931
The Van Suyden Sapphires, by Charles Carey. Dodd, 1905

WADDELL, CHARLES CAREY; see WADDEL, CHARLES CAREY

WADDELL, ELEANOR LEE (M)
Murder at Drake's Anchorage. Dutton, 1949

WADDELL, MARTIN (D)
Otley. Hodder, 1966; Stein, 1966
Otley Pursued. Hodder, 1966; Stein, 1967

WADE, ALAN (M)
Isle of Peril. Mystery House, 1957

WADE, BOB; see MILLER, BILL

WADE, GARRISON, pseud. (M)
Alias John Smith. Vantage, 1966

WADE, HARRISON (M)
So Lovely to Kill. Graphic, 1956

WADE, HENRY, pseud; see AUBREY-FLETCHER, HENRY LANCELOT

WADE, JONATHAN (S)
Back to Life. Pantheon, 1962
Running Sand. Collins, 1962; Random, 1963

WADE, KATHLEEN (M)
Cloak for Malice. Hutchinson, 1949
Crime at Gargoyles. Hutchinson, 1947

WADELTON, MAGGIE OWEN (M)
Sarah Mandrake. Paperback Lib., 1966

WADHAM, RUTH (M)
Weekend in Bagdad. Gollancz, 1958; Macmillan, 1959

WADSWORTH, LEDA ABIGAIL (M)
The Lost Moon Mystery. Museum Press, 1950

WAER, JACK (M)
Murder in Las Vegas. Avon, 1955
Seventeen and Black. Viking, 1954

WAGNAILS, MABEL (M)
Mad-Song. Funk, 1926

WAGNER, CONSTANCE (M)
The Major Has Seven Guests. Stokes, 1940

WAGNER, ESTHER; see WAGNER, JOHN

WAGNER, GEOFFREY (S)
Born of the Sun. Popular Lib., 1956
The Passionate Land. S & S, 1953; Pyramid, 1964; Mayflower, 1966
Seasons of Assassins. GM, 1961; Quadriga, 1964
The Venables. Murray, J., 1952; S & S, 1952

WAGNER, JOHN and ESTHER WAGNER (M)
The Gift of Rome. Little, 1961

WAGONER, DAVID (M)
The Man in the Middle. Harcourt, 1954

WAHL, ALBERTA ELIZABETH HUGHES (D)
Handsome But Dead. Howell, Soskin, 1942

WAHLÖÖ, PER (M)
The Assignment. Knopf, 1961; Joseph, M., 1965
The Murder on the Thirty-first Floor. Joseph, M., 1964 (U.S title: The Thirty-first Floor. Knopf, 1967)
Roseanna, with Maj Sjowall. Pantheon, 1967
The Thirty-first Floor; see Murder on the Thirty-first Floor

WAINWRIGHT, JOHN (D)
The Crystalized Carbon Pig. Collins, 1966; Walker & Co., 1967
Death in a Sleeping City. Collins, 1965
Evil Intent. Collins, 1966
Talent For Murder. Walker & Co., 1967
Ten Steps to the Gallows. Collins, 1966

WAITT, ISABEL WOODMAN (D)
Death à la King. Phoenix, 1943

WAKEFIELD, HERBERT RUSSELL (M)
Belt of Suspicion. Collins, 1938
The Clock Strikes Twelve. Jenkins, 1940; Arkham, 1946
The Green Bicycle Case. Allen, P., 1932
Hearken to the Evidence. Doubleday, Doran, 1934
Hostess to Death. Collins, 1940
The Strayers from Sheal. Arkham, 1961

WAKEFIELD, JOHN (D)
Death the Sure Physician. Constable, 1965; Dodd, 1966

WAKEFIELD, R. I. (M)
You Will Die Today. Dodd, 1953

WALCOTT, EARLE ASHLEY (M)
Blindfolded. Bobbs, 1906

WALES, KIRK (D)
Six Were to Die. Mystery House, 1941

WALK, CHARLES EDMONDS (M)
The Crimson Cross. McClurg, 1913
The Green Seal. McClurg, 1914
The Paternoster Ruby. McClurg, 1910
The Yellow Circle. McClurg, 1909

WALKER, CHARLES MAURICE (M)
Death of a Jazz King. Paul, S., 1936

WALKER, DAVID ESDAILE (M)
Diamonds for Danger. Harper, 1953 (English title: Diamonds for Moscow. Chapman, 1953)

WALKER, DAVID HARRY (M)
Storm and the Silence. Houghton, 1949; Cape, 1950
Winter of Madness. Collins, 1964; PB, 1965

WALKER, GERTRUDE (M)
Diamonds Don't Burn. Jenkins, 1955
So Deadly Fair. Putnam, 1948

WALKER, HARRY, pseud; see WAUGH, HILLARY BALDWIN

WALKER, IRA, pseud; see WALKER, IRMA RUTH RODEN

WALKER, IRMA RUTH RODEN (M) (Pseudonym: Ira Walker)
The Man in the Driver's Seat. Abelard, 1964
Someone's Stolen Nellie Grey. Abelard, 1963

WALKER-TAYLOR, PHILIP NEVILLE (D)
Murder in the Flagship. Mill, 1937
Murder in the Game Reserve. Butterworth, T., 1937
Murder in the Suez Canal. Butterworth, T., 1937
Murder in the Taj Mahal. Butterworth, T., 1938

WALL, JOHN (M)
Guardian Angel in the Underworld. Vantage, 1958

WALL, JOHN W. (M) (Pseudonym: "Sarban")
The Doll Maker. Ballantine, 1960
Ringstones. Coward, 1951; Ballantine, 1960

WALLACE, BRYAN EDGAR
Murder on the Night Ferry. Hodder, 1965

WALLACE, C. H. (M)
E.T.A. for Death. Belmont, 1967
Highflight to Hell. Belmont, 1966
Tailwind to Danger. Belmont, 1966

WALLACE, CARLETON (D)
Death of a Libertine. Long, 1936
Devil Breathes But Once. Long, 1937
Mr. Death; see Mr. Death Walks Abroad
Mr. Death Walks Abroad. Long, 1933 (U.S. title: Mr. Death. Doubleday, Doran, 1934)
Sinister Alibi. Doubleday, Doran, 1934; Long, 1934

WALLACE, EDGAR (Full name: Richard Edgar Horatio Wallace) (M-D-S)
The Admirable Carfew. Ward, Lock, 1914
The Adventures of Heine. Ward, Lock, 1919, 1930
Again Sanders. Hodder, 1928; Doubleday, Doran, 1931
Again the Ringer. Hodder, 1929 (U.S. title: The Ringer Returns. Doubleday, Doran, 1931)
Again the Three Just Men. Hodder, 1929 (Also published as: Again the Three. Hodder, 1930. U.S. title: The Law of the Three Just Men. Doubleday, Doran, 1931)
Angel, Esquire. Holt, H., 1908; Small, 1927; Readers' Lib., 1928
The Angel of Terror. Hodder, 1922; Small, 1922 (Also published as: The Destroying Angel)
The Arranways Mystery; see Coat of Arms
The Avenger. Long, 1926 (Also published as: The Hairy Arm. Small, 1925 and The Extra Girl)
Barbara on Her Own. Newnes, 1926
Beyond Recall; see The Blue Hand
Big Foot. Long, 1927

Big Four. Readers' Lib., 1929 (Also published as: The Crooks of Society)
The Black; see The Man From Morocco
The Black. Queensway, 1935 (Also published as: Blackmailers I Have Foiled)
The Black Abbot. Hodder, 1926; Doubleday, Page, 1927
The Black Tenth; see The Yellow Snake
Blackmail and The Iron Grip. Readers' Lib., 1940
Blackmailers I Have Foiled; see The Black
The Blue Hand. Small, 1925; Ward, Lock, 1925 (Also published as: Beyond Recall)
Bones. Ward, Lock, 1915
Bones in London. Ward, Lock, 1921
Bones of the River. Newnes, 1923
The Book of All-Power. Ward, Lock, 1921
The Books of Bart. Ward, Lock, 1923
Bosambo of the River. Ward, Lock, 1914
The Brigand. Hodder, 1927
The Calendar. Collins, 1930; Doubleday, Doran, 1931
Captain Tatham of Tatham Island. Gale, 1909 (Also published as: Eve's Island. Newnes, 1926 and The Island of Galloping Gold. Newnes, 1916)
Captains of Souls. Small, 1922; Long, 1923
The Cat Burglar. Newnes, 1929
Chick. Ward, Lock, 1923
Children of the Poor; see The Gunner
Circumstanial Evidence. Newnes, 1929; World Syndicate, 1934 (Also published as: Fighting Snub Reilly. Newnes, 1929)
The Clever One; see The Forger
The Clue of the New Pin. Hodder, 1923; Small, 1923
The Clue of the Silver Key. Hodder, 1930 (U.S. title: The Silver Key. Doubleday, Doran, 1930)
The Clue of the Twisted Candle. Small, 1916; Newnes, 1918
Coat of Arms. Hutchinson, 1931 (U.S. title: The Arranways Mystery. Doubleday, Doran, 1932)
The Colossus; see The Joker
The Council of Justice. Ward, Lock, 1908
The Counterfeiter; see The Forger
The Crime Book of J.G. Reeder. Burt, 1935 (Contains: Terror Keeps, Red Aces, and Mr. Reeder Returns)
The Crimson Circle. Doubleday, Doran, 1929; Hodder, 1932; Macfadden, 1967
The Croakers; see The Dark Eyes of London
Crooks of Society; see The Big Four
The Daffodil Murder; see The Daffodil Mystery
The Daffodil Mystery. Ward, Lock, 1920; Small, 1921 (Also published as: The Daffodil Murder)
The Dark Eyes of London. Ward, Lock, 1924; Doubleday, Doran, 1929 (Also published as: The Croakers)
The Daughters of the Night. Newnes, 1928
The Day of Uniting. Hodder, 1926; Mystery League, 1930
A Debt Discharged. Ward, Lock, 1916
The Devil Man. Collins, 1931; Doubleday, Doran, 1931 (Also published as: Sinister Street, The Life and Death of Charles Peace, and Silver Steel)
The Diamond Men; see The Face in the Night
Diana of Kara-Kara; see Double Dan
The Door with Seven Locks. Doubleday, Page, 1926; Hodder, 1926
The Double. Doubleday, Page, 1927; Hodder, 1928 (Also published as: Sinister Halls)
Double Dan. Hodder, 1924 (Also published as: Diana of Kara-Kara. Small, 1924)
Down Under Donovan. Ward, Lock, 1918
The Duke in the Suburbs. Ward, Lock, 1909
The Edgar Wallace Foursome. Long, 1933 (Contains: The Man from Morocco, Captains of Souls, The Hand of Power, and The Mixer)
The Edgar Wallace Police Van. Hodder, 1930 (Contains: The Green Archer, The Forger, The Double, and The Flying Squad)
The Edgar Wallace Race Special. Collins, 1932 (Contains: Educated Evans, More Educated Evans, Good Evans and The Calendar)
The Edgar Wallace Reader. World Pub., 1943
The Edgar Wallace Second Book. Newnes, 1931
Educated Evans. Collins, 1929
Elegant Edward. Readers' Lib., 1928
Eve's Island; see Captain Tatham of Tatham Island
The Extra Girl; see The Avenger
The Face in the Night. Long, 1924; Doubleday, Doran, 1929 (Also published as: The Diamond Men and The Ragged Princess)
The Feathered Serpent. Hodder, 1927; Doubleday, Doran, 1928 (Also published as: Inspector Wade and Inspector Wade and the Feathered Serpent)
The Fellowship of the Frog. Ward, Lock, 1925; Doubleday, Doran, 1928
Fighting Snub Reilly; see Circumstantial Evidence
Flat 2. Garden City Pub., 1924; Long, 1927

The Flying Fifty-Five. Hutchinson, 1922
The Flying Squad. Hodder, 1928; Doubleday, Doran, 1929
For Information Received. Newnes, 1929
The Forger. Hodder, 1929 (U.S. title: The Clever One. Doubleday, Doran, 1928. Also published as: The Counterfeiter)
Forty-eight Short Stories. Newnes, 1929
Four Complete Novels. Newnes, 1930
The Four Just Men. Tallis, 1905; Small, 1920
Four Square Jane. World Wide, 1928; Readers' Lib., 1929 (Also published as: The Fourth Square)
The Fourth Plague. Ward, Lock, 1913; Doubleday, Doran, 1930
The Fourth Square; see Four Square Jane
The Frightened Lady. Hodder, 1932; Musson, 1933 (U.S. title: The Mystery of the Frightened Lady. Doubleday, Doran, 1933)
The Gallows Hand; see The Terrible People
The Gangsters Come to London; see When the Gangs Come to London
The Gaol Breakers; see We Shall See
The Gaunt Stranger. Hodder, 1925 (U.S. title: The Ringer. Doubleday, Page, 1926. Also published as: Police Work)
The Ghost of Downhill. Readers' Lib., 1929
The Girl from Scotland Yard; see The Square Emerald
The Golden Hades. Collins, 1929 (Also published as: Stamped in Gold)
Good Evans. Collins, 1929
The Governor of Chi-Foo. Newnes, 1929; World Syndicate, 1933
The Green Archer. Hodder, 1923; Small, 1924; Norton, 1965
The Green Pack, with Robert G. Curtis. Doubleday, Doran, 1933
The Green Ribbon. Hutchinson, 1929; Doubleday, Doran, 1930
Green Rust. Ward, Lock, 1919, 1934; Small, 1920
Grey Timothy. Ward, Lock, 1913 (Also published as: Pallard the Punter. Ward, Lock, 1914)
Gunman's Bluff; see The Gunner
The Gunner. Long, 1928 (U.S. title: Gunman's Bluff. Doubleday, Doran, 1929. Also published as: Children of the Poor)
The Guv'nor and Other Stories. Collins, 1932 (U.S. title: Mr. Reeder Returns. Doubleday, Doran, 1932)
The Hairy Arm; see The Avenger
The Hand of Power. Long, 1929; Mystery League, 1930 (Also published as: The Proud Sons of Ragusa)
The India Rubber Men. Doubleday, Doran, 1930; Hodder, 1930 (Also published as: The Pool and Wolves of the Waterfront)
Inspector Wade; see The Feathered Serpent
Inspector Wade and the Feathered Serpent; see The Feathered Serpent
The Iron Grip. Readers' Lib., 1930 (Also published as: Wireless Bryce)
The Island of Galloping Gold; see Captain Tatham of Tatham Island
Jack o'Judgment. Ward, Lock, 1920; Small, 1921
The Joker. Hodder, 1926 (U.S. title: The Colossus. Doubleday, Doran, 1932. Also published as: The Park Lane Mystery)
The Just Men of Cordova. Ward, Lock, 1917, 1931
Kate, Plus Ten. Burt, 1930; Ward, Lock, 1931
The Keepers of the King's Peace. Ward, Lock, 1917
Killer Kay. Newnes, 1930
A King by Night. Long, 1925; Doubleday, Page, 1926
The Lady Called Nita. Newnes, 1930
The Lady of Ascot. Hutchinson, 1930
The Lady of Little Hell. Newnes, 1929
The Last Adventure. Hutchinson, 1934
The Law of the Four Just Men. Hodder, 1921
The Law of the Three Just Men; see Again the Three Just Men
Lieutenant Bones. Ward, Lock, 1918
The Life and Death of Charles Peace; see The Devil Man
The Little Green Man. Newnes, 1929
The Lone House Mystery. Collins, 1929
The Mammoth Mystery Book. Doubleday, Doran, 1929 (Contains: Gaol Breakers, Just Men of Cordova, and King by Night)
The Man at the Carlton. Hodder, 1931; Doubleday, Doran, 1932 (Also published as: His Devoted Squealer and The Mystery of Mary Greer)
The Man from Morocco. Long, 1926 (U.S. title: The Black. Doubleday, Doran, 1930. Also published as: Souls in Shadows)
The Man Who Bought London. Ward, Lock, 1915
The Man Who Changed His Name, with Robert G. Curtis. Hodder, 1929; Hutchinson, 1934
The Man Who Knew. Small, 1918; Newnes, 1919
The Man Who Was Nobody. Ward, Lock, 1927
The Melody of Death. Readers' Lib., 1928; Doubleday, Doran, 1934
The Million Dollar Story. Newnes, 1926

The Mind of Mr. J. G. Reeder. Hodder, 1925 (U.S. title: The Murder Book of J. G. Reeder. Doubleday, Doran, 1929)
The Missing Million. Long, 1923; Small, 1925
Mr. Commissioner Sanders; see Sanders
Mr. J. G. Reeder Returns; see Guv'nor and Other Stories
Mr. Justice Maxwell. Ward, Lock, 1922 (Also published as: Take-a-Chance Anderson)
The Mixer. Long, 1927
More Educated Evans. Collins, 1930
The Mouthpiece, with Robert G. Curtis. Dodge, 1936
Mrs. William Jones—and Bill. Newnes, 1930
The Murder Book of J. G. Reeder; see The Mind of Mr. J. G. Reeder
The Mystery of Mary Grier; see The Man at the Carlton
The Mystery of the Frightened Lady; see The Frightened Lady
New Mammoth Mystery Book. Burt, 1932 (Contains: The Four Just Men, The Secret House and The Man Who Knew)
Nig Nog. World Pub., 1934
The Nine Bears. Ward, Lock, 1912 (Also published as: Silinski, Master Criminal. World Syndicate, 1930 and The Other Man. Dodd, 1911)
Nobby. Newnes, 1916 (Also published as: Smithy's Friend Nobby. "Town Topics," Dec., 1914)
The Northing Tramp. Hodder, 1926; Doubleday, Doran, 1929
Number Six. 1922 (Also published as: Number Six and the Borgia)
Number Six and the Borgia; see Number Six
On the Spot. Doubleday, Doran, 1931; Long, 1931
The Orator. Hutchinson, 1928
The Other Man; The Nine Bears
Pallard the Punter; see Grey Timothy
The Park Lane Mystery; see The Joker
Penelope of the Polyantha. Hodder, 1926
The People of the River. Ward, Lock, 1912
Police Work; see The Gaunt Stranger
The Pool; see The India Rubber Men
The Prison Breakers. Newnes, 1929
Private Selby. Ward, Lock, 1930
The Proud Sons of Ragusa; see The Hand of Power
Ragged Princess; see The Face in the Night
Red Aces. Hodder, 1929; Doubleday, Doran, 1931
The Reporter. Readers' Lib., 1929 (Also published as: Wise Y. Simon)
The Ringer; see The Gaunt Stranger
The Ringer Returns; see Again the Ringer
The River of Stars. Ward, Lock, 1913
Room 13. Long, 1924
Sanctuary Island, with R. J. Curtis. 1936
Sanders. Hodder, 1926 (U.S. title: Mr. Commissioner Sanders. Doubleday, Doran, 1930)
Sanders of the River. Ward, Lock, 1911, 1933; Doubleday, Doran, 1930
Sandi, the King-Maker. Ward, Lock, 1922
Scotland Yard Book of Edgar Wallace. Burt, 1932; Doubleday, Doran, 1932
Scotland Yard's Yankee Dick; see When the Gangs Come to London
The Secret House. Ward, Lock, 1917; Small, 1919
Sergeant Dunn C.I.D.; see Sergeant Sir Peter
Sergeant Sir Peter. Chapman, 1932; Doubleday, Doran, 1933 (Also published as: Sergeant Dunn C.I.D.)
The Sign of the Leopard; see The Squeaker
Silinski, Master Criminal; see The Nine Bears
The Silver Key; see The Clue of the Silver Key
Silver Steel; see The Devil Man
Sinister Halls; see The Double
The Sinister Man. Hodder, 1924; Small, 1925
Sinister Street; see The Devil Man
Smithy. Tallis, 1905
Smithy Abroad. E. Hulton, 1909
Smithy and the Hun. Pearson, 1915
Smithy's Friend Nobby; see Nobby
The Square Emerald. Hodder, 1926 (U.S. title: The Girl from Scotland Yard. Burt, 1927; Doubleday, Page, 1927)
The Squeaker. Hodder, 1927 (U.S. title: The Squealer. Doubleday, Doran, 1929. Also published as: The Sign of the Leopard)
The Squealer; see The Squeaker
Stamped in Gold; see The Golden Hades
The Steward. Collins, 1932
The Strange Countess. Hodder, 1925; Small, 1926
Stranger Than Fiction. Howell, Soskin, 1947
The Stretelli Case and Other Mystery Stories. World Syndicate, 1930
Take-a-Chance Anderson; see Mr. Justice Maxwell
Tam o' the Scoots. Small, 1919
The Terrible People. Doubleday, Page, 1926; Hodder, 1926 (Also published as: The Gallows Hand)
The Terror. Collins, 1929
Terror Keep. Doubleday, Page, 1927; Hodder, 1927
Thief in the Night. World Wide, 1930

The Three Just Men. Hodder, 1926; Doubleday, Doran, 1929
The Three Oak Mystery. Ward, Lock, 1924
The Tomb of Ts'in. Ward, Lock, 1916
The Traitor's Gate. Doubleday, Page, 1927; Hodder, 1927
The Twister. Long, 1928; Doubleday, Doran, 1929
The Valley of Ghosts. Small, 1923; Hodder, 1925
We Shall See. Hodder, 1928 (U.S. title: The Gaol-Breakers. Doubleday, Doran, 1931)
When the Gangs Came to London. Doubleday, Doran, 1932; Long, 1932 (Also published as: The Gangsters Come to London and Scotland Yard's Yankee Dick)
White Face. Hodder, 1930; Doubleday, Doran, 1931
Wireless Bryce; see The Iron Grip
Wise Y. Simon; see The Reporter
Wolves of the Waterfront; see The India Rubber Men
The Woman from the East. Hutchinson, 1934
The Yellow Snake. Hodder, 1926 (Also published as: The Black Tenth)

WALLACE, F. L. (D)
Three Times a Victim. Ace, 1957

WALLACE, FLOYD (D)
Wired for Scandal. Ace, 1959

WALLACE, MARY (M)
From This Death Forward. Arcadia, 1959

WALLACE, RICHARD EDGAR HORATIO; see WALLACE, EDGAR

WALLACE, ROBERT (S)
The Body on the Beach. Watt, G., 1932
The Broadway Murders. Regency, 1965 (Phantom series, #5)
The Daggers of Kali. Regency, 1965 (Phantom series, #6)
Death Glow. Regency, 1966
Fangs of Murder. Regency, 1966
The Green Glare Murders. Regency, 1966 (Phantom series, #12)
The Jig-saw Murder Case. Gabriel, 1933
Murder Trail. Popular Lib., 1965 (Phantom series, #10)
Murder Under the Big Top. Regency, 1965 (Phantom series, #7)
The Phantom Detective. Regency, 1966 (Phantom series, #1)
Seven Men Are Murdered. Fiction League, 1933
Yellow Shadows of Death. Corinth, 1966 (Phantom series, #9)

WALLER, LESLIE (S) (Pseudonym: C. S. Cody)
Bed She Made, by C. S. Cody. Dial, 1951
'K'. GM, 1963
Witching Night, by C. S. Cody. World Pub., 1952

WALLING, ROBERT ALFRED JOHN (D)
The Bachelor Flat Mystery. Morrow, 1934; Burt, 1936
Behind the Yellow Blind. Hodder, 1932
Bury Him Deeper. Hodder, 1937
By Hook or by Crook; see By Hook or Crook
By Hook or Crook. Morrow, 1941 (English title: By Hook or by Crook. Hodder, 1941)
Castle Dinas; see The Corpse with the Eerie Eye
The Cat and the Corpse; see The Corpse in the Green Pyjamas
The Coroner Doubts. Hodder, 1938
A Corpse by Any Other Name. Morrow, 1943 (English title: The Doodled Asterisk. Hodder, 1943)
Corpse in the Coppice. Morrow, 1935 (English title: Mr. Tolefree's Reluctant Witnesses. Hodder, 1936)
The Corpse in the Crimson Slippers. Hodder, 1936; Morrow, 1936
The Corpse in the Green Pyjamas. Morrow, 1935 (English title: The Cat and the Corpse. Hodder, 1935)
The Corpse with the Blistered Hand. Morrow, 1939 (English title: Dust in the Vault. Hodder, 1939)
The Corpse with the Blue Cravat. Morrow, 1938
The Corpse with the Dirty Face. Morrow, 1936 (English title: The Crime in Cumberland Court. Hodder, 1938)
The Corpse with the Eerie Eye. Morrow, 1942 (English title: Castle Dinas. Hodder, 1942)
The Corpse with the Floating Foot. Morrow, 1936 (English title: The Mystery of Mr. Mock. Hodder, 1937)
The Corpse with the Grimy Glove. Morrow, 1938
The Corpse with the Missing Watch. Morrow, 1949
The Corpse with the Red-Headed Friend. Morrow, 1939 (English title: They Liked Entwhistle. Hodder, 1939)
The Corpse Without a Clue. Hodder, 1944; Morrow, 1944
Cries in the Night. Dutton, 1933
The Crime in Cumberland Court; see The Corpse with the Dirty Face
Dinner-party at Bardolph's. Jarrolds, 1927 (U.S. title: That Dinner at Bardolph's. Morrow, 1928)

The Doodled Asterisk; see A Corpse by Any Other Name
Dust in the Vault; see The Corpse with the Blistered Hand
Eight to Nine. Hodder, 1934
The Fatal Five Minutes. Hodder, 1932; World Pub., 1942
Five Suspects; see Fatal Legacy
Follow the Blue Car; see In Time for Murder
In Time for Murder. Morrow, 1933 (English title: Follow the Blue Car. Hodder, 1933)
The Late Unlamented. Hodder, 1948; Morrow, 1948
The Legacy of Death. Morrow, 1934 (English title: Five Suspects. Hodder, 1935)
The Man with the Squeaky Voice. Methuen, 1930; Morrow, 1930
Marooned with Murder. Morrow, 1937
Mr. Tolefree's Reluctant Witnesses; see The Corpse in the Coppice
More Than One Serpent. Hodder, 1938
Murder at Midnight. Morrow, 1932
Murder at the Keyhole. Methuen, 1929; Morrow, 1929
Murder Mansion. Dutton, 1934
The Mystery of Mr. Mock; see The Corpse with the Floating Foot
Prove It, Mr. Tolefree. Morrow, 1933 (English title: Tolliver Case. Hodder, 1934)
The Spider and the Fly. Morrow, 1940 (English title: Why Did Trethewy Die? Hodder, 1940)
The Stroke of One. Morrow, 1931
The Strong Room. Jarrolds, 1927
That Dinner at Bardolph's; see Dinner-party at Bardolph's
They Liked Entwhistle; see The Corpse with the Red-headed Friend
The Tolliver Case; see Prove It, Mr. Tolefree
The Walling Omnibus. Blue Ribbon, 1939
Why Did Trethewy Die?; see The Spider and the Fly
The Woman He Chose. Dutton, 1934

WALLIS, A. J.; see BLAIR, CHARLES F., JR.

WALLIS, JAMES H. (M)
Capital City Mystery. Dutton, 1932; Jarrolds, 1933
Cries in the Night. Jarrolds, 1935
The House of Murder; see Murder Mansion
Murder by Formula. Dutton, 1931; Jarrolds, 1932
Murder Mansion. Dutton, 1934 (English title: The House of Murder. Jarrolds, 1934)
The Mystery of Vaucluse. Dutton, 1933
The Niece of Abraham Pein. Dutton, 1943; Jarrolds, 1944
Once Off Guard. Dutton, 1942; Jarrolds, 1943
The Servant of Death. Dutton, 1932; Jarrolds, 1933

WALLIS, RUTH OTIS SAWTELL (D)
Blood from a Stone. Dodd, 1945
Cold Bed in the Clay. Dodd, 1945
Forget My Fate. Dodd, 1950
No Bones About It. Dodd, 1944
Too Many Bones. Dodd, 1943; Dell

WALPOLE, HORACE (S)
The Castle of Otranto. Oxford, 1964

WALSH, GOODWIN (D)
The Voice of the Murderer. Putnam, 1926

WALSH, JAMES MORGAN (D-M)
(Pseudonym: H. Haverstock Hill)
Bandits of the Night. Hamilton, 1933
The Black Cross. Hamilton, 1928; Withy Grove, 1941
Black Dragon. Collins, 1938
The Black Ghost. Hamilton, 1930; Brewer, 1931
Bullets for Breakfast. Collins, 1939
Chalk-Face. Hodder, 1937
The Company of Shadows. Hamilton, 1926
The Crime of Cleopatra's Needle. Hamilton, 1928
Danger Zone. Collins, 1942
Death at His Elbow. Collins, 1941
Dial 999. Collins, 1938
Exit Simeon Hex. Hamilton, 1930
Express Delivery. Collins, 1946
Face Value. Collins, 1944
A Girl of the Islands. Hamilton, 1932
The Hairpin Mystery. Hamilton, 1926; Withy Grove, 1941
Half Ace. Collins, 1936
The Hand of Doom. Hamilton, 1927
Images of Man. Hamilton, 1927
Island Alert. Collins, 1943
Island of Spies. Collins, 1937
The King of Tiger Bay. Collins, 1952
The King's Enemies. Collins, 1939
The King's Messenger. Collins, 1933; Low, 1949
Lady Incognito. Collins, 1932
The League of Missing Men. Hamilton, 1932
The Man Behind the Curtain. Hamilton, 1931
The Man from Whitehall. Collins, 1934
The Man Who Grew Bulbs. Vallancey, 1945
Mutton Dressed as Lamb and Live Bait. Polybooks, 1944
Mystery House. Hamilton, 1931

The Mystery Man. Hamilton, 1929; Mellifont, 1942
The Mystery of the Crystal Skull. Hamilton, 1929
The Mystery of the Green Caterpillars. Hamilton, 1929; Withy Grove, 1944
Next, Please. Collins, 1951
Once in Tiger Bay. Collins, 1947
The Purple Stain. Hamilton, 1928; Mellifont, 1944
Return to Tiger Bay. Collins, 1950
The Secret Service Girl. Collins, 1933; Low, 1947
Secret Weapons. Collins, 1940
The Silent Man. Collins, 1935
The Silver Greyhound. Hamilton, 1928; Withy Grove, 1941
Spies Are Abroad. Collins, 1933; Low, 1947
Spies from the Skies. Collins, 1941
Spies in Pursuit. Collins, 1934; Low, 1949
Spies in Spain. Collins, 1937; Odhams, 1937
Spies Never Return. Collins, 1935
Spies' Vendetta. Collins, 1936
The Tempania Mystery. Hamilton, 1929
Tiger of the Night. Collins, 1935
Time to Kill. Collins, 1949
Vandals of the Void. Hamilton, 1931
Walking Shadow. Collins, 1948
The Whisperer. Hamilton, 1931
Whispers in the Dark. Collins, 1945
White Mask. Doran, 1927; Hamilton

WALSH, MAURICE (D)
Danger Under the Moon. Lippincott, 1957
The Man in Brown. Chambers, 1945
Nine Strings to Your Bow. Lippincott, 1945
The Small Dark Man. Chambers, 1929; Stokes, 1929

WALSH, PAUL G. (M)
K K K. Avon, 1956
Murder in Baracoa. Avon, 1958
The Murder Room. Avon, 1957

WALSH, ROBERT (S)
The Violent Hours. Signet, 1958

WALSH, THOMAS (D-M)
The Action of the Tiger. S & S, 1958
Dangerous Passenger. Little, 1959
The Dark Window. Little, 1956
The Eye of the Needle. S & S, 1961; Cassell, 1962; Dell, 1967
The Face of the Enemy. S & S, 1967
Nightmare in Manhattan. Little, 1950; Hamilton, H., 1951; Macfadden, 1964
The Night Watch. Hamilton, H., 1952; Little, 1952; Transworld, 1954
The Resurrection Man. S & S, 1966; Cassell, 1967
The Tenth Point. S & S, 1965
A Thief in the Night. S & S, 1962; Cassell, 1963; Award, 1965
To Hide a Rogue. S & S, 1964; Award 1966

WALTER, ALEXIA E.; see WALTER, HUBERT CONRAD

WALTER, ELIZABETH (S)
Snowfall and Other Chilling Events. Stein, 1966

WALTER, HUBERT CONRAD (M)
Betrayal. Dutton, 1930; Methuen, 1931
The Patriot, with Alexia E. Walter. Dutton, 1928; Methuen, 1928

WALTER, HUGH
A Bullet for Charles. MacDonald & Co., 1955

WALTON, FRANCIS, pseud; see HODDER, ALFRED

WALZ, MRS. AUDREY (D) (Pseudonym: Francis Bonnamy)
Blood and Thirsty. Duell, 1949; Gryphon, 1952
Dead Reckoning, Duell, 1943; Penguin, 1948
Death by Appointment. Doubleday, Doran, 1931
Death on a Dude Ranch. Doubleday, Doran, 1937; Gryphon, 1953
The King Is Dead on Queen Street. Penguin, 1948
The Man in the Mist. Duell, 1951; Gryphon, 1952
Portrait of an Artist as a Dead Man. Duell, 1947
A Rope of Sand. Duell, 1944; Penguin, 1947
Self-Portrait of Murder. Gryphon, 1951

WARD, ARTHUR SARSFIELD (M) (Pseudonym: Sax Rohmer)
The Bat Flies Low. Doubleday, Doran, 1935; Cassell, 1936
Bat-Wing. Cassell, 1921; Doubleday, Page, 1921
Bimbâshi Barûk of Egypt. McBride, 1944 (English title: Egyptian Nights. Hale, R., 1944)
The Book of Fu Manchu. Hurst, 1929
The Bride of Fu Manchu. Cassell, 1933; Pyramid, 1962 (Also published as: Fu Manchu's Bride. Doubleday, Doran, 1933)
Brood of the Witch Queen. Pearson, 1918; Pyramid, 1966
The Daughter of Fu Manchu. Cassell, 1931; Pyramid, 1964

The Day the World Ended. Cassell, 1930; Ace, 1964
The Devil Doctor. Methuen, 1916
Dope. Cassell, 1919; McBride, 1919
The Dream Detective. Jarrolds, 1920; Doubleday, Page, 1925; Pyramid
The Drums of Fu Manchu. Cassell, 1939; Doubleday, Doran, 1939; Pyramid, 1962
Egyptian Nights; see Bimbâshi Barûk of Egypt
Emperor Fu Manchu. GM, 1959; Pyramid
The Emperor of America. Cassell, 1929; Collier, 1929
The Exploits of Captain O'Hagan. Jarrolds, 1916
The Fire Goddess. GM, 1952
Fire-Tongue. Cassell, 1921; Doubleday, Page, 1922
Fu Manchu's Bride; see The Bride of Fu Manchu
The Golden Scorpion. Methuen, 1919; McBride, 1920
The Green Eyes of Bast. Cassell, 1920; McBride, 1920
Grey Face. Cassell, 1924; Doubleday, Page, 1924
The Hand of Fu Manchu. Burt, 1917; Pyramid, 1962
Hangover House. Graphic, 1949; Jenkins, 1950
The Haunting of Low Fennel. Pearson, 1924
The Insidious Dr. Fu Manchu. McBride, 1913; Pyramid, 1963 (Also published as: The Mystery of Fu Manchu. Methuen, 1913)
The Island of Fu Manchu. Cassell, 1941; Doubleday, Doran, 1941; Pyramid, 1963
The Mask of Fu Manchu. Doubleday, Doran, 1932; Cassell, 1933; Pyramid, 1962
The Moon Is Red. Jenkins, 1954
Moon of Madness. Cassell, 1927; Doubleday, Page, 1927
The Mystery of Fu Manchu; see The Insidious Fu Manchu
The Orchard of Tears. Methuen, 1918
President Fu Manchu. Cassell, 1936; Doubleday, Doran, 1936; Pyramid, 1963
The Quest of the Sacred Slipper. Pearson, 1919, 1925; Pyramid, 1967
Re-enter Fu Manchu. GM, 1957, 1964
Return of Fu Manchu. McBride, 1916; GM, 1961; Pyramid, 1961
Return of Sumuru. GM, 1954
Salute to Bazarada and Other Stories. Cassell, 1939
Sand and Satin. Jenkins, 1955
Seven Sins. McBride, 1943; Cassell, 1944
The Shadow of Fu Manchu. Doubleday, 1948; Jenkins, 1949; Pyramid, 1963
She Who Sleeps. Cassell, 1928
The Si-Fan Mysteries. Methuen, 1917
The Sinister Madonna. GM, 1956
The Sins of Severac Bablon. Cassell, 1914
Sins of Sumuru. Jenkins, 1950
Slaves of Sumuru. Jenkins, 1952
Sumuru. GM, 1951
Tales of Chinatown. Cassell, 1922; Doubleday, Page, 1922
Tales of East and West. Cassell, 1932; Burt, 1933
Tales of Secret Egypt. Methuen, 1918; McBride, 1919
The Trail of Fu Manchu. Cassell, 1934; Doubleday, Doran, 1934; Pyramid, 1964
Virgin in Flames. Jenkins, 1953
White Velvet. Cassell, 1936; Doubleday, Doran, 1936
The Yellow Claw. Burt, 1915; Methuen, 1915; Pyramid
Yellow Shadows. Cassell, 1925
Yu'an Hee See Laughs. Cassell, 1932; Doubleday, Doran, 1932

WARD, COLIN (M)
The House Party Murder. Collins, 1933; Morrow, 1934

WARD, ERNEST (M)
Five for Bridge. Crowell, 1940

WARD, GERALD (M)
Time to Kill. Jarrolds, 1958

WARD, HAROLD (M)
The Blood of Buddha. Melrose, 1937
Murder of a Painted Lady. Melrose, 1937
The Vulture. Pearson, 1936
The Vulture Strikes. Pearson, 1936

WARD, HERBERT D. (M)
White Crown. Houghton, 1894

WARD, JULIAN, pseud. (D)
Death Sleeps in Kensington. Hodder, 1951

WARD, STEVE (M)
Odds Against Linda. Ace, 1960

WARD, WILLIAM (M)
The Passenger from Scotland Yard. Economy Book League, 1933

WARDEN, FLORENCE, pseud; see JAMES, FLORENCE ALICE PRICE

WARDEN, GERTRUDE (M)
As a Bird to the Snare. Arrowsmith, 1888
Beyond the Law. Ward, Lock, 1902

WARDEN, LEWIS (M)
Death on Wheels. Bouregy, 1964

WARE, JUDITH (S)
Detour to Denmark. Paperback Lib., 1967
The Faxon Secret. Paperback Lib., 1966
Fear Place. Paperback Lib., 1967
Quarry House. Paperback Lib., 1965
Thorne House. Paperback Lib., 1965

WARE, WALLACE (S)
The Charka Memorial. Doubleday, 1954

WARING, MOLLY (M)
After the Verdict. Wright & Brown, 1951

WARMAN, ERIK (M)
Soft at the Centre. Dakers, 1953

WARNER, DOUGLAS (D)
Death of a Bogey. Cassell, 1962
Death of a Dreamer. Cassell, 1964; Walker & Co., 1965
Death of a Nude. Cassell, 1964; Corgi, 1966
Death of a Snout. Cassell, 1961; Walker & Co., 1962
Death of a Tom. Cassell, 1963; Macmillan, 1964

WARNER, OLIVER (M)
The Secret of the Marsh. Chatto, 1927; Dutton, 1927

WARREN, CHARLES MARQUIS (M)
Deadhead. Coward, 1949; Boardman, T. V., 1950

WARREN, JAMES (M)
Brush of Death. Collins, 1958
Cold Steel. Collins, 1957
The Disappearing Corpse. Washburn, 1958
No Sleep at All. Alliance, 1941; Collins, 1941
Prowl No More Lady. Collins, 1942
Runaway Corpse. Collins, 1947
She Fell Among Actors. Collins, 1944; Doubleday, Doran, 1944

WARREN, JOHN RUSSELL (M) (Pseudonym: Gilbert Coverack)
ATS Mystery. Hurst, 1943, Macmillan, 1944
Bride for Bombay. Ward, Lock, 1931
Castle Enigma. Ward, Lock, 1930
Gas Mask Murder. Heinemann, 1939 (U.S. title: Murder in the Blackout. Sheridan, 1940; World Pub., 1943)
Half a Clue. Ward, Lock, 1930
The Magpie Murder. Sheridan, 1942; Earl, 1947
Missing from His Home. Melrose, 1950
Murder from Three Angles. Furman, 1939; Heinemann, 1940
Murder in the Blackout; see Gas Mask Murder
Mystery Mine. Ward, Lock, 1930
Princess Proxy. Ward, Lock, 1932
Snow Upon the Desert. Ward, Lock, 1932
This Inward Horror; see This Mortal Coil
This Mortal Coil. Melrose, 1947 (U.S. title: This Inward Horror. Dutton, 1948)
Time for a Murder. Hurst, 1941; Sheridan, 1941

WARREN, PAULETTE (S)
Ravenkill. Lancer
Some Beckoning Wraith. Lancer, 1965

WARREN, VERNON (D)
Appointment in Hell. Gifford, 1956
Back Lash. Gifford, 1960
Blue Mauritius. Gifford, 1954
Brandon Returns. Gifford, 1954
Brandon Takes Over. Gifford, 1953
Bullets for Brandon. Gifford, 1955
By Fair Means or Foul. Gifford, 1956
Farewell by Death. Gifford, 1961
Invitation to Kill. Gifford, 1963
Mister Violence. Gifford, 1961
No Bouquets for Brandon. Gifford, 1955
Runaround. Gifford, 1958; Thriller Book Club, 1958
Stopover Danger. Gifford, 1959
Three Steps to Hell. Gifford, 1957

WARRINER, THURMAN (M) (Pseudonym: Simon Troy)
Cease Upon the Midnight, by Simon Troy. Gollancz, 1964; Macmillan, 1965
Death's Bright Angel. Hodder, 1956
Death's Dateless Night. Hodder, 1952
Don't Play with the Rough Boys, by Simon Troy. Macmillan, 1954
The Doors of Sleep. Hodder, 1955; Penguin, 1961
Drunkard's End, by Simon Troy. Doubleday, 1960; Gollancz, 1960
Ducats in Her Coffin. Hodder, 1951
Golden Lantern. Hodder, 1958
Halfway to Murder, by Simon Troy. Gollancz, 1955
Heavenly Bodies. Hodder, 1960
Method in His Murder. Hodder, 1950; Macmillan, 1951
Second Cousin Removed, by Simon Troy Gollancz, 1961; Macmillan, 1962
She Died, of Course. Hodder, 1958
Tonight and Tomorrow, by Simon Troy. Gollancz, 1957
Waiting for Oliver, by Simon Troy. Gollancz, 1962; Macmillan, 1963

WARWICK, CHESTER (S)
My Pal, the Killer. Ace, 1961

WARWICK, PAULINE, pseud; see DAVIES, BETTY EVELYN

WASHBURN, ROBERT COLLYER (M)
The Jury of Death. Doubleday, Doran, 1930

WASSERMAN, JACOB (M)
The Maurizius Case. Liveright, 1929; Pyramid, 1964

WATEN, JUDAH LEON (M)
Shares in Murder. Australasian Book Society, 1957

"WATERS," pseud; see RUSSELL, WILLIAM

WATKINS, ALEX (M) (Pseudonym: J. Lane Linklater)
The Bishop's Cap Murder. Foulsham, 1949
Black Opal. Boardman, T. V., 1949
Shadow for a Lady. Boardman, T. V., 1948
She Had a Little Knife. Foulsham, 1950
A Tisket, a Casket. Bouregy, 1959

WATKINS, RICHARD HOWELLS (M-S)
The Air Murders. Doubleday, Doran, 1929; Selwyn, 1929
Half a Clew. Clode, 1927
The Master of Revels. Doubleday, Doran, 1928

WATKINSON, VALERIE (M)
The Sped Arrow. Scribner, 1964

WATSON, COLIN (D-S)
Bump in the Night. Eyre, 1960; Walker & Co., 1961; Penguin, 1963
Coffin Scarely Used. Eyre, 1958; Penguin, 1962; Putnam, 1967
Hopjoy Was Here. Eyre, 1962; Penguin, 1963; Walker & Co., 1963
Lonelyheart 4122. Putnam, 1967

WATSON, H. B. MARRIOTT (M)
High Toby. Methuen, 1906
King's Highway. Mills & Boon, 1910

WATSON, JOHN REAY; see REES, ARTHUR JOHN

WATSON, KEITH WEST-; see WEST-WATSON, KEITH

WATSON, P. W. (S)
Bride's Castle. Farrar & Rinehart, 1944

WATSON, SELWYN VICTOR (M) (Pseudonym: "Selwyn")
Operation Ballerina. Hodder, 1953

WAUGH, HILLARY BALDWIN (D) (Pseudonym: H. Baldwin Taylor, Harry Walker)
Born Victim. Doubleday, 1962; Gollancz, 1963; Avon, 1964
The Case of the Missing Gardener, by Harry Walker. Arcadia, 1954
Death and Circumstance. Doubleday, 1963; Gollancz, 1963; Avon, 1966
The Duplicate, by H. Baldwin Taylor. Doubleday, 1964
The Eighth Mrs. Bluebeard. Doubleday, 1958; Crest, 1959; Foulsham, 1959
End of a Party. Doubleday, 1965
Girl on the Run. Doubleday, 1965
The Girl Who Cried Wolf. Doubleday, 1959; Dell, 1960
Hope to Die. Coward, 1948
Last Seen Wearing. Doubleday, 1952; Gollancz, 1953
The Late Mrs. D. Doubleday, 1962; Avon, 1964
Madam Will Not Dine Tonight. Coward, 1947; Boardman, T. V., 1949
The Missing Man. Doubleday, 1964; Gollancz, 1964
Murder on the Terrace, by Harry Walker. Foulsham, 1961
The Odds Run Out. Coward, 1949; Boardman, T. V., 1950
Prisoner's Plea. Doubleday, 1963; Gollancz, 1964
Pure Poison. Doubleday, 1966; Gollancz, 1967
Rag and a Bone. Doubleday, 1954; Foulsham, 1955
Rich Man, Dead Man. Doubleday, 1954 (English title: Rich Man, Murder. Foulsham, 1956)
Rich Man, Murder; see Rich Man, Dead Man
Road Block. Doubleday, 1960; Gollancz, 1961; Popular Lib., 1965
Sleep Long, My Love. Doubleday, 1959; Gollancz, 1960; Dell, 1964
That Night It Rained. Doubleday, 1961
The Triumvirate. Doubleday, 1966
The Trouble with Tycoons, by H. Baldwin Taylor. Doubleday, 1967

WAY, ELIZABETH P. FENWICK; see FENWICK, ELIZABETH P.

WAY, ISABEL STEWART (S)
Fleur Macabre. Tower, 1967

WAYE, CECIL (M)
The End of the Chase. Hodder, 1932
The Figure of Eight. Hodder, 1931
Murder at Monk's Barn. Hodder, 1931
The Prime Minister's Peril. Hodder, 1933

WAYLAND, PATRICK, pseud; see O'CONNOR, RICHARD

WEATHERLY, MAX (M)
The Mantis and the Moth. Houghton, 1964; PB, 1965

WEAVER, ROBERT G. and SOL RUBINSTEIN (M) (Pseudonym: Rubin Weber)
Gravemaker's House. Harper & Row, 1964; Avon, 1966

WEAVER, WARD, pseud; see MASON, FRANCIS VAN WYCK

WEBB, DOROTHY ANNA (D-M) (Pseudonym: Jermyn March)
Dear Traitor. Hurst, 1925
The Man Behind the Face. Hurst, 1927
Rust of Murder. Hurst, 1924
The Scarlet Thumb. Henkle, 1929

WEBB, JACK (D) (Pseudonym: John Farr)
The Bad Blond. Rinehart, 1956; Boardman, T. V., 1957
The Big Sin. Rinehart, 1952; Boardman, T. V., 1953
The Brass Halo. Rinehart, 1957; Boardman, T. V., 1958
The Broken Doll. Rinehart, 1955; Boardman, T. V., 1956
The Damned Lovely. Rinehart, 1954
The Deadly Combo, by John Farr. Ace, 1958
The Deadly Sex. Rinehart, 1959; Boardman, T. V., 1960
The Delicate Darling. Rinehart, 1959; Boardman, T. V., 1960
Don't Feed the Animals, by John Farr. Abelard, 1955 (Also published as: The Zoo Murders. Foulsham, 1956)
The Gilded Witch. Boardman, T. V., 1963; Regency, 1963
The Lady and the Snake, by John Farr. Ace, 1957
Make My Bed Soon. Holt, 1963; Boardman, T. V., 1964; Avon, 1965
Naked Angel. Rinehart, 1953 (Also published as: Such Women Are Dangerous. Boardman, T. V., 1954)
One for My Dame. Holt, 1961; Avon, 1964
Such Women Are Dangerous; see Naked Angel
The Zoo Murders; see Don't Feed the Animals

WEBB, JEAN FRANCIS (M)
Murder's Hex Sign. Macmillan, 1950
No Match for Murder. Macmillan, 1942

WEBB, JOHN EDGAR (S)
Four Steps to the Wall. Dial, 1948

WEBB, RICHARD WILSON and HUGH CALLINGHAM WHEELER (Pseudonyms: Q. Patrick, Patrick Quentin, Jonathan Stagge)
Black Widow, by Patrick Quentin. S & S, 1952
Call a Hearse, by Jonathan Stagge. Joseph, M., 1942
Cottage Sinister, by Q. Patrick. Swain, 1931; Longmans, 1932 (Written by Richard W. Webb and Martha Mott Kelley)
Danger Next Door, by Patrick Quentin. S & S, 1950; Cassell, 1951
Darker Grows the Valley. Cassell, 1935
Death and the Dear Girls; see Death, My Darling Daughters
Death and the Maiden, by Q. Patrick. Cassell, 1939; S & S, 1939
Death for Dear Clara, by Q. Patrick. Cassell, 1937; S & S, 1937
Death Goes to School. Cassell, 1936; Random, 1936
Death in Bermuda; see Return to the Scene
Death in the Dovecote. Cassell, 1934
Death, My Darling Daughters, by Jonathan Stagge. Doubleday, Doran, 1945 (English title: Death and the Dear Girls. Joseph, M., 1946)
Death's Old Sweet Song, by Jonathan Stagge. Doubleday, 1946; Joseph, M., 1947
Dogs Do Bark. Doubleday, Doran, 1937 (English title: Murder Gone to Earth. Joseph, M., 1937)
Family Skeletons, by Patrick Quentin. Gollancz, 1965; Random, 1965 (Written by Hugh C. Wheeler only)
Fatal Woman, by Patrick Quentin. Gollancz, 1953
File on Claudia Cragge. Jarrolds, 1938; Morrow, 1938
File on Fenton and Farr. Morrow, 1937; Jarrolds, 1938
The Follower, by Patrick Quentin. Gollancz, 1950; S & S, 1950; Penguin, 1955
Funeral for Five, by Jonathan Stagge. Joseph, M., 1940
Girl on the Gallows. GM, 1954
Green-eyed Monster, by Patrick Quentin. Gollancz, 1960; Random, 1960
Grindle Nightmare. Hartney, 1935; Ballantine
Light from a Lantern, by Jonathan Stagge. Joseph, M., 1943
Man in the Net, by Patrick Quentin. Gollancz, 1956; S & S, 1956
Man with Two Wives, by Patrick Quentin. Gollancz, 1955; S & S, 1955
Murder at Cambridge. Farrar & Rinehart, 1933 (English title: Murder at the 'Varsity. Longmans, 1933)
Murder at the 'Varsity; see Murder at Cambridge

Murder at the Women's City Club. Swain, 1932 (Written by Richard W. Webb and Martha Mott Kelley)
Murder by Prescription, by Jonathan Stagge. Doubleday, Doran, 1938 (English title: Murder or Mercy. Joseph, M., 1937)
Murder Gone to Earth; see Dogs Do Bark
Murder in the Stars; see Stars Spell Death
Murder or Mercy; see Murder by Prescription
My Son the Murderer, by Patrick Quentin. S & S, 1954; Avon, 1965 (English title: Wife of Ronald Sheldon. Gollancz, 1954)
The Ordeal of Mrs. Snow and Other Stories, by Patrick Quentin. Gollancz, 1961; Random, 1961; New English Lib., 1964 (Written by Hugh C. Wheeler only)
Puzzle for Fiends, by Patrick Quentin. S & S, 1946; Gollancz, 1947; Penguin, 1955; New English Lib., 1962
A Puzzle for Fools, by Patrick Quentin. Gollancz, 1936; S & S, 1936; World Pub., 1943
Puzzle for Pilgrims, by Patrick Quentin. S & S, 1947; Gollancz, 1948
Puzzle for Players, by Patrick Quentin. S & S, 1938; Gollancz, 1939
Puzzle for Puppets, by Patrick Quentin. S & S, 1944; Gollancz, 1945
Puzzle for Wantons, by Patrick Quentin. S & S, 1945; Gollancz, 1946
Return to the Scene, by Q. Patrick. S & S, 1941 (English title: Death in Bermuda. Cassell, 1941)
Run to Death, by Patrick Quentin. Gollancz, 1948; S & S, 1948; New English Lib., 1962
Scarlet Circle, by Jonathan Stagge. Doubleday, Doran, 1943
Shadow of Guilt, by Patrick Quentin. Gollancz, 1959; Random, 1959
S.S. Murder. Farrar & Rinehart, 1933; Gollancz, 1933
Stars Spell Death, by Jonathan Stagge. Doubleday, Doran, 1939 (English title: Murder in the Stars. Joseph, M., 1940)
Suspicious Circumstances, by Patrick Quentin. S & S, 1957; Gollancz, 1958
The Three Fears, by Jonathan Stagge. Doubleday, 1949; Joseph, M., 1949
Turn of the Table, by Jonathan Stagge. Doubleday, Doran, 1940
Wife of Ronald Sheldon; see My Son the Murderer
Yellow Taxi, by Jonathan Stagge. Doubleday, Doran, 1942

WEBER, RUBIN, pseud; see WEAVER, ROBERT

WEBSTER, FREDERICK ANNESLEY MICHAEL (D)
Beneath the Mask. Skeffington, 1948
Black Shadow. Nisbet, 1922; Warne, 1930
Crime Scientist. Warne, 1930; Wright & Brown, 1930
The Gathering Storm. Wright & Brown, 1933
Old Ebbie. Warne, 1930
Old Ebbie, Detective Up-to-date. Chapman, 1923; Warne, 1930
Old Ebbie Returns. Chapman, 1925

WEBSTER, H. M. (M)
The Ballycronin Mystery. Hurst, 1947
Tontine Treasure. Hurst, 1951

WEBSTER, HENRY KITCHELL (M)
The Alleged Great Aunt. Bobbs, 1935; Paul, S., 1935
The Clock Strikes Two. Bobbs, 1928
The Corbin Necklace. Bobbs, 1926 (English title: The Mystery of the Corbin Necklace. Hamilton, 1929)
The Man with the Scarred Hand. Bobbs, 1930
The Mystery of the Corbin Necklace; see The Corbin Necklace
The Quartz Eye. Bobbs, 1928; Hodder, 1928
The Sealed Trunk. Bobbs, 1929; Paul, S., 1929
The Whispering Man. Appleton, D., 1908; Nash, 1908
Who Is the Next? Bobbs, 1931

WEBSTER, J. (M)
Four-pools Mystery. Century, 1908; Hodder, 1916

WEEKES, AGNES RUSSELL and ROSE KIRKPATRICK WEEKES (M) (Pseudonym: Anthony Pryde)
Emerald Necklace. Dodd, 1931; Ward, Lock, 1931
The Figure on the Terrace. Ward, Lock, 1933
Secret Room. Dodd, 1929

WEEKES, ROSE KIRKPATRICK; see WEEKES, AGNES RUSSELL

WEEKS, JACK (M)
The Grey Affair. Dell, 1961

WEEKS, WILLIAM RAWLE (S)
Knock and Wait Awhile. Houghton, 1957; Bantam

WEES, FRANCES SHELLEY JOHNSON (M)
The Country of the Strangers. Doubleday, 1960

Dangerous Deadline. Ward, Lock, 1961
Detectives, Ltd. Eyre, 1933
The Faceless Enemy. Doubleday, 1966; Cassell, 1967
The Keys of My Prison. Doubleday, 1956
The Maestro Murders. Mystery League, 1931
M'Lord, I Am Not Guilty. Doubleday, 1954; Jenkins, 1954; Pyramid, 1967
The Mystery of the Creeping Man. Macrae Smith, 1931; Eyre, 1934
This Necessary Murder. Jenkins, 1957
Where Is Jenny Now? Doubleday, 1958; Jenkins, 1958

WEINER, HENRI, pseud; see LONGSTREET, STEPHEN

WEINSTEIN, SOL (M)
Loxfinger. PB, 1965
On the Secret Service of His Majesty the Queen. PB, 1966

WEINTRAUB, SIDNEY (M)
Mexican Slay Ride. Abelard, 1962; Hale, R., 1962
The Siamese Coup Affair. Boardman, T. V., 1963

WEIR, HUGH COSGRO (D)
Miss Madelyn Mack, Detective. Page, 1914

WEISSEL, AUGUST (M)
The Mystery of the Green Car. Nelson, 1913

WELCOME, JOHN, pseud; see BRENNAN, JOHN

WELLARD, JAMES HOWARD (S)
Action of the Tiger. Avon, 1955; St. Martin's, 1955
Moment in Time. Dodd, 1947
The Snake in the Grass. Dodd, 1942
Spotlight on Murder. Foulsham, 1949

WELLES, ORSON (M)
Mr. Arkadin. Crowell, 1957

WELLMAN, MANLY WADE (M)
Find My Killer. Farrar, Straus, 1947

WELLS, ANNA MARY (M)
Fear of Death. Wingate, 1951
Murder's Choice. Knopf, 1943; Hammond, 1950
The Night of May Third. Doubleday, 1956; Foulsham, 1957
Sin of Angels. S & S, 1948; Hammond, 1951
A Talent for Murder. Knopf, 1942; Hammond, 1948

WELLS, CAROLYN (D) (Pseudonym: Rowland Wright)
Adventures of the Clothes-line. Doran, 1923
The Affair at Flower Acres. Doran, 1923
All at Sea. Lippincott, 1927
Anybody But Anne. Lippincott, 1914
Anything But the Truth. Lippincott, 1925
The Beautiful Derelict. Lippincott, 1935
The Black Night Murders. Lippincott, 1941
Bride of a Moment. Doran, 1916
The Broken O. Lippincott, 1933
The Bronze Hand. Lippincott, 1925
Calling All Suspects. Lippincott, 1939
A Chain of Evidence. Lippincott, 1912
The Clue. Lippincott, 1909; Hodder, 1920
Clue of the Eyelash. Lippincott, 1933; Laurie, 1936
The Come-Back. Doran, 1921; Hodder, 1921
The Crime in the Crypt. Lippincott, 1928
Crime Incarnate. Lippincott, 1940
Crime Tears On. Lippincott, 1939
The Curved Blades. Lippincott, 1916
The Daughter of the House. Lippincott, 1925
The Deep-Lake Mystery. Doubleday, Doran, 1928
The Devil's Work. Lippincott, 1940
The Diamond Pin. Lippincott, 1919
The Disappearance of Kimball Webb, by Rowland Wright. Dodd, 1920
The Doomed Five. Lippincott, 1930
The Doorstep Murders. Doubleday, Doran, 1930
Eyes in the Wall. Lippincott, 1934
Face Cards. Putnam, 1925
Faulkner's Folly. Doubleday, Page, 1917; Grosset, 1919
Feathers Left Around. Lippincott, 1922
For Goodness' Sake. Lippincott, 1935
The Fourteenth Key. Putnam, 1924
Fuller's Earth. Lippincott, 1932
The Furthest Fury. Lippincott, 1924
Ghosts' High Noon. Lippincott, 1930
Gilt-Edged Guilt. Lippincott, 1938
The Gold Bag. Lippincott, 1911
Horror House. Lippincott, 1931
The Huddle. Lippincott, 1936
The Importance of Being Murdered. Lippincott, 1939
In the Onyx Lobby. Doran, 1920; Hodder, 1921
In the Tiger's Cage. Lippincott, 1934
The Killer. Lippincott, 1938
The Luminous Face. Doubleday, Page, 1921
The Man Who Fell Through the Earth. Doran, 1919; Harrap, 1924

Mark of Cain. Lippincott, 1917; Hodder, 1920
The Master Murderer. Lippincott, 1933
The Maxwell Mystery. Lippincott, 1913
The Missing Link. Lippincott, 1938; Triangle, 1939
Money Musk. Lippincott, 1936
More Lives Than One. Boni & Liveright, 1923
The Moss Mystery. Doubleday, Page, 1924
Murder at the Casino. Lippincott, 1944
Murder in the Bookshop. Lippincott, 1936
Murder on Parade. Lippincott, 1940
Murder Plus. Lippincott, 1940
Murder Will In. Lippincott, 1942
The Mystery Girl. Lippincott, 1922
Mystery of the Sycamore. Lippincott, 1921
Mystery of the Tarn. Lippincott, 1937
Omnibus Fleming Stone. Lippincott, 1932
Prillilgirl. Lippincott, 1924
Radio Studio Murder. Lippincott, 1937
Raspberry Jam. Lippincott, 1920
The Red-haired Girl. Lippincott, 1926
The Roll-top Desk Mystery. Lippincott, 1932
The Room with the Tassells. Doran, 1918
The Sixth Commandment. Doubleday, Page, 1927
The Skeleton at the Feast. Doubleday, Doran, 1931
Sleeping Dogs. Doubleday, Doran, 1929
Spooky Hollow. Lippincott, 1923
The Tannahill Tangle. Lippincott, 1928
The Tapestry Room Murder. Lippincott, 1929
Triple Murder. Lippincott, 1929
The Umbrella Murder. Lippincott, 1931
The Vanishing of Betty Varian. Doubleday, Page, 1922; Collins, 1924
The Vanity Case. Putnam, 1926
Vicky Van. Lippincott, 1918; Hodder, 1920
The Visiting Villain. Lippincott, 1934
Wheels Within Wheels. Doran, 1923
Where's Emily? Lippincott, 1927
The White Alley. Lippincott, 1912; Hodder, 1920
Who Killed Caldwell? Lippincott, 1942
The Wooden Indian. Lippincott, 1935

WELLS, CHARLIE (M)
The Last Kill. Signet, 1955
Let the Night Cry. Abelard, 1953

WELLS, HERBERT GEORGE (S)
The Inexperienced Ghost. Bantam, 1965
The Invisible Man. Pearson, 1897; Longmans, 1936; Popular Lib., 1964
The Island of Dr. Moreau. Heinemann, 1896; Ballantine, 1963
The Plattner Story and Others. Methuen, 1897
The Stolen Bacillus. Methuen, 1895; Macmillan, 1920

WELLS, SUSAN, pseud; see SIEGEL, DORIS

WELLS, TOBIAS, pseud; see FORBES, DeLORIS STANTON

WEMPE, IRENE (S)
Come to My Funeral. Ballantine, 1967

WENTWORTH, PATRICIA, pseud; see TURNBULL, DORA AMY DILLON

WENZELL, ISABEL d'ESTE (S)
Dragon's Lair. Lancer, 1967

WERRY, RICHARD R. (M)
Hammer Me Home. Dodd, 1955

WERTENBAKER, LAEL TUCKER (S)
The Eye of the Lion. Little, 1964

WEST, CAROL (M)
Laughing Malefactor. Vantage, 1964

WEST, ELLIOT (S)
Man Running. Little, 1959; Ace
The Night Is a Time for Listening. Random, 1966; Bantam, 1967

WEST, GEOFFREY PHILIP (M)
How Did Elmer Die? Longmans, 1938

WEST, JOHN B. (D)
Bullets Are My Business. Signet, 1960
Cobra Venom. Signet, 1959
Death on the Rocks. Signet, 1959
An Eye for an Eye. Signet, 1959
Never Kill a Cop. Signet, 1961
A Taste for Blood. Signet, 1960

WEST, JOYCE; see SCOTT, MARY CLARKE

WEST, KEITH, pseud; see LANE, KENNETH WESTMACOTT

WEST, MORRIS L. (D) (Pseudonym: Michael East)
Backlash. Morrow, 1958
The Big Story; see The Crooked Road
The Crooked Road. Morrow, 1957 (English title: The Big Story. Heinemann, 1957)
Gallows in the Sand. Angus, 1956
McCreary Moves In, by Michael East. Heinemann, 1958
The Naked Country, by Michael East. Dell, 1961
The Second Victory. Heinemann, 1958

WEST, NICHOLSON (M)
The Mysterious Millionaire. Greening, 1906

WESTALL, WILLIAM (M)
Very Queer Business. Chatto, 1904

WESTBIE, CONSTANCE LOVEALL (M)
The Birdcage Murders. Bouregy, 1964

WESTBROOK, PERRY D. (M)
It Boils Down to Murder. Arcadia, 1953

WESTERHAM, S. C.; see ALINGTON, CYRIL A.

WESTHEIMER, DAVID (S) (Pseudonym: Z. Z. Smith)
A Very Private Island, by Z. Z. Smith. Signet
Von Ryan's Express. Joseph, M., 1964; Signet, 1965; Pan, 1966

WESTLAKE, DONALD E. (M) (Pseudonyms: Tucker Coe, Richard Stark)
The Busybody. Random, 1966
The Damsel, by Richard Stark. Macmillan, 1967
The Fugitive Pigeon. Random, 1965; Dell, 1968
God Save the Mark. Random, 1967
The Green Eagle Score, by Richard Stark. GM, 1967
The Handle, by Richard Stark. PB, 1966
The Hunters, by Richard Stark. PB, 1963 (Also published as: Point Blank! GM, 1967)
The Jugger, by Richard Stark. PB, 1965
The Killing Time. Random, 1961; Boardman, T. V., 1962 (Also published as: The Operator. Dell, 1964)
Killy. Random, 1963; Boardman, T. V., 1964
Kinds of Love, Kinds of Death, by Tucker Coe. Random, 1967
The Man with the Getaway Face, by Richard Stark. PB, 1963
The Mercenaries. Random, 1960; Boardman, T. V., 1961
The Mourner, by Richard Stark. PB, 1963
Murder Among Children, by Tucker Coe. Random, 1968
The Outfit, by Richard Stark. PB, 1963
The Operator; see The Killing Time.
Pity Him Afterwards. Random, 1964
Point Blank; see The Hunters
The Rare Coin Score, by Richard Stark. GM, 1967
The Score, by Richard Stark. PB, 1964
The Seventh, by Richard Stark. PB, 1964
The Spy in the Ointment. Random, 1966
361. Boardman, T. V., 1962; Random, 1962

WESTON, ALLEN, pseud; see NORTON, ALICE MARY

WESTON, GARNETT JAMES (M)
Dead Men Are Dangerous. Hutchinson, 1937; Stokes, 1937
Death Never Forgets. Hutchinson, 1935
The Hidden Portal. Doubleday, 1946; Collier
The Legacy of Fear. Mill, 1950
The Man with the Monocle. Doubleday, Doran, 1943
Murder in Haste. Stokes, 1935
Murder on Shadow Island. Farrar & Rinehart, 1933; Hutchinson, 1933
Poldrate Street. Messner, 1944
The Wondering Moon. Dodd, 1926
The Undertaker Dies. Hutchinson, 1940

WESTON, HELEN GRAY (S)
House of False Faces. Paperback Lib., 1967
Mystic Manor. Paperback Lib., 1966

WEST-WATSON, KEITH CAMPBELL (M) (Pseudonym: Keith Campbell)
Born Beautiful. MacDonald & Co., 1951
Broken Branch. Rich, 1944
Darling, Don't. MacDonald & Co., 1950
Goodbye Gorgeous. MacDonald & Co., 1950
Last Journey. Rich, 1941
Listen, Lovely. MacDonald & Co., 1949
Pardon My Gun. MacDonald & Co., 1954
That Was No Lady. MacDonald & Co., 1952

WETHERELL, JUNE (S)
House on Cobra. Belmont, 1966

WEYMOUTH, ANTHONY, pseud; see COBB, IVO GEIKIE

WHALEY, FRANCIS JOHN (M)
Challenge to Murder. Skeffington, 1937
Death at Datchets. Hale, R., 1941
Enter a Spy. Hale, R., 1941
The Mystery of Number Five. Hale, R., 1940
Reduction of Staff. Skeffington, 1936
Southern Electric Murder. Skeffington, 1938
Swift Solution. Hale, R., 1939
This Path Is Dangerous. Hale, R., 1938
Trouble in College. Skeffington, 1936

WHARTON, ANTHONY, pseud; see McALLISTER, ALISTER

WHARTON, EDITH (M)
Ghosts. Appleton-Century, 1937

WHEATLEY, DENNIS (S)
Bill for the Use of a Body. Hutchinson, 1964
Black August. Hutchinson, 1934
Black Baroness. Hutchinson, 1940
Code Word—Golden Fleece. Hutchinson, 1951
Contraband. Hutchinson, 1936
Curtain of Fear. Hutchinson, 1953
Dangerous Inheritance. Hutchinson, 1965
The Devil Rides Out. Hutchinson, 1935
The Eunuch of Stamboul. Hutchinsı 1935; Little, 1935
The Fabulous Valley. Hutchinson, 1934
Faked Passports. Macmillan, 1943; Hutchinson, 1963
File on Bolitho Blane. Morrow, 1936 (English title: Murder Off Miami. Hutchinson, 1936)
File on Robert Prentice. Greenberg, 1937 (English title: Who Killed Robert Prentice? Hutchinson, 1937)
The Forbidden Territory. Hutchinson, 1933; Dutton, 1935
Golden Spaniard. Hutchinson, 1938
Gunmen, Gallants, and Ghosts. Hutchinson, 1943
Island Where Time Stands Still. Hutchinson, 1954
Launching of Roger Brook. Hutchinson, 1947
Man Who Killed the King. Hutchinson, 1951; Putnam, 1965
Murder Off Miami; see File on Bolitho Blane
Prisoner in the Mask. Hutchinson, 1957
Quest of Julian Day. Hutchinson, 1939
Rising Storm. Hutchinson, 1952
The Satanist. Hutchinson, 1960
The Scarlet Imposter. Macmillan, 1942
The Second Seal. Macmillan, 1944
The Secret War, with J. G. Links. Hutchinson, 1937
Shadow of Tyburn Tree. Hutchinson, 1948
Such Power Is Dangerous. Hutchinson, 1933
The Sword of Fate. Macmillan, 1944
They Found Atlantis, with J. G. Links. Hutchinson, 1936
Uncharted Seas, with J. G. Links. Hutchinson, 1964
Vendetta in Spain. Hutchinson, 1961
Who Killed Robert Prentice?; see File on Robert Prentice

WHEELER, BENSON and CLAIRE LEE PURDY (M)
The Riddle of the Eighth Quest. Speller, 1936

WHEELER, E. L. (M)
Fritz to the Front. Westbrook

WHEELER, H. E. (M)
Dead Men Turn Green. Jenkins, 1939
Death Calls the Jester Jenkins, 1936
Death Takes a Ride. Jenkins, 1942
No Crime Is Perfect. Jenkins, 1935
The Syndicate of Death. Jenkins, 1937
The Third Attempt. Jenkins, 1946

WHEELER, HUGH CALLINGHAM; see WEBB, RICHARD WILSON

WHEELOCK, DOROTHY (M)
Dead Giveaway. Phoenix, 1942
Murder at Montauk. Phoenix, 1940

WHELTON, PAUL (M)
Angels Are Painted Fair. Lippincott, 1947
Call the Lady Indiscreet. Lippincott, 1946
Death and the Devil. Lippincott, 1944
In Comes Death. Lippincott, 1951
Pardon My Blood. Lippincott, 1950
Women Are Skin Deep. Lippincott, 1948

WHIPPLE, KENNETH (M)
Fire at Fitch's Folly. Crowell, 1935
Murders at Loon Lake. King, A. H., 1933

WHISHAW, FRED (M)
Diamonds of Evil. Long, 1902
The Informer. Long, 1908

WHITE, ARED (S)
Agent B-7. Houghton, 1934
Seven Tickets to Singapore. Houghton, 1939
The Spy Net. Burt, 1930

WHITE, EDWARD LUCAS (M)
Lukundoo. Doran, 1927

WHITE, ETHEL LINA (D-S)
An Elephant Never Forgets. Collins, 1937; Harper, 1938
Fear Stalks the Village. Ward, Lock, 1932; Harper, 1942; Paperback Lib., 1966
First Time He Died. Collins, 1935 (English title: Midnight House. Collins, 1942)
Her Heart in Her Throat. Harper, 1942; Grosset, 1944 (Also published as: The Unseen. Paperback Lib., 1966)
The Lady Vanishes; see The Wheel Spins
The Man Who Loved Lions; see The Man Who Was Not There
The Man Who Was Not There. Collins, 1943; Harper, 1943; Grosset, 1945

(Also published as: The Man Who Loved Lions. Collins, 1943)
Midnight House; see Her Heart in Her Throat
Put Out the Light. Ward, Lock, 1935; Harper, 1943 (Also published as: Sinister Light. Paperback Lib., 1966)
She Faded Into Air. Collins, 1941; Harper, 1941; Popular Lib., 1967
Sinister Light; see Put Out the Light
Some Must Watch. Ward, Lock, 1934; Harper, 1941 (Also published as: The Spiral Staircase. World Pub., 1946; Popular Lib., 1965)
The Spiral Staircase; see Some Must Watch
Step in the Dark. Collins, 1938; Harper, 1939; Paperback Lib., 1966
They See in Darkness. Collins, 1944
The Third Eye. Collins, 1937; Harper, 1937; Paperback Lib., 1967
The Unseen; see Her Heart in Her Throat
Wax. Collins, 1935; Doubleday, Doran, 1935; Paperback Lib., 1967
The Wheel Spins. Collins, 1936; Harper, 1936; Books, 1945 (Also published as: The Lady Vanishes. Paperback Lib., 1966)
While She Sleeps. Harper, 1940; Paperback Lib., 1966

WHITE, FRED M. (M)
A Crime on Canvas. Fenno, 1909

WHITE, GRACE, M.; see DEAKIN, HILDA L.

WHITE, HERBERT OLIVER (M) (Pseudonym: Oliver Martyn)
The Body in the Pound. Eldon, 1933
The Man They Couldn't Hang. Morrow, 1933

WHITE, JAMES DILLON (Pseudonym: Felix Krull)
The Village Pub Murders. Ward, Lock, 1962

WHITE, LESLIE TURNER (D)
Five Thousand Trojan Horses. World's Work, 1943
Harness Bull. Harcourt, 1937; Hamilton, H., 1938
Homicide. Harcourt, 1937; Hamilton, H., 1938
Me, Detective. Harcourt, 1936
River of No Return. Macrae Smith, 1941; World's Work, 1947
Six Weeks South of Texas. World's Work, 1948

WHITE, LIONEL (M)
Before I Die; see To Find a Killer
The Big Caper. GM, 1955
Clean Break. Boardman, T. V., 1955; Dutton, 1955 (Also published as: The Killing. Tower, 1964)
Coffin for a Hood. GM, 1958
The Crimshaw Memorandum. Dutton, 1967
A Death at Sea. Dutton, 1961; Ace, 1962; Boardman, T. V., 1962
Death Takes the Bus. GM, 1957
Flight into Terror. Dutton, 1955; Boardman, T. V., 1957; Tower, 1965
A Grave Undertaking. Dutton, 1961 Boardman, T. V., 1962
Hostage to a Hood. GM, 1957
The House Next Door. Dutton, 1956; Lancer, 1966
The House on K Street. Dutton, 1965; Boardman, T. V., 1966
Invitation to Violence. Boardman, T. V., 1958; Dutton, 1958
The Killing; see Clean Break
Lament for a Virgin. GM, 1960
The Merriweather File. Dutton, 1959; Boardman, T. V., 1960
The Money Trap. Dutton, 1963; Boardman, T. V., 1964; Monarch, 1964
The Night of the Rape. Dutton, 1967
Obsession. Dutton, 1962; Boardman, T. V., 1963; Monarch, 1963
Operation Murder
Party to Murder. GM, 1966
Rafferty. Dutton, 1959; Bantam, 1960; Boardman, T. V., 1960
The Ransomed Madonna. Dutton, 1964; Boardman, T. V., 1965
Right for Murder. Boardman, T. V., 1957
Run, Killer, Run; see Seven Hungry Men
Seven Hungry Men. 1952 (Also published as: Run, Killer, Run. Avon)
The Snatchers. Avon, 1953, 1961
Steal Big. GM, 1960
The Time of Terror. Dutton, 1960; Boardman, T. V., 1961; Ace, 1962
To Find a Killer. Dutton, 1954; Signet (Also published as: Before I Die. Tower)
Too Young to Die. GM, 1958

WHITE, REGINALD JAMES (M)
The Smartest Grave. Doubleday, 1964

WHITE, STEWARD EDWARD (M)
The Sign of Six. Bobbs, 1912

WHITE, WILLIAM ANTHONY PARKER; see BOUCHER, ANTHONY

WHITE, WILLIAM J.
One for the Road. Cape, 1956

WHITE, WILLIAM PATTERSON (M)
Cloudy in the West. Hodder, 1928; Little, 1928

WHITECHURCH, VICTOR LORENZO (M)
Canon in Residence. Unwin, 1904
The Crime at Diana's Pool. Duffield, 1927; Unwin, 1927
Murder at Exbridge; see Murder at the College
Murder at the College. Collins, 1932 (U.S. title: Murder at Exbridge. Dodd, 1932)
Murder at the Pageant. Collins, 1930; Duffield, 1931
Robbery at Rudwick House. Duffield, 1929
Shot on the Downs. Unwin, 1927; Duffield, 1928
Templeton Case. Clode, 1924; Long, 1924
Thrilling Stories of the Railway. Pearson, 1912

WHITEHEAD, HENRY S. (M)
Jumbee. Arkham, 1944

WHITEHORNE, EARL (S)
Supercargo. Funk, 1939

WHITEHOUSE, ARCH; see WHITEHOUSE, ARTHUR GEORGE JOSEPH

WHITEHOUSE, ARTHUR (ARCH) GEORGE JOSEPH (M)
Crime on a Convoy Carrier. World's Work, 1943

WHITELAW, DAVID (M)
I Could a Tale Unfold. Jenkins, 1959; Roy Pubs., 1959
The Imposter. Hodder, 1915
Murder Calling. Bles, 1934; Kendall, 1934
Presumed Dead. MacDonald & Co., 1952
The Ryecroft Verdict. MacDonald & Co., 1946

WHITFIELD, RAOUL (M)
Death in a Bowl. Knopf, 1931
Green Ice. Knopf, 1930
Virgin Kills. Knopf, 1932; Grosset, 1933

WHITNEY, J. L. H. (S)
The Whisperer of Shadows. Ace, 1964

WHITNEY, JANET (S)
The Quaker Bride. Pyramid, 1966

WHITNEY, PHYLLIS AYAME (S-Gothic)
Black Amber. Appleton, 1964; Crest, 1965
Blue Fire. Appleton, 1961; Bantam, 1965
Columbella. Doubleday, 1966
The Moonflower. Appleton, 1958; Lancer, 1964
The Quicksilver Pool. Appleton, 1955
Red Carnelian; see Red Is for Murder
Red Is for Murder. Ziff-Davis, 1943 (Also published as: Red Carnelian. Paperback Lib., 1968)
Sea Jade. Appleton, 1964; Crest, 1964, 1966
Seven Tears for Apollo. Appleton, 1963; Crest, 1964
Silverhill. Doubleday, 1967
Skye Cameron. Appleton, 1957; Paperback Lib., 1964
Step to the Music. Berkley Pub., 1959; Ace, 1962
Thunder Heights. Appleton, 1960
The Trembling Hills. Appleton, 1956; Ace, 1963
Window on the Square. Appleton, 1962; Crest, 1962

WHITTAKER, F. (M)
Red Rajah. Westbrook

WHITTEN, LESLIE H. (D-S)
Moon of the Wolf. Doubleday, 1967
Progeny of the Adder. Doubleday, 1965; Hodder, 1966; Ace, 1968

WHITTINGTON, HARRY (M)
Brute in Brass. GM, 1956
The Doomsday Affair. Ace, 1965 (The Man from U.N.C.L.E. series #2)
Haven for the Damned. GM, 1962
The Humming Box. Ace, 1956
One Deadly Dawn. Ace, 1957
Play for Keeps. Abelard, 1957
Strangers on Friday. Abelard, 1959
Ticket to Hell. GM, 1959
Web of Murder. GM, 1958
You'll Die Next. Ace, 1954

WIBBERLY, LEONARD PATRICK O'CONNOR (D) (Pseudonym: Leonard Holton)
Deliver Us from Wolves. Dodd, 1963; Dell, 1966
Flowers by Request. Dodd, 1964
Out of the Depths, by Leonard Holton. Dodd, 1966; Dell, 1967
A Pact With Satan, by Leonard Holton. Dodd, 1960
The Saint Maker, by Leonard Holton. Dodd, 1959; Hale, R., 1960
The Secret of the Doubting Saint, by Leonard Holton. Dodd, 1961; Dell, 1965

WICKER, MARY STUART (M)
And Where's Mr. Bellamy? Hutchinson, 1948

WICKER, TOM (M)
The Devil Must. Harper, 1957
The Judgment. Sloane, 1957

WICKERS, N. (M)
The Mystery of Sun Dial Court. Penn, 1926

WICKHAM, HARVEY (D)
The Boncoeur Affair. Clode, 1923
The Clue of the Primros Petal. Brentano, 1923
Scarlet X. Clode, 1922
The Trail of the Squid. Clode, 1924

WICKWARE, FRANCIS SILL (S)
Dangerous Ground. Doubleday, 1946

WIDDER, ARTHUR (S)
Adventures in Black. Scholastic, 1965

WIEGAND, WILLIAM (D)
At Last, Mr. Tolliver. Rinehart, 1950

WIENER, WILLARD (S)
Four Boys, a Girl and a Gun. Dial, 1944; Longmans, 1944

WIGHT, NATALIE (M)
Death in the Inner Office. Phoenix, 1938

WILCOX, COLLIN (D)
The Black Door. Dodd, 1967

WILCOX, HARRY (M) (Pseudonym: Mark Derby)
Afraid in the Dark; see Malayan Rose
The Bad Step; see Out of Asia Alive
The Big Water. Collins, 1953; Viking, 1953
The Dark. Collins, 1962
Echo of a Bomb. Viking, 1957
Element of Risk. Collins, 1952
Five Nights in Singapore. Collins, 1961
The Ghost Blonde. Viking, 1960
Malayan Rose. Collins, 1951 (U.S. title: Afraid of the Dark. Viking, 1952)
Out of Asia Alive. Collins, 1954 (U.S. title: The Bad Step. Viking, 1954; Permabooks)
Sun in the Hunter's Eye. Viking, 1958
The Sunlit Ambush. Collins, 1955; Viking, 1955; Dell, 1959
The Tigress. Collins, 1959 (U.S. title: Womanhunt. Viking, 1959; Ace)
Womanhunt; see The Tigress

WILCOX, JESS (S)
Kill Me, Sweet. Monarch, 1960

WILDE, OSCAR (M)
The Canterville Ghost. Luce, J. W., 1906
Lord Savile's Crime and Other Stories. Osgood, 1891
The Picture of Dorian Gray. Ward, Lock, 1891

WILDE, PERCIVAL (D)
Design for Murder. Random, 1941; Gollancz, 1942
Inquest. Gollancz, 1939; Random, 1940
Mystery Weekend. Gollancz, 1938; Harcourt, 1938
P.P. Moran, Operative. Gollancz, 1947; Random, 1947
Rogues in Clover. Appleton, D., 1929
Tinsley's Bones. Random, 1942; Gollancz, 1943

WILDER, ROBERT (S)
Fruit of the Poppy. Putnam, 1965
Walk with Evil. Crest, 1957

WILEY, HUGH (M)
Copper Mask. Knopf, 1932
Jade. Knopf, 1921
Manchu Blood. Knopf, 1927

WILHELM, KATE (M-S)
More Bitter Than Death. S & S, 1963; Tower
The Nevermore Affair. Doubleday, 1966

WILKINSON, BURKE (M)
Last Clear Chance. Hodder, 1954; Little, 1954
Night of the Short Knives. Scribner, 1964; Hodder, 1965; Popular Lib., 1966
Run, Mongoose. Little, 1950; Hodder, 1951

WILKINSON, ELLEN C. (M)
The Divison Bell Mystery. Harrap, 1932

WILKINSON, RODERICK (M)
Big Still. Long, 1958; British Book Centre, 1959; Walker & Co., 1967

WILLARD, JOSHUA (D)
The Thorne Theatre Mystery. Phoenix, 1937

WILLETT, E. NODALL (M)
The Sitting Emperor. Gardner, 1930

WILLIAMS, ALAN (S)
Barbouze. Blond, A., 1963 (U.S. title: False Beards. Harper & Row, 1963; Signet, 1966)
False Beards; see Barbouze
Long Run South. Little, 1962; Avon, 1967
Snake Water. Blond, A., 1965

WILLIAMS, ALEXANDER HAZARD (M)
Death over Newark. Payson, W. F., 1933
Jinx Theatre Murder. Payson, W. F., 1933
Murder in the W.P.A. McBride, 1937

WILLIAMS, BEN AMES (M)
The Bellmer Mystery; see Death on Scurvy Street
Death on Scurvy Street. Dutton, 1929 (English title: The Bellmer Mystery. Paul, S., 1930)
Dreadful Night. Dutton, 1928; Paul, S., 1929
End to Mirth. Dutton, 1931
Hostile Valley. Dutton, 1934
Lady in Peril; see Money Mask
Money Mask. Dutton, 1932 (Also published as: Lady in Peril. Popular Lib., 1968)
The Pirate's Purchase. Dutton, 1931
Silver Forest. Dutton, 1926

WILLIAMS, BRAD (S)
A Borderline Case. Mill, 1960
Death Lies in Waiting. Jenkins, 1961
Make a Killing. Mill, 1961
A Stranger to Herself. Doubleday, 1964; Pyramid, 1966
A Well-Dressed Skeleton. Mill, 1962; Jenkins, 1963

WILLIAMS, BROCK (M)
The Earl of Chicago. Harrap, 1937

WILLIAMS, CHARLES (S)
Aground. Viking, 1960; Cassell, 1961; Crest, 1961
The Big Bite. Dell, 1956; Cassell, 1957
The Catfish Tangle. Cassell, 1963
The Concrete Flamingo. Cassell, 1960; Viking, 1960
Dead Calm. Viking, 1963; Avon, 1965 (Sequel to: Aground)
The Girl Out Back. Dell, 1958
Go Home, Stranger. GM, 1953
Hell Hath No Fury. GM, 1953
The Long Saturday Night. GM, 1962; Cassell, 1964
Man in Motion. Cassell, 1959 (Also published as: Man on the Run. GM, 1959)
Man on the Run; see Man in Motion
Nude on Thin Ice. Avon, 1961
Operator. Cassell, 1958
The Sailcloth Shroud. Cassell, 1961; Dell, 1961; Viking, 1961
The Scorpion Reef. Macmillan, 1955; Cassell, 1956
Stain of Suspicion. Cassell, 1959
A Touch of Death. GM, 1953
Uncle Sagamore and His Girls.
The Wrong Venus. New Amer. Lib., 1966

WILLIAMS, CHRISTOPHER HODDER-; see HODDER-WILLIAMS, CHRISTOPHER

WILLIAMS, DAVID
Agent from the West. Cape, 1956

WILLIAMS, ERIC (S)
The Borders of Barbarism. Heinemann, 1961; Coward, 1962
Dragoman Pass. Collins, 1951; Coward, 1959

WILLIAMS, GEORGE VALENTINE; see WILLIAMS, VALENTINE

WILLIAMS, H. S. (M)
Witness of the Sun. Doubleday, Page, 1920

WILLIAMS, HARPER (M)
The Thing in the Woods. McBride, 1924

WILLIAMS, KIRBY (M)
C.V.C Murders. Doubleday, Doran, 1929; Hutchinson, 1929
The Opera Murders. Scribner, 1933

WILLIAMS, LAWRENCE (S)
The Fiery Furnace. S & S, 1960

WILLIAMS, MARGARET WETHERBY; see WILLIAMS, WETHERBY

WILLIAMS, ROBERT V. (M)
Run with the Devil.

WILLIAMS, STEPHEN DANIEL (D-Satire)
The Adventures of Shylar Homes. Carlton, 1966

WILLIAMS, VALENTINE (Full name: George Valentine Williams) (M) (Pseudonyms: Douglas Valentine, "Vedette")
The Clock Ticks On. Hodder, 1932
Clubfoot the Avenger. Collier, 1923; Houghton, 1924
The Clue of the Rising Moon. Houghton, 1924; Hodder, 1925
The Crouching Beast. Houghton, 1928; Hodder, 1929
The Curiosity of Mr. Treadgold. Houghton, 1937 (English title: Mr. Treadgold Cuts In. Hodder, 1937)
Dead Man Manor. Hodder, 1936; Houghton, 1936 (Serial title: "Footsteps in the Night")
Death Answers the Bell. Hodder, 1932; Houghton, 1932
"Deeds of the Fox"; see The Fox Prowls
The Eye in Attendance. Hodder, 1927; Houghton, 1927
Fog, with Dorothy Rice Sims. Hodder, 1933; Houghton, 1933
"Footsteps in the Night;" see Dead Man Manor
The Fox Prowls. Houghton, 1939 (Published in Cavalcade as "Deeds of the Fox")

The Gold Comfit Box. Hodder, 1932
Island Gold. Houghton, 1926
The Key Man. Houghton, 1926; Hodder, 1935
The Knife Behind the Curtain. Houghton, 1930; Hodder, 1931
The Man with the Club Foot. Houghton, 1931; Jenkins, 1931
Masks Off at Midnight. Hodder, 1934; Houghton, 1934
Mr. Ramosi. Hodder, 1926; Houghton, 1926
Mr. Treadgold Cuts In; see The Curiosity of Mr. Treadgold
The Mysterious Miss Morrison. Houghton, 1930
The Mystery of the Gold Box. Houghton, 1932
Okewood of the Secret Service. Grosset, 1925
The Orange Divan. Houghton, 1923; Jenkins, 1926
The Pigeon House. Hodder, 1926
The Portcullis Room. Hodder, 1934; Houghton, 1934
Red Mass. Houghton, 1925; Hodder, 1930
The Skeleton out of the Cupboard. Hodder, 1946
The Spider's Touch. Houghton, 1936
Three of Clubs. Hodder, 1924; Houghton, 1924
The Yellow Streak. Houghton, 1922; Jenkins, 1932

WILLIAMS, WETHERBY (Full name: Margaret Wetherby Williams) (M-D) (Pseudonym: Margaret Erskine)
And Being Dead. Bles, 1938
Case with Three Husbands, by Margaret Erskine. Doubleday, 1967
Dead by Now. Hammond, 1950; Doubleday, 1954
The Dead Don't Speak. 1955
The Death of Our Dear One. Hammond, 1952 (U.S. title: Look Behind You. Doubleday, 1952)
The Disappearing Bridegroom. Hammond, 1950
The Family at Tammerton. Doubleday, 1966
Fatal Relations. Hammond, 1955 (U.S. title: Old Mrs. Ommanney Is Dead. Doubleday, 1955; Ace, 1967)
Give Up the Ghost. Doubleday, 1949; Hammond, 1949
A Graveyard Plot. Doubleday, 1959
The House in Belmont Square. Hodder, 1963 (U.S. title: No. 9, Belmont Square. Doubleday, 1963; Ace, 1967)
The House of the Enchantress. Hodder, 1959
I Knew Macbean. Hammond, 1948; Doubleday, 1949
The Limping Man. Doubleday, Doran, 1939
Look Behind You, Lady; see The Death of Our Dear One
No. 9, Belmont Square; see The House in Belmont Square
Old Mrs. Ommanney Is Dead; see Fatal Relations
Silver Ladies. Doubleday, 1951; Ace, 1967
Sleep No More. Hodder, 1958
The Voice of Murder. Doubleday, 1956; Hodder, 1956
The Voice of the House; see The Whispering House
The Whispering House. Hammond, 1947 (U.S. title: The Voice of the House. Doubleday, 1947)
The Woman at Belguard. Doubleday, 1961; Ace, 1968; Penguin

WILLIAMSON, A. M.; see WILLIAMSON, CHARLES NORRIS

WILLIAMSON, BEATRICE GLYNN (D)
Death Stalks the Ward. Hutchinson, 1942

WILLIAMSON, CHARLES NORRIS and A. M. WILLIAMSON (M)
The Great Pearl Secret. Burt, 1921; Methuen, 1921
The Lion's Mouth. Burt, 1919
The Night of the Wedding. Doubleday, Page, 1923
The Scarlet Runner. Methuen, 1908
The Second Latchkey. Doubleday, Page, 1920

WILLIAMSON, HUGH ROSS (M)
The Day They Killed the King. Macmillan, 1957

WILLIS, GEORGE ANTHONY ARMSTRONG (M) (Pseudonym: Anthony Armstrong)
He Was found in the Road. Methuen, 1952
No Higher Mountain. Methuen, 1951
Poison Trail. Benn, 1933
A Room at the Hotel Ambre. Doubleday, 1956
The Secret Trail. Methuen, 1928
The Strange Case of Mr. Pelham. Doubleday, 1957
The Trail of Fear. Macrae Smith, 1927; White House, 1929; Methuen, 1931
The Trail of the Black King. Macrae Smith, 1931; Methuen, 1931
The Trail of the Lotto. Methuen, 1929; Macrae Smith, 1930

WILLIS, TED (M)
The Blue Lamp. Convoy, 1950

WILLOCK, COLIN DENNISTOUN (M)
Death at Flight. Heinemann, 1956

Death at the Strike. Heinemann, 1957
Death in Covert. Heinemann, 1961; Penguin, 1963

WILLOCK, RUTH (M)
The Night of the Visitor. Ace, 1965

WILLOTT, HILDA (D)
Diamonds of Death. Longmans, 1930
Murder at the Party. Paul, S., 1931
Tragedy in Pewsewy Chart. Longmans, 1929

WILLOUGHBY, JOHN (M)
Crimsoned Millions. Clode, 1927

WILLS, CECIL MELVILLE (D)
The Case of the Empty Beehive. Hale, R., 1959
The Clue of the Golden Ear-ring. Hodder, 1950
The Clue of the Lost Hour. Hodder, 1949
The Colonel's Foxhound. Hale, R., 1960
The Dead Voice. Hodder, 1952
Death at the Pelican. Heritage, 1934
Death in the Dark. Hutchinson, 1955
Death of a Best Seller. Hale, R., 1959
Death on the Line. Hutchinson, 1959
Defeat of a Detective. Hodder, 1936
It Pays to Die. Hodder, 1953
Mere Murder. Hale, R., 1958
Midsummer Murder. Hutchinson, 1956
The Tiger Strikes Again. Hutchinson, 1957
What Say the Jury? Hodder, 1952
Who Killed Brother Treasurer? Hodder, 1951

WILLS, HELEN; see MURPHY, ROBERT W.

WILLS, RONALD, pseud; see THOMAS, RONALD WILLS

WILLS, THOMAS; pseud; see ARD, WILLIAM

WILLSON, MITCHELL A. and ABRAHAM POLANSKY (M) (Pseudonym: Emmett Hogarth)
Goose Is Cooked. Doubleday, Doran, 1940

WILMER, DALE, pseud; see MILLER, BILL

WILMOT, EILEEN (M)
Dangerous Search. Wright & Brown, 1959
Holiday with Danger. Wright & Brown, 1959

WILMOT, JAMES REGINALD (M) (Pseudonym: Ralph Trevor)
The Ace of Clubs Murder. Wright & Brown, 1939
Behind the Green Mask. Wright & Brown, 1940
The Corpse in the Caravan. Wright & Brown, 1939
Death Burns the Candle. Wright & Brown, 1938
Death Comes Too Late. Wright & Brown, 1938
Death in the Stalls. Nicholson, 1934 (U.S. title: Death in the Theatre. Kendall, 1934)
Death in the Surgery. Wright & Brown, 1937
Death in the Theatre; see Death in the Stalls
The Deputy Avenger. Wright & Brown, 1938
Easy for the Crook. Wright & Brown, 1939
The Eyes Through the Mask. Wright & Brown, 1935
Front Page Murder. Wright & Brown, 1942
The Ghost Counts Ten. Wright & Brown, 1938
The Girl in the Crimson Cloak. Wright & Brown, 1940
High Spy. Wright & Brown, 1942
The House of Silence. Wright & Brown, 1935
Invitation to Murder. Wright & Brown, 1936
Meet Doctor Death. Wright & Brown, 1940
The Monday Night Murder. Wright & Brown, 1935
The Moorcroft Manor Maystery. Wright & Brown, 1935
Murder for Two. Wright & Brown, 1939
A Murder Has Been Arranged. Wright & Brown, 1942
Murder in Silk. Wright & Brown, 1937
Murder in the Fifth Column. Wright & Brown, 1940
Murder Without Regret. Wright & Brown, 1937
Night Tide. Nicholson, 1936
On the Night of the Ninth. Wright & Brown, 1935
The Phantom Raider. Wright & Brown, 1941
Red Stands for Danger. Wright & Brown, 1941
Sky-High Terror. Wright & Brown, 1940
Some Person Unknown. Wright & Brown, 1935
Under Suspicion. Wright & Brown, 1936
Viper's Vengeance. Wright & Brown, 1938
Who Killed the Crooner? Wright & Brown, 1941

WILMOT, ROBERT PATRICK (D)
Blood in Your Eye. Lippincott, 1952

Death Rides a Painted Horse. Lippincott, 1954
Murder on Monday. Lippincott, 1953

WILSON, ALEXANDER D. (M)
The Death of Dr. Whitelaw. Longmans, 1930
The Devil's Cocktail. Longmans, 1928
Murder Mansion. Longmans, 1929
The Mystery of Tunnel 51. Longmans, 1928

WILSON, CAROLYN (S)
Scent of Lilacs. Ace, 1966

WILSON, CHRISTOPHER (M)
The Missing Millionaire. Blackwood, 1911

WILSON, COLIN (S)
The Glass Cage. Barker, 1966; Random, 1967
Necessary Doubt. Trident, 1964; PB, 1966
Ritual in the Dark. Houghton, 1960; Popular Lib., 1961

WILSON, DANA (D)
Make with the Brains, Pierre. Messner, 1946
Scenario for Murder. Foulsham, 1949

WILSON, DAVID (M)
The Search for Geoffrey Goring. Jenkins, 1962

WILSON, GARNETT (M)
The Man with a Monocle. Doubleday, Doran, 1943

WILSON, GERTRUDE MARY BRYANT (D)
Bury That Poker. Hale, R., 1957
I Was Murdered. Hale, R., 1957; Walker & Co., 1961
It Rained That Friday. Hale, R., 1960
Murder on Monday. Hale, R., 1963
Nightmare Cottage. Hale, R., 1963
Roberta Died. Hale, R., 1962
Shadows on the Landing. Hale, R., 1959
Shot at Dawn. Hale, R., 1964
Thirteen Stannergate. Hale, R., 1958
Three Fingered Death. Hale, R., 1961
Witchwater. Hale, R., 1961

WILSON, GROVE (M)
Monster of Snowden Hall. Washburn, 1932; Skeffington, 1933
Mysterious Wife. Frank-Maurice, 1927
Sport of the Gods. Frank-Maurice, 1926

WILSON, HUGH LAURENCE (M)
Dark Echo. Rinehart, 1949

WILSON, JACK (M)
Adam Grey. Muller, 1964

WILSON, JOHN ANTHONY (S) (Pseudonym: Anthony Burgess)
Tremor of Intent. Norton, 1966; Ballantine, 1967

WILSON, JOHN ROWAN (M)
Means to an End. Doubleday, 1959
Round Voyage. Doubleday, 1957

WILSON, LEE, pseud; see LEMMON, LAURA LEE

WILSON, MITCHELL (M)
Footsteps Behind Her. S & S, 1942
Live with Lightning. Little, 1949; Allen, W. H., 1950; Popular Lib., 1966
The Panic-Stricken. S & S, 1946; Dell
Stalk the Hunter. S & S, 1943

WILSON, PHILIP W. (M)
The Black Tarn. Farrar & Rinehart, 1945
The Bride's Castle. Rinehart, 1944
The Old Mill. Rinehart, 1946

WILSON, ROBERT McNAIR (D) (Pseudonym: Anthony Wynne)
Blue Vesuvius. Hutchinson, 1930; Lippincott, 1931
The Case of the Gold Coins. Hutchinson, 1933; Lippincott, 1934; Burt
The Case of the Green Knives; see Green Knife
The Case of the Red-haired Girl; see The Cotswold Case
The Cotswold Case. Lippincott, 1933 (English title: The Case of the Red-haired Girl. Hutchinson, 1932)
The Dagger. Lippincott, 1929; Hutchinson, 1931
Death of a Banker. Hutchinson, 1934; Lippincott, 1934
Death of a Golfer. Hutchinson, 1937; Lippincott, 1937
Death of a King; see Murder Calls Dr. Hailey
Death of a Shadow. Hutchinson, 1952
Death out of the Night. Lippincott, 1933 (English title: Loving Cup. Hutchinson, 1933)
Door Nails Never Die. Hutchinson, 1939; Lippincott, 1939
Double Thirteen Mystery. Hutchinson, 1925; Lippincott, 1925; Burt
Emergency Exit. Hutchinson, 1941
Fourth Finger. Lippincott, 1929; Hutchinson, 1931
Green Knife. Lippincott, 1932; Burt, 1933 (English title: The Case of the Green Knife. Hutchinson, 1932)

Holbein Mystery; see Red Lady
Horseman of Death. Lippincott, 1927; Hutchinson, 1930
The House on the Hard. Hutchinson, 1940
Loving Cup; see Death out of Night
Murder Calls Dr. Hailey. Lippincott, 1938 (English title: Death of a King. Hutchinson, 1938)
Murder in the Church. Hutchinson, 1942
Murder in the Morning. Hillman, 1937
Murder in Thin Air. Hutchinson, 1936; Lippincott, 1936
Murder of a Lady. Hutchinson, 1931
Mystery of the Ashes. Hutchinson, 1927; Burt, 1929
Mystery of the Evil Eye. Hutchinson, 1925
Red Lady. Lippincott, 1935 (English title: Holbein Mystery. Hutchinson, 1935)
Red Scar. Lippincott, 1928; Hutchinson, 1931
The Room with Iron Shutters. Hutchinson, 1929; Lippincott, 1930
The Sign of Evil. Lippincott, 1925; Burt
Silver Arrow. Hutchinson, 1931 (U.S. title: White Arrow. Lippincott, 1932)
Silver Scale Mystery. Lippincott, 1931
Sinners Go Secretly. Hutchinson, 1927; Burt, 1930; Lippincott
Toll-house Murder. Hutchinson, 1934; Lippincott, 1935
White Arrow; see Silver Arrow
Yellow Crystal. Hutchinson, 1929; Lippincott, 1930

WILSON, RUTH (M)
The Town Is Full of Rumors. S & S, 1941

WILSON, STANLEY KIDDER (M)
Scream of the Doll. Duffield, 1931

WILSTACH, JOHN (M)
Under Cover Man. Burt, 1931

WIMHURST, CECIL GORDON (D)
(Pseudonym: Nigel Brent)
Golden Angel. Muller, 1958
The Leopard Died Too. Muller, 1957
Murder Swings High. Muller, 1956
No Space for Murder. Muller, 1960
The Scarlet Lily. Muller, 1953

WINCHELL, PRENTICE (D) (Pseudonyms: Dev Collans, Spencer Dean, Jay DeBekker, Stewart Sterling, Dester St. Clair)
The Affair of the California Cutie; see Dead Sure
The Affair of the Kentucky Casanova; see Dead of Night
The Affair of the Virginia Widow; see Dead Wrong
Alarm in the Night, by Stewart Sterling. Dutton, 1949
Alibi Baby, by Stewart Sterling. Washburn, 1955; Boardman, T. V., 1955
The Big Ear, by Stewart Sterling. Dutton, 1953; Boardman, T. V., 1955
The Body in the Bed, by Stewart Sterling. Lippincott, 1959
A Candle for a Corpse, by Stewart Sterling. Lippincott, 1957
Credit for a Murder, by Spencer Dean. Doubleday, 1961; Permabooks, 1963
Danger! Detectives Working. Coward, 1955
Dead Certain. Ace, 1960
Dead of Night; the Affair of the Kentucky Casanova, by Stewart Sterling. Dutton, 1950
Dead Right, by Stewart Sterling. Lippincott, 1956
Dead Sure; the Affair of the California Cutie, by Stewart Sterling. Dutton, 1949; Locke, 1951
Dead to the World, by Stewart Sterling. Lippincott, 1958
Dead Wrong; the Affair of the Virginia Widow, by Stewart Sterling. Lippincott, 1947
Dishonor Among Thieves, by Spencer Dean. Doubleday, 1958; PB
Down Among the Dead Men, by Stewart Sterling. Putnam, 1943; Gardner, 1949
Dying Room Only. Ace, 1960
Fire on Fear Street, by Stewart Sterling. Lippincott, 1959
Five Alarm Fire, by Stewart Sterling. Putnam, 1942; Ace, 1961
Frightened Fingers, by Spencer Dean. Washburn, 1954; Boardman, T. V., 1955
Hinges of Hell, by Stewart Sterling. Washburn, 1955
I Was a House Detective, by Dev Collans with Stewart Sterling. Dutton, 1954
The Lady's Not for Living, by Dester St. Clair. GM, 1953
Marked Down for Murder, by Spencer Dean. Doubleday, 1956
The Merchant of Murder, by Spencer Dean. Doubleday, 1959; PB, 1960
Murder After a Fashion, by Spencer Dean. Doubleday, 1960
Murder on Delivery, by Spencer Dean. Doubleday, 1957
Nightmare at Noon, by Stewart Sterling. Dutton, 1951; Dell
Price Tag for Murder, by Spencer Dean. Doubleday, 1959; PB, 1961
Scent of Fear, by Spencer Dean. Washburn, 1954
Too Hot to Handle, by Stewart Sterling. Random, 1961; Boardman, T. V., 1962

Where There's Smoke, by Stewart Sterling. Lippincott, 1946; Dell

WINCOR, RICHARD (D)
St. Ives Murder. Oceana, 1958

WINN, PATRICK (D)
Colour of Murder. Hale, R., 1965
Invisible Evidence. Hale, R., 1963
Postscript to Murder. Hale, R., 1964

WINNER, PERCY (M)
Scene in the Ice-blue Eyes. Harcourt, 1947

WINSLOW, HORATIO G.; see QUIRK, LESLIE

WINSLOW, JOAN (M)
Griffen Towers. Ace

WINSOR, G. MacLEOD (M)
Mysterious Disappearance. Faber, 1926
Vanishing Men. Morrow, 1927

WINSTON, DAOMA (S-Gothic)
Carnaby Curse. Belmont, 1967
Castle of Closing Doors. Belmont, 1967
Mansion of Smiling Masks. Signet, 1967
The Secrets of Cromwell Crossing. Lancer, 1965
Shadow of an Unknown Woman. Lancer, 1967
Sinister Stone. Paperback Lib., 1966

WINSTON, PETER (S)
The ABC Affair. Award, 1967 (Adjustors series #2)
Assignment to Bahrein. Award, 1967 (Adjustors series #1)

WINTER, BEVIS (M) (Pseudonyms: Al Bocca, Peter Cagney, Gordon Shayne)
All or Nothing. Milestone, 1953
And So to Death, by Gordon Shayne. Jasmit Pub., 1952
Blondes End Up Dead. Jenkins, 1959
A Corner in Corpses, by Al Bocca. Milestone, 1953
Darker Grows the Street. Jenkins, 1953
The Dead Sleep for Keeps. Jenkins, 1953
Dressed to Kill. Milestone, 1952
A Grave for Madam, by Peter Cagney. Jenkins, 1961
Hear the Stripper Scream, by Peter Cagney. Jenkins, 1966
Let the Lady Die. Jenkins, 1957
Next Stop - the Morgue. Jenkins, 1955
The Night Was Made for Murder. Jenkins, 1958
No Room at the Morgue, by Al Bocca. Milestone, 1952
A Noose of Emeralds. Mystery House, 1956
Redheads Cool Fast. Jenkins, 1952
Sleep Long, My Lovely. Jenkins, 1958
Ticket to Eternity, by Gordon Shayne. Jasmit Pub., 1952
Ticket to San Diego, by Al Bocca. Scion, 1952
Trouble Calling, by Al Bocca. Milestone, 1953

WINTERTON, PAUL (M-D) (Pseudonyms: Roger Bax, Andrew Garve, Paul Somers)
The Ashes of Loda, by Andrew Garve. Cassell, 1964; Harper & Row, 1965
Beginner's Luck, by Paul Somers. Harper, 1958
Blueprint for Murder, see The Trouble with Murder
Broken Jigsaw, by Paul Somers. Harper, 1961
By-Line for Murder, by Andrew Garve. Harper, 1951; Lancer, 1964 (English title: A Press of Suspects. Collins, 1951)
Came the Dawn; see Two If by Sea.
The Cuckoo Line Affair, by Andrew Garve. Collins, 1953; Harper, 1953; Lancer, 1963
Death and the Sky Above, by Andrew Garve. Collins, 1953; Harper, 1953; Lancer, 1963
Death Beneath Jerusalem, by Roger Bax. Nelson, T., 1938
The Disposing of Henry, by Roger Bax. Harper, 1947; Hutchinson, 1947
End of the Track, by Andrew Garve. Collins, 1956; Harper, 1956; Lancer, 1963
The Far Sands, by Andrew Garve. Harper, 1960; Collins, 1961
Fontego's Folly, by Andrew Garve. Harper, 1950 (English title: No Mask for Murder. Collins, 1950)
Frame-Up, by Andrew Garve. Collins, 1964; Harper & Row, 1964
The Galloway Case, by Andrew Garve. Collins, 1958; Harper, 1958
The Golden Deed, by Andrew Garve. Doubleday, 1961; Lancer, 1967
A Grave Case of Murder, by Roger Bax. Harper, 1951; Hutchinson, 1951
A Hero for Leanda, by Andrew Garve. Hutchinson, 1952; Doubleday, 1961
Hide and Go Seek, by Andrew Garve. Harper, 1966
A Hole in the Ground, by Andrew Garve. Collins, 1952; Harper, 1952; Lancer, 1964
The House of Soldiers, by Andrew Garve. Harper, 1961; Collins, 1962; Lancer, 1963
The Megstone Plot, by Andrew Garve. Collins, 1956; Harper, 1956

Murder in Moscow, by Andrew Garve. Collins, 1950; Fontana, 1954 (U.S. title: Murder Through a Looking Glass. Harper, 1951; Lancer, 1966)
Murder Through a Looking Glass; see Murder in Moscow
Murder's Fen, by Andrew Garve. Collins, 1966
The Narrow Search, by Andrew Garve. Collins, 1957; Harper, 1957
No Mask for Murder; see Fontego's Folly
No Tears for Hilda, by Andrew Garve. Collins, 1950; Harper, 1951; Lancer, 1964
Operation Piracy, by Paul Somers. Harper, 1948
A Press of Suspects; see By-Line for Murder
The Prisoner's Friend, by Andrew Garve. Collins, 1962; Harper & Row, 1963
Red Escapade, by Roger Bax. Skeffington, 1940
The Riddle of Samson, by Andrew Garve. Collins, 1954; Harper, 1954
The Sea Monks, by Andrew Garve. Collins, 1963; Harper & Row, 1963; Lancer, 1964
The Shivering Mountain, by Paul Somers. Harper, 1960
The Trouble with Murder, by Roger Bax. Harper, 1948 (English title: Blueprint for Murder. Hutchinson, 1948)
Two If by Sea, by Roger Bax. Harper, 1949 (English title: Came the Dawn. Hutchinson, 1949)
A Very Quiet Place, by Andrew Garve. Collins, 1967; Harper & Row, 1967

WINTHROP, WILMA (S)
Tryst with Terror. Lancer, 1965

WISE, ARTHUR (M)
The Death's Head. Cassell, 1962

WITHERS, E. L.; pseud; see POTTER, GEORGE WILLIAM

WITHERS, JULIA (S)
Echo in a Dark Wind. Signet, 1966

WITNEY, FREDERICK (S)
Grand Guignol. Constable, 1947

WITTING, CLIFFORD (D)
A Bullet for Rhino. Hodder, 1950
The Case of the Busy Bees. Hodder, 1952
The Case of the Michaelmas Goose. Hodder, 1938
Catt out of the Bag. Hodder, 1939
Crime in Whispers. Hodder, 1964
Dead on Time. Hodder, 1948
Driven to Kill. Hodder, 1961
Let X Be the Murderer. Hodder, 1947
Measure for Murder. Hodder, 1941
Midsummer Murder. Hodder, 1937
Mischief in the Offing. Hodder, 1958
Murder in Blue. Hodder, 1937
Silence After Dinner. Hodder, 1953
Subject-Murder. Hodder, 1945
There Was a Crooked Man. Hodder, 1960; British Book Centre, 1962
Villainous Saltpetre. Hodder, 1962

WODEN, GEORGE, pseud; see SLANEY, GEORGE WILSON

WOGAN, CHARLES (M)
Cyanide for the Chorister. Long, 1950
Hangman's Hands. Long, 1947
Horror at Warden's Hall. Long, 1949

WOLF, MARI (S)
The Golden Frame. Permabooks, 1961

WOLFE, B. (M)
The Great Prince Died

WOLFE, KATHERINE (M)
The Attic Room. Morrow, 1942
Tall Man Walking. Doubleday, Doran, 1936

WOLFE, WINIFRED (S)
Never Step on a Rainbow. Harper & Row, 1965

WOLFF, WILLIAM ALMON (M)
Manhattan Night. Minton, 1930
Murder at Ender. Minton, 1933; Putnam, 1933
The Trial of Mary Dugan. Doubleday, Doran, 1928

WOLFSON, VICTOR (S) (Pseudonym: Langdon Dodge)
The Lonely Steeple. Lancer, 1966
Midsummer Madness, by Langdon Dodge. Doubleday, 1950

WOLLHEIM, DONALD (M)
More Macabre. Ace, 1961

WOLSELEY, FAITH (M)
Which Way Came Death. Murray, J., 1936

WOOD, CLEMENT (D)
The Corpse in the Guest Room. Arcadia, 1945
Death in Ankara. Mystery House, 1944
Death on the Pampas. Arcadia, 1944; McLeod, 1944
Double Jeopardy. Arcadia, 1947
The Shadow from the Bogue. Dutton, 1928
The Tabloid Murders. Macaulay, 1930

WOOD, ELLEN PRICE (M)
The Englishman of the Rue Cain. Chatto, 1889
Johnny Ludlow. Bentley, 1874
The Night of the Third Ult. Lovell, 1890
Passenger from Scotland Yard. Chatto, 1888
Shadow of Ashlydyat. Bentley, 1863

WOOD, ERNEST (M)
Feloniously and Wilfully. Long, 1947

WOOD, JAMES (M)
Fire Rock. Vanguard, 1966
Northern Mission. Duckworth, 1954
Rain Islands. Duckworth, 1957
The Sealer. Vanguard, 1960

WOOD, LESLIE (M)
Hardship Our Garment. Hutchinson, 1947

WOOD, SALLY (D)
Death in Lord Byron's Room. Morrow, 1948
Murder of a Novelist. S & S, 1941

WOOD, SAMUEL ADAM
Red Square. Dutton, 1934

WOODBURY, DAVID OAKES (S)
Five Days to Oblivion. Devin-Adair, 1963
Mr. Faraday's Formula. Devin-Adair, 1965

WOODHOUSE, MARTIN (S)
The Tree Frog. Coward, 1966; Signet, 1967

WOODROW, NANCY MANN (M)
The Black Pearl. Appleton, D., 1912
Burned Evidence. Putnam, 1925
Come Alone. Macaulay, 1929
Hornet's Nest. Little, 1917
The Moonhill Mystery. Macaulay, 1930
Pawns of Murder. Smith, R. R., 1932; Paul, S., 1933

WOODRUFF, PHILIP (M)
Call the Next Witness. Harcourt, 1946

WOODS, KATHERINE (M)
Murder in a Walled Town. Houghton, 1934

WOODS, SARA, pseud; see BOWEN-JUDD, SARA HULTON

WOODTHORPE, RALPH CARTER (M)
Dagger in Fleet Street. Nicholson, 1934
Death in a Little Town. Doubleday, Doran, 1935; Nicholson, 1935
Death Wears a Purple Shirt. Doubleday, Doran, 1934 (English title: Silence of a Purple Shirt. Nicholson, 1934)
The Necessary Corpse. Doubleday, Doran, 1939; Nicholson, 1939
Public School Murder. Nicholson, 1932
Rope for a Convict. Nicholson, 1939; Doubleday, Doran, 1940
The Shadow on the Downs. Doubleday, Doran, 1935; Nicholson, 1935
Silence of a Purple Shirt; see Death Wears a Purple Shirt

WOODWARD, EDWARD (M)
Bill Marshall, Turf Sleuth. Mellifont, 1942
Dead Man's Plaything. Kemsley, 1950
Death Amidst Satin. Long, 1940
Gentlemen at Large. Long, 1948
House of Terror. Mystery League, 1930; Paperback Lib., 1967

WOODWARD, HELEN (M)
Bowling Green Murder, with Frances Amherst. Random, 1940
Money to Burn. McKay, 1945

WOODWARD, LILLIAN (M)
Nurse Frayne's Strange Quest. Hale, R., 1960

WOODY, WILLIAM (M)
Mistress of Horror House. Ace, 1959

WOOLFOLK, WILLIAM (M)
Blacker Than Murder. Hale, R., 1958
Run While You Can. Popular Lib., 1957; Hale, R., 1958

WOOLL, EDWARD (M)
Libel. Blackie & Son, 1935; Macrae Smith, 1936

WOOLRICH, CORNELL, pseud; see HOPLEY-WOOLRICH, CORNELL

WORKMAN, JAMES (M)
The Apologetic Tiger. Hodder, 1958
The Face of Fortune. Hodder, 1961

WORLEY, WILLIAM (M)
My Dead Wife. S & S, 1948

WORMSER, RICHARD (D)
The Body Looks Familiar. Dell, 1958
The Communists' Corpse. Gollancz, 1935; Smith, H., 1935
Drive East on 66. GM, 1961
The Late Mrs. Fine. GM, 1961
The Man With the Wax Face. Smith, H., 1934
A Nice Girl Like You. GM, 1963
Perfect Pigeon. GM, 1962
The Torn Curtain. Dell, 1966

WORSLEY-GOUGH, BARBARA (M)
Alibi Innings. Joseph, M., 1954; Penguin, 1958
Lantern Hill. Joseph, M., 1957

WORTH, CEDRIC (D)
The Corpse That Knew Everybody. Dutton, 1951
The Trail of the Serpent. Dutton, 1940

WORTHINGTON-STUART, BRIAN ARTHUR (M-S) (Pseudonyms: Peter Meredith, Brian Stuart)
Checkmate, by Peter Meredith. Ward, Lock, 1950
The City of Shadows, by Peter Meredith. Warne, 1952
The Crocodile Man, by Peter Meredith. Ward, Lock, 1951
The Denzil Emeralds, by Peter Meredith. Ward, Lock, 1954
Floodwater, by Peter Meredith. Ward, Lock, 1950
Invitation to a Ball, by Peter Meredith. Ward, Lock, 1949
Knock-out Kavanagh, by Brian Stuart. Ward, Lock, 1948
The Mysterious Monsieur Moray, by Brian Stuart. Ward, Lock, 1950
Oasis, by Peter Meredith. Ward, Lock, 1951
Sands of the Desert, by Peter Meredith. Ward, Lock, 1953
The Serpent's Fangs, by Brian Stuart. Ward, Lock, 1951
The Silver Phantom Murder, by Brian Stuart. Ward, Lock, 1950

WORTS, GEORGE F. (M) (Pseudonym: Loring Brent)
The Blue Lacquer Box. Kinsey, 1939; Hurst, 1940
The Dangerous Young Man. Hurst, 1940; Kinsey, 1940
The Greenfield Mystery. Whitman, 1929
The House of Creeping Horror. King, A. H., 1934
Laughing Girl. Kinsey, 1941
The Monster of the Lagoon. Popular Publications, 1947
No More Corpse, by Loring Brent. King, A. H., 1932
Peter the Brazen. Lippincott, 1919
The Phantom President. Cape, 1932
Silver Fang. McClurg, 1930

WRAY, I., pseud. (M)
Murder and Ariadne. Methuen, 1931
Vye Murder. Methuen, 1930

WREN, PERCIVAL C. (M)
Beau Geste. Murray, J., 1924; Stokes, 1925; PB, 1961
The Cardboard Castle. Houghton, 1938; Murray, J., 1938

WRENN, HAROLD A. (M)
Due to Expire. Hale, R., 1958
The Lady Prefers Murder. Hammond, 1959

WRIGHT, ELSIE N. (D)
The Strange Murders at Greystones. World Syndicate, 1931

WRIGHT, JUNE (D)
The Devil's Caress. Hutchinson, 1952
Makeup for Murder. Long, 1966
Murder in the Telephone Exchange. Hutchinson, 1948
Reservation for Murder. Long, 1958

WRIGHT, MASON (M)
The Army Post Murders. Farrar & Rinehart, 1931
Murder on Polopel, with William R. Kane. Doubleday, Doran, 1929

WRIGHT, OLIVER (M)
Riverport Mail. Nash, 1912

WRIGHT, ROWLAND, pseud; see WELLS, CAROLYN

WRIGHT, SYDNEY FOWLER (M) (Pseudonym: Sydney Fowler)
The Adventure of the Blue Room. Rich, 1945
The Adventure of Wyndham Smith. Jenkins, 1938
Arresting Delia. Jarrolds, 1933; Macaulay, 1933
The Attic Murder. Butterworth, T., 1936
The Bell Street Murders. Harrap, 1931; Macaulay, 1931
Beyond the Rim. Jarrolds, 1932
A Bout with the Mildew Gang. Eyre, 1941
By Saturday. Lane, 1931
The Case of Anne Bickerton. Boni, 1930 (Also published as: The King Against Anne Bickerton. Harrap, 1930 and Rex vs Anne Bickerton. Penguin, 1947)
Crime and Company. Macaulay, 1931 (English title: The Handprint Mystery. Jarrolds, 1932)
Dinner in New York. Eyre, 1943
The End of the Mildew Gang. Eyre, 1944
Four Callers in Razor Street. Jenkins, 1937
The Handprint Mystery; see Crime and Company
The Hanging of Constance Hillier. Jarrolds, 1931; Macaulay, 1932
The Hidden Tribe. Hale, R., 1938
The Jordan's Murder. Jenkins, 1938
Justice and the Rat. Books for Today, 1945
The King Against Anne Bickerton; see The Case of Anne Bickerton

Lord's Right in Languedoc. Jarrolds, 1933; Wetzel, 1934
Megiddo's Ridge. Hale, R., 1937
The Murder in Bethnal Square. Jenkins, 1938
New Gods Lead. Jarrolds, 1937
The Ordeal of Barata. Jenkins, 1939
Post-mortem Evidence. Butterworth, T., 1936
Power. Jarrolds, 1933
Prelude in Prague. Newnes, 1935
Rex vs. Anne Bickerton; see The Case of Anne Bickerton
The Riding of Lancelot. Wright & Brown, 1929
The Rissole Mystery. Rich, 1941
The Screaming Lake. Hale, R., 1937
The Second Bout with the Mildew Gang. Eyre, 1942
The Secret of the Screen. Jarrolds, 1933
The Spider's War. Abelard, 1954
Three Witnesses. Butterworth, T., 1935
The Throne of Saturn. Arkham, 1949; Heinemann, 1951
Too Much for Mr. Jollipot. Eyre, 1945
Was Murder Done? Butterworth, T., 1936
Who Else But She? Jarrolds, 1934
Who Murdered Reynard? Rich, 1947
The Wills of Jane Kanwhistle. Jenkins, 1939
Witchfinder and Other Tales. Books for Today, 1946
With Cause Enough. Harvill, 1954

WRIGHT, WADE JOHN (M)
Blood in the Ashes. Hale, R., 1964
A Hearse Waiting. Hale, R., 1965
Shadows Don't Bleed. Hale, R., 1967
Suddenly You're Dead. Hale, R., 1964
Until She Dies. Hale, R., 1965

WRIGHT, WILLARD HUNTINGTON (D) (Pseudonym: S. S. Van Dine)
The Benson Murder Case. Scribner, 1926; Burt, 1928; Cassell, 1931
The Bishop Murder Case. Scribner, 1929; Grosset, 1930; Cassell, 1931 (Also included in Death and Detection. Benn, 1957; McClelland, 1957)
The Canary Murder Case. Scribner, 1927; Benn, 1930; Cassell, 1932
The Casino Murder Case. Cassell, 1934; Scribner, 1934
The Dragon Murder Case. Scribner, 1933; Cassell, 1935; Grosset, 1937
The Garden Murder Case. Cassell, 1937; Scribner, 1938; Paperback Lib., 1963
The Gracie Allen Murder Case. Scribner, 1938; Cassell, 1940
The Greene Murder Case. Benn, 1928; Scribner, 1928; Grosset, 1929
The Kennel Murder Case. Cassell, 1931; Scribner, 1933; Grosset, 1937
The Kidnap Murder Case. Cassell, 1936; Scribner, 1936
Philo Vance Murder Cases. Scribner, 1936
Philo Vance Weekend: The Canary, Green & Bishop Murder Cases. Grosset, 1937
The Scarab Murder Case. Scribner, 1930; Cassell, 1932; Grosset, 1937; Paperback, 1963
The Winter Murder Case. Scribner, 1939

WUORIO, EVA-LIS (S)
Midsummer Lokki. Holt, 1967
The Woman with the Portuguese Basket. Dobson, 1963; Holt, 1964; Lancer, 1966
Z for Zaborra. Holt, 1966; Lancer, 1966

WYKES, ALAN (M)
Pen-Friend. Duckworth, 1950
Pursuit Till Morning. Random, 1947 Duckworth, 1948

WYLIE, IDA ALEXA ROSS (M)
Rogues and Company. Lane, 1921

WYLIE, NOEL (D)
Dumb Witness. Hammond, 1959
Saddle a Killer. Hammond, 1960

WYLIE, PHILIP GORDON (D)
The Corpses at Indian Stones. Farrar & Rinehart, 1943; Popular Lib., 1967
Danger Mansion. Popular Lib., 1966
Experiment in Crime. Lancer, 1965
Five Fatal Words, with Edwin Balmer. Long, 1932; Smith, R. R., 1932
The Golden Hoard, with Edwin Balmer. Stokes, 1934
The Murder Invisible. Farrar & Rinehart, 1932; Popular Lib., 1967
Nine Rittenhouse Square. Popular Lib., 1959, 1966
The Shield of Silence, with Edwin Balmer. Stokes, 1936
A Resourceful Lady. Popular Lib., 1966
The Smuggled Atom Bomb. Lancer, 1965
Three to Be Read. Rinehart, 1948

WYMARK, EDWARD (S)
As Good as Gold. Coward, 1967

WYND, OSWALD (S-D) (Pseudonym: Gavin Black)
Black Fountains. Doubleday, 1947
Dead Man Calling, by Gavin Black. Random, 1962; Dolphin, 1965

Death the Red Flower. Cassell, 1965; Harcourt, 1965; Signet, 1968
The Devil Came on Sunday. Doubleday, 1961
A Dragon for Christmas, by Gavin Black. Harper & Row, 1963; Collins, 1964; Banner, 1967
The Eyes Around Me, by Gavin Black. Collins, 1964; Harper & Row, 1964
Friend of the Family. Doubleday, 1950
The Gentle Private. Doubleday, 1951
Moon of the Tiger. Doubleday, 1958
Red Sun South. Doubleday, 1948
Suddenly at Singapore, by Gavin Black. Collins, 1961
Summer Can't Last. Cassell, 1959
A Walk in the Long Dark Night. Cassell, 1962
Walk Softly, Men Praying. Harcourt, 1967
A Wind of Death, by Gavin Black. Harper & Row, 1967
You Want to Die, by Gavin Black. Harper & Row, 1966

WYNDHAM, JOHN, pseud; see HARRIS, JOHN BEYNON

WYNNE, ANTHONY, pseud; see WILSON, ROBERT McNAIR

WYNNE, FRED E. (M)
The Mediterranean Mystery. Duffield, 1923; Jenkins, 1923

WYNNTON, PATRICK (S)
The Agent Outside. Longmans, 1931
The Black Turret. Hodder, 1925
The Honourable Pursuit. Hodder, 1930
The Lost Mark. Hodder, 1929
Spider's Parlour. Longmans, 1933
The Ten Jewels. Hodder, 1931
The Third Messenger. Hodder, 1926; Doran, 1927
Zia. Hodder, 1928

XANTIPPE, pseud. (M)
Death Catches Up with Mr. Kluck. Doubleday, Doran, 1935

YAFFE, JAMES (S)
Nothing But the Night. Little, 1957; Bantam, 1959

YARDLEY, HERBERT O. (M)
The Blonde Countess. Faber, 1934; Longmans, 1934
Crows Are Black Everywhere, with Carl Grabo. Putnam, 1945
Red Sun of Nippon. Longmans, 1934

YATES, ALAN GEOFFREY (S-D) (Pseudonym: Carter Brown) (All published by Horwitz Publications, Ltd., Sidney, Australia)
Angel. Signet, 1962
Baby, You're Guilt-edged. Signet, 1956
Bella Donna Was Poison. Signet, 1957
Bid the Babe By-By. Signet, 1956
The Black Lace Hangover. Signet, 1966
The Blonde. Signet, 1958
Blonde on a Broomstick. Signet, 1966
The Body. Signet, 1958, 1964
The Bombshell. Signet, 1960
The Brazen. Signet, 1960
Bullet for My Baby. Signet, 1955
The Bump and Grind Murders. Signet
Caress Before Killing. Signet, 1957
Catch Me a Phoenix. Signet, 1965
Charlie Sent Me. Signet, 1963
Chorine Makes a Killing. 1957
The Cold Dark House. Barker, 1958; Signet, 1958
The Corpse. Signet, 1958, 1965
A Corpse for Christmas. Signet
Curtains for a Chorine. Signet, 1955
Curves for the Coroner. Signet, 1955
The Dame. Signet, 1959, 1965
The Dance of Death. Signet, 1964
The Deadly Kitten. Signet, 1967
Delilah Was Deadly. Signet, 1956
The Desired. Signet, 1960
Donna Died Laughing. 1957
The Dream Is Deadly. Signet, 1960
The Dumdum Murder. Signet, 1962
Eve, It's Extortion. 1957
The Ever-Loving Blues. Signet, 1961
The Exotic. Signet, 1961
The Frame Is Beautiful. 1953
The Fraulein Is Feline. 1953
The Girl from Outer Space. Signet, 1965
The Girl in a Shroud. Signet, 1963
The Girl Who Was Possessed. Signet, 1963
Graves I Dig. Signet, 1960
Guilt-Edged Case. Signet
The Hammer of Thor. Signet, 1965
The Hellcat. Signet, 1962
High Fashion in Homicide. 1958
Homicide Hoyden. 1954
Honey, Here's Your Hearse. 1955
The Hong Kong Caper. Signet, 1962
The Hoodlum Is a Honey. 1955
House of Sorcery. Signet, 1967
Ice-Cold in Ermine. 1958
Ice-Cold Nude. Signet, 1962
The Jade-Eyed Jungle. Signet
The Killer Is Kissable. 1954
Kiss and Kiss. 1955
The Lady Has No Convictions. 1956
The Lady Is Available. Signet, 1962
The Lady Is Transparent. Signet, 1962
Lament for a Lousy Lover. Signet, 1960
Lead Astray. 1955
Lipstick Larceny. 1955
Long Time No Leola. Signet, 1967
The Lover. Signet, 1959
Lover, Don't Come Back. Signet, 1962
The Loving and the Dead. Signet, 1959

Madam, You're Mayhem. 1957
Maid for Murder. 1954
Man on the Stairs
Meet Murder. 1956
The Million Dollar Babe. Signet, 1961
Miss Called Murder. 1955
The Mistress. Signet, 1959
Model of No Virtue. 1957
A Morgue Amour. 1954
Murder by Misdemeanor. 1955
Murder in the Key Club. Signet, 1962
Murder Is a Package Deal. Signet, 1964
Murder—Paris Fashion. 1954
Murder Wears a Mantilla. Signet, 1962
The Murderer Is Among Us. Signet, 1962
My Mermaid Murmurs Murder. 1953
The Myopic Mermaid. Signet, 1961
Nemesis Wore Nylons. 1954
The Never-was Girl. Signet
No Blonde Is an Island. Signet, 1965
No Body She Knows. 1958
No Future Fair Lady. 1958
No Halo for Hedy. 1956
No Harp for My Angel. 1956
No Tears from the Widow. Signet, 1966
None But the Lethal Heart. Signet, 1959
Nude-with a View. Signet
Nymph to the Slaughter. Signet
The Passionate. Signet, 1959, 1964
The Passionate Pagan. Signet, 1963
Play Now-Kill Later. Signet, 1966
The Plush-Lined Coffin. Signet, 1967
The Sad-Eyed Seductress. Signet, 1961
The Savage Salome. Signet, 1961
Scarlet Flush. Signet, 1963
Seidlitz and the Super-Spy. Signet, 1967
Shady Lady. 1954
Shamus, Your Slip Is Showing. 1955
The Silken Nightmare. Signet, 1963
Sinner, You Slay Me. 1957
Small Change
So What Killed the Vampire? Signet, 1966
The Sob-Sister Cries Murder. 1955
The Sometime Wife. Signet, 1965
Strictly for Felony. 1956
The Stripper. Signet, 1961
Suddenly by Violence. Signet, 1959
Swan Song for a Siren. 1955
Sweetheart, This Is Homicide. 1957
Target for Their Dark Desire. Signet, 1966
The Temptress. Signet, 1960
Terror Comes Creeping. Signet, 1959
The Tigress. Signet, 1961
Tomorrow Is Murder. Signet, 1960
Trouble Is a Dame. 1954
The Two-Timing Blonde. 1955
The Unorthodox Corpse. Signet, 1961
Until Temptation Do Us Part. Signet, 1967
The Velvet Vixen. Signet
Venus Unarmed. 1953
The Victim. Signet, 1959
Walk Softly, Witch. Signet, 1959, 1964
The Wanton. Signet, 1959
The Wayward Wahnie. Signet, 1960
The Wench Is Wicked. 1955
The White Bikini. Signet, 1963
Who Killed Dr. Sex? Signet, 1964
Widow Bewitched. 1958
The Wildcat
The Wind-Up Doll. Signet
Wreath for a Redhead. 1957
Zelda. Signet, 1961

YATES, DORNFORD, pseud; see MERCER, CECIL WILLIAM

YATES, GEORGE WORTHING (M)
(Joint pseudonym with Charles Hunt Marshall: Peter Hunt)
The Body That Came by Post. Davies, 1937; Morrow, 1937
The Body That Wasn't Uncle. Davies, 1939; Morrow, 1939; Dell
Gale Warning. Ward, Lock, 1939
If a Body. Morrow, 1941
Murder Among the Nudists, by Peter Hunt. Vanguard, 1934
Murder for Breakfast, by Peter Hunt. Vanguard, 1934
Murders at Scandal House, by Peter Hunt. Appleton-Century, 1933
There Was a Crooked Man. Davies, 1936; Morrow, 1936; Triangle, 1939

YATES, LIONEL and HONOR GOODHART (M)
The Eclipse of James Trent, D.I. Murray, 1924

YATES, MARGARET TAYLER (M-D)
Death Sends a Cable. Macmillan, 1938; Davies, 1939
Hush-Hush Murders. Macmillan, 1937; Dickson, 1938
Midway to Murder. Macmillan, 1941
Murder by the Yard. Macmillan, 1942

YATES, MARGARET POLK and PAULA BRAMLETTE (M)
Death Casts a Vote. Dutton, 1948
Widow's Walk. Dutton, 1945

YORCK, RUTH L. (M)
So Cold the Night. Harper, 1948

YORK, ANDREW, pseud; see NICOLE, CHRISTOPHER

YORK, JEREMY, pseud; see CREASEY, JOHN

YOUD, CHRISTOPHER SAMUEL (S)
Holly Ash. Cassell, 1955 (U.S. title: The Opportunist. Harper, 1957)

YOUNG, EDWARD PRESTON (M)
The Fifth Passenger. Harper & Row, 1963

YOUNG, ERIC BRETT (M) (Pseudonym: Eric Leacroft)
Dancing Beggars. Hutchinson, 1929; Lippincott, 1929
Murder at Fleet. Hutchinson, 1927; Lippincott, 1928

YOUNG, ERNEST A. (D) (Pseudonym: Harry Rockwood)
Abner Terret, the Lawyer Detective, by Harry Rockwood. Ogilvie, 1883
Clarice Dyke, the Female Detective. Ogilvie, 1883
Donald Dyke, the Yankee Detective, by Harry Rockwood. Street, 1900
File No. 114. Ogilvie, 1886 (A Sequel to File 113 by Emile Gaboriou)
Harry Sharpe, the New York Detective, by Harry Rockwood. Ogilvie, 1893
Lake Darby, the "World" Detective; or Romance of the Dexter, Maine Bank Robbery and Murder, by Harry Rockwood. Ogilvie, 1887
Mrs. Donald Dyke, Detective, by Harry Rockwood. Street, 1900
Nat Foster, the Boston Detective. A Thrilling Story of Detective Life, by Harry Rockwood. Ogilvie, 1883
Neil Nelson, the Veteran Detective; or, Tracking Mail Robbers, by Harry Rockwood. Ogilvie, 1885
The Railway Detective, by Harry Rockwood. Street, 1900

YOUNG, FRANCIS BRETT (M-S)
Black Diamond. Collins, 1921; Dutton, 1921
Cold Harbour. Collins, 1924; Knopf, 1925
A Man About the House. Heinemann, 1942; Reynal, 1942

YOUNG, G. R. (M)
Crooked Shadows. Garden City Pub., 1924

YOUNG, GEORGE (M)
Code-Name Caruso. Hutchinson, 1961
A Man Called Lenz. Hutchinson, 1954; Coward, 1955

YOUNG, GORDON RAY (M)
The Devil's Passport. Century, 1933; Cassell, 1934

YOUNG, KENDALL, pseud; see YOUNG, PHYLLIS BRETT

YOUNG, PHYLLIS BRETT (S) (Pseudonym: Kendall Young)
The Ravine. Allen, W. H., 1962
Undine. Longmans, 1964; Putnam, 1964; Crest, 1964

YOUNG, ROSE EMMET (M)
Murder at Manson's. Day, 1927

YOUNGER, ELIZABETH HELY (M)
Dominant Third; see I'll Be Judge, I'll Be Jury
I'll Be Judge, I'll Be Jury. Scribner, 1959; Dell, 1962 (English title: Dominant Third. Heinemann, 1959; British Book Centre, 1959)
A Mark of Displeasure. Scribner, 1960

YOUNGER, WILLIAM (M)
Goodbye Is Not Worthwhile. McClelland, 1956
Skin Trap. Eyre, 1957
You Pay for Pity. Dodd, 1958

YUDKOFF, ALVIN (M)
Circumstances Beyond Control. Rinehart, 1955

ZANGWILL, ISRAEL (D)
The Big Bow Mystery. Henry, 1892; Rand, 1895
The Grey Wig. Heinemann, 1903; Macmillan, 1903

ZARABICA, MLADIN (D)
Scutari. Farrar, 1967

ZHDANOV, ALEXANDER IVANOVICH, pseud. (S)
Shadow of Peril. Doubleday, 1963

ZINBERG, LEN (D-M) (Pseudonym: Ed Lacy)
Be Careful How You Live; see Time Wounds All Heels
The Best That Ever Did It. Harper, 1955; Hutchinson, 1957
The Big Fix. Pyramid, 1960; Boardman, T. V., 1961
Breathe No More, My Lady. Avon, 1958
Bugged for Murder. Avon, 1961
Dead End; see Time Wounds All Heels
A Deadly Affair. Hillman, 1960
Death in Passing. Boardman, T. V., 1959
Devil for the Witch. Boardman, T. V., 1958
Double Trouble. Harper & Row, 1964; Boardman, T. V., 1965
Enter Without Desire. Macfadden, 1964
The Freeloaders. Berkley Pub., 1961; Boardman, T. V., 1962
Go for the Body. Boardman, T. V., 1959; Avon
Harlem Underground. Pyramid, 1965
Keep an Eye on the Body; see Lead with Your Left
Lead with Your Left. Boardman, T. V., 1957; Harper, 1957 (Also published as: Keep an Eye on the Body. Mercury Mystery)

Listen to the Night; see Shakedown for Murder
The Men from the Boys. Harper, 1956; Boardman, T. V., 1960; Macfadden, 1967
Moment of Untruth. Boardman, T. V., 1965
Pity the Honest. Boardman, T. V., 1964; Macfadden, 1965
Room to Swing. Harper, 1957; Boardman, T. V., 1958
The Sex Castle. Paperback Lib., 1963
Shakedown for Murder. Avon, 1959 (Also published as: Listen to the Night)
Sin in Their Blood. Macfadden, 1966
Sleep in Thunder. Grosset, 1964
Strip for Violence. Macfadden, 1965
Time Wounds All Heels. Boardman, T. V., 1958 (Also published as: Be Careful How You Live. Harper, 1959 and Dead End. Pyramid, 1960)
Two Hot to Handle. Paperback Lib., 1963
The Woman Aroused. Avon

ZUGSMITH, LEANE; see RANDAU, CARL

ZUKAS, EDGAR V. (M)
A Handful of Stars. Vantage, 1964

PART II

A Bibliographic Guide to Mystery Fiction

1

SUBJECT GUIDE TO MYSTERIES

Have you ever wondered what goes on behind the doors of a large advertising agency? Or just what an archaeologist does when he is out in the field? Do actors and artists really lead the depraved lives you've always imagined they did?

There is one way to find out and enjoy a good mystery, detective or suspense story at the same time. Not satisfied merely with creating intriguing characters and unique settings, today's writers go to considerable lengths to portray accurately the subjects they are dealing with. There are too many experts around nowadays for any conscientious writer to make the flubbs they used to get by with in the good old days. Whether you are interested in ballet, bees, atomic research or communism, there is an author somewhere who has blended his love for the mystery with carefully researched information from his own field. When a Helen Traubel writes *The Metropolitan Opera Murders,* you can bet she knows the background she is writing about. When ex-jockey Dick Francis writes those superb stories about the racing world, it's from his own vast experience that the facts are garnered. History has been re-created in one type of mystery novel that has become extremely popular in the past few years. Especially noteworthy in this genre are the novels of John Dickson Carr, who combines a keen ear for the sounds of history with a mastery of the techniques of detection. You can go backstage with actors in TV, in the theatre and in the movies; and even the world of sports has been investigated by the curious writer. Many true murder cases have become the basis for mystery novels, and the taboo subjects of a few years ago are now becoming common topics for the mystery writer.

Advertising

The world of advertising with its high pressures, keen competition and fragile friendships has become a popular setting for murder mysteries. Those who are interested in this field might try:

Eichler, Alfred, *Death of an Artist*
———. *Death of an Ad Man*
———. *Hearse for the Boss*
———. *Murder in the Radio Department*
Goldsmith, Gene, *Layout for a Corpse*

Gribble, Leonard, *Don't Argue with Death*
Herber, William, *Death Paints a Portrait*
Iams, Jack, *Prematurely Gay*
Keating, H. R. F., *Death and the Visiting Fireman*
McMullen, Mary, *Death of Miss X*
Moyes, Patricia, *Murder à la Mode*
Oleskar, Harry, *Now Will You Try for Murder?*
Sayers, Dorothy, *Murder Must Advertise*
Wilkinson, Roderick, *The Big Still*

Amnesia

Whether real or feigned amnesia is always an intriguing theme for a mystery novel.
Alan, Marjorie, *Murder in a Maze*
Alexander, David, *Most Men Don't Kill*
Allingham, Margery, *Traitor's Purse*
Appleby, John, *Aphrodite Means Death*
Armstrong, Anthony, *He Was Found in the Road*
Bentley, Edmund C., *Elephant's Work*
Blizard, Marie, *The Dark Corner*
Boileau, Pierre and Thomas Narcejac, *The Evil Eye*
Brown, Frederic, *We All Killed Grandma*
Chance, John N., *The Man with No Face*
Davis, Stratford, *The Troubled Mind*
Dodge, Davis, *The Lights of Skaro*
Fuller, Roy B., *Fantasy and Fugue*
Gault, William C., *The Canvas Coffin*
Gilbert, Anthony, *Give Death a Name*
Jarvie, C. G., *He Would Provoke Death*
Kane, Henry, *Edge of Panic*
Kennington, Alan, *The Lost One*
Little, Constance and Gwenyth Little, *Blackout*
Marsh, Jean, *Identity Unwanted*
Orgill, Douglas, *Man in the Dark*
Perdue, Virginia, *Alarum and Excursion*
Prescott, H. F. M., *Dead and Not Buried*
Quentin, Patrick, *Puzzle for Fiends*
Stewart, Mary, *Thunder on the Right*
Stout, Rex, *Black Mountain*
Warren, Charles M., *Deadhead*
Wentworth, Patricia, *The Case of William Smith*

Antiques and Objets D'Art

The world of antiques and rare objects which are always tempting to thieves is an ideal source of material for the mystery writer. After you look behind the title page to see if it's still that first edition you're reading, try one of these:
Alexander, David, *Paint the Town Black*
Benson, Ben, *Beware the Pale Horse*
Brent, Nigel, *Golden Angel*
Bush, Christopher, *The Case of the Purloined Picture*
Dickson, Carter, *The Curse of the Bronze Lamp*
Kyle, Elizabeth, *The Regent's Candlesticks*
McLean, Alistair, *Deadly Honeymoon*
Manton, Peter, *Policeman's Triumph*
Martin, Shane, *Twelve Girls in the Garden*
Page, Marco, *Fast Company*
Pollard, A. O., *Sinister Secret*
Powell, Richard, *Lay That Pistol Down*
———. *Shoot If You Must*
Punshon, Ernest R., *The Golden Dagger*
Sims, George, *The Terrible Door*
Spiller, Andrew, *As They Shall Sow*

Archaeology

From the "digs" of ancient worlds to the halls of musty museums, the murderer is often an invisible companion.
Bell, Josephine, *Bones in the Barrow*
Blackstock, Charity, *Foggy, Foggy Dew*
Blake, Nicholas, *Widow's Cruise*
Canning, Victor, *The Golden Salamander*
Christie, Agatha, *Murder in Mesopotamia*
Clare, Marguerite, *Pierce the Gloom*
Cory, Desmond, *Height of Day*
Courtier, Sidney H., *One Cried Murder*
Farrer, Katherine, *The Cretan Counterfeit*
Fitt, Mary, *The Late Uncle Max*
———. *Sweet Poison*
Garve, Andrew, *Riddle of Samson*
Gruber, Frank, *The Greek Affair*
Harvester, Simon, *Paradise Men*
Hawton, Hector, *The Nine Singing Apes*

Martin, Shane, *The Man Made of Tin*
———. *The Saracen Shadow*
———. *The Third Shadow*
———. *Twelve Girls in the Garden*
Mitchell, Gladys, *Come Away, Death*
Munslow, Bruce J., *Deep Sand*
Orgill, Douglas, *The Death Bringers*
Peters, Ellis, *Death Mask*
Stein, Aaron Marc, *Moonmilk and Murder*
Tranter, Nigel, *The Enduring Flame*
———. *Stone*
Trench, John, *Beyond the Atlas*
———. *Dishonored Bones*
———. *The Docken Dead*
Wallis, Ruth S., *Blood from a Stone*
———. *Too Many Bones*

Arson

Like blackmail it attracts the unscrupulous and may lead to murder.

Bingham, John, *The Paton Street Case*
Blayn, Hugo, *Flashpoint*
Brock, Alan St. H., *Inquiries by the Yard*
Burton, Miles, *Smell of Smoke*
Cameron, Owen, *Fire Trap*
Carnac, Carol, *Burning Question*
Cross, Mark, *Third Time Unlucky*
Dudley, Ernest, *The Crooked Straight*
Goodis, David, *Fire in the Flesh*
Graham, Winston, *Fortune Is a Woman*
Grierson, Francis, *The Strange Case of Edgar Heriot*
Kelland, Clarence B., *Where There's Smoke*
Monig, Christopher, *Burned Man*
Sterling, Stewart, *Candle for a Corpse*
———. *Fire on Fear Street* (*See* Comprehensive Bibliography for other Ben Pedley stories)
Williams, Lawrence, *The Fiery Furnace*

Artists

Like actors, they are a volatile lot and things happen when their ambitions are threatened.

Allingham, Majorie, *Black Plumes*
Duncan, Francis, *So Pretty a Problem*
Farrar, Stewart, *Death in the Wrong Bed*
Gardiner, Stephen, *Death Is an Artist*
Hunter, Alan, *Gently with the Painters*
Iams, Jack, *Death Draws a Line*
Innes, Michael, *Private View*
King, Frank, *Case of the Vanishing Artist*
Lorac, E. C. R., *Checkmate to Murder*
Newman, T., *Raphael Resurrection*
Pim, Sheila, *Brush with Death*
Queen, Ellery, *The Glass Village*
Quentin, Patrick, *The Man in the Net*
Ransome, Stephen, *I'll Die for You*
Reilly, Helen, *The Canvas Dagger*
Rhode, John, *An Artist Dies*
Sayers, Dorothy L., *Five Red Herrings*
Usher, Frank, *Death in Error*
———. *Death Is Waiting*
———. *Die, My Darling*
———. *First to Kill*
———. *Ghost of a Chance*
———. *Lonely Cage*
———. *Portrait of Fear*
———. *Price of Death*
Warren, James, *Brush of Death*

Atomic Research

Behind the security there still lurks danger and intrigue and mystery writers have taken full advantage of the possibilities.

Betteridge, Don, *Not Single Spies*
Durbridge, Francis, *Back Room Girl*
Gask, Arthur, *Vaults of Backarden Castle*
Gordon, Donald, *Flight of the Bat*
Groom, Pelham, *The Fourth Seal*
Haggard, William, *Slow Burner*
Hamilton, Donald, *The Steel Mirror*
Hastings, Michael, *Twelve on Endurance*
Hawton, Hector, *Case of the Crazy Atom*
Hodder-Williams, Christopher, *Chain Reaction*
Hough, Stanley B., *Mission in Guemo*
Lee, Austin, *Miss Hogg and the Squash Club Murder*
Mackenzie, Nigel, *In Great Danger*
MacLean, Alastair, *Ice Station Zebra*
Mars, Alastair, *Atomic Submarine*
Marsh, Patrick, *Breakdown*
Nelson, Hugh L., *Murder Comes High*

Newman, Bernard, *Dead Man Murder*
Noel, Sterling, *Few Die Well*
Postgate, Raymond, *The Ledger Is Kept*
Strutton, B., *Jury of Angels*
Teilhet, Darwin, *The Big Runaround*
Wood, James, *Northern Mission*

Ballet

Like the theatre, the world of ballet is one apart from that of normal life. Here we have a group of people strictly devoted to their art and highly jealous of anyone who threatens it. Naturally it becomes an interesting background for a murder story.

Box, Edgar, *Death in the Fifth Position*
Brahms, Caryl, *A Bullet in the Ballet*
———. *Casino for Sale*
Conyn, Cornelius and Jon C. Marten, *The Bali Ballet Murder*
Cores, Lucy, *Corpse de Ballet*

Bees

We think of them chiefly as producers of a delicacy for the breakfast table, but they can also become killers in the wrong hands.

Heard, H. F., *A Taste for Honey*
Pims, Sheila, *Hive of Suspects*
Vivian, Francis, *The Singing Masons*

Blackmail

Perhaps there is no lower individual on earth than the blackmailer and he is a ripe victim for murder.

Alington, Cyril A., *Blackmail in Blankshire*
Annesley, Michael, *The Lights That Did Not Fail*
Atiyah, Edward, *The Crime of Julian Masters*
Axelrod, George, *Blackmailer*
Bridges, Victor, *Secrecy Essential*
Cecil, Henry, *Natural Causes*
Chance, John N., *Dead Man's Knock*
Christie, Agatha, *The Secret of Chimneys*
Clevely, Hugh, *Public Enemy*
Connington, J. J., *Death at Swaythling Court*
Corrigan, Mark, *Madame Sly*
Costello, Paul, *Red Beard*
Crofts, Freeman W., *Anything to Declare?*
Cumberland, Marten, *The Man Who Covered Mirrors*
Curtiss, Ursula, *Voice Out of Darkness*
Daniel, Roland, *Dangerous Moment*
Dudley, Ernest, *Whistling Sands*
Duncan, Francis, *Question of Time*
Easton, Nat, *Bill for Damages*
———. *Book for Banning*
Ernst, Paul, *The Bronze Mermaid*
Fair, A. A., *Some Slips Don't Show*
Fenisong, Ruth, *Blackmailer*
———. *Widow's Blackmail*
Ferrars, Elizabeth, *The Clock That Wouldn't Stop*
———. *A Tale of Two Murders*
Flynn, Thomas T., *It's Murder*
Fox, James M., *Death Commits Bigamy*
Gardner, Erle Stanley, *The Case of the Green-eyed Sister*
———. *The D.A. Holds a Candle*
Garve, Andrew, *End of the Track*
———. *The Narrow Search*
Gask, Arthur, *The Silent Dead*
Gilbert, Anthony, *Footsteps Behind Me*
Graham, A., *No Sale for Haloes*
Graham, Neill, *The Quest of Mr. Sandyman*
Gregg, Cecil F., *Chief Constable*
Grierson, Francis, *Blackmail in Red*
———. *Sign of the Nine*
Haddow, Dennis, *Hanged by a Thread*
Heberden, Mary V., *Murder Goes Astray*
Herber, William, *King-sized Murder*
Hocking, Anne, *Epitaph for a Nurse*
Hopley, George, *Fright*
Horler, Sidney, *The Menace*
———. *Scarlett-Special Branch*
Irish, William, *I Married a Dead Man*
Joseph, George, *Swan Song for a Thrush*
King, Frank, *Big Blackmail*
———. *Death of a Cloven Hoof*
Lloyd, Lavender, *The Linton Memorial*
Macdonald, Philip, *Guest in the House*
Mackenzie, Andrew, *The Reaching Hand*
Mackenzie, Donald, *Dangerous Silence*

Marsh, Ngaio, *Death in a White Tie*
Mason, A. E. W., *The House in Lordship Lane*
Matheson, Jean, *Dire Departed*
Meynell, Laurence, *One Step from Murder*
Mitchell, James, *Way Back*
Morris, Shayne, *Horse of Many Colors*
Morton, Anthony, *Black for the Baron*
Mosely, Dana, *Dead of Summer*
Muir, Dexter, *Rosemary for Death*
O'Farrell, William, *The Devil His Due*
O'Sullivan, James B., *Nerve-Beat*
Pollard, A. O., *Deal in Death*
Ransome, Stephen, *Night Drop*
Rattray, Simon, *Knight Sinister*
Rhode, John, *Open Verdict*
Robertson, Colin, *You Can Keep the Corpse*
Rutledge, Nancy, *Cry Murder*
Shearing, Joseph, *For Her to See*
Simenon, Georges, *Negro*
Straker, J. F., *Pick up the Pieces*
Strange, John S., *Uneasy Is the Grave*
Symons, Julian, *Gigantic Shadow*
Truss, Leslie S., *Put Out the Light*
Wallace, Edgar, *Missing Million*
Wentworth, Patricia, *Mr. Zero*
———. *Out of the Past*

Children

There used to be a taboo about using children in mystery and detective stories. If they appeared at all, it was only as victims of kidnapping and were invariably returned safely to their parents at the end of the story. Nowadays children are not only kidnapped; they are also brutal victims of sadistic killers or vicious killers in their own right. Readers who are interested in books which feature children as principal characters might turn to some of the following:

Armstrong, Charlotte, *Incident at a Corner*
Aswell, Mary L., *Far to Go*
Bagby, George, *Cop Killer* (A 15-year-old juvenile delinquent)
———. *Evil Genius*
Barry, Jerome, *Extreme License* (A 17-year-old girl involved in murder)
Bates, Herbert, *Dear Life*
Bawden, Nina, *Devil by the Sea* (A child caught in the web of her own make-believe)
Bell, Josephine, *Bones in the Barrow* (A young boy witnesses a scene of terror)
———. *Easy Prey*
Benson, Ben, *The Girl in the Cage*
Blake, Nicholas, *The Whisper in the Gloom*
Blankfort, Michael, *The Widow-Makers*
Brackett, Leigh, *The Tiger Among Us* (Five young hoodlums tracked by their victim)
Brewer, Gill, *And the Girl Screamed*
Brinton, Henry, *Coppers and Gold* (A 14-year-old girl detective)
Butler, Gwendoline W., *The Dull Dead*
Caldwell, Taylor, *Wicked Angel* (A vicious child killer who looks like an angel)
Carleton, Majorie C., *The Night of the Good Children*
Chamberlain, Anne, *The Tall Dark Man* (A little girl is witness to murder)
Chance, John N., *Little Crime*
Christie, Agatha, *They Do It with Mirrors*
Clewes, Winston, *Troy and the Maypole*
Comstock, Caroline, *Bandar-log Murder*
Cullingford, Guy, *The Whipping Boys*
De Jong, Dola, *The Whirligig of Time*
Deming, Richard, *Juvenile Delinquent*
Doubtfire, Dianne, *Lust for Innocence*
Dürrenmatt, Fredric, *The Pledge* (Effect of a child's murder on the career of a police detective)
Echard, Margaret, *I Met Murder on the Way* (The terror of a 14-year-old girl)
Ellin, Stanley, *The Dreadful Summit*
Ellison, Harlan, *The Deadly Streets*
———. *Tomboy*
Eustis, Helen, *Fool Killer*
Farris, John, *When Michael Calls*
Fast, Julius, *Street of Fear*
Ferrars, E. X., *The Sleeping Dogs* (A child murder)
Fleming, Joan M., *The Chill and the Kill*
Forbes, Stanton, *Relative to Death*
French, E. T., *Never Smile at Children* (A 5-year-old girl's shocked reaction to murder)
Fuller, Roy B., *With My Little Eye*
Garve, Andrew, *End of the Track*
Graaf, Peter, *Dust and the Curious Boy* (Search for a missing boy)
Greene, Graham, *Brighton Rock* (A 17-year-old murderer)
Grubb, Davis, *Night of the Hunter* (Two children stalked by a vicious killer)
Henry, Charles, *The Hostage* (The disappearance of a 6-year-old girl)
Hobson, Hank, *The Mission House Murder*
Kendall, Carol, *Baby Snatcher*
———. *Black Seven*

Lees, Hannah, *Death in the Doll's House*
Linington, Elizabeth, *No Evil Angel* (A 13-year-old girl involved in brutal murders)
Lyon, Dana, *The Frightened Child*
———. *The Lost One*
McBain, Ed, *King's Ransom*
MacDonald, Philip, *Murder Gone Mad* (A mad child killer on the loose)
MacDonald, Ross, *The Far Side of the Dollar* (A search for a missing boy)
McShane, Mark, *The Girl Nobody Knows*
March, William, *The Bad Seed* (A vicious 12-year-old murderess)
Marric, J. J., *Gideon's Fire* (A strangled child)
Masterson, Whit, *A Shadow in the Wild*
Millar, Margaret, *The Fiend*
Moore, Philips, *Once Upon a Friday* (A 17-year-old schizophrenic boy and the brutal murder of a child)
O'Donnell, Lillian, *Babes in the Woods* (Death of a 7-year-old child)
Parker, Richard, *Gingerbread Man*
———. *Harm Intended*
Patrick, Q., "Little Boy Lost," *Ellery Queen Mystery Magazine* (October, 1947)
———. *The Man in the Net* (Five children help to solve a crime)
———. "Portrait of a Murderer," *Harper's* (April, 1942)
Pentecost, Hugh, "The Children Vanished" in *Hit Parade of Mystery Stories*
Peters, Ellis, *Death and the Joyful Woman*
———. *Death Mask*
Phillips, Conrad, *The Empty Cot* (A normal boy who suddenly becomes a homicidal maniac)
Proctor, Maurice, *The Pennycross Murders*
Queen, Ellery, *Inspector Queen's Own Case: November Song* (A kidnapping case)
Ross, Ivan, *Requiem for a Schoolgirl*
Shenkin, Elizabeth, *Midsummer Nightmare*
Stout, Rex, *The Mother Hunt*
Tickell, Jerrard, *The Hunt for Richard Thorpe* (Kidnapping of a 12-year-old)
Wade, Henry, *The Litmore Snatch*
Whitney, Phyliss, *A Window on the Square*

Christmas

Considering the ingenuity of mystery writers, it's not surprising that they've even been able to find a dark side to Christmas. Here are some good examples:

Alexander, David, *Shoot a Sitting Duck*
Black, Gavin, *A Dragon for Christmas*
Christie, Agatha, *Hercule Poirot's Christmas*
Delaney, Joseph, *The Christmas Tree Murders*
Eberhart, Mignon G., *Postmark Murder*
Erskine, Margaret, *House of the Enchantress*
Farrell, Kathleen, *Mistletoe Malice*
Foley, Rae, *Where Is Mary Bostwick?*
Gunn, Victor, *Death on Shivering Sand*
Hardwick, Richard, *The Season to Be Deadly*
Hare, Cyril, *An English Murder*
Heyer, Georgette, *Envious Casca*
Iams, Jack, *Do Not Murder Before Christmas*
Innes, Michael, *Christmas at Candleshoes*
Kane, Henry, *A Corpse for Christmas*
Kelly, Mary C., *The Christmas Egg*
Kitchin, C. H. B., *Crime at Christmas*
Lambert, Elisabeth, *The Sleeping House Party*
Miers, Earl, *The Christmas Card Murders*

Clergy

The clergy also have their temptations. And not too surprisingly, they also like to play the detective game when the opportunity presents itself.

Alington, Cyril A., *Archdeacons Ashore*
———. *Blackmail in Blankshire*
———. *Gold and Gaiters*
Allen, Mabel E., *Murder at the Flood*
Bentley, Edmund C., *Elephant's Work: An Enigma*
Burton, Miles, *Death Takes the Living*
Caruso, Joseph, *The Priest*
Dick, Alexandra, *Crime in the Close*
DuBois, Theodora, *The Listener*
Eisinger, Jo, *The Walls Came Tumbling Down*
Gilbert, Michael, *Close Quarters*
Heard, Gerald, *Black Fox*
Hubbard, Margaret, *Murder Takes the Veil*

Keneally, T., *The Place at Whitton*
Lee, Austin, *Miss Hogg and the Dead Dean*
Rogers, Kerk, *With Intent to Destroy*
Warriner, Thurman, *Heavenly Bodies*
Wills, Cecil M., *Midsummer Murder*
See also:
Catalan, Henri, The Soeur Angele stories
Chesterton, G. K., The Father Brown stories
Herr, Dann and Joel Wells, eds., *Bodies and Souls* (Detective and murder stories with a religious background)
Holton, Leonard, The Father Bredder stories
Kemelman, Harry, The Rabbi Small stories
Scherf, Margaret, The Rev. Martin Buell stories
Webb, Jack, The Father Shanley and Sergeant Golden stories

Communism

The battleground of all the *isms* is a natural for the mystery writer.
Bennett, Kem, *The Devil's Current*
Bryan, John, *The Man Who Came Back*
Buchan, John, *Huntingtower*
Clements, Eileen H., *Honey for the Marshal*
Cory, Desmond, *Pilgrim at the Gate*
———. *Pilgrim on the Island*
Deighton, Len, *Funeral in Berlin*
———. *The Ipcress File*
Foley, Rae, *Man in the Shadow*
Fox, James M., *No Dark Crusade*
Gainham, Sarah, *The Stone Roses*
Graham, Winston, *Greek Fire*
Haggard, William, *The Telemann Touch*
Hamilton, D., *Murder Twice Told*
Harling, Robert, *The Enormous Shadow*
Harvester, Simon, *Flight in Darkness*
MacCutchan, Philip, *Moscow Coach*
MacInnes, Helen, *North from Rome*
McPartland, John, *Danger for Breakfast*
Marquand, John P., *Stopover Tokyo*
Parker, Robert, *Ticket to Oblivion*
Savage, Richard, *Innocents*
Slater, Humphrey, *The Conspirator*
Strachan, Tony S., *The Short Week-end*
Wheatley, Dennis, *Curtain of Fear*
Wormser, Richard, *The Torn Curtain*

Gambling

Although they deal with the subject, you as a reader can't lose by trying any of these:
Brown, Fredric, *Compliments of a Fiend*
Carrier, Warren, *Bay of the Damned*
Dolph, Jack, *Murder Is Mutuel*
Fleming, Ian, *Casino Royale*
———. *Moonraker*
Hammett, Dashiell, *The Glass Key*
Kathrens, William H., *The Lady Makes News*
Lee, Edward, *Fish for Murder*
Leslie, Jean, *The Man Who Held Five Aces*
Murray, Max, *Good Luck to the Corpse*
Rabe, Peter, *Kill the Boss Goodbye*

Historical Novels

One of the most interesting trends in recent years is that of the mystery, detective and suspense novelist taking leave of his own century and going back into history to find his material. Some fascinating books have come out of these re-creations.
Berckman, Evelyn, *Lament for Four Brides* (Modern and feudal France merge)
———. *Strange Bedfellow* (A search for a ruby which has been lost for two hundred years)
Blackstock, Lee, *All Men Are Murderers* (The shadow of an ancient murder set in 17th century Scotland)
Bullett, Gerald, *Trouble at Number Seven*
Carr, John Dickson, *The Bride of Newgate* (1815)
———. *Captain Cut-Throat* (1675)
———. *The Demoniacs* (1757)
———. *The Devil in Velvet* (1675)
———. *Fear Is the Same* (1795)
———. *Fire, Burn* (1829)
———. *Most Secret* (1670)
———. *Scandal at High Chimneys* (1865)

———. *The Witch at the Low-Tide* (1907)
Christie, Agatha, *Death Comes as the End* (Egypt, 2000 B.C.)
Cooper, John C., *The Haunted Strangler* (1880)
De La Torre, Lillian, *Detections of Dr. Sam: Johnson* (18th century)
———. *Dr. Sam: Johnson, Detector* (18th century)
———. *Elizabeth Is Missing* (18th century)
Disney, Doris M., *Dark Lady* (A modern author solves an old crime)
Eberhart, Mignon G., *The Cup, the Blade, or the Gun* (1863)
Fitt, Mary, *Case for the Defence* (1896–1919)
Graham, Winston, *The Wreck of the Grey Cat* (1898)
Gray, Charles E., *Murder Defies the Roman Emperor* (Hadrian's Rome, 135 A.D.)
Heard, Gerald, *The Black Fox* (1870)
Horler, Sidney, *The Blanco Case*
Kelland, Clarence B., *The Lady and the Giant* (1869)
Langton, Jane, *The Transcendental Murder* (The ghosts of Thoreau, Emerson and Alcott)
Luhr, Victor, *The Longbow Murder* (Richard the Lion-Hearted)
Mathieson, Theodore, *The Devil and Ben Franklin* (Philadelphia in 1734)
———. *The Great Detectives* (The great men of history as detectives)
Pentecost, Hugh, *The Assassins* (New York City during the Civil War)
Queen, Ellery, *A Study in Terror* (Ellery Queen aids Sherlock Holmes in solving the mystery of Jack the Ripper)
———. *The Finishing Stroke* (A murder solved 27 years after it was committed)
Roscoe, Theodore, *Only in New England* (1911)
Smith, Shelley, *An Afternoon to Kill*
Tey, Josephine, *The Daughter of Time* (A detective reopens the case of Richard III)
Wagner, John, *The Gift of Rome* (Rome, 66 B.C.)
Wallace, Edgar, *Devil Man* (England, 1875–1879)

Homosexuals and Lesbians

The world of the homosexual and the lesbian, which has long been a taboo subject, has just recently been explored by mystery, detective and suspense writers.

Baxt, George, *A Queer Kind of Death*
———. *Swing Low, Sweet Harriet*
Fast, Julius, *The Street of Fear*
Levin, Meyer, *Compulsion*
Linington, Elizabeth, *Greenmask*
Mills, Carley, *The Nearness of Evil*
O'Farrell, William, *The Snakes of St. Cyr*
Racker, Vin, *The Evil Friendship*
Rand, Lou, *Gay Detective*
Spicer, Bart, *Act of Anger*
Stone, Hampton, *The Murder That Wouldn't Stay Solved*
Thorp, Rodney, *The Detective*
Yaffe, James, *Nothing But the Night*

Hospitals

The world of hospitals, doctors and nurses where the battle between life and death never ceases has become a favorite locale for the detective, mystery and suspense writer.

Allen, Clifford, *Dark Places*
Archer, Margaret, *Gentle Rain*
Austwick, J., *Highland Homicide*
———. *The Hubberthwaite Horror*
Bayne, Isabella, *Death and Benedict*
Birch, Bruce, *Subway in the Sky*
Blackwood, Algernon, *John Silence*
Borgenicht, Miriam, *Don't Look Back*
Brand, Christianna, *Green for Danger*
Bryant, Michael, *Intent to Kill*
Burke, John F., *The Poison Cupboard*
Candy, Edward, *Bones of Contention*
———. *Which Doctor?*
Cannan, Joanna, *And Be a Villain*
Carnac, Carol, *Long Shadows*
Clements, Eileen, H., *Uncommon Cold*
Drachman, Theodore S., *Something for the Birds*
Fast, Julius, *Street of Fear*
Finney, Jack, *The Body Snatchers*
Fleming, Joan, *The Deeds of Dr. Deadcert*
Garve, Andrew, *Fontego's Folly*
Godey, John, *This Year's Murder*

Halliday, Michael, *Thicker Than Water*
Heberden, Mary V., *To What Dread End*
Hocking, Anne, *The Wicked Flee*
———. *Epitaph for a Nurse*
Horler, Sidney, *The Charlatan*
King, Frank, *Only Half the Doctor Died*
Maguire, P. P., *Certain Dr. Mellor*
Matheson, Jean, *So Difficult to Die*
Messenger, Elizabeth M., *Dive Deep for Death*
Murray, Max, *The Doctor and the Corpse*
Plummer, Thomas A., *The Murder of Dr. Grey*
———. *Murder in the Surgery*
Rhode, John, *Dr. Goodwood's Locum*
Sansom, J., *The Man Who Could Cheat Death*
Scott, Sutherland, *Diagnosis: Murder*
———. *Doctor Dodd's Experiment*
———. *The Mass Radiography Murders*
———. *Tincture of Murder*
See also:
Bachmann, Lawrence, The Dr. Coffee novels and stories
Brand, Max, The Dr. Kildare novels
Eberhart, Mignon G., The Nurse Keate novels
Rhode, John, The Dr. Priestley novels
Rinehart, Mary Roberts, The Miss Pinkerton novels

Impersonation

E. Phillips Oppenheim's *The Great Impersonation* was one of the great suspense stories of all times. With its resounding success, it is no surprise that other writers have tried their hand at this same theme. There are many variations as these stories will reveal:

Armstrong, Anthony, *The Strange Case of Mr. Pelham*
Armstrong, Charlotte, *The Dream-Walker*
Ashe, Gordon, *Double for Death*
Audemars, Pierre, *Two Imposters*
Avallone, Michael, *Spitting Image*
Bayne-Powell, Rosamund, *The Crime at Porches Hill*
Berckman, Evelyn, *Blind Villain*
Boileau, Pierre and Thomas Narcejac, *Prisoner*
Carr, John Dickson, *The Crooked Hinge*
Corrigan, Mark, *The Girl from Moscow*
Curtiss, Ursula, *Widow's Web*
Davis, Howard C., *Renegade from Russia*
Du Maurier, Daphne, *The Scapegoat*
Duncan, David, *The Bramble Bush*
Eberhart, Mignon G., *Unknown Quantity*
Fair, A. A., *Bats Fly at Dusk*
Fleming, Ian, *Moonraker*
Fredericks, Ernest J., *Lost Friday*
Friend, Oscar, *Mississippi Hawk*
Graffy, Joseph, *The Man Who Was Not Himself*
Grant, Richard, *Threat of the Cloven Hoof*
Highsmith, Patricia, *The Talented Mr. Ripley*
Hill, Vincent, *The Lady from Hamburg*
Horler, Sidney, *The Man Who Died Twice*
Innes, Michael, *Hare Sitting Up*
Irish, William, *I Married a Dead Man*
Lancaster, Vicky, *Royal Deputy*
Landon, Christopher G., *Hornet's Nest*
———. *Mirror Room*
Lorac, E. C. R., *Ask a Policeman*
McCloy, Helen, *Alias Basil Willing*
———. *Through a Glass Darkly*
Masur, Harold Q., *The Big Money*
Oppenheim, E. Phillips, *Anna the Adventuress*
———. *The Great Impersonation*
Punshon, Ernest R., *The Secret Search*
Ransome, Stephen, *I'll Die for You*
Roth, Holly, *Mask of Glass*
Tey, Josephine, *To Love and Be Wise*
Wallace, Edgar, *Double Dan*

Insurance

Insurance, especially when there is a lot of it involved, is a temptation to the unscrupulous. Various themes have been divised by writers from the misuse of a usually protective device.

Cain, James M., *Double Indemnity*
Carmichael, Harry, *Dead of the Night*
———. *Deadly Nightcap*
———. *James Knowland: Deceased*
———. *Justice Enough*
———. *Or Be He Dead*
———. *Question of Time*
———. *Seeds of Hate*
———. *Stranglehold*
Chaber, M. E., *Hearse of Another Color*
Chase, James Hadley, *Double Shuffle*

Disney, Doris M., *Halloween Murder*
———. *Quiet Violence*
Gilbert, Michael, *The Doors Open*
Graham, Winston, *Fortune Is a Woman*
Hastings, MacDonald, *Cork and the Serpent*
———. *Cork in the Doghouse*
———. *Cork on the Water*
Knox, Ronald A., *Three Taps*
Malcolm-Smith, George, *The Trouble with Fidelity*
Mason, Howard, *The Body Below*
Merwin, Samuel, *Matter of Policy*
Meynell, Laurence W., *Danger Round the Corner*
Monig, Christopher, *Abra-cadaver*
———. *Burned Man*
Pearson, William, *Hunt the Man Down*
Sanborn, B. X., *The Doom-maker*
Waugh, Hillary B., *The Eighth Mrs. Bluebeard*

Lawyers

Perhaps the best known of the lawyer-detectives is Perry Mason whose numerous cases may be found in the Comprehensive Bibliography. Try these also:

Ashford, Jeffrey, *Counsel for the Defense*
———. *Forget What You Saw*
Carr, John Dickson, *Patrick Butler for the Defense*
Fish, Robert L., *Trials of O'Brien*
Gilbert, Anthony, *A Nice Cup of Tea*
Green, Anne K., *The Leavenworth Case*
Grierson, Francis, *The Second Man*
Hare, Cyril, *Tragedy at Law*
Hart, Frances N., *The Bellamy Trial*
Mills, Osmington, *No Match for the Law*
Ransome, Stephen, *The Frazer Acquittal*
Rice, Craig, *Double Frame*
———. *My Kingdom for a Hearse*
Underwood, Michael, *False Witness*
———. *Murder Made Absolute*
Woods, Sara H., *Bloody Instructions*

Libraries

A library, especially one of those turn-of the-century relics, is as good a place for a mystery of a gothic castle. Even during the day, with its air of quietness, it is a place where dark things might happen.

Austwick, John, *Mobile Library Murders*
———. *Murder in the Borough Library*
Bell, Josephine, *Death on the Borough Council*
Blackstock, Charity, *Dewey Death*
Boyd, Marian M., *Murder in the Stacks*
Flynn, Brian, *Out of the Dusk*
Garve, Andrew, *The Galloway Case*
Johnson, W. B., *The Widening Stain*
Langton, Jane, *The Transcendental Murder*
Symons, Julian, *The Color of Murder*

Police

The modern trend toward giving the police credit where credit is due is a healthy sign. Books in which departments rather than individuals are emphasized are included among the following:

Benson, Ben, *The Running Man*
Brean, Herbert, *A Matter of Fact*
Brock, Alan, *Browns of the Yard*
———. *Inquiries by the Yard*
Brown, Fredric, *The Lenient Beast*
Crawley, J. C., *Investment in Crime*
Dekobra, Maurice, *Operation Magali*
Deming, Richard, *Case of the Courteous Killer*
Dineen, Joseph F., *Anatomy of a Crime*
Dürrenmatt, Fredric, *The Pledge*
Farmer, Bernard J., *Death at the Cascades*
———. *Death of a Bookseller*
———. *Murder Next Year*
Gilbert, Michael F., *Blood and Judgment*
Godfrey, Peter, *Death Under the Table*
The Gordons, *Case File: FBI*
———. *Case of the Talking Bug*
Graeme, Bruce, *Just an Ordinary Case*
Grierson, Francis, *He Had It Coming to Him*
Harrington, Joseph, *The Last Known Address*

Henry, Jack, *Flannelfoot, Phantom Crook*
Highsmith, Patricia, *The Blunderer*
Hobart, Robertson, *The Case of the Shaven Blond*
Howard, Leigh, *Blind Date*
Hume, Fergus, *Mystery of a Hansom Cab*
Jessup, Richard, *Man in Charge*
Krasney, Samuel A., *Death Cries in the Street*
Linington, Elizabeth, *Greenmask*
McBain, Ed, *Ten Plus One*
McGivern, William P., *The Big Heat*
———. *The Seven File*
McNamara, Ed, *Once Over Deadly*
Marric, J. J., *Gideon's Day*
Pike, Robert L., *Police Blotter*
Shannon, Dell, *With a Vengeance*
Sheldon, Walt, *The Man Who Paid His Way*
Treat, Lawrence, *V as in Victim*
Vickers, Roy, *The Department of Dead Ends*
Wade, Henry, *Be Kind to the Killer*
———. *Diplomat's Folly*
———. *Gold Was Our Grave*
———. *Here Comes the Copper*
———. *The Litmore Snatch*
Willis, Ted, *The Blue Lamp*
Young, George, *A Man Called Lenz*
See also:
Benson, Ben, The Massachusetts State Police series
Egan, Lesley, The Glendale Police Force series
McBain, Ed, The 87th Precinct series
Marric, J. J., The Gideon stories
Pike, Robert L., The 52nd Precinct series
Proctor, Maurice, Inspector Martineau series (Granchester Police Force)
Shannon, Dell, The Wilcox Place Police Station stories

Railroads

Right from the beginning the railroad with its limitless possibilities for excitement and intrigue has appealed to the writer of mystery, detective and suspense fiction.

Blochman, Lawrence Goldtree, *Bombay Mail*
Chalmers, Stephen, *The Crime in Car 13*
Davis, Tech, *Full Fare for a Corpse*
Denbie, Roger, *Death on the Limited*
The Gordons, *Campaign Train*
Greene, Graham, *The Orient Express*
Highsmith, Patricia, *Strangers on a Train*
Hitchens, Hubert and Dolores Beale Hitchens, *End of the Line*
———. *F.O.B. Murder*
———. *The Grudge*
———. *The Man Who Followed Women*
———. *One-Way Ticket*
Kendrick, Baynard Hardwick, *The Last Express*
Leverage, Henry, *The Purple Limited*
MacVeigh, Sue, *Grand Central Murder*
———. *Murder Under Construction*
———. *Streamlined Murder*
Nebel, Frederick, *Sleepers East*
Packard, Frank Lucius, *The Wire Devils*
Post, Melville Davisson, *Walker of the Secret Service*
Propper, Milton Morris, *The Ticker Tape Murder*
Reilly, Helen Kieran, *Compartment K*
Rinehart, Mary Roberts, *The Man in Lower Ten*
Ross, Barnaby, *The Tragedy of X*
Tucker, Arthur Wilson, *Last Stop*

Romans A Clef

It is not a secret any longer that many mystery, detective, and suspense novels are based on the lives of real people and on many true, famous criminal cases. Some such books listed in the Comprehensive Bibliography are:

Abbot, Anthony, *About the Murder of the Clergyman's Mistress* (Based on the Halls-Mills Case)
Berkeley, Anthony, *Murder in the Basement* (Based on the career of the murderer George Joseph Smith)
———. *Wychford Poisoning Case* (Based on the famous Maybrick Case in 1889)
Boucher, Anthony, *The Case of the Solid Key* (Based on the H. H. Holmes Case)
Cain, James, *Double Indemnity* (Based somewhat on the Snyder-Gray Case)
Carr, John Dickson, *The Burning Court* (Based on the historical figures Mme.

la Marquise de Brinvilliers and Captain Sainte-Croix)
Chaber, M. E., *The Gallows Garden* (Based on the Galindez Case)
Dreiser, Theodore, *An American Tragedy* (Based on the Chester Gillette Case)
Endore, Guy, *Werewolf of Paris* (Based on the trial of Sergeant Bertrand in 1848)
Goodchild, George and Bechhofer Roberts, *The Dear Old Gentleman* (Based on the Sandyford mystery of 1862)
Greene, Ward, *Death in the Deep South* (Based on the Leo Frank Case in 1915)
Levin, Meyer, *Compulsion* (Based on the Leopold-Leob Case)
Longstreet, Stephen, *The Crime* (Based on the Halls-Mills Case)
Marlowe, Stephen, *Murder Is My Dish* (Based on the Galindez Case)
Rinehart, Mary Roberts, *The Afterhouse* (Based on murders committed aboard the *Herbert Fuller* in 1896)
Stevenson, Robert Louis, *The Body Snatchers* (Possibly suggested by the Burke and Hare Case)
Van Dine, S. S., *The Canary Murder Case* (Suggested by the murder of Dot King in 1923)
Yaffe, James, *Nothing But the Night* (Based on the Leob-Leopold Case)

The famous Jack the Ripper case has inspired a number of novels in this genre:
Alexander, David, *Terror on Broadway*
Brown, Fredric, *The Screaming Mimi*
Capon, Paul, *The Seventh Passenger*
Desmond, Hugh, *Death Let Loose*
———. *A Scream in the Night*
Hamilton, Patrick, *Hangover Square*
Lowndes, Marie, *The Lodger*
Marsh, Ngaio, *Singing in the Shrouds*
Morland, Nigel, *Death for Sale*
Queen, Ellery, *A Study in Terror*
Wilson, Colin, *Ritual in the Dark*
Bibliography:
Sandoe, James, "Criminal Clef: Tales and Plays Based on Real Crimes," *Wilson Library Bulletin* (December, 1946).
Walbridge, Earle F., *Literary Characters Drawn from Life.* H. W. Wilson, 1936.

Satire

The detective story lends itself beautifully to satire. Many of the detective characters with their know-all attitudes and eccentricities make perfect targets for the satirists. There is a world of difference, however, between a clever satire and one of the spoofs or parodies that we are bombarded with today on television and in the movies. Readers who wish to sample the real thing might try some of these:
Aldrich, Thomas B., *The Stillwater Tragedy*
Alington, Cyril A., *Gold and Gaiters*
Audemars, Pierre, *Two Imposters*
Bangs, John K., *Mrs. Raffles*
Berkeley, Anthony, *The Poisoned Chocolates Case*
Bierce, Ambrose, *Can Such Things Be?*
Black, J. M., Jr., "There Is No Sleuth Like Holmes," *Rotarian* (August, 1947)
Burgess, Eric A., *Divided We Fall*
Davey, Jocelyn, *Undoubted Deed*
Ford, Corey, *The John Riddell Murder Case: A Philo Vance Parody*
Gregory, Harry, *The Man from M.O.T.H.E.R.*
Haggard, William, *Closed Circuit*
Johnstone, C., "The Detective Story's Origin," *Harper's* (February 12, 1910)
Leacock, Stephen, *Here Are My Lectures and Stories.* Read "Murder at $2.50 a Crime" (Dodd, Mead, 1937)
———. "The Irreducible Detective Story," *Golden Book* (May, 1932)
———. "Twenty Cents Worth of Murder," *Saturday Review of Literature* (July 8, 1939)
Lieberman, E., "What Ails the Whodunit?" *Saturday Review of Literature* (June 21, 1947)
Perelman, S. J., "Farewell, My Lovely Appetizer," *Ellery Queen Mystery Magazine* (August, 1945)
Symons, Julian, *The Thirty-first of February*
———. *The Immaterial Murder Case*
Ward, C., "The Pink Murder Case" by S. S. Veedam, *Saturday Review of Literature* (November 2, 1929)

Sports

Although not widely represented, the world of sports has begun to appear as a background for mystery, detective and suspense stories. Especially good are the stories of ex-jockey Dick Francis, whose novels of the horse-racing world have stimulated a great deal of interest. Also read the novels of William Campbell Gault whose speciality is professional football—*The Day of the Ram* is a good one. Ellery Queen has an anthology called *Sporting Blood* which covers the whole field. If you can still find them in the library or the second-hand bookstores, the older novels of Cortland Fitzsimmons deal with various sports such as hockey and football. *The American Gun Mystery,* another one by Queen, has a rodeo in Madison Square Garden as a background. Michael Avallone handles the world of baseball in *Dead Game;* the world of cricket is explored in Barbara Worsley-Gough's *Alibi Innings.* Jack Dolph in *Murder Is Mutuel* depicts the world of bigtime gambling and the race tracks. Two mysteries dealing with hockey and tennis respectively are *Foul Play* by Jeremy Potter and *Two Sets to Murder* by Ludovic Peters.

Theatre and the Movies

The performing arts, whose inhabitants live on charged emotions, offer a rich field for the writer of detective, mystery and suspense fiction. Besides offering a good story, these novels usually are rich in background materials.

Allingham, Margery, *Deadly Duo*
Ames, Delano, *She Wouldn't Say Who*
Benson, Theodora, *Rehearsal for Death*
Broun, Daniel, *From Nine O'Clock to Jamaica Bay*
Brown, Carter, *The Girl from Outer Space*
Bryant, Matt, *Cue for Murder*
Bude, John, *Death Steals the Show*
Chambers, Peter, *Dames Can Be Deadly*
Chance, John N., *Fatal Fascination*
Cores, Lucy, *Painted for the Kill*
Corrigan, Mark, *The Wayward Blonde*
Cox, William, *Death on Location*
Coxe, George H., *Venturesome Lady*
Crispin, Edmund, *The Case of the Gilded Fly*
———. *Obsequies at Oxford*
Cumberland, Marten, *On the Danger List*
Desmond, Hugh, *Death by Candlelight*
Gault, William C., *Blood on the Boards*
———. *Death out of Focus*
———. *Vein of Violence*
Kane, Frank, *Bare Trap*
Kane, Henry, *Dangling Man*
———. *Fistful of Death*
Latimer, Jonathan, *Black Is the Fashion for Dying*
Lee, Elsie, *Dark Moon, Lost Lady*
Lee, Gypsy Rose, *The G-String Murders*
Loraine, Philip, *Exit with Intent*
McLean, Allan C., *Murder by Invitation*
Marsh, Ngaio, *Enter a Murderer*
———. *Final Curtain*
———. *Killer Dolphin*
———. *Night at the Vulcan*
———. *Vintage Murder*
Peters, E., *Where There's a Will*
Philips, Judson, *Killer on the Catwalk*
Plummer, Thomas A., *Death Haunts the Repertory*
Quentin, Patrick, *Suspicious Circumstances*
Rinehart, Mary Roberts, *The Case of Jennie Brice*
Roby, Mary L., *Still as the Grave*
Roth, Holly, *The Crimson in the Purple*
Rutledge, Nancy, *Cry Murder*
Tack, Alfred, *A Murder Is Staged*
Wentworth, Patricia, *Rehearsal for Death*

Universities and Colleges

The campus with its shady walks, its buildings with long, dark corridors and laboratories with their secrets—all of these in recent years have become familiar to the mystery reader.

Armstrong, Charlotte, *The Better to Eat You*
———. *A Dram of Poison*
———. *The Witch's House*
Asimov, Isaac, *The Death Dealers*

Blake, Nicholas, *The Morning After Death*
Burning, Michael and Althen Grey, *Dusty Death*
Burton, Miles, *Murder Out of School*
Carr, John Dickson, *Dead Man's Knock*
Crispin, Edmond, *The Case of the Gilded Fly*
———. *The Moving Toyshop*
Cross, Amanda, *In the Last Analysis*
———. *The James Joyce Murder*
Daniels, Harold R., *The Accused*
Davies, Leslie P., *The Paper Dolls*
Eustis, Helen, *The Horizontal Man*
Farrer, Katherine D., *Gownsman's Gallows*
Fenwick, Elizabeth P., *A Long Way Down*
Fuller, Timothy, *Harvard Has a Homicide*
Hocking, Anne, *The Simple Way of Poison*
Hodgin, M. R., *The Student Body*
Innes, Michael, *Death at the President's Lodgings*
———. *The Long Farewell*
———. *Old Hall, New Hall*
———. *Operation Pax*
———. *Seven Suspects*
Kelly, Mary C., *Dead Man's Riddle*
Kyd, Thomas, *Cover His Face*
Langley, Lee, *Osiris Died in Autumn*
Langton, Jane, *The Transcendental Murder*
Levin, Ira, *A Kiss Before Dying*
Lockridge, Frances & Richard, *Murder Is Served*
MacDonald, Ross, *The Chill*
Mainwaring, Marion, *Murder at Midyears*
Martin, Robert B., *Death Takes a Sabbatical*
Masterman, John C., *The Case of the Four Friends*
———. *The Oxford Tragedy*
Mitchell, Gladys, *Laurels Are Poison*
Owen, Hans C., *Ways of Death*
Post, Mortimer, *Candidate for Murder*
Rogers, Samuel, *Don't Look Behind You*
Simmons, Addison, *Death on the Campus*
Wakefield, R. I., *You Will Die Today*
Waugh, Hillary B., *Last Seen Wearing*
Wylie, Philip, *Experiment in Crime*

2

THE MYSTERY NOVEL ON THE SCREEN

Along with the Western, the mystery, detective and suspense story has been one of the staples of the motion picture industry since its infancy. Unlike the Western, however, which has been coddled and molded until it has almost become an art form, the detective story has been largely ignored and neglected. On the other hand, because of its excellent technical ingenuity, Hollywood occasionally has turned out superb mystery and suspense thrillers.

In my own opinion, the movies and the stage are poor media for the detective story. It is, essentially, a reading exercise which loses a great deal of its effectiveness when translated into sight and sound. It is a puzzle in which the author pits his wits against those of the reader, and the more ingenious the writer is, the more able he is to outwit his opponent, even though he plants all the clues needed to solve the crime. A good example of this is in the motion picture version of Ira Levin's *A Kiss Before Dying*. It was a very good suspense picture for those who had not read the book, but a great disappointment to those who had. The whole effectiveness of the story lies in the girl discovering the identity of her sister's murderer. In the book we never learn exactly who he is until the final chapter; in the film we see him almost at the beginning of the picture, and there is very little doubt at any time who he really is.

Hollywood is twice guilty, in my estimation, when it comes to this type of literature. They have an almost neurotic need to take an already well-plotted story and hand it to a screenwriter who mutilates it beyond recognition, and an irritating insistence on changing titles so that the reader is not aware that a picture has been made from a favorite story. Some of the classics in the field have ended up with such trite titles that they keep the public away. Evidently the motion picture producers are still not aware that 40% of the American reading public reads this kind of literature and is very knowledgeable about it.

A very recent example comes to mind. One can only wonder why Ross MacDonald, the creator of Lew Archer, allowed the screenwriters to change his character's name to Harper when it served no useful purpose. You now have the amusing experience of being able to buy a pocket edition of *The Moving Target* on the newsstand. The book is called *Harper,* but no one by that name appears in the book.

Because television has made it possible to see many of the old films again, this portion of the book is devoted to the literature as it has made its transition to the screen. The Selected Filmography, arranged by author, gives some idea of the types of mystery, detective and suspense fiction that have been adapted for films and of the transformation they have undergone in the transition to an entirely different medium. The Film and Book Cross Index is a listing, by no means complete, of the novels and short stories in this genre that have been made into motion pictures. In the first two columns of this section the original names of the books are listed along with their authors. In the third column appears the title under which it was made into a film. The reader should be warned, however: there may be still further title changes. To complicate matters even further, those who edit the films for TV have also gotten into the habit of changing the titles again. Happy hunting!

Selected Filmography by Author

Michael Arlen

It seems ironic now that a character created for one obscure short story was to become a favorite character in fifteen movies while other more durable ones, such as Gardner's Perry Mason and Dannay and Lee's Ellery Queen, found little favor with movie fans. From 1941 to 1949, fifteen movies based on Michael Arlen's Falcon were produced. George Sanders and Tom Conway played the character. In one picture, *The Falcon's Brother,* Conway played the Falcon, while Sanders played the brother.

Here is a list of the Falcon pictures. Except for *The Falcon Takes Over,* which was Raymond Chandler's *Farewell, My Lovely* in its first screen treatment, the others were original screen treatments:

1941	*A Date with the Falcon*
	The Gay Falcon
1942	*The Falcon's Brother*
1943	*The Falcon Takes Over*
	The Falcon and the Co-eds
	The Falcon in Danger
	The Falcon Strikes Back
1944	*The Falcon in Hollywood*
	The Falcon in Mexico
	The Falcon Out West
1945	*The Falcon in San Francisco*
1946	*The Falcon's Alibi*
1947	*The Falcon's Adventure*
1948	*Appointment with Murder*
	The Devil's Cargo
1949	*Search for Danger*

Earl Derr Biggers

Earl Derr Biggers was well represented on the screen during the heyday of his popularity. Five versions of *Seven Keys to Baldpate* were produced between 1917 and 1947. Two versions of *The Agony Column* were made, and in typical Hollywood fashion were given new titles so that the mystery fan would never know that his favorite story might have been filmed. The 1917 version was called *Blind Adventure,* and the 1930 version *The Second Floor Mystery.* Both of them seem rather trite titles and no great improvement over the original.

It was Biggers' Chinese detective hero, Charlie Chan, who was to create the greatest stir. After the success of *Behind That Curtain* in 1929, more than thirty-five features and serials were produced with the Charlie Chan character. After the original novels had been filmed and re-filmed, the rest of the scripts were original screenplays and stories adapted from the works of other writers. *Charlie Chan in Reno,* produced in 1939, was adapted from a Philip Wylie story, "Death Makes a Decree."

Charlie Chan was to continue to appear

on radio and television for many years, and even now the old features can often be seen on the late show.

1917 *Blind Adventure*
Seven Keys to Baldpate
1925 *Seven Keys to Baldpate*
1927 *The Chinese Parrot*
1929 *Behind That Curtain*
1930 *Seven Keys to Baldpate*
1931 *The Black Camel*
Charlie Chan Carries On
Charlie Chan's Chance
1933 *Charlie Chan's Greatest Case.* Based on *The House Without a Key.*
Charlie Chan's Secret
1934 *Charlie Chan's Courage.* Based on *The Chinese Parrot.*
Charlie Chan in London
1935 *Charlie Chan in Egypt*
Charlie Chan in Paris
Charlie Chan in Shanghai
Seven Keys to Baldpate
1936 *Charlie Chan at the Circus*
Charlie Chan's Secret
1937 *Charlie Chan at the Opera*
Charlie Chan at the Olympics
Charlie Chan at the Race Track
Charlie Chan on Broadway
1938 *Charlie Chan at Monte Carlo*
1939 *Charlie Chan at Treasure Island*
Charlie Chan in the City in Darkness
Charlie Chan in Honolulu
Charlie Chan in Reno. Based on "Death Makes a Decree" by Philip Wylie.
1940 *Charlie Chan at the Wax Museum*
Charlie Chan in Panama
Charlie Chan's Murder Cruise (Remake of *Charlie Chan Carries On*)
Murder over New York
1941 *Charlie Chan in Rio*
Dead Men Tell
1944 *Charlie Chan in the Secret Service*
1945 *The Jade Mask*
The Red Dragon
The Scarlet Clue
1946 *Dangerous Money*
Dark Alibi
Shadows over Chinatown
The Trap
1947 *The Chinese Ring*
Seven Keys to Baldpate
1948 *Docks of New Orleans*
The Golden Eye
1949 *The Sky Dragon*

Jack Boyle

Another favorite fictional character popular with movie audiences from 1918 to 1949 was Boston Blackie, created by Jack Boyle. The character was a great boost to the career of Chester Morris, who played the role in a number of the later films.

1918 *Boston Blackie's Little Pal*
1919 *Blackie's Redemption*
1922 *Missing Millions.* Based on "A Problem in Grand Larceny" and "An Answer in Grand Larceny."
1941 *Meet Boston Blackie*
1942 *Alias Boston Blackie*
Boston Blackie Goes Hollywood
Boston Blackie Goes to Washington
Confessions of Boston Blackie
1943 *After Midnight with Boston Blackie*
The Chance of a Lifetime
One Mysterious Night
1945 *Boston Blackie Booked on Suspicion*
Boston Blackie's Rendezvous
1946 *Boston Blackie and the Law*
Close Call for Boston Blackie
The Phantom Thief
1948 *Trapped by Boston Blackie*
1949 *Boston Blackie's Chinese Venture*

Raymond Chandler

Considering his position in the detective field today and the great contributions he made, Raymond Chandler has been rather shabbily treated by the movie industry.

Farewell, My Lovely was first produced in 1942 as a B picture. Philip Marlowe became the Falcon, and the picture was called *The Falcon Takes Over.* It was filmed again in 1944. This time the title was changed to *Murder, My Sweet.* Dick Powell played the private eye. The critics liked this one, and it helped Dick Powell's career, who up to this time had been primarily a singing juvenile.

The first version of *The High Window* was a B picture called *Time to Kill.* This time Philip Marlowe had become Mike Shayne, and was played by Lloyd Nolan. The second version was called *The Brasher Doubloon* with George Montgomery playing Philip Marlowe. Montgomery was not an effective Marlowe, and the critics were not kind.

Lady in the Lake was filmed in 1946

with Robert Montgomery as Philip Marlowe. This is an interesting film because the director experimented by having the audience follow the picture through the eyes of the hero. In effect the camera was the real hero and we didn't see much of Montgomery/Marlowe in the film.

In *The Big Sleep* Humphrey Bogart played Philip Marlowe and managed through sheer personality to raise a rather confused drama to an entertaining level. Bogart came the closest, perhaps, to being the ideal Marlowe.

Leslie Charteris

Although popular with mystery readers, Charteris' Saint was only a minor success with movie fans. In the late thirties and early forties, he made a few appearances in B pictures. George Sanders, Hugh Sinclair and Louis Hayward were playing the role, and they might as well have been called the Falcon or the Lone Wolf, because many of these pictures had a dreary sameness to them. In the early sixties, Roger Moore appeared as the Saint in a British TV series. It was extremely popular in England, and later became equally popular with American viewers.

1938 *The Saint in New York,* Louis Hayward

1939 *The Saint in London,* George Sanders

The Saint Strikes Back, George Sanders. Based on *Angels of Doom.*

1940 *The Saint's Double Trouble,* George Sanders

The Saint Takes Over, George Sanders

1941 *The Saint in Palm Springs,* George Sanders

The Saint's Vacation, Hugh Sinclair. Based on *Getaway.*

1943 *The Saint Meets the Tiger,* Hugh Sinclair. Based on *Meet the Tiger.*

1954 *The Saint's Girl Friday*

Agatha Christie

The First Lady of Crime was another writer who was treated rather shabbily by the motion picture producers. Considering their incessant cries for stories that had plots to them, it is a wonder that they could ignore her ingenious ones so completely.

In a recent interview Mrs. Christie expressed her disapproval of what the industry had done to her stories. The only one she was really satisfied with was *The Witness for the Prosecution.* She told of her refusal in recent years to sell her books for fear of what might be done with them. When she was finally persuaded to part with them, she did so expecting them to be made into TV films, but they were again turned into some rather ghastly films. She enjoyed immensely the bad reviews they got from the critics. Her chief complaint was the usual one of the mystery writer. The studios turned her stories over to writers who proceeded to change the plots. Stories about Hercule Poirot were turned into a vehicle for an actress playing Miss Marple.

In 1945, *And Then There Were None* was made into a better than average mystery film, after it had been a successful stage play, *Ten Little Indians.* In 1965, it was remade under this latter title, and the setting was changed to the Swiss Alps for reasons buried in the mind of the screenwriter. It claimed to have a different ending than the original 1945 film, but this was only partially true. The order in which the victims died was changed slightly, but the same person turned out to be the murderer in both versions. It carried a gimmick: a sixty-second break was given the audience. During this brief period a series of quick flashbacks was supposed to give the viewer time enough to solve the crime. All in all, it was a disappointing picture.

A short story, "Philomel Cottage," was the basis for a successful stage play, *Love from a Stranger.* It was made into a fairly suspenseful film in 1947 with Sylvia Sydney and John Hodiak in the leading roles.

Another short story from the Mr. Quin adventures was turned into a full feature-length film, then re-written in 1929 into a novel called *The Passing of Mr. Quin* by G. Roy McRae.

Margaret Rutherford made a personal success as Miss Marple in a series of pictures, *Murder at the Gallop, Murder, She Said,* and *Murder Ahoy,* but they were not critical successes, and Mrs. Christie did not approve of them herself.

In 1966, Tony Randall appeared as Hercule Poirot in *The Alphabet Murders* based on *The ABC Murders.* This was not particularly successful either.

Len Deighton

The ideal combination of a great series character and a fine actor was sure to be potent box-office. Len Deighton's *The Ipcress File* was a sensation in England, and repeated some of that success in the United States. The movie version with Michael Caine in the leading role turned out to be a real surprise, and it was followed in 1966 with *Funeral in Berlin.* As this is being written, Caine is filming *Billion Dollar Brain* which will carry on the adventures of the intrepid Mr. Palmer. A fourth novel, *An Expensive Place to Die,* without Harry Palmer, but with a host of other interesting characters, has been bought for the screen.

Frederic Dannay and Manfred Lee

Again the movie producers failed to take advantage of material which, had it been given the right treatment, could have made exciting motion pictures. Ellery Queen caused only a small flurry of interest in the late thirties and the early forties. Too many different actors playing Ellery Queen may have been one of the reasons, but the screen treatments were also at fault, doing injustice to many of the stories.

1935 *The Spanish Cape Mystery.* Donald Cook as Ellery Queen.

1936 *The Mandarin Mystery.* Eddie Quillan as Ellery Queen. Based on *The Chinese Orange Mystery.*

1937 *The Crime Nobody Saw.* This was supposedly based on a play entitled *Men Working* by Ellery Queen and Lowell Brentano. Ellery Queen did not appear as a character in it.

1940 *Ellery Queen, Master Detective.* Ralph Bellamy appeared as Ellery Queen in an original screenplay that Edward Connor in his *Film in Review* article thought might possibly be based on *The Door Between.* Published in 1941 as *Ellery Queen, Master Detective.* See Bibliography at the end of this section.

1941 *Ellery Queen's Penthouse Mystery.* Ralph Bellamy again played Ellery Queen.

Ellery Queen and the Perfect Crime. Ralph Bellamy.

Ellery Queen and the Murder Ring. Ralph Bellamy. Based on *The Dutch Shoe Mystery.*

1942 William Gargan appeared as Ellery Queen in three films in this year:

A Close Call for Ellery Queen. Based on *The Dragon's Teeth.*

A Desperate Chance for Ellery Queen. Adapted from a radio script.

Enemy Agents Meet Ellery Queen. Based on *The Greek Coffin Mystery.*

Sir Arthur Conan Doyle

It will come as no great surprise to anyone that perhaps more movies have been made from the Sherlock Holmes stories of Sir Arthur Conan Doyle than from any other author's. Even as recently as March, 1966, *Variety* reported that the Doyle estate, along with Bernard Shaw's and Ian Fleming's, was the richest literary estate in the world, and that plans were going ahead to make even more motion pictures and television plays from the stories.

The popularity of the stories is attested to by the fact that there have been 106 Sherlock Holmes films, including 17 versions of *The Hound of the Baskervilles.* Forrest Holger-Madsen, a Danish actor, was the first to play Holmes on the screen. The most famous, and perhaps the most popular Sherlock Holmes, was Basil Rathbone. In one series of twelve pictures, he played Holmes and Nigel Bruce played Dr. Watson.

The movie makers have been fairly faithful in their adaptations of the work of the master, although some of the films made with Basil Rathbone in the forties used only the character and had original stories. We even had the experience of seeing Sherlock Holmes outwitting Nazi spies in Washington, D.C. during World War II. In England a TV series starring Ronald Howard, the son of Leslie Howard, was very popular, and Holmes even took on a new role as a singer when the Broadway musical, *Baker Street,* appeared in the early sixties. Fritz Weaver sang the part of Sherlock Holmes in the musical. The most recent Sherlock Holmes film is *A Study in*

Terror, which is an original screenplay. In this adventure he solves the mystery of Jack the Ripper. In the paperback edition, Ellery Queen has somehow gotten into the act, and we have the experience of watching two great detectives solving the same crime generations apart.

1903 *Sherlock Holmes Baffled.* Earliest Holmes film known.
1905 *Adventures of Sherlock Holmes*
1908 *Rival Sherlock Holmes* (Italian)
Sherlock Holmes in the Great Murder Mystery
Sherlock Holmes
Sherlock Holmes in the Gas Chamber
1910 *The Murder in Baker Street* and nine other one-reelers using the Holmes character but not the stories.
1912 *The Speckled Band* (Anglo-French)
The Adventures of Sherlock Holmes. Eight one-reelers based on the stories.
1913 *Sherlock Holmes Solves the Sign of the Four.* Harry Benham as Sherlock Holmes.
1914 *A Study in Scarlet.* Fred Paul as Sherlock Holmes.
1916 *Sherlock Holmes.* William Gillette as Sherlock Holmes.
1917 *Der Hund von Baskervilles* (German)
1922 *Sherlock Holmes* (English title: *Moriarty*). John Barrymore as Sherlock Holmes and Roland Young as Watson.
The Hound of the Baskervilles (English). Eille Norwood as Sherlock Holmes.
Fifteen two-reel productions based on the stories produced by Educational Pictures.
1929 *Der Hund* (Sudfilm). Last silent Holmes film.
The Return of Sherlock Holmes. First talking picture with Sherlock Holmes played by Clive Brook.
Talking short with A. Conan Doyle talking about the Holmes stories and his fans.
1930 *Sherlock Holmes' Fatal Hour* (English title: *The Sleeping Cardinal*). Based on the short stories "The Final Problem" and "The Empty House."
1931 *The Speckled Band.* Raymond Massey as Sherlock Holmes.
1932 *The Sign of the Four.* Arthur Wontner as Sherlock Holmes.
The Missing Rembrandt. Based on "The Adventures of Charles Augustus Milverton."
The Hound of the Baskervilles. Robert Rendel as Sherlock Holmes.
Sherlock Holmes. Clive Brooks again as Sherlock Holmes.
1933 *A Study in Scarlet.* Only the title was used. Reginald Owen played Sherlock Holmes.
1935 *Triumph of Sherlock Holmes.* Based on *The Valley of Fear.*
Murder at the Baskervilles (English title: *Silver Blaze*). Loosely based on "Adventure of Silver Blaze."
1936 *Der Hund von Baskervilles* (German). Peter Voss played Sherlock Holmes.
1937 *Die Graue Dame* (German). The Holmes character was used but it was not based on any of the known stories.
1939 *Hound of the Baskervilles.* Basil Rathbone as Sherlock Holmes.
Adventures of Sherlock Holmes. Basil Rathbone as Sherlock Holmes.
1941 *Murder at the Baskervilles.* Based on the short story "Silver Blaze."
1942 *Sherlock Holmes and the Voice of Terror.* Basil Rathbone as Sherlock Holmes. Based on *His Last Bow.*
Sherlock Holmes and the Secret Weapon. Basil Rathbone as Sherlock Holmes. Based on the short story "Dancing Men."
1943 *Sherlock Holmes in Washington.* An original story. Basil Rathbone.
Sherlock Holmes Faces Death. Based on the short story "Musgrave Ritual."
1944 *The Scarlet Claw.* An original story.
Pearl of Death. Miles Mander as Sherlock Holmes. Based on the short story "Six Napoleans."
1945 *House of Fear.* Based on "The Five Orange Pips."
The Woman in Green. An original story.
Pursuit to Algiers. An original story.
1946 *Terror by Night*
Dressed to Kill

1959 *The Hound of the Baskervilles* (English)

1966 *A Study in Terror.* John Neville as Sherlock Holmes solves the Jack the Ripper case.

Davis Dresser

Michael Shayne was played by Lloyd Nolan in a series of B pictures from 1940 to 1944, when Hugh Beaumont carried on the role. As usual the scripts were not all fashioned from the Brett Halliday stories of Davis Dresser. *Time to Kill* was Raymond Chandler's *The High Window,* and Philip Marlowe had become Mike Shayne. *Sleepers West* was adapted from a Frederick Nebel novel called *Sleepers East.* This picture was a sleeper, that is, a low budget picture that turned out to be the critics' delight and a box office bonanza. It was remade a few years later under another title, but Mike Shayne was no longer in it.

1941 *Blue, White and Perfect*
Dressed to Kill. Based on *The Dead Take No Bows* by Richard Burke.
Michael Shayne, Private Detective
Sleepers West. Based on *Sleepers East.*

1942 *Just Off Broadway*
Time to Kill. Based on *The High Window.*

1946 *Blonde for a Day*
Larceny in Her Heart

1947 *Three on a Ticket*
Too Many Winners

Mignon G. Eberhart

The early novels of Mignon G. Eberhart had a brief popularity on America's screens during the decade between 1935 and 1945. Although they were constantly entertaining, they were never more than another B picture on the bottom half of a double feature.

1935 *While the Patient Slept*
The White Cockatoo

1936 *The Murder of Dr. Harrigan.* Based on *From this Dark Stairway.*
Murder by an Aristocrat

1937 *The Great Hospital Mystery.* Based on "Dead Yesterday."

1938 *Mystery House.* Based on *Mystery of Hunting's End.*
The Patient in Room 18

1945 *Three's a Crowd.* Based on *Hasty Wedding.*

Ian Fleming

A casual word from the late President Kennedy that Ian Fleming was one of his favorite writers was enough to ignite the blaze that was to sweep around the world. It was inevitable that the movies would discover James Bond and in the person of Sean Connery the world has found a new hero. David Niven played Bond in *Casino Royale* which was really a spoof of the whole series.

1962 *Goldfinger*

1963 *From Russia with Love*

1965 *Dr. No*

1966 *Thunderball*

1967 *Casino Royale*
You Only Live Twice

Erle Stanley Gardner

Despite the tremendous popularity of Erle Stanley Gardner's books, they were not a great success in the movies. Four actors played Perry Mason in the film versions, but none of them seemed to have made the impact that Raymond Burr did when he played him on TV for nine years. All of these were B pictures and were usually used to fill a second spot on a screen program.

1934 *The Case of the Howling Dog*

1935 *The Case of the Curious Bride*
The Case of the Lucky Legs

1936 *The Case of the Black Cat.* Based on *The Case of the Caretaker's Cat.*
The Case of the Velvet Claws
Special Investigator

1937 *The Case of the Stuttering Bishop*

Graham Greene

The novels and original screenplays of Graham Greene have graced the screens of the world since 1934. Except for a few clinkers, most of the pictures have received good reviews and some of them are considered superb examples of screen suspense. *The Third Man* brought thousands of tourists flocking to Vienna to visit the famous ferris wheel in the Prater and to listen to the zither music that was one of the popular parts of the soundtrack.

1934 *The Orient Express*
1942 *This Gun for Hire*
1944 *The Ministry of Fear*
Forty-eight Hours
1945 *Confidential Agent*
1948 *Brighton Rock* (Also filmed as *Young Scarface* in 1951)
The Smugglers. Based on *The Man Within.*
The Fallen Idol
1949 *The Third Man*
1951 *Young Scarface*. Based on *Brighton Rock.*
1956 *Loser Takes All*
1957 *Short Cut to Hell.* Book title: *Gun for Sale*
1958 *Across the Bridge*. Based on short story entitled "Across the Bridge."
1960 *Our Man in Havana*

Dashiell Hammett

After *The Thin Man* was released in 1934, the whole country became enamored with Nick and Nora Charles, played with wit and grace by William Powell and Myrna Loy. They continued to appear in original screenplays, many of which Hammett wrote himself, until 1947.

The Maltese Falcon first appeared as a motion picture in 1931 as a feature starring Ricardo Cortez as Sam Spade. Bebe Daniels and Dudley Digges were also in the cast. It was remade in 1936, re-titled *Satan Met a Lady,* and this time the cast included Warren William and Bette Davis. The best and most popular version came out in 1941 and reverted to the original title. Humphrey Bogart was Sam Spade, and the cast also included Mary Astor, Sydney Greenstreet and Peter Lorre.

The Glass Key first appeared in 1935 and starred Edward Arnold and George Raft. It was remade under the same title in 1942 and starred Alan Ladd, Brian Donlevy and Veronica Lake.

1931 *City Streets*
The Maltese Falcon
1934 *The Thin Man*
Woman in the Dark
1935 *The Glass Key*
Mister Dynamite. Based on a screen story entitled "On the Make."
1936 *After the Thin Man*
Satan Met a Lady. Based on *The Maltese Falcon.*
1939 *Another Thin Man*
1941 *Shadow of the Thin Man*
The Maltese Falcon
1944 *The Thin Man Goes Home*
1947 *Song of the Thin Man*

John LeCarré

Another name that came up big in the suspense field was John LeCarré whose *The Spy Who Came in from the Cold* was a welcome diversion from the phoney spy stories that had been flooding the market. Richard Burton's sensitive portrayal on the screen gave a new stature to this type of film. Another LeCarré story, *Call for the Dead,* gave a starring role to James Mason. On the screen it was called *The Deadly Affair* and it, too, was an outstanding example of the suspense genre on the screen.

Herman Cyril McNeile

In the years between 1929 and 1939, Herman Cyril McNeile's Bulldog Drummond made frequent appearances on American and world screens and was a popular hero of the movie audiences. In 1966, he reappeared in the guise of Richard Johnson in a film called *Deadlier Than the Male,* but according to the critics, he had lost much of his zing.

1929 *Bulldog Drummond*
1934 *Bulldog Drummond Strikes Back*
1935 *The Return of Bulldog Drummond.* Based on *The Black Gang.*
Alias Bulldog Drummond

1937 *Bulldog Drummond at Bay*
Bulldog Drummond Comes Back. Based on *The Female of the Species.*
Bulldog Drummond Escapes. Based on the play *Bulldog Drummond Again.*
Bulldog Drummond's Revenge. Based on *Return of Bulldog Drummond.*
1938 *Arrest Bulldog Drummond.* Based on *The Final Count.*
Bulldog Drummond in Africa. Based on *The Challenge.*
Bulldog Drummond's Peril. Based on *The Third Round.*
1939 *Bulldog Drummond's Bride.* Based on *Bulldog Drummond and the Oriental Mind.*
Bulldog Drummond's Secret Police. Based on *Temple Tower.*
Mr. and Mrs. Bulldog Drummond
1948 *The Challenge.* Based on the novel *The Challenge.*
1951 *Calling Bulldog Drummond.* Based on a story by Gerald Fairlie.
1966 *Deadlier Than the Male.* Based on the McNeile characters with Bulldog Drummond as a secret agent.

John P. Marquand

In 1965, Mr. Moto returned to the screen as a secret agent for Interpol with Henry Silva playing the wily Oriental sleuth. Almost twenty-six years had gone by since Peter Lorre played the detective in the three Moto films that were made in 1939.

1937 *Look Out Mr. Moto*
Thank You, Mr. Moto
Think Fast Mr. Moto
1938 *Mr. Moto Takes a Chance*
Mr. Moto's Gamble
The Mysterious Mr. Moto
Mr. Moto in Danger Island. Based on *Murder in Trinidad* by John W. Vandercook.
1939 *Mr. Moto Takes a Vacation*
Mr. Moto's Last Warning
Danger Island. The story was taken from a novel by John W. Vandercook.
1966 *The Return of Mr. Moto.* An original screen play starring Henry Silva as Mr. Moto, now a secret agent.

E. Phillips Oppenheim

The impressive output of E. Phillips Oppenheim was not overlooked by the motion picture producers between the years 1915 and 1938. The most popular of his stories was *The Great Impersonation,* first filmed in 1921, and then remade in 1942.

1915 *Master Mummer*
Mr. Grex of Monte Carlo
1916 *Under Suspicion*
1917 *The Silent Master*
The Sleeping Memory
1919 *The Cinema Murder*
The Illustrious Prince
The Long Arm of Mannister
Test of Honor
1921 *Behind Masks*
The Great Impersonation
Mystery Road
Pilgrims of the Night
1924 *Behold the Woman*
1926 *The Golden Web*
The Millionaires
The Passionate Quest
The Prince of Tempters
1931 *The Lion and the Lamb*
1934 *Monte Carlo Nights.* Based on "Numbers of Death."
1936 *Amazing Quest.* Based on *The Amazing Quest of Mr. Ernest Bliss.*
1937 *Romance and Riches.* Based on *The Amazing Quest of Mr. Ernest Bliss.*
1938 *Strange Boarders.* Based on *The Strange Boarders of Palace Crescent.*
1942 *The Great Impersonation*

Edgar Allan Poe

If Poe were alive today, it is almost certain that he would have been a screenwriter, or at least recognized the possibilities of the screen for telling the kind of story which he could write so well.

The first Poe film appeared exactly one

hundred years after his birth (1809), and they have been appearing quite regularly ever since. In the beginning many of them had Poe himself as the main character with scenes from his stories. Many films were made which were faithful adaptations of the original tales. There have also been many poor ones which merely retained a title or a character from one of the stories. They have also been a great source for some interesting experimental films. The Poe treasury has not been exhausted by any means so we should be able to look forward to many more and better films in the future.

1909 *Edgar Allan Poe*. Directed by D. W. Griffith and starring Herbert Yost as Poe.

Le Système du Dr. Goudron et du Professeur Plume (French). Based partly on a Poe story.

1912 *The Raven*. Guy Oliver played Poe. This picture contained a number of scenes from Poe's short stories.

1913 *The Pit and the Pendulum*

The Bells. A melodramatic picture in which the bells were used as symbols.

Der Student von Prag. German film starring Paul Wegener, based on "William Wilson."

1914 *Murders in the Rue Morgue*

The Avenging Conscience. Directed by D. W. Griffith, and starring Henry B. Walthall.

1915 *The Raven*. Starring Henry B. Walthall.

1917 *Isle of Oblivion*. A Russian film partly based on a Poe story.

1923 *A Spectre Haunts Europe*. Based on "The Masque of the Red Death."

1926 *Der Student von Prag*. Second German version starring Conrad Veidt. It was released in the U.S. under the title *The Man Who Cheated Life*, 1929.

1927 *The Tell-Tale Heart*. Directed by Charles F. Klein.

1928 *The Fall of the House of Usher*. American film by James Sibley Watson and Melville Webber.

La Chute de la Maison Usher. A French film directed by Jean Epstein.

1932 *Murders in the Rue Morgue*. Directed by Robert Florey.

1934 *The Black Cat*. Starring Bela Lugosi and Boris Karloff. Only the title had any reference to the Poe story.

The Bucket of Blood. A British film based on the "Tell-Tale Heart."

The Crime of Dr. Crespi. Based on "The Premature Burial."

The Tell-Tale Heart

1935 *The Raven*. Starring Boris Karloff.

1940 *The Living Dead*. Based on two short stories by Edgar Allan Poe, "The Black Cat" and "The System of Doctor Tarr and Professor Feather," and on "The Suicide Club" by Robert Louis Stevenson.

1941 *The Black Cat*. Starring Basil Rathbone.

The Tell-Tale Heart. An M-G-M short starring Joseph Schildkraut.

1942 *The Fall of the House of Usher*. 8mm experimental film.

The Mystery of Marie Rogêt. With Maria Montez.

The Loves of Edgar Allan Poe. With Linda Darnell and John Shepperd.

The Raven. A Paramount animated cartoon.

1948 *Histoires Extraordinaires* (French film)

The Raven. A short subject made by Westport-International.

1950 *Heartbeat*. A television production starring Richard Hart.

1951 *The Man with a Cloak*. Based on John Dickson Carr's story, "Gentleman from Paris." Supposedly the main character was Poe.

1952 *The Fall of the House of Usher* (British film)

1954 *Phantom of the Rue Morgue*. Starring Karl Malden.

The Raven. A short experimental film.

1955 *The Tell-Tale Heart*. A surrealistic animated cartoon released by UPA.

1956 *Manfish*. Based on "The Gold Bug" and "Tell-Tale Heart," starring John Bromfield.

Black Cat (UCLA, 16mm short)

1960 *House of Usher*. Starring Vincent Price.

1962 *The Tell-Tale Heart*

The Raven

Louis Joseph Vance

The Lone Wolf created by Louis Joseph Vance had a brief popularity in the forties. Most of the pictures were B ones, produced without much imagination and receiving very little critical attention. Louis Hayward, Francis Lederer and Warren Williams played the Lone Wolf at various times.

1922 *The Black Bag*
1929 *The Lone Wolf's Laughter*
1936 *The Lone Wolf Returns*
1938 *The Lone Wolf in Paris*
1939 *Lone Wolf Spy Hunt*
1940 *The Lone Wolf Keeps a Date*
The Lone Wolf Meets a Lady. Based on *The Lone Wolf.*
Lone Wolf Strikes
1941 *Lone Wolf Takes a Chance*
1947 *Lone Wolf in London*
Lone Wolf in Mexico
1949 *Lone Wolf and His Lady*

S. S. Van Dine

Extremely popular in the late twenties and early thirties, S. S. Van Dine was the first mystery writer to make the best seller lists. It was inevitable that Hollywood would quickly discover him. In William Powell they had the perfect Philo Vance, but before the series was to run its course, eight other actors were to portray the erudite detective. *The Kidnap Murder Case* and the *Winter Murder Case* were never made into films. The following is a brief history of the S. S. Van Dine saga on the screen.

1929 *The Canary Murder Case.* William Powell as Philo Vance.
The Greene Murder Case. William Powell as Philo Vance.
The Bishop Murder Case. William Powell as Philo Vance.
1930 *The Benson Murder Case.* William Powell as Philo Vance.
Scarab Murder Case
1933 *The Kennel Murder Case.* William Powell's last appearance as Philo Vance.
1934 *The Dragon Murder Case.* Warren William as Philo Vance.
1935 *The Casino Murder Case.* Paul Lukas as Philo Vance.
1936 *The Garden Murder Case.* Edmund Lowe as Philo Vance.
1937 *Night of Mystery.* Remake of *The Greene Murder Case* with Grant Richards as Philo Vance.
1939 *The Gracie Allen Murder Case.* With Warren William as Philo Vance.
1940 *Calling Philo Vance.* Remake of *The Kennel Murder Case.* James Stephenson played Philo Vance.
1947 *Philo Vance's Gamble.* Original story. Alan Curtis starring as Vance.
Philo Vance Returns. Original story. Alan Curtis.
Philo Vance's Secret Mission. Original story. Alan Curtis.

Cornell Woolrich

Woolrich's contribution to the screen has ranged from A pictures such as *The Rear Window* in which James Stewart starred, to a series of pictures made under the Republic bannerhead and which were fillers of little consequence. All of his stories, though, have the qualities that producers seek and it is surprising that more of them haven't been used. Mysteries, it seems, lurk in many other places besides mystery stories.

1938 *Convicted.* Based on the short story "Face Work."
1942 *The Street of Chance.* Based on *The Black Curtain.*
1943 *The Leopard Man.* Based on *Black Alibi.*
1944 *Mark of the Whistler.* Not an original Woolrich story.
The Phantom Lady
1946 *The Black Angel*
The Chase. Based on *The Black Path of Fear.*
Deadline at Dawn
1947 *Fall Guy.* Based on the short story "Cocaine."
Fear in the Night. Based on *Nightmare.*
The Guilty. Based on the short story "Two Men in a Furnished Room."

1948 *I Wouldn't Be in Your Shoes*
The Window. Based on the short story "The Boy Cried Murder." Remade in 1956 and entitled *Nightmare*.
The Night Has a Thousand Eyes
The Return of the Whistler. Not an original Woolrich story.

1950 *No Man of Her Own*. Based on *I Married a Dead Man*.
1954 *Rear Window*. Based on the short story "Rear Window" in *After Dinner Story*.
1956 *Nightmare*

Film and Book Cross-Index

NAME OF BOOK	AUTHOR	NAME OF FILM AND PRINCIPAL STAR
The ABC Murders	Agatha Christie	*The Alphabet Murders*, 1966, Tony Randall
About the Murder of the Circus Queen	Anthony Abbot	*The Circus Queen Murder*, 1933, Greta Nissen
About the Murder of the Night Club Lady	Anthony Abbot	*Night Club Lady*, 1932, Adolph Menjou
Above Suspicion	Helen MacInnes	*Above Suspicion*, 1943, Joan Crawford
Account Rendered	Pamela Barrington	*Account Rendered*, 1957, Griffith Jones
"The Adventure of Charles Augustus Milverton"	A. Conan Doyle	*The Missing Rembrandt*, 1932
"Adventure of Silver Blaze"	A. Conan Doyle	*Murder at the Baskervilles*, 1935, 1941, Peter Voss
"Adventure of the Speckled Band"	A. Conan Doyle	*The Speckled Band*, 1931, Raymond Massey
Adventures of Sherlock Holmes	A. Conan Doyle	*Adventures of Sherlock Holmes*, 1939, Basil Rathbone
After the Funeral	Agatha Christie	*Murder at the Gallop*, 1963, Margaret Rutherford
The Agony Column	Earl Derr Biggers	*Blind Adventure*, 1917 *The Second Floor Mystery*, 1930
"Aloha Means Goodbye"	Robert Carson	*Across the Pacific*, 1942, Humphrey Bogart
Alter Ego	Arch Oboler	*Bewitched*, 1944, Phyllis Thaxter (Based on radio program)
The Amateur Cracksman	Ernest W. Hornung	*Raffles, The Amateur Cracksman*, 1917, 1925 *Raffles*, 1930, 1940
The Amateur Gentleman	John Jeffrey Farnol	*The Amateur Gentlemen*, 1936
The Amazing Quest of Mr. Ernest Bliss	E. Phillips Oppenheim	*Amazing Quest*, 1936 *Romance and Riches*, 1937
The Amboy Dukes	Irving Shulman	*The City Across the River*, 1949, Stephen McNally
Anatomy of a Murder	Robert Traver	*Anatomy of a Murder*, 1959, James Stewart
And Then There Were None	Agatha Christie	*And Then There Were None*, 1945, Barry Fitzgerald *Ten Little Indians*, 1965, Hugh O'Brien
Angels of Doom	Leslie Charteris	*The Saint Strikes Back*, 1939
Arsène Lupin	Maurice LeBlanc	*Arsène Lupin*, 1916, 1917, 1932
Arsène Lupin Returns	Maurice LeBlanc	*Arsène Lupin Returns*, 1938
Ashenden	W. Somerset Maugham	*Secret Agent*, 1936
The Asphalt Jungle	William R. Burnett	*The Asphalt Jungle*, 1950, Sterling Hayden

NAME OF BOOK	AUTHOR	NAME OF FILM AND PRINCIPAL STAR
Assault on a Queen	Jack Finney	*Assault on a Queen,* 1966, Frank Sinatra
Assignment in Brittany	Helen MacInnes	*Assignment in Brittany,* 1942, Jean-Pierre Aumont
At the Villa Rose	Alfred E. W. Mason	*The House of Mystery,* 1941
Background to Danger	Eric Ambler	*Background to Danger,* 1943, George Brent
Backlash	Frank Gruber	*Backlash,* 1956
Backstage Mystery	Octavus Roy Cohen	*Curtain at Eight,* 1933
Bad Day at Black Rock	Howard Breslin	*Bad Day at Black Rock,* 1946, Spencer Tracy
The Bad Seed	William March	*The Bad Seed,* 1956, Nancy Kelly
Badge of Evil	Whit Masterson	*A Touch of Evil,* 1958
The Bat	Mary Roberts Rinehart	*The Bat,* 1926 *The Bat Whispers,* 1931
Be Still My Love	June Truesdale	*The Accused,* 1948, Loretta Young
The Beast with Five Fingers	William Fryer Harvey	*The Beast with Five Fingers,* 1947, Peter Lorre
Beat the Devil	James Helvick	*Beat the Devil,* 1954, Humphrey Bogart
Beau Geste	Percival C. Wren	*Beau Geste,* 1927, 1939, 1966
Bedelia	Vera Caspary	*Bedelia,* 1946, Margaret Lockwood
Before I Wake	Hal Debrett	*Shadow of Fear,* 1956, Mona Freeman (English title: *Before I Wake*)
Before the Fact	Francis Iles	*Suspicion,* 1941, Cary Grant
Behind That Curtain	Earl Biggers	*Behind That Curtain,* 1929
Behind the Headlines	Robert Chapman	*Behind the Headlines,* 1956
The Bellamy Trial	Frances Noyes Hart	*The Bellamy Trial,* 1928
The Benson Murder Case	S. S. Van Dine	*The Benson Murder Case,* 1930, William Powell
Betrayal from the East	Alan Hynd	*Betrayal from the East,* 1945, Lee Tracy
Beware of the Dog	Roald Dahl	*36 Hours,* 1964, James Garner
Beyond This Place	A. J. Cronin	*Web of Evidence,* 1959, Van Johnson
The Big Boodle	Robert Sylvestre	*The Big Boodle,* 1957
The Big Bow Mystery	Israel Zangwill	*The Perfect Crime,* 1928 *The Crime Doctor,* 1934 *The Verdict,* 1946
The Big Caper	Lionel White	*The Big Caper,* 1947
The Big Clock	Kenneth Fearing	*The Big Clock,* 1948, Ray Milland
The Big Heat	William P. McGivern	*The Big Heat,* 1953, Glenn Ford
The Big Night; see *Dreadful Summit*		
The Big Sleep	Raymond Chandler	*The Big Sleep,* 1946, Humphrey Bogart
Billion Dollar Brain	Len Deighton	*Billion Dollar Brain,* 1967
"The Birds"	Daphne Du Maurier	*The Birds,* 1963, Tippi Hedren
Bishop Murder Case	S. S. Van Dine	*Bishop Murder Case,* 1930
Black Alibi	Cornell Woolrich	*The Leopard Man,* 1943, Dennis O'Keefe
The Black Angel	Cornell Woolrich	*The Black Angel,* 1946, Dan Duryea
The Black Bag	Louis Joseph Vance	*The Black Bag,* 1922
The Black Camel	Earl Derr Biggers	*The Black Camel,* 1931
"The Black Cat"	Edgar Allan Poe	*The Black Cat,* 1934, Boris Karloff; 1941, Basil Rathbone *The Living Dead,* 1940
The Black Curtain	Cornell Woolrich	*The Street of Chance,* 1942

NAME OF BOOK	AUTHOR	NAME OF FILM AND PRINCIPAL STAR
The Black Gang	H. C. McNeile	*The Return of Bulldog Drummond*
Black Path of Fear	Cornell Woolrich	*The Chase,* 1946, Robert Cummings
Black Widow	Patrick Quentin	*Black Widow,* 1954, Ginger Rogers
Blanche Fury	Joseph Shearing	*Blanche Fury,* 1948, Valerie Hobson
The Blank Wall	Elizabeth Sanxay Holding	*The Reckless Moment,* 1949, James Mason
Blindfold	Lucille Fletcher	*Blindfold,* 1966, Rock Hudson
Blonde Died Dancing	Kelley Roos	*Come Dance With Me,* 1960
Blood on Her Shoe	Medora Field	*The Girl Who Dared,* 1944, Lorna Gray
Body Snatcher	Robert Louis Stevenson	*Body Snatcher,* 1945, Boris Karloff
Bombay Mail	Lawrence G. Blochman	*Bombay Mail,* 1934
Bonadventure (Play)	Charlotte Hastings	*Thunder on the Hill,* 1951, Claudette Colbert
Boston Blackie	Jack Boyle	*After Midnight with Boston Blackie,* 1943, Chester Morris
		Alias Boston Blackie, 1942, Chester Morris
		Boston Blackie and the Law, 1946, Chester Morris
		Boston Blackie Booked on Suspicion, 1945, Chester Morris
		Boston Blackie Goes Hollywood, 1942, Chester Morris
		Boston Blackie's Chinese Venture, 1949, Chester Morris
		Boston Blackie's Rendezvous, 1945, Chester Morris
		Close Call for Boston Blackie, 1946, Chester Morris
Boy on a Dolphin	David Devine	*Boy on a Dolphin,* 1957, Alan Ladd
"The Boy Who Cried Murder"	Cornell Woolrich	*The Window,* 1949, Bobby Driscoll
The Break in the Circle	Philip Loraine	*Break in the Circle,* 1957
The Bride Wore Black	Cornell Woolrich	*The Bride Wore Black,* 1968, Jeanne Moreau
Brighton Rock	Graham Greene	*Brighton Rock,* 1948
		Young Scarface, 1951
Build My Gallows High	Geoffrey Homes	*Out of the Past,* 1947, Robert Mitchum
Bulldog Drummond	H. C. McNeile	*Bulldog Drummond,* 1929
Bulldog Drummond and the Oriental Mind	H. C. McNeile	*Bulldog Drummond's Bride,* 1939
Bulldog Drummond at Bay	H. C. McNeile	*Bulldog Drummond at Bay,* 1937
Bulldog Drummond Strikes Back	H. C. McNeile	*Bulldog Drummond Strikes Back,* 1934
Bunny Lake Is Missing	Evelyn Piper	*Bunny Lake Is Missing,* 1965, Carol Lynley
Burn, Witch, Burn	Abraham Merritt	*The Devil Doll,* 1936
The Burning Court	John Dickson Carr	*The Burning Court,* 1963
Busman's Honeyman	Dorothy L. Sayers	*Haunted Honeymoon,* 1940, Robert Montgomery (English title: *Busman's Holiday*)
The Busybody	Donald Westlake	*The Busybody*
Cabin B-16	John Dickson Carr	*Dangerous Crossing,* 1953, Jeanne Crain
Call for the Dead	John Le Carré	*The Deadly Affair,* 1966, James Mason

NAME OF BOOK	AUTHOR	NAME OF FILM AND PRINCIPAL STAR
Calling Bulldog Drummond	Gerald Fairlie	*Calling Bulldog Drummond,* 1951, Walter Pidgeon
Calling Dr. Kildare	Max Brand	*Calling Dr. Kildare,* 1939, Lew Ayres
Calling Mr. Callaghan	Peter Cheyney	*The Amazing Mr. Callaghan,* 1953
The Campanile Murders	Whitman Chambers	*Murder on the Campus,* 1934
Campbell's Kingdom	Hammond Innes	*Campbell's Kingdom,* 1958
The Canary Murder Case	S. S. Van Dine	*The Canary Murder Case,* 1929, William Powell
The Canterville Ghost	Oscar Wilde	*The Canterville Ghost,* 1943, Charles Laughton
The Caper of the Golden Bulls	William P. McGivern	*The Caper of the Golden Bulls,* 1967
Carmilla	Sheridan Le Fanu	*Blood and Roses,* 1961, Mel Ferrer
The Case Against Mrs. Ames	Arthur Somers Roche	*The Case Against Mrs. Ames,* 1936
Case File: FBI	The Gordons	*Down Three Dark Streets,* 1954, Broderick Crawford
Case of the Caretaker's Cat	Erle Stanley Gardner	*Case of the Black Cat,* 1936
The Case of the Constant God	Rufus King	*Love Letters of a Star,* 1936
The Case of the Curious Bride	Erle Stanley Gardner	*The Case of the Curious Bride,* 1935
The Case of the Howling Dog	Erle Stanley Gardner	*The Case of the Howling Dog,* 1934
The Case of the Lucky Legs	Erle Stanley Gardner	*The Case of the Lucky Legs,* 1935
The Case of the Stuttering Bishop	Erle Stanley Gardner	*The Case of the Stuttering Bishop,* 1937
The Case of the Velvet Claws	Erle Stanley Gardner	*The Case of the Velvet Claws,* 1936
The Case of the Weird Sisters	Charlotte Armstrong	*Three Weird Sisters,* 1948
The Casino Murder Case	S. S. Van Dine	*The Casino Murder Case,* 1935, Paul Lukas
Casino Royale	Ian Fleming	*Casino Royale,* 1967
Castle Minerva	Victor Canning	*Masquerade,* 1965
The Catacombs	Jay Bennett	*Woman Who Wouldn't Die,* 1965, Gary Merrill
The Challenge	H. C. McNeile	*Bulldog Drummond in Africa,* 1938 *The Challenge,* 1948
Charlie Chan Carries On	Earl Biggers	*Charlie Chan Carries On,* 1931 *Charlie Chan's Murder Cruise,* 1940
The Chinese Orange Mystery	Ellery Queen	*The Mandarin Mystery,* 1936, Eddie Quillan
The Chinese Parrot	Earl Biggers	*The Chinese Parrot,* 1927 *Charlie Chan's Courage,* 1934
Chronicles of Cleek	Thomas W. Hanshew	*Chronicles of Cleek,* 1913–14
Cinema Murder	E. Phillips Oppenheim	*Cinema Murder,* 1919
The Cipher	Gordon Cotler	*Arabesque,* 1966, Gregory Peck
Circle of Danger	Philip MacDonald	*Circle of Danger,* 1951, Ray Milland
Circular Staircase	Mary Roberts Rinehart	*Circular Staircase,* 1915
Clean Break	Lionel White	*The Killing,* 1956, Sterling Hayden
"Cocaine"	Cornell Woolrich	*Fall Guy,* 1947, Robert Armstrong
Coffin for Dimitrios	Eric Ambler	*Mask for Dimitrios,* 1944, Peter Lorre

NAME OF BOOK	AUTHOR	NAME OF FILM AND PRINCIPAL STAR
The Commissioner	Richard Doughty	*Madigan,* 1968
Compulsion	Meyer Levin	*Compulsion,* 1959, Dean Stockwell
Confidential Agent	Graham Greene	*Confidential Agent,* 1945, Charles Boyer
The Conspirator	Humphrey Slater	*The Conspirator,* 1949, Robert Taylor
The Conspirators	Frederick Prokosch	*The Conspirators,* 1944, Hedy Lamarr
The Counterfeit Traitor	Alexander Klein	*Counterfeit Traitor,* 1960, William Holden
Covenant with Death	Stephen Becker	*A Covenant with Death,* 1967
The Crack in the Mirror	Marcel Haedrich	*Crack in the Mirror,* 1960, Juliette Greco
The Creaking Chair	Lawrence Meynell	*Shadow Man,* 1953, Caesar Romero
"Crime Without Passion"	Ben Hecht	*Crime Without Passion,* 1934
Criss-Cross	Don Tracy	*Criss-Cross,* 1948, Burt Lancaster
Cry in the Night	Whit Masterson	*Cry in the Night,* 1956
Cry Wolf	Marjorie Carleton	*Cry Wolf,* 1947, Errol Flynn
"Dancing Men"	A. Conan Doyle	*Sherlock Holmes and the Secret Weapon,* 1942, Basil Rathbone
A Dandy in Aspic	Derek Marlowe	*A Dandy in Aspic,* 1968
Danger Signal	Phyllis Bottome	*Danger Signal,* 1945, Faye Emerson
Danger Island	John W. Vandercook	*Danger Island,* 1939
Dark Hazard	William R. Burnett	*Dark Hazard,* 1934, Edward G. Robinson
Dark Passage	David Goodis	*Dark Passage,* 1947, Humphrey Bogart
Dark Waters	Frank and Marian Cockerell	*Dark Waters,* 1944, Merle Oberon
Day of the Arrow	Philip Loraine	*Eye of the Devil,* 1966, Deborah Kerr
The Day the Fish Came Out	Michael Cacoyannis	*The Day the Fish Came Out,* 1967
The Dead Don't Care	Jonathan Latimer	*The Last Warning,* 1938
Dead Men Tell No Tales	E. W. Hornung	*Dead Men Tell No Tales,* 1920
The Dead Take No Bows	Richard Burke	*Dressed to Kill,* 1941
"Dead Yesterday"	Mignon G. Eberhart	*The Great Hospital Mystery,* 1937
Deadlier Than the Male	James Gunn	*Born to Kill,* 1947, Claire Trevor
Deadline at Dawn	William Irish	*Deadline at Dawn,* 1946, Susan Hayward
The Deadly Game	Nicholas Bentley	*The Deadly Game,* 1954
Death at Broadcast House	Val Gielgud	*Death at Broadcast House,* 1935
Death Catches Up with Mr. Kluck	Xantippe	*Danger on the Air,* 1938
Death from the Sanskrit	Lawrence G. Blochman	*Quiet, Please, Murder,* 1942, George Sanders
Death Has Deep Roots	Michael Gilbert	*Guilty,* 1956
Death in the Deep South	Ward Greene	*They Won't Forget,* 1937, Lana Turner
Death in the Doll's House	Lawrence Bachmann and Hannah Lees	*Shadow on the Wall,* 1950
"Death Makes a Decree"	Philip Wylie	*Charlie Chan in Reno,* 1939
Death on the Diamond	Cortland Fitzsimmons	*Death on the Diamond,* 1934
"Death Watch"	Edgar Wallace	*Before Dawn,* 1933
Deeds of Dr. Deadcert	Joan Fleming	*Family Doctor,* 1957 *Prescription for Murder,* 1958
D'Entre les Morts	Pierre Boileau and Thomas Narcejec	*Vertigo,* 1958, Kim Novak
Department K	Hartley Howard	*Assignment K*

NAME OF BOOK	AUTHOR	NAME OF FILM AND PRINCIPAL STAR
The Desperate Hours	Joseph Hayes	*The Desperate Hours,* 1955, Humphrey Bogart
Desperate Moment	Martha Albrand	*Desperate Moment,* 1953, Dirk Bogarde
The Detective	Roderick Thorp	*The Detective,* 1968, Frank Sinatra
The Devil Rides Out	Dennis Wheatley	*The Devil Rides Out,* 1968
The Devil's Own	Peter Curtis	*The Witches,* 1966, Joan Fontaine
The Diamond Master	Jacques Futrelle	*The Diamond Queen,* 1921 (Serial)
Diamonds for Danger	David Walker	*A Man Could Get Killed,* 1965, James Garner
The Disappearance of Roger Tremayne	Bruce Graeme	*Missing Ten Days,* 1941
Dr. Jekyll and Mr. Hyde	Robert Louis Stevenson	*Dr. Jekyll and Mr. Hyde,* 1920, 1932, 1941
Dr. No	Ian Fleming	*Dr. No,* 1965, Sean Connery
Dog Show Murder	Frank Gruber	*Death of a Champion,* 1939, Donald O'Connor
Don Among the Dead Men	Colwym E. Vulliamy	*They All Died Laughing,* 1964, Leo McKern
Donovan's Brain	Curt Siodmak	*Donovan's Brain,* 1953, Lew Ayres
Double Indemnity	James Cain	*Double Indemnity,* 1944, Fred MacMurray
Double Jeopardy	Joe Pagano	*Murder Without Tears,* 1953, Craig Stevens
The Double Take	Roy Huggins	*I Love Trouble,* 1948, Franchot Tone
Dracula	Bram Stoker	*Dracula,* 1931, Bela Lugosi *Dracula's Daughter,* 1936, Gloria Holden *Horrors of Dracula,* 1957
The Dragon Murder Case	S. S. Van Dine	*The Dragon Murder Case,* 1934, Warren William
The Dragon's Teeth	Ellery Queen	*Close Call for Ellery Queen,* 1942, William Gargan
Dreadful Summit	Stanley Ellin	*Big Night,* 1952, John Barrymore, Jr.
Dutch Shoe Mystery	Ellery Queen	*Ellery Queen and the Murder Ring,* 1941, Ralph Bellamy
The Eastern Dinner	Donald Downes	*The Pigeon That Took Rome,* 1962, Charlton Heston
The Eliminator	Andrew York	*Danger Route,* 1968
The Emperor's Candlesticks	Baroness Orczy	*The Emperor's Candlesticks,* 1937, William Powell
Emperor's Snuffbox	John Dickson Carr	*That Woman Opposite,* 1957 *City After Midnight,* 1959
"The Empty House"	A. Conan Doyle	*Sherlock Holmes' Fatal Hour,* 1931 (Also based on "The Final Problem")
"The Enemy"	Charlotte Armstrong	*Talk About a Stranger,* 1952 (Original title: *The Enemy*)
Enter Sir John	Clemence Dane and Helen Simpson	*Murder,* 1930
Epitaph for a Spy	Eric Ambler	*Hotel Reserve,* 1944, James Mason
Escape	Ethel Vance	*Escape,* 1940, Norma Shearer
The Executioners	John D. MacDonald	*Cape Fear,* 1961, Gregory Peck
Experiment Perilous	Margaret Carpenter	*Experiment Perilous,* 1944, Hedy Lamarr
Face the Music	Ernest Borneman	*The Black Glove,* 1954, Alex Nicol
"Face Work"	Cornell Woolrich	*Convicted,* 1938

NAME OF BOOK	AUTHOR	NAME OF FILM AND PRINCIPAL STAR
"The Fall of the House of Usher"	Edgar Allan Poe	*The Fall of the House of Usher,* 1942, 1952
		House of Usher, 1960, Vincent Price
Fallen Angel	Howard Fast	*Jigsaw,* 1968
Fallen Angel	Marty Holland	*Fallen Angel,* 1946, Alice Faye
The Fallen Idol	Graham Greene	*The Fallen Idol,* 1948, Ralph Richardson
The Fallen Sparrow	Dorothy B. Hughes	*Fallen Sparrow,* 1943, John Garfield
Family Skeleton	Doris Miles Disney	*Stella,* 1950
Farewell, My Lovely	Raymond Chandler	*Falcon Takes Over,* 1942
		Murder, My Sweet, 1944, Dick Powell
Fast Company	Marco Page	*Fast Company,* 1938, Melvin Douglas (TV title: *Rare Book Murder*)
Father Brown, Detective	G. K. Chesterton	*The Detective,* 1955, Alec Guiness
Fear No More	Leslie Edgley	*Fear No More,* 1961
The Female of the Species	H. C. McNeile	*Bulldog Drummond Comes Back,* 1937
File No. 113	Emile Gaboriau	*File No. 113,* 1915
The Final Count	H. C. McNeile	*Arrest Bulldog Drummond,* 1938
"The Final Problem"	A. Conan Doyle	*Sherlock Holmes' Fatal Hour,* 1931 (Also based on "The Empty House")
The First Train to Babylon	Max Ehrlich	*The Naked Edge,* 1961, Gary Cooper
Five Against the House	Jack Finney	*Five Against the House,* 1955, Kim Novak
Five Fragments	George Dyer	*Spy Ship,* 1942 (Original title: *Caught in the Fog*)
"The Five Orange Pips"	A. Conan Doyle	*House of Fear,* 1945
Five Steps to Danger	Donald Hamilton	*Five Steps to Danger,* 1957, Sterling Hayden
The Floating Dutchman	Nicholas Bentley	*The Floating Dutchman,* 1953
The Florentine Dagger	Ben Hecht	*The Florentine Dagger,* 1935
The Fool Killer	Helen Eustis	*The Fool Killer,* 1965, Tony Perkins
For Her to See	Joseph Shearing	*So Evil, My Love,* 1948, Ray Milland
Fortune Is a Woman	Winston Graham	*She Played with Fire,* 1958, Arlene Dahl
4:50 from Paddington	Agatha Christie	*Murder, She Said,* 1961, Margaret Rutherford
Frankenstein	Mary Shelley	*Frankenstein,* 1932, Boris Karloff
		Bride of Frankenstein, 1935, Elsa Lanchester
The French Key	Frank Gruber	*The French Key,* 1946, Albert Dekker
The Frightened Child	Dana Lyon	*The House on Telegraph Hill,* 1951, Richard Basehart
The Frightened Stiff	Kelley Roos	*A Night to Remember,* 1942
From Russia with Love	Ian Fleming	*From Russia with Love,* 1963, Sean Connery
From This Dark Stairway	Mignon G. Eberhart	*The Murder of Dr. Harrigan,* 1936
Fruit of the Poppy	Robert Wilder	*Sol Madrid,* 1968
Fugitive Lady	Doris Miles Disney	*Fugitive Lady,* 1951
The Full Treatment	Ronald Scott Thorn	*Stop Me Before I Kill,* 1961, Claude Dauphin
Funeral in Berlin	Len Deighton	*Funeral in Berlin,* 1966, Michael Caine
The Garden Murder Case	S. S. Van Dine	*The Garden Murder Case,* 1936
"The Gay Falcon"	Michael Arlen	*A Date with the Falcon,* 1941
The Gentleman from Paris	John Dickson Carr	*The Man with a Cloak,* 1951, Joseph Cotten
Getaway	Leslie Charteris	*The Saint's Vacation,* 1941

NAME OF BOOK	AUTHOR	NAME OF FILM AND PRINCIPAL STAR
"The Ghost of John Holling"	Edgar Wallace	*Mystery Liner,* 1934
Gideon's Day	J. J. Marric	*Gideon of Scotland Yard,* 1959, Jack Hawkins
The Girl Hunters	Mickey Spillane	*The Girl Hunters,* 1963
The Girl in the Cage	Ben Benson	*Running Wild,* 1955, William Campbell
The Glass Key	Dashiell Hammett	*The Glass Key,* Edward Arnold, 1935; Alan Ladd, 1942
The Gold Bag	Carolyn Wells	*Mystery of West Sedgewick,* 1913
"The Gold Bug"	Edgar Allan Poe	*Manfish,* 1956, John Bromfield. Also based on "The Tell-Tale Heart" (English title: *Calypso*)
The Golden Salamander	Victor Canning	*The Golden Salamander,* 1950, Trevor Howard
Goldfinger	Ian Fleming	*Goldfinger,* 1964, Sean Connery
The Gracie Allen Murder Case	S. S. Van Dine	*The Gracie Allen Murder Case,* 1939, Warren William
Grand Central Murder	Sue MacVeigh	*Grand Central Murder,* 1942
The Great Impersonation	E. Phillips Oppenheim	*The Great Impersonation,* 1921; 1942, Edmund Lowe
The Greek Coffin Mystery	Ellery Queen	*Enemy Agents Meet Ellery Queen,* 1942, William Gargan
"The Greek Poropulos"	Edgar Wallace	*Born to Gamble,* 1935
Green for Danger	Christianna Brand	*Green for Danger,* 1947, Sally Gray
The Green Man	Edgar Wallace	*The Green Man,* 1957, Alistair Sim
The G-String Murders	Gypsy Rose Lee	*Lady of Burlesque,* 1943, Barbara Stanwyck
Gun for Sale	Graham Greene	*Short Cut to Hell,* 1957
Hammer the Toff	John Creasey	*Hammer the Toff,* 1952
Hangover Square	Patrick Hamilton	*Hangover Square,* 1945, Laird Creger
Hasty Wedding	Mignon G. Eberhart	*Three's a Crowd,* 1945
Having Wonderful Crime	Craig Rice	*Having Wonderful Crime,* 1945, Pat O'Brien
He Was Found in the Road	Anthony Armstrong	*The Man in the Road,* 1957
Headed for a Hearse	Jonathan Latimer	*The Westland Case,* 1937, Preston Foster
Hearses Don't Hurry	Stephen Ransome	*Who Is Hope Schuyler,* 1942
The Heat of the Day	Thomas Sterling	*The Honey Pot,* 1967
Hell on Frisco Bay	William P. McGivern	*Hell on Frisco Bay,* 1956, Alan Ladd
Hide and Seek	Marcus Magill	*It's a Bet*
High Sierra	William R. Burnett	*High Sierra,* 1941, Ida Lupino *I Died a Thousand Times,* 1955, Shelley Winters
The High Window	Raymond Chandler	*Time to Kill,* 1942, Lloyd Nolan *The Brasher Doubloon,* 1947, George Montgomery
Highly Dangerous	Eric Ambler	*Highly Dangerous,* 1951, Dane Clark
His First Offense (Play)	J. Storer Clauston	*Bizarre, Bizarre,* 1939
His Last Bow	A. Conan Doyle	*Sherlock Holmes and the Voice of Terror,* 1942, Basil Rathbone
Home Sweet Homicide	Craig Rice	*Home Sweet Homicide,* 1946, Randolph Scott
Hound of the Baskervilles	A. Conan Doyle	*The Hound of the Baskervilles,* 1922, Eille Norwood as Sherlock Holmes; 1932, Robert Rendel as Sherlock

NAME OF BOOK	AUTHOR	NAME OF FILM AND PRINCIPAL STAR
		Holmes; 1939, Basil Rathbone as Sherlock Holmes; 1959, Peter Cushing
The House of Doctor Edwards	Francis Beeding	*Spellbound,* 1945, Ingrid Bergman
The House of Secrets	Sidney Horler	*The House of Secrets,* 1936
The House of the Arrow	Alfred E. W. Mason	*The House of the Arrow,* 1954, Oscar Homolka
The House Without a Key	Earl Biggers	*Charlie Chan's Greatest Case,* 1933
Hue and Cry	Marjorie Carleton	*Hue and Cry,* 1948, Alistair Sim (Produced from a screen play)
Huntingtower	John Buchan	*Huntingtower,* 1928
I Married a Dead Man	William Irish	*No Man of Her Own,* 1950
I, The Jury	Mickey Spillane	*I, The Jury,* 1953, Biff Elliot
I Wake Up Screaming	Steven G. Fisher	*Hot Spot,* 1941, Betty Grable *Vicki,* 1953, Jeanne Crain
I Wouldn't Be in Your Shoes	Cornell Woolrich	*I Wouldn't Be in Your Shoes,* 1948, Don Castle
"If I Should Die"	Hugh Pentecost	*Appointment with a Shadow,* 1958
If the Shroud Fits	Kelley Roos	*Dangerous Blondes,* 1943, Evelyn Keyes
I'll Get You for This	James Hadley Chase	*Lucky Nick Cain,* 1951, George Raft
In the Heat of the Night	John Ball	*In the Heat of the Night,* 1967
The Interruption	William W. Jacobs	*Footsteps in the Fog,* 1955, Jean Simmons
Invitation to a Murder (Play)	Rufus King	*The Hidden Hand,* 1942
The Ipcress File	Len Deighton	*The Ipcress File,* 1965, Michael Caine
Jeane of the Marshes	E. Phillips Oppenheim	*Behind Masks,* 1932
Jim Hanvey, Detective	Octavus Roy Cohen	*Jim Hanvey, Detective,* 1937
Journey into Fear	Eric Ambler	*Journey into Fear,* 1942, Orson Welles
Judge Priest	Irvin S. Cobb	*Judge Priest,* 1934, Will Rogers
The Juggernaut	Alice Campbell	*The Juggernaut,* 1937
The Jury	Gerald Bullett	*The Last Man to Hang,* 1956
The Kennel Murder Case	S. S. Van Dine	*The Kennel Murder Case,* 1933, William Powell *Calling Philo Vance,* 1940, James Stephenson
Key Witness	Frank Kane	*Key Witness,* 1960, Jeffrey Hunter
Killing a Mouse on Sunday	Emeric Pressburger	*Behold a Pale Horse,* 1964, Gregory Peck
A Kiss Before Dying	Ira Levin	*A Kiss Before Dying,* 1956
Kiss Me Deadly	Mickey Spillane	*Kiss Me Deadly,* 1955, Ralph Meeker
Kiss of Death	Eleazar Lipsky	*Kiss of Death,* 1947, Richard Widmark
Kiss the Blood Off My Hands	Gerald Butler	*Kiss the Blood Off My Hands,* 1948, Burt Lancaster (English title: *Blood on My Hands*)
Lady in the Lake	Raymond Chandler	*Lady in the Lake,* 1947, Robert Montgomery
The Lady in the Morgue	Jonathan Latimer	*Lady in the Morgue,* 1938, Preston Foster
The Last Express	Baynard H. Kendrick	*Last Express,* 1938
The Last Trap	Sinclair Gluck	*The Dark Hour,* 1936
Laura	Vera Caspary	*Laura,* 1944, Gene Tierney
The League of Gentlemen	John Boland	*The League of Gentlemen,* 1961

NAME OF BOOK	AUTHOR	NAME OF FILM AND PRINCIPAL STAR
Legacy of a Spy	Henry S. Maxfield	*The Double Man,* 1967
The Light of Day	Eric Ambler	*The Man in the Middle,* 1963
The Lion and the Lamb	E. Phillips Oppenheim	*The Lion and the Lamb,* 1931
Lions at the Kill	Simon Kent	*Seven Thieves,* 1960, Edward G. Robinson
The Liquidator	John Gardner	*The Liquidator,* 1966, Rod Taylor
The List of Adrian Messenger	Philip MacDonald	*The List of Adrian Messenger,* 1963, Dana Wynter
Little Caesar	William R. Burnett	*Little Caesar,* 1930, Edward G. Robinson
The Lock and the Key	Frank Gruber	*Man in the Vault,* 1957
The Lodger	Mrs. Belloc Lowndes	*The Lodger,* 1932
		The Lodger, 1944, George Sanders
		The Man in the Attic, 1953, Jack Palance
The Lone Wolf	Louis Joseph Vance	*The Lone Wolf Meets a Lady,* 1940
"The Lone Wolf in Paris"	Louis Joseph Vance	*The Lone Wolf in Paris,* 1938
The Lone Wolf Returns	Louis Joseph Vance	*The Lone Wolf Returns,* 1936
The Lone Wolf Spy Hunt	Louis Joseph Vance	*The Lone Wolf Spy Hunt,* 1939
The Lonely Skier	Hammond Innes	*Snowbound,* 1947, Dennis Price
The Long Wait	Mickey Spillane	*The Long Wait,* 1954, Anthony Quinn
Love in Amsterdam	Nicholas Freeling	*Amsterdam Affair,* 1968
Macbeth	William Shakespeare	*Joe Macbeth,* 1956, Paul Douglas
Mad with Much Heart	Gerald Butler	*On Dangerous Ground,* 1951, Robert Ryan
The Maltese Falcon	Dashiell Hammett	*The Maltese Falcon,* 1931, Ricardo Cortez; 1941, Humphrey Bogart
		Satan Met a Lady, 1936, Warren William
The Man Inside	M. E. Chaber	*The Man Inside,* 1958
The Man Within	Graham Greene	*The Smugglers,* 1948, Michael Redgrave
A Man Without Friends	Margaret Echard	*Lightning Strikes Twice,* 1951
The Manchurian Candidate	Richard Condon	*The Manchurian Candidate,* 1962, Frank Sinatra
Marnie	Winston Graham	*Marnie,* 1965, Tippi Hedren
The Mask of Fu Manchu	Sax Rohmer	*Mask of Fu Manchu,* 1933, Boris Karloff
The Master Mummer	E. Phillips Oppenheim	*The Master Mummer,* 1915
The Master of Ballantrae	Robert Louis Stevenson	*Master of Ballantrae,* 1933, Errol Flynn
Meet Mr. Callaghan	Peter Cheyney	*Meet Mr. Callaghan,* 1954, Derrick De Marney
Meet the Tiger	Leslie Charteris	*The Saint Meets the Tiger,* 1943
The Megstone Plot	Andrew Garve	*A Touch of Larceny,* 1960
Miami Mayhem	Marvin H. Albert	*Tony Rome,* Frank Sinatra
Michael Shayne, Private Detective	Brett Halliday	*Michael Shayne, Private Detective* 1940, Lloyd Nolan
The Midwich Cuckoos	John Wyndham	*Village of the Damned,* 1960, George Sanders
Mildred Pierce	James M. Cain	*Mildred Pierce,* 1945, Joan Crawford
"The Million Pound Day"	Leslie Charteris	*Saint in London,* 1939
The Mind of Mr. J. G. Reeder	Edgar Wallace	*The Mysterious Mr. Reeder,* 1940
The Ministry of Fear	Graham Greene	*The Ministry of Fear,* 1944, Ray Milland
Mirage	Howard Fast	*Mirage,* 1965, Gregory Peck

NAME OF BOOK	AUTHOR	NAME OF FILM AND PRINCIPAL STAR
Mischief	Charlotte Armstrong	*Don't Bother to Knock,* 1952, Marilyn Monroe
Mr. Arkadin	Orson Welles	*Confidential Report,* 1955 *Mr. Arkadin,* 1962
Mister Buddwing	Evan Hunter	*Mr. Buddwing,* 1966, James Garner
Modesty Blaise	Peter O'Donnell	*Modesty Blaise,* 1966, Monica Vitti
The Moonspinners	Mary Stewart	*The Moonspinners,* 1965, Hayley Mills
Moss Rose	Joseph Shearing	*Moss Rose,* 1947, Peggy Cummins
"The Most Dangerous Game"	Richard Connell	*The Most Dangerous Game,* 1932, Joel McCrae *A Game of Death,* 1946, John Loder *Run for the Sun,* 1956, Richard Widmark
The Moving Target	Ross MacDonald	*Harper,* 1966, Paul Newman
Mrs. McGinty's Dead	Agatha Christie	*Murder Most Foul,* Margaret Rutherford
Murder at Glen Athol	Norman Lippincott	*Murder at Glen Athol,* 1935
Murder by an Aristocrat	Mignon G. Eberhart	*Murder by an Aristocrat,* 1936
Murder by Proxy	Helen Nielsen	*Blackout,* 1953
Murder by the Clock	Rufus King	*Murder by the Clock,* 1931
Murder for the Millions	Robert Chapman	*Murder Reported,* 1956
Murder in the Surgery	James G. Edwards	*Mystery of the White Room,* 1939
Murder in Trinidad	John W. Vandercook	*Mr. Moto in Danger Island,* 1939 *Caribbean Mystery,* 1945
Murder Lady; see *Once Too Often*		
Murder Mistaken	Leonard Gribble and Janet Green	*Cast a Dark Shadow,* 1958
Murder of Steven Kester	Harriette Ashbrook	*Green Eyes,* 1934
Murder on the Blackboard	Stuart Palmer	*Murder on the Blackboard,* 1934
Murder with Pictures	George Harmon Coxe	*Murder with Pictures,* 1936
Murderer's Row	Donald Hamilton	*Murderer's Row,* 1966, Dean Martin
"Murders in the Rue Morgue"	Edgar Allan Poe	*Murders in the Rue Morgue,* 1932, Bela Lugosi *Phantom of the Rue Morgue,* 1954, Karl Malden
Museum Piece No. 13	Rufus King	*The Secret Beyond the Door,* 1948
"Musgrave Ritual"	A Conan Doyle	*Sherlock Holmes Faces Death,* 1943
"My Brother Down There" (Later published as: *The Running Target*)	Steven Frazee	*The Running Target,* 1956
My Cousin Rachel	Daphne Du Maurier	*My Cousin Rachel,* 1952, Olivia de Haviland
My Gun Is Quick	Mickey Spillane	*My Gun Is Quick,* 1957, Robert Bray
Mystery of a Hansom Cab	Fergus Hume	*Mystery of a Hansom Cab,* 1915
Mystery of Edwin Drood	Charles Dickens	*Mystery of Edwin Drood,* 1935, Claude Rains
Mystery of Hunting's End	Mignon G. Eberhart	*Mystery House,* 1938
"Mystery of Marie Roget"	Edgar Allan Poe	*Mystery of Marie Roget,* 1942, Maria Montez
Mystery of Number 47	J. Storer Clouston	*Mystery of Number 47,* 1917
Mystery of Orcival	Emile Gaboriau	*Mystery of Orcival,* 1916
Mystery of the Boule Cabinet	Burton E. Stevenson	*In the Next Room,* 1930
Mystery of the Dead Police	Philip MacDonald	*Mystery of Mr. X,* 1934
Mystery of the Yellow Room	Gaston Leroux	*Mystery of the Yellow Room,* 1913, 1919

NAME OF BOOK	AUTHOR	NAME OF FILM AND PRINCIPAL STAR
The Naked Runner	Francis Clifford	*The Naked Runner,* 1967, Frank Sinatra
The Nanny	Evelyn Piper	*The Nanny,* 1965, Bette Davis
"Night Call"	Irwin and David Shaw	*Take One False Step,* 1949, William Powell
The Night Has a Thousand Eyes	George Hopley	*The Night Has a Thousand Eyes,* 1948
Night Must Fall	William Drummond	*Night Must Fall* (from the play by Emlyn Williams), Robert Montgomery, 1936; Albert Finney, 1964
Night of the Generals	Hans Hellmut Kirst	*Night of the Generals,* 1967, Peter O'Toole
The Night of the Hunter	Davis Grubb	*Night of the Hunter,* 1955, Robert Mitchum
"The Night Runner"	Owen Cameron	*The Night Runner,* 1957, Ray Danton
Night Without Sleep	Elick Moll	*Night Without Sleep,* 1952, Gary Merrill
Night Without Stars	Winston Graham	*Night Without Stars,* 1953, David Farrar
Nightmare	Anne Blaisdell	*Die, Die, My Darling,* 1965
Nightmare	Cornell Woolrich	*Fear in the Night,* 1947, Paul Kelly *Nightmare,* 1956, Edward G. Robinson
No Coffin for a Corpse	Clayton Rawson	*Man Who Wouldn't Die*
No Hands on the Clock	Geoffrey Homes	*No Hands on the Clock,* 1941
No Orchids for Miss Blandish	James Hadley Chase	*No Orchids for Miss Blandish,* 1948, Jack La Rue
No Way to Treat a Lady	William Goldman	*No Way to Treat a Lady,* 1967
The Norths Meet Murder	The Lockridges	*Mr. and Mrs. North,* 1941, Gracie Allen
The Norwich Victims	Francis Beeding	*Dead Men Tell No Tales,* 1939
Notorious Miss Lisle	Gertrude M. Reynolds	*Notorious Miss Lisle,* 1921
"Notorious Sophie Lang"	Frederick Irving Anderson	*Notorious Sophie Lang,* 1934
"Numbers of Death"	E. Phillips Oppenheim	*Monte Carlo Nights,* 1934
Odd Man Out	Eric Ambler	*Odd Man Out,* 1947, James Mason
Odds Against Tomorrow	William P. McGivern	*Odds Against Tomorrow,* 1959, Robert Ryan
Odor of Violets	Baynard H. Kendrick	*Eyes in the Night,* 1942, Edward Arnold
The Old Dark House	J. B. Priestley	*The Old Dark House,* 1932, Boris Karloff
The Oldest Confession	Richard Condon	*Once a Thief,* 1961, Rita Hayworth
Once Off Guard	J. H. Wallis	*Woman in the Window,* 1944, Joan Bennett
Once Too Often	Whitman Chambers	*Blonde Ice,* 1948, Leslie Brooks
The Other One	Catherine Turney	*Back from the Dead,* 1957
Our Mother's House	Julian Gloag	*Our Mother's House,* 1967
Out of the Dark	Ursula Curtiss	*I Saw What You Did,* 1965, Joan Crawford
Outrun the Constable	Selwyn Jepson	*Stage Fright,* 1950, Marlene Dietrich
The Outsiders	A. E. Martin	*The Glass Tomb,* 1955, John Ireland
Panther's Moon	Victor Canning	*Spy Hunt,* 1950
Passport to Oblivion	James Leasor	*Where the Spies Are,* 1965, David Niven

NAME OF BOOK	AUTHOR	NAME OF FILM AND PRINCIPAL STAR
The Patient in Room 18	Mignon G. Eberhart	*The Patient in Room 18,* 1938, Ralph Bellamy
Penelope	E. V. Cunningham	*Penelope,* 1966, Natalie Wood
The Penguin Pool Murder	Stuart Palmer	*The Penguin Pool Murder,* 1932, Edna Mae Oliver
The Penthouse Mystery	Ellery Queen	*Ellery Queen's Penthouse Mystery,* 1941
People Against O'Hara	Eleazar Lipsky	*People Against O'Hara,* 1951, Spencer Tracy
The Perfect Case	Anthony Abbot	*Boomerang,* 1947, Dana Andrews
The Perfect Crime	Ellery Queen	*Ellery Queen and the Perfect Crime,* 1941
The Phantom Lady	Cornell Woolrich	*The Phantom Lady,* 1944, Franchot Tone
Phantom of the Opera	Gaston Leroux	*Phantom of the Opera,* 1925, Lon Chaney; 1930, Claude Rains; 1962
"Philomel Cottage"	Agatha Christie	*Love from a Stranger,* 1947, Sylvia Sydney, John Hodiak
The Phoenix	Lawrence P. Bachmann	*Ten Seconds to Hell,* 1959
The Postman Always Rings Twice	James Cain	*The Postman Always Rings Twice,* 1946, Lana Turner
"The Premature Burial"	Edgar Allan Poe	*The Crime of Dr. Crespi,* 1934
The President's Mystery story	Franklin D. Roosevelt	*The President's Mystery,* 1936
Psycho	Robert Bloch	*Psycho,* 1960, Anthony Perkins
"The Purple Hieroglyph"	Murray Leinster	*Murder Will Out,* 1930
Puzzle of the Briar Pipe	Stuart Palmer	*Murder on a Bridle Path,* 1936
Puzzle of the Pepper Tree	Stuart Palmer	*Murder on a Honeymoon,* 1935
The Quarry	John Moroso	*The City of Silent Men,* 1921
Queen in Danger	Simon Rattray	*Man in Hiding,* 1953, Paul Henreid (English title: *Man Trap*)
Quiller Memorandum	Adam Hall	*Quiller Memorandum,* 1966, Alec Guiness
"Rear Window"	William Irish	*Rear Window,* 1950, James Stewart
Rebecca	Daphne Du Maurier	*Rebecca,* 1940, Joan Fontaine
Red Harvest	Dashiell Hammett	*Roadhouse Nights,* 1930
Return from the Ashes	Hubert Monteilhet	*Return from the Ashes,* 1965, Ingrid Thulin
Return of Bulldog Drummond	H. C. McNeile	*Bulldog Drummond's Revenge,* 1937
The Return of Sherlock Holmes	A. Conan Doyle	*The Return of Sherlock Holmes*
"Return of Sophie Lang"	Frederick Irving Anderson	*The Return of Sophie Lang,* 1936
Rich Is the Treasure	Maurice Procter	*The Diamond Wizard,* 1953, Dennis O'Keefe
Ride the Pink Horse	Dorothy B. Hughes	*Ride the Pink Horse,* 1947, Robert Montgomery
"Road to Carmichael's"	Richard Wormser	*The Big Steal,* 1949, Robert Mitchum
"Rodolphe et la Revolver"	Noel Calef	*Tiger Bay,* 1960, Hayley Mills
Rogue Cop	William P. McGivern	*Rogue Cop,* 1954, Robert Taylor
Rogue Male	Geoffrey Household	*Man Hunt,* 1941, Walter Pidgeon
A Rope of Sand	Francis Bonnamy	*Rope of Sand,* 1949, Peter Lorre
Rosemary's Baby	Ira Levin	*Rosemary's Baby,* 1968, Mia Farrow
The Running Target; see "My Brother Down There"		

NAME OF BOOK	AUTHOR	NAME OF FILM AND PRINCIPAL STAR
The Saint in New York	Leslie Charteris	*Saint in New York,* 1938, Louis Hayward
The Scapegoat	Daphne Du Maurier	*The Scapegoat,* 1958, Alec Guiness
The Scarab Murder Case	S. S. Van Dine	*Scarab Murder Case,* 1930
Scent of Mystery	Kelley Roos	*Scent of Mystery,* 1959, Peter Lorre
Scorpio Letters	Victor Canning	*Scorpio Letters,* Alex Cord
Séance on a Wet Afternoon	Mark McShane	*Séance on a Wet Afternoon,* 1964, Kim Stanley
Secret Agent	Joseph Conrad	*Sabotage,* 1937
Seven-Eleven-Officer Needs Help	Whit Masterson	*The Warning Shot,* 1966, David Janssen
Seven Keys to Baldpate	Earl Derr Biggers	*Seven Keys to Baldpate,* 1917, 1925, 1930, 1935, 1947
Seven Thunders	Rupert Croft-Cooke	*Seven Thunders,* 1957 *The Beasts of Marseilles,* 1959, Stephen Boyd
Seventy Thousand Witnesses	Cortland Fitzsimmons	*Seventy Thousand Witnesses,* 1932
Shadows over Elveron	Michael Kingsley	*Shadows over Elveron,* 1967
She Died Young	Alan Kennington	*Mystery of the Downs,* 1956
Shield for Murder	William P. McGivern	*Shield for Murder,* 1954, Edmund O'Brien
Sign of the Four	A. Conan Doyle	*Sign of the Four,* 1932, Arthur Wontner
Sign of the Ram	Margaret Ferguson	*Sign of the Ram,* 1948, Susan Peters
The Silencers	Donald Hamilton	*The Silencers,* 1966, Dean Martin
"Silver Mask"	Hugh Walpole	*Kind Lady,* 1935, Aline MacMahon; 1951, Ethel Barrymore
Simon Lash, Private Detective	Frank Gruber	*Accomplice,* 1946
Sing a Song of Homicide	James R. Langham	*A Night in New Orleans,* 1942, Preston Foster
Sinister Errand	Peter Cheyney	*Diplomatic Courier,* 1952, Tyrone Power
"Sire de Maletroit's Door"	Robert Louis Stevenson	*The Strange Door,* 1951, Boris Karloff
"Six Napoleans"	A. Conan Doyle	*Pearl of Death,* 1944
Sleepers East	Frederick Nebel	*Sleepers West,* 1941, Lloyd Nolan
The Soft Touch	John D. MacDonald	*Deadlock,* 1961, Jeffrey Hunter
Some Must Watch	Ethel Lina White	*The Spiral Staircase,* 1946, Dorothy McGuire
"Sophie Lang Goes West"	Frederick Irving Anderson	*Sophie Lang Goes West,* 1937
Sorry, Wrong Number	Lucille Fletcher	*Sorry, Wrong Number,* 1948, Barbara Stanwyck
The Spanish Cape Mystery	Ellery Queen	*The Spanish Cape Mystery,* 1935, Donald Cook
Special Investigator	Erle Stanley Gardner	*Special Investigator,* 1937
Spin the Glass Web	Max Simon Ehrlich	*The Glass Web,* 1953, Edward G. Robinson
The Spy	Paul Thomas	*The Defector,* 1966, Montgomery Clift
The Spy in Black	Joseph Storer Clouston	*The Spy in Black,* 1938
Spy in the Room	Dennison Clift	*Secrets of Scotland Yard*
Spy Who Came in from the Cold	John Le Carré	*Spy Who Came in from the Cold,* 1961, Richard Burton
The Squeaker	Edgar Wallace	*Murder on Diamond Row,* 1937, Edmund Lowe
Stamboul Train	Graham Greene	*Orient Express,* 1934

NAME OF BOOK	AUTHOR	NAME OF FILM AND PRINCIPAL STAR
Story of Ivy	Mrs. Belloc Lowndes	*Ivy,* 1947, Joan Fontaine
Strange Boarders of Palace Crescent	E. Phillips Oppenheim	*Strange Boarders,* 1938
Strangers on a Train	Patricia Highsmith	*Strangers on a Train,* 1951, Farley Granger
The Straw Man	Doris Miles Disney	*The Straw Man,* 1953
A Study in Terror	Ellery Queen	*A Study in Terror,* 1966, John Neville
Sudden Fear	Edna Sherry	*Sudden Fear,* 1954, Joan Crawford
"The Suicide Club"	Robert Louis Stevenson	*The Living Dead,* 1940
Sylvia	E. V. Cunningham	*Sylvia,* 1965, Carroll Baker
"The System of Doctor Tarr and Professor Feather"	Edgar Allan Poe	*The Living Dead,* 1940
Take My Life	Winston Graham	*Take My Life,* 1947, Hugh Williams
The Talented Mr. Ripley	Patricia Highsmith	*Purple Noon,* 1961
Taste for Honey	H. R. Heard	*The Deadly Bees,* 1967, Suzannah Leigh
"The Tell-Tale Heart"	Edgar Allan Poe	*Bucket of Blood,* 1934
		The Tell-Tale Heart, 1934; 1941 (short), Joseph Schildkraut; 1962
		The Manfish, 1956, John Bromfield. Also based on "The Goldbug." (English title: *Calypso*)
Temple Tower	H. C. McNeile	*Bulldog Drummond's Secret Police,* 1939
10:30 from Marseille	Sebastien Japrisot	*The Sleeping Car Murder,* 1966, Simone Signoret
Term of Trial	James Barlow	*Term of Trial,* 1962, Lawrence Olivier
Thank You, Mr. Moto	John P. Marquand	*Thank You, Mr. Moto,* 1937
That Darn Cat	The Gordons	*That Darn Cat,* 1966, Suzanne Pleschette
Thieves Like Us	Edward Anderson	*Your Red Wagon.* (English title: *The Twisted Road*)
The Thin Man	Dashiell Hammett	*Thin Man,* 1934, William Powell
		They Live by Night, 1948
Think Fast Mr. Moto	John P. Marquand	*Think Fast Mr. Moto,* 1937
The Third Man	Graham Greene	*The Third Man,* 1949, Orson Welles
The Third Round	H. C. McNeile	*Bulldog Drummond's Peril,* 1938
The Thirty-Nine Steps	John Buchan	*The Thirty-Nine Steps,* 1935, Robert Donat; 1960, Kenneth More
Through the Wall	Cleveland Moffett	*Through the Wall,* 1916
Thunderball	Ian Fleming	*Thunderball,* 1966, Sean Connery
The Tiger Among Us	Leigh Brackett	*13 West Street,* 1962, Alan Ladd
To Catch a Thief	David Dodge	*To Catch a Thief,* 1954, Cary Grant
"Tom Sawyer, Detective"	Samuel L. Clemens	*Tom Sawyer, Detective,* 1938
Trent's Last Case	E. C. Bentley	*Trent's Last Case,* 1952
Trial	Don Mankiewicz	*Trial,* 1955, Glenn Ford
Trial by Terror	Paul Gallico	*Assignment Paris,* 1952, Dana Andrews
Turn of the Screw	Henry James	*The Innocents,* 1962, Deborah Kerr
"Twelve Coins of Confucius"	Harry Stephen Keeler	*Mysterious Mr. Wong,* 1935
Twenty Plus Two	Frank Gruber	*Twenty Plus Two,* 1962, David Janssen
"Two Men in a Furnished Room"	Cornell Woolrich	*The Guilty,* 1947

NAME OF BOOK	AUTHOR	NAME OF FILM AND PRINCIPAL STAR
Two O'Clock Courage	Gelett Burgess	*Two in the Dark,* 1936 *Two O'Clock Courage,* 1945
Uncle Silas	Sheridan Le Fanu	*The Inheritance,* 1949, Jean Simmons
Uncommon Danger; see *Background to Danger*		
Uneasy Terms	Peter Cheyney	*Uneasy Terms,* 1948, Michael Rennie
The Uninvited	Dorothy Macardle	*The Uninvited,* 1944, Ray Milland
The Unseen	Ethel Lina White	*The Unseen,* 1945, Joel McCrea
The Unsuspected	Charlotte Armstrong	*The Unsuspected,* 1947, Claude Rains
The Valley of Fear	A. Conan Doyle	*Triumph of Sherlock Holmes*
Vanity Row	William R. Burnett	*Accused of Murder,* 1957, Vera Ralston
Velvet Fleece	Lois C. Eby and John C. Fleming	*Larceny,* 1948, John Payne
Venetian Affair	Helen MacInnes	*Venetian Affair,* 1966, Elke Sommer
Venetian Bird	Victor Canning	*The Assassin,* 1952, Richard Todd
"Victoria Docks at 8"	Rufus King and Charles Beahan	*White Tie and Tails,* 1946, Dan Duryea
Wallingford and Blackie Daw	George Randolph Chester	*Adventures of Wallingford,* 1931
The Walls Came Tumbling Down	Jo Eisinger	*Walls Came Tumbling Down,* 1946, Lee Bowman
Wanton Murder	Peter Godfrey	*The Girl in the Black Stockings,* 1957
Warrant for X	Philip MacDonald	*25 Paces to Baker Street,* 1938
The Way Ahead	Eric Ambler	*The Way Ahead,* 1943, David Niven
The Way to the Gold	Wilbur Daniel Steel	*The Way to the Gold,* 1957, Jeffrey Hunter
Whatever Happened to Baby Jane?	Henry Farrell	*Whatever Happened to Baby Jane?,* 1963, Bette Davis
While the Patient Slept	Mignon G. Eberhart	*While the Patient Slept,* 1935
The Whispering Window	Cortland Fitzsimmons	*The Longest Night,* 1936
The White Cockatoo	Mignon G. Eberhart	*The White Cockatoo,* 1935
Who Killed Aunt Maggie?	Medora Field	*Who Killed Aunt Maggie?,* 1940
Witness for the Prosecution	Agatha Christie	*Witness for the Prosecution,* 1958, Charles Laughton
The Woman in Red	Anthony Gilbert	*My Name Is Julia Ross,* 1945, Nina Foch
Woman in White	Wilkie Collins	*Woman in White,* 1948, Alexis Smith
The Woman Who Was No More	Pierre Boileau and Thomas Narcejac	*Diabolique*
Wreck of the Mary Deare	Hammond Innes	*Wreck of the Mary Deare,* 1959, Gary Cooper
The Wrong Box	Robert Louis Stevenson	*The Wrong Box,* 1966, John Mills
You Only Live Twice	Ian Fleming	*You Only Live Twice,* 1967
You're Best Alone	Peter Curtis	*Guilt Is My Shadow,* 1951, Elizabeth Sellars

Film Detectives

A listing of the stage and screen stars who have at one time or another portrayed the great detective creations.

Boston Blackie
  Chester Morris
Sexton Blake
  Geoffrey Toone
James Bond
  Sean Connery
  David Niven
Nick Carter
  Walter Pidgeon

Charlie Chan
  J. Carroll Nash
  Warner Oland
  Sydney Toland
Nick Charles
  William Powell
Nora Charles
  Myrna Loy
Thatcher Colt
  Adolphe Menjou
Bill Crane
  Preston Foster
Nancy Drew
  Bonita Granville
Bulldog Drummond
  Ronald Colman
  Walter Pidgeon
  Richard Johnson
The Falcon
  Tom Conway
  George Sanders
Dr. Fu Manchu
  Boris Karloff
Peter Gunn
  Craig Stevens
Mike Hammer
  Robert Bray
  Biff Elliot
  Ralph Meeker
  Anthony Quinn
Hanaud
  Oscar Homolka
Harper (Lew Archer)
  Paul Newman
Matt Helm
  Dean Martin
Sherlock Holmes
  John Barrymore (American)
  Harry Benham (English)
  Carlyle Blackwell (American)
  Clive Brook (English)
  Peter Cushing (English)
  William Gillette (American)
  Forrest Holger-Madsen (Danish)
  Ronald Howard (English)
  Miles Mander (English)
  Raymond Massey (Canadian)
  Eille Norwood (English)
  Fred Paul (English)
  Basil Rathbone (English)
  Robert Rendell (English)
  M. Treville (French)
  Fritz Weaver (American)
  Arthur Wontner (English)
The Lone Wolf
  Louis Hayward
  Francis Lederer
  Warren William
Philip Marlowe
  Humphrey Bogart
  George Montgomery
  Robert Montgomery
  Dick Powell
Miss Marple
  Margaret Rutherford
Perry Mason
  Raymond Burr (TV)
  Ricardo Cortez
  Henry Stephenson
  Warren William
  Donald Woods
Mr. Moto
  Peter Lorre
  Henry Silva
Boysie Oakes
  Rod Taylor
Hercule Poirot
  Tony Randall
Ellery Queen
  Ralph Bellamy
  Lee Bowman (TV)
  Donald Cook
  William Gargan
  Richard Hart (TV)
  Hugh Marlowe (TV)
  George Nader (TV)
  Lee Philips (TV)
  Eddie Quillan
The Saint
  Louis Hayward
  Roger Moore (TV)
  George Sanders
  Hugh Sinclair
Mike Shayne
  Lloyd Nolan
Sam Spade
  Humphrey Bogart
Philo Vance
  Alan Curtis
  Edmund Lowe
  Paul Lukas
  William Powell
  Basil Rathbone
  Grant Richards
  James Stephenson
  Warren William
  William Wright
Honey West
  Anne Francis
Peter Wimsey
  Robert Montgomery
Hildegarde Withers
  Edna Mae Oliver
Mr. Wong
  Boris Karloff

Bibliography on Films

Behlmer, Rudy. "Chaney's Phantom," *Films in Review* (October, 1962). Notes on the first *Phantom of the Opera.*

Connor, Edward. "The Four Ellery Queens," *Films in Review* (June–July, 1960).

———. "The Nine Philo Vances," *Films in Review* (March, 1958).

———. "Sherlock Holmes on the Screen," *Films in Review* (August–September, 1961).

Dimmitt, Richard B. *A Title Guide to the Talkies.* New York: Scarecrow Press, 1965.

Jacobs, Jack. "William Powell," *Films in Review* (November, 1958). Films in which Powell created Philo Vance and Nick Charles among other detective characters.

Miller, Don. "Crime of Passion Films," *Films in Review* (October, 1962).

———. "Horror Films on TV," *Films in Review* (March, 1958).

Nolan, Jack Edmund. "Graham Greene's Movies," *Films in Review* (January, 1964).

"Parade of Violence," in the *Penguin New Writing, No. 30.* New York, London: Penguin Books, 1947.

Roman, Robert C. "Poe on the Screen," *Films in Review* (October, 1961).

Ross-Maclaren, J. "A Brief Survey of British Feature Films," in *Penguin New Writing, No. 29.* New York, London: Penguin Books, 1945. Discusses many of the older mystery films.

Walbridge, Earl F. "Films à Clef," *Films in Review* (March, 1958).

3

MYSTERY PLAYS

Suddenly the lights go out, and there is a hushed silence. Then a shot breaks the quiet of the night, followed by a harrowing scream. When the lights come on, a body lies in full view of the audience. Now they can breathe easier again, sit back and relax. The show is on.

Almost as early as the mystery novel itself came the mystery play, and hardly a year goes by without an example of this genre appearing on the Broadway or London stage. The thriller has long been a staple of the London season, while the early mystery melodramas such as *The Cat and the Canary* and *The Bat* thrilled thousands in their original runs on Broadway before they became popular in stock and amateur productions. In my opinion the stage offers a better medium than the motion picture for presenting the mystery story because of the close proximity of the audience to the players. The nearness to the peril at hand adds that extra fillip which is all but lacking in the coldness which emanates from a movie screen.

As in the books, every device has been used to catch the audience's attention. *On Trial* in 1913 was the first play to use the flashback as a means of telling its story. *The Night of January 13th* used the audience as a jury, and had two endings depending on which verdict they brought in. Another long-running hit, *The Spider,* had action that took place in the audience as well as on the stage.

Many mystery stage plays are original stories, and the novelizations, usually written by another author, come after the play has been written and successfully produced. Many of the famous mystery novels of our time have been adapted for the stage, but they are not always completely successful when transferred to this new medium.

For each play there is an indication of the number of male (m) and female (f) characters and of the copyright holders, i.e., Samuel French (F) or Dramatist Play Service (DPS).

Amber for Anna, Arthur Watkyn. 6m, 5f. (F) A group of people returning from a thriller relive another at home.

Anatomy of a Murder, Elihu Winer, based on a novel by Robert Traver. 16m, 2f. (F)

Angel Street (English title: *Gaslight*), Patrick Hamilton. 2m, 3f. (F) A gaslight thriller which became *Gaslight* on the screen.

Arsenic and Old Lace, Joseph Kesselring. 11m, 3f. (DPS) Two sweet old ladies who murder out of the goodness of their hearts.

The Aspern Papers, Michael Redgrave. 2m, 4f. (F) An American publisher seeks information on a writer long dead. Based on the story by Henry James.

The Bad Seed, Maxwell Anderson. 7m, 5f, 1 child. (DPS) Adapted from William March's novel about a child murderess.

The Bat, Mary Roberts Rinehart and Avery Hopwood. 7m, 3f. (F) A typical and popular mystery play of the twenties.

Blind Alley, James Warwick. 7m, 4f. (F) This play was the first of its kind to use modern psychology.

Brother Orchid, Leo Brady. 11m. (F) A gangster who is "on the spot" takes refuge with an order of monks.

The Burning Man, Tim J. Kelly. 4m, 3f. (F) The shadow of an old murder hovers over a group gathered in a gloomy lodge.

The Caine Mutiny Court-Martial, Herman Wouk. 19m. (F) The trial scene from the famous novel abounds in suspenseful scenes.

Calculated Risk, Joseph Hayes, based on a play by George Ross and Campbell Singer. 11m, 3f. (F)
The New York World-Telegram called it "a lively whodunit at the corporation level."

The Cat and the Canary, John Willard. 6m, 4f. (F) A typical 1929 thriller of a group of heirs called together to hear the reading of a will.

Catch Me If You Can, Jack Weinstock and Willie Gilbert. 5m, 2f. (F) The *New York Post* called it "a resourceful and amusing comedy mystery."

The Chalk Garden, Enid Bagnold. 2m, 7f. (F) One of the characters is a woman involved in a famous murder case.

A Clean Kill, Michael Gilbert. 5m, 3f. (F) The eternal triangle leads to murder!

The Clutching Claw. R. T. Kettering. 6m, 7f. (DPS) A web of lies leads to a murder in which innocent people are involved.

Cock Robin, Philip Barry and Elmer Rice. 8m, 4f. (F) Murder takes place during the actual performance of a play.

The Creaking Chair, Allene Tupper Wilkes. 8m, 4f. (F) The play was based on the fate that overtook members of the crew who investigated King Tut's tomb.

Criminal at Large, Edgar Wallace. 11m, 2f. (F) A typical English thriller.

Cuckoos on the Hearth, Parker W. Fennelly. 7m, 5f. (DPS) A daffy comedy in which the author has written two different versions of the same incident.

Cue for Passion, Elmer Rice. 4m, 3f. (DPS) A modernized version of Shakespeare's *Hamlet.*

Dangerous Corner, J. B. Priestley. 3m, 4f. (F) A combination mystery play and psychological study.

The Dark House, Wall Spence. 8m, 5f. (DPS) An eccentric, a queer will, and a murder!

Daughter of Silence, Morris L. West. 18m, 5f. (F) A courtroom drama with psychological overtones.

Dead on Nine, Jack Popplewell. 4m, 3f. (F) A marital quartet plays a dangerous murder game.

Dead Pigeon, Leonard Kantor. 2m, 1f. (F) Two detectives guard a murder witness in a hotel room.

A Dead Secret, Rockney Ackland. 9m, 5f. (F) Miss Lummis dies of arsenic poisoning and the mystery begins.

The Deadly Game, James Yaffee. 6m, 2f. (DPS) Based on Frederic Dürrenmatt's *Traps*

Design for Murder, George Batson. 4m, 6f. (F) A drawing room whodunit.

The Desperate Hours, Joseph Hayes. 11m, 3f. (F) Escaped convicts hold a family prisoner in their own home.

Detective Story, Sidney Kingsley. 24m, 8f. (DPS) A detective who can only divide the law between right and wrong.

Dial M for Murder, Frederick Knott. 5m, 1f. (DPS) A husband who plans to murder his wife for her money.

Dilemma, Joan Brampton. 3m, 3f. (DPS) Murder for money is also the theme of this suspenseful play.

The Donovan Affair, Owen Davis. 11m, 6f. (F) Death strikes fast when the lights go out.

Double Door, Elizabeth McFadden. 7m, 5f. (F) A young wife pitted against a hateful mother-in-law.

Dracula, Hamilton Deane and J. L. Balderston. 6m, 2f. (F) Based on the famous vampire novel by Bram Stoker.

Duet for Two Hands, Mary Hayley Bell. 2m, 3f. (F) The New York *Herald Tribune* called it "an upper-class British thriller."

Edwina Black, William Dinner and William Morum. 2m, 2f. (F) It was called *The Late Edwina Black* in England and is a gripping thriller.

Gaslight; see *Angel Street*

The Gazebo, Alex Coppel. 9m, 3f. (DPS) The body is buried under the foundation of the gazebo, but refuses to remain there.

The Ghost Train, Arnold Ridley. 7m, 4f. (F) A lonely railway station and a phantom train that haunts the area.

The Gorilla, Ralph Spence. 9m, 2f. (F) A popular mystery comedy of the twenties.

Hangman's Noose, George Batson. 4m, 6f. (F) Another one where all the heirs gather to hear the will being read.

The Haunted House, Owen Davis. 8m, 3f. (F) A fabulously successful mystery comedy of the Golden Era.

High Ground (Bonaventure), Charlotte Hastings. 3m, 8f. (F) A nursing convent is the novel setting for this play.

The Hollow, Agatha Christie. 6m, 6f. (F) Murder stalks a country home near London in the great Christie manner.

Home at Seven, R. C. Sherriff. 5m, 2f. (F) Murder invades the lives of an ordinary family.

House Without Windows (The Tin Cup). 3m, 4f. (DPS) A perfect crime is committed—almost.

Houseparty, Kenneth Phillips Britton and Roy Hargrave. 9m, 9f. (F) Death invades a college fraternity.

I Killed the Count, Alec Coppel. 10m, 3f. (F) A murder is committed, and everybody confesses to being the killer.

I Want a Policeman, Rufus King and Milton Lazarus. 11m, 3f. (DPS) Murder among the upper classes in novelist King's best style.

Incognito, N. Richard Nusbaum. 7m, 12f. (F) Murder on the high seas with nine women as murder suspects.

The Innocents, William Archibald. 1m, 2f, 2 children. (F) Henry James' famous story of haunting and terror.

An Inspector Calls, J. B. Priestley. 4m, 3f. (DPS) A psychological study which ends where it begins.

Invitation to a Murder, Rufus King. 8m, 3f. (F) Murder against the background of an old Southern California estate.

The Jade God, William Edwin Barry. 6m, 4f. (F) A novelist turns detective to clear his fiancée.

Kill Two Birds, Philip Levene. 8m, 2f. (F) Considered one of England's top melodramas.

Kind Lady, Edward Chodorov. 6m, 8f. (F) Based on a short story by Hugh Walpole about a lady kept prisoner in her own home by a gang of crooks.

Laburnum Grove, J. B. Priestley. 6m, 3f. (F) Is George Radfern a member of a counterfeit ring or not?

Ladies in Retirement, Edward Percy and Reginald Denham. 1m, 6f. (DPS) A housekeeper murders her mistress to protect her mentally retarded sisters.

Lady in Danger, Max Afford and Alexander Kirkland. 8m, 3f. (F) A lady mystery novelist is accused of a crime similar to one in her book.

The Last Warning, Martin Fallon. 10m, 4f. (F) Murder strikes during a theatrical performance.

Laura, Vera Caspary and George Sklar. 5m, 3f. (DPS) A detective falls in love with a dead woman.

The Locked Room, Herbert Ashton. 9m, 4f. (F) One of mysterydom's classic devices used in a stage play.

Love from a Stranger, Frank Vosper. 4m, 4f. (F) Vosper also acted in this thriller based on an Agatha Christie story.

The Man, Mel Dinelli. 5m, 2f. (DPS) A housewife is trapped in her own home by a psycho handyman.

Margin for Error, Clare Boothe. 7m, 2f. (DPS) A Jewish policeman is assigned to guard the German embassy in New York City.

Meet a Body, Frank Lander and Sidney Gilliat. 8m, 4f. (F) A vacuum cleaner salesman is innocently drawn into a murder case.

Miss Pell Is Missing, Leonard Gershe. 4m, 3f. (F) A private detective is hired to find the missing Miss Pell.

Monique, Dorothy and Michael Blankfort. 5m, 6f. (F) Based on a novel by Pierre Boileau and Thomas Narcejac.

The Mousetrap, Agatha Christie. 5m, 3f. (F) This is the one that has been running in London for sixteen years.

Mr. and Mrs. North, Owen Davis. 16m, 4f. (F) A top Broadway mystery comedy based on the Lockridge characters.

A Murder Has Been Arranged, Emlyn Williams. 4m, 5f. (F) A writer suddenly realizes that a chapter from his book has become a suicide confession.

Murder in a Nunnery, Emmet Lavery. 5m, 12f. (F) Murder strikes in a convent school.

Murder in the Old Red Barn; see *Murder of Maria Marten*

Murder, My Sweet Matilda, Janet Green. 9m, 3f. (DPS) The play which was the basis for Doris Day's film *Midnight Lace.*

Murder of Maria Marten, or The Red

Barn, Brian J. Burton. 8m, 8f. (F) An old-time melodrama based on a true English murder case. There are several versions of this play.

Murder Without Crime, J. Lee Thompson. 2m, 2f. (F) The eternal triangle takes on a murderous twist.

Mystery at Greenfingers, J. B. Priestley. 4m, 6f. (F) A group of travelers get stranded in a storm-bound hotel.

Night Must Fall, Emlyn Williams. 4m, 5f. (F) A classic about Dan, the murdering bellhop.

Nine Pine Street, John Colton and Carlton Miles. 7m, 9f. (F) Based on a play by William Miles and Donald Blackwell who got the idea from the famous Lizzie Borden case.

The Ninth Guest, Owen Davis. 7m, 3f. (F) The title refers to Death, and you can go on from there.

Not Herbert, Howard Irving Young. 7m, 5f. (F) An apparent shrinking violet is a notorious thief.

Not in the Book, Arthur Watkyn. 7m, 1f. (F) A thriller in the best English tradition.

The Oblong Circle, Harold P. Rednour. 9m, 3f. (F) A mystery which uses a new and unique method of presentation.

On Trial, Elmer Rice. (F)

The Perfect Alibi, A. A. Milne. 7m, 3f. (F) We know at once whodunit, but how will they be caught?

Portrait in Black, Ivan Goff and Ben Roberts. 5m, 3f. (F) The *New York Sun* called it "a chill and shudder drama."

The Post Road, Wilbur Daniel Steele and Norma Mitchell. 7m, 8f. (F) Charlotte Greenwood played in this one under the title *Leaning on Letty.*

The Potting Shed, Graham Greene. 6m, 5f. (F) A super-intellectual mystery drama.

Prescription: Murder, William Link and Richard Levinson. 4m, 3f. (F) A cat-and-mouse game between a psychiatrist and a detective.

Ransom, Cyril Hume and Richard Maibaum. 11m, 4f. (F) A kidnapping brings on a nightmare for an average family.

Ramshackle Inn, George Batson. 9m, 6f. (F) Zazu Pitts played this on Broadway and the road and it was a great hit.

Rope, Patrick Hamilton. 6m, 2f. (F) A thriller based on the Loeb-Leopold case.

Seven Keys to Baldpate, George M. Cohan. 9m, 4f. (F) Adapted from Earl Derr Biggers' famous novel.

The Shop at Sly Corner, Edward Percy. 6m, 4f. (DPS) Murder and blackmail become a part of an old antique shop.

A Shot in the Dark, Marcel Achard, adapted by Harry Kurnitz. 5m, 3f. (F) Julie Harris had one of her great Broadway triumphs in this hilarious mystery.

Shred of Evidence, R. C. Sherriff. 6m, 3f. (F) An English thriller which builds to a terrific climax.

Signpost to Murder, Monte Doyle. 6m, 1f. (F) Margaret Lockwood starred in this thriller on the London stage.

A Slight Case of Murder, Damon Runyon and Howard Lindsay. 11m, 3f. (DPS) A comedy mystery about a gangster who tries to go legitimate.

The Sound of Murder, William Fairchild. 4m, 2f. (F) The *London Sunday Pictorial* called it "the most ingenious and liveliest murder yarn for years."

Speaking of Murder, Audrey and William Roos. 3m, 4f. (F) The team who write mystery novels under the pseudonym of Kelley Roos show they are at home in this medium as well.

The Spider, Fulton Oursler and Lowell Brentano. 21m, 3f. (F) A popular play where the murder takes place in the audience.

The Spider's Web, Agatha Christie. 8m, 3f. (F) Margaret Lockwood and Agatha Christie teamed to thrill London.

The Spiral Staircase, F. Andrews Leslie. 4m, 4f. (DPS) A play adapted from the successful film of the same name.

Suspect, Edward Percy and Reginald Denham. 4m, 4f. (DPS) A psychological drama concerning a woman trying to live down a past.

The Tavern, George M. Cohan. 10m, 4f. (F) The most famous of the Cohan productions in the mystery vein.

Ten Little Indians, Agatha Christie. 8m, 3f. (F) An old nursery rhyme and a calculating murderer with all the Christie flair.

Thérèse, Thomas Job. 4m, 4f. (F) This is a dramatization of an Emile Zola novel and a real spellbinder.

The Thirteenth Chair, Bayard Veiler. 10m, 7f. (F) Murder goes to a séance in a famous old mystery play.

Towards Zero, Agatha Christie and Gerald Verner. 7m, 4f. (DPS) Murder invades a house party but don't expect the usual with Christie around to lead you through the maze.

The Traitor, Herman Wouk. 15m, 3f. (F) A prominent scientist plans to turn over secret plans to the enemy.

The Trial of Mary Dugan, Bayard Veiler. 20m, 7f. (F) One of the most famous of all courtroom dramas.

The Two Mrs. Carrolls, Martin Vane. 3m, 5f. (F) When Mr. Carroll is attracted to a beautiful neighbor, he plans to kill his current wife.

Wait Until Dark, Frederic Knott. 6m, 2f. (DPS) A young blind wife is terrorized by a gang seeking loot hidden in a doll.

Whistling in the Dark, Laurence Gross and Edward Childs. 10m, 2f. (F) A writer is forced to work out his ingenious plots for the use of gangsters.

Witness for the Prosecution, Agatha Christie. 17m, 5f. (F) This probably has the most stunning ending ever conceived for a thriller.

BIBLIOGRAPHY

Drames à Clef. New York: New York Public Library, 1956. A list of plays, many of them mysteries, which are based on true murder cases and real people.

Wilson, A. D. "Crime and the Stage," *Spectator* (April 10, 1936).

4

SCENE OF THE CRIME

In the good old days murders were committed in only two places: picturesque old English country houses and lavish Manhattan penthouses. Or so it must have seemed to the inveterate reader of detective stories. Considering how ingenious the writers were in creating bizarre methods for killing off their victims, these same creators were quite unimaginative in finding new and interesting places in which to have them die.

Sometimes, of course, murders took place in such isolated places as London, Paris, Chicago, or Southern California; but the reader was not really on familiar ground until he returned to the security of Massacre Manor where Sir John Solvit had gathered all the suspects together in the library around the fireplace and was about to explain to them how a bullet made of solid ice had been fired from the grandfather's clock exactly at the hour of midnight. If the reader was not an intellectual and wanted something a little more lurid, he could always find beautiful blonde chorus girls who got mixed up with nasty underworld characters and got strangled for their indiscretions. These crimes, incidentally, were invariably solved by lone wolves who were called in by the New York Police Department when it was unable to solve the case.

World War II changed all this—fortunately. The global war made millions of people aware of places and names which previously had been unfamiliar references in the geography books. The GI's and the correspondents who came home to civilian jobs were as familiar with Calcutta and Penang as they were with Jersey City and Sacramento. They had traveled, undergone unusual experiences, and knew people of many races. They were no longer satisfied with the routine or the mundane and wanted the real thing in their reading as well as in their daily living.

Naturally the movie industry became aware of this trend too. No longer were the films produced on the back lots of Hollywood; the producers moved all over the face of the earth in search of authenticity.

The change of scene in the mystery, suspense and detective story came as a welcome relief, as did many other innovations. Many of the old taboos were gone, too. Love stories, or even suggestions of romance, were almost unknown back in those good old days. In fact one cardinal rule set down by S. S. Van Dine, Ronald Knox and many others was that a love affair should never be allowed to interfere with the problems of detecting. How things have changed! Today's secret agent and troubleshooter is so busy flitting from bed to bed that it is almost miraculous that he gets any work accomplished. It is a rare story today that does not have at least a glamorous blonde, a smouldering brunette, or a stunning redhead popping up to divert the hero at every turn of event. Today's hero must have a way with women as well as a way with his fists and his guns if he is to succeed.

For the detective fan who wants a different background to add spice to the murders and intrigues, and to the armchair traveler who wants to add a little excitement to his usual fare, these suggestions are offered. It is virtually a trip around the world with violence, murder and intrigue as boon companions.

One final word—it is interesting to note that whether the victim is killed in Bangkok, Calcutta or Tokyo, he is still invariably an Anglo-Saxon. That much is still true and unchanging in the fascinating world of the mystery, detective and suspense novel.

Afghanistan

Harvester, Simon, *Silk Road*

Africa

Aarons, Edward, *Assignment-Madelaine* (Algiers)
Allen, Clifford, *Dark Places* (West Africa)
Allen, Eric, *Death on Delivery* (North Africa)
Ashe, Gordon, *Death in Diamonds* (Kalahari)
Ashley, Kate, *The Cinnabar Shroud*
Caillou, Alan, *Rogue's Gambit* (Ethiopia)
Canning, Victor, *Black Flamingo* (Central Africa)
———. *The Golden Salamander* (Morocco)
Carr, John D., *Behind the Crimson Blind* (Tangier)
Carstairs, John P., *No Wooden Overcoat* (Tangier)
Christie, Agatha, *So Many Steps to Death* (Morocco)
Clifford, Francis, *The Green Fields of Eden*
Cobb, Belton, *Corpse at Casablanca*
Corrigan, Mark, *Madame Sly* (Morocco)
Cory, Desmond, *High Requiem* (North Africa)
Crane, Frances, *Coral Princess Murders* (Tangier)
Croft-Cooke, Rupert, *Barbary Night* (Tangier)
Crofts, Freeman W., *Death of a Train* (North Africa)
———. *Groote Park Murders* (South Africa)
Daniel, Roland, *The Kenya Tragedy*
Deane, Norman, *Look at Murder* (Natal-Durban)
Dembo, Samuel, *Kalhari Kill* (Bechuanaland)
Desmond, Hugh, *Jacaranda Murders* (Natal-Durban)
Douglas, Malcolm, *Prey by Night* (Tangier)
Drummond, June, *The Black Unicorn* (Transvaal)
———. *Welcome, Proud Lady* (Cape Town)
Dryer, Bernard, *Port Afrique* (North Africa)
Edqvist, Dagmar, *Black Sister* (Tanganyika)
Fearon, Diana, *Nairobi Nightcap* (Nairobi)
Fergusson, Bernard, *The Rare Adventure* (Algiers, Tunisia)
Fores, John, *Forgotten Place* (North Africa)
Freestone, Basil, *The Golden Drum* (West-Africa)
Fry, Pete, *Grey Sombrero* (Tangier)
Fullerton, Alexander, *Bury the Past* (Cape Town)
Garve, Andrew, *Hero for Leanda* (Ghana)
Godfrey, Peter A., *Death Under the Table* (Cape Town)

Goodchild, George, *Last Secret* (North Africa)
Gray, Dulcie, *Baby Face* (North Africa)
Hardinge, Rex, *Murder on the Veld*
———. *Secret of the Sheba*
Harman, Neal, *Peace and Peter Lamont* (North Africa)
———. *Yours Truly, Angus MacIvor* (Transvaal)
Harris, Peter, *Letters of Discredit* (Cape Town)
Harvester, Simon, *Sheep May Safely Graze* (Kenya)
Hayles, Kenneth, *The Purple Sheba* (Algiers)
Head, Matthew, *Cabinda Affair*
———. *Devil in the Bush* (Congo)
Hurst, Ida, *African Heartbeat*
Huxley, Êlspeth, *Incident at the Merry Hippo* (East Africa)
Iams, Jack, *The Body Missed the Boat*
Innes, Hammond, *The Naked Land* (Morocco)
Jacobs, Thomas Curtis Hicks, *Let Him Stay Dead*
Jenkins, Geoffrey, *A Twist of Sand* (Southwest Africa)
———. *A River of Diamonds* (South Africa)
Kaye, H. B., *Death Is a Black Camel* (East Africa)
Kaye, Mary, *The House of Shade* (Zanzibar)
———. *Later Than You Think* (Kenya)
———. *Night on the Island* (East Africa)
Lejeune, Anthony, *Duel in the Shadows* (Ghana)
Leonard, Charles, *Fanatic of Fez* (Morocco)
Leslie, Norman, *Death Comes to Kenya*
Lloyd, Lavander, *Linton Memorial* (East Africa)
Long, E. Laurie, *River Passage* (West Africa)
McCutcheon, Hugh, *Yet She Must Die* (Morocco)
Mackenzie, Nigel, *The Dark Night*
———. *Murder for Two*
———. *Pyramid of Death*
Mackinnon, Clark, *Flame Lily* (Cape Province)
Mason, F. Van Wyck, *Zanzibar Intrigue*
Maugham, Robert, *The Man with Two Shadows* (North Africa)
Meredith, Peter, *Crocodile Man* (West Africa)
Monig, Christopher, *Once Upon a Crime* (Transvaal)
Moodie, Edwin, *Great Shakes* (Transvaal)
Morrison, Emmeline, *Tale Untold* (Tangier)
Mullally, Frederic, *Marianne*
Mulvihill, William, *The Mantrackers* (Tanganyika)
Murray, Audrey A., *The Blanket*
O'Brine, Padraic M., *Deadly Interlude* (Tangier)
O'Neill, Kerry, *Death at Dakar* (Senegal)
Packer, Joy, *The Man in the Mews* (South Africa)
Pendower, Jacques, *Million in Tunis*
Rabe, Peter, *The Spy Who Was Three Feet Tall*
Rougvie, Cameron, *Tangier Assignment*
Royce, Kenneth, *The Soft-footed Moor* (Tangier)
Scobie, Alastair, *The Cape Town Affair*
———. *Murder à la Mozambique*
Shannon, Carl, *Fatal Footsteps* (Liberia)
Sheckley, Robert, *Live Gold* (Sahara)
Sibly, John, *Girl on the Run* (Kenya)
Sprigg, C. St. John, *The Corpse with the Sunburned Face*
Temple, Paul, *East of Algiers* (Tunis)
Thomas, Ross, *The Seersucker Whipsaw*
Trench, John, *Beyond the Atlas* (Ethiopia)
Vance, John H., *The Man in the Cage* (Algiers)
Van Rensburg, Helen and Louwrens, *Death in a Dark Pool* (Swaziland)
———. *Man with Two Ties* (Transvaal)
Wainwright, John, *The Crystalized Carbon Pig*
Weston, Garnett, *The Hidden Portal*
Wheatley, Dennis, *The Fabulous Valley* (Bechuanaland)
Williams, Alan, *Long Run South* (Morocco)
Wren, Percival C., *Beau Geste*
Wuorio, Eva-Lis, *Z for Zaborra* (Marrakech)

Albania

Bridges, Ann, *Singing Waters*
Fallon, Martin, *Keys of Hell* (Albanian Coast)
Wellard, James, *Action of the Tiger*

Andorra

Appleby, John, *The Secret Mountains*

Arctic and Antarctic

Lester, Frank, *Death and the South Wind*
MacLean, Alastair, *Ice Station Zebra*
Muir, Thomas, *Death Below Zero*

Around the World

Castle, Dennis, *The Fourth Gambler*

Australia

Antill, Elizabeth, *Death on the Barrier Reef* (Great Barrier Reef)
Armstrong, Raymond, *Sinister Widow Down Under*
Atkinson, Hugh, *The Reckoning*
Backhouse, Elizabeth, *Mists Came Down* (Western Australia)
———. *Web of Shadows* (Western Australia)
Batchelor, Denzil, *Everything Happens to Hector* (Sydney)
Bateson, David, *I'll Go Anywhere*
Berrow, Norman, *Don't Jump, Mr. Boland* (Sydney)
Bunce, Sydney, *Take This Life*
Campbell, Ronald, *Marked for Murder*
Carlon, Patricia, *The Price of an Orphan*
Corrigan, Mark, *Big Boys Don't Cry*
———. *Cruel Lady* (Melbourne)
———. *Sydney for Sin*
Courtier, Sidney, *Come Back to Murder*
———. *Death in Dream Time* (Queensland)
———. *Now Seek My Bones* (Northern Territory)
———. *One Cried Murder*
———. *Shroud for Unlac*
———. *Who Dies for Me*
Creasey, John, *The Toff Down Under*
———. *Murder—London–Australia*
Desmond, Hugh, *Calling Alan Fraser* (Perth)
Elliott, Peers, *Mystery of the Black Dagger* (Queensland, Northern Territory)
Flower, Pat, *Goodbye, Sweet William* (Sydney)
———. *Wax Flowers for Gloria* (Sydney)
Fowler, Helen, *Hold a Bright Mirror* (Sydney)
———. *Shades Will Not Vanish*
Gardiner, Heather, *Murder in Haste* (Sydney)
———. *Money on Murder* (Melbourne)
Graham, Nancy, *Black Swan* (Western Australia)
———. *Purple Jacaranda*
Gray, Dulcie, *Murder in Melbourne*
Grierson, Linden, *Sunken Garden* (New South Wales)
Hamilton, Ian, *The Persecutor*
Hardy, Lindsay, *Nightshade Ring*
Hobart, Robertson, *Case of the Shaven Blonde*
———. *Dangerous Cargoes*
Hume, Fergus, *Mystery of a Hansom Cab* (Melbourne)
James, Henry C., *The Green Opal*
Jay, Charlotte, *A Knife Is Feminine*
Kelly, Vince, *The Greedy Ones* (Sydney)
Keneally, Thomas, *The Place at Whitton*
Kimmins, Anthony, *Lugs O'Leary*
Little, Constance and Gwenyth, *The Great Black Kamba*
McCutchan, Philip, *Redcap*
Mace, Helen, *House of Hate* (Tasmania)
———. *Murder Among Those Present* (Tasmania)
Martin, Archibald E., *Chinese Bed Mysteries* (Queensland)
———. *Curious Crime*
———. *The Outsiders* (Sydney)
———. *Sinners Never Die*

Murray, Max, *The Right Honorable Corpse* (Canberra)
Neville, Margot, *Divining Rod for Murder*
———. *Flame of Murder* (Sydney)
———. *Murder and Gardenias* (Sydney)
———. *Murder and Poor Jenny* (Sydney)
———. *Murder Before Marriage* (Sydney)
———. *Murder in a Blue Moon* (Sydney)
———. *Murder in Rockwater* (Sydney)
———. *Murder of a Nymph* (New South Wales)
———. *Murder of the Well-Beloved* (Sydney)
———. *Murder to Welcome Her* (Sydney)
———. *Sweet Night for Murder* (Sydney)
North, Eric, *Chip on My Shoulder* (Melbourne)
———. *Nobody Stops Me*
Salter, Elizabeth, *The Will to Survive*
Singer, Bant, *Don't Slip, Delaney* (Sydney)
———. *You're Wrong, Delaney* (Sydney)
Stivens, Dallas, *Jimmy Brockett* (Sydney)
———. *Wide Arch* (Sydney)
Upfield, Arthur W., *An Author Bites the Dust*
———. *Bachelors of Broken Hill* (Broken Hill)
———. *Battling Prophet* (Adelaide)
———. *Bony and the Black Virgin* (New South Wales)
———. Bony and Kelly Gang
———. *Bony and the Mouse* (Western Australia)
———. *Bony Buys a Woman* (Northern Territory)
———. *Cake in the Hat Box* (Northern Territory)
———. *Death of a Lake*
———. *Death of a Swagman*
———. *Devil's Step* (Victoria)
———. *Lure of the Bush*
———. *Man of Two Tribes* (Nullarbor Plain)
———. *Mountains Have a Secret*
———. *Murder Must Wait* (New South Wales)
———. *Mystery of Swordfish Reef* (New South Wales)
———. *New Shoe* (Victoria)
———. *No Footprints in the Bush* (Queensland)
———. *Sands of Windee* (New South Wales)
———. *Sinister Stones*
———. *Venom House*
———. *Widow of Broome* (Northern Territory)
———. *Wings Above the Diamantina*
Watkinson, Valerie, *The Sped Arrow*
West, Morris L., *Gallows in the Sand* (Great Barrier Reef)
Workman, James, *Face of Fortune*
Wright, June, *Devil's Caress*

Austria

Albrand, Martha, *A Call from Austria* (Vienna)
Ames, Delano L., *Crime out of Mind* (Tyrol)
Callas, Theo, *City of Kites* (Vienna)
Carnac, Carol, *Crossed Skiis*
Carr, Glyn, *Corpse in the Crevasse* (Tyrol)
Cobden, Guy, *I Saw Murder*
Corrigan, Mark, *Cruel Lady*
Cory, Desmond, *Dead Man Falling*
Daniels, Norman, *Some Die Running*
Gainham, Sarah, *The Mythmaker*
———. *Time Right Deadly* (Vienna)
Gibbs-Smith, C., *Escape and Be Secret*
Gilbert, Michael, *After the Fine Weather* (Southern Austria)
———. *Be Shot for Sixpence*
Greene, Graham, *The Third Man* (Vienna)
Hall, Geoffrey, *Watcher at the Door*
Halliday, Leonard, *Smiling Spider*
———. *Top Secret*
Innes, Hammond, *Fire in the Snow*
Kades, Hans, *House of Crystal* (Tyrol)
Lorac, E. C. R., *Murder in Vienna* (Vienna)
McCutcheon, Hugh, *Suddenly in Vienna*
Marlowe, Stephen, *Passport to Peril* (Vienna)
Oppenheim, E. Phillips, *The Last Train Out*
Ross, Marilyn, *Assignment: Danger*
Sereny, Gitta, *The Medallion* (Vienna)
Stern, Richard M., *Search for Tabatha Carr*
———. *The Kessler Legacy*
Stewart, Mary, *Airs Above the Ground*
Storm, Joan, *Bitter Rubies*
Trefus, Victor, *But No Man Seen* (Vienna)
Yates, Dornford, *Storm Music*
———. *An Eye for a Tooth* (Pre-War Austria)

Balkans

Ambler, Eric, *Judgment on Deltchev*
Ballinger, Bill, *Beacon in the Night*
Milner, George, *Scarlet Fountains*
Williams, David, *Agent from the West*
See also individual countries

Belgium

Acland, Alice, *Person of Discretion*
Albrand, Martha, *Meet Me Tonight*
Baggaley, James, *Shadow of the Eagle* (Ardennes)
Cory, Desmond, *The Phoenix Sings* (Antwerp)
Freeling, Nicholas, *A Question of Loyalty*
Melides, Nicholas, *Buns from the Gutter*
Reed, Eliot, *Tender to Danger* (Brussels)
Shapiro, Lionel, *Torch for a Dark Journey*
Simenon, Georges, *Burgomasters of Furnes*
Weeks, William, *Knock and Wait Awhile* (Brussels)

Burma

Aarons, Edward S., *Assignment-Burma Girl*
Harvester, Simon, *Dragon Road*
Hastings, Michael, *Death in Deep Green*
Mason, F. Van Wyck, *Trouble in Burma*
Phillips, James A., *Pagoda*

Cambodia

Ballinger, Bill, *Spy at Angkor Wat*
Casey, Robert J., *Cambodian Quest*

Canada

Bagley, Desmond, *Festival for Spies* (British Columbia)
Bindloss, Harold, *Lone Hand*
Binns, Ottwell, *Lady of North Star*
Bonnamy, Francis, *The Man in the Mist*
Brett, Martin, *The Darker Traffic* (Montreal)
———. *Exit in Green*
———. *Hot Freeze* (Montreal)
Bryan, Michael, *Intent to Kill* (Montreal)
Castle, John and Arthur Hailey, *Flight into Danger* (Winnipeg to Vancouver)
Cushing, E. Louise, *Murder's No Picnic*
Disney, Doris, *The Seventeenth Letter* (Nova Scotia)
Fry, Pamela, *Harsh Evidence* (Ontario)
Hamilton, Donald, *The Ravagers*
Harris, John N., *The Weird World of Wes Beattie*
Innes, Hammond, *Campbell's Kingdom* (Alberta)
Johnson, Lilian, *The Medallion*
Keirstad, Burton and Donald Campbell, *Brownsville Murders*
Kelland, Clarence B., *Case of the Nameless Corpse* (Alberta)
Kennedy, Milward, *Escape to Quebec*
Mayse, Arthur, *Desperate Search*
———. *Perilous Passage*
Millar, M., *Iron Gates*
———. *Fire Will Freeze*
O'Donnell, Lillian, *Deathschuss*
O'Grady, Rohan, *Let's Kill Uncle*
Paul, John, *Oil by Murder*
Reilly, Helen, *Compartment K* (Trans-Canada)
Stringer, Arthur J., *Ghost Plane*
Thayer, Lee, *Still No Answer*
Thurley, Norgrove, *Murder Strikes North* (Yukon Territory)
Wees, Frances S., *Country of the Strangers*
Weston, Garnett, *Murder on Shadow Island*
Williams, Valentine, *Dead Man Manor*

Canary Islands

Cadell, Elizabeth, *Canary Yellow*
Mair, George, *Miss Turquoise*
Mitchell, Gladys, *Twenty-Third Man*

Caribbean

Barbour, Ralph H., *Death in the Virgins*
Bennett, Dorothy, *Carrion Crows*
Booth, Charles G., *Mr. Angel Comes Aboard*
Burnham, David, *Last Act in Bermuda*
Cave, H. B., *The Cross on the Drum*
Chaber, M. E., *Gallows Garden*
Chambers, Whitman, *Dangerous Water* (Bahamas)
———. *Dry Tortugas*
Charteris, Leslie, *Saint on the Spanish Main*
Cheyney, Peter, *Dark Bahama*
Christie, Agatha, *A Caribbean Mystery*
Clifford, Francis, *The Hunting Ground*
Coxe, George H., *Man on a Rope*
———. *Man Who Died Twice* (Barbados)
———. *Uninvited Guest* (Barbados)
Cronin, Michael, *Ask for Trouble* (Quirico)
Dark, James, *Operation Scuba*
Desmond, Hugh, *Fear Walks the Island*
Douglass, Donald M., *Rebecca's Pride*
DuBois, William, *Case of the Frightened Fish* (Bahamas)
Eberhart, Mignon G., *Enemy in the House* (Jamaica)
———. *House of Storm*
Ellington, Richard, *Stone Cold Dead*
Flagg, John, *The Paradise Gun*
Fleming, Ian, *Man with the Golden Gun* (Jamaica)
———. *Live and Let Live*
———. *Dr. No*
Footner, Hulbert, *The Obeah Murders*
Ford, Leslie, *The Bahamas Murder Case* (Nassau)
Fuller, William, *Brad Dolan's Blonde Cargo*
Garve, Andrew, *Fontego's Folly*
Gaskin, Catherine, *The Tilsit Inheritance*
Grierson, Linden, *The Senorita Penny*
Haggard, William, *The Telemann Touch*
Hayles, Kenneth, *The Volcano*
Hoffenberg, Jack, *A Thunder at Dawn*
Holding, Elizabeth S., *Strange Crime in Bermuda* (Bermuda)
Johnston, Ronald, *Danger at Bravo Key*
Kraslow, David, *A Certain Evil*
Langmaid, Kenneth, *Mystery Cruise*
McCloy, Helen, *Goblin Market*
MacDonald, John D., *A Man of Affairs* (Bahamas)
Mansfield, Paul, *Final Exposure*
Marquand, John, *Last Laugh, Mr. Moto*
Mason, F. Van Wyck, *Castle Island Case* (Bermuda)
Mason, Howard, *Body Below* (Guadeloupe)
Mole, William, *Goodbye Is Not Worthwhile* (Barbados)
Muir, Thomas, *Death in the Soundings*
Quirk, Jon, *The Tournament* (Grand Bahama)
Root, Pat, *Evil Became Them*
Saxby, Charles, *Even Bishops Die*
Shannon, Dell, *Mark of Murder* (Bermuda)
Sharp, Willoughby, *Murder in Bermuda* (Bermuda)
Siller, Van, *Bermuda Murder* (Bermuda)
———. *Last Resort*
Smith, Shelley, *This Is the House*
Stribling, Thomas S., *Clues of the Caribees*
Thayer, Lee, *The Prisoner Pleads Not Guilty* (Bermuda)
Thorne, E. P., *Moon Dance* (Haiti)
Walsh, Paul E., *Murder in Baracoa*
Wilkinson, B., *Run Mongoose*
Vandercook, J. W., *Murder in Trinidad*
See also Cuba

Central America

Coles, Manning, *Dangerous by Nature*
Franklin, Charles, *Trembling Thread*
Graeme, Roderic, *Blackshirt Meets the Lady*

Halliday, Brett, *Fit to Kill*
Knight, K. M., *Bells for the Dead* (Guatemala)
———. *Fatal Harvest*
———. *Trademark of a Traitor*
Usher, Frank H., *Portrait of Fear*
See also Panama

Ceylon

Marlowe, Dan J., *Route of the Red Gold*
Marsh, Jean, *Death Among the Stars*

China

Berges, M. L., *Woman of Shanghai* (Shanghai)
Black, Gavin, *A Dragon for Christmas* (Peking)
Carter, Nick, *Operation Starvation*
Crossen, Kendall F., *Tortured Path*
Daniels, Norman, *Operation "K"*
Dekobra, M., *Chinese Puzzle*
———. *Honeymoon in Shanghai*
Dodge, Steve, *Shanghai Incident*
Esmond, Sidney, *Peacock's Feather*
Fleischman, A. S., *Shanghai Flame*
Goldsmith, Louis C., *Streamlined Dragon*
Gulik, Robert H. Van, *Chinese Bell Murders*
———. *Chinese Gold Murders*
———. *Chinese Lake Murders*
———. *Emperor's Pearl*
———. *The Haunted Monastery*
———. *Murder in Canton*
See also Author entry in Comprehensive Bibliography
Harvester, Simon, *Flight in Darkness*
Johnston, George H., *Death Takes Small Bites* (Yunnan)
Long, E. Laurie, *Dope Ship*
McCutchan, Philip, *Dead Line* (London to China)
———. *On Course for Danger*
MacSwan, Norman, *Inn with the Wooden Door*
Marquand, John P., *Thank You, Mr. Moto* (Peking)
Mason, F. Van Wyck, *The Shanghai Bund Murders*
Morland, Nigel, *Sing a Song of Cyanide* (Shanghai)
Norman, James, *Murder Chop Chop*
———. *Nightwalkers*
Rohmer, Sax, *Emperor Fu Manchu* (Szechwan)
Smith, Don, *China Coaster*
Starrett, Vincent, *Murder in Peking*
Teilhet, Hildegarde, *The Assassins*
Tregaskis, Richard, *China Bomb*
Wynd, Oswald, *Death, the Red Flower*

Cuba

Coxe, George H., *Woman at Bay*
Dudley, Frank, *The Havana Hotel Murders*
Greene, Graham, *Our Man in Havana*
James, Leigh, *The Chameleon File*
Lockridge, Frances and Richard, *Voyage into Violence*
Marlowe, Hugh, *Passage by Night*
Richards, Clay, *The Gentle Assassin*
Sylvester, Robert, *Big Boodle*

Cyprus

Appleby, John, *The Bad Summer* (Nicosia)
Annesley, Michael, *Spy Island*
Blackstock, Charity, *Mr. Christopoulos*
Buttenshaw, Diana, *Violence in Paradise*
Greenfield, G., *At Bay*
Hocking, Anne, *So Many Doors*
Kaye, Mary M., *Death Walked in Cyprus*
Wills, Cecil M., *Clue of the Golden Earring*

Czechoslovakia

Copp, De Witt, *The Pursuit of Agent M*
Davidson, Lionel, *Night of Wenceslas* (Prague)
Gainham, Sarah, *The Stone Roses* (Prague)
Hostovský, Egon, *Missing* (Prague)
Sherwood, John, *Mr. Blessington's Imperialistic Plot*
Wheatley, Dennis, *Curtain of Fear*

Denmark

Albrand, Martha, *Nightmare in Copenhagen*
Capit, Eline, *Run from the Sheep*
McGurk, Slater, *Denmark Bus*
Nielsen, Helen, *Stranger in the Dark* (Copenhagen)
Ware, Judith, *Detour to Denmark*
York, Andrew, *The Coordinator*

Egypt

Aarons, Edward S., *Assignment—The Cairo Dancers*
Caillou, Âlan, *Alien Virus* (Cairo)
Canning, Victor, *Twist of the Knife* (Cairo)
Christie, Agatha, *Death on the Nile*
Dickson, Carter, *The Curse of the Bronze Lamp* (Cairo)
Harvester, Simon, *Treacherous Road*
Heckstall-Smith, Anthony, *Man with Yellow Shoes*
Hocking, Anne, *Nile Green* (Cairo)
Jarvis, Henry W., *House of Silence* (Cairo)
Jefferies, Ian, *Thirteen Days*
Leonard, Charles, *Expert in Murder* (Cairo)
MacKenzie, Nigel, *Murder over Karnak*
McKinley, Frances, *Death Sails the Nile*
Manchester, William, *Beard the Lion* (Cairo)
Mason, F. Van Wyck, *The Cairo Garter Murders*
Munslow, Bruce, *Deep Sand*
———. *No Safe Road*
O'Brine, Padraic M., *Corpse to Cairo*
Parsons, Anthony, *Death by the Nile* (Cairo)
Sheraton, N., *Cairo Ring*
Sherwood, J., *Undiplomatic Exit*
Wheatley, D., *Quest of Julian Day*

Europe (Continental)

Adams, Nathan, *The Fifth Horseman*
Albrand, Martha, *The Linden Affair* (Central Europe)
Ambler, Eric, *Background to Danger*
———. *The Schirmer Inheritance*
Bagby, George, *Body in the Basket*
Baker, W. Howard, *Departure Deferred*
Betteridge, Don, *The Package Holiday Spy Case*
Brunner, John, *Wear the Butcher's Medal*
Calvin, Henry, *It's Different Abroad*
Canning, Victor, *Scorpio Letters*
———. *The Whip Hand*
Chaber, M. E., *Wanted: Dead Men*
Cross, James, *To Hell for Half-a-Crown*
Ferguson, John, *Stealthy Terror*
Fox, James M., *Dark Crusade*
Freeling, Nicholas, *King of the Rainy Country*
Gill, Elizabeth, *What Dread Hand?*
Greene, Graham, *Orient Express* (London–Istanbul)
Highsmith, Patricia, *The Two Faces of January*
Jones, Philip, *Month of the Pearl*
Lyall, Gavin, *Midnight Plus One*
Mario, C., *Six Graves to Munich*
Maugham, W. Somerset, *Ashenden*
Mullally, Frederic, *Marianne*
Murray, Paul, *Free Agent*
Nielsen, Helen, *False Witness*
Roth, Holly, *Shadow of a Lady*
Sims, George, *The Terrible Door*
Sinstadt, Gerald, *The Fidelio Score*
Wood, James, *Rain Islands*
Wuorio, Eva-Lis, *Z for Zaborra*

Fiji Islands

Arthur, Frank, *Another Mystery in Suva*
———. *Suva Harbor Mystery*
Vandercook, John W., *Murder in Fiji*

Finland

Gordon, Donald, *The Flight of the Bat*
Long, E. Laurie, *Lumber Ship*
Lyall, Gavin, *The Most Dangerous Game*
Wuorio, Eva-Lis, *Midsummer Lokki*

France

Abdullah, Achmed, *Trail of the Beast*
Abro, Ben, *Assassination* (Paris)
Adams, Herbert, *Mystery and Minette* (French Coast)
Albrand, Martha, *The Mask of Alexander* (Paris)
Allingham, Margery, "Last Act" in *Deadly Duo*
Ambler, Eric, *Epitaph for a Spy* (Riviera)
———. *Kind of Anger* (Paris)
———. *To Catch a Spy* (Riviera)
Ames, Delano, *Corpse Diplomatique* (Provence)
———. *Murder Maestro, Please*
Arley, Catherine, *Dead Man's Bay* (Brittany)
Armstrong, Anthony, *A Room at the Hotel Ambre* (Paris)
Atkey, Philip, *Juniper Rock*
Audemars, Pierre, *Streets of Grass*
———. *Temptations of Hercules*
———. *The Turns of Time* (Paris)
———. *Two Imposters*
Aveline, Claude, *The Fountain at Marlieux*
Baron, Stanley W., *End of the Line*
Beeding, Francis, *Eleven Were Brave*
———. *There Are Thirteen*
Bell, Josephine, *The House Above the River* (Brittany)
Bellairs, George, *Bones in the Wilderness* (Camargue)
———. *Death in High Provence*
———. *Death in Room 5*
Bennett, Kem, *Passport for a Renegade*
Berckman, Evelyn, *Lament for Four Brides*
Berry, John, *Don't Betray Me* (Paris)
Boileau, Pierre and Thomas Narcejac, *Prisoner*
———. *Sleeping Beauty*
Braun, M. G., *Operation Jealousy* (French resort town)
Brickhill, Paul, *War of Nerves* (Paris)
Broad, Peter, *Death on the Beach* (Brittany)
Bude, John, *Another Man's Shadow*
———. *Death on the Riviera*
Burke, Richard, *The Frightened Pigeon*
Calin, Hal J., *Rocks and Ruin* (Paris)
Calvin, Henry, *It's Different Abroad*
Campbell, Alice, *Murder in Paris*
Canning, Victor, *Green Battlefield*
———. *A Handful of Silver*
———. *Limbo Line*
Carey, Wymond, *"No. 101"* (Paris)
Carr, Glyn, *Ice Axe Murders* (Mont Blanc)
Carr, John D., *Captain Cut-Throat*
———. *Emperor's Snuff-Box*
Carstairs, John P., *Gardenias Bruise Easily* (Provence)
Catalan, Henri, *Soeur Angele and the Embarrassed Ladies* (Paris)
———. *Soeur Angele and the Ghosts of Chambord* (Paris)
Chaber, M. E., *So Dead the Rose* (Paris)
Cheyney, Peter, *I'll Say She Does* (Paris)
———. *Ladies Won't Wait*
Clements, Eileen H., *Back in Daylight* (Brittany)
———. *Let or Hindrance* (Calais)
Coles, Manning, *Concrete Crime*
———. *Death of an Ambassador*
———. *Knife for the Juggler* (Paris)
———. *Night Train to Paris*
———. *Three Beans*
Condon, Richard, *An Infinity of Mirrors*
Conte, Manfred, *Jeopardy* (Paris)
Cory, Desmond, *Name of the Game Is Death* (South of France)
———. *This Traitor, Death* (Paris)
Crane, Frances, *Death in the Blue Hour* (Paris)
Crofts, Freeman W., *The Pit-Prop Syndicate*

Cross, Beverly, *The Nightwalkers* (Paris)
Cross, James, *Grave of Heroes* (Paris)
Cumberland, Marten, *Fade Out the Stars* (Paris)
———. *Far Better Dead*
———. *Grave Consequences* (Paris)
———. *House in the Forest*
———. *Murmurs in the Rue Morgue* (Paris)
———. *Out of This World*
———. *Quislings over Paris*
Dodge, David, *Carambola* (Cannes)
———. *To Catch a Thief* (Riviera)
Ellin, Stanley, *The House of Cards* (Paris)
Ely, David, *Trot* (Paris)
Fairlie, Gerald, *Double the Bluff* (Paris)
Farrer, Katherine, *Gownsman's Gallows*
Ferrars, E. X., *Hunt the Tortoise*
Fielding, Archibald, *The Cluny Problem*
Fleming, Ian, *Casino Royale*
Fleming, Joan, *The Good and the Bad*
Flower, Pat, *Wreath of Water Lilies* (Provence)
Franklin, Charles, *Handful of Sinners* (Provence)
———. *Stop That Man*
Freyer, Frederic, *Black, Black Hearse* (Paris)
Gaboriau, Emile, *see* complete listing in Comprehensive Bibliography
Gardner, John, *The Liquidator*
Garth, David, *The Tortured Angel*
"Georgius," *My Fair Lady* (Paris)
Gérard, Francis, *The Mark of the Moon*
Gilbert, Michael, *Death Has Deep Roots*
Gouze, Roger, *A Quiet Game of Bambu* (French Alps)
Graeme, Bruce, *Lady in Black* (Paris)
Graffy, Joseph, *Man Who Was Not Himself*
Gray, Berkeley, *The Big Brain*
Greig, Maysie, *Date with Danger*
Hambledon, Phyllis, *Invitation to Terror* (Dinard)
Head, Matthew, *Murder at the Flea Club* (Paris)
Healey, Ben, *Waiting for a Flea* (Riviera)
Hely, Elizabeth, *I'll Be Judge, I'll Be Jury*
Highsmith, Patricia, *Two Faces of January* (Paris)
Holt, Deben, *Sinner Takes All* (Brittany)
Holt, Victoria, *The King of the Castle* (Southern France)
Home, Michael, *Auber File*
Howatch, Susan, *Call in the Night*
Hunt, Howard, *Violent Ones*
Jacobs, Thomas Curtis Hicks, *Cause for Suspicion* (Pyrenees)
Japrisot, Sebastien, *A Trap for Cinderella* (French resort)
———. *10:30 from Marseilles*
Jepson, Selwyn, *Noise in the Night* (Paris)
Joseph, George, *Needle in the Haystack* (Corsica)
Kane, Frank, *Maid in Paris* (Paris)
Keith, David, *A Matter of Iodine* (Brittany)
Knight, Kathleen, *High Rendezvous*
Lacy, Ed, *Go for the Body* (Paris)
Laflin, Jack, *Spy in White Gloves*
Landon, Christopher, *Shadow of Time* (Loire Inférieure)
Laurent, Cecil St., *The Cautious Maiden*
LeBlanc, Maurice, *see* complete listing in Comprehensive Bibliography
Levene, Philip, *Ambrose in Paris*
Leyford, Henry, *Murder Moon* (Riviera)
Linn, Kay, *Laughing Mountain* (French village)
Lister, Stephen, *Delorme in Deep Water* (Alps)
Lodwick, John, *Love Bade Me Welcome*
Loraine, Philip, *Day of the Arrow* (Auvergne)
Lowndes, Marie, *End of Her Honeymoon* (Paris)
Lyall, Gavin, *Midnight Plus One*
Macardle, Dorothy, *Dark Enchantment* (South of France)
McConnor, Vincent, *French Doll* (Paris)
McGerr, Patricia, *Fatal in My Fashion* (Paris)
MacInnes, Helen, *Double Image* (Paris)
Mackinnon, Allan, *Danger By My Side* (Provence)
Malo, V. G., *And Why Not?* (Paris)
———. *Murder on the Mistral* (Marseilles)
Marlowe, Stephen, *Search for Bruno Heidler*
Marsh, Ngaio, *Spinsters in Jeopardy* (Riviera)
Martin, Shane, *Saracen Shadow* (Gironde)
Mason, John W., *Saboteurs*
Masson, René, *Landru* (Paris)
Mayo, James, *Rebound*
———. *A Season of Nerves*
Merrick, William, *Packard Case* (Paris)
Monteilhet, Hubert, *Return to the Ashes* (Paris)
———. *Road to Hell* (French village)
Munro, James, *The Man Who Sold Death*
Murray, Max, *Good Luck to the Corpse*
———. *A Corpse for Breakfast*
———. *King and the Corpse*
Newman, Bernard, *The Otan Plot* (Paris)
———. *Papa Pontivy and the Maginot Murder*
O'Farrell, William, *The Snakes of St. Cyr* (Marseilles)

Orgill, Douglas, *Man in the Dark* (French coast)
Palmer, Bruce, *Flesh and Blood* (Arles)
Parker, Robert, *Ticket to Oblivion* (Paris)
Paul, Elliot, *Hugger-Mugger in the Louvre* (Paris)
———. *Mysterious Mickey Finn* (Paris)
———. *Mayhem in B Flat* (Paris)
Radford, Edwin and Mona A., *Death at the Château Noir*
Reed, Eliot, *Charter to Danger* (Cannes)
Reynaud-Fourton, Alain, *The Reluctant Assassin*
Robertson, Colin, *Calling Peter Gayleigh*
———. *Peter Gayleigh Flies High* (Provence)
Robinson, Ethelbert, *Death Designs a Dress* (Paris)
Ronald, E. B., *Sort of Madness* (Paris)
Royce, Kenneth, *My Turn to Die*
Rushton, Charles, *Devil's Power* (Paris)
Rutherford, Douglas, *Creeping Flesh* (Paris)
Sanders, Bruce, *To Catch a Spy*
Sayers, Dorothy L., *Clouds of Witness*
Shearing, Joseph, *Spider in the Cup*
Sherwood, John, *Ambush for Anatol* (Paris)
Simenon, Georges, *see* early novels in Comprehensive Bibliography
Slater, Humphrey, *Three Among Mountains*
Stafford, Marjorie, *Death Plays the Gramophone* (Paris)
Stein, Aaron M., *Moonmilk and Murder* (Dordogne)
Stewart, Mary, *Madam, Will You Talk?* (Provence)
———. *Thunder on the Right*
———. *Nine Coaches Waiting* (Haute-Savoie)
Strange, John Stephen, *Handful of Silver* (Paris)
Summerton, Margaret, *Nightingale at Noon* (Camargue)
Teilhet, Darwin and Hildegarde, *Double Agent*
Teilhet, Hildegarde, *Private Undertaking* (Riviera)
Toussaint-Samat, Jean, *Shoes That Walked Twice* (Marseilles)
Usher, Frank, *Death in Error*
———. *Death in Waiting*
———. *Price of Death* (Provence)
Vestal, Stanley, *Wine Room Murder*
Wallis, Ruth, *Blood from a Stone* (Hautes-Pyrénées)
Warriner, Thurman, *Death's Dateless Night*
Welcome, John, *Run for Cover* (Provence)
West, Elliot, *Man Running*
Wheatley, Dennis, *Launching of Roger Brook*
———. *Man Who Killed the King*
———. *Prisoner in the Mask* (Paris)
———. *Rising Storm*
———. *Shadow of Tyburn Tree*

Germany

Allain, Marcel, *The Yellow Document; or, Fantômas of Berlin*
Angellotti, Marion, *Three Black Bags*
Berckman, Evelyn, *The Evil of Time*
———. *The Strange Bedfellow*
Betteridge, Don, *Case of the Berlin Spy*
———. *Potsdam Murder Plot*
Birch, Bruce, *Subway in the Sky*
Blair, Charles and A. J. Wallis, *Thunder Above*
Braun, M. G., *Operation Atlantis* (Berlin)
Brown, Carter, *The Girl from Outer Space*
Burnett, Hallie, *Watch on the Wall* (Berlin)
Cargill, Leslie, *Lady Was Elusive*
Chaber, M. E., *No Grave for March* (East Berlin)
———. *Splintered Man* (East Berlin)
Coles, Manning, *All That Glitters*
———. *Green Hazard*
———. *No Entry*
———. *Now or Never*
Copp, DeWitt, *Pursuit of Agent M* (East Germany)
Cory, Desmond, *Pilgrim at the Gate*
———. *Pilgrim on the Island*
Cross, James, *The Dark Road* (West Germany)
Deighton, Len, *Funeral in Berlin*
Dibner, Martin, *A God for Tomorrow*
Fry, Pete, *The Red Stockings*
Fullerton, Alexander, *Bury the Past*
Gainham, Sarah, *The Cold Dark Night*
Haggard, William, *Venetian Blind* (Düsseldorf)
Hall, Adam, *The Quiller Memorandum* (Berlin)
Hardy, Lindsay, *Faceless Ones*
Hughes, K., *Long Echo*
Hunter, Jack D., *One of Us Works for Them*
Innes, Hammond, *Air Bridge*

Kathrens, William, *Benny Went First*
Kaye, Mary, *Death Walked in Berlin*
Kielland, Axel, *Dangerous Honeymoon*
Kirst, Hans, *Brothers in Arms*
Lakin, Richard, *The Body Fell on Berlin*
Le Carré, John, *The Looking Glass War*
———. *Call for the Dead*
———. *Spy Who Came in from the Cold*
Lee, Elsie, *Dark Moon, Lost Lady*
Longstreth, T. Morris, *Dangerline* (Berlin)
McDougall, Murdoch, *Chase the Snowman*
———. *Soft as Silk*
McGovern, James, *Berlin Couriers*
MacKenzie, Donald, *Double Exposure* (Düsseldorf)
Malcolm, Jean, *Discourse with Shadows* (Frankfort)
Marlowe, Derek, *Dandy in the Aspic* (Berlin)
Morrison, Emmeline, *Tale Untold*
Raine, Richard, *The Corder Index*
Roth, Holly, *Content Assignment*
Sawkins, Raymond, *Snow in Paradise*
Shearing, Joseph, *Moss Rose*
Storm, Joan, *Dark Emerald*
Underwood, Michael, *The Unprofessional Spy* (Berlin)
West, Elliot, *The Night Is a Time for Listening*

Greece

Appleby, John, *Aphrodite Means Death*
———. *Arms of Venus*
———. *Captive City*
Ayrton, Elizabeth, *Silence in Crete*
Bell, Josephine, *The Catalyst*
Blake, Nicholas, *The Widow's Cruise*
Ferrars, E. X., *No Peace for the Wicked*
Graham, Winston, *Greek Fire* (Athens)
Gruber, Frank, *The Greek Affair* (Athens)
Hay, Frances, *There Was No Moon* (Crete)
Highsmith, Patricia, *Two Faces of January* (Athens)
Lee, Elsie, *Spy at the Villa Miranda*
MacInnes, Helen, *Decision at Delphi*
———. *Double Image* (Mykonos)
Marlowe, Hugh, *Passage by Night*
Martin, Shane, *The Third Statue*
Mitchell, Gladys, *Come Away, Death*
Parker, Richard, *Only Some Had Guns*
Patterson, Henry, *The Dark Side of the Island*
Stewart, Mary, *My Brother Michael* (Delphi)
———. *The Moon-Spinners* (Crete)
———. *This Rough Magic* (Corfu)
Whitney, Phyllis, *Seven Tears for Apollo*

Hawaii

Adams, Cleve F., *And Sudden Death*
Biggers, Earl D., *see* complete listing in Comprehensive Bibliography
Corrigan, Mark, *Honolulu Snatch*
Davis, Mildred, *Strange Corner*
Fair, A. A., *Some Women Won't Wait*
Ford, Leslie, *Honolulu Story*
Hamilton, Donald, *The Betrayers*
Horn, F. S., *The Twin Serpents*
Huntsberry, William, *Harbor of Little Boats*
Sheridan, Juanita, *Kahuna Killer*
———. *Mamo Murders*
———. *Waikiki Widow*
———. *What Dark Secret?*

Holland (Netherlands)

Aarons, Edward S., *Assignment–Lowlands* (Amsterdam)
Albrand, Martha, *No Surrender*
Canning, Victor, *House of Seven Flies*
Coles, Manning, *Diamonds to Amsterdam*
Freeling, Nicholas, *Because of the Cats*
———. *Double Barrel*
———. *Death in Amsterdam*
———. *A Question of Loyalty*
Fry, Pete, *The Red Stockings* (Amsterdam)
Graham, Winston, *The Little Walls*
Hartog, Jan de, *The Inspector* (Amsterdam to Israel)
Miller, Sigmund, *The Snow Leopard*
Simenon, Georges, *Maigret Abroad*
Weeks, William, *Knock and Wait Awhile*

Hong Kong

Black, Gavin, *The Eyes Around Me*
Boswell, John, *Blue Pheasant*
Chaber, M. E., *Man in the Middle*
Chase, James Hadley, *Coffin from Hong Kong*
Cooke, David C., *The 14th Agent*
Daniels, Norman, *Baron of Hong Kong*
Dark, James, *Assignment-Hong Kong*
Gann, Ernest, *Soldier of Fortune*
Harvester, Simon, *Bamboo Screen*
McCutchan, Philip, *Skyprobe*
Mason, F. Van Wyck, *Hong Kong Airbase Murders*
Page, Michael, *Spare the Vanquished*
Peters, Bryan, *Hong Kong Kill*

Hungary

Aarons, Edward S., *Assignment–Budapest*
———. *Assignment–Stella Marni*
Desmond, Hugh, *The Strangler*
Fagyas, M., *The Fifth Woman* (Budapest)
———. *The Widow-Maker*
Gallico, Paul, *Trial by Terror* (Budapest)
Jeffries, Ian, *It Wasn't Me*
MacLean, Alistair, *Secret Ways*
Mason, F. Van Wyck, *Budapest Parade Murders*
Parker, Robert B., *Passport to Peril* (Budapest)
Pollard, A. O., *Death Parade*

Iceland

Cousins, Edmond G., *Untimely Frost*
Fry, Pete, *The Bright Green Waistcoat*

India

Allison, William, *Turnstiles of Night*
Blochman, Lawrence, *Bombay Mail*
———. *Red Snow at Darjeeling*
Cooke, David C., *c/o American Embassy*
Harvester, Simon, *Tiger in the North*
Jay, Charlotte, *Yellow Turban*
Kaye, Mary, *Death Walked in Kashmir*
———. *Shadow of the Moon*
Keating, H. R. F., *The Perfect Murder* (Bombay)
Leasor, James, *Spylight* (Himalayas)
Mason, F. Van Wyck, *Himalayan Assignment*
Mather, Berkley, *Pass Beyond Kashmir*
———. *The Gold of Malabar*
Mundy, Max, *Death Is a Tiger*
Parsons, Anthony, *Death of a Governor*
Robinson, Philip, *Pakistani Agent* (Bombay)
Rushton, Charles, *Dark Amid the Blaze* (Native States)
St. John, David, *Towers of Silence* (Bombay)
Stuart, Alan, *Unwilling Agent*
Thorne, E. P., *Sinister Sanctuary*
Webster, F. A. M., *Beneath the Mask*

Indonesia

Ambler, Eric, *State of Siege*
Ballinger, Bill, *Spy in the Java Sea*

Iran

Aarons, Edward, *Assignment–Moon Girl*
Stewart, Desmond, *Leopard in the Grass*

Iraq

Christie, Agatha, *They Came to Baghdad*
Mackinnon, A., *Assignment in Iraq*
———. *Red-winged Angel*
———. *Summons from Baghdad*
Wadham, Ruth, *Weekend in Baghdad*

Ireland

Bamford, Francis and Viola Bankes, *Vicious Circle*
Cleeve, Brian, *Death of a Painted Lady* (Dublin)
———. *Vote X for Treason*
Dillon, Ellis, *Death at Crane's Court* (Galway)
———. *Sent to His Account*
DuBois, Theodora, *The Cavalier's Corpse*
———. *Shannon Terror*
Fitzgerald, Nigel, *Black Welcome*
———. *The Candles Are All Out*
———. *Day of the Adder* (Rural Ireland)
———. *House Is Falling*
———. *Midsummer Malice*
———. *Rosy Pastor*
———. *Student Body* (Dublin)
———. *Suffer a Witch*
Gaines, Robert, *The Invisible Evil*
Garve, Andrew, *House of Soldiers*
Guinness, Katherine, *Fishermen's End* (Kerry)
Helvick, James, *The Horses*
Kenyon, Michael, *May You Die in Ireland*
Landon, Christopher, *Dead Men Rise Up Never*
Loraine, Philip, *Nightmare in Dublin*
O'Neill, Desmond, *Life Has No Price*
O'Sullivan, James B., *Someone Walked over My Grave*
Pim, Sheila, *A Hive of Suspects*
Piper, Peter, *Woman Delia* (Northern Ireland)
Pollard, M., *Thicker Than Water*
———. *Minutes of a Murder*
Redmond, Liam, *Death Is So Kind* (Dublin)
Rodney, Bryan, *Owl Flies Home*
St. John, David, *On Hazardous Duty*
Stein, Aaron M., *Shoot Me Dacent*
Stewart, J. I. M., *Case of the Journeying Boy*
Walsh, Maurice, *Danger Under the Moon*
Webster, H. M., *Tontine Treasure*
———. *Ballycronin Mystery*
White, William J., *One for the Road* (Dublin)

Israel

Hesky, Olga, *The Serpent's Smile*
Jefferies, Ian, *Thirteen Days*
Manchester, William, *Beard the Lion* (Gaza Strip)
Munslow, Bruce, *No Safe Road*
Murray, Paul, *The Free Agent*
Spark, Muriel, *The Mandelbaum Gate*
Young, George, *Man Called Lenz*

Italy

Aarons, Edward S., *Assignment–Sorrento Siren*
———. *Assignment–Palermo*
———. *Assignment–Lili Lamaris* (Rome)
Albrand, Martha, *After Midnight*
———. *Mask of Alexander* (Venice)
———. *Without Orders*
Allen, Eric, *The Man Who Chose Death*
Ambler, Eric, *Cause for Alarm*
Andersch, Alfred, *The Redhead* (Milan–Venice)
Appleby, John, *Venice Preserve Me*
Black, Ian Stuart, *Passionate City* (Rome)
Blackburn, Barbara, *City of Forever* (Rome)
Brand, Christianna, *Tour de Force*
Bryan, John, *Contessa Came Too*
Caillou, Alan, *Who'll Buy My Evil* (Rome)

Calvin, Henry, *The Italian Gadget*
Canning, Victor, *Bird of Prey*
———. *The Chasm*
Chaber, M. E., *A Lonely Walk* (Rome)
Coffman, Virginia, *The Demon Tower* (Napoleonic Italy)
Cohen, Octavus, *Florian Slappey Goes Abroad*
Creasey, John, *Death of an Assassin* (Milan)
Deane, Norman, *Double for Murder*
Donati, Sergio, *The Paper Tomb*
Douglas, Malcolm, *Rain of Terror* (Naples)
Downes, Donald, *The Eastern Dinner* (Rome)
Dudley, Ernest, *Dr. Morelle and Destiny*
Ellin, Stanley, *The House of Cards*
Evans, Alfred J., *All's Fair on Lake Garda*
Ferrars, E. X., *Alibi for a Witch*
Gair, Malcolm, *Sapphires on Wednesday*
Gardner, Alan, *Six Day Week* (Rome)
Gardner, John, *Amber Nile* (Lake Maggiore)
Gibbs-Smith, Charles, *The Caroline Affair* (Venice)
Glanville, Brian, *After Rome, Africa*
Graham, Winston, *Little Walls*
———. *Night Without Stars*
Haggard, William, *Venetian Blind*
Halliday, Leonard, *Devil's Door*
Harling, Robert, *The Endless Colonnade* (Rome)
Highsmith, Patricia, *Those Who Walk Away*
Hotchner, A. E., *The Dangerous American*
Innes, Hammond, *Dead and Alive*
King, Francis, *Dividing Stream*
Knight, Kathleen, *Invitation to Vengeance* (Sicily)
Lebherz, Richard, *Altars of the Heart* (Rome)
Lett, Gordon, *Many-Headed Monster*
Lorac, E. C. R., *Murder on a Monument*
McGivern, William, *Margin of Terror* (Rome)
McGuire, Paul, *Enter Three Witches*
MacInnes, Helen, *North from Rome*
Marshall, Raymond, *Mission to Sienna*
———. *Mission to Venice*
———. *You Find Him, I'll Fix Him*
Moyes, Patricia, *Dead Men Don't Ski*
Rabe, Peter, *A House in Naples*
Revell, Louisa, *See Rome and Die*
Rutherford, Douglas, *Long Echo*
Sheers, James, *The Counterfeit Courier*
Stein, Aaron M., *Sitting Up Dead*
Sterling, Thomas, *The Evil of the Day* (Venice)
Stern, Richard M., *The Bright Road to Fear*
Stone, David, *The Tired Spy* (Florence, Elba)
Storm, Joan, *Deadly Diamond*
Townsend, Paul, *Died O' Wednesday*

Japan

Aarons, Edward S., *Assignment–Manchurian Doll*
Bellah, James, *Brass Gong Tree*
Bender, W., Jr., *Tokyo Intrigue*
Black, Gavin, *Dead Man Calling* (Tokyo)
Dark, James, *Assignment in Tokyo*
Fleming, Ian, *You Only Live Twice*
Harvester, Simon, *Copper Butterfly*
MacPartland, John, *Tokyo Doll*
Marquand, John P., *Mr. Moto's Three Aces*
———. *Stopover Tokyo*
Middleton, Ted, *Operation Tokyo*
Munro, James, *Die Rich, Die Happy*
Norman, Earl, *Kill Me in Shimbashi*
———. *Kill Me in Yokohama*
———. *Kill Me in Yoshiwara*
Roberts, James H., *The Q Document*
St. John, David, *One of Our Agents Is Missing* (Tokyo)
Seward, Jack, *Cave of the Chinese Skeletons* (Tokyo)
Wynd, Oswald, *Walk Softly, Men Praying*

Java

Crisp, Frank, *Fazackerly's Millions*
———. *The Java Wreckmen*

Jordan

Christie, Agatha, *Appointment with Death*
Gruber, Frank, *The Bridge of Sand* (Galilee)

Korea

Harvester, Simon, *The Flying Horse* (North Korea)

Lapland

Lyall, Gavin, *The Most Dangerous Game*

Lebanon

Alan, Roy, *My Bonnie Lies Under the Sea*
Atiyeh, Edward, *The Cruel Fire*
Griswold, George, *Red Pawns*
Jay, Charlotte, *Arms for Adonis*
Stewart, Mary, *The Gabriel Hounds*

Malaya

Ambler, Eric, *A Passage of Arms*
Black, Gavin, *A Wind of Death*
Corrigan, Mark, *Singapore Downbeat*
Dark, James, *The Bamboo Bomb*
Derby, Mark, *Five Nights in Singapore*
———. *Big Water*
———. *Malayan Rose* (Singapore)
———. *Out of Asia Alive*
———. *Sun in the Hunter's Eye*
———. *The Sunlit Ambush*
———. *The Tigress*
East, Michael, *McCreary Moves In*
Harvester, Simon, *The Golden Fear*
———. *An Hour Before Zero*
———. *Yesterday Walkers*
Hastings, Michael, *Death in Deep Green*
———. *Man Who Came Back*
Mason, F. Van Wyck, *Singapore Exile Murders*
Meade, Dorothy C., *Fatal Shadows*
Sherwood, John, *Two Died in Singapore*
Tannock, Malcolm, *Uneasy Money*
Thorne, E. P., *Red Bamboo*
Trevor, Elleston, *Pesang Run*

Malta

Betteridge, Don, *Gibraltar Conspiracy*
Butler, Gwendoline, *Coffin in Malta*
Wills, Cecil M., *The Dead Voice*

Manchuria

Aarons, Edward S., *Assignment–Manchurian Doll*

Mediterranean

Bagley, Desmond, *The Golden Keel*
Brand, Christianna, *Tour de Force*
Hambledon, Phyllis, *Passports to Murder*
Lyall, Gavin, *The Wrong Side of the Sky*
Martin, Shane, *Mourner's Voyage*
Mayo, James, *Hammerhead*
Wynne, Fred E., *The Mediterranean Mystery*

Mexico

Ayer, Frederick, *The Man in the Mirror*
Baker, Charlotte, *House of Roses*
———. *Sombrero for Miss Brown*
Blanc, Suzanne, *The Green Stone*
———. *The Rose Window*
———. *The Yellow Villa*
Buckingham, Bruce, *Boiled Alive*
Cain, James, *Serenade*
Chambers, Whitman, *Action at World's End*
Chandler, Raymond, *The Long Goodbye*
Crane, Frances, *Ultra-Violet Widow*
Downing, George Todd, *The Last Trumpet*
———. *Murder on Tour*
———. *Murder on the Tropic*
———. *Night Over Mexico*
Eberhart, Mignon G., *Wings of Fear*
Highsmith, Patricia, *A Game for the Living*
Home, Geoffrey, *Street of the Crying Woman* (Mexico City)
Hughes, Dorothy, *The Candy Kid*
Knight, Kathleen, *Birds of Ill Omen*
———. *Blue Horse of Taxco*
———. *Dying Echo*
———. *Stream Sinister*
Koehler, Robert, *The Hooded Vulture Murders*
MacNeil, Neil, *Mexican Slay Ride*
Markson, David, *Miss Doll, Go Home* (Artist's colony)
Millar, Margaret, *The Listening Walls* (Mexico City)
Murray, Cromwell, *Day of the Dead*
Olsen, D. B., *Bring the Bride a Shroud*
Palmer, Stuart, *Puzzle of the Blue Banderilla*
Prather, Richard S., *Pattern for Panic*
Quentin, P., *The Follower*
———. *Run to Death*
Rayter, Joe, *Stab in the Dark*
Russell, Charlotte M., *Ill Met in Mexico*
Stein, Aaron M., *The Dead Thing in the Pool*
———. *Death Meets 400 Rabbits* (Acapulco)
———. *Second Burial*
———. *Three with Blood*
———. *Mask for Murder* (Yucatan)
Waer, Jack, *Seventeen and Black* (Mexico City)
Weintraub, Sidney, *Mexican Slay Ride*

Middle East

Aarons, Edward, *Assignment–Zoraya*
Alan, Roy, *My Bonnie Lies Under the Sea*
Barton, Donald R., *Once in Aleppo*
Caillou, Alan, *Journey to Orassia*
Gruber, Frank, *Bridge of Sand*
Haggard, William, *Powder Barrel*
Harvester, Simon, *Lucifer at Sunset*
———. *Treacherous Road* (Yemen)
Leasor, James, *Passport to Oblivion*
Parker, Richard, *Only Some Had Guns*
Sherwood, John, *Undiplomatic Exit*
Tranter, Nigel, *The Enduring Flame*
Winston, Peter, *Assignment to Bahrein*
See also individual countries.

Monaco

Albrand, Martha, *A Day in Monte Carlo*
Armstrong, Anthony, *The Strange Case of Mr. Pelham*
Heckstall-Smith, Anthony, *Where There Are Vultures*
Irving, Peter, *An Italian Called Mario*
Mason, A. E. W., *At the Villa Rose*
Oppenheim, E. Phillips, *Murder at Monte Carlo*

Netherlands *see* Holland

New Guinea

Harvester, Simon, *The Paradise Men*
Jay, Charlotte, *Beat Not the Bones*
Muir, Dennis, *Death Defies the Doctor*
Vandercook, John W., *Murder in New Guinea*

New Zealand

Courtier, Sidney, *Mimic a Murderer*
Eden, Dorothy, *Bride by Candlelight*
———. *Lamb to the Slaughter*
Jay, Simon, *Death of a Skin Diver*
———. *Hank of Hair*
Marsh, Ngaio, *Colour Scheme*
———. *Died in the Wool*
———. *Vintage Murder*
Messenger, Elizabeth, *Dive Deep for Death*
———. *Growing Evil*
———. *Light on Murder*
———. *Material Witness*
———. *Murder Stalks the Bay*
Rhodes, Denys, *Fly Away, Peter*
Salter, Elizabeth, *Death in a Mist*

Norway

Innes, Hammond, *Blue Ice*
Landon, Christopher, *Hornet's Nest*

Pakistan

Aarons, Edward S., *Assignment–Karachi*
Mather, Berkley, *The Pass Beyond Kashmir*
Robinson, Philip, *The Pakistani Agent*

Panama

Amos, Alan, *Fatal Harvest*
———. *Panic in Paradise*
Coxe, George H., *Death at the Isthmus*

Philippines

Archer, Frank, *The Malabang Pearl*
Chamberlain, E., *Appointment in Manila*
———. *Manila Hemp*
Coxe, George H., *Dangerous Legacy*
Knight, Clifford, *Affair of the Circus Queen*

Poland

Clifford, Francis, *The Naked Runner* (Warsaw)
Cory, Desmond, *Pilgrim at the Gate*
Garve, Andrew, *The Ashes of Loda*

Iams, Jack, *A Shot of Murder*
Kirst, Hans, *Night of the Generals* (Warsaw)
MacInnes, Helen, *While Still We Live*
Marshall, Bruce, *Month of Falling Leaves*
Wheatley, Dennis, *Codeword–Golden Fleece*
Wuorio, Eva-Lis, *Z for Zaborra*

Portugal

Ainsworth, Harriet, *Shadow on the Water*
Brennan, Frederick, *Memo to a Firing Squad* (Lisbon)
Bridge, Ann, *The Portuguese Escape*
Cadell, Elizabeth, *Shadows on the Water* (Lisbon)
Fleming, Joan, *Death of a Sardine*
Footner, Hulbert, *Unneutral Murder* (Lisbon)
Lee, Babs, *Passport to Oblivion*
Lee, Elsie, *Curse of Carranca* (Lisbon)
Telfair, Richard, *Target for Tonight*
Walker, David E., *Diamonds for Danger*
Wuorio, Eva-Lis, *Woman with the Portuguese Basket*

Puerto Rico

Gayle, Newton, *Murder at 28:10*
Knight, Adam, *Sunburned Corpse*
O'Donnell, Lillian, *Murder Under the Sun*

Romania

Mason, F. Van Wyck, *The Bucharest Ballerina Murders*
Williams, Eric, *Dragoman Pass*

Scotland

Acland, Alice, *Person of Discretion*
Austwick, John, *Highland Homicide*
Bindloss, Harold, *Lone Hand*
Blackstock, Lee, *All Men Are Murderers* (Highlands)
Boland, John, *The Catch*
Bridge, Ann, *The Dangerous Islands* (Hebrides)
Caird, Janet, *Murder Reflected*
———. *Perturbing Spirit*
Calvin, Henry, *It's Different Abroad*
Cleaton, Irene, *The Outsider* (Edinburgh)
Devine, David, *His Own Appointed Day*
Elgin, Mary, *Highland Masquerade*
Gardiner, Dorothy K., *The Seventh Mourner*
Glaister, John, *The Power of Poison*
Gray, Berkeley, *Conquest in Scotland*
Gunn, Neil M., *Lost Chart*
Hamilton, Henrietta, *At Night to Die*
Hastings, MacDonald, *Cork on the Water*
Hely, Elizabeth, *A Mark of Displeasure* (Edinburgh)
Howarth, David, *Thieves' Hole*
Howatch, Susan, *The Waiting Sands* (Northern Scotland)
Johns, William E., *Man Who Lost His Way*
Kellier, Elizabeth, *Nurse to a Stranger*
Kelly, Mary, *Dead Man's Riddle* (Edinburgh)
Knox, Bill, *see* listing in Comprehensive Bibliography
McCloy, Helen, *The One That Got Away*
McCutcheon, Hugh, *And the Moon Was Full*
McKelway, St. Clair, *The Edinburgh Caper*
MacLean, Alistair, *When Eight Bells Toll*
McTyre, Paul, *Bar Sinister*
Malloch, Peter, *Fugitives Road*
Marsh, J., *Small and Deadly*
Mitchell, Gladys, *My Bones Will Keep* (Edinburgh)
Muir, Augustus, *Dark Adventure*
Murray, William H., *Appointment in Tibet*

Sayers, Dorothy L., *Five Red Herrings*
Tey, Josephine, *The Singing Sands*
Walling, Robert, *Marooned with Murder*
Walsh, Maurice, *Nine Strings to Your Bow*

South America

Atlee, Philip, *The Irish Beauty Contract*
Ayala, Francisco, *Death as a Way of Life*
Bagley, Desmond, *High Citadel* (Andes)
Chaber, M. E., *The Gallows Garden*
———. *Six Who Ran* (Brazil)
Charteris, Leslie, *Senor Saint*
Clifford, Francis, *Act of Mercy*
Collins, Norman, *Flames Coming Out of the Top*
Cory, Desmond, *Johnny Goes South* (Argentina)
———. *Johnny Goes West*
Coxe, George H., *Assignment in Guiana*
———. *One Minute Past Eight* (Venezuela)
Cumberland, Marten, *Nobody Is Safe* (Buenos Aires)
Desmond, Hugh, *Doorway to Death* (Buenos Aires)
Dodge, David, *The Long Escape* (Chile)
———. *Plunder of the Sun* (Chile, Peru)
———. *The Red Tassel* (Bolivia)
Dundas, Lawrence, *He Liked Them Murderous* (Andes)
East, Roger, *The Pearl Choker* (Venezuela)
Fish, Robert L., *Brazilian Sleigh Ride* (Brazil)
———. *Isle of the Snakes* (Brazil)
———. *The Shrunken Head*
———. *Diamond Bubble* (Brazil)
Haggard, William, *Closed Circuit*
Hall, Adam, *The Volcanoes of San Domingo*
Hiscock, Robin, *The Killer Wind*
Holbrook, Marion, *Crime Wind*
Hough, Stanley B., *Mission in Guemo*
Kelsey, Vera, *The Owl Sang Three Times*
Laflin, Jack, *The Spy in White Gloves* (Jungles)
Lawrence, H. L., *The Sparta Medallion*
Leonard, Charles, *Pursuit in Peru*
Levey, Robert, *Murder in Lima*
Meynell, Lawrence, *Danger Round the Corner*
Pattinson, James, *Contact Mr. Delgado*
Paul, Elliot, *Summer in December*
Pollard, Alfred O., *Deal in Death*
Priestley, J. B., *Saturn Over the Water*
Quirk, John, *Survivor* (Jungles)
Roby, Mary L., *Afraid of the Dark* (Rio)
Sage, Dana, *The Moon Was Red* (LaPaz, Bolivia)
Silliphant, Sterling, *Maracaibo* (Venezuela)
Spinelli, Marcus, *Assignment Without Glory* (Brazil)
Sutherland, Neil, *The Pawn*
Tranter, Nigel, *Rio d'Oro*
Winston, Peter, *The ABC Affair* (La Paz)
Wood, Clement, *Death on the Pampas* (Buenos Aires)
Wood, James, *The Sealer* (Tierra del Fuego)
Woolrich, Cornell, *Black Alibi*

Southeast Asia

Aarons, Edward S., *Assignment–Cong-Hai Kill*
———. *Assignment–Sulu Sea*
See also individual countries

South Seas

Bellah, James W., *Seven Must Die*
Stevenson, Robert Louis, *The Wrecker* (Marquesas Islands)
Stewart, J. I. M., *Lament for a Maker*

Spain

Allen, Eric, *Perilous Passport*
Ames, Delano, *Landscape with Corpse*
———. *Man in the Tricorn Hat*
———. *Man with Three Chins*

———. *Man with the Three Jaguars*
———. *No Mourning for the Matador* (Barcelona)
Bagby, George, *The Body in the Basket*
Ballard, K. G., *The Bar Sinister*
———. *The Coast of Fear*
Bonett, John and Emery, *Better Off Dead*
———. *The Private Face of Murder*
Bryan, Michael, *Murder in Majorca*
Burke, Richard, *The Frightened Pigeon*
Canning, Victor, *Manasco Road*
Chaber, M. E., *The Man Inside*
Clifford, Francis, *Third Side of the Coin*
Cory, Desmond, *Stranglehold*
———. *Deadfall*
———. *Undertow*
Costello, Paul, *Cat and the Fiddle*
Crockett, A., *Toys of Desperation*
Deane, Norman, *Death in the Spanish Sun*
Douglas, Malcolm, *Prey by Night*
Fitzgerald, Kevin, *Quiet Under the Sun*
Fry, Pete, *The Black Beret*
Hamilton, Donald, *The Wrecking Crew*
Hocking, Anne, *Killing Kin*
———. *Murder at Mid-day*
Jacobs, T. C. H., *Deadly Race*
Lee, Babs, *Passport to Oblivion*
McGivern, William, *A Choice of Assassins*
———. *The Caper of the Golden Bulls*
———. *Seven Lies South*
McGuire, Paul, *Enter Three Witches*
Mara, Bernard, *Bullet for My Lady* (Barcelona)
Marlowe, Stephen, *Drum Beat–Madrid*
Mercer, Ian, *Mission to Majorca*
Perowne, Barry, *Tilted Moon*
Pressburger, Emerick, *Killing a Mouse on Sunday*
Robertson, Colin, *Smuggler's Moon*
Roos, Kelley, *A Few Days in Madrid*
Rougvie, Cameron, *Medal from Pamplona*
Sanderson, Douglas, *Cry Wolfram*
———. *Mark It for Murder*
Spicer, Bart, *Day of the Dead*
Story, Jack T., *Money Goes Round and Round*
Strachan, Tony S., *Short Weekend*
West, Elliot, *Man Running*

Sweden

Aarons, Edward, *Assignment–Black Viking*
Page, Michael F., *Innocent Bystander*
Starnes, Richard, *Requiem in Utopia*
Tranter, Nigel, *Man Behind the Curtain*
Walter, Hugh, *Bullet for Charles*
York, Andrew, *The Eliminator*

Switzerland

Aarons, Edward, *Assignment–School for Spies*
Albrand, Martha, *Hunted Woman*
———. *None Shall Know*
Audemars, Pierre, *A Woven Web*
Bennett, Dorothea, *Under the Skin* (Ski resort)
Bridge, Ann, *Numbered Account* (Geneva)
Carr, Glyn, *Murder on the Matterhorn*
Carr, John D., *In Spite of Thunder* (Geneva)
Carter, Nick, *The Eyes of the Tiger*
Cleeve, Brian, *Assignment to Vengeance*
Daniels, Norman, *Operation "N"*
"Diplomat," *Slow Death at Geneva*
Dürrenmatt, Frederic, *The Judge and His Hangman*
———. *The Pledge*
Fletcher, Lucille, *And Presumed Dead* (Swiss resort)
Gardner, Erle Stanley, *Case of the Musical Cow*
Gaskin, Catherine, *File on Devlin*
Griswold, George, *The Pinned Man*
Halliday, Leonard, *The Smiling Spider*
Knight, Kathleen, *High Rendezvous*
Leasor, James, *Spylight*
MacInnes, Helen, *Pray for a Brave Heart*
Mathews, Nieves, *She Died Without Light*
Moyes, Patricia, *Dead Men Don't Ski* (Dolomites)
———. *Death on the Agenda* (Geneva)
Snell, Edmund, *Murder in Switzerland*
Summerton, Margaret, *Ring of Mischief*

Syria

Maddock, Stephen, *Overture to Trouble*

Tahiti

Gardner, Alan, *Assignment–Tahiti*

Simenon, Georges, *Stowaway*

Thailand

Aarons, Edward S., *Assignment–Cong-Hai Kill*

Blackstock, Charity, *When the Sun Goes Down*

Corrigan, Mark, *Menace in Siam*

Hall, Adam, *The Ninth Directive* (Bangkok)

Harvester, Simon, *Dragon Road*

Mason, F. Van Wyck, *Secret Mission to Bangkok*

Trieste

Cory, Desmond, *Intrigue*

Harvester, Simon, *Delay in Danger*

Howe, Russell W., *Behold, the City*

King, Clifford, *A Place to Hide*

Rutherford, Douglas, *Flight into Peril*

Tunisia

Fergusson, Bernard, *The Rare Adventure*

Turkey

Aarons, Edward S., *Assignment–Ankara*

Ambler, Eric, *Journey into Fear*

———. *Coffin for Dimitrios*

———. *Light of Day* (Istanbul)

Bridge, Ann, *The Dark Moment*

Carter, Nick, *Istanbul*

Castle, John, *The Seventh Fury*

Fleming, Ian, *From Russia with Love*

Fleming, Joan, *Nothing Is the Number When You Die* (Istanbul)

———. *When I Get Rich* (Istanbul)

Greene, Graham, *Orient Express* (London–Istanbul)

Mason, F. Van Wyck, *Dardanelles Derelict*

Rathbone, Julian, *Diamonds Bid* (Ankara)

Rosten, Leo, *A Most Private Intrigue* (Istanbul)

Wheatley, Dennis, *The Eunuch of Stamboul*

Whitney, Phyllis, *Black Amber*

Wood, Clement, *Death in Ankara*

U.S.S.R.

Aarons, Edward, *Assignment–Suicide*

Bax, Roger, *Came the Dawn*

Behn, Noel, *The Kremlin Letter*

Bruce, J., *Deep Freeze*

Daniels, Norman, *Spy Ghost*

Davis, Howard C., *The Renegade from Russia*

Frayn, Michael, *Russian Interpreter*

Garve, Andrew, *Ashes of Loda*

———. *Murder in Moscow*

Harvester, Simon, *Red Road*

Kendrick, Baynard, *Murder Made in Moscow*

Laflin, Jack, *The Reluctant Spy*

Luther, Jack, *Intermind*

McCutchan, Philip, *Moscow Coach*

MacKenzie, Nigel, *Red Light*
Mair, George B., *Death's Foot Forward* (Moscow)
Marsh, John, *Brain of Paul Menoloff*
Pattinson, James, *Mystery of the Gregory Kotovsky*
Pollard, Alfred O., *The Iron Curtain*
Reed, Eliot, *Maras Affair*
Rosten, Leo, *A Most Private Intrigue*
"Selwyn," *Operation Ballerina*
Semyonov, Julian, *Petrovka 38*
Simenon, Georges, *Window Over the Way* (Batum)
Walker, David E., *Diamonds for Danger*
Wees, Frances S., *Country of the Strangers*
Wood, Samuel A., *Red Square*
Wuorio, Eva-Lis, *Woman with the Portuguese Basket*

Vietnam

Carter, Nick, *Hanoi*
Daniels, Norman, *Operation "VC"*
Harvester, Simon, *Battle Road*
Mason, F. Van Wyck, *Saigon Singer*

Virgin Islands

Douglass, Donald M., *Many Brave Hearts*

Wales

Blaisdell, Anne, *Nightmare*
Boore, Walter H., *The Valley and the Shadow*
Brand, Christianna, *Cat and Mouse*
Carnac, Carol, *Impact of Evidence*
Crofts, Freeman W., *The Sea Mystery*
Kennington, Alan, *Young Man with a Scythe*
Philpotts, Eden, *Deed Without a Name*
Priestley, J. B., *The Old Dark House*

Yugoslavia

Canning, Victor, *A Forest of Eyes*
———. *The Whip Hand*
Dodge, David, *Lights of Skaro*
Durrell, Lawrence, *White Eagles over Serbia*
Gainham, Sarah, *The Silent Hostage*
Kyle, Elizabeth, *The Other Miss Evans*
Sanderson, Douglas, *Final Run*
Sidgwick, C., *Manhunt in Dalmatia*
Stout, Rex, *Black Mountain*
Strachan, T. S., *No Law in Illyria*

Locales

Along with the characters they have created, authors in this field have also devised their own environments with cities and places which have become as familiar as one's own home town. Do you remember these and can you guess what real city or place the author had in mind at the time he was writing about it?

Bay City, Raymond Chandler
Deer Lick, A. B. Cunningham
87th St. Precinct, Ed McBain
Farrington, Sweet Grass, Montana, Margaret Scherf
Laurel Falls, Rufus King
Madison City, Erle Stanley Gardner
Orchid City, James Hadley Chase
Stockford, Connecticut, Hillary Waugh
Wilcox Place Police Station, Elizabeth Linington
Wrightsville, Connecticut, Ellery Queen

5

HEROES, VILLAINS–AND HEROINES

Of the creating of detectives, it seems, there is no end. Like a well-known brand of canned and bottled foods, there are many varieties.

There are male detectives (Sherlock Holmes); female detectives (Miss Marple) and neutrals. Did you know that there is a Gay Detective, Francis Morley, whose agency specializes in crushing blackmail rings which prey on homosexuals?

There are boy detectives (P. J. Davenant); girl detectives (Nancy Drew) and even children (Emil and the Detectives).

The animal kingdom has also gotten into the act. There is Phut Phat, the cat; Chang, the police dog; and Freddy, the Pig.

There are detectives who are lawyers (Perry Mason); doctors (Dr. Priestley); teachers (Julia Tyler); ministers (Rev. Martin Buell); priests (Father Brown); nuns (Soeur Angele); rabbis (David Small); nurses (Miss Keate); fire marshals (Ben Pedley) and spinsters (Miss Silver).

There are private eyes who are a bit passé now, and if you read enough mysteries, you'll even find a bona fide police officer and a police department that has sense enough to solve a crime occasionally. It used to be almost entirely the talented amateurs' game, but it is refreshing to note that in recent years the trend has changed and that police departments are given the credit they so richly deserve. The police procedural books of Dell Shannon and J. J. Marric are good examples of cases solved by men working as teams and using scientific methods.

Detective story writers are as whimsical about naming their characters as they are their books. Who but mystery writers could get by with naming their detectives Montague Migglewade and Diddymus Demetrius Duckworthy? Surely they must have tongue in cheek when they give characters such names as "Tiger" Wragge, "Copper" Penny, and "Cotton" Moon.

The following dictionary is a listing of detectives, criminals, and organizations found in the literature of mystery, detective, and suspense fiction. Wherever possible a representative novel follows to give the librarian an easier approach to his task. When the character appears mainly in short stories, a representative title follows enclosed by quotation marks. These short stories may be found in the numerous anthologies or in back issues of such periodicals as the *Ellery Queen Mystery Magazine*. If no listing is given, it means that examples were not available to the compiler because these are characters mainly in British mysteries, many of which are not available in the U.S.A.

This list is by no means complete, but I believe it is the most comprehensive one compiled to date. The serious student of the literature is referred to Ellery Queen's *The Detective Short Story: A Bibliography* for a further listing of the earlier detective creations, most of which can no longer be found on the library shelves, but which will be of historical interest to the scholar. Such persons should contact the Occidental College Library of Los Angeles which will be the future home of the famous E. T. Guymon, Jr. Collection, and the Texas University home of the Ellery Queen Short Story Collection.

CHARACTER	AUTHOR	TITLE
Aakonen, Paavo	Mabel H. Seeley	*The Chuckling Fingers*
Abbershaw, George	Marjorie Allingham	*The Crime at Black Dudley*
Abbott, Frank	Patricia Wentworth	*The Fingerprint*
Abbott, Mrs. Jean	Frances Crane	*Black Cypress*
Abbott, Patricia	Mary Roberts Rinehart	*The Great Mistake*
Abbott, Patrick	Frances Crane	*The Yellow Violet*
Abbott, Sammy and Ethel	James R. Langham	*Sing a Song of Homicide*
Ablewhite, Godfrey	Wilkie Collins	*The Moonstone*
Abner, Uncle	Melville Davisson Post	*Uncle Abner, Master of Mysteries*
"The Ace" (Justin March)	Sidney Horler	*Enter the Ace*
Ackroyd, Roger	Agatha Christie	*The Murder of Roger Ackroyd*
Adams, Adelaide ("The Old Battle-Axe")	Anita Blackmon	*Murder à la Richelieu*
Adams, Anthony	Timothy Brace	*Murder Goes Fishing*
Adams, Bradley	Maurice Dekobra	
Adams, Detective-Constable	Roland Daniel	
Adams, Detective-Inspector	Josephine Bell	*Death in Retirement*
Adams, Donald O'Keefe (Don O'K)	Dana Sage	*The Moon Was Red*
Adams, Nurse ("Miss Pinkerton")	Mary Roberts Rinehart	*Miss Pinkerton*
Adams, Peter	Forrester Hazard	*The Hex Murder*
"The Adjusters"	Peter Winston	*The ABC Affair*
Adler, Irene	Sir Arthur Conan Doyle	"A Scandal in Bohemia"
Agent 64	Charles Rushton	
Aiken, Leo	Bruno Fischer	*Bleeding Scissors*
Ainsley, John	Arthur Somers Roche	"The Jeweled Casket"
Ainsworth, Milo	Milo Ainsworth	*Murder Is Catching*
Alcazar, Dr.	Philip MacDonald	*The Green and Gold String*
Allain, Inspector Pierre	Bruce Graeme	*The Mystery of the Stolen Hats*
Allan, Sheriff Rocky	Virginia Rath	*Ferryman, Take Him Across*
Allen, Janet; *see* Barron, Mrs. Peter		
Allen, Peter	Lindsay Anson	*Such Natural Deaths*
Allenby, Inspector	M. P. Muir and E. D. H. Tollemache	
Alley, Inspector	Raymond Boyd	*Murder Is a Furtive Thing*
Alleyn, Chief Inspector Roderick	Ngaio Marsh	*Overture to Death*
Alleyn, Mrs. Roderick; *see* Troy, Agather		

CHARACTER	AUTHOR	TITLE
Allhoff, Inspector	D. L. Champion	"A Corpse Grows in Brooklyn"
Allison, Sir William	Sidney Horler	
Allwright, Superintendent Dudley	Philip MacDonald	*Escape*
Allyn, Troy	Ngaio Marsh	*Final Curtain*
Almack	E. H. Cragg	*Almack, the Detective*
Almsford, Peter	Max Murray	*The Queen and the Corpse*
Alwyn, Mark	Headon Hill	*The Golden Temptress*
Amayat	Henry DeVere Stackpoole	*The Mystery of Uncle Ballard*
Amber, Joan (later Mrs. Reggie Fortune)	Henry C. Bailey	*Mr. Fortune Objects*
Ambo, Mr.	Thurman Warriner	*Death's Bright Angel*
"Ambrose"	D. Brown	
"Ambrose" (Ambrose West)	Philip Levene	*Ambrose in London*
Ameny, Major	Edgar Wallace	
Ames, Martin	Alfred Eichler	*Moment for Murder*
Ames, Professor	Farraday Keene	*Pattern in Black and Red*
Ames, Russell	Frank Stevens	*She Left a Silver Slipper*
Ames, Sid	Henry W. Roden	*One Angel Less*
Amour; *see* Saint-Amour		
Anderson, Detective	Mary Roberts Rinehart and Avery Hopwood	*The Bat*
Anderson, Pike	Carl M. Chapin	*Three Died Beside the Marble Pool*
Anderson, Scott (Chief of Police)	Dashiell Hammett	"Two Sharp Knives"
Andradas, Manuel ("The Photographer")	James Holding	"The Photographer and the Professor"
Andrews, Inspector	Herman C. McNeile ("Sapper")	
"The Angel of the Lace Curtains"; *see* Wolff, Commissioner		
Angele, Soeur	Henri Catalan	*Soeur Angele and the Embarrassed Ladies*
Anglesea, Ronald	G. Milner	
Ankers, Inspector	Pagan Muat	
Anson, Captain Michael	F. L. Wheeler	
Anson, Ross	V. Hill	
Ansthruther, Bill	J. Nicholas	
Ansthruther, Sir George	Carter Dickson	
Anton, Joe	Evelyn Piper	*The Motive*
Antonia	E. T. A. Hoffman	*The Tales of Hoffman*
Antonin, M.	Paul Tabori	*Perditas End*
APE	Norman Daniels	*Spy Ghost*
Appleby, Assistant Commissioner Sir John	Michael Innes	*Seven Suspects*
Appleby, Detective-Sergeant	Alex Atkinson	*Exit Charlie*
April, Johnny	John Roscoe and Michael Ruso	*Death Is a Round Black Ball*
Apthorpe, Howard	Kate Ashley	*Cinnabar Shroud*
Aragon, Jose	Dorothy B. F. Hughes	*The Candy Kid*
Arbuthnot, Hon. Freddy	Dorothy Sayers	*Strong Poison*

CHARACTER	AUTHOR	TITLE
Arbuthnot, Hon. Ludovick ("Sandy"), later Lord Clanroyden	John Buchan	*Pilgrims Way*
"The Archdeacon"	Thurman Warriner	*Death's Bright Angel*
Archer (G-Man)	Jean Francis Webb	*Murder's Hex Sign*
Archer, Inspector	Ernest Dudley	
Archer, Jill	Stephen Ransome	*Death Checks In*
Archer, Lew (Harper)	John Ross MacDonald	*The Moving Target*
Archer, Maxwell	Hugh Clevely	*No Peace for Archer*
Archer, Oceola	Joseph Baker Carr	*The Man with Bated Breath*
Archer, Thomas	M. Frazer	
Arden, Captain Christopher	Leslie Charteris	*Daredevil*
Ark, Simon	Edward D. Hoch	"Flame at Twilight"
Arlen, Bob	A. Mackenzie	
Armine, Bron	Kenneth O'Hara	*Underhandover*
Armiston, Oliver	Frederick Irving Anderson	*The Book of Murder*
Armitage, Detective-Sergeant	Bryan Briandeeve	*I Never Miss Twice*
Armour, Mr.	John MacDonald	
Armstrong, Assistant Commissioner Sir Herbert	John Dickson Carr	
Armstrong, Lord Richard	Roland Daniel	
Arnholt	Gordon Latta	*Arnholt Makes His Bow*
Arnold, Sergeant Frank	T. A. Plummer	
Arnold, Inspector Henry	Miles Burton	*Death in Shallow Water*
Arnold, Robert	Constance and Gwenyth Little	
Arnold, Shadrack	Vern Chute	*Never Trust the Obvious*
Aron, Simon	Dennis Wheatley	
Arran, Toby	John Creasey	
Arrow, Inspector	Paul Mansfield	*Final Exposure*
Artside, Mrs. Liz	Michael Gilbert	*The Country House Burglar*
Ash, Chief Superintendent	Francis Grierson	
Ashby, Chief Inspector Hugh	P. Manton	
Ashe, Saxon	Saxon Ashe	*I Am Saxon Ashe*
Ashenden	W. Somerset Maugham	*Ashenden, or the British Agent*
Ashley, T.	George Allan England	"The Case of Jane Cole, Spinster"
Ashton, Detective-Inspector	Elizabeth Antill	*Murder in Mid-Atlantic*
Ashton, Inspector	Clodagh G. Jarvie	*Vicious Circuit*
Ashton, J. Dabney	David Alexander	*Murder Points a Finger*
Ashton-Kirk	John T. MacIntyre	*Ashton-Kirk, Criminologist*
Ashwin, Dr. John	Anthony Boucher	*The Case of the Seven of Cavalry*
Asnum, Mr.	H. Hawton	
"A.S.P."; *see* Pennington, Hon. Arthur		
Assche, Brian and Veronica	Marjorie Alan	*Murder Next Door*
Asterbrook, Detective-Sergeant	John Boland	
Astley, Simon	Val Gielgud	

CHARACTER	AUTHOR	TITLE
Astro; *see* Kerby		
Austen, Detective Chief Inspector William	Anne Hocking	*Poison in Paradise*
The Avenger	Walter B. Gibson	
Avon, Domoney	V. Hill	
AXE	Nick Carter	*The China Doll*
B., Inspector (G. 7)	Georges Simenon	*The Secret of Fort Bayard*
Babbing, Walter	Harvey J. Higgins	"The Blackmailers"
Bablon, Severac	Sax Rohmer	*Sins of Severac Bablon*
The Baccarat Club	Jessie Louisa Rickard	*The Baccarat Club*
Bagby, George	George Bagby	*The Body in the Basket*
Bagshot, Chief Inspector	Manning Coles	*With Intent to Deceive*
Bahl; *see* De Bahl		
Bailey, Carleton	Joseph Cottin Cooke	*Vera Gerard Case*
Bailey, Hilary Dunsany III ("Dunsany Brooke")	Hilea Bailey	*The Smiling Corpse*
Bailey, Hilea	Hilea Bailey	*Give Thanks to Death*
Bailey, Stuart	Roy Huggins	*The Double Take*
Bain, Joe (Acting Sheriff)	John Holbrook	*The Fox Valley Murders*
Bain, Stephen	Robert Sheckley	*Time Limit*
Baines, Scattergood	Clarence Budington Kelland	*Scattergood Baines*
Baker, Chief Inspector	Osmington Mills	*At One Fell Swoop*
Baker, Diane	Leslie Ford	
Baker, Lieutenant Jeff	The Gordons	
Baker, Ronald	George Gibbs	
Baley, Elijah	Isaac Asimov	*The Naked Sun*
Ballantyne, Brian	W. E. Johns	
Ballard, Guy	K. D. Guiness	
Ballmeyer; *see* Larsan, Frederic		
Balm, Gilead	Bernard Caper	*Gilead Balm, Knight Errant*
Bamford, Inspector John	Francis Vivian	
Bancroft, Charles Duke	Melville Burt	*The Yellow Robe Murders*
Banion, Dan	Robert Finnegan	*The Bandaged Nude*
Banner, Inspector	N. Graham	
Banner, Rex	Robert Chapman	*Murder for the Million*
Banning, Bill	Nat Easton	*A Book for Banning*
Bannion, Burns	Earl Norman	*Kill Me in Shimbashi*
Bannion, Sergeant Dave	William P. McGivern	*Big Heat*
Barcello, Lieutenant Lee	Stephen Ransome	*The Hidden Hour*
Baring, Martella (later Lady Saumerez)	Clemence Dane and Helen Simpson	*Enter Sir John*
Barlach, Police Commissioner	Frederic Dürrenmatt	*The Judge and His Hangman*
Barnard, Detective-Inspector	T. C. H. Jacobs	
Barne, Colonel	Edmund G. Cousins	
Barnes, Bookee	Bruce Cassiday	
Barnes, Bromley	George Barton	*The Strange Adventures of Bromley Barnes*
Barnett, George	M. Cronin	
Barnett, Inspector	B. Cobb	

CHARACTER	AUTHOR	TITLE
Barnett, Jim; *see* Lupin, Arsène		
Barney, Detective; *see* Cook, Barney		
Barnum, Dave	George Harmon Coxe	*Never Bet Your Life*
The Baron	Anthony Morton	*Meet the Baron*
Baron, Peter	Bruce Cassaday	"The Mendoza Memorandum"
Barr, Black	Erle Stanley Gardner	
Barr, Ronald	Robert Murphy	*Murder in Waiting*
Barrabel, Chief Inspector	Edgar Wallace	
Barraclough, Inspector	George Dilnot	*The Pink Edge*
Barret, Peter	P. Campion	
Barrett, Selwyn	C. T. Stoneham	
Barron, Insurance Detective	F. J. Price	*Mind Wreckers Limited*
Barron, Peter	Ruth Darby	*Death Conducts a Tour*
Barron, Mrs. Peter (née Janet Allen)	Ruth Darby	*Death Conducts a Tour*
Barry, Herbert	Edwin Baird	"The Mystery of the Locked Door"
Bart, "Easy"	F. Orlin Tremaine	*I'll Kill You Often*
Bartlett, Hal	Lawrence Dwight Smith	
Bartlett, Nell	D. Elias	
Barton, Susan	Robert George Dean	*Three Lights Went Out*
Baskerville, Sir Henry	Sir Arthur Conan Doyle	*The Hound of the Baskervilles*
Baskerville, John; *see* Stapleton, John		
Bass, Inspector	George Selmark	*Murder in Silence*
Bassadag, Inspector	M. Cronin	
Bassett, Chief Inspector	Clive Ryland	
Bassett, Sheriff	Jacqueline Cutlip	"The Black Cloud"
Bastion, Professor Luther	Gavin Holt	"The Aztec Skull"
Bastion, Chief Inspector "Plumber"	Richard M. Harrison	*Brickbats for Bastion*
Bat, Black Tony Quinn	G. Wayman Jones	*Markets of Treason*
Bates, Lieutenant	Louisa Revell	*No Pockets in a Shroud*
Bates, Pincher	W. Shand	
Bathgate, Nigel	Ngaio Marsh	*Artists in Crime*
Bathhurst	Lawrence Lynch	*The Diamond Coterie*
Bathhurst, Anthony	Brian Flynn	*The Crime at the Crossways*
Battle, Superintendent	Agatha Christie	*Seven Dials Mystery*
"Battling Beaucaire"; *see* Puyster, Reginald de		
Batts, Assistant Fire Marshal Craig	Clarence Budington Kelland	*Where There's Smoke*
Batts, Singer	Thomas B. Dewey	*Mourning After*
Baum, Lisl	Ian Fleming	*For Your Eyes Only*
Baxall, Inspector	S. Miles	
Baxter	Lawrence Treat	"Harlequin's Death Mask"
Bayley, Patrick	Anthony Lejeune	
Bayliss, Pete	Blair Treynor	*Widow's Pique*
Baynes, Dr.	V. Bell	*Death and the Night Watches*
Beagle, Amanda	Torrey Chanslor	*Our First Murder*
Beagle, Lutie	Torrey Chanslor	*Our First Murder*
Beagle, Otis	Frank Gruber	*The Lonesome Badger*
Bean, Sawney	Scottish folklore	*Sawney Bean*

CHARACTER	AUTHOR	TITLE
Beasley, Eliot	Mignon G. Eberhart	
Beaton, Ian	P. Malloch	
"Beaucaire, Battling"; *see* Puyster, Reginald de		
Beaumont, Ned	Dashiell Hammett	*The Glass Key*
Beaumont, Trevor	Alan Mackenzie	
"The Beautiful Gunner" (Norma Lee)	Norma Lee	*Beautiful Gunner*
Beck, Paul	McDonnell Bodkin	*The Rule of Thumb Detective*
Beddingfield, Anne	Agatha Christie	*The Man in the Brown Suit*
Bedford, Daniel	Robert P. Hansen	
Bedison, Detective-Inspector	T. Cobb	
Beedel, Inspector	Ernest Bramah	*The Eyes of Max Carrados*
Beef, Sergeant William	Leo Bruce	*Case for Sergeant Beef*
Beever of Scotland Yard	J. Cockin	
Behrens, Mr.	Michael Gilbert	"The Future of the Service"
Belamy, Peter	B. Stanley	
Belcourt, Robert	Cameron Rougvie	*Tangier Assignment*
Bell, Chief Inspector	Neil Graham	
Bell, Inspector	G. Morgan	
Bell, M.	Mrs. L. T. Meade and Robert Eustace	*The Sanctuary Club*
Bell, Sergeant	Ernest Robert Punshon	*The Unexpected Legacy*
Bell, Superintendent	Henry C. Bailey	"The Little House"
Bellamy, Professor Akers	George Goodchild	*Dear Old Gentleman*
Bellamy, Chief Superintendent John	T. C. H. Jacobs	*Broken Alibi*
Bellamy, Nick	Peter Cheyney	
Bellona Club	Dorothy L. Sayers	*The Unpleasantness at the Bellona Club*
Belman, Margaret (later Mrs. J. G. Reeder)	Edgar Wallace	*The Mind of J. G. Reeder*
Belmore, J. Montagne	N. Berrow	
Belsize, Chris	Vernon Rendall	*London Nights of Belsize*
Bemmister, Mr.	Max Dalman	*Elusive Nephew*
Ben of the Merchant Service	Joseph J. Farjeon	*No. 17*
Benasque, Michael	Alan Caillou	*Who'll Buy My Evil*
Bencolin, Henri	John Dickson Carr	*The Lost Gallows*
Bendilow, Ex-Superintendent	C. Wallace	
Bendon, Wing Commander David ("Jason")	John N. Chance	*The Jason Affair*
Bendovid, Tante Fayga	Viola Brothers Shore	" 'Bye, 'Bye, Bluebeard"
Benedict, Bill	Bryant Ford	
Benham, Detective-Senior Sergeant	P. Elliott	
Benham, John	M. Home	
Bennett, Geoffery ("Lord" Broghville)	George Worthing Yates	*There Was a Crooked Man*
Bennett, Hugh	Julian Symons	*Progress of a Crime*

CHARACTER	AUTHOR	TITLE
Bennett, Jim	Robert L. Martin	*Catch a Killer*
Bennett, Ted	James M. Ullman	"The Stock Market Mystery"
Benning, Luke	Muriel Bradley	*Devil in the Sky*
Bennion, Roger	Herbert Adams	*Roger Bennion's Double*
Benoit	P. Irving	
Bensinger, Paula	James Hadley Chase	
Benskin, Peter	E. Phillips Oppenheim	"The Great West Raid"
Benson, John	Sue B. Hays	*Go Down, Death*
Benson, Mrs. Philip (née Elsie Ritter)	Molly E. Corne	*Death at a Masquerade*
Benson, Philip	Molly E. Corne	
Bent, John	Henry C. Branson	*The Pricking Thumb*
Bentiron, Dr. Thaddeus	Ernest M. Poate	*Dr. Bentiron: Detective*
Bentley, John	Hamish Boyd	*One Night of Murder*
Bentley, Steve	Robert Dietrich	*Mistress to Murder*
Bercolin	John Dickson Carr	*It Walks by Night*
Beresford, Tommy and Tuppence	Agatha Christie	*Partners in Crime*
Bernadone, Inspector Peter	Frank P. Grady	*Sergeant Death*
Bernard, Inspector	S. Esmond	
Berthelotte, Superintendent	Helen Robertson	*The Crystal Gazers*
Bessy, Miss	Hilda Lawrence	*Death of a Doll*
Best, Petunia	Bridget Chetwynd	*Rubies, Emeralds and Diamonds*
Bestoso, Lieutenant	Leslie Ford	
Betteredge, Gabriel	Wilkie Collins	*The Moonstone*
Betts, Sergeant	N. Mackenzie	
Beverly, Hon. Bill	G. Brandon	
Bey, Nuri	Joan Fleming	*When I Get Rich*
Bidders, Charlie	N. Thurley	
Big, Mr. Buonaparte Ignace Gallia	Ian Fleming	*Live and Let Die*
Big Nick; *see* Morro, "Big" Nick		
Bigelow, Antony	Burton Stevenson	*The Red Carnation*
Biles, Inspector	Anthony Wynne	*Sinners Go Secretly*
"Bill, The Bloodhound"; *see* Dawson, Chief Inspector William		
Bindon, Major	D. Divine	
Binks, Detective-Inspector	W. F. Temple	
Bird, Chief Inspector	H. Long	
Bird, Colonel	Gordon Gaskill	"Murder on Skiis"
Birdseye, Miriam	Nancy Spain	*Not Wanted on Voyage*
Birdsong, Dr. Tom	Leslie Ford	*Three Bright Pebbles*
Birnick, Jim	Thomas Polsky	
Birrell, Detective-Sergeant Aloysius	Charles P. Snow	*Death Under Sail*
Bishop, Hugo	Simon Rattray	*Queen in Danger*
Bishop, Robin	Geoffrey Homes	*The Doctor Died at Dusk*
Bixby, Zebediah	Mike Teagle	*Murders in Silk*
Bjelke, Superintendent	Jonas Lie	
"The Black"; *see* Morlake, James		
Black, Carlos	George Harmon Coxe	*No Time to Kill*

CHARACTER	AUTHOR	TITLE
Black, Henry (Lord Fortworth)	Bertram Atkey	*Arsenic and Gold*
Black, Colonel Jarvis	Peter Coffin	*The Search for My Great-Uncle's Head*
Black, Jet	Robert Glover	*Murderer's Maze*
"Black Maria" (Maria Black)	John Slate	*Black Maria, M.A.*
Black, Reginald ("Beauty")	Edward Ronns	*The Corpse Hangs High*
Blackburn, Jeffrey	Max Afford	*Death's Mannikins*
Blackett, Major	James Ronald	
Blackie, Boston	Jack Boyle	*Boston Blackie*
Blackshirt	Bruce Graeme	*Blackshirt*
Blackwood, Riley	Vincent Starrett	*Midnight and Percy Jones*
Blagdon, Superintendent	Edgar Wallace	
Blaikie, Inspector	G. D. H. and M. I. Cole	
Blaine, Will	Rufus King	"To Remember You By"
Blair, Andy	Lee Sheridan Cox	"The Great Halloween Mystery"
Blair, Spencer	Roland Daniel	*Spencer Blair, G-Man*
Blair, Susan	Allan Vaughan Elston	"The Perfect Secretary"
Blaise, Ellie	Marco Page	*Fast Company*
Blaise, Modesty	Peter O'Donnell	*Modesty Blaise*
Blake, Alan	J. Mason	
Blake, Andy and Arab (Arabella)	Richard Powell	*And Hope to Die*
Blake, Edward	S. Gardiner	
Blake, Franklin	Wilkie Collins	*The Moonstone*
Blake, Captain Kenwood	Carter Dickson	*Unicorn Murders*
Blake, Red	Edward Lee	*A Fish for Murder*
Blake, Sexton	Union Jack Library	
Blake the Butler	William Le Queux	*Blake, the Butler*
Blakeley; *see* Dowell-Blakeley, Captain Leigh		
Blakeley, Dr. Frederick Holmes	Ernest M. Poate	
Blakiston, Rodney	E. Messenger	
Blampignon, Inspector	John Bude	*Death on the Riviera*
Blatchington, Everard	G. D. H. and M. I. Cole	*The Blatchington Tangle*
Blathers	Charles Dickens	*Oliver Twist*
Blenkiron, John S.	John Buchan	*Greenmantle*
Blessington, Mr.	John Sherwood	*Dr. Bruderstein Vanishes*
Bligh, Chief Inspector	Edward C. Bentley	*Trent's Last Case*
Bliss, Superintendent	Edgar Wallace	"The Man with the Red Beard"
Blood, Colonel	Howard Charles Davis	*The Big Heist*
Blood, Johnny	Bruce Cassiday	*The Death Rehearsal*
Blossom, Detective-Sergeant "Cherry"	C. M. Wills	
Blott, Detective-Inspector Erasmus	T. C. H. Jacobs	
Blount, Inspector	Nicholas Blake	*The Beast Must Die*
Blow, Dr. William	Kenneth Hopkins	*Body Blow*
"The Blue Mask"; *see* Mannering, John		
Blunder, Mark	Simon Harvester	

CHARACTER	AUTHOR	TITLE
Blunt's Brilliant Detectives; *see* Beresford, Tommy		
Bly, Doirit	Frank Bunce	*Rehearsal for Murder*
Blythe, Maxwell	Judson P. Philips	*Death Delivers a Postcard*
Boas, Harryboy	Alexander Baron	*The Lowlife*
Bogarders, Chief Inspector Nicholas	Neil Graham	
Bogart, Ruth	John P. Marquand	*Stopover Tokyo*
Bohun, Henry	Michael Gilbert	"If You Know How"
Bolt, Sam	G. G. Fickling	*Bombshell*
"Bombi"	Max Brand	*The Death of Love*
Bonaparte, Napoleon	Arthur W. Upfield	*The Bushman Who Came Back*
Bond, Christopher	W. Martyn	
Bond, James	Ian Fleming	*Casino Royale*
Bondurant, Inspector Victor	James G. Edwards	*The Private Pavilion*
Bone, Inspector	G. Mitcham	
"Bones"; *see* Tibbits, Lieutenant Francis Augustus		
Bonnamy, Francis	Francis Bonnamy	*Death by Appointment*
Bonnarbel, M.	Charles Rushton	
Bonner, Theodolina ("Dol")	Rex Stout	*The Hand in the Glove*
Bonnet, Mrs.	C. L. Taylor	
Boom	Marion Randolph	
Borden, Mr.	J. Coggin	
Borden, Hilary	Richard Keverne	*He Laughed at Murder*
Borel, Narcisse	Eugene Sue	
Borges, Inspector	John and Emery Bonett	*The Private Face of Murder*
Bottwink, Dr.	Cyril Hare	*An English Murder*
Boudet, Inspector	Phyllis Hambledon	
Bounty, Sheriff Peter	George Todd Downing	*Death Under the Moonflower*
Bourne, Inspector "Daddy"	G. V. Galwey	
Bourne, Molly	Paul Somers	*Operation Piracy*
Bouvard, Monsieur	Franklin L. Gregory	*Cipher of Death*
Bowen, Geoffrey	Francis Lockridge	*Catch as Catch Can*
Bowman, Floyd	Robert McDowell	"Hound's Teeth"
Bowman, Glenn	Hartley Howard	*The Bowman Touch*
Boxruud, Sheriff Carl	Mabel Seeley	*Crying Sisters*
Boyd, Danny	Carter Brown	*Sometime Wife*
Boyd, Felix	Scott Campbell	*Below the Dead-line*
Boyd, Nile	D. Chambers	
Boyd, Samuel	Benjamin L. Farjeon	*Samuel Boyd of Catchpole Square*
Boyle	Cyril Alington	*Mr. Evans*
Boyle, P. C.	Carol Carnac	
Boyne, Laggan	Simon Still	"Kelman's Eyes"
Bozzy	Lillian De La Torre	"The Banquo Trap"
Bracegirdle, Millicent	Stacy Aumonier	*Miss Bracegirdle and Others*
Bradbury, Superintendent	Norman Longmate	
Brade, Professor Louis	Isaac Asimov	*Death Dealers*
Brade, Simon	Lady Harriette Campbell	*The String Glove Mystery*
Bradfield, Peter	C. Witting	
Bradford, Mrs. Joseph	Robert Player	*The Ingenious Mr. Stone*
Bradford, Peter	Ben Benson	*The Black Mirror*

CHARACTER	AUTHOR	TITLE
Bradford, Ring	William Huntsberry	*Dangerous Harbor*
Bradley, Mrs. Adela	Gladys Mitchell	*When Last I Died*
Bradley, Dame Beatrice Lestrange	Gladys Mitchell	*Come Away, Death*
Bradley, Inspector Luke	Hugh Pentecost	*The 24th Horse*
Bradley of the Flying Squad	Edgar Wallace	*The Flying Squad*
Bradley, Rupert	E. B. Ronald	
Bradley, Sam	C. Conrad	
Bradshaw, Noah	Madeleine Johnston	*Comets Have Long Tails*
Bradstreet, Inspector	Leonard A. G. Strong	*Murder Plays an Ugly Scene*
Brady, Bat	L. Bell	
Brady, Inspector Franklin	Allan McRoyd	*The Golden Goose Murders*
Bragg, Inspector John	Henry Wade	*Here Comes the Copper*
Braid, Inspector Peter	William M. Duncan	
Brailey, Detective-Sergeant Jim	D. Haddow	
Brain, Colonel	Henry Cecil	*According to the Evidence*
Brand, Colonel	Alan Caillou	
Brand, Inspector	C. Robertson	
Brand, Delia	Rex Stout	*The Mountain Cat Murders*
Brand, Gala	Ian Fleming	*Moonraker*
Brand, Helene (later Mrs. Jake Justus)	Craig Rice	*The Wrong Murder*
Brand, Mark ("The Counsellor")	J. J. Connington	*The Two Ticket Puzzle*
Brand, Pete	Harry Olesker	*Now Will You Try for Murder*
Brander, Olivia	E. Chamberlain	
Brandon, Dal	L. White	
Brandon, Mark	Vernon Warren	*Runaround*
Brandon, Mike	Gordon Ashe	*Introducing Mr. Brandon*
Brandon, Sheriff Rex	Erle Stanley Gardner	*The D.A. Breaks an Egg*
"Brandt, Dirk"; *see* Kingston, Michael		
"Brandt, Hendrik"; *see* Hambledon, Thomas Elpinstone		
Brann, Willie	Benton Braden	"Signals of Death"
Brannigan, Superintendent	Alan Mackenzie	
Branson, Al	Robert P. Koehler	*Steps to Murder*
Brant, Mason	Nevil Monroe Hopkins	*The Strange Cases of Mason Brant*
Brass, John	Henri Weiner	*Crime on the Cuff*
Braxton, Colonel	Melville Davisson Post	*The Silent Witness*
Breakes, Johnnie	M. Cronin	
Bream, Superintendent	M. Halliday	
Bredder, Father	Leonard Holton	*A Pact with Satan*
Brede, Michael	Francis Grierson	
Bredon, Miles	Ronald A. Knox	*Footsteps at the Lock*
Bredon; *see* Wimsey, Lord Peter		
Breeze, Benedict	Isabella Bayne	*Death and Benedict*
"Brendan, George"; *see* Wour, Hazlitt		
Brendel, Ernest	John C. Masterman	*The Case of the Four Friends*
Brennan, Captain	John Dickson Carr	
Brennan, Chief Tim	Clarissa Fairchild	

CHARACTER	AUTHOR	TITLE
Brent, Bill	Frederick C. Davis	"Thanks for the Lovely Funeral"
Brent, "Bundles"	Agatha Christie	*The Seven Dials Mystery*
Brent, George	Alfred Tack	
Brent, Hilary	M. Annesley	
Brent, Inspector	David Whitelaw	
Brent, Detective-Inspector James	H. Kemp	
Brent, Mr.	Gilderoy Davison	*Exit Mr. Brent*
Brent, Superintendent	C. Hogarth	
Brett	Arthur Morrison	*Martin Hewett, Investigator*
Brett, Brian	Christopher Monig	*Lonely Graves*
Brett, Chico	Kevin O'Hara	
Brett, Jeffrey	Leonard Ross	*Adventure in Washington*
Brett, Marcus	Mrs. Baillie Reynolds	*The Intrusive Tourist*
Brett, Mike	K. Campbell	
Brett, Reginald	Louis Tracy	*The Albert Gate Mystery*
Brewster, Amy	Samuel Merwin, Jr.	*A Matter of Policy*
Brewster, Fredrika ("Ricky")	Marie Blizard	*Conspiracy of Silence*
Briar, Inspector Robin	J. Sandys	
Brice, Secret Agent	M. Home	
Brickley, Bella	Hulbert Footner	*The Casual Murderer*
Bridie, Detective-Inspector Ian Alexander	Margery Allingham	*Black Plumes*
Briercliffe, Ronald	Francis Beeding	*Hell Let Loose*
Briffett, Mervyn	Julian Symons	"The Wimbledon Mystery"
"The Brigand"; *see* Newton, Anthony		
Brigg, Detective-Inspector	J. Corbett	
Brincourt, Blaise de	Dennis Allan	*Dead to Rights*
Brisband, Sergeant	J. Bentley	
Briscoe, Chief Mike	Charles Saxby	*Death Joins the Woman's Club*
Bristow, Superintendent William	Anthony Morton	*Deaf, Dumb and Blonde*
Britain, Captain Bill	John Courage	*Spooks Sometimes Sing*
Britten, Rod	F. Brown	
Britton, Rocky	D. Holt	
Brixan, Mike	Edgar Wallace	*The Hairy Arm*
Brock, Inspector	Reginald J. White	*The Smartest Grave*
Brockett, Mathilda	Carolyn Byrd Dawson	*The Lady Wept Alone*
Brocklesdowne, Lord	Ralph Inchbald	
Brodie, Sergeant	G. Dickson	
Brodney, Philip	Henry Carstairs	
Broghville, "Lord"; *see* Bennett, Geoffery		
Brook, Sergeant	George Goodchild	*Death on the Center Court*
"Brooke, Dunsany"; *see* Bailey, Hilary Dunsany III		
Brooke, Loveday	C. L. Perkis	*The Experiences of Loveday Brooke: Lady Detective*
Brooke, Peter	Peter Manton	
Brooks, G. B.	William Tucker	*A Man in My Grave*
Brooks, Luther	A. Eichler	
Brooks, Martin	Frances and Richard Lockridge	*Think of Death*

CHARACTER	AUTHOR	TITLE
Brown, Benvenuto	Elizabeth Gill	*What Dread Hand?*
Brown, Bill	Rae Foley	
Brown, Chief Inspector	Peter Broad	*Death on the Beach*
Brown, Dagobert	Delano Ames	*Landscape with Corpse*
Brown, Father	G. K. Chesterton	*The Innocence of Father Brown*
Brown, Captain Hurley	Edgar Wallace	
Brown, Deputy Sheriff Jake	Owen Cameron	*The Fire Trap*
Brown, Jane	Delano Ames	*Landscape with Corpse*
Brown, Dr. Jimmy	Henry Harrison Kroll	*The Ghosts of Slave Drivers Bend*
Brown, Milly	A. Lee	
Brown, Quiribus	Harry S. Keeler	
Brownhall, Sergeant	Cecil Freeman Gregg	
Browning, Commissioner Peter	"Sea-Lion"	*Sea of Troubles*
Bruce, Claude	Gordon Holmes	*Arncliffe Puzzle*
Bruff, Matthew	Wilkie Collins	*The Moonstone*
Brummel, Inspector	R. Verron	
Brunnell, Paul	Richard Bennett	*Whispering Money*
Brush, Dr. Lucas	Frank Dudley	*Havana Hotel Murders*
Bryant, John	R. Grayson	
Bryant, Steve	P. George	
Bryce, Emily and Henry	Margaret Scherf	*Green Plaid Pants*
Bryden, Steve	G. Joseph	
Buchanan, George	Paul McGuire	*A Funeral in Eden*
Buck, Sergeant Phineas T.	Leslie Ford	*The Woman in Black*
Buck, Zebulion	Hugh L. Nelson	
Bucket, Inspector	Charles Dickens	*Bleak House*
Buckley, George Stanhope	Lawrence Meynell	
Budd, Barnabas	John Brophy	
Budd, Superintendent Robert	Gerald Verner	*The Crooked Circle*
Buell, Reverend Martin	Margaret Scherf	*The Cautious Overshoes*
Bull, Sir George	Milward Kennedy	*Bull's Eye*
Bull, Homer	Lawrence Lariar	
Bull, Inspector J. Humphrey	David Frome	*The Hammersmith Murders*
Bullot, Inspector	Edgar Wallace	
Bulmer, Sergeant Thomas	Wilkie Collins	"The Biter Bit"
Bunce, Dr. Nathaniel	Elizabeth M. Curtiss	*Nine Doctors and a Madman*
"Bundle"	Agatha Christie	*Secret of Chimneys*
Bunn, Smiler	Bertram Atkey	*Smiler Bunn, Gentleman-Adventurer*
"Bunny"; *see* Manders, "Bunny"		
Bunt, Joe	Laurence Donovan	"Coiffeured to Kill"
Bunter, Mervyn	Dorothy Sayers	*Whose Body?*
Bureau X	Sterling Noel	*Few Die Well*
Burgess, Detective	William Irish	*The Phantom Lady*
Burgess, Jeff	Thomas T. Flynn	*Murder Caravan*
Burgess, Richard	Alfred O. Pollard	
Burke, Amos	Roger Fuller	*Who Killed Madcap Millicent?*
Burke, Chief	Robert Orr Chipperfield	*The Second Bullet*
Burke, Gerald	Benge Atlee	*Black Feather*
Burke, Inspector	Cortland Fitzsimmons	*Sudden Silence*

CHARACTER	AUTHOR	TITLE
Burke, Jerry	Asa Baker	*The Kissed Corpse*
Burke, Joe	William Campbell Gault	
Burke, Shamus	H. M. Webster	
Burke, Terry	Cortland Fitzsimmons	*Death on the Diamond*
Burman, Area-Suprintendent	John G. Brandon	
Burman, Detective-Inspector Cheviot	Geoffrey Belton Cobb	*The Missing Scapegoat*
Burnham, "Breeze"	Sinclair Gluck	
Burnley, Inspector	Freeman Wills Crofts	*The Cask*
Burns, Larry	Sloane Callaway	
Burr, Jason	David Kent	*Jason Burr's First Case*
Burrell, Jacob	Guy Boothby	*Mystery of the Clasped Hands*
Burrows, Inspector	J. Ronald	
Burton, Dick	R. S. Braun	
Burton, Jerry and Joanna	Agatha Christie	
Burton, Mary J. ("Polly")	Baroness Orczy	*The Old Man in the Corner*
Burwell, Richard	Cleveland Moffett	"The Mysterious Card"
Butler, Michael	Elizabeth Ferrars	
Butler, Patrick	John Dickson Carr	*Patrick Butler for the Defense*
Butt, Johnny	Henry Carstairs	
Butterworth, Amelia	Anna Katherine Green	*That Affair Next Door*
Butts, Archie	Clarence Budington Kelland	
Buxton, Chief Inspector	James Byron	*Or Be He Dead*
Byrd, Horace	Anna Katherine Green	*Hand and Ring*
Byrnes, Inspector	A. E. Costello	"Inspector Byrnes"
Byrnes, Inspector	Julian Hawthorne	*An American Penman*
Cabot, Philip	Roman McDougal	*Deaths of Lora Karen*
Caddee, Don	Spencer Dean	*The Merchant of Murder*
Cade, Anthony	Agatha Christie	*Secret of Chimneys*
Cadman, Detective-Inspector	Charles Rushton	*No Beast So Fierce*
Cadmus, Judge John	Helen McCloy	"The Outer Darkness"
Cadover, Detective-Inspector Thomas	Michael Innes	*One-Man Show*
Cadrichet	Eugene Chavette	*L'Heritage d'un Pique-Assiette*
Caine, Inspector Fred	Charles G. Given	*The Jig-Time Murders*
Cairo, Joel	Dashiell Hammett	*The Maltese Falcon*
Cairsdale, Godfrey	Valentine Williams	
Calder, Mr.	Michael Gilbert	"The Future of the Service"
Caldwell, Superintendent Mark	Paul Mansfield	*Final Exposure*
Calhoun, Bert	Weed Dickinson	*Dead Man Talks Too Much*
Callaghan, James	Lord Charnwood	*Tracks in the Snow*
Callaghan, "Slim"	Peter Cheyney	*Dark Duet*
Callahan, Andy	Pat McGerr	*Save the Witness*
Callahan, Brock ("The Rock")	William Campbell Gault	*Vein of Violence*
Callaway, Inspector	Frank Swinnerton	"Soho Night's Entertainment"
Cam, Inspector	Joan Cockin	
Camberwell, Roger	Joseph S. Fletcher	*Murder of a Banker*
Cameron, Janice	Juanita Sheridan	*Waikiki Widow*
Cameron, Paul	H. Hunt	
Campbell	Manning Coles	*With Intent to Deceive*
Campbell, Ed	Stephen Marlowe	*Passport to Peril*

CHARACTER	AUTHOR	TITLE
Campbell, Humphrey	Geoffrey Homes	*Build My Gallows High*
Campbell, Major John	Mignon G. Eberhart	
Campbell, Quessy	Gail Stockwell	*Death by Invitation*
Campbell, Pat	Eli Colter	*Cheer for the Dead*
Campenhaye, Paul	Joseph S. Fletcher	*Paul Campenhaye: Specialist in Criminology*
Campion, Albert	Margery Allingham	*Death of a Ghost*
Canalli, Bill	Bill Peters	*Blondes Die Young*
"Candid Camera Kid"; *see* Wade, Jerry		
Candy, Inspector Eve	B. J. Farmer	
Cane, David	John Courage	
Canfield, David	E. Allen	
Canning, Detective-Inspector	John N. Chance	
Cannon, Curt	Curt Cannon	*I'm Cannon for Hire*
Cape, Patrol Officer Sam	Dirk Sabre	*Murder by Bamboo*
Caranac, Dr.	Abraham Merritt	*Creep, Shadow*
Carberry, Jane	B. Symons	
Cardani, Paul	Joseph T. Shaw	
Cardby, Ex-Chief Detective	David Hume	*Dangerous Mr. Dell*
Cardby, Mick	David Hume	*Dangerous Mr. Dell*
Cardew, Gordon	Edgar Wallace	
Cardew, Jimmy	J. Corbett	
Carella, Steve	Ed McBain	*Killer's Choice*
Carey, Mark	John G. Brandon	
Carilla, Mickey	N. McGuire	
Carlisle, Kenneth	Carolyn Wells	*The Skeleton at the Feast*
Carlton, Substitute-Inspector Jim	Edgar Wallace	
Carlyle, Louis	Ernest Bramah	*The Eyes of Max Carrados*
Carmichael, Superintendent	Edwin and Mona A. Radford	
Carnacke	William Hope Hodgson	*Carnacke, the Ghost-Finder*
Carner, Mary	Zelda Popkin	*Dead Man's Gift*
Carnes & Stanhope	Lawrence Lynch	*The Slender Clue*
Carnon, John	G. Hoster	
Carolus, Lucian	E. Ascher	
Carpenter, Cassandra; *see* Price, Mrs. Cassandra		
Carpenter, Colonel Rutherford B.	Alice Tilton	*Beginning with a Bash*
Carr, A. B.	Erle Stanley Gardner	*The D.A. Breaks an Egg*
Carr, Ruston	A. Parsons	
Carrados, Max (born Max Wynn)	Ernest Bramah	*Max Carrados*
Carrick, Webb	Bill Knox	*Blacklight*
Carrington, F. T.	J. Storer Clouston	*Carrington's Cases*
Carrington, Giles	Georgette Heyer	*Merely Murder*
Carruthers, Dr.	H. Blayn	
Carruthers, Inspector John	John Dickson Carr	
Carson, Andrew	D. Rutherford	
Carstairs (Great Dane)	Norbert Davis	*Sally's in the Alley*
Carstairs, Susan	Elizabeth Linington	*No Evil Angel*

CHARACTER	AUTHOR	TITLE
Carter, Anthony	Jacques Pendower	
Carter, Horace	Margaret P. Yates and Paula Bramlette	*Widow's Walk*
Carter, Inspector	Ernest R. Punshon	*The Unexpected Legacy*
Carter, Martin	E. Burgess	
Carter, Nick	John Coryell	"The Old Detective's Pupil"
Carter, Philip	Florence Ryerson and C. C. Clements	*Seven Suspects*
Carter, Stephen	Amelia R. Long	*The House with Green Shudders*
Carteret, Michael	Richard Keverne	
Carteret, Owen	Victor Bridges	
Carteret, Tiny	"Sapper"	*Tiny Carteret*
Carver, Bruce	Denis Allen	*Brandon Is Missing*
Carver, Inspector	Edgar Wallace	*Clue of the New Pin*
Carver, Margot	Esther Haven Fonseca	*The 13th Bed in the Ballroom*
Carver, Rex	Victor Canning	*Doubled in Diamonds*
Carver, Stewart and Stella	S. Carver	
Cary, Lieutenant	Henry W. Roden	*Wake for a Lady*
Caryll, Diana	C. Robertson	
Case, John	V. White	
Case, Paul	Jason Manor	
Case, Tiffany	Ian Fleming	*Diamonds Are Forever*
Casement, Sarah	Helen Reilly	
Casey, "Flashgun" Jack	George Harmon Coxe	*Error of Judgement*
Cassel, Nigel	Margaret Bonham	*House Across the Water*
Cassidy, Ray	Thomas Walsh	*The Dark Window*
Castle, Johnny	C. S. Montague	"Murder in Mink"
Catalyst Club	George Dyer	*The Long Death*
Catchpole, Inspector	Brian Flynn	
Cates, Sam	Ernest J. Fredericks	*Lost Friday*
Catherick, Anne	Wilkie Collins	*The Woman in White*
Catlin, Police Captain	F. Van Wyck Mason	
Cator, Robert	Walt Sheldon	*The Man Who Paid His Way*
Catt, Tom	J. Gannett	*Murder After Dark*
Caution, "Lemmy"	Peter Cheyney	*I'll Say She Does*
Cavanagh, Detective Mike	Frank O'Malley	*The Best Go First*
Cavendish, Cavendish	G. H. Johnson	
Cavendish, Georgia; *see* Strangeways, Mrs. Nigel		
Cellini, Dr. Emmanuel	Kyle Hunt	*Wicked as the Devil*
Chace, Christopher	Jean Lilly	*Death in B-Minor*
Chadlington, Colonel	Victor L. Whitechurch	*Shot on the Downs*
Chadwick, John	Guy Cobden	*I Saw Murder*
Chafik, Inspector	Charles B. Child	"The Thumbless Man"
Challenger, Professor	Sir Arthur Conan Doyle	*The Poison Belt*
Challis, Professor	Martin Shane	*Twelve Girls in the Garden*
Chaloner, Silas	V. Smith	
Chambers, Peter	Henry Kane	*Trinity in Violence*
Chambrun, Pierre	Hugh Pentecost	*The Shape of Fear*
Chan, Charlie	Earl Derr Biggers	*The House Without a Key*
Chance, Mr.	John N. Chance	*Death Stalks the Cobbled Square*
Chance, Christopher ("Kit")	Stephen Ransome	*Hearses Don't Hurry*
Chandler, Cliff	Baynard Kendrick	"The Eye"
Chandler, Colonel	T. X. Pantcheff	

CHARACTER	AUTHOR	TITLE
Chandler, Detective-Inspector	Josephine Bell	*Port of London Murders*
Chandler, Joe	Marie A. Lowndes	*The Lodger*
Chandos, Richard	Dornford Yates	
Chaney	Joseph S. Fletcher	*Murder of a Banker*
Chaney, Ben	Vera Caspary	*Bedelia*
Chang, Mr.	A. E. Apple	*Mr. Chang of Scotland Yard*
Channing, Peter	L. Shapiro	
Chant, Chief Jeremy	Dorothy Camoron Disney	*Strawstack*
Chanways, Lord Montague	J. G. Brandon	
Chaplin, Constable	Ralph Arnold	*Skeletons and Cupboards*
Chapman, Steve	Graham Hastings	*Twice Checked*
Chard, Peter	G. Verner	
Charlemagne	Daniel Roselle	"Charlemagne and the Secret Plans"
Charles, Nicholas ("Nick") and Nora	Dashiell Hammett	*The Thin Man*
Charlesworth, Mr.	Christianna Brand	*Death in High Heels*
Charlton, Inspector	C. Witting	
Chase, Sheriff Ernest	Timothy Brace	*Murder Goes Fishing*
Chatham, Bill	C. Williams	
Chauvet, M.	Freeman Wills Crofts	*The Cask*
Chavasse, Paul	Martin Fallon	*The Keys of Hell*
Chaviski, Joe	Edwin P. Hicks	"Town Hero"
Cheese, Inspector	Nicholas Bentley	*Gammon and Espionage*
Chennault Investigations	Peter Cheyney	*Dark Bahamas*
Cheri-Bibi	Gaston Leroux	*New Idol*
Cherrington, Sir Richard	Glyn Daniel	*Welcome Death*
Chertsy, Gilbert	Sidney Horler	*The Black Heart*
Chess, Victoria	N. M. Newton	
Chetwynd, Anthony	J. L. Morrissey	
Cheung, Y.	Harry Stephen Keeler	*Y. Cheung: Business Detective*
Cheviot, Detective-Superintendent	John Dickson Carr	*Fire, Burn*
Cheyne, Evelyn	Carter Dickson	*Unicorn Murders*
Chickener, Captain	F. Arthur	
"The Chill"	Edward C. Bentley	*Elephant's Work*
Chin Chinn	Albert W. Aiken	*Chin Chinn, Private Detective*
"China Man"; *see* Gar, Joe		
Chipstead, "Bunny"	Sidney Horler	*Secret Agent*
Chitterwick, Ambrose	Anthony Berkeley	*Trial and Error*
Chizmadia, Arthur	Judson P. Phillips	
Christensen, Chief Kurt	Ruth Darby	*Death Boards the Lazy Lady*
Christie, Bill	J. Cassells	
Christie, Lieutenant	Robert P. Wilmot	
Christopher, Jimmy (Operator 5)	Curtis Steele	*Legions of the Death Master*
Chucky, Inspector	Christianna Brand	*Cat and Mouse*
Church, Alice	Elizabeth Ferrars	
Chuska, Hosteen	The Gordons	*Captive*
Cibber, Mike	Lovat Marshall	
Cibo, Comus ("Monsieur Zero")	Nellie Tom-Gallon	"The Middle Dozen"
Cirret, M.	Elizabeth Hely	*A Mark of Displeasure*

CHARACTER	AUTHOR	TITLE
Clack, Drusilla	Wilkie Collins	*The Moonstone*
Claghorn, Tony	Percival Wilde	"The Adventure of the Fallen Angels"
Clairval, Samson	Roger Francis	
Clancy, Lieutenant	Robert L. Pike	*Police Blotter*
Clancy, Peter	Lee Thayer	*Dead Reckoning*
Clane, Terry	Erle Stanley Gardner	*Murder Up My Sleeve*
Clanroyden, Lord Ludovick ("Sandy"); *see* Arbuthnot, Hon. Ludovick		
Clapp, Lieutenant Austin	Wade Miller	*Deadly Weapon*
Clark, Bob ("The Crimson Mask")	Frank Johnson	*Traffic in Murder*
Clark, C. Clark	Samm Sinclair Baker	*Murder Very Dry*
Clark, Conway	John Cotton	*The Devil's Pigeons*
Clarke, Inspector	Patrick Quentin	
Clary, Cayce	Mignon G. Eberhart	
Claw	Nick Carter	
Clay, Colonel	Grant Allen	"The Diamond Links"
Clay, Detective-Inspector	Gavin Holt	
Clay, Sam	Jonathan Latimer	*Sinners and Shrouds*
Clay, Sergeant	William G. Beyer	*Murder by Arrangement*
Clay, Stephen	Sidney E. Porcelain	
Claymore, Tod	Tod Claymore	*This Is What Happened*
Claypole	Francis Beeding	*The Little White Hag*
Claythorne, Sergeant	John Slate	
Clayton, Roger	N. Thurley	
Cleek, Hamilton (Alias "George Headland," "The Man of Forty Faces," "Prince of Mauravania," etc.)	Thomas W. Hanshew	*The Man of the Forty Faces*
Clegg, Gerry	A. Fraser	
Clements, Bill	A. Stuart	
Clements, Cy	John Farr	*Zoo Murders*
Clements, Frank	John Rhode	*Story of a Great Conspiracy*
Clerkenwell, Molly	Martin Joseph	
Clevedon, Howard	Alfred O. Pollard	
Cleveland, Job	M. S. Michel	
Clewth, Superintendent	Henry Wade	*High Sheriff*
Cliff, Ex-Professor Copey	Eric Heath	*Murder in the Museum*
Climpson, Alexandra Katherine	Dorothy Sayers	*Unnatural Death*
Clinton, Detective-Sergeant James	Leonard Gribble	*Tragedy in E Flat*
Club of Queer Trades	G. K. Chesterton	*The Club of Queer Trades*
"Clubfoot"; *see* Grundt, Dr. Adolph		
Cluer, Daniel J.	William B. M. Ferguson	*Shayne Case*
Clume, Asoph	Raymond L. Goldman	*Murder Behind the Mike*
Clunk, Joshua	Henry C. Bailey	*The Garston Murder Case*
Clutha	Hugh Munro	*Clutha Plays a Hunch*
Clutterbuck, John	Alfred Henry Ruegg	*John Clutterbuck, C. W.*
Clyde, Murray	Sterry Browning	*Crime at Cape Folly*

CHARACTER	AUTHOR	TITLE
Clye, Oliver	Francis Beeding	
Cobb, Dr. Emma	Richard Connell	"Doc Em Lives"
Cobb, Inspector	Jonathan Stagge	*Death's Old Sweet Song*
Cobb, Sergeant	R. Armstrong	
Cobb, Shuttlebury	R. Austin Freeman	*The Surprising Experience of Mr. Shuttlebury Cobb*
Cochet, Armand ("The White Eagle")	Arthur Somers Roche	"The Jeweled Casket"
Cockrill, Inspector	Christianna Brand	*Heads You Lose*
Coffee, Dr. Daniel Webster	Lawrence G. Blochman	*Diagnosis: Homicide*
Coffey, Phaudric	H. M. Webster	
Coffin, Inspector	Gwendoline Butler	*Coffin in Malta*
Coffin, Peter	Peter Coffin	*Search for My Great Uncle's Head*
Cohen, Marty	Emmet Hogarth	*Goose Is Cooked*
Colby, Al	David Dodge	*The Red Tassel*
Coldwell, Inspector	Edgar Wallace	
Cole, Schyler	Frederick C. Davis	*Lilies in Her Garden Grew*
Coll, Lieutenant	Rufus King	"A Little Cloud . . . Like a Man's Hand"
Collett, Chief Inspector T.B.	Edgar Wallace	*The Arranways Mystery*
Collin, Mr. Philip	Frank Heller	*Perilous Transactions of Mr. Collin*
Collins, Inspector	Bruce Graeme	
Collins, Railroad Police Agent	Bert and Dolores Hitchens	*FOB Murder*
Collinson, Andy	Henry Holt	*Ace of Spades*
Colman, Seth	Lewis Padgett	*The Brass Ring*
Colt, Commissioner Thatcher	Anthony Abbot	*About the Murder of the Night Club Lady*
Colton, Thornley	Clinton H. Stagg	*Thornley Colton: Blind Detective*
Conacher, Steve	Adam Knight	*Murder for Madame*
Confidential Investigation Services	R. P. Wilmot	*Confidential Investigation Services*
Conners, Le Droit	Samuel Gardenshire	*The Long Arm*
Connor, Doc	Jack Dolph	*Murder Makes the Mare Go*
Connor, "Lefty"	Brad Shannon	*Bury the Guy!*
Connors, Dorinda	E. L. Cushing	
Conover, Mr. and Mrs. John Henry	Wade Miller	
Conquest, Norman	Berkeley Gray	*Crime Marches On*
Conrad, Clive ("The Dormouse")	Frank King	*Enter the Dormouse*
Conrad Detective Agency	Frank King	*Enter the Dormouse*
Conray, Philip	K. Hayles	
Conrigan, Superintendent Garry	G. Dilnot	
Considine, Steve	Robert P. Wilmot	*Blood in Your Eye*
Continental OP	Dashiell Hammett	"The Continental OP"
Conway, Sir Brian Dinsmore	S. Stone	
Conway, Detective-Inspector Clive	E. Laurie Long	
Conway, K. C.	S. Stone	
Cook, Barney	Harvey J. O'Higgins	*Adventures of Detective Barney*
Cook, Madge	Margaret Tayler Yates	*Murder by the Yard*
Cool, Mrs. Bertha	Erle Stanley Gardner	*Lam to the Slaughter*

CHARACTER	AUTHOR	TITLE
Copley, Detective-Inspector	Philip MacDonald	
Coquenil, Paul	Cleveland Moffett	*Through the Wall*
Corbin, Ben	Robert Crane	*Paradise Trap*
Corby, Lieutenant	Patricia Highsmith	*The Blunderer*
Cordell, Geoffrey	Leslie Bridgmont	*Unbriefed Mission*
Cordell, Matt	Evan Hunter	"Now Die in It"
Cordry, Jason	James O'Hanlon	*Murder at Coney Island*
Coritts, Tom	L. Hardy	
Cork, Montague	MacDonald Hastings	*Cork in Bottle*
Corless, Jock	S. H. Courtier	
Cornell, Chief Inspector	Leo Grex	
Cornell, Inspector	Hugh Clevely	
Cornford, Inspector	Milward Kennedy	*Corpse on the Mat*
Cornforth, A.	P. Capon	
Corning, Ken	Erle Stanley Gardner	
Cornish, Alexander	John August	*Troubled Star*
Cornish, Kay	Virginia Hanson	*Death Walks the Post*
Cornish, Ex-Detective Inspector Nicholas	A. MacKenzie	
"Corrector of Destinies"; *see* Mason, Randolph		
Corridon, "Brick-Top"	R. Marshall	
Corrigan, Mark	M. Corrigan	
Corrigan, Captain Tim	Ellery Queen	*How Goes the Murder?*
Corry, Bruce	Michael Halliday	
Cortland, Corporal	Erle Stanley Gardner	"The Case of the Murderer's Bride"
Cossins, Detective-Sergeant	Cyril A. Alington	
Costaine, Tony	Neil McNeil	*The Spy Catchers*
Costello	J. Nicholson	
Cotterel, Martin	John Trench	*What Rough Beast*
Cotton, Gunston	Rupert Grayson	*Death Rides the Forest*
Cotton, Larry	B. Vane	
Cotton, Neal	Sam S. Taylor	*So Cold, My Bed*
Coulson, Detective	Jack Mann	*Coulson Alone*
"The Counsellor"; *see* Brand, Mark		
Counterpol	John Boland	*Counterpol*
Counterstroke; *see* Nicholson, Lloyd		
Courtenay, Amanda	Christopher Reeve	*Lady, Be Careful*
Cowper, John	Francis Beeding	*The Black Arrows*
Cox, Superintendent	Belton Cobb	
Coyle, Danny	Judson P. Phillips	*The 14th Trump*
Crabtree, John Carter	Leslie Ford	
Cragg, Sam	Frank Gruber	*The French Key*
Craggs, Emma	Henry R. F. Keating	*Death of a Fat God*
Craig, John	I. Jeffries	
Craig, Nat	Ernest Dudley	
Craig, Robert	C. Cullen	
Craig, Steve	Bevis Winter	*Noose of Emeralds*
Craig, Walter	H. Innes	
Craigie, Gordon	John Creasey	
Craine, Paul	Eugene P. Healey	*Craine's First Case*
Cramer, Inspector	Rex Stout	*The Mother Hunt*

CHARACTER	AUTHOR	TITLE
Crane, William ("Bill") and Ann	Jonathan Latimer	*The Lady in the Morgue*
Crankshaw, Inspector	E. X. Ferrars	*Depart This Life*
Cranston, Inspector	J. Corbett	
Crawford, Bruce	N. Deane	
Crawford, Inspector John	G. M. Wilson	
Crawford, Liane	Susan Gilruth	
Creed, John	Anthony Marsden	
Creevy, Colonel Winston	Jeremy Lord	*The Bannerman Case*
Creighton	F. Britten Austin	"Diamond Cuts Diamond"
Crichton, Peter	Sidney Horler	
"The Crime Doctor"; *see* Dollar, Dr.		
Crime Haters	John Creasey	*The Crime Haters*
Crimp, Hetty	J. Matheson	
Crimson Clown	Johnston McCulley	*The Crimson Clown*
"The Crimson Mask"; *see* Clark, Bob		
Crisp, Colonel	Roy Vickers	
Cristo, Lieutenant Johnny	Lee Costigan	*Never Kill a Cop*
Crittenden, Joseph J.	William Wiser	
Croft, Detective-Inspector	J. Corbett	
Croft, Superintendent	Joseph S. Fletcher	*The Murder in the Pallant*
Croker, Danby	R. Austin Freeman	"The Brazen Serpent"
Crole, Simon	Robert H. Leitfred	*The Corpse That Spoke*
Cromwell, Chief Inspector "Ironsides"	Victor Gunn	*Ironsides Sees Red*
Cromwell, Sergeant	George Bellairs	*Death Before Breakfast*
Crook, Arthur	Anthony Gilbert	*The Innocent Bottle*
Crosby, David	Harry Stephen Keeler	*The Amazing Web*
Crosby, Herbert	Mary Semple Scott	*Crime Hound*
Crosby, Mark	Eleanor Blake	*Death Down East*
Cross, Howard	John Ross MacDonald	*Meet Me at the Morgue*
Cross, Inspector	John Donovan	*The Case of the Talking Dust*
Cross, Ex-Detective Inspector John	F. J. Lowe	*Killer from the Grave*
Crow	George Norworthy	
Crow, Anderson	George Barr McCutcheon	*Anderson Crow, Detective*
Crow, Sergeant George	Roger Simons	*Gamble with Death*
Crowder, Uncle George	Hugh Pentecost	"My Dear Uncle Sherlock"
Crumlish, Father Francis Xavier	Alice Scanlan Reach	"The Gentle Touch"
Crump, Officer Homer	Robert Twohy	"Routine Investigation"
Crusit, Myra	Joseph C. Lincoln	
Cuff, Sergeant	Wilkie Collins	*The Moonstone*
Cumberledge, Hubert	Grant Allen	
Cummings, Joel	J. Brogan	
Cummings, Ronnie	John Dellbridge	
Cunliffe, Dr.	H. Frankish	*Dr. Cunliffe, Investigator*
Cunningham, Detective-Sergeant	Michael Halliday	
Cunningham, Major "Brains"	E. P. Thorne	

CHARACTER	AUTHOR	TITLE
Cupples, Nathaniel Burton	Edmund C. Bentley	*Trent's Last Case*
Currie, Colin	E. Maschwitz	
Currie, Inspector	Neil Graham	
Curry, Eleanor	March Evermay	*They Talked of Poison*
Curry, Splash	Carter Brown	
Curtis, Ellen	Babs Lee	*Passport to Oblivion*
Curtis, Hugh	Paul Somers	*Operation Piracy*
Curtis, Lyle	Emma Lou Fetta	
Curwen, Detective-Inspector	Roy Vickers	"The Dacey Affair"
Cyr, Dr. Jacques	Donald Q. Burleigh	*Kristiana Killers*
Czissar, Dr. Jan	Eric Ambler	"The Case of the Emerald Sky"
D-	Graham Greene	*The Confidential Agent*
D— (Minister)	Edgar Allan Poe	"The Purloined Letter"
"D.A."; *see* Selby, "D.A." Douglas		
Daburon, M.	Emile Gaboriau	*L'Affaire Lerouge*
Daggart, Brinton	Mark Saxton	
Dagobert	Baldwin Groller	*Detective Dagobert's Deeds and Adventures*
Dain, Stephen	Robert Sheckley	*Live Gold*
Dale, Gregory	K. Hayles	
Dale, Ex-Superintendent James	J. C. Cooper	
Dale, Jimmy	Frank L. Packard	*The Adventures of Jimmy Dale*
Dale, John	Jeremy York	
Dale, Kenneth	Raymond Allen	"A Happy Solution"
Dale, Mr.	John Chance	
D'Alessandro, Sergeant John	Milton K. Ozaki	
Dallow, Shane	G. Joseph	
Dalmas, John	Raymond Chandler	"Red Wind"
Daly, Ken	Roderick Wilkinson	*The Big Still*
Daly, Professor	E. Dillon	
Damian, Paul	Paul Walsh	*Murder Room*
Damman, Captain	Mark Saxton	
Dan, Lingo	Percival Pollard	*Lingo Dan*
Danavan, Mat	James Warner	
Dane, Major	Mary Roberts Rinehart	*The Yellow Room*
Dane, Timothy	William Ard	*Perfect Frame*
Danforth, Carol	James Holding	"The Hong Kong Jewel Mystery"
Danforth, King	James Holding	"The Hong Kong Jewel Mystery"
Daniels, Charmian	Jennie Melville	*Come Home and Be Killed*
Daniels, Mr.	Q. Patrick	*S.S. Murder*
Daniels, Mohawk	William L. Rohde	*High Red for Dead*
Danning, Colonel David	Don Von Elsner	*Don't Just Stand There, Do Some-one*
Dante, Paul	D. Muir	
Dantry, Captain Nick	John Hunter	*The Man Behind*
Danvers, Detective-Inspector	David Whitelaw	
Dapertutte	E. T. A. Hoffmann	*Weird Tales*
Darch, Superintendent	B. Rodney	
D'Arcy, Detective	Elizabeth Linington	*No Evil Angel*
Dare, Susan	Mignon G. Eberhart	*Introducing Susan Dare*
Dark, Algy	Ernest Dudley	

CHARACTER	AUTHOR	TITLE
Darnley, Superintendent	Alan Brock	*Inquiries by the Yard*
Darrell, Jeffrey	Harry Stephen Keeler	
Darrow, Inspector Caesar	John Mason Bigelow	*Death Is an Early Riser*
Daryl, Middleton	Edward Acheson	
Daryl, Mike	L. Wilkinson	
Dash, Speed	Erle Stanley Gardner	
DaSilva, Captain Jose (Ze)	Robert L. Fish	*Brazilian Sleigh Ride*
Datchery, Dick	Charles Dickens	*The Mystery of Edwin Drood*
"Daubreuil, Paul"; *see* Lupin, Arsène		
Davenant, P. J.	Lord Frederic Hamilton	*Holiday Adventures of Mr. P. J. Davenant*
Davenport, Anne; *see* McLean, Mrs. Hugh		
Daventree, James	C. D. E. Francis	*Portrait of a Killer*
Daw, Blackie	George Randolph Chester	*Young Wallingford*
Dawe, Archer	Joseph S. Fletcher	*The Adventures of Archer Dawe, Sleuthhound*
Dawes, Sergeant Freddie	Margaret Erskine	*Sleep No More*
Dawkins, Chief Inspector	G. Dilnot	
Dawle, Superintendent	Henry Wade	*The Hanging Captain*
Dawlish, Patrick and Felicity	Gordon Ashe	*Man Who Laughed at Murder*
Dawn, Paul	James Yaffe	"The Problem of the Emperor's Mushroom"
Dawson, Inspector	Kenneth Laing	*Shadow People*
Dawson, Captain Jack	"Sea-Lion"	
Dawson, Superintendent	Milward Kennedy	*Poison in the Parish*
Dawson, Chief Inspector William (Alias "Bill the Bloodhound," "Cholmondeley Jones")	Bennet Copplestone	*The Diversions of Dawson*
Dax, Commissioner Saturnin	Marten Cumberland	*Murmurs in the Rue Morgue*
Day, Julian	Dennis Wheatley	
Deacon, Bethany	Nigel Morland	
Deakin, Sheriff Clem	J. E. Barry	
Dean, Garry	Paul Whelton	*Pardon My Blood*
Dean, Herbert Ranchester	Mary Roberts Rinehart	*The Album*
Dean, Sally	Bruce Sanders	*To Catch a Spy*
Deane, Robert	John W. Vandercook	*Murder in Fiji*
Deane, Tony	Victor Bridges	
Deans, Sergeant Sally	Leonard Gribble and G. Laws	*Sally of Scotland Yard*
De Bahl, Baron Alexis ("The Fox")	Valentine Williams	*The Fox Prowls*
Debenham, Detective-Inspector	C. Brooks	
Decker, Lieutenant Bill	Lawrence Treat	*F as in Flight*
Dee, Judge	Robert Van Gulik	*The Chinese Bell Murder*

CHARACTER	AUTHOR	TITLE
Dee, Mr.	Desmond Cory	*The Name of the Game Is Death*
Deene, Carolus	Leo Bruce	*Such Is Death*
Deering, John	C. Brooks	
Deglin, Lieutenant	W. L. Stuart	
DeHaviland, Evelyn	John N. Chance	*Wheels in the Forest*
DeKlerk, Detective-Inspector	Hugh Desmond	
Delagardie, Honoria; *see* Denver, Honoria		
Delahanty, Police Chief	John Stephen Strange	*Night of Reckoning*
DeLancy (King of Thieves)	Harry Stephen Keeler	*Thieves' Night*
Delaney, Denis	Denis Delaney	*Cat in Gloves*
Delaney, Denis Aloysius	Bart Singer	*You're Wrong, Délaney*
Delaney, Eddie	A. Graham	
Delaney, Mike	C. E. Maine	
Delaroy, "Steeley"	William E. Johns	*Steeley Flies Again*
Delevan, Danny	Frederick C. Davis	*The Graveyard Never Closes*
DeLobo, Senor Arnaz	Erle Stanley Gardner	
Delorme, Father	Stephen Lister	*Delorme in Deep Water*
Deming, Richard	R. L. F. McCombs	
Dempster, Ruth	Sidney Horler	
Dene, Dorcas	George R. Sims	*Dorcas Dene: Detective*
Dene, Sir John	Herbert Jenkins	*Malcom Sage, Detective*
Dene, Michael	G. Verner	
Dene, Trevor	Valentine Williams	*Masks Off at Midnight*
Denning, Superintendent	H. Blayn	
Denny, Hal	Lucian Austin	
Denton, Daniel	Leslie Cargill	
Denver, Gerald Christian Wimsey (Viscount St. George)	Dorothy Sayers	*Strong Poison*
Denver, Dowager Duchess Honoria Lucasta Wimsey (née Delagardie)	Dorothy Sayers	*Clouds of Witness*
Department of Concealed Communications	Edward D. Hoch	"The Spy Who Took the Long Route"
Department of Dead Ends	Roy Vickers	"The Man Who Murdered in Public"
Department of Queer Complaints	Carter Dickson	*Scotland Yard: The Department of Queer Complaints*
Department Z	John Creasey	*Sabotage*
Deran, Jacques	J. Gearson	*Velvet Well*
De Raven, Carter	Walter Ripperger	"The Affair of the Dancing Skeleton"
Derry, Nigel	John Bude	
Destime, Smithin	Dennis Wheatley	
"Detective Barney"; *see* Cook, Barney		
De Wet, Inspector	N. Mackenzie	
Dewin, Peter	Edgar Wallace	
Dexter, Inspector	Bruce Graeme	*No Clues for Dexter*
Diavolo, Don	Stuart Towne	
Digburn, Ward	Bruce Sanders	*To Catch a Spy*
Dill, "Daffy"	Richard Sale	*A Nose for News*

CHARACTER	AUTHOR	TITLE
Dillon, Sheriff Steve	Anna Katherine Green	*Miss Hurd: An Enigma*
Di Marco, Jeff	Doris Miles Disney	*Method in Madness*
"The Disguiser"	Sidney Horler	*The Man Who Died Twice*
"Disher"	Will Scott	*The Mask*
Dix, Constantine	Barry Pain	*Stories in the Dark*
Dix, Francis	Mary E. Wilkins Freeman	*The Long Arm*
Dixon, Dr. Herbert	Erle Stanley Gardner	"The Case of the Murderer's Bride"
Dixon, P. C. George	Ted Willis	*The Blue Lamp*
Dixon, Tom	H. J. Hultman	
Dixon, "Totem"	Mary Richart	*Murder in the Town*
"Dizzy Duo" (Snooty and Scoop)	Joe Archibald	"Slip Service"
Doan	Norbert Davis	*Sally's in the Alley*
Doane, Liz	Frances S. Wees	*The Country of the Strangers*
Dobson, Inspector	Henry Wade	*The Verdict of You All*
Dodd, Cedric	Kenneth Livingston	*The Dodd Cases*
Dodd, Septimus	Sutherland Scott	*Doctor Dodd's Experiment*
Dodd, Superintendent	Henry Wade	*Missing Partners*
"Dodo"	Anne Nash	*Death by Design*
Dolan, Brad	William Fuller	*Brad Dolan's Blonde Cargo*
Doleman, Inspector	John Bude	
Dollar, Dr. ("The Crime Doctor")	Ernest W. Hornung	*The Crime Doctor*
Dollops	Thomas W. Hanshew	*Cleek, The Master Detective*
Donahue, "Donny"	Frederic Nebel	"Dead Date"
Donaldson, Inspector	G. Verner	
Donan, Sheriff Gil	Margaret P. Hood	*The Scarlet Thread*
Donaque, Monsieur	Arthur Train	*Monsieur Donaque*
Donnell, Bill	G. Dickson	
Donny, Sheriff Pete	Mignon G. Eberhart	
Donovan, Claude ("Harvard")	Judson P. Phillips	*The 14th Trump*
Donovan, Dick	Joyce Emerson Muddock	*The Man from Manchester*
Donovan, Eli	J. Rubel	
Donovan, Lieutenant Jerome	Elizabeth Dean	
Doome, Sheridan	Stephen Gould	*Murder of the Admiral*
Doonh, Langa	Reginald T. M. Scott	*Secret Service Smith*
Doowinkle, John ("D.A.")	Harry Klingsberg	*Doowinkle, D.A.*
"The Dormouse"; *see* Conrad Clive		
Dorn, Michael	Edgar Wallace	*The Strange Countess*
Dornfell, Inspector	J. J. Connington	
"The Double-C Man"; *see* Rand		
Douglas, Ian	A. MacKinnon	
Douglas, Kirk	Octavus Roy Cohen	
Douglin, Mackay Solomon	Carl Shannon	*Fatal Footsteps*
Doulan, Mr.	Norman Leslie	
Dove, Fidelity	Roy Vickers	"The St. Jocasta Tapestries"
Dover, Chief Inspector Wilfred	Joyce Porter	*Dover One*
Dowell-Blakeley, Captain Leigh	Edward Acheson	*Murder to Hounds*
Downey, Corporal	James B. Hendryx	*Outlaws of Halfaday Creek*
Downs, Jerry	Leo Grex	*The Man from Manhattan*

CHARACTER	AUTHOR	TITLE
Doyle, Chief Detective-Inspector Larry	Francis Grierson	
Doyle, Lieutenant	Richard Lakin	*The Body Fell on Berlin*
Doyle, Patrick Michael	Audrey Newell	*Who Killed Cavelotti?*
Dracula, Count	Bram Stoker	*Dracula*
Drake, Callie	Constance and Gwenyth Little	
Drake, Desmond	"Sea-Lion"	*Damn Desmond Drake*
Drake, Detective-Inspector	K. Wade	
Drake, Dexter	Elsa Barker	*The C.I.D. of Dexter Drake*
Drake, John	Wilfred McNeilly	*No Way Out*
Drake, Jonathan	Ralph Oppenheim	"The Death Chair Murders"
Drake, Captain Martin	Carter Dickson	*Skeleton in the Clock*
Drake, Paul	Erle Stanley Gardner	*The Case of the Sulky Girl*
Drake, Steve ("The Ripper")	Richard Ellington	*Just Killing Time*
Dransfield, Chief Inspector	Frank King	*The Ghoul*
Draper, Sergeant	John Rhode	
Drax, Sir Hugo	Ian Fleming	*Moonraker*
Drayton, George	Vincent McConnor	"Just Like Inspector Maigret"
"The Dreamer"; *see* Reamer, Donald		
Dred, Michael	Marie and Robert Leighton	*Michael Dred: Detective*
Dreist (Police Dog)	Baynard Kendrick	*Reservations for Death*
Drew, Major Adam	Virginia Hanson	*Mystery for Mary*
Drew, Gordon	H. Blayn	
Drew, Nancy	Carolyn Keene	*The Clue in the Crumbling Wall*
Drexel, Detective-Superintendent	G. Usher	
Drexel, Roger	Lawrence Lynch	*Moina*
Driffield, Sir Clinton	J. J. Connington	*Death at Swaythling Court*
Driscoll, Sheriff "Stuff"	Rufus King	"The Seeds of Murder"
Drood, Edwin	Charles Dickens	"The Mystery of Edwin Drood"
Druce, Inspector	Hugh Desmond	
Drum, Chester	Stephen Marlowe	*Murder Is My Dish*
Drummond, Captain Hugh ("Bulldog")	Herman C. McNeile	*Bulldog Drummond*
Duane	John Benton	*Duane and the Art Murders*
Duble, Sam	George Harmon Coxe	*Fashioned for Murder*
"Ducharme, Professor Paul"; *see* Valmont, Eugene		
Duckett, George	Valentine Williams	
Duckworthy, Diddymus Demetrius	Philip G. Larbalestier	
Dudley, John and Jane	Paul Dobbins	*Death in the Dunes*
Duff	Charles Dickens	*Oliver Twist*
Duff, John	Harvey J. O'Higgins	*Detective Duff Unravels It*
Duffy, Cornelius	William G. Beyer	*Murder by Arrangement*
Duffy, Father	Dorothy Salisbury Davis	*A Gentle Murderer*
Duffy, Lieutenant	Burton E. Stevenson	
Duffy, Superintendent	Nigel Fitzgerald	*Echo Answers Murder*
Duker, Casson	William Mole	*Skin Trap*
Dukovski	Anton Chekov	*The Shooting Party*
Dulcet, Dove	Christopher Morley	"Codeine (7 per cent)"

CHARACTER	AUTHOR	TITLE
Duluth, Jake	Patrick Quentin	*My Son, The Murderer*
Duluth, Peter	Patrick Quentin	*Puzzle for Fiends*
Dumm, Virgil	Val Roser	*Murder in the Wind*
Dunbar, Peter	Helen McCloy	*The One That Got Away*
Duncan, Hugh	Archibald E. Fielding	*Murder in Suffolk*
Duncan, Matt	H. H. Holmes	*Nine Times Nine*
Duncan, Robbie	Dan Billany	*It Takes a Thief*
Dundas, Michael	Virginia Roth	*Death Breaks the Ring*
Dundee, James F.	Anne Austin	*Murder Backstairs*
Dunlap, Constance	Arthur B. Reeve	*Constance Dunlap, Woman Detective*
Dunn, Jim	H. L. Nelson	*The Sleep Is Deep*
Dunn, Dr. Peter	John A. Ferguson	*Death Comes to Perigord*
Dunn, Sir Peter	Edgar Wallace	*Sergeant Sir Peter*
Dunning, Ex-Detective-Inspector	Hugh Desmond	
Dupin, C. Auguste	Edgar Allan Poe	"Murder in the Rue Morgue"
Dupuy, M.	Anthony Gilbert	*The Man in Button Boots*
Durand, Red	J. T. Story	
Durea, Frank	Erle Stanley Gardner	*Case of the Smoking Chimney*
Durkin, Lieutenant Dan	Arthur M. Chase	*Twenty Minutes to Kill*
Durrant, Sergeant	N. Mackenzie	
Durrell, Sam	Edward S. Aarons	*Assignment-Ankara*
Dusen; *see* Van Dusen, Prof. Augustus		
Dust, Joe	Peter Graaf	*Daughter Fair*
Duval, Inspector Henri	Leonard Gribble	
Duveen, Dulcie (later Mrs. Arthur Hastings)	Agatha Christie	*Murder on the Links*
Duveen, Michael	Eden Phillpotts	*Black, White and Brindled*
DuVivien, Natasha	Nancy Spain	*Not Wanted on Voyage*
Dwayne, Inspector	Joseph S. Fletcher	*Bartenstein Case*
Dwyer, Ethan	Robert P. Hansen	*Mark Three for Murder*
Dyke, Toby	E. X. Ferrars	*Remove the Bodies*
Dynes, Inspector	H. Robertson	
Dyson, Dr. Anne	J. S. Story	
Dyson, Sergeant	Andrew Garve	*Hide and Go Seek*
Eady, Quentin	E. P. Thorne	
Early, Inspector	Leslie Sands	*Something to Hide*
East, Mark	Hilda Lawrence	*Death of a Doll*
Eastabrook, Robert	Louis Dodge	*Whispers*
Easterbrook, Mark	Agatha Christie	*The Pale Horse*
Eastwood, Anthony	Agatha Christie	"The Mystery of the Spanish Shawl"
Eaton, Richard	Dennis Wheatley	
Edward, "Elegant"	Edgar Wallace	*Elegant Edward*
Edwards, Inspector	William LeQueux	*The Man from Downing Street*
Edwards, Jane Amanda	Charlotte Murray	*Hand Me a Crime*
Edwards, Johnny	Richard Powell	*Shot in the Dark*
Edwards, Kathie	Eleanor Blake	*Death Down East*
Edwards, Sergeant	Mary E. Wilkins Freeman	
Egerton, Scott	Anthony Gilbert	
Egg, Montague	Dorothy Sayers	*Sleuths on the Run*
Ego, Inspector	G. R. Mallach	"In Confidence"
Egypt, Harry	Daniel Brown	*The Subject of Harry Egypt*
Eldon, Sheriff Bill	Erle Stanley Gardner	"The Clue of the Hungry Horse"
Elizabeth	Florence A. Kilpatrick	*Elizabeth the Sleuth*

CHARACTER	AUTHOR	TITLE
Elk, Inspector	Edgar Wallace	*The Twister*
Ellerdine, Detective-Superintendent Roger	Cecil M. Wills	*Clue of the Golden Earring*
Ellis, Kay	Ruth Otis Wallis	*Too Many Bones*
Ellis, Sergeant	F. Vivian	
Elton, Brian	Joseph J. Farjeon	
Elver, Horace Augustus	George Dilnot	
Elyot, Toby	Sarah Gainham	*The Stone Roses*
Emeny, Arnold	Max Murray	
Emery, Justin	Elizabeth Ferrars	
Emery, Val	George Dilnot	
Emil; *see* Tischbein, Emil		
Emmons, Matt	Edward S. Aarons	
Emp, H. ("Rope")	Sidney Horler	*Master of Venom*
Enderby, Peter	N. Mackenzie	
"Engel, George"; *see* Wolff, Commissioner		
English, Jeff	Sterling Noel	
Entwistle, Ebbie ("Old Ebbie")	Frederick A. M. Webster	*Old Ebbie Returns*
Erridge, Matt	Aaron Marc Stein	*Blood on the Stars*
Errol, Mark and Michael	John Creasey	
Erskine, Professor	Michael Burning and Althen Grey	*Dusty Death*
Essington, Mandell	Joseph Storer Clouston	*Lunatic at Large Again*
Estees, Brigit	L. Lewis	
Evans, Dan	Ernest Dudley	
Evans, Homer	Elliot Paul	*Hugger-Mugger in the Louvre*
Evans, Inspector	M. Gallie	
Evans, John	Raymond Chandler	*Killer in the Rain*
Evans, Sam	Frederic Brown	
Everhard, Don	Gordon Young	*The Devil's Passport*
Eversleigh, Bill	Agatha Christie	
Ewe-all (Goat)	Richard Starnes	*Another Mug for the Bier*
Exendene	John F. Byrne	"The Mystery of the Third Mustache"
Eylesbarrow, Lucy	Agatha Christie	*What Mrs. McGillicuddy Saw*
Fair, Prosper	Barry Perowne	
Fairbanks, Henry ("Hank")	Elizabeth Dean	*Murder Is a Collector's Item*
Fairbrother, Inspector	Maurice Procter	
Fairfax	Guy Boothby	*My Strangest Case*
Fairfax, Colin	Victor Bridges	
Fairford, Inspector Tom	G. D. H. and M. I. Cole	*The Brothers Sackville*
Faithfull, Detective-Inspector	Ernest Dudley	
The Falcon	Drexel Drake	*The Falcon's Prey*
Falcon, Superintendent	Dornford Yates	
Falkenstein, Jesse	Leslie Egan	*My Name Is Death*
Falmouth, Superintendent	Edgar Wallace	
Fandor	Marcel Allain	*Juve in the Docks*

CHARACTER	AUTHOR	TITLE
Fane, Martin and Richard	Michael Halliday	*Man on the Run*
Fang, Wu	Roland Daniel	*Wu Fang*
Fanshawe, Sergeant Denis	Hugh Desmond	
Fansler, Professor Kate	Amanda Cross	*In the Last Analysis*
Fantômas	Marcel Allain	*Juve in the Docks*
Farland, Bill	Holly Roth	*The Crimson in the Purple*
Farley, Jerome	Maurice Walsh	*Danger Under the Moon*
Farling, Hornsby	C. F. Nicolet	
Farne, Inspector	R. Grant	
Farnham	Norbert Davis	"Do a Dame a Favor"
Farnsworth, Dr.	Francis Leo Golden	"The Testimony of Dr. Farnsworth"
Farquhar, Sir Robert	Sidney Horler	
Farr, Kate	L. Lewis	
Farrant, Chief Inspector Michael	Philip G. Larbalestier	
Farrar	Robert A. J. Walling	*The Fatal Five Minutes*
Farrar, Johnny	James Hadley Chase	
Farrar, Teddy	Edmund Snell	"Farrar Fits In"
Farrel, Railroad Policeman	Bert and Dolores Hitchens	*End of the Line*
Farrell-Knox	Brian Flynn	
Farris, Jean	Rex Stout	
Fathom	Peter Anthony	*Withered Murder*
Faulkner, Christmas	Paul Capon	
Fauntley, Lorna	Anthony Morton	*Deaf, Dumb and Blonde*
Faversham, Alice	Frank King	
Fayle, Lewis	M. Mountford	
Fayne, Richard	S. Bunce	
Fearing, Patricia	Ian Fleming	*Thunderball*
Featherstone, Captain Jim	Edgar Wallace	
Fedora, Johnny	Desmond Cory	*Undertow*
Feen, Colonel Brian	Christopher Bush	
Feenix, Detective-Inspector	Joan Fleming	
Felix, M.	Benjamin L. Farjeon	*The Mystery of M. Felix*
Fell, Dr. Gideon	John Dickson Carr	*The Arabian Nights Murder*
Fellowes, Commissioner	Gilbert Charles North	
Fellows, Police Chief Fred	Hillary Waugh	*The Late Mrs. D.*
Felse, Dominic and Bunty	Ellis Peters	*Who Lies Here*
Felse, Detective-Inspector George	Ellis Peters	*Who Lies Here*
Felstead, Charles Medway	Lawrence W. Meynell	
Felton, Ray	John Marsh	*Small and Deadly*
Fen, Gervase	Edmund Crispin	*Love Lies Bleeding*
Fenby, Inspector	Richard Hull	*The Murders of Monty*
Fenner, Maxwell	Louis F. Booth	*Broker's End*
Fenstrom, Charley	Charles H. Snow	*Buckhorn Murder Case*
Fenton, Laurie	Michael Annesley	*Fenton of the Foreign Office*
Ferenc, Dr.	R. Savage	
Fergus, Sara	Helen Joan Hultman	*Find the Woman*

CHARACTER	AUTHOR	TITLE
Ferguson, District Attorney	James Eastwood	
Ferguson, Sergeant Alec	Thomas Walsh	"Cop on the Prowl"
Ferrara, Mr.	A. Scobie	
Ferrars, Francis	Lawrence Lynch	*The Last Stroke*
Ferrers, Lon	Peter Cheyney	
Ferribly, Inspector	Miles Burton	
Ferrieres, Magistrate	J. Guil and J. Baneal	*One Crime Too Many*
Ferrison, Roger	E. Phillips Oppenheim	
Feston, Bernard	Kevin Fitzgerald	*Dangerous to Lean Out*
Fey, Sheridan	F. Duncan	
Field, Fabian	Dick Donovan	*Triumphs of Fabian-Field: Criminologist*
Fiennes, Evelyn	Michael Gilbert	*After the Fine Weather*
Finbow	Charles P. Snow	*Death Under Sail*
Finch, Inspector Septimus	Margaret Erskine	*The Whispering House*
Findlater, Iain	N. Tranter	
Findlay, Dr.	Harry Kemp	
Finlay of the Sentinel	Cecil F. Gregg	*Finlay of the Sentinel*
Finnegan, Barney	D. Rutherford	
Finnegan, John	Norman Forrest	*Death Took a Greek God*
Finney, Dr. Mary	Matthew Head	*Murder at the Flea Club*
Finsbury, Michael	Robert L. Stevenson and Lloyd Osbourne	*The Wrong Box*
Firebrace, Captain	"Seafarer"	*Captain Firebrace*
Firth, Ian	Ludovic Peters	*Two Sets to Murder*
Fisher, Horne	G. K. Chesterton	*The Man Who Knew Too Much*
Fiske, Lee	Lee Roberts	*The Case of the Missing Lovers*
Fitzbrown, Dr.	Mary Fitt	*Clues to Cristobel*
Fitzgerald, Brian	Fergus Hume	*The Mystery of a Hansom Cab*
Fitzgerald, Mrs.	Anne Hocking	*Old Mrs. Fitzgerald*
Fitzwilliam, Luke	Agatha Christie	*Easy to Kill*
Flack, Colonel Humphrey	Everett Rhodes Castle	"The Colonel Gives a Party"
Flagg, Paul	Bruno Fischer	*The Angels Fell*
Flagg, Superintendent	John Cassells	*Enter Suprintendent Flagg*
Flagg, Webster	Veronica Parker Johns	*Servant's Problem*
Flambeau	G. K. Chesterton	"The Secret of Flambeau"
Flater, Cyrus	August Derleth	*Death by Design*
Fleet, Inspector	M. Maytham	
Fletcher, Alec	Jack Hoffenberg	
Fletcher, Johnny	Frank Gruber	*The French Key*
Flixworth, Superintendent	Miles Burton	
Flock, Ray	Jack Iams	
Flocon	Major Arthur Griffith	*The Rome Express*
Floyd, Inspector	Albert Harding	*Death on Raven's Scar*
Flynn, Captain	Ernest Laurie Long	*The Blindness of Flynn*
Folly, Superintendent	Jeremy York	*Run Away to Murder*
Fontaine, Solange	F. Tennyson Jesse	*Solange Stories*
Forain, Paul	G. K. Chesterton	"The Five of Swords"
Foran, Mark	W. T. Ballard	*Murder Las Vegas Style*
Forbes, Andrew	L. Halliday	
Forbes, Detective	H. Gardiner	
Forbes, Sir Graham	Francis Durbridge	
Forbes, Kenneth	Paul Capon	

CHARACTER	AUTHOR	TITLE
Ford, Brad	Hank Hobson	
Fordinghame, Sir Brian	Sidney Horler	*Vivanti*
Forester, Lieutenant-Colonel Adrian	B. Stuart	
Forester, Stet	G. Hoster	
Forgan	Manning Coles	*With Intent to Deceive*
Forrest, John	A. Fullerton	
Forrest, Richard	Anthony Heckstall-Smith	
Forstmann, Dr.	Helen Eustis	*The Horizontal Man*
Forsyth, Gideon	Robert Louis Stevenson	*The Wrong Box*
Forsythe, Captain John	Christopher Hale	*Midsummer Nightmare*
Fortune, Ann; *see* Crane, William		
Fortune, Dan	Michael Collins	*Act of Fear*
Fortune, Dr. Reginald ("Reggie")	Henry C. Bailey	*Call Mr. Fortune*
Fortune, Mrs. Reginald; *see* Amber, Joan		
Fortune, Temple	T. C. H. Jacobs	*Dangerous Fortune*
Fortworth, Lord; *see* Black, Henry		
Fosco, Count	Wilkie Collins	*The Woman in White*
Foster, Captain	George Malcolm-Smith	*If a Body Meet a Body*
"The Four Adjusters"	Mark Cross	*Challenge to the Four*
"Four Just Men"	Edgar Wallace	*Four Just Men*
Four Square Jane	Edgar Wallace	*Four Square Jane*
Fowler, Dan	Norman A. Daniels	*G-Men Strike Hard*
Fowler, Timothy	Anne Colyer	*Going to St. Ives*
"The Fox"; *see* De Bahl, Baron		
Fox, Anatole	Bruce Sanders	
Fox, Inspector	Ngaio Marsh	*Artists in Crime*
Fox, Larry	J. Marsh	
Fox, Tecumseh	Rex Stout	*Double for Death*
Foxlihough, Granius; *see* Toft		
Foyle, Assistant Chief Inspector	Helen McCloy	*Dance of Death*
Frame, Reynold	Herbert Brean	*Wilders Walk Away*
Frampton, Inspector Andrew	Thomas Arthur Plummer	*The Dumb Witness*
Francine, Ken	Ed Lacy	
Frant, Miss Arabella	D. Fearon	
Franzino, Lieutenant	Ed Lacy	*The Best That Ever Did It*
Fraser, Ex-Superintendent Alan	Hugh Desmond	*Calling Alan Fraser*
Fraser, Alan	N. Mackensie	
Fraser, Daird	Victor Canning	
Fraser, Sergeant	J. W. Mason	
Fraser, Inspector Tom	William M. Duncan	
Frayle, Miss	Ernest Dudley	*Meet Dr. Morelle*
Frayley, Detective-Inspector	Alfred Tack	
Frazer, Graham	Joseph Graffy	*Man Who Was Not Himself*
Freddy the Frog	Charles Brooks	*The Swimming Frog*
Freeland, Detective-Inspector	H. Ainsworth	

CHARACTER	AUTHOR	TITLE
Freeman, Jub	Lawrence Treat	*V as in Victim*
Freeman, Noah	Stanley Ellin	"The Crime of Ezechiele Coen"
French, Lieutenant Bill	Christopher Hale	*Midsummer Nightmare*
French, Chief Superintendent Joseph	Freeman Wills	*Inspector French's Greatest Case*
French, Michael	Victor Bridges	
Freyberger, Gustave	Henry de V. Stacpoole	
Friar, Inspector Robin	J. Sandys	
Friday, Joe	Richard Deming	*The Lineup*
Friker, Inspector Paul	Mignon G. Eberhart	*Speak No Evil*
Frobisher, Detective-Sergeant	Joanna Cannan	
Frobisher, Timothy	Constance and Gwenyth Little	
Froget, Monsieur	Georges Simenon	"The Case of Arnold Schultringer"
Frost, Gerald ("Nighthawk")	Sidney Horler	*Return of Nighthawk*
Frost, Inspector	Herbert Maynard Smith	*Inspector Frost in Crevenna Cove*
Frost, Mr.	Mary Fitt	
Frost, Chief Inspector Roger "Tey"	Francis Grierson	
Frost, Sergeant	Eleanor Daly Boylan	"The Methodical Man"
Fry, Pete and Betsy	Pete Fry	*The Grey Sombrero*
Fuller, Inspector	Mary Roberts Rinehart	
Fu Manchu, Dr.	Sax Rohmer	*The Insidious Dr. Fu Manchu*
Furey, Lee	Ernie Weatherall	
Furlong, Jim	George Griswold	*A Checkmate by the Colonel*
Furneaux, Inspector	Louis Tracy	*The Strange Disappearance of Lady Delia*
Furniss, Chief Inspector	Alex Atkinson	*Exit Charlie*
Furze, Jimmy	Leslie Cargill	
Fylton, Bernard	John D. Beresford	*Instrument of Destiny*
G—	Edgar Allan Poe	"The Mystery of Marie Roget"
G. 7; *see* B, Inspector		
Gabriel, Bill	Lawrence G. Blochman	
Gaden, Detective-Superintendent	P. H. Powell	
"Gaffer"	Avran Davidson	"The Affair at Lahore Cantonment"
Galbraith, De	Frances Duncombe	*Death of a Spinster*
Gale, Gabriel	G. K. Chesterton	*The Poet and the Lunatics*
Gale, Nicholas	Peter Cheyney	*Try Anything Twice*
Gale, Simon	G. Verner	
Gall, Joe	Philip Atlee	"The Irish Beauty Contract"
Gallagher, Gale	Gale Gallagher	*Chord in Crimson*
Galleon, J.	McKnight Malmar	*Fog Is a Shroud*
"Galloping Dick"; *see* Ryder, Richard		
Galore, Pussy	Ian Fleming	*Goldfinger*
Galpin, Charles	Jeremy York	*Sentence of Death*
Galt, Bob	David X. Manners	*Memory of a Scream*
Gamadge, Henry	Elizabeth Daly	*Death and Letters*
Gammond, Lieutenant Roger	T. Muir	
Gang-Smasher	Hugh Clevely	*The Gang-Smasher*
Ganimard, Chief Inspector	Maurice Leblanc	"The Red Silk Scarf"
Ganns, Peter	Eden Phillpotts	*The Grey Room*

CHARACTER	AUTHOR	TITLE
Gantt, Bernard ("Barney") and Muriel	John Stephen Strange	*Look Your Last*
Gar, Joe ("China Man")	Raoul Whitfield	"Death in the Pasig"
Gardella, Inspector	Judson P. Philips	
Garet, Fontaine	Evelyn Cameron	*Malice Domestic*
Garfield, Grant	Charles Franklin	*Escape to Death*
Garfin, Mike	Martin Brett	*Murder Came Tumbling*
Garner, George	Roy Fuller	*Second Curtain*
Garrett, Lieutenant Ed	Muriel Bradley	*Death for My Neighbor*
Garrett, Inspector	J. Turner	
Garrett, Matt	Josephine Gill	*The House That Died*
Garrett, Sheldon	Philip MacDonald	*Warrant for X*
Garron, Detective	Jacques Futrelle	*The Statement of the Accused*
Garth	Wadsworth Camp	*Communicating Door*
Garth	Harrison J. Holt	*Midnight at Mears House*
Garth, Inspector	H. Blayn	
Garth, Inspector	Ernest Dudley	
Garvin, Mr.	Leslie T. Shortell	*The Hounds Are Restless Tonight*
Gaspard, "Papa"	E. P. Thorne	
Gates, Ben	Robert Kyle	*Some Like It Cool*
Gates, Dan	Vance C. Criss	"Two More for Hell"
Gault, Captain	William Hope Hodgson	"The Red Herring"
Gault, "The Goldfish"	Joseph Gollomb	*The Curtain of Storm*
Gaunt, Jeremy	Marion Randolph	
Gaunt, John	Carter Dickson	*The Bowstring Murders*
Gaunt, Rufus	Peter Cheyney	
"Gay Detective"; *see* Morley, Francis		
Gayleigh, Peter	Colin Robertson	*Calling Peter Gayleigh*
Gaylord, Jan	Mary Hastings	*Cork and the Serpent*
Gazely, Hilda	Elizabeth Ferrars	
Gee	Jack Mann	*Gee's First Case*
Gelignite Gang	John Creasey	*The Gelignite Gang*
Genther, Baron Von	Quentin Reynolds	"The Bluebird Murders"
Gently, Superintendent	Alan Hunter	*Gently Go Man*
Gentry, Police Chief Will	Brett Halliday	*The Blonde Cried Murder*
"George"	Elizabeth Ferrars	
Gerard, Colonel Etienne	Sir Arthur Conan Doyle	*Exploits of Brigadier Gerard*
Gerard, Jim	Jack Hoffenberg	
Gerhlich, Inspector	Lee Fredericks	"Hijack Haul"
Gernon, Nigel	Clement Wood	*Death in Ankara*
Gethryn, Colonel Anthony Ruthven	Philip MacDonald	*The Rasp*
Gevrol, Inspector "General"	Emile Gaboriau	*L'Affaire Lerouge*
Ghent, Inspector	Basil Francis	*Death in Act IV*
Ghost, Walter	Vincent Starrett	*Murder on B Deck*
Ghote, Inspector	Herbert R. F. Keating	*The Perfect Murder*
Gibbs, Grumpy	Bliss Lomax	*The Leather Burners*
Gibbs, James	Francis Hobson	*Death on a Back-Bench*
Gibbs, James Augustus ("Jag")	Means Davis	*The Chess Murders*
Gibson, Detective-Lieutenant Andrew	T. Muir	

CHARACTER	AUTHOR	TITLE
Gibson, Chris	Ione Montgomery	*The Golden Dress*
Gibson, "Gibby"	Hampton Stone	*The Girl with a Hole in Her Head*
Gibson, Glen	J. Bentley	
Gibson, Assistant District Attorney Jeremiah X.	Hampton Stone	*Man Who Had Too Much to Lose*
Gideon, Commander	J. J. Marric	*Gideon's Fire*
Gidleigh, Inspector	Selden Truss	*In Secret Places*
Gilbert, Adam	N. Cromarty	
Gilbert, Kevin	Wade Miller	*Deadly Weapon*
Gill, Constable	Nigel Morland	"All in the Night's Work"
Gill, Eve	Selwyn Jepson	*The Hungry Spider*
Gilles, Superintendent	Jacques Decrest	*Meet a Body*
Gillespie, Ian	Michael Halliday	
Gillespie, Dr. Leonard	Max Brand	*Young Dr. Kildare*
Gillespie, Superintendent	George Bellairs	
Gillingham, Anthony	A. A. Milne	*The Red House Mystery*
Gillman, Steve	Elizabeth Backhouse	*Mists Came Down*
Gilly, Mr.	William M. Duncan	*The Crime Master*
Gilman, Dick	Cornell Woolrich	"I Won't Take a Minute"
Gilmartin, Inspector	Charles Barry	*The Wrong Murder Mystery*
Gilmore, Jimmy (Alias "Mr. Death")	G. Wayman Jones	*Alias Mr. Death*
Gilmour, Inspector	MacLeod Winsor	
Giuletta	E. T. A. Hoffman	*The Tales of Hoffman*
Glaister	William M. Duncan	*The Crime Master*
Glass, Constable	Georgette Heyer	
Glass, Joel and Gerda	Marco Page	*Fast Company*
Gleason, Sergeant	Brett Halliday	"Second Honeymoon"
Glenman Brothers (Nick)	MacKinlay Kantor	"The Hunting of Hemingway"
Gloom, Superintendent	F. King	
Glover, Daniel	Maurice Walsh	
Glover, Inspector	March Evermay	*This Death Was Murder*
Gluch, Baron	Virgil Markham	
Goade, Nicholas	E. Phillips Oppenheim	*Nicholas Goade, Detective*
Godahl, "The Infallible"	Frederick Irving Anderson	"The Infallible Godahl"
Godfrey, Jim	Burton E. Stevenson	*The Mystery of the Boule Cabinet*
Gold, Lieutenant Max	Octavus Roy Cohen	
Golden, Sergeant Sammy	Jack Webb	*The Delicate Darling*
Goldfinger, Auric	Ian Fleming	*Goldfinger*
"The Goldfish"; *see* Gault, "The Goldfish"		
Goldsmith, Sergeant	Dorothy Salisbury Davis	*A Gentle Murderer*
Goliath	Emile Zola	"La Débâcle"
Gonsalez	Edgar Wallace	*Three Just Men*
Goodnight, Mary	Ian Fleming	*The Man with the Golden Gun*
Goodwin, Archie	Rex Stout	*Fer-de-lance*
The Gorbals Diehards	John Buchan	*Huntingtower*
Gorby	Fergus Hume	*The Mystery of a Hansom Cab*
Gordon, Ben	Ivan T. Ross	*Murder Out of School*
Gordon, Fanny	Edith MacVane	
Gordon, Inspector Hugh	Susan Gilruth	

CHARACTER	AUTHOR	TITLE
Gordon, Hugh	Gene Goldsmith	*Murder on His Mind*
Gordon, Richard	Edgar Wallace	
Gordon, Sergeant	William M. Duncan	
Gore, Hastings	Van Siller	
Gore, Sheriff	Charles Saxby and Louis Molnar	*Death Cuts the Film*
Gore, Colonel Wyckham	Lynn Brock	*The Stoat*
Gorringe, Miss	Simon Rattray	
Gott, Dr. Giles ("Gilbert Pentreith")	Michael Innes	
Gould, Bart	Joseph Milton	*President's Agent*
Gower, Sergeant	Henry Wade	*The Duke of York's Steps*
Gowrie, Jimmy	David Whitelaw	
Grace, Detective Jason	Dell Shannon	*Coffin Corner*
Grady, Lieutenant Francis Byron	Ione Sandberg Shriber	*Head over Heels in Murder*
Graham, Detective-Inspector	Hugh Desmond	
Graham, Gordon	Mariam Allen de Ford	"I Murdered a Man"
Graham, Jack	Hillary Waugh	*Eighth Mrs. Bluebeard*
Graham, Nancy	Marjorie Bennett	
Graham, Professor Nigel	Victor Bridges	
Graham, Richard	John Welcome	*Hard to Handle*
Granby, Colonel Alistair	Francis Beeding	*Eight Crooked Trenches*
Granger, Ernest	Harrington Hext	*Number 87*
Granitsky, Donovan Grant ("Granit")	Ian Fleming	*From Russia with Love*
Grant, Inspector Alan	Josephine Tey	*The Daughter of Time*
Grant, Basil	G. K. Chesterton	*The Club of Queer Trades*
Grant, Chief Inspector Charles	Andrew Garve	
Grant, Dr. David	George Mair	*Miss Turquoise*
Grant, David	R. Armstrong	
Grant, Inspector	Gerard Fairlie	
Grant, Inspector	G. Heyer	
Grant, Jim	M. McLaren	
Grant, Kirby	Clay Richards	*Death of an Angel*
Grant, Michael	Roland Daniel	
Grant, Phineas	H. Gray	
Grant, Roddy	Roy Sonin	
Grant, Tony	Paul McGuire	*The Spanish Steps*
Grant, Victor	John B. Ethan	*Murder on Wall Street*
Grant, Dr. Victoria	Dorothy Cameron Disney	*Hangman's Tree*
Grass, Harry	Owen Cameron	*The Butcher's Wife*
Graves, Sam	N. M. Newton	
Gray, Colin	Mark Channing	
Gray, Inspector	Peter Piper	*The Corpse That Came Back*
Gray, Michael	Henry Kuttner	*The Murder of Eleanor Pope*
Gray, Neil	Jacques Pendower	
Gray, Packard	William R. Weeks	*Knock and Wait Awhile*
"Gray Phantom"	Herman Landon	*The Gray Phantom*
"The Gray Seal"; *see* Dale, Jimmy		
Grayle, Barnaby	W. W. Sayer	
Grayling, Tony	Alfred O. Pollard	

CHARACTER	AUTHOR	TITLE
Green, Colonel	E. Phillips Oppenheim	
Green, Charles	Arthur M. Chase	*No Outlet*
Green, Horatio	Beverly Nichols	*Murder by Request*
Green, Jeff	Carlton Keith	*Rich Uncle*
"The Green Shadow"	Herman Landon	*The Green Shadow*
Greene, Ex-Superintendent "Tubby"	R. Goyne	
Greenleaf	Herbert O. Yardley	*Red Sun of Nippon*
Greenslade, Wilfred	Alfred O. Pollard	
"Greensleeves"; *see* Leslie, Ludovic		
Greer, James	Newton Gayle	*Death Follows a Formula*
Gregg, Sammy	Harold Kemp	
Gregory, George	J. E. Barry	
Gregory, Lieutenant	Medora Field	*Who Killed Aunt Maggie?*
Gregson, Inspector Tobias	Sir Arthur Conan Doyle	*A Study in Scarlet*
Grendon, Paul	Frank King	"Death on the 8–45"
Grenier, Colonel	B. Stuart	
Grenville, Richard	J. Ward	*Death Sleeps in Kensington*
Gretton, Beverly	Herbert Cadett	*Adventures of a Journalist*
Greve, Inspector	Dennis Haddow	
Grey, Calwyn	Arthur J. Rees	*Greymarsh*
Grey, Cyriack Skinner	Arthur Porges	"The Scientist and the Vanished Weapon"
Grey, Lindy	Desmond Cory	
Grey, Tony	M. Halliday	
"Greybreek"; *see* MacLeod, Alastair		
Griddle, L. F. ("Scoop")	Thomas Polsky	*Curtains for the Judge*
Grief, Inspector	Norman Forrest	*Death Took a Greek God*
Griff, Sidney	Erle Stanley Gardner	*Clue of the Forgotten Murder*
Griffith, William	Robert George Dean	*Murder Makes a Merry Widow*
Grim, James Schyler ("Jimgrim")	Talbot Mundy	*The Mystery of Khufu's Tomb*
Grodman, George	Israel Zangwill	*The Big Bow Mystery*
Grodnik, Jack	Bart Spicer	*Black Sheep, Run*
Grogan, Inspector	Margot Neville	
Groode, Mr.	George Griswold	*The Pinned Man*
Gross, Nathaniel Ironsides	Colin Willock	
Grundt, Dr. Adolph ("Clubfoot")	Valentine Williams	*The Mystery of the Gold Box*
Gryce, Ebenezer	Anna Katherine Green	*The Leavenworth Case*
Guant, Mike	George Braddon	
Gubb, Philo	Ellis Parker Butler	"Philo Gubb's Greatest Case"
Guest, Superintendent	Milward Kennedy	*Half-Mast Murder*
Guild, John	A. Campbell	
Gulliver, Jim	William Campbell Gault	
Gutman, Caspar	Dashiell Hammett	*The Maltese Falcon*
Guy, Brian	Jason Ridgeway	*The Treasure of the Cosa Nostra*
"H.M."; *see* Merrivale, Sir Henry		
Habershon, Bruce	Roy Vickers	
Hadden, Chief Inspector	John Dickson Carr	
Hadden, Detective	Charles Gibbon	*A Hard Knot*

CHARACTER	AUTHOR	TITLE
Hadley, Superintendent Daird	John Dickson Carr	*Till Death Do Us Part*
Hagen, Mort	Whit Masterson	*Dead, She Was Beautiful*
Hagg, Inspector Charles	Angus MacVicar	
Hailey, Dr. Eustace	Anthony Wynne	*Sign of Evil*
Haki, Colonel	Eric Ambler	*Journey into Fear*
Halcombe, Marian	Wilkie Collins	*The Woman in White*
Hale, Ed	Weed Dickinson	*Dead Man Talks Too Much*
Hale, Max	K. Sandford	
Hale, Maxfield Chauncey	George Harmon Coxe	*The Lady Is Afraid*
Hale, Monty	Victor Gunn	
Hale, Spenser	Robert Barr	"The Absent-Minded Coterie"
Hale, Warner	A. Miller	
Hall, Inspector	Henry C. Bailey	
Hall, Pete	Sonia Cole	
Hall, "Satan"	Carroll J. Daly	*Murder at Our House*
Hall, Detective-Inspector "Tubby"	Phillis Hambledon	
Halliday, David	H. Baldwin Taylor	*The Triumvirate*
Halliday, Policewoman Lys	D. Black	
Halper, Bernie	Charles Green	"The One and Only Bernie"
Halstead, Arthur	William Edward Hayes	*The Black Doll*
Hambledon, Sir Rubert	John Dellbridge	*Searchlight on Hambledon*
Hambledon, Thomas ("Tommy") Elphinstone (Alias "Hendrik Brandt," "Klaus Lehmann")	Manning Coles	*The Exploits of Tommy Hambledon*
Hammer, Mike	Mickey Spillane	*I, the Jury*
Hammers, Al	William L. Rohde	
Hammersley, Cyril	George Gibbs	*The Yellow Dove*
Hammond, Lieutenant	Charlotte Murray Russell	*Clue of the Naked Eye*
Hammond, Sheriff Tim	Carolyn Byrd Dawson	*The Lady Wept Alone*
Hampden, Clive	Pete Fry	*Harsh Evidence*
Hanaud, Inspector	Alfred E. W. Mason	*At the Villa Rose*
Hand, Christopher	Stanley Hart Page	*Fool's Gold*
"Handsome"; *see* Kusak, "Handsome"		
"Handsome"; *see* West, Inspector Roger		
Hanford, Bill	Russell R. Philips	*Death Smiles*
Hannah	Dwight V. Babcock	*A Homicide for Hannah*
Hannasyde, Superintendent	Georgette Heyer	*They Found Him Dead*
Hannay, Richard	John Buchan	*The Adventures of Richard Hannay*
Hannen, "Mute"	George Braddon	
Hanrahan, Policewoman	Thomas Walsh	"Lady Cop"
Hanslet, Superintendent	John Rhode	*Murder at the Motor Show*
Hanson, Captain Mark	Joseph C. Lincoln	*Blair's Attic*
Hanvey, James H. ("Jim")	Octavus Roy Cohen	*Jim Hanvey, Detective*
Harbottle, Inspector	Georgette Heyer	
Hardcastle, Peter	Eden Phillpotts	*The Grey Room*

CHARACTER	AUTHOR	TITLE
Hardcastle, Superintendent	Lord Gorell	
Harder, Dan	Richard Deming	"The Taipei Affair"
Harder, Lomax	Arnold Bennett	"Murder"
Hardin, Bart	David Alexander	*Dead, Man, Dead*
Harding, Inspector	Georgette Heyer	
Harding, Major	Victor Bridges	*The Man Who Vanished*
Hardy, Bren	William J. Elliott	*Bren Hardy, Tough Dame*
Hardy, Tony	N. Deane	
Harford, Matt	John Boland	
Harker, Colonel	M. Black	
Harland, John	Rae Foley	*An Ape in Velvet*
Harley, John	Alfred Tack	
Harley, Paul	Sax Rohmer	*Bat Wing*
Harman, Inspector "Big" Mike	J. M. Walsh	
Harmas, Steve	James Hadley Chase	*Tell It to the Birds*
Harnold, Pierre	Maurice Dekobra	
Harper; *see* Archer, Lew		
Harper, Bill	Paul Ernst	
Harper, Steve	Walter C. Brown	*Murder at Mocking House*
Harper, Superintendent	Ngaio Marsh	
Harpinger, Ernest	Henry Carstairs	*Harpinger's Hunch*
Harrigan	Patrick O'Malley	*The Affair of John Donne*
Harrington, John	J. Ward	
Harrington, Superintendent	E. Maschwitz	
Harris, Inspector	Elizabeth and John Rosenberg	*Out, Brief Candle*
Harris, Paul	Gavin Black	*The Eyes Around Me*
Harris, Red	Marten Cumberland	
Harrison, Clay	Clifton Robbins	*Methylated Murder*
Harrison, Danny	Adam Hobhouse	*The Hangover Murders*
Harrison, Detective-Constable	Roland Daniel	
Harrison, Inspector	Hugh Desmond	
Harrison, Inspector	Mary Roberts Rinehart	*The Door*
Harrison, Paul	Dorothy Sayers and Robert Eustace	*The Documents in the Case*
Harrison, Secret Agent	Simon Harvester	
Harry, "Smallpox"	Rufus King	"The Seeds of Murder"
Harry, the Hat	Philip MacDonald	"Two Exploits of Harry the Hat"
Hartley, Derek	George Lett	*The Many Headed Monster*
Harty, Sergeant	Joel Y. Dane	*The Cabana Murders*
Harvard, Paul	Charles H. Gibbs-Smith	*The Caroline Affair*
Harvey, Gail	George Gibbs	
Harvey, Paul	Robert Orr Chipperfield	*The Second Bullet*
Harwell, James Trueman	Anna Katherine Green	*The Leavenworth Case*
Haskell, Mark	Hugh Pentecost	*The Shape of Fear*
Hassal, Gracie	Hugh Clevely	
Hastings, Captain Arthur	Agatha Christie	*Murder on the Links*
Hastings, Mrs. Arthur; *see* Duveen, Dulcie		
Hastings, Jefferson	James Hay, Jr.	*No Clue*
Hastings, Jimmy	Charles G. Givens	*The Rose Petal Murders*

CHARACTER	AUTHOR	TITLE
Hastings, Lady Lupin	Joan Coggin	*Dancing with Death*
Hastings, Spencer	Philip MacDonald	*The Rasp*
Haswell, Jimmy	Herbert Adams	*The Body in the Bunker*
Hatch, Professor Cyrus	Frederick C. Davis	*Coffins for Three*
Hatch, Hutchinson	Jacques Futrelle	"The Problem of Cell 13"
Hatch, Commissioner Mark	Frederick C. Davis	*Coffins for Three*
Hatch, Sergeant	J. Marsh	
Hathway, Michael	E. Allen	
Hatton	John D. Beresford	"The Artificial Mole"
Havelock, Judy	Ian Fleming	*For Your Eyes Only*
Havilland, Anthony	Val Gielgud	
Havoc, Johnny	John Jakes	*Johnny Havoc*
Haw, Raffles	A. Conan Doyle	*The Doings of Raffles Haw*
Hawk	Richard Hardwick	*Hawk*
Hawkes, "A.B.C."	C. E. Bechhofer Roberts	"The Persistent House-Hunters"
Hawks, Joaquin	Bill S. Ballinger	*The Spy at Angkor Wat*
Hayward, Inspector	Bruce Sanders	
Hazard, Dixon	Lee Crosby	*Terror by Night*
Hazell, Thorpe	Victor L. Whitechurch	*Thrilling Stories of the Railway*
Hazelton, Alexander	A. Hazelton	
Hazlerigg, Chief Inspector Bobby	Michael Gilbert	*Close Quarters*
Headcorn, Chief Inspector	Alice Campbell	*They Hunted a Fox*
"Headland, George"; *see* Cleek, George		
Headley, Inspector	Thomas B. Morris	
Heald, Max	H. Hossent	
Healy, Dan	Hunter Stinson	"A Killer Needs Brains"
Hearle, Eric	Archie Joscelyn	*The Golden Bowl*
Heat, Inspector	Joseph Conrad	*The Secret Agent*
Heath, Sergeant Ernest	S. S. Van Dine	*The Benson Murder Case*
Heath, Evan	Robert Hare	*The Hand of the Chimpanzee*
Heatherwick, Mr.	Joseph S. Fletcher	*The Charing Cross Mystery*
Heaton, Bill	Edward Woodward	*Gentlemen at Large*
Hebdon, Detective-Superintendent	Peter Graaf	*The Sapphire Conference*
Heck, Brian Young	Bruce Graeme	
Hedley, Paul	Ben Healey	*Waiting for a Tiger*
Hefferman, Hooky	Lawrence Meynell	*Too Clever by Half*
Heimrich, Captain M. T.	Francis Richards	*Burnt Offerings*
Heine	Edgar Wallace	*The Adventures of Heine*
Heinsheimer, Inspector August	Zelda Popkin	
Heldar, Sally and Johnny	H. Hamilton	
Hellier, Richard	Henry de V. Stacpoole	
Hellis, Inspector	Simon Harvester	
Helm, Ben	Bruno Fischer	*Stripped for Murder*
Helm, Matt	Donald Hamilton	*The Wrecking Crew*
Helston, David	M. F. Page	
Hemingway, Chief Inspector	Georgette Heyer	*Envious Casca*
Hemsley, Detective-Inspector	Hugh Desmond	
Henderson, David	Francis Durbridge	

CHARACTER	AUTHOR	TITLE
Henderson, Mark	E. Chamberlain	
Henderson, Shep	William Pearson	
Hennessy, Inspector	G. D. H. and M. I. Cole	
Henry, Gilmore	Cornelius W. Grafton	*The Rat Began to Gnaw the Rope*
Henry, Rush	Joe Barry	*The Triple Cross*
Hepburn, Alan	John Dickson Carr	
Herald, Simon	John Welcome	
Hercules, Esq.	Gwyn Evans	*Hercules, Esq.*
Heriot, Detective-Inspector	Francis A. Symonds	*Smile and Murder*
Hern, Dr. Audre Metcalf	A. Gask	
Hern, Rowland	Nicholas Olde	*The Incredible Adventures of Rowland Hern*
Hero, Alexander	Paul Gallico	
Heron, Inspector	Headon Hill	*Guilty Gold*
Herrick, A. Z.	Whitman Chambers	
Herridge, Lissa Vickers	Constance and Gwenyth Little	
Herrington, Chief Detective-Inspector	Colin Robertson	
Herrivell, Sir Richard	John Bentley	*The Whitney Case*
Herrold, Dr. John	Means Davis	*The Hospital Murders*
Heskell, Inspector	Henry Wade	
Hewitt, Martin	Arthur Morrison	*Martin Hewitt: Investigator*
Hickory	Anna Katherine Green	*Hand and Glove*
Hicks	Frederick A. M. Webster	*Old Ebbie Returns*
Hicks, Alfred	Ralph C. Woodthorpe	
Hicks, "Alphabet"	Rex Stout	"By His Own Hand"
Hieronomo, Anne	Dorothy Cameron Disney	*The Balcony*
Higgins, Inspector Cuthbert	Cecil F. Gregg	*Dead on Time*
Higgins, Lieutenant	T. Middleton	
Higgins, Matt	Means Davis	*Chess Murders*
Highway	Garnett Weston	*Dead Men Are Dangerous*
Hildreth, Barnabas	Vincent Cornier	"The Smell That Killed"
Hill, Asmun	H. Hawton	
Hill, Murray	Frank Gruber	
Hilliard, Detective-Inspector	William H. L. Crauford	
Hilton, Inspector Rodney	Mary Durham	
Hinkle, Ambrose (Little Amby)	Thomas McMorrow	*The Sinister History of Ambrose Hinkle*
Hinton, Superintendent	Henry Carstairs	
Hite, Quinny	Richard Burke	*The Fourth Star*
Hobart, Lieutenant	Ione Montgomery	
"The Hobo Detective"; *see* Thorne, Tommy		
Hoeffler	Patrick O'Malley	*The Affair of John Donne*
Hogan, Hard Rock	Erle Stanley Gardner	
Hogan, Mr.	R. MacLean	
Hogarth, Inspector	Joseph J. Farjeon	
Hogarth, Lieutenant	Henry W. Roden	*Wake for a Lady*
Hogg, Miss Flora	Austin Lee	*Miss Hogg and the Dead Dean*
Holbrook, Bill	Edgar Wallace	
Holcomb, Sergeant	Erle Stanley Gardner	*The Case of the Black-Eyed Blonde*

CHARACTER	AUTHOR	TITLE
Holleran, Cornelius	Thomas Walsh	"Girl in Danger"
Holley, Herman	Richard Sale	*Monkey in the Morgue*
Holliday, Felix	A. E. Jones	
Holliday, Hiram	Paul Gallico	*The Adventures of Hiram Holliday*
Hollis, Inspector	Josephine Pullein-Thompson	
Holly, Inspector	Raymond Postgate	*Somebody at the Door*
Holm, Patricia	Leslie Charteris	*Arrest the Saint*
Holman, Matthew	Richard Marsh	*The Beetles*
Holman, Rick	Carter Brown	*The Girl from Outer Space*
Holmes, Mycroft	Sir Arthur Conan Doyle	"The Final Problem"
Holmes, Raffles	John Kendrick Bangs	*R. Holmes and Co.*
Holmes, Sherlock	Sir Arthur Conan Doyle (*see also* Adrian C. Doyle and John Dickson Carr)	*Adventures of Sherlock Holmes*
Holmes, William	Conrad Voss Bark	*Mr. Holmes Goes to Ground*
Holroyd, Detective-Inspector	Edwin and Mona A. Radford	
Holt, Assistant District Attorney	Whit Masterson	
Holt, Father	Henry Thackeray	*Henry Esmond*
Holt, Jasper	Sinclair Lewis	"The Willow Walk"
Holt, Larry	Edgar Wallace	*Dark Eyes of London*
Holt, Mr.	Norman Lippincott	*Murder at Glen Athol*
Holtz, Nicholas	Alexander Laing	*The Motives of Nicholas Holtz*
Homes, Schlock	Robert L. Fish	"The Adventures of the Ascot Tie"
Homes, Shylock	John Kendrick Bangs	*The Posthumous Memoirs of Shylock Homes*
Honneger, Captain George	John Stephen Strange	*All Men Are Liars*
Hood, Mark	James Dark	*Assignment in Tokyo*
Hoong, Sergeant	Robert Van Gulik	*The Chinese Bell Murders*
Hooper, Lieutenant	Ursula Curtiss	*Voice out of Darkness*
Hope, Jefferson	Sir Arthur Conan Doyle	*A Study in Scarlet*
Hopkins, Chief Inspector	R. Daniel	
Hopkins, Joan	David Burnham	*Last Act in Bermuda*
Hopkins, Inspector Stephen	David Burnham	*Last Act in Bermuda*
Hopley, Victor	Henry C. Bailey	
Horace, Chief Inspector James	Seldon Truss	*One Man's Enemies*
Horne, Charles	Wilson Tucker	*Red Herring*
Hornleigh, Inspector	Haus Wolfgang Priwin	
Hostage, Christopher	Noel Cromarty	
Howard, Anthony	Hugh D. McCutcheon	*Murder at the Angel*
Howard, Graham	E. H. Clements	
Howard, Michael	John Blackburn	*A Sour Apple Tree*
Howard, Tony	Arthur Applin	*Sweeter Than Honey*
Howard, Wallace	Frederica De Laguna	*The Arrow Points to Murder*
Howden, Sir John	W. Mills	
Howell, Martin	William Woolfolk	*Run While You Can*
Howes, Dave	Vincent G. Malo	
Hoye, Ex-Detective-Superintendent James	N. Bell	
Hudson, Mrs.	Sir Arthur Conan Doyle	*The Sign of Four*
Hudson, Doris	Lawrence G. Blochman	*Clues for Dr. Coffee*

CHARACTER	AUTHOR	TITLE
Hudson, Robert	Victor Canning	
Hughes, Inspector	Elizabeth Ferrars	
Hughes, Inspector	D. W. F. Hardie	
Hughes, Sandra	H. Long	
Hughes, Sergeant	Osmington Mills	*At One Fell Swoop*
Huish, Superintendent	Agatha Christie	*Ordeal by Innocence*
Hull, Miss "Scraps"	Ione Montgomery	*The Golden Dress*
"The Human Encyclopedia"; *see* Quade, Oliver		
Humble, Mr.	Frank Bunce	*So Young a Body*
Humblethorne, Inspector	Lord Gorell	*In the Night*
Humbly, Inspector	Edmund Crispin	"Merry Go-Round"
Hume, Inspector Laurice	William M. Duncan	*The Murder Man*
Hume, Hamp and Carmel	Brandon Bird	*Death in Four Colors*
Hunt, Elsie Mae	Aaron Marc Stein	*Death Meets 400 Rabbits*
Hunt, Frederick	Lillian Day and Norbert Lederer	
Hunt, Laura	Vera Caspary	*Laura*
Hunt, Lucius	J. Wellard	
Hunt, Will	Nina Bawden	*Odd Flamingo*
Hunter, Ambrose	Frederic Brown	*The Fabulous Clipjoint*
Hunter, Anthony ("Tony")	Robert George Dean	*Affair at Lover's Leap*
Hunter, Ed	Frederic Brown	*The Late Lamented*
Hunter, Jimmy	Mary Stimson	
Hunter, Chief Inspector Max	D. Muir	
Hunter, Superintendent Philip	Maurice Procter	*The Ripper*
The Hunters	Paul Tabori	*The Doomsday Brain*
Hurst, Susan and Roger	Michael Halliday	
Huxford, Rex	Cromwell Gibbons	*Murder in Hollywood*
Hyde, Barney	N. Brent	
Hyde, Detective-Inspector	Anthony Heckstall-Smith	*Murder on the Brain*
Hyer, Henry ("Hank")	Kurt Steel	*Judas Incorporated*
Hyland, Terry	Reginald Davis	
I Am (Cat)	Manning Long	*Dull Thud*
ICE (International Combine of Endeavor)	Bruce Cassiday	"Deep Sleep"
Ignatius, Brother	F. Vivian	
"Infallible Godahl"; *see* Godahl		
Ingram, Detective-Inspector	N. Mackenzie	
Ingram, John and Rae	Charles Williams	*Dead Calm*
Innes, Rachel	Mary R. Rinehart	*The Circular Staircase*
"The Inspector"	Mark Van Doren	"The Luminous Face"
Intertrust	James Dark	*Come Die with Me*
Ipps, Inspector	C. Brooks	
Ipswitch, Inspector	Reginald Davis	*Nine Days Panic*
Irish, Jerry	Nellise Childe	*The Diamond Ransom Murders*
Ironside, Inspector	Henry R. F. Keating	*Is Skin Deep, Is Fatal*

CHARACTER	AUTHOR	TITLE
Irving, Paul	Leo Grex	*The Madison Murder*
Ives, Chief Inspector	Clive Ryland	
Ives, Janet	B. Stanley	
Ivy, Frances Bascom	Charles Ventura	"Killers Corridor"
Ixell, Barron	Oscar Schisgall	*Baron Ixell, Crime Breaker*
"Jack O'Judgment"	Edgar Wallace	*Dark Eyes of London*
Jack O' Lantern	George Goodchild	*Jack O' Lantern*
Jackson, Inspector	David Lindsay	
Jackson, John	C. F. Gregg	
Jackson, Lieutenant A.	Anthony Boucher	"Elsewhen"
Jackson, Nick (Swami Mirza Baba)	Paul Gallico	*Hurry, Hurry, Hurry*
Jacobs, Morris	Seldon Truss	
James, Inspector	William H. L. Crauford	
James, Inspector	N. Mackenzie	
James, Michael Dane	James M. Ullman	"The Stock Market Mystery"
James, Mike	D. Scott	
James, Walter	Wade Miller	*Deadly Weapon*
Jameson, Walter	Arthur B. Reeve	"The Poisoned Pen"
Jamieson	Mary Roberts Rinehart	*The Circular Staircase*
Jamieson, Superintendent	Anthony Berkeley	*Dead Mrs. Stratton*
Jannock, Chief Inspector	S. Fox	
Janvier, Inspector	Georges Simenon	
Japp, Inspector	Agatha Christie	"Murder in the Mews"
Jarrell, David	Leo Grex	
Jarvis, Jimmie	Dorothy Salisbury Davis	*Old Sinners Never Die*
"Jason"; *see* Bendon, Wing-Commander David		
Javert	Victor Hugo	*Les Miserables*
Jeacock, Meg	Elizabeth Ferrars	
Jean, M.	Fortuné du Boisgobey	*Le Coup de Ponce*
"Jeanniot, Captain"; *see* Arsène, Lupin		
"Jeff"	Carlton Keith	*Diamond-Studded Typewriter*
Jefferson, Ray	P. P. Muir and E. D. H. Tollemache	
Jellipot	Sidney Fowler	*The Jordans Murder*
Jendell, Detective	V. Kelly	
Jenkins, Ed ("The Phantom Crook")	Erle Stanley Gardner	
Jenkins, Hepzibah ("Happy")	Henry Barnard Safford	
Jennings, Ezra	Wilkie Collins	
Jentry, Inspector Auguste	Bruce Graeme	
Jericho, John	Hugh Pentecost	"Jericho and the Silent Witness"
Jerningham, Ted	"Sapper"	
Jervis, Dr. Christopher	Richard Austin Freeman	*The Red Thumb Mark*
Jervis, Inspector	J. Patrick	
Jervois, Captain Gerald	John Russell Warren	*Murder in the Blackout*
Jessup, Inspector Courtney	Ryley Cooper	"Suspect Unknown"
Jewle, Chief Inspector	Christopher Bush	*Case of the Heavenly Twin*
"Jimgrim"; *see* Grim, James Schyler		

CHARACTER	AUTHOR	TITLE
Jocelyn, Robert	Lawrence Lynch	*The Unseen Hand*
John, Sheriff	Talmage Powell	"A Break in the Weather"
John, Sir; *see* Saumarez, Sir John		
Johnny	Shaun MacCarthy	*Johnny Goes East*
Johns, Detective-Inspector	S. Miles	
Johnson, Coffin Ed	Chester Himes	*Cotton Comes to Harlem*
Johnson, Hope	Vincent Starrett	*Murder in Peking*
Johnson, Dr. Sam	Lillian De La Torre	*Dr. Sam: Johnson, Detector*
Johnson, Steve	Hugh L. Nelson	*Dead Giveaway*
Johnstone	C. E. Bechhofer Roberts	"The English Filter"
Joly, Inspector	Arthur Sherburne Hardy	*Diane and Her Friends*
"Jonah and Co."; *see* Mansel		
Jonas, Jonas P.	E. X. Ferrars	"The Case of the Blue Bowl"
Jonathan, Martin	Michael Halliday	
Jones, Adrian Van Reypen Egerton ("Average")	Samuel Hopkins Adams	*Average Jones*
Jones, Inspector Athelney	Sir Arthur Conan Doyle	*The Sign of the Four*
Jones, Bobby and Frankie	Agatha Christie	*The Boomerang Club*
Jones, "Careful"	"Pat Hand" (Thomas B. Costain)	
"Jones, Cholmondeley"; *see* Dawson, Chief Inspector William		
Jones, "Curly"	David Knox Patton	
Jones, Sheriff Davey	Francis W. Bronson	*Nice People Don't Kill*
Jones, Edmund ("Jupiter")	Timothy Fuller	*Harvard Has a Homicide*
Jones, Inspector Evan	C. Franklin	
Jones, "Grave Digger"	Chester Himes	*Cotton Comes to Harlem*
Jones, Hemlock	Bret Harte	*The Stolen Cigar Case*
Jones, Kennedy	Norman Klein	*The Destroying Angel*
Jones, Lancelot	Shelby Smith	*An Afternoon to Kill*
Jones, "Meddlesome"	Sir Basil Thomson	"The Hanover Court Murder"
Jones, Morrocco	Jack Baynes	*The Case of the Syndicate Hoods*
Jones, Sam	Thomas Kyd	*Blood on the Bosom Divine*
Jones, Superintendent	Edwin and Mona A. Radford	
Jones, Victoria	Agatha Christie	
Jones, Detective Walter	Wade Miller	
Jones, Xenius ("X")	Harry Stephen Keeler	*X Jones of Scotland Yard*
Jonquelle ("Prefect of Police of Paris")	Melville Davisson Post	*Monsieur Jonquelle, Prefect of Police*
Jordan, Dan	Harlan Reed	*The Case of the Crawling Cockroach*
Jordon	William Holder	"What's the Percentage?"
Jordon, Allie	F. S. Wees	
Jordon, Jack	William DuBois	*Case of the Deadly Diary*
Jordon, Scott	Harold J. Masur	"Build Another Coffin"
Jordon, "Tiger" Tim	Edgar Wallace	*The Man at the Carleton*
Jordon, Timothy	Edgar Wallace	

CHARACTER	AUTHOR	TITLE
Josephine, Joseph; *see* Rouletabille, Joseph		
Joss, Detective-Inspector	Henry Wade	
Josselin	Andrew Cassels Brown	*Josselin Takes a Hand*
Joyce, Michael (Agency)	Louis Cornell	*Poison Case No. 10*
Jucker, Garnet	Harry S. Keeler	
"Julia"	Peter Cheyney	
Julyn, Colonel	Daphne Du Maurier	*Rebecca*
"The Just Men"	Edgar Wallace	*The Four Just Men*
Justus, Mrs. Helene; *see* Brand, Helene		
Justus, Jake	Craig Rice	*The Wrong Murder*
Juve	Marcel Allain	*Juve in the Dock*
Kames, Sir Bruton	Douglas G. Browne	*Too Many Cousins*
Kane, Doris	George Gibbs	
Kane, Fred	Charles Saxby	
Kanc, Inspector	Roger Scarlett	*In the First Degree*
Kane, Michael	Peter Cheyney	
Kane, Peter	Hugh B. Cave	"The Dead Don't Swim"
Kane, "Sugar"	Lovat Marshall	*Sugar for the Lady*
Kang, Dr.	Victor Canning	"Death in Italy"
Kaplin, Inspector	Henry De V. Stacpoole	"The Rope of Pearls"
Kar, Kevin	Man Van Der Veer	"The Agents"
Karmesin	Gerald Kersh	"Karmesin: Racketeer"
Kaspir, Colonel	C. Philip Donnel	"The Body Travels East"
Kastellane, Anna	E. Phillips Oppenheim	*The Ostrekoff Jewels*
"The Kat"	Nancy Spain	*Kat Strikes*
Kavanagh, Major Robin	Brian Stuart	*Knock-Out Kavanagh*
Kaz; *see* Von Kaz, Baron Franz		
Kearns, Sergeant	G. Malcolm-Smith	
Keate, Nurse Sarah	Mignon G. Eberhart	*The Patient in Room 18*
Keeble, Magnus	A. Wood	
Keen, Franklyn	H. Long	
Keen, Major Gregory	L. Hardy	
Keith, Harrison	Nicholas Carter	*Adventures of Harrison Keith, Detective*
Keith, John	Norman Daniels	*Spy Ghost*
Kells, Gerry	Paul Cain	*Fast One*
Kells, Michael	Peter Cheyney	*Ladies Won't Wait*
Kelly, Aloysius	Barbara Worsley-Gough	*Alibi Innings*
Kelly, Homer	James Langton	
Kelly, Joe	Robert Avery	
Kelly, Johnny	J. M. Walsh	
Kelly, Midge	J. Marsh	
Kelly, "Muggs"	Donald Bayne Hobart	"Pardon Death's Glove"
Kelly, Robert Emmet	Thomas Walsh	"Always a Stranger"
Kelly, "Slot-Machine"	Dennis Lynds	"The Hero"
Kelly, Steven	E. Burton	
Kelly, Terence	Frances Steegmüller	*Blue Harpsichord*
Kelstern, Ruth	Edgar Jepson	"The Tea Leaf"
Kelton, Matthew	Richard Connell	*Murder at Sea*
Kempson, Superintendent	E. C. R. Lorac	*People Will Talk*
Kendall, Inspector	Joseph J. Farjeon	*Thirteen Guests*

CHARACTER	AUTHOR	TITLE
Kennedy	Frederick Nebel	*Winter Kill*
Kennedy, Bill	Leslie Charteris	*X Esquire*
Kennedy, Professor Craig	Arthur B. Reeve	*The Silent Bullet*
Kennedy, Inspector	Jeremy York	*Missing*
Kennedy, Mr.	H. R. Hays	
Kennedy, Storm	Sax Rohmer	
Kennedy, Lieutenant Tom	York Smith	
Kennington, Raymond	James Byrom	
Kenny, Inspector Mike	E. Dillon	
Kent, Celia	Elizabeth Ferrars	*Hunt the Tortoise*
Kent, Christopher	John Boswell	*Lost Girl*
Kent, Harry	Christopher G. Landon	*Unseen Enemy*
Kent, Wally	Charlotte Murray	
Kenton, Malcolm	Simon Harvester	
Kenway, Inspector	Edwin and Mona A. Radford	
Kenyon, Clayton	Headon Hill	*The Comlyn Alibi*
Keogh, Dinny	Larry Holden	
Kerby, Astrogen ("Astro")	Gelett Burgess	*Master of Mysteries*
Kerim, Darko	Ian Fleming	*From Russia with Love*
Kerman, Jack	James Hadley Chase	
Kernehan, Mike	Bert and Dolores Hitchens	*The Man Who Followed Women*
Kerr, Bill	John Creasey	
Kerrigan, Lieutenant	Joseph Harrington	*Blind Spot*
Kerrigan, Peter	Esther Haven Fonseca	*Death Below the Dam*
Kerrigan, Peter	Neil Gordon	*Shakespeare Murders*
Kerry, Inspector	Clive Ryland	
Ketcham, John	Frank P. Grady	*Sergeant Death*
Kettner, Professor	Ernest Harrison	"English Lesson"
KGB	Ian Fleming	*The Man with the Golden Gun*
Kidd, Superintendent	James Veitch	*Live Till Tomorrow*
Kilbane, Detective	Thomas Walsh	"Once Over, Not Too Lightly"
Kilby, Mark	Robert Caine Frazer	*The Secret Syndicate*
Kildare, Dr. James	Max Brand	*Young Dr. Kildare*
Kilgerrin, Paul	Charles Leonard	*Search for a Scientist*
Kill, Hendrik Van; *see* Van Kill, Hendrik		
Killain, Johnny	Dan J. Marlowe	*Shake a Crooked Town*
Killmaster; *see* Carter, Nick		
Kilsip, Detective	Fergus Hume	*Mystery of a Hansom Cab*
Kincaid, Roger	Hake Talbot	*Rim of the Pit*
Kindersley, Richard	Alfred O. Pollard	
King, Amenu	Roger Manvell	*The Dreamers*
King, Bill	B. J. Maylon	
King, Inspector Charles	Joseph L. Bonney	*Death by Dynamite*
King, Peter	Cortland Fitzimmons and John Mulholland	*Girl in the Cage*
King, Superintendent	John Rhode	*The House on Tollard Ridge*
Kingston, Michael (Alias "Dirk Brandt," "Bill Sanders")	Manning Coles	*Drink to Yesterday*
Kinkaid, Jeff	Carl Henry Rathjen	"Touch and Blow"
Kinnerton, Paul	William H. L. Crauford	

CHARACTER	AUTHOR	TITLE
Kinross, Dr. Dermot	John Dickson Carr	*The Emperor's Snuffbox*
Kinso, Inspector Harvey	William Woolfolk	*Run While You Can*
Kirby, Mrs. Astrogen; *see* Stewart, Valeska		
Kirby, Joseph ("Joe")	Dwight V. Babcock	*A Homocide for Hannah*
Kirby, "Silk"	G. Wayman Jones	"Markets of Treason"
Kirk, Ashton	John T. McIntyre	*Ashton Kirk: Investigator*
Kirk, Bill	William M. Duncan	
Kirk, General	John Blackburn	*Broken Boy*
Kirk, Murray	Stanley Ellin	*The Eighth Circle*
Kirtland, Detective-Inspector	Frances P. Keyes	
Kirtland, Inspector	Frances P. Keyes	
Kitty (McGarry's Mouse)	Matt Taylor	"McGarry and the Box-office Bandits"
Klaw, Moris	Sax Rohmer	*The Dream Detective*
Kleb, Rosa	Ian Fleming	*From Russia with Love*
Kling, Sergeant Bert	Ed McBain	*Killer's Choice*
Klump, Detective Willie	Joe Archibald	"It Couldn't Happen to Willie"
Knell, Inspector	George Bellairs	*Corpse at the Carnival*
Kneller, Inspector	William H. L. Crauford	
Kneller, Superintendent	Henry Wade	
Knight, Bill	Maurice Procter	*The Pub Crawler*
Knight, David	N. Lee	
Knight, John Arden	Henry W. Roden	*Too Busy to Die*
Knollis, Gordon	Frances Vivian	*Darkling Death*
Knollis, Superintendent	F. Vivian	
Knook, Mr.	Sidney Horler	*The Prince of Plunder*
Knox, Honourable Algernon	E. Phillips Oppenheim	*The Hon. Algernon Knox, Detective*
Koa, Komako	Max Long	*Murder Between Dark and Dark*
Koharik, Lieutenant Larry	John M. Eshleman	*The Long Chase*
Koko (Cat)	Lilian Jackson Braun	*The Cat Who Ate Danish Modern*
Koluchy, Madame	L. T. Mead and Robert Eustace	*The Brotherhood of the Seven Kings*
Koravitch, Captain Ivan	Victor L. Whitechurch	*The Adventures of Captain Ivan Koravitch*
Kozminski, Detective-Inspector Abraham	Q. Downes	
Kramer, August Frankfurter ("Gus")	Cedric Worth	
Kramer, Ben	Louise Revelle	
Kramer, Phil	Paul Kruger	*Weave a Wicked Web*
Krasinsky, Mr.	Peter Cheyney	"Sweet Murder at Figg's End"
Krespel	E. T. A. Hoffman	*Weird Tales*
Krest, Liz	Ian Fleming	*For Your Eyes Only*
Krook, Dr.	Arthur Mallory	
Kuelz, Oscar	Erich Kastner	*Emil and the Detectives*
Kung	Keith West	*Hanging Waters*
Kuryakin, Illya	Michael Avallone	*The Man from U.N.C.L.E.*
Kusak, "Handsome"	Craig Rice	*The April Robin Murders*
Kwang	Frank V. Martinek	*Don Winslow, U.S.N. in Ceylon*
Kynnersley, Sir John	Arthur C. Fox-Davies	*The Mauleverer Murders*
Kyra; *see* Sokratescu, Kyra		
Labbe, M.	Georges Simenon	

CHARACTER	AUTHOR	TITLE
Laidman, Detective-Inspector Martin	S. Seaton	
Laing, Patrick	Patrick Laing	*The Lady Is Dead*
Lake, Quentin	Leslie Beresford	*Murder Can Be Such Fun*
Lake, Stan	Whitman Chambers	*Dead Men Leave No Fingerprints*
Lam, Donald	A. A. Fair	*Lam to the Slaughter*
Lamb, Captain	Leslie Ford	*The Woman in Black*
Lamb, Detective	Robert Dundee	*Pandora's Box*
Lamb, Inspector	Patricia Wentworth	*The Blind Side*
Lamb, Sergeant John	John Donovan	*The Case of the Talking Dust*
Lamb, Martin	Anthony Boucher	*Case of the Seven of Calvary*
Lamont, Nick "The Kick"	John Jakes	"Dr. Sweetkill"
Lancey, Markade	Barbara Frost	*The Corpse Died Twice*
Lancing, Inspector	Carol Carnac	
Land, Marty	David Alexander	*Bloodstain*
Landers, Peter	Victor Canning	
Landervorne, Sir John	John Dickson Carr	
Landles, Detective-Sergeant	Elizabeth Backhouse	*Mists Came Down*
Landon, Inspector	A. F. Grey	*Momentary Stoppage*
Lane, Drury	Barnaby Ross	*The Tragedy of X*
Lane, James	Florence Ryerson and C. C. Clements	*Blind Man's Buff*
Lane, Jeff	George Harmon Coxe	*One Minute Past Eight*
Lang, Andrew	Charles J. Finger	*Adventures of Andrew Lang*
Lang, Sophie	Frederick Irving Anderson	*The Notorious Sophie Lang*
Langer, Judd	J. Foster	
Langholm, Charles	Ernest W. Hornung	*The Shadow of the Rope*
Langley, Tom	J. Monmouth	
Langton, Detective-Inspector	M. Dare	
Langtry, Jimmy	Francis Leslie	*Second Stroke*
Lanigan, Tim	Robert P. Hansen	*Dead Pigeon*
Lanyard, Michael ("The Lone Wolf")	Louis Joseph Vance	*The Lone Wolf*
Largo, Emilio	Ian Fleming	*Thunderball*
Larigan, Jeff	Hugh Pentecost	"The Girl Who Lived Dangerously"
Larkin, Bill	Glen M. Barns	
Larkin, Glen	Lawrence G. Blochman	*Midnight Sailing*
Larkin, The Juggler	Erle Stanley Gardner	
Larose, Gilbert	Arthur Gask	*The Hidden Door*
Larrabee, Lieutenant Kirk	Adam Bliss	*Murder Upstairs*
Larsan, Frederic	Gaston Leroux	*The Mystery of the Yellow Room*
Larson, Lieutenant	Samuel A. Krasney	*Death Cries in the Street*
La Salle, Peter	S. Noel	
Lash, Simon	Frank Gruber	"Death on Eagle's Crag"
Laspiza, Bucky	Ed Lacy	*Be Careful How You Live*
Latham, Mrs. Grace	Leslie Ford	*The Woman in Black*
Latimer, Charles	Eric Ambler	*A Coffin for Dimitrios*
Latin, Max	Norbert Davis	"Don't Give Your Right Name"
La Touches, Georges	Freeman Wills Crofts	*The Cask*
Latour, Deputy Sheriff Andy	D. Keene	
Latrelle, Simone; *see* Solitaire		
Laud, Superintendent	Nigel Fitzgerald	*This Won't Hurt You*

CHARACTER	AUTHOR	TITLE
Laurance, Bluey	A. Scobie	
Lavender, James Eliot ("Jimmie")	Vincent Starrett	*The Casebook of Jimmie Lavender*
Law, Inspector	John Cassells	
Lawrence, Jim	Lawrence G. Blochman	*Rather Cool for Mayhem*
Lawson, Tuck	Charles T. Stoneham	
Leach, Martin	"Sea-Lion"	
League of Gentlemen	John Boland	*League of Gentlemen*
Leamas, Alex	John Le Carré	*The Spy Who Came in from the Cold*
Leather, Danny	David Lawrence	*Dead Orchid*
Leborgne, Joseph	Georges Simenon	*The Three Rembrandts*
Le Briton, Dr. Miles	John Esteven	*By Night at Dinsmore*
Lecain, Dominique	Roger Francis Didelot	*Death of the Deputy*
Le Chiffre	Ian Fleming	*Casino Royale*
Lecoq, Monsieur	Emile Gaboriau	*Monsieur Lecoq*
Lee, George	Fergus Hume	*The Miser's Well*
Lee, Gerry	K. Hopkins	
Lee, Gypsy Rose	Gypsy Rose Lee	*G-String Murders*
Lee, Judith	Richard Marsh	*Judith Lee: Some Pages from Her Life*
Lee, Detective-Inspector Lawrence	D. Fisher	
Lee, Norma ("The Beautiful Gunner")	Norma Lee	*Beautiful Gunner*
Lee, Sergeant First Class Robert E. ("Lonesome")	John McPartland	
Leek, Sergeant	G. Verner	
Lefarge, M.	Freeman Wills Crofts	*The Cask*
Legrand, William	Edgar Allan Poe	"The Gold Bug"
"Lehmann, Klaus"; *see* Hambledon, Thomas		
Leiter, Felix	Ian Fleming	*Casino Royale*
Leith, Gwynn	Viola Brothers Shore	"The Mackenzie Case"
Leith, Sergeant James	Peter Drax	
Leith, Lester	Erle Stanley Gardner	"Bird in Hand"
Leith, Marion	Elizabeth Messenger	
Leithen, Sir Edward	John Buchan	*Powerhouse*
Leland, Quinn	Franklin M. Davis, Jr.	*Secret: Hong Kong*
Lemeurier, Mrs. Lucia Masterson (later Mrs. Anthony Ruthven Gethryn)	Philip MacDonald	*The Rasp*
Lemoine	Agatha Christie	*The Secret of Chimneys*
Lennox, Bill	Willis T. Ballard	"Murder Is a Swell Idea"
Lennox, Marg	Helen J. Hultman	
Lenz, Dr.	Patrick Quentin	*Puzzle for Players*
Leonard, Miriam ("Miss Montana")	Elliot Paul	*Hugger-Mugger in the Louvre*
Leopold, Captain	Edward D. Hoch	
Le Roux, Rolf	Peter Godfrey	*Death Under the Table*
Leroy, Martin and Helen	James Holding	"The Hong Kong Jewel Mystery"
Leslie, Ludovic ("Greensleeves")	William M. Duncan	
Lessing, Detective-Superintendent Roger	Stella Claydon	*A Lesson in Murder*

CHARACTER	AUTHOR	TITLE
Lester, Captain "Tiger"	Don Betteridge	*Contact Man*
Lestrade, Inspector	Sir Arthur Conan Doyle	*A Study in Scarlet*
Lethbury, Dr. Arnold	Michael Gilbert	"Professional Riposte"
Letord, Superintendent	Manning Coles	*Search for a Sultan*
Leveret, M.	Jean Touissaint-Samat	*The Dead Man at the Window*
Leverett	Anthony Marsden	"Heredity"
Levine, Abraham	Donald Westlake	"The Death of a Bum"
Lewis, Inspector	C. Little	
Lewker, Sir Abercrombie	Glynn Carr	*The Youth Hostel Murders*
Leyland, Inspector	Ronald A. Knox	*The Three Taps*
"The Liberator"	Norman Deane	*Return to Adventure*
Licorice (Licensed Organization for International Crime and Espionage)	Richard L. Hershatter	*The Man Who Hated Licorice*
Liddell, Johnny	Frank Kane	*Grave Danger*
Liddon, Mark	Patrick Quentin	*The Follower*
"The Lieutenant"	Nicholas Di Minno	"Case of the Night Club Chanteuse"
Linden, Barry	Inigo Jones	*Clue of the Hungry Corpse*
Lindley, Donald	Alex Gaby	"D.A.'s Dream Case"
Lindquist, Michael	Esther Haven Fonseca	*The Affair at the Grotto*
Lindsay, Ralph	Ben Benson	*End of Violence*
Linley, Mr.	Lord Dunsany	"Two Bottles of Relish"
Lintock, Hamish	Bruce Sanders	
Linton, John	Hugh McCutcheon	
Linz, Baroness Clara	E. Phillips Oppenheim	*Advice Ltd.*
Lister, Detective-Sergeant Johnny	Victor Gunn	*Murder at the Hotel*
Little Amby; *see* Hinkle, Ambrose		
Littlejohn, Superintendent	George Bellairs	*Death Drops the Pilot*
Llorca, Juan	Delano Ames	*The Man with Three Jaguars*
Lobo, Pepe	Peter Romsey	*The Lidless Eye*
Locke, Major Kim	Kendell F. Crossen	*The Tortured Path*
Locke, Sherry	Willetta Ann Barber and R. F. Schabelitz	*Deed Is Drawn*
Loddon, Dick	Nigel Morland	
Loftus, Bill	John Creasey	
Loftus, Phoebe	Rose Finnegan	"Paid in Full"
Logan, Professor Hilary	George F. Worts	*Laughing Girl*
Logan, Mike	Henry Holt	
Lognon, Inspector	Georges Simenon	
Lomas, Honourable Sidney	Henry C. Bailey	*The Long Dinner*
Lombard, Dr. Anthony	Julius Fast	*Street of Fear*
Lombard, John	Cornell Woolrich	*Phantom Lady*
London, Jimmie	J. Rowland	
"The Lone Wolf"; *see* Lanyard, Michael		
Long, Inspector Arnold	Edgar Wallace	*The Terrible People*
Long, Detective-Sergeant	J. M. Fox	
Long, Lydford	Henry Carstairs	
Longworth, Algy	Herman C. McNeile	*The Third Round*
Longworth, Deputy Sheriff Bill	Robert Wilder	*Walk with Evil*

CHARACTER	AUTHOR	TITLE
"Lord" Broghville; *see* Bennett, Geoffrey		
Lord, Inspector	David Frome	*Scotland Yard Can Wait*
Lord, Inspector Michael	C. Daly King	*Arrogant Alibi*
Lord Peter; *see* Wimsey, Lord Peter		
Lord Plimsoll; *see* Plimsoll, Lord Simon		
Loring, Captain	Dolan Birkeley	*The Blue Geranium*
Lorne, Michael	Richard Keverne	*He Laughed at Murder*
Lorrimer, Spencer	William H. L. Crauford	
Lott, Inspector	Henry Wade	*The Dying Alderman*
Lottie	Thurman Warriner	*Death's Bright Angel*
Louden, Max	R. Mann	*Nothing to Declare*
Louis	E. Phillips Oppenheim	*Pulpit in the Grill Room*
Love, Dr. Jason	James Leasor	*Passport to Oblivion*
Love, Pharaoh	George Baxt	*A Queer Kind of Death*
Loveapple, Miss	Ethel Lina White	*While She Sleeps*
Lovick, Ambrose	G. M. Wilson	
Low, Ambrose	Henry Cecil	*According to the Evidence*
Lowe, Selby	Edgar Wallace	*King by Night*
Lowell, Bill	Whitman Chambers	*Bright Star of Danger*
Lucas, Ben	Helen Nielsen	"This Man Is Dangerous"
Lucas, Captain Ben	Royce Howes	*Murder at Maneuvers*
Luccan, Detective-Inspector Andy	Nigel Morland	
Lucias, Captain Ben	Royce Howes	*Death Rides a Hobby*
Lucifer, Wilbur K.	James Workman	
Luck, Simon	J. Marsh	
Ludlow, Johnny	Mrs. Henry Wood	"The Ebony Box"
Lugg, Magersfontein	Margery Allingham	"The Case of the Late Pig"
Luke, Chief Inspector Charles	Margery Allingham	*The Beckoning Lady*
Lumsden, Archie	Max Saltmarsh	*The Clouded Moon*
Lumsden, Mike	Michael Halliday	
Lund, Sam	Ed Lacy	*The Best That Ever Did It*
Lundy, Inspector	Philip Loraine	
Lupin, Arsène (alias "Jim Barnett," "Paul Daubreuil," "Captain Jeanniot," "Prince Renine," "Horace Velmont")	Maurice LeBlanc	*The Eight Strokes of the Clock*
Lydney, George	S. Fox	
Lyle, Samuel	Arthur Crabb	*Samuel Lyle, Criminologist*
Lymington, John	John N. Chance	
Lynch, Bertram	John W. Vandercook	*Murder in Fiji*
Lynd, Vesper	Ian Fleming	*Casino Royale*
Lynn, Shasta	Wade Miller	*Deadly Weapon*
Lynton, Richard	M. Tannock	
Lyson, Major	E. Phillips Oppenheim	*The Milan Grill Room*
M (Head of British Secret Service, full name unknown)	Ian Fleming	*Casino Royale*
Mabuse, Dr.	Norbert Jacques	*Dr. Mabuse, Master of Mystery*
"Mac"	Thomas B. Dewey	*Portrait of a Dead Heiress*
MacAlastair, Alastair	Sibyl Ericson	*The Curate's Crime*

CHARACTER	AUTHOR	TITLE
MaCall, Johnny and Moira	Gerard Fairlie	*Deadline for MaCall*
MacAllister, Sergeant	William M. Duncan	
McAlpine, Dr. Barbara	J. Austwick	
McAlpine, Philip	Adam Diment	*The Bang Bang Birds*
McAndrew, Dr. Ian	T. C. H. Jacobs	
MacAvoy, Bill	Gordon Volk	*Meeting by Moonlight*
McBain, Sergeant	Anne Littlefield	*Which Mrs. Bennett*
McBain, Vicky	Colin Robertson	*Venetian Mask*
McBride, Rex	Cleve F. Adams	*Sabotage*
McCall, Andy	William M. Duncan	
MacCallum, Chief Inspector Duncan	Allan MacKinnon	*Murder, Repeat, Murder*
McCarthy, Cathy	Melville Burt	*Case of the Laughing Jesuit*
McCarthy, Detective-Inspector	John G. Brandon	
McCarty, Inspector Timothy	Isabel Ostrander	*McCarty Incog.*
Macclesfield, Detective-Inspector	Michael Halliday	*Hilda, Take Heed*
McClint, Inspector Colin	Hugh Munro	
McClure, Kerry	Mary V. Heberden	
McConn, Sergeant Patrick	Richard M. Baker	*Death Stops the Manuscript*
McCorkle	Ross Thomas	*The Cold War Swap*
MacCormack, Tim	R. Hansen	
McCoy	Whit Masterson	
McCoy, Lieutenant	Sinclair Gluck	*The Blind Fury*
McCunn, Dickson	John Buchan	
MacDonald, Captain	Nigel Mackenzie	
MacDonald, Detective-Sergeant Kenneth	Angus MacVicar	
McDonald, Lynn	Kay Cleaver Strahan	*The Meriwether Mystery*
MacDonald, Superintendent	E. C. R. Lorac	*The Last Escape*
McDowell, Nick	Hugh Kimberley	
McDuff, Inspector Angus	John Mersereau	
MacDuffy, Inspector Angus	Edwin Balmer and Philip Wylie	
McGarrah, Inspector	Charles C. Nicolet	
McGarry, Dan	Matt Taylor	"McGarry and the Box-office Bandits"
McGee, "Squiller"	A. A. Archer	*The Weekend Murders*
McGee, Travis	John D. MacDonald	*Bright Orange for the Shroud*
MacGillicuddy	Robert George Dean	*Murder by Marriage*
McGorr, Policewoman Alice	Arthur W. Upfield	
McGovern, Phil	D. S. Davis	
McGovern, Sergeant	Lillian Day and Norbert Lederer	
MacGowan, Lieutenant Will	Shirley and Adele Seifert	
McGrath, Steve	Lawrence Lariar	*Friday for Death*
McGraw, Inspector	Gelett Burgess	*Master of Mysteries*
MacGregor, Echo; *see* Ware, Mrs. Anthony		

CHARACTER	AUTHOR	TITLE
MacGregor, Etienne	Peter Cheyney	
McGregor, Inspector	Henry Kane	*Laughter in the Alehouse*
MacGregor, Sergeant	Joyce Porter	*Dover One*
McGuire, Inspector Aloysius	John Russell Warren	*Murder from Three Angles*
McGuire, Patrick	Patrick O. McGuire	*A Time for Murder*
MacIlroy, Detective-Inspector	Peter Cheyney	
McIntosh, Superintendent William	A. MacVigar	
McIntyre, Chief "Mac"	Molly E. Corne	*Death at the Manor*
MacIvor, Angus	Neal Harman	*Yours Truly, Angus MacIvor*
Mack, Dr. Johnny	Theodore S. Drachman	*Something for the Birds*
Mackail, Mr.	David Lockwood	
McKay, Captain	Lawrence G. Blochman	
McKay, Chief Inspector Ellis	Leonard A. G. Strong	*Which I Never*
McKay, Randle; *see* Wren, Lassiter		
McKay, Tony	Sax Rohmer	*Emperor Fu Manchu*
McKechnie, Railroad Police Agent	Bert and Dolores Hitchens	*The Man Who Followed Women*
McKee, Inspector Christopher	Helen Reilly	*Compartment K*
M'Kellar, Detective-Inspector	Hugh McCutcheon	*Murder at the Angel*
McKelvie, Graydon	Marion Harvey	
McKinnon, Clay	Steve Brackeen	*Delfina*
McKinnon, Todd	Lenore Glen Offord	*The Skeleton Key*
McLaggan, Donald	M. Tannock	
MacLain, Captain Duncan	Baynard H. Kendrick	*Blind Man's Bluff*
MacLaird, Mrs.	William C. White	*Career*
McLean, Chief Inspector	George Goodchild	*McLean Sees It Through*
McLean, Lieutenant-Commander Hugh ("Davvie")	Margaret Taylor Yates	*Death Sends a Cable*
McLean, Mrs. Hugh (née Anne Davenport)	Margaret Taylor Yates	*The Hush-Hush Murders*
MacLean, Roy	Bill Gaston	*Death Crag*
McLean, Tucker	M. Corrigan	
MacLeod, Alastair ("Greybreek")	Angus MacVicar	*Greybreek*
MacLeod, Dr. Andrew ("Tully")	Edgar Wallace	
McLeod, Chief Inspector	Roland Daniel	
MacLeod, David and Sadie	Colin Robertson	
MacLeod, George	David Dodge	
McLeod, Neill	Allan C. McLean	*The Carpet Slipper Murder*
MacLevy, Oscar	Bruno Fischer	
McManus, Sergeant	Belton Cobb	
McMillan, Brian	Kenneth Allsop	*The Leopard-Paw Orchid*
Macmorran, Inspector	Brian Flynn	*The Spiked Lion*

CHARACTER	AUTHOR	TITLE
McMurdo, Chief Inspector Andy	Nigel Morland	
MacNab	John Cassells	
MacNab, Alastair	James Ronald	*They Can't Hang Me*
MacNab, Francis	John A. Ferguson	"The White Line"
McNamara, Detective	John Bentley	
McNeece, Jim	Carroll Cox Estes	*Moon Gate*
McNeill, Dr. Jeffrey and Anne	Theodora DuBois	*The McNeills Chase a Ghost*
MacNeill, Superintendent	William M. Duncan	
Macomber, Elisha	Kathleen Moore Knight	*The Trouble at Turkey Hill*
McPherson, Mark	Vera Caspary	*Laura*
McQueen, Mickey	Harvey J. O'Higgins	
Macrae, Inspector	Alan Mackinnon	
Macready, Sheriff	Hugh Holman	*Slay the Murderer*
MacTavish, Alonzo	Peter Cheyney	
MacVeigh, Captain Andy and Sue	Sue MacVeigh	*Murder Under Construction*
MacVeigh, Peter	Theodora DuBois	*High Tension*
Madden, Con	Maurice Walsh	*Nine Strings to Your Bow*
Madden, "Chief" Jerome	Thomas Polsky	*Curtains for the Judge*
Madden, Jerry	J. Marsh	
Madden, Postal Inspector	Doris Miles Disney	*Unappointed Rounds*
Maddison, John	Frank Chittenden	
Maddox	J. H. Chase	*Tell It to the Birds*
Maddox, Ivor	Elizabeth Linington	*No Evil Angel*
Maddox, Mr.	Thomas T. Flynn	"Hayseed Homicide"
Madgin, James	Thomas W. Speight	*Under Lock and Key*
Madigan, Lieutenant	Edwin Lanham	
Madigan, Sherry	Clarence Budington Kelland	*Stolen Goods*
Madrid, Sol	Robert Wilder	*Fruit of the Poppy*
Magill, Sheriff Moss	Dorothy Gardiner	*Lion in Wait*
Magruder, Inspector	Jerome and Harold Prince	"The Man in the Velvet Hat"
Maguire, Finke	Elliot Paul	*Murder on the Left Bank*
Maguire, Johnny	Richard Himmel	*The Chinese Keyhole*
Mahan, Betty	Timothy Fuller	*Two Thirds of a Ghost*
Mahoun, Nicky	C. Smith	
Maidment, Richard ("The Pilgrim")	Michael Cronin	*Begin with a Gun*
Maigret, Inspector	Georges Simenon	*The Patience of Maigret*
Mais, Inspector	Leslie Beresford	*Murder Can Be Such Fun*
Maitland, Anthony	Sara Woods	*Enter Certain Murderers*
Maitland, Jim	R. Daniel	
Maitland, Jim	"Sapper"	*Jim Maitland*
Maitland, Miss Tania	"Sea-Lion"	*When Danger Threatens*
Maland, Sheriff Eric	Mabel Seeley	*The Whispering Cup*
Malcolm, James "Solo"	Neill Graham	*Murder Makes It Certain*
Mallard, Chief Superintendent "Duck"	Andrew Spiller	*Birds of a Feather*
Mallett, Inspector John	Cyril Hare	*Untimely Death*
Mallett, Superintendent	Mary Fitt	*Clues to Cristobel*
Mallory, Dennis	Howard C. Huston	*The Blind Saw Murder*
Mallory, Detective	Jacques Futrelle	*The Superfluous Finger*
Mallory, Lieutenant	Ross Graham	*Death on a Smoke Boat*

CHARACTER	AUTHOR	TITLE
Malloy, Vic	James Hadley Chase	*Too Dangerous to Be Free*
Malone, John J.	Craig Rice	*The Lucky Stiff*
Malone, Policeman Johnny	Ferguson Findley	*Handful of Murder*
Malone, Mr.	Nigel Morland	
Malone, Robert	Henry C. James	
Malone, "Rube"	Thomas Walsh	"Women-Pests or Poison"
Maltby, Edward	Joseph J. Farjeon	
Maltby, Inspector	H. Hawton	
Malvern, Steve	A. Graham	
"Man in the Corner"; *see* "The Old Man in the Corner"		
"The Man of Forty Faces"; *see* Cleek, Hamilton		
Manby, Charles	Lawrence W. Meynell	
Manchenil, Bolivar	Donald McNutt Douglas	*Many Brave Hearts*
Manchu; *see* Fu Manchu, Dr.		
Manciple, Professor	Kenneth Hopkins	*She Died Because*
Mancuso	H. B. Dickey	"No Trouble at All"
Manders, "Bunny"	Ernest W. Hornung	*The Amateur Cracksman*
Manderson, Mrs. Mabel Domecq (later Mrs. Philip Marsham Trent)	Edmund C. Bentley	*Trent's Last Case*
Mandeville, Klyde	Kathleen C. Groom	*The Folly of Fear*
Manfred	Edgar Wallace	*Three Just Men*
Manfred, Judge	Alec R. Hilliard	*Outlaw Island*
Manleigh, Chief Inspector	Stanley P. Toye	
Mann, Mr.	Edgar Wallace	*The Man Who Knew*
Mann, Patrick	David Duff	*Traitor's Pass*
Mann, "Tiger"	Mickey Spillane	*Day of the Guns*
Mannering, John ("The Blue Mask")	Anthony Morton	*The Return of the Blue Mask*
Manners, Hartley	Charles I. Dutton	*Black Fog*
Manners, Hector	Denzil Batchelor	*Everything Happens to Hector*
Manning, Charles Hendesley	Herbert De Hamel	*Many Thanks—Ben Hassett*
Manning, Detective-Sergeant	M. Neville	
Manning, Fire Marshal	Carl Henry Rathjen	"Full Moon Tonight"
Manning, Superintendent	Belton Cobb	*The Secret of Superintendent Manning*
Manrique, Ramon	Leslie Charteris	
Mansel, George	A. Parsons	
Mansel, Jonathan	Dornford Yates	*Were Death Denied*
Manson, Dr.	Edwin and Mona A. Radford	
Manson, Helen	Harvey J. O'Higgins	
Manton, Detective-Superintendent	Michael Underwood	*Adam's Case*
Mappin, Amos Lee	Hulbert Footner	*Death of the Saboteur*
Maquis, Johnny	V. Warren	
March, Colonel	Carter Dickson	*The Department of Queer Complaints*

CHARACTER	AUTHOR	TITLE
March, Danny	Frances S. Wees	
March, Erik	G. G. Fickling	
March, Justin; *see* "The Ace"		
March, Larry	Whitman Chambers	
March, Milo	M. E. Chaber	*A Hearse of Another Color*
March, Chief Constable Randal	Patricia Wentworth	*The Brading Collection*
Marchmont, Inspector	Hugh Desmond	
Marcus, Lieutenant Joe	Fletcher Flora	"The Dead Don't Speak"
Marden, Tony	H. C. Davis	
Marfleet, Inspector	Headon Hill	*The Man from Egypt*
Marin, Mr.	Edgar Wallace	*The Island of Galloping Gold*
Markham, John F-X	S. S. Van Dine	*The Benson Murder Case*
Markham, Philip	Lawrence W. Meynell	
Marks, Jonathan	Glen M. Barnes	*Murder Is a Gamble*
Marlow, Dick	John Bentley	*Mr. Marlow Chooses Wine*
Marlow, Nicholas	Eric Ambler	*Cause for Alarm*
Marlow, Superintendent	G. Dickson	
Marlowe, Philip	Raymond Chandler	*The Big Sleep*
Marlowe, Piers	Piers Marlowe	
Marlowe, Sarah	Patricia Wentworth	
Marlowe, Simon	James Baggaley	*Shadow of the Eagle*
Marly, Dr. Richard	Mignon G. Eberhart	"Murder at the Dog Show"
Marmouset	Ponson du Terrail	*Les Exploits de Rocambole*
Marple, Miss Jane	Agatha Christie	*A Murder Is Announced*
Marples, Roger	Francis Beeding	
Marquis, Sir Henry	Melville Davisson Post	*The Sleuth of St. James Square*
Marr, Dick	Stephen Maddock	*Public Mischief*
Marrowfat, Superintendent	Dennis Wheatley	
Marsden, Detective-Inspector	Elizabeth Backhouse	*The Night Has Eyes*
Marsh, Alan	George Harmon Coxe	"There Is Still Tomorrow"
Marsh, Lieutenant Eddie	Jack Dolph	*Murder Is Mutuel*
Marsh, Emma	Elizabeth Dean	*Murder Is a Serious Business*
Marshall, Gary	George Harmon Coxe	*No Time to Kill*
Marshall, Johnny	James M. Fox	*A Shroud for Mr. Bundy*
Marshall, Nick	Gilroy Mitcham	
Marshall, Superintendent	Bernard Newman	
Marshall, Suzy	James M. Fox	*A Shroud for Mr. Bundy*
Marshall, Terence	H. H. Holmes	*Nine Times Nine*
Martens, Commissioner	August Weissl	*Mystery of the Green Car*
Martin, Anthony	William Francis	*Bury Me Not*
Martin, Bill	Charles T. Stoneham	
Martin, Blain	Michael Dare	*Murder Incognito*
Martin, Dick	Edgar Wallace	*Door with Seven Locks*
Martin, Edmund H.	E. Phillips Oppenheim	*Mysteries of the Riviera*
Martin, Frank and Elspeth	J. Paul	
Martin, Inspector George	Francis Beeding	*He Could Not Have Slipped*
Martin, Inspector	Wallace Jackson	*Diamonds of Death*
Martin, Superintendent John	S. Miles	

CHARACTER	AUTHOR	TITLE
Martin, "Pulp"	Jeremy Slate	
Martin, Commander Reid	Nard Jones	*The Case of the Hanging Lady*
Martin, Slade	Jacques Pendower	
Martin, Sylvia	Erle Stanley Gardner	
Martin, Detective-Inspector "Tubby"	Phyllis Hambledon	
Martineau, Detective-Inspector	Maurice Proctor	*Killer at Large*
Marvin, Pete	B. Edmunds	
Mason, Chief Detective-Inspector	Edgar Wallace	
Mason, Chief Inspector Dick	R. Armstrong	
Mason, Francis	William Haggard	
Mason, Perry	Erle Stanley Gardner	*The Case of the Sulky Girl*
Mason, Peter	J. Norwood	
Mason, Philip	Hugh Clevely	
Mason, Randolph	Melville Davisson Post	*The Strange Schemes of Randolph Mason*
Massey, Oliver	Henry C. Beck	
Masters, Chief Inspector Humphrey	Carter Dickson	*The Reader Is Warned*
Masters, Jigger	Anthony Rud	*The Stuffed Men*
Masterson, Jill	Ian Fleming	*Goldfinger*
Masterton, Guy	William M. Duncan	
Matthai, Inspector	F. Dürrenmatt	
Matthews, John	Leonard A. G. Strong	
Matthews, Ward	M. Miller	
Mattingly, Lieutenant	Norman Stanley Bartner	
"Mauravania, Prince of"; *see* Cleek, Hamilton		
Maury, Inspector	J. M. Walsh	
Mawley, Adrian	Lawrence W. Meynell	
Mawson, James Levitt	Ralph Henry Barbour	*Death in the Virgins*
Maxwell, Justice	Edgar Wallace	*Mr. Justice Maxwell*
Mayfair, Sergeant	James B. Hendryx	
Mayhew, Philip	Peter Campion	
Mayhew, Lieutenant Stephen	D. B. Olsen	*The Cat Saw Murder*
Maynard, Garrett	Howard Swiggett	*Hidden and the Hunted*
Mayo, Asey	Phoebe Atwood Taylor	*The Cape Cod Mystery*
Mayo, Superintendent George	Bruce Sanders	
Mead, Lieutenant Valentine	Joseph Storer Clouston	
Meadow, Squeakie (Desdemona)	Margaret Manners	"Squeakie's First Case"
Meadows, Peter	Richard Powell	
Meatyard, Lieutenant	Stanley Casson	*Murder by Burial*
Medway, Jason	P. Marlowe	
Meech, "Spider"	Clifford Orr	*Dartmouth Murders*
Meers, Police Chief	Ruth Fenisong	
Mellanby, Robina	Elizabeth Ferrars	
Mellish, Inspector	J. Day	
Mellsonby, Thomas	J. Fleming	
Melrose, "Hawk"	John H. Knox	"Riddle of the Barking Boy"

CHARACTER	AUTHOR	TITLE
Mendel, Lieutenant	H. E. Helseth	
Mendoza, Lieutenant Luis	Dell Shannon	*Coffin Corner*
Menendes, Inspector	Suzanne Blanc	*The Green Stone*
Menzies, Laura	Gladys Mitchell	*Spotted Hemlock*
Menzies, Chief Inspector Weir	Frank Froest	*Maelstrom*
Mercer, Edward	Victor Canning	*Bird of Prey*
Meredith, Sir John (formerly Chief Inspector)	Francis Gerard	*The Concrete Castle Murders*
Meredith, Assistant Commissioner T. X.	Edgar Wallace	
Merefield, Harold	John Rhode	
Merlini	Clayton Rawson	*Footprints on the Ceiling*
Merrill, Jonathan	F. E. Wees	
Merriman, John and Joan	Milward Kennedy	
Merrion, Desmond	Miles Burton	*Death in Shallow Water*
Merrivale, Sir Henry ("H.M.")	Carter Dickson	*The Plague Court Murders*
Merrowdene, Mrs.	Agatha Christie	"Accident"
Mertin	Eric Bayley	*Secret of Scotland Yard*
Merton, Detective-Inspector	C. Ashton	
Messenger, John	C. L. Reid	
"Meticulous Michael"; *see* Morlant, Sergeant Michael		
Metz, Fred	Allan McRoyd	
Meynard, Katheren Lutetia (later Mrs. Hazlitt Woar)	George Worthing Yates	
Michel, Vivienne	Ian Fleming	*Spy Who Loved Me*
Micklem, Don	R. Marshall	
Middle, Sergeant	William M. Duncan	
"The Midnight Cavalier"; *see* Stone, J. Rockingham		
Midnight, Steve	John Butter	"The Saint in Silver"
Midwinter, Inspector Bertram	Harrington Hext	*The Thing at Their Heels*
Migglewade, Montague	E. Hale	
Mildenhall, Charles	E. Phillips Oppenheim	*Last Train Out*
Miles, Charlie	Hillary Waugh	*Eighth Mrs. Bluebeard*
Miles, Philip	James Remington McCarthy	*Special Agent*
Milk, Miss Jessie	Guy Cullingford	*Conjurer's Coffin*
Miller, Alan	Peter Hunt	*Murder Among the Nudists*
Miller, "Doc"	Herman Peterson	*Murder R.F.D.*
Miller, John	Clarence Budington Kelland	*Murder Makes an Entrance*
Miller, Joseph; *see* Muller, Joe		
Millet, Inspector	George R. Sims	*Tinkletop's Crime*
Milligan, "Sailor"	T. C. H. Jacobs	
Milliken	A. H. Z. Carr	"The Man Who Understood Women"

CHARACTER	AUTHOR	TITLE
Milton, Chief Inspector	Frank King	
Milton, Henry Arthur ("The Ringer")	Edgar Wallace	*Again the Ringer*
Minerva Club	Victor Canning	"A Stroke of Genius"
Minot, Sam	Freeman Dana	*Murder at the New York World's Fair*
Minter, Superintendent Patrick J.	Edgar Wallace	
Miquet, Carl (later Baroness Von Katz)	Darwin and Hildegarde Teilhet	*The Crimson Hair Murders*
"Miss Montana"; *see* Leonard, Miriam		
"Mister Death"; *see* Gilmore, Jimmy		
Mitchell, Bill	Harold A. Wrenn	
Mitchell, Chief Inspector	Freeman Wills Crofts	*Inspector French and the Starvel Tragedy*
Mitchell, Inspector	Josephine Bell	*Port of London Murders*
Mitchell, Max	Ernest Dudley	
Mitchell, Peter	G. W. Cooke	
The Mixer; *see* Smith, Anthony		
Moffatt, Barney	Lee Herrington	*Carry My Coffin Slowly*
Moffatt, Dan	Rex Hardinge	
Mohune, Peter	Pelham Groom	*Mohune's Nine Lives*
Moidart, Chief Constable	Clive Ryland	
Moine, Vic	Bert and Dolores Hitchens	*One-Way Ticket*
Molloy, "Chance"	Lester Dent	*Dead at the Take-Off*
Molly, Lady	Baroness Orczy	*Lady Molly of Scotland Yard*
Mom	James Yaffee	"Mom Makes a Wish"
Moneypenny, Miss	Ian Fleming	*Casino Royale*
Monk, Inspector	P. Manton	
Monroe, Crete	Dwight Marfield	
"Monsieur Zero"; *see* Cibo, Comus		
"Montana, Miss"; *see* Leonard, Miriam		
Montmaront, Yvonne de	John Creasey	
Mookerji, Dr. Motilal	Lawrence G. Blochman	*Clues for Dr. Coffee*
Moon, Cotton	Rufus King	*Holiday Homicide*
Moon, Manville	Richard Deming	"No Pockets in a Shroud"
Mooney, Jerry	Kerry O'Neil	*Ninth Floor: Middle City Tower*
Moore, Inspector	Torrey Chanslor	*Our First Murder*
Moore, Toussaint	Ed Lacy	*Room to Swing*
Moran, Jigger	John Roeburt	*There Are Dead Men in Manhattan*
Moran, P.	Percival Wilde	"P. Moran, Diamond Hunter"
Mordant, Detective-Inspector	J. Corbett	
Mordiford, Mr.	Cyril A. Alington	*Nabob's Jewel*
Morel	Frederick Irving Anderson	"The House of Many Mansions"
Morelle, Dr.	Ernest Dudley	*Meet Dr. Morelle*
Moresby, Chief Inspector	Anthony Berkeley	*The Poisoned Chocolates Case*
Morgan, Detective-Chief Inspector Chris	Charles Dixon	

CHARACTER	AUTHOR	TITLE
Morgan, Christopher	Sinclair Gluck	*The Blind Fury*
Morgan, Inspector Elwyn	Stewart Farrar	*The Snake on 99*
Morgan, Inspector	John Bingham	*Inspector Morgan's Dilemma*
Morgan, Inspector	Jeremy Slate	
Morgan, Inspector	Oswald Crawfurd	*Revelations of Inspector Morgan*
Morgan, Oscar	Geoffrey Homes	*The Doctor Died at Dusk*
Morgan, Ruff	Jimmy Shannon	*Devil's Passkey*
Morgan and Avon	V. Hill	
Morgan the Raider	Mickey Spillane	*The Delta Factor*
Morlake, James ("The Black")	Edgar Wallace	*The Black*
Morlant, Sergeant Michael ("Meticulous Michael")	Frank King	
Morlay, John	Edgar Wallace	
Morley, Al	R. Cocking	
Morley, Francis ("Gay Detective")	Lou Rand	*Rough Trade*
Morphew, Harriet	Mary Allerton	*Shadow and the Web*
Morriarty, Professor James	Sir Arthur Conan Doyle	"The Final Problem"
Morris, Hugh	William Targ and Lewis Herman	*The Case of Mr. Cassidy*
Morris, Sergeant	Rufus King	*Lethal Lady*
Morrison, Dan	Joseph Shallit	*Kiss the Killer*
Morrison, Detective	Dorothy Ogburn	*The Will and the Deed*
Morro, "Big" Nick	Prosper Buranelli	*The News-Reel Murder*
Morrough, Guy	Nigel Fitzgerald	*Imagine a Man*
Morston, Mary; *see* Watson, Mrs. John H.		
Mortimer, Superintendent Frederick	A. A. Milne	"Once a Murderer"
Mortimer, Dr. James	Sir Arthur Conan Doyle	*The Hound of the Baskervilles*
Mortimer, Sergeant	J. Corbett	
Moss, Inspector Phil	Bill Knox	*The Taste of Proof*
Mosson, Major	Leslie Cargill	
Motcomb, Martin and Rosalind	Phyllis Hambledon	
Moto, T. A.	John P. Marquand	*Mr. Moto's Three Aces*
Mott, Daisy Jane	Jennifer Jones	
Mott, Lucie	E. Phillips Oppenheim	*Ask Miss Mott*
Mowry, James	E. F. Russell	
Much, Dr. Peter	Simon Jay	*Death of a Skindiver*
Muir, Peter	Max Brand	*The Face and the Doctor*
Muir, Rex	Simon Harvester	
Muir, Superintendent	Francis Grierson	
Muldoon, Hart	Jonathan Flagg	*Lovely Mask*
Muller, Joe	Grace I. Colbron and Augusta Groner	*The Crippled Hand*
Mulligan, Mr. Patrick	Baroness Orczy	*Skin o' My Tooth*
Mulligan, Tim	Aaron Marc Stein	*Death Meets 400 Rabbits*
Mullins, Sergeant	Frances and Richard Lockridge	*Dead as a Dinosaur*
Mundy, Todd	Brook Hastings	*The Demon Within*
Munn, Wolfgang Amadeus	J. C. Snaith	

CHARACTER	AUTHOR	TITLE
Munson, Scott	Thorne Smith	*Did She Fall?*
Munt, Mr.	Hugh Clevely	*Mr. Munt Carries On*
Munting, John	Dorothy Sayers and Robert Eustace	*The Documents in the Case*
Murch, Inspector	Edmund C. Bentley	"The Inoffensive Captain"
Murdoch, Bruce	Norman Deane	*Secret Errand*
Murdock, "Captain"	Carl McK. Saunders	"When Hell Blows Its Lid"
Murdock, Kent	George Harmon Coxe	*Triple Exposure*
Murdock, Miles ("The Purple Scar")	John S. Endicott	*Night of Murder*
Murdock, Rachel	D. B. Olsen	*Cats Don't Smile*
Murmur, Heron	Simon Harvester	*The Chinese Hammer*
Mustard, Buddy	R. Daniel	
Mycroft, Mr.	Gerald Heard	*A Taste for Honey*
Myers, Inspector	C. Franklin	
Myrl, Dora	M. McDonnell Bodkin	*Dora Myrl: The Lady Detective*
Myrtle, Chief Inspector	Henry Wade	
Mysterious Traveler	Mutual Broadcasting Station	
"The Nailer"	Peter O'Donnell	*Modesty Blaise*
Nalon, Mark	Robert Hansen	*Mark Three for Murder*
Narkom, Superintendent Maverick	Thomas W. Hanshew	*Cleek, the Master Detective*
Narrocott, Inspector	Agatha Christie	*Murder at Hazelmoor*
Nash, Aulrey	Tech Davis	*Terror at Compass Lake*
Nason, Jerry	George Harmon Coxe	*Fashioned for Murder*
Nason, Inspector Nick	J. Manor	
Naughton, Phil	Bruce Sanders	
Neel, Mark	H. Gray	
Neill, Henry F.	Dashiell Hammett	*Red Harvest*
"Nell"	Anne Nash	*Death by Design*
Nelson, Inspector Gridley	Ruth Fenisong	*Dead Weight*
Netterly, Colonel	Henry Wade	*A Dying Fall*
Newall, Sergeant "Know-all"	John Cassells	*Waters of Sadness*
Newberry, Millicent	Jeanette Lee	
Newman, Bernard	Bernard Newman	
Newton, Anthony ("The Brigand")	Edgar Wallace	*The Brigand*
Nichol, Nicholas	C. B. Smith	
Nicola	Guy Boothby	*Dr. Nicola*
Nicoloson, Lloyd (Counterstroke)	Patrick Wayland	*Double Defector*
Nield, Chief Inspector	Andrew Garve	*Hide and Go Seek*
"Night Wind"	Varick Vanardy	*Alias the Night Wind*
"Nighthawk"; *see* Frost, Gerald		
Nightingale, Chief Inspector Brett	Mary C. Kelly	*The Christmas Egg*
Nikolls, Windermere	Peter Cheyney	"A Matter of Cooperation"
No, Dr.	Ian Fleming	*Dr. No*
Noble, Nick	Anthony Boucher	"Black Murder"
Nolan, John and Prue	Charles Nicolai	
Noon, Ed	Michael Avallone	"The Thing in Evening Dress"
Noonan, Inspector	Willard Rich	*Brain Waves and Death*
Noonan, Mike	S. J. Perelman	"Farewell, My Lovely Appetizer"

CHARACTER	AUTHOR	TITLE
Norman, Detective-Inspector	Lawrence Meynell	
Norman, Brigadier Felix	Marten Cumberland	*Hate for Sale*
Norris, Mrs. Annie	Dorothy Salisbury Davis	"Mrs. Norris Visits the Library"
Norroy, Yorke	George Bronson Howard	*Norroy, Diplomatic Agent*
North, Inspector Edward	C. Robertson	
North, Gerald	Frances and Richard Lockridge	*Murder Is Suggested*
North, Gilbert	Guy Cullingford	
North, Colonel Hugh	F. Van Wyck Mason	*Saigon Singer*
North, Nigel	R. Grant	
North, Pamela (Mrs. Gerald North)	Frances and Richard Lockridge	*Patterns of Murder*
North, Richard	Pearl Foley	*The Yellow Circle*
Northeast, Inspector Guy	Joanna Cannon	
Norton (T-Man)	Maurice Procter	"The Million Dollar Mystery"
"November Joe"	Hesketh Prichard	*November Joe*
Oakes, Boysie	John Gardner	*Understrike*
Oates, Inspector Stanislaus	Margery Allingham	*More Work for the Undertaker*
The Obelists	Charles Daly King	*The Obelists at Sea*
Obituary Club	Hugh Pentecost	*The Obituary Club*
O'Breen, Fergus	Anthony Boucher	*The Case of the Seven Sneezes*
O'Brien, Inspector	K. D. Guines	
O'Brien, Neil	Dennis Allen	*Born to Be Murdered*
O'Brien, "Obie"	Joseph R. Marshall	*Murder in an Artist's Colony*
O'Brien, Pierre	Whitman Chambers	*Dog Eat Dog*
O'Brien, Terrence	Mary Roberts Rinehart	*The Swimming Pool*
O'Connell, Daniel Roe	Desmond O'Neill	*Life Has No Price*
O'Connor, Chief Inspector	Philip Loraine	
O'Connor, Jim	Charles Rushton	
O'Day, Terence	Peter Cheyney	*One of Those Things*
Odeen, Detective-Sergeant	John and Ward Hawkins	
Odell, Philip	L. Powell	
Odell, Ross	Wreford Paddon	
O'Donovan, Inspector	Brian Cleeve	*Death of a Wicked Servant*
O'Dowd, Captain	C. Hogarth	
O'Hagen, Sergeant Simon	George Dyer	*The Five Fragments*
O'Hanlon, Lucius	Marten Cumberland	
O'Hara, Caryl	Peter Cheyney	
O'Hara, Terence	Paul Costello	*The Blue Diamond*
O'Hearn, Tim	Ben Ames Williams	
O'K, Don; *see* Adams, Donald O'Keefe		
O'Keefe, Police Officer Kerry	Leslie Ford	*Girl from the Mimosa Club*
O'Kelly, Michael	Manning O'Brine	
Okewood, Major Francis	Valentine Williams	
"The Old Battle-Axe"; *see* Adams, Adelaide		
"Old Calamity"	Joseph Fulling Fishman	"Old Calamity Tries a Bluff"

CHARACTER	AUTHOR	TITLE
"Old Ebbie"; *see* Entwhistle, Ebbie		
"The Old General"; *see* Wharton, George		
"The Old Man"	Dashiell Hammett	*The Dain Curse*
"The Old Man in the Corner"	Baroness Orczy	*The Old Man in the Corner*
"Old Sharon"	Wilkie Collins	*My Lady's Money*
O'Leary, Detective-Lieutenant Joseph	S. Toune	
O'Leary, Lance	Mignon G. Eberhart	*The Patient in Room 18*
O'Leary, Lugs	Anthony M. Kimmins	*Lugs O'Leary*
Olivaw, R. Daneel	Isaac Asimov	*Naked Sun*
Oliver, Mrs. Ariadne	Agatha Christie	*The Third Girl*
Olympia	E. T. A. Hoffmann	*The Tales of Hoffmann*
O'Malley, Officer	William B. MacHarg	"Too Many Enemies"
O'Mara, Shaun Aloysius	Peter Cheyney	*The Dark Street*
O'More, Mary	Whitman Chambers	*Bright Star of Danger*
O'Neill, Jim	Doris Miles Disney	*Fire at Will*
O'Neill, Tip	James Edward Grant	*The Green Shadow*
Opera, Christie	Dorothy Uhnak	*The Bait*
"The Orator"; *see* Rater, Inspector O.		
Ord, Detective-Inspector	Austen Allen	*Menace to Mrs. Kershaw*
ORGY (Organization for the Rational Organization of Youth)	Ted Marks	*My Son, the Double Agent*
Ormac, Inspector Emil	T. C. H. Jacobs	
Ormiston, Colonel	J. M. Walsh	
Ormond, Inspector Daniel	John Brophy	
O'Rourke, Campbell	Max Brand	*Murder Me*
Orr, Nan	Anita Bontell	
Orton, John	Francis Beeding	
Orville, Philip	Constance Rutherford	*Door Without a Key*
Osborne, Harry	W. Goodman	
Osborne, Tom	Allan C. McLean	
Osgood, Sergeant	Helen Nielsen	*Woman on the Roof*
O'Shaunessey, Mike	Will Oursler	"The Shadow and the Shadowed"
O'Sullivan, Johnny	Jerome Odlum	*Nine Lives Are Not Enough*
Otley	Martin Waddell	*Otley*
Ourney, Mal	Raoul Whitfield	
Owen, Sergeant Bobby	Ernest R. Punshon	*Information Received*
Owl	Bryan Rodney	*Owl Flies Home*
Pace, Dr.	Roger Denbie	*Death on the Limited*
Padillo	Ross Thomas	*The Cold War Swap*
"The Padre"	Richard Goyne	
Pagan, Ralph	A. Wood	
Page, Detective-Inspector	J. Corbett	
Page, Dinah	J. Marsh	
Page, James	Selwyn Jepson	*Noise in the Night*
Page, Susan	Dorothy Cameron Disney	
Painter, Lenny	George Malcolm-Smith	*The Trouble with Fidelity*
Painter, Peter	Brett Halliday	*Counterfeit Wife*
Palfrey, Dr.	John Creasey	*The League of Light*

CHARACTER	AUTHOR	TITLE
Palgrave, Kitty	Brian Cleeve	*I Never Miss Twice*
Palliser, Sir Edward	Agatha Christie	"Sing a Song of Sixpence"
Pancho, Don	B. Buckingham	
Pao, Magistrate	Leon Comber	*The Strange Cases of Magistrate Pao*
"Papa" Pontivy; *see* Pontivy		
Pardasse, Henri	Frank King	
Pardoe, Inspector Dan	Dorothy Bowers	*Dead Without a Name*
Paris, Wade	Ben Benson	*Beware the Pale Horse*
Parker, Chief Inspector Charles	Dorothy Sayers	"Absolutely Elsewhere"
Parker, Mrs. Charles; *see* Wimsey, Lady Mary		
Parker, Detective-Inspector	John Austwick	*Highland Homicide*
Parker, Lieutenant	Henry Kane	*Hang by Your Neck*
Parker, Noel	Lawrence W. Meynell	
Parker, Peter	Richard Goyne	
Parkinson	Ernest Bramah	"The Ghost at Massingham Mansions"
Parmelee, Bill	Percival Wilde	*Rogues in Clover*
Parr, Deputy	Frederick Irving Anderson	*The Book of Murder*
Parr, Inspector	Edgar Wallace	
Parrock, Mr. Justice	Donn Russell	*Difference in Death*
Parrott, Gordon and Liz	Manning Long	*Dull Thud*
Partington, Ex-Group Captain George	Alfred O. Pollard	
Partridge, Dr.	John Dickson Carr	*Nine Wrong Answers*
Pascal, Lieutenant	Hugh Pentecost	"Tomorrow Is Yesterday"
Paschal, Mrs.	"Anonyma"	*The Experiences of a Lady Detective*
Patapon	Eugene Chavette	*Le Roi des Limiers*
"The Patent Leather Kid"	Erle Stanley Gardner	
Paternoster, Colonel	Ralph Inchbald	
Patterson, Dr.	Harrison R. Steeves	*Goodnight, Sheriff*
Patterson, Mark	Nigel Morland	
Paul, Dr. Stephen	J. Leslie	
Paulson, Don	Joy F. Hutton	*Too Good to Be True*
Paxton, Humphrey	John I. M. Stewart	*The Case of the Journeying Boy*
Paxton, Leo	R. Arnold	
Peace, Addington	Bertram Fletcher Robinson	*Chronicles of Addington Peace*
Peace, Lieutenant Commissioner Geoffrey	Geoffrey Jenkins	*Twist of Sand*
Peachy, Dr. St. George	Richard Starnes	*Another Mug for the Bier*
Peake, Inspector	Gavin Holt	
Pearson, Chief Inspector Andrew William	Eric Shepherd	*Murder in a Nunnery*
Peck, Anson	Charlotte Murray Russell	
Peck, Judge Ephraim Peabody	August W. Derleth	*Murder Stalks the Wakely Family*
Pedley, Fire Marshal Ben	Stewart Sterling	*Where There's Smoke*
Pedro	Union Jack Library	

CHARACTER	AUTHOR	TITLE
Peel, Emma	John Garforth	*The Laugh Was on Lazarus*
Peel, Mordaunt	John Stephen Strange	*For the Hangman*
Pelchek, Steve	Jack Usher	*Brothers and Sisters Have I None*
Pelham, Pel	A. E. Martin	*The Outsiders*
Pellew, Gregory	Val Gielgud	*The Goggle-Box Affair*
Pelts	Frederick Irving Anderson	"The Door Key"
Penberthy, Elisha	Kathleen Moore Knight	
Pendlebury	Anthony Webb	
Pendleton, Geoffrey	N. Deane	
Pendower, Inspector Fillet	Henry Brinton	*Coppers and Gold*
Penge, Brenton	Carleton Darve	*Crackswoman*
Penk, Inspector	William Gore	
Pennington, Honourable Arthur Stukesley ("A.S.P.")	John G. Brandon	
Pennoyer, Miles ("The Psychic Doctor")	M. Lawrence	
Penny, Mrs. Alice	Adam Bliss	
Penny, Inspector "Copper"	C. Barry	
Penny, Eleanor	Francis Grierson	
Pennyfeather, Dr.	D. B. Olsen	*Love Me in Death*
Penrose, Inspector	F. Duncan	
"Pentreith, Gilbert"; *see* Gott, Dr. Giles		
Pepper, Mr.	Sir Basil Thomson	*Mr. Pepper, Investigator*
Pepper, Sergeant	Brett Halliday	
Pepper, William	George Griswold	*Red Pawns*
Percival, Inspector	Richard Hull	
Peregrine, Rufus ("The Red Falcon")	David J. Gammon	*Meet the Falcon*
Perine, Effie	Dashiell Hammett	"A Man Called Spade"
Perkins, Bruce	Jean Lilly	
Perkins, Marvin	Ralph Henry Barbour	*Death in the Virgins*
Perkins, Willie	Lee Sheridan Cox	"The Male 10 Glasses"
Perkins, Willis	Philip Wylie	"Perkins First Case"
Perks, Matilda	Ralph C. Woodthorpe	*Shadow on the Downs*
Pete, Blue	Luke Allan	*Blue Pete, Detective*
Peter the Scribe	Victor Luhrs	*The Longbow Murder*
Peters	Eden Phillpotts	"Peters, Detective"
Peters, Detective-Inspector	D. Gray	
Peters, Jeff	O. Henry	"A Personal Magnet"
Peterson, Carl	"Sapper"	*The Final Count*
Peterson, Ralph	J. Corbett	
Petrella, Detective-Sergeant Steve	Michael Gilbert	*Blood and Judgment*
Petrie, Amos	John Victor Turner	*Below the Clock*
Petrie, Dr.	Sax Rohmer	*The Insidious Dr. Fu Manchu*
Petrie, Detective Soc	G. T. Fleming-Roberts	*Homicide Hostess*
Pettigrew, Francis	Cyril Hare	*Death Walks the Woods*
Pettigrew, James Nathaniel	I. Mercer	
Pettingell, Inspector	Anne Rowe	*Curiosity Killed a Cat*
Peyton, Jane	Elizabeth Messenger	
"The Phantom Crook"; *see* Jenkins, Ed		

CHARACTER	AUTHOR	TITLE
"The Phantom Detective"; *see* Van Loan, Richard		
Phelan, Sam	Thomas Kyd	*Blood on the Bosom Divine*
Phillpotts, Freddy	Alfred Betts Caldwell	*No Tears Shed*
Phipps, Miss	Phyllis Bentley	"Miss Phipps Goes to School"
Phloi, Madame	Lilian Jackson Braun	"Phut Phat Concentrates"
"The Photographer"; *see* Andradas, Manuel		
Phut Phat (Cat)	Lilian Jackson Braun	"Phut Phat Concentrates"
"The Picaroon"; *see* Saxon, Ludovic		
Pickering, John	M. Parker	
Pickett, Mrs.	Jack Iams	*What Rhymes with Murder*
Picon, Mons	Leo Bruce	*A Case for Three Detectives*
Picot, Lieutenant	Mignon G. Eberhart	*With This Ring*
Pierce, Inspector	R. A. J. Walling	
Pike, Suprintendent Arnold	Philip MacDonald	*Murder Gone Mad*
"The Pilgrim"; *see* Maidment, Richard		
Pilgrim, Professor and Mrs. Stephen	Dexter Muir	*Pilgrims Meet Murder*
Pillguard, Harry	S. Graham	
Pimme, Patrick Perigord	Francis Grierson	
Pinaud, M.	Pierre Audemars	*The Turns of Time*
Pine, Paul	Howard Browne	*The Taste of Ashes*
Pine, Paul	John Evans	*Halo for Satan*
Pink, Norman	Mark McShane	*Night's Evil*
Pinkerton, Evan	David Frome	*The Hammersmith Murders*
"Pinkerton, Miss"; *see* Adams, Nurse		
Pinkley, Sylvester Horatio	C. M. Wills	
Piper, John	Harry Carmichael	*Post Mortem*
Piper, Katherine	Amelia Reynolds Long	*Murder Goes South*
Piper, Inspector Oscar	Stuart Palmer	"The Riddle of the Dangling Pearl"
Piper, Peter	Nancy Barr Mavity	*The Fate of Jane Mackenzie*
Pitou, Joseph	Benjamin L. Farjeon	*Samuel Boyd of Catchpole Square*
Pitt, Inspector	John F. Straker	
Place, Detective Inspector	J. W. Mason	
Platt, Sergeant	Bruce Graeme	
Plett, Detective-Sergeant	Henry Wade	
Plimsoll, Lord Simon	Leo Bruce	*A Case for Three Detectives*
Plunkett, Roy	Mary Kelly	
Poe, Christopher	Robert Carlton Brown	*The Remarkable Adventures of Christopher Poe*
Poggioli, Professor Henry	Thomas S. Stribling	*Clues of the Caribbees*
Poiccart	Edgar Wallace	*The Three Just Men*
Pointer, Chief Inspector	Archibald E. Fielding	*In the Night*
Poirot, Hercule	Agatha Christie	*The Mysterious Affair at Styles*
Polden, Lancelot	John Courage	

CHARACTER	AUTHOR	TITLE
Polkinghorn, Amos	Charlotte Armstrong	"Ten Clues for Mr. Polkinghorn"
Pollard, Inspector	John G. Brandon	
Polton, Nathaniel	R. Austin Freeman	*The Red Thumb Mark*
Pond	G. K. Chesterton	*The Paradoxes of Mr. Pond*
Pond, Beulah	Hilda Lawrence	*Death of a Doll*
Pons, Solar	August Derleth	*The Adventures of Solar Pons*
Ponsonby, Loelia (Secretary of 00 Section)	Ian Fleming	
Ponsonby, Peter	Jean Leslie	*One Cried Murder*
Pontivy, "Papa"	Bernard Newman	"Death at the Wicket"
Poole, Inspector John	Henry Wade	*Be Kind to the Killer*
Poole, Major	H. Hawton	
Popeau, Hercules	Mrs. Belloc Lowndes	"A Labor of Hercules"
Porkreth, Detective	V. Kelly	
Porlock, Paul	David Stone	*The Tired Spy*
Port, Daniel	Peter Rabe	*The Out Is Death*
Porter, Nikki	Ellery Queen	"The Thanksgiving Day Mystery"
Potter, Miss Abigail	B. L. Reynolds	
Potter, Mr. Hiram	Rae Foley	*Repent at Leisure*
Potter, Inspector	Edgar Lustgarten	
Potts, George	Marjorie Carleton	"I.O.U.—One Life"
Potts, Lieutenant Hake	Bryant Ford	
Powel, P.O. Inspector Thomas	John Steven Strange	
Powell, Mike	James Francis Bonnell	*Death over Sunday*
Power, Nelson	N. Thurley	
Powers, Johnny	Joe Rayter	*The Victim Was Important*
Preece, Sergeant	Joseph S. Fletcher	
Preed, Mr.	Ladbroke L. D. Black	*Mr. Preed Investigates*
Prendergast, Dr. Michael	G. D. H. and M. I. Cole	*Superintendent Wilson's Holiday*
Prentice, Lieutenant John	"Sea-Lion"	*When Danger Threatens*
Prentiss, Judge	Veronica Parker Johns	
Prentiss, Steve	H. Whittington	
Prescott, Detective	William Irish	
Prescott, Diana	Constance and Gwenyth Little	*The Black Shrouds*
Prescott, Captain Louis	Josiah E. Greene	*Madmen Die Alone*
Preston, Alan	L. Halliday	
Preston, John	Peter Chester	*Killing Comes Easy*
Preston, Mark	Peter Chambers	*Always Take the Big Ones*
Price, Mrs. Cassandra ("Cassie") (née Carpenter)	Alica Tilton	*Cold Steal*
Price, Detective-Inspector Ronald	Joanna Cannan	*All Is Discovered*
Priest, Giles	Simon Harvester	*Shadows in a Hidden Land*
Priest, Judge William	Irvin S. Cobb	*Old Judge Priest*
Priestley, Dr.	John Rhode	*The Paddington Mystery*
Priggley, Rupert	L. Bruce	
Primrose, Colonel John	Leslie Ford	*The Woman in Black*
Prince, David	G. Webb	
Prince Detective Agency	John Creasey	*Man on the Run*
Prince, Henry	Cecil F. Gregg	*Henry Prince in Action*
Prince, Nicholas	Bernard Newman	

CHARACTER	AUTHOR	TITLE
"Prince of Mauravania"; *see* Cleek, Hamilton		
"Prince Renine"; *see* Lupine, Arsène		
Pringle, Romney	Clifford Ashdown	*Adventures of Romney Pringle*
Proctor, Chief Inspector	William M. Duncan	
Pronty, Dr. Samuel	Ellery Queen	*The Adventures of Ellery Queen*
Prosper, Clem	Bruno Fischer	
Protection Ltd.	N. Harman	
"The Psychic Doctor"; *see* Pennoyer, Miles		
Puckle, Mr.	Ralph Arnold	*Fish and Company*
Pujol, Aristedes	William J. Locke	*The Joyous Adventures of Aristedes Pujol*
Puma, Joe	William Campbell Gault	*Dead Hero*
Purbright, Detective-Inspector	Colin Watson	*Bump in the Night*
Purdy, Miss	Gertrude M. Wilson	
"The Purple Scar"; *see* Murdock, Miles		
Purvis, Probation Officer Rosa	Hugh Desmond	
Puyster, Reginald de ("Battling Beaucaire")	Rufus King	"The Man Who Didn't Exist"
Pybus, V. I.	Nigel Morland	"Introducing V. I. Pybus"
Pye, Detective-Inspector	K. Hopkins	
Pye, Superintendent	E. L. White	
Pyke, Inspector	Georges Simenon	
Pym, John	David Christie Murray	*The Investigations of John Pym*
Pym, Miss	Josephine Tey	*Miss Pym Disposes*
Pym, Deputy Assistant Commissioner Mrs. Palmyra Evangeline	Nigel Morland	*Clue of the Bricklayer's Aunt*
Pym, Special Investigator	Henry Stratton	*The Blanket*
Pyne, Parker	Agatha Christie	*Parker Pyne, Detective*
"Q.Q."; *see* Quayne, Quentin		
Quade, Calamity	Richard Sale	*Monkey in the Morgue*
Quade, Marty	Emile C. Tepperman	"Parade of the Wooden Kimonos"
Quade, Oliver ("The Human Encyclopedia")	Frank Gruber	"Ask Me Another"
Quarles, Christopher	Percy Brebner	*Christopher Quarles, Master Detective*
Quarles, Francis	Julian Symons	*Murder, Murder*
Quayle, Captain	Mignon G. Eberhart	*Escape the Night*
Quayle, Everard Peter	Peter Cheyney	*Dark Bahama*
Quayle, Richard	D. Gray	
Quayne, Quentin ("Q.Q.")	Frederick Britten Austin	"Diamond Cut Diamond"
Queen, Ellery	Ellery Queen	*The Roman Hat Mystery*
Queen, Inspector Richard	Ellery Queen	*The Roman Hat Mystery*

CHARACTER	AUTHOR	TITLE
Quell, Peter	William J. Makin	
Quentin, Sergeant Mike	Neil Graham	*Queer Mr. Quell*
Quest, Gregory	William C. MacDonald	
Quex, Miss Queenie	C. F. Gregg	
Quick, Orson	Kurt Steel	
Quigley, Michael	Edgar Wallace	*White Face*
Quill, Inspector Adam	Caryl Brahms and S. J. Simon	*Murder à la Stroganoff*
Quill, Detective-Inspector	E. P. Thorne	
Quin, Christopher	Sidney Horler	
Quin, Harley	Agatha Christie	*The Mysterious Mr. Quin*
Quin, Sebastian	Sidney Horler	*The Screaming Skull*
Quinlan	Whit Masterson	
Quinn	Harry Carmichael	*Vendetta*
Quinn, Joe	Margaret Millar	
Quinn, Tony	G. Wayman Jones	"Markets of Treason"
Quint, Lieutenant Peter D.	Hugh Austin	*It Couldn't Be Murder*
Quinto, Gimiendo	James Norman	*The Nightwalkers*
Quist, Alan	Hugh Pentecost	"The Girl Who Lived Dangerously"
Qwilleran, Mr.	Lilian Jackson Braun	*The Cat Who Ate Danish Modern*
Race, Captain Charles	Henry Wade	
Race, Christopher	Charles N. and A. M. Williamson	*Scarlet Runner*
Radford, Stuart	Rex Hardinge	
Radigan, Lieutenant	Hulbert Footner	
Radin, John	F. Miller	
Raeburn, Mark	Malcolm Gair	*Snow Job*
Rafferty, Red	Harold B. Kaye	*Red Rafferty*
Raffles, A. J.	Ernest W. Hornung	*Raffles, the Amateur Cracksman*
Raffles, Mrs.	John Kendrick Bangs	*Mrs. Raffles*
Ralston, Detective-Sergeant	Hal Debrett	*A Lonely Way to Die*
Rambeau, Monsieur	Hans Kades	*House of Crystal*
Ramos, Frank	Frederic Brown	*Lenient Beast*
Ramsey, Steve	C. H. Wallace	*Tailwind to Danger*
Rand ("The Double-C Man")	Edward D. Hoch	"The Spy Who Took the Long Route"
Rand, Colonel Theodore	Anthony Boucher	"The Clue of the Knave of Diamonds"
Randall, "Guffy"	Margery Allingham	
Randall, Knox	George Harmon Coxe	*Inland Passage*
Randall, Colonel "Rip"	Eric Leyland	*Challenge*
Randall, William Wilson	C. Franklin	
Randolph, Lucy	Leslie Ford	*The Town Cried Murder*
Random, Guy	Oliver Anderson	*Random at Random*
Random, Roderick ("Drawers")	C. Kendall	
Ranger, Captain Ian	Leonard A. Knight	
Rankin, Inspector	Timothy Fuller	*Harvard Has a Homicide*
Rankin, Tommy	Milton Propper	*The Divorce Court Murder*
Ransom, Glen	V. Warren	
Ransome, Arnold	Hugh Desmond	
Ransome, Stephen	Stephen Ransome	
Rant, Chief Detective-Inspector	H. E. Wheeler	*Death Takes a Ride*

CHARACTER	AUTHOR	TITLE
Raoul, Monsieur	Hilary St. George Saunders	*The Sleeping Bacchus*
Raphael, Dr. Louis	Augustus Muir	*The Third Warning*
Rapp, Inspector	Edward J. Millward	*The House of Wraith*
Rasselas	Michael Gilbert	"The Future of the Service"
Rastin, Grandfather	Lloyd Biggler, Jr.	"The Great Alma Mater Mystery"
Rater, Inspector O. ("The Orator")	Edgar Wallace	*The Orator*
Ratislow, Superintendent	C. M. Wills	
Raven	Graham Greene	*This Gun for Hire*
Raven, Detective-Inspector Paul	Douglas Warner	*Death of a Bogey*
Ravenhill, Anthony	Reginald Francis Foster	*Anthony Ravenhill, Crime Merchant*
Rawlins, Detective-Inspector	R. Marshall	
Rawlins, Inspector Humphrey	John Palmer	*Man in the Purple Gown*
Rawson, Howard	R. Grant	
Rayder, Stan	Jonathan Craig	*The Case of the Silent Stranger*
Raymond, Bohemund (Bo)	Gerald Kersh	"The Haunted Typewriter"
Raymond, Sergeant Christopher	Norman R. Longmate	
Raymond, Everett	Anna Katherine Green	*The Leavenworth Case*
Raymond, Nimrod	Clayton W. Cobb	*The Mountaineer Detective*
Rayne, Dick	Richard Sheldon	*Poor Prisoner's Defense*
Reamer, Superintendent Donald ("The Dreamer")	Duncan W. Murdock	*Meet the Dreamer*
Rector, Captain Pete	Van Siller	*Good Night, Ladies*
Reddick, Sergeant Cliff	Gil Brewer	
"The Red Falcon"; *see* Peregrine, Rufus		
Reed, Anthony	S. P. Toye	
Reed, Lal	Clement Wood	*Death in Ankara*
Reed, Rufus	Raymond L. Goldman	*Murder Behind the Mike*
Reeder, J. G.	Edgar Wallace	*The Mind of J. G. Reeder*
Reeder, Mrs. J. G.; *see* Belman, Margaret		
Reese, Johnny	Zelda Popkin	
Reeves, Chief Inspector	E. C. R. Lorac	*Policemen in the Precinct*
Reeves, Mordaunt	Ronald A. Knox	*The Viaduct Murder*
Regan, Lieutenant	Alfred Tack	
Regan, Inspector Mickey and Pam	E. Hale	
Regan, Paddy	D. Rutherford	
Regent, Detective Archie	Dorothy Bennett	*Carrion Crows*
Rehm, Jimmy	William Herber	*King-Sized Murder*
Reisen, Adelbert	Pelham Groom	*Fourth Seal*
Remington, Dick	Benjamin L. Farjeon	*The Great Porter Square*
"The Remover"	Roland Daniel	*The Remover*
Renfrew, Mark	N. Deane	
"Renine, Prince"; *see* Lupin, Arsène		
Renn, David	Margaret Storm Jameson	*Before the Crossing*

CHARACTER	AUTHOR	TITLE
Rennert, Hugh	Todd Downing	*The Cat Screams*
Rennett, Carl	Edgar Wallace	*Arranways Mystery*
Repton, Helen	Brian Flynn	
Return, David	Manly Wade Wellman	"A Star for a Warrior"
Revel, Michael and Fleur	Norman Berrow	
Reynolds, Claire	Helen Woodward and Frances Amherst	*Bowling Green Murder*
Reynolds, Nancy	Dorothy Cole Meade	*Death over Her Shoulder*
Rhodes, Rocky	Pat McGerr	*Catch Me if You Can*
Rhyce, Jack	John P. Marquand	
Ricardo, Julius	Alfred E. W. Mason	*At the Villa Rose*
Rice, Stanley	Baynard H. Kendrick	*Death Beyond the Go Thru*
Richards, Paul	Duncan Dallas	*Paul Richards, Detective*
Richardson, Constable (later Inspector and Superintendent)	Sir Basil Thomson	*Richardson Goes Abroad*
Richleau, Duc de	Dennis Wheatley	
Richmond, Mrs. Sally	Clarissa Fairchild Cushman	*I Wanted to Murder*
Rickett, Detective-Inspector	Peter Cheyney	
Riddle, Sergeant Kit	Carol Carnac	
Rider, "Honeychile"	Ian Fleming	*Dr. No*
Riesner, Lieutenant Hank	E. Sherry	
Riggs, Bingo	Craig Rice	*The April Robin Murders*
"The Ringer"; *see* Milton, Henry Arthur		
Ringrose, Inspector John	Eden Phillpotts	"Prince Charlie's Dirk"
Ringway, Stephen	Stanley M. Lott	
Ringwood, Dr.	J. J. Connington	
Ringwood, Inspector Richard	K. Farrer	
Rip (Police Dog)	Erle Stanley Gardner	"The Case of the Scattered Rubies"
Ripley, Special Agent John	The Gordons	*Case File: FBI*
Ripley, Rainbow	Bliss Lomax	*The Leather Burners*
"The Ripper"; *see* Drake, Steve		
Ripple, Chief Inspector	John Victor Turner	*Below the Clock*
Ritchie, Colonel	R. Marshall	
Ritchie, Kay	John Mersereau	
Ritter, Elsie; *see* Benson, Mrs. Philip		
Ritter, Lieutenant Max	Laurence G. Blochman	*Diagnosis: Homicide*
"River Joe"	William Donald Bray	*The Palace Sinks at Midnight*
Rivers, Chief Inspector	Carol Carnac	*Over the Garden Wall*
Rivers, David	J. Muir	
Rivers, Ed	Talmage Powell	*Start Screaming Murder*
Riviere, Inspector Simon	Claude Aveline	*Double Death of Frederic Belot*
Rizzi, Captain	Thomas Sterling	*The Silent Siren*
Robbins, Dave	Henry Slesar	*The Gray Flannel Shroud*
Roberts, Eddie	Ed Lacy	"The Real Sugar"
Robertson, Andrew	Hugh Desmond	
Robinson, Inspector	Alan Peters	*Who Killed the Doctors?*

CHARACTER	AUTHOR	TITLE
Robinson, Kelly	John Tiger	*Masterstroke*
Robinson, Rob	R. Glover	*Murderer's Maze*
Robson, Inspector	Benjamin L. Farjeon	*Samuel Boyd of Catchpole Square*
Rocambole	Alexis de Ponson (Ponson du Terrail)	*Les Exploits de Recambole*
Rockwell, City Editor	Jack Iams	*Do Not Murder Before Christmas*
Roden, Sheriff Jess	Albert B. Cunningham	*The Killer Watches the Manhunt*
Rodriquez, Joe	Tom H. Moriarty	"The Million Dollar Road"
Rodriquez, Lieutenant	Elizabeth Linington	*No Evil Angel*
Rogers, "Bull"	A. Brede	
Rogers, Dirk	Frank Crisp	
Rogers, Professor Huntoon	Clifford Knight	*The Affair of the Scarlet Crab*
Rogers, Lieutenant	Samuel Elkin	"Survival of the Fittest"
Rohan and Post	Dorothy Dunn	*Murder's Web*
Roland, Dr. Andrew	Ethel Fleming	
Roldan, Maximo	Antonio Helu	*The Compulsion Murder*
Rolfe, Simon	Joseph L. Bonney	*Death by Dynamite*
Rollison, Hon. Richard; *see* "The Toff"		
Romano, Lieutenant	David Alexander	*Shoot a Sitting Duck*
Romanova, Tatiana	Ian Fleming	*From Russia with Love*
Rook, Howard	Stuart Palmer	*Unhappy Hooligan*
Rooke, Terry	David Alexander	*Murder in Black and White*
Root, Lieutenant	Arthur Littlefield	*Which Mrs. Bennett?*
Roper, Sergeant	Neil Graham	
Rosegarland, Peter	Robert Brennan	*The Man Who Walked Like a Dancer*
Ross, Gordon	Lord Gorell	
Ross, Ian	James Wood	*The Sealer*
Ross, Robert	C. Landon	
Ross, Sergeant	Geoffrey Belton Cobb	*Sergeant Ross in Disguise*
Ross, Superintendent	J. J. Connington	*Two Tickets Puzzle*
Rossiter, Pat	John Dickson Carr	
Rostetter, Tommy	Alice O. Campbell	*Desire to Kill*
Rouben	Frank Swinnerton	"Soho Night's Entertainment"
Rouletabille, Joseph (born Joseph Josephine)	Gaston Leroux	*The Mystery of the Yellow Room*
Rountree, Stonewall	Jesse Carmack	*The Tell-Tale Clock Mystery*
Rover Club	Arthur B. Maurice	*The Riddle of the Rovers*
Rowlands, Chief Superintendent Bill	N. Lucas	
Royden, Phil	Esther Haven Fonseca	*The Thirteenth Bed in the Ballroom*
Rudd, Hugh	H. C. Davis	
Ruddock, Sergeant	Francis Beeding	
Ruff, Peter	E. Phillips Oppenheim	"The Little Lady from Servia"
Ruggdale, Paul	Carl M. Chapin	
Ruggles, Tolly	Mari Ervin	*Death in the Yew Alley*
Rummel, "Beau"	Ellery Queen	
Runford, Chief Inspector	Diana Fearon	
Rusby, Inspector Myles	Virgil Markham	*Inspector Rusby's Finale*
Russell, Alan	Neil Fitzgerald	
Russell, Charles	William Haggard	*Powder Barrel*
Russell, Franklin	Richard M. Baker	*Death Stops the Manuscript*
Russell, Jim	George Harmon Coxe	*Death at the Isthmus*
Russell, Mary Ann	Ian Fleming	*For Your Eyes Only*

CHARACTER	AUTHOR	TITLE
Russell, Rocky	N. Sheraton	
Rutland, Detective-Inspector	Patrick Leyton	*Silent Death*
Rutledge, Elizabeth	Julius Fast	*A Model for Murder*
Ryan, O'Neill	Herbert Brean	*A Matter of Fact*
Ryan, Sean	Brian Cleeve	*Vice Isn't Private*
Ryan, Detective-Sergeant Tim	Lee Fredericks	*Hyack Haul*
Ryde, Merton	E. North	
Ryde, Sergeant Peggy	Francis Grierson	
Ryder, Inspector	Sax Rohmer	
Ryder, Richard ("Galloping Dick")	H. B. Marriott Watson	"The Galloping Assizes"
Ryder, Stephen	Mary Hastings Bradley	*Nice People Murder*
Rye, William	John Spain	*Dig Me a Grave*
Saber, Joel	Gavin Holt	*The Theme Is Murder*
Sabin, Mr.	E. Phillips Oppenheim	*The Mysterious Mr. Sabin*
Sackler, Rex	D. L. Champion	*The Corpse Pays Cash*
Sage, Malcom	Herbert Jenkins	*Malcom Sage, Detective*
Sage, Constable Orlo	Frederick Irving Anderson	*The Book of Murder*
Sage, Sergeant	William M. Duncan	
Sail, Oscar	Lester Dent	"Tropical Disturbance"
"The Saint"; *see* Templar, Simon		
Saint, Philip	Sidney Horler	
Saint-Amour, Lieutenant Bob	Donald Clough Cameron	*Murder's Coming*
St. George, Colonel Ivor	Philip MacDonald	*Guest in the House*
Saintonge	Fortuné du Boisgobey	*Cornaline la Dompteuse*
Salinger, J.	Joan Hewett	*Women Are Dynamite*
Sallust, Gregory ("The Scarlet Imposter")	Dennis Wheatley	*The Scarlet Imposter*
Salmond, Andrew	Lawrence Dundas	*Spider at the Elvira*
Salt, Sergeant	Dorothy Bowers	*Deed Without a Name*
Samson, Captain	Gavin Douglas	*The Obstinate Captain Samson*
Sanchez, Dr. Xenophen Quintero	Thomas S. Stribling	"The Cablegram"
Sanctuary Club	Mrs. L. T. Meade	*The Sanctuary Club*
"Sanders, Bill"; *see* Kingston, Michael		
Sanders, Commissioner	Edgar Wallace and Francis Gerard	*Sanders of the River*
Sanders, Joe	F. Goldsmith	
Sanders, Dr. John	Anne Austin	
Sanders, Dr. John	Carter Dickson	*The Reader Is Warned*
Sanders, Lee	G. W. Cooke	
Sands, Dr. Adrian	Henry Brinton	*An Apple a Day*
Sands, Inspector	Margaret Millar	*The Iron Gates*
Sands, Milton	Edgar Wallace	
Sands, "Whispering"	Erle Stanley Gardner	"The Desert Detective"
Sandyman, Superintendent	Neil Graham	*The Amazing Mr. Sandyman*
Sandys, Jacob	Julian Maclaren-Ross	*Until the Day She Dies*
Sara, Madame	Mrs. L. T. Meade	*The Sorceress of the Strand*
Sardcrow, Lieutenant-Commissioner John	D. Rooksby	
Sarel, Colonel Richard	John Bryan	*The Difference to Me*

CHARACTER	AUTHOR	TITLE
Sergeant, Peter Cutler III	Edgar Box	*Death in the Fifth Position*
Sargent, Sergeant	O. Downes	
Satin, Mr.	Bruce Cassiday	"Deep Sleep"
Satterly, Commissioner	Peter Motte and Reginald Campbell	
Satterthwaite, Mr.	Agatha Christie	*Mysterious Mr. Quin*
Saturday, Johnny	Lawrence Goldman	*Fall Guy for Murder*
Sault, Ambrose	Edgar Wallace	
Saumerez, Sir John (born Jonathan Simmonds)	Clemence Dane and Helen Simpson	*Re-enter Sir John*
Saumerez, Lady; *see* Baring, Martella		
Saunders, Chief Detective-Inspector	A. Carr	
Saunders, Michael	M. Mountford	
Saunders, Miss	Anna Katherine Green	*The Mayor's Wife*
Saunders, Railroad Policeman	Bert and Dolores Hitchens	*End of the Line*
Sauzas	Patricia Highsmith	
Savage, Anthony	Thomas T. Flynn	*Murder Caravan*
Savage, "Doc"	Kenneth Robeson	*The Mystic Mullah*
Savage, Rampion	James E. Turner	*Frontiers of Death*
Savoy, Paul	Jackson Gregory	*A Case for Mr. Paul Savoy*
Saxon, Ludovic ("The Picaroon")	John Cassells	*Enter the Picaroon*
Saxon, Peter	Robert George Dean	
Scales, John	Dorothy L. Sayers	"Blood Sacrifice"
Scaramanga	Ian Fleming	*The Man with the Golden Gun*
Scarfe, Paul	Raymond Boyd	*Murder Is a Furtive Thing*
Scarle, Sir Benjamin	J. Donovan	
"The Scarlet Imposter"; *see* Sallust, Gregory		
Scarlet, Postal Inspector Will	Clarence Budington Kelland	*Great Mail Robbery*
Scarlett, Dr.	Alexander Laing	*Doctor Scarlett*
Scarlett, Peter	Sidney Horler	*Scarlett-Special Branch*
Schmidt, Imperator	Robert George Dean	
Schmidt, Inspector	George Bagby	*Drop Dead*
Schnucke (Seeing-eye dog)	Baynard Kendrick	*Reservations for Death*
Schofield, Pete	Thomas B. Dewey	*And Where She Stops*
Scone, Matthew	Newton Hill	*The Body Drank Coffee*
"Scoop"; *see* Griddle, L. F.		
Scott, Alexander	John Tiger	*Masterstroke*
Scott, Len	Colin Robertson	
Scott, Nelson	Eric Lennox	"Advertisements for Murder"
Scott, Shell	Richard S. Prather	*Kill the Clown*
Scott, Tony	J. Corbett	
Scotter, John Franklin Cornelius	Thurman Warriner	*Method in His Murder*
Seabright, Ruth	Elizabeth Ferrars	
Seabright, Superintendent	Frederick Britten Austin	"Diamond Cut Diamond"
Seal, Quentin	S. Smith	
Seaton, Mark	T. B. Morris	

CHARACTER	AUTHOR	TITLE
Sebastian, Professor	Grant Allen	
"Secret Agent X"	Brant House	*Corpse Contraband*
"Secret Service Smith"; *see* Smith, Aurelius		
Seddicombe, Rev. Selwyn	C. M. Wills	
Seegrave, Superintendent	Wilkie Collins	*The Moonstone*
Seidlitz	Carter Brown	*Tomorrow Is Murder*
Selborne, Charity	Mary Stewart	*Madame, Will You Talk*
Selby, "D.A." Douglas	Erle Stanley Gardner	*The D.A. Holds a Candle*
Selby, Chief Inspector Martin	Charles Bidmead	*Man in the Shadows*
Selby, Pete	Jonathan Craig	*The Case of the Silent Stranger*
Selfridge, Jason	Frederick Irving Anderson	"The Door Key"
Selwyn, Murray	Ernest Dudley	
Semlake, Inspector	John Varnam	*Death Rehearses*
Senstrom, Sergeant	Philip Clark	*The Dark River*
"Sergeant Sir Peter"; *see* Dunn, Sir Peter		
Severn	Edmund C. Bentley	*Elephant's Work*
Severson, Knute	Tobias Wells	*What Should You Know of Dying?*
Sevrel, Inspector Paxton	Cedric Worth	*The Trail of the Serpent*
Seymour, Anne (later Mrs. John Webb)	Frank G. Presnell	*No Mourners Present*
Shad (Short for Shadow)	Cornel Woolrich	"Hot Water"
"The Shadow"	Maxwell Grant	*The Mark of the Shadow*
"The Shadowers Inc."	David Fox	*The Doom Dealer*
"Shakespeare, Bill"; *see* Witherall, Leonidas		
Shale, Sergeant	John Cassells	
Shand, Dale	Douglas S. Enefer	*The Last Door*
Shand, Russell	Mary Roberts Rinehart	*The Wall*
Shand, Tony	Willetta Anna Barber and R. Schabelitz	*Murder Draws a Line*
Shane, Michael (*see also* Shayne, Michael)	Brett Halliday	*Call for Michael Shane*
Shane, Peter	Francis Bonnamy	*Death on a Dude Ranch*
Shanley, Father	Jack Webb	*The Bad Blonde*
Shannahan, Red	Norman Leslie	
Shannon, Desmond	Mary V. Heberden	*That's the Spirit*
Shannon, Detective	William H. L. Crauford	
Shannon, Michael	Gerald Bowman	*The Sawdust Angel*
Shapiro, Lieutenant Nathan	Francis Lockridge	*Murder and Blueberry Pie*
Shard, David	Sidney Horler	
Sharpin, Matthew	Wilkie Collins	"The Biter Bit"
Shatterhand, Dr.	Ian Fleming	*You Only Live Twice*
Shaw, Andrew	George Woden	
Shaw, Commissioner	Philip D. McCutchan	*Redcap*
Shaw, Mertie	H. Taylor Baldwin	*The Duplicate*
Shaw, Sergeant	John Bingham	*Inspector Morgan's Dilemma*
Shawney, Inspector	W. Shand	
Shayne, Michael (*see also* Shane, Michael)	Brett Halliday	*This Is It, Michael Shayne*

CHARACTER	AUTHOR	TITLE
Shears, Holmlock	Maurice Leblanc	*Holmlock Shears Arrives Late*
Shelley, Inspector	J. Rowland	
Shelton, Tony	Sidney Horler	
Sheppard, Dr. James	Agatha Christie	*The Murder of Roger Ackroyd*
Sheriffe, Sir Rowland	C. Reeve	
Sheringham, Roger	Anthony Berkeley	*The Poisoned Chocolates Case*
Sherwood, Ned	Robert Sylvester	*The Big Boodle*
Sherwood, Thomas	F. Hoyle	
Shinn, Johnny	Ellery Queen	*The Glass Village*
Shipton, Charley	C. H. Simpson	*Life in the Far West*
Shirley, Constable	Osmington Mills	*Enemies of the Bride*
Shirley, John	K. Wake	
Shomar, Lieutenant Shomri	Henry Klinger	*Wanton for Murder*
Shott, Chief Inspector	Nigel Morland	
Sibley, Michael	John Bingham	*My Name Is Michael Bingham*
Sickel, Ebon	Robert P. Hansen	*Trouble Comes Double*
Silence, Dr. John	Algernon Blackwood	*John Silence*
"Silent Sam"; *see* Simons, Samuel S.		
Silk, Dorian	Simon Harvester	*Assassin's Road*
Silk, Steve	James B. O'Sullivan	*I Die Possessed*
Silver, Inspector	William M. Duncan	
Silver, Inspector	Henry Holt	*Don't Shoot Darling*
Silver, Jennifer	Mary Stewart	*Thunder on the Right*
Silver, John Quick	R. Daniel	
Silver, Miss Maude	Patricia Wentworth	*The Gazebo*
Silverface	Harman Long	*Silverface*
Simmonds, Jonathan; *see* Saumerez, Sir John		
Simons, Samuel S. ("Silent Sam")	Hal K. Wells	"Code for Killing"
Simpson, Arthur Abdel	Eric Ambler	*The Light of Day*
Simpson, Bob	K. Lowe	
Sims, Fred	G. G. Fickling	*Bombshell*
Sims, Superintendent	Francis Grierson	*Murder in Black*
Sinclair, Sir Arthur	Walter S. Masterman	*2 LO*
Sinclair, Harry	Hugh L. Nelson	*Dead Giveaway*
Sinclair, Toby	"Sapper"	
Skarle	Erle Stanley Gardner	
Skirment, Tommy	Harry S. Keeler	
Slade	Richard Essex	*Slade of the Yard*
Slade, Inspector Anthony	Leonard R. Gribble	*Death Pays the Piper*
Slade, Geoffrey	F. Lester	
Slade, Nicholas	Ralph C. Woodthorpe	*Death Wears a Purple Shirt*
Sladey, Michael	Noel Cromarty	
Slane, Sir Jasper	E. Phillips Oppenheim	*Slane's Long Shots*
Slappy, Florian	Octavus Roy Cohen	*Florian Slappy, Private Eye*
Slater, Bill	Henry S. Maxfield	*Legacy of a Spy*
Slater, Martin	J. Patrick	"Portrait of a Murderer"
Slidenberry, Customs Officer	Thomas S. Stribling	*Clues of the Caribbees*
Sloan, Charley	Glen M. Barns	
Sloan, John	N. Deane	

CHARACTER	AUTHOR	TITLE
Sloane, P. H.	Mignon G. Eberhart	
Slocum, Eddie	Frank Gruber	
Small, Caspar	C. Brooks	
Small, Detective-Officer	Michael Halliday	
Small, Rabbi	Harry Kemelman	*Friday the Rabbi Slept Late*
Small, Jonathan	Sir Arthur Conan Doyle	*Sign of the Four*
Smarles	MacGregor Urquhart	*The Bluebottle*
Smiley, George	John Le Carré	*Call for the Dead*
Smiling, John	John Dolland	*A Gentleman Hangs*
"Smith"	E. North	
Smith, Anthony (The Mixer)	Edgar Wallace	"The Seventy-Fourth Diamond"
Smith, Arnold	H. Rutland	
Smith, Aurelius ("Secret Service Smith")	R. T. M. Scott	"Underground"
Smith, Benbow Collingwood Horatio	Patricia Wentworth	*Down Under*
Smith, Cellini	Robert Reeves	*Cellini Smith, Detective*
Smith, Daye	F. Usher	
Smith, Sir Denis Nayland (formerly Commissioner)	Sax Rohmer	*The Insidious Dr. Fu Manchu*
Smith, Emery	John August	*Troubled Star*
Smith, Federal Agent	Cleve Franklin Adams	*Up Jumped the Devil*
Smith, Frank	Richard Deming	*The Lineup*
Smith, Howard	Victor Canning	
Smith, Inspector	Simon Troy	*Cease Upon the Midnight*
Smith, Dr. John	Hugh Pentecost	*Where the Snow Was Red*
Smith, Dr. Jonas	Leslie Ford	*Date with Death*
Smith, Kim	John Boland	*Counterpol in Paris*
Smith, Detective-Inspector Lancelot Carolus	Norman Berrow	
Smith, Lex; *see* Smith, Socrates		
Smith, Marco Polo	John Jakes	*Devil Has Four Faces*
Smith, Nayland; *see* Smith, Denis Nayland		
Smith, Peter J.		*Crooks in Clover*
Smith, Socrates and Lex	Edgar Wallace	
Smith, Chief Inspector "Surefoot"	Edgar Wallace	*The Nine Bears*
Smith, Chief Commissioner T. B.	Edgar Wallace	*Silinski, Master Criminal*
Smithers, Mr.	Henry R. F. Keating	*Death and the Visiting Firemen*
Smitty	Steve Fisher	"Goodbye, Hannah"
Smyth, F. Millard	Eunice Mays Boyd	*Murder Breaks Trail*
Snell, Cynthia	Hugh Clevely	
Snell, Inspector	E. Phillips Oppenheim	*Sir Adam Disappeared*
Snewin, Superintendent	S. Gardiner	
Snooty and Scoop; *see* "Dizzy Duo"		
Soames, Tilly	Ian Fleming	*Goldfinger*
Sober, Martin	Paul Cade	*Death Slams the Door*
Socrates	Breni James	"Socrates Solves Another Murder"
Sokratescu, Kyra	Gilbert Frankau	"Who Killed Castelvetri?"

CHARACTER	AUTHOR	TITLE
Solan, Jeremy ("Thunder")	Dornford Yates	
Solange; *see* Fontaine, Solange		
Solitaire (Simone Latrelle)	Ian Fleming	*Live and Let Die*
Solo, Napoleon	Michael Avallone	*The Man from U.N.C.L.E.*
Somers, Sergeant	Ernest Dudley	
Soryden, Clarissa	Isabella Bayne	*Cruel as the Grave*
South, Joseph ("Joe")	Gentry Nyland	
Southern, James	Milward Kennedy	
Spade, Sam	Dashiell Hammett	*The Maltese Falcon*
Spain, Sir Roger	Selwyn Jepson	*Keep Murder Quiet*
Spalanzani	E. T. A. Hoffmann	*Weird Tales*
Spalding, Nat	Paul Capon	
Spang Bros. (Jack and Seraffimo)	Ian Fleming	*Diamonds Are Forever*
Spangled Mob	Ian Fleming	*Diamonds Are Forever*
Spargo, Frank	Joseph S. Fletcher	*The Middle Temple Murders*
Sparks, Ben	William Manchester	*Beard the Lion*
"The Sparrow"	Edgar Wallace	
Sparton, Sheriff	Christine Noble Govan	*Plantation Murder*
Speare, Lucas	Frederick C. Davis	*Lilies in Her Garden Grew*
Spearman, Rosanna	Wilkie Collins	*The Moonstone*
Spearpoint, Inspector	F. Arthur	
Spears, Tom	William Campbell Gault	
SPECTRE (Special Executive for Counterintelligence, Terrorism, Revenge, and Extortion)	Ian Fleming	*From Russia with Love*
Speedon, Mike	Hulbert Footner	
Speke, Sergeant	Lord Charnwood	*Tracks in the Snow*
Spence, Philip	A. Fraser	
Spencer, Detective-Sergeant Jack	Bruce Graeme	
Spencer, Mr.	J. Jowett	
Spinder, Joe	Thomas B. Dewey	*Mourning After*
Spinnet, Phineas	Andrew Soutar	*Museum Mystery*
Spinosa, Ben	Herzl Fife	"Pattern for Murder"
Sprague, "Scientific"	Francis Lynde	*Scientific Sprague*
Springfield, Mr.	J. Sandys	
Sprules, Inspector	Herbert Adams	*The Body in the Bunker*
S.P.Y. (Satellite for Photographic Intelligence)	Bruce Cassiday	"S.P.Y. in the Sky"
Spyess, Jem	Samuel Duff	"The Bow-Street Runner"
Squeakie; *see* Meadow, Squeakie		
Stacey, Don	S. Browning	
Stacey, Sandy	S. Scott	
Stack, Chip	Tighe Jarrett	"The Case of the Clever Contessa"
Stacker, Sergeant	John Cassells	
Stacpoole, Detective-Inspector	B. Maxwell	
Staines	Joan Coggins	*Dancing with Death*
Staines, Detective-Inspector	Edgar Wallace	*The Double*

CHARACTER	AUTHOR	TITLE
Stammers, Detective-Inspector	Allan MacKinnon	*House of Darkness*
Standish, Roland	"Sapper"	*Roland Standish*
Standish, Tiger	Sidney Horler	*Tiger Standish Does His Stuff*
Standish, Hon. Timothy Overbury ("Tiger")	Sidney Horler	*The Grim Game*
Stanhope; *see* Carnes & Stanhope		
Stanley, Anne	Josiah E. Green	
Stanley, Bert	Rufus King	*Holiday Homicide*
Stanley, Hagar	Fergus Hume	
Stannard, Barry	M. Tannock	
Stanner	Allan MacKinnon	*Murder, Repeat, Murder*
Stanton, Hugh	Roy Vickers	
Stanton, Jimmy	Sidney Horler	
Stapleton, John (alias of "John Baskerville"; also known as "John Vanderleur")	Sir Arthur Conan Doyle	*The Hound of the Baskervilles*
Stark, Peter	William Herber	
Stark, Philip	Helen McCloy	*The Goblin Market*
Starmer, Alec	Mary Kelly	
Starr, Inspector Bill	Nigel Morland	
Starr, Dr. Colin	Rufus King	*Diagnosis: Murder*
Stauffer, Lieutenant John T.	A. H. Z. Carr	"The Nameology Murder"
Stayne, Colonel John	"Seamark"	
Steed, John	John Garforth	*The Laugh Was on Lazarus*
Steel, Fletcher	Donald Barr Chidsey	*The Thing's Dynamite*
Steele, Argus	Babs Lee	*Passport to Oblivion*
Steele, James	Dana Chambers	*Too Like the Lightning*
Steele, Rocky	John B. West	*Never Kill a Cop*
Steele, Stephen	Kirke Mechem	*A Frame for Murder*
Steele, Ted	Q. Patrick	
Stein, Jacob	Jeremy York	
Stevens, Blooey	Peter Cheyney	
Stevens, Superintendent	Bruce Graeme	*Epilogue to "The Mystery of Edwin Drood"*
Stevenson, William	Andrew Salmond	
Stewart, Duncan	Margot Bennett	*Farewell Crown and Goodbye King*
Stewart, Michael	Edwin Lanham	
Stewart, Valeska (later Mrs. Astrogen Kirby)	Gelett Burgess	*Astro, Master of Mysteries*
Stirling, Allan	William M. Duncan	
Stockton, Gregory	James Reach	
Stole, Sebastian	Charles Wogan	
Stone, Clara	Clara Stone	*Death in Cranford*
Stone, Curt	Jack Seward	*The Cave of the Chinese Skeletons*
Stone, Fleming	Carolyn Wells	*The Clue*
Stone, J. Rockingham ("The Midnight Cavalier")	Raymond Armstrong	*The Midnight Cavalier*
Stone, Nate	William F. Schwartz	
Stone, "Rolling"	Kenneth Laing	*Shadow People*
Storey, Madame Rosika	Hulbert Footner	*Madame Storey*
Storke, Dr. Archibald	Anita Boutell	*Death Brings a Stork*
Storm, Christopher ("Kit")	Willetta Ann Barber	*Drawn Conclusion*

CHARACTER	AUTHOR	TITLE
Storm, Jack and Lola	Dorothy Cameron Disney	
Storm, John	Francis K. Allan	*First Come, First Kill*
Storm, Larry	Hugh Pentecost	*Cancelled in Red*
Storm, Lee	Edward Ronns	
Storm, Lieutenant Mark	G. G. Fickling	*Bombshell*
Storme, Carrie	Audrey Gaines	*The Old Must Die*
Stout, Sergeant	Neil Graham	
Straight, Ricky	G. Morgan	
Straker, Inspector	Wallace Jackson	*Diamonds of Death*
Strang, Inspector	Carol Carnac	
Strang, John, M. P. and daughter Sally	Henry Brinton	*Apprentice to Fear*
Strange	Sir Edward J. Reed	*Fort Minister*
Strange, Violet	Anna Katherine Green	*The Golden Slipper*
Strangely, Peter	Elizabeth Best Black	*The Ravenell Riddle*
Strangeways, Nigel	Nicholas Blake	*The Beast Must Die*
Strangeways, Mrs. Nigel (née Georgia Cavendish)	Nicholas Blake	*Head of a Traveler*
Strawn, Captain	Carter Dickson	
Street, Della	Erle Stanley Gardner	*The Case of the Sulky Girl*
Stroganoff, Vladimir	Caryl Brahms and S. J. Simon	*Murder à la Stroganoff*
Strom, Lieutenant Peter	Mabel Seeley	*The Listening House*
Strong, Paul and Mary	Dorothy Cameron Disney	
Stroode, Major	Ralph Inchbald	
Strutt, Superintendent George	W. Mole	
Stuart, Mrs. Molly	Delia Van Deusen	*Murder Bicarb*
Stuart, Sally	Medora Field	*Who Killed Aunt Maggie?*
Stuart, William J.	Richard Pitts Powell	*Shell Game*
Styles, Peter	Judson P. Philips	*Black Glass City*
"Subway Sam"; *see* Tham, Thubway		
Sugar	Lovat Marshall	*Sugar on the Kill*
Sugg, Calvin	Dick Donovan	*Tracked to Doom*
Suicide Club	Robert Louis Stevenson	*New Arabian Nights*
Sullivan, Barry	Judson P. Phillips	
Sullivan, Inspector James	Virginia Rath	
Summers, Steve	Jason Manor	*The Pawn of Fear*
Sunday, Aunt	Joseph Farjeon	*Aunt Sunday Takes Command*
"Surefoot"; *see* Smith, "Surefoot"		
Suresne, Inspector	E. Phillips Oppenheim	
SuSu (Superior Suda of Siam)	Lilian Jackson Braun	"SuSu and the 8:30 Ghost"
Suzuki, Kissy	Ian Fleming	*You Only Live Twice*
Swainson, Chief Inspector Tom	Bruce Sanders	
Swami Mirza Baba; *see* Jackson, Nick		
Sweeney, Mickey	Lincoln Steffens	
Sweeney, William	Frederic Brown	*The Screaming Mimi*
Sweetwater, Caleb	Anna Katherine Green	*Initials Only*
Swift, Leighton	Charles Reed Jones	*The King Murder*
"Swindle Sheet"	Gerald Kersh	"The Haunted Typewriter"

CHARACTER	AUTHOR	TITLE
Swinton, Detective-Inspector	Pat Flower	
Sylvia	Erle Stanley Gardner	*The D.A. Breaks an Egg*
Syme, Gabriel	G. K. Chesterton	*The Man Who Was Thursday*
Tabaret, Père ("Tir-au-clair")	Emile Gaboriau	*L'Affaire Lerouge*
Taggett, Mr.	Thomas B. Aldrich	*The Stillwater Tragedy*
Taine, Colonel Roger	Geoffrey Household	*A Rough Shoot*
Tairlaine, Dr. Michael	Carter Dickson	
Talbot, Peter	Patricia Wentworth	*Rolling Stone*
Taliaferro, Hooper	John E. Canaday	*The Cabinda Affair*
Tallboys, Colonel	Ernest R. Punshon	
Tancred, Dr. Benjamin	G. D. H. and M. I. Cole	*Dr. Tancred Begins*
Tanner, Chief Inspector	Edgar Wallace	
Tanner, Inspector	Freeman Wills Crofts	*The Ponson Case*
Tarleton, Brett and Marilyn	H. B. Kaye	
Tarling, Mr.	Edgar Wallace	
Tarrant, Detective-Sergeant Frank	Hugh Desmond	
Tarrant, Mr. Trevis	Charles Daly King	*The Curious Mr. Tarrant*
Taunton, Inspector	John Bude	*The Night the Fog Came Down*
Taylor, Gene	Hillary Waugh	*Eighth Mrs. Bluebeard*
Taylor, Mitch	Lawrence Treat	*V as in Victim*
Taylor, Pete	Robert D. Abrahams	*Death After Lunch*
Teacher, Sergeant	William M. Duncan	
Teal, Chief Inspector Eustace	Leslie Charteris	*The Saint—Wanted for Murder*
Tellford, Jeff and "Ma"	D. Fisher	
Tempest, Bill	William Shand	*Man Called Tempest*
Tempest, Kate	D. Eden	
Templar, Simon ("The Saint")	Leslie Charteris	*The First Saint Omnibus*
Temple, Paul and Steve	Paul Temple	
Templeton, Paul	Richard Goyne	
Templewaite, Bruce	Allan Cecil	*Turquoise Clues*
Tennent, Jim	Michael Reyes	*The Dead Parrot*
Tennente, Major	Thomas Flanagan	"The Cold Winds of Adesta"
Terence, Michael and "Terry"	G. Brandon	
Terhune, Theodore I.	Bruce Graeme	*Seven Clues in Search of a Crime*
Terhune, Wade	Isabel Ostrander	
Terningham	Isabel Briggs Myers	*Give Me Death*
Terrell, Sam	William P. McGivern	*Night Extra*
Terry, Paula	B. Knox	
Thackeray, Chief Inspector	Lee Spencer	*Furtive Men*
Tham, Thubway ("Subway Sam")	Johnston McCulley	"Thubway Tham, Thirlian"
Thames, Sydney	Clinton H. Stagg	
Thane, Detective-Inspector Colin	Bill Knox	*The Grey Sentinels*
Thane, Mel	Vern Chute	*Blackmail*
Tharp, Guy	Dashiell Hammett	"Ruffian's Wife"
Theakstone, Chief Inspector Francis	Wilkie Collins	"The Biter Bit"
Thingbottom, Detective	W. Tucker	

CHARACTER	AUTHOR	TITLE
"The Thinking Machine"; *see* Van Dusen, Prof. Augustus		
Thomas, Ethel	Cortland Fitzsimmons	*The Moving Finger*
Thompson, Detective-Sergeant	J. W. Mason	
Thompson, Sheriff Jake	Evelyn Cameron	*Malice Domestic*
Thompson, Chief Inspector James	Peter Drax	*Crime to Music*
Thompson, Paul Andrew	Robert George Dean	*Three Lights Went Out*
Thompson, Tommy	Paul Gallico	"The Roman Kid"
Thorndyke, Dr. John Evelyn, M.D., F.R.C.P.	R. Austin Freeman	*The Red Thumb Mark*
Thorne, Dr. Abel	Eden Phillpotts	
Thorne, Tommy ("The Hobo Detective")	Charles H. Snow	*The Buckhorn Murder Case*
Thorne, "Slip"	Peter Boyd	*Slip Sees Red*
Thornley, Robin	William H. L. Crauford	
Thornton, Bill	Edison Marshall	
Thornton, Colin	Lawrence Meynell	
Thorpe, Andy	Q. Patrick	
Thorpe, Robert	Carol Carnac	
"The Three Just Men"	Edgar Wallace	*The Three Just Men*
Thrush	Michael Avallone	*The Thousand Coffins Affair*
Thundersley, Asta	Gerald Kersh	
Thurloe	T. Herd	*Death of a Convict*
Thursday, Max	Wade Miller	*Shoot to Kill*
Thuum, Inspector	Ellery Queen	*The Tragedy of Y*
Tibbitts, Lieut. Francis Augustus ("Bones")	Edgar Wallace and Francis Gerard	
Tibbs, Virgil R.	John Ball	*In the Heat of the Night*
Tierney, James	John A. Moroso	*The Listening Man*
Tilbury, Margaret	Dorothy Cameron Disney	
Tilyar, Hamish	G. Joseph	
Tinker	Union Jack Library	
Tintagel, Ginger	F. Draco	*Cruise with Death*
Tiny, Gene	H. Kane	
"Tir-au-clair"; *see* Tabaret, Père		
Tischbein, Emil	Eric Kastner	*Emil and the Detectives*
Tish	Mary Roberts Rinehart	"The Treasure Hunt"
Tobin, Inspector	Dorothy B. Hughes	*So Blue Marble*
Tobin, Mitchell	Tucker Coe	*Kinds of Love, Kinds of Death*
Tobin, Neil	B. Strutton	*Jury of Angels*
Toby, Dr. Quentin	Sturges Mason Schley	*Dream Sinister*
Todd, Jerry	Martin Joseph Freeman	*The Case of the Blind Mouse*
Todhunter, Detective	Helen Reilly	*The Dead Can Tell*
Todhunter, Laurence	Anthony Berkeley	*Trial and Error*
"The Toff" (Hon. Richard Rollison)	John Creasey	*Makeup for the Toff*
Toft (The Venerable Granius Foxlihough, Archdeacon of Tanchester)	Thurman Warriner	
Toledo, Mike	Leo Grex	

CHARACTER	AUTHOR	TITLE
Tolefree, Philip	Robert A. J. Walling	*The Fatal Five Minutes*
Tollies, Vincent	G. Morgan	
Tolliver, Dr.	William Wiegand	*At Last, Mr. Tolliver*
Tomlin, Henry	C. Conrad	
Tope, Sergeant Edward	H. C. Davis	
Toplitt, Kingsley	Gail Stockwell	*Death by Invitation*
Tor, Nelson	Barbara Malim	
Torrent, Captain	Lucy Cores	*Painted for the Kill*
Tort, Julius	Alan Caillou	
Tott, Sergeant	Gray Usher	
Touche, Georges La	Freeman Wills Crofts	*The Cask*
Tower, Mrs. Boylston (Daisy)	Freeman Dana	
Townsend, Mathilda	Arthur M. Chase	*No Outlet*
Townsend, Flight Lieutenant Robert "Peel"	Alfred O. Pollard	
Tracy, Bill	Frederic Brown	*Murder Can Be Fun*
Tracy, La Comtesse Teresa di Vicenzo	Ian Fleming	*On Her Majesty's Secret Service*
Tracy, Inspector Noel	Alex Fraser	*Constables Don't Count*
Tracy, Philip ("Spike")	Harriette Ashbrook	*Purple Onion Mystery*
Tragg, Lieutenant	Erle Stanley Gardner	*The Case of the Velvet Claws*
Trant, Lieutenant	Patrick Quentin	*Death and the Maiden*
Trant, Luther	Edgar Balmer and William MacHarg	*The Achievements of Luther Trant*
Trask, Lieutenant	Arthur Porges	"The Scientist and the Bagful of Water"
Travener, Inspector	Agatha Christie	*Crooked House*
Travers, Inspector	Pamela Barrington	*Among Those Present*
Travers, Ludovic	Christopher Bush	*The Case of the Tudor Queen*
Treadgold, Horace B.	Valentine Williams	*The Curiosity of Mr. Treadgold*
Tredegar, Detective-Inspector	Leslie Cargill	
Treen, Katey	Phoebe F. Gaye	*Treen and Wild Horses*
Trees, Peter	John Quirk	*Survivor*
Trelawney, Edward	Amelia Reynolds Long	*Murder Three Times*
Tremaine, Mordecai	F. Duncan	
Tremayne, Caroline	"Sea-Lion"	
Tremayne, Tommy	James Dark	*Throne of Satan*
Trent, Anthony and Patricia	Wyndham Martyn	*Return of Anthony Trent*
Trent, David	J. Corbett	
Trent, Gregory	Adele Seifert	*Deeds Ill Done*
Trent, Katy	Geraldine Trotta	*Veronica Died Monday*
Trent, Patricia; *see* Trent, Anthony		
Trent, Philip Marsham	Edmund C. Bentley	*Trent's Last Case*
Trent, Mrs. Philip Marsham; *see* Manderson, Mrs. Mabel		
Trenton, Garway	John P. Carstairs	*Gardenias Bruise Easily*
Trenton, Rob	Erle Stanley Gardner	*The Case of the Musical Cow*
Trevelyon, Mr.	James Workman	
Trevening, Augustine and Ruth	Philip Whitwell Wilson	*Black Tarn*
Treves, Mr.	Agatha Christie	
Trevor, Carole	Judson P. Philips	*Death Delivers a Post Card*
Trevor, Dr. Harrison	Ben Roy Redman	"The Perfect Crime"

CHARACTER	AUTHOR	TITLE
Trevor, Inspector	S. Smith	
Trevor, Dr. John	Henry Barnard Safford	
Trevor, Lord	Clarence Herbert New	*The Unseen Hand*
Trill, Vincent	Dick Donovan	*The Records of Vincent Trill*
Trimble, Detective-Superintendent	Cyril Hare	*Death Walks the Woods*
Trimble, Superintendent	Lord Gorell	
Trivett, Superintendent Bill	Gordon Ashe	
Trotter, Detective-Sergeant	T. C. H. Jacobs	
Troy, Agather (later Mrs. Roderick Alleyn)	Ngaio Marsh	*Artists in Crime*
Troy, Davis	Alan Gardner	*Six Day Week*
Troy, Jeff and Haila	Kelley Roos	*Ghost of a Chance*
Truax, Phil	Dashiell Hammett	"Laughing Masks" (Also called "When Luck's Running Good")
Truckes, Sergeant	H. F. M. Prescott	*Dead and Not Buried*
Trumbull, Harriet	Margaret Armstrong	*Murder in Stained Glass*
Tuck, Richard	L. Lewis	
Tucker, Andy	O. Henry	*The Gentle Grafter*
Tucker, Sheriff	Rose Finnegan	"Paid in Full"
Tudor, Mark	Anne Nash	*Death by Design*
Tuke, Harvey	Douglas G. Browne	*Too Many Cousins*
Tuller, Mike	J. M. Walsh	
Tully, Jasper	Dorothy Salisbury Davis	*A Gentleman Called*
Tuppence; *see* Beresford, Tommy		
Turley, Chief Inspector	Roy Vickers	
Turnbull, Inspector	John Creasey	
Turner, Tommy	Alfred Tack	
Turtle, Superintendent Mark	Philip G. Larbalestier	
Tutt, Ephraim	Arthur Train	*Mr. Tutt at His Best*
Tuttle, Gregory	Sarah Rider	*Misplaced Corpse*
Twist, Bleeker	David Duncan	*The Madrone Tree*
"Twisted Face"	Gilderoy Davison	*Twisted Face, the Avenger*
"The Twister"	Edgar Wallace	*The Twister*
Twombley, Jabez	Sidney C. Williams	*The Murder of Miss Betty Sloane*
Twotoes, Tommy	David Alexander	*Most Men Don't Kill*
Tyler, Bill	J. S. Masher	
Tyler, Dennis	John Franklin Carter	*Murder in the Embassy*
Tyler, Julia	Louisa Revell	*See Rome and Die*
Tyler, Ritzy	Gavin Holt	*Send No Flowers*
Tyson, Judge Henry	Frederick Arnold Kummer	*The Twisted Face*
Unc	John Jakes	"Unc Foils Show Foe"
Uncle Abner; *see* Abner		
Underhill, Bruce	Lawrence Treat	
Uniatz, "Hoppy"	Leslie Charteris	*The Saint Bids Diamonds*
Universal Export (Secret Headquarters of British Secret Service)	Ian Fleming	*Casino Royale*
Upjohn, Inspector	E. X. Ferrars	*The March Hare Murders*
Upwood, Robin	Newton Gayle	
Urizar, Captain Miguel	Helen McCloy	*She Walks Alone*

CHARACTER	AUTHOR	TITLE
Ursula, Sister Mary O.M.B.	Anthony Boucher	*The Stripper*
Usher, Ambrose	Jocelyn Davey	*A Touch of Stage Fright*
Vachell, Superintendent	Elspeth Huxley	*Murder at Government House*
Val, Inspector	Alfred Henry Lewis	*Confessions of a Detective*
Valcour, Lieutenant	Rufus King	*Murder Challenges Valcour*
Vale, Sergeant	Clive Ryland	
Valentin, Aristede	G. K. Chesterton	*The Innocence of Father Brown*
Valentine, Captain	Carleton S. Montayne	*The Blue Cross*
Valeska; *see* Stewart, Valeska		
Valk, Van der	Nicholas Freeling	*Criminal Conversation*
Vallon, Johnny	Peter Cheyney	*Lady Beware*
Valmont, Eugene ("Professor Paul Ducharme")	Robert Barr	*The Triumphs of Eugene Valmont*
Vance, Philo	S. S. Van Dine	*The Benson Murder Case*
Vandam, Inspector	Freeman Wills Crofts	
"Vandeleur, John"; *see* Stapleton, John		
Van Doren, Hannah	Dwight V. Babcock	*Homicide for Hannah*
Vandrift, Sir Charles	Grant Allen	
Van Dusen, Professor Augustus, S.F.X., Ph.D., LLD, F.R.S., M.D.S. ("The Thinking Machine")	Jacques Futrelle	"The Problem of Cell 13"
Vane, Adam	William E. Johns	
Vane, Dr.	Desmond Cory	
Vane, Harriet (later Lady Peter Wimsey)	Dorothy Sayers	*Strong Poison*
Vane, Jocelyn	S. Browning	
Vaness, Richard	M. Black	
Vanessa, Sarah	Joan Storm	*The Deadly Diamond*
Van Horn, Carey	Queena Mario	*Murder in the Opera House*
Van Kaz, Baron Franz Maximilian Karagoz	Darwin and Hildegarde Teilhet	*The Feather Cloak Murders*
Van Kill, Hendrik Peter Minuit ("Hal")	Spencer Bayne	*Agent Extraordinary*
Van Loan, Richard Curtis ("The Phantom Detective")	Robert Wallace	*The Thousand Island Murders*
Vanne, Toby	John F. Straker	
Vanner, Rick	Mary V. Heberden	*The Sleeping Witness*
Van Ryn, Rex	Dennis Wheatley	
Varallo, Detective Vic	Lesley Egan	*Detective's Due*
Vardon, Roger	Gerard B. Lambert	*Murder in Newport*
Vargas	Norbert Davis	"Do a Dame a Favor"
Varley, Cosmo	R. Grant	
Varney, Emily	M. E. Allen	
Vaughan, Mr.	Mary Fitt	
Vautrin	Honoré de Balzac	*Father Goriot*
Velie, Sergeant Thomas	Ellery Queen	*There Was an Old Woman*
"Velmont, Horace"; *see* Lupin, Arsène		
Velvet, Nick	Edward D. Hoch	"The Theft of the Clouded Tiger"
Venable, Charles	Christopher St. J. Sprigg	
Vencel, Platt	Steve Frazee	

CHARACTER	AUTHOR	TITLE
Venner	Clarence Hedley Barker	
Verek, Lieutenant	Nancy Rutledge	
Verinder, Rachel	Wilkie Collins	*The Moonstone*
Verity, Detective-Inspector Arnold	S. Scott	
Verity, Mr.	Peter Antony	*Woman in the Wardrobe*
Verloc, Mr.	Joseph Conrad	*The Secret Agent*
Verner, Richard	Christopher Anvil	"The Problem Solver and the Spy"
Verney, George	Andrew Garve	*Murder Through the Looking Glass*
Verney, Mrs.	H. Ainsworth	
Vernon, Inspector John	Rosamond Bayne-Powell	*Crime at Cloysters*
Vernon, Larry	David Bateson	*It's Murder, Senorita*
Verrey, Tony	Vivian Meik	*The Curse of Red Shiva*
Vestry, Mr.	Joseph Krumgold	*Thanks to Murder*
Vickary, Grant	Robertson Hobart	*The Case of the Shaven Blonde*
Villiers, Captain Derek	B. Stuart	
Vine, Gil	Stewart Sterling	*Dead to the World*
Vine, Dr. Richard	Dana Chambers	
Vinsen, Tad ("Skipper")	T. Kenyon Cook	
Vitali, Domino	Ian Fleming	*Thunderball*
Vivanti, Paul	Sidney Horler	*Vivanti*
Von Flanagan, Captain	Craig Rice	*The Right Murder*
Von Katz, Baroness; *see* Miquet, Carl		
Von Leeuw, Bengal	Lorenz Heller	*Murder in Makeup*
Vorobeitchik, Wenceslas	Andre Steeman	*The Night of the 12th–13th*
Vorst, Master	"Seamark"	*Master Vorst*
Voss, Abelard	Donald Clough Cameron	*Grave Without Grass*
Vulkan, Johnny	Len Deighton	*Funeral in Berlin*
Wace, Chief Inspector Fadiman	Roger Simons	*Gamble with Death*
Wade, Hilda	Grant Allen	*Hilda Wade*
Wade, Jerry ("Candid Camera Kid")	John L. Benton	*Appointment with Murder*
Wade, John	William R. Cox	"Pursuit of Murder"
Wade, Sergeant	Ernest Dudley	
Wade, Sergeant	Joseph J. Farjeon	
Waghorn, Inspector Jimmy	John Rhode	*An Artist Dies*
Wait, Jacob	Mignon G. Eberhart	*The Pattern*
Waldron, Anthony V.	George Clinton Bester	*The Corpse Came Calling*
Wale, "Cash"	Peter Paige	"Local Corpse Makes Good"
Walker ("Of the Secret Service")	Melville Davisson Post	*Walker of the Secret Service*
Wallace, Captain Jeffrey	Stephen Ransome	
Wallingford, "Get-Rich-Quick"	George Randolph Chester	*Get-Rich-Quick Wallingford*
Walsh, Denzil	Simon Harvester	
Walsh, Lionel	R. Grant	
Walter, Howell	Dick Donovan	*The Mystery of Jamaica Terrace*
Walter, Detective James	Wade Miller	*Deadly Weapon*
Walton, Rex	Edgar Wallace	
Wantage, Geoffrey	"Taffrail"	
War, Inspector	Peter Manton	

CHARACTER	AUTHOR	TITLE
Warbrook, Jonathan	Ronald Simpson	*The Return of Colonel Pho*
Ward, Martin	Michael Cronin	
Wardlaw, Henry	J. A. Kitchin	
Ware, Anthony	Susan Wells	*Murder Is Not Enough*
Ware, Mrs. Anthony (née Echo MacGregor)	Susan Wells	*Footsteps in the Air*
Warlock, Mike	Paul Haggard	*Death Talks Shop*
Warner, Inspector	E. C. R. Lorac	
Warren, Aunt Isabelle	Constance and Gwyneth Little	
Warren, James	James Warren	*She Fell Among Actors*
Warrender, Mr. and Mrs. James	G. D. H. and M. I. Cole	*Mrs. Warrender's Profession*
Warwick, Chief Inspector	Maurice Procter	"The Million Dollar Mystery"
Warwick, Roger	John N. Chance	
Washington, Johnny	Francis Durbridge	*Beware of Johnny Washington*
"Waters"	William Russell	*Recollections of a Detective Police-Officer*
Waters, Sergeant	Amelia Reynolds Long	
Watney, Peter	Sidney Horler	
Watson, Harry F.	Joseph L. Bonney	
Watson, Dr. John H.	Sir Arthur Conan Doyle	*A Study in Scarlet*
Watson, Mrs. John H. (née Mary Morstan)	Sir Arthur Conan Doyle	"The Final Problem"
Watt, Reginald Fortescue	F. King	
Watts, Walter A. (Wally)	Paul W. Fairmen	"Wally, the Watchful Eye"
Wayne, Morgan	M. Blood	*The Avenger*
Wayne, Rodney	Lawrence W. Meynell	
Wayward, Deputy Sheriff Carl	Lawrence Treat	*H as in Hangman*
Weathergay, Dean	Alvin Pevehouse	"The Bay of the Dead"
Weaver, Sergeant Bill	Lee Spencer	*Furtive Men*
Weaver, George	F. Brown	
Weaver, T. S.	David Keith	
Webb, John	Frank G. Presnell	*Send Another Coffin*
Webb, Mrs. John; *see* Seymour, Anne		
Webley, Inspector	Douglas Furber	*Just Another Murder*
Webster, Dallas	D. Sanford	
Webster, Lieutenant	David Dodge	*Death and Taxes*
Wedderburn	Miriam Allen De Ford	"Something to Do with Figures"
Weeke, Aunts Sunday, Wednesday and Thursday	Joseph J. Farjeon	*Aunt Sunday Sees It Through*
Weigand, Lieutenant William	Frances and Richard Lockridge	*Murder Is Suggested*
Weissman, Lieutenant	Stewart Sterling	
Welch, Agatha	Veronica Parker Johns	*Murder by the Day*
Wellard, Chief Inspector	Clive Ryland	
Wells, Professor Clifford	Norman Stanley Bortner	*Bond Grayson Murdered*
Welpton, Sam	John A. Saxon	

CHARACTER	AUTHOR	TITLE
Wembury, Detective-Inspector Alan	Edgar Wallace	
Wenk	Norbert Jacques	*Dr. Mabuse: Master of Mystery*
Wentworth, Barbara	C. Franklin	
Werner, Superintendent	Malcolm Gair	
Wesley, Diana and Sheridan	Hillary Waugh	
West, Ambrose; *see* "Ambrose"		
West, Honey ("Best Stacked Private Eye Alive")	G. G. Fickling	*Honey and Blood*
West, Dr. Martin	Andrew Garve	*Fontego's Folly*
West, Inspector Roger ("Handsome")	John Creasey	*Death of a Postman*
Westborough, Professor Theocritus Lucius	Clyde B. Clason	*The Man from Tibet*
Westcloss, "Aunt" Emily	Robert George Dean	
Westcott, Thorne	Anne Nash	
Westfall, Vance	W. Pearson	
Westlake, Dawn	Jonathan Stagge	*Death, My Darling Daughter*
Westlake, Dr. Hugh	Jonathan Stagge	*The Yellow Taxi*
Westlake, Robert	Michael Cronin	
Weston, Inspector	Alan Mackenzie	
Weston, James	James Warren	*The Disappearing Corpse*
Weston, Peter	Henry La Garde	
Weston, Peter	T. X. Pantcheff	
Westow, Detective-Constable	Seldon Truss	*Always Ask a Policeman*
Wetherbee, Admiral	Allen R. Bosworth	*Full Crash Dive*
Wharton, Superintendent George ("The Old General")	Christopher Bush	*The Case of the Tudor Queen*
Wheat, Chief Inspector Septimus	John Cassells	
Wheeler, Al	Carter Brown	*The Victim*
Wheeler, Sergeant	J. Corbett	
"The Whispering Man"	Henry Kitchell Webster	*The Whispering Man*
"The White Eagle"; *see* Cochet, Armand		
White, Inspector	Gordon Holmes	*Arncliffe Puzzle*
White, Lieutenant Lace	Jeanette Covert Nolan	*Profile in Guilt*
Whitehall, Lieutenant	Maurice Beam and Sumner Gritton	*Murder in a Shell*
Whitelock, Nashe	Nat Easton	
Whiting, Alex	Dorothy Salisbury Davis	*The Judas Cat*
Whiting, Lieutenant Percival	Jeremy Lord	
Whitney, Detective James	David Dodge	*Bullets for the Bridegroom*
Whittaker, Christopher	Zelda Popkin	
Whyte, Professor Chattin ("Chat") and Sarah	Wesley C. Clark	*Murder Goes to Bank Night*
Wibley, "Flash George"	John G. Brandon	
Wicher, Inspector Jonathan	John Dickson Carr	

CHARACTER	AUTHOR	TITLE
Wickham, Colonel	Anthony Wynne	*Death Out of the Night*
Wickley, Mrs. Mabel	Marjorie Boniface	*Murder as an Ornament*
Wickwire, Mr. James	Mignon G. Eberhart	"Mr. Wickwire Adds and Subtracts"
Widgeon, Inspector	A. Thomas	
Wigan, Sergeant Jack	Benjamin J. Farmer	
Wiggars	Lee Thayer	*No Holiday for Death*
Wiggins	Sir Arthur Conan Doyle	*A Study in Scarlet*
Wigmore, Sir Barnard	John Collier	"A Matter of Taste"
Wilbur, Keigthley	Frank Danby	*The Story Behind the Verdict*
Wilcox, Jackson	R. Daniel	
Wilde, Brian	R. Daniel	
Wilde, Carney	Bart Spicer	*Blues for the Prince*
Wilde, Jonas	Andrew York	*The Eliminator*
Wilde, "Tubby"	William E. Johns	
Wilding, Ex-Superintendent Nick	M. Richmond	
Wilkie, Nurse	William Fryer Harvey	*The Arm of Mrs. Egan*
Wille, Superintendent	Edgar Wallace	
Williams, Caleb	William Godwin	*Things as They Are*
Williams, D. J.	Menna Gallie	
Williams, "Doc"	Jonathan Latimer	
Williams, Race	Carroll John Daly	*Murder from the East*
Williams, Superintendent	B. Gray	
Willing, Dr. Basil	Helen McCloy	*The One That Got Away*
Willis, Inspector	Freeman Wills Crofts	*The Pit-Prop Syndicate*
Wilson, Detective-Inspector Bill	B. Knox	
Wilson, Superintendent Eric	E. P. Thorne	
Wilson, Ex-Superintendent Henry	G. D. H. and M. I. Cole	*The Brooklyn Murders*
Wilson, Detective-Inspector James	R. S. Daniel	
Wilson, Lieutenant	G. Goldsmith	
Wimburn, Clive	William H. L. Crauford	
Wimp, Edward	Israel Zangwill	*The Big Bow Mystery*
Wimperis, Freddy	Michael Cronin	
Wimsey, Lady Mary (later Mrs. Charles Parker)	Dorothy Sayers	*Clouds of Witness*
Wimsey, Lady Peter; *see* Vane, Harriet		
Wimsey, Lord Peter Death Bredon	Dorothy Sayers	*The Nine Tailors*
Windermaine, Gerry	"Seamark"	
Windward, Bruce	Stephen Bandolier	*Murder Manana*
Wineglass, Colonel	Michael Arlen	*Hell! Said the Duchess*
Winkley	Harriet Rutland	*Knock, Murderer, Knock*
Winkman, Jake	Don Von Elsner	*How to Succeed at Murder Without Really Trying*
Winn, Wheatley	John C. Masterman	
Winslow, Chief Constable	Clive Ryland	
Winslow, Don	Frank O. Martinek	*Don Winslow, USN, in Ceylon*
Winston, Peter	Peter Winston	*The ABC Affair*
Winter, Inspector	G. Butler	

CHARACTER	AUTHOR	TITLE
Winter, Chief Superintendent James Leander	Louis Tracy	*The Strange Disappearance of Lady Delia*
Winter, Mark	Jack Siegal	*Dawn at Kahlenberg*
Winters, Lieutenant	Edgar Box	*Death in the Fifth Position*
Winters, Matt	Inez Dellrichs	*Kettel Mill Mystery*
Wintino, Dave	Ed Lacy	*Lead with Your Left*
Wintringham, Dr. David	Josephine Bell	*Murder in Hospital*
Wirrall, Chief Inspector	Paul Capon	
Wise, Bill	Peter Boyd	*Slip Sees Red*
Wiston, Ex-Superintendent Archie	Lindsay Anson	*I Don't Like Cats*
Witherall, Leonidas ("Bill Shakespeare")	Alice Tilton	*The Cut Direct*
Withers, "Big Bill"	John G. Brandon	
Withers, Hildegarde	Stuart Palmer	*Four Lost Ladies*
Woar, Hazlitt George Brendan	George Worthing Yates	*The Body That Came by Post*
Woar, Mrs. Hazlitt; *see* Meynard, Katheren		
Wolf, Sir William	Eden Phillpotts	*The Mystery of Sir Henry Wolf*
Wolfe, Nero	Rex Stout	*Fer-de-Lance*
Wolff, Commissioner (alias "George Engel," "The Angel of the Lace Curtains")	Dietrich Thedan	*The Long Miracle*
Wong, Mei	Dan Ross	"The Mi Lo Diamonds"
Woode, Teak	Julian Symons	*The Immaterial Murder Case*
Woodhead, Alister	E. H. Clements	
Woody	John Jakes	"Unc Foils Show Foe"
Woolcott, Mr.	J. Jowett	
Woolrich, Tony	Milton M. Raison	
Worden, Pete	William Campbell Gault	*Don't Cry for Me*
Worthington, Inspector	Joseph J. Farjeon	
Wragge, "Tiger" and Jill	Paul Capon	
Wraithlea	P. N. Walker-Taylor	
Wrayne, Daphne	Mark Cross	*Challenge to the Four*
Wreford, Guy	D. Clarke	
Wu, Lily	Juanita Sheridan	*Chinese Shop*
Wyatt, Chief Inspector and Sally	Francis Durbridge	
Wyatt, Joseph	Alfred E. W. Mason	*The Dean's Elbow*
Wycherley, Boyce	Dennis Dean	*Emerald Murder Case*
Wyckoff, Captain	Ernest Ward	*Five for Bridge*
Wynn, Max; *see* Carrados, Max		
Wynnton, Robert	Sidney Horler	
X Club	Ben Hecht	"The Fifteen Murderers"
Yale, Derrick	Edgar Wallace	
Yardley, Bill	F. Lester	
Yarrow, Inspector	Richard Hull	
Yates, Susan	Emma Lou Fetta	*Murder in Style*
Yeo, Mrs. Georgia	Ethel Lina White	*Step in the Dark*
Zacharias, Mike	Robert P. Wilmot	*Blood in Your Eye*
Zaleski, Prince	Mathew P. Shiel	*Prince Zaleski*

CHARACTER	AUTHOR	TITLE
Zambra, Sebastian	Headon Hill	*Cabinet Secrets*
Zenon, Mathieu	H. Long	
Zoom, Sidney	Erle Stanley Gardner	"The Case of the Scattered Rubies"
Zordan, Anna	James Eastwood	*The Chinese Visitor*

6

ANTHOLOGIES AND COLLECTIONS

"Variety's the very spice of life, that gives it all its flavour." William Cowper might well have been talking about the anthologies and collections found in the realm of detective, mystery and suspense fiction for this field is certainly rich with them. In recent years writers have wandered the globe in search of exotic locales and unique characters to people them. A glance at "The Scene of the Crime" and "Heroes, Villains—and Heroines" will attest to that. There is another way, however, in which the armchair traveler may broaden his horizon without stirring from the magic carpet in his living room. Does he wish to survey a century of crime in a single evening? Mingle with the master poisoners of the past? Read a choice lot of the world's best mysteries in a single sitting? Is he interested only in the female species of the criminal? The possibilities are endless if you will look over the following list and savor the feast that has been set before you.

Somebody, somewhere, at one time or another has had the idea for seemingly every possible type of anthology or collection, and there should be one to suit every taste. *Bodies and Souls* is a collection of murder stories which will be of particular interest to Catholic readers because of the unique backgrounds of the stories. Sometimes the only thing anthologies have in common is that they are collections of mystery, detective or suspense stories and even that is enough to satisfy the most avid fan.

Adams, A. K. (ed.). *Favorite Trial Stories, Fact and Fiction.* Dodd, 1966.

Ainsworth, Norma Ruedi (ed.). *Hit Parade of Mystery Stories. Scholastic Magazine,* 1963. Seven stories especially chosen for teen-agers.

———. *Stories of Suspense. Scholastic Magazine,* 1963.

*Alexander, David (ed.). *Tales for a Rainy Night.* Holt, 1961; Crest, 1964; Dobson, 1967. MWA anthology.

Allen, M. C. (ed.). *Shock!* Popular Lib., 1965.

Arthur, Robert (ed.). *Cloak and Dagger.* Dell, 1967.

Asbury, Herbert (ed.). *Not at Night.* Vanguard, 1928.

Ask a Policeman. Morrow, 1933. Contributions by Anthony Berkeley, Gladys Mitchell and Dorothy Sayers.

Avon Mystery Story Teller. Avon, 1946.

Baffling Detective Stories by Masters of Mystery. Black, 1928.

Bayer, Eleanor and Leo Bayer (eds.). *Cleveland Murders.* Duell, 1947.

Bayer, Leo; *see* Bayer, Eleanor.

Bayer, Oliver Weld, pseud; *see* Bayer, Eleanor.

Beach, Stewart (ed.). *This Week's Stories of Mystery and Suspense.* Random, 1957; Berkley Pub., 1962. Abridged Berkley edition contains 16 stories.

Beaumont, Charles (ed.). *The Fiend in*

You. Ballantine, 1962. 16 stories of criminals and the supernatural.

Beecroft, John; *see* Costain, Thomas; *see also* Haycraft, Howard.

Benedict, Stewart H. (ed.). *The Crime Solvers*. Dell, 1966.

———. *Tales of Horror and Suspense*. Dell, 1963.

Bentley, Edmond C. (ed.). *The Second Century of Detective Stories*. Hutchinson, 1938.

Best Detective Stories of the Year. 21 annual volumes. Various editors and publishers.

Best Murder Stories. Faber, 1935–1951.

Big Book of Detective Stories. William Clowes. No date.

Bisserov, George (ed.). *An Omnibus of British Mysteries*. Juniper, 1960.

———. *An Omnibus of Continental Mysteries*. Juniper, 1960.

Bleiler, Everett F. (ed.). *Three Gothic Novels and a Fragment*. Dover, 1965. Contains: *The Castle of Otranto, Vathek*, and *The Vampire*.

Bond, Raymond Tostevin (ed.). *Famous Stories of Code and Cipher*. Rinehart, 1947; Collier, 1965.

———. *Handbook for Poisoners*. Rinehart, 1951. A collection of great poison stories with a 78 page preface on poisons.

Book of a Thousand Thrills. Allied Newspapers, 1923.

Boucher, Anthony (ed.). *Best Detective Stories of the Year*. 18th–19th Annual Collections. Dutton, 1963–1966. English title: *Best American Detective Stories of the Year*. Boardman, T. V., 1963–1964.

———. *Best Detective Stories of the Year*. 22nd Annual Collection. Dutton, 1967.

*———. *Four and Twenty Bloodhounds*. S & S, 1950. MWA anthology.

———. *Great American Detective Stories*. World Pub., 1945.

———. *The Quintessence of Queen: Best Prize Stories from Twelve Years of Ellery Queen's Mystery Magazine*. Random, 1962. English title: *A Magnum of Mysteries*. Gollancz, 1963.

———. *The Quintessence of Queen #2*. Avon, 1963. Includes 10 stories from the 1962 Random House edition.

Bradbury, Ray (ed.). *The Circus of Dr. Lao and Other Improbable Tales*. Bantam, 1956. 12 stories.

Bull, Randolph Cecil (ed.). *Great Stories of Detection*. Barker, 1960.

———. *Great Tales of Mystery*. Hill & Wang, 1960.

———. *Great Tales of Terror*. Hamilton, 1963; Panther.

Burnett, Hallie; *see* Burnett, Whit.

Burnett, Whit and Hallie Burnett (eds.). *Nineteen Tales of Terror*. Bantam, 1957.

———. *Things and Claws*. Ballantine, 1961. Horror stories by Daphne Du Maurier, Stuart Cloete, Jesse Stuart and others.

———. *The Tough Ones*. Popular Lib. An anthology of realistic short stories, some with a criminous theme.

***Butcher's Dozen*. Heinemann, 1956. A Crime Writers' Association anthology.

Cannell, J. C. (ed.). *One Hundred Mysteries for Armchair Detectives*. Long, 1932.

Cantor, Hal (ed.). *Ghosts and Things*. Berkley Pub., 1962.

A Century of Thrillers. 3 vols. President Press, 1937.

A Century of Thrillers: From Poe to Arlen. Daily Express Publications, 1934. Foreword by James Agate.

A Century of Thrillers. Second series. Daily Express Publications, 1935.

Cerf, Bennett (ed.). *Three Famous Murder Novels*. Random, 1942. Contains: *Before the Fact,* by Francis Illes; *Trent's Last Case,* by E. C. Bentley; and *The House of the Arrow,* by A. E. W. Mason.

———. *Three Famous Spy Novels*. Random, 1942. Contains: *The Great Impersonation,* by E. Phillips Oppenheim; *Journey into Fear,* by Eric Ambler; and *The Confidential Agent,* by Graham Greene.

———. *The Unexpected*. Bantam, 1948. Abridged edition: *Stories Selected from the Unexpected*. Bantam, 1963.

Chesterton, G. K. (ed.). *A Century of Detective Stories*. Hutchinson, 1935. Never published in the United States.

Cheyney, Peter (ed.). *Best Stories of the Underworld*. Faber, 1949.

***Choice of Weapons*. Hodder, 1958. A Crime Writers' Association anthology.

Collins, Charles M. (ed.). *Fright: Six Tales of the Unknown Calculated to Induce Fright*. Avon, 1963.

Comber, Leon (ed.). *Strange Cases of Magistrate Pao*. Tuttle, 1964.

Congdon, Don (ed.). *Stories for the Dead of Night*. Dell, 1957.

———. *Tales of Love and Horror*. Ballantine, 1961.

——— and Michael Congdon (eds.). *Alone by Night*. Ballantine, 1967.

Congdon, Michael; *see* Congdon, Don.

Conklin, Groff (ed.). *The Graveyard Reader*. Ballantine, 1958, 1965. 12 terrifying tales.

———. *In the Grip of Terror*. Permabooks, 1951; Doubleday, 1954. 25 nightmarish tales.

——— and Dr. Noah Fabricant (eds.). *Great Detective Stories About Doctors*. Collier, 1965.

Cooke, David (ed.). *Best Detective Stories of the Year*. Dutton, 1950–1960.

———. *My Best Murder Story*. Merlin, 1955; Boardman, T. V., 1959.

Costain, Thomas and John Beecroft (eds.). *Thirty Stories to Remember*. Doubleday, 1962. Mixed anthology containing some stories in the mystery, suspense category.

*Coxe, George Harmon (ed.). *Butcher, Baker, Murder-Maker*. Knopf, 1954. MWA anthology.

**Cream of the Crime*. Holt, 1962; Harrap, 1964. Foreword by Hugh Pentecost. MWA anthology.

*Creasey, John (ed.). *Crimes Across the Sea*. Harper & Row, 1964; Longmans, 1964. MWA anthology.

———. *The Mystery Bedside Book*. First-Sixth Series. Hodder, 1960–1965.

**Crime Club Golden Book of Best Detective Stories*. Doubleday, Doran, 1934. MWA anthology.

Crime Writers' Association. Annual anthologies. See individual entries marked by a double asterisk (**).

Crispin, Edmond, pseud; *see* Montgomery, Robert Bruce.

*Crossen, Kendall Foster (ed.). *Murder Cavalcade*. Collins, 1946; Duell, 1946; Hammond, 1953, 1957. Introduction by Richard Lockridge. Also published as: *Great Murder Stories*. Penguin, 1948. MWA anthology.

Cuppy, Will (ed.). *Murder Without Tears*. Sheridan, 1946.

———. *World's Great Detective Stories*. World Pub., 1943.

———. *The World's Great Mystery Stories*. World Pub., 1943.

Dahlin, Ragnar (ed.). *Detectives and Ghosts*. Svenska Bókförlaget, 1956.

Davenport, Basil (ed.). *Deals with the Devil*. Ballantine.

———. *Invisible Men*. Ballantine, 1960.

———. *Tales to Be Told in the Dark*. Dodd, 1953.

———. *Thirteen Ways to Dispose of a Body*. Dodd, 1965; Faber, 1967.

———. *Thirteen Ways to Kill a Man: An Anthology*. Dodd, 1965.

*Davis, Dorothy Salisbury (ed.). *Choice of Murders*. Scribner, 1958 (contains 23 stories); MacDonald & Co., 1960 (contains 18 stories). MWA anthology.

De Ford, Miriam Allen (ed.). *The Theme Is Murder: An Anthology of Mysteries*. Abelard, 1967.

De La Torre, Lillian, pseud; *see* McCue, Lillian Bueno.

Derleth, August (ed.). *Dark Mind, Dark Heart*. Arkham, 1962. Supernatural and terror stories.

———. *The Night Side: Masterpieces of the Strange and Terrible*. Rinehart, 1947.

———. *Over the Edge*. Arkham, 1964.

———. *Sleep No More*. Farrar, Straus, 1944; Murray Hill, 1944. 20 horror stories.

*Dewey, Thomas Blanchard (ed.). *Sleuths and Consequences*. S & S, 1966. MWA anthology.

Dresser, Davis (ed.). *Best Detective Stories of the Year*. 17th Annual Collection. Dell, 1964. English title: *Best American Detective Stories of the Year*. 11th Annual Collection. Boardman, T. V., 1962.

*———. *Big Time Mysteries*. Dodd, 1958. MWA anthology.

*——— and Helen McCloy (eds). *Twenty Great Tales of Murder*. Random, 1951; Hammond, 1952. MWA anthology.

Dudley, Ernest (ed.). *The Armchair Detective Reader*. Boardman, T. V., 1948.

———. *The Second Armchair Reader*. Boardman, T. V., 1950.

Eckberg, Arno (ed.). *An Omnibus of Continental Mysteries*. Juniper, 1961.

Edwards, Eleanor Middleton (ed.). *Great Mystery Stories*. Hart, 1962.

Eenhoorn, Michael (ed.). *Omnibus of American Mysteries*. Juniper, 1959.

Eliot, George Fielding (ed.). *Executioner's Signature*. Great Amer. Pub., 1960.

Evans, Pauline Rush (ed.). *Good Housekeeping's Best Book of Mystery Stories*. Prentice-Hall, 1958.

The Evening Standard Book of Strange Stories. Hutchinson, 1934.

The Evening Standard Detective Book. 1st and 2nd series. Gollancz, 1950–1951.

Fabricant, Dr. Noah; *see* Conklin, Groff.

Famous Detective Stories. Black, 1928.

Fast, Julius (ed.). *Out of This World*. Penguin, 1944.

Fifth Mystery Book; see *The Mystery Book*.

Fifty Masterpieces of Mystery. Odhams, 1935.

*Fischer, Bruno (ed.). *Crooks' Tour.* Dodd, 1953; MacDonald & Co., 1954. MWA anthology.

Fourth Mystery Book; see *The Mystery Book.*

Fraser, Phyllis; *see* Wise, Herbert A.

French, Joseph Lewis (ed.). *Best Ghost Stories.* Boni & Liveright, 1919.

———. *The Ghost Story Omnibus.* Dodd, 1953.

———. *Ghosts, Grim and Gentle.* Dodd, 1926.

———. *The Gray Shadow.* Century, 1931.

———. *Great Detective Stories.* 3 vols. MacVeagh, 1924. Contents: Vol. I. *Great Detective Stories from Voltaire to Poe.* Vol. II. *Great Detective Stories from Dickens to Gaboriau.* Vol. III. *Great Detective Stories from Costello to Stevenson.*

———. *Great Ghost Stories.* Dodd, 1918.

———. *Masterpieces of Mystery.* 4 vols. Doubleday, Page, 1920. Includes *Riddle Stories.*

———. *Tales of Terror.* Small, 1925.

Furman, Abraham Louis (ed.). *The Fourth Mystery Companion.* Lantern Press, 1947.

———. *The Mystery Companion.* Gold Label, 1943; Popular Lib., 1941. 14 great detective stories.

———. *The Second Mystery Companion.* Gold Label, 1944.

———. *The Third Mystery Companion.* Gold Label, 1945.

*Gardiner, Dorothy (ed.). *For Love or Money.* Doubleday, 1957; MacDonald & Co., 1959. MWA anthology.

Gawsworth, John (ed.). *Crimes, Creeps and Thrills: Forty-five New Stories of Detection, Horror and Adventure by Eminent Modern Authors.* Grant, E., 1937.

*Gordon, Gordon and Mildred Gordon (eds.). *A Pride of Felons.* Macmillan, 1963. MWA anthology.

Gordon, Mildred; *see* Gordon, Gordon.

Greene, Graham and Hugh Greene (eds.). *The Spy's Bedside Book.* Hart-Davis, 1958.

Greene, Hugh; *see* Greene, Graham.

Greenfield, Louis; *see* Stout, Rex.

Haining, Peter (ed.). *The Gentlewomen of Evil: An Anthology of Rare Supernatural Stories from the Pens of Victorian Ladies.* Taplinger, 1967.

Halliday, Brett; pseud; *see* Dresser, Davis.

Hanlon, Jon, pseud; *see* Kemp, Earl.

Harré, Thomas Everett (ed.). *Beware After Dark.* Macaulay, 1929; Emerson, 1945.

Harrington, Henry; *see* Knox, Ronald A.

Hawthorne, Julian (ed.). *Library of the World's Best Mystery and Detective Stories.* 6 vols. Review of Reviews, 1908.

Haycraft, Howard (ed.). *The Boys' Book of Great Detectives.* Harper, 1938. A book for teen-age boys featuring the best known fictional detective characters of our time.

———. *The Boys' Second Book of Great Detective Stories.* Harper, 1940; Berkley Pub., 1964.

——— and John Beecroft (eds.). *A Mystery Omnibus: Three Times Three.* Doubleday, 1964.

———. *Ten Great Mysteries.* Doubleday, 1959.

———. *A Treasury of Great Mysteries.* 2 vols. S & S, 1957.

Herr, Dann and Joel Wells (eds.). *Bodies and Souls.* Doubleday, 1961; Dell, 1963. Murder stories of particular interest to Catholics because of the authors' viewpoint or the background of the stories.

———. *Bodies and Spirits.* Doubleday, 1964.

Hirsch, Phil (ed.). *Death House.* Pyramid, 1966.

———. *A Mad Passion for Murder.* Pyramid, 1966.

Hitchcock, Alfred (ed.). *Alfred Hitchcock Presents: A Baker's Dozen of Suspense Stories.* Dell, 1963.

———. *Alfred Hitchcock Presents: Fear and Trembling.* Dell, 1948, 1963.

———. *Alfred Hitchcock Presents: More of My Favorites in Suspense.* Dell, 1964.

———. *Alfred Hitchcock Presents: More Stories for Late at Night.* Dell, 1962.

———. *Alfred Hitchcock Presents: My Favorites in Suspense.* Random, 1959. Also published as: *My Favorites in Suspense.* Reinhardt, 1960.

———. *Alfred Hitchcock Presents: Once Upon a Dreadful Time.* Dell, 1964.

———. *Alfred Hitchcock Presents: Sixteen Skeletons from My Closet.* Dell, 1963.

———. *Alfred Hitchcock Presents: Stories for Late at Night.* Random, 1961. Also published as: *Stories for Late at Night.* Reinhardt, 1962.

———. *Alfred Hitchcock Presents: Stories My Mother Never Told Me.* Random,

1963. Also published as: *Stories My Mother Never Told Me.* Reinhardt, 1964.

———. *Alfred Hitchcock Presents: Stories Not for the Nervous.* Random, 1965; Dell, 1966.

———. *Alfred Hitchcock Presents: Stories That Scared Even Me.* Random, 1967.

———. *Alfred Hitchcock Presents: Twelve Stories They Wouldn't Let Me Do on TV.* Reinhardt, 1957; S & S, 1957; Pan, 1960; Dell, 1964.

———. *Alfred Hitchcock's Fourteen Suspense Stories to Play Russian Roulette By.* Dell, 1963.

———. *Anti-Social Register.* Dell, 1965.

———. *Bar the Doors!* Dell, 1946.

———. *The Fireside Book of Suspense.* S & S, 1947.

———. *Hangman's Dozen.* Dell, 1962.

———. *Hard Day at the Scaffold.* Dell, 1967.

———. *Haunted Houseful.* Random, 1961; Reinhardt, 1962.

———. *Hold Your Breath.* Dell, 1947.

———. *Noose Report.* Dell, 1966.

———. *Suspense Stories Collected by Alfred Hitchcock.* Dell, 1945.

———. *Thirteen More Stories They Wouldn't Let Me Do on TV.* S & S, 1957; Dell, 1959.

———. *Witches' Brew.* Dell, 1965.

Hodapp, William (ed.). *Crazy Mixed-up Kids.* Berkley Pub., 1955. An anthology of the crazy, mixed-up behavior of the young.

Hodge, James (ed.). *Final Selection.* Penguin.

Hurwood, Bernhardt J. (ed.). *Monsters and Nightmares.* Belmont, 1967.

———. *Monsters Galore.* GM, 1965.

Kahn, Joan (ed.). *The Edge of the Chair.* Harper & Row, 1967.

Kaplan, Arthur (ed.). *The Fine Art of Espionage.* Award, 1967.

Karloff, Boris (ed.). *Boris Karloff's Favorite Horror Stories.* Avon, 1965.

Karp, Marvin Allen (ed.). *The Spy in the Shadows.* Popular Lib., 1965.

———. *Suddenly—Great Stories of Suspense and the Unexpected.* Popular Lib., 1965.

———. *To Catch a Spy.* Popular Lib., 1965.

Kemp, Earl (ed.). *Death's Loving Arms and Other Terror Tales.* Corinth, 1966.

———. *The House of Living Death and Other Terror Tales.* Corinth, 1966.

———. *Stories from Dr. Death and Other Terror Tales.* Corinth, 1966.

Knox, Ronald A. and Henry Harrington (eds.). *Best English Detective Stories of 1928.* First series. Liveright, 1929.

Lee, Elizabeth (ed.). *Murder Mixture.* Elek, 1963.

Lie, Jonas (ed.). *Weird Tales from Northern Seas.* Paul, 1893.

*Lockridge, Frances and Richard Lockridge (eds.). *Crime for Two.* Lippincott, 1955; MacDonald & Co., 1957. MWA anthology.

Lockridge, Richard; *see* Lockridge, Frances.

McCloy, Helen; *see* Dresser, Davis.

McCue, Lillian Bueno (ed.). *Villainy Detected.* Appleton-Century, 1947.

*MacDonald, John D. (ed.). *The Lethal Sex.* Collins, 1962. MWA anthology.

MacGowan, Kenneth (ed.). *Sleuths: 23 Great Detectives of Fiction and Their Best Stories.* Harcourt, 1931.

McSpadden, J. W. (ed.). *Famous Detective Stories.* Crowell, 1935.

**Maiden Murders.* Harper, 1952. Introduction by John Dickson Carr. MWA anthology.

Margolies, Joseph Aaron (ed.). *Strange and Fantastic Stories: 50 Tales of Terror, Horror, and Fantasy.* McGraw, 1946.

Margulies, Leo (ed.). *Back Alley Jungle.* Crest, 1961. An anthology of teen-age hoods and tramps.

———. *Dames, Danger, Death.* Pyramid, 1960.

———. *The Ghoul Keepers.* Pyramid, 1965.

———. *Master Murder Stories.* Hampton, 1945.

———. *Mike Shayne's Torrid Twelve.* Dell, 1961. 12 stories from *Mike Shayne's Mystery Magazine,* 1956–1959.

———. *Mink Is for a Minx.* 1st annual edition. Subtitle: The Best from Mike Shayne's Mystery Magazine. Dell, 1964.

———. *Weird Tales.* Pyramid, 1964.

———. *Worlds of Weird.* Pyramid, 1965.

———. *Young and Deadly.* Fawcett, 1959. An anthology of teen-age rebels.

———. *The Young Punks.* Pyramid, 1957. An anthology of violence-crazed youths.

Meredith, Scott and Sidney Meredith (eds.). *The Best from Manhunt.* Permabooks, 1958. 13 of the toughest stories ever written.

———. *The Bloodhound Anthology.* Boardman, T. V., 1959.

Meredith, Sidney; *see* Meredith, Scott.

Merrill, Judith (ed.). *Galaxy of Ghouls.* Lion, 1935.

———. *Shot in the Dark.* Bantam, 1950.

Merson, J. G. M. (ed.). *Modern Detective Stories.* Longmans, 1955.

———. *Six Detective Stories.* Longmans, 1960.

Methold, Kenneth (ed.). *Modern Tales of Mystery and Detection.* Hamilton, H., 1960.

Montgomery, Robert Bruce (ed.). *Best Detective Stories.* Faber, 1959.

Morley, Christopher (ed.). *Murder with a Difference.* Random, 1946. Includes Richard Hull's *Murder of My Aunt,* Gerald Heard's *A Taste for Honey,* and Patrick Hamilton's *Hangover Square.*

Morris, Louis (ed.). *Masterpieces of Adventure.* Hart, 1966.

———. *Masterpieces of Suspense.* Hart, 1966.

Morris, Rosamund (ed.). *Great Suspense Stories.* Hart, 1962.

———. *Masterpieces of Horror.* Hart, 1966.

———. *Masterpieces of Mystery and Detection.* Hart, 1965.

———. *Masterpieces of Suspense.* Hart, 1966.

Morrison, Henry (ed.). *Come Seven, Come Death.* PB, 1965.

My Best Detective Story. Faber, 1931.

My Best Mystery Story. Faber, 1939.

My Best Spy Story. Faber, 1938.

My Best Thriller. Faber, 1933. 26 stories chosen by their authors.

The Mystery Book. Farrar & Rinehart, 1939. Includes: "About the Disappearance of Agatha King," by Anthony Abbot; "Death Stops at a Tourist Camp," by Leslie Ford; "Mr. Pinkerton: Passage for One," by David Frome; "The Curve of the Catanary," by Mary Roberts Rinehart; and *Red Threads,* by Rex Stout.

Other anthologies in this series are: *The Second Mystery Book* (1940); *The Third Mystery Book* (1941); *The Fourth Mystery Book* (1942); and *The Fifth Mystery Book* (1944). All published by Farrar & Rinehart.

The Fifth Mystery Book includes Philip Wylie's "Stab in the Back"; Agatha Christie's "Tape Measure Murder"; Hugh Pentecost's "Dead Man's Tales"; and Ethel Gayles' *Murder Buys a Rug.*

Mystery Writers of America. Annual anthologies. Various editors and publishers. *See* titles marked by an asterisk (*).

Neale, Arthur (ed.). *Detective Stories for Boys.* Clode, 1930.

———. *Great Weird Stories.* Duffield, 1929.

———. *Master Detective Stories.* Clode, 1929.

Nelson, James (ed.). *The Complete Murder Sampler.* Doubleday, 1946. A collection which presents the main varieties of mystery storytelling.

Netherwood, B. A. (ed.). *Medley Macabre.* Hammond, 1966.

Norton, Alden T. (ed.). *Horror Times Ten.* Berkley Pub., 1967.

101 Worlds' Great Mystery Stories. Blue Ribbon Books, 1929.

Oursler, Will (ed.). *As Tough as They Come.* Doubleday, 1951. Also published as: *17 Hardboiled Stories of Murder.* Permabooks, 1951.

Owen, Frank (ed.). *Fireside Mystery Book.* Lantern Press, 1947.

———. *Murder for the Millions.* Fell, 1946.

Peck, Ira (ed.). *A Treasury of Great Ghost Stories.* Popular Lib., 1965.

***Planned Departures.* Hodder, 1960. A Crime Writers' Association anthology. Introduction by Elizabeth Ferrars.

The Playboy Book of Crime and Suspense. Trident, 1966; PB, 1967.

The Playboy Book of Horror and the Supernatural. Trident, 1967.

The Pocketbook of Great Detectives. PB, 1941.

Postgate, Raymond (ed.). *Detective Stories of Today, 1940.* Faber, 1940.

Powell, Talmadge (ed.). *Best Detective Stories of the Year.* Dutton, 1961.

Protter, Eric (ed.). *Monster Festival.* Vanguard, 1965.

Queen, Ellery (ed.). *Anthologies from Mystery Magazine.* Published biannually in paperback format.

———. *Best Stories from Ellery Queen's Mystery Magazine.* Little, 1944.

———. *Challenge to the Reader.* Stokes, 1938; Blue Ribbon Books, 1940.

———. *Ellery Queen's All-Star Lineup.* 22nd Awards Annual. New Amer. Lib., 1967.

———. *Ellery Queen's Double Dozen.* 19th Awards Annual. Random, 1964.

English title: *Ellery Queen's 19th Mystery Annual.* Gollancz, 1965.

———. *Ellery Queen's 15th–16th Mystery Annual.* Random, 1960–1961; Gollancz, 1961–1962.

———. *Ellery Queen's 14th Annual.* Random, 1959. English title: *Ellery Queen's Choice.* Collins, 1961.

———. *Ellery Queen's Lethal Black Book.* Dell, 1965. 13 stories of avarice and mayhem.

———. *Ellery Queen's Mystery Mix.* 18th Awards Annual. Random, 1963; Gollancz, 1964.

———. *Ellery Queen's 13th Annual.* Random, 1958. English title: *Ellery Queen's Choice.* Collins, 1960.

———. *Ellery Queen's 20th Anniversary Annual: 20 Stories from Ellery Queen's Mystery Magazine.* Random, 1965.

———. *Ellery Queen's 21st Annual Crime Carousel: 21 Stories from Ellery Queen's Mystery Magazine.* New Amer. Lib., 1966. English title: *Ellery Queen's Crime Carousel.* Gollancz, 1967.

———. *The Female of the Species: A Collection of Stories About Women in Crime.* Little, 1943. English title: *Ladies in Crime.* Faber, 1947. Also published as: *The Great Women Detectives and Criminals.* Blue Ribbon Books, 1946.

———. *The Literature of Crime.* Little, 1950; Cassell, 1952. 26 world famous authors try crime fiction. Also published as: *Ellery Queen's Book of Mystery Stories.* Pan, 1964.

———. *The Misadventures of Sherlock Holmes.* Little, 1944.

———. *Murder by Experts.* Little, 1947; Low, 1950.

———. *101 Year's Entertainment: The Great Detective Stories, 1841–1941.* Little, 1941; Garden City Pub., 1945; Random, 1946.

———. *The Queen's Awards.* 1st–12th Awards Annual. Little, 1946–1954; Gollancz, 1948–1955; S & S, 1956–1957; Collins, 1956–1960. The 9th and 10th Annuals were entitled: *Ellery Queen's Awards.*

———. *Rogue's Gallery: The Great Criminals of Detective Fiction.* Little, 1945; Faber, 1947; Sun Dial, 1947; Dell, 1966.

———. *Sporting Blood.* Little, 1942. English title: *Sporting Detective Stories.* Faber, 1946. Also published as: *Great Sports Detective Stories.* Blue Ribbon Books, 1946.

———. *To Be Read Before Midnight.* 17th Awards Annual. Random, 1962.

———. *To the Queen's Taste.* Little, 1946; Faber, 1955. First Supplement to *101's Years Entertainment.*

———. *Twentieth Century Detective Stories.* World Pub., 1948; Popular Lib., 1964. Includes Queen's Quorum, a list and description of the 100 most important detective short story anthologies since 1845.

*Radin, Edward D. (ed.). *Masters of Mayhem.* Morrow, 1965. MWA anthology.

Rathbone, Basil (ed.). *Basil Rathbone Selects Strange Tales.* Belmont, 1965.

Reader's Digest Anthology of Mystery and Suspense. Reader's Digest Assn., 1959.

Reynolds, Francis Joseph (ed.). *Master Tales of Mystery.* 2 vols. Collier, 1915.

Rhode, John, pseud; *see* Street, Cecil John.

Rhys, Ernest; *see* Scott, Catherine.

Rice, Craig (ed.). *The Los Angeles Murders.* Duell, 1947.

Ripley, Harold Austin. (ed.). *How Good a Detective Are You?* Stokes, 1934. A collection of minute mysteries.

Sandoe, James (ed.). *Murder, Plain and Fanciful.* Sheridan, 1948.

Santesson, Hans Stefan (ed.). *The Award Espionage Reader.* Award, 1965.

———. *The Saint Magazine Reader.* Doubleday, 1966.

Sarlat, Noah (ed.). *The Spy in Black Lace.* Lancer.

Saul, George Brandon (ed.). *Owl's Watch.* Crest, 1965.

Sayers, Dorothy L. (ed.). *The Great Short Stories of Detection, Mystery, and Horror.* First–Third series. Gollancz, 1929–1934. Published in the U.S. as: *The First Omnibus of Crime.* Harcourt, 1929; *The Second Omnibus of Crime.* Coward, 1932; and *The Third Omnibus of Crime.* Coward, 1935; Blue Ribbon Books, 1937. Published in a two vol. set by Harcourt in 1961.

———. *Human and Inhuman.* Macfadden, 1963. Stories from the *Omnibus of Crime.*

———. *Stories of the Supernatural.* Macfadden, 1963. Stories from the *Omnibus of Crime.*

———. *Tales of Detection.* Dent, 1936.

Schwartz, H. S. (ed.). *Contemporary French Stories of Mystery and Fantasy.* Knopf, 1926.

Scott, Catharine and Ernest Rhys (eds.). *Mystery Stories, Old and New.* Appleton, D., 1927.

The Second Mystery Book; see *The Mystery Book.*

Serling, Rod (ed.). *Rod Serling's Triple W: Witches, Warlocks & Werewolves.* Bantam, 1963.

Shaw, Joseph T. (ed.). *The Hard-Boiled Omnibus: Early Stories from Black Mask.* S & S, 1946; PB, 1952.

Shayne, Mike (ed.). *Dangerous Dames.* Dell, 1965. 12 stories of women involved in murder.

———. *Murder in Miami.* Dell, 1959. 10 murder cases with a Miami background.

Singer, Kurt (ed.). *The Gothic Reader.* Ace, 1966.

———. *More Spy Stories.* Allen, W. H., 1955.

———. *World's Best Stories, Fact and Fiction.* Funk, 1954.

***Some Like Them Dead.* Hodder, 1960. A Crime Writers' Association anthology.

Spector, Robert Donald (ed.). *Seven Masterpieces of Gothic Horror.* Bantam, 1963.

Starrett, Vincent (ed.). *Fourteen Great Detective Stories.* Modern Lib., 1928.

———. *The World's Great Spy Stories.* World Pub., 1944.

Stefan, Hans (ed.). *The Award Espionage Reader.* Award, 1966.

Stern, Philip Van Doren (ed.). *Great Tales of Fantasy and Imagination.* Holt, H., 1942. Also published as: *The Moonlight Traveler.* Doubleday, Doran, 1943.

———. *A Midnight Reader: Great Stories of Haunting and Horror.* Holt, H., 1942.

*Stout, Rex (ed.). *Eat, Drink—and Be Buried.* Viking, 1965. Abridged edition: *For Tomorrow We Die.* MacDonald & Co., 1958. MWA anthology.

——— and Louis Greenfield (eds.). *Rue Morgue Number One.* Creative Age Press, 1946.

Street, Cecil John (ed.). *Detection Medley.* Hutchinson, 1939. U.S. titles: *The Lineup.* Dodd, 1940 and *The Avon Book of Modern Crime Stories.* Avon, 1942.

Tales from the Crypt. Ballantine, 1964.

Tales of the Incredible. Ballantine, 1965.

Tales of the Uncanny. Panther.

Tales of the Supernatural. Panther.

Terrors: A Collection of Uneasy Tales. Allan, P., 1933.

Third Mystery Book; see *The Mystery Book.*

Thomson, Christine Campbell (ed.). *More Not at Night.* Arrow Books, 1961.

———. *Not at Night: Tales That Freeze the Blood.* Selwyn, 1925; Arrow Books, 1960.

Thomson, Henry Douglas (ed.). *Great Book of Thrillers.* Odhams, 1935.

———. *The Mystery Book.* Collins, 1935; Odhams, 1935.

Thrills. Twenty Specially Selected New Stories of Crime, Mystery and Horror. Associated Newspapers, Ltd. No date.

Thwing, Eugene (ed.). *World's Best One Hundred Detective Stories.* Funk, 1929.

*Treat, Lawrence (ed.). *Murder in Mind.* Dutton, 1967. MWA anthology.

Treble, Henry A. (ed.). *Treasuries of Modern Prose: Modern Detective Stories.* First–Second series. Univ. of London Press. Second series appeared in 1932.

Van Dine, S. S., pseud; *see* Wright, Willard Huntington.

Van Thal, Herbert (ed.). *The Book of Strange Stories.* Pan, 1954.

———. *Famous Tales of the Fantastic.* Hill & Wang, 1965.

———. *The Pan Book of Horror Stories.* Pan, 1959; GM, 1966.

———. *The Fifth Pan Book of Horror Stories.* Pan, 1964.

———. *The Fourth Pan Book of Horror Stories.* Pan, 1963.

———. *The Second Pan Book of Horror Stories.* Pan, 1960.

———. *The Striking Terror.* Barker, 1963.

———. *The Third Pan Book of Horror Stories.* Pan, 1962.

———. *Told in the Dark.* Pan, 1950.

Vickers, Roy (ed.). *Best Detective Stories.* Faber, 1965.

———. *Best Police Stories.* Faber, 1966.

**———. *Crime Writers' Choice.* Hodder, 1964. A Crime Writers' Association anthology.

Wagenknecht, Edward (ed.). *Murder by Gaslight: Victorian Tales.* Prentice-Hall, 1949.

———. Six Novels of the Supernatural. Viking, 1944.

Wallace, William (ed.). *Tales of Mystery and Crime.* Ward, E., 1948.

Ward, Don (ed.). *Favorite Stories of Hypnotism.* Dodd, 1965.

Wells, Carolyn (ed.). *American Detective Stories.* Oxford, 1927.

———. *American Mystery Stories.* Oxford, 1927.

Wells, Joel; *see* Herr, Dann.

Westlake, Donald E. and William Tenn

(eds.). *Once Against the Law.* Macmillan, 1967.

Wheatley, Dennis (ed.). *A Century of Spy Stories.* Hutchinson, 1938.

Widmer, Harry (ed.). *The Hardboiled Lineup.* Lion, 1957.

Williams, Blanche Colton (ed.). *Mystery and the Detective.* Appleton-Century, 1938.

Williams, Herbert (ed.). *Terror at Night: 13 Tales of Mystery and Imagination.* Avon, 1947.

Wise, Herbert A. and Phyllis Fraser (eds.). *Great Tales of Terror and the Supernatural.* Random, 1944 (Modern Lib. Giant, 1947).

World's Great Detective Stories. Black, 1928.

World's 101 Best Detective Stories. Black, 1928.

Wright, Lee (ed.). *The Pocketbook Mystery Reader.* PB, 1942.

———. *The Pocketbook of Mystery Stories.* PB, 1941.

———. *These Will Chill You.* Bantam, 1967.

———. *Wake Up Screaming.* Bantam, 1967.

———. *Wicked Women: The Deadlier Sex.* PB, 1960. 12 stories concerning criminal females.

Wright, Willard Huntington (ed.). *Great Detective Stories.* Scribner, 1927. Also published as: *The World's Great Detective Stories,* ed. by S. S. Van Dine. Blue Ribbon Books, 1931.

Wrong, Edward M. (ed.). *Stories of Crime and Detection.* Oxford, 1926. One of the most famous collections with an outstanding introduction.

7

AWARD-WINNING MYSTERIES

In Hollywood it's the Oscar. On TV it's the Emmy. In the detective, mystery and suspense fields the equivalents are the Edgars, the Ravens, and the Silver Daggers.

Every field of endeavor desires to recognize the achievements of its finest craftsmen and to make this acknowledgment public. Once a year a committee chosen by the Mystery Writers of America picks five or six books as nominees for the various categories for which the awards are given. Edgars are awarded in these categories: best mystery novel, the best first mystery novel, the best fact crime book, the best juvenile mystery, the best mystery short story, the best mystery motion picture, the best television mystery, and the best mystery book jackets of the year.

In addition to the Edgars, special awards called Ravens are given for outstanding contributions to the mystery field. On one occasion in 1958, a special scroll was presented to Mrs. Eleanor Roosevelt honoring her husband as "a distinguished mystery fan." Another special award, the Blunt Instrument, has been given to the mystery reader of the year.

In England, it is the Silver Dagger award which is bestowed upon the authors of the four best crime books of the year by the Crime Writers' Association. In 1966 something new was added: a Sherlock Holmes calabash pipe was given to the winner of the special award created for the Detective of the Year.

Mystery Writers of America Edgar Allan Poe Awards

BEST MYSTERY NOVEL

1953 Charlotte Jay, *Beat Not the Bones*
1954 Raymond Chandler, *The Long Goodbye*
1955 Margaret Millar, *The Beast in View*
1956 Charlotte Armstrong, *A Dram of Poison*
1957 Ed Lacy, *Room to Swing*
1958 Stanley Ellin, *The Eighth Circle*
1959 Celia Fremlin, *The Hours Before Dawn*
1960 Julian Symons, *The Progress of a Crime*
1961 J. J. Marric, *Gideon's Fire*
1962 Ellis Petters, *Death and the Joyful Woman*
1963 Eric Ambler, *The Light of Day*
1964 John Le Carré, *The Spy Who Came in from the Cold*
1965 Adam Hall, *The Quiller Memorandum*

1966 Nicholas Freeling, *The King of the Rainy Country*
1967 Donald Westlake, *God Save the Mark*

BEST FIRST MYSTERY NOVEL

1945 Julius Fast, *Watchful at Night*
1946 Helen Eustis, *The Horizontal Man*
1947 Frederic Brown, *The Fabulous Clipjoint*
1948 Mildred Davis, *The Room Upstairs*
1949 Alan Green, *What a Body*
1950 Thomas Walsh, *Nightmare in Manhattan*
1951 May McMullen, *Strangle Hold*
1952 William Campbell Gault, *Don't Cry for Me*
1953 Ira Levin, *A Kiss Before Dying*
1954 Jean Potts, *Go, Lovely Rose*
1955 Lane Kauffmann, *The Perfectionist*
1956 Donald McNutt Douglass, *Rebecca's Pride*
1957 William R. Weeks, *Knock and Wait Awhile*
1958 Richard Martin Stern, *The Bright Road to Fear*
1959 Henry Slesar, *The Grey Flannel Shroud*
1960 John Holbrook Vance, *The Man in the Cage*
1961 Suzanne Blanc, *The Green Stone*
1962 Robert L. Fish, *The Fugitive*
1963 Cornelius Hirschberg, *Florentine Finish*
1964 Harry Kemelman, *Friday, the Rabbi Slept Late*
1965 John Ball, *In the Heat of the Night*
1966 Thomas Ross, *The Cold War Swap*
1967 Michael Collins, *Act of Fear*

SHORT STORY

1947 Ellery Queen for *To the Queen's Taste* and editing of *Ellery Queen's Mystery Magazine*
1948 William Irish
1949 Ellery Queen
1950 Lawrence G. Blochman for *Diagnosis: Homicide*
1951 John Collier for *Fancies and Goodnights*
1952 Philip MacDonald for *Something to Hide*
1953 Roald Dahl for *Someone Like You*
1954 Stanley Ellin for "The House Party" (*Ellery Queen's Mystery Magazine*)
1955 Philip MacDonald for "Dream No More" (*Ellery Queen's Mystery Magazine*. Included in collection *The Man Out in the Rain*)
1956 Stanley Ellin for "The Blessington Method" (*Ellery Queen's Mystery Magazine*)
1957 Gerald Kersh for "The Secret of the Bottle"
1958 William O'Farrell for "Over There Darkness" (*Sleuth*)
1959 Roald Dahl for "The Landlady" (*New Yorker*)
1960 John Durham
1961 Avram Davidson for "Affair at Lahore Cantonment" (*Ellery Queen's Mystery Magazine*)
1962 David Ely for "The Sailing Club" (*Cosmopolitan*)
1963 Leslie Ann Brownrigg
1964 Lawrence Treat for "H as in Homicide" (*Ellery Queen's Mystery Magazine*)
1965 Shirley Jackson for "The Possibility of Evil"
1966 Rhys Davies for "The Chosen One"

FACT CRIME

1947 Edward D. Radin, *Twelve Against the Law* (Duell)
1948 Marie Rodell
1949 Joseph Henry Jackson, *Bad Company* (Harcourt)
1950 Edward D. Radin for editorship of *Detective* magazine
1951 St. Clair McKelway, *True Tales from the Annals of Crime and Rascality* (Random)
1952 Erle Stanley Gardner, *Court of Last Resort* (Sloane)
1953 John Bartlow Martin, *Why Did They Kill?* (Ballantine)
1954 Charles Boswell and Lewis Thompson, *The Girl with the Scarlet Brand* (GM)
1955 Manly Wade Wellman, *Dead and Gone* (Univ. of North Carolina Press)
1956 Charles and Louise Samuels, *Night Fell on Georgia* (Dell)
1957 Harold R. Danforth and James D. Horan, *The D.A.'s Man* (Crown)

1958 Wenzell Brown, *They Died in the Chair* (Popular Lib.)
1959 Thomas Gallagher, *Fire at Sea* (Rinehart)
1960 Miriam Allen De Ford, *The Overbury Affair* (Chilton)
1961 Barrett Prettyman, Jr., *Death and the Supreme Court* (Harcourt)
1962 Francis Russell, *Tragedy in Dedham* (McGraw)
1963 Gerold Frank, *The Deed* (S & S)
1964 Anthony Lewis, *Gideon's Trumpet* (Random)
1965 Truman Capote, *In Cold Blood* (Random)
1966 Gerold Frank, *The Boston Strangler*
1967 Victoria Lincoln, *A Private Disgrace* (Putnam)

JUVENILE

1960 Phyllis A. Whitney, *The Haunted Pool* (Westminster)
1961 Edward Fenton, *The Phantom of Walkaway Hill* (Doubleday)
1962 Scott Corbett, *Cutlass Island* (Little)
1963 Phyllis A. Whitney, *Mystery of the Hidden Hand* (Westminster)
1964 Marcella Thum, *Mystery at Crane's Landing* (Dodd)
1965 Leon Ware, *The Mystery of 22 East* (Westminster)
1966 Kin Platt, *Sinbad and Me* (Chilton)
1967 Gretchen Sprague, *Signpost to Terror* (Dodd)

CRITIC

1945 Anthony Boucher
1946 William Weber. Reviewer for *Saturday Review of Literature* under name Judge Lynch
1947 Howard Haycraft for reviews in *Ellery Queen's Mystery Magazine*
1948 James Sandoe, Clayton Rawson
1949 Anthony Boucher
1950 Dorothy B. Hughes
1951 *The San Francisco Chronicle*
1952 Anthony Boucher and *The New York Times*
1953 Brett Halliday and Helen McCloy
1954 Drexel Drake of the *Chicago Tribune*
1956 Curtis W. Casewit, *Denver Post*
1960 James Sandoc, *New York Herald-Tribune*
1963 Hans Stefan Santesson. Reviewer for *Saint Mystery Magazine*
1966 John T. Winterich, *Saturday Review*

MOTION PICTURES

1945 *Murder, My Sweet*
1946 *The Killers*
1947 *Crossfire*
1948 *Call Northside 777*
1949 *The Window*
1950 *The Asphalt Jungle*
1951 *Detective Story*
1952 *Five Fingers*
1953 *The Big Heat*
1954 *Rear Window*
1955 *The Desperate Hours*
1956 No prize
1957 *Twelve Angry Men*
1958 *The Defiant Ones*
1959 *North by Northwest*
1960 *Psycho*
1961 *The Innocents*
1962 No prize
1963 *Charade*
1964 *Hush, Hush, Sweet Charlotte*
1965 *The Spy Who Came in from the Cold*
1966 *Harper*
1967 *In the Heat of the Night*

FOREIGN FILM

1948 *Jenny Lamour* (Special award)
1955 *Diabolique* (Special award)
1958 *Inspector Maigret*
1959 *Sapphire*
1960 No prize
1961 *Purple Noon*
1962 No prize
1963 *Any Number Can Play*
1964 *Séance on a Wet Afternoon*
1965 *The Ipcress File*

TELEVISION

1951 *The Web*
1952 *Dragnet*
1953 Jerome Ross, "Crime at Blossoms" (*Studio One*)
1954 Gore Vidal, "Smoke" (*Suspense*)
1955 Alvin Sapinsley, Jr., "The Sting of Death," adapted from H. F. Heard's novel *A Taste for Honey* (*Elgin Hour*)
1956 Sidney Carroll, "The Fine Art of Murder" (*Omnibus*)
1957 Howard Swanton, "Mechanical Manhunt" (*Alcoa Hour*)
1958 James Lee, "Capital Punishment" (*Omnibus*); and Adrian Spies, "Edge of Truth" (*Studio One*)
1959 David Karp, "The Empty Chair" (*The Untouchables*)
1960 Kelley Roos, "The Case of the Burning Court"; Bill Ballinger, "The Day of the Bullet"
1961 Leigh Vance and John Lemont, "Witness in the Dark"
The Defenders series (Special Raven award)
1962 A. A. Roberts, "The Problem of Cell 13"
1963 Luther Davis, "End of the World, Baby"
1964 *The Fugitive* series
1965 James Bridges, "An Unlocked Window"
1966 Jerome Ross, "Operation Rogesh" (*Mission: Impossible*)
1967 Harold Gast and Leon Tokatyn, "Tempest in a Texas Town" (*Judd for the Defense*)

RADIO

1945 Ellery Queen for *Adventures of Ellery Queen* and the Lockridges for *Mr. and Mrs. North*
1946 *The Adventures of Sam Spade*
1947 *Suspense*
1948 *Inner Sanctum*
1949 "Murder by Experts"
1950 *Dragnet*
1951 *Dragnet*
1952 *The Mysterious Traveler*
1953 E. Jack Newman, "The Shot" (*Suspense*)
1954 Stanley Niss, "The Tree" (*21st Precinct*)
1955 No prize
1956 No prize
1957 Jay McMullen, "The Galindez-Murphy Case"
1958 William N. Robson for *Suspense*

JACKET

1954 Dell Books
1955 Charles Scribner's Sons
1956 Doubleday & Co. for *Inspector Maigret and the Burglar's Wife* by Georges Simenon
1957 Harper & Bros.
1958 Dell Books
1959 Simon & Schuster
1960 Charles Scribner's Sons for Elizabeth Hely's *A Mark of Displeasure;* Dell Books for John Dickson Carr's *The Three Coffins*
1961 Walker & Co. for general excellence
1962 Crime Club (Doubleday) and Collier Books
1963 Random House and Bantam Books
1964 Crime Club (Doubleday) and Bantam Books
1965 Random House and Dell Books
1966 Crowell-Collier; Ballantine for *Some of Your Blood* by Theodore Sturgeon; and Crime Club (Doubleday) for *The Crimson Madness of Little Doom* by Mark McShane
1967 Crime Club (Doubleday) for *Perturbing Spirit* by Janet Caird and Ballantine Books for *Johnny Underground* by Patricia Moyes

GRAND MASTER

1957 Vincent Starrett
1958 Rex Stout
1960 Ellery Queen
1961 Erle Stanley Gardner
1962 John Dickson Carr
1963 George Harmon Coxe
1965 Georges Simenon
1966 Baynard Kendrick

Past Special Awards

THE EDGAR

1948 Clayton Rawson
Arthur A. Stoughton
1949 Sidney Kingsley for play *Detective Story*
John Dickson Carr for *Life of Arthur Conan Doyle*
1951 Ellery Queen
1952 Frederick Knott
1953 Mary Roberts Rinehart
1954 Agatha Christie for play *Witness for the Prosecution*
Berton Roueché for *Eleven Blue Men*. Medical detection (Little)
1956 Meyer Levin for *Compulsion*
1958 Olive Woolley Burt
1959 Lucille Fletcher
Ray Brennan
David Cooke
1960 Elizabeth Daly
1961 Thomas McDade
Frederick Knott for play *Write Me a Murder*
1962 Patrick Quentin for short story collection *Ordeal of Mrs. Snow*
E. Spencer Shew for *Companion to Murder*
Philip Reisman for documentary "Cops and Robbers"
1963 Philip Durham for *Down These Mean Streets* about Raymond Chandler (Univ. of North Carolina Press)

THE RAVEN

1952 E. T. Guymon, Jr.
1953 Thomas A. Gonzalez
Dr. Harrison Martland
Tom Lehrer for ballads parodying mystery and crime
1958 Lawrence G. Blochman
Frederic Melcher
1959 Gail Patrick Jackson for *Perry Mason* series
1960 Charles Addams
Philip Wittenberg
1961 Herbert Brodkin
1965 Rev. O. C. Edwards for article "The Gospel According to 007" (*Living Church*)
1966 *Ellery Queen's Mystery Magazine*

MYSTERY READER

1956 Dorothy Kilgallen
1959 Phyllis McGinley
1966 Richard Watts, Jr.

A SCROLL

1958 Mrs. Franklin D. Roosevelt

Dodd, Mead Awards

Between the years 1936 and 1954, Dodd, Mead & Company offered a prize of $2,500 against royalties for the best mystery and detective novel by an author previously unpublished under their Red Badge imprint. This award, which was judged by Dodd, Mead's editorial staff, was offered on a semi-annual basis, but prizes were not always awarded.

1936 Clifford Knight, *The Affair of the Scarlet Crab*
1937 Marco Page, *Fast Company*
1938 Hugh Pentecost, *Cancelled in Red*
1939 David Keith, *A Matter of Iodine*
1940 Susannah Shane, *Lady in Lilac*
1941 Eleanor Kelly Sellars, *Murder à la Mode*
1942 James Wellard, *The Snake in the Grass*
1943 Christianna Brand, *Heads You Lose*
Ruth Sawtell Wallis, *Too Many Bones*
1944 Lawrence Lariar, *The Man with the Lumpy Nose*
1945 Elinor Chamberlain, *Appointment in Manila*
Franklin Pell, *Hangman's Hill*
1946 Lee Wilson, *This Deadly Dark*
1947 Helen Steers, *Death Will Find Me*
1948 William P. McGivern, *But Death Runs Faster*
Ursula Curtiss, *Voice Out of Darkness*
1949 Bart Spicer, *The Dark Light*
1950 Brandon Bird, *Death in Four Colors*

1951 No prize
1952 No prize
1953 No prize
1954 Evelyn Berckman, *The Evil of Time*
Oliver Gard, *The Seventh Chasm*

The Crime Writers' Association Awards

1955 Winston Graham, *The Little Walls.* Runners-up: Leigh Howard for *Blind Date,* Ngaio Marsh for *Scales of Justice,* and Margot Bennett for *The Man Who Didn't Fly.*

1956 Edward Geierson, *The Second Man.* Runners-up: Sarah Gainham for *Time Right Deadly,* Arthur Upfield for *Man of Two Tribes,* and J. J. Marric for *Gideon's Week.*

1957 Julian Symons, *The Colour of Murder.* Runners-up: Ngaio Marsh for *Off with His Head,* George Milner for *Your Money and Your Life,* and Douglas Rutherford for *The Long Echo.*

1958 Margot Bennett, *Someone from the Past.* Runners-up: Margery Allingham for *Hide My Eyes,* James Byrom for *Or Be He Dead,* and John Sherwood for *Undiplomatic Exit.*

1959 Eric Ambler, *A Passage of Arms.* Runners-up: James Mitchell for *The Way Back,* and Menna Gallie for *Strike for a Kingdom.* (Runners-up reduced from three to two).

1960 Lionel Davidson, *The Night of Wenceslas.* Runners-up: Mary Stewart for *My Brother Michael,* and Julian Symons for *The Progress of a Crime.*

1961 Mary Kelly, *The Spoilt Kill.* Runners-up: John Le Carré for *Call for the Dead* and Allan Prior for *One Away.*

1962 Joan Fleming, *When I Grow Rich.* Runners-up: Eric Ambler for *The Light of Day* and Colin Watson for *Hopjoy Was Here.*

1963 John Le Carré, *The Spy Who Came in from the Cold.* Runners-up: Nicholas Freeling for *Guns Before Butter* and William Haggard for *The High Wire.*

1964 H. R. F. Keating, *The Perfect Murder* (best British crime novel), and Patricia Highsmith, *The Two Faces of January* (best foreign crime novel). Runners-up: Gavin Lyall for *The Most Dangerous Game* and Ross Macdonald for *The Chill.*

1965 Gavin Lyall, *Midnight Plus One* (best British crime novel), Ross Macdonald, *The Far Side of the Dollar* (best foreign crime novel). Runners-up: Dick Francis for *For Kicks* and Emma Lathen for *Accounting for Murder.*

GRAND PRIX DE LITTÉRATURE POLICIÈRE

The Grand Prix de Littérature Policière is awarded in two categories: French detective stories and foreign detective stories translated into French. The awards were created in June, 1948 under the title: Grand Prix du Club des Detectives. The prizes are exclusively honorary and are given annually. Thirteen copies of the work must be submitted; a maximum of two titles. There is a jury of a dozen persons which makes the final choices.

1948 Leo Malet, *Le cinquième procédé* (S.E.P.E.)
Francis Noyes Hart, *Le procès Bellamy.* Published in English as: *The Bellamy Trial* (Le Portulan)

1949 Odette Sorenson, *La parole est au mort* (Le Portulan)
Patrick Quentin, *Puzzle au Mexique.* Published in English as: *Puzzle for Pilgrims* (Presses de la Cité)

1950 Géo-Charles Veran, *Jeux pour mourir*
Martha Albrand, *Les morts ne parlent plus.* Published in English as: *After Midnight*

1951 Germaine et Jacques Decrest, *Fumées sans feu* (Flore)
Joel T. Rogers, *Jeux de massacre* (Flammarion)

1952 André Piljean, *Passons la monnaie* (Editions Gallimard)
Pat MacGerr, *Bonnes à tuer* (Flammarion)

1953 J. P. Conty, *Operation odyssée* (Editions de la Porte Saint-Martin)
Geoffrey Hall, *L'Homme de nulle part* (Flammarion)

1954 François Brigneau, *La beauté qui meurt* (André Martel)
William Irish, *Un pied dans la tomb* (Presses de la Cité)
1955 M. G. Morris, *Assassin mon frère* (Presses de la Cité)
Michael Gilbert, *Un mort dans le tunnel* (Editions René Julliard)
1956 Joseph Hayes, *Terreur dans la maison.* Published in English as: *The Desperate Hours.* (Librairie Hachette)
Guy Venayre, *Les petites mains de la justice* (Editions Denoël)
Michel Lebrun, *Pleins feux sur Sylvie* (Presses de la Cité)
Charles Williams, *Peaux de bananes* (Editions Gallimard)
1957 Frédéric Dard: *Le bourreau pleure* (Editions Fleuve Noir)
Patricia Highsmith: Monsieur Ripley. Published in English as: *The Talented Mr. Ripley* (Calmann-Lévy Editeur)
1958 Fred Kassak, *On n'enterre pas le dimanche* (Editions de L'Arabesque)
Chester Himes, *La reine des pommes* (Editions Gallimard)
1959 Paul Gerard, *Devil en rouge* (Presses de la Cité)
Donald Downes, *Bourreau, fais ton metier* (Editions Gallimard)
1960 Hubert Monteilhet, *Les mantes religieuses.* Published in English as: *The Praying Mantises.* (Editions Donoël)
Thomas Sterling, *Le tricheur de Venise.* Published in English as: *The Evil of the Day* (Editions de Trévise)
1962 Pierre Forquin, *Le procès du diable* (Editions Denoël)
Susan Blanc, *Feu vert pour la mort* (Presses de la Cité)
1963 Sébastien Japrisot, *Piège pour Cendrillon.* Published in English as: *A Trap for Cinderella* (Editions Denoël)
Shelley Smith, *La fin des fins* (Presses de la Cité)
1964 Michel Carnal, *La jeune morte* (Editions Fleuve Noir)
John MacDonald, *La tete sur le billot* (Gallimard)
1965 Marc Delory: *Bateau en Espagne* (Editions Denoël)
Nicolas Freeling, *Frontière belge* (Librairie Plon)
1966 Lawrence Oriol, *Interne de Service*

Source of information: *Guide de prix litteraires,* Cercle de la Librairie, Paris.

8

WRITINGS ON THE MYSTERY NOVEL

For the mystery fan, the next best thing to reading a detective story is to read about one. Ever since Poe wrote that first tale back in 1841, there has always been someone around to tell you (1) Why you should like it; (2) Why you shouldn't like it; (3) What's wrong with it; (4) What's right about it; (5) Why you are fascinated by them; (6) Why they bore the daylights out of you; (7) Why they can't possibly last much longer; (8) Why they will go on forever; (9) Why there must be fixed rules for writing them; and (10) Why a critic is so delighted when a new author breaks them.

For a type of literature that has been popular for more than a hundred years, the critical writing about it is not at all extensive. From 1841 to 1878, the references were fleeting indeed. Poe's work, as popular as it was, did not attract any imitators at home. Most of the critical attention came from abroad. Even after *The Leavenworth Case,* the critics limited themselves to an occasional pot shot at the general field. It was a rare American or English anthology which even referred to this type of literature. It is only in recent years that any serious critical attention has been given to the specific contributions to this form of literary achievement.

Not until recently did the mystery, detective and suspense fans get something they had been searching for for a long time. In October, 1967, the first issue of *The Armchair Detective* appeared. Its editor is Allen J. Hubin, who has a private collection of about seven thousand books. The first issue contained articles by the late William S. Baring-Gould on Sax Rohmer; G. C. Ramsey telling about the book he wrote on Agatha Christie; James Keddie, Jr. reminiscing about the life of a detective story collector. After its first appearance, Anthony Boucher spoke highly of it in the *New York Times Book Review,* and orders began to pour into Mr. Hubin by the hundreds. Its future is assured, and any readers wishing to subscribe to the magazine, can send $3 to Allen J. Hubin, 3656 Midland, White Bear Lake, Minnesota, 55110, and get on the mailing list.

The material in the following section is divided into two parts: First, the critical material in books; second, the critical material in periodicals and pamphlets. Included among the books are Haycraft's *Murder for Pleasure* and *The Art of the Mystery Story,* which should be required reading for anyone seriously interested in this field. Included also are Murch's *The Development of the Detective Story,* Thomson's *Masters of Mystery,* and Carolyn Wells' *Technique of the Mystery Story.* These five are the major works in this area. This compiler hopes that with the help of the following material someone will be sufficiently inspired to do comprehensive research on this fascinating subject.

(I)

American Detective Stories. London: Pilot Press, 1944. Read the introduction by Maurice Richardson.

Barzun, Jacques (ed.). *The Delights of Detection.* New York: Criterion Books, 1961. Read the introduction by the editor, "Detection and the Literary Art."

———. *The Energies of Art.* New York: Harper & Bros., 1956. See "From Phedre to Sherlock Holmes."

Bates, George, Booksellers, London. *Catalogue* of rare and interesting books illustrating the detective and mystery story, offered by George Bates. London, 1935.

Bell, J. *et al. Crime in Good Company; Essays on Criminals and Crime-Writing.* London: Constable & Co., 1959.

Birthday Tribute to Rex Stout. New York: Viking Press, 1965. Pamphlet.

Block, Eugene B. *The Wizard of Berkeley.* New York: Coward, McCann, Inc., 1958. This is a true case history of a real private eye.

Boucher, Anthony. *Ellery Queen: A Double Profile.* Boston: Little, Brown, 1951. Pamphlet.

——— (ed.). *Great American Detective Stories.* Cleveland: World Publishing Co., 1945. Read the introduction by the editor.

Bruccoli, Matthew J. *Raymond Chandler: A Checklist.* Kent, Ohio: Kent State University Press, 1968.

Cambiaire, Celestin P. *The Influence of Edgar Allan Poe in France.* New York: G. E. Stechert & Co., 1927. Chapters on the early history of detective fiction.

Carr, John Dickson. *Three Coffins.* New York: Harper & Bros., 1935 (Published in England as: *The Hollow Man.* London: William Collins Sons & Co., 1935). See "The Locked Room Lecture." Also in Haycraft's *Art of the Mystery Story.* Simon and Schuster, 1946.

Carter, John. *Books and Book-Collectors.* Cleveland: World Publishing Co., 1957. See "Collecting Detective Fiction." This may also be found in Haycraft's *Art of the Detective Story.* Simon and Schuster, 1946.

Chandler, F. W. *The Literature of Roguery.* Boston: Houghton, Mifflin, 1907. Read "The Literature of Crime Detection."

Chesterton, G. K. *Autobiography.* London: Hutchinson & Co., 1949.

——— (ed.). *A Century of Detective Stories.* London: Hutchinson & Co., 1935. Read the introduction by Chesterton.

———. *The Defendant.* London: Brimley Johnson & Ince, Ltd., 1901. See the essay "A Defense of the Detective Story."

Comber, Leon (ed.). *The Strange Cases of Magistrate Pao, Chinese Tales of Crime and Detection.* Rutland, Vt.: Charles E. Tuttle, 1964. Read the introduction which is an explanation of the long life and history of the Chinese detective story.

Cox, Anthony Berkeley. *The Second Shot.* New York: Doubleday, Doran, 1931. Read the foreword.

Crouse, Russell. *Murder Won't Out.* New York: Doubleday, Doran, 1932. See "The Murder of Mary Cecilia Rogers." A true account of the real murder on which Poe based his short story "The Mystery of Marie Rogêt," one of the cornerstones of detective literature.

Cruse, A. *After the Victorians.* London: George Allen & Unwin, 1938. See "Crime Fiction."

Cullen, Tom. *Autumn of Terror, Jack the Ripper: His Crimes and Times.* London: Bodley Head, 1965.

Cuppy, Will (ed.). *Murder Without Tears.* New York: Sheridan House, 1946. Read the introduction by the editor.

———. *World's Great Mystery Stories.* Cleveland: World Publishing Co., 1943. Read the introduction by the editor.

Davis, David Brian. *Homicide in American Fiction, 1798–1860.* Ithaca, New York: Cornell University Press, 1957. Data on early novelists who wrote murder and detective stories in the 19th century.

Dickens, Charles. *Letters.* New York: Macmillan, 1893. These letters reveal Dickens' keen interest in police methods being developed in London.

Doyle, A. Conan. *The Complete Sherlock Holmes.* New York: Garden City Publishing Co., 1938. Read the introduction by Christopher Morley.

Felstead, S. Theodore. *Shades of Scotland Yard*. London: John Long, 1950. A true account of the yard. Provides an interesting background to fictional accounts.

Fiedler, Leslie A. (ed.). *Art of the Essay*. New York: Thomas Y. Crowell Co., 1958. Read the essay by George Orwell, "Raffles and Miss Blandish."

Forbes, Anita P. (ed.). *Essays for Discussion*. New York: Harper & Bros., 1931. See "Cold Chills of 1928."

Ford, Ford Madox. *The March of Literature*. New York: Dial Press, 1938. See pp. 831–833.

Freeman, Richard Austin. *Dr. Thorndyke's Crime File*. New York: Dodd, Mead, 1941. Omnibus edition, edited by P. M. Stone. See "The Art of the Detective Story" and "Thorndykiana" by Freeman and P. M. Stone.

Gant, Richard. *Ian Fleming: The Man with the Golden Pen*. New York: Lancer, n.d.

Gardiner, Harold Charles. *In All Conscience*. New York: Doubleday, 1959. See "The Barbarians are Within the Gates."

Gass, Sherlock Bronson. *The Crier of the Shops*. Boston: Marshall Jones, 1925. Read "Desipere in Loco."

Gollomb, Joseph. *Scotland Yard*. London: Hutchinson, 1926. An accurate account of Scotland Yard, in contrast to the many distorted versions found in the fiction of the day.

Graves, Robert and Alan Hodge. *The Long Weekend*. New York: Macmillan Co., 1941. See pp. 289–291 on crime writers in Great Britain.

Gruber, Frank. *The Pulp Jungle*. Los Angeles: Sherbourne Press, 1947.

Hardy, Thomas J. *Books on the Shelf*. London: Philip Allan & Co., 1934. See "The Romance of Crime."

Harrison, Richard. *C.I.D. and F.B.I.* London: Muller, 1956.

Hart, J. D. *The Popular Book; a History of America's Literary Taste*. New York: Oxford University Press, 1950.

Hawthorne, Julian (ed.). *Library of the World's Best Mystery and Detective Stories*. New York: Review of Reviews Company, 1907. 6 vols. Read the introduction by Charles Johnston in the Oriental Volume.

———. *The Lock and Key Library*. New York: Review of Reviews Company, 1909. Read the introduction, "Riddle Stories."

Haycraft, Howard (ed.). *The Art of the Mystery Story: A Collection of Critical Essays*. New York: Simon and Schuster, 1946. With a commentary by Mr. Haycraft. This was the first collection in book form of the critical writings about mystery, crime and detective stories. Contains essays by Nicholas Blake, Issac Anderson, Anthony Boucher, Judge Lynch, etc. Many of the introductions to other books listed in the bibliography can be found here if the original book cannot be obtained.

———. *The Boys' Book of Great Detective Stories*. New York: Harper & Bros., 1938. Read the preface and the introductions to individual stories. Also the *Boys' Second Book of Great Detective Stories*. New York: Harper & Bros., 1940. Read the introduction and "About the Author and the Story" at the beginning of each story.

———. *Murder for Pleasure: The Life and Times of the Detective Story*. New York: Appleton-Century, 1941. The most comprehensive history of the detective story ever written in America. Contains an excellent introduction by Nicholas Blake, "The Detective Story—Why?" Also in Haycraft's *Art of the Mystery Story*. Simon and Schuster, 1946.

Honce, C. *Mark Twain's Associated Press Speech*. New York: Privately printed, 1940.

———. *A Sherlock Holmes Birthday*. New York: Privately printed, 1938.

Hughes, Rupert. *The Complete Detective*. New York: Sheridan House, 1950. Read the first chapter, "The Detective in Fact and Fiction."

Indianapolis (Ind.) Public Library. *Some Less Known Detective Stories*. Indianapolis, n.d.

Jesse, F. Tennyston. *Solange Stories*. New York: Macmillan Co., 1931. Read the foreword.

Johnston, Alva. *The Case of Erle Stanley Gardner*. New York: William Morrow & Co., 1947.

Knox, Ronald A. and Henry Harrington (eds.). *The Best English Detective Stories of 1928*. New York: Liveright Publishing Corp., 1929. Read the introduction which includes the editors' "A Detective Story Decalogue" which may also be found in Haycraft's *Art of the Mystery Story*. New York: Simon and Schuster, 1946.

Landmarks in Medicine: Laity Lectures. New York: Appleton-Century, 1929. See "Dr. Watson and Sherlock Holmes" by H. S. Martland.

Leacock, Stephen. *Here Are My Lectures and Stories*. New York: Dodd, Mead, 1937. Read "Murder at $2.50 a Crime." This essay is also in Haycraft's *Art of the Mystery Story*. Simon & Schuster, 1946.

Leonard, Sterling A. and R. C. Pooley (eds.). *Introducing Essays*. Chicago: Scott, Foresman, 1933. See "On the Floor of the Library" by Simeon Strunsky.

Lucas, Edward V. *A Fronded Isle and Other Essays*. New York: Doubleday, Doran, 1928. See "Murder and Motives."

———. *Only the Other Day*. Philadelphia: Lippincott, 1937. See "My Murder Story." This essay may also be found in Haycraft's *Art of the Mystery Story*. Simon and Schuster, 1946.

Mabbott, Thomas Ollive. *The Pleasures of Publishing*. New York: Columbia University Press, 1941.

MacDonald, John M. *The Murderer and His Victim*. Springfield, Ill.: Charles C. Thomas, Publishers, 1961. See "Homicide in Fiction" by Stuart Boyd.

MacGowan, K. (ed.). *Sleuths: Twenty-three Great Detectives of Fiction and Their Best Stories*. New York: Harcourt, 1931. Read the introduction and "Who's Who" accounts of detectives preceding each story.

Martienssen, Anthony. *Crime and the Police*. Penguin, 1951. A knowledgeable critique of the methods of detective story writers.

Masterman, Walter S. *The Wrong Letter*. New York: E. P. Dutton & Co., 1926. See the preface by G. K. Chesterton.

Matthews, Brander. *Inquiries and Opinions*. New York: Charles Scribner's Sons, 1907. See "Poe and the Detective Story."

Meet the Detective. London: George Allen & Unwin, 1935. These are reprints of BBC broadcasts. 15 English detective writers tell about their creations.

Milne, A. A. *By Way of Introduction*. New York: E. P. Dutton & Co., 1929. See "Introducing Crime."

———. *If I May*. New York: E. P. Dutton & Co., 1921. See "The Watson Touch."

Murch, Alma E. *The Development of the Detective Novel*. London: Peter Owen, 1958.

Nash, Odgen. *The Face Is Familiar*. Boston: Little, Brown, 1940. Read "Don't Guess, Let Me Tell You." Reprinted from *The New Yorker*.

Nelson, James (ed.). *The Complete Murder Sampler*. New York: Doubleday & Co., 1946. Read the introduction.

Noyes, Edward S. (ed.). *Readings on the Modern Essay*. Boston: Houghton, Mifflin Co., 1933. See "On Detective Novels" by G. K. Chesterton.

Odell, Robin. *Jack the Ripper in Fact and Fiction*. London: Harrap, 1965.

Overton, Grant M. *American Nights' Entertainment*. New York: D. Appleton & Co., 1923. See "A Breathless Chapter."

Pearson, Edmund L. *Books in Black or Red*. New York: Macmillan Co., 1923. See "With Acknowledgments to Thomas De Quincey."

Pearson, John. *The Life of Ian Fleming*. New York: McGraw-Hill Book Co., 1966.

Peck, Harry T. *Studies in Several Literatures*. New York: Dodd, Mead, 1909. See "The Detective Story."

Pence, Raymond W. (ed.). *Essays by Present-Day Writers*. New York: Macmillan Co., 1924. See "On the Floor of the Library," by Simeon Strunsky.

Pope-Hennessy, Una. *Edgar Allan Poe, A Critical Biography*. New York: Macmillan Co., 1934.

Pritchard, Francis Henry (ed.). *Essays of Today: An Anthology*. Boston: Little, Brown & Co., 1924. See "A Defense of Detective Stories" by G. K. Chesterton. This essay may also be found in Haycraft's *Art of the Mystery Story*. Simon and Schuster, 1946.

Queen, Ellery (ed.). *Challenge to the Reader: An Anthology*. New York: Frederick A. Stokes Co., 1936. See the introduction, and afterwords to the individual stories.

———. *The Literature of Crime*. Boston: Little, Brown & Co., 1950. See the introduction.

———. *101 Years' Entertainment: The Great Detective Stories, 1841–1941.* Boston: Little, Brown & Co., 1941. The introductory essay may be found also in Haycraft's *Art of the Mystery Story.* Simon and Schuster, 1946.

———. *Queen's Quorum: A History of the Detective-Crime Short Story as revealed by the 106 most important books published in the field since 1845.* Boston: Little, Brown & Co., 1951.

———. *Rogue's Gallery, The Great Criminals of Modern Fiction.* Boston: Little, Brown & Co., 1945. See the foreword and other essays.

Rawson, Clayton. *Death from a Top Hat.* New York: G. P. Putnam's Sons, 1938. See the first chapter for a critique of the detective story.

Reynolds, Francis Joseph (ed.). *Master Tales of Mystery.* New York: P. F. Collier & Co., 1915. 2 vols. Read the introduction.

Reynolds, Quentin. *Police Headquarters.* London: Cassell, 1956.

Rhodes, John (ed.). *A Detection Medley.* London: Hutchinson & Co., 1939. (Also published as *The Line-up.* New York: Dodd, Mead, 1940.) The essays are by the various members of the Detection Club such as John Rhode, A. A. Milne, etc.

Roberts, Denys K. (ed.). *Titles to Fame.* London: Thomas Nelson & Sons, 1937. Read the essay by Dorothy L. Sayers entitled "Gaudy Night" which is an account of the creation of her well-known fictional character, Lord Peter Wimsey. This essay may also be found in Haycraft's *Art of the Mystery Story.* Simon and Schuster, 1946.

Roberts, Kenneth L. *For Authors Only and Other Gloomy Essays.* New York: Doubleday, Doran, 1935. See the title essay, "For Authors Only."

Robinson, Henry Morton. *Science Versus Crime.* London: George Bell & Sons, 1937.

Rodell, Marie. *Mystery Fiction; Theory and Techniques.* London: Hammond & Co., 1954.

Roe, Frederick C. *Modern France.* London: Longmans, 1955. Contains considerable material on the French detective novel.

Rosenbach, A. S. W. *A Book Hunter's Holiday.* Boston: Houghton Mifflin Co., 1936. See "The Trail of Scarlet."

Russell, William ("Waters"). *Recollections of a Detective Police Officer.* London: J. and C. Brown, 1856.

Sandoe, James (ed.). *Murder: Plain and Fanciful With Some Milder Malefactions.* New York: Sheridan House, 1948. Read the foreword.

Sayers, Dorothy L. (ed.). *Great Short Stories of Detection, Mystery and Horror.* 3 vols. London: Victor Gollancz, Ltd., 1928–1932. (Also published as: *The Omnibus of Crime.* New York: Harcourt, Brace & Co., 1929; *The Second Omnibus of Crime.* New York: Coward-McCann, 1932; and *The Third Omnibus of Crime.* New York: Coward-McCann, 1935.) Read the introduction which is a fine short history of the mystery story.

———. *Tales of Detection.* London: J. M. Dent & Sons, 1936. Read the introduction. This may also be found in Haycraft's *Art of the Mystery Story.* Simon and Schuster, 1946.

Scott, Sir Harold (ed.). *The Concise Encyclopedia of Crime and Criminals.* New York: Hawthorn Books, 1961.

Scribner's Detective Fiction: A Collection of First and a Few Early Editions. New York: Scribner Book Store, 1934.

Seaborne, Edward A. (ed.). *The Detective in Fiction: A Posse of Eight.* London: George Bell & Sons, 1931. Read the introduction.

Shiel, Matthew P. *Science, Life and Literature.* London: Williams & Norgate, 1950. See the author's explanation of how "Prince Zaleski" was created.

Snelling, O. F. *007—James Bond: A Report.* London: The Holland Press, 1964. (Published in the U.S. by Signet, 1965). An in-depth report on the truly amazing James Bond.

Solmes, Alwyn. *The English Policeman, 1871–1935.* London: George Allen & Unwin, 1935. Contains material on English crime fiction.

Starrett, Vincent. *Books Alive.* New York: Random House, 1940. See "From Poe to Poirot."

———. *The Private Life of Sherlock Holmes.* New York: Macmillan Co., 1933. The title essay from the book may be found in Haycraft's *Art of the Mystery Story.* Simon and Schuster, 1946.

——— (ed.). *Fourteen Great Detective Stories.* New York: Modern Library, 1928. Read the essay, "Of Detective Literature."

———. *World's Great Spy Stories.* Cleveland: World Publishing Co., 1944. Read the introduction, and the brief forewords to individual stories.

Stevenson, William Bruce (comp.). *Detective Fiction.* London: Cambridge University Press, 1958.

Stout, Rex. "Crime in Fiction." In *Saturday Review Reader, An Anthology.* New York: Bantam Books, 1951.

Strunsky, Simeon. *Sinbad and His Friends.* New York: Henry Holt & Co., 1921. See "On the Floor of the Library." *See also,* entries for Anita P. Forbes, Sterling A. Leonard, and Raymond W. Pence.

The Sunday Times (London). *The Hundred Best Crime Stories.* Compiled by Julian Symons. London: 1959. Good introduction by Symons.

Sutherland, Scott. *Blood in Their Ink.* London: Stanley Paul & Co., 1953.

Swinnerton, Frank A. *The Georgian Literary Scene.* London: Hutchinson & Co., 1938. See "A Postwar Symptom."

Symons, Julian. *The Detective Story in Britain.* London: Longmans, Green & Co., 1962. A very good short history of detective fiction.

Thomson, Sir Basil. *The Story of Scotland Yard.* London: Grayson & Grayson, Ltd., 1935. See introduction.

Thomson, Henry Douglas. *Masters of Mystery: A Study of the Detective Story.* London: William Collins Sons & Co., 1931. One of the earliest studies of the detective story. A selection from the opening chapter may be found in Haycraft's *Art of the Mystery Novel.* Simon and Schuster, 1946.

Tinsley, William. *Random Recollections of an Old Publisher.* Simpkin, Marshall, Hamilton, Kent & Co., Ltd., 1900. Contains material on publishing of detective fiction.

Van Dine, S. S., pseud; *see* Wright, Willard Huntington.

Vollmer, August and A. E. Parker. *Crime, Crooks and Cops.* New York: Funk & Wagnalls Co., 1937.

Vries, P. H. de. *Poe and After; the Detective Story Investigated.* Amsterdam: Bakker, 1956.

Wagenknecht, Edward (ed.). *Murder by Gaslight: Victorian Tales.* New York: Prentice-Hall, 1949. Read the introduction by the author.

Warren, Dale (ed.). *What Is a Book?* Boston: Houghton Mifflin Co., 1935. Read "On Crime Fiction," by Valentine Williams.

Wells, Carolyn. *Technique of the Mystery Story.* Springfield, Mass.: Home Correspondence School, 1929.

Wilson, Edmund. *A Literary Chronicle, 1920–50.* New York: Farrar, Straus and Cudahy, 1950. Read "Why Do People Read Detective Stories?," "Who Cares Who Killed Roger Ackroyd?," and "Mr. Holmes, They Were the Footprints of a Gigantic Hound!"

Wood, C. W. *Memorials of Mrs. Henry Wood.* London: Bentley, 1894. Memoirs of one of the earliest and most prolific of detective story writers.

Wright, Lee (ed.). *The Pocket Book of Great Detectives.* New York: Pocket Books, 1941. Read the introduction by Alfred Hitchcock.

Wright, Willard Huntington. *The Great Detective Stories.* New York: Charles Scribner's Sons, 1927. Read the introduction. This may also be found in Haycraft's *The Art of the Mystery Story.* Simon and Schuster, 1946.

———. *Philo Vance Murder Cases.* (Omnibus vol.) London and New York: Charles Scribner's Sons, 1936. Includes the 20 rules for writing detective stories. The rules may also be found in Haycraft's *Art of the Mystery Story.* Simon and Schuster, 1946.

Wrong, Edward Murray (ed.). *Crime and Detection.* London and New York: Oxford University Press, 1926. Read the introduction. This may also be found in Haycraft's *Art of the Mystery Story.* Simon and Schuster, 1946.

(II)

Abbot, A. "True Story Haunted Him," *Reader's Digest* (October, 1945).

Adams, C. F. "Motivation in Mystery Fiction," *Writer* (May, 1942).

Adams, E. R. "Meet the Private Detective," *Canadian Business* (February, 1949).

Adams, J. "Detective-Fiction Game," *Overland Monthly* (August, 1932).

Allan, A. K. "I Write Puzzling Stories," *Profitable Hobbies* (August, 1953).

Allingham, Margery. "Party of One," *Holiday* (September, 1963).

"American View of English Detective Fiction," *Bookman* (London), (July, 1932).

Amis, Kingsley. "My Favorite Sleuths," *Playboy* (December, 1966). A dossier on fiction's most famous detectives.

"And Is It Ever True?" *Times Literary Supplement* (London), (June 23, 1961).

"Antecedents and Past Performance and Future Plans of Hugh North," *Publishers' Weekly* (August 23, 1941).

Auden, W. H. "Guilty Vicarage: Notes on the Detective Story by an Addict," *Harper* (May, 1948). Also in *The Art of the Essay*. New York: Thomas Y. Crowell Co., 1958.

Aydelotte, W. O. "Detective Story as a Historical Source," *Yale Review* (September, 1949).

Bainbridge, J. "Ellery Queen: Crime Made Him Famous and His Authors Rich," *Life* (November, 1943).

Barzun, Jacques. "Detection and the Literary Art," *The New Republic* (April 24, 1961).

———. "Party of One," *Holiday* (July, 1958).

———. "Suspense Suspended," *American Scholar* (Fall, 1958).

Bauer, H. C. "Seasoned to Taste," *Wilson Library Bulletin* (June, 1957).

Bazelon, David T. "Dashiell Hammett's Private Eye: No Loyalty Beyond the Job," *Commentary* (May, 1949).

Beattie, A. B. "Whet Your Wits on a Clue," *Survey* (July 15, 1930).

Becker, M. L. "Reader's Guide: Plots for Mystery Stories," *Saturday Review of Literature* (March 25, 1933).

Benét, Stephen. "Bigger and Better Murders," *Bookman* (May, 1926).

Benét, William Rose. "Here's to Crime," *Saturday Review of Literature* (February 8, 1928).

Bester, A. "Writing the Radio Mystery," *Writer* (December, 1951).

Bishop, J. P. "Georges Simenon: Adventures of Maigret," *The New Republic* (March 10, 1941).

Black, J. M., Jr. "There Is No Sleuth Like Holmes," *Rotarian* (August, 1947).

"Blood and Thunder Yen," *Literary Digest* (June 21, 1930).

Bogan, Louise. "Time of the Assassins," *The Nation* (April 22, 1944). "Discussion," *The Nation* (May 27, 1944).

"Bookbag of Thrillers," *Vogue* (December, 1965).

Boucher, Anthony. "Ethics of the Mystery Novel," *Tricolor* (October, 1944). Also in Haycraft's *Art of the Mystery Novel.*

———. "It's Murder, Amigos: The Mystery Story Takes Root in Latin America," *Publishers' Weekly* (April 19, 1947).

———. "Murder Up-to-date," *Writer* (July, 1954).

———. Reply on "Thinker and the Tough Guy," *Commonweal* (December 23, 1949).

Boutell, C. B. "England's Other Crisis," *Publisher's Weekly* (April 15, 1939). How Howard Spring of the *Evening Standard* wrestled with mystery fiction.

Boynton, H. W. "Adventures and Riddles," *Bookman* (May, 1919).

Bremner, M. "Crime Fiction for Intellectuals," *20th Century* (September, 1954).

Brisbane, P. "A Poll of Mystery Fans," *Publishers' Weekly* (August 10, 1940).

——— and Carpenter, C. "Mouthpiece for Murder," *Publishers' Weekly* (March 15, 1941). Increasing circulation of mysteries in a rental library.

Brophy, B. "Detective Fiction: A Modern Myth of Violence?" *Hudson Review* (Spring, 1965).

Brown, H. "Sherlock Holmes and the Pygmies," *Woman's Home Companion* (November, 1930).

Brown, W. "Defense of the Bedside Pad," *Writer* (September, 1965).

Burack, A. S. "Writing Detective and Mystery Fiction," *Writer* (July, 1945, rev., 1967).

Campbell, A. "Thrillers for Eggheads," *The New Republic* (July 3, 1965).

Carr, John Dickson. "Murder-Fancier Recommends," *Harper* (July, 1965).

——— and Taylor, R. L. "Profiles: Two Authors in an Attic," *The New Yorker* (September 15, 1951).

"Case of the Mystery Writer," *Saturday Review* (July 16, 1958). An account of Erle Stanley Gardner's success as a mystery writer.

Casey, R. J. "Oh, England! Full of Sin as Discovered by a Chronic Reader of English Detective and Mystery Stories," *Scribner's Magazine* (April, 1937). Also found in Haycraft's *The Art of the Mystery Story*. New York: Simon and Schuster, 1946.

"Century of Thrills and Chills: Ellery Queen Meets the Critics," *Wilson Library Bulletin* (April, 1942). Transcription of a *Speaking of Books* broadcast.

Chandler, Raymond. "The Simple Art of Murder," *Saturday Review* (April 15, 1950). Also in *The Art of the Essay*. New York: *Crowell,* 1946, and in Haycraft's *The Art of the Mystery Story*. New York: Simon and Schuster, 1946.

———. "Casual Notes on the Mystery Novel," *Writer* (July, 1963).
Charteris, Leslie. "Saint Goes West," *Life* (May 19, 1941).
———. "The Saint on TV," *Saint Mystery Magazine* (August, 1965). Also condensed in *Writer* (February, 1966).
Chesterton, C. "Art and the Detective," *Temple Bar* (London), (October, 1906). Also in *Living Age* (November 24, 1906).
Chevally, A. "Letter from France," *Saturday Review of Literature* (December 13, 1930).
"The Chinese Apathy Toward Crime Detection," *Literary Digest* (September 23, 1933).
Cohen, R. "Private Eyes and Public Critics," *Partisan Review* (Spring, 1957).
Colburn, Grace I. "Detective Story in Germany and Scandinavia," *Bookman* (December, 1909).
Collins, H. "Your Literary IQ: Ten More Famous Detectives," *Saturday Review of Literature* (January 29, 1940).
"Columbia Surveys the Pleasures of Mystery Reading," *Publishers' Weekly* (April 26, 1941).
Connell, S. M. "Crime Does Pay," *Wilson Library Bulletin* (November, 1951).
Corbett, J. E. "Art of Writing Thrillers," *Contemporary Review* (October, 1952).
Coxe, G. H. "Characters for Mystery Fiction," *Writer* (September, 1959).
———. "Starting That Mystery Book," *Writer* (December, 1940).
Crane, F. "Crime Pays Two Cents a Word," *Writer* (May, 1941).
———. "Innocent Ones: Finding Characters," *Writer* (December, 1953).
———. "Research for the Mystery Writer," *Writer* (February, 1965).
Creasey, John. "Mystery the World Over," *Rotarian* (December, 1957).
"Crime and the Reader," *Nation* (February 13, 1908).
"Crime, Detection and Society," *Times Literary Supplement* (London), (June 23, 1961).
"Crime Should Be Credible," *Saturday Review of Literature* (October 8, 1932).
"Crime Wave," *Time* (June 4, 1960).
Cuff, S. "Chacun à son mystère, with list," *Saturday Review* (January 24, 1953).
———. "Good Mysteries for Summer," *Saturday Review* (June 15, 1957).
———. "Prime Crimes of 1956," *Saturday Review* (December 22, 1956).
———. "Toughie Submerged." *Saturday Review* (December 24, 1955).
———. "Year of Crime," *Saturday Review* (December 25, 1954).
Cummings, J. C. "Detective Stories," *Bookman* (January, 1910).
Cuppy, Will. "How to Read a Whodunit," *Mystery Book Magazine* (January, 1946). Also in Haycraft's *Art of the Mystery Novel.* New York: Simon and Schuster, 1946.
Cushing, C. P. "Who Writes These Mystery Yarns?," *Independent* (April 9, 1927).

Daly, E. "Are You Sure They Are All Horrid?," *Writer* (June, 1948).
Dane, Daniel C. "Best Detective Story in the World," *Bookman* (October, 1932).
Darnton, C. "American Legal Processes" (Letter), *New Statesman & Nation* (October 13, 1951).
Darwin, B. "Multiple Murder," *Nation* (London), (August 10, 1928).
Davenport, Basil. "The Devil Is Not Dead," *Saturday Review of Literature* (February 15, 1936).
Davey, J. "Mysteryland Revisited," *Reporter* (April 16, 1959).
Davis, Elmer. "The Real Sherlock Holmes," *Saturday Review of Literature* (December 2, 1933).
DeFord, M. A. "Psychology of Mystery Story Writing," *Writer* (June, 1964).
"Detective Fiction." *Times Literary Supplement* (London), (February 25, 1955).
"Detective Story Is in Danger of Getting Played Out," *Time* (January 13, 1947).
"Detectiveness in Fiction." *Nation* (August 15, 1912).
"Detectives," *Saturday Review of Literature* (May 5, 1883).
"Detectives in Fiction: A Study in Literary Fashions," *Living Age* (September, 1926).
DeVoto, Bernard. "Alias Nero Wolfe," *Harper* (July, 1954).
———. "Easy Chair Reply to Edmund Wilson," *Harper* (December, 1944).
Dickens, Charles. "Poe Forecasts Ending of 'Barnaby Rudge.' " *Saturday Evening Post* (May 1, 1841).
———. "Poe's Criticism of 'Barnaby Rudge' and How the Plot Should Have Developed," *Graham's Magazine* (February, 1842).

"Ellery Queen Builds Collection of Rare Detective Short Stories," *Publishers' Weekly* (November 20, 1943).
Ellin, S. "The Irony of It" *Writer* (November, 1957).

———. "Planning a Mystery Back to Front," *Writer* (December, 1966).

———. "Viewpoint and the Mystery Short Story," *Writer* (May, 1963).

———. "Writing a Mystery Novel," *Writer* (November, 1960).

Elwin, M. "Psychology of the Thriller," *Saturday Review of Literature* (August 26, 1933).

"Emile Gaboriau," *Times Literary Supplement* (London), (November 2, 1935).

Evans, D. W. "Casebook of T. S. Eliot," *Modern Language Notes* (November, 1956). Influence of crime fiction on Eliot's work.

Evans, W. "Is Sherlock Holmes Alive?" *Reader's Digest* (August, 1954).

Ewart, S. T. "Murder in (and of) a Library," *Library World* (November, 1937).

Fadiman, Clifton. "On Reading Mysteries," *Good Housekeeping* (February, 1943).

Farrar, J. "Have You a Detective in Your Home? Today's Craze for a Crime in Fiction and Its Causes," *Century* (1929).

Fickling, S. "Take It Seriously," *Writer* (May, 1966).

Field, L. M. "Philo Vance & Co. Benefactors," *North American Review* (March, 1933).

Fiscalani, J. "Elementary, My Dear Watson," *Commonweal* (October 27, 1961).

Fish, H. D. "All Children Love a Secret," *Library Bulletin* (October, 1946).

"$5,000,000 Worth of Crime," *Publishers' Weekly* (July 24, 1937).

"Five Writers in One: The Versatility of Agatha Christie," *Times Literary Supplement* (London), (February 25, 1955).

Fleming, Mrs. Ian. "How James Bond Destroyed My Husband," *Ladies Home Journal* (October, 1966).

"Footnotes to Romans à clef," *Saturday Review of Literature* (July 13, 1935).

Frank, W. "Mystery Tale," *New Republic* (October 13, 1926).

Freeman, R. Austin. "Art of the Detective Story," *19th Century* (May, 1924).

Gardiner, D. "No Mirrors, Please," *Writer* (January, 1964).

Gardner, Erle Stanley. "Getting Away with Murder," *Atlantic Monthly* (January, 1965).

Gardner, R. "Baker Street and the Bible; Sherlock Holmes and the Historical Jesus," *Hibbert Journal* (April, 1952).

Gawsworth, John. "Intro to Thrills, Crimes and Mysteries," *Associated Newspapers* (1936).

Gerhardt, Mia I. "Homicide West: Some Observations on the Nero Wolfe Stories of Rex Stout," *English Studies* (April, 1968).

Gerould, K. F. "A Grave Literary Crisis," *Saturday Review* (London), (February 22, 1930).

———. "Men, Women, and Thrillers," *Yale Review* (June, 1930).

———. "Murder for Pastime," *Saturday Review of Literature* (August 3, 1935).

"Golden Sunset for Private Eyes," *Punch* (February 22, 1961).

"Goodbye, Old Cat," *Punch* (April 24, 1957). A memoir of Dr. Nikola and his cat, Apollyon.

Gordon, M. "First Whodunit," *Writer* (February, 1947).

"Gory Goulash," *Newsweek* (August 15, 1960).

Gruber, Frank. "Mystery Writer Can Make Money," *Publishers' Weekly* (April 5, 1941).

Hamilton, D. H. "Detective Story and the Manuscript," *Hobbies* (July, 1957).

Hamilton, K. M. "Murder and Mystery Stories: An Interpretation of Detective Fiction," *Dalhousie Review* (Summer, 1953).

Hammett, Dashiell. "Review of 'The Benson Murder Case,' " *Saturday Review of Literature* (January 15, 1927).

Harvey, F. B. "Pre-eminent Victorians: A Gossip on Sherlock Holmes," *London Quarterly Review* (April, 1944).

Harwood, H. C. "Detective Stories," *Outlook* (London), (January 1, 1927).

———. "Holiday Homicide," *Saturday Review* (London), (August 17, 1929).

———. "Murder of Late," *Saturday Review* (London), (February 2, 1929).

Haycraft, Howard. "Corpse with the Raised Eyebrows," *Publishers' Weekly* (August 9, 1941).

———. "Decennial Detective Digest: With Haycraft-Queen List of Detective-Crime-Mystery Fiction," *Wilson Library Bulletin* (November, 1951).

———. "Dictators, Democrats, and Detectives," *Saturday Review of Literature* (October 7, 1939). Also in *Spectator* (London), (November 17, 1939). Translated in *Kort en Goed* (Johannesburg), (April, 1940). Also reprinted in part as Chapter XV of *Murder for Pleasure*. New York: Appleton-Century, 1941.

———. "Father of the Detective Story; E. A. Poe," *Saturday Review of Literature* (August 23, 1941).

———. "From Poe to Hammett: A Foundation List of Detective Fiction," *Wilson Library Bulletin* (February, 1938).

———. "Mystery Writers, Professional and Amateur Reply to Frank Gruber, *Publishers' Weekly* (April 19, 1941).

———. "Whodunit in World War II and After," *New York Times Book Review* (August 12, 1945).

Hecht, Ben. "Whistling Corpse," *Ellery Queen Mystery Magazine* (September, 1945). Satire. Also in Haycraft's *The Art of the Mystery Story*. New York: Simon and Schuster, 1946.

"Hedunit," *Newsweek* (May 15, 1961).

"Hedunit," *Time* (June 20, 1949).

Hendricks, D. "Red Herrings Are Bad Business," *Publishers' Weekly* (July 5, 1941).

Herman, L. "I Spy a Mystery," *Mademoiselle* (July, 1964).

Highsmith, P., "Suspense Rules and Non-Rules," *Writer* (November, 1964).

———. "The Suspense Short Story," *Writer* (March, 1966).

Hobshawn, E. "Criminal as Hero and Myth," *Times Literary Supplement* (London), (June 23, 1961).

Hoskins, Percy. "Crime Reporting and Its Sale," *Times Literary Supplement* (London), (June 23, 1961).

Howard, J. E. "Homage to Holmes," *New Stateman* (January 23, 1954). "Discussion" (February 27, 1954; March 6, 1954).

Howe, Sir Ronald, "A Personal Reaction," *Times Literary Supplement* (London), (February 25, 1955). A professional view of the detective story.

Hughes, D. B. "Challenge of Mystery Fiction," *Writer* (May, 1947).

Hutchinson, H. G. "Detective Fiction," *Quarterly* (July, 1929).

Hyans, E. "Small Hours Reading," *New Statesman* (April 4, 1953).

Iams, J. "You, Too, Can Get Away with Murder," *Writer* (May, 1950).

"The Images of Horror: The Unknown and Familiar," *Times Literary Supplement* (London), (February 25, 1955).

Innes, M. "Death as a Game," *Esquire* (January, 1965).

Jacobs, J. "Simenon's Mosaic," *Reporter* (January 14, 1965).

Jarrett, C. "Jane Austen and Detective Stories," *Saturday Review of Literature* (December 7, 1935).

Johnston, R. W. "Death's Fair-Haired Boy," *Life* (June 23, 1952).

Johnstone, C. "The Detective Story's Origin," *Harper's Magazine* (February 12, 1910).

Kahn, J. "Editing the Mystery and Suspense Novel," *Writer* (July, 1966).

Kellett, E. E. "Marginal Comments," *Spectator* (February 26, 1937).

Kendrick, B. "It's a Mystery to Me," *Writer* (September, 1947).

Kennedy, F. "From Whodunits to Poetry," *Saturday Review of Literature* (October 18, 1941).

Kilpatrick, C. E. (Compiler). "Roundup of Westerns, Mysteries, Horror and Science Fiction," *Library Journal* (February, 1958; October, 1958).

Knox, R. "Ten Rules for a Good Detective Story," *Publishers' Weekly* (October 5, 1929).

Krutch, Joseph Wood. "Only a Detective Story," *Nation* (November 25, 1944). Also in Haycraft, H. *The Art of the Mystery Story*. New York: Simon and Schuster, 1946.

Kubie, Lawrence S., M.D. "The Literature of Horror," *Saturday Review of Literature* (October 20, 1934).

Kunitz, S. J. "Crime of the Century," *Wilson Library Bulletin* (May, 1941).

Lacey, E. "Have Typewriter, Should Travel," *Writer* (April, 1964).

———. "Whodunit? You?" *Writer* (February, 1959).

Langsbaum, R. "Crime in Modern Literature," rev., *American Scholar* (Summer, 1957).

Laurence, H. "Domesticating the Murder," *Saturday Review of Literature* (February 17, 1945). Also in *Writer* (July, 1945).

"Lawyer and a Mystery Writer Trade Blows," *Literary Digest* (October 26, 1929).

Leacock, Stephen. "The Irreducible Detective Story," *Golden Book* (May, 1932).

———. "Twenty Cents Worth of Murder," *Saturday Review of Literature* (July 8, 1939).

Lejeune, Anthony. "Age of the Great Detective," *Times Literary Supplement* (London), (June 23, 1961).

Lewis, K. W. "Checklist of Detectives," *Publishers' Weekly* (August 9, 1941).

Lieberman, E. "What Ails the Whodunit?" *Saturday Review of Literature* (June 21, 1947).

"Life Guide," *Life* (December 22, 1962).

Little, L. T. "Mystery Story in the Hospital," *Libraries* (October, 1929).

Lockridge, R. "Some Like It Crude: Some Like It Subtle," *Writer* (October, 1961).

Long, J. "Guilty as Hell, But—" *Writer* (March, 1941).

"Looking Backward: Detective Stories," *Literary Review* (November 24, 1923).

"Looking for a Raven," *Newsweek* (May 2, 1955).

Lynch, Judge. "Autopsy in April: Crimes of 1945, First Quarter," *Saturday Review of Literature* (May 5, 1945).

———. "Blotter for 1939," *Saturday Review of Literature* (December 30, 1939).

———. "Come, Sweet Death: Roundup of Whodunits, 1940," *Saturday Review of Literature* (December 7, 1940).

———. "Corpse Under the Xmas Tree," *Saturday Review of Literature* (December 21, 1946).

———. "Crime Blotter for 1947," *Saturday Review of Literature* (December 27, 1947).

———. "Crime of the First Quarter," *Saturday Review of Literature* (May 1, 1948).

———. "Death Takes a Holiday: 1924 to 1944," *Saturday Review of Literature* (August 5, 1944).

———. "Most Deserving Murders of 1949," *Saturday Review of Literature* (December 31, 1949).

———. "Murder at the Half," *Saturday Review of Literature* (July 31, 1948).

———. "Spring Comes to Life with Death," *Saturday Review of Literature* (April 5, 1941).

———. "Spring Styles in Homicide: A Survey," *Publishers' Weekly* (May 30, 1942).

McCarthy, Mary. "Murder and Karl Marx: Class-conscious Detective Stories," *Nation* (March 25, 1936). Reply by W. Seagle (April 15, 1936).

McCloy, Helen. "Whodunits, Still a Stepchild," *New Republic* (October 31, 1955).

———. "Writing and Selling of Mysteries," *Writer* (April, 1947).

McDonald, J. "Crime That Pays," *Writer* (May, 1951).

McElroy, C. F. "The Cliché of the Mystery Writers," *Saturday Review of Literature* (January 13, 1940).

McGerr, P. "There's a Dividend in Mysteries," *Writer* (April, 1965).

McGill, V. J. "Henry James, Master Detective," *Bookman* (November, 1930).

McKay, H. C. "Camera in Contemporary Literature," *American Photography* (October, 1945).

Mackenzie, D. "Without Bent Wire or Stethoscope," *Writer* (August, 1961).

McLinhan, H. M. "Footprints in the Sands of Crime," *Sewanee Review* (October, 1946).

Mallalieu, J. P. W. "From Wandsworth Gaol," *Spectator* (July 6, 1951).

———. "Shady Mr. Holmes," *Spectator* (February 27, 1953).

Marion, D. "Detective Novel," *Living Age* (November, 1939).

Marlowe, D. J., "Stike a Note and Hold It," *Writer* (August, 1963).

Marshburn, J. H. "Cruell Murder Donne in Kent and Its Literary Manifestations," *Studia Philaletica* (April, 1949).

Mason, A. E. W. "Detective Novels," *Nation & Athenaeum* (London), (February 7, 1925).

Masur, H. Q. "That Mystery Novel," *Writer* (January, 1950).

Matthews, B. "Poe and the Detective Story," *Scribner's Magazine* (September, 1907).

Maugham, W. S. "Give Me a Murder," *Saturday Evening Post* (December 28, 1940). Summary in *Saturday Review of Literature* (January 4, 1941).

Maurice, A. B. "The Detective in Fiction," *Bookman* (May, 1902).

Mercier, V. "Defective Detectives," *Nation* (November 16, 1964).

Michel, M. S. "Hardboiled Detective Novel," *Writer* (April, 1944).

Milne, A. A. "Books and Writers," *Spectator* (June 30, 1950).

———. "Modern Detective Novel, *Spectator* (April 6, 1951).

Mochrie, M. "They Make Crime Pay," *Delineator* (February, 1937).

Morley, Christopher. "Adjectives and Whodunits, Reply to Judge Lynch," *Saturday Review of Literature* (May 3, 1941).

———. "Dr. Watson's Secret," *Saturday Review of Literature* (December 15, 1934).

———. "Granules from an Hour Glass," *Saturday Review of Literature* (March 10, 1928).

———. "Mystery—Detective Stories of an Earlier Vintage," *Saturday Review of Literature* (January 13, 1940).

———. "Was Sherlock Holmes an American?" *Saturday Review of Literature* (July 21, 1934; July 28, 1934).

Morris, T. "Suggestible Offender," *Times Literary Supplement* (London), (June 23, 1961).

Morton, C. W. "Accent on Living," *Atlantic Monthly* (May, 1957).

Muhlen, H. "Thinker and the Tough Guy," *Commonweal* (November 25, 1949).

Mumford, E. W. "The Perfect Crime," *Atlantic Monthly* (March, 1932).

"Murder Business," *Newsweek* (October 31, 1949).

"Murder in Midsummer," *Time* (August 10, 1959).

"Murder Market," *Time* (February 28, 1938).

"Murder Most Foul; Ingenious Means of Murder Devised by Mystery," *Reader's Digest* (October, 1936).

"Mysteries for Firelight," *Newsweek* (December 5, 1955).

"Mysteries in Reprint: A Dislocated Market," *Publishers' Weekly* (January 10, 1948).

"Mystery Medley," *Newsweek* (September 6, 1954).

"New Mysteries," *Time* (December 5, 1955; March 19, 1956).

"The New School of Murder Mystery," *Literary Digest* (September 1, 1934).

"New Thrill for Armchair Detectives with a Crimefile of Clues, the Fan Works Out Own Solution," *Literary Digest* (October 3, 1936).

Nicolson, H. "Detective Novels," *Spectator* (December 8, 1950).

———. "Reading Detective Fiction," *Spectator* (March 23, 1951).

Nicolson, M. "The Professor and the Detective," *Atlantic Monthly* (April, 1929).

"No Ghost for Edgar Wallace," *Literary Digest* (March 19, 1932). A follow-up report on this prolific writer which appeared after his death.

"Noble Art of Mystery," *Nation* (September 14, 1927).

Ocampo, V. "Detective Story," *Books Abroad* (January, 1942).

Odell, R. "Mystery Fiction (Whodunit, Whydunit, Howdunit)," *American Speech* (December, 1950).

O'Faolain, S. "Give Us Back Bill Sikes," *Spectator* (February 15, 1935).

"Old Mystery Books," *Saturday Evening Post* (September 5, 1931).

Olney, C. "Literacy of Sherlock Holmes," *University of Kansas City Review* (March, 1956).

"On Intellectual Thrillers," *Bookman* (March, 1933).

O'Neill, D. "Too Many Murders," *Saturday Review of Literature* (February 11, 1939).

O'Riordan, C. "Vicious Circle," *New Statesman* (June 28, 1930).

Orr, C. "Miss Clink and Mr. Crump Talk Mysteries," *Publishers' Weekly* (July 20, 1929).

Osborne, E. A. "Collecting Detective Fiction," *Bookman* (London), (February, 1932).

"Outstanding Recent Mysteries," *New Republic* (October 31, 1955).

Parsons, L. "On the Novels of Raymond Chandler," *Fortnightly Review* (May, 1954).

———. "Simenon & Chandler," *Contemporary Review* (January, 1960).

Patrick, Q. "So You're Going to Write a Mystery?" *Writer* (February, 1942).

Paul, E. "Whodunit; Mystery Stories in the Making," *Atlantic Monthly* (July, 1941).

Pearson, E. "Spring, Three One Hundred," *Outlook* (August 3, 1927).

Pember, J. E. "Clichés in Mystery Stories," *Writer* (August, 1943).

Perelman, S. J. "Farewell, My Lovely Appetizer," *Ellery Queen Mystery Magazine* (August, 1945).

Peterson, J. "Cosmic View of the Private Eye," *Saturday Review* (August 22, 1953). Reply with rejoinder by A. Boucher (October 31, 1953).

Philmore, R. "Second Inquest on Detective Stories," *Discovery* (September, 1938). Also in Haycraft, H. *The Art of the Mystery Story*. New York: Simon and Schuster, 1946.

——— and Yudkin, J. "Inquest on Detective Stories," *Discovery* (April, 1938). Also in Haycraft, H. *The Art of the Mystery Story*. New York: Simon and Schuster, 1946.

Popkin, Z. "Corpse Can't Lear," *Writer* (October, 1942).

Portugal, E. "Death to the Detectives," *Bookman* (London), (April, 1933).

Post, M. "Crimes of a Month," *New Republic* (May 12, 1941).

Powell, R. "How to Get Away with Murder," *Writer* (December, 1948).

Powys, J. C. "Crime Wave in Fiction," *World's Work* (September, 1929).

Priestley, J. B. "On Holiday with the Bodies," *Saturday Review of Literature* (July 3, 1926). Reply by V. Rendall (July 10, 1926).

———. "Too Many Corpses in Detective Fiction," *Literary Digest* (February 27, 1932). A plea for fewer corpses and newer forms of detective fiction.

"Printed Murder Is Valued at $5,000,000 a Year," *Newsweek* (June 19, 1937).

Pritchett, V. S. "Lineage of the Detective Story," *New Statesman and Nation* (June 16, 1951).

"The Publisher's Share," *Times Literary Supplement* (London), (June 23, 1961).

Queen, E. "Detective's Dictionary: Some Definitions from a Work Being Compiled," *Good Housekeeping* (February, 1944).

———. "Detective Short Story," *Saturday Review* (November 22, 1941).

Quincunx. "In General: The Cult of Detective Stories, *Saturday Review* (London), (December 6, 1930).

Quinton, A. "The Decadence of Detection," *Encounter* (May, 1955).

Quiz, Quintus. "Mental Holidays," *Christian Century* (July 25, 1934).

———. "A Resolution and a Protest," *Christian Century* (February 8, 1939).

"Radio Program Builds Audience for Inner Sanctum Mysteries," *Publishers' Weekly* (July 4, 1942).

Raynor, H. "Decline and Fall of the Detective Story," *Fortnightly Review* (February, 1953).

"Read 'em and Creep," *Publishers' Weekly* (July 20, 1929).

"The Red Hand." *Times Literary Supplement* (London), (June 23, 1961).

Redman, B. R. "Decline and Fall of the Whodunit?" *Saturday Review* (May 31, 1952).

Reeve, A. B. "In Defense of the Detective Story," *Independent* (July 10, 1913).

Reeve, Wybert. "Recollections of Wilkie Collins," *Chambers Journal,* Vol. IX.

Rhodes, H. T. F. "Detective in Fiction—and in Fact," *Cornhill* (January, 1958).

Rinehart, Mary Roberts. "Repute of the Crime Story," *Publishers' Weekly* (February 1, 1930).

Roberts, D. M. "Red-Headed League and the Rue Morgue," *Scholastic* (February 26, 1938).

Roberts, K. L. "For Authors Only: Mysteries Easily Solved in English Detective Stories," *Saturday Evening Post* (September 24, 1932).

Robbins, L. H. "They Get Away with Murder," *New York Times Magazine* (November 17, 1940).

Rodell, M. F. "Murder for Rent, Murder for Sale," *Publishers' Weekly* (February 15, 1941).

Rosenbach, A. S. W. "The Trail of Scarlet," *Saturday Evening Post* (October 1, 1932).

Russell, D. C. "Chandler Books," *Atlantic Monthly* (March, 1945).

Rutledge, N. "Writing a Mystery," *Writer* (January, 1957).

Sander, R. N. "They Kill and Tell: Isabelle Taylor Tell About the Woman Whodunit Writers," *Independent Women* (October, 1943).

Sandoe, James. "Case of the Respectable Corpse," *Publishers' Weekly* (February 20, 1943).

———. "Dagger of the Mind," *Poetry Magazine* (June, 1946). Also in Haycraft, H. *The Art of The Mystery Story.* New York: Simon and Schuster, 1946.

———. "Red Herrings Make Good Reading: Reply to D. Hendricks," *Publishers' Weekly* (August 2, 1941).

Sayers, D. L. "Sport of the Noble Minds," *Saturday Review of Literature* (August 3, 1929).

"School of Cruelty," *Saturday Review of Literature* (March 21, 1931).

"School of Detective Yarns Needed," *Literary Digest* (September 23, 1922).

Scott, James R. A. "Detective Novels," *London Mercury* (February, 1939).

Scrutton, M. "Addiction to Fiction," *20th Century* (April, 1956).

Seagle, W. "Murder, Marx and McCarthy: A Reply to Mary McCarthy," *Nation* (April 15, 1936).

"Secret Attraction," *Times Literary Supplement* (London), (February 25, 1955). Discusses the attraction that the detective story has for the reader.

Seldes, G. "Diplomat's Delight," *Bookman* (September, 1927).

———. "Van Dine and His Public," *New Republic* (June 19, 1929).

Shannon, D. "Writing the Police-Routine Novel," *Writer* (March, 1967).

"Sherlock Holmes and After," *Saturday Review of Literature* (July 19, 1930).

"Sherlock Holmes at Home—in Effigy: The Famous Room in Baker Street Recreated," *Illustrated London News* (June 2, 1951).

"Shifting the Apology," *Saturday Review of Literature* (September 11, 1926).

Shrapnel, Norman. "The Literature of Violence and Pursuit," *Times Literary Supplement* (London), (June 23, 1961).

"The Silver Age, Crime Fiction from Its Heyday Until Now," *Times Literary Supplement* (London), (February 25, 1955).

Simpson, H. "Down Among the Dead Men," *Bookman* (London), (December, 1934).

Sington, D. "Raymond Chandler on Crime and Punishment," *20th Century* (May, 1959).

Sisk, J. P. "Crime and Criticism," *Commonweal* (April 20, 1956). Reply by G. Cashman (May 18, 1956); Rejoinder (June 15, 1956).

Sister Maura. "Detective Fiction," *Dalhousie Review* (January, 1951).

Smith, H. "New Detectives," *Good Housekeeping* (September, 1947).

Sparrell, A. "Fiction and Cookery: An Interview with Carolyn Wells," *Christian Science Monitor Magazine* (October 21, 1939).

Sprague, P. W. "A Plea for Mystery Relief," *Atlantic Monthly* (June, 1933).

Sproul, K. "Here's to Crime," *Saturday Review* (August 18, 1951).

———. "Therapeutics of Murder," *Writer* (February, 1949).

Squires, J. "Man Who Created Sherlock Holmes; Review of *The Life of Sir A. C. Doyle,* by J. D. Carr," *Illustrated London News* (February 5, 1949).

Squires, P. C. "Charles Dickens as Criminologist," *Journal of Criminal Law* (July, 1938).

Steel, Kurt. "A Literary Crisis," reply to Quiz, Quintus (*supra*), *Christian Century* (May 17, 1939).

Steeves, H. R. "A Sober Word on the Detective Story," *Harper's* (April, 1941). Also in Haycraft, H. *The Art of the Mystery Story*. New York: Simon and Schuster, 1946.

Stern, P. V. D. "The Case of the Corpse in the Blind Alley," *Virginia Quarterly Review* (Spring, 1941). Also in Haycraft, H. *The Art of the Mystery Story*. New York: Simon and Schuster, 1946.

Stevens, G. "Death by Misadventure: Centennial of the Detective Story," *Saturday Review of Literature* (October 18, 1941).

Stirling, S. "Strictly Phoney," *Publishers' Weekly* (March 21, 1942).

Stolper, B. J. R. "Who Done It?" *Scholastic* (October 22, 1938).

———. "Who Done It?" *Scholastic* (April 8, 1946).

Stone, E. "Caleb Williams and Martin Faber: A Contrast," *Modern Language Notes* (November, 1947).

Stone, P. M. "Long Life: To Some Detectives," *Bookman* (London), (June, 1933). Reply to E. Portugal.

Storr, Anthony. "A Black and White World," *Times Literary Supplement* (London), (June 23, 1961).

Stout, Rex. "Grim Fairy Tales," *Saturday Review of Literature* (April 2, 1949).

———. "Watson Was a Woman," *Saturday Review of Literature* (March 1, 1941).

———. "We Mystery Writers Don't Kid Ourselves," *Publishers' Weekly* (December 28, 1940).

Symons, Julian and Edmund Crispin. "Is the Detective Story Dead?" *Times Literary Supplement* (London), (June 23, 1961).

Tanasoca, D. "Honeysuckle for Hummingbird," *Wilson Library Bulletin* (November, 1951).

Taylor, F. S. "Corpus Delecti: Secret Disposal of the Body," *Living Age* (July, 1937).

———. "The Crux of a Murder: Disposal of the Body," *Spectator* (April 9, 1937). Also in Haycraft, H. *Art of the Mystery Story*. New York: Simon and Schuster, 1946.

Taylor, I. "Mysteries Don't Just Grow," *Library Journal* (August, 1951).

———. "Just Mysteries and Proud of It!" *Publishers' Weekly* (Feburary 22, 1941).

"Thriller-Writer's Diary and Compendium of Useful Information," *Punch* (November 3, 1958).

"Throw out the Detective," *Saturday Review of Literature* (December 1, 1928).

Tiffany, H. R. "Pacifying the Public with Mysteries," *Publishers' Weekly* (August 24, 1935).

Tobin, D. "Come Off It, Sister," *Collier's* (July 1, 1950).

"Tram Cars or 'Dodgems': Detection, Thrills and Horror," *Times Literary Supplement* (February 25, 1955).

"T.V.'s 'Private Eyes' Send Business to the Real McCoy," *Financial Post* (November 30, 1963).

Ullman, A. G. "Making Crime Pay," *Publishers' Weekly* (July 7, 1934).

———. "Serving the Mystery Fan," *Publishers' Weekly* (August 18, 1934).

"Ultimate Source of Sherlock Holmes," *Bookman* (April, 1908). Traces origin back to Persian literature.

Van Dine, S. S. "I Used to Be a Highbrow But Look at Me Now," *American Magazine* (September, 1928).

Veedam, S. S. "The Pink Murder Case," *Saturday Review of Literature* (November 2, 1929). Satire on Van Dine novels.

Very, Pierre. "Murder on Parnassus," *Living Age* (April, 1935). The French view of the mystery story. Also in Haycraft, H. *The Art of the Mystery Story.* New York: Simon and Schuster, 1946.

"Vintage Chillers," *Newsweek* (July 5, 1954).

"Voracious Readers' Swiftly Changing Tastes Keep Publishers on Jump," *Literary Digest* (January 2, 1937).

Waite, J. B. "If Judges Wrote Detective Stories," with reply by R. Denbie. *Scribners* (April, 1934).

——— and M. W. Kimball. "Lawyer Looks at Detective Fiction," *Bookman* (August, 1929). Same condensed, *Literary Digest* (October 26, 1929), together with a reply by S. S. Van Dine. Also in Haycraft, H. *The Art of the Mystery Story*. New York: Simon and Schuster, 1946.

Webb, J. "Do-it-yourself Homicides," *Writer* (October, 1963).

Webb, K. W. and H. C. Wheeler. "Mystery Short Short," *Writer* (January, 1951).

Weber, W. C. "Survey of Sleuths," *Publishers' Weekly* (January 30, 1937).

Wells, Carolyn. "Technique of the Mystery Story," *Nation* (July 9, 1914).

Wells, W. H. "New Blood Whets More Customers' Appetites for Murder," *Publishers' Weekly* (August 13, 1938).

"What Policemen Read," *Times Literary Supplement* (London), (June 23, 1961).

"What the Police Read," *Literary Digest* (June 14, 1914).

"What's in a Book Title?" *Saturday Review of Literature* (July 6, 1935; August 10, 1935).

"What's the Lure of Detective Stories?" *Literary Digest* (January 24, 1931). Real detectives and writers of detective fiction ponder the lure of this type of fiction.

Whipple, L. "Nirvana for Two Dollars," *Survey* (May 1, 1929).

Whiteside, T. "Murder a Minute," *Collier's* (February 5, 1949).

Whitney, P. A. "Writing the Gothic Novel," *Writer* (February, 1967).

"Who Done It as Dickens Did It," *Collier's* (March 14, 1953).

"Who Done It? Detectives in Fiction," *Wilson Library Bulletin* (June, October, 1940; January, 1941).

"Why Do People Read Detective Stories?" *New Yorker* (October 14, 1944).

Williams, G. "Chills for Children; with Graded List," *Publishers' Weekly* (October 24, 1942).

Williams, H. L. "The Germ of the Detective Novel," *Bookbuyer* (November, 1900).

Williams, V. "Detective Fiction," *Bookman* (July, 1928).

———. "Detective in Fiction," *Fortnightly Review* (September, 1930).

———. "Putting the Shock into Shockers," *Bookman* (November, 1927).

Wilson, A. D. "Crime and the Stage," *Spectator* (April 10, 1936).

Wilson, E. "Who Cares Who Killed Roger Ackroyd? Second Report on Detective Fiction," *New Yorker* (January 20, 1945).

Wimsatt, W. K. "Poe and the Mystery of Mary Rogers," *PMLA* (March, 1941).

Winterich, J. T. "Homicide for the Holidays; a Selection of Choice Crime Books," *Saturday Review* (December 23, 1961).

Wise, W. "For Vicarious Adventures, a Suspenseful Springtime," *Saturday Review* (April 9, 1960).

Wodehouse, P. G. "About These Mystery Stories," *Saturday Evening Post* (May 25, 1929).

Wood, A. "Crime and Contrition in Literature," *Contemporary Review* (July, 1960).

Woollcott, A. "President's Crime Shelf; with List," *Reader's Digest* (April, 1941).

Wright, L. "Dividends for Death," *Writer* (September, 1945).

———. "Murder for Profit," *Publishers' Weekly* (April 10, 1937).

———. "Mysteries Are Books," *Publishers' Weekly* (January 25, 1941).

Wright, R. "Forgotten Dentures: Molars and Murders in Old New York," *Saturday Review of Literature* (January 1, 1944).

Wright, W. H. "The Detective Novel," *Scribner's Magazine* (November, 1926).

———. "How I Get Away with Murder," *Reader's Digest* (July, 1936).

"Write Me a Murder, and the Authors Oblige," *Newsweek* (January 1, 1962).

Wylie, Philip. "Crime of Mickey Spillane," *Good Housekeeping* (February, 1955).

Wyndham, H. "The Lure of the Crime Book," *Saturday Review* (London), (July 8, 1933).

Zegel, S. "Whodunit—Soviet Style," *Atlas* (May, 1965).

APPENDIX

MURDER MISCELLANY

Webster defines miscellany as "a mixture of various things"—"a collection of writings on various subjects"—"separate studies or writings collected in one volume." Strictly speaking a miscellany is something that has various traits "dealing with or interested in unrelated topics or subjects."

For you—the reader—this is the bonus—the extras that were left when the research has been collected, sorted out and organized. You will find here the odd facts that always come to light in any kind of research: the historical facts that pertain to the field; a short dictionary of mystery terms, strictly for the novice, naturally; the pulp magazines where many of the greatest writers got their finest training. Here, too, are some of the great, and the near-great, who, like yourself, are mystery buffs. Here is the absorbing story of the collaborations which abound in the mystery fields, and another mystery in itself—why pseudonyms? You will learn of the organizations and societies in the field, and learn why the titles of books change as they cross oceans or go from one medium to another. Last but not least you'll learn what is going on in other countries of the world as far as mysteries are concerned.

Origins

When C. Auguste Dupin solved "The Murders in the Rue Morgue" in 1841, "The Mystery of Marie Rogêt" in 1843, and the enigma of "The Purloined Letter" in 1845, he was to become the first in a long line of detectives continuing to the present day. As the creator of Dupin, Edgar Allan Poe became the father of the detective story as we know it today. Despite his great contribution to the field, Poe cannot, however, be given complete credit for its enormous growth and popularity.

Records show that there is not a single period in the history of man when he has not been intrigued by the mysterious and the unknown. There is little doubt that Poe had read Voltaire's *Zadig,* written in 1748. Voltaire, in turn, as a literary man, is likely to have been familiar with Chevalier de Mailly's *Le Voyage et les aventures des trois Princes de Serendip, traduit du Persan,* published in Paris in 1719. Mailly borrowed his plot from *Pereginaggio dei Tre Giovanni Figliuoli del Re di Saren-*

dippo, printed in Venice in 1557. This Italian story can be traced to the *A Thousand and One Nights* and to ancient Greek texts. It is interesting to note that Dorothy L. Sayers in her very fine collection, *The Omnibus of Crime,* opens the book with two short selections from the *Apocryphal Scriptures:* "The History of Bel" and "The History of Susanna."

In 1764, *The Castle of Otranto* was first published in England, masked as a translation from the Italian. In reality it was the work of Horace Walpole, then a little-known English writer. It had all the familiar touches that we associate with today's popular Gothic novel: the gloomy surroundings, the helpless heroine, the menacing villain. It is also very possible that Poe had read *The Castle of Otranto* and been influenced by it. Certainly it was to have a great effect on later works, and is one of the precursors of the modern detective novel.

Poe must have also read François Eugene Vidocq's *Memoires de Vidocq,* published in Paris in 1828. This real-life detective writing of his own sensational exploits enjoyed a tremendous popularity with French readers. It is interesting today to realize that it was the French and English who further developed the detective story after Poe had set the example. While Poe's stories created a great deal of interest at home and were widely read, they had very little effect on other American writers who made no attempt to imitate them or develop the form.

In France, however, where Poe has always been very popular, Emile Gaboriau wrote a series of detective stories based on actual police records and featuring the detective, Monsieur Lecoq.

At the same time in England, Wilkie Collins wrote *The Woman in White* (1860) and *The Moonstone* (1868), the first examples of the detective novel to appear in that country. Charles Dickens, who was interested in the new police methods being introduced in London, used a detective as a character in *Bleak House* in 1852 and was writing *The Mystery of Edwin Drood* at the time of his death in 1870. Another book published in England (1856) attracted a great deal of attention. The success of *Recollections of a Detective Police-Officer* by "Waters" (William Russell) indicated that the English reading public was ready for a major detective character to appear on the literary scene.

It wasn't until almost thirty-three years after Poe that an American writer was to seriously continue his work. During this period, writers such as Mrs. Henry Wood, best known for *East Lynne* (1861), and Mary Elizabeth Braddon, whose *Lady Audley's Secret* (1862) was extremely popular, produced wildly romantic tales that have elements of the modern mystery and suspense story. The first American writer to give the detective novel its present formula and popularity was Anna Katherine Green. *The Leavenworth Case,* written in 1878, is still considered one of the great classics in the crime field, although it sounds a little stilted and old-fashioned today. Some of her other books, *The Amethyst Box, House in the Mist,* and *The Millionaire Baby,* though less successful than *The Leavenworth Case,* were still very popular with readers in the eighties and nineties.

Another aspect in the development of the detective story was the dime novel. The first dime novel detective, Harlan Page Halsey's "Old Sleuth," appeared in America in 1872, and was to be followed by such immortals as Nick Carter and Sexton Blake. Nick Carter was the brainchild of John Russell Coryell who wrote hundreds of stories about him, beginning with *The Old Detective's Pupil* in 1886. Later many other writers used the name and wrote thousands of short stories and novelettes about him. The character has appeared on the radio, stage, television and in the movies. The old stories are available in pocket editions today and new authors are currently writing full-length novels about his escapades. In tune with the times, he is now a secret agent. Sexton Blake stories have also been appearing all over the world for seventy-two years, and have been and still are written by a score of writers. He has also appeared in motion pictures.

In 1887, there appeared a book which was to become one of the first huge successes in the mystery field. Fergus Hume, an Australian, after carefully studying the works of Gaboriau, wrote a novel called *The Mystery of a Hansom Cab.* Only moderately popular in his home country, it was sold to a London group which reissued the novel and sold more than 400,000 copies of it. It is rather dull by today's standards, but should be read by any serious student for its historical interest.

One of the major fictional detectives was ready to make his bow. There will be no attempt made here to repeat the entire fantastic story of Sir Arthur Conan Doyle's immortal creation. Sherlock Holmes, appearing in the 1890's, has become a household word and model for hundreds of fictional characters. The highest honor which can be bestowed on a writer has been given to Doyle by the Baker Street Irregulars, an exclusive club of Holmes devotees. One of the strict rules of the club is that during meetings Doyle's name is never mentioned. He has created such a memorable character that there are actually many people who believe that Holmes was a living person. To meet the demands of these fans a replica of the chambers in Baker Street was opened and is still one of the tourist sights of London.

The full flood was not yet ready to break, but a steady trickle was beginning to appear. In the late nineties and early years of the century such books as these were published: Israel Zangwill's *The Big Bow Mystery* in 1892; E. W. Hornung's *The Amateur Cracksman* in 1899; Jacques Futrelle's *The Thinking Machine,* Maurice Le Blanc's *Arsène Lupin,* R. Austin Freeman's *The Red Thumb Mark,* all published in 1907; Erskine Childer's *The Riddle of the Sands* in 1903. This latter book quite accurately predicted Germany's attempts to invade England almost forty years before the event actually took place. It has been called the classic secret service novel, and many of our present-day examples of the genre seem pretty insipid in comparison.

In 1908, Mary Roberts Rinehart wrote a mystery called *The Circular Staircase* and founded the "Had-I-But-Known" school which was to become so popular with the lady readers of the lending library. The same technique was to be adapted with great success in the confession magazines which owe more than they know to the early writers of detective fiction.

World War I was to bring to a halt the publication of mystery novels in England, but it was only a temporary situation. After peace had been declared, the public demanded more of their favorite reading matter, and there were the old masters and a lot of promising apprentices ready to satisfy the almost insatiable appetite of a greedy public.

The high tide of detective story popularity came between 1925 and 1945. Among the writers were S. S. Van Dine, whose erudition lent a new dimension to the detective novel. *The Benson Murder Case* was one of the first detective novels to become a best-seller. This was followed by *The Canary Murder Case, The Greene Murder Case,* and many others.

Earl Derr Biggers created the Chinese detective Charlie Chan in such books as *Behind That Curtain, The House Without a Key,* and *The Chinese Parrot.* Charlie Chan was to appear on radio, television, and in the movies hundreds of times before his popularity faded. He is also the only famous detective character who cannot be found in a short story. Agatha Christie, who had made her first appearance in 1920 with *The Mysterious Affair at Styles,* was to continue the stream of books which appeared regularly up to the present.

In the early thirties a quiet revolution began in the detective field. Dashiell Hammett was the innovator of the realistic and hard-boiled school which was to take over almost completely after World War II had made the old-time detective story pallid in comparison to the real life tragedy which had just occurred. Hammett's Continental Op, a blood brother to Fleming's James Bond, and Sam Spade became the new idols of the mystery fans. Hammett also introduced Nick Charles and his wife Nora, creating an entirely new kind of detective novel in *The Thin Man.* Raymond Chandler continued to mine the vein by creating Philip Marlowe in *The Big Sleep, Lady in the Lake, The High Window* and other similar novels.

The golden age of the detective mystery also included these memorable characters: John P. Marquand's Mr. Moto; Agatha Christie's Hercule Poirot and Miss Marple (now played on the screen by Margaret Rutherford); G. K. Chesterton's Father Brown; Rex Stout's Nero Wolfe; Erle Stanley Gardner's Perry Mason, Douglas Selby, Bertha Cool, and Donald Lam.

Today the trend is toward the novel of suspense. The detective is no longer the central character; the private eye has become obsolete, a parody if he appears at all. New police methods and cooperation between different bureaus of a modern police department have made the lone wolf operator an oddity. The police procedural novels of Dell Shannon and John Creasey are good examples of whole groups of men working together for the common good.

More often than not, it is the spy or the secret agent who works alone now. This is the new hero of our time, but considering the great number of parodies that have appeared recently he too perhaps has had his day.

I should like to think that in the novels of Patricia Moyes, and a few other newcomers who are brightening up the present scene, that at long last we are going to come full circle to the novel of detection once again. We can only wait and see.

Mystery Buffs

John Carter in his essay "Collecting Detective Fiction" in *Books and Book-Collectors* states: "For quite apart from the distinguished authors scattered up and down its history, it is notorious that the detective story is the favourite reading of statesmen, of dons in our older universities, and in fact of all that is most intellectual in the reading public." Among the prominent people that he mentions are Lord Rosebery, who possessed a first edition of *The Memoirs of Sherlock Holmes;* the late Montague Rhodes James, Provost of Eton, was an acknowledged authority on this subject; Mr. Desmond MacCarthy who was a prominent Holmesian scholar; and Mr. S. C. Roberts, a Master of Pembroke College, Cambridge, and responsible for the standard life of Doctor Watson. E. M. Wrong, Fellow of Magdalen College, Oxford and a distinguished historian, wrote an essay entitled *Crime and Detection* for the World's Classic series which is still considered one of the best ever written on the subject. Other writers on this subject have been Willard Huntington Wright, better known to mystery fans as S. S. Van Dine, Miss Dorothy L. Sayers, and Mr. H. Douglas Thomson, all of whom have also distinguished themselves in other fields.

American presidents, too, have helped the cause. Franklin D. Roosevelt was a great fan, and even suggested a plot that was developed into *The President's Mystery*. President Woodrow Wilson was the man partly responsible for the popularity of J. S. Fletcher. A reporter, noticing the President reading a book in bed, asked him the title of it. It was J. S. Fletcher's *The Middle Temple Murder,* and it brought instant and lasting fame to its author. Without a casual word from the late President Kennedy, it is doubtful whether James Bond would have become a national folk hero. President Lincoln is said to have won a law case by referring to a detective story.

John Foster Dulles, former Secretary of State, was an Erle Stanley Gardner fan. Also included among his fans were Einstein, James F. Byrnes, another former Secretary of State, and Chief Justice Fred Vinson.

Bertrand Russell, one of the great minds of our time, has this to say about the detective story: "Anyone who hopes that in time it may be possible to abolish war should give serious thought to the problem of satisfying harmlessly the instincts that we inherit from long generations of savages. For my part I find a sufficient outlet in detective stories, where I alternately identify myself with the murderer and the huntsman-detective."

Included among the fans must be the collectors. Ned Guymon of San Diego, California, is the owner of the largest private collection of detective and mystery stories in the world. It contains hundreds of original manuscripts and valuable first editions. A friend of many of the prominent writers in the field, his library has always been open to the researcher as this writer can testify. The present collection is being given to his Alma Mater, Occidental College in Los Angeles, California.

Organizations and Societies

Baker Street Irregulars

The Baker Street Irregulars, which derives its name from the street gang that used to help Sherlock Holmes with some of his cases, was founded by Christopher Morley in 1934. It is a loosely organized literary society devoted to the study of Sherlock Holmes. There are no formal entrance requirements, but all members must have a thorough knowledge of the Sherlock Holmes stories. As older members die, their names (derived from the titles of the short stories) are passed on to new members. Thus the Irregulars' membership is maintained at fifty-two. Members keep in touch with each other and informed of developments by considerable personal correspondence and by reading a quarterly called *The Baker Street Journal.* The annual subscription is $4.00 and it may be obtained by writing to Julian Wolff, Commissionaire, 33 Riverside Drive, New York, New York 10023. In this manner, interested Sherlockians are gradually absorbed into the society.

Main activities of the organization are the Silver Blaze Handicap, run at Aqueduct some time in September, and the annual dinner held each January. Attendance at the dinner is limited to Investitured Irregulars who have received the Irregular Shilling for service and demonstrated interest over a period of years.

In addition to the parent society, there are Scion Societies all over the country. The Second Scion Society is called the Speckled Band of Boston and was organized in April, 1940. Another Scion group is the Five Orange Pips which has Westchester for its home base. There are also the Norwegian Explorers of Minneapolis and St. Paul and the Sons of Copper Beeches in Philadelphia.

There is also a business affiliate, The Baker Street Irregulars, Inc., Sycamores, Spring Valley Road, Morristown, New Jersey, which issues lists of Sherlockian books that it has for sale.

The Detection Club

The Detection Club (commonly called the London Detection Club) was founded in 1928 by Anthony Berkeley who put the organization, under a thinly disguised title, in a book called *The Poisoned Chocolates Case*. Its first President (or Ruler) was G. K. Chesterton who called it a "small society of writers of detective stories." He served the club until his death in 1936. He was succeeded by E. C. Bentley, the author of *Trent's Last Case,* who occupied the chair for some years. The membership of the club is kept by charter relatively small, but includes the most distinguished names in British detective fiction. Among the members have been John Dickson Carr, Agatha Christie, Freeman Wills Crofts, F. Austin Freeman and Dorothy L. Sayers. Election to membership is a coveted professional recognition. The dues are nominal, and the club maintains premises and a criminological library from the proceeds of occasional anthologies to which the members contribute, with the royalties accruing to the organization.

The Crime Writers' Association

The Crime Writers' Association was founded in 1953 by John Creasey and Nigel Morland. The membership is limited to authors who have published fiction or non-fiction books with a crime theme, writers of TV and radio scripts that have been performed, and writers of short stories. There is also an associate membership for publishers, reputable agents, reviewers, and producers of plays, etc., with a crime theme. There are monthly meetings in London at which time members can talk shop and exchange ideas and news.

The chairman serves for only one year, but the secretary and treasurer can be reelected to office as many times as the members wish. Each year since 1955, they have presented the Association's Annual Critics Awards. Initially a best book was chosen and three runners-up; in 1959, however, the runners-up were reduced from three to two. In 1964, the Committee made a further change in the rules. If the best crime novel of the year was by a British author, then there would be a second Silver Dagger given for the best crime novel by a foreign author. If, however, the best crime novel of the year was by a foreigner, then the second dagger would go to the best British crime novel, these to be followed by two runners-up.

The Crime Writers' Association winners are selected by a panel of leading newspaper and magazine critics and are not influenced in any way by the officials or members of the Association. In fact, although leading critic Julian Symons is always invited to sit on the panel, he resigns from it when it becomes known that one of his books has appeared in the short list. The list of the associations awards to date can be found under Award-Winning Mysteries.

This material was kindly furnished by Mrs. Bonney Harris, secretary of the Crime Writers' Association.

The Mystery Writers of America

The Mystery Writers of America was founded in 1945, and is a non-profit organization of mystery and crime writers in all categories, established ". . . to promote and protect the interests and to increase the earnings of mystery story writers . . . to maintain and improve the esteem and recognition of mystery writing in the publishing industry and among the reading public . . . to disseminate helpful and rewarding information among the membership, and to foster the benefits of stimulating association with others having this common interest and uncommon talent."

The organization has a national office at Suite 125, Hotel Seville, 29th St. & Madison Ave., New York, N.Y. 10016 and is open to all members. Publishers, television and radio producers, advertising agencies, movie and theatrical producers, foreign businessmen and others call and write to MWA about writers, materials, services, or activities connected with the mystery field.

There are four regional chapters: New York which has members from Maine to Florida; Chicago which is headquarters for the Midwest Chapter; San Francisco which is home base for the Northern California Chapter; and Los Angeles which is headquarters for Southern California.

Each year a MWA anthology is issued and the proceeds go to the organization. Members contribute stories for this special volume. A monthly publication, *The Third Degree,* is sent to all members. Each year in April an Annual Awards Dinner is held in New York City. A complete listing of these awards will be found in the awards section of this book.

Sherlock Holmes Foundation

On April 19, 1966, The Conan Doyle Foundation was opened in Lausanne, Switzerland, by Adrian Doyle, the son of Sir Arthur Conan Doyle. The Château de Lucens, which is on the principal route between Berne and Lausanne, is a feudal château with a dungeon of the Louis XIII period and a gothic chapel. There is a replica of the Baker Street Chambers of Sherlock Holmes similar to the one in London. There is also one of the most complete libraries on Sherlock Holmes. Also included in the château are ancient instruments of torture, and a collection of trophies that Adrian Doyle has collected on his various expeditions to the tropics.

The President's Mystery Story

In 1935, while Franklin D. Roosevelt was President, he confided to a group of friends one evening that he had carried the plot for a mystery story in his mind for many years. When one of the guests, Fulton Oursler (also known to mystery fans by his pseudonym, Anthony Abbot) asked him why he had never written it down, the President answered simply that he had never been able to find a logical solution for it, and neither had anyone else to whom he had told it. The problem was: "How can a man disappear with $5,000,000 in any negotiable form and not be traced?" Oursler suggested some possible solutions, but the President found something wrong with all of them. When Oursler suggested that some of America's top mystery writers and perhaps the American public could find a solution for it, the President gave Oursler permission to use the plot.

Oursler assigned a number of the popular writers of the day to do parts of the book, not telling most of them the origin of the plot. Rupert Hughes, who had been told about it, agreed to do the opening chapter. Then followed chapters by Samuel Hopkins Adams, Rita Weiman, S. S. Van Dine, John Erskine, and Mr. Oursler himself writing under his pseudonym, Anthony Abbot. "The President's Mystery Story. Plot by Franklin D. Roosevelt" was first published in *Liberty Magazine* in November, 1935, and later as a hardcover book. The book had a moderate success, and the President's share of the royalties was turned over to his favorite charity. For today's readers who may be interested in the book, it has been reissued by Prentice-Hall in a new edition intended for the camp generation.

Collaborations

Perhaps in no other field of literature has there been such collaboration as there is in that of the mystery, detective and suspense novel. Your favorite writer may in actuality be two friends writing under one pseudonym, a husband and wife team, two brothers, two cousins, two sisters, or a father and son team.

Some of the better known collaborations are those of John Leslie Palmer and Hilary Aidan St. George Saunders who wrote under the name of Francis Beeding and Adelaide Frances Oke Manning and Cyril Henry Coles who wrote under the pseudonym of Manning Coles. Bob Wade and Bill Miller may be better known to you as Wade Miller and Whit Masterson. Richard Webb and Hugh C. Wheeler wrote under the joint pseudonyms Q. Patrick, Patrick Quentin and Jonathan Stagge. Charles Rodda and Eric Ambler, both great mystery writers in their own right, also collaborated under the pseudonym Eliot Reed.

Some of the better known husband and wife teams are the Gordons, the Teilhets, the Hanshews, and the Lockridges, all writing under their own name. Bart Spicer and his wife Betty have produced some novels under the pseudonym of Jay Barbette. Dolores Hitchens, who is also D. B. Olsen, has written a number of novels with her husband Bert. Audrey and William Roos write under the name of Kelley Roos. Sister teams include such names as the Littles and the Goyders; cousin teams include Frederic Dannay and Manfred Lee who write under the famous name of Ellery Queen.

A good example of a brother team is John and Ward Hawkins. Philip MacDonald and his father Ronald MacDonald produced one book under the pseudonym Oliver Fleming. Bruce Graeme, author of the "Blackshirt" novels, gave his character to his son Roderic, who now writes the books with great success.

Pseudonyms

The reasons for choosing a pseudonym are as varied as people themselves. Many writers prefer not to use their own names for their professional writing. Some have names which are too difficult, too simple, or which have been used before. Some writers are so prolific that no publisher will publish everything they write under one name. John Creasey, for example, writes under some 19 pseudonyms, not all of them in the mystery field. Two writers wishing to collaborate on a book will often write under a single name. Women writers frequently use male names—the old ways die hard. Publishers once believed that the public would not buy detective stories written by women authors. That is why there are so many writers with names that are sexless as far as the reader can determine.[1]

[1] For an interesting chapter on the use of pseudonyms read *In the Queen's Parlor,* by Ellery Queen. See also Deborah Kassmans' "What's in a Pen Name?," *Writer* (May, 1957).

Title Changes

One of the minor irritations in doing research on this book was the problem of title changes. In most cases the titles of English detective stories are changed when they are published in the United States, and vice versa. The changes are understandable in the main, because the titles usually contain references to things and places which are unknown outside the country of origin. More annoying, however, is the practice of pocket book publishers changing the title a third or fourth time when a book becomes available in a pocket edition. One of the extreme examples I found concerned one of Agatha Christie's books. The original title of the book was *4:50 from Paddington,* serialized as "Eye Witness to Murder." When it was published in the United States, it was retitled *What Mrs. McGillicuddy Saw*. When this book was made into a motion picture, it was called *Murder, She Said,* and was published under that title as a pocket book. Another Christie book is known under three titles: *Ten Little Niggers, Ten Little Indians,* and *And Then There Were None.* Few of the Christie books escape title changes when they cross the Atlantic and in many of John Creasey's books we not only have a title change, but a pseudonym change as well.

Some Critics

Many of our leading mystery, detective, and suspense writers have been critics as well as writers of fiction. It all began, of course, with Edgar Allan Poe, the father of the detective story. He was a distinguished critic whose criticisms have stood the test of time quite well. In our own time, Anthony Boucher, before his death in 1968 the mystery critic of the *New York Times,* has quite an impressive list of novels to his credit, one of which, *The Case of the Baker Street Irregulars* has become a classic in the field. He wrote mysteries also under the pseudonym of H. H. Holmes, and has compiled a number of detective and mystery anthologies. A neighbor and friend of Mr. Boucher's, Lenore Glen Offord, the creator of Tod Downing, conducts "The Gory Road" in the *San Francisco Chronicle.* Dorothy B. Hughes was the reviewer for the late New York *Herald Tribune's Book Week.* Among modern British critics is Julian Symons of the London *Times.* He is also on the committee which chooses the best books of the genre each year, and when one of his own books appears on the list, which happens quite frequently, he temporarily withdraws from the committee. His books usually win anyway. Edmund Crispin is presently reviewing mysteries for the *Sunday Times.* In Holland, Ab Visser is not only one of their most able novelists, but a translator and critic as well.

Best Sellers

70 Years of Best Sellers by Alice Payne Hackett, published by the R. R. Bowker Company in 1967, contains a great deal of information of interest to the reader of mystery, detective and suspense fiction.

Of the 151 books in this field which have sold a million or more copies, 91 are by Erle Stanley Gardner, followed by Richard Prather (16), Ellery Queen (13), Mickey Spillane (12), Ian Fleming (11), Agatha Christie (4), Dashiell Hammett and John D. MacDonald (2). The first title on the list chronologically is Mary Roberts Rinehart's *The Circular Staircase* (first published in 1908) and the last two are *The Spy Who Came in from the Cold* by John LeCarré and *You Only Live Twice* by Ian Fleming, both published in 1964.

Publication of mystery, suspense and detective stories has been increasing. In 1956 there were 448 titles, plus reprints, while in 1965 there were 785.

Brett Halliday's Mike Shayne stories have had paperback sales of 35 million, Agatha Christie and Richard Prather 25 million, and Mary Roberts Rinehart 15 million.

Here are the top 11 mystery titles in all U.S. editions:

	Title	Copies
1.	*I, the Jury,* by Mickey Spillane	5,390,105
2.	*The Big Kill,* by Mickey Spillane	5,089,472
3.	*My Gun Is Quick,* by Mickey Spillane	4,916,074
4.	*One Lonely Night,* by Mickey Spillane	4,873,563
5.	*The Long Wait,* by Mickey Spillane	4,835,966
6.	*Kiss Me, Deadly,* by Mickey Spillane	4,828,044
7.	*Vengeance Is Mine,* by Mickey Spillane	4,637,734
8.	*Thunderball,* by Ian Fleming	4,186,935
9.	*Goldfinger,* by Ian Fleming	3,642,411
10.	*The Case of the Lucky Legs,* by Erle Stanley Gardner	3,499,948
11.	*You Only Live Twice,* by Ian Fleming	3,283,000

Dictionary

The world of the detective, mystery and suspense novel has developed its own vocabulary over the years. Here are some of the terms most frequently used to describe various aspects of this kind of fiction:

Cliff-Hanger

The expression originated in the days of the early movie serials when each episode ended in a suspenseful moment which was to lure the customer back the next week. It is used variously nowadays to describe any melodramatic story, play, book or movie which leaves the audience waiting to see how the situation will resolve itself.

Clue or Clew

In detective stories any pertinent information which the detective has which helps him solve the crime. The better the plot is, the more elusive the clue is to the reader.

Cui Bono

Literally "to whose advantage." It fastens the crime on a character who has a great deal to gain from its perpetration.

Detective Story

One in which a detective or detectives solve the crime.

Gothics

Just a new name for the old "damsel in distress" novel.

Gunsel

A gunman in hard-boiled detective fiction. Originated in Dashiell Hammett's *The Maltese Falcon*.

Had-I-But-Known

The story seen in retrospect—a favorite with the ladies.

Howdunit

The emphasis is on the method by which the crime is committed.

Inverted Detective Story

A detective story in which the criminal is known, but where the solution to the problem lies in some other aspect of the characters or the motive.

LSP

The Least Suspected Person. Maybe the butler?

Mystery Story

A story in which the emphasis is on an event or a thing rather than on the people trying to solve it.

Police Procedural

A fairly recent innovation in which the whole police department works together as a team and no one individual gets the credit.

Private Eye

A private detective working alone; not directly connected with any law enforcement agency, but generally cooperating with them. Don't look for them in the newer books, as they are quite an anachronism.

Red Herring

A misleading clue.

Shamus

A slang expression for a private eye or a policeman. Originally the name given to the custodian of a synagogue.

Suspense Story

A story in which the reader's interest is held by the precarious situation in which the principal character finds himself. The emphasis seems to be most often on the situations themselves, rather than the characters who, very often, are not much more than stock figures. A favorite plot is to have a very ordinary person find himself in a situation from which it seems impossible that he will extricate himself. When you have a very lovely young girl in a brooding mansion on the moorlands, you have the type of novel we call gothic.

Thriller

Primarily an English term, this is a less sophisticated and more melodramatic story than a plain mystery. Emphasis is predominantly on thrilling incidents and lots of action. E. C. R. Lorac's *Death of an Author* mentions a "thriller merchant," a slang expression for a writer of this type of fiction. Actually many of the books listed in the Comprehensive Bibliography are of this classification, but have usually been included in other categories for identification purposes.

Whodunit

A story in which the emphasis is on the solution of a crime or mystery, usually murder. The word originated about 1928.

Whydunit

A story in which the emphasis is on why the murder took place. Greatly influenced by the growth of psychology.

Quotations

"The detective story is the normal recreation of noble minds."

ATTRIBUTED TO PHILIP GUEDALLA

"My theory is that people who don't like mystery stories are anarchists."

REX STOUT

"It will be found that the ingenious are always fanciful, and the truly imaginative never otherwise than analytic."

EDGAR ALLAN POE in "THE MURDERS IN THE RUE MORGUE"

"The history of the detective story begins with the publication of 'The Murders in the Rue Morgue.' "

BRANDER MATTHEWS

"Do you feel an uncomfortable heat on the pit of your stomach, Sir? And a nasty thumping at the top of your head? I call it detective fever."

WILKIE COLLINS in *The Moonstone*

"It should be possible, I thought, to write a detective story in which the detective was recognizable as a human being."

E. C. BENTLEY in *Those Days*

"So far the most fascinating attempt made to renovate the detective story consists in assigning a more important role to psychology."

DENIS MARION

"The literature of crime detection is of recent growth because the historical conditions on which it depends are modern."

F. W. CHANDLER in *The Literature of Roguery*

"Poe transported the detective story from the group of tales of adventure into the group of portrayals of character. By bestowing upon it a human interest he raised it to a literary scale."

BRANDER MATTHEWS in "POE AND THE DETECTIVE STORY"

"The writer is left with only one quality, that of intellectual acuteness with which to endow his hero."

SIR ARTHUR CONAN DOYLE

"The crime story is almost the only novel worth reading today because it deals with the fundamental conflict of mankind; the conflict of good and bad. At its best it is the morality play of our age."

JOHN CREASEY

"Detective stories have appeared in every kind of physical form from the full-dress three-volume novel down to the Detective Supplement of the Union Jack."

JOHN CARTER, "COLLECTING DETECTIVE FICTION" in *Books and Book Collecting*

"The detective story is in danger of being played out. Stories are getting cleverer and cleverer, but the readers are getting cleverer and cleverer, too. It is almost impossible at the moment to think up any form of bluff which the really seasoned reader will not see through."

RONALD A. KNOX in *Tablet* (LONDON), 1947

"The puzzle element, or at least the element of suspense, of uncertainty, must be there . . . readers demand it, and there is something in crime writers that demands it too. Given that necessity, it is possible to construct stories that mirror some sort of psychological reality in our tangled and morally disordered society."

JULIAN SYMONS, LONDON *Times* MYSTERY CRITIC

"A good detective story is the answer to Lowell's question, 'What is so rare as a day in June?' "

FRANKLIN D. ROOSEVELT

"The true detective story is the most moral story there is. Sin gets punished, virtue triumphs, and if these things don't happen, you're not reading anything but a problem novel."

LEWIS NICHOLS, *New York Times,* APRIL 27, 1958

". . . it is notorious that the detective story is the favorite reading of statesmen, of dons in our older universities, and in fact of all that is most intellectual in the reading public . . ."

JOHN CARTER

". . . it is one of the hectic pleasures of reading about crime that we can switch sides constantly. We can commit murder in the morning and catch ourselves in the afternoon . . ."

Times Literary Supplement, FEBRUARY, 1955

"There certainly does seem a possibility that the detective story will sometime come to an end, simply because the public will have learnt all the tricks . . ."

DOROTHY L. SAYERS

"Clearly, there could be no detective stories until there are detectives. This did not occur until the nineteenth century . . ."

HOWARD HAYCRAFT in *Murder for Pleasure*

"The trouble in the matter is that many people do not realize that there is such a thing as a good mystery story; to them it is like speaking of a good devil."

G. K. CHESTERTON

"What we want in our detective fiction . . . is deep mystery and conflicting clues."

E. M. WRONG

"The less love in a detective story the better . . ."

DOROTHY L. SAYERS

"Perhaps art in general should have no moral purpose, but the art of the detective story is a study as fascinating as it is deserving of serious attention, and from a collector's point of view it has a host of attractive features."

JOHN CARTER

"No detective has been so successfully eccentric as he (Holmes) was . . ."

E. M. WRONG

". . . the reading of detective stories, like the smoking of pipes and the flogging of trout streams, became in a flash one of the outward signs of respectability . . ."

Times Literary Supplement, FEBRUARY, 1955

". . . the perishable format in which so many of the most covetable detective items first appeared ensures them a permanent standard of scarcity in any sort of decent condition."

JOHN CARTER

"If we err, therefore, in our liking of detective stories, we err with Plato."

JOHN CARTER

"The detective story has proved capable of high development and has become a definitive art."

E. M. WRONG

"Just as a devotee of cricket will spend happy winter evenings compiling imaginary teams of the greatest ever, so will the detection-addict set himself up as a one-man selection committee to choose the classics of his kind."

C. DAY LEWIS

"Murder witnessed from the soft cushions of an evening train, murder lying quiet behind a glass of port and a cigar, murder under the eiderdown: in such circumstances all of us can cope with crime . . ."

ANONYMOUS

"In its severest form, the mystery story is pure analytical exercise, and, as such, may be a highly finished work of art, within its highly artificial limits . . ."

DOROTHY L. SAYERS

"The vogue for collecting detective first editions has come a long way since the days of the now historic 1934 catalogue issued by Scribner's of New York."

Times Literary Supplement,
DECEMBER 8, 1966

"It is fortunate for the mystery-monger that, whereas up to the present there is only one known way of getting born, there are endless ways of getting killed . . ."

DOROTHY L. SAYERS

"The detective story shows every sign of having come to stay."

JOHN CARTER, 1934

Pulp Magazines

Many of our most famous writers in the field of mystery, detective and suspense got their start in the old pulp magazines of yesterday. Many of the old titles which should bring back memories are here along with some of the current favorites still found on the newsstands.

Adventure
Ainslee's Magazine
Alfred Hitchcock Mystery Magazine
Argosy
Black Book Detective
Black Cat
Black Mask
Clues
Crack Detective
Detective Novels
Detective Tales
Dime Detective Magazine
Doc Savage Magazine
Double Action Detective
Ed McBain's Mystery Book
Edgar Wallace Mystery Magazine
Ellery Queen's Mystery Magazine
Exciting Detective
Famous Story
Flynn's (later *Detective Fiction Weekly*)
The Girl from U.N.C.L.E.
G-Men Detective
Golden Book
Hampton's
London Mystery Magazine
McClure's
MacKill's Mystery Magazine
Mammoth Detective
The Man from U.N.C.L.E.
Manhunt
Mike Shayne Mystery Magazine
Munsey's Magazine
Mystery
Mystery League
Mystery Stories
New Detective Magazine
Pearson's
Phantom Detective
Popular Detective
Red Star Detective
Saint's Mystery Magazine
Secret Agent X
Short Stories
Sleuth
Smart Set
Smashing Detective
Street and Smith's *Detective Story*
Ten Detective Aces
Thrilling Detective
Top Notch Detective
Tower's Mystery Magazine
Triple Detective
Undercover Detective
Variety Detective

Mystery Novel Abroad

Although mystery, detective, and suspense novels are written primarily in the United States and Great Britain, they are read in almost every country of the world. Authors such as Agatha Christie and Ian Fleming have a world-wide popularity that must be the envy of the so-called literary clique. The number of translations made from these books runs into the millions, but it is almost a one-way situation. The number of foreign books translated into English is miniscule in comparison, and the contributions from these countries, with the exception of France, could almost be counted on the fingers of both hands. This is sheer exaggeration, of course, but I am trying to say that none of these other countries have as great a stake in this type of literature as the United States and Great Britain.

France

France's contribution to the field began shortly after the publication of Poe's short stories in the 1840's. It seems incredible now that Poe's tales made such a slight impression on American readers, and hardly any on Americal writers, who failed to follow his example which would have been a sure sign of success. In France, however, the stories were hailed with great acclaim.

Even before the appearance of Poe's stories in France, *The Memoirs of Vidocq, Principal Agent of the French Police* had been popular with the French public. With the interest aroused by Poe's short stories, Emile Gaboriau caught the fancy of French readers and his novels, beginning with *L'Affaire Lerouge* published in 1866, were widely read. This novel did not appear in the United States, however, until 1891. *The Crime of the Opera House* by Fortuné Du Boisgobey, a follower of Gaboriau, was published earlier in the United States in 1881 and provided the incentive for Harlan P. Halsey to introduce the detective and the detective story as the main elements in the dime novel.

Rocambole, a fictional character, was created by Pierre Alexis de Ponson, known as Ponson du Terrail. Rocambole, one of the first of the juvenile detectives, was only twelve years old and appeared in twenty-two stories. Tiring of his creation, the author had him killed off. Public demand, however, had him resurrected in 1862, and once again as a man in 1866. The same thing was to happen in England in 1905 when Sir Arthur Conan Doyle, having killed off Sherlock Holmes, was forced to bring him back to life because of an avid public's clamor.

Although the detective story continued its popularity, only two writers arose to distinguish themselves in the field: Maurice LeBlanc and Gaston Leroux. Leroux's *The Mystery of the Yellow Chamber* is considered to be the masterpiece of French detective fiction, and the only classic novel of detective writing outside the United States and Great Britain. Not until 1932, when we were introduced to Georges Simenon, did we find a writer to reach the stature of Leroux and LeBlanc.

In recent years, France has given us Roger Francis Didelot, author of *Death of the Deputy* and *Murder in the Bath;* Jean Toussaint-Samat, author of *Ships Aflame, The Dead Man at the Window,* and *The Shoes That Walked Twice;* Stanislaus-Andre Steeman's *The Night of the 12th–13th;* Simone D'Erigney's *The Mysterious Madame S;* and Jean Hougron's *A Question of Character.* More recently we have had the work of Sebastien Japrisot whose *10:30 from Marseilles* and *A Trap for Cinderella* have aroused interest here. *10:30 from Marseilles* was made into a movie called *The Sleeping Car Murders.*

There is also the work of Hubert Monteilhet which includes *The Praying Mantises* and *Return from the Ashes* and Roger Gouze's *A Quiet Game of Bambu.* In the suspense field we have Noel Calef's *Frantic,* Emmanuel Robles' *Dawn on Our Darkness* and Jean-Jacques Gautier's *Triple Mirror.* This does not exhaust the field but does give a small idea of what is available from French writers.

The Black River Enterprise, which offers 24 cheap paperback titles each month, reaches a wider and less discriminating audience. Among its huge stable of writers was the late Jean Bruce who has just recently been translated and is beginning to appear on American newsstands. Many of the leading French publishers: Plon, Denoël, Presses de la Cité, Fayard, Le Masque, and Gallimard are bringing out huge printings of English and American authors.

Germany

Next to France, Germany has been the most represented in the detective and suspense field. In the early part of this century such authors as Augusta Groner, who was translated by Grace Isabel Colbron, appeared with such works as *The Lady in Blue, Joe Muller, Detective, The Crippled Hand, Murdered?, The Golden Bullet, Why She Put Out the Lamp, By a Thread,* and *The Ninety-Seventh.* Groner's detective creation, Joseph Muller, has received a modicum of fame, and is known to collectors and mystery buffs if not to the general public.

Other German writers known here are Karl Peter Rosner and his *The Versegy Case;* Dietrich Thedan's *The Counsel for the Defense;* Johann Heinrich Daniel Kaulbach for his *White Carnation;* Frederick Thieme; August Schrader's *Not Guilty;* Zschokkes' *The Dead Guest;* Wilhelm Hauff's *The Singer;* Baroness de la Motte Fouqe's *The Revolutionist;* E. T. A. Hoffman, whose "Mlle. de Scudery" and "The Deserted House" influenced Edgar Allan Poe; Paul Lindau's *Helene Jung;* and Adam Ernst Wildenbruch's *The Wandering Light.* Although available in the U.S., these were not always in translation and would be difficult to find today. Just recently, however, Hans Hellmut Kirst has received good critical reaction in this country with *The Night of the Generals* which has been made into a motion picture with Peter O'Toole.

Norway

A recent mystery novel in Norway has been Gerd Nyqvist's *Avdøde Ønsket Ikke Blomster* (*The Dead Don't Need Flowers*) which has been read quite widely for the past two years. Waldemar Brogger and O. Selmar collaborated on *Skriftemalet* in 1965 and *Døden Kommer Baffra* in 1963. Torolf Elster was represented by *Piken Men Unharet.* None of these, unfortunately, has been translated into English. One of Norway's writers of detective stories who received attention away from his homeland was Andre Bjerke, who under the pseudonym of Bernhard Borge, had his novel, *Death in the Blue Lake* translated into English and published in 1961. It received a fair amount of critical attention.

Among the popular writers currently appearing in Norwegian detective magazines are Walter Gun, Fred Freddy, John Bell, Finn Arneson, and Stein Wang. These are probably pseudonyms if Norwegian publishers follow the patterns set down by their American and British counterparts.

Translations of American and British mystery, detective, and suspense novels are also popular in Norway, and because so many Norwegians read English these days many of these books are sold in their original versions. This is also true of many other foreign countries where English is widely understood.

Denmark

The Danish writers of mystery, detective, and suspense fiction have made little impact on the American and British markets. Steen Steensen Blicher has authored *The Rector of Veilbye* which is available in English translation. Baron Palle Rosenkrantz has had two of his novels translated into English, one of which, *What the Forest Pool Hid,* was popular some years ago.

Sweden

Recently two of Sweden's most popular mystery writers have been translated into English. Per Wahloo's, *The 31st Floor, Roseanna,* and *The Assignment* have received considerable critical attention in both England and the United States. Per, or Peter, Wahloo, writes his books with his wife, Maj Sjowall. Their detective creation, Chief Inspector Jensen, is as popular as Chief Inspector Christer Wick, the brainchild of another Swedish writer, Maria Lang, who is just now being published in the United States. Her novel, *A Wreath for the Bride,* was published late in 1968.

Italy

Italy has made very little contribution to the American and British mystery scene. Only a handful of novels have appeared in recent years, and one of them curiously enough has an American scene. Giuseppe Collizzi's *The Night Has Another Voice* is hardly distinguishable from an American novel of the same kind. Dino Buzzati's *Larger Than Life* and Sergio Donati's *The Paper Tomb* are two other Italian writers who have been translated into English. Neither has made a terrific impact on the reading public.

Holland

Perhaps the outstanding figure on the Netherlands scene is Ab Visser, novelist, critic and translator. He is also a popular columnist for Amsterdam's *De Telegraaf.* Visser's three novels, *Uitnodiging Tot Moord* (*Invitation to Murder*); *De Samenzwering* (*The Conspirators*); and *De Kat and de Rat* (*The Cat and the Rat*) are, unfortunately, not available in English, but they should be along with his *Kain Sloeg Abel: Een Handleiding Voor De Detective-Lezer,* a survey of the mystery and detective field somewhat similar to Haycraft's *Murder for Pleasure.* He recently completed *Onder de Gordel; Erotiek in de Misdaadroman,* a study of the erotic elements of the detective story.

Others on the local scene, but not translated into English are Joop van de Broek, who writes under the pseudonym Jan Van Gent, Pim Hopdorp, Eline Capit, Van Eemlandt, H. J. Oolbekkink, Hellinger (Hellinga), Willi Corsari, and Martin Treffer. Better known to American and British readers are the late Robert Van Gulik and Nicholas Freeling. In Holland, Freeling's Dutch detective is not considered particularly Dutch, but more an American's idea of what a Dutch detective should be.

Switzerland

From this rugged land comes the superior work of Frederic Dürrenmatt whose *The Judge and His Hangman* and *The*

Pledge have been translated into English and have received high critical praise.

Japan

While American and British translations are very popular in Japan, they have sent us very little in return. Haro Tirai, who is one of their popular writers, has a volume, *Japanese Tales of Mystery and Imagination* which has been translated into English. Another popular writer in Japan was the late Kodo Nomura who wrote many stories about a detective called Zenigata Heiiji. These stories were set in samurai days, and have never been published in English.

Russia

Russia's contribution to the mystery, detective, and suspense field has been very slight, and this is a field which it can be truly said they can not claim to have invented. The *Ellery Queen Mystery Magazine* has published a couple of their short stories, but the mystery elements are very slight, and do not show the imagination used by our very best creators. Readers wishing to sample their style might try Anton Chekov's short stories, "The Cook's Wedding" and "The Hunting Party."

Mexico

Perhaps the most important figure to emerge out of Mexico in recent years is Antonio Helu who was first introduced to the American public through the pages of the *Ellery Queen Mystery Magazine* in November, 1944. His greatest creation is Maximo Roldan, a Mexican detective, who is also a thief of some ability.

Latin America and Spain

Spain has provided one or two examples and a little more is forthcoming, but it is not impressive. Latin America shows little interest in this type of literature, but translations of American and British books are quite widely read. Jorge Luis Borges' philosophical mysteries *Ficciones* and *Labyrinths* show the trend of the mystery story in these countries and are the only good examples we have of this kind of writing. Marco Denevi wrote a mystery in Spanish called *Rosaura a las diez*. This was translated in 1964 and published by Holt under the title *Rosa at Ten O'Clock*.

Necrology

Many of the luminaries who brought the mystery, detective, and suspense field to its present eminence are no longer with us. This part of the book is dedicated to their memory.

Abdullah, Achmed, 1881–1945
Allen, Grant, 1848–1899
Allingham, Marjory, 1904–1966
Andrew, Clifton R., 1892–1963
Armstrong, Margaret Neilson, 1867–1944
Asbury, Herbert, 1891–1963
Atkinson, Alex, 1916–1962

Barr, Robert, 1850–1912
Bellamann, Henry, 1882–1945
Bentley, Edmund Clerihew, 1875–1956
Bierce, Ambrose, 1842–1914?
Biggers, Earl Derr, 1884–1933
Bindloss, Harold, 1866–1945
Blackwood, Algernon, 1869–1951
Blixen, Karen (Isak Dinesen), 1885–1962
Bok, Curtis, 1897–1962
Bower, Bertha M., 1871–1940
Braddon, Mary Elizabeth, 1837–1915
Brennan, Frederick Hazlitt, 1902–1962
Brochet, Jean (Jean Bruce), 1921–1963
Buchan, John, 1875–1940
Bulwer-Lytton, Edward Thomas, 1803–1873
Burgess, Gelett, 1866–1951
Burke, Richard, 1886–1962
Burke, Thomas, 1887–1945
Burroughs, Edgar Rice, 1875–1950

Caine, Sir Hall, 1853–1931
Campbell, William Edward March (William March), 1893–1954
Chambers, Robert William, 1865–1933
Chandler, Raymond, 1888–1959
Chesterton, Gilbert Keith, 1874–1936
Cheyney, Peter, 1896–1951
Christ, Jay Finley, 1884–1963
Clad, Noel, 1923–1962
Cobb, Irvin Shrewsbury, 1876–1944
Collins, William Wilkie, 1824–1889
Costain, Thomas Bertram (Pat Hand), 1885–1965
Crofts, Freeman Wills, 1879–1957
Cunningham, Albert Benjamin (Estil Dale), 1882–1962

Dickens, Charles, 1812–1870
Doyle, Sir Arthur Conan, 1859–1930

Du Boisgobey, Fortuné Hippolyte Auguste, 1821–1891

Faulkner, William, 1897–1962
Fleming, Ian, 1908–1964
Fletcher, Joseph Smith, 1863–1935
Freeman, Mary E., 1852–1930
Freeman, Richard Austin, 1862–1943
Futrelle, Jacques, 1875–1912

Gaboriau, Emile, 1833–1873
Gollomb, Joseph, 1881–1950
Green, Anna Katherine, 1846–1935
Gregory, Jackson, 1882–1943
Gresham, William Lindsay, 1909–1962

Hamilton, Patrick, 1904–1962
Hammett, Dashiell, 1894–1961
Hanshew, Thomas W., 1857–1914
Hart, Mrs. Frances Newbold, 1890–1943
Hawkins, Sir Anthony Hope (Anthony Hope), 1863–1933
Hawthorne, Julian, 1846–1934
Hilton, James, 1900–1954
Hitchens, Robert Smythe, 1864–1950
Hornung, Ernest William, 1866–1921
Hume, Fergus, 1859–1932
Huxley, Aldous, 1894–1963

Jackson, Shirley, 1919–1965
Jacobsson, Per, 1894–1963
Jerome, Jerome Klapka, 1859–1927
Jesse, Friniwyd Tennyson, 1898?–1958

Kersh, Gerald, 1911–1968
King, Charles Daly, 1895–1963
Kipling, Rudyard, 1865–1936
Knox, Ronald, 1888–1957

La Farge, Oliver, 1901–1963
LeBlanc, Maurice, 1864–1941
Lee, Norman, 1900–1962
LeFanu, Joseph Sheridan, 1814–1873
LeQueux, William, 1864–1927
Leroux, Gaston, 1868–1927
Lockridge, Mrs. Frances Louise, 1896–1963
London, Jack, 1876–1916
Long, Gabrielle Margaret Vere Campbell (Joseph Shearing), 1886–1952
Lovecraft, Howard Phillips, 1880–1937
Lowndes, Mrs. Marie Adelaide Belloc, 1868–1947

McCutcheon, George Barr, 1866–1928
MacGowan, Kenneth, 1888–1963
McGrath, Harold, 1871–1932
Machen, Arthur, 1863–1947
Mackintosh, Elizabeth (Josephine Tey), 1897–1952
McNeile, Herman Cyril (Sapper), 1888–1937
Marquand, John Phillips, 1893–1960
Mason, Alfred Edward Woodley, 1865–1948
Maugham, William Somerset, 1874–1965
Meade, L. T., 1854–1914
Moffett, Cleveland, 1863–1926
Morgan, Robert S., 1905–1962
Morrison, Arthur, 1863–1945

O'Farrell, William, 1904–1962
O'Higgins, Harvey Jerrold, 1876–1929
Oppenheim, Edward Phillips, 1866–1946
Orczy, Baroness Emmuska, 1865–1947
Ostrander, Isabel Egenton, 1885–1924
Oursler, Fulton (Anthony Abbot), 1893–1952

Packard, Frank Lucius, 1877–1942
Pain, Barry, 1862–1928
Palmer, John Leslie (Francis Beeding), 1885–1944
Poe, Edgar Allan, 1809–1849
Porter, William Sydney (O. Henry), 1862–1910
Post, Melville Davisson, 1871–1930
Prichard, Hesketh V. H., 1876–1922

Reeve, Arthur B., 1880–1936
Reilly, Helen, 1891–1962
Rinehart, Mrs. Mary Roberts, 1876–1958
Roche, Arthur Somers, 1883–1935

Saunders, Hilary Aidan St. George, 1898–1951
Sayers, Dorothy Leigh, 1893–1957
Smith, Ernest Bramah (Ernest Bramah), ?–1942
Stoker, Bram, 1847–1912
Strachey, John, 1901–1963

Terrall, Robert, ?–1963
Thompson, J. C., 192?–1962
Tracy, Louis, 1863–1928

Upfield, Arthur William, 1888–1964

Vandercook, John W., 1902–1963
Vidocq, François Eugene, 1775–1857

Wallace, Edgar, 1875–1932
Walling, Robert Alfred Jones, 1869–1949
Wells, Carolyn, 1870–1942
Wilde, Percival, 1887–1953
Williams, Valentine, 1883–1946
Wood, Mrs. Henry, 1814–1887
Wright, Willard Huntington (S. S. Van Dine), 1888–1939

Zangwill, Israel, 1864–1926

Index to the Comprehensive Bibliography, 1841-1967